WHAT TO EXPECT® THE FIRST YEAR

D0901753

Also available from What to Expect®

What to Expect® When You're Expecting

What to Eat When You're Expecting

The **What to Expect® When You're Expecting** *Pregnancy Organizer*

What to Expect® Pregnancy Planner

The What to Expect® Baby-Sitter's Handbook

What to Expect® the Toddler Years

WHAT TO EXPECT® THE FIRST YEAR

••••

Heidi Murkoff

with Sharon Mazel

POCKET
BOOKS
LONDON • SYDNEY • NEW YORK • TORONTO

To Emma and Wyatt, Rachel, Ethan and Elizabeth for the
magical, memorable first years each of you gave us

To our partners in parenting, Erik, Howard and Tim, without
whom we couldn't have made it through those first years

This 2nd edition published by Pocket Books, 2010
An imprint of Simon & Schuster UK Ltd
A CBS COMPANY

3 5 7 9 10 8 6 4

Simon & Schuster UK Ltd
1st Floor
222 Gray's Inn Road
London WC1X 8HB

www.simonandschuster.co.uk

Simon & Schuster Australia
Sydney

A CIP catalogue record for this book is available from the British Library

ISBN 978-1-84983-165-9

Typeset by M Rules
Printed and bound by CPI Group (UK) Ltd, Croydon, CR0 4YY

A SECOND ROUND OF THANKS

I f there's anything harder than writing a book, it's rewriting a book. Like reinventing the wheel (how can we do it better?), it takes a lot of reevaluating, a lot of revisiting, and a lot of second-guessing (What works well already? What used to work but doesn't any more? What never really worked in the first place? What could work – with a little work?). It also takes a lot of help, from a whole bunch of people. From friends, colleagues, academics, health care professionals – and some special folks who fit into all four categories at the same time, some who have supported us from the first draft of the first edition, others who have only recently joined the team; many more wonderful people than we could possibly list here, that is, without running even farther over the expected page count in this second edition than we already have. We gratefully thank all of you, including:

Suzanne Rafer, a wonderful editor and even better friend, who has gamely waded through thousands and thousands of *What to Expect* manuscript pages over the last twenty years, shepherding sentences gone astray (and puns gone bad), deftly deleting words (the extraneous ones, that is), relentlessly waving her pink flags until we surrender to her better judgment – for everything you do, and for always being there.

Peter Workman, a publisher of uncommon (at least these days) character, skill and, most of all, faith – for standing behind us from the humble beginnings of *What to Expect.* We share every success with you and with . . .

Lisa Hollander, for making every book look its best, and Barbara Balch, for giving her a hand with this one; Judith Cheng, for another beautiful US cover (and another memorable baby), and Judy Francis, for her adorable (and

illuminating!) illustrations. Anne Cherry, for smoothing out the kinks in the manuscript. Robyn Schwartz, for good humour and fast reflexes. Carolan Workman, Suzie Bolotin, David Schiller, Jenny Mandel, Sarah Edmond, Jim Eber, Kate Tyler, Bruce Harris, Pat Upton, Saundra Pearson, Beth Doty and all the other wonderful members of the Workman family – lots of hugs and kisses to each and every one of you, for all your hard work, support and love. Thanks also to all of you who worked on the first edition but have since moved on.

Sharon Mazel, for absolutely everything you do (and for the amazing speed with which you do it all; it probably helps that you never sleep): favourite e-mail companion (you've got mail – again!), tireless researcher (who takes her research seriously – and has Kira and Sophia to show for it) and writer, steadfast gatekeeper of TMI – you're half of our one-two punch, and I treasure you. Thanks, too, to Dr Jay Mazel – not just for sharing Sharon but for offering endless after hours medical advice – and to the four (and counting?) Mazel girls: Daniella, Arianne, Kira and especially timely Sophia. Special thanks to the girls' paediatrician, Dr Jeffrey Bernstein, who patiently answered the hundreds of *First Year* questions Sharon snuck into well-baby visits. And Aliza Graber, for getting us organized.

Dr Mark Widome, Professor of Paediatrics at The Penn State Children's Hospital and star of both paediatric practice (we envy those kids in your care!) and the *Today* show, and our extraordinary medical adviser. Not only for your invaluable knowledge, wisdom and insights, which make us look good, but for your humour, empathy and compassion, which make us feel even better.

Your attention to detail (through every word on every last page of manuscript) always went above and beyond – and we can't thank you enough.

Lisa Bernstein, Executive Director of the What to Expect Foundation, for your determined dedication to the health and well-being of all babies – and always, for your love, support and friendship. (And, of course, to Zoe, Teddy and Dan Dubno.) Marc Chamlin, Ellen Goldsmith-Vein and Alan Nevins – for protecting me, standing up for me and, most of all, for caring about me. Medora Heibron, for her invaluable insights on adoption. All the dedicated, wonderful people at the American Academy of Pediatrics, whom we can always count on for the most up-to-date (and most balanced) facts and positions. And to the countless AAP members who have answered questions, offered feedback, and helped make this book the best it could be.

With love, to my husband, best friend, partner in parenting, partner in business, and partner in life, Erik Murkoff, for making everything possible. I couldn't begin to do it without you, and I'd never want to try. And to Emma and Wyatt, my inspiration and (real live) guinea pigs; I love you guys.

To two of the best husbands and fathers around, Howard Eisenberg and Tim Hathaway, to those amazing Hathaway kids, Rachel, Ethan and Liz. And to Mildred and Harry Scharaga, Victor Shargai and John Aniello, for your love and support.

To Arlene Eisenberg, for everything; your legacy lives on in the hearts of so many. We'll always love you and miss you.

With admiration, to all the doctors, PNPs and nurses everywhere who take care of babies – and their nervous parents. And to our readers – our inspiration, our favourite resource, and the reason we do what we do – and keep doing (and redoing) it.

– *HEIDI MURKOFF*

CONTENTS

————————— *Part 1* —————————

THE FIRST YEAR

Facts Favouring Breastfeeding ♦ *Breastfeeding Myths* ♦ Facts Favouring Formula Feeding ♦ Factoring in Feelings ♦ When You Can't or Shouldn't Breastfeed ♦ *Adoption and Breastfeeding*

Coping with Motherhood ♦ *Mother Care* ♦ A Changing Lifestyle ♦ *This Book's for You, Too* ♦ Whether or Not to Go Back to Work ♦ *Leave: It's Not Just for Mothers Any More* ♦ Grandparents ♦ A Lack of Grandparents ♦ A Maternity Nurse or Doula ♦ Other Sources of Help ♦ Which Nappies to Use ♦ Quitting Smoking ♦ A Name for Baby ♦ Preparing the Family Pet ♦ Preparing Your Breasts for Breastfeeding ♦ *Don't Express Yourself – Yet*

What it's Important to Know:

What Kind of Practice Is Perfect? ♦ Making Sure Dr Right is Right for You ♦ *A Good Alternative?* ♦ Your Partnership with Dr Right

---

Part 2

OF SPECIAL CONCERN

Chapter 22: The Adopted Baby 657

--- *Part 3* ---

FOR THE FAMILY

Chapter 23: For Mum:
Enjoying the First Year 668

What it's Important to Know:

— *Part 4* —
READY REFERENCE

A PARENTING BOOK
THAT STANDS ALONE

When, some fifteen years ago, the authors of this book's popular predecessor, *What to Expect When You're Expecting,* decided to venture beyond pregnancy to publish a book for new parents, they must have known that they were stepping into crowded and competitive territory. Since Benjamin Spock published his first edition of *Baby and Child Care* in 1946, many authors had tried their hand at writing a book to help us raise happier and healthier children. Among authors following in Dr Spock's footsteps, there was no shortage of experts: paediatricians, child psychologists, academics and assorted specialists. Ironically, these authorities were following in the footsteps of a person who repeatedly reminded parents that, when raising children, one should not rely too heavily on experts; that it is often better to trust your instincts.

What to Expect the First Year was different. It was a project that was both bold in scope and unique in perspective. It promised to explain 'everything parents needed to know about the first year of life'. And rather than being written by experts, it was written by a team of accomplished authors whose only real claim to our attention was that they were parents like ourselves. They set out to provide for other parents answers to questions that they themselves had – or might have had – about raising their own children.

What to Expect the First Year has been very well received and extraordinarily successful. With over 7 million copies in print, it delivers on its promise, and readers have surely validated its parent-centred approach. But its suc-

cess – and the success of this revision – is due, I believe, not only to its broad coverage and unique approach, but also to the careful research that has gone into each topic, the thoughtful and reasoned discussions of everyday problems, and an attention to detail that is often striking.

Written from a parent's point of view, *First Year* offers the kind of advice that parents often appreciate but that professionals seldom think to include. Heidi Murkoff, who originated the idea for *What to Expect When You're Expecting* when she was pregnant with her daughter Emma, no doubt got many of the ideas for this book as she was figuring out how to best feed Emma, dealing with her crying spells, and watching and wondering as Emma grew and progressed through the developmental milestones of the first year. Were Heidi and her co-authors paediatricians as well as parents, they could have drawn on clinical experience and thinking, but perhaps at the expense of their experience and thinking as parents. They may have still mentioned all of the advantages of breastfeeding and the rationale of not starting baby foods until a baby is developmentally ready. But would they have covered the advantages of choosing a name for a baby that is easy to say and to spell, and avoiding names that are trendy or political? They would still have talked about the foods that comprise the 'Baby Daily Dozen' to help assure good nutrition, but would they have told us about saving empty baby food jars to warm and serve small portions? They stress the importance of taking the full dose of a prescribed medicine with all the conviction of your child's doctor, but they add that you might consider chilling the medicine, a trick to make it more palatable without affecting potency. And try using a shallow medicine spoon . . . well, you can read about why.

The scope of *What to Expect the First Year* puts it almost in a category of its own. While some authors do quite well with medical advice, they skimp on the developmental side, or fail to go beyond the basics of nutrition. Others that emphasize child development are unconvincing – and therefore unreassuring – on issues of physical health and disease prevention. This book covers almost everything a parent could want to know about raising an infant. Whether you are preparing formula, removing splinters, considering the advantages of teaching a baby sign language, or are curious about whether the rash is due to fifth disease (slapped-cheek), this book will be of help. It may not always replace more definitive and specialized sources of information, but it probably will. More often than not, *First Year* will get you through until morning!

Readers will appreciate the attention to detail in *First Year*. Among the list of environmental hazards are the seldom-mentioned sewing and knitting supplies that are too small and too sharp to safely occupy the same space as an active and inquisitive eight-month-old. If you want to know about baby acne, how and where to find good in-home child care, what the outlook is for a premature baby with chronic lung disease, or just need a dosage chart for common fever medicines, it's here. The authors' time-tested month-by-month approach, including

the reassuring 'What your child may be doing' section, remains in this second edition. There is also a special section on seasonally appropriate advice, a section on first aid, on premature babies, and on adopted babies. There is special advice for fathers and for siblings. And, as in the past, there is an excellent reference section that covers recipes, home remedies, and common illnesses.

While most of what made the first edition of *First Year* so popular remains, many sections have had important updates. This second edition updates child safety seat information, child CPR recommendations, information for parents of children with special needs, including small prematures, and there is updated information on immunizations and common childhood illnesses. Chapters such as 'Becoming a Father', 'The Adopted Baby', and 'The First Postpartum Days' continue to provide parents with the kinds of practical, reassuring information that keeps this book a top seller year after year.

What to Expect the First Year has not only aged well, it has got better. I have long advised new parents to keep several books on their reference shelf, if possible. But if they had to choose just one book to keep on hand, this should be the one. *What to Expect the First Year* stands alone as well as, if not better than, any current book on infant care.

– *Mark D. Widome, MD, MPH*
Professor of Pediatrics
The Penn State Children's Hospital
Hershey, Pennsylvania

A SECOND BABY IS BORN

How time flies when you've been raising children and writing books. Though it seems like just yesterday (okay, maybe the day before yesterday) when my husband, Erik, and I brought our first baby, Emma, home from the hospital, it's actually been over twenty years (eighteen since we brought home her brother, Wyatt). And though it seems like just yesterday that my co-authors and I delivered the first edition of *What to Expect the First Year,* it's actually been nearly a decade and a half.

Time for another baby? Don't think so (though I'm admittedly tempted whenever a warm bundle gets within cuddling distance, I've become a little too attached to uninterrupted sleep). Time for another edition of *First Year?* Absolutely.

Which brings to mind a question I get a lot: Why would you need to write another edition of *What to Expect the First Year?* Have babies really changed all that much in the last fifteen years?

It's true, though every baby is unique (as second-time parents are quick to discover), as a group today's babies aren't all that different than babies born when *First Year* was (though they are, on average, a bit bigger). They still spend a good amount of time eating, sleeping and crying. They still don't have a whole lot of hair or a whole lot of teeth. They still go through plenty of nappies. They still smell sweeter than any perfume. They're still round and soft and (for lack of a better word) yummy. They still have the same basic needs: food, comfort and lots of love. And because they still don't come with instructions, they still keep their parents guessing (and turning to books like this one) – a lot.

But while babies haven't changed all that much, how we care for them has. From the way we put them to sleep (backs, please, not tummies) to the way we soothe them (how about a massage, baby?) to the way we communicate with them (baby talk out, baby signs in). From guidelines on feeding (breastfeed longer, start solids later) to guidelines on immunization (combined vaccines mean fewer tears) to guidelines on car seat safety (babies now stay rear-facing until their first birthday, no matter how big they get before then). Figure in the explosion of baby products (from nursing pillows to hands-free breast pumps, from angled bottles to spill-proof cups, from high-tech baby monitors to low-tech baby slings), and it's clearly time for a revision.

What can you expect from this second edition? Plenty that's new and improved; dozens of new questions and answers, many of them inspired by reader's letters; expanded sections on a multitude of topics (from understanding your newborn to stimulating your older baby, from juggling career and family to mediating sibling squabbles); a new chapter devoted to breastfeeding; the latest information and the latest trends on everything baby: more illustrations – all of them new.

But because some things about babies never change, you can expect that some things about *What to Expect the First Year* haven't changed, either. The easy-to-use format, the no-question-is-too-silly-to-ask philosophy, the familiar reassurance that breeds comfort – and hopefully, all the help that you'll need to see you and baby happily and healthily through those remarkable (and exhausting) first twelve months.

Wishing you a wonderful First Year!

– *Heidi Murkoff*

THE FIRST YEAR

Get Ready, Get Set

After nearly nine months of wait- ing, there's finally a light at the end of the tunnel (perhaps, even, effacement and dilatation at the end of the cervix). But with just weeks to go before D-day, have you come to terms with your baby coming to term? Will you be ready for your baby's arrival when he or she is ready to arrive?

Even former Girl Guides will find there's no way to be completely prepared for the time when baby makes three (or more). But there are a myriad of steps that can be taken to make the transition a smoother one – from selecting the right baby name to selecting the right hospital, from deciding between breast and bottle to deciding between cloth nappies and disposables, from psyching yourself up for the changes the new arrival will bring to preparing the family dog. The flurry of activity as you attempt to get ready and set may occasionally seem frenzied, but you'll find it good preparation for the even more hectic pace that awaits you after baby's born.

FEEDING YOUR BABY: Breast or Formula, or Both

Perhaps there's never been a ques- tion for you. When you close your eyes and summon up a day- dreamed snapshot of life with baby, you clearly see yourself suckling your pre- cious bundle at the breast or, just as clearly, cuddling your newborn as he or she takes a bottle. Whatever your rea- sons – practical, emotional or medical – your mind was made up about baby feeding early in pregnancy, perhaps even before conception.

Or maybe that snapshot isn't quite so well focused. Maybe you can't exactly see yourself breastfeeding, but you've heard so much about how breast milk is better for baby that you can't see yourself bottle feeding either. Or maybe you'd really like to give breastfeeding a try but fear that it won't mix well with working, or with sleeping, or with romance. Or maybe it's your spouse's mixed feelings – or a friend's, or your mother's – that are giving you second thoughts.

No matter what's causing your indecision, or your ambivalence, or your confusion about the right baby-feeding method for you, the best way to bring that fuzzy picture into focus is to explore the facts, as well as your feelings. First of all, what are the facts?

FACTS FAVOURING BREASTFEEDING

No matter how far technology advances, there will always be some things that nature does better. Among them: formulate the best food and best food delivery system for babies – a system that is at the same time good for mothers. As Oliver Wendell Holmes Senior said well over a century ago, 'A pair of substantial mammary glands has the advantage over the two hemispheres of the most learned professor's brain in the art of compounding a nutritious fluid for infants.' Today, paediatricians, obstetricians, midwives, even manufacturers of infant formula concur: under most circumstances, breast is best by far. Here are just some of the reasons why:

It's custom-made. Tailored to the needs of human infants, breast milk contains at least 100 ingredients that are not found in cow's milk and that can't be synthesized in the laboratory. Moreover, unlike formula, the composition of breast milk changes constantly to meet a baby's ever-changing needs: it's different in the morning than it is in the late afternoon; different at the beginning of a feeding than at the end; different the first month than the seventh; different for a premature baby than for a term baby. The nutrients in breast milk are matched to an infant's needs and his or her ability to handle them. For example, breast milk contains less sodium than cow's milk

formula, making it easier for a baby's kidneys to handle.

It goes down easily. Breast milk is designed for a human baby's sensitive and still-developing digestive system, rather than for a young calf's. Its protein (mostly lactalbumin) and its fat are more easily handled by the baby than are the protein (mostly caseinogen) and fat in cow's milk. Infants also have an easier time absorbing the important micronutrients in breast milk than those in cow's milk (in which, again, nutrients are designed to be absorbed by the young calf). The practical result: Breastfed babies may be less likely to suffer from gas and excessive spitting up.

It's safe. You can be sure that the milk served up from your breasts isn't improperly prepared, spoiled or contaminated (assuming that you don't have an illness that would make breastfeeding unsafe for baby; few illnesses do).

It keeps allergies on hold. Babies are almost never allergic to breast milk. Though an infant may be sensitive to something a mother has eaten that has passed into her milk, breast milk itself is virtually always tolerated well. On the other hand, more than one out of ten infants, after an initial exposure, turn out to be allergic to cow's milk formula. (A switch to a soya or hydrolysate formula usually solves the problem – though such formulas stray even farther from the composition of human milk than cow's milk formula.[1]) Some studies also show that breastfed babies may be less likely to get childhood asthma and eczema than those babies fed formula.

---

1. Soya *milks,* however, are not nutritionally adequate and should not be used for infant feeding. Neither is cow's milk; babies should be fed formula only.

It's a tummy soother. Because of breast milk's naturally laxative effect and because of the easier digestibility of breast milk, infants who nurse are almost never constipated. Also, though their movements are normally very loose, diarrhoea is rarely a problem. In fact, breast milk appears to reduce the risk of digestive upset both by destroying harmful microorganisms and by encouraging the growth of beneficial ones.

It keeps nappy rash away. The breast-fed baby's sweet-smelling movements are less likely to cause nappy rash, though this advantage (as well as the less objectionable odour) disappears once solids are introduced.

It's an infection preventer. From the first time to the last time infants suckle at their mothers' breasts, they get a healthy dose of antibodies to bolster their immunity to disease. In general, they will come down with fewer colds, ear infections, lower respiratory tract infections, urinary tract infections, and other illnesses than bottle-fed infants, and when they do, they will usually recover more quickly and with fewer complications. Breastfeeding also improves the immune response to immunizations for most diseases (such as tetanus, diphtheria and polio). Plus, it may offer some protection against Sudden Infant Death Syndrome (SIDS).

It's a fat flattener. Breastfed infants are often less chubby than their bottle-fed peers. That is, in part, because breast-feeding puts baby's appetite in charge of consumption. A breastfed baby is likely to stop when satiated, while a bottle-fed infant may be urged to continue sucking until the bottle's emptied. In addition, breast milk is actually calorie controlled. The hindmilk (the milk a baby gets at the end of a nursing session) is higher in calories than the milk at the beginning and tends to make a baby feel full – a signal to stop sucking. Nursing also appears to somewhat lower the risk of obesity during childhood and later in life. Recent studies show that children who are mostly breastfed as infants are less likely to be overweight as teenagers than their formula-fed peers. The studies also found that the longer an infant was breastfed, the less likely he or she is to be overweight. Breastfeeding may also be linked to lower cholesterol readings in adulthood.

It's a brain booster. Breastfeeding appears to slightly increase a child's IQ, at least through age fifteen, and possibly into adulthood. This may be related not only to the brain-building fatty acids (DHA) in breast milk but also to the closeness and mother-baby interaction that is built into breastfeeding, which possibly fosters intellectual development.

More sucking satisfaction. A baby can continue sucking at a nearly empty breast once a feeding is over. This non-nutritive sucking comes in especially handy if baby is distressed and needs to be calmed down. An empty bottle does not allow for continued sucking.

It builds stronger mouths. Mother's nipples and baby's mouth are a perfect match (though it often doesn't seem so the first time mother and baby try to work together). Even the most scientifically designed artificial teat fails to give a baby's jaws, gums, teeth and palate the workout he or she would get at mother's breast – a workout that ensures optimum oral development and some perks for baby's future teeth. Babies who are breastfed are less likely to get cavities later on in childhood than those who were not.

There are also breastfeeding benefits for the mother (and father):

Convenience. Breast milk is the ultimate convenience food, always in stock, ready to use, clean and consistently at the perfect temperature. No formula to run out of, shop for, or lug around, no bottles to clean or refill, no powders to mix, no feedings to warm. Wherever you are – in bed, on the road, at a restaurant, on the beach – all the nourishment your baby needs is always ready and waiting. Should baby and mother be apart for the night, the day, or even the weekend, breast milk can be expressed in advance and stored in the refrigerator or freezer for bottle feedings.

Lower cost. Breast milk is free, whereas bottle feeding can be an expensive proposition. With breastfeeding, there are no bottles or formula to buy; there are no half-emptied bottles or opened cans of formula to waste.

Quicker postpartum recovery. All your motivations for breastfeeding don't have to be selfless ones. Because breastfeeding is part of the natural cycle of pregnancy-childbirth-mothering, it is designed to be better not just for baby but for you as well. It will help your uterus shrink back to prepregnancy size more quickly (that's the increased cramping you'll likely feel during the first postpartum days as your baby suckles), which in turn will reduce your flow of lochia (the postpartum discharge) more rapidly, which means less blood loss. And it will help you shed leftover pregnancy weight by burning upwards of 500 extra calories a day. Some of this weight was laid down in the form of fat reserves especially to help you produce milk; now's your chance to use it.

***Some* protection against pregnancy.** Ovulation and menstruation are suppressed in most (though not all) nursing mothers at least until their babies begin to take significant supplementation (whether in the form of formula or solids), often until weaning, and sometimes for several months afterwards. (Which doesn't mean that you can't become pregnant. Since ovulation can quietly precede your first postpartum period, you can never be certain as to when the protection you've been receiving from breastfeeding will stop. See page 697 for more on birth control.)

Cancer risk reduction. Feeding your baby via the breast can reduce your risk of some cancers down the road. Women who breastfeed have a slightly lower risk of developing uterine cancer, ovarian cancer and premenopausal breast cancer.

Bone building. Women who nurse have a lower risk of developing osteoporosis later in life than women who have never breastfed.

Enforced rest periods. Breastfeeding ensures frequent breaks in your day, especially at first (sometimes more frequent than you'd like). Whether or not you feel you have the time to relax, your postpartum body needs the time off your feet that breastfeeding forces you to take.

Less complicated night-time feedings. Even parents who can't get enough of their adorable infants during the day don't always look forward to seeing them at 2 AM (or at any other time between midnight and dawn). But baby's night-time waking can be a lot easier to take when comfort is as close as your breasts, instead of far off in the refrigerator, needing to be poured into a bottle. (It's even easier on mum if dad completes the transfer of baby from cot to breast and back again.)

BREASTFEEDING MYTHS

MYTH: You can't breastfeed if you have small breasts or flat nipples.
Reality: In no way does outward appearance affect the production of milk or a mother's ability to dispense it. Breasts and nipples of all shapes and sizes can satisfy a hungry baby. Inverted nipples that don't become erect when stimulated don't even usually need any preparation to make them fully functional; see page 26.

MYTH: Breastfeeding is a lot of trouble.
Reality: Never again will it be so easy to feed your children (once you get the hang of it). Breasts, unlike bottles, are ready when baby is. You don't have to remember to take them with you when you're planning a day at the beach, lug them in a changing bag, or worry about the milk inside them spoiling in the hot sun.

MYTH: Breastfeeding ties you down.
Reality: It's true that breastfeeding is naturally better suited to mothers who plan to be with their babies most of the time. But those who are willing to make the effort to express and store milk, or who prefer to supplement with formula, can satisfy both their need to work – or see a movie, or go to an all-day seminar – and their desire to breastfeed. And when it comes to stepping out with baby, it's the breastfeeding mother who is more mobile, always having an ample supply of food along no matter where she goes or how long she plans to stay.

MYTH: Breastfeeding will ruin your breasts.
Reality: Much to the surprise of many people, it's not breastfeeding that affects the shape or size of your breasts but rather pregnancy itself. During pregnancy, your breasts prepare for lactation, even if you don't end up nursing – and these changes are sometimes permanent. Excessive weight gain during pregnancy, hereditary factors, age or poor support (going bra-less) can also result in breasts that are less firm. Breastfeeding is blame free.

MYTH: Breastfeeding didn't work the first time so it won't work again.
Reality: Even if you had trouble breastfeeding your first baby, research shows that you'll likely produce more milk and have an easier time breastfeeding the second time around. The adage 'If at first you don't succeed, try, try again' emphatically applies to nursing.

MYTH: Breastfeeding excludes dad.
Reality: A father who wants to be involved in the care of his nursing infant can find ample opportunity – for bathing, nappy changing, holding, rocking, playing with, bottle feeding with expressed milk or supplemental formula, and, once solids are introduced, spooning those 'trains into the tunnel'.

Eventually, easier multitasking. Once you become proficient at nursing – and master the one-arm manoeuvre – you'll find that you can nurse and do just about anything else at the same time – page through a magazine, check your e-mail, or read your toddler a favourite book. (Just make sure that you spend plenty of nursing time interacting with your baby, too.)

Strong mother-baby bond. As almost any mother who's ever breastfed will tell you, the breastfeeding benefit you're likely to treasure most is the bond it nurtures between mother and child. There's skin-to-skin and eye-to-eye contact, and the opportunity to cuddle, baby-babble and coo built right into the breastfeeding experience. True, you can enjoy the same pleasures when bottle feeding, but it takes more of a conscious effort (see page 104), since you may frequently be faced with the temptation to relegate the feeding to others when you're tired, for example, or to prop the bottle when you're busy. Another benefit for breast-feeding mums: Research suggests that women who breastfeed are somewhat less likely to suffer from postnatal depression.

FACTS FAVOURING FORMULA FEEDING

If there were no advantages to bottle feeding, no one who was able to breastfeed would ever turn to formula. But there are some very real advantages, and for some mothers (and some fathers) they are compelling, even in light of breastfeeding's many benefits:

Longer satisfaction for baby. Infant formula made from cow's milk is more difficult to digest than breast milk, and the large rubbery curds it forms stay in a baby's stomach longer, giving a feeling of satiety that can last several hours, extending the period between feedings to three or four hours even early on. Because breast milk is easily and quickly digested, on the other hand, many nursing newborns feed so often that it sometimes seems as though they're permanently attached to their mothers' breasts. Though this frequent nursing serves a practical purpose – it stimulates the production of milk and improves the supply – it can be time-consuming for mum.

Easy monitoring of intake. You know just how much a bottle-fed baby is taking. Because breasts aren't calibrated to measure baby's intake, a nursing mother may worry that her newborn isn't getting enough to eat (though that's rarely the case – especially once nursing is established – since breastfed babies tend to eat as much as they need). The bottle-feeding mother has no such problem – a glance at the bottle tells her exactly what she wants to know. (This can be a disadvantage, however, if anxious parents push babies to take more than they want.)

More freedom. Formula feeding doesn't tie the mother to baby day and night. Want to take in dinner and a show with your spouse? Or even get away for a romantic weekend? A grandparent or a baby-sitter can stand in. Intend to go back to work when the baby is three months old? No weaning or expressing breast milk will be necessary – just a daily supply of bottles and formula for the child-care provider to use to feed your baby. (Of course, these options are also open to breastfeeding mums who express milk or supplement with formula.)

Fewer demands. The woman exhausted by a difficult labour may be grateful to have the option of sleeping through middle-of-the-night or crack-of-dawn feedings. Dad, grandma (if she's come to stay), a baby nurse, a doula or anyone else on hand can take over those honours. There's also less of a physical drain on a newly delivered mother's resources if she doesn't have to add milk production to her many daily – and nightly – challenges.

More participation for father. Dads can share in the pleasures of baby feeding when baby is bottle fed in a way that's impossible with the breastfed infant, unless you pump regularly or supplement with formula.

More participation for older siblings. An older child will feel very much involved in taking care of his or her 'new baby' when giving a bottle. (Again, this option is also open to breastfeeders who supplement with expressed milk or formula.)

No interference with fashion. A bottle-feeding mother can dress as she pleases. The nursing mother's wardrobe is not quite as limited as it was when she was pregnant, but most of the time she won't be able to put fashion before practicality. She'll have to forgo one-piece dresses that don't button up the front. (Try accommodating a hungry baby by lifting your dress over your waist and you'll see why.)

Less restriction on birth control methods. A breastfeeding mother has to limit her choice of contraception to those methods that are safe during lactation (but there are many; see page 697). The formula-feeding mum has no such restrictions.

Fewer dietary demands and restrictions. A formula-feeding mother can stop eating for two. Unlike the nursing mum, she can give up the extra protein and calcium, and she can forget about her prenatal vitamin supplements. She can have a few drinks at a party, take prescription medicine, eat all the spicy foods and cabbage she wants (though many babies won't object to these tastes in breast milk), without worrying about the possible effect on her baby. After the first six weeks postpartum (but not before, when her body is still in the recovery phase), she can diet somewhat more strenuously to take off any pregnancy weight that lingers. This is something that the breastfeeding mother can't do until baby is weaned – though, because of the calories milk production requires, she may not have to diet at all to reach her goal.

Less embarrassment for the modest. While the nursing mother may receive curious (or unfortunately, sometimes glaring) glances when she chooses to breastfeed in public, no one will look twice or askance at a woman bottle-feeding her baby. Neither will the bottle-feeding mother need to worry about the sometimes awkward procedure of redressing (refastening bra flaps, retucking in shirts, rebuttoning buttons) after the feeding is done. (These hang-ups, though, are often quickly hung up; many women who opt to try to breast-feed soon find it becomes second nature – even in crowded restaurants.)

Potentially, more lovemaking. After months of making love under somewhat less than ideal conditions, many couples look forward to picking up where they left off before conception. For some breastfeeding women, a vagina left dry by the hormonal changes of lactation, teamed with sore nipples and leaky breasts, can make lovemaking a challenge. For the bottle-feeding mother, once she's recovered from delivery, nothing (except for an unexpectedly awake and crying baby) need stand between her and her mate.

FACTORING IN FEELINGS

The facts are before you; you've read them and reread them, considered them and reconsidered them. And yet perhaps you're still left undecided. That's because, as with many other decisions you're making these days, the decision between breast and formula doesn't depend just on facts. It also depends on feelings.

Do you feel that you really want to breastfeed but believe it's impractical because you're planning to go back to work soon after your baby is born? Don't let circumstances deprive you and your baby of the experience. A few weeks of nursing are better than none at all; both of you stand to benefit from even the briefest encounter with it. And with a little extra dedication and planning (okay, maybe a lot of extra dedication and planning), you should be able to work out a system for continuing to breastfeed even after you've returned to your job (see page 246).

Do you feel fundamentally negative about breastfeeding yet find the facts in favour of it too convincing to ignore? Here again, you might give nursing a try. If your feelings don't take a shift towards the positive, you can quit. At least your baby will have reaped the benefits of breastfeeding for a short time (which is better than no time at all), and you'll know that you tried, erasing those nagging doubts. (It's best not to quit before you've given nursing your best shot, however. A really fair trial would last at least a month, or better six weeks, since for some women it could take that long to establish a good nursing relationship even under the best of circumstances.)

Do you feel fundamentally uncomfortable with – even averse to – the idea of breastfeeding? Or have you previously breastfed and not enjoyed it? Even under these circumstances, it would still be wise to seriously consider a six-week trial run, which will give your child some of the benefits of breastfeeding and give you a chance to put your feelings to the test. If after this attempt, you still feel breastfeeding is not for you, you can turn to formula without regret.

Do you fear that you won't be able to nurse because of a highly-strung (can't-sit-still) temperament, but agree that breast milk is best for baby? Again, you have nothing to lose by trying, and you have everything to gain should your personality turn out to be more compatible with breastfeeding than you thought. Don't judge the situation too early in the game, however. Even women ordinarily graced with saint-like calm can find the first few weeks of

breastfeeding (or motherhood, for that matter) a time of high anxiety. Many, however, are surprised to find that once a smoothly working breastfeeding relationship is established, nursing is stress-reducing rather than stress-producing – the hormones released as baby suckles actually enhance relaxation, and the experience itself is one of the healthiest routes to tension relief. (At the beginning, give yourself the best chance of success by unwinding with some relaxation techniques before nursing your newborn.) Keep in mind that you can always switch to formula later, should your initial instincts prove correct.

If dad feels jealous or unsettled at the thought of your breastfeeding, have him read the facts, too. They may persuade him that his loss (which, after all, is only a temporary one) or his distaste (which will also be temporary; once breastfeeding begins, most fathers find they watch in wonder) will be baby's gain. Also show him the section on breastfeeding and fathers in chapter 24. It may help to bring in a paediatrician, family doctor or lactation consultant to reinforce the facts. Talking to other fathers whose babies have breastfed will also help him feel more comfortable, while contributing to your already compelling case. Keep in mind that his support is extremely important and worth winning over. Though you can certainly breastfeed without it, studies show that women who have the wholehearted support of their partners during breastfeeding are far more likely to stick with it.

No matter the reasons that bring them to breastfeeding, most women ultimately find it an overwhelmingly positive experience – joyful, exhilarating and incomparably fulfilling (at least, once they and their babies get the hang of it). Even those women who begin to breastfeed out of duty often continue to do it because of the pleasure it brings them. Many who, before baby arrives, can't imagine engaging in such an intimate act in the company of strangers live to eat their words and to lift their shirts at the sound of baby's first cry – on an aeroplane, in a crowded park, at a restaurant.

In the end, however, if you opt not to breastfeed (with or without a trial run), don't feel guilty. Almost nothing you do for your baby is right if it doesn't feel right for you – and that includes breastfeeding. Even babies who were born yesterday are wise enough to sense feelings of uneasiness in their mothers; a bottle given lovingly can be better for your infant than a breast offered grudgingly.

WHEN YOU CAN'T OR SHOULDN'T BREASTFEED

For some women, the pros and cons of breastfeeding and formula feeding are academic. They don't have the option of nursing their new babies, either because of their own health or their baby's. The most common maternal factors that *may* prevent or interfere with breastfeeding include:

◆ Serious debilitating illness (such as heart or kidney disease, or severe anaemia), or extreme underweight (your body needs fat stores to produce milk) – though some women do manage to overcome these obstacles and breastfeed their babies.

◆ Serious infection, such as active, untreated tuberculosis (after two weeks of treatment, breastfeeding should be okay); or AIDS or HIV infection, which can be transmitted via body fluids, including breast milk. You *can* nurse if you are infected with hepatitis A (after baby receives gamma globulin) or hepatitis B (after baby receives gamma globulin and the hepatitis B vaccine).[2]

◆ A condition requiring regular medication that passes into the breast milk and might be harmful to the baby, such as anticancer, some antithyroid or antihypertensive drugs; lithium, tranquillizers or sedatives. A temporary need for medications, such as penicillin, even at the time you begin nursing, should not interfere with breastfeeding. Women who need antibiotics during labour or because of a breast infection (mastitis) can continue to breastfeed while on the medication. Always check with baby's doctor before starting a new medicine during lactation.

◆ Drug abuse – including the use of tranquillizers, amphetamines, barbiturates or other pills, heroin, methadone, cocaine, marijuana, or the abuse of alcohol (an occasional drink is okay; see page 91).

◆ Exposure to certain toxic chemicals in the workplace. To determine whether you have been exposed to toxic chemicals in your workplace, check with the Health and Safety department of your local council.

◆ Inadequate glandular tissue in the breasts (this has nothing to do with the size of your breasts) or damage to the nerve supply to the nipple (as from injury or surgery). In some cases you may be able to attempt

2. If you develop an infection while nursing, by the time the diagnosis has been made, the baby has already been exposed. Continue nursing so your baby receives your antibodies from your breast milk.

ADOPTION AND BREASTFEEDING

Just because you haven't given birth to your baby doesn't necessarily mean that you can't breastfeed. With plenty of advance planning and preparation, adopting mothers can sometimes suc-cessfully breastfeed their infants (though usually not without supplementation) if they get started within a few days after birth. See page 661 for tips on breast-feeding an adopted baby.

---

breastfeeding, but under careful medical supervision, to be certain your baby is thriving. If you've had surgery for breast cancer in one breast, ask your doctor about the possibility of nursing from the other.

Some conditions in the newborn may make breastfeeding difficult, but not impossible (with the right medical support). They include:

◆ A metabolic disorder, such as PKU or lactose intolerance, that makes the baby unable to digest both human and cow's milk. Treatment for babies with PKU involves supplementing with a phenylalanine-free formula. Formula feedings can be combined with breast-feeding as long as blood levels are carefully monitored and the amount of breastfeeding is controlled. In the case of lactose intolerance (which is extremely rare in infancy), expressed mother's milk can be treated with lac-tase to make it digestible.

◆ Cleft lip and/or cleft palate that interferes with suckling at the breast. In some cases, especially when only cleft lip is present, it is possible to breastfeed. Using a special mouth appliance can allow a baby with a cleft palate to breastfeed. Ask to see a lactation consultant before you make a feeding decision. It may also be feasible to express breast milk until after surgery (usually per-formed during the first few weeks of life), and to begin breastfeeding then.

If you can't breastfeed, or if you just don't wish to, be assured that a commercial baby formula will almost certainly nourish your baby adequately (rare exceptions would include infants with multiple allergies who require spe-cial formulas). Millions of healthy, happy babies (possibly, you among them) have been raised on the bottle, and your baby can be, too.

What You May Be Concerned About

COPING WITH MOTHERHOOD

'Everything's ready for the baby – except me. I just can't picture myself as a mother.'

Even those women who pictured themselves as mothers from the first time they held a baby doll often start to doubt the validity of their calling when it threatens to become a round-the-clock reality. Those who spurned dolls for

---

MOTHER CARE

Whether you're still impatiently awaiting baby's arrival, or you've just brought your brand-new bundle of joy home, you probably have almost as many questions about how to care for yourself in the postpartum period as you do about how to care for your newborn. Turn to chapter 23 for information on the first postpartum year.

---

relationships with trucks and footballs, mowed lawns instead of baby-sitting, and rarely gave passing buggies more than a passing glance (until the day their pregnancy test came back positive) may face delivery day with even greater trepidation.

But not only is this ninth-month crumbling of confidence normal, it's healthy. Strolling into motherhood (or parenthood, for that matter) blithely self-assured may only set you up for a swift and unsettling jolt of reality when the job turns out to be more overwhelming than you'd imagined – which it almost always is, at least at first.

So if you don't feel ready for motherhood, don't worry. But do prepare. Read at least the first few chapters in this book and everything else you can about newborns and infants (always keeping in mind that babies don't always go 'by the book'). Spend some time, if possible, with newborns or young babies; hold them, even change their nappies as you get the scoop (and the poop) from their parents about the pleasures and challenges of caring for an infant. Taking a parenting course will also help prepare you for the toughest (and ultimately, the most fulfilling) job you'll ever love. (All of this advice also applies for soon-to-be fathers approaching this new role with some trepidation.)

Most of all, realize that mothers (and fathers) are not born – they're created on the job. A woman who's gained some experience with other people's infants may be somewhat more comfortable at

first than the mother who's a complete novice, but by the six-week checkup it will be difficult to tell them apart.

A CHANGING LIFESTYLE

'I really look forward to having my baby. But I worry that the lifestyle my spouse and I have grown accustomed to will completely change.'

To be sure, nappies aren't the only things that will be changing around your house once baby arrives. Most everything about your lifestyle – from your priorities to your attitudes, from your sleeping patterns to your eating patterns, from the way you spend your days and nights to the way you spend your weekends, from romance to finance – will change, at least to some degree. For instance, you may still be able to eat some lunches and dinners out (especially if you're going back to work), but fewer of them may be at candlelit French bistros and more of them at family-style eateries with high chairs and a high tolerance for peas and carrots ground into the carpeting. Late nights in are likely to take the place of late nights out; breakfast in bed is likely to take on a whole new meaning (a 5 AM nursing session, rather than coffee, croissants and the weekend paper at 11); lovemaking is less likely to be inspired by passion than scheduled around baby's nap (if it's scheduled at all). Silk blouses and wool trousers will probably be tucked away in the back of the cupboard to make room for washables that can weather encounters with spit-up and leaky nappies; more movies will be seen on DVD than in cinemas (and chances are once you do get back to the cinema on a regular basis, it will be to catch the first runs of the latest animated blockbuster).

In other words, little babies make a big difference in how you live your life. But while every couple finds that their lifestyle changes somewhat once they become parents, just how much yours will change will depend on you, your spouse and, most of all, your baby. Some parents find they don't miss their child-free lifestyles all that much; for the most part, cocooning as a cozy threesome suits them. Some parents find they don't miss it as much as they thought they would, but also find they crave a little nightlife with their home life (in which case, regular Saturday-night baby-sitters can accommodate that craving). Some babies turn out to be more adaptable (which means they can be easily toted on evenings out and weekend excursions); others turn out to be slaves to their feeding and eating schedules (which means their parents will probably have to be, too).

So while the lifestyle changes are ones you're better off preparing for now – at least emotionally – it's hard to predict until parenthood is upon you how extensive yours will be and how you'll feel about them. It helps to keep in mind that change, while always challenging, can be exciting, too. Though there's no doubt your life will be different, there's also no doubt that it will be – in so many ways – richer and better than ever. Just ask any parent.

WHETHER OR NOT TO GO BACK TO WORK

'Every time I talk to a friend or read an article on the subject, I change my mind about whether or not to go back to work soon after my baby is born.'

Today's expectant working woman has it all to look forward to: all the satisfaction of a fulfilling career, all the joy of raising a family – and all the guilt, anxiety and confusion inherent in deciding which of the two will hold priority in her life after delivery.

But while it seems as though this is a choice you should make now, it really isn't. Deciding, while you're still pregnant, whether you'll stay home or go back to work (and when) after baby is born is like choosing between a job you're familiar with and one you know nothing about. Instead, assuming you have the options, keep them open until you've spent some time at home with your baby. You may find that nothing you've ever done – including your

---

THIS BOOK'S FOR YOU, TOO

As you read *What to Expect the First Year*, you'll notice many references to traditional family relationships – to 'wives', 'husbands', 'spouses'. These references are not meant to exclude mothers and fathers who are single, who have same-sex partners, or who have chosen not to marry their live-in partners. These terms are, rather, a way of avoiding phrases (for instance 'your husband or significant other') that may be more inclusive but also more cumbersome to read. Please mentally edit out any phrase that doesn't fit and replace it with one that's right for you and your situation.

LEAVE: IT'S NOT JUST FOR MOTHERS ANY MORE

There's no better way for a fledgling family to get to know each other than by spending the first few weeks at home, undisturbed by work or other distracting obligations. It's also the best way for new mums and dads to learn the ropes of the parenting business. And that's why more and more fathers are taking advantage of the new paternity leave rights (which came into effect in April 2003). Eligible employees can choose to take either one week or two weeks' paternity leave (though not odd days), either from the date of the baby's birth or from a chosen number of days or weeks after the birth. Some family-friendly companies offer even better plans for new parents. Check with your company, and see page 721 for more details.

job – has ever given you as much satisfaction as caring for your newborn does, and you may postpone going back to work indefinitely. Or you may find that, as much as you enjoy being a mother, you're not cut out for full-time parenting – you miss your career too much. Or you may find that you'd like to combine the best of both worlds by taking a part-time position, job sharing with another parent, or working from home full- or part-time. Keep in mind that there are no 'right' decisions when it comes to this very personal question – only the decision that's right for you. Remember, too, that you can always change your mind if the decision you think is right turns out to be all wrong. (See page 716 for some advice on making the decision once baby appears on the scene.)

GRANDPARENTS

'My mother has her bags packed and is ready to fly in "to give me a hand" the moment the baby arrives. The idea makes me nervous because my mother tends to take over, but I don't want to hurt her feelings and tell her not to come.'

Whether it's loving and warm, distant and frosty, or tottering on the brink somewhere in between, a woman's relationship with her mother (or mother-in-law) is one of the most complicated in her life. It becomes even more so when daughter becomes mother, and mother becomes grandmother. Though there may be hundreds of times in the next couple of decades when your wishes will come into conflict with those of your parents, this may be the one situation that will set the precedent for those to come.

In other words, the timing of the first grandparents' visit is one of the first decisions you'll make as parents. You should base it, like most decisions you'll make as parents, on what's right for the two of you and for your new arrival. If you feel that yours is a threesome that wouldn't benefit from company right now – particularly the kind of company that tends to bring a lot of baggage (and we're not talking just suitcases) – then your decision should reflect this. Let your parents (and your in-laws, too, if necessary) know that you and your spouse need to spend some time alone with the baby before they pay their first visit.

Explain that this time will allow you to become more comfortable in your new roles, to adjust to your new life, and to bond with your new family member. Assure them that their company and their help with the baby and around the house will be most welcome in a few weeks. Remind your mother, too, that the baby will be more responsive, more interesting, more awake and more photogenic by then (sleeping babies all tend to look alike, anyway).

Your mother may feel a little hurt at first, even a little rejected or angry – and she may even deploy that not-so-secret maternal weapon, guilt. But don't worry (and don't cave in). Once she holds her grandchild in her arms, chances are all will be forgiven and forgotten. What won't be forgotten is that you and your spouse are the ones who set the rules for your family, an important concept to relay to parents and in-laws early (particularly those with the tendency to take charge).

On the other hand, many new mums and dads feel an urge to renew or strengthen the bonds with their own parents during pregnancy and afterwards. And some new parents welcome the experience, the extra sets of hands, and perhaps the hot dinners and vacuumed carpets that come with a postpartum visit from grandparents. Just as those who feel the need to say, 'Mother, I'd rather do it myself,' shouldn't be plagued by guilt, those who feel they need the help shouldn't have qualms about saying, 'I'd rather *not* do it myself.' The decision that's right for you is the right decision to make.

'My in-laws have opinions on everything to do with our baby and how we're going to raise her – from feeding and sleeping schedules to whether I should go back to work. I love them, but how do I get them to butt out?'

It's not an easy concept to grasp at first (though it does sink in eventually, usually in the middle of a 3 AM feeding or a four-hour colic bout): you are the parents now. It's a job that comes with enormous pleasures, but also with enormous responsibilities. And one of the first responsibilities you'll have is letting your in-laws know that you and your spouse are responsible for the care, feeding and raising of your new daughter. The sooner you convey this message, the sooner everyone can start feeling comfortable in their new roles (you as parents, your in-laws as grandparents).

Say it early (and often, if necessary), say it firmly, but most of all, say it lovingly. Explain to your well-meaning but interfering in-laws that they did a great job of raising your spouse, and now it's his turn and yours to be the parents. There will be times when you'll welcome their advice (especially if grandma has catalogued somewhere in her vast reserves of experience a sure-fire trick for calming a crying newborn), but other times when you'll want to learn from your paediatrician, your baby books and your mistakes – much as they probably did. Explain, too, that not only is it important for you to set the rules (as they did when they first became parents), but that many of the rules have changed (babies are no longer put to sleep on their tummies or fed on a schedule) since they were in the parenting game, which is why their way of doing things may no longer be recommended. And don't forget to say it with humour. Point out that chances are, the changing tables will turn once again when your daughter becomes a parent – and accuses you of dispensing old-fashioned advice.

That said, keep two things in mind. Firstly, the wisdom that grandparents bring with them is invaluable. Whether you feel your parents (or your spouse's) did a great job raising you or just a fair one, there is always something to be learned from their experience, even if it's only what not to do. Though plenty of fine-tuning and refashioning is inevitably necessary, there's no point in completely reinventing the wheel – or parenting practices – with every generation. And secondly, if parenthood is a responsibility, grandparenthood is the reward – one you will someday want to enjoy yourself. As you assert your independence as parents, be sure you don't deprive your in-laws of their reward.

A LACK OF GRANDPARENTS

'My spouse's parents are deceased. Mine are elderly and live several hundred miles away. I feel I have no family to talk to about my pregnancy and about the baby. I think it will be worse when she arrives.'

You're not alone in feeling alone. While in generations past the extended family rarely extended beyond the county line (and often no further than the house next door), millions of couples in today's mobile society live hundreds or thousands of miles from parents and family. Never is this separation more keenly felt – on both sides – than when a new generation is being added.

Keeping in touch with your parents by phone, e-mail, videos, photos and regular visits will help fill the gap between far-flung generations, and will also help your baby get to know her grandparents as she grows. But for the kind of emotional and practical support you'll be craving after the baby's born, and might otherwise get from your parents if they lived nearby, you'll

need to find surrogates. Parent groups, which sometimes evolve out of antenatal or exercise classes, or simply develop spontaneously among casual acquaintances, can provide that kind of support (plus a plethora of swapped baby-care tips). So can places of worship, especially those with a strong sense of community and lots of young families. You might also consider spending time with a senior citizen (or senior couple) in your area who is far from his or her family, too, and misses the company of grandchildren as much as you miss the company of a grandparent. Weekly visits and joint outings can give you and your baby a sense of family, while giving your 'adopted' grandparent or grandparents a sense of being needed – filling the void all around.

A MATERNITY NURSE OR DOULA

'Some of my friends hired maternity nurses when their babies were born. Do I need one, too?'

If you've determined there's enough money in your budget for a baby nurse (they don't come cheap), you'll need to consider several other factors before deciding whether or not to hire one. Here are some reasons why you might opt for the help:

◆ To get some hands-on training in baby care. If you haven't had experience or taken a parenting class and feel you'd rather not learn from the mistakes you make on the job and on your baby, a good baby nurse will be able to instruct in such basics as bathing, burping, changing nappies and even breastfeeding. If this is your reason for hiring a nurse, however, be sure that the person you hire is as interested in teaching as you are in learning. Some won't tolerate novice parents peeping over their shoulders; one with such a dictatorial take-charge attitude can leave you as inexperienced and unsure when she departs as you were when she arrived.

♦ To avoid getting up in the middle of the night for feedings. If you're formula feeding and would rather sleep through the night, at least in the early weeks of postpartum fatigue, a baby nurse, on duty twenty-four hours a day or hired just for nights, can take over or share this feeding responsibility with you and your spouse.

♦ To spend more time with an older child. Some parents hire a baby nurse so that they can be more available to their older children, and hopefully spare them the pangs of jealousy that are often provoked by new arrivals. Such a nurse might be hired to work just a few hours a day during the time you want to spend with your older child. If this is your major reason for hiring a nurse, however, keep in mind that her presence will probably serve only to postpone feelings of sibling jealousy. See chapter 25 for sibling issues.

♦ To give yourself a chance to recuperate after a Caesarean or difficult vaginal birth. Since you probably won't know if you're going to have a difficult time beforehand, it's not a bad idea to do some scouting around for nurses in advance, just in case. If you have the name of a potential nurse or two, or at least have spoken to an agency, you can call shortly after you deliver and have a helper hired before you get home.

A baby nurse may not be the best solution to your postpartum needs if:

♦ You're breastfeeding. Since a nurse can't feed a nursing newborn, and feeding is one of the most time-consuming tasks in the care of a young baby, she may not prove to be all that helpful. For the nursing mother, household help – someone to cook, clean and do laundry – is probably a wiser investment, unless you can find a nurse who will do these chores and also offer breastfeeding tips.

♦ You're not comfortable with a stranger living in your home. If the idea of having a non-family member sharing your bathroom, your kitchen and your table twenty-four hours a day makes you uneasy, hire a part-time nurse rather than a live-in, or opt for one of the other sources of help described below.

♦ You'd rather do it yourself. If you want to be the one to give the first bath, catch sight of the first smile (even if they say it's only gas), soothe your baby through the first bout of crying (even if it's at 2 AM), don't hire a nurse, hire household help to free you up for fun with baby.

♦ Dad would rather do it, too. If you and your spouse are planning to share baby care, a nurse may get in the way. There may also not be much left for her to do – except to collect her paycheque – especially if dad's around full-time while he's enjoying paternity leave. In that case, the money could probably be more sensibly spent on cleaning help.

If you decide that a baby nurse is right for you, the best way to go about finding one is to ask for recommendations from friends who've used one. Be sure to find out if the nurse in question has the qualifications and qualities you're looking for. Some cook, some don't. Some will do light housework and laundry, others won't. Some are gentle, motherly women who will nurture your innate mothering ability and leave you feeling more confident; others are bossy, cold and patronizing and will leave you feeling totally inadequate. Many are qualified nurses; some have also been trained specifically in caring for mother as well as baby, in mother-child relations, and in teaching breastfeeding and child-care basics. A personal interview is extremely important, since it's the only way to know whether you are going to feel comfortable with a particular candidate. But excellent references (do check them out) are a must. A nurse hired through an agency should be registered. It's also very important that a nurse – or anyone else you hire who may come in contact with the baby – has been screened for TB. She should also be trained in CPR and child safety, as well as be up-to-date on baby-care practices (putting baby to sleep face up; keeping toys, pillows and blankets out of the cot, and so on).

You might also consider a postpartum doula. Like a baby nurse, a doula helps a new mother with the baby. Unlike most nurses, she'll also take charge of the household care. She'll set up the nursery, give baby-care tips, cook, clean, run errands, help care for an older child (or spend time caring for the newborn so you have more time to baby your older child) and more, depending on your needs. She will also likely be a good source of breastfeeding tips and will nurture you, the new mother (much as a labour doula does), so you can better nurture your baby. In other words, a doula mothers the mother, providing a sympathetic ear and serving as an antidote for the isolation many new mothers experience. Postpartum doulas usually charge by the hour (unlike nurses, who usually charge by the week), so they can get costly – but if you use her time effectively, a doula can be well worth the price.

For more information on doulas or to locate one in your area, contact Doula UK: PO Box 26678, London N14 4WB, www.doula.org.uk.

OTHER SOURCES OF HELP

'With the loss of my income, we just can't afford the expense of a maternity nurse. Since I may need a Caesarean – my baby's in a breech position – I wonder if I will be able to manage without help.'

Just because you can't afford – or don't want to hire – a maternity nurse doesn't mean you have to go it alone. Most women, in fact, rely on other sources of help, at least one of which is probably available to you:

The new father. If your spouse can arrange his schedule so that he can be with both of you for the first few weeks (by taking advantage of paternity leave rights, see page 721), he is probably your best helper. Together and without outside assistance or interference, you'll both learn more about your baby and baby care than you would any other way. No experience is necessary for the job; you'll both catch on quickly. Do take a baby-care class together at a local hospital or community centre (there are also classes for dads only), and read a child-care book or two before baby arrives to pick up some of the basics beforehand. Consider turning to family, friends, the baby's doctor, the hospital nursery staff, the NCT and other sources of information and advice to fill in the blanks. Your partner-in-parenting should also be prepared to perform more than his share of the household chores in those first six weeks postpartum, when you'll still be recovering no matter how you end up delivering.

A grandma. If you have a mother or mother-in-law whom you'd be comfortable having around on a live-in or come-in basis for the first weeks (and who you think can 'help out' without 'taking over' – a fine line that some grandparents have trouble not crossing), this may provide another good solution. Grandmothers (and many grandfathers) have at least 101 uses: they can rock a crying baby, cook a splendid supper, wash and fold the laundry, do the shopping and much, much more. This kind of arrangement works particularly well if you can handle a little well-meant interference good-naturedly. Of course, if the grandparent in question has an already busy life and isn't interested in revisiting the changing table, this won't be an option.

Your freezer. You won't be able to put baby on ice when you're tired, but you will be able to pull meals out of the deep freeze if you prepared some during the last weeks of pregnancy when, if you weren't working, you may have had too much time on your hands anyway. A few nutritious casseroles, a roasted chicken ready to reheat, or a prepared pasta sauce will ease the pressure of having to feed yourself and the rest of your family nightly. Then you can focus more on feeding baby (which you may find a full-time job for a while if you're nursing). Don't hesitate to stock up on frozen vegetables, too; they take little preparation time and are nutritious as well.

Your favourite take-away. If you don't have the time or the opportunity (or the energy or the ambition) to prepare meals in advance, you still won't have to cook in those busy postpartum days. Nearly every neighbourhood has one or more take-aways where you can get meats, chicken, sometimes fish, and side dishes ready to heat and eat – and, increasingly, fresh salads that require only a fork and an appetite to enjoy. Put favourite take-away restaurants on speed dial, and don't forget the salad bar at your local supermarket.

Paper goods. When dinner is over, whether home-prepared or take-away, there are always dishes to do – unless you rely on paper plates, plastic cutlery and disposable cups. Disposables will also come in handy for serving snacks to visitors who have come to admire the baby. (Keep such entertaining to a minimum, however, if you want to survive the postpartum period.)

Cleaning help. If there's one job that most new parents would gladly relinquish, it's cleaning. Give it up – to a cleaning service, a cleaning person, someone you've used before, or someone new – anyone who can vacuum and dust, mop floors and scour bathrooms, so that you and your spouse can have more time and energy to devote to baby, any older children, yourselves, and each other. This is a good route for parents who want to do most of the newborn care themselves but don't want to sacrifice their health, sanity or the condition of their home in the deal.

Remember, even if you hire help, and most especially if you don't, there will inevitably be things that don't get done during those early weeks. As long as caring for your baby and getting rest for yourself aren't among them, don't worry – but do get used to it. Though a certain amount of order will eventually be restored to your home, life with children will almost always include living with at least a few untied ends – not to mention a few unwashed dishes in the sink . . . a few dust balls under the coffee table . . . a few loads of laundry that still need folding . . .

WHICH NAPPIES TO USE

'Everyone I know uses disposable nappies, and they do seem a lot less of a mess than cloth ones. But are they as good for baby?'

Ever since Eve, parents have had to confront the problem of how to cover baby's bottom. And over the millennia, some ingenious – though not necessarily convenient – solutions evolved. For instance, American Indian mothers apparently kept their babies (and their own backs) dry and comfortable by packing their papoose boards with the soft shredded insides of reeds.

Luckily, as a parent in the twenty-first century, you won't have to wade daily into the marshes to choose the softest and most absorbent reeds to pad your Snugli. But you will have to choose among a plethora of possibilities, ranging from several types of cloth nappies (to launder yourself or order from a nappy service) to a bewildering and ever-changing array of disposables.

The choice that's right for you and your baby may be different from the one that's right for your neighbours and their infants. Personal factors will be of major significance since, scientifically and economically, there's no conclusive winner in the nappy derby. Consider the following in making your choice:

Disposable nappies. The parents' choice by far, disposables are most often selected for their convenience. And for busy parents (is there another kind?), that's a major advantage. There

are no dirty nappies to collect, tote around, and pile up for weekly pickup or laundry. Disposables also save a certain amount of time and effort; they're faster and easier to put on and take off (especially important if your baby is a wriggler). Newer (and more costly) styles are increasingly more absorbent and theoretically less likely to cause nappy rash. They're trimmer, better fitting, and less apt to leak.

These desirable features also add up to a distinct disadvantage: since disposables soak up so much urine and often 'feel' dry when they're far from it, parents are less likely to change nappies frequently enough, and infrequent changes can lead to nappy rash. The super absorbency of these nappies also makes it hard to tell how much your newborn is urinating, to gauge if his or her milk intake is sufficient. Additionally, the new superbreed of nappy keeps babies so comfortable when wet that toilet learning may eventually be more difficult to accomplish. Also on the minus side is the effect that paper nappies have on the environment as they're loaded into landfills. (Though cloth nappies also take a toll on Mother Nature in terms of power and water use, as well as soap runoff.) Having to shop for and lug the nappies home is also a potential disadvantage, when weighed against the convenience of a nappy service, but this drawback can be avoided if you order by phone or on-line.

Home-delivered cloth nappies. To those who are reluctant to encase their infant's bottom in paper and plastic, soft, comfortable, sterilized and possibly ecologically preferable cotton nappies are appealing, especially when they are delivered to the door weekly. Some studies (which nappy services are fond of quoting) show a lower incidence of nappy rash with such nappies; others (cited by paper nappy manufacturers) show superabsorbent disposables yielding a lower incidence of rash. If cloth nappies are continued into toddlerhood (many parents switch to paper before this), toilet learning may be easier to accomplish, because direct contact between a sopping wet cloth nappy and skin makes a child very uncomfortable, more aware of being wet, and, hopefully, more inspired to use the potty.

There are disadvantages, however. Separate waterproof pants are usually needed to avoid having to change baby, cot and often parent's clothes every time baby wets (though there are 'all-in-ones' – fitted cloth nappies with the waterproof cover already sewn on). These waterproof pants increase the risk of rash by keeping air out and moisture in, though breathable nappy pants or wraps made of cotton or wool (sometimes with airy mesh linings and/or absorbent foam fillings) can reduce or even eliminate this problem. Because there's more fussing and fiddling involved (though technical advances in the cloth arena – such as fitted nappies and easier fasteners – continue to reduce this drawback significantly), nappy changes are generally more trouble with cloth nappies, particularly as baby becomes more proficient in squirming. Because absorbency is more limited, double nappies are usually needed at night, and, for some heavy wetters, during the day. Boys, who concentrate their urine in front, may need paper nappy liners. And then there are the plastic bags of soiled nappies to be carried home from outings and the ever-present bucket of dirty nappies, which is never truly odour free (though the same can be said for disposable nappies if kept for too long in a nappy bucket).

Finally, though cloth nappies don't end up in landfills, their laundering does have a negative impact on the environment; whether it's as significant as the impact from disposables is debatable.

Home-laundered cloth nappies. These may be the clear loser compared to the other two choices. Because they can't be adequately sanitized, home-laundered nappies are, according to studies, more likely to cause nappy rash. And though they seem to be far less expensive than either of the other nappy choices, they are only slightly so, when one considers the cost of soap, water and power used. In addition, they demand a greater expenditure of time and effort – to soak, wash, dry and fold between uses.

Some parents decide to use cloth nappies for the first few months, a time when baby usually spends more time at home than on the go, and then graduate to disposables as the logistics of toting cloth become too much like hard work. They will often, however, use disposables on outings and, sometimes, at night (because their greater absorbency keeps baby more comfortable longer and may ensure a better night's sleep) from the start.

Whichever nappy you decide on now, you may find that your baby develops nappy rash frequently later. This could point to a sensitivity to your choice. If this occurs, don't fight it – switch. Try a different type of nappy (switch from cloth to paper or vice versa) or a different brand of disposable. Also see tips for preventing and treating nappy rash on page 265.

QUITTING SMOKING

'Except for the first few months of pregnancy, when I couldn't smoke because it made me queasy, I never managed to give it up entirely – and neither has my spouse. How much will smoking around our baby affect her?'

Nothing you can buy in a layette department, splurge on in a toy store, or put away into a trust fund can match the gift to your newborn of growing up in a smoke-free environment. Smoking by parents has been linked to an increased risk of Sudden Infant Death Syndrome (SIDS), to more respiratory illnesses (colds, flu, bronchiolitis, asthma) and ear infections during the first year of life, to impaired lung function and reduced lung capacity, as well as to an increased risk of tooth decay later on in childhood. Not only are the children of smokers sick more often than children of non-smokers, but their illnesses also last longer. They are also more likely to be hospitalized in the first three years of life. The more smokers in the household, the more severe the negative effects, since the amount of smoke a child inhales is related to the number of smokers she is exposed to on a regular basis. And the risks aren't eliminated even when parents step outside the house to light up. Researchers have found that children in households with smokers who smoke only outside are *still* exposed to 70 per cent more damaging lung particles than those in non-smoking households.

Perhaps worst of all, offspring of smokers are more likely to become smokers than children whose parents don't smoke. So quitting may not only keep your child healthier in childhood, it may, by lessening the chance of your child smoking later in life, also keep her alive and well longer. And if that's not motivation enough, keep this in mind, too: by quitting you'll be giving your baby the gift of healthier parents.

If you haven't been able to quit up until now, it obviously won't be easy. As they would with any drug addiction (particularly such a powerful one), your body and your mind will align against

you. But if you're determined to fight back – for your sake and your baby's – you can triumph over both. And the best time to do it is now, before baby is born. Giving up smoking before delivery will increase the oxygen available to your baby during childbirth. And your newborn will come home from the hospital to clean, breathable air and, if you're breastfeeding, to nicotine-free milk. If you are still in the early months of pregnancy, quitting now will also reduce the risk of premature delivery and of having a low-birthweight baby. (Any time, however, is a good time to quit, especially when there's a new set of lungs in the house. If you don't manage to do it before delivery, redouble your efforts once baby's sharing the air in your home.)

A NAME FOR BABY

'I've always been unhappy with my name. How can we be sure our son won't be unhappy with the name we choose?'

What's in a name? To a newborn baby, not much. Feed him, clothe him, comfort and entertain him, and you can call him 'Rover' for all he'll care. Once friends and the outside world begin to play a bigger role in your child's life, however (usually early in primary school), antipathy to the name you selected may develop. Though there's no way to guarantee baby will love for a lifetime the name you choose, careful and sensitive selection will lessen the chance of a name turning out to be Trouble. Here are some tips to keep in mind when selecting a name for your baby:

◆ Make sure both you and your spouse like the name – the way it sounds and looks, and the connotations it carries. Ask yourselves, 'Would I like it if it were my name?'

◆ Select a meaningful name – name your baby after a loved family member, a respected historical or biblical character, or a favourite character in literature. Such a name gives the child a sense of belonging, of being part of an extended family or of the greater world.

◆ Select a name that fits. Melanie, for example, which means 'black' or 'dark', would be fitting for a dark-haired girl; Dustin, 'a fighter', might be appropriate for a boy who made it through a difficult delivery. Or one that fits you spiritually, symbolizing, perhaps, a quality you wish for him or her, such as Hope, or Faith, or Christian. Or that reflects your feelings about the birth – Joy, for example, or Ian ('gracious gift of God'). A fitting name can make a child feel extra special, though to match baby up with such a name you may have to postpone the decision until after birth.

◆ How will the name sound to others? Are there any possible hidden meanings or soundalike words that might someday make the name embarrassing to your child? Check the initials; do they spell something that could make your child the butt of jokes or teasing? The name Anna Samantha Smith, for example, just might be the source of playground torment for a child. What about possible nicknames? Could they trigger childish insults? If it's an extremely unusual name, or one that's very ethnic, consider whether it may be difficult for your child to live with later on.

◆ Include a middle name so that if your child turns out to be unhappy with his first name, the middle name can be substituted.

◆ Consider choosing a name that's easy to say and spell. A very unusual name that teachers are always mispronouncing or a name that's always being misspelled could become a burden – not only in school but also later on in life. On the other hand, some children (and later, adults) ultimately enjoy having an unusual name because it will separate them from the pack.

◆ Avoid the trendy or the political. Don't saddle your child with this year's hot name (after a TV or film star or politician who's making every magazine cover). When the famous namesake turns out to be a flash in the pan or worse, the name may become outdated or place your child in a light that is uncomfortable.

◆ Use a real name instead of a diminutive (Robert, not Bob; Elizabeth instead of Liz.) You can use the diminutive form throughout childhood, but your child then has the option of switching to the more dignified version when he or she ventures out into adulthood.

◆ If you don't want your child to be one of six Emilys or seven Sams in the class, avoid picking a name from the year's Top Ten. Many parenting magazines and websites run an annual piece on the subject of popular names, so check the Internet for this year's winners. You can also gauge which are the most popular names in your neighbourhood by reading the birth announcements, or taking a stroll in the playground and listening to the (proper) names parents call their children.

◆ Consider family feelings, but don't let them dominate. If there's a family name that you don't love but your parents would like to see perpetuated out of either tradition or sentiment, try it as a middle name, alter it so that it's more appealing to you, choose another form of the same name (most names actually have several forms), or select a name with the same meaning. A good baby name book will be helpful here. And remember, no matter what names you choose, your parents and grandparents will love the kids – even if they're not happy with the names at first.

◆ Be sure the name or names are euphonic with the last name and with each other. A good general rule: a short last name goes well with a long first name (Abigail Jones) and vice versa (James Martinez), while two-syllable firsts usually complement two-syllable lasts (Hannah Kramer).

PREPARING THE FAMILY PET

'Our dog is intensely jealous of my affections – she always tries to come between me and my spouse when we hug. I'm worried about how she'll react to the new baby.'

It's hard for a dog who's always been treated like a baby to roll over and play dog when a real baby appears on the scene. But that's exactly what she'll have to do when her place in your heart has to be shared by that tiny but threatening new human you'll soon be bringing home from the hospital. Though a little initial moping around may be unavoidable, you'll want to do whatever you can to prevent excessive jealousy and, of course, any aggressive reactions. Start now.

◆ Invest in an obedience training programme for your dog if she isn't trained already – and even if you've never felt there was the need for it before. Friskiness and puppy-like exuberance aren't usually a problem in a childless home, but they could be in one with a new baby. Particularly because the baby's behaviour won't be controllable or predictable, your dog's must be. Obedience training won't take the spirit out of your pet, but it will make her more stable, and thus less likely to harm your baby.

◆ Get your dog used to babies now, if you can. Invite friends with babies over to the house, or let her (under careful supervision, and if the parent is willing) sniff near a baby in the park or be petted by a toddler, so that she can become familiar with their smells and their moves.

◆ Get your dog used to life with a baby in the house. Use a baby-size doll as a prop in her training (it'll also be helpful in yours). Put a nappy on the doll; carry, sing to, and rock it; 'nurse' it; put it to bed in the cot; take it for a walk in the pram (if you don't mind the neighbours staring). Now and then, play a tape of a baby crying.

◆ Get your dog used to sleeping alone, if that's what the postpartum arrangement will be, so that the change doesn't come as a shock. Fix up a comfortable doggie bed in a corner – with a favourite pillow or blanket for company. Consider keeping it in a baby-free zone; a crawling baby's invasion of her sleeping space can provoke an aggressive reaction in the friendliest of canines.

◆ Take your dog for a complete medical checkup. Be sure that your dog is flea- and tick-free (ask your vet about using a pill or another method that's effective against these pests yet safe to use around your baby). Also be sure to have your dog checked for worms of any kind.

◆ If your baby will have a separate room, train your dog to stay out of it while you're not there. A gate to block the doorway will help discourage unsolicited visits. If your baby's cot will be in your room or in a corner of the living room, train your dog not to go under the cot, since she could accidentally unlock the side, letting it fall.

◆ If your dog's feeding station is one your baby will later be able to get to easily, move it to the cellar, garage or some other area that doesn't invite a curious crawler, since even an easy-going dog can become vicious when her food is threatened. If you live in a small apartment, get your dog on an evening feeding schedule and remove her food dish during the day. Don't even leave her food around when the dog is safely outside, because those tasty nuggets taste good not only to canines – many babies love sampling them, too, and they pose a choking hazard. And use a small non-tip water bowl unless you enjoy mopping the floor frequently.

◆ After delivery, but while you're still in the hospital or birthing centre, have your spouse bring home an unwashed piece of clothing your newborn has worn so that your pet can become familiar with the baby's scent. When you arrive home, let your spouse hold the baby while you greet your pet. Then to satisfy her curiosity, let the dog sniff the baby – who should be well swaddled, with

head and face protected by your arms. Once the baby's snug in the cot, break out a special treat for the dog and spend a little time alone with her.

◆ Be attentive to your new baby, of course, but don't act overprotective around your dog. This will only make the animal more jealous and insecure. Instead, as you would with a human sibling (though on a different level, naturally), try to get your pet involved with the new addition and let her know she's still a loved member of the family. Pet her while you nurse, walk her while you take the baby out in the pram, allow her into the baby's room while you're there. Try to make a point of spending at least five minutes every day alone with her. But should she show even the slightest aggressiveness towards your baby, reprimand her immediately.

◆ If, despite your efforts to prepare and reassure her, your dog seems hostile towards the new arrival, keep her tied up and away from the baby until you're sure she's worked out her feelings. Just because a dog has never bitten before doesn't mean she's not capable of it under duress. If tying up the dog only adds to her hostility, you may have to consider finding another home for her. (With male dogs, neutering may reduce aggressiveness.)

'I worry that our cat, who has always slept with us, may be jealous of the new baby.'

Even friendly cats can undergo personality changes when a baby arrives. And since cats are just as capable of harming an infant as dogs are, with their claws as well as with their jaws, it's as important to make sure they are well prepared for the family expansion. Most of the above tips for preparing a dog can work for a cat as well. Be particularly careful to reassure your cat – through plenty of attention – that he is still a family favourite. And because cats usually love to cuddle next to a warm body and can quickly scale the sides of a cot, be sure to attach a specially designed mesh cot net securely over it to keep yours from bedding down with baby – a friendly gesture that could end in tragedy. Also keep cats (and dogs) from licking your infant's face or any broken skin.

PREPARING YOUR BREASTS FOR BREASTFEEDING

'I have a friend who insists that I should toughen my nipples in preparation for nursing. Is that a good idea?'

Female nipples are designed for nursing. And, with very few exceptions, they come to the job fully qualified, without the need for prior preparation. In fact, in some cases the procedures that used to be recommended for toughening up or otherwise readying the nipples for breastfeeding can do more harm than good. For instance, applying alcohol, witch hazel, or tincture of benzoin can dry the nipples and make them more, rather than less, likely to crack and fissure; even soap can be drying, and its use on the nipples should be avoided during the last trimester of pregnancy and during lactation itself. Ditto using a brush on nipples, which can irritate tender tissues, making them more – not less – likely to crack under the pressures of nursing. Massaging or using a breast pump to prepare nipples isn't just

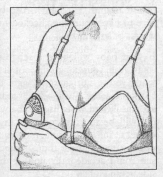

BREAST SHELLS

Breast shells exert constant yet painless pressure, which draws out inverted or flat nipples.

counterproductive, it can be dangerous; such manipulations can stimulate contractions and occasionally even trigger a breast infection.

While the vast majority of nipples don't need any preparation for breastfeeding, a predelivery exam by your practitioner can screen your breasts for any anatomical features that might prove problematic once breastfeeding begins, such as underdeveloped glandular tissue or inverted nipples.

If you do have inverted nipples (your nipples retract into the breast tissue instead of sticking out when you're cold or when you compress your breast with your fingers at the edge of the areola), ask your practitioner if they'll need any preparation for breastfeeding. Though research shows that such preparation isn't usually necessary (once breastfeeding is initiated, most inverted nipples do their job as well as any others), some practitioners continue to recommend the use of breast shells. These plastic shells gradually draw out

**DON'T EXPRESS
YOURSELF – YET**

It may be tempting to try to express colostrum antenatally to see if it's there – but don't. Not only can such nipple manipulation cause uterine contractions, but it might also result in some loss of the valuable elements of this premilk. For more on colostrum, see page 72.

flat or inverted nipples (see illustration) by exerting painless pressure on the breasts. On the downside, breast shells can be embarrassingly conspicuous and may also cause sweating and rashes.

More important than preparing your breasts for breastfeeding is preparing your mind. Learn all you can about breastfeeding: take a antenatal course, if possible; read chapter 3 and books on the subject; get in touch with your local NCT group or La Leche League (both of which are invaluable sources of advice and support) or check out their websites at www.nctpregnancyandbabycare.com and www.laleche.org.uk; get tips and feedback from breastfeeding friends; and consider using a lactation consultant.

What it's Important to Know:
SELECTING THE RIGHT DOCTOR

Breast or bottle? Cloth or paper? The Pooh curtains or the bunny ones? With all the dozens of decisions you'll need to make before that bundle of joy arrives, there's one that should definitely top the list: choosing the right doctor for your baby.

Assuming you stay in the community and are relatively satisfied with the care, the doctor you choose for your baby could well be seeing baby – and you – through some eighteen years of runny noses, earaches, sore throats, high fevers, upset stomachs, bumps and bruises, maybe even broken bones; through dramatic physical and psychological developmental milestones that will both thrill and bewilder you; through moments you can't now even conceive of. You won't be living with your baby's doctor during those years (though there will be times, particularly nights and weekends, when you'll wish

you were), but you'll still want someone with whom you feel comfortable and compatible. Someone you wouldn't hesitate to waken at 2 AM when your nine-month-old's fever hits a new high, someone you wouldn't be embarrassed to ask about your six-month-old's sudden fascination with his genitals, someone you would feel free to question when you aren't sure an antibiotic that's been prescribed is necessary.

In other words, it's best to look before you leap into a GP's office with your newborn in tow. Though it's not a decision that can't be undone – you can change your GP at any time, without offering an explanation (and this works both ways; you can be struck off a GP's list) – it's one that shouldn't be made lightly.

As you begin your search for Doctor Right, think locally – not only for logistical reasons (dragging even healthy babies long distances isn't fun; dragging sick ones can be a nightmare for all involved), but for practical ones (most GPs won't accept you as patients if you live out of the area). For a list of likely candidates, check your local health authority – which can provide you with the names of doctors who live in your area, along with details on their specialties and interests.

Of course, your best source of leads when it comes to tracking down the right doctor for your baby is other parents. No one can tell you more about a doctor's bedside manner than his or her satisfied (or dissatisfied) patients. Recommendations are most helpful when they come from friends or acquaintances who mirror you in temperament and child-rearing philosophy. Otherwise, the very qualities that make them swear by their doctor may make you want to swear at him or her.

WHAT KIND OF PRACTICE IS PERFECT?

To some parents, the type of practice may be almost as important as the type of doctor. There are several options; the one most appealing to you will depend on your personal preferences and priorities.

The solo practitioner. In such a practice, a doctor works alone, using another doctor to cover when he or she is away or otherwise unavailable. The major advantage of a solo practitioner is that such a doctor has the opportunity to build close one-to-one relationships with each of his or her patients. But there's also a disadvantage to this: solo practitioners aren't likely to be on call around the clock and around the calendar. They'll be around for scheduled appointments (unless called to an emergency), and on call most of the time, but they will take holidays and occasional nights and weekends off, leaving patients who require emergency care or consultation to a covering doctor (locum) who may be unfamiliar to them. If you do select a solo practitioner, ask about who will be covering at such times, and be sure that in an emergency, your child's records will be available even when the doctor is not.

The partnership. Sometimes two doctors are better than one. If one isn't on call, the other almost always is. If you see them in rotation, you and your child often can, thanks to the frequent well-child visits during the first year, build good relationships with both. Though partners will probably concur on most major issues and will likely share similar philosophies of practice, they may occasionally offer different opinions. Having more than one opinion may in some instances be confusing, but hearing two approaches to a particularly confounding problem can be useful. (If one doesn't seem to be able to solve your baby's sleeping problems, maybe the other will.)

An important question to ask before deciding on a partnership: can you schedule appointments with the doctor of your choice? If not, and if you discover you like one but not the other, you may spend half your visits with a doctor with whom you're not comfortable. Even if you can choose the preferred doctor for checkups, sick children must usually be seen by whoever is available at the time.

The group practice. If two are good, will three or more be better? In some ways probably yes; in others, possibly no. A group is more likely to be able to provide twenty-four-hour coverage by doctors in the practice, but less likely to ensure close doctor-patient relationships – again, unless you can select the same doctor (or two) for regular checkups. The more doctors a child will be exposed to on well-child and sick-call visits, the longer it may take to feel comfortable with each one, though this will be much less of a problem if all the doctors are warm and caring practitioners. Also a factor here: if you rotate doctors, contradictory advice can either enlighten or confound. In the long run, more important than the number of doctors in a practice will be the confidence you have in them individually and as a group.

MAKING SURE DR RIGHT IS RIGHT FOR YOU

Other considerations you may want to bear in mind when choosing Dr Right include the following:

Surgery location. Lugging a size-42 belly with you everywhere you go may seem like a struggle now, but it's travelling light compared to what you'll be carrying around after delivery. Going unwalkable distances will require more planning than just hopping on a bus or train or into a car, and the further you have to go, particularly in foul weather, the more complicated outings will become. When you're dealing with a sick or injured child, a nearby surgery is not just a convenience; it can also mean faster care and treatment. But when you make your decision, keep in mind: a truly one-of-a-kind practitioner may be worth a lengthier trip.

Surgery hours. What constitutes convenient surgery hours will depend on your own schedules. If one or both of you have 9-to-5 jobs, some early

morning, evening or weekend hours may be a major requirement.

Atmosphere. You can tell a lot about the atmosphere of a surgery before you even see it. If you're treated curtly on the phone, chances are in-surgery experiences won't be any more pleasant. If, on the other hand, you're greeted by a cheerful welcoming voice, you're likely to be met with concern and kindness when you come in with a sick, injured or anxious child. You can gain further insight when you make your first visit to the surgery. Is the receptionist friendly, or is her manner crisp and sterile? Is the staff responsive to and patient with its young clients, or is communication with them limited to 'Get down', 'Don't touch', and 'Keep quiet'?

Decor. A baby doctor needs more than a couple of magazines on the table and a few Expressionist prints on the wall to make the 'Right' design statement in the waiting room. On your reconnaissance visit, look for features that will make waiting less painful for both you and your expected: a comfortable play area for toddlers as well as a waiting area for older children (if space permits); a selection of clean, well-maintained toys and books appropriate for a range of ages; low chairs or other sitting space designed for little bodies. Wallpaper in bold colours and intriguing patterns (orange kangaroos and yellow tigers rather than tastefully understated earth tones) and bright pictures (in both the waiting room and the examining rooms) will also give uneasy minds something comforting to focus on while anticipating or experiencing the poking and prodding of a checkup. (But keep in mind, not every good doctor is a Disney buff.) A welcome addition in the family practitioner's surgery: separate waiting areas for adults only and adults with children.

Waiting time. A forty-five-minute wait when you're pacing with a fussy infant or trying to distract a restless toddler with yet another picture book can be a trying experience for all involved. Yet such waits are not uncommon when the surgery is really busy. For some parents a long wait may merely be an inconvenience; for others it is something their schedules simply can't accommodate.

In trying to gauge the average waiting time in a particular surgery, ask the receptionist, and if her answer is vague or noncommittal, pose the question to a few waiting parents.

A long average wait can be a sign of disorganization in the surgery, of overbooking, or of a doctor's having more patients than he or she can handle. But it doesn't tell you much about the quality of medical care. Some very good doctors are not very good managers. They may end up spending more time with each patient than allotted (something you will appreciate in the examining room but not in the waiting room). Or they may not like to turn down requests to fit sick children into an already full schedule (something you will definitely appreciate when it's your child who's sick).

All waiting doesn't take place in the waiting room. The most uncomfortable wait is often in the examining room, holding an unhappy, undressed baby, with no space to pace, or trying to distract a frightened toddler without benefit of the toy collection just outside. While long waits in the examining room may not alone be sufficient reason for rejecting a doctor, if they do prove to be a problem, be sure to make a point of letting the nurse know that you would prefer to do most of your waiting in the waiting room.

House calls. Yes, GPs still make them. Most of the time, however, as your doctor will probably explain, house calls are not only unnecessary, they aren't best for baby. At the surgery, a doctor can use equipment and perform tests that can't be stashed in a little black bag. Still, occasions may arise when you will appreciate very much the doctor who is willing to put his or her bedside manner to work literally – as when junior is home from nursery school with a bad stomach flu, baby's down with a high fever and a bronchial cough, and you're on duty at home alone in a snowstorm.

Protocol for taking phone queries. If new parents rushed to the doctor's surgery every time they had questions about their babies' health or development, doctors' surgeries would be jammed day and night. That's why many queries can be answered and worries assuaged via the telephone. And why you'll want to know in advance how your prospective baby doctor handles such calls. Some parents prefer the call-hour approach: a particular time is set aside each day for the doctor to field phone calls. No patients are seen during this time and distractions are few. This ensures almost immediate access to the doctor – though there may be several bouts with a busy signal or a brief wait for a callback. Other parents find it difficult to confine their worries to between 7 and 8 in the morning or 11 and noon, or worse, to wait until tomorrow's call hour for relief from today's worries. They prefer the doctor callback system: They call when a problem or question arises, and the doctor calls back when there's a free moment between patients. Even if the callback doesn't come for hours (in a non-emergency, of course), callers can at least unburden themselves on – and sometimes be reassured or counselled by – the person who takes the call. And there is the comfort of knowing they will talk to the doctor by the end of the day.

Style. When you're in the market for a doctor, as when you're shopping for baby furniture, the style that's right will depend on your style. Do you prefer a doctor who is easygoing and informal, formal and businesslike, or somewhere in between? Are you most comfortable with a father (or mother) figure, or with a doctor who treats you as a partner in your child's care? Do you want a doctor who gives the impression of having all the answers, or one who is willing to admit, 'I don't know, but I'll find out'.

Just as there are certain features all parents look for in a cot or pushchair (quality, workmanship, value), there are certain traits they all want in a prospective baby doctor: the ability to listen (without eyeing the next name in the appointment book); an openness to questions and a willingness to respond to them fully and clearly (without becoming defensive or feeling threatened); and, most of all, a genuine fondness for children.

Philosophy. Even in the best of marriages, spouses don't always agree, and even in the best of doctor-patient relationships there may be points of difference. But, as with marriages, doctor-patient relationships are most likely to succeed if both partners agree on a majority of major issues. Seek an appointment to ask about the doctor's positions on any of the following that you consider important:

◆ Breastfeeding. If you're eager to nurse, a doctor who is only luke-warm towards or confesses to little knowledge of the subject may not provide the support and assistance novice nursers need.

◆ Vegetarianism. If you and your family don't eat meat or fish, it's useful to have a doctor who not only

accepts that but also knows something about meeting a growing child's nutritional needs on a vegetarian or vegan diet.

◆ Preventive medicine. If you believe in more than an ounce of prevention, it's a good idea to select a doctor who shares that philosophy – emphasizing the 'well' in baby care (good nutrition, physical activity, immunizations, and so on).

A GOOD ALTERNATIVE?

Looking for an alternative to traditional medical care? More and more Britons are. And the ranks of alternative practitioners are rapidly growing to meet that demand. There are now 40,000 alternative practitioners in the UK – compared with 36,000 GPs. But – and this is an important 'but' – far from all of these practitioners are properly trained or qualified, which makes seeking their care for yourself or your child potentially bad medicine. If you'd like to consult with an alternative therapist to complement the care of your traditional GP, first do your homework. Check with the Institute of Complementary Medicine (020 7237 5165, www.icmedicine.co.uk) that they are on the British Register of Complementary Practitioners. Also look for recommendations – from other parents, as well as from your GP (who may, in some cases, be able to refer you). And since you'll likely be paying out of your own pocket (alternative therapies are only occasionally available on the NHS), always ask for cost estimates in advance.

◆ Antibiotics. It's a good idea to select a doctor who's up-to-date on the latest recommendations for when and how often to prescribe antibiotics. Research indicates that many doctors prescribe antibiotics too frequently, often when the situation doesn't warrant it (usually at the parents' request).

◆ Complementary and alternative medicine. If a more holistic approach to your family's health care is important to you, look for a doctor who is familiar with alternative and complementary medicine and open to incorporating nonconventional therapies that are safe and effective into your child's care.

YOUR PARTNERSHIP WITH DR RIGHT

Once you've chosen Dr Right, you can't just drop your baby's health care into his or her lap, sit back with a waiting room magazine and relax, assured of the right results. As parents, you, and not your doctor, have the most significant impact on your baby's health. If you don't hold up your part of the partnership, even the best of doctors won't be able to provide the best of care for your baby. To be the right patient-parent for Dr Right, you have a long list of responsibilities.

Follow surgery etiquette. Arrive for appointments on time or, if the surgery perpetually runs late, call half an hour in advance of a scheduled appointment and ask how much later you can safely arrive; try to give at least twenty-four hours' notice when cancelling; and keep to arranged payment agreements. Remember, patients (or in this case, parents of patients) are partly responsible

for the smooth operation of a doctor's surgery.

Practice prevention. Though it's wise to select a doctor who believes in preventive medicine and concentrates on well-baby care, the burden for keeping baby healthy will fall more heavily on you than on the doctor. It's you who must see that baby gets proper nutrition, enjoys a wholesome balance of rest and active play, is not exposed unnecessarily to infection or cigarette smoke, and is kept as safe as possible from accidental injury. It's you who must help your baby establish good health and safety habits that can last and give benefit for a lifetime.

Put your worries on paper. Many of the questions you'll come up with between checkups are worthy of your concern without being worthy of a special phone call ('Why doesn't he have any teeth yet?' or 'How can I get him to enjoy his bath?'). Jot these down as they occur to you, before they have a chance to escape in the course of a typically hectic day with baby. Then ask them at your next visit.

Take notes. The doctor gives you instructions about what to do if your baby has a reaction to her first injections. You get home, she has a fever, and you panic. What was it she said? It's not surprising you've forgotten – the baby was crying after the injection and you could barely hear the instructions as you struggled to dress her, never mind remember them. The remedy for parental memory loss: always bring a pen and paper to your doctor visits and jot down diagnoses, instructions and any other information you may want to refer to later. This may not be easy while balancing baby on your lap (that's why two-parent visits are ideal), but it's worth the contortions that may be involved. Or, ask the doctor or nurse if they can jot down some of the information for you.

Take notes at telephone 'visits', too. Though you're positive you'll remember the name of the over-the-counter ointment the doctor recommended for baby's rash or the dosage of paracetamol prescribed for teething pain, these details can easily escape your mind when you hang up the phone to the sight of baby smearing carrot purée all over the kitchen wall.

Pick up the phone. Thanks to Alexander Graham Bell, the relief for your worries is only a phone call away. But don't use your baby's doctor as a ready reference; before making a call, try to find the answers to your questions in this or in another baby book on your shelf. If you're unsuccessful, however, don't hesitate to call for fear of abusing your telephone privileges. In the early months, doctors expect a lot of telephone calls, especially from first-time parents. Don't call cold, however. Make the most of the conversation by glancing over the Before Calling the Doctor checklist starting on page 534 and call prepared.

Follow doctor's advice. In any good partnership, both sides contribute what they know or do best. In this partnership, your baby's doctor will be contributing years of training and experience. To get the most benefit from those contributions, it makes sense to take the doctor's advice when feasible, and to inform him or her when you don't intend to, or for some reason, can't. This is particularly vital in medical situations. Say an antibiotic has been prescribed for baby's earache. The baby spits up the medication and won't touch another drop. Since the earache seems better anyway, you give up trying to force it down his or her little throat and

don't bother to let the doctor know. Then, two days later, baby's temperature is up. What the doctor would have told you, had you called, is that once the medication is begun the baby may start to improve, but unless the full course of treatment is completed, the illness can return with greater force. He or she might also have been able to advise you on better ways of getting the medication down or of alternative ways of medicating.

Speak up. To say that it's important to follow doctor's advice is not to say that mother or father doesn't sometimes know best – even better than doctor. Sometimes, parental instincts are as keenly accurate in picking up symptoms of illness as any instrument in a doctor's black bag. If you sense the doctor's diagnosis or treatment is off, say so (calmly and rationally, not in a challenging way). You may learn something from each other.

Speak up, too, if you've heard about a new treatment for colic or for runny noses, or anything else that you feel might benefit your baby. If it's something you've read, bring in the source when possible. Perhaps the doctor has already heard about this advance and can give you additional information for or against it. If the doctor is unfamiliar with it, he or she will probably want to learn more about it before offering an opinion. Be aware, however, that medical reporting (especially on the Internet) can be uneven. With your doctor's help, you should be able to sort out the useful from the useless.

End a relationship that's not right. There's no such thing as a perfect doctor (any more than there's such a thing as a perfect parent). And, again, even in the best of partnerships, there's bound to be some disagreement. But if there seems to be more discord than harmony, try talking things out with the doctor before you consider ending the relationship. You may find that there's a misunderstanding rather than serious philosophical differences behind the rift, in which case you may be able to make a fresh start with the same doctor. If the doctor you've chosen turns out to be truly Dr Wrong, you will begin the search for a new doctor a lot wiser and, hopefully, end up with better results. To make sure you don't leave your baby without a doctor while you shop around again, avoid terminating your current relationship until you've found a replacement. When you have, be sure all of your child's medical records are transferred promptly.

◆◆◆

CHAPTER 2

Buying for Baby

You've resisted the temptation for months. Passed wistfully by the Layette Department on your way to Maternity, not daring to run as much as a finger over the lacy rompers and handknit sweaters, casting no more than a longing glance at the musical mobiles and cuddly teddies. But now, at long last, with delivery only weeks away, it's not only okay to stop resisting and start buying, it's absolutely necessary.

Do, however, fight the urge to belly up to the counter and put yourself in the hands of the grandmotherly saleswoman who's waiting to sell you everything she has in stock and several other things she's ready to order at the drop of a credit card. Her voice-of-experience sales pitch may make you forget that you'll be getting some hand-me-downs from your sister-in-law, that dozens of gifts will soon come pouring in, and that you will be doing laundry frequently. And you may end up with shopping bags loaded with more tiny outfits, toys and paraphernalia than your baby will ever be able to use before outgrowing them.

Instead, do your homework before starting your shopping. Calculate your minimum needs (you'll always be able to fill in later) using the shopping list beginning on page 44, and face that saleswoman armed with these basic guidelines:

- ◆ Don't buy a complete layette as espoused by the store or any list; use lists merely as a guide. Just as every baby is different, every baby's (and parent's) needs are different.

- ◆ Keep in mind how many times a week you (or someone else) will be doing the laundry. If you will be washing almost every day, buy the smallest suggested number of items on the list; if you will have to lug loads down to the local Suds 'n Spin and can do it only weekly, then buy the largest number.

- ◆ Gratefully accept any hand-me-down baby clothes given to you by friends or family. Your baby is likely to go through two or three outfits a day in the first few months. At that rate, your wallet will be mightily stretched as you try to keep up with his or her wardrobe needs. Even if all the hand-me-downs aren't exactly your style, it'll be nice to have them standing by for those days when the laundry doesn't quite get done (again). Check off items borrowed or handed down before finalizing your shopping list.

◆ If friends and family ask what you'll need, don't be embarrassed to tell them. They really would rather buy you something you'll use rather than something you'll have to cart back to the store postpartum. Suggest a few items in various price ranges to give them freedom of choice, but don't suggest the same items to different people. Better still, register for your baby's needs to make the giving and receiving easier and more efficient (see box on facing page).

◆ Hold off on buying items you won't need right away (a high chair, a baby seat for the bathtub, toys too advanced for infants) and items you may end up not needing (the full quota of pyjamas, towels, T-shirt sets) until you've received all your gifts. When the Post Office van stops making its daily gifts drop-off, recalculate your needs and head out for the store once more.

◆ Buy mostly six- to nine-month sizes. You may want a couple of three-month-size shirts and maybe an outfit or two for dress-up that fit just right, but for the most part it's more practical to roll up sleeves and endure a slightly blousy look for a few weeks until baby starts to fill out the larger sizes (which happens seemingly overnight). And as irresistible as it may be to unpack your purchases into baby's new dresser, hold back. Keep all baby clothes (even the set you're planning to take baby home in) tagged or in their original packages. That way, if baby checks in at 4.7 kg (10 lb 6 oz), your spouse, mother or a friend can exchange at least some of those tiny items for the six-month size while you're still in the hospital or birthing centre, and the others soon after. Likewise, if your baby arrives early,

weighing just 2.25 kg (5 lb), some of the larger sizes can be exchanged.

In general, buy at least one size ahead (most six-month-old babies wear nine- or twelve-month sizes; some even fill out eighteen-month sizes), but eyeball before purchasing because some styles (particularly imported ones) can run much larger or smaller than average. When in doubt, buy big, keeping this in mind: children grow and clothes (if they're cotton) shrink.

◆ Keep the season in mind as you shop. If baby is expected on the cusp of a season, buy just a few tiny items for the immediate weather and larger ones for the weather expected in the months ahead. Continue to consider the seasons as baby grows. That adorable appliquéd August-perfect sunsuit at half price may be difficult to pass up, but if it's a twelve-month size and your baby will be a year old next May, it's a purchase you'll eventually regret.

◆ When selecting baby clothes, consider convenience and comfort first, fashion second. Tiny buttons at baby's neckline may be darling, but the struggle to fasten them with baby squirming on the changing table won't be. An organdy party frock may look fetching on the hanger but may have to stay there if it irritates baby's delicate skin. An imported sailor suit may look smart – until you have to change baby and find no access to the nappy area. A lace collar might be beautiful, but when your baby spits up all over it, it will be a pain in *your* neck to wash.

Always look for outfits made of soft, easy-care fabrics, with poppers instead of buttons (inconvenient, and should baby manage to chew or pry one off, unsafe), head openings that

REGISTER FOR YOUR BABY NEEDS

It may be the thought that counts when it comes to baby presents – that is, until you end up with three baby baths, twenty-seven size three-month onesies, and four identical baby carriers at your baby shower. Since gift givers are as anxious to give you gifts you want as you are to receive them, help them and yourselves out by signing up with a baby registry. Baby registries are available at most stores that sell baby products (and on-line) and allow expectant parents to register their wish lists before delivery, just as engaged couples register their wish lists before their weddings. Registering will help assure that you'll get what you do want, won't get what you don't want or don't need (multiples of the same item, for instance), and that you won't have to spend your postpartum days running from store to store, returning and exchanging.

are roomy (or have poppers at the neck), and bottoms that open conveniently for nappy changing. Shun long strings or ribbons, which are potentially hazardous (none should be longer than 15 cm/6 in), and rough seams, which are potentially uncomfortable. Room for growth is another important feature: adjustable shoulder straps, stretch fabrics, undefined waistlines on one-piece garments, elasticized waistlines, double rows of poppers on sleepwear, trousers that can be rolled up, wide hems that can be taken down, tucks, pleats or yokes. Pyjamas with 'feet' should be the right length, or should have elasticized ankles to keep them in place.

◆ If you haven't learned the gender of your baby through antenatal testing, don't buy everything in yellow or green (unless you're crazy about those colours), particularly since many infants don't have the complexion to carry off these shades. Both boys and girls can wear reds, blues, navys, whites and creams. If you wait on some purchases until baby arrives, you'll be able to indulge in some dainty pinks for a daughter or some more distinctly boy styles for a son.

At some stores, you can order a layette and not pick it up until after the baby is born – at which time you can specify the colour. This will work only if dad, grandma or a friend can pick up your order while you're in the hospital or birthing centre, or if it can be delivered before you arrive home.

◆ When buying baby furniture, practicality and safety should supersede style. An antique cradle, either purchased or passed down, may lend that heirloom look to the nursery – but you could be setting your baby up for a fall should the bottom not prove strong enough to support his or her weight, or for a lead overdose if the paint job, too, is antique. If you have a dog, a cradle may be too close to the ground for comfort. Keep in mind, too, that many hand-me-down cots and cradles do not meet current safety standards. A plush Rolls-Royce of buggy may evoke a lot of smiles when you walk down the street but a lot of frowns when you hold up the bus line while struggling to fold it and lug it, baby and changing bag, up the steps. For other features to favour in baby furnishings, see page 43.

◆ When buying toiletries for baby, buy only what you need (see list on page 40), rather than one of everything you see. When comparing products, look for those that are alcohol free (alcohol is drying to a baby's skin) and contain the fewest artificial colours, preservatives and other chemical additives.

◆ When stocking the medicine chest, however, err on the side of excess, filling it, just in case, with everything you might need in an emergency (and hope you'll never have to use). Otherwise, you may find yourself helpless when your baby wakes in the middle of the night, burning up with fever, and you have no medication on hand to bring it down. Or when baby's stuffy nose is keeping him or her (and you) up, and you realize you never got around to buying a nasal aspirator.

BABY'S WARDROBE

By far the most fun you'll have preparing for baby will be buying those tiny, cute clothes. In fact, it may take considerable reserves of willpower to avoid overfilling your baby's cupboard with too many adorable outfits (particularly those that are as impractical as they are irresistible). Here are some general guidelines; again, you may *need* more or fewer of all of these; how many you'll *want* is another story altogether:

Three to ten vests/onesies. For your newborn, your best bet are the vests that open in the front, with poppers on the sides. These are easier to get on your baby in the first few weeks, and until your baby's umbilical stump falls off, it's better not to have tight clothes rubbing against it. Once

the stump does fall off, you can switch to the pullover onesie style, which is smoother and more comfortable for baby. These one-piece body suits snap on the bottom and don't ride up, keeping tummies covered in cold weather.

Four to seven stretchies with feet, for an autumn or winter baby, but just three or four for a late-spring or summer arrival. Footed outfits keep tootsies toasty without socks, making them especially practical (as you'll soon find out, socks and booties rarely stay put for long). Make sure they have poppers (or zips) at the crotch for easy access to baby's bottom, which you'll be visiting quite often – otherwise you'll be undressing and redressing at every nappy change.

Two-piece outfits. These are less practical, so try to limit yourself (it will be hard!) to one or two of them. Look for ones that snap together at the waist so the trousers don't fall off and the shirt doesn't ride up.

Three to six rompers (one-piece, short-sleeved, snap-at-the-crotch outfits without legs), for a late-spring or summer baby.

Three to six nightgowns with elastic bottoms. While stretchies can also stand in as sleepwear, some parents prefer nightgowns for their babies, especially in the early weeks, when the easy-open bottoms make those middle-of-the-night nappy changes more convenient. Nightgowns that close at the bottom with drawstrings (most have elastic instead) shouldn't be used once your baby becomes more active (removing the string eliminates any choking or strangulation risk, but if you do, the gown will creep up during the night). Sleepwear for children must meet government standards for flame resistance; there will usually be a label on the sleepwear advising parents whether or not that particular item meets safety standards.

Two to three blanket sleepers, for late-autumn or winter babies. These sleepers keep baby cuddly warm without a duvet or blanket (which should be avoided because of the risk of suffocation or Sudden Infant Death Syndrome – SIDS – see page 256). Bag sleepers shouldn't be used past five months.

One to three sweaters. One lightweight sweater will do in summer; heavier ones will be needed in cold weather. Look for ones that are washable and dryable as well as easy on, easy off.

One to three hats. Summer babies need at least one lightweight hat with a brim (for sun protection). Winter babies need one or more heavier-weight hats (a lot of the body's heat escapes through the head, and since a baby's head is disproportionately large, there's a lot of potential for heat loss). The hats should be shaped to cover the ears snugly but not too tightly.

One bunting or snowsuit with attached mittens, for a late autumn or winter baby. If you're buying a sleeping bag, look for one that has a slot on the bottom for a car seat strap, to make buckling up easier and more secure.

Two to three pairs of booties or socks. As you'll soon find out, these are often kicked off within moments after they're put on (something you don't usually notice until you're halfway down the street or on the other side of the shopping centre), so look for styles that promise to stay put.

Three washable bibs. Even before you bring on the puréed peas and strained

carrots, you'll need these to protect clothes from spit-up and drool.

Three to four waterproof pants, nappy covers or nappy wraps, if you're planning to use cloth nappies. If you're using disposables, you might consider one pretty pair for special occasions (though probably only if your baby's a girl and will be wearing dresses).

BABY'S LINENS

Whatever colours and patterns you choose, when it comes to linens, size matters. Sheets and mattress pads must fit the mattresses you'll be using *tightly.* That way they won't come loose and pose a safety risk.

Three to four fitted sheets each, for cot, carrycot and/or pram. All sheets should fit *very snugly,* so they can't be pulled out. You might also consider half-sheets that tie or snap onto the cot bars and go on top of the fitted sheet. If your baby spits up a lot, it'll be easier to change just the half-sheet instead of removing the hard-to-remove fitted sheet. Be sure the half-sheets are securely attached.

Two to six waterproof pads, for protecting cot, pram, furniture and laps.

Two quilted mattress pads, for cot (to protect the mattress). Again, the fit should be very snug.

Two washable cot or carrycot blankets (optional). These are fine for use in the pram or over a baby who's buckled into a car seat (or a baby who's otherwise being supervised). But blankets should be avoided for sleep (especially after the first month) because such bedding is a risk factor for SIDS. It's much safer to dress your baby in blanket sleepers or other warm nightclothes instead. If you do choose to use a blanket, it should be lightweight and not densely woven, without any long fringes or with a loose weave that might unravel; it should be tucked under the mattress and only reach baby's underarms. Once baby's able to move around more (sometime after the first month, though possibly earlier or later), a blanket shouldn't be used at all for sleep.

One to two blankets for pram or buggy. Just one lightweight blanket for a summer baby.

Two to three terry-cloth towels. Hooded towels are best, since they keep baby's head warm after a bath.

Two to three soft flannels.

A dozen square cloth nappies or 'muslins' (burping cloths), for protecting your shoulders when burping baby, to protect sheets when baby spits up, for emergency bibs, and much more.

Two to five swaddling blankets, depending on the season. Newborns like to be swaddled, and swaddling or 'receiving' blankets are useful when trying to make your baby cozy. See page 144 for tips on how to swaddle your baby safely.

Nappies. If you're using disposable nappies, buy one or two packets of the newborn size and then wait until after baby is born (so you'll know how big your baby is) before purchasing several dozen nappies in the right size. If you're using cloth nappies and plan to wash them yourself, purchase two to five dozen prefolded cloth ones, plus two dozen disposable nappies (once you know how big the baby is) so you can use them for outings and emergencies. If you are planning on using a nappy service, sign up in your eighth month and they will be ready to deliver as soon as you do. You might also want to buy some nappy liners to pad the front of the nappy if you're expecting a boy (a boy's concentrated flow is more likely to lead to leaks) or just for extra night-time protection.

BABY'S GROOMING NEEDS

Babies smell pretty terrific naturally, and as far as their grooming needs are concerned, less is almost always more. So buy products that have as few additives and fragrances as possible (remember, baby skin is very tender), and keep in mind that many products marketed to parents of infants aren't even necessary. Even some of the following are optional. Items needed for nappy changes should be kept on a shelf high enough above the changing table to prevent baby's grabbing for them but low enough for you to reach easily.

Baby soap or bath liquid or foam, to be used sparingly. Look for a gentle formula.

No-tears baby shampoo. For young infants, no-tears baby bath or foam (which may be easier to control because it stays put) can be used for shampoo.

Baby oil. This can come in handy if you need to gently clean a sticky bowel movement off a sore bottom. It's also often prescribed for cradle cap.

Baby powder, optional. Contrary to popular belief, babies don't really need to be powdered (though a little is nice in warm weather). But if you choose to powder, use a cornflour-, not talc-based product.

Ointment or cream for nappy rash. Ask the doctor for a recommendation.

DON'T GO NUTS

When buying lotions for your baby, read labels carefully and don't buy those that contain peanut oil. Researchers have found that infants (particularly those with skin conditions) who are rubbed with such creams may be at a higher risk of developing peanut allergies by age two. Luckily, most baby lotions made in the UK don't contain peanut oil, but some foreign-made baby products do, and so do some domestically made creams not specifically marketed for infants.

Petroleum jelly, such as Vaseline, for lubricating rectal thermometers. Do not use to treat nappy rash.

Baby wipes, for nappy changes, hand washing on the go, cleanups after spit-ups and leaky nappy incidents, and dozens of other uses. But use cotton wool balls and plain water for cleansing baby's bottom during the first few weeks and whenever nappy rash is a problem.

Sterile cotton wool balls, for cleaning baby's eyes, for nappy changes in the first few weeks, and when baby has a nappy rash.

Baby nail scissors or clippers. Never use sharp adult scissors; babies are squirmy and cuts can easily result.

Baby brush and comb, which hairless babies won't need for a few months at least. If baby ends up having lots of hair, use only a wide-toothed comb for hair that's wet and tangled.

Eight nappy pins, if you'll be using them. Metal heads are better than plastic, which can crack.

BABY'S MEDICINE CABINET

Have these supplies on hand rather than waiting to buy them when you need them (usually in the middle of the night and/or the middle of a snowstorm). Ask your baby's doctor for recommendations on brands and dosages. Most importantly, store them out of reach of infants and children.

Liquid aspirin substitute, such as Calpol (paracetamol).

Antiseptic ointment or cream, for minor cuts and scrapes.

Hydrogen peroxide, for cleaning cuts. A non-stinging spray that numbs or relieves pain as it cleans can make the job even easier.

Calamine lotion or hydrocortisone cream (0.5 per cent), for mosquito bites and itchy rashes.

Rehydration fluid (such as Dioralyte), if the baby's doctor recommends it for treatment of diarrhoea.

Sunscreen, which is now recommended even for infants under six months old when sun protection is otherwise impossible. Look for a gentle made-for-baby formulation.

Rubbing alcohol, for swabbing on umbilical stump or for cleaning thermometers, but not for rubdowns.

Calibrated spoon, dropper and/or oral syringe, for administering medications. (Whenever possible, use the one that comes with a medication.)

Sterile bandages and gauze pads, in a variety of sizes and shapes.

Adhesive tape, for securing gauze pads.

Tweezers, for pulling out splinters.

Nasal aspirator, a bulb syringe for clearing a stuffy nose (see page 547).

Ear syringe, for removing wax buildup, if baby's doctor recommends it.

Cool mist humidifier. Humidifiers can help a baby sleep when his or her nose is stuffed up, though they're not a necessity. Cool mist is the best – warm mist or steam humidifiers can lead to burns – but keep in mind that they must be cleaned thoroughly and according to the manufacturer's directions to avoid the growth of mould and bacteria.

A digital thermometer. It is no longer recommended that parents use glass mercury thermometers because of the dangers of mercury exposure. Tympanic (ear) thermometers are less reliable in infants than rectal or axial (armpit) ones. The newer temporal artery thermometers that take the temperature on the forehead, have been shown in studies to be very accurate; they may become more widely available and affordable. (See page 568 for more on thermometers.)

Small penlight, to check throat for inflammation or pupils after a head injury (see page 585).

Tongue depressors, for examining the throat.

Heating pad and/or hot-water bottle, for soothing a colicky tummy or relieving sore muscles.

BABY FEEDING SUPPLIES

You'll need to stock up on more of these supplies, of course, if you'll be bottle feeding, either exclusively or in combination with breastfeeding. But even exclusive breastfeeders will have to invest in a few of the following, if only for backup.

Four bottles, 120-ml (4-fl oz) size, and ten to twelve bottles, 250-ml (8-fl oz) size, with teats and rings, if you're bottle feeding; four to six bottles, 250-ml (8-fl oz) size with teats and rings if you're supplementing; one bottle, 250-ml (8-fl oz) size with teat and ring for emergency supplementary feeding if you're breastfeeding exclusively. Opt for BPA-free bottles if possible. Bottles come in three types: *traditional-style* bottles have straight necks and bodies; bottles with *angled necks* are designed to reduce baby's air intake by keeping the teat filled with liquid (less air equals less gas; some say the angle may reduce the incidence of ear infections by keeping baby in a more upright position during feedings); *disposable* systems consist of a reusable holder with disposable liners or plastic bags, which collapse as baby feeds, also minimizing air swallowing.

Teats come in several shapes (including the orthodontic shape and those with a wide base to mimic a mother's nipple) and with different hole sizes (smaller for younger babies, larger for older ones). Silicone teats are odour and taste free, don't get gummy, are dishwasher safe, and are see-through (so you can see if they're clean). Try several types to see which work best for your baby.

Utensils for formula preparation, if you're bottle feeding. Exactly which items you'll need will depend on the type of formula you plan to use, but the shopping list will usually include bottle and teat brushes, large measuring jug, measuring cup, possibly a can opener, long-handled mixing spoon, and a dishwasher basket to keep teats and rings (collars) from being tossed around the dishwasher.

A breast pump, if you're breastfeeding and want to express milk so someone else can feed the baby while you're at work or away for a few hours. See page 150 for information on the types of

breast pumps available and advice on choosing one.

A dummy, if you decide to use one. It's not technically a feeding supply, but it will satisfy your baby's oral needs when he or she wants to suck but isn't hungry. Look for sturdy construction and ventilation holes in the shield. Like teats, dummies also come in easy-to-clean silicone. Never attach a cord or ribbon that's more than 15 cm (6 in) long to a dummy.

Nursery Necessities and Niceties

A baby's needs are basic: a pair of loving arms to be cuddled and rocked in, a set of breasts (or a bottle) to feed from, and a safe, secure environment. In fact, many of the multitudes of products, furnishings and accessories marketed for the nursery aren't even necessary. Still, you'll be doing plenty of buying when it comes to baby's new room. Decor won't much matter to that room's resident (at least, not at first). Though you'll likely spend hours agonizing over it, your newborn won't care whether the bumpers are adorned with jumping bunnies or shooting stars, or whether the wallpaper coordinates with the sheets. What does matter, however, is that the nursery provides the safe, secure environment your baby needs. Which means, among other things, a cot that meets current safety standards, a bumper that fits snugly, a changing table that won't take a tumble, and lead-free paint on everything. When choosing furniture for your baby's nursery, as you've undoubtedly already noticed in your first forays to the store, there are endless styles,

colours, finishes and features to pick from. Though you can certainly make choices with an eye towards style (and budget, of course), your first allegiance should be to selecting the products that will be safest and most efficient.

In general, look for items that have only lead-free paint; sturdy non-tip construction; smooth edges and rounded corners; and safety restraint straps at the crotch and waist, where appropriate. And while most, if not all, manufacturers comply with safety guidelines, when shopping, you should avoid choosing any items that have rough edges, sharp points, or small parts that might break loose; exposed hinges or springs; or attached strings, cords or ribbons. Be sure to follow the manufacturer's directions for use and maintenance of all items and to regularly check baby's cot, infant seat and other equipment for loose screws, frayed straps, supports that have snapped, and other signs of wear. Also, always send in your product registration card so that you can be notified in case of a recall.

Cot. Your baby's cot is one of the more important pieces of furniture you'll buy. You'll want it to be safe, comfortable, practical and durable (not only so it will survive the two or three years your baby will be sleeping in it, but also so that you can reuse it for any future siblings). There are two basic types of cots: *standard* cots can come with single or double drop sides, though most manufacturers have stopped making cots with dropped sides because of safety concerns. Some models have a drawer on the bottom for storage. A *convertible* cot can theoretically take your infant from baby all the way to teenager (if it lasts that long), converting from a cot to a toddler bed and then to a day or full-size bed.

When choosing a cot, look for a label stating that safety standards have been met; cot slats that are no more than 6 cm (2⅜ in) apart (smaller than the diameter of a fizzy drink can), with no splinters or cracks in the wood; minimum rail height of 66 cm (26 in) when the mattress is at its lowest position; at least 23 cm (9 in) between the mattress support and the top of the drop side when lowered; a secure locking mechanism for the drop side; and no peeling paint, rough corners or posts or knobs that protrude. You should also look for a cot that has a metal mattress support (which will support a jumping toddler better than wood), adjustable mattress height so the mattress can be lowered as your baby grows, casters (with a wheel lock) for mobility, and a plastic covering on teething rails (so your baby doesn't chew on the wood).

Do not use antiques or cots older than ten years. Old cots (especially those made before 1973, but even some made in the 1980s and 1990s) may be charming or of great sentimental value, but they do not meet current safety standards. They might have slats that are too far apart, may contain lead in the paint, may have cracked or splintered wood, may have been recalled, and may have other dangers.

Cot mattress. Because your baby will likely be spending twelve to sixteen hours (or more) a day sleeping on it, you'll want to make sure the cot mattress you select is not only safe and comfortable, but also high quality. There are two types of cot mattresses: *innerspring* and *foam*. An innerspring mattress is heavier than a foam one and will usually last longer and keep its shape better, offering better support. It's also more expensive than a foam mattress. A good (though not an absolute) rule of thumb when choosing an innerspring mattress is to look for one with a high number of coils. The higher the count (usually 150 or more), the firmer (and better quality, and safer) the mattress. A foam mattress, made of polyester or polyether, weighs less than the innerspring mattress (making changing sheets – which you'll be doing often – much easier). If you're buying foam, look for a mattress with high foam density, which will mean more support and safety for your baby. More important than the type of mattress you choose is that it be firm and fit snugly in the cot, with no more than two adult-finger widths between cot and mattress.

Bumper. From pink-and-white gingham to Winnie-the-Pooh, boldly coloured choo-choo trains to dainty flowers, parents today have no problem finding a cot bumper that suits their taste and nursery decor. But while you may appreciate the bumper for the design statement it makes, it's not a necessity (baby won't really get hurt if his or her arms or legs get momentarily caught between the cot slats), nor is it always safe (though there are breathable mesh bumpers that lower the risk of suffocation should an infant press his or her face up against them). If you do choose to use a bumper, be sure it has a snug (not floppy) fit around the entire perimeter of the cot. There should also be at least six ties or sets of poppers for fastening it to the cot rails. The ties should not be longer than 15 cm (6 in) to avoid any risk of strangulation.

At most baby stores, bumpers are sold as part of a bedding set; the bumper, cot sheet and duvet come packaged together. While it might look very coordinated, using the duvet as a blanket for your baby is not a good idea. To reduce the risk of suffocation or SIDS, soft bedding, pillows and fluffy blankets or duvets should *never* be used in your baby's cot (see page 257). Use the duvet and pillow as decoration elsewhere in your baby's room, or save them for when your baby graduates to a bed.

Carrycot or cradle. Because you don't really need a carrycot or cradle (they can be used for only the first four months or so; you can skip them and go directly to a cot), they don't fall into the 'necessary' category. Still, they sure can be nice to have in the early weeks, when baby may enjoy their cozy quarters and you may appreciate their convenience. Another advantage of the carrycot or cradle is that its height is usually fairly close to that of your bed, allowing you to reach over and comfort (or lift out) your baby in the middle of the night, without even getting out of bed. A carrycot is also lightweight and can be moved from room to room. Some can hit the road, too, folding neatly for travel. A cradle is less mobile, but most will rock back and forth, providing the soothing motion that babies crave (though most experts agree that the more effective rocking direction is the head-to-toes motion of a rocking chair and not the side-to-side motion of a cradle). Some cradles come with a battery-operated vibrating feature to help soothe babies to sleep. Look for a lock that keeps the cradle from moving around when baby's sleeping.

When shopping for a carrycot or cradle, resist antiques or heirlooms, which may be unsafe. Look for one that has a sturdy stable base, is an adequate size to hold your baby, has a firm mattress that fits snugly, has rigid (not soft) sides, and meets all current safety standards. Cradle sides should be at least 20 cm (8 in) high (when measured from the mattress to the top). You will appreciate a cradle that has wheels, but if it does, look for one that also has wheel locks. If it is a folding model, learn how to securely lock the legs; if it has a hood, make sure it folds back (so that you can easily put your sleeping baby in it). Some cradles convert to bedside sleepers (see below).

Bedside sleepers. Another item not in the 'necessity' category, a bedside sleeper is nice to have if you want to co-sleep with your baby, are nursing, or just want to reach over in the middle of the night for a reassuring pat. The bedside sleeper has a high padded rim on three sides and one open side that fits flush against your bed mattress at the same height as an adult bed, allowing for easy access to baby.

Changing space. By the time your baby reaches his or her first birthday, chances are you'll have changed nearly 2,500 nappies (without even winning any honours

in the *Guinness Book of World Records*).
With that staggering number in mind,
you'll want to set up a comfortable place
to change those nappies – one that is also
convenient, safe, and easy to clean.
Though it's nice to buy a table designed
specifically for changing baby, it's not
really necessary. You can actually turn an
ordinary dresser or table into a changing
space. If you go that route, you'll need to
shop for a thick pad with a safety strap to
place on the dresser to keep it protected
and to keep baby secure and comfortable. Make sure, too, that the dresser
height is comfortable for you (and whoever else will be doing nappy duty) and
that the pad doesn't slide off the dresser
top when you're changing a squirmy
baby.

If you're planning to buy a changing table, you'll have two options: a
stand-alone changing table (look for one
that is sturdy and has solid legs, a protective guardrail, safety straps, washable
padding, nappy storage within your
reach, and toiletry storage out of baby's
reach), or a *combination* dresser/chang-
ing table, which has an oversize top or a
flip-open top with a pad. If using the
flip-open type of changing table, do not
place baby's weight on the outer edge:
That can cause the entire chest to
topple. As with the stand-alone changing table, look for one that is sturdy and
has safety straps, a washable pad and
adequate storage space for nappies,
wipes, creams and other items.

If you do opt for the stand-alone
style, be sure to purchase (or have on
hand) a chest of drawers or other type of
storage unit for baby's clothes.

Nappy bucket. Your baby's bottom is
sure to be sweet and adorable. But what
comes out of it probably won't be.
Luckily, nappies are there to catch it all.
But to catch all those dirty nappies,
you'll need a nappy bucket designed to

whisk away and store the evidence (and
odour). If you're using disposable nappies, you can choose a fancy nappy
bucket that tightly seals (or even coils)
nappies in an odour-preventing plastic
liner. Or look for one that uses ordinary
refuse bags (because the special liner
refills can get expensive). Whichever
type you use, remember to empty the
bucket often (but hold your nose when
you do, because the stench of stored
nappies can knock you off your feet).

If you are using cloth nappies,
choose a bucket that is easy to wash and
has a tight-fitting top that a baby or toddler can't pry open. If you're using a
nappy service, the service will usually
provide you with a deodourized nappy
bucket and cart away the stinky contents weekly.

Baby bath. New babies are slippery
when wet – not to mention squirmy. All
of which can serve to unnerve even the
most confident parents when it comes
time for that first bath. To make sure it's
fun and safe to rub-a-dub-dub when
your infant's in the tub, invest in or
borrow a baby bath – most are designed
to follow a newborn's contours and
offer support while preventing him or
her from sliding under the water. They
come in a myriad of styles: plastic, foam
cushions, mesh sling, and so on. Some
'grow' with your baby and can be used
all the way through the toddler years
(when placed in a regular bathtub).

When buying a baby bath, look for
one that has a non-skid bottom and a
smooth rounded edge that will retain its
shape when filled with water (and baby);
is easy to wash; has quick drainage, a
roomy size (large enough for your baby at
four or five months, as well as now), support for baby's head and shoulders,
portability, and has a mildew-resistant
foam pad (if applicable). Another alternative to the baby bath is a thick sponge

specially designed to cushion the baby in a sink or a tub.

Infant seat. Bouncer seats, baby rockers or infant activity seats (designed for newborns to age eight or nine months) can be invaluable for parents of young babies, not only because they can calm a fussy baby, but also because they can give parents' arms a rest. An infant seat will allow you to have your baby safely nearby (but not on your shoulder) while you cook, fold laundry, use the computer, take a shower, or do just about anything else. And since such infant seats are lightweight and take up little room, they can be moved from kitchen to bathroom to bedroom quite easily. And your baby will appreciate being propped up at a gentle incline, allowing him or her a great view for watching you (baby's favourite entertainment) as you go about your daily routine.

There are two basic types of infant seat: the lightweight *framed* seat (also known as a bouncer seat), which has a flexible frame covered with a fabric seat and bounces or rocks back and forth using your baby's weight and movement; and the hard-shelled *battery-operated* infant seat, which, with the flip of a switch, provides a constant rocking or vibrating motion. Both kinds of infant seat often come with sunshade canopies (useful if you'll be using it outdoors) and a removable toy bar that can provide entertainment and activities for your baby. Some models have a sounds-and-music feature. There are even infant seats that double as travel cots, while still others that can be transformed into a toddler seat when your baby gets older.

When choosing an infant seat, look for one with a wide, sturdy, stable base; non-skid bottom; safety restraints that go around baby's waist and between his or her legs; comfortable padding; and a removable padded insert so the seat can be used for your newborn and then later for your older infant. Choose one that is lightweight and portable and, if battery operated, has an adjustable speed. For optimum safety, never leave an infant, even a very young one, in an infant seat at the edge of a table or counter or near something (such as a wall) he or she could push off from. Be sure to always keep your baby safely strapped in. Don't carry the seat with your baby in it, and never use an infant seat as a car seat.

Rocking chair or glider. The traditional rocking chair that has been around for years (chances are there's one that's been passed down in your family) has, in recent years, been usurped in popularity by the glider-rocker, which 'rocks' you and your baby in a smooth horizontal gliding motion. Gliders are safer in a nursery than rocking chairs because they don't have runners, which children can get caught under. While a glider is optional, many parents find it's great for feeding and for calming baby. Many come with matching gliding ottomans so you can kick up your tired feet as you glide. An advantage of a glider-rocker is that it's a purchase that will continue to be used even as baby grows (you can read to your toddler on it, use it yourself while watching TV, and so on).

There are many different designs to choose from when buying a glider; most have seat and back cushions; some have arm pads (which your weary arms will appreciate). Glide before you buy; try it out in the store to find the one that's most comfortable for you.

Baby monitor. A baby monitor allows parents to keep tabs on a sleeping infant without standing guard over the cot (though, realistically, you'll be doing plenty of that in the first few weeks, too). It's ideal if your baby's room is out of earshot of your bedroom or other parts of the house. During the day, a baby monitor allows you the freedom to do things around the house while your baby naps; at night you can sleep in another room, yet still hear when your baby wakes for a feeding.

There are two types of monitors: audio and audio-video. The basic *audio* monitors transmit sound only. The transmitter is left in your baby's room, and the receiver either goes where you go (battery operated and clipped on) or plugs in to an outlet in the room you'll be in. Some monitors have two receivers so both parents can listen in (or you can keep one receiver in your bedroom and the other in the kitchen, for example). An added feature to the audio monitor is the 'sound-and-light' feature. Such a monitor has a special LED display that enables you to 'see' the sound level of your baby. The *audio-video* model allows you to see and hear your baby on a TV screen using a small camera placed near the baby's cot. High-tech models have infrared technology so you can see your baby even if it is dark in the nursery.

When choosing a baby monitor, you'll first have to determine if you'll need one with low-range frequency (49 MHz) or high-range frequency (900 MHz). If you live in a high-rise apartment building or a densely populated area, you're likely to experience interference from other sources such as mobile phones, cordless phones, or radios if you choose one with low frequency. So choose a 900 MHz one (or the newer 2.4 GHz for even more clarity), and look for one that offers more than one channel (so you can change channels if you're picking up your neighbour's phone conversation instead of your baby's cries, as interesting as the former might prove). Also look for models that can use batteries and A/C adapters; have a low-battery indicator; volume control (so you can decide if you want to hear your baby's every breath or just his or her cries); compact size; and are safe (no exposed parts that can cause electrocution). Remember to keep both the transmitter and receiver out of baby's (and older children's) reach.

Baby swing. Ask most parents to name the single best piece of baby equipment they purchased, and chances are they'll say the baby swing. Baby swings can be nothing short of miraculous when it comes to soothing a fussy baby; they can also give parents some much-needed time off from rocking baby in their arms. (Some babies dislike the swing and are not comforted by it; before you buy one, test it out – with your baby in it – at a friend's house or in the store.) Swings either have a windup mechanism or are battery operated (something you'll certainly appreciate if your baby really loves the swing). There are also portable swings that are lightweight and easy to carry (in case you think your baby will need the swing while visiting grandma).

When selecting a swing, look for a sturdy frame; a wide base; secure safety straps; smooth surfaces free of sharp edges, hinges that can catch little fingers, or small parts that can break off; a seat that reclines for a young infant; an activity tray for diversion; adjustable speeds; quiet motor or quiet crank mechanism; and easy accessibility. Check if the swing you're purchasing is safe for babies under six weeks old (some aren't), and stop using the swing when your baby reaches 6.8 to 9 kg (15 to 20 lb) (check the manufacturer's weight recommendations). Never use the swing as a substitute for supervision; use it only when baby's in the same room as you. Also, limit the amount of time your baby spends in the swing, especially at high speeds; some babies can get dizzy from a lot of swinging time.

Night-light. As you stumble out of bed for yet another middle-of-the-night feeding, you'll be thankful for a night-light (or a lamp with a dimmer) in your baby's room. Not only will it keep you from tripping over that stuffed giraffe you left in the middle of the floor, but it will also keep you from having to turn on a bright light (which will be jarring for you and baby, disturbing the sleepy darkness and making a return to dreamland more elusive). Look for a plug-in model that can safely be left on, and remember to put it in an outlet that baby can't reach.

Travel cot. If you plan on travelling often to places where such equipment will not be available (or may not meet safety standards), you should consider a travel cot. Travel cots are smaller than full-size cots, fold up easily, fit in the boot of a car, and are available in wood, plastic or with mesh sides. If buying one, look for easy folding, storage, and portability. See Playpen, page 59 for more on safety features.

Equipment for Outings

Because you're not going to want to *literally* be a stay-at-home parent – even if you're not going back to work – you'll need to prepare for taking your baby out of the house by getting (at a minimum) a buggy and a car seat. As with nursery furniture, when choosing outing equipment there are endless styles, colours, finishes and features to pick from. Once again, your job is to make sure whatever you choose for your baby is chosen with safety, comfort and your budget in mind. You'll also want to take into account your lifestyle (Are you in and out of your car often? Do you walk to the corner grocery store to do your shopping? Will you be boarding buses with baby daily?) before selecting outing equipment.

In general, look for items that meet safety standards and have adequate safety straps at the crotch and waist, where appropriate. You should avoid choosing any items that have rough edges, sharp points or small parts that might break loose; exposed hinges or springs; or attached strings, cords or ribbons. Be sure to follow the manufacturer's directions for use and maintenance of all items and to regularly check baby's buggy, car seat and other equipment for loose screws, frayed straps, supports that have snapped, and other signs of wear. Also, always send in your product registration card so that you can be notified in case of a recall.

Pushchair and/or pram. The right buggy (or pushchair) can make your daily life with baby – from the proverbial walk in the park to that hike to the shops – much more manageable and much less exhausting. But wading through the dozens of choices (and price tags) in the store can be overwhelming, to say the least. Because there are so many different types of buggies, prams, travel systems, joggers and pushchair/pram combinations available, you'll need to consider your lifestyle in order to find the one (or ones) right for you. Will you be taking long, leisurely strolls with your baby on quiet suburban streets (or in that park)? Or will you be hitting the jogging trails with junior? Do you spend a lot of time getting in and out of your car? Or more time climbing in and out of buses or railway stations? Will you be taking mostly short walks to the corner shop, or will you also be taking long trips with your baby on aeroplanes or trains? Do you have a toddler at home who still likes to be in a buggy? Are you (or your spouse or caregiver) very tall or very short? Do you live in a small walk-up apartment, a flat or a house with many steps at the front door? Once you've answered these questions, you're armed with enough information to make your choice. And, depending on your budget, you might consider buying more than one type for more flexibility. The basic pushchairs and prams available include:

♦ *Classic pram:* Considered the 'limousine' of baby carriages, this type of baby toter is similar to the kind grandma used to use. These are typically very sturdy, have large (non-swivelling) wheels for a smooth ride, shock-absorbing suspension, and elegant canopies and fabrics. In most, the carriage component snaps into the chassis (and can double as a carrycot) and the baby faces the parent. Prams are large, heavy (weighing around 18 kg/40 lb), extremely durable (can be passed down to all your children), and usually expensive. They are a great choice if you'll be taking long strolls with baby but won't have to be navigating flights of stairs on your way in and out of your home.

♦ *Convertible pram-pushchairs:* Because only prams (with their flat surface) or pushchairs that recline are appropriate for a baby under three

months, a convertible pram-pushchair can be a good choice for parents who want the sturdiness and comfort of a pram but also the convenience and manoeuvrability of a pushchair. The convertible models recline fully to a flat surface, allowing a parent to look down into the pram at their newborn. Once the baby gets a little older (four to six months), the handle is flipped, the seat back pushed up, and presto, you've got yourself a front-facing pushchair. Most models fold relatively compactly, and while they are heavier and more cumbersome than standard pushchairs (see below), they are also very durable and will last many years (and through many babies, if you're so inclined).

♦ *Standard pushchair:* These models are designed to be portable and fold compactly. Most are made of aluminum (generally weighing just over 6.8 kg (15 lb)); are sturdy and easy to fold; have a reclining seat; and provide a smooth ride. Although they are heavier and more cumbersome when travelling (or hopping in and out of buses or subways) than buggies (see below), they are a good choice for parents looking for durability and comfort.

♦ *Buggy.* Buggies (which are sometimes referred to as 'umbrella' pushchairs because of their curved handlebars) are feather-light (usually weighing between 2.25 to 6.8 kg/5 to 15 lb) and exceptionally easy to fold. When folded, they are extremely compact for convenient carrying and storing. Since most do not recline or offer sufficient padding or support, they can't be used for small babies, but they're ideal for older children, especially when travelling, using public transport, or getting in and out of a car often. You may want to hold off on buying a buggy until your baby's big enough to use it. (A kickstand is a great addition to a buggy; it can keep a bag-laden buggy from tipping backwards when you lift baby out.)

◆ *Travel system pushchair:* Travel system pushchairs are convenient 'all-in-ones', combining car seat and pushchair in one package. The base is a standard pushchair that allows an infant car seat to be snapped on top. Parents find this especially convenient because they can move a sleeping baby from car to pushchair without waking him or her up. And once your baby outgrows the infant car seat, the bottom part can be used as a stand-alone pushchair, similar to the standard pushchair described above. These travel system pushchairs are usually heavier than standard pushchairs (even though the pushchair base is not usually as sturdy as a standard pushchair), but are a good choice for those looking for car convenience. There are also lightweight pushchair *frames* available that allow any brand of infant car seat to be clipped on, providing the same advantages as those of the larger pushchair system, though when the baby gets too big for the car seat, the frame can't be used as a stand-alone pushchair.

◆ *Jogger pushchair:* Looking for a way to get back into shape and bring baby along? If you're an avid jogger or enjoy long walks in the country, a jogger pushchair might be the right choice for you. These pushchairs have three large wheels, great suspension, provide a smooth ride for your child on all terrains, and are

lightweight. Many have a braking system, come with wrist straps and a storage pouch or basket, and are easy to manoeuvre (though they should be used only on smooth terrain). Most aren't designed to tote newborns, so if you're looking to hit the jogging path sooner rather than later, choose one that comes with an infant seat attachment so baby can recline in comfort and safety while you sweat that pregnancy weight off.

◆ *Double (or triple) buggy:* If you're expecting baby number two and you have a toddler at home, or if you are having twins, you'll need a double buggy (or triple if you're expecting triplets, have a toddler and new twins, or have twin toddlers and a new baby). Double buggies offer the convenience of pushing two children as comfortably (almost) as pushing one. The two types of double buggy are the side-by-side model or tandem (one seat in front of the other). If you're buying a side-by-side model, look for one that has reclining seats and can fit through doorways and aisles (most do, but some are too wide for narrow passageways). A tandem model is great for a newborn and a toddler but can be heavy to push, and when baby gets bigger, your children may fight over who gets the 'front seat'. Another option if you have an older child: a pushchair that has a sitting ledge or standing platform in the front or back so you can push both children together.

Regardless of which type of pushchair you buy, be sure it meets current safety standards. Look for one with a wide wheel base and swivel wheels (if applicable) for easy manoeuvrability, and good wheel brakes. Keep in mind

WHAT'S IN A BUCKLE?

The five-point harness has five straps: two at the shoulders, two at the hips, and one at the crotch. Experts usually rate this type of harness as safest because it offers more points of protection. Look for this type if choosing a convertible car seat; a newborn fits best in this type of harness.

that better-quality nylon or metal (and thus more expensive) wheels will last much longer, are easier to manoeuvre, and provide a smoother ride than those made of soft plastic. A good brand will also have buckles that are easy for you (but not your crafty toddler) to latch and unlatch. Buckles should also fit snugly around your baby's waist and crotch, be adjustable, and be comfortable. A jogging pushchair should have a five-point harness (with shoulder straps) for maximum safety. Plastic buggies are light and easy to carry but are not as sturdy (and won't last as long) as those made from aluminum. Steel ones are also sturdy but can be quite heavy. Washable fabric and padding that is removable is a plus, as you'll find out the first time the nappy leaks or the juice spills.

Each type of pushchair comes with

its own set of bells and whistles. Decide from the many available features what you won't be able to live without, what you'll find useful, and what you probably won't end up needing at all: a large basket or storage area to tote nappy bag, groceries or baby toys (don't overload handles with bags or other items, since the weight could tip the pushchair over and baby with it); adjustable handle height if anyone who will be pushing the pushchair is very tall; a rain cover; child feeding tray; a tray for parents complete with cup holder (for your latte); changing bag hooks; removable weather boot; sun canopy or parasol; canopy with sunroof; adjustable footrest; one-handed fold; one-handed steering.

Pushchairs that have reclining seats are necessary for a small infant and advantageous for when your toddler falls asleep. If you'll be folding your pushchair often (to store in your house, to put in the car, to get on a bus), you'll want one that has an easy open and close mechanism, and one that you can fold and unfold while holding your baby.

Finally, before buying any pushchair, take it for a test drive in the store to see how easy it is to handle, if it is comfortable for you and your baby, and how it folds and unfolds.

Child car seat. Car seats aren't just for your peace of mind and your baby's safety, they're required by law. In fact, most hospitals won't even let you take your baby home unless you have an infant car seat securely strapped into your car's backseat. Even if you don't own a car, you'll need a car seat if you ever plan to get into a cab, go for a drive in someone else's car, or rent a car. More than any other item on your shopping list, this is the one you'll need to have before that first contraction hits.

When choosing a child car seat, be sure it meets government safety

REAR-FACING INFANT SEAT

*A rear-facing seat should be used until a baby is at least one year old and 9 kg (20 lb). The harness slots should be at or below your baby's shoulders; the harness chest clip should be at the infant's armpit level. Check the instructions to see how the carrying handle should be positioned during travel. **Never** place any rear-facing infant seat in the front seat of a vehicle, particularly one equipped with air bags.*

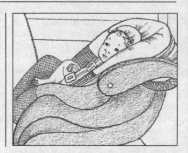

standards. Never borrow an older car seat or use one that's already been in an accident. Also be sure to send in the registration card so the manufacturer can notify you if there is a recall on your car seat. See page 132 for information on installing your baby's car seat properly and more safety tips.

There are many types of car seats available. The right type of safety seat will depend on your child's age, size and weight. Features within each category vary from manufacturer to manufacturer, so decide which model works best for your situation, then choose a seat that's easy to use and that fits well in your vehicle.

◆ *Rear-facing infant car seats:* These seats, designed to support a baby's head, neck and back, are installed rear-facing (facing the back window of your vehicle) in the backseat and recline at a 45-degree angle. You can choose either a three- or five-point harness buckling system, though five-point provides by far the best protection and is favoured by safety experts. Many models have a stay-in-car detachable base that allows for quick installation and easy removal.

After buckling your baby into the seat, you simply lock the seat into the base. (This feature is also helpful if you're using a travel system pushchair, see page 51.) These seats can also be used without the base. Rear-facing car seats usually have carrying handles that vary in style and ease of use. Angle indicators, built-in angle adjusters and head support systems are standard on most infant car seats. A rear-facing seat should be used until your baby is *at least* one year old *and* 9 kg (20 lb). Children who reach 9 kg (20 lb) before the first birthday (many babies reach that weight by nine months or even sooner), or who outgrow the infant seat height-wise (they're 68.5 cm/27 in tall and/or their head has reached the top of the car seat back) still need to stay in the rear-facing position until they're a year old. Some rear-facing infant car seats can be used up to 13.5 to 16 kg (30 to 35 lb), making it easier for you to keep a big baby rear-facing the full year, or you can switch to a convertible seat (and use it in the rear-facing position) when baby's outgrown the infant seat.

◆ *Infant-toddler convertible seats:* These

THE LATCH SYSTEM

This safety seat attachment system makes child safety seats easier to use and safer than ever. The system, called Lower Anchors and Tethers for CHildren (LATCH), makes correct installation much less complicated because you don't need to use seat belts to secure the safety seat.

The system requires that the car seat be equipped with top tether strap attachments. The adjustable tether strap is a belt that better stabilizes the car seat and reduces the potential for your child's head to be thrown forward in a collision. The tether strap is anchored to the upper back of the child car seat and hooks into the rear shelf area, the ceiling, or the floor of your vehicle. The majority of cars, minivans and light trucks built after model year 2000 can accommodate the tether strap; tether kits are also available for most older car seats.

The majority of vehicles made after model year 2002 also have lower anchors located between the vehicle's seat cush-

ion and seat back, which enables a car seat (made after year 2002) to be snapped into the anchors for a secure fit. Together, the lower anchors and upper tethers make up the LATCH system. Remember, if you have a car seat and/or car made before model year 2002, you still *must* use your car's seat belts to secure the car seat.

---

seats can be used in the rear-facing position for babies under one year and 9 kg (20 lb) and in the front-facing position for children up to 18 kg 18 kg (40 lb) (around four years old; weight specifications vary from model to model, so read the information on their packaging carefully). One advantage to this type of seat is that your baby can use it from birth right through the toddler years. Another advantage is that it can accommodate babies who are too tall or heavy for most infant seats, keeping them in the recommended rear-facing position until at least the first birthday. The drawback is that it provides a less secure fit for the newborn than the rear-facing infant seat.

If you do choose a convertible car seat, make sure your baby can recline comfortably in the seat in the rear-facing position.

♦ *Toddler-only forward-facing seats:* These car seats are used for children *at least* one year old *and* over 9 kg (20 lb) and can be used, depending on the model, until your toddler is 18 to 27 kg (40 to 60 lbs). These usually are available with the five-point harness (which is considered by far the safest), the T-shield, or the overhead (or tray) shield. Some models convert to a belt-positioning booster seat when your child is over 18 kg (40 lb).

CONVERTIBLE SEAT/ FORWARD-FACING SEAT

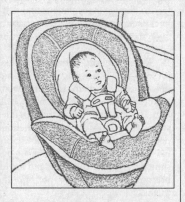 

Designed for children from birth to 18 kg (40 lb), this unit faces the rear in a semi-reclining position for infant use, then can be switched to an upright, front-facing position when baby is older. When in the front-facing position, the car seat (like a toddler-only forward-facing car seat) should be in *the upright position, and the shoulder straps should be moved to the slots above your child's shoulders. The harness chest clip should be at your child's armpit level. Place this seat (and all children under the age of thirteen) in the rear seat of the vehicle.*

◆ *Booster seats:* An adult lap-shoulder belt does not fit properly (and therefore isn't safe) until a child is at least eight years and is approaching 145 cm (57 in) tall. So from the time your child is 18 kg (40 lb) and outgrows the toddler (or convertible) seat until he or she is tall enough and mature enough to sit safely in an adult safety belt, you'll need to use a booster seat. A belt-positioning booster seat is used with the car's lap/shoulder belts. It raises your child so that the adult seat belts fit properly, assuring that your child's upper body and head will be protected in a collision. (The shield booster, an older-model booster designed to be used with a lap belt only, does not provide enough upper body protection, according to most experts, and is no longer certified for use in children weighing more than 18 kg/40 lb.)

Your child should continue to use a booster until he or she can sit all the way back against the vehicle seat with his or her knees bending comfortably at the edge of the seat cushion; the lap portion of the belt should fit tightly across the top of the thighs (and not ride up over the belly), and the shoulder portion should fit tightly over the shoulder (and not cut into the neck or face). You won't need a booster seat until your child has graduated from the toddler or convertible seat, and since models change from year to year, you're much better holding off on this purchase. (For more on booster seats and safety, see *What to Expect the Toddler Years*).

♦ *Integrated safety seats:* Some vehicles on the market feature front-facing child safety seats that are built in, or integrated, into the vehicle's seat itself and can accommodate a child up to 27 to 29.5 kg (60 or 65 lb). These seats are very convenient, eliminating the need to install and remove the safety seat (and the possibility of installing it incorrectly). Keep in mind, however, that you'll still need a rear-facing infant car seat for your baby and a booster seat for when he or she gets older.

Baby carrier or sling. Marsupials (such as kangaroos) and many human cultures have known for millennia the benefits of 'wearing' a baby: convenience (no pushchair or pram to push), efficiency (parental hands are freed up for any number of multitasks, from doing laundry, to checking e-mail, to carting groceries, to eating dinner), enhanced comfort for baby (babies who are worn cry less), and enhanced pleasure for parents (nothing beats having a sweet, warm baby snuggled at your breast). For those reasons and for dozens of others, most every parent will appreciate having a baby carrier or sling on hand in the first year of life and beyond. There are as many styles of carriers and slings to choose from as there are reasons for buying or borrowing one:

Front carriers consist of a fabric compartment supported by two shoulder straps. They are designed so your baby can either face inwards (especially useful for when baby is sleeping or for a newborn who doesn't have good head control) or face outwards (so baby can enjoy the same sights as you). They feature adjustable straps that distribute weight evenly so that your back and shoulders share the load. Most can accommodate an infant up to 13.5 kg (30 lb), though many parents find that a backpack works better once baby is over six months. Some front carriers convert to backpacks.

When choosing a front carrier, look for one that is easy to hook up and detach without help and that won't require you to wake up your baby to slip him or her out; adjustable, padded straps that don't dig into your shoulders; easy washability; breathable fabric (so baby won't overheat); head and shoulder support for baby; and a wide bottom that supports bottom and thighs.

A *sling carrier* is a wide swath of fabric that slings across your body, supported by a shoulder strap. Infants are able to lie down comfortably in them or face outwards. An older baby can straddle your hip while being supported by the sling. An additional plus for nursing mothers: slings allow discreet and convenient breastfeeding. When choosing a sling, look for washable, breathable fabric; a well-padded and comfortable strap; and trimness (one that isn't bulky with extra fabric).

A *framed carrier* is a backpack frame made of metal or plastic with a fabric seat. Unlike front carriers, which distribute baby's weight on your shoulders and neck, a backpack carrier places the weight on your back and waist. This type of carrier is not recommended for babies under six months old but can be used for children up to 18 kg (40 lb) and age three (depending on the model). When choosing one, look for models that have a built-in stand, which helps make loading and mounting easier; are moisture resistant; and have: cleanable fabric, adjustability, safety straps or harness to prevent your child from climbing out, firm and thick shoulder strap padding, lumbar support to help distribute the weight down towards your hips, and storage pockets for baby paraphernalia (so you don't have to lug a separate changing bag on your shoulder as well). A heavy-duty backpack is necessary for long hikes. A lightweight model is fine for errands. A backpack that converts to a pushchair could come in quite handy.

Carriers should not be used while driving, jogging, exercising or cooking. Always bend at the knees to pick something up when 'wearing' your baby (so he or she doesn't slide out), and stay off stools and ladders. *Never* use a carrier instead of a car seat, and never leave a child unattended and propped up in a back carrier – even for a moment.

Changing bag. Have baby, will travel – but you won't get far without a changing bag. A changing bag is, for most parents, something they don't leave home without . . . ever. But with so many on the market, how do you choose? Simple: the best changing bag for you is the one that best suits your needs. For example, if you're doing any bottle feeding, you'll want a changing bag that has a separate insulated bottle holding area. Also consider size and carrying comfort. You don't want one that can't fit more than one nappy and a bottle in it; on the other hand, a very large one will be too unwieldy to lug around. Look for one in a moisture-resistant material such as nylon or vinyl with multiple roomy compartments (so you can keep nappies, especially dirty ones, away from bottles and food); a shoulder strap or backpack style; a zip closing for the main compartment; a detachable changing pad; style, if that's important to you (some parents prefer the kind of sleek, sophisticated changing bag that could pass as a large handbag; others like one that screams 'baby' – complete with pastel ducks or alphabet blocks, while still others seek a bag to match their pushchair or baby blanket). You can also adapt any other carrier (such as a gym bag, backpack or over-size handbag) for carrying baby gear.

When Baby Gets Older

Already overwhelmed by the length (and expense) of your shopping list? Here's some good news: the following items won't be needed until baby's older, which means you can safely put off purchasing them. However, you may still want to register for the big-ticket items in case a close friend or relative (or a group of friends or relatives chipping in together) opt to buy them for you now.

High chair. You won't need a high chair until your baby is on solids (usually around six months old; babies who start solids earlier can be fed in an infant seat).

Still, next to the cot and the car seat, the high chair is one of the most indispensable of baby furnishings. Again, you'll find a staggering number of models to choose from, with a variety of features; some have adjustable height, others recline (which makes them perfect for feeding babies under six months), while still others fold up for storage.

When choosing a high chair, look for one that meets government safety standards with a wide, sturdy, non-tip base; a tray that can be easily removed or locked in place with one hand; a wide lip to catch spills; a seat back high enough to support baby's head; comfortable

BUYING FOR BABY'S FUTURE

Now that you've bought the truckloads of baby paraphernalia you'll need for the first year (and then some), it's time to put some thought into the kind of planning that's not sold in any stores – planning that will protect your baby's future.

Write a will. Many adults do not have a will. Being without a will is always a risky proposition, but it can result in especially unfortunate circumstances in the case of young families, whose children might be left unprotected if their parents pass away. Even if you don't have many financial assets, you'll need to name at least one guardian who will be able to raise your child (or children) if you and your spouse die before they reach the age of eighteen. If you don't have a will stating your preferences, the courts will determine who gets custody of your children.

Start saving. As much as you think it will cost to raise your child, it will probably cost a lot more. The sooner you start putting money away for your child's future expenses (especially education) the better, because your initial investment, even if it's small, will have more time to grow. Start now, with your next pay cheque; eighteen years from now, you'll be glad you did.

Buy life insurance for yourself (not baby). But make sure it's the right kind. Financial planners advise that parents buy term life insurance to protect the rest of your family in case you die. Such insurance provides a benefit upon death without any cash accumulation. You should also consider disability insurance, since younger adults are more likely to be disabled (and thus unable to earn sufficient income) than to die prematurely.

padding; safety straps; a crotch post to keep baby from slipping down; wheels that lock; a secure locking device if the chair folds; and no sharp edges. Also important: make sure the high chair you choose is easy to clean (plastic or vinyl seat, plastic tray).

There are plenty of hand-painted wooden high chairs available (at high cost) for style-conscious parents; however, they often get low marks in practicality once less-style-conscious baby starts smearing them with apple purée and mashed bananas.

Portable feeding seat. Also called *booster seats,* these are invaluable when you're visiting friends or relatives or dining at restaurants that don't provide them; otherwise your baby will be dining on your lap. They also come in handy when your toddler's ready to move to the

table with you but isn't quite ready for prime-time seating. (Once they start walking – and sometimes before – toddlers lose patience with being confined in tight spaces, such as high chairs, and appreciate the relative freedom of a booster.) A booster seat is a plastic seat that can be strapped onto a regular chair. Many have adjustable seat levels; some have attachable trays.

Another option is the seat that locks directly onto a table, though some question the safety of these hook-on types; there is the risk that your child might unhook the chair by pushing back with his or her feet. And not all tables can accommodate hook-on models. When buying a portable feeding seat, look for a comfortable seat; sturdy design; safety straps to prevent baby's slipping out; portability; if applicable, a removable tray; and a locking mechanism to prevent falls. See page 330 for safety tips.

Bath seat. Once baby outgrows the baby bath, but before he or she is big enough to comfortably sit in the big bath, a bath seat can come in handy. Look for safety straps and a suction bottom. Most importantly, never leave your child unattended in a bath seat, and always keep him or her within arm's reach. A child can slip under the water and drown in the time it takes to fetch a towel or answer a telephone.

Playpen. These are usually rectangular in shape, with a floor, mesh sides and rails that lock and unlock for easy (but safe) collapsibility and folding. Most fold into a long rectangle and come with a carrying case for easy transport. Some have wheels; others have removable padded changing stations that fit on top, built-in cradles for newborns, side storage areas, and even a canopy for shade (useful if you bring the playpen outdoors). Playpens can also be used as travel cots when travelling. When choosing a playpen, make sure it meets government safety standards and has fine-mesh netting that won't catch fingers or buttons; removable fitted sheets for easy cleanup; tough pads that won't tear easily; padded metal hinges; a babyproof collapse mechanism; quick setup; easy folding; and portability.

Safety gate. As soon as junior starts to crawl (or starts getting around another way, such as creeping or cruising), you should install safety gates wherever potential hazards might lurk (doorways to rooms that are unsafe for baby; the top and bottom of stairs). *Pressure-mounted* gates consist of two sliding panels that adjust to the size of the doorway and then lock into place by wedging against the doorposts. Such a gate shouldn't be used on stairs.

Another option is the *wall-mounted* gate, which attaches directly to the wall using screws and can withstand a lot more force than the pressure-mounted ones. This type of gate usually has a swinging door plus a latch that locks it shut. When choosing a safety gate, look for a label indicating it meets government safety standards; expandability (to fit all size doorways and stairs); sturdiness; slats (if there are any) no more than 6 cm (2⅜ in) apart; a latch that is easy to open and close (or you may neglect to close it), preferably with a one-handed release. Do not use an old accordion-style gate – they are unsafe.

Stationary entertainers (ExerSaucer). Mobile walkers are no longer recommended because of the risk of injury and even death. Instead, parents have the option of purchasing a stationary entertainment toy (commonly called an ExerSaucer) that allows a baby to bounce, jump, spin and play while staying safely in one place. When choosing, look for one with height adjustment (so it can grow with baby); a padded, washable seat that spins in a full circle; a sturdy stationary base; and a wide selection of attached toys and activities. If you do opt for an ExerSaucer, make sure you do not leave your baby in it for long periods of time (see page 331 for reasons why).

◆ ◆ ◆

CHAPTER 3

Breastfeeding Basics

They make it look so easy, those nursing mothers you've seen. Without skipping a beat of conversation or a bite of salad, they lift their shirts and put their babies to breast. Deftly, nonchalantly, as though it were the most natural process in the world.

The fact is, however, that while the source may be natural, nursing comfort and know-how – especially for first-time mothers – are often not. Sometimes there are physical factors that foil those first few attempts; at other times, it's just a simple lack of experience on the part of both participants.

Your early nursing experiences might be blissful – with baby latching on quickly and suckling until satiated. Or, more likely, they might go something like this: even with your most concerted efforts, you can't seem to get baby to hold on to your nipple, never mind to suck on it. The baby's fussy; you're frustrated; soon you're both in tears.

If that second scenario has been playing out for you and your baby as you begin breastfeeding, don't throw in the nursing bra. You're not failing, you're just getting started. Nursing, like most other fundamentals of parenting, is learned, not instinctive. After a little time, and a little instruction, it won't be long before your baby and breasts are in perfect synch. Some of the most mutually satisfying breast-baby relationships begin with several days, or even weeks, of fumbling, of bungled efforts, and of tears on both sides. Before you know it, you'll be making it look easy – and natural, too.

Getting Started Breastfeeding

There's no magic formula (so to speak) for a successful breastfeeding relationship. But there are plenty of steps you can take, right from the very beginning, to give you and your baby an edge in breastfeeding success:

Get an early start. Early-bird nursers tend to catch on sooner, not to mention latch on sooner. If both you and baby are up to it, nurse as soon as possible after birth – right in the birthing or delivery room is best. Babies show an eagerness and readiness to suck during the first two hours after birth, with the sucking reflex most powerful about thirty minutes after delivery. But don't worry if you and baby aren't successful right off the bat. Trying to force the feeding when you're both exhausted from a difficult delivery only sets the stage for a disappointing experience. Cuddling at the breast can be just as satisfying as nursing in the first few moments of your baby's life. If you don't get around to feeding right after delivery, ask to have the baby brought to you for nursing as soon as possible after all necessary nursery procedures have been completed. Keep in mind, too, that even an early start doesn't guarantee instant success. No matter when you first get going, plenty of practice may be needed before you and your baby make perfect.

Beat the system. Many hospitals and most birthing centres recognize the importance of getting a mother and baby off to a good breastfeeding start. But even the most enlightened hospitals are usually run for the greater good – which sometimes doesn't coincide with the needs of the breastfeeding mother and baby. To make sure you aren't thwarted in your efforts by arbitrary regulations, ask your doctor *in advance* to make your preferences (demand feeding, no bottles, no dummies) known to the staff, or explain them to the nurses yourself.

Get together. Making sure you and your baby are together most or all of the time can give early breastfeeding a much better chance of success, which is why rooming-in can be ideal. If you're tired from a difficult delivery, or don't feel confident enough yet to deal with the baby on a twenty-four-hour basis, partial rooming-in (days, but not nights) may be preferable. With this system you can have your baby with you all day for demand feeding, and have a nurse bring you the baby for night feedings when he or she wakes, perhaps allowing you to get much-needed sleep.

If twenty-four-hour rooming-in isn't available, isn't possible (some hospitals allow rooming-in only in private rooms or when both patients in a shared room want to keep their babies with them), or doesn't appeal to you, you can ask to have the baby brought to you when he or she is awake and hungry, or at least every two to three hours.

Ban the bottle. Make sure your baby's appetite and sucking instincts aren't sabotaged. Some hospital nurseries still try to quiet a crying baby between breastfeeding sessions with a bottle of sugar water. Even a few sips of sugar water will satisfy tender appetites and early sucking needs, leaving baby more sleepy than hungry when brought to you later. You may also find your baby reluctant to struggle with the breast nipple after a few encounters with an artificial one, which yields results with a lot less effort. Worse still, if your breasts aren't stimulated to produce enough milk, a vicious cycle begins – one that interferes with the establishment of a good demand-and-supply system.

Dummies and formula feedings can also interfere with nursing. So issue strict orders through your baby's doctor that supplementary feedings and dummies not be given to your baby in the nursery unless medically necessary. You may even want to put a sign on the baby's cot that reads: 'Breastfeeding only – no bottles please.'

Take requests. Feeding on demand – when baby is hungry, not when a schedule dictates – is generally best for breastfeeding success. But in the early days, when baby's less hungry than sleepy, chances are there won't be much demand, and you'll have to initiate most of the feedings. Strive for at least eight to twelve feedings a day, even if the demand isn't up to that level yet. Not only will this keep your baby happy but it will also increase your milk supply to meet the demand as it grows. Imposing a four-hour feeding schedule, on the other hand, can worsen breast engorgement early on and result in an undernourished baby later.

Don't let sleeping babies lie. Some babies, especially in the first few days of life, may be a lot more interested in sleeping than feeding and may not wake for nourishment often enough. Although babies don't need that much milk (or colostrum) in the first few days, your breasts need all the stimulation they can get to make sure that when your week-old baby does wake up for his feedings, you'll have enough milk to combat his or her hunger. For tips on waking a sleeping baby for feeding, see page 115.

Know the signs. Ideally, you should feed your baby when he or she first shows the signs of hunger or interest in sucking, which might include mouthing the hands or rooting around for the nipple, or just being particularly alert. Crying is not a feeding cue, so try not to wait until frantic crying – a late sign of hunger – begins. But if crying has started, do some rocking and soothing before you start nursing. Or offer your finger to suck on until baby calms down. After all, it's hard enough for an inexperienced sucker to find the nipple when calm; when your baby has worked up to a full-fledged frenzy, it may be impossible.

Practice, practice, practice. Consider the feedings before your milk comes in as 'dry runs', and don't be concerned that baby is getting very little in the way of nourishment. Your milk supply is tailored to your baby's needs. Right now those needs are minimal. In fact, the newborn stomach can't tolerate a lot of food, and the tiny quantity of colostrum you're

producing is just right. Use those initial feeding sessions to work on your nursing technique rather than to fill baby's belly, and be assured that he or she isn't starving while you're both learning.

Give it time. No successful breastfeeding relationship was built in a day. Baby, fresh out of the womb, is certainly inexperienced – and so are you if this is your first time. You both have a lot to learn, and you'll both have to be patient while you learn it. There will be plenty of trial and even more error before supplier and demander are working in concert. Even if you've successfully nursed another baby before, each newborn is different, and the road to breastfeeding harmony may take different turns this time around.

Keep in mind that things may go even more slowly if one or both of you had a difficult time during labour and delivery, or if you had anaesthesia. Drowsy mothers and sluggish infants may not be up to tackling the art of breastfeeding just yet. Sleep it off (and let baby do the same) before getting serious about the task ahead of you.

Don't go it alone. Get some professional help, if you can. Hopefully, a breastfeeding specialist will join you during at least a couple of your baby's first feedings to provide hands-on instruction, helpful hints and perhaps literature – as is routine in some hospitals and many birthing centres. If this service isn't offered to you, ask if a lactation consultant or a nurse who is knowledgeable about breastfeeding can observe your technique and redirect you if you and your baby are not on target. If you leave the hospital or birthing centre before getting help, someone with breastfeeding expertise – either the baby's doctor, a home midwife or an outside lactation consultant – should evaluate your technique within a few days.

You can also find empathy and advice by calling either your local NCT

GETTING HELP

There are many resources for the breast-feeding mum. Here are some places to contact for help and more information:

♦ Association of Breastfeeding Mothers
PO Box 207
Bridgwater TA6 7YT
08444 122 949
24-hour helpline for breastfeeding mothers.
www.abm.me.uk

♦ www.breastfeeding.co.uk
Support and information on all aspects of breastfeeding, and the chance to chat on-line with mothers about their experiences of breast-feeding.

♦ National Breastfeeding Helpline
0300 100 0212 (9.30 AM to 9.30 PM, 7 days a week)

♦ La Leche League
PO Box 29
West Bridgford
Nottingham NG2 7NP
0845 120 2918
(those who take the calls are mothers like you, answering the phone in their own home, so only call in the evenings or at weekends if it's urgent)
www.laleche.org.uk

♦ National Childbirth Trust Breastfeeding Line
0300 330 0771
(8 AM to 10 PM, 7 days a week)
Can put you in touch with a local NCT breastfeeding counsellor. You do not need to be an NCT member to get this help.
www.nct.org.uk

group or La Leche League chapter. Volunteers at both organizations are experienced nursing mothers who are trained to become accredited leaders. They hold regular meetings and are available for telephone consultations. Or enlist the support of friends, relatives, and others who have breastfed successfully.

Keep your cool. This isn't easy to do when you're a brand-new mother, but it's vital for breastfeeding success. Tension can inhibit the let-down of milk, which means that even if you are producing milk, it may not be dispensed until you relax. If you're feeling edgy, banish visitors from the room before you feed your baby. Do relaxation exercises if you feel they might help, pick up a book or magazine, or just close your eyes and listen to soft music for a few minutes.

Breastfeeding basics

Building a successful breastfeeding relationship with your baby will depend on proper technique and know-how. Understanding how lactation works, learning how to properly position your baby at the breast, being sure that your baby is correctly latched on, and knowing when a feeding is over or when baby needs another meal will all gradually lead to a growing sense of confidence, the comforting feeling that you're 'doing it right'. To enhance your chances of success, boost your nursing savvy before you put baby to breast by taking this minicourse first.

HOW LACTATION WORKS

Lactation, or breastfeeding, is the natural completion of the reproductive cycle; here's how it works:

◆ **How it's made.** The process of milk production is automatically initiated the instant you push out the placenta, as your body, which has spent nine months feeding your baby inside you, busily gears up for the shifts in hormones that will allow you to feed baby from the outside. The levels of the hormones oestrogen and progesterone decline dramatically in the moments after delivery, and the level of the hormone prolactin (one of the hormones responsible for lactation) rises dramatically, activating the milk-producing cells of your breasts. But while hormones trigger the start of lactation, they can't keep milk production going without some help – and the help comes in the form of a tiny mouth, namely your baby's. As that tiny mouth suckles at your breast, your prolactin level increases, stepping up milk production. Just as important, a cycle begins – one that ensures that a steady production of milk will continue: Your baby removes milk from your breasts (creating demand), your breasts produce milk (creating supply). The more the demand, the more the supply. Anything that keeps your baby from removing milk from your breasts will inhibit the supply. Infrequent feeding, feedings that are too brief, or ineffective suckling can all quickly result in diminished milk production. Think of it this way: the more milk the baby takes, the more milk the breast will make.

◆ **How it flows.** It's not enough to produce milk; if it's not released from the tiny sacs where the milk is manufactured, baby doesn't get fed and further production is suppressed. That's why the single most important function that affects the success of breastfeeding is the let-down reflex, which allows the milk to flow. Let-down occurs when your baby suckles, prompting the release of the hormone oxytocin, which in turn stimulates the flow of milk. Later on, when your breasts get the hang of let-down, it may occur whenever suckling seems (at least, to your body) imminent – as when your baby's due for a feeding, or even when you're just thinking about your baby.

◆ **How it changes.** The milk your baby gets is not a uniform fluid in the way that formula is. The composition of your milk changes from feeding to feeding and even within the same nursing session. The first milk to flow when your baby starts suckling is the foremilk. This milk has been dubbed the 'thirst quencher' because it is dilute and low in fat. As the nursing session progresses, your breast produces and secretes hind milk – milk that is high in protein, fat and calories. If you cut a nursing session short, your baby will be getting only the foremilk and not the fattier, more nutritious hind milk, causing hunger to strike sooner, and even inhibiting weight gain. Be sure at least one breast is well drained at each feed to guarantee your baby is getting the hind milk. You'll be able to tell if baby has emptied enough of the breast if it feels much softer when the feeding is finished than it did when you began. (Keep in mind that a lactating breast is never truly empty; there's always some milk available, and there's always some being produced.) You'll also notice the milk flow has decreased to a trickle and your baby swallows less often than when your breast was full of milk.

BEGINNING TO BREASTFEED

Here's how to make sure the milk gets where it's supposed to go:

◆ Seek some peace and quiet. Until breastfeeding becomes second nature to you and baby (and it will!), you'll need to focus as you feed. To do this, set yourselves up in an area that has few distractions and a low noise level. As you become more comfortable with breastfeeding, you can keep a book or magazine handy to occupy you during long feeding sessions. (But don't forget to put your reading material down periodically so you can interact with your nursing infant; that's not just part of the fun of nursing, it's part of the benefit for baby.) Talking on the telephone can be too distracting in the early weeks, so turn down the ringer and let voice mail or the answer phone pick up messages. You may also want to avoid watching television during feedings until you get the hang of breastfeeding.

◆ Get comfy. Settle into a position that's comfortable for you and your baby. Try sitting on the living room sofa (as long as it's not too deep), a glider in the baby's room, an armchair, or propped up in bed. You can even nurse lying down in bed. If you're sitting up, a pillow across your lap will help raise your baby to a comfortable height. Plus, if you've had a Caesarean, the pillow prevents baby from putting pressure on your

scar. Make sure, too, that your arms are propped up on a pillow or chair arms; trying to hold 2.7 to 4 kg (6 to 9 lb) without support can lead to arm cramps and pain. Elevate your legs, too, if you can. Experiment to find the position that works best for you – preferably one you can hold for a long time without feeling strained or stiff.

◆ Quench your own thirst. Have a drink – of milk, juice or water – by your side to replenish fluids as you nurse. Avoid hot drinks (which could scald you or your baby, should they spill). If you don't feel like having a cold drink, opt for something lukewarm. And add a healthy snack if it's been a while since your last meal; the better fed you are, the better fed baby will be.

BREASTFEEDING POSITIONS

There are plenty of positions you and your baby can eventually explore while breastfeeding. But the most important one to know is the 'basic' position, the one from which most other positions take form: position your baby on his or her side, facing your nipple. Make sure that baby's whole tiny body is facing you – you're tummy to tummy – with his or her ear, shoulder and hip in a straight line. You don't want your baby's head turned to the side; rather it should be straight in line with his or her body. (Imagine how difficult it would be for you to drink and swallow while turning your head to the side. It's the same for your baby.)

Lactation specialists recommend two nursing positions during the first few weeks: the crossover hold and the clutch hold. Once you're more comfortable

Crossover hold

Clutch hold

Cradle hold

Side-lying position

with breastfeeding, you can add the cradle hold and the side-lying position. So get into your starting position, and try:

◆ *Crossover hold:* Hold your baby's head with the hand opposite to the breast from which you'll be nursing (if you're nursing on the right breast, hold your baby's head with your left hand). Your wrist should rest between your baby's shoulder blades, your thumb behind one ear, your other fingers behind the other ear. Using your right hand, cup your right breast, placing your thumb above your nipple and areola at the

spot where your baby's nose will touch your breast. Your index finger should be at the spot where your baby's chin will touch the breast. *Lightly* compress your breast. This will give your breast a shape that more closely matches the shape of your baby's mouth. You are now ready to have the baby latch on.

◆ *Clutch hold:* This position is especially useful if you've had a Caesarean and you want to avoid placing your baby against your abdomen, if your breasts are large, if your baby is small or premature, or if you're nursing twins. Position your baby at your side in a semi-sitting position facing you, with baby's legs under your arm (your right arm if you are nursing on the right breast). Use pillows to bring the baby up to the level of your nipple. Support your baby's head with your right hand and cup your breast with your left hand as you would for the crossover hold.

♦ *Cradle hold:* In this classic breast-feeding position, your baby's head rests in the bend of your elbow and your hand holds your baby's thigh or buttocks. Baby's lower arm (if you're nursing from your right breast, it's baby's left arm) is tucked away, under your arm and around your waist. Cup your breast with your left hand (if nursing from the right breast) as in the crossover hold.

♦ *Side-lying position:* This position is a good choice when you're nursing in the middle of the night or when you need some rest (or, rather, when you can have some rest; you'll always need it). Lie on your side with a pillow supporting your head. Position your baby on her side facing you, tummy to tummy. Make sure her mouth is in line with your nipple. Support your breast with your hand as in the other nursing positions. You may want to put a small pillow behind your baby's back to hold her close.

Whichever position you choose, be sure you bring baby to the breast – not breast to the baby. Many latching-on problems occur because mum is hunched over baby, trying to shove her breast in baby's mouth. Instead, keep your back straight and bring your baby to the breast.

A Proper Latch

A good position is a great place to start. But for breastfeeding to succeed, a proper latch – making sure that baby and breast hook up just right – is a skill you'll have to master. For some mothers and infants it's effortless; for others, it takes a lot of practice.

♦ What a good latch looks like: a proper latch encompasses both the nipple and the areola (the dark area surrounding the nipple). Baby's gums need to compress the areola and the milk sinuses located underneath it in order to start the flow. Sucking on just the nipple will not only leave your infant hungry (because the glands that secrete the milk won't be compressed) but will also make your nipples sore and even cracked. Be sure, too, that your baby hasn't completely missed the mark and started sucking on another part of the breast entirely. Newborns are eager to suck even if no milk is forthcoming and can cause a painful bruise by gumming sensitive breast tissue.

♦ Get ready for a good latch: once you and your baby are in a comfortable position, gently tickle your baby's lips with your nipple until his or her mouth is open very wide – like a yawn. Some lactation specialists suggest directing your nipple towards your baby's nose and then down to the lower part of the upper lip to get your baby to open his or her mouth very wide. This prevents the lower lip from getting tucked in during nursing. If your baby isn't opening up, you might try to squeeze some colostrum (and later on, milk) onto his or her lips to encourage latching on.

Tickling baby's lip

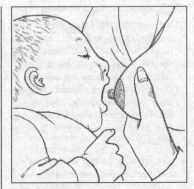

Baby opens wide

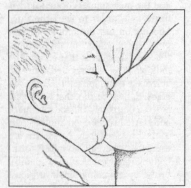

Latching on

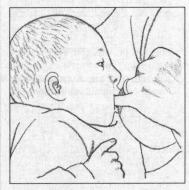

Breaking suction

If your baby turns away, gently stroke the cheek on the side nearest you. The rooting reflex will make baby turn his or her head towards your breast. (Don't press on both cheeks to open your baby's mouth; that will just cause confusion.) Once baby gets the hang of nursing, just the feel of the breast, and sometimes even the smell of milk, will cause him or her to turn towards your nipple.

♦ Seal the deal: once the mouth is open wide, move your baby closer. Do not move your breast towards the baby, and don't push your baby's head into your breast. And be sure not to stuff your nipple into your baby's unwilling mouth; let your baby take the initiative. It might take a couple of attempts before your baby opens his or her mouth wide enough to latch on properly. Remember to keep your hold on your breast until baby has a firm grasp and is suckling well; don't let go of your breast too quickly.

♦ Check the latch: you'll know your baby is properly latched on when the chin and the tip of the nose are

SUCKING VERSUS SUCKLING

It's a subtle distinction that can make all the difference in the success of breastfeeding. To make sure your baby is suckling (that is, extracting milk from your breast), not just sucking (gumming your breast with no results), watch for a strong, steady, suck-swallow-breath pattern. You'll notice a rhythmic motion in baby's cheek, jaw and ear. Later, when your milk comes in, you'll also want to listen for the sound of swallowing (sometimes even gulping) that will let you know that suckling is in progress.

touching your breast. As your baby nurses, your nipple will be drawn to the rear of his or her throat, and those tiny gums will be compressing your areola. Baby's lips should be flanged outwards, like fish lips, rather than tucked in. Also check to be sure your baby isn't sucking his or her own lower lip (newborns will suck on anything) or tongue (because your nipple is positioned underneath the tongue instead of over it). You can check by pulling the lower lip down during nursing. If it does seem to be the tongue that's being sucked, break the suction with your finger, remove your nipple, and make certain baby's tongue is lowered before you start again. If it's the lip, gently ease it out while baby suckles.

Breastfeeding will not be painful if your baby is latched on properly (unless, of course, you have a cracked nipple or a breast infection; see pages 77 and 82). If you feel nipple pain

while nursing, your baby is probably chewing on your nipple instead of gumming the entire nipple and areola. Take the baby off your breast (see below) and latch him or her on again. Your baby is also not latched on properly if you hear clicking noises.

◆ Give baby some room to breathe: if your breast is blocking your baby's nose once he or she's latched on, *lightly* depress the breast with your finger. Elevating your baby slightly may also help provide a little breathing room. But as you manoeuvre, be sure not to loosen that latch you both worked so hard to achieve.

◆ Unlatch with care: if your baby has finished suckling but is still holding on to your breast, pulling it out abruptly can cause injury to the nipple. Instead, break the suction first by putting your finger into the corner of the baby's mouth to admit some air and gently pushing your finger between his or her gums until you feel the release.

HOW LONG TO FEED

It used to be thought that keeping initial feedings short (five minutes on each breast) would prevent sore nipples by allowing them to toughen up gradually. Sore nipples, however, result from improper positioning of the baby on the breast and have little to do with the length of the feeding. As long as your positioning is correct, there is no need to limit the time your baby spends at the breast. Instead, let your baby be your guide; all babies set their own nursing patterns, and following that pattern will help ensure both baby and breasts are satisfied. Expect feedings to be marathon

WHAT TYPE OF NURSER IS YOUR BABY?

Just as every baby has a unique personality, so does each baby have a unique nursing style. Your baby may fall into one of these categories classified by researchers. Or you may find your baby has developed a nursing persona all his or her own.

Barracuda: Your baby's nursing style is barracuda-like if he or she latches on to the breast tenaciously and suckles voraciously for ten to twenty minutes. A barracuda baby doesn't dawdle – feeding time is no-nonsense for him or her. Occasionally, a barracuda baby's suck is so vigorous that it actually hurts at first. If your nipples fall victim to your barracuda baby's strong suck, don't worry – they'll toughen up quickly as they acclimate to nursing with the sharks. (See tips for soothing sore nipples on page 77).

Excited Ineffective: If your baby becomes so wound up with excitement when presented with a breast that he or she often loses grasp of it – and then screams and cries in frustration – it's likely you have an excited ineffective on your hands. Mothers of this type of nurser have to practise extra patience; you'll need to get your baby nice and calm before putting him or her back on the job. Usually, excited ineffectives become less excited and more effective as they get the hang of nursing, at which point they'll be able to hold on to the prize without incident.

Procrastinator: Procrastinators do just that – procrastinate. These slowpoke babies show no particular interest or ability in sucking until the fourth or fifth day, when the milk comes in. Forcing a procrastinator to feed before he or she's game will do no good (as forcing one to do homework before the last minute will surely backfire, but you'll find that out later on). Instead, waiting it out seems to be the best bet; procrastinators tend to get down to the business of nursing when they're good and ready.

Gourmet: If your baby likes to play with your nipple, mouth it, taste a little milk, smack his or her lips, and then slowly savour each mouthful of milk as though composing a restaurant review, he or she is likely a gourmet. As far as the gourmet is concerned, breast milk is not fast food. Try to rush gourmets through their meals and they'll become thoroughly furious – so let them take their time enjoying the feeding experience.

Rester: Resters like to nurse a few minutes and then rest a few minutes. Some even prefer the nip-and-nap approach: nurse for fifteen minutes, fall asleep for fifteen minutes, then wake to continue the feeding. Nursing this type of baby will take time and it will take patience, but hurrying a rester through his or her courses, like hurrying a gourmet, will do no good.

sessions at first. Some newborns can take up to forty-five minutes to complete a feeding (though the average time is twenty to thirty minutes). So don't pull the plug just because your baby has fed for fifteen minutes on breast number one. Wait until he or she seems ready to quit, then offer the second breast, but don't force it.

Ideally, at least one breast should be emptied at each feeding (though, again, your breast is never truly 'empty', just well drained). This is more important than being sure that baby feeds from both breasts. Then you can be certain your baby gets the hind (or fatty) milk that comes at the end of a feeding, and not just the foremilk that comes at the start (see page 64).

The best way to end a feeding is to wait until your baby lets go of the nipple. If your baby does not let go of the nipple (babies often drift off to sleep on the job), you'll know to end the feeding when the rhythmic suck-swallow pattern slows down to four sucks per one swallow. Often, your baby will fall asleep at the end of the first breast and either awaken to nurse from the second (after a good burp, see page 134) or sleep through until the next feeding. Start the next feeding on the breast that baby didn't nurse on at all last time or didn't drain thoroughly. As a reminder, you can fasten a safety pin to your nursing bra on the side you started with at the previous feeding, or you can tuck a nursing pad or tissue in the bra cup on that side. The pad also will absorb any leakage from the breast you're not nursing on (which will be letting down with anticipation).

How Often to Feed

At first, you'll need to nurse often – *at least* eight to twelve times in twenty-four hours (sometimes even more if baby demands it), draining at least one breast at each feeding. Break that down, and it means you'll be nursing every two to three hours (counting from the beginning of each nursing session). But don't let the clock be your guide. Follow your baby's lead (unless he or she is not waking up for feedings), keeping in mind that feeding patterns vary widely from baby to baby. Some newborns will need to nurse more often (every one and a half to two hours), others a little less frequently (every three hours). If you have a more frequent nipper, you may be going from one feeding to the next with only a little over an hour in between – not much rest for your weary

breasts. But don't worry. This frequency is only temporary, and as your milk supply increases and your baby gets bigger, the breaks between feedings will get longer.

How regularly spaced your baby's feedings are may vary, too, from those of the baby down the street. Some thoughtful babies feed every one and a half hours during the day, but stretch the time between night feedings to three or even four hours. Consider yourself lucky if your baby falls into that category – just be sure to keep track of your baby's wet nappies to ensure he or she is getting enough milk with all that sleep (see page 158). Other babies might operate like clockwork around the clock – waking every two and a half hours for a feeding whether it's the middle of the morning or the middle of the night. Even these babies will settle down into a more civilized pattern over the next few months; as they begin to differentiate between day and night, their grateful parents will welcome the gradually longer stretches between night-time feedings.

But while the temptation will be great to stretch out the time between feedings early on, resist. Milk production is influenced by the frequency, intensity and duration of suckling, especially in the first weeks of life. Cutting down on that necessarily frequent demand – or cutting nursing sessions short – will quickly sabotage your supply. So will letting baby sleep through feedings when he or she should be eating instead; if it's been three hours since your newborn last fed, then it's time for a wake-up call. (See page 115 for techniques to wake your baby.)

What You May Be Concerned About

COLOSTRUM

'I just gave birth a few hours ago; I'm beat and my daughter's really sleepy. Do I really need to nurse right away? I don't even have any milk yet.'

The sooner you nurse, the sooner you'll have milk to nurse with, since milk supply depends on milk demand. But nursing early and often does more than ensure that you'll be producing milk in the coming days; it also ensures that your baby will receive her full quota of colostrum, the ideal food for the first few days of life. This thick yellow (or sometimes clear) liquid, dubbed 'liquid gold' for its potent formula, is rich with antibodies and white blood cells that can defend against harmful bacteria and viruses and even, according to researchers, stimulate the production of antibodies in the newborn's own immune system. Colostrum also coats the inside of baby's intestines, effectively preventing harmful bacteria from invading her immature digestive system, and protecting against allergies and digestive upset. And if that's not enough, colostrum stimulates the passage of your baby's first bowel movement (meconium; see page 125) and helps to eliminate bilirubin, reducing any potential jaundice in your newborn (see page 123).

A little colostrum goes a long way. All in all, your baby will extract only teaspoons of it – but amazingly, that's all she needs. And since colostrum is easy to digest – it's high in protein, vitamins and minerals, and low in fat and sugar – it serves as the perfect appetizer to the alimentary adventures that lie ahead.

Suckling on colostrum for a few days satisfies your baby's tender appetite while getting her off to the healthiest start in life. But it also stimulates the production of the next course: transitional milk. Transitional milk, which your breasts serve up between colostrum and mature milk, often resembles milk mixed with orange juice (fortunately, it tastes much better than that to new babies) and is the milk that appears when your milk 'comes in'. It contains lower levels of immunoglobulins and protein than colostrum does, but it has more lactose, fat and calories. Mature milk, arriving between the tenth day and second week postpartum, is thin and white (sometimes appearing slightly bluish). Though it looks like watery skimmed milk, it's actually power packed with all the fat and other nutrients that growing babies need.

ENGORGED BREASTS

'Since my milk came in today, my breasts are swollen to three times their normal size, hard and so painful I can barely stand it. How am I supposed to nurse this way?'

They grew and grew through nine months of pregnancy – and just when you thought they couldn't get any bigger (at least, without visiting a plastic surgeon), that's exactly what happens in the first postpartum week. And they hurt, a lot – so much so that putting on a bra can be agonizing. What's worse, now that the milk's finally arrived, nursing can actually be even more challenging than it was before the milk was there – not just because your breasts are painfully tender, but also because they're so hard and swollen that the nipples may be flat and difficult for your baby to get a grasp on.

The engorgement that accompanies the arrival of a mother's milk (and which can be worse when nursing gets off to a slow start) comes on suddenly and dramatically, in a matter of a few hours. It most often occurs on the third or fourth day postpartum, though occasionally as early as the second day or as late as the seventh. Though engorgement is a sign that your breasts are beginning to fill up with milk, the pain and swelling are also a result of blood rushing to the site, ensuring that the milk factory is in full swing.

Engorgement is more uncomfortable for some women than for others, is typically more pronounced with first babies, and also occurs later with first babies than with subsequent ones. Some lucky women (usually second- and third-timers) get their milk without paying the price of engorgement, especially if they're nursing regularly from the start.

Fortunately, engorgement is blessedly temporary; it gradually diminishes as a well-coordinated milk supply-and-demand system is established. For most women, the swelling and pain last no longer than twenty-four to forty-eight hours, though some suffer through it for as long as a week.

Until then, there are some steps you can take to reduce the discomfort:

◆ Use heat *briefly* to help soften the areola and encourage let-down at the *beginning* of a nursing session. To do this, place a flannel dipped in warm, not hot, water on just the areola, or lean into a bowl of warm water. You can also encourage milk flow by gently massaging the breast your baby is suckling.

◆ Use ice packs *after* nursing to reduce engorgement. And though it may sound a little strange and look even stranger, chilled cabbage leaves may also prove surprisingly soothing (use large outer leaves, rinse and pat dry, and make an opening in the centre of each for your nipple). Or use specially designed cooling bra inserts.

◆ Wear a well-fitting nursing bra (with wide straps and no plastic lining) round the clock. Pressure against your sore and engorged breasts can be painful, however, so make sure the bra is not too tight. And wear loose clothing that doesn't rub against your sensitive breasts.

◆ The best treatment for engorgement is breastfeeding frequently, so don't be tempted to skip or skimp on a feeding because of pain. The less your baby sucks, the more engorged your breasts will become, and the more pain you'll have to suffer. The more you nurse your newborn, on the other hand, the more quickly engorgement will subside. If your baby doesn't nurse vigorously enough to relieve the engorgement in both breasts at each feeding, use a breast pump to do this yourself. But don't pump too much, just enough to relieve the engorgement. Otherwise, your breasts will produce more milk than the baby is taking, leading to an off-balance supply-and-demand system and further engorgement.

◆ Hand-express a bit of milk from each breast before nursing to lessen the engorgement. This will get your milk flowing and soften the nipple so that your baby can get a better hold on it.

◆ Alter the position of your baby from one feeding to the next (try the clutch hold at one feeding, the cradle hold at the next; see page 65). This will ensure that all the milk ducts are being emptied and may help lessen the pain of engorgement.

♦ For severe pain, you might consider taking paracetamol or another mild pain reliever prescribed by your doctor. If you do take a pain reliever, be sure to take it just after a feeding.

'I just had my second baby. My breasts are much less engorged than with my first. Does this mean I'm going to have less milk?'

No, it means that you're going to have less pain and less difficulty nursing – a good thing all around. Though some veteran mums are unlucky enough to experience the same amount of engorgement, or occasionally more, with their second baby than with their first, it's much more common for the breasts to engorge less with the second and subsequent pregnancies. Perhaps it's because your breasts, having been there and done that before, are having less trouble adjusting to the influx of milk. Or perhaps it's because your experience has resulted in more efficient nursing (and draining of the breasts) right from the start. After all, the sooner a baby begins breastfeeding well, the less engorgement typically occurs.

Very rarely, a lack of engorgement and of a sensation of milk let-down does indicate inadequate milk production, but only in first-time mothers. And even most first-timers who don't experience engorgement turn out to have copious milk supplies nevertheless. In fact, there's no reason to worry that a milk supply might not be up to par unless a baby isn't thriving (see page 157).

OVERABUNDANT MILK

'Even though my breasts are no longer engorged, I have so much milk that my baby chokes every time she nurses. Could I have too much?'

Though it may seem right now like you have enough milk to feed the entire neighbourhood – or, at least, a small day care centre – rest assured, you'll soon have just the right amount to feed one hungry baby, namely yours. Many women find there's too much of a good thing in the first few weeks of nursing, often so much that their babies have a hard time keeping up with the flow and end up gasping, sputtering and choking as they attempt to swallow all that's pouring out. You may find, too, that the overflow causes leaking and spraying, which can be uncomfortable and embarrassing (especially when it occurs in public). It may be that you're producing more milk than the baby needs right now, or it may be that you're just letting it down more quickly than your baby can drink it. Either way, your supply and delivery system are likely to work out the kinks gradually over the next month or so, becoming more in synch with your baby's demand, which means that the overflowing will taper off. Until then, keep a towel handy for drying you and baby during feedings, and try these techniques for slowing the flow:

♦ If your baby gulps frantically and gasps just after you have let-down, try taking her off the breast for a moment as the milk rushes out. Once the flood slows to a steady stream she can handle, put baby back to the breast.

♦ Nurse from only one breast at a feeding. This way, your breast will be drained more completely and your baby will be inundated with the heavy downpour of milk only once in a feeding, instead of twice.

◆ Gently apply pressure to the areola while nursing to help stem the flow of milk during let-down.

◆ Reposition your baby slightly so that she sits up more. Some babies will let the overflow trickle out of their mouth to alleviate the problem.

◆ Try nursing against gravity by sitting back slightly or even nursing while lying on your back with your baby on top of your chest (though this may be unwieldy to do often).

◆ Pump before each feeding just until the initial heavy flow has slowed. Then you can put your baby to the breast knowing she won't be flooded with milk.

◆ Don't be tempted to decrease your fluid intake. Neither increasing nor decreasing your fluid intake has any correlation to milk production. Drinking less will not cause you to produce less milk, but it can lead to health problems for you.

Some women continue to be prodigious producers of milk throughout lactation. If that turns out to be the case with you, don't worry. As your baby becomes bigger, hungrier and a more efficient nurser, chances are she'll eventually learn to go with the flow.

LEAKING AND SPRAYING

'I seem to be leaking milk from my breasts all the time. Is this normal? Is it going to last?'

There's no contest when it comes to wet T-shirts (and wet sweatshirts, and wet sweaters, and wet nightgowns, sopping wet bras, and even wet pillows): Newly nursing mothers win hands down. The first few weeks of nursing are almost always very damp ones, with milk leaking, dripping or even spraying frequently. The leaks spring anytime, anywhere, and usually without much warning. Suddenly, you'll feel that telltale tingle of let-down, and before you can grab a new nursing pad to stem the flow or a towel or sweater to cover it up, you'll look down to see yet another wet circle on one or both breasts.

Because let-down is a physical process that has a powerful mind connection, you're most likely to leak when you're thinking about your baby, talking about your baby, or hearing your baby cry. A warm shower may sometimes stimulate the drip, too. But you may also find yourself springing spontaneous leaks at seemingly random times – times when baby's the last thing on your mind (like when you're sleeping or paying bills), and times that couldn't be more public or less opportune (like when you're waiting in a queue at the post office or about to give a presentation at work or in the middle of making love). Milk may drip when you're late for a feeding or in anticipation of it (especially if baby has settled into a somewhat regular feeding schedule), or it may leak from one breast while you nurse from the other.

Living with leaky breasts certainly isn't fun, and it can be uncomfortable, unpleasant and endlessly embarrassing, too. But this common side effect of breastfeeding is completely normal, particularly early on. (Not leaking at all or leaking only a little can be just as normal, and in fact, many second-time mothers might notice that their breasts leak less than they did the first time around.) Over time, as the demand for milk starts meeting the supply, and as breastfeeding becomes better regulated, breasts begin to leak considerably less. While you're waiting for that dryer day to dawn, try these tips:

◆ Keep a stash of nursing pads. These can be a lifesaver (or, at least, a shirt saver) for women who leak. Put a supply of nursing pads in the nappy bag, in your handbag and next to your bed, and change them whenever they become wet, which may be as often as you nurse, sometimes even more often. Don't use pads that have a plastic or waterproof liner. These trap moisture, rather than absorbing it, and can lead to nipple irritation. Experiment to find the variety that works for you; some women favour disposables, while others prefer the feel of washable cotton pads.

◆ Don't wet the bed. If you find you leak a lot at night, line your bra with extra nursing pads before going to bed, or place a large towel under you while you sleep. The last thing you'll want to be doing now is changing your sheets every day – or worse, shopping for a new mattress.

◆ Opt for prints, especially dark ones. You'll soon figure out that these clothes camouflage the milk stains best. And as if you're looking for another reason to wear washable clothes when there's a newborn around, leaking should seal it.

◆ Don't pump to prevent leaking. Not only will extra pumping not contain the leak, it will also encourage it. After all, the more your breasts are stimulated, the more milk they produce.

◆ Apply pressure. When nursing is well established and your milk production has levelled off (but not before), you can try to stem the leak when you feel it starting by pressing your nipples (probably not a good idea in public) or folding your arms tightly against your breasts. Don't do this often in the first few weeks, however, because it may inhibit milk let-down and can lead to a clogged milk duct.

LET-DOWN

'Every time I put my baby to the breast, I feel a strange sensation in my breasts as my milk starts to come out. Is this normal?'

The feeling you're describing is what's known in the breastfeeding business as 'let-down'. Not only is it normal, it's also a necessary part of the nursing process – a signal that milk is being released from the ducts that produce it. Let-down can be experienced as a tingling sensation, as pins and needles (sometimes uncomfortably sharp ones), and often as a full or warm feeling. It's usually more intense in the early months of breastfeeding (and at the beginning of a feeding, though several let-downs may occur each time you nurse) and may be somewhat less noticeable as your baby gets older. Let-down can also occur in one breast when your baby is suckling on the other, in anticipation of nursing, and at times when nursing's not even on the schedule (see previous question).

Let-down may take as long as a few minutes (from first suckle to first drip) in the early weeks of breastfeeding. Once breast and baby get the hang of nursing, let-down usually occurs within a few seconds. Later, as milk production decreases (when you introduce solids or formula, for instance), let-down may once again take longer.

Stress, anxiety, fatigue, illness or distraction can inhibit the let-down reflex, as can large amounts of alcohol. So if you're finding your let-down reflex isn't optimal or is taking a long time to get going, try doing some relaxation techniques before putting baby to breast, choosing a quiet locale for feeding sessions, and limiting yourself to only a single occasional alcoholic drink. Gently stroking your breast before nursing may also stimulate the flow. But don't worry about your let-down. True let-down problems are extremely rare.

A deep, shooting pain in your breasts right after a nursing session is a sign that they're starting to fill up with milk once again; generally those post-feeding pains don't continue past the first few weeks. Stinging or burning pain *during* nursing may be related to thrush (an infection passed from baby's mouth to mother's nipples; see page 122). Nipple pain during nursing can usually be linked to incorrect latching (see page 67).

CLUSTER FEEDINGS

'My two-week-old baby had been nursing pretty regularly – every two to three hours. But all of a sudden, he's demanding to be fed every hour. Does that mean he's not getting enough?'

Sounds like you have a hungry boy on your hands – or, rather, at your breast. He might be going through a growth spurt (most common at three weeks and again at six), or he might just need more milk to keep him satisfied. Either way, what he's doing to make sure he gets that milk is called 'cluster feeding'. His instincts tell him that nursing for twenty minutes every hour is a more efficient way of coercing your breasts to produce the extra milk he needs than nursing for thirty minutes every two or three hours. And so he treats you like a snack bar rather than a restaurant. No sooner does he happily finish a meal than he's rooting around again, looking for something to eat. Put him to the breast again, and he'll do another feed.

Such marathon sessions are exhausting – you may begin to feel as though your baby is permanently attached to your breast. But the good news is that the cluster feeding usually lasts only a day or two, the time it takes for your milk supply to catch up with your growing baby's demand; he's then likely to return to a more consistent – and civilized – pattern of nursing. In the meantime, bring on the feed as often as your little bottomless pit seems to want it.

SORE NIPPLES

'Breastfeeding is something I always wanted to do. But my nipples have become so excruciatingly sore that I'm not sure I can continue nursing my daughter.'

At first you wonder if your newborn will ever catch on to nursing; then, before you know it, she's suckling so vigorously your nipples become sore, even painful. And such tender nipples can make nursing a miserable – and frustrating – experience. Fortunately, most women don't suffer for long; their nipples toughen up quickly, and breastfeeding stops being a pain and starts being a pleasure. But some women, particularly those whose babies are incorrectly positioned, and those who have a 'barracuda baby' (one with a very vigorous suck, see page 70), have continued trouble, with soreness and cracking so painful they may come to dread each feeding. There are, however, routes to relief from sore nipples:

BUMPS ON THE ROAD TO SUCCESS?

Although you may have had access to a lactation specialist in the hospital right after delivery, chances are (unless you had a Caesarean) that you left the hospital within two days of childbirth and before nursing was well established (and even before your milk came in). Unfortunately, most nursing problems don't crop up when help is still as close as the call button next to the hospital bed. They surface once you're home, usually in the first week or two postpartum. If you find the road to breastfeeding success is lined with more bumps than you'd anticipated, don't give up. Instead, pick up the phone and ask for a home visit with a breastfeeding consultant. Many new mothers who experience difficulties with breastfeeding find such visits immensely beneficial, putting them back on the road to success and making them better equipped to handle the bumps along the way. Don't wait, hoping things will get better on their own; the earlier breastfeeding problems are managed, the less likely they'll be to spiral into something less manageable (such as insufficient milk production or baby not getting enough), and the less likely you'll be to give up nursing before you have to. So consider getting help before you consider throwing in the towel. You and your baby deserve it.

♦ Be sure your baby is correctly positioned, facing your breast with the entire areola (not just the nipple) in her mouth when nursing, Not only will her sucking on the nipple alone leave you sore, it will also leave her frustrated, since she won't get much milk. If engorgement makes it difficult for her to grasp the full areola, express a little milk manually or with a breast pump before nursing to reduce the engorgement and make it easier for her to get a good grip.

♦ Expose sore or cracked nipples to the air briefly after each feeding. Protect them from clothing and other irritations and surround them with a cushion of air by wearing breast shells (not shields). Change nursing pads often if leaking milk keeps them wet. Also, make sure the nursing pads don't have a plastic liner, which will only trap moisture and increase irritation.

♦ If you live in a humid climate, wave an electric hair dryer, set on warm, across the breast (about 15 to 20 cm/6 to 8 in away) for two or three minutes (no more). In a dry climate, moisture will be more helpful – let whatever milk is left on the breast after a feeding dry there. Or express a few drops of milk at the end of a feeding and rub it on your nipples, making sure to let your nipples dry before putting your bra back on.

♦ Nipples are naturally protected and lubricated by sweat glands and skin oils. But using a commercial preparation of modified lanolin can prevent and/or heal nipple cracking. After nursing, apply ultrapurified, medical grade lanolin, but avoid petroleum-based products and petroleum jelly itself (Vaseline) and other oily products. Wash nipples only with water – whether your nipples are sore or not. Never use soap, alcohol, tincture of benzoin or premoistened towelettes. Your baby is already protected from your germs, and the milk itself is clean.

- Wet tea bags with cool water and place them on your sore nipples. The properties in the tea will help to soothe and heal them.

- Vary your nursing position so a different part of the nipple will be compressed at each feeding; but always keep baby facing your breasts.

- Don't favour one breast because it is less sore or because the nipple isn't cracked. Try to use both breasts at every feeding, even if only for a few minutes, but nurse from the less sore one first, since the baby will suck more vigorously when hungry. If both nipples are equally sore (or not sore at all), start off the feeding with the breast you used last and didn't drain thoroughly.

- Relax for fifteen minutes or so before feeding. Relaxation will enhance the let-down of milk (which will mean that baby won't have to suck as hard), whereas tension will hinder it. If the pain is severe, ask your doctor about taking an over-the-counter pain medication to relieve it.

- If your nipples are cracked, be especially alert to signs of breast infection, which can occur when germs enter a milk duct through a crack in the nipple. See page 82 for information on clogged ducts and mastitis.

TIME SPENT BREASTFEEDING

'Why didn't somebody tell me I'd be nursing my baby twenty-four hours a day?'

Maybe because you wouldn't have believed it. Or because nobody wanted to discourage you. Either way,

now you know. Nursing is, for many mothers, a nearly round-the-clock job in the early weeks. But take heart; as time passes, you'll spend less of it as a captive of your baby's eager suckling. As breast-feeding becomes solidly established, the number of feedings will begin to trail off. By the time your baby's sleeping through the night, you'll probably be down to five or six feedings, taking a total of only three or four hours out of your day.

In the meantime, put everything else that's clamouring to be done out of your mind; relax and savour these special moments that only you can share with your baby. Make double use of them by keeping a baby journal, reading a book, or scheduling your day on paper. Chances are that once your baby is weaned, you'll look back and think how much you miss those many hours of nursing.

NURSING FASHIONS

'When I was pregnant I couldn't wait to get back into my normal clothes. But now that I'm nursing my son, I'm finding that I'm still limited in what I can wear.'

It hardly seems fair. Now that you've finally got something that resembles a waist back (sort of), what you wear is still an issue. Fortunately, your fashion options are a lot less limited when you're breastfeeding than they were while you were expecting. True, your wardrobe may need some adjusting, especially from that waist up. But with an eye towards practicality, it is possible to satisfy your baby's appetite for milk and your appetite for style with the same wardrobe.

The right bra. Not surprisingly, the most important item in your breast-feeding wardrobe is the one only you, your baby, and your spouse will be seeing: a good nursing bra, or more likely, several. Ideally, you should purchase at least one nursing bra before your baby is born so that you'll be able to use it right away in the hospital. But some mothers find their breast size expands so much once their milk comes in that buying a bra before then isn't cost effective.

There are many different styles of nursing bras available – with or without underwires, no-nonsense and no-frills or lacy (though probably not racy), with cups that unhook on the shoulders or in the centre of the bra, or those that just pull to the side. Try on a variety, making your decision with comfort and convenience top priorities – and keeping in mind that you'll be unhooking the bra with one hand while holding a crying, hungry baby in the other. Whichever style you choose, make sure the bra is made of strong, breathable cotton, and that it has room to grow as your breasts do. A too-tight bra can cause clogged ducts, not to mention discomfort when breasts are engorged and nipples are sore.

Two-piece outfits. Two-piece is the fashion statement to make when you're breastfeeding – especially when you can pull up the top of the outfit for nursing access (but avoid tight shells). Shirts or dresses that button or zip down the front can also work (though you may be exposing more than you'd like in public if you need to unzip from the top for baby to reach his target; unbuttoning from the bottom is usually a better bet). You might also want to look for nursing dresses and tops that are designed with hidden flaps to facilitate discreet nursing and easy access for pumping. Such nursing wear is also designed to fit a nursing mother's larger bust size, a big plus.

Stay away from solids. Solid colours, whites and anything sheer will show milk leaks more obviously than dark patterns, which will mask not only your wet secrets but also the lumpiness of your breast pads.

Wear washables. Between leaking milk and baby spit-up, your local dry cleaner will be as happy as you are that there's a new baby in your house – unless you wear clothes you can toss in the washing machine and dryer. And after a few incidents with your good silk blouses, chances are washables will be all you'll be wearing.

Don't forget to pad your bra. A breastfeeding mother's most important accessory is the nursing pad. No matter what else you're wearing, always tuck one or two inside your bra (see page 76 for details).

NURSING IN PUBLIC

'I'm planning to breastfeed my daughter for at least six months, and I know I can't stay in my house all the time. But I'm not so sure about nursing in public.'

In most parts of the world, a mother nursing her baby doesn't attract any more attention than a mother bottle feeding her infant. But in the United Kingdom, acceptance of public breastfeeding has been slower in coming. Ironically, although the breast is celebrated in movies, in magazines and on the catwalk, it can still be a tough sell when there's a baby feeding from it.

Happily, nursing in public is becoming more accepted – and easier to do in more and more places. So just because you're nursing doesn't mean you'll have to be cooped up for the duration. With a little practice, you'll learn how to breastfeed so discreetly that only you and your daughter will know she's having lunch.

Using a blanket to nurse in public

To make public breastfeeding more private :

◆ Dress the part. With the right outfit (see previous question), you can breastfeed your baby in front of a crowd without exposing even an inch of skin. Unbutton your blouse from the bottom, or lift your shirt up slightly. You baby's head will cover any part of your breast that may be exposed.

◆ Practice in front of a mirror before venturing out in public. You'll see that, with strategic positioning, you'll be completely covered up. Or enlist your spouse (or a friend) to watch you as you feed the baby the first few times in public; he can monitor for any mishaps.

◆ Drape a blanket, shawl or nursing cover (aka hooter hider) over your shoulder (see illustration) to form a tent over your baby. But be careful not to cover your baby completely. She'll still need to breathe, so be sure her tent is well ventilated. When you and baby are eating out together, you can also use a large napkin.

◆ Wear your baby. A sling makes breastfeeding in public extremely discreet; wearing your baby this way, you can eat, watch movies, even walk around while nursing. People will just think your baby is sleeping.

◆ Create your own privacy zone. Find a bench under a tree, pick a corner with a roomy chair in a department store, or sit in a booth in a restaurant. Turn away from people while your baby is latching on, and turn back once your baby is well positioned at your breast.

◆ Look for special accommodations. Many large stores, shopping centres, airports and even amusement parks have rooms set aside for nursing mothers, complete with comfortable rocking chairs and changing tables. Or, seek out a bathroom with a separate lounge area for your baby's dining pleasure. If none of these are options where you'll be going, and you prefer to nurse without a crowd, feed baby in your parked car before heading out to your destination, temperature permitting.

◆ Feed before the frenzy. Don't wait until your baby becomes hysterical to start nursing her. A screaming baby only attracts the attention you don't want when you're nursing in public. Instead, watch for your baby's hunger cues, and whenever possible, preempt crying with a meal.

◆ Do what comes naturally. Although mothers have no legal right to breastfeed in public in the UK, if feeding your baby in public feels right, go ahead and do it. If it doesn't, even after some practice, opt for privacy whenever you can.

LUMP IN BREAST

'I've suddenly discovered a lump in my breast. It's tender and a little red. Could it be related to nursing – or something worse?'

Finding a lump in a breast strikes concern in any woman. But fortunately, what you describe is almost certainly related to nursing – a milk duct has probably become clogged, causing milk to back up. The clogged area usually appears as a lump that is red and tender. Though not serious in itself, a clogged duct can lead to breast infection, so it shouldn't be neglected. The basis of treatment is to keep milk flowing:

◆ Drain the affected breast thoroughly at each feeding. Offer it first, and encourage baby to take as much milk as possible. If there still seems to be a significant amount of milk left after nursing (if you can express a stream, rather than just a few drops), express the remaining milk by hand or with a breast pump.

◆ Keep pressure off the clogged duct. Be sure your bra isn't too tight or your clothes too constricting. Rotate your nursing positions to put pressure on different ducts at each nursing.

◆ Enlist baby for a massage. Positioning your baby's chin so that it massages the clogged duct during suckling will help clear it.

◆ Put warm compresses on the clogged duct before each feeding. Gently massage the duct before and during the feeding.

◆ Be sure that dried milk isn't blocking the nipple. Clean any away with warm water.

◆ Don't stop nursing. Now is not the time to wean your baby, or to cut back on nursing. This would compound the problem.

◆ Occasionally, in spite of best efforts, an infection can develop. If the tender area becomes increasingly painful, hard and red, and/or if you develop a fever, call your doctor (see next question).

MASTITIS

'My little boy is an enthusiastic nurser, and though my nipples were a little cracked and sore, I thought everything was going pretty well. Now, all of a sudden, one breast is very tender and hard – worse than when my milk first came in.'

For most women the course of breast-feeding, after a shaky initial startup, is relatively smooth. But for a few – and it sounds like you're one of them – mastitis (an inflammation of the breast) comes along to complicate matters. This infection can occur anytime during lactation, but it is most common between the second and sixth postpartum weeks.

Mastitis is usually caused by the entry of germs, often from the baby's mouth, into a milk duct through a crack in the skin of the nipple. Since cracked nipples are more common among first-time breastfeeders, whose nipples are not used to the rigours of infant sucking, mastitis strikes these women more often. The symptoms of mastitis include severe soreness, hardness, redness, heat and swelling over the affected duct, with generalized chills and usually fever of about 38.3° to 38.9°C (101° to 102°F) – though occasionally the only symptoms are fever and fatigue. Prompt medical treatment is important, so report any such symptoms to your doctor immediately. Prescribed therapy will include antibiotics and possibly bed rest, pain relievers and heat applications.

Though nursing from the affected breast will be painful, you should not avoid it. In fact, you should let your baby nurse frequently to keep the milk flowing and avoid clogging. Empty the breast thoroughly by hand or with a pump after each feeding if your baby doesn't do a thorough job himself. Don't worry about transmitting the infection to your baby; the germs that caused the infection probably came from his mouth in the first place.

Delay in treating mastitis could lead to the development of a breast abscess, the symptoms of which are excruciating, throbbing pain; swelling, tenderness and heat in the area of the abscess; and temperature swings between 37.8° to 39.4° (100° and 103°F). Treatment generally includes antibiotics and, frequently, surgical drainage under local anaesthesia. If you develop an abscess, breastfeeding on the affected breast must be halted temporarily, though you should continue to empty it with a pump until healing is complete and nursing can resume. In the meantime, baby can continue nursing on the unaffected breast.

BREASTFEEDING DURING ILLNESS

'I've just come down with the flu. Can I still breastfeed my baby without her getting sick?'

B reastfeeding your baby is the best way to strengthen her resistance to your germs (and other germs around her) and to keep her healthy. She can't catch cold germs through your breast milk, though she can become infected through other contact with you. To minimize the spread of infection, always wash your hands before handling your baby or her belongings and also before feedings; if she ends up getting sick in spite of your precautions, see the treatment tips starting on page 548.

To speed your own recovery as well as keep up your milk supply and your strength while you have a cold or flu, drink extra fluids (a cup of water, juice, soup or decaffeinated tea every hour while you're awake), be sure to take your vitamin supplement, and eat as balanced a diet as you can under the circumstances. Check with your doctor if you need medication – but don't take any without medical approval.

If you come down with a 'stomach virus', or gastroenteritis, you should again take precautions against infecting your baby – though the risk is small, since breastfed babies appear to be protected against most such infections. Wash your hands, especially after you've gone to the bathroom, before touching your baby or anything that she might put into her mouth. Take plenty of fluids (such as diluted fruit juices or decaffeinated teas) to replace those lost through diarrhoea or vomiting.

BREASTFEEDING WHILE MENSTRUATING

'My period has returned early even though I'm nursing. Will my milk be affected by my period? Can I still nurse my son?'

W hile it's true that many women who are exclusively nursing don't begin menstruating until they wean (or partially wean) their babies, some women, like you, find their period returning as early as three to six months postpartum.

The return of menstruation does not mean the end of breastfeeding. You can, and should, continue to breastfeed

BIRTH CONTROL AND THE BREASTFEEDING MOTHER

In the past, nursing mothers had to rely on a barrier method of contraception such as the diaphragm or condom. But today, women who are breastfeeding have the option of taking the 'minipill' – a progestin-only version of the Pill – as well as other hormonal methods that are safe for use during lactation. For more on birth control postpartum and while breastfeeding, see page 697.

EXERCISE AND NURSING

'Now that my baby is six weeks old, I'd like to resume my exercise routine. But I've heard exercise will make my milk turn sour.'

What you've heard about exercise and breast milk (that increased levels of lactic acid after exercise may sour milk) is now old news. Happily, the latest research shows that moderate to high-intensity exercise (such as an aerobic routine four or five times a week) doesn't turn milk sour or cause babies to turn up their noses at mum's breast after a workout.

So by all means, hit the running trail (or the step climber, or the pool). Just be careful not to overdo it (exercising to the point of exhaustion actually might increase lactic acid levels enough to sour your milk). To play it extra safe, try to schedule your workout for immediately after a feeding, so that in the very unlikely event that lactic acid levels reach milk-souring heights, they won't affect baby's next meal. Another advantage to exercising right after a feeding: your breasts will not be as uncomfortably full. If for some reason you can't fit a feeding in before a very strenuous exercise session, try to pump and store your milk ahead of time, and then feed the pre-exercise milk in a bottle when your baby is ready. And since salty milk doesn't taste any better than sour milk, if you're breastfeeding after a workout, hit the showers first (or, at least, wash the remnants of salty sweat off your breasts).

Keep in mind that if you exercise *excessively* on a regular basis, you might have trouble maintaining your milk supply. This may have more to do with persistent motion of the breasts and excessive friction of clothes against the nipples than the actual exertion of the

your baby even if you've started menstruating, even while you have your period. However, you might experience a temporary drop in your milk supply, probably because of the hormonal changes that occur during menstruation. Continuing to nurse your baby frequently, especially at the beginning of your cycle, may help, but this temporary reduction in supply may just be par for the menstruating course. Your supply will return in a few days once your hormone levels return to normal. The taste of your milk may also change slightly, just before or during your period, again, because of hormonal changes. Your baby may be unaffected by this (some infants are less picky eaters than others), or he may nurse less often or less enthusiastically, reject one breast or both, or just be more fussy than usual. Another way your cycle may affect breastfeeding: You may find your nipples are more tender during ovulation, during the days before your period, or at both times.

exercise. So be sure to wear a firm sports bra made of cotton any time you work out. Also, since strenuous arm exercises can cause clogged milk ducts in some women, pump iron with caution.

Finally, remember to drink a glass of water (or other liquid) before and after a workout to replace any fluid lost while exercising, especially during hot weather.

COMBINING BREAST AND BOTTLE

'I am aware of all the benefits of breastfeeding, but I'm not sure I want to nurse my daughter exclusively. Is it possible to combine breastfeeding and formula feeding?'

Though all might agree that exclusive breastfeeding is by far the best choice for baby, some women find that it's unrealistic for their lifestyle (too many business trips away from home), too difficult (they experience extremely sore and cracked nipples, or suffer from multiple breast infections or chronic breast milk shortage), too time-consuming (between work and other obligations) or just plain exhausting. For these women, combining breastfeeding with formula-feeding may be the best choice. Though it's not an option that's often put on the table (women tend to assume that breastfeeding and formula-feeding are all-or-nothing propositions), it's one that can offer the best of both feeding arrangements in some situations. Keep in mind that *any* breast milk is better for a baby than none at all.

There are important things to remember, however, if you're going to 'do the combo':

Put off the bottle. Try to delay giving your baby a formula bottle until breastfeeding is established – at least two to three weeks. This way, your milk

supply will be built up and your baby will be used to breastfeeding (which takes more effort) before the bottle (which takes less effort) is introduced.

Go slow. Don't switch to the combo abruptly; instead, make the transition slowly. Introduce the first formula bottle an hour or two after a breastfeeding session (when baby's hungry but not starving). Gradually build up to more frequent bottles and decrease nursing sessions, preferably allowing a few days in between each new bottle addition, until you are offering a bottle instead of a breast every other feeding (or as often as you choose). Taking the slow approach to eliminating a breastfeed avoids clogged ducts and breast infections.

Keep an eye on the supply. When you do begin supplementing, the decrease in demand for your breast milk may quickly result in a diminished supply. You'll need to make sure that you fit in enough breastfeedings so that your milk supply doesn't drop too much. (For most women, six thorough breastfeeds in a twenty-four-hour period is enough to maintain adequate milk production for a newborn). You might also need to pump occasionally to keep your milk supply up. If your baby doesn't nurse enough (or if you're not pumping to make up those missed nursings), you may find you don't have enough milk to continue breastfeeding – and the combo can backfire.

Choose the right nipple. You've got the right teat for the breastfeedings; now choose the right one for the bottle, too. Pick a teat that resembles those made by nature, one with a wide base and a slow flow. The shape of such a teat enables your baby to form a tight seal around the base, rather than just sucking the tip. And the slow flow ensures that your baby has to work for the milk, much as she has to when breastfeeding.

NIPPLE CONFUSION GOT YOU CONFUSED?

Maybe you'd like to try the 'combo' of breast and bottle. Or maybe you'd just like to introduce a bottle so you have the option of falling back on one every now and then. But you've heard that bringing on the bottle too soon or in the wrong way can cause 'nipple confusion', and now you're unsure how to proceed. Though many breastfeeding consultants do warn new mothers about the perils of nipple confusion – arguing that starting a bottle before baby has mastered breastfeeding may sabotage nursing (though other experts contend there is no such thing as nipple confusion) – it is possible to train an infant to switch effortlessly between breast and bottle.

Timing is key (bring the bottle on too soon, and baby may balk at the breast, because it suddenly seems like too much hard work; bring it on too late in the game, and baby may already be too attached to mum's nipple to sample the factory-made variety). But personality plays a part, too (some babies are more open to new experiences, some are stubborn creatures of habit). Most important, however, is perseverance (yours and baby's). While your baby may well be puzzled by the bottle at first, and may even reject the first few attempts, chances are he or she will soon get the hang of working the combo. Do keep in mind, however, that there are some babies who develop an inflexible preference for one method of feeding over the other and remain resistant to combining them. For more on introducing a bottle, see page 211.

RELACTATION

'I've been feeding my ten-day-old baby both formula and breast milk since birth, but now I want to breastfeed him exclusively. Is this possible?'

It won't be easy – even this short period of supplementing has cut down on supply – but it'll definitely be possible. With time, dedication, patience – and a cooperatively hungry baby – you will soon be able to make the switch from the combo back to breast alone. The key to weaning your baby off formula will be to produce enough milk to make up the difference. Here's how you can pump up your milk supply, and make a successful transition from partial breastfeeding to exclusive breastfeeding:

◆ Go for empty. Because frequent and regular stimulation of your breasts is critical to milk production (the more you use, the more you'll make),

you'll need to drain your breasts (either by nursing your baby or by pumping) *at least* every two and a half hours during the day and every three to four hours at night.

◆ Top off with the pump. Finish each nursing session with five to ten minutes of pumping to ensure that your breasts are thoroughly drained, stimulating even further milk production. Either freeze the pumped milk for later use (see page 156) or feed it to your baby along with any supplemental formula.

◆ Ease off the formula. Don't take your baby off formula cold turkey. Until full milk production has been established, your baby will need supplemental feedings, but offer the bottle only after a nursing session. As your own milk supply increases, gradually feed less formula in each bottle. If you write down the amount of formula your baby takes daily, you should see a slow decrease in that amount as your milk supply increases.

◆ Consider a supplementer. Using a supplemental nutrition system (SNS) may make your transition from breast and bottle to breast alone a lot smoother. Such a system enables you to feed your baby formula while he sucks at the breast (see page 161). This way, your breasts get the stimulation they need and your baby gets all the food he needs.

◆ Do nappy counts. Remember to keep track of your baby's wet nappies and bowel movements to make sure he's getting enough to eat (see page 158). Also, keep in touch with your baby's doctor and have the baby weighed often to make sure he's getting enough to eat during the transition.

◆ Possibly, try medication. There are herbal options (some breastfeeding consultants recommend fenugreek in small amounts to stimulate milk production), but, as with all herbs and medications, do not take anything to stimulate your milk production without the knowledge and direction of

your doctor and/or a registered breastfeeding consultant familiar with your particular situation. And don't even consider taking them unless you're really struggling with milk production.

◆ Be patient. Relactation is a time-consuming process, and your success is dependent on a good support system. Enlist help from your spouse, family and friends, if possible. Get support and advice from a breastfeeding consultant. You can find one through the hospital, your doctor, or midwife, or by contacting either your local NCT or La Leche League.

Relactating will take round-the-clock effort on your part for at least a few days and as long as a few weeks. Though at times it may prove frustrating, chances are that it will ultimately be rewarding. Once in a while, however, even with best efforts, relactating doesn't take. If that does end up being the case with you, and you end up having to bottle feed either partially or completely, don't feel guilty. Your efforts to nurse should make you proud. And remember, any breastfeeding – even for a short time – benefits your baby greatly.

What it's Important to Know:
KEEPING YOUR MILK HEALTHY AND SAFE

Feeding your baby outside the womb doesn't require quite the degree of dietary dedication – or monitoring – that feeding your baby inside the womb did. But for as long as you're breastfeeding, you'll need to pay a certain amount of attention to what goes into you in order to ensure that everything that goes into your baby is healthy and safe.

WHAT YOU EAT

Tired of watching your diet like an expectant hawk? Here's some news you'll be happy to hear: compared to pregnancy, nursing actually makes minimal demands on your diet. The basic fat-protein-carbohydrate composition of human milk isn't directly dependent on what a mother eats. In fact, all over the

CAN FOODS MAKE MILK?

Every breastfeeding mother has heard about at least one: foods, drinks and herbal potions with the supposed power to increase milk production. They run the gamut – from milk and beer, to teas made from fennel, blessed thistle, anise, nettle, and alfalfa; from checkpeas and liquorice, to potatoes, olives and carrots. Though some mothers swear by these cultural traditions and old wives' standards, some experts say that the effects of such 'milk-making potions' are largely psychological. If a mother believes that what she eats or drinks will make milk, she'll be relaxed. If she's relaxed, she'll have a good let-down. If her let-down reflex is good, she'll interpret it to mean she has more milk, and that the potion worked its magic after all. Remember: the best – and only proven – way to increase your milk supply is to have your baby nurse frequently.

world, women produce adequate and abundant milk on inadequate diets. That's because if a mother doesn't consume enough calories and protein to produce milk, her body will tap its own stores of nutrients to fuel milk production – that is, until those stores are depleted.

But just because you can make milk on an inadequate diet doesn't mean you should. Clearly, no matter how many nutrients your body may have stockpiled, the goal when you're nursing should never be to deplete those stores – that's too risky, setting you up for a variety of health problems, including the potential later in life for osteoporosis. So be sure to eat (no matter how eager you are to shed weight), and eat well (see the Postpartum Diet, page 669). But take comfort in the fact that nursing mothers – unlike expectant ones – don't have to be quite as careful about what they eat and don't eat. (There still are restrictions for safety's sake, however; read about them on page 91.)

In fact, eating a wide variety of foods appears to be beneficial to your nursing baby, and not just from a nutrition standpoint. Because what you eat affects the taste and smell of your breast milk, your breastfed baby is exposed to different flavours well before he or she is ready to sit down at the dinner table, which may help shape future eating habits. The very early flavour experiences a breastfed baby has may actually provide the foundation for cultural and ethnic preferences in cuisine. A young Indian toddler, for instance, typically has no problem wolfing down curried food – probably because he or she has been exposed to it as a foetus (through the amniotic fluid) and as a nursing infant. For the same reason, a young Mexican child may be more accustomed to the smell and taste of hot salsas. On the other hand, a child whose mother ate a bland diet while she was pregnant and nursing may be more likely to push away a bowl of peppery chili once it's time for solids.

Occasionally, a baby with a particularly discriminating palate may snub his or her mother's milk after mum has eaten something with a distinctive taste, like garlic (again, possibly, because the flavour is unfamiliar). Others, perhaps because they became used to an infusion of garlic during their stay in the uterus, may even relish mum's milk more when she's been hitting the pesto and scampi. And if you'd like to give your child a taste for vegetables, here's something else to chew on: in one study, infants whose mothers drank carrot juice when they were pregnant and breastfeeding lapped up cereal mixed with carrot juice more eagerly than infants of mothers who stayed away from carrots – evidence that what you eat now can have a positive effect on your nursing baby's future eating habits, which is yet another good reason to eat your vegetables. Another plus: your breastfed baby may have a leg up on his formula-fed contemporaries when it comes time to take a seat in the high chair. Breastfed babies have been shown to have an easier time transitioning to solid foods, probably because they've already acclimatized to different flavours from drinking their mother's milk.

But chances are that not all of what you eat will have a happy ending in baby's tummy. Some mothers, after eating foods like cabbage, broccoli, onions, cauliflower or Brussels sprouts, find their nursing babies get gassy (though scientific studies have failed to back up this anecdotal evidence). Colic in some babies has been linked to dairy products, caffeine, onions, cabbage or beans in their mother's diet. A maternal diet that's heavy on melons, peaches and other fruits can cause diarrhoea in some babies. Chilli can cause a rash in some breastfed infants. Other babies are actually allergic to foods in their mother's diets, with the most common offenders being cow's milk, eggs, citrus fruits, nuts or wheat (see page 171 for more on allergies in breastfed babies). What you eat can also change the colour of your milk, and even the colour of your baby's urine. For instance, a mum who drinks orange soda may find her breast milk a pink-orange colour and her baby's urine bright pink (pretty harmless, but definitely anxiety-producing). Kelp, seaweed (in the tablet form), and other natural vitamins from health food sources have been associated with green breast milk (fine for St Patrick's Day, but probably not something you'd want to see on a regular basis).

It takes between two and six hours from the time you eat a certain food until it affects the taste and odour of your milk. So, if you find your baby is gassy, spits up more, rejects the breast, or is fussy a few hours after you eat a certain food, try eliminating that food from your diet for a few days and see if your baby's symptoms or reluctance to nurse disappear.

What You Drink

How much do you have to drink to make sure your baby gets enough to drink? Actually, no more than you have to drink at any other time in your adult life. Nursing mothers do not have to drink any more than those eight daily glasses – of water, milk or other fluids – in order to ensure a good milk supply. In fact, too much fluid can actually decrease the amount of milk you make.

That said, most adults don't drink their full fluid requirement every day, and nursing mothers are no exception. One way to make sure you drink your quota is to keep a bottle or glass of water close by when you're nursing (which will be at least eight times a day at first); when your baby drinks, so should you. If you're not drinking enough, your milk supply won't tell you (it won't decrease unless you're seriously dehydrated), but your urine will; it will become darker and more scant. As a general rule, waiting until you're thirsty to drink means you're going too long without fluids. (You may be thirstier than usual after you deliver your baby, because of fluid loss and inadequate fluid intake during labour; replenishing those fluids is important for your health.)

There are some drinks you should

avoid, or at least limit, when you're breastfeeding. See page 91 for more.

WHAT MEDICATION YOU TAKE

Most medications – both over-the-counter and prescription – don't have an effect on the quantity of milk a nursing mother makes or the well-being of her baby. While it's true that what goes into your body usually does make its way into your milk supply, the amount that ultimately ends up in your baby's meals is generally a tiny fraction of what you ingest. Many drugs appear to have no effect on a nursing baby at all, others a mild, transient effect, and a very few can have a significant detrimental effect. But since not enough is known about the long-term effects of medications on the nursing infant, you'll need to practise prudence when it comes to taking over-the-counter or prescription drugs while you're breastfeeding.

All medications that pose even a theoretical risk to the nursing baby carry a warning – on the label, the packet, or both. When the benefits outweigh the possible risks, your doctor will probably okay the occasional use of certain drugs without medical consultation (certain cold medications and mild pain relievers, for example) and prescribe others when your health requires it. Like an expectant mother, a nursing mother does neither herself nor her baby a favour by refusing to take prescribed medication under such circumstances. Do be sure, of course, that any doctor who prescribes a medication for you knows that you're breastfeeding.

For the most up-to-date information on which drugs are believed safe during lactation and which aren't, check with your child's doctor or health visitor. The most recent research indicates that most medicines (including paracetamol, ibuprofen, most sedatives, antihistamines, decongestants, some antibiotics, antihypertensives, antithyroid drugs and even some antidepressants) are compatible with nursing. Some, however, including anticancer drugs, lithium and ergots (drugs used to treat migraines) are clearly harmful. Others are suspect. In some cases, a medication can safely be discontinued for the duration of nursing; in others, it is possible to find a safer substitute. When medication that is not compatible with breastfeeding is needed short-term, nursing can be interrupted temporarily (with breasts pumped and milk discarded). Or dosing can be timed for just after nursing or before baby's longest sleep period. As always, take medicines – and that includes herbals and supplements – only with your doctor's approval.

WHAT YOU SHOULD AVOID

Though nursing mothers have considerably more leeway when it comes to their diet and their lifestyle than pregnant women do, there are still a number of substances that are smart to avoid – or at least, cut back on – while you're breastfeeding. Many are ones that you've probably already weaned yourself off of in preparation for or during pregnancy.

Nicotine. Many of the toxic substances in tobacco enter the bloodstream and eventually your milk. Heavy smoking (more than a pack a day) decreases milk production and can cause vomiting, diarrhoea, rapid heart rate and restlessness in babies. Though the long-term effects of these poisons on your baby aren't known for sure, one can safely speculate that they aren't positive. On top of that, it is known that secondhand

(and even third-hand) smoke from parental smoking can cause a variety of health problems in offspring, including colic, respiratory infections and an increase in the risk of SIDS (see page 256). If you can't stop smoking, your baby's still better off being breastfed than being bottle-fed; do, however, try cutting back on the number of cigarettes you smoke each day, and don't smoke just before breastfeeding.

Alcohol. Alcohol does find its way into your breast milk, though the amount your baby gets is considerably less than the amount you drink. While it's probably fine to have a few drinks a week (though no more than one in a single day), you should try to limit your consumption of alcoholic drinks in general while nursing.

Heavy drinking has other drawbacks as well. In large doses, alcohol can make baby sleepy, sluggish, unresponsive and unable to suck well. In very large doses, it can interfere with breathing. Too many drinks can also impair your own functioning (whether you're nursing or not), making you less able to care for, protect and nourish your baby, and can make you more susceptible to depression, fatigue and lapses in judgment. Also, it can weaken your let-down reflex. If you do choose to have an occasional drink, take it right after you nurse, rather than before, to allow a couple of hours for the alcohol to metabolize.

Caffeine. One or two cups of caffeinated coffee, tea or cola a day won't affect your baby or you – and during those early sleep-deprived postpartum weeks, a little jolt from your local coffee bar may be just what you need to keep going. More caffeine probably isn't a good idea; too many cups could make one or both of you jittery, irritable and sleepless (something you definitely don't want). Caffeine has also been linked to reflux in

---

NO PEANUTS WHILE FEEDING YOUR LITTLE PEANUT?

If you have a family history of peanut – or other – allergies, it's probably wise to avoid peanuts and foods that contain them while breastfeeding. Research has found that peanut allergens may be passed through breast milk from the mother to the nursing baby. It has been theorized that this early exposure to peanut allergens may cause the baby to become sensitized to them, eventually leading to potentially serious allergies later in childhood. If you have allergies, or if you have a family history of allergies, speak to your baby's doctor or your allergist to determine what foods, if any, you should avoid while breastfeeding.

---

some babies. Keep in mind that babies can't get rid of caffeine as efficiently as adults, so it can build up in their systems. So limit your caffeine while you're breastfeeding, or switch over to or supplement with caffeine-free drinks.

Herbs. Although herbs are natural, they aren't always safe, especially for breastfeeding mothers. They can be just as powerful – and just as toxic – as some drugs. Like drugs, chemical ingredients from herbs do get into breast milk. Even herbs like fenugreek (which has been used for centuries to increase a nursing mother's milk supply, and is sometimes recommended in small amounts by breastfeeding consultants, though the scientific studies have been mixed) can have a very potent effect on blood pressure and heart rate when taken in large doses. In general, little is known about how herbs affect a nursing baby, because few studies have been done. Play it safe and consult with your doctor before taking any herbal remedy. Think twice before drinking herbal tea, too. For now, stick to reliable brands of herbal teas that are thought to be safe during lactation (these include orange spice, peppermint, raspberry, red bush and rose hip), read labels carefully to make sure other herbs haven't been added to the brew, and drink them only in moderation.

Chemicals. Eating a diet high in added chemicals is never a particularly good idea; during breastfeeding, as during pregnancy, it may be a particularly bad one. While it isn't necessary to be obsessed about reading labels, a little prudence is warranted. Remember: many of the substances that are added to your foods will be added, through you, to your baby's. As a general rule, try to avoid processed foods that contain long lists of additives, and try the following tips for safer eating:

◆ Sweeten safely. Aspartame is probably a better bet than saccharin (only tiny amounts of aspartame pass into breast milk), but since the long-term health consequences of the sweetener, if any, aren't yet known, excess is definitely not best. (Don't use aspartame at all if you have PKU or your baby does.) Sucralose (Splenda), however, is made from sugar and is considered safe and a good all-round calorie-free sugar substitute.

◆ Go organic. Certified organic fruits and vegetables are now widely available in supermarkets, as are organic dairy products and organic poultry, meat and eggs. But don't feel you have to drive yourself crazy (or drive yourself all over town) in order to protect your baby's milk from pesticides. Do what you can to avoid incidental pesticides (and choosing organic is the best way to do this), but realize that a certain amount will end up in your diet, and thus in your milk, despite your best efforts – and that these amounts won't be harmful. When organic isn't available, or you just don't want to pay the higher price, peel or scrub fruits and vegetable skins well (use produce wash for extra protection).

◆ Stay low-fat. As it was during pregnancy, it's smart to choose fat-free or low-fat dairy products, as well as lean meats and poultry without the skin, for two reasons. First, a low-fat diet will make it easier to shed your pregnancy weight gain. Two, the pesticides and other chemicals ingested by animals are stored in their fat (and in their organs, such as liver, kidneys and brain, which is why you should eat these meats only rarely while you're breastfeeding). Organic dairy and meat products, of course, don't pose the same potential risk – a good reason to select them when you can.

◆ Fish selectively. The same guidelines on fish safety that apply to pregnant women apply to breastfeeding ones. So to minimize your (and your baby's) exposure to mercury avoid eating shark, swordfish, marlin, king mackerel and tilefish, and limit your consumption to 340 g (12 oz) (total) per week of salmon, sea bass, flounder, sole, haddock, halibut, ocean perch, pollack, cod and farm-raised trout. The FSA also advises that you don't eat more than 280 g (drained weight) of canned tuna, or one fresh tuna steak (170 gram, 140 g cooked) per week.

◆ ◆ ◆

CHAPTER 4

Your Newborn Baby

The wait is over. Your baby – the little person you've been eagerly expecting for nine months – is finally here. As you hold this tiny warm bundle for the first time, you're bound to be flooded by a thousand and one emotions, running the confusing gamut from excitement and exhilaration to apprehension and self-doubt. And, especially if you're a first-time parent, you're also likely to be overwhelmed by (at least) a thousand and one questions. Why is her head such a funny shape? Why does he have acne already? Why can't I get her to stay awake long enough to breastfeed? Why won't he stop crying?

As you search around for the operating instructions (don't babies come with them?), here's something you need to know: yes, you've got a lot to learn (after all, nobody's born knowing how to care for an umbilical stump or massage a clogged tear duct), but give yourself half a chance, and you'll be surprised to find how much of this parenting thing actually comes naturally (including the most important operating instruction of all: love your baby). So find the answers to your questions in the chapters that follow, but as you do, don't forget to tap into your most valuable resource of all – your own instincts.

What Your Baby May Be Doing

Within a few days of birth your baby will probably be able to:

- lift head briefly when on the tummy (which baby should be on only when supervised)

- move arms and legs on both sides of the body equally well

- focus on objects within 20 to 38 cm (8 to 15 in) (especially your face!)

What You Can Expect at Hospital Checkups

Your baby's very first checkup will take place moments after his or her arrival, in the delivery or birthing room. Here, or later on in the nursery, you can expect that a doctor or nurse will do some or all of the following:

◆ Clear baby's airways by suctioning his or her nose (which may be done as soon as the head appears or after the rest of the baby is delivered).

◆ Clamp the umbilical cord in two places and cut between the two clamps – although dad may do the cutting honours. (Antibiotic ointment or an antiseptic may be applied to the cord stump, and the clamp is usually left on for at least twenty-four hours).

◆ Assign baby an Apgar score (rating of baby's condition at one and five minutes after birth; see page 97).

◆ Administer antibiotic ointment to the eyes (see page 111) to prevent gonococcal or chlamydial infection.

◆ Weigh baby (average weight is 3.4 kg/7½ lb; 95 per cent of full-term babies weigh in at between 2.5 and 4.5 kg/5½ and 10 lb).

◆ Measure baby's length (average length is 51 cm/20 in; 95 per cent of newborns are between 46 and 56 cm/18 and 22 in).

◆ Measure head circumference (average is 35 cm/13.8 in; normal range is from 33 to 37.3 cm/12.9 to 14.7 in).

◆ Count fingers and toes, and note if baby's observable body parts and features appear normal.

◆ Assess gestational age (time spent in the uterus) in babies born before term.

◆ Hand baby to you for breastfeeding and/or cuddling.

◆ Before baby leaves the delivery or birthing room, place ID bands on baby. Baby's footprints and mum's fingerprint may also be obtained for future identification purposes (the ink is washed off your baby's feet, and any residual smudges you may note are only temporary).

The baby's doctor will perform a more complete examination of the new arrival sometime during the next 24 hours. If you can arrange to be present, this is a good time to start asking the thousands of questions you're sure to have. The doctor will check the following:

◆ Weight (it will probably have dropped since birth, and will drop a little more in the next couple of days), head circumference (may be larger than it was at first, as any moulding of the head begins to round out), and length (which won't actually have changed, but might seem to have because measuring a baby – who can't stand or cooperate – is a highly inexact procedure).

◆ Heart sounds and respirations

◆ Internal organs, such as kidneys, liver and spleen, by palpation (examining by touch, externally)

◆ Newborn reflexes

◆ Hips, for possible dislocation

NEWBORN HEARING SCREENING

Babies learn everything about their environment from their senses – from the sight of daddy's smiling face, to the feel of warm skin as they're cradled in loving arms, to the smell of a flower, to the sound of mummy's voice as she matches coo for coo. But for 1–3 out of every 1,000 babies born in the UK each year, the sense of hearing – so integral to the development of speech and language skills – is impaired.

Until recently, hearing loss usually went undetected in young children until delays in those important skills were noticed, often not until the preschool years, sometimes not until much later. Today, however, it is possible to screen newborn babies for hearing loss.

One test, called otoacoustic emissions (OAE), measures response to sound by using a small probe inserted in the baby's ear canal. In babies with normal hearing, a microphone inside the probe records faint noises coming from the baby's ear in response to the auditory stimulation. This test can be done while the baby is sleeping, is completed within a few minutes, and causes no pain or discomfort. A second screening method, called auditory brainstem response (ABR), uses electrodes placed on the baby's scalp to detect activity in the brain stem's auditory region in response to 'clicks' sounded in the baby's ear. ABR screening requires the baby to be awake and in a quiet state, but it is also quick and painless. If your baby doesn't pass the initial screening, the test will be repeated to avoid false-positive results.

Unfortunately, these tests are not yet routine in the UK but are becoming more available. If you think your baby is at risk of hearing loss, however, make sure you ask about having him or her screened before you leave hospital. Though hearing loss can affect anyone, risk factors include NICU (Neonatal Intensive Care Unit) admission for two or more days; syndromes known to include hearing loss, such as Usher's syndrome or Waardenburg's syndrome; family history of childhood hearing loss; as well as congenital infections, such as toxoplasmosis, syphilis, rubella, cytomegalovirus and herpes.

- Hands, feet, arms, legs, genitals
- The umbilical stump

During your baby's hospital stay, the nurses and/or doctors will:

- Record passage or lack of passage of urine and/or stools (to rule out any problems in the elimination department).

- Administer vitamin K injection, to enhance the clotting ability of baby's blood.

- Obtain blood from infant's heel (with a quick prick), to be screened for phenylketonuria (PKU) and hypothyroidism. Blood can also be tested for certain metabolic disorders.

- Possibly, with your consent, administer the first dose of hepatitis B vaccine sometime before hospital discharge. This is routine in some hospitals, and necessary if an infant's mother tests positive for hep-B. If you're not a carrier, the first dose may be given anytime during the first two months, or the paediatrician may suggest giving the DTaP-polio-hep B combination vaccine starting at two months. Babies who've had the birth dose can also receive the combination vaccine; the extra dose of hep-B isn't a problem. Follow the doctor's recommendations.

PORTRAIT OF A NEWBORN

Despite the oohs and aahs they elicit from excited friends and families, most freshly delivered babies aren't exactly the dimpled, advertisement-ready bundles of cuteness most first-time parents expect to be handed. Loveable, yes. Ready for their close-up, usually not.

For starters, the average new arrival's head looks too large for its body (it's about one quarter of baby's total length), and its legs are usually more chicken-scrawny than baby-round. If the trip through the birth canal was a particularly tight squeeze, the head may be somewhat moulded – sometimes to the point of being 'cone' shaped. A bruise might also have been raised on the scalp during delivery.

Newborn hair may be practically nonexistent, limited to a sprinkling of fuzz, or so full it looks like it's already due for a trim; it may lie flat or stand up straight in spikes. When hair is thin, blood vessels may be seen as a blue road map across baby's scalp, and the pulse may be visible at the soft spot, or fontanel, on the top of the head.

Many newborns (like their mothers) appear to have gone a few rounds in the ring after a vaginal delivery. (Babies who arrive by Caesarean, especially if they didn't go through the compression of labour first, often have a significant edge in the looks department.) Their eyes may appear squinty because of the folds at the inner corners, swelling from delivery and, possibly, because of the infection-protecting eye ointment gooping them up. Their eyes may also be bloodshot from the pres-

sures of labour (which is often the case with mum, too). The nose may be flattened and the chin unsymmetrical or pushed in from being squeezed through the pelvis, adding to the boxer-like appearance.

Because a newborn's skin is thin, it usually has a pale pinkish cast (even in non-Caucasian babies) from the blood vessels just beneath it. Right after delivery, it's most often covered with the remains of the vernix caseosa, a cheesy coating that protects foetuses during the time spent soaking in the amniotic fluid (the earlier a baby arrives, the more vernix is left on the skin). Babies born late may have skin that's wrinkled or peeling (because they had little or no vernix left to protect it). Babies born late are also less likely than early babies to be covered with lanugo, a downy prenatal fur that can appear on shoulders, back, forehead and cheeks and that disappears within the first few weeks of life.

Finally, because of an infusion of female hormones from the placenta just before birth, many babies, both boys and girls, have swollen breasts and/or genitals. There may even be a milky discharge from the breasts and, in girls, a vaginal discharge (sometimes bloody).

Be sure to capture those newborn features on film quickly (as if you'll need to be told to grab the camera!), because they're all temporary. Most are gone within the first few days, the rest within a few weeks, leaving nothing but dimpled, picture-pretty cuteness in their place.

◆ Conduct a hearing screening (see box, page 95).

APGAR TEST

The first test most babies are given – and which most pass with good scores – is the Apgar, developed by anaesthesiologist Virginia Apgar. The scores, recorded at one minute and again at five minutes after birth, reflect the newborn's general condition and are based on observations made in five assessment categories. Babies who score between 7 and 10 are in good to excellent condition and usually require only routine postdelivery care; those scoring between 4 and 6, in fair condition, may require some resuscitative measures; and those who score under 4, in poor condition, will require immediate and maximal lifesaving efforts. Research shows that even babies whose scores remain low at five minutes usually turn out to be completely normal and healthy.

YOUR NEWBORN'S REFLEXES

Mother Nature pulls out all the stops when it comes to newborn babies, providing them with a set of inborn reflexes designed to protect these especially vulnerable creatures and ensure their care (even if the new parents' instincts haven't fully kicked in yet).

Some of these primitive behaviours are spontaneous, while others are responses to certain actions. Some seem intended to shield a baby from harm (such as when a baby swipes at something covering his or her face, a reflex that is meant to prevent suffocation). Others seem to guarantee that a baby will get fed (as when a baby roots for a nipple). And while many of the reflexes have obvious value as survival mechanisms, nature's intentions are more subtle in others. Take the fencing reflex. Though few newborns are challenged to a duel, some theorize that they take this challenging stance while on their backs in order to prevent them from rolling away from their mothers.

APGAR TABLE

SIGN	POINTS		
	0	1	2
Appearance (colour)	Pale or blue	Body pink, extremities blue	Pink
Pulse (heartbeat)	Not detectible	Below 100	Over 100
Grimace (reflex irritability)	No response to stimulation	Grimace	Lusty cry
Activity (muscle tone)	Flaccid (weak or no activity)	Some movement of extremities	A lot of activity
Respiration (breathing)	None	Slow, irregular	Good (crying)

Startle, or Moro, reflex. When startled by a sudden or loud noise, or a feeling of falling, the Moro reflex will cause the baby to extend the legs, arms and fingers, arch the back, draw the head back, then draw the arms back, fists clenched, into the chest.

Duration: Four to six months.

Babinski's, or plantar, reflex. When the sole of a baby's foot is gently stroked from the heel to toe, the baby's toes flare upwards and the foot turns in.

Duration: Between six months and two years, after which toes curl downwards.

Rooting reflex. A newborn whose cheek is gently stroked will turn in the direction of the stimulus, mouth open and ready to suckle. This reflex helps the baby locate the breast or bottle and secure a meal.

Duration: About three to four months, though it may persist when baby is sleeping.

Walking, or stepping, reflex. Held upright on a table or other flat surface, supported under the arms, a newborn may lift one leg and then the other, taking what seem to be 'steps'. This 'practice walking' reflex works best after the fourth day of life.

HOSPITAL PROCEDURES
FOR BABIES BORN AT HOME

Having your baby at home means that you'll have more control over the birth – plus no bags to pack – but it also means you'll have more responsibilities afterwards. Some procedures that are routine in hospitals and birthing centres may just be bureaucratic red tape that you and your baby can easily skip; others, however, are necessary for your baby's health and future well-being; still others are required by law. Give birth in a hospital, and the following are automatically taken care of; give birth at home, and you'll need to:

◆ Give some thought to eye ointment. Some midwives allow the parents of a newborn to give informed consent not to administer antibiotic eye ointment (which protects babies from infection should their mother have a venereal disease) after birth. Though the ointment used is no longer irritating to baby's eyes, it can blur vision, making that first eye-to-eye contact in

mummy's and daddy's arms less clear. Discuss this option with your practitioner before delivery.

◆ Plan for routine shots and tests. All babies born in a hospital receive their first dose of hepatitis B vaccine, and all receive a shot of vitamin K (to improve blood clotting) shortly after delivery. They're also given a heel stick to screen for PKU and hypothyroidism, and in some hospitals or at the parent's request, for a variety of other conditions. Speak to your baby's doctor about when these procedures can be performed on your newborn. It's also a good idea to arrange a hearing test, typically administered to newborns before they leave the hospital (see page 95).

◆ Be sure to contact your doctor immediately after the birth to arrange an appointment for your baby as soon as possible.

Duration: Variable, but typically about two months. (This reflex does not forecast early walking.)

Sucking reflex. A newborn will reflexively suck when the roof of his or her mouth is touched, such as when a nipple is placed in the mouth.

Duration: Present at birth and lasts until two to four months, when voluntary sucking takes over.

Palmar grasping reflex. Touch the palm of your baby's hand, and his or her fingers will curl around and cling to your finger (or any object). An interesting bit of baby trivia: a newborn's grasp may be powerful enough to support full body weight – but don't try this at home (or anywhere else, for that matter). Some more trivia: This reflex curls babies' feet and toes, too, when they're touched.

Duration: Three to six months.

Tonic neck, or fencing, reflex. Placed on the back, a young baby will assume a 'fencing position', head to one side, with arms and legs on that side extended and the opposite limbs flexed. *En garde!*

Duration: Varies a lot. It may be present at birth or may not appear for at least two months, and disappear at about four to six months – or sooner, or later.

For fun, or out of curiosity, you can try checking your baby for these reflexes – but keep in mind that your results may be less reliable than those of a doctor or other trained examiner. A baby's reflexes may be less pronounced, too, if he or she is hungry or tired. So try again another day, and if you still can't observe the reflexes, mention this to your baby's doctor, who probably has already tested your baby successfully for all newborn reflexes and will be happy to repeat the demonstrations for you at the next clinic visit.

Feeding Your Baby:
GETTING STARTED FORMULA FEEDING

The actual process of feeding a baby a bottle, oddly enough, typically comes more naturally – or at least more easily – than breastfeeding. Babies have little trouble learning to suckle from an artificial nipple, and parents have little difficulty at the delivery end. (Which is why mothers who choose to do the 'combo' should hold off on bottles until they and their babies are well established in their breastfeeding routine.) Getting to the feeding, however, may take a little more effort and a lot more know-how. After all, while breast milk is ready to serve, formula must be selected, purchased, sometimes prepared, and often stored.

Whether you're formula feeding exclusively or just supplementing, you'll need to know how to get started. (See page 42 for tips on choosing teats and bottles for your formula-fed baby.)

SELECTING A FORMULA

Formulas can't precisely replicate nature's recipe for breast milk (for instance, they can't pass along antibodies), but they do come closer to that gold standard of baby feeding than they ever have before. In fact, all of today's formulas are made with types and proportions of proteins, fats, carbohydrates, sodium, vitamins, minerals, water and other nutrients similar to breast milk's, and must meet government standards. So just about any iron-containing formula you choose for your baby will be nutritionally sound. Still, the vast selection of formulas on your local supermarket or chemist shelf can be dizzying – and more than a little confusing. Before you contemplate that selection, consider the following formula facts:

◆ Your baby's doctor and health visitor know a thing or two about formula. In your search for the perfect formula for your baby, start with a call to either of them. He or she can help steer you to a formula that is closest to human milk in composition, as well as the one that best fits your baby's needs.

◆ Cows make the best formula for most human babies. That's why the majority of formulas are made with cow's milk that has been modified to meet the nutritional needs of human babies. (Do not feed your baby regular cow's milk until after his or her first birthday; it's not as easily digested or absorbed as formula and doesn't provide the proper nutritional elements a growing infant needs.) In infant formulas, cow's milk proteins are made more digestible, more lactose is added (so that it's closer to breast milk in

composition), and butterfat is replaced with vegetable oils.

◆ Soya-based formulas should be used only in certain circumstances. In these formulas, soya beans are modified with vitamins, minerals and nutrients to approximate breast milk. Since they stray further from human milk than cow's milk formulas do, and because research shows that infants on soya are more likely to develop a peanut allergy later on, soya formulas are not usually recommended unless there are special health considerations for the baby, such as a cow's milk allergy. Vegans may also choose to go soya from the start, without any medical indications.

◆ Special formulas are best for some special babies. There are formulas available for premature babies, babies who turn out to be allergic to cow's milk and soya, as well as those with metabolic disorders, such as PKU. There are also lactose-free formulas, as well as hypoallergenic formulas designed to trigger fewer allergies in those babies prone to them. For some babies, these formulas are easier to digest than standard formulations; not surprisingly, they are much more expensive. You don't need to use them unless your baby's doctor has recommended them. There are also some organic formulas that are produced from milk products untouched by growth hormones, antibiotics or pesticides.

◆ Follow-ups are not always best. Follow-up formulas are designed for babies older than four months who are also eating solid foods. Check with your baby's doctor before using follow-up formula; some doctors don't recommend them.

NEED HELP AT THE BREAST?

If you're breastfeeding – either exclusively or in combination with the bottle – you'll find everything you need to know in chapter 3, beginning on page 63.

DHA: THE SMART CHOICE IN BABY FORMULAS?

Just when formula companies think they've come as close as they can to simulating the composition of breast milk, another discovery about what makes breast best sends them back to the formulating tables. The most recent is the importance of the omega-3 fatty acids found naturally in breast milk: DHA (docosahexaenoic acid) and ARA (arachidonic acid). These headline-making nutrients have been recognized by scientists as enhancing mental and visual development in infants, and as playing a pivotal role in brain function.

Scientists have found that infants accumulate DHA/ARA in their brains and retinas most rapidly between the third trimester of pregnancy (when they receive a supply of the fatty acid courtesy of the placenta) and age 18 months – not coincidentally, the period of greatest growth in young brains. Research so far has shown that infants benefit significantly from an adequate intake of DHA/ARA, though a direct link to boosted IQ and other developmental edges – while widely speculated – has yet to be clearly established.

Even without DHA and RHA supplementation, full-term infants already have some of these valuable fatty acids stored up from their stint in the womb. They also appear able to manufacture some DHA and ARA from other oils already in formula (though some studies suggest that the amount they can make themselves may not be enough to foster optimal brain and visual development). Premature babies, who missed out on all or part of the third trimester, are at a distinct disadvantage in the fatty acid department, since they have no reserves to tap into.

♦ Iron-fortified is best. While formulas come in low-iron formulations, they aren't considered a healthy option. Most doctors recommend that babies be given iron-fortified formula from birth until one year.

♦ For best results, look to your baby. Different formulas work well for different babies at different times. Coupled with the advice of your doctor, your baby's reaction to the formula you're feeding will help you assess what's best.

Once you've narrowed your selection down to a general type, you'll need to choose, too, between the different forms those formulations come in:

Ready-to-use. Premixed ready-to-go formula comes in 200-ml (7-fl oz) and 500-ml (17½-fl oz) cartons. It doesn't get easier than this, but it does get less expensive (see options below).

Ready-to-pour. Available in cartons of various sizes, this liquid formula need only be poured into the bottle of your choice to be ready for use. It's less expensive than single-serving feedings, but the formula left in the carton needs to be stored properly. You'll also pay more for the convenience of ready-to-pours than formulas that need to be mixed.

Powder. The least expensive option, yet the most time-consuming and potentially messy, powered formula is reconstituted with a specified amount of water. It's available in cans or single-serving packets. Besides the low cost, another compelling reason to opt for

HOW MUCH FORMULA IS LIKE A FEAST?

How much formula does your baby need? A lot depends on your baby's weight, age and, once solids are being taken, how much he or she is eating. As a general rule, infants under six months (those not supplementing with solids) should be taking 60 to 70 ml (2 to 2½ fl oz) of formula per 450 g (1 lb) of body weight over a twenty-four-hour period. So, if your baby weighs, that would translate to 570 to 710 ml (20 to 25 fl oz) of formula a day; in a twenty-four-hour period, you'll be feeding your baby around 85 to 115 ml (3 to 4 fl oz) every four hours.

But because these are just rough guidelines, and because every baby is different (and even the same baby's needs are different on two different days), you shouldn't expect your infant to follow this formula (so to speak) with mathematical precision. How much your baby needs to take may vary somewhat – from day to day and feeding to feeding – and may stray significantly from what baby's peers need.

Keep in mind, too, that your baby's consumption will depend not just on weight but also on age. A large newborn, for example, probably won't be able to drink as much as a small three-month-old – even if their weights are the same. So start your newborn out slow, with 30 to 60 ml (1 to 2 fl oz) or so at each feeding for the first week every three to four hours (or on demand). Gradually up the amount, adding more as the demand becomes greater, but never push baby to take more than he or she wants. After all, your baby's tummy is the size of his or her fist (not yours). Put too much in the tummy, and it's bound to overflow – in the form of excessive spit-up.

Most of all, remember that bottle-fed babies, just like breastfed babies, know when they've had enough – and enough, for a newborn, is like a feast. Take your cues from baby's hunger, and you're sure to find the perfect formula for feeding your baby. As long as your baby is gaining enough weight, is wetting and dirtying enough nappies, and is happy and healthy (see page 158), you can be sure you're on target. For more reassurance, check with your baby's doctor or health visitor on formula intake.

---

powder (at least when you're out and about with baby) is that it doesn't need to be refrigerated until it's mixed.

SAFE BOTTLE FEEDING

Formula feeding has never been safer – as long as you take just a few precautions:

- Always check the expiration date on formula; do not purchase or use any formula that has expired. Don't buy or use dented, leaky or otherwise damaged cans or other containers.

- Wash your hands thoroughly before preparing formula.

- Before opening, wash the tops of formula cans with detergent and hot water; rinse well and dry. Shake, if the label specifies.

- Use clean scissors to open cartons of liquid formula. Wash the scissors after each use. Most powdered formula cans come with special pull-open tops, making the use of a can opener unnecessary.

- Boil the water used to mix formula first, and allow to cool before mixing. (Test the temperature by shaking a few drops on your inner wrist.)

♦ Bottles and teats don't need to be sterilized with special equipment. Dishwashers (or sink washing with detergent and hot water) get them clean enough. Some doctors recommend submerging bottles and teats in a pot of boiling water for a few minutes before the first use.

♦ But here's a step you should never skip: follow the manufacturer's directions precisely when mixing formula. *Always* check cans to see if formula needs to be diluted: diluting a formula that shouldn't be diluted, or not diluting one that should be, could be dangerous. Formula that is too weak can stunt growth. Formula that is too strong can lead to dehydration.

♦ Bottle warming is a matter of taste, namely baby's. There is no health reason to warm formula before feedings, though some babies prefer it this way, especially if that's what they've become accustomed to. In fact, you might consider starting your baby out on formula that's been mixed with room temperature water or even a bottle right out of the fridge; if he or she gets used to it that way, you can save yourself the time and the hassle of warming bottles (something you'll especially appreciate in the middle of the night or when your baby's frantic for a feed). If you do plan to serve the bottle warm, place it in a pot or bowl of hot water or run hot water over it. Check the temperature of the formula frequently by shaking a few drops on your inner wrist; it's ready for baby when it no longer feels cold to the touch – it doesn't need to be very

warm, just body temperature. Once it's warmed, use formula immediately, since bacteria multiply rapidly at lukewarm temperatures. Never heat formula in a microwave oven – the liquid may warm unevenly, or the container may remain cool when the formula has got hot enough to burn baby's mouth or throat.

♦ Throw out formula remaining in the bottle after a feeding. It's a potential breeding ground for bacteria, even if you refrigerate it, and should never be reused, tempting as that might be.

♦ Rinse bottles and teats right after use, for easier cleaning.

♦ Cover opened cartons of liquid formula tightly and store them in the refrigerator for *no longer* than the times specified on the labels, usually forty-eight hours. Opened cans of dry formula should be covered and stored in a cool, dry place for use within the month.

♦ Store unopened cartons of liquid formula at between 12.8° and 23.9° (55° and 75°F). Don't use unopened liquid for long periods at temperatures at or below 0°C (32°F) or in direct heat above 35°C (95°F). Also, don't use formula that has been frozen (soya products freeze more quickly) or that shows white specks or streaks even after shaking.

♦ Keep prepared bottles of formula refrigerated until ready to use. If you are travelling away from home, store previously prepared bottles in an insulated container or in a plastic bag with a small ice pack or a dozen ice cubes (the formula will stay fresh as long as most of the ice is frozen); or pack the bottles with a small carton or can of juice that you've prefrozen (not only will the formula stay fresh, but you'll have a cold drink handy, too). Do *not* use formula that is no longer cold to the touch (unless, of course, it's ready-to-serve and hasn't been opened or is powdered formula that has just been mixed with warm or room temperature water). You can also take along ready-to-use bottled formula, or bottles of water and single-serving formula packets to mix with them.

BOTTLE FEEDING WITH LOVE

Whether you've chosen to feed your baby exclusively with formula or to mix it up with breast, the most important ingredient in any feeding session is love. Though you'll always feel

FROM BOTTLE, WITH LOVE

Bottle feeding gives dad and other family members the chance to get close to baby. Use the time for cuddling and interaction; nourishment needn't come from the breast to come with love.

that love, it's also essential that you communicate it to your baby. The kind of skin-to-skin, eye-to-eye contact that's linked to optimum brain development and attachment in a newborn is a built-in feature of breastfeeding. With bottle feeding, that contact takes a conscious effort, and many well-meaning but harried bottle-feeding parents at least occasionally give in to feeding shortcuts that compromise closeness for convenience. To make sure you keep in touch with your baby while you're bottle feeding:

Don't prop the bottle. For a young baby, who is as hungry for emotional gratification in the form of cuddling as for oral gratification in the form of food, propping is very unsatisfying. And besides the emotional drawbacks, there are physical ones as well. For one thing, the risk of choking is always present when you prop, even if your baby is in a reclining high chair or infant seat. Prop with baby lying down, and he or she may also be more susceptible to ear infections. Once teeth come in, letting a baby fall asleep with a bottle in his or her mouth (which wouldn't happen if you were administering the feeding) can lead to tooth decay, since the formula is left to pool in the mouth. So avoid the temptation to prop the bottle and leave your baby during a feeding, even if it means the million and one things you have to do won't get done.

Go skin to skin, when possible. There are piles of research to show the developmental benefits of regular close contact with a newborn. But no research is as convincing as the satisfaction both you and your baby will get by sharing the warmth and intimacy of skin-to-skin contact. So whenever possible (it won't work in public, but it will in private), open your shirt and nestle your baby close to you when you bottle feed. Breasts aren't necessary to achieve the desired effect, either; dads can cuddle their babies cheek-to-chest just as effectively during an open-shirt feeding.

Switch arms. Breastfeeding also builds in this feature (alternating breasts means alternating arms); with bottle feeding, you'll have to remember to switch. A switch midfeeding serves two purposes: firstly, it gives your baby a chance to see the world from different perspectives. Secondly, it gives you a chance to relieve the aches that can develop from staying in one position for so long.

Let baby call it quits. When it comes to feedings, your baby's the boss. If you see only 90 ml (3 fl oz) have been emptied when the usual meal is 120 ml (4 fl oz), don't be tempted to push the rest. A healthy baby knows when to stop. And it's this kind of pushing that often leads bottle-fed babies to become too plump – much more often than breast-fed babies, who eat to appetite.

Take your time. A nursing baby can keep suckling on a breast long after it's been drained, just for comfort and sucking satisfaction. Your bottle-fed baby can't do the same with an empty bottle, but there are ways you can supply some of the same satisfactions. Extend the pleasure of the feeding session by socializing once the bottle is drained – assuming he or she hasn't dropped off into a milk-induced sleep. If your baby doesn't seem satisfied with the amount of sucking each feeding's providing, try using teats with smaller holes, which will ensure that your baby will get to suck longer for the same meal. Or finish off feedings by offering a dummy briefly. If your baby seems to be fussing for more at meal's end, consider whether you're

offering enough formula. Increase it by 30 to 60 ml (2 to 3 fl oz) to see if it's really hunger that's making your baby fretful.

Feel good about bottle feeding. If you were eager to breastfeed and for some reason couldn't – or couldn't keep it up – don't feel guilty or frustrated. Such negative feelings can be unwittingly transmitted to your baby during feedings, and keep you both from enjoying what should be a treasured ritual. Remember: filled with the right formula and given the right way, a bottle can be used to pass along good nutrition and lots of love.

BOTTLE FEEDING WITH EASE

If you've had some experience bottle feeding a young infant – either a sibling, a baby-sitting charge or a friend's baby – chances are the correct technique will come back to you (like riding a bike) virtually the moment you hold your baby in your arms. If you're a first-timer – or if you just want to bone up on bottle- feeding basics – the following step-by-step tips should help:

◆ Give notice. Let baby know that 'formula's on' by stroking his or her cheek with your finger or the tip of the teat. That will encourage your baby to 'root', turning in the direction of the stroke. Then place the teat gently between baby's lips and, hopefully, sucking will begin. If baby still doesn't get the picture, a drop of formula on the lips should clue him or her in.

◆ Make air the enemy. Tilt the bottle up so that formula always fills the teat completely. If you don't, and air fills part of it, baby will be chasing formula down with air – a recipe for gassiness, which will make both of you miserable. Anti-air precautions aren't necessary, however, if you're using disposable bottle liners, which automatically deflate (eliminating air pockets), or if you're using angled bottles that keep the formula pooled near the teat.

◆ Start slow. Don't be concerned if your baby doesn't seem to take much formula at first. The newborn's need for nutrition is minimal for a few days after birth – a breastfed baby, on orders from Mother Nature, receives only a teaspoonful of colostrum at each feeding during this time. If you're in the hospital, the nursery will probably provide you with full 120 ml (4 fl oz) bottles, but don't expect them to be drained. A baby who falls asleep after taking (15 ml (½ fl oz) or so is probably saying, 'I've had enough'. On the other hand, if baby doesn't fall asleep but turns away from the bottle fussily after just a few minutes of nipping, it's more likely a matter of gas than overfilling. In that case, don't give up without a bubble. If after a good burping (see page 134) the teat is still rejected, take that as your signal the meal is over. (See page 102 for more details on how much formula to feed.)

◆ Check your speed. Be certain that formula isn't coming through the teat too quickly or too slowly. Teats are available in different sizes for babies' different sizes and age; a newborn teat dispenses milk more slowly, which is usually perfect for a baby who's just getting the hang of sucking (and whose appetite is still tender). You can check the speed of the teats you're using by giving the bottle, turned upside down, a few quick shakes. If milk pours or spurts out, it's flowing too quickly; if just a drop or two escapes, too slowly. If you get a little spray, and then some drops, the flow is just about right. But the very best way to test the flow is by observing the little mouth it's flowing into. If there's a lot of gulping and sputtering going on, and milk is always dripping out of the corners of baby's mouth, the flow is too fast. If baby seems to work very hard at sucking for a few moments, then seems frustrated (possibly letting go of the teat to complain), the flow's too slow. Sometimes, a flow problem has less to do with the size of the teat than with the way the cap is fastened. A very tight cap inhibits flow by creating a partial vacuum; loosening it up a bit may make the formula flow more freely.

◆ **Minimize midnight hassles.** Make night feedings less of an ordeal by investing in a bedside bottle holder, which keeps baby's bottle safely chilled until ready to use and then warms it to room temperature in minutes. Or keep a bottle on ice, champagne-style, in the nursery (or by your bed), ready to serve cold or to warm under the bathroom tap when baby starts fussing for a feeding.

What You May Be Concerned About

BIRTHWEIGHT

'My friends all seem to be having babies that weigh 3.6 and 4 kg (8 and 9 lb) at birth. Mine weighed in at a little over 2.9 kg (6½ lb) at full term. She's healthy, but she seems so small.'

Just like healthy adults, healthy babies come in all kinds of packages – long and lanky, big and bulky, slight and slender. And more often than not, a baby can thank the adults in her life for her birth stats; the laws of genetics dictate that large parents generally have large children and small parents generally have small children (though when dad's large and mum's small, the progeny are more likely to follow in mum's smaller footsteps, at least at birth). Mum's own birthweight can also influence her offspring's. Still another factor is a baby's sex: girls tend to weigh in lighter and measure in shorter than boys do. And though there is a laundry list of other factors that can affect a baby's size at birth – such as what mum ate during pregnancy and how much weight she gained – the only factor that matters now is that your baby is completely healthy. And, in fact, a petite 2.9-kg (6½-lb) baby can be every bit as vigorous as a chubby 3.6- or 4-kg (8- or 9-lb) one.

Keep in mind, too, that some babies who start out small quickly outpace their peers on the growth charts as they start catching up to their genetic potential. (For more on this, see page 299.) In the meantime, enjoy your healthy baby while she's still a relatively light load. It won't be long before just hearing the words 'Carry me!' from your strapping toddler will make your back start aching.

BONDING

'I had an emergency Caesarean and they whisked my baby away to the ICU before I had a chance to bond with her. Could this affect our relationship?'

Bonding at birth is an idea whose time has come – and, by now, should be gone. That's because the theory, first suggested in the 1970s, that a mother-baby relationship will be better when the two spend sixteen hours of the first twenty-four in close loving contact, just hasn't held up in research or in practice.

Without a doubt, good things have come from the bonding theory. Because of it, hospitals now encourage new parents to hold their babies moments after birth, and to cuddle and nurse them for anywhere from ten minutes to an hour or more, instead of dispatching the newborn off to the nursery the instant the cord is cut. This encounter gives mother, father and baby a chance to make early contact, skin to skin, eye to eye – definitely a change for the better. On the other hand, the concept leaves many parents who aren't able to hold their babies immediately after birth (either because they had emergency surgical deliveries or traumatic vaginal births, or because the infants arrived in need of special care) feeling as though they've missed the chance of a lifetime to foster a close relationship with their offspring.

But not only do many experts believe that bonding doesn't have to be firmly established at birth, most dispute that it can be. Freshly delivered infants come equipped with all their senses; they're capable of making eye contact – and even of recognizing their mother's voice (though they won't recognize her face until somewhere around three months). They're also alert in the hour right after birth, which makes this an especially good time for that first official get-together with their parents. But because they're not capable of retaining these experiences – as wonderful as they are – those first few moments can't make or break future relationships. A new mother will certainly remember that special first meeting, but she may not feel an immediate bond with her baby for a variety of reasons: exhaustion from a long labour and delivery, grogginess from medication, pain from cramping or an incision, a feeling of being over-whelmed by the enormous responsibility that's just been handed her, or simply a lack of preparation for the experience of holding and caring for a newborn.

The first few moments a parent and baby spend together after birth are important – but no more important than the hours, and days, and weeks, and years that lie ahead. They mark only the beginning of the long and complex process of getting to know and love each other. And this beginning can just as well take place hours after birth in a hospital bed, or through the portholes of an incubator, or even weeks later at home. When your parents and grand-parents were born, they probably saw little of their mothers and even less of their fathers until they went home (usu-ally ten days after birth), and the vast majority of that generation grew up with strong, loving family ties. Mothers who have the chance to bond at birth with one child and not with another usually report no difference in their feelings towards the children. And adoptive par-ents, who often don't meet their babies until hospital discharge (or even much later), can foster bonds as strong as those of birth parents who met their infants moments after delivery.

The kind of love that lasts a lifetime can't magically evolve in a few hours, or even a few days. In fact, experts believe that it doesn't completely take hold until somewhere in the second half of the baby's first year. The first moments after birth may become a cherished memory for some, but for others they may be just a blur. Either way, these moments don't indelibly colour the character and qual-ity of your future relationship.

The complicated process of parent-child bonding actually begins for parents during pregnancy, when atti-tudes and feelings towards the baby start developing. The relationship con-tinues to evolve and change all through infancy, childhood and adolescence, and even into adulthood. So relax. There's lots of time to tie those bonds that bind.

'I've been told that bonding at birth brings mother and baby closer together. I held my new daughter for nearly an hour right after delivery, but she seemed like a stranger to me then, and still does now, three days later.'

Love at first sight is a concept that flourishes in novels and movies but rarely materializes in real life. The kind of love that lasts a lifetime usually requires time, nurturing and plenty of patience to develop and deepen. And that's just as true for parental love as it is for romantic love.

Physical closeness between parent and child immediately after birth does not guarantee instant emotional close-ness. Those first postpartum moments aren't automatically bathed in a glow of maternal (or paternal) love. In fact, the first sensation a woman experiences after birth is just as likely to be relief as it is love – relief that the baby is normal and, especially if her labour was difficult, that the ordeal is over. It's not at all unusual to regard that squalling and unsociable infant as a stranger with very little connection to the cozy, idealized baby you carried for nine months – and to feel little more than neutral towards her. One study has found that it took an average of over two weeks (and often as long as nine weeks) for mothers to begin having strongly positive feelings towards their newborns.

Just how a woman reacts to her newborn at their first meeting may depend on a variety of factors: the length and intensity of her labour; whether she received medication during labour; her previous experience (or lack of it) with infants; her feelings about having a child; her relationship with her spouse, extraneous worries that may preoccupy her; her general health; and probably most important of all, her personality.

Your reaction is normal for *you*. And as long as you feel an increasing sense of comfort and attachment as the days go by, you can relax. Some of the best relationships get off to the slowest starts. Give yourself and your baby a chance to get to know and appreciate each other, and let the love grow unhurriedly.

If you don't feel a growing closeness after a few weeks, however, or if you feel anger or antipathy towards your baby, talk to your doctor. It's possible that you're suffering from postnatal depression, especially if you're experiencing other symptoms of the condition. If that's the case, treatment is important not just for your health but also for the well-being of your baby and your relationship with her. See page 676 for more.

WEIGHT LOSS

'I expected my baby to lose some weight in the hospital, but she dropped from 3.4 kg (7½ lb) to 3.1 kg (6 lb 14 oz). Isn't that excessive?'

FOR FATHERS ONLY: BECOMING ENGROSSED

While bonding is a process that involves both parents, fathers apparently have their own way of becoming close to their new infants – and researchers have even given it a name of its own: engrossment. Engrossment applies not only to what a father does for his baby (such as holding, comforting, rocking, massaging) and the unique way that he does it (fathers have a touch that's different from mothers', a difference babies respond to), but also what the baby does for his or her father (such as bringing out his sensitive, nurturing side). For more on fathering, see chapter 24.

New parents, eager to start issuing reports on their baby's progress in the weight-gain department, are often disappointed when their babies check out of the hospital weighing considerably less than when they checked in. But nearly all newborns are destined to lose some of their birthweight (usually between 5 and 10 per cent) in the first five days of life – not as a result of fad dieting in the nursery, but because of normal postdelivery fluid loss, which is not immediately recouped, since babies need and take in little food during this time. Breastfed babies, who consume only teaspoons at a time of the premilk colostrum, generally lose more than bottle-fed babies. Most newborns have stopped losing by the fifth day and have regained or surpassed their birthweight by ten to fourteen days of age – when you can start issuing those bulletins.

BABY'S LOOKS

'People ask me whether the baby looks like me or my husband. Neither one of us has a pointy head, puffy eyes, an ear that bends forward, and a pushed-in nose. When will he start looking better?'

There's a good reason why two- and three-month-old babies are used to portray newborns in movies and television commercials: most newborns are not exactly photogenic. And though parental love is blinder than most, even parents who are head over heels can't help but notice the many imperfections of their newborn's appearance. Fortunately, most of the newborn characteristics that will keep your baby from costarring in films and selling nappies on TV are temporary.

The features you're describing weren't inherited from some distant pointy-headed, puffy-eyed, flap-eared relative. They were acquired during your baby's stay in the cramped quarters of your uterus, during the stormy passage through your bony pelvis in preparation for birth, and during his final traumatic trip through the narrow confines of your birth canal during delivery.

If it weren't for the miraculous design of the foetal head – with the skull bones not fully fused, allowing them to be pushed and moulded as the baby makes its descent – there would be many more surgical deliveries. So be thankful for the pointy little head that came with your vaginal delivery, and rest assured that the skull will just as miraculously return to cherubic roundness within a few days or so.

The swelling around your baby's eyes is also due, at least in part, to the beating he took on his fantastic voyage into the world. (Another contributing factor might be the antibiotic ointment placed in your baby's eyes to prevent gonococcal or chlamydial infection.) Some have postulated that this swelling serves as natural protection for newborns, whose eyes are being exposed to light for the first time. The worry that the puffiness may interfere with a baby's ability to see mummy and daddy, making that first eye-to-eye contact impossible, is unfounded. Though he can't distinguish one from another, a newborn can make out blurry faces at birth – even through swollen lids.

The bent ear is probably another outcome of the crowding your baby experienced in the uterus. As a foetus grows and becomes more snugly lodged in his mother's cozy amniotic sac, an ear that happens to get pushed forward may stay that way even after birth. But this is only temporary. Taping it back won't help, say the experts, and the tape might cause irritation, but you can speed the return to normal ear positioning by being sure the ear is back against the head when putting baby (supervised) on his side to play. Some ears, of course, are genetically destined to stand out – but if that's the case, both generally do, right from the start.

The pushed-in nose is very likely a result of a tight squeeze during labour and delivery, and should return to normal naturally. But because baby noses are so different from the adult variety (the bridge is broad, almost nonexistent, the shape often nondescript), it may still be a while before you can tell whose nose your baby has.

EYE COLOUR

'I was hoping my baby would have green eyes like my husband, but her eyes seem to be a dark greyish colour. Is there any chance that they'll turn?'

The favourite guessing game of pregnancy – will it be a boy or a girl? – is replaced by another in the first few months of a baby's life – what colour will her eyes turn out to be?

It's definitely too early to call now. Most Caucasian babies are born with dark blue or slate-coloured eyes; most dark-skinned infants with dark, usually brown, eyes. While the dark eyes of the darker-skinned babies will stay dark, the eye colour of Caucasian babies may go through a number of changes (making the betting more lively) before becoming set somewhere between three and six months, or even later. And since pigmentation of the iris may continue increasing during the entire first year, the depth of colour may not be evident until around baby's first birthday.

BLOODSHOT EYES

'The whites of my newborn's eyes look bloodshot. Is this an infection?'

It's not the late hours that newborns keep that often give their eyes that bloodshot look (no, that would be why *your* eyes will be looking so red for the next few months). Rather, it's a harmless condition that occurs when there is trauma to the eyeball – often in the form of broken blood vessels – during a vaginal delivery. (Actually, many new mothers who put in a lot of pushing time during delivery sport matching broken blood vessels in their eyes.) Like a skin bruise, the discolouration disappears in a few days and does not indicate there has been any damage to your baby's eyes.

EYE OINTMENT

'Why does my newborn have ointment in his eyes, and how long will it blur his vision?'

There are a lot of factors standing between a newborn baby and a clear view of his surroundings: the fact that his eyes are puffy from delivery; that they're still adjusting to the bright lights of the outside world after spending nine months in a dark womb; that they're naturally nearsighted; and, finally, as you've noticed, that they're gooey with ointment. But the ointment serves an important purpose that makes a little increased blurriness well worthwhile: it is administered to prevent a gonococcal or chlamydial infection. Once a major cause of blindness, such infections have been virtually eliminated by this preventive treatment. The antibiotic ointment, usually erythromycin, is mild and not as potentially irritating to the eyes as the silver nitrate drops that were once the treatment of choice (and are still used in a few hospitals). Doctors found that the silver nitrate drops caused redness and inflammation, as well as a tendency for infants to develop a chemical conjunctivitis, characterized by swelling and a yellowish discharge.

The slight swelling and oozy blurriness of your newborn's eye will last only a day or two. Tearing, swelling or infection that begins after that may be caused by a blocked tear duct (see page 202).

ROOMING-IN

'Having the baby room-in with me sounded like heaven before I gave birth. Now it seems more like hell. I can't get the baby to stop crying, yet what kind of mother would I be if I asked the nurse to take her back to the nursery?'

You would be a very human mother (which, by the way, you might as well get used to being). Considering the challenge you've just been through (childbirth), and the one you're about to undertake (parenting), it's not surprising you're more in the mood for sleep than you are for a crying baby. And it's nothing to feel guilty about, either (remember, you're only human).

Sure, some women handle round-the-clock rooming-in with ease, right from the first night. They may have had deliveries that left them feeling exhilarated instead of exhausted. Or they may have had some experience caring for newborns, their own or other people's. For these women, an inconsolable infant at 3 A.M. may not be a joy, but it's not a nightmare, either. For a woman who's been without sleep for forty-eight hours, however, whose body has been left limp from an enervating labour, and who's never been closer to a baby than a nappy ad, such predawn bouts can leave her wondering tearfully: Why did I ever decide to become a mother?

Playing the martyr can raise motherly resentments, feelings baby will be likely to sense. If, instead, the baby is taken back to the nursery between feedings at night, mother and child, both well rested, may find getting acquainted easier when morning comes. And morning is the best time to take advantage of one of the major advantages of daytime rooming-in: the chance to learn how to care for your new baby while there's still experienced help just down the hallway if you need it. Remember, even if you've opted to have the baby with you during the day, you shouldn't feel like you can't call on the nursery staff to give you a hand. That's what they're there for.

When night falls again, and if you feel rested enough, try keeping the baby and see how things go. She may surprise you by doing more sleeping than crying, and you may surprise yourself by feeling more comfortable with her. Or if the second night turns out to be a repeat of the first, or if you're still not up to

working the evening shift, feel free to take advantage of the nursery again. Full-time rooming-in is a wonderful option in family-centred maternity care – but it's not for everyone. You are *not* a failure as a mother if you don't enjoy, or you're too exhausted for, rooming-in. Don't be pushed into it if you don't think you want it; and once you've committed yourself, don't feel you can't change your mind and go part-time.

Be flexible. Focus on the quality of the time you spend with your baby in the hospital rather than the quantity. Round-the-clock rooming-in will begin soon enough at home. By then, if you don't overdo now, you should be emotionally and physically ready to deal with it.

PAIN MEDICATION

'I've been having some pretty bad pain from my Caesarean incision. My obstetrician has prescribed some pain medication, but I'm worried about the drug getting into my milk.'

You don't need to suffer in order to keep your baby safe. In fact, not taking medication for your pain can actually do you both more harm than good. The tension and exhaustion that can result from unrelieved post-Caesarean (or vaginal birth) pain will only interfere with your ability to establish a good nursing relationship with your baby (you need to be relaxed) and a good milk supply (you need to be rested). Besides which, the medication will appear only in very minuscule amounts in your colostrum; by the time your milk supply comes in, you probably won't need narcotic pain relief. And if your baby does receive a small dose of medication, he or she will sleep it off easily, with no ill effects.

HAVE YOU HEARD THE ONE . . .

You haven't been a parent for forty-eight hours yet, and already you've been on the receiving end of so much conflicting advice (on everything from umbilical stump care to feeding) that your head's in a tailspin. The hospital staff tells you one thing, your sister (veteran of two newborns) has a completely different take, and both clash with what you seem to recall baby's paediatrician telling you.

The fact is that the facts about infant care (at least, the most up-to-date facts) aren't easy to sort out – especially when everyone (and their mother) is telling you something different. Your best bet when all that contradicting counsel leaves you in doubt about any infant care issue (or when you need a deciding vote you can count on): stick with the doctor's advice.

Of course, in listening to others, don't forget that you've got another valuable resource you can trust – your own instincts. Often parents, even the really green ones, do know best – and usually, much more than they think they do.

If your pain is not extremely severe – or once it starts to ease up – you might consider asking the nurse for extra-strength paracetamol, the pain reliever of choice during breastfeeding.

BABY'S SLEEPINESS

'My baby seemed very alert right after she was born, but ever since, she's been sleeping so soundly I can hardly wake her to eat, much less to socialize.'

You've waited nine long months to meet your baby – and now that she's here, all she does is sleep. Don't worry, though, this chronic sleepiness is no reflection on your feeding or socializing skills – it's just a sign that baby's doing what comes naturally. Wakefulness for the first hour or so after birth followed by a long stretch, often twenty-four hours, of pronounced drowsiness is the normal newborn pattern (though she won't sleep for twenty-four hours straight). It is a pattern probably designed to give babies a chance to recover from the exhausting work of being born, and their mothers a chance to recover from giving birth. (You will need to make sure that your baby fits feedings into her sleep schedule,

however; see page 116 for some waking techniques.)

Don't expect your newborn to become much more stimulating company once those twenty-four hours of sleepiness are over, either. Here's approximately how you can expect it to go: in the first few weeks of life, her two- to four-hour-long sleeping periods will end abruptly with crying. She'll rouse to a semi-awake state to eat, probably doing a fair amount of dozing while she's feeding (shaking the teat around in her mouth will get her sucking again when she drifts off midmeal). Once she's satiated, she'll finally fall more soundly asleep, ready for yet another nap.

At first, your little sleepyhead will be truly alert for only about three minutes of every hour during the day, and less (you hope) at night, a schedule that will allow a total of about an hour a day for active socializing. Though that may be frustrating for you (after all, how long have you waited to try out your peek-a-boo prowess?), it's just what Mother Nature ordered for your baby. She's not mature enough to benefit from longer periods of alertness, and

A NEWBORN STATE OF MIND

It may seem to the casual observer – or the brand-new parent – that infants have just three things on their minds: eating, sleeping and crying (not necessarily in that order). In fact, however, researchers have shown that infant behaviour is actually at least twice as complex as that and can be organized into six states of consciousness. Learn to observe and understand these states, and you'll be able to decipher the messages your baby's sending you, and even figure out what he or she wants.

Quiet Alert. This state is a baby's secret agent mode. When babies are in quiet alert, their motor activity is suppressed, so they rarely move. Instead, they spend all their energy watching (with their eyes wide open, usually staring directly at someone) and listening intently. This behaviour makes quiet alert the perfect time for one-on-one socializing. Newborns by the end of their first month typically spend two and a half hours a day in this state.

Active Alert. The motor's running when babies are in active alert – with arms moving and legs kicking. They may even make some small sounds. Though they'll be doing a lot of looking around in this state, they're more likely to be focused on objects than on people – your cue that baby's more interested in taking in the big picture than in doing any serious socializing. Babies are most often in this newborn state of mind before they eat or when they are borderline fussy. You may be able to preempt full-fledged fussiness at the end of an active alert period by feeding or doing some soothing rocking.

Crying. This is, of course, the state newborns are best known for. Crying occurs when babies are hungry, uncomfortable, bored (not getting enough attention) or just plain unhappy. While crying, babies will contort their faces, move their arms and legs vigorously, and shut their eyes tightly.

Drowsiness. Babies are in this state, not surprisingly, when they're waking up or nodding off to sleep. Drowsy babies will make some moves (such as stretching upon waking) and make a variety of adorable but seemingly incongruous facial gestures (that can run the gamut from scowling to surprised to elated), but the eyelids are droopy and the eyes will appear dull, glazed and unfocused.

Quiet Sleep. In this state, baby's face is relaxed and the eyelids are closed and still. Body movement is rare, with just occasional startles or mouth movements, and breathing is very regular. Quiet sleep alternates every thirty minutes with active sleep.

Active Sleep. Half of the time babies sleep, they are in the active sleep state. In this restless sleep state (which is actually a lot more restful for baby than it looks), the eyes, though closed, can often be seen moving under the lids – thus the name REM, or rapid eye movement sleep. Breathing is not regular; babies may move their mouths in a sucking or chewing motion or even smile; arms and legs may also shift around a great deal.

these periods of sleep – particularly of REM (or dream state) sleep – apparently help her develop.

Gradually, your baby's periods of wakefulness will grow longer. By the end of the first month, most babies are alert for about two to three hours every day, most of it in one relatively long stretch, usually in the late afternoon (at which point, you can start testing out your baby-entertaining material on her). And some of their evening 'naps', instead of being two or three hours long, may last as long as six or six and a half hours.

In the meantime, you may continue to be thwarted in your attempts to get to know your baby. But instead of standing over the cot waiting for her to wake up for a play session, try to use her sleeping time to store up a few zzz's of your own. You'll need them for the days (and nights) ahead, when she'll probably be awake more than you'd like.

EMPTY BREASTS

'It's been two days since I gave birth to my little girl, and nothing comes out of my breasts when I squeeze them, not even colostrum. I'm worried that she's starving.'

Not only is your baby not starving, she isn't even hungry yet. Infants aren't born with an appetite, or even with immediate nutritional needs. And by the time your baby begins to get hungry for a breast full of milk, usually around the third or fourth postpartum day, you will almost certainly be able to oblige.

Which isn't to say that your breasts are empty now. Colostrum (which provides your baby with nourishment and with important antibodies her own body can't yet produce, while helping to empty her digestive system of meconium and excess mucus) is almost certainly present, though in very tiny amounts (first feedings average less than a half-teaspoon; by the third day, less than three tablespoons per feeding over ten feedings). But colostrum isn't that easy to express manually. Even a day-old baby, with no previous experience, is better equipped to extract this pre-milk than you are.

GAGGING AND CHOKING

'When they brought my baby to me this morning, he seemed to gag and choke and then spit up some liquidy stuff. I hadn't nursed him yet, so it couldn't have been spit-up. What's wrong?'

Your baby spent the last nine months, more or less, living in a liquid environment. He didn't breathe air, but he did suck in a lot of fluid. Though a nurse or doctor probably suctioned his airways clear at birth, there may have been additional mucus and fluid in his lungs, and this gagging and choking is your baby's way of clearing out what remains. It's perfectly normal, and nothing to worry about.

SLEEPING THROUGH MEALS

'The doctor says I should feed my baby every two to three hours, but sometimes I don't hear from him for five or six. Should I wake him up to eat?'

Some babies are perfectly happy to sleep through meals, particularly during the first few days of life. But letting a sleeping baby lie through his feedings means that he won't be getting enough to eat, and if you're nursing, that your milk supply won't be getting the jump start it needs. If your baby is a sleepy baby, try these rousing techniques at mealtime:

◆ Choose the right sleep to wake him from. Baby will be much more easily roused during active, or REM, sleep. You'll know your baby is in this light sleep cycle (it takes up about about 50 per cent of his sleeping time) when he starts moving his arms and legs, changing facial expressions and fluttering his eyelids.

◆ Unwrap him. Sometimes, just unswaddling your baby will wake him up. If it doesn't, undress him right down to the nappy (room temperature permitting) and try some skin-to-skin contact.

◆ Go for a change. Even if his nappy is not that wet, a change may be just jarring enough to wake him for his meal.

◆ Dim the lights. Though it may seem that turning on the high-voltage lamps might be the best way to jolt baby out of his slumber, it could have just the opposite effect. A newborn's eyes are sensitive to light; if the room is too bright, your baby may be more comfortable keeping them tightly shut. But don't turn the lights all the way off. A too-dark room will only lull baby back off to dreamland.

◆ Try the 'doll's eyes' technique. Holding a baby upright will usually cause his or her eyes to open (much as a doll's would). Gently raise your baby into an upright or sitting position and pat him on the back. Be careful not to jackknife him (fold him forward).

◆ Be sociable. Sing a lively song. Talk to your baby and, once you get his eyes open, make eye contact with him. A little social stimulation may induce him to stay awake.

◆ Rub him the right way. Stroke the palms of your baby's hands and soles of his feet; massage his arms, back and shoulders. Or do some baby aerobics: move his arms, and pump his legs in a bicycling motion.

◆ If sleepyhead still won't rise to the occasion, place a cool (not cold) flannel on his forehead or rub his face gently with the flannel.

Of course, getting baby up doesn't mean you'll be able to keep baby up – especially not after a few nips of sleep-inducing milk. A baby that's still drowsy may take the teat, suckle briefly, then promptly fall back asleep, long before he's managed to make a meal of it. When this happens, try:

◆ A burp – whether baby needs a bubble or not, the jostling may rouse him again.

◆ A change – this time, of feeding position. Whether you're nursing or bottle feeding, switch from the cradle hold to the clutch hold (which babies are less likely to sleep in).

◆ A dribble – some breast milk or formula dribbled on baby's lips may whet his appetite for his second course.

◆ A jiggle – jiggling the breast or bottle in his mouth or stroking his cheek may get the sucking action going again.

◆ And repeat – Some young babies alternate sucking and dozing from the start of the meal to the finish. If that's the case with your baby, you may find you'll have to burp, change, dribble and jiggle at least several times to get a full feeding in.

It's fine to occasionally let your baby sleep when he's dropped off to dreamland after just a brief appetizer, and all efforts to tempt him into his entrée have failed. But for now, don't let him go more than three hours without a full meal if he's nursing or four hours if he's formula fed. It's also not a good idea to let your baby nip and nap at fifteen- to thirty-minute intervals all day long. If that seems to be the trend, be

CRACKING THE CRYING CODE

Sure, crying is a baby's only form of communication – but that doesn't mean you'll always know exactly what he or she is trying to say. Not to worry. This cheat sheet can help you figure out what those whimpers, wails, and shrieks really mean:

'I'm hungry'. A short and low-pitched cry that rises and falls rhythmically and has a pleading quality to it (as in 'Please, please feed me!') usually means that baby's in the market for a meal. The hunger cry is often preceded by hunger cues, such as lip smacking, rooting or finger sucking. Catch on to the clues, and you can often avoid the tears.

'I'm in pain'. This cry begins suddenly (usually in response to a stimulus – for instance, the jab of a needle at shot time) and is loud (as in ear-piercing), panicked, and long (with each wail lasting as long as a few seconds), leaving the baby breathless. It's followed by a long pause (that's baby catching his or her breath, saving up for another chorus) and then repeated, long, high-pitched shrieks.

'I'm bored'. This cry starts out as coos (as baby tries to get a good interaction going), then turns into fussing (when the attention he or she is craving isn't forthcoming), then builds to bursts of indignant crying ('Why are you ignoring me?') alternating with whimpers ('C'mon, what's a baby got to do to get a cuddle around here?'). The boredom cry stops as soon as the baby is picked up.

'I'm overtired or uncomfortable'. A whiny, nasal, continuous cry that builds in intensity is usually baby's signal that he or she has had enough (as in 'Nap, please!' or 'Nappy change, pronto!' or 'Can't you see I've had it with this infant seat?').

'I'm sick'. This cry is often weak and nasal sounding, with a lower pitch than the 'pain' or 'overtired' cry – as though baby just doesn't have the energy to pump up the volume. It's often accompanied by other signs of illness and changes in the baby's behaviour (for example, listlessness, refusal to eat, fever and/or diarrhoea). There's no sadder cry in baby's repertoire than the 'sick' cry, nor one that tugs harder at parental heartstrings.

relentless in your attempts to waken him when he dozes off during a feed.

If chronic sleepiness interferes so much with eating that your baby isn't thriving (see page 159 for signs), consult the doctor.

NON-STOP FEEDING

'I'm afraid my baby is going to turn into a little blimp. Almost immediately after I put her down, she's up, crying to be nursed again.'

Your baby may indeed be destined for the Goodyear fleet if you feed her again immediately after she's had a full meal. Babies cry for reasons other than hunger, and it may be that you are misreading the signals she's sending (see box, above). Sometimes, crying is a baby's way of unwinding for a few minutes before she falls asleep. Put her back to the breast, and you may not just be overfeeding her but also interrupting her efforts to settle down for a nap. Sometimes, crying after a meal may be a cry for companionship – a signal that baby's in the mood for some socializing, not another meal. Sometimes, crying means that baby is having trouble calming herself down, in which case a little rocking and a few soft lullabies may be just what she's fussing for. And

TIPS FOR SUCCESSFUL FEEDING SESSIONS

Whether it's a breast or a bottle that will be your newborn's ticket to a full tummy, the guidelines that follow should help make the trip a smoother one:

Minimize the mayhem. While you're both learning the ropes, you and your baby will have to focus on the feeding, and the fewer distractions from that job, the better. Turn off the television (soft music is fine), and let the answer phone pick up the phone at baby's mealtimes. Retire to the bedroom to feed baby when you have guests or when the general atmosphere in the living room rivals that of a three-ring circus (which in many homes, is around the clock). If you have other children, chances are you'll already be pretty proficient at feeding – the challenge will be keeping your older ones and your baby happy at the same time. Try diverting their attentions to some quiet activity, like colouring, that they can settle down with at your side, or take this opportunity to read them a story.

Make a change. If your baby is relatively calm, you've got time for a change. A clean nappy will make for a more comfortable meal and reduce the need for a change right after – a definite plus if your baby has nodded off to dreamland and you'd rather he or she stay there for a while. But don't change before middle-of-the-night feedings if baby's only damp (sopping's another story); such a disruption makes falling back to sleep more difficult, especially for infants who are mixing up their days and nights.

Wash up. Even though you won't be doing the eating, it's your hands that should be washed with soap and water before your baby's meals.

Get comfy. Aches and pains are an occupational hazard for new parents who use unaccustomed muscles to carry growing babies around. Feeding baby in an awkward position will only compound the problem. So before putting baby to breast or bottle, be sure you're comfortable, with adequate support both for your back and for the arm under baby.

Loosen up. If your baby is tightly swaddled, unwrap him or her so you can cuddle while you feed.

Cool down a fired-up baby. A baby who's upset will have trouble settling down to the business of feeding, and even more trouble with the business of digesting. Try a soothing song or a little rocking first.

Sound reveille. Some babies are sleepy at mealtimes, especially in the early days, and a concerted effort is required to rouse them to the task of nursing at breast or bottle. If your little one is a dinner dozer, try the wake-up techniques on page 116.

Break for a burp. Midway through each feeding, make a routine of stopping for a burp. Burp, too, any time baby seems to want to quit feeding prematurely or starts fussing at the nipple – it may be gas, not food, that's filling that little tummy. Bring up the bubble, and you're back in business.

Make contact. Cuddle and caress your baby with your hands, your eyes and your voice. Remember, meals should fill your baby's daily requirements not just for nutrients but for parental love as well.

sometimes, it's just a simple matter of gas (which more feeding would only compound). Bringing up the bubble may bring her the contentment she's craving.

If you've ruled out all of the above scenarios – as well as done a quick check for a dirty or uncomfortably wet nappy – and your baby's still crying, then consider that perhaps she really hasn't had enough to eat. It's possible that a growth spurt may be temporarily sending her appetite into overdrive. But keep in mind that offering your daughter food every time she cries after eating won't just blimp her out but may also get her hooked on a snack-and-snooze habit that will be difficult to break her of later on.

Do be sure, however, that your baby is gaining weight at an adequate rate. If she isn't, she may indeed be crying out of chronic hunger – which may be a sign that you're not producing enough milk. (See pages 159–162 if your baby doesn't seem to be thriving.)

QUIVERING CHIN

'Sometimes, especially when he's been crying, my baby's chin quivers.'

Though your baby's quivering chin may look like another one of his ingenious inborn ploys for playing at your heartstrings, it's actually a sign that his nervous system, like those of his newborn peers, is not fully mature. Give him the sympathy he appears to be craving, and enjoy the quivering chin while it lasts – which won't be for long.

STARTLING

'I'm worried that there's something wrong with my baby's nervous system. Even when she's sleeping, she'll suddenly seem to jump out of her skin.'

Assuming your baby hasn't been overdoing the black coffee, the jumpiness you notice is due to her startle reflex, one of the many very normal (though seemingly peculiar) reflexes newborns are born with. Also known as the Moro reflex, it occurs more frequently in some babies than in others, sometimes for no apparent reason, but most often in response to a loud noise, jolting or a feeling of falling – as when a young infant is picked up or placed down without adequate support. Like many other reflexes, the Moro is probably a built-in survival mechanism designed to protect the vulnerable newborn; in this case, it's likely a primitive attempt to regain perceived loss of equilibrium. In a Moro, the baby typically stiffens her body, flings her arms up and out symmetrically, spreads her usually tightly clenched fists wide open, draws her knees up, then finally brings her arms, fists clenched once again, back to her body in an embracing gesture – all in a matter of seconds. She may also cry out.

While the sight of a startled baby often startles her parents, a doctor is more likely to be concerned if a baby doesn't exhibit this reflex. Newborns are routinely tested for startling, the presence of which is actually one reassuring sign that the neurological system is functioning well. You'll find that your baby will gradually startle less frequently and less dramatically, and that the reflex will disappear fully somewhere between four and six months. (Your baby may occasionally startle, of course, at any age – just as adults can – but not with the same pattern of reactions.)

BIRTHMARKS

'I've just noticed a raised bright red blotch on my daughter's stomach. Is this a birthmark? Will it ever go away?'

Long before your daughter starts petitioning parental powers for her first bikini, that strawberry birthmark – like most birthmarks – will be a part of her childish past, leaving her belly ready (even if her parents aren't) for beach baring. Of course, when you look at a newborn's birthmark – which can be quite large and quite vibrant – this often seems hard to believe. Sometimes the mark (which often appears not at birth but rather in the first few weeks of life) grows a bit before fading. And when it does begin to shrink or fade, the changes from day to day are often difficult to see. For that reason, many doctors document birthmark changes by photographing and measuring the mark periodically. If your baby's doctor doesn't, you can do so just for your own reassurance.

Birthmarks come in a variety of shapes, colours and textures and are usually categorized in the following ways:

Strawberry haemangioma. This soft, raised, strawberry red birthmark, as small as a freckle or as large as a coaster, is composed of immature veins and capillaries that broke away from the circulatory system during foetal development. It may rarely be visible at birth but typically appears suddenly during the first few weeks of life, and is so common that one out of ten babies will probably have one. Strawberry birthmarks grow for a while but eventually will start to fade to a pearly grey and almost always finally disappear completely, sometime between ages five and ten. Although parents may be tempted to demand treatment for a very obvious strawberry mark, particularly on the face, such birthmarks are often best left untreated unless they continue to grow, repeatedly bleed or become infected, or interfere with a function, such as vision. Treatment apparently can lead to more complications than a more conservative let-it-disappear-on-its-own approach.

If your child's doctor determines treatment is advisable, there are several options. The simplest are compression and massage, both of which seem to hasten its retreat. More aggressive forms of therapy for strawberry haemangiomas include the administration of steroids, surgery, laser therapy, cryotherapy (freezing with dry ice), and injection of hardening agents (such as those used in treating varicose veins). Many experts believe few of these birthmarks require such therapies (though if it is decided that a strawberry mark needs to be removed, it will be easier to treat when it is small). When a strawberry, reduced by either treatment or time, leaves a scar or some residual tissue, plastic surgery can usually eliminate it.

Occasionally a strawberry mark may bleed, either spontaneously or because it was scratched or bumped. Applying pressure will stem the flow of blood.

Much less common are cavernous (or venous) haemangiomas – only one or two out of every hundred babies has one. Often combined with the strawberry type, these birthmarks tend to be deeper and larger, and are light to deep blue in colour. They regress more slowly and less completely than strawberry haemangiomas, and are more likely to require treatment.

Salmon patch, or nevus simplex ('stork bites'). These salmon-coloured patches can appear on the forehead, the upper eyelids, and around the nose and mouth, but are most often seen at the nape of the neck (where the fabled stork carries the baby, thus the nickname 'stork bites'). They invariably become lighter during the first two years of life, becoming noticeable only when the child cries or exerts herself. Since more than 95 per cent of the lesions on the face fade completely, these cause less concern cosmetically than other birthmarks.

Port-wine stain, or nevus flammeus. These purplish red birthmarks, which may appear anywhere on the body, are composed of dilated mature capillaries. They are normally present at birth as flat or barely elevated pink or reddish purple lesions. Though they may change colour slightly, they don't fade appreciably over time and can be considered permanent, though treatment with a pulse-dyed laser anytime from infancy through adulthood can improve appearance.

Café au lait spots. These flat patches on the skin, which can range in colour from tan (coffee with a lot of milk) to light brown (coffee with a touch of milk), can turn up anywhere on the body. They are quite common, apparent either at birth or during the first few years of life, and don't disappear. If your child has a large number of café au lait spots (six or more), point this out to her doctor.

Mongolian spots. Blue to slate grey, resembling bruises, Mongolian spots may turn up on the buttocks or back, and sometimes the legs and shoulders, of nine out of ten children of African, Asian or Indian descent. These ill-defined patches are also fairly common in infants of Mediterranean ancestry but are rare in blond-haired, blue-eyed infants. Though most often present at birth and gone within the first year, occasionally they don't appear until later and/or persist into adulthood.

Congenital pigmented nevi. These moles vary in colour from light brown to blackish and may be hairy. Small ones are very common; larger ones, 'giant pigmented nevi', are rare but carry a greater potential for becoming malignant. It is usually recommended that large moles, and suspicious smaller ones, be removed if removal can be accomplished easily, and that those not removed be followed carefully by a dermatologist.

COMPLEXION PROBLEMS

'My baby seems to have little white pimples all over his face. Will scrubbing help to clear them?'

No need to break out the Clearasil yet. Though parents may be dismayed to find a sprinkling of tiny whiteheads on their newborn's face (particularly around the nose and chin, occasionally on the trunk or extremities, or even on the penis), these blemishes are temporary and not a signal of complexion troubles to come. The best treatment for these milia, which are caused by clogging of the newborn's immature oil glands, is no treatment at all. As tempting as it may be to squeeze, scrub or treat them, don't. They'll disappear spontaneously, usually within a few weeks, leaving your son's skin clear and smooth – at least until secondary school.

'There are red blotches with white centres on my baby's face and body. Are these anything to worry about?'

Rare is the baby who escapes the newborn period with skin unscathed.

The newborn complexion woe that caught your baby is also one of the most common: erythema toxicum. Despite its ominous-sounding name and alarming appearance – blotchy, irregularly shaped reddened areas with pale centres – erythema toxicum is completely harmless and short-lived. It looks like a collection of insect bites and will disappear without treatment.

MOUTH CYSTS OR SPOTS

'When my baby was screaming with her mouth wide open, I noticed a few little white bumps on her gums. Could she be getting teeth?'

Don't alert the media (or the grandparents) yet. While a baby very occasionally will sprout a couple of bottom central incisors six months or so before schedule, little white bumps on the gums are much more likely to be tiny fluid-filled papules, or cysts. These harmless cysts are common in newborns and will soon disappear, leaving gums clear in plenty of time for that first toothless grin.

Some babies may also have yellowish white spots on the roof of their mouth at birth. Like the cysts, they are neither uncommon nor of any medical significance in newborns. Dubbed 'Epstein's pearls', these spots will disappear without treatment.

EARLY TEETH

'I was shocked to find my baby was born with two front teeth. The doctor says she'll have to have them pulled – why?'

Every once in a while, a newborn arrives on the scene with a tooth or two. And though these tiny pearly whites may be cute as can be – and fun to show off – they may need to be removed if they're not well anchored in the gums, to keep her from choking on or swallowing them. Such extra-early teeth may be preteeth, or extra teeth, which, after they've been removed, will be replaced by primary teeth at the usual time. But more often they are primary teeth, and if they must be extracted, temporary dentures may be needed to stand in for them until their secondary successors come in.

THRUSH

'My baby seems to have a white curd in her mouth. I thought it was spit-up milk, but when I tried to brush it away, her mouth started to bleed.'

There's a fungus among you – or, more accurately, between you. Though the fungus infection known as thrush is causing problems in your baby's mouth, it probably started in your birth canal as a monilial infection – and that's where your baby picked it up. The causative organism is *Candida albicans,* which is a normal inhabitant of the mouth and vagina. Kept in check by other microorganisms, it usually causes no problem. But should this arrangement be upset – by illness, the use of antibiotics or hormonal changes (such as in pregnancy) – conditions become favourable for the fungus to grow and cause symptoms of infection.

Thrush appears in elevated white patches that look like cottage cheese or milk curds on the insides of a baby's cheeks, and sometimes on the tongue, roof of the mouth and gums. If the patches are wiped away, a raw red area is exposed, and there may be bleeding. Thrush is most common in newborns, but occasionally an older baby, particularly one taking antibiotics, will become infected. Call the doctor if you suspect thrush.

A breastfeeding mother can also develop thrush on her nipples, characterized by pink, itchy, flaky, crusty or burning nipples, and if the thrush is not treated by antifungal agents, baby and mum can continue to reinfect each other. Breastfeeding need not be interrupted if one or both of you have been diagnosed with thrush (though the condition, because it's painful, can interfere with baby's feeding if it's not treated). You'll just both be treated at the same time for one to two weeks until the symptoms have cleared.

JAUNDICE

'The doctor says my baby is jaundiced and has to spend time under the bililights before she can go home. He says it isn't serious, but anything that keeps a baby in the hospital sounds serious to me.'

Walk into any newborn nursery, and you'll see that more than half the babies have begun to yellow by their second or third days – not with age, but with newborn jaundice. The yellowing, which starts at the head and works its way down toward the toes, tinting even the whites of the eyes, comes from an excess of bilirubin in the blood. (The process is the same in black- and brown-skinned babies, but the yellowing may be visible only in the palms of the hands, the soles of the feet, and the whites of the eyes.)

Bilirubin, a chemical formed during the normal breakdown of red blood cells, is usually removed from the blood by the liver. But newborns often produce more bilirubin than their immature livers can handle. As a result, the bilirubin builds up in the blood, causing the yellowish tinge and what is known as normal, or physiologic, newborn jaundice.

In physiologic jaundice, yellowing usually begins on the second or third day of life, peaks by the fifth day, and is substantially diminished by the time baby is a week or ten days old. It appears a bit later (about the third or fourth day) and lasts longer (often fourteen days or more) in premature babies because of their extremely immature livers. Jaundice is more likely to occur in babies who lose a lot of weight right after delivery, in babies who have diabetic mothers, and in babies who arrived via induced labour.

Mild to moderate physiologic jaundice usually requires no treatment. Usually a doctor will keep a baby with high physiologic jaundice in the hospital for a few extra days for observation and phototherapy treatment under fluorescent light, often called a bililight. Light alters bilirubin, making it easier for a baby's liver to get rid of it. During the treatment, babies are naked except for nappies, and their eyes are covered to protect them from the light. They are also given extra fluid to compensate for the increased water loss through the skin, and may be restricted to the nursery except for feedings. Freestanding units or fibre-optic blankets wrapped around baby's middle allow more flexibility, often permitting baby to go home with mum.

In almost all cases, the bilirubin levels (determined through blood tests) will gradually diminish in a baby who's been treated, and the infant will go home with a clean bill of health.

Rarely, the bilirubin increases further or more rapidly than expected, suggesting that the jaundice may be non-physiologic. This type of jaundice usually begins either earlier or later than physiologic jaundice, and levels of bilirubin are higher. Treatment to bring down abnormally high levels of bilirubin is important to prevent a buildup of the substance in the brain, a condition known as kernicterus. Signs of kernicterus are weak crying, sluggish reflexes, and poor sucking in a very jaundiced infant (a baby who's being treated under lights may also seem sluggish, but that's from being warm and understimulated – not from kernicterus). Untreated, kernicterus can lead to permanent brain damage or even death. Some hospitals are taking steps to monitor the level of bilirubin in babies' blood through blood tests and follow-up visits to ensure that these extremely rare cases of kernicterus are not missed.

The paediatrician will also check baby's colour at the first visit to screen for non-physiologic jaundice. The treatment of non-physiologic jaundice will depend on the cause but may include phototherapy, blood transfusions, or

---

NEWBORN SECURITY

To make sure that you go home from the hospital with your baby and not someone else's, hospital personnel will check your hospital ID bracelet against your baby's (the ones that were put on immediately after birth) any time you take the baby from the nursery and on your way out the hospital door. Some hospitals have colour-coded badges given only to family members who have been authorized to visit the baby. And others place special detectors on the baby that will sound an alarm if the baby is removed from the maternity floor without permission.

---

surgery. Drug therapy is rarely used, and home phototherapy treatments are no longer considered a standard treatment.

'I've heard that breastfeeding causes jaundice. My baby is a little jaundiced – should I stop nursing?'

Blood bilirubin levels are, on the average, higher in breastfed babies than in bottle-fed infants, and they may stay elevated longer (as long as six weeks). Not only is this exaggerated physiologic jaundice nothing to worry about, but it's also not a reason to consider weaning. In fact, interrupting breastfeeding and/or giving glucose water feedings seem to increase rather than decrease bilirubin levels, and can also interfere with the establishment of lactation. It's been suggested that breastfeeding in the first hour after birth can reduce bilirubin levels in nursing infants.

True breast milk jaundice is suspected when levels of bilirubin rise rapidly *late* in the first week of life and non-physiologic jaundice has been ruled out. It's believed to be caused by a substance in the breast milk of some women that interferes with the breakdown of bilirubin, and is estimated to occur in about 2 per cent of breastfed babies. In most cases, it clears up on its own within a few weeks without any treatment and without interrupting breastfeeding. In very severe cases, when levels are extremely high, some doctors may advise supplementing with formula (or even stopping breastfeeding for a day, while mum pumps to keep her milk supply up), and/or using light therapy.

STOOL COLOUR

'When I changed my baby's nappy for the first time, I was shocked to see that his stools were greenish black.'

THE SCOOP ON NEWBORN POOP

So you think if you've seen one dirty nappy, you've seen them all? Far from it. Though what goes into your baby at this point is definitely one of two things (breast milk or formula), what comes out can be one of many. In fact, the colour and texture of your baby's poop can change from day to day – and bowel movement to bowel movement – causing even the seasoned parent to worry. Here's the scoop on what the contents of your baby's nappy may mean:

Sticky, tar-like; black or dark green. Meconium – a newborn's first few stools

Grainy; greenish yellow or brown. Transitional stools – which start turning up on the third or fourth day after birth

Seedy, curdy, creamy or lumpy; light yellow to mustard or bright green. Normal breast milk stools

Slightly formed; light brownish to bright yellow to dark green. Normal formula stools

Frequent, watery; greener than usual. Diarrhoea

Hard, pellet-like; mucous or blood streaked. Constipation

Black. Iron supplementation

Red streaked. Rectal fissures or milk allergy

Mucousy; green or light yellow. A virus such as a cold or stomach bug

This is only the first of many shocking discoveries you will make in your baby's nappies during the next year or so. And for the most part, what you will be discovering, though occasionally unsettling to the sensibilities, will be completely normal. What you've turned up this time is meconium, the tarry greenish black substance that gradually filled your baby's intestines during his stay in your uterus. That the meconium is now in his nappy instead of his intestines is a good sign – now you know that his bowels are unobstructed.

Sometime after the first twenty-four hours, when all the meconium has been passed, you will see transitional stools, which are dark greenish yellow and loose, sometimes 'seedy' in texture (particularly among breastfed infants), and may occasionally contain mucus. There may even be traces of blood in them, probably the result of a baby's

swallowing some of his mother's blood during delivery (just to be sure, save any nappy containing blood to show to a nurse or doctor).

After three or four days of transitional stools, what your baby starts putting out will depend on what you've been putting into him. If it's breast milk, the movements will often be mustard-like in colour and consistency, sometimes loose, even watery, sometimes seedy, mushy or curdy. If it's formula, the stool will be soft but better formed than a breastfed baby's, and anywhere from pale yellow to yellowish brown, light brown or brown-green. Iron in baby's diet (whether from formula or vitamin drops) can also lend a black or dark green hue to movements.

Whatever you do, don't compare your baby's nappies to those of the baby in the next bassinet. Like fingerprints, no two stools are exactly alike. And unlike fingerprints, they are different

GOING HOME

In the 1950s, new babies came home from the hospital after ten days. In the 1980s stays of between two and four days were common. By the 1990s, many mothers were opting to go home after only one night – and in some cases sooner. The decision about when to go home is best made on a case-by-case basis with a doctor's input. Early discharge is safest when an infant is full-term; is an appropriate weight; has started feeding well; and is going home with a parent (or parents) who knows the basics and is well enough to provide care. If for any reason you have concerns about early discharge, speak to your child's doctor.

Once home, you will be visited by a community midwife, who will continue to visit for the next ten days as necessary. She will be on the lookout for newborn problems such as yellowing of the skin* and the whites of the eyes (a sign of jaundice); refusal to eat; dehydration (fewer than six wet nappies in twenty-four hours, or dark yellow urine); constant crying, or moaning instead of crying; fever; red or purple dots anywhere on the skin.

*To check for jaundice in light-skinned babies, press your newborn's arm or thigh with your thumb. If the area beneath the pressure turns yellowish rather than white, jaundice may be present.

---

not only from baby to baby, but also from day to day (even movement to movement) in any one baby. The changes, as you will see when baby moves on to solids, will become more pronounced as his diet becomes more varied.

DUMMY USE

'I've always hated seeing older kids with dummies, and I'm afraid that will happen to my daughter if she gets a dummy in the nursery.'

Being quieted with a dummy during the few days your baby spends in the hospital nursery will not get her hooked – she's too young to become a habitual sucker yet. There are, however, some sound reasons why you might prefer that the nurses find another way of comforting her, and that she pass on the dummy for now:

♦ If you're nursing, dummy use might cause nipple confusion (sucking on the artificial nipple requires a different motion than suckling at the breast) and interfere with the establishment of breastfeeding.

♦ Whether you're breast or bottle feeding, your baby may get sufficient sucking satisfaction from the dummy and refuse to suckle at feeding times.

♦ Your newborn is better off having her needs attended to – in the form of a meal, a cuddle, a little rocking, a clean nappy – when she cries than having a dummy plugged in.

If you decide you'd rather the nursery staff not give your baby a dummy, tell them so. If she's not rooming-in, ask them to bring her to you for a feeding when she cries (or if she's just finished a feeding, to try some other comfort measures). Or see if you can switch to rooming-in. If your baby seems to need more between-meal sucking once you're at home, and you're considering dummy use, see page 187.

What it's Important to Know: THE BABY CARE PRIMER

Put the nappy on backwards? Took five minutes to get baby positioned for a productive burp? Forgot to wash under the arms at bath time? Don't worry. Babies are not only forgiving – they also usually don't even notice. Nevertheless, every new parent wants to do everything, or at least as much as possible, right. This Baby Care Primer will help guide you to that goal. But remember, these are only suggested ways to care for baby. You may come up with some of your own that are even better. As long as it's safe and loving, do what works for you.

BATHING BABY

Until a baby starts getting down and dirty on all fours, a daily bath isn't a necessity. As long as adequate spot cleaning is done during nappy changes and after feedings, a bath two or three times a week in the precrawling months will keep baby sweet smelling and presentable. Such a light bathing schedule can be particularly welcome in the early weeks when the ritual is often dreaded by both bather and bathee. Babies who don't soon become fond of the bath (many eventually come to love it) can continue to be bathed two or three times a week, even when dirt begins to accumulate. Daily spongings, in such critical places as face, neck, hands and bottom, can stand in between dunks (see page 354 for tips on reducing fear of the bath). For those babies, however, who find it a treat, a daily bath becomes a treasured ritual.

Just about any time of the day can be the right time for a newborn bath, though bathing just before bedtime will help induce the more relaxed state conducive to sleep. (Once baby's spending the days getting dirty, night-time baths will just make the most sense on all fronts – and backsides.) Avoid baths just after or just before a meal, since spitting up could be the result of so much handling on a full tummy, and baby may not be cooperative on an empty one. Allot plenty of undivided time for the bath, so it won't be hurried and you won't be tempted to leave baby unattended even for a second to take care of something else. Let the answer phone pick up the phone during the bath.

While you are using a portable bath, any room in the house can accommodate the procedure, though with all the splashing and dripping, the kitchen or bathroom provides the most suitable setting. Your work surface should be at a level that's easy for your manoeuvring and roomy enough for all the paraphernalia it must hold. For baby's comfort, especially in the early months, turn off fans and air conditioners until the bath is over, and be sure the room you choose is warm (24° to 27°C/75° to 80°F, if possible) and draught free. If you have a hard time achieving such a temperature range, try warming the bathroom first with shower steam.

The sponge bath. Until the umbilical cord and circumcision, if any, are healed (a couple of weeks, more or less) bath baths will be taboo, and a flannel will be your baby's only route to getting clean. For a thorough sponge bath, follow these steps:

1. Select a bath site. The changing table, a kitchen counter, your bed or the baby's cot (if the mattress is high enough) are all suitable locations for a sponge bath; simply cover your bed or the cot with a waterproof pad or the counter with a thick towel or pad.

2. Have all of the following ready *before* undressing baby:

- baby soap and shampoo, if you use it

- two flannels (one will do if you use your hand for soaping)

- sterile cottonwool balls for cleaning the eyes

- towel, preferably with a hood

- clean nappy and clothing

- ointment or cream for nappy rash, if needed

- rubbing alcohol and cotton swabs or alcohol pads for the umbilical cord (if recommended, see page 145)

- warm water, if you won't be within reach of the sink

3. Get baby ready. If the room is warm, you can remove all of baby's clothing before beginning, covering him or her loosely with a towel while you work (most babies dislike being totally bare); if it's cool, undress each part of the body as you're ready to wash it. No matter what the room temperature, don't take off baby's nappy until it's time to wash the bottom; a baby without a nappy (especially a boy) should always be considered armed and dangerous.

4. Begin washing, starting with the cleanest areas of the body and working toward the dirtiest, so that the flannel and the water you're using will stay clean. Soap with your hands or a flannel, but use a clean cloth for rinsing. This order of business usually works well:

- Head. Once or twice a week, use soap or baby shampoo, rinsing very thoroughly. On interim days, use just water. A careful hold (see illustration, page 131) at the sink's edge can be the easiest and most comfortable way to rinse baby's head. Gently towel-dry baby's hair (for most babies this takes just a few seconds) before proceeding.

- Face. First, using a sterile cottonwool ball moistened in warm water, clean baby's eyes, wiping gently from the nose outwards. Use a fresh ball for each eye. No soap is needed for the face. Wipe around the outer ears but not inside. Dry all parts of the face.

- Neck and chest. Soap is not necessary, unless baby is very sweaty or dirty. Be sure to get into those abundant folds and creases, where dirt tends to accumulate. Dry.

- Arms. Extend the arms to get into the elbow creases, and press the palms to open the fist. The hands will need a bit of soap, but be sure to rinse them well before they are back in baby's mouth. Dry.

- Back. Turn baby over on the tummy with head to one side, and wash back, being sure not to miss those neck folds. Since this isn't a dirty area, soap probably won't be necessary. Dry, and dress the upper body before continuing if the room is chilly.

- Legs. Extend the legs to get the backs of the knees, though baby will probably resist being unfurled. Dry.

- Nappy area. Follow directions for

Covering baby's bottom while you wash baby's top keeps baby warm and comfortable while you work; and it protects you, particularly if baby is a boy, from a sudden spurt.

care of the circumcised penis or the uncircumcised penis (see page 143) and, if recommended, the umbilical stump (see page 145) until healing is complete. Wash girls front to back, spreading the labia and cleaning with soap and water. A white vaginal discharge is normal; don't try to scrub it away. Use a fresh section of the flannel and clean water or fresh water poured from a cup to rinse the vagina. Wash boys carefully, getting into all the creases and crevices with soap and water, but don't try to retract the foreskin on an uncircumcised baby. Dry the nappy area well, and apply ointment or cream if needed.

5. Put on a nappy and dress baby.

The baby bath. A baby is ready for a bath as soon as both umbilical cord stump and circumcision, if any, are healed. If baby doesn't seem to like being in the water, go back to sponge baths for a few days before trying again. Be sure the water temperature is com-

fortable and that baby is held firmly to combat any reflexive fear of falling.

1. Select a site for the portable baby bath. The kitchen or bathroom sink or counter or the big bath (though the manoeuvring involved when bathing a tiny baby while bending and stretching over a bath can be tricky) are all good candidates. Be sure you will be comfortable and have plenty of room for the bath and bath paraphernalia. The first couple of times you give a bath, you might want to omit the soap – wet babies are always slippery, but soapy, wet babies are extra slippery.

2. Have all of the following ready *before* undressing baby and filling the bath:

♦ bath, basin or sink scrubbed and ready to fill

♦ baby soap and shampoo, if you use it

♦ two flannels (one will do if you use your hand for soaping)

♦ sterile cottonwool balls for cleaning the eyes

The nappy area will require the most concentrated cleaning effort, and should be saved for last so any germs from the region won't be spread to other parts of the body.

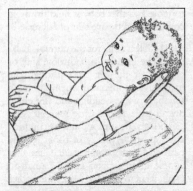

Most babies are very tentative, even tearful, the first few times they're in a bath. So go out of your way to offer support – with reassuring words and a strong, steady grip.

If the bath doesn't offer adequate support for your baby's slippery body and floppy head, you'll need to do so. Gently but firmly does it.

- towel, preferably with a hood
- clean nappy and clothing
- ointment or cream for nappy rash, if needed

3. Run water into the baby bath (enough so that part of baby's body is

Until baby's neck gains more control over the head, you'll have to hold it steady with one hand while you use your other hand to wash the back.

in the water but not too much); test with your elbow to be sure it's comfortably warm. Never run the water with baby in the bath because a sudden temperature change might occur. Don't add baby soap or bubble bath to the water, as these can be drying to baby's skin.

4. Undress baby completely.

5. Slip baby gradually into the bath, talking in soothing and reassuring tones to minimize fear, and holding on securely to prevent a startle reflex. Support the neck and head with one hand unless the bath has built-in support, or if your baby seems to prefer your arms to the bath's support, until good head control develops. Hold baby securely in a semi-reclining position – slipping under suddenly could provide a bad scare.

6. With your free hand, wash baby, working from the cleanest to the dirtiest areas. First, using a sterile cottonwool ball moistened in warm water, clean baby's eyes, wiping gently from the nose outwards. Use a fresh ball for each eye. Then wash face, outer ears and neck. Though soap won't usually be necessary elsewhere every day (unless your baby tends to have allover 'accidents'), do use it on hands and the nappy area daily. Use it every couple of days on arms, neck, legs, and abdomen as long as baby's skin doesn't seem dry – less often if it does. Apply soap with your hand or with a flannel. When you've taken care of baby's front parts, turn him or her over your arm to wash back and buttocks.

7. Rinse baby thoroughly with a fresh flannel.

8. Once or twice a week, wash baby's scalp, using mild baby soap or baby shampoo. Rinse very thoroughly and towel-dry gently.

9. Wrap baby in a towel, pat dry, and dress.

SHAMPOOING BABY

This is a fairly painless process with a young baby. But to help forestall future shampoo phobias, avoid getting even tearless soap or shampoo in your baby's eyes from the first. Shampoo only once or twice a week, unless cradle cap or a particularly oily scalp requires more frequent head cleanings.

1. Wet baby's hair with a gentle spray from the sink hose or by pouring a little water from a cup. Add just a drop of baby shampoo or baby soap (more will make rinsing difficult), and rub in lightly to produce a lather. A foam product may be easier to control.

2. Hold baby's head (well supported) over the sink and rinse thoroughly with a gentle spray or two or three cupfuls of clean water.

Once baby has graduated to a big bath, you can try giving the shampoo at the end of the bath – right in the bath. Since most babies (and young children) don't like to put their heads back for a shampoo – it makes them feel too vulnerable and often leads to tears and, later, tantrums – use a spray nozzle if your bath has one, and if your child doesn't find it too frightening. A specially designed shampoo visor (available from chemists and from mail-order or on-line catalogues) that guards the eyes from flowing water and soap, but leaves the hair exposed for washing, is ideal if your child will wear it – some won't. If your baby resists both sprays and visors, you can continue shampooing (or at least rinsing, after doing the lathering in the bath) at the sink until he or she is more cooperative in the bath. Though the process isn't perfect (and it can grow awkward as the child grows larger), it's quick and consequently minimizes the period of suffering for both of you.

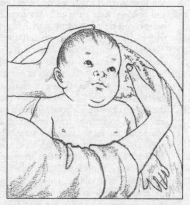

Sometimes rinsing off shampoo is best done with a few gentle wipes with a flannel.

SAFE SEATING

New parents taking their babies out for the first time are always careful to bundle them up (often overbundling them) against the elements, fearful of the consequences of a sudden gust of wind or sprinkle of rain. Yet many of these same parents fail to protect their offspring well enough where it counts – in the car. Though a little bad weather is unlikely to harm a newborn, riding without the protection of a safety seat or riding in a safety seat that is improperly secured can. Car crashes injure and kill more children yearly than all of the major childhood illnesses combined. Nationally, over 16,000 children (0–14) are injured while travelling in cars.

So for that first ride home from the hospital – and every ride after that – be sure an infant safety seat is *properly* installed in your car, and your baby properly secured in it. Even if your destination is literally just a few streets away (most accidents occur within twenty-five miles of home and not, as is often believed, on motorways). Even if you're driving slowly (a crash at thirty miles per hour creates as much force as a fall from a third-storey window). Even if you're wearing a seat belt and holding your baby tight (in a crash, baby could be crushed by your body or whipped from your arms, possibly flying through the windshield). Even if you're driving very carefully (you don't actually have to crash for severe injuries to result – many occur when a car stops short or swerves to avoid an accident). Every time the car is in motion – whether it's for a trip across the country or from one space to another in the same car park – your baby needs to be buckled up safely.

Getting your baby used to a safety seat from the very first ride will help make later acceptance of it almost automatic. And children who ride in safety restraints regularly are not only safer but also better behaved during drives – something you'll appreciate when you're riding with a toddler.

In addition to checking that a seat meets government safety standards, be sure that it is appropriate for your baby's age and weight and that you install and use it correctly:

◆ Follow manufacturer's directions for installation of the seat and securing of your baby. Check before each ride that the seat is property secured and the seat belts, or LATCH system (see page 54) holding it are snugly fastened. Use locking clips, available with most seats, to secure lap/shoulder belts that don't stay tight (mostly needed in vehicles manufactured before 1996). The car seat should not wobble, pivot, slide side to side, tip over or move more than 2.5 cm (1 in) when you push it from front to back or side to side; instead, when properly installed it should stay tight. (You'll know the rear-facing infant seat is installed tightly enough if, when you hold the top edge of the car seat and try to push it downwards, the back of the seat stays firmly in place at the same angle.) To make sure you've installed the car seat correctly, check it out with a local garage that is part of the Fit Safe Sit Safe Scheme. For more information, contact your council Road Safety Unit.

◆ Infants should ride in a rear-facing car seat (reclining at a 45-degree angle) until they reach 9 kg (20 lb) *and* at least a year old. Even babies who pass the 9-kg (20-lb) mark before their first birthday (many do) or have outgrown the infant seat heightwise (they're 68.5 cm/27 in tall and/or the top of their head is the same height as the back of the car seat) should stay in a rear-facing car seat until they're a year old. Before that milestone, baby's spine and neck are not strong enough to withstand a forceful back-and-forth motion (as in a car crash). If baby has outgrown the infant seat but isn't ready to face forward, use a convertible seat, which can accommodate larger babies (as heavy as 13.5 to 16 kg/30 to 35 lb and taller than 68.5 cm/27 in) in the *rear-facing* position. After your baby has turned a year (and reached 9 kg/20 lb), you can switch the convertible seat to the front-facing position or invest in a toddler seat.

◆ Place the infant safety seat, if at all possible, in the middle of the backseat – the safest spot in the car. *Never* put an ordinary rear-facing infant seat in the front seat of a car equipped with a passenger-side air bag; if the air bag is inflated (which could happen even at slow speeds in a fender bender), the force could seriously injure or kill a baby. In fact, the safest place for all children under thirteen is in the backseat – older children should ride up front only when absolutely necessary and when safely restrained and sitting as far from the passenger-side air bag as possible. (New air bag–compatible car seats are being marketed that can be safely used in the front seat when there is no backseat available – as in a pickup truck or two-seater sports car. Even those seats, however, provide greatest safety in the backseat.)

◆ Adjust the shoulder harness to fit your baby. The harness slots on a rear-facing safety seat should be at or below your baby's shoulders; the harness chest clip should be at armpit level. The straps should lie flat and untwisted, and should be tight enough so that you can't get more than two fingers between the harness and your baby's collarbone. Check the instructions to see how the carrying handle should be positioned during travel, if applicable.

◆ Dress your baby in clothes that allow straps to go between his or her legs. In cold weather, place blankets on top of your strapped-in baby (after adjusting the harness straps snugly), rather than dressing baby in a snowsuit. A heavy snowsuit can come between your baby and an adequately tight harness.

◆ Most infant seats come with special cushioned inserts to keep a very young baby's head from flopping around. If not, pad the sides of the car seat and the area around the head and neck with a rolled blanket.

◆ Be sure that large or heavy items, such as suitcases, are firmly secured so that they can't become hazardous flying objects during a short stop or crash.

◆ For older babies, attach soft toys to the seat with plastic links or very short cords. Loose toys tend to be flung around the car or dropped, upsetting baby and distracting the driver. Or use toys designed specifically for baby car seat use.

◆ Many infant car seats can lock into shopping trolleys – something that's sure to be convenient but is also potentially dangerous. The weight of the baby and car seat makes the shopping trolley top-heavy and more likely to tip over. So be extra vigilant when placing your baby's car seat on a shopping trolley; or for optimum safety use a sling, baby carrier or pushchair when shopping.

◆ The Civil Aviation Authority (CAA) recommends that when flying, children be securely fastened in child safety seats (secured with the aeroplane seat belt) until they are four years old. Most infant, convertible and forward-facing seats are certified for use on aeroplanes.

◆ See chapter 2 for more on choosing an infant safety seat, types of harnesses available and other safety information.

◆ The most important rule of car seat safety is: *Never make an exception.* Whenever the car is moving, everyone in the car should be safely and appropriately buckled up.

SAFETY FROM ALL SIDES?

The safest place in any vehicle is the middle of the backseat, which is why, when you have the choice, that's where your baby should be sitting. But if that seat's not always available (because you have more than one baby, for instance), or if your vehicle doesn't have a middle seat in the back, a seat on either side of the back (in a correctly installed and used child safety seat) is the next safest thing.

But what if your car comes equipped with side air bags, as more and more vehicles do? Though the data isn't available yet to show that side air bags can injure young children when they inflate, crash tests show that they may. To play it safe – the only way to play it when there's a baby onboard – ask your dealer about turning your side air bags off. (Side-curtain air bags, however, don't appear to pose a risk to young children.)

BURPING BABY

Milk isn't all baby swallows when sucking on a nipple. Along with that nutritive fluid comes non-nutritive air, which can make a baby feel uncomfortably full before he or she's finished a meal. That's why burping baby to bring up any excess air that's accumulated – every 60 ml (2 fl oz) or so when bottle feeding, and between breasts when breastfeeding (or midbreast, if a young infant is managing only one breast at a time) – is such an important part of the feeding process. There are three ways this is commonly done – on your shoulder, face-down on your lap, or sitting up – and it's a good idea to try them all to see which works most efficiently for both you and baby. Though a gentle pat or rub may get the burp up for most babies, some need a slightly firmer hand.

On your shoulder. Hold baby firmly against your shoulder, firmly supporting the buttocks with one hand and patting or rubbing the back with the other.

Face-down on your lap. Turn baby face-down on your lap, stomach over one leg, head resting on the other. Holding him or her securely with one hand, pat or rub with the other.

Sitting up. Sit baby on your lap, head leaning forward, chest supported by your arm as you hold him or her under the chin. Pat or rub, being sure not to let baby's head flop backwards.

An over-the-shoulder burp yields best results for many babies, but don't forget to protect your clothes.

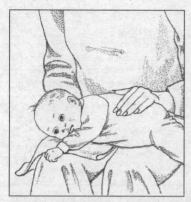

The lap-burp position has the added benefit of being soothing to some colicky infants.

CHANGING BABY

Especially in the early months, the time for a change can come all too often – sometimes hourly during baby's waking hours. But as tedious a chore as it can be for both baby and you, frequent changes (taking place, at the very least, before or after every daytime feeding

Even a newborn can sit up for a burp – but be sure the head gets adequate support.

and whenever there's a bowel movement) are the best way to avoid irritation and nappy rash on that sensitive bottom. Telling when it's time for a change is easier if you're using cloth nappies, since they feel wet when they are wet. If you're using disposable nappies, however, you'll probably have to take a closer look (and sniff) to gauge wetness; since they're much more absorbent, they tend not to feel wet until they're seriously saturated. Waking a sleeping baby to change a nappy is hardly ever necessary, and unless baby's very wet and uncomfortable or has had a bowel movement, you don't need to change nappies at night-time feedings; the activity and light involved can interfere with baby's getting back to sleep.

To ensure a change for the better whenever you change your baby's nappy:

1. Before you begin to change a nappy, be sure everything you need is at hand, either on the changing table or, if you're away from home, in your changing bag. Otherwise, you could end up removing a messy nappy only to find out you have nothing to clean the mess with. You will need all or some of the following:

♦ a clean nappy

♦ cottonwool balls and warm water for babies under one month (or those with nappy rash) and a small towel or dry flannel for drying; baby wipes for other babies

♦ a change of clothes if the nappy has leaked (it happens with the best of them); clean nappy wraps or waterproof pants if you're using cloth nappies

♦ ointment or cream, if needed, for nappy rash; lotions and powders are

Disposables make quick work of nappy changing. Once baby is in place, simply bring the front of the nappy through baby's legs and fasten, making sure the tabs are pressed down securely.

unnecessary. Be careful with nappy creams because if you get some on the tabs of the disposable nappy, it can interfere with their sticking power (this, of course, is not an issue if you're using nappies with Velcro tabs).

2. Wash and dry your hands before you begin, if possible, or give them a once-over with a baby wipe.

3. Have baby entertainment available – live or otherwise. Live shows (cooing, funny faces, songs) can be provided by the nappy changer or by siblings, parents or friends on hand. Diversion can also come in the form of a mobile hanging over the changing table, a stuffed toy or two in baby's range of vision (and later, within reach), a music box, a mechanical toy – whatever will hold your baby's interest long enough for you to take off one nappy and put on another. But don't use items such as powder or lotion containers for distraction, since an older baby may grab and mouth or upend them.

4. Spread a protective cloth nappy or a changing mat if you are changing baby anywhere but on a changing table.

Wherever you make the change, be careful not to leave baby unattended, not even for a moment. Even strapped to a changing table, your baby shouldn't be out of arm's reach.

5. Unfasten the nappy, but don't remove it yet. First survey the scene. If there's a bowel movement, use the nappy to wipe most of it away, keeping the nappy over the penis as you work if your baby is a boy. Now fold the nappy under baby with the unsoiled side up to act as a protective surface, and clean baby's front thoroughly with warm water or a wipe, being sure to get into all the creases; then lift both legs, clean the buttocks, and slip the soiled nappy out and a fresh nappy under before releasing the legs. (Keep a fresh nappy over a penis for as much of this process as possible, in self-defence. Baby boys often get erections during nappy changes; this is perfectly normal, and not a sign that they're being over-stimulated.) Pat baby dry if you used water. Make sure baby's bottom is completely dry before putting on his or her nappy or any ointments or creams. If you note any irritation or rash, see page 265 for treatment tips.

6. If you're using cloth nappies, they're probably prefolded and ready to use. But you may have to fold them further until your baby is a bit bigger. The extra fabric should be in the front for boys and the back for girls. To avoid sticking baby when using pins (there are pins made especially to minimize this possibility), hold your fingers under the layers of nappy as you insert the pin. Sticking the pins in a bar of soap while you're making the change will make them slip more smoothly through the fabric. Once a pin becomes dull, discard it. Better still, look for nappies or nappy covers with Velcro fasteners. See page 20 for other options.

If you're using paper nappies with sticky tabs be careful not to let the tape stick on baby's skin. Or look for those that use Velcro fasteners instead, so you can open and close them with ease.

Nappies and protective pants should fit snugly to minimize leaks, but not so snugly that they rub or irritate baby's delicate skin. Telltale marks will warn you that the nappy is too tight.

Wetness will be less likely to creep up to drench vest and clothing on boys if the penis is aimed downward as the nappy is put on. If the umbilical stump is still attached, fold the nappy down to expose the raw area to air and keep it from getting wet.

7. Dispose of nappies in a sanitary way. Used disposable nappies can be folded over, tightly reclosed, and dropped into a nappy bucket or the dustbin. Used cloth nappies should be kept in a tightly covered nappy bucket (your own, or one supplied by the nappy service) until pickup or wash day. If you're away from home, they can be held in a plastic bag or scented nappy sack until you get home.

8. Change baby's clothing and/or bed linen as needed.

9. Wash your hands with soap and water, when possible, or clean them thoroughly with a baby wipe.

DRESSING BABY

With floppy arms, stubbornly curled-up legs, a head that invariably seems larger than the openings provided by most baby clothes, and an active dislike for being naked, an infant can be a challenge to dress and undress. But there are ways of making these daily tasks less of a chore for both of you:

Putting clothes over baby's head

Putting baby's arms in sleeves

1. Select clothes with easy-on, easy-off features in mind. Wide neck openings or necks with popper closings are best. Poppers or a zipper at the crotch make dressing and nappy changes easier. Sleeves should be fairly loose, and a minimum of fastening (particularly up the back) should be necessary. Clothes made of stretch or knit fabrics are often easier to put on than stiff garments with less give.

2. Make changes only when necessary. If you find the odour from frequent spit-ups offensive, sponge the spots lightly with a baby wipe rather than changing outfits every time baby has a productive burp. Or try guarding against such incidents by putting a large bib on baby during and after feedings.

3. Dress baby on a flat surface, such as a changing table, bed or cot mattress. And have some entertainment available.

4. Consider dressing time a social time, too. Light, cheerful conversation (a running commentary on what you're doing, for instance) can help distract baby from the discomforts and indignities of being dressed and make cooperation more likely. Making a learning game out of pulling on clothes will team distraction with stimulation. And punctuating your commentary with loud kisses (a smooch for each adorable hand and foot as it appears from the sleeve or trouser leg) can add to the fun for both of you.

5. Stretch neck openings with your hands before attempting to get baby into a garment. Ease, rather than tug, them on and off, keeping the opening as wide as possible in the process and trying to avoid snagging the ears or nose. Turn the split second during which baby's head is covered, which might otherwise be scary or uncomfortable, into a game of peeka-boo ('Where is Mummy? Here she is!' and then, as baby gets old enough to realize that he or she is equally invisible to you, 'Where is Daniella? Here she is!').

6. Try to reach into sleeves and pull baby's hands through, rather than trying to shove rubbery little arms into limp cylinders of cloth. A game here, too ('Where is Brandon's hand? Here it is!'), will help distract and educate when baby's hands temporarily disappear.

7. When pulling a zip up or down, draw the garment away from baby's body to avoid pinching tender skin.

EAR CARE

The old adage 'Never put anything smaller than your elbow in your ears' is advocated not only by grandmothers but also by modern medical authorities as well. They agree that putting anything in the ear that fits – whether it's a coin inserted by a curious toddler or a cotton swab inserted by a well-meaning parent – is dangerous. Do wipe your baby's outer ears with a flannel or cottonwool ball, but don't try to venture into the ear canal itself with swabs, fingers or anything else. The ear is naturally self-cleaning, and trying to remove wax by probing may only force it further into the ear. If wax seems to be accumulating, ask the doctor about it at the next visit.

LIFTING AND CARRYING BABY

For those who have never carried a tiny baby, the experience can, at first, prove very unnerving. But it can be

Be sure to carefully support the neck and back with your arm when lifting a baby who is lying face-up.

Slip one hand under the chin and neck and the other under the bottom to pick up a baby lying face-down.

equally unnerving for the baby. After months of being moved gently and securely in the snug uterine cocoon, being plucked up, wafted through the open air, and plunked down can come as quite a shock. Particularly when adequate support isn't provided for the head and neck, this can result in baby having a frightening sensation of falling and, consequently, a startle reaction. So a good infant-carrying technique aims at carrying baby not only in a way that is safe, but also in a way that *feels* safe.

You'll eventually develop techniques for carrying your baby that are comfortable for both of you, and carrying will become a completely natural experience. While you are sorting laundry, using the computer, or reading labels in the supermarket, baby will be casually slung over your shoulder or under your arm, feeling as secure as he or she did in utero. In the awkward interim, however, these tips will help:

Picking baby up. Before you even touch your baby, make your presence known through voice or eye contact. Being lifted unaware by unseen hands to an unknown destination can be unsettling.

Let baby adjust to the switch in support from mattress (or other surface) to arms by slipping your hands under him or her (one under head and neck, the other under bottom) and keeping them there for a few moments before actually lifting.

Slide the hand under baby's head down the back so that your arm acts as a back and neck support, and your hand cradles the buttocks. Use the other hand to support the legs and lift baby gently towards your body, caressing as you go. By bending over to bring your body closer, you will limit the distance your baby will have to travel in midair – and the discomfort that comes with it.

Carrying baby comfortably. A small baby can be cradled very snugly in just one arm (with your hand on baby's bottom, and your forearm supporting back, neck and head) if you feel secure that way.

With a larger baby, you both may be more comfortable if you keep one hand under legs and buttocks and the other supporting back, neck and head (your hand encircling baby's arm, your wrist under the head).

The front carry is a favourite with babies, since it allows them a view of the world.

Some babies prefer the shoulder carry, all the time or some of the time. It's easy to get baby up there smoothly with one hand on the buttocks, the other under head and neck. Until baby's head becomes self-supporting, you will have to provide the support. But this can be done even with one hand if you tuck baby's bottom into the crook of your elbow and run your arm up the back with your hand supporting the head and neck.

Even fairly young babies enjoy the

When baby gets older and can carry his or her own weight well, the hip carry leaves the carrier with a free hand.

front-face carry, in which they can watch the world go by, and many older babies prefer it. Face your baby out, keeping one hand across his or her chest, pressed back against your own, and the other supporting baby's bottom.

The hip carry gives you freedom to use one hand for chores while carrying an older baby resting on your hip. (Avoid this hold if you have lower-back problems.) Hold baby snugly against your body with one arm, resting his bottom on your hip.

Putting baby back down. Hold baby close to your body as you bend over the cot or pram (again to limit the midair travel distance), one hand on baby's bottom, one supporting back, neck and head. Keep hands in place for a few moments until baby feels the comfort and security of the mattress, then slip them out. A few light pats or a bit of gentle hand pressure (depending on what seems to please your baby most), a few parting words if baby's awake, and you're ready to make the break. (For more tips on putting a sleeping baby down without waking him or her, see page 180.)

NAIL TRIMMING

Although trimming a newborn's tiny fingernails may make most new parents uneasy, it's a job that must be done. Little hands with little control and long fingernails can do a lot of damage, usually in the form of scratches on his or her own face.

An infant's nails are often overgrown at birth (it's hard to get a trim in utero) and so soft that cutting through them is nearly as easy as cutting through a piece of paper. Getting your baby to hold still for the procedure, however, won't be so easy. Cutting a baby's nails while he or she is sleeping may work if you've got a sound sleeper or if you don't mind waking him or her. When baby's awake, it's best to trim the nails with the help of an assistant who can hold each hand as you cut. Always use a special baby nail scissor or baby nail clipper which has rounded tips – if baby starts to bolt at the wrong moment, no one will be jabbed with a sharp point. To avoid nipping the skin as you clip the nail, press the finger pad down and out of the way as you cut. Even with this precaution you may, however, occasionally draw blood – most parents do at one time or another. If you do, apply pressure with a sterile gauze pad until bleeding stops; a plaster probably won't be needed.

NOSE CARE

As with the inside of the ears, the inside of the nose is self-cleaning and needs no special care. If there is a discharge, wipe the outside, but do not use cotton swabs, twisted tissues or your fingernail to try to remove material from inside the nose – you may only push the matter back farther into the nose, or even scratch delicate membranes. If baby has a lot of mucus due to a cold, suction it out with an infant nasal aspirator (see page 547).

OUTINGS WITH BABY

Never again will you be able to leave the house empty-handed – at least not when baby's along. In general, you'll need some or all of the following whenever you go out:

A changing bag. Don't leave home without it. Keep the bag packed and ready, restocking it regularly, so you can just pick up and go. (See page 57 for tips on choosing a nappy bag.)

A changing mat. If your changing bag doesn't have one, pack a waterproof pad. You can use a towel or a cloth nappy in a pinch, but they won't adequately protect carpeting, beds or furniture when you're changing baby during a visit.

Nappies. How many depends on how long your outing will be. Always take at least one more than you think you'll need – you'll probably need it if you don't.

Baby wipes. A small convenience pack is easier to carry than a full-size container, but it must be refilled frequently. Or you can use a small zip-lock plastic sandwich bag to tote a mini-supply. Wipes are handy, incidentally, for washing your own hands before feeding baby and before and after changes, as well as for removing spit-up and baby-food stains from clothing or furniture.

Zip-lock plastic bags and nappy sacks. You'll need these for disposing of dirty disposable nappies, particularly when no dustbin is available, as well as for carrying wet and soiled baby clothes home.

Formula. If you are going to be out past the next feeding with a bottle-fed baby, or might be, you'll have to bring a meal along. No refrigeration will be necessary if you take along an unopened bottle of ready-to-use formula or a bottle of water to which you will add powdered formula. If, however, you bring along formula you've prepared at home, you will have to store it in an insulated container along with a small ice pack or ice cubes.

Shoulder nappies. Your friends may enjoy holding your baby – but not being spit up on. A handy cloth nappy or 'muslin' will prevent embarrassing moments and smelly shoulders.

A change of baby clothes. Baby's outfit is picture-perfect and you're off to a special family gathering. You arrive, lift your bundle of cuteness from the car seat, and find a pool of loose, mustardy stools has added the outfit's 'finishing touch'. Just one reason why you need to carry along an extra – and for extended outings, two extra – sets of clothing. And lots of baby wipes.

An extra blanket or sweater. Particularly in transitional seasons, when temperatures can fluctuate unpredictably, the additional covering will come in handy.

A dummy, if baby uses one. Carry it in a clean plastic bag.

Entertainment. Something to provide visual stimulation is appropriate for very young babies – particularly for the car seat or pushchair. For older babies, lightweight toys they can swat at poke at, and mouth will fill the bill.

Sunscreen. If adequate shade is not available, use a small amount of baby-safe sunscreen on baby's face, hands and body (now recommended even on babies under six months) year-round (in winter, snow and sun can combine to cause serious burns).

A snack for mum. If you're breastfeeding or will be out for a long stretch and may not be able to find a nutritious snack easily, take one along: a piece of fruit; some cheese; whole-grain crackers or bread; a bag of dried fruit. A container or can of fruit juice or a thermos containing a hot or cold drink is a nice addition if your outing will be to a park where no liquid refreshment is available.

A snack (or two, or three) for baby. Once solids are introduced, bring along jars of baby food (no refrigeration is needed before they're open, no heating up is needed before serving) if you'll be out during mealtime; a spoon stashed in a plastic bag (save the bag to bring the dirty spoon home in); a bib; and plenty of paper towels. Later, a selection of finger foods (non-perishable if you'll be out in hot weather) such as fresh fruit, crackers or oat cakes will ward off hunger between meals, while providing baby with a wholesome activity during your outing. Beware, however, of using snacks to ward off boredom or to keep baby from

---

BABY BUSINESS

It's hard to believe that a newborn baby will ever have any business to take care of (besides eating, sleeping, crying and growing). But there is one very important document that your baby will need periodically throughout life, and it should be registered for now – a birth certificate.

A birth certificate will be needed as proof of birth and citizenship when (and all of these will come sooner than you think) registering for school and applying for a driver's licence, passport, marriage licence or Social Security benefits. When you collect the birth certificate, examine it carefully to be sure it's accurate – mistakes are sometimes made. If there are errors, or if you hadn't quite settled on a name for your baby before leaving the hospital and want to add it now (you should), call the registrar for instructions on how to make the necessary corrections or additions. Once you have a correct birth certificate, make a few copies and file them in a safe place.

crying – the pattern of eating for the wrong reasons in childhood can continue as an undesirable habit later on.

Miscellaneous toiletries and first aid items. Depending on any particular health needs your child may have as well as on where you're going, you may also want to carry: nappy rash ointment or cream; plasters and antiseptic ointment (especially once baby has started crawling or walking); any medication your baby is taking (if you will be out when the next dose is due; if refrigeration is required, pack with an ice pack in an insulated container).

PENIS CARE

At birth, the foreskin (the continuous layer of skin that covers the penis) is firmly attached to the glans (the rounded end of the penis). Over time in an uncircumcised penis, foreskin and glans begin to separate, as cells are shed from the surface of each layer. The discarded cells, which are replaced throughout life, accumulate as whitish, cheesy 'pearls' that gradually work their way out via the tip of the foreskin.

Usually by the end of the second year for nine out of ten uncircumcised boys, but sometimes not until they are five, ten or more years old, foreskin and glans become fully separated. At this point the opening is sufficiently large that the foreskin can be pushed back, or retracted, uncovering the glans.

Care of the uncircumcised penis. Contrary to what was once believed, no special care is needed for the uncircumcised penis in infancy – soap and water, applied externally, just as the rest of the body is washed, will keep it clean. Not only is it unnecessary to try to forcibly retract the foreskin, or clean under it

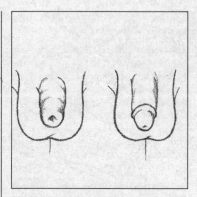

Neither the uncircumcised penis (left) nor the circumcised penis, from which the foreskin has been removed, requires special care in infancy.

with cotton swabs, irrigation or antiseptics – it can also actually be harmful. Once the foreskin has clearly separated, you can retract it occasionally and clean under it. By the age of puberty most foreskins will be retractable, and at that time a boy can learn to retract his and clean under it himself.

Care of the circumcised penis. The only care the circumcised penis will ever need, once the incision is healed, is ordinary washing with soap and water. For care during the recovery period, see page 193.

SLEEPING POSITION

The safest way to place your baby down to sleep is on his or her back. Babies placed on their stomachs to sleep are at greater risk of Sudden Infant Death Syndrome (SIDS). The incidence of SIDS is highest in the first six months, although the recommendation of 'back to sleep' applies for the whole first year. (Once baby starts rolling over, however,

Tuck the blanket's corner under baby's back.

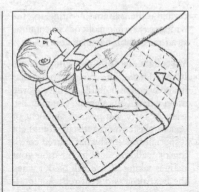

Lift the blanket's bottom corner over baby's body.

Bring the last corner of the blanket over baby's body.

SWADDLING BABY

For some newborns, swaddling is soothing and may reduce crying, especially during colicky periods; others very much dislike the lack of freedom that comes with being wrapped up tightly. Swaddling does not increase the risk of SIDS, as long as baby is placed on the back to sleep and isn't overheated. In fact, some research is even showing that swaddling may reduce the SIDS risk by keeping babies safely on their backs when they sleep. (And because many babies are more comfortable on their backs when they're swaddled, another happy result may be less crying in that position.) Here's how to swaddle:

1. Spread a receiving blanket on a cot, a bed or a changing table, with one corner folded down about six inches. Place baby on the blanket diagonally, head above the folded corner.

2. Take the corner near baby's left arm and pull it over the arm and across the baby's body. Lift the right arm, and

he or she may prefer to sleep on the stomach; still, continue to put your baby down on the back and let him or her decide about flipping.) You should also never place baby on soft bedding (firm mattresses only, with no 'pillow-top'), or in a cot (or parents' bed) with pillows, duvets or fluffy blankets, or stuffed animals because of the risk of suffocation. See page 256 for more on SIDS.

tuck the blanket corner under baby's back on the right side. (If you have a swaddling blanket with Velcro tabs, no tucking is needed.)

3. Lift the bottom corner and bring it up over baby's body, tucking it into the first swathe.

4. Lift the last corner, bring it over baby's right arm, and tuck it in under the back on the left side.

If your baby seems to prefer more hand mobility, wrap below the arms, leaving hands free. Because being wrapped up can interfere with development as baby gets older, and because a blanket that a swaddled baby kicks off can pose a safety hazard in the cot, stop swaddling once baby becomes more active.

UMBILICAL STUMP CARE

The last remnant of a baby's close attachment to his or her mother in the uterus is the stump of the umbilical cord. It turns black a few days after birth and can be expected to drop off anywhere between one and four weeks later. You can hasten healing and prevent infection by keeping the area dry and exposed to air. The following will help accomplish this:

1. When putting on baby's nappy, fold the front of it down below the navel to keep urine off and let air in. Fold the vest up.

2. Skip bath baths and avoid wetting the navel when sponging, until the cord falls off.

3. Though it's been traditional to keep swabbing the stump with alcohol once baby gets home, recent studies show that healing is faster without continued use of alcohol, and there is no increased risk of infection. Ask your doctor or midwife what he or she recommends. If you do apply alcohol, using a cotton swab will prevent irritation of tender surrounding skin.

4. If the area around the navel turns red, or the site oozes or has a foul smell, call the doctor.

◆ ◆ ◆

CHAPTER 5

The First Month

You've brought your baby home and you're giving parenthood everything you've got. Yet you can't help wondering: Is everything you've got enough? After all, your schedule (and life as you seem to recall knowing it) is upended; you're holding your baby as if he or she were made of glass; and you can't remember the last time you've showered or slept more than two hours in a row.

As your baby grows from a cute but largely unresponsive newborn to a full-fledged cuddly infant, your sleepless nights and hectic days will likely be filled not only with pure joy but also with exhaustion – not to mention new questions and concerns: Is my baby getting enough to eat? Why does he spit up so much? Are these crying spells considered colic? Will she (and we) ever sleep through the night? And how many times a day can I actually call the doctor? Not to worry. Believe it or not, by month's end you'll have settled into a comfortable routine with baby, one that's still exhausting but much more manageable. You'll also feel like a seasoned pro in the baby-care game (at least compared to what you feel like today) – feeding, burping, bathing and handling baby with relative ease.

What Your Baby May Be Doing

All babies reach milestones on their own developmental time line. If your baby seems not to have reached one or more of these milestones, rest assured, he or she probably will very soon. Your baby's rate of development is almost certainly normal for your baby. Keep in mind, too, that skills babies perform from the tummy position can be mastered only if there's an opportunity to practise. So make sure your baby spends supervised playtime on his or her belly. If you have concerns about your baby's development, check with the doctor. Premature infants generally reach milestones later than others of the same birth age, often achieving them closer to their adjusted age (the age they would be if they had been born at term), and sometimes later.

WHAT YOUR BABY MAY BE DOING THIS MONTH

All parents want to know if their babies are developing well. The problem is that when they compare their babies to the 'average' baby of the same age, they find that their own child is usually ahead or behind – few are exactly average.

To help you determine whether your baby's development fits within the wide range of normal rather than just into the limited range of 'average', we've developed a monthly span of achievements into which virtually all babies fall, based on the Denver Developmental Screening Tests and on the Clinical Linguistic and Auditory Milestone Scale (CLAMS). In any one month, a full 90 per cent of all babies will have mastered the achievements in the first category, 'What your baby should be able to do'. About 75 per cent will have gained command of those in the second category, 'What your baby will probably be able to do'. Roughly half will have accomplished the feats in the third category, 'What your baby may possibly be able to do'. And about 25 per cent will have pulled off the exploits in the last category, 'What your baby may even be able to do'.

Most parents will find their babies achieving in several different categories at any one time. A few may find their offspring staying constantly in the same category. Some may find their baby's development uneven – slow one month, making a big leap the next. All can relax in the knowledge that their babies are perfectly normal.

Only when a baby is not achieving what a child of the same age 'should be able to do' on a *consistent* basis, need a parent be concerned and consult the doctor. Even then, no problem may exist – baby may just be marching (or rolling over, or pulling up) to a different drummer.

Use the What Your Baby May Be Doing sections of the book to check progress monthly, if you like. But don't use them to make assessment of your baby's abilities now or in the future. They are far from predictive. If checking your baby against such lists becomes anxiety-provoking rather than reassuring, by all means ignore them. Your baby will develop just as well if you never look at them – and you may be a lot happier.

By one month, your baby . . . should be able to:

◆ lift head briefly when on stomach on a flat surface

◆ focus on a face

. . . will probably be able to:

◆ respond to a bell in some way, such as startling, crying, quieting

. . . may possibly be able to:

◆ lift head 45 degrees when on stomach

By the end of this month, a baby should be able to focus on a face.

- vocalize in ways other than crying (e.g. cooing)
- smile in response to your smile

. . . may even be able to:

- lift head 90 degrees when on stomach
- hold head steady when upright
- bring both hands together
- smile spontaneously

WHAT YOU CAN EXPECT AT THIS MONTH'S CHECKUP

Well-baby checkups will be events you'll come to look forward to; not only as an opportunity to see how much your baby's grown, but to ask the dozens of questions that have come up since the last visit to the clinic but didn't rate an immediate frantic phone call (there will be plenty of those, too). Make sure you keep a list of these questions and bring them along to appointments (they'll be tough to recall when you're dealing with sleep deprivation and a squirming, naked infant).

Each health visitor (and doctor, who will most likely see you on your first visit) will have his or her own approach to well-baby checkups. The overall organization of the physical exam, as well as the number and type of assessment techniques used and procedures performed, will also vary with the individual needs of the child. But, in general, you can expect the following at a checkup when your baby is between one and four weeks old. (The first visit may take place earlier, or there may be more than one checkup in the first month, under special circumstances, such as when a newborn has had jaundice, was premature, or when there are any problems with the establishment of breastfeeding.)

- Questions about how you and baby and the rest of the family are doing at home, and about baby's eating, sleeping, bowel movements and general progress.
- Measurement of baby's weight, length, and head circumference and plotting of progress since birth.
- Vision and hearing assessments.
- A report on results of neonatal screening tests (for PKU, hypothyroidism and other inborn errors of metabolism), if not given previously. If the doctor doesn't mention the tests, the results were very likely normal, but do ask for them for your own records. If your baby was released from the hospital before these tests were performed, or if they were done before he or she was seventy-two hours old, they will probably be performed or repeated now.
- A physical exam. The doctor or health visitor will examine and assess all or most of the following, although some evaluations will be carried out by the experienced eye or hand, without comment:
  - ❖ heart sounds with a stethoscope, and visual check of the heartbeat through the chest wall
  - ❖ abdomen, by palpation (feeling outside), for any abnormal masses
  - ❖ hips, checking for dislocation by rotating the legs
  - ❖ hands and arms, feet and legs, for normal development and motion
  - ❖ back and spine, for any abnormalities
  - ❖ eyes, with an ophthalmoscope and/or a penlight, for normal reflexes and focusing, and for tear duct functioning

❖ ears, with an otoscope, for colour, fluid, movement

❖ nose, with otoscope, for colour and condition of mucous membranes

❖ mouth and throat, using a wooden tongue depressor, for colour, sores, bumps

❖ neck, for normal motion, thyroid and lymph gland size (lymph glands are more easily felt in infants, and this is normal)

❖ underarms, for swollen lymph glands

❖ the fontanels (the soft spots on the head), by feeling with the hands

❖ respiration and respiratory function, by observation, and sometimes with stethoscope and/or light tapping of chest and back

❖ the genitalia, for any abnormalities, such as hernias or undescended testicles; the anus for cracks or fissures; the femoral pulse in the groin, for a strong, steady beat

❖ healing of the umbilical cord and circumcision (if applicable)

❖ the skin, for colour, tone, rashes and lesions, such as birthmarks

❖ reflexes specific to baby's age

❖ overall movement and behaviour, ability to relate to others

◆ Guidance about what to expect in the next month in relation to feeding, sleeping, development and infant safety.

◆ Possibly the second dose of the hepatitis B vaccination, if baby won't be getting the combined DTaP-hepB-IPV vaccine (Pediarix) starting at two months.

Before the visit is over, be sure to:

◆ Ask for guidelines for calling when baby is sick. (What would necessitate a call in the middle of the night? How can the doctor be reached outside of regular surgery times?)

◆ Express any concerns that may have arisen over the past month – about baby's health, behaviour, sleep, feeding, and so on.

◆ Jot down information and instructions from the doctor so you don't forget.

When you get home, record all pertinent information (baby's weight, length, head circumference, blood type, test results, birthmarks) in a permanent health record.

Feeding Your Baby This Month: EXPRESSING BREAST MILK[1]

Though this early in the parenting game you and your baby probably haven't been apart for more than an hour or two (if that), there

---

1. If you're breastfeeding. Bottle-feeding issues are covered starting on page 99.

comes a time in every nursing mother's life when she needs, or wants, more flexibility than round-the-clock breastfeeding can provide. When she can't breastfeed her baby – because she's working, travelling, or just out for the evening – but still wants her baby to be fed breast milk. Enter expressed milk.

WHY MOTHERS EXPRESS MILK

It's not so much a law of physics as it is a law of busy motherhood: you can't always count on your baby and your breasts being at the same place at the same time. There is a way, however, to feed your baby breast milk (and keep your milk supply up) even if you and baby are miles apart: by expressing milk.

There are many situations (short- or long-term, on a regular schedule or just occasionally) when a mother might need or want to express breast milk, usually by pumping. The most common reasons why women pump are to:

◆ Relieve engorgement when the milk comes in

◆ Collect milk for feedings when working

◆ Provide relief bottles when away from home

◆ Increase or maintain the milk supply

◆ Store milk in the freezer for emergencies

◆ Prevent engorgement and maintain milk supply when nursing is temporarily halted because of illness (mother's or baby's)

◆ Maintain milk supply if nursing needs to be stopped temporarily because mother is taking medication that is incompatible with nursing

◆ Provide breast milk for a hospitalized sick or premature baby

◆ Provide milk for bottle or tube feeding when a baby (premature or otherwise) is too weak to nurse or has an oral defect that hinders nursing

◆ Stimulate relactation, if a mother changes her mind about nursing or if a baby turns out to be allergic to cow's milk after early weaning

◆ Induce lactation in an adopting mother, or in a biological mother whose milk is slow in coming in

CHOOSING A PUMP

At one time, the only way to express milk was by hand, a long and tedious process that often failed to produce significant quantities of milk (and, frankly, hurt – a lot). Today, spurred by the resurgence of breastfeeding, manufacturers are marketing a variety of breast pumps – ranging from simple hand-operated models that cost a few pounds to pricey hospital-grade electric ones (that are now more affordable for home use) – to make pumping easier and more convenient. Though an occasional mother will still express by hand, at least to relieve engorgement, most will invest in either an electric, battery-operated, or manual pump.

Before deciding which type of pump is best for you, you'll need to do a little homework:

◆ Consider your needs. Will you be pumping regularly because you're going back to work or will be out of the house on a daily basis? Will you pump only once in a while to provide a relief bottle? Or will you be pumping full-time to provide nourishment for your sick or premature baby, who may be in the hospital for weeks or months?

♦ Weigh your options. If you'll be pumping several times a day for an extended period of time (such as when working or to feed a preterm infant), a double electric pump will probably be your best bet. If you need to pump only for occasional outings, a single electric, battery or manual pump will fill your needs (and those few bottles). If you're planning on expressing only when you're engorged or for a rare bottle feeding, you can probably get away with expressing by hand (though an inexpensive manual pump may still make sense; it can take a lot of squeezing by hand to fill even one bottle).

♦ Investigate. Talk to friends who use pumps to see which they prefer. Not all pumps are created equal – not even among the electric ones. Some electric pumps can be uncomfortable to use, and some hand pumps painfully slow (and sometimes just plain painful) for expressing large quantities of milk. Also, discuss the options with a breastfeeding consultant or your doctor. Research the types of pumps available (call up the manufacturers, check their websites), and consider your wallet as well as the models' features before choosing one.

All About Pumps

All pumps use a breast cup or shield that's placed over your breast, centred over your nipple and areola. Whether you're using an electric or manual pump, suction is created when the pumping action is begun, mimicking baby's suckling. Depending on the

pump you use (and how fast your letdown is), it can take anywhere from ten to forty-five minutes to pump both breasts. Pumping shouldn't hurt; if it does, make sure you're pumping correctly. If you are, and it still hurts, the fault might lie with the pump; consider making a switch.

Electric pump. Powerful, fast and easy to use (usually), a fully automatic electric pump closely imitates the rhythmic suckling action of a nursing baby. Many electric pumps allow for double pumping – a great feature if you're pumping often. Not only does pumping both breasts simultaneously cut pumping time in half, it stimulates an increase in prolactin, which means you'll actually produce more milk faster. Hospital-grade electric pumps are usually expensive, but if time is an important consideration, one may be well worth the investment. (Also, when you weigh it against the cost of formula, you may break even or possibly come out ahead.)

Many women rent hospital-grade electric pumps from hospitals, pharmacies, or NCT or La Leche groups; some buy or rent jointly with other women, or buy them, use them and then sell them (or lend them). Electric pumps also come in portable models that are inconspicuous (the black carrying cases are designed to look like backpacks or shoulder bags) and are also less expensive, smaller than and just as efficient as

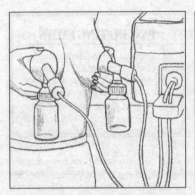

Double pumping is quick, efficient and comfortable.

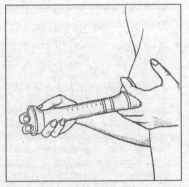

Though tough on the arm that's doing the pumping, the syringe pump is a convenient way to express milk.

the hospital-grade ones. Some also come with a car adapter and/or battery pack so you don't have to plug them in.

Battery-operated pump. Less powerful than the electric pumps, more expensive than the manual pumps, battery-operated pumps promise portability and efficient operation, but not all models deliver. They are usually moderately priced, but the speed at which some eat batteries makes them expensive to use and of questionable practicality.

Taking convenience to another level entirely are battery-operated pumps that are 'wearable'. They come with soft breast cups about the size of a doughnut that are placed inside your bra and hooked up to small collection bags that lie flat against your body. Because the system is so discreet, you can wear it at the office, pumping while you work, without anyone being the wiser. And since it's completely hands free, it's the multitasker's dream come true; you can pump while typing at the computer, talking on the phone, even cooking dinner. Check with your local NCT group or La Leche League for the latest scoop on these.

Manual pump. These hand-operated pumps come in several styles; some are better than others:

♦ A *syringe pump* is composed of two cylinders, one inside the other. The inner cylinder is placed over the nipple and the outer, when pushed in and pulled out, creates suction that draws milk into it.

♦ A *trigger-operated pump* creates suction with each squeeze of the handle.

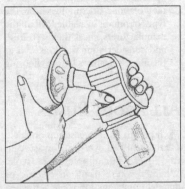

A trigger pump can efficiently stimulate let-down, making expressing milk an easy task.

PUMPING PRACTICE MAKES PERFECT

No matter what method of expressing you choose, you may find it difficult to extract much milk the first few times. Consider those initial pumping sessions to be practice – your goal should be to figure out how to use the pump, not necessarily to score large quantities of milk. Milk probably won't be flowing in copious amounts during early sessions anyway, for two reasons: Firstly, you're not producing that much milk yet (if your baby is still less than a month or two old); secondly, a pump (especially as wielded by a novice pumper) is much less effective in extracting milk than a baby is. But with perseverance (and practice, practice, practice), you'll become an expert pumper in no time.

One popular type includes petal massage cushions designed to simulate the infant's compression on the areola, which stimulates let-down.

- A *bulb or 'bicycle-horn' pump*, which suctions milk from breasts with each squeeze of the bulb, is not recommended because it is very inefficient, uncomfortable and extremely unsanitary (breeding bacteria that can contaminate the breast milk). It can also lead to sore nipples and damage breast tissue.

Both the syringe and trigger pumps are popular because they are fairly simple to use, moderate in price, easy to clean, portable and can also double as feeding bottles.

PREPARING TO PUMP

Whenever you pump (and no matter what type of pump you're using), there are basic preparation steps you'll need to take to ensure a safe and easy pumping session:

- Time it right. Choose a time of day when your breasts are ordinarily full. If you're pumping because you're away from your baby and missing feedings, try to pump at the same times you would normally feed, about once every three hours. If you're home and want to stock the freezer with breast milk for emergencies or relief bottles, pump one hour after baby's first morning feeding, since most women have more milk earlier in the day. (Late afternoon or early evening, when women typically have the least milk, thanks to exhaustion and end-of-the-day stress, is usually a particularly unproductive time to pump.) Or pump from one breast while nursing your baby from the other one; the natural let-down action your body produces for your suckling baby will help stimulate milk flow in the pumped breast as well. (But don't try this until you're skilled at both nursing and expressing, since this can be a tricky manoeuvre for a beginner).

- Wash up. Wash your hands and make sure that all your pumping equipment is clean. Washing your pump immediately after each use in hot, soapy water will make the job of keeping it clean easier. If you use your pump away from home, carry along a bottle brush, detergent and paper towels for washup.

- Keep it quiet. Choose a quiet, comfortably warm environment for

(TELL)TALES FROM THE OTHER SIDE

If you're not double pumping, the breast not being pumped will start getting into the action ahead of time and will leak accordingly. To avoid a mess, make sure the breast that's being ignored is well packed with breast pads (especially if you'll be going back to your desk after pumping), or take advantage of every drop of milk and collect whatever leaks in a bottle, a clean cup or breast shell.

pumping, where you won't be interrupted by phones or doorbells and where you will have some privacy. At work, a private office, an unoccupied meeting room, or the women's lounge can serve as your pumping headquarters. If you're at home, wait until baby's naptime, or hand baby over to someone else so you can be free to concentrate on pumping (unless you're pumping while nursing).

◆ Get comfy. Make yourself comfortable, with your feet up, if possible. Relax for several minutes before beginning. Use meditation or other relaxation techniques, music, TV or whatever you find helps you unwind.

◆ Hydrate. Drink some water, juice, milk, decaffeinated tea or coffee, or broth just before beginning.

◆ Encourage let-down. Think about your baby, look at baby's photo and/or picture yourself nursing, to help stimulate let-down. If you're home, giving baby a quick cuddle just before you start pumping could do the trick. If you're using a 'wearable' pump or an electric pump that

leaves your hands free (by using a special 'bra' devised to keep the pumps in place), you can even hold the baby – though many babies balk at being so near and yet so far from the source of their food ('Hey . . . why's that machine having all the fun?'). Applying hot soaks to your nipples and breasts for five or ten minutes, taking a hot shower, doing breast massage, or leaning over and shaking your breasts are other ways of enhancing let-down.

HOW TO EXPRESS BREAST MILK

Though the basic principle of expressing milk is the same whichever pump you use (stimulation and compression of the areola draws milk from the ducts out through the nipples), there are subtle differences in techniques depending on the type of pump (or, in the case of hand expression, non-pump) you're using.

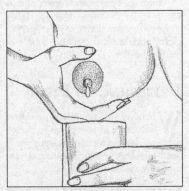

Expressing breast milk by hand is a slow process. This method is best for expressing only small amounts, as when the breast is too engorged for baby to get a comfortable mouthful.

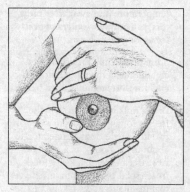

To massage your breast, place one hand underneath your breast, the other on top. Slide the palm of one hand or both from the chest gently towards the nipple and apply mild pressure. Rotate your hands around the breast, and repeat in order to reach all the milk ducts.

Expressing milk by hand. To begin, place your hand on one breast, with your thumb and forefingers opposite each other around the edge of the areola. Press your hand in towards your chest, gently pressing thumb and forefinger together while pulling forwards slightly. (Don't let your fingers slip onto the nipple.) Repeat rhythmically to start milk flowing, rotating your hand position to get to all milk ducts. Repeat with the other breast, massaging in between expressions, as needed. Repeat with the first breast, then do the second again.

If you want to collect the milk expressed, use a clean wide-topped cup under the breast you're working on. You can collect whatever drips from the

2. Breast shells are intended to correct inverted nipples. However, they can also be used during a feeding to catch and collect milk that leaks from one breast while the baby nurses from the other or while pumping. Place the breast shell inside your bra on the alternate breast.

other breast by placing a breast shell[2] over it inside your bra. Collected milk should be poured into bottles or storage bags and refrigerated as soon as possible (see page 156).

Expressing milk with a manual pump. Follow the directions for the pump you are using. You might find moistening the outer edge of the flange with water or breast milk will ensure a good suction, but it's not a necessary step. The flange should surround the nipple and areola, with all of the nipple and part of the areola in it. Use quick, short pulses at the start of the pumping session to closely imitate baby's sucking action. Once let-down occurs, you can switch to long, steady strokes. If you want to use a hand pump on one breast while nursing your baby on the other, prop the baby at your breast on a pillow (being sure he or she can't tumble off your lap).

Expressing milk with an electric pump. Follow the directions for the

WHERE DOES THE MILK GO?

Many pumps come with containers that can be used as storage and feeding bottles; others allow you to use a standard feeding bottle to collect the milk. Special breast milk storage bags are convenient for freezing milk. (Disposable bottle liners are made of thinner plastic than the milk storage bags and can break more easily.) Some pumps allow you to collect the expressed milk directly into the storage bags, so you don't need the extra step of transferring the milk from bottle to bag before storing. Be sure to wash any containers or bottles used for milk collection in hot soapy water or a dishwasher after you're done.

QUICK TIP

Fill breast milk storage containers or bags for the freezer only three-fourths full to allow for expansion, and label with the date (always use the oldest milk first).

pump you are using. Double pumping is ideal because it saves time and increases milk volume. You might want to moisten the outer edge of the flange with water or breast milk to ensure a good suction. Start out on the minimum suction and increase it as the milk begins to flow, if necessary. If your nipples are sore, keep the pump at the lower setting. You might find you get more milk from one breast than the other when you double pump – that's normal, because each breast functions independently of the other.

STORING BREAST MILK

Keep the milk that you expressed fresh and safe for baby by keeping these storage guidelines in mind:

♦ Refrigerate expressed milk as soon as you can; if that's not possible, breast milk will stay fresh at room temperature (but away from radiators, sun or other sources of heat) for as long as six hours.

♦ Store breast milk for up to forty-eight hours in the refrigerator, or chill for thirty minutes, then freeze.

♦ Breast milk will stay fresh in the freezer for anywhere from a week or two in a single-door refrigerator, to about three months in a two-door frost-free model that keeps foods frozen solid, to six months in a freezer that maintains a $-17.7°C$ ($0°F$) temperature.

♦ Freeze milk in small quantities, 90 to 120 ml (3 to 4 fl oz) at a time, to minimize waste and allow for easier thawing.

♦ To thaw breast milk, shake the bottle or bag under lukewarm tap water; then use within thirty minutes. Or thaw in the refrigerator and use within twenty-four hours. Do not thaw in a microwave oven, on the top of the stove, or at room temperature; and do not refreeze.

When your baby has finished feeding on a bottle, discard the remaining milk. Also discard any milk that has been stored for periods longer than those recommended above.

What You May Be Concerned About

'BREAKING' BABY

'I'm so afraid of handling the baby – he's so tiny and fragile looking.'

Newborn babies may look as fragile as porcelain dolls, but they're not. In fact, they're really pretty sturdy. As long as their heads are well supported, they can't be harmed by normal handling – even when it's a little clumsy and tentative, as is often the case when the handling's being done by a first-time parent. You'll gradually learn what's comfortable for your baby and for you, since handling styles vary greatly from parent to parent. Soon you'll be toting your baby as casually as a bag of groceries – and often *with* a bag of groceries. For handling instructions, see pages 138–140.

THE FONTANELS

'I'm so nervous when I handle my baby's head – that soft spot seems so vulnerable. Sometimes it seems to pulsate, which really makes me nervous.'

That 'soft spot' – actually there are two and they are called fontanels – is tougher than it looks. The sturdy membrane covering the fontanels is capable of protecting the newborn from the probing of even the most curious sibling fingers (though that's definitely not something you'd want to encourage) and certainly from everyday handling.

These openings in the skull, where the bones haven't yet grown together, aren't there to make new parents nervous about handling baby (though that's often the upshot) but, rather, for two very important reasons. During childbirth, they allow the foetal head to mould to fit through the birth canal, something a solidly fused skull couldn't do. Later, they allow for the tremendous brain growth of the first year.

The larger of the two openings, the anterior fontanel, is on the top of the newborn's head; it is diamond shaped and may be as wide as 5 cm (2 in). It starts to close when an infant is six months old and is usually totally closed by eighteen months.

The fontanel normally appears flat, though it may bulge a bit when baby cries and if baby's hair is sparse and fair, the cerebral pulse may be visible through it (which is completely normal and nothing to worry about). An anterior fontanel that appears *significantly* sunken is usually a sign of dehydration, a warning that the baby needs to be given fluids promptly. (Call the baby's doctor immediately to report this symptom.) A fontanel that bulges persistently (as opposed to a little bulging with crying) may indicate increased pressure inside the head and also requires immediate medical attention.

The posterior fontanel, a smaller triangular opening towards the back of the head less than 1.3 cm (½ in) in diameter, is much less noticeable and may be difficult for you to locate. It generally is completely closed by the third month. Fontanels that close prematurely (they rarely do) can result in a misshapen head and require medical attention.

SKINNY BABY

'At three weeks, my baby seems skinnier than when he was born. What could be wrong?'

Occasionally, an infant who had a lot of facial swelling at birth begins to look thinner as the swelling goes down. Most, however, have started to fill out by three weeks, looking less like scrawny chickens and more like rounded babies. In most cases, you can expect a breastfed baby to regain his birthweight by two weeks and then gain roughly (170 to 225 g (6 to 8 oz) a week for the next couple of months. But your eyes are not necessarily a reliable gauge of your baby's weight gain (sometimes those who see a baby every day are less likely to notice his growth than those who see him less often). If you have some doubt about whether your baby's making that kind of progress, call the doctor's surgery and ask if you could bring him in for an impromptu weighing.

If baby's tipping the scales just fine, then chances are he's being fed just fine. If his weight isn't up to speed, it's possible that he's not getting enough to eat (see page 159).

HAVING ENOUGH BREAST MILK

'*When my milk came in, my breasts were overflowing. Now that the engorgement is gone, I'm not leaking any more and I'm worried I don't have enough milk for my son.*'

Since the human breast doesn't come equipped with millimetre/ounce calibrations, it's virtually impossible to discern with the eye how adequate your milk supply is. Instead, you'll have to use your baby as a guide. If he seems to be happy, healthy and gaining weight well, you're producing enough milk. You don't have to spray like a fountain or leak like a tap to nurse successfully; the only milk that counts is the milk that goes into your baby. If at any time your baby doesn't seem to be thriving, more frequent nursing plus the other tips on the opposite page should help you produce more milk.

'*My baby was nursing about every three hours and seemed to be doing very well. Now, suddenly, she seems to want to nurse every hour. Could something have happened to my milk supply?*'

Unlike a well, a milk supply is unlikely to dry up if it's used regularly. In fact, quite the opposite is true: the more your baby nurses, the more milk your breasts will produce. A much more plausible explanation for your baby's frequent trips to the breast is a growth or appetite spurt. These occur most commonly at three weeks, six weeks and three months, but can occur at any time during an infant's development. Sometimes, much to parental dismay, even a baby who has been sleeping through the night begins to wake for a middle-of-the-night feeding during a growth spurt. In this case, a baby's active appetite is merely nature's way of ensuring that her mother's body increases milk production to meet her growth needs.

Just relax and keep your breasts handy until the growth spurt passes. Don't be tempted to give your baby formula (or even worse, solids) to appease her appetite, because a decrease in frequency of nursing would cut down your supply of milk, which is just the opposite of what the baby ordered. Such a pattern – started by baby wanting to nurse more, leading to mum becoming anxious about the adequacy of her milk supply and offering a supplement, followed by a decrease in milk production – is one of the major causes of breastfeeding being abandoned early on.

Sometimes a baby begins to demand more daytime feedings temporarily when she begins to sleep through the night, but this, too, shall pass with time. If, however, your baby continues to want to nurse hourly (or nearly so) for more than a week, check her weight gain (and see below). It could mean she's not getting enough to eat.

BABY GETTING ENOUGH BREAST MILK

'*How can I be sure that my breastfed son is getting enough to eat?*'

When it comes to bottle feeding, the proof that baby's getting enough to eat is in the bottle – the empty bottle. When it comes to breastfeeding, determining whether baby's well fed takes a little more digging. Luckily, there are several signs you can look for to reassure yourself that your breastfed baby is getting his fair share of food:

He's having at least five large, seedy, mustardy bowel movements a day. Fewer than five movements a day in the early weeks could indicate inadequate food intake. (Though later on, around age six weeks to three months, the rate could slow down to one a day or even one every two to three days.)

His nappy is wet when he's changed before each feeding. A baby who urinates more than eight to ten times a day is getting adequate fluid.

His urine is colourless. A baby who is not getting enough fluids passes urine that is yellow, possibly fishy smelling and/or contains urate crystals (these look like powdered brick, give the wet nappy a pinkish red tinge and are normal before the mother's breast milk comes in but not later).

You hear a lot of gulping and swallowing as your baby nurses. If you don't, he may not be getting much to swallow. Don't worry, however, about relatively silent eating if baby is gaining well.

He seems happy and content after most feedings. A lot of crying and fussing or frantic finger sucking after a full nursing could mean a baby is still hungry. Not all fussing, of course, is related to hunger. After eating, it could also be related to gas, an attempt to push out a bowel movement or to settle down for a nap, or a craving for attention. Or your baby could be fussy because of colic (see pages 182–184).

You experienced breast engorgement when your milk came in. Engorgement is a good sign you can produce milk. And breasts that are fuller when you get up in the morning and after three or four hours without nursing than they are after nursing indicate they are filling with milk regularly – and also that your baby is draining them. If baby is gaining well, however, lack of noticeable engorgement shouldn't concern you.

You notice the sensation of let-down and/or experience milk leakage. Different women experience let-down differently (see page 76), but feeling it when you start nursing indicates that milk is coming down from the storage ducts to the nipples ready to be enjoyed by your baby. Not every woman notices let-down when it occurs, but its absence (in combination with signs of baby's failure to thrive) should raise a warning flag.

You don't start menstruating during the first three months postpartum. The period usually doesn't return in a woman who is exclusively breastfeeding, particularly in the first three months. Its premature return may be due to changing hormone levels, reflecting inadequate milk production.

'I thought my baby was getting enough to eat, but the doctor says the baby isn't gaining weight quickly enough. What could be the problem?'

There are a number of possible reasons why your baby may not be thriving on breast milk. Many of them can be easily remedied, so that baby can continue nursing and start gaining weight faster:

Possible problem: *You're not feeding baby often enough.*
Solution: Increase feedings to at least eight to ten times in twenty-four hours. Don't go more than three hours during

the day or four at night between feedings (four-hour daytime schedules were devised for bottle-fed babies). That means waking up a sleeping baby so that he won't miss dinner or feeding a hungry one even if he just finished a meal an hour earlier. If your baby is 'happy to starve' (some newborns are) and never demands feeding, it means taking the initiative yourself and setting a busy feeding schedule for him. Frequent nursings will not only help to fill baby's tummy (and fill out his frame), they will also stimulate your milk production.

Possible problem: *You're not draining at least one breast at each feeding.*
Solution: Nursing for at least ten minutes at the first breast should drain it sufficiently; if your baby accomplishes this task, let him nurse for as long (or as little) as he likes on the second. Remember to alternate the starting breast at each feeding.

Possible problem: *You're limiting the amount of time spent at the breast.* Switching breasts after only five minutes (or before baby is ready to let go) can deprive baby of the rich, fatty hindmilk necessary for weight gain.
Solution: Watch your baby – and not the clock – to ensure that he gets not only the foremilk but also the hindmilk.

Possible problem: *Your baby is a lazy or ineffective suckler.* This may be because he was preterm, is ill, or has abnormal mouth development (such as a cleft palate or tied tongue).
Solution: The less effective the suckling, the less milk is produced, setting baby up for failure to thrive. Until he's a strong suckler, he will need help stimulating your breasts to provide adequate milk. This can be done with a breast pump, which you can use to empty the breasts after each feeding (save any milk you collect for future use in bottles). Until milk production

is adequate, your doctor will very likely recommend supplemental bottle feedings of formula (given after breastfeeding sessions) or the use of a supplemental system, or SNS (see illustration on facing page). The SNS has the advantage of not causing nipple confusion because it doesn't introduce an artificial nipple.

If your baby tires easily, you may be advised to nurse for only a short time at each breast (you can pump the rest later to empty the breast), then follow with a supplement of expressed milk or formula given by bottle or the supplemental nutrition system, both of which require less effort by the baby.

Possible problem: *Your baby hasn't yet learned how to coordinate his jaw muscles for suckling.*
Solution: An ineffective suckler will also need help from a breast pump to stimulate his mother's breasts to begin producing larger quantities of milk. In addition, he will need lessons in improving his suckling technique; the doctor may recommend you get help from a breastfeeding consultant and possibly even a speech/language pathologist. While your baby is learning, he may need supplemental feedings (see above). For further suggestions on improving suckling technique, call your local NCT group or La Leche League.

Possible problem: *Your nipples are sore or you have a breast infection.* Not only can the pain interfere with your desire to nurse, reducing nursing frequency and milk production, it can actually inhibit milk let-down.
Solution: Take steps to heal sore nipples or cure mastitis (see pages 77 and 82). But do not use a nipple shield, as this can interfere with your baby's ability to latch on to your nipples, compounding your problems.

Possible problem: *Your nipples are flat or inverted.* It's sometimes difficult for a

Supplemental Nutrition System: This apparatus can supply baby with supplementary feedings while stimulating mother's milk production. A feeding bottle hangs around the mother's neck; slim tubes leading from the bottle are taped down her breasts, extending slightly past the nipples. The bottle is filled with mother's own milk, collected with a breast pump, with breast milk from a milk bank, or with the formula recommended by the baby's doctor. As baby nurses at the breast, he takes the supplement through the tube. This system avoids the nipple confusion that arises when supplementary feedings are given in a bottle (a baby must learn to suck differently at bottle than *at breast) and stimulates the mother to produce more milk even as she is supplementing artificially.*

baby to get a firm hold on such nipples. This situation sets up the negative cycle of not enough suckling, leading to not enough milk, to even less suckling and less milk.

Solution: Help baby get a better grip during nursing by taking the outer part of the areola between your thumb and forefinger and compressing the entire area for his sucking. Use breast shells between feedings to make your nipples easier to draw out, but avoid breast shields during nursing, which, though they can draw nipples out, can prevent baby from properly grasping your nipple and sets up a longer-term problem.

Possible problem: *Some other factor is interfering with milk let-down.* Let-down is a physical function that can be inhibited as well as stimulated by your state of mind. If you're embarrassed or anxious about breastfeeding in general, or in a particular situation, not only can let-down be stifled, but the volume and calorie count of your milk can be affected.

Solution: Try to feed baby where you are most at ease – in private, if nursing around other people makes you tense. To help you relax, sit in a comfortable chair, play soft music, have something nonalcoholic to drink, try meditation or relaxation techniques. Massaging the breasts or applying warm soaks also encourages let-down, as does opening your shirt and cuddling baby skin to skin.

Possible problem: *Your baby is getting sucking satisfaction elsewhere.* If your baby is getting most of his sucking satisfaction from a dummy or other non-nutritive source, he may have little interest in the breast.

Solution: Toss out the dummy and nurse baby when he seems to want to suck. And don't give him supplementary bottles of water, which not only supply non-nutritive sucking but can dampen appetite and, in excess, alter blood sodium levels.

Possible problem: *You're not burping baby between breasts.* A baby who's swallowed air can stop eating before he's had enough because he feels uncomfortably full.

Solution: Bringing up the air will give him room for more milk. Be sure to burp baby between breasts (or even mid-breast if nursing is taking a while) whether he seems to need it or not, more often if he fusses a lot while nursing.

Possible problem: *Your baby is sleeping through the night.* An uninterrupted night's sleep is great for your looks but not necessarily for your milk supply. If baby is going seven or eight (or even ten) hours a night without nursing, your milk may be diminishing and supplementation may eventually be needed.

Solution: To make sure this doesn't happen, you may have to wake your little sleepyhead once in the middle of the night. He shouldn't be going longer than four hours at night without a feeding during the first month.

Possible problem: *You've returned to work.* Returning to work – and going eight to ten hours without nursing during the day – can also decrease the milk supply.

Solution: One way to prevent this is to express milk at work at least once every four hours you're away from baby (even if you're not using the milk for feeding).

Possible problem: *You're doing too much too soon.* Producing breast milk requires a lot of energy. If you're expending yours in other ways and not getting adequate rest, your breast milk supply may diminish.

Solution: Try a day of almost complete bed rest, followed by three or four days of taking it easy and see if your baby isn't more satisfied.

Possible problem: *You're sleeping on your stomach.* When you sleep on your stomach, something a lot of women are eager to do after the later months of

pregnancy when they couldn't, you also sleep on your breasts. And the pressure on your breasts could cut down on your milk production.

Solution: Turn over, at least partway, to take the pressure off those mammary glands.

Possible problem: *You can use some help.*

Solution: Breastfeeding doesn't come easily to every mother and every baby – and chances are some guidance from a knowledgeable source, such as a breastfeeding consultant, can put you back on course (see page 63).

Possible problem: *You're harbouring placental fragments in your uterus.* Your body won't accept the fact that you've actually delivered until all the products of pregnancy have been expelled, including the entire placenta. Until it's thoroughly convinced that baby's living on the outside now, your body may not produce adequate levels of prolactin, the hormone that stimulates milk production.

Solution: If you have any abnormal bleeding or other signs of retained placental fragments, contact your doctor at once. A dilatation and curettage (D & C) could put you and your baby on the right track to successful breastfeeding, while avoiding the danger a retained placenta can pose to your own health.

Even with your best efforts, under the best conditions, with ample support from your doctor, a breastfeeding consultant, your spouse and your friends, it may turn out that you're still unable to provide all the milk your baby needs. A small percentage of women are simply unable to breastfeed their babies without supplementation and a very few can't breastfeed at all. The reason may be physical, such as a prolactin deficiency, insufficient mammary glandular tissue, markedly asymmetrical breasts, or damage to the nerves to the nipple caused by breast surgery. Or it could be due to excessive stress, which can inhibit let-down. Or, occasionally, it may not be pinpointed at all. An early clue that your breasts may not be able to produce adequate milk is their failure to enlarge at all during pregnancy – though it's not an infallible clue and is often less reliable in second and subsequent pregnancies than in first ones.

If your baby isn't thriving and unless the problem appears to be one that can be cleared up in just a few days, his doctor is almost certain to prescribe supplemental formula feedings. Don't despair. What's most important is adequately nourishing your baby, not whether you give breast or bottle. In most cases, when supplementing, you can have the benefits of the direct parent-baby contact that nursing affords by letting baby suckle at your breast for pleasure (his and yours) after he's finished his bottle, or by using a supplemental nursing system.

Once a baby who is not doing well on the breast is put on formula, he almost invariably thrives. In the rare instance that he doesn't, a return trip to the doctor is necessary to see what it is that is interfering with adequate weight gain.

NURSING BLISTERS

'Why does my baby have a blister on her upper lip? Is she sucking too hard?'

For a baby with a hearty appetite, there's no such thing as sucking too hard – although a new mother with tender nipples may disagree. And though 'nursing blisters', which develop on the centre of the upper lips of many newborns, both breast and bottle fed,

are caused by vigorous suckling, they have no medical significance, cause the infant no discomfort and will disappear without treatment within a few weeks to months. Sometimes, they even seem to disappear between feedings.

FEEDING SCHEDULE

'I seem to be nursing my new daughter all the time. Whatever happened to the four-hour schedules I've heard about?'

Apparently, your baby (like all the other nursing babies you'll notice nipping at their mothers' breasts almost continuously in the first few months of life) hasn't heard about the four-hour schedule. Hunger calls and she wants to eat – a lot more often than most 'schedules' would permit her to.

Let her – at least for now. Three- and four-hour schedules are based on the needs of bottle-fed newborns, who usually do very well on such regimens. But most breastfed babies need to eat more often than that. That's because breast milk is digested more quickly than formula, making them feel hungry again sooner and because frequent nursing helps establish a good milk supply – the foundation of a successful breastfeeding relationship.

Nurse as frequently as baby seems to want to during the early weeks. But if your baby is still demanding food every hour at three weeks of age or so, check with the doctor to see if her weight gain is normal. If it isn't, seek advice from the doctor and see Baby Getting Enough Breast Milk, page 158. If she seems to be thriving, however, it's time to start making demands of your own. Hourly nursing is not only too much of an emotional strain for you, it's a physical strain as well, making you

DOUBLE THE TROUBLE, DOUBLE THE FUN

Today, most expectant parents of twins see double on the ultrasound screen early in pregnancy, making mad postpartum dashes to the store for a second set of everything rare. But even with seven or eight months' notice, it may be impossible to prepare completely for the day when babies make four (or, if siblings are already on the scene, more). Knowing how to plan and what to expect can provide a greater sense of control over what may seem (at least initially) a fundamentally uncontrollable situation.

Be doubly prepared. Since double blessings often come early (full term for twins may be 37 weeks, rather than 40), it's a good idea to start organizing for the babies' arrival well in advance. Try to have every child-care item in the house and ready for use before you go to the hospital. But while it makes sense to devote a lot of time to preparations, it doesn't make sense to exhaust yourself (particularly if your doctor has given you specific orders to take it easy). Get plenty of rest before the babies arrive – you can expect it to be a rare luxury once they do.

Double up. Do as much as possible for your babies in tandem. That means waking them at the same time so they can be fed together, putting them in the bath (once they're able to sit) together, walking them in the pushchair together. Double burp them together across your lap, or with one on your lap and the other your shoulder. When you can't double up, alternate. At an early age, daily baths aren't necessary, so bathe one one night, the other the next. Or bathe them every second or third night and sponge in between. Putting them foot to foot in the same cot during the early weeks may help them sleep better – but ask your doctor first. Some experts warn that tandem sleeping can increase the SIDS risk once the twins are able to roll over.

Split up. The work, that is. When both parents are around, divide the household chores (cooking, cleaning, laundry, shopping) and the babies (you take over one baby, your spouse the other). Be sure that you alternate babies so that both children get to know both parents well, and vice versa.

Try the double-breasted approach. Nursing twins can be physically challenging but eliminates fussing with dozens of bottles and endless amounts of formula. Nursing simultaneously will save time and avoid a daily breastfeeding marathon. You can hold the babies, propped on pillows, in the clutch position with their feet behind you (see page 66), or, with one at each breast, their bodies crossed in front of you. Alternate the breast each baby gets at every feeding to avoid creating favourites (and to avoid mismatched breasts, should one baby turn out to be a more proficient sucker than the other, or one baby getting less to eat if one breast turns out to be a less productive provider). If you find it too difficult to breastfeed your twins exclusively, you can nurse one while you bottle feed the other – again alternating from feeding to feeding. To keep up both your energy and your milk supply, be sure to get super nutrition (including 400 to 500 extra calories per baby) and adequate rest.

Plan to have some extra hands on hand, if you're bottle feeding. Bottle feeding twins requires either an extra set of hands or great ingenuity. If you find yourself with two babies and just two hands at feeding time, you can sit on a sofa between the babies with their feet towards the back and hold a bottle for each. Or hold them both in your arms with the bottles in bottle proppers raised to a comfortable height by pillows. You can also occasionally prop the bottle for one in a baby seat (but never lying down), while you feed the other the traditional way. Feeding them one after the other is another possibility, but that will significantly cut into the already tiny amount of time you'll have for other activities. This procedure will also put the babies on somewhat different napping schedules if they sleep after eating, which can be good if you'd like some time alone with each, or bad if you depend on that tandem sleeping time to rest or get things done around the house.

Double the help. All new parents need help – you need it twice as much. Accept all the help you can get, from any willing source.

Double up on equipment. When you don't have another pair of hands around to help, utilize such conveniences as baby carriers (you can use a large sling for two babies, use two slings, or tote one baby in a carrier and one in your arms), baby swings (some models can't be used until a baby is six weeks old), and infant seats. A playpen is a safe playground for your twins as they get older, and because they'll have each other for company, they will be willing to be relegated to it more often and for longer periods than a singleton would. Select a double buggy to meet your needs (if you will be traversing narrow grocery aisles, for example, a back-to-front model will be more practical than a side-by-side one); you will probably find a pram a waste of money. And don't forget that you will need two car seats. Put both in the backseat of the car.

Keep twice as many records. Who took what at which feeding, who was bathed yesterday, who's scheduled for today? Unless you keep a log (in a notebook posted on the nursery wall, or on a blackboard), you're sure to forget. Also make note in a permanent record book of immunizations, illnesses, and so on. Though most of the time, the babies will both get everything that's going around, occasionally only one will – and you may not remember which one.

Don't split zzz's. Sleep will necessarily be scarce for the first few months, but it will be scarcer if you allow your babies to waken at random during the night. Instead, when the first cries, wake the second and feed them both. Any time that both your little darlings are napping during the day, catch a few winks yourself – or at least put your feet up.

Go one-on-one. Though it won't be easy (at least in the beginning), there are ways to find that special one-on-one time with each child during the day. When you're better rested yourself, stagger naptime – put one child down 15 minutes before the other – so you can shower some individualized attention on the one who's awake. Or take only one child on an errand and leave the other one with a sitter or your spouse. Join a playgroup or mother-and-baby group and alternate which child you bring along each week. Even everyday baby chores, such as nappy changing or dressing, can become special one-on-one time for each child.

Double up on support. Other parents of twins will be your best source of advice and support; be sure to tap them. Find a parents-of-twins support group in your neighbourhood or, if one is lacking, start one. But avoid becoming too clannish, socializing with only the parents of twins and having your babies participate in twins-only play groups. Though there's something indisputably different about being a twin, excluding your children from relationships with singletons will discourage normal social development with peers – the majority of whom will not be twins.

Be doubly alert, once your twins are mobile. You'll find, as your babies begin crawling and cruising, that what one of them doesn't think of in the way of exploits, the other will. So they will need to be watched twice as carefully.

Expect things to get doubly better. The first four months with twins are the most challenging. Once you begin to work out the many logistics, you'll find yourself falling into an easier rhythm. Keep in mind, too, that twins are often each other's best company – many have a way of keeping each other busy that parents of demanding singletons find enviable, and which will free you up more and more in the months and years to come.

exhausted and may actually lead to decreased milk supply. Neither is it best for your baby, since she needs longer periods of sleep and longer periods of wakefulness when she should be looking at something other than a breast. Keep in mind, too, that crying doesn't always signal hunger; babies also cry when they're sleepy, bored, or just in the mood for attention (for help interpreting your baby's cries, see page 117).

Assuming your milk supply is well established, you can start slightly stretching the periods between feedings (which may also help your baby sleep better at night). When baby wakes crying an hour after feeding, don't rush to feed her. If she still seems sleepy, try to get her back to sleep without nursing her. Before picking her up, pat or rub her or turn on a musical toy and see if she'll drift back off. If not, pick her up, sing softly to her, walk with her, rock her, again with the goal of getting her back to sleep. If she seems alert, change her, talk to her, distract her in some other way, even take her for a stroll outdoors. She may become so interested in you and the rest of the world that she actually forgets about your breasts – at least for a few minutes.

When you finally do nurse, don't accept the snack-bar approach some babies try to take; encourage her to nurse at least ten minutes on each side. If she falls off to sleep, try to waken her to continue the meal. If you can manage to stretch the periods between nursings a little more each day, eventually you and baby will be on a more reasonable schedule: two to three hours and eventually four or so. But it should be a schedule based on her hunger, not the clock.

TIMING IS EVERYTHING

Like labour contractions, intervals between feedings are timed from the beginning of one to the beginning of the next. So a baby who nurses for forty minutes starting at 10 AM, then sleeps for an hour and twenty minutes before eating again, is on a two-hour schedule, not a one-hour-and-twenty-minute one.

CHANGING YOUR MIND ABOUT BREASTFEEDING

'I've been breastfeeding my son for three weeks and I'm just not enjoying it. I'd like to switch to a bottle, but I feel so guilty.'

Beginning breastfeeding can be a frustrating series of trials and (plenty of) errors. As far as enjoyment goes, it can be elusive on both sides of the breast in this early adjustment period. It's very possible that your dissatisfaction with breastfeeding is just the result of a bumpy start (which almost always turns into a smooth ride by the middle of the second month). So it might make sense to hold off on your decision until your baby is six weeks old (or even two months), by which time he will have received many of the benefits of breastfeeding (though there are a lot of benefits to extended breastfeeding, see page 264) and breastfeeding generally will have become much easier and more satisfying for both participants. Then, if you're still not enjoying nursing, feel free – and free of remorse – to wean. Remember, if it doesn't feel right for you and your baby, it probably isn't. Trust your feelings and your instincts.

Too Much Formula

'My baby loves his bottle. If it were up to him, he'd drink all day. How do I know when to give him more formula or when to stop?'

Because their intake is regulated both by their appetite and by an ingenious supply-and-demand system, breastfed babies rarely get too much – or too little – of a good thing. Bottle-fed babies, whose intake is regulated instead by their parents, can. As long as your baby is healthy, happy and gaining adequate weight, you know he's getting enough formula. But he can be taking in more than he needs – especially if his bottle becomes the liquid equivalent of an all-you-can eat buffet, continuously refilled by well meaning parents even after his appetite is satisfied.

Too much formula can lead to a too chubby baby (which, research shows, can lead to a too chubby child and a too chubby adult). But it can also lead to other problems. If your baby seems to be spitting up a lot (more than normal, see page 170), if he has abdominal pain (he draws his legs up onto a tense abdomen immediately after a feeding) and/or is gaining weight excessively, he might be taking too much formula. Your health visitor will be able to tell you what his rate of gain should be and how much formula (approximately) he should be getting at each feeding (see page 102). If he does seem to be taking too much, try offering smaller-volume feedings and stop when baby seems full instead of pushing him to take more; burp more often to relieve any abdominal discomfort he may have; and ask the doctor about whether you can give him an occasional small bottle of water (to quench his thirst without filling him up). Keep in mind, too, that it may just be the sucking (not the formula that comes with it) that he's craving; some babies need to suck more than others. If that's the case, consider using a dummy during the next couple of months, while this need to suck is strongest (see page 187), or help him find his fingers or fist to suck on.

Supplementary Water

'I'm wondering if I should give our daughter bottles of water instead of nursing her so often.'

Sorry, but a bottle of water is no substitute – or supplement – for your breasts right now. A baby who is exclusively breastfed gets all the fluids she needs from breast milk and that's exactly where she should be getting them from. Not only doesn't she need supplementary water under normal circumstances, she shouldn't be offered any. First of all, bottles of water (particularly early on in breastfeeding) can satisfy her appetite and her need to suck, sabotaging nursing efforts. Second of all, too much water can dangerously dilute a baby's blood, causing chemical imbalances. This second potential problem also holds true for bottle-fed babies who are fed too much water. Though it's fine to give a little water to a bottle-fed baby in very hot weather, it's not usually necessary. Giving an older infant (over age four months) small sips of water from a cup, however, is fine (they won't be able to take too much from a cup, only from a bottle). Children on solids can handle more water, whether they're breastfed or formula-fed.

If you're wondering whether your baby is nursing too frequently, see page 158.

SUPPLEMENT SENSE

Here's a guide to the most common supplemental nutrients your baby's doctor may prescribe:

Vitamin D. This vitamin, which is necessary for proper bone development and protects against diseases such as rickets, is naturally manufactured by the skin when it is exposed to sunlight. But because most babies don't get enough sun to fill their vitamin D quota (about 15 minutes a week for fair-skinned babies, more for dark-skinned babies) due to protective clothing, sunscreen and long winter months in certain instances, and because breast milk contains only a small amount of D, some doctors recommend vitamin D supplementation for infants who are breastfed – often in the form of ACD drops (which contain vitamins A, C and D) – beginning at birth.

Since all the vitamins and minerals a baby needs (including D) are provided by commercial baby formula, bottle-fed infants who receive more than 450 ml (16 fl oz) of formula a day do not need any additional supplementation. (Too much vitamin D can be toxic.)

Iron. Since iron deficiency during the first eighteen months of life can cause serious developmental and behavioural problems, it's important that babies get enough iron. Your newborn, unless premature or low birth-weight, probably arrived with a considerable iron reserve, but this will be depleted somewhere between four and six months of age.

If you're formula feeding, iron-fortified formula will fill baby's needs. Breast milk contains sufficient iron during the first six months, so if you're nursing, there's no need for supplemental iron until the half-year mark is reached. Once solids are started, you can guarantee that your baby will continue to fill his or her requirement for this vital mineral by serving up foods that contain supplemental iron, such as enriched cereals, meats and green vegetables. Adequate vitamin C intake will improve iron absorption, and once your baby begins taking a lot of

VITAMIN SUPPLEMENTS

'Everybody we talk to has a different opinion on vitamins for babies. We can't decide whether or not to give them to our new son.'

The science of nutrition is still in its relative infancy – and that includes the study of vitamins (they weren't even given that name until 1912). With lots more to learn and with new information being uncovered each day, it's not surprising that recommendations on giving vitamins seem to be ever-changing and ever-conflicting. And it's not surprising that consumers – including new parents – are often left wondering how to proceed.

What's clear is that babies who are formula-fed don't need supplemental vitamins of any kind, because all the nutrients they need are already in the formula (just read the label and you'll see). The picture's less clear when it comes to babies who are exclusively breastfed. Current research indicates that healthy breastfeeding infants get most (though not all) of the vitamins and minerals they are believed to need from breast milk (if their mothers are eating a good diet and taking a pregnancy-breastfeeding supplement daily). The vitamins that are missing from breast milk, most notably vitamin D, can be obtained from supplemental drops (see box on pages 168–169).

Some infants may need even more

solids, it's a good idea to give a vitamin C food at each meal so that the benefits of any iron taken are maximized (see page 315). Supplemental iron drops are not a first choice for babies (though they may be recommended for premature babies) because they are not well tolerated and can cause staining on the teeth. Also, the mineral can be toxic in large doses, so paediatricians use drops only when necessary.

Fluoride. Most doctors agree that babies do not need fluoride supplementation during the first six months of life. After six months, a fluoride supplement should be given if there isn't adequate fluoride in your water system. If you're uncertain of the fluoride levels in your tap water, your baby's doctor may be able to advise you. Or you can call your local water company or water authority. If your water is from a well or other private source, you can have its fluoride content checked by a lab (ask the health department how to have this done). Then check with your doctor to see if any additional fluoride is necessary.

With fluoride, as with most good things, too much can be bad. Excessive intake while the teeth are developing in the gums, such as might occur when a baby drinks fluoridated water (either plain or mixed with formula) *and* takes a supplement, can cause 'fluorosis', or mottling (white striations appearing on the teeth). Excessive intake can also occur if a baby or young child uses fluoridated toothpaste, which they tend to swallow. The lesser forms of mottling are not noticeable or aesthetically unattractive. More serious mottling, however, is not only disfiguring, but the pitting can predispose the teeth to decay, eliminating the good that fluoride is supposed to do.

Babies and young children, because of their small size and because their teeth are still developing, are particularly susceptible to fluorosis. So be wary of overdose. Once brushing is started, don't use toothpaste unless your baby insists (and then use a tiny drop, or you can choose an unfluoridated baby toothpaste). Cap the paste whenever it's not in use, and put it out of baby's reach – some babies and toddlers love to eat the stuff.

in the way of supplemental nutrients – for instance, babies who have health problems that compromise their nutritional status (those who are not able to absorb certain nutrients well from their foods and/or are on restricted diets) and babies of breastfeeding vegans who eat no animal products and take no supplements themselves. The latter should receive, at the very least, vitamin B_{12}, which may be totally absent in their mother's milk and probably folic acid as well; but a complete vitamin-mineral supplement with iron is usually a good idea.

Healthy older children with adequate diets, on the other hand, probably do not need routine vitamins – even if one day the baby cereal ends up on the floor, most of the yogurt appears to be smeared on the high chair tray and the evening offering of puréed chicken is tentatively tasted, then spat out. Some doctors nevertheless recommend giving vitamin drops daily, as health insurance and probably will recommend an over-the-counter supplement that supplies no more than the recommended daily allowance of vitamins and minerals for your older baby. Don't give your baby any additional vitamin, mineral, or herbal supplements unless recommended by your doctor.

QUICK TIP

Keep a small plastic bottle of water mixed with a little baking soda handy for spit-up spot cleaning. Rubbing a cloth moistened with the mixture on spots will keep them from setting and will eliminate most of the odour. Or use a baby wipe.

SPITTING UP

'My baby spits up so much that I'm worried she's not getting enough nourishment.'

Although it may seem all that's going into your daughter is coming back up, that's almost certainly not the case. What looks like a mealful of milk to you is probably no more than a tablespoon or two, mixed with saliva and mucus – certainly not enough to interfere with your baby's nourishment. (To see how much a little bit of liquid can look like, spill a couple of tablespoons of milk on your kitchen counter.) Spitting up is extremely common in infancy and although it's messy and smelly, it's not usually a cause for concern. (Doctors are fond of saying that spit-up is a laundry problem, not a health problem.)

Most babies spit up at least occasionally; some spit up with every feeding. The process in newborns may be related to an immature sphincter between the oesophagus and the stomach and to excess mucus that needs to be cleared. In older babies, spitting up occurs when milk mixed with air comes back up with a burp. Sometimes a baby wisely spits up because she's eaten too much.

The material your baby spits up will be relatively unchanged from the form in which it entered her mouth if it went only as far as the oesophagus before coming back up. But if it travelled down to the stomach before its return trip, it will look curdled and smell like sour milk.

There are no sure cures for spitting up. But you can try to minimize the air gulping around mealtimes that can contribute to it: don't feed her when she's crying (take a break in the action to calm her down); keep her as upright as possible while feeding and for a while afterwards; if bottle feeding, be sure bottle teats are neither too large nor too small and that bottles are tilted so that formula (not air) fills the teat (or use an angled bottle or one with disposable liners). It may also be helpful to avoid bouncing her around while she's eating or just afterwards (when possible, strap her in a baby seat or pushcahair for a while after feedings). And don't forget to burp her during a meal, instead of waiting until the end of the meal, when one big bubble may bring up the works.

Accept, however, that no matter what you do, if your baby's a spitter, she's going to spit – and you're going to have to live with it for at least six months. (The living will be a little neater, however, if you keep a precautionary nappy on your shoulder or lap whenever you're on baby duty.) Most babies ease up on their spitting when they start sitting upright, although a few will continue causing malodorous mayhem well up until their first birthdays.

While ordinary spitting is normal and no cause for concern, some kinds of spitting up do, however, signal possible problems. Call the doctor if your baby's spitting up is associated with poor weight gain or prolonged gagging and coughing, if it seems severe (gastroesophageal reflux or GER), or if her vomit is brown or green in colour or shoots out a metre or so (2 or 3 ft) (projectile vomiting). These could indicate a medical problem, such as an intestinal obstruction or pyloric stenosis (treatable by surgery). For more information on these conditions, see pages 559 and 651. Also call if the spitting seems to be causing baby discomfort. Most babies are 'happy spitters'; if your baby is having pain with spitting, it may be because it's causing an irritation in her oesophagus.

BLOOD IN SPIT-UP

'When my two-week-old spit up today after I nursed her, there were some reddish streaks in with the curdled milk. I'm really worried about her.'

Any blood that seems to be coming from a two-week-old baby, particularly when it's found in her spit-up, is bound to be alarming. But before you panic, try to determine whose blood it actually is. If your nipples are cracked, even very slightly, it's probably your blood, which baby could be sucking in (and then spitting up) along with the milk each time she nurses.

If your nipples aren't obviously the cause (they may be, even if you can't see the tiny cracks), or if you're not breastfeeding, call your doctor to help you figure out the source of the blood in your baby's spit-up.

MILK ALLERGY

'My baby is crying a lot and I'm wondering if he might be allergic to the milk in his formula. How can I tell?'

As eager as you might be to uncover a cause (and an easy cure) for your baby's crying, milk is not a likely suspect. Milk allergy is the most common food allergy in infants, but it is less common than most people believe (only about one in a hundred babies will develop a true intolerance to milk). Most doctors believe it an unlikely possibility in a child whose parents don't have allergies and in one whose only symptom is crying. A baby who is having a severe allergic response to milk will usually vomit frequently and have loose, watery stools, possibly tinged with blood. Less severe reactions may include occasional vomiting and loose mucousy stools. Some babies who are allergic to milk may also have eczema, hives, wheezing and/or a nasal discharge or stuffiness when exposed to milk protein.

Unfortunately, there's no way to test for milk allergy, except through trial and error. If you suspect milk allergy, discuss the possibility with your baby's doctor before taking any action. If there is no history of allergy in your family and if there are no symptoms other than the crying, then it is likely the doctor will suggest you treat the crying spells as ordinary colic (see pages 182–184).

If there are family allergies or symptoms other than crying, a trial change of formula – to hydrolysate (in which the protein is partly broken down or predigested) or soya – may be recommended. A rapid improvement in the colicky behaviour and the disappearance of other symptoms, if any, would suggest the possibility of an allergy to milk – or it could just be a coincidence. Reinstating the milk formula is one way of verifying the diagnosis; if the symptoms return with the milk, allergy is likely.

In many cases, there's no change when a baby is switched to a soya formula. This may mean he's also allergic to soya, has a medical condition that has nothing to do with milk and that needs to be diagnosed, or simply has an immature digestive system. A switch from soya to hydrolysate formula should help if the baby seems to be sensitive to both soya and milk.

Very rarely, the problem is an enzyme deficiency – an infant is born unable to produce lactase, the enzyme needed to digest the milk sugar lactose. Such a child has persistent diarrhoea from the start and fails to gain weight. A formula containing little or no lactose will usually resolve the problem. Unlike a temporary lactose intolerance that sometimes develops during a bout with an intestinal bug, a congenital lactase deficiency is usually permanent. The baby will probably never be able to tolerate ordinary milk products – though he is likely to be fine on those that are lactose reduced.

If the problem is not traced to milk allergy or intolerance, it's probably best to stay with – or switch back to – a cow's milk formula, since it is the better breast milk substitute.

Infant allergy to cow's milk is usually outgrown by the end of the first year and almost always by the end of the second. If your baby is taken off cow's milk formula, his doctor may suggest trying it again after six months on a substitute formula, or may suggest waiting until the first birthday.

MILK ALLERGY IN BREASTFED BABIES

'I'm breastfeeding my son exclusively and when I changed his nappy today, I noticed some streaks of blood in his bowel movement. What can that mean?'

Babies are virtually never allergic to their mother's milk, but, very rarely, a baby can be allergic to something in his mother's diet that ends up in her milk – often cow's milk proteins. And it sounds as if this might be the case with your very sensitive infant.

Symptoms of such an allergy, known as allergic colitis, include blood in baby's stool; fussiness or crankiness; lack of, or minimal (or no) weight gain; vomiting and/or diarrhoea. Your baby could have one or all of these symptoms. Researchers suspect that some babies may become sensitized to certain foods mother eats while baby is still in utero, causing such allergies after birth.

While cow's milk and other dairy products are a common culprit in these reactions, they're not the only ones. Other possibilities include soya, nuts, wheat and peanuts. A quick check with your baby's doctor will probably lead you to this course of action: to determine what in your diet is causing your baby's allergy, try eliminating all potentially offending foods for a week (or until your baby's symptoms disappear) and then slowly reintroduce them into your diet while you monitor your baby's reaction.

Usually, you'll quickly see which of the foods you eat cause problems for your baby. Occasionally, no correlation between foods and allergic symptoms is found. In that case, your baby might just have had a gastrointestinal virus that caused the streaks of blood in his stool. Or there might be small cracks or fissures in his anus that caused the bleeding. Monitoring by your baby's doctor should solve the mystery.

BOWEL MOVEMENTS

'I expected one, maybe two, bowel movements a day from my breastfed baby. But she seems to have one in every nappy – sometimes as many as ten a day. And they're very loose. Could she have diarrhoea?'

Your baby isn't the first breastfed infant ever who seemed to be bent on beating the world record for dirtying nappies. Not only is such an active elimination pattern not a bad sign in a breastfed newborn, it's a good one. Since the amount that's coming out is related to the amount going in, any breastfeeding mother whose newborn has five or more movements daily can be assured that her baby is getting sufficient nourishment. (Mothers of nursing newborns who have fewer movements should see page 159.) The number of movements progressively decreases and may dwindle down to no more than one a day, or every other day, next month, though some babies continue to have several movements a day for the entire first year. It's not necessary to continue keeping count – the number may vary from day to day and that's perfectly normal, too.

Normal, also, for breastfed infants is a very soft, sometimes even watery, stool. But diarrhoea – frequent stools that are liquidy, smelly and may contain mucus, often accompanied by fever and/or weight loss – is less common among children who dine on breast milk alone. If they do get it, they have fewer, smaller movements than bottle-fed babies with diarrhoea and recover more quickly, probably because of the antibacterial properties of breast milk.

EXPLOSIVE BOWEL MOVEMENTS

'My son's bowel movements come with such force and such explosive sound, I'm worried that he has some digestive problem. Or maybe something's wrong with my breast milk.'

Breastfed newborns are rarely discreet when it comes to making bowel movements. The noisy barrage that fills the room as they fill their nappies can often be heard in the next room and can alarm first-time parents. Yet these movements and the surprising variety of sounds that punctuates their passing are normal, the result of gas being forcefully expelled from an immature digestive system. Things should quiet down in a month or two.

PASSING GAS

'My baby passes gas all day long – very loudly. Could she be having stomach troubles?'

The digestive exclamations that frequently explode from a newborn's tiny bottom, at least as emphatically as the grown-up variety, can be unsettling – and sometimes embarrassing – to parents. But, like explosive bowel movements, they are perfectly normal. Once your newborn's digestive system works out the kinks, the gas will pass more quietly and less frequently. Until then, you can always blame the dog (that is, if you have one handy).

CONSTIPATION

'I'm worried that my baby is constipated. He's been averaging only one movement every two or three days. Could it be his formula?'

Childhood constipation has been flippantly defined as having movements less often than your parent. But that's an unreliable gauge, since each individual has a personal pattern of elimination and it's not necessarily a case of 'like parent, like child'. Some bottle-fed babies go three or four days between movements. But they're not considered to be constipated unless those infrequent movements are firmly formed or come out in hard pellets, or if they cause pain or bleeding (from a fissure or crack in the anus as a result of pushing). If your baby's movements are soft and cause no problems, don't worry. But if you suspect constipation, consult his doctor. Giving baby a little water (only with the doctor's okay) might help. (For babies older than four months, a small amount of prune juice may ease constipation; check with the doctor before offering it.) Rarely, a milk allergy can cause constipation, in which case a switch of formulas might do the trick (again, only with the doctor's approval). And don't take any other steps, such as giving laxatives (even mineral oil), enemas, or herbal teas without medical advice.

'I thought breastfed babies were never constipated – but my daughter grunts and groans and strains whenever she has a bowel movement.'

It's true that breastfed babies are rarely constipated, because breast milk is just the right match for the human baby's digestive tract. But it's also true that some have to push and strain to get their movements out, even though the movement comes out soft and seems as though it should have been easy to pass.[3] Why this is so isn't certain. Some have theorized it's because the soft stool of the breastfed baby doesn't put adequate pressure on the anus. Others speculate that the muscles of the newborn anus are neither strong enough nor coordinated enough to eliminate any stool easily. Still others point to the fact that young babies, who usually have bowel movements lying down, get no help from gravity.

Whatever the reason, the difficulty should ease up when solids are added to your baby's diet. But, in the meantime, don't worry. And don't use laxatives (even

mineral oil), enemas or any other home remedies for the problem – because it really isn't one. When an adult is constipated, walking often helps alleviate the problem; you might try flexing and extending your baby's legs in a bicycling motion while she's on her back to assist her when she seems uncomfortable.

SLEEPING POSITIONS

'My parents say they always put me to sleep on my tummy. But the doctor says our baby should sleep on her back. I'm confused.'

When your parents were putting you to sleep, tummy was indeed the position of choice. That's because experts used to believe that being tummy down prevented babies from choking on their spit-up while they slept. But more recent research indicates that the back position is the safest position of all. Studies have shown that back sleepers have fewer fevers, fewer problems with nasal congestion and fewer ear infections than tummy sleepers and are no more likely to spit-up during the night (or choke on their spit-up). But by far the most important reason why back sleeping is safer: placing babies to sleep on their backs sharply reduces the risk of cot death (SIDS). This compelling evidence has prompted the Back to Sleep campaign, which recommends that all healthy infants be put to sleep on their backs.[4]

Start your baby sleeping on her back right away, so that she'll get used to and feel comfortable in that position from the beginning (most babies naturally prefer being tummy down). Some babies fuss a

---

3. If your breastfed baby has very infrequent bowel movements and is not gaining well, then see page 159 and check with your doctor. It's possible she isn't getting enough to eat and thus has not much to eliminate.

4. Some case-by-case exceptions might be made for infants with severe gastroesophageal reflux or those with airway malformations.

lot on their back; because their flailing arms and legs don't have the mattress to snuggle against, they may feel less cozy and secure. Because of that, you'll probably find that your baby startles more often during sleep, which may lead to slightly more frequent wakings. (Swaddling baby early on may make her more comfy – and content – on her back; see page 194.) It's also possible that she will develop a flat or bald spot from always facing in the same direction – usually because she is focusing on the same spot (often a window) – while lying on her back. To minimize this problem, alternate her position (head at one end of the cot one night, the other the next). If in spite of your efforts her head flattens or a bald spot develops, don't worry. These problems will gradually correct themselves as she gets older. Severe cases can be corrected with a special headband or helmet.

Putting baby on her tummy to play when she's awake (and watched) will minimize flattening while allowing her to develop muscles and practise gross motor skills (see page 205). Remember: *Back to sleep, tummy to play.*

SLEEPING PATTERNS

'I thought newborns were supposed to sleep all the time. Our three-week-old daughter hardly seems to sleep at all.'

Newborns often seem not to know what they're 'supposed to do'. They nurse erratically when they're 'supposed to' be on a three- or four-hour schedule, or they sleep twelve hours a day (or twenty-two) when they're 'supposed to' sleep sixteen and a half hours. That's because they know what we often forget – that there's almost nothing a baby is supposed to do at any specific time. 'Average' babies, who do everything by the book,

do exist – but they're in the minority. The sixteen and a half hours that reflects the average sleeping time for babies in their first month of life takes into account babies who sleep twelve hours a day and others who sleep twenty-three, as well as all those in between. The baby who falls at either end of the spectrum is no less normal than one who falls near the average. Some infants, like some adults, appear to need more sleep than others, some less.

So assuming your baby seems healthy and happy in every way, don't worry about her wakefulness, but do get used to it. Infants who sleep very little tend to grow into children who sleep very little – with parents who, not coincidentally, also sleep very little.

'My baby gets up several times a night. My mother says if I don't get her into a regular sleeping pattern now, she may never develop good sleep habits. She says I should let her cry it out instead of feeding her all night.'

Any experienced parent, particularly whose experience has included coping with a child who wouldn't sleep through the night or who had trouble falling asleep, knows the importance of fostering good sleep habits in children at an early age. But the first month of life is way too early. Your baby is just beginning to learn about the world. The most important lesson she needs to learn now is that when she calls, you will be there – even at 3 AM, and even when she's up for the fourth time in six hours. There are many methods that can be used by parents who want to help their baby figure out how to fall asleep by herself, but not for several months yet – not until she begins to feel more secure and more in control of her environment.

If you're breastfeeding, trying to institute a sleeping schedule now could also interfere with establishing a good milk supply – and with your baby's growth. Breastfed newborns need to eat more frequently than bottle-fed babies, often every two or three hours, which generally prevents them from sleeping through the night until somewhere between the third and sixth month. Like the time-honoured four-hour feeding schedule, the belief that babies should sleep through the night by two months is based on the developmental behaviour of formula-fed infants and it's often unrealistic for those who are nursing.

So while there's no harm in thinking ahead about fostering good sleep habits in your child, it's too early to put those plans into action.

RESTLESS SLEEP

'Our baby, who shares our room, tosses and turns all night. Could our being near be keeping him from sleeping soundly?'

Although the phrase 'sleeping like a baby' is often equated with enviably peaceful rest, particularly by the manufacturers of mattresses and sleep aids, babies' sleep isn't peaceful at all. Newborns do sleep a lot, but they also wake up a lot in the process. That's because much of their sleep is REM (rapid eye movement) sleep, an active sleep with dreaming and a lot of movement. At the end of each REM sleep period, the sleeper usually awakens briefly. When you hear your baby fuss or whimper at night, it's probably because he's finishing a REM period, not because you share a room with him.

As he gets older, his sleeping patterns will mature. He will have less REM sleep and longer periods of the much sounder 'quiet sleep', from which it's harder to rouse him. He will continue to stir and whimper periodically, but less frequently.

Though your being in the same room with baby probably isn't disturbing his sleep at this stage, it certainly is disturbing yours. Not only do you waken at every moan, but you are also tempted to pick him up more often than necessary during the night. Try to ignore your baby's midnight murmurings; pick him up only when he begins to cry steadily and seriously. You'll both sleep better. If you find that difficult, then perhaps you should consider separate sleeping quarters – if you have the space and aren't choosing to co-sleep for other reasons.

Do be alert, however, for sudden waking and crying, unusual restlessness, or other changes in sleeping patterns that don't seem to be related to events in baby's life (such as teething or an over-stimulating day). If you note them, check for signs of illness such as fever, appetite loss or diarrhoea (see chapter 18). Call your doctor if the symptoms persist.

MIXING UP OF NIGHT AND DAY

'My three-week-old sleeps most of the day and wants to stay up all night. How can I get her to reverse her schedule so we all can get some rest?'

Babies who work (or play) the night shift, getting most of their sleep by day, can turn normally active, alert parents into barely functioning zombies. Happily, this blissful ignorance of the difference between day and night isn't a permanent condition. The newborn who, before her arrival in the world of daytime light and night-time darkness, was kept in the dark for nine months just needs a little time to adjust.

Chances are your baby will stop

mixing up her days and nights within the next few weeks on her own. If you'd like to help speed the process, try limiting her daytime naps to no more than three or four hours each. Although waking a sleeping infant can be tricky, it's usually possible. Try holding her upright, eliciting a burp, stripping off her clothes, rubbing under her chin or massaging her feet. Once she's somewhat alert, try to further stimulate her: talk to her, sing lively songs, dangle a toy within her range of vision, which is about 20 to 35 cm (8 to 14 in). (For other tips on keeping baby awake, see page 116.) Don't, however, try to keep her from napping at all during the day, with the hope that she'll sleep at night. An overtired and perhaps overstimulated, baby is not likely to sleep well at night.

Making a clear distinction between day and night may help. If she naps in her room, avoid darkening it or trying to keep the noise level down. When she wakens, ply her with stimulating activities. At night, do the opposite. When you put baby to bed, strive for darkness (use room-darkening shades), relative quiet and inactivity. No matter how tempting it may be, don't play with or talk to her when she wakens during the night; don't turn on the lights or the TV while you're feeding her; keep communications to a whisper or softly sung lullabies; and be certain when she's back in her cot that sleeping conditions are ideal (see Better Sleep for Baby, page 179).

Although it may seem like a dubious blessing, consider yourself lucky that your baby sleeps for long stretches – even if it is during the day. It's a good sign that she's capable of sleeping well and that once she's got her internal clock set correctly, she will sleep well at night.

NOISE WHEN BABY IS SLEEPING

'I have a friend who turns off the phone when her son is sleeping, has a note on the door asking people to knock instead of ring and tiptoes around the apartment at naptime. Is this a good idea?'

By attempting to turn off all the sound in her baby's life, your friend is programming him to be able to sleep only under controlled conditions. The problem is, this programming, though well intentioned, will probably make it difficult for her child to get a good night's shut-eye later on in life when he has to sleep in the real world – a world where phones and doorbells ring.

And what's more, her efforts will probably be counterproductive. Though a sudden loud sound may waken some babies, others can sleep through fireworks, wailing sirens and barking dogs. For most, however, a steady hum of background noise – from a TV or stereo, a fan or air conditioner, a musical toy or one that imitates uterine sounds or from a white-noise machine – appears to be more conducive to restful sleep than perfect silence, particularly if the baby has fallen asleep to the beat of such sounds.

Just how much noise, as well as what kinds of noise, a baby can sleep through depends partly on the sounds he became accustomed to before birth and partly on individual temperament (some babies are much more sensitive to stimulus than others). So parents have to take their cues from their babies in determining how far they must go to protect them from noise during naps and at night. If a baby turns out to be especially sound-sensitive during sleep, it's probably wise to turn the phone down to low, to change the doorbell to a less abrasive ring and to play the radio or TV more softly. Such tactics are unnecessary, however, if a baby sleeps through everything.

BABY'S BREATHING

'Every time I watch my newborn sleep, her breathing seems irregular, her chest moves in a funny way and frankly it frightens me. Is something wrong with my baby?'

No, your baby is perfectly normal – and you are, too, for worrying (and for standing over her cot watching her breathing – something most new parents do frequently in the first few weeks of their babies' lives; see next question).

A newborn's normal breathing rate is about forty times each minute during waking hours; when your baby sleeps, however, it may slow down to as few as twenty times per minute. But what's alarming you – and what often alarms new parents – is how irregular an infant's breathing pattern is while she's sleeping. Your baby might breathe fast, with repeated rapid and shallow breaths, lasting 15 to 20 seconds and then pause (that is, stop breathing – and this is where it gets really scary), usually for less than 10 seconds (though it might seem forever to you) and then, after that brief respiratory respite, breathe again (which is generally when her parents can start breathing again, too). This type of breathing pattern, called periodic breathing, is normal and is due to your baby's immature (but, for her age, developmentally appropriate) breathing control centre in the brain.

You may also notice your baby's chest moving in and out while she is sleeping. Babies normally use their diaphragm (the large muscle below the lungs) for breathing. As long as your baby shows no blueness around the lips and resumes normal shallow breathing without any parental intervention, you have nothing to worry about.

Half of a newborn's sleep is spent in REM (rapid eye movement) sleep, a time when she breathes irregularly, grunts and snorts and twitches a lot – you can even see her eyes moving under the lids. The rest of her slumber is spent in quiet sleep, when she breathes very deeply and quietly and seems very still, except for occasional sucking motions or startling. As she gets older, she will experience less REM sleep and the quiet sleep will become more like the non-REM sleep of adults.

In other words, what you're describing is normal baby breathing. If, however, your baby takes more than sixty breaths per minute, flares her nose, makes grunting noises, looks blue or sucks in the muscles between the ribs with each breath so that her ribs stick out, call the doctor immediately.

'Everybody always jokes about sneaking into the baby's room to hear if he's breathing. Well, now I find myself doing just that – even in the middle of the night.'

A new parent neurotically checking a baby's breathing does seem like good comic material – until you become a new parent. And then it's no laughing matter. You wake in a cold sweat to complete silence after putting baby to bed five hours earlier. Could something be wrong? Why didn't he wake up? Or you pass his cot and he seems so silent and still that you have to poke him gingerly to be sure he's okay. Or he's grunting and snorting so hard you're sure he's having trouble breathing. You . . . and millions of other new parents.

Not only are your concerns normal, but your baby's varied breathing patterns when he snoozes are, too. You

BETTER SLEEP FOR BABY

Whether a good sleeper or a not so good one, your baby can be helped to sleep to potential with some or all of the following sleep enhancers, many of which help re-create some of the comforts of home in the womb:

Cozy sleeping space. A cot is a great modern invention – but in the early weeks many newborns somehow sense its vastness and balk when sentenced to solitude, smack in the centre of its mattress, so clearly removed from its distant walls. If your baby seems uncomfortable in the cot, a cradle, a moses basket or a carrycot can be used for the first few months to provide a snugger fit that's closer to the nine-month-long embrace in the uterus. For added security, swaddle your infant (but not once he or she becomes more active; see page 144), or use a baby sleeping bag.

Controlled temperature. Being too warm or too cold can disturb a baby's sleep. For tips on keeping baby comfortable in warm weather, see page 510; for tips in cold weather, see page 519.

Soothing movement. In the uterus, babies are most active when their mothers are at rest; when their mothers are up and on the go, they slow down, lulled by the motion. Out of the womb, movement still has a soothing effect. Rocking, swaying and patting will all contribute to contentment – and sleep.

Soothing sound. For many months, your heartbeat, the gurgling of your tummy, and your voice entertained and comforted your baby. Now sleeping may be difficult without some background noise. Try the hum of a fan, the soft strains of music from a radio or stereo, the tinkling of a music box or musical mobile, or one of those baby soothers that imitate uterine or heartbeat sounds.

A peaceful place. Babies sleep better in their own room because you'll be less likely to pick them up at the littlest whimper. However, since research suggests a parent's proximity may reduce the risk of SIDS during the first six to twelve months, experts now recommend that babies sleep in the same room as their parents (if you're comfortable doing so), preferably in a bassinet or co-sleeper (bed sharing presents other safety risks; see page 261). Either way, try not to pick your baby up at every toss or turn. And if baby does bunk alone, be close enough – or use a monitor – to hear the cries before they turn into ear-piercing wails.

Routine. Since your newborn will fall asleep most of the time while nursing or bottle feeding, a bedtime routine might seem unnecessary. But it's never too early to begin such a routine, and certainly by the age of six months it should top off every evening. The ritual of a warm bath, followed by being dressed in nightclothes, a little quiet playtime on your bed, a singsong story or nursery rhyme from a picture book, can be soothing and soporific for even the youngest babies. The breast or bottle can be last on the agenda for babies who still fall asleep that way, but can come earlier for those who have already learned to doze off on their own.

Adequate daytime rest. Some parents try to solve the night-time sleeping problems of their babies by keeping them awake during the day, even at times when their baby wants to sleep. This is a big mistake (though it's all right to limit the length of daytime naps a little in order to maintain the contrast between day and night), because an overtired baby sleeps more fitfully than a well-rested one.

will eventually become less panicky about whether he's going to wake up in the morning and more comfortable with both you and him sleeping eight hours at a stretch.

Still, you may never totally be able to abandon the habit of checking on your child's breathing (at least once in a while) until he's off to college out of sight, though not out of mind.

MOVING A SLEEPING BABY TO BED

'I'm a nervous wreck when I try to put my sleeping baby down in her cot. I'm always afraid she'll wake up – and she usually does.'

She's finally asleep – after what seems like hours of nursing on sore breasts, rocking in aching arms, lullabying in an increasingly hoarse voice. You rise ever so slowly from the glider and edge cautiously to the cot, holding your breath and moving only the muscles that are absolutely necessary. Then, with a silent but fervent prayer, you lift her over the edge of the cot and begin the perilous descent to the mattress below. Finally, you release her, but a split second too soon. She's down – then she's up. Turning her head from side to side, sniffing and whimpering softly, then sobbing loudly. Ready to cry yourself, you pick her up and start all over.

The scenario's the same in almost every home with an infant. If you're having trouble keeping a good baby down, wait ten minutes until she's in deep sleep, then try:

A high mattress. If you were a gorilla, you might be able to set your baby down in a cot with a low mattress without having to scale the rail or, alternatively, drop her the last 15 cm (6 in). Since you're only human, you will find it much easier if you set the mattress at the highest possible level (at least 10 cm (4 in) from the top of the rail); just be sure to lower it by the time your baby is old enough to sit up. If your cot has the option, lower the side rail before putting baby down to avoid having to bend over a high railing. Or, for the first few weeks, use a cot substitute such as a moses basket, carrycot or cradle, all of which may be easier to lift a baby into and out of. Often these offer the important plus of being rockable, so the rocking motion that started in your arms can continue after you bed baby down.

A little light. Though it's a good idea to get baby to sleep in a darkened room, be sure there's enough light (a nightlight will do) for you to see your way to the cot without bumping into a dresser or tripping over a toy – which is sure to jar you and your baby.

Close quarters. The longer the distance between the place where baby falls asleep and the place where you are going to put her down, the more opportunity for her to awaken on the way. So feed or rock her as close to the cradle or cot as possible.

A seat you can get out of. Always feed or rock your baby in a chair or sofa that you can rise from smoothly, without disturbing her.

The right side. Or the left. Feed or rock baby in whichever arm will allow you to put her in the cot most easily. If she falls asleep prematurely on the wrong arm, gently switch sides and rock or feed some more before attempting to put her down.

Constant contact. When baby is comfortable and secure in your arms, suddenly being dropped into open space, even for an inch or two, startles – and awakens. Cradle baby all the way down, back first, easing your bottom hand out from under just before you reach the mattress. Maintain a hands-on pose for a few moments longer, gently patting if she starts to stir.

A lulling tune. Hypnotize your baby to sleep with a traditional lullaby (she won't object if you're off-key) or an improvised one with a monotonous beat ('aah-ah aah-ah ba-by, aah-ah aah-ah ba-by'). Continue as you carry her to her cot, while you're putting her down and for a few moments afterwards. If she begins to toss, sing some more, until she's fully quieted.

CRYING

'We congratulated ourselves in the hospital on having such a good baby. We were home hardly a week when she started howling.'

If one- and two-day-old babies cried as much as they were destined to a couple of weeks later, new parents would doubtless think twice about checking out of the hospital with their newborns. Once they're safely ensconced at home, babies don't seem to hesitate to show their true colours, with all doing some crying, and many doing a considerable amount. Crying is, after all, the only way infants have of communicating their needs and feelings – their very first baby talk. Your baby can't tell you that she's lonely, hungry, wet, tired, uncomfortable, too warm, too cold or frustrated any other way. And though it may seem impossible now, you will soon be able (at least part of the time) to decode your baby's different cries and know what she's asking for (see page 117).

Some newborn crying, however, seems entirely unrelated to basic needs. Eighty to 90 per cent of all babies, in fact, have daily crying sessions of from fifteen minutes to an hour that are not easily explained. These periodic crying spells, like those associated with colic, a more severe and persistent form of unexplained crying, most often occur in the evening. It may be that this is the most hectic time of day in the home, with dinner being prepared, parents and siblings coming home from work and school, the family trying to eat, other children, if any, vying for attention; the hustle-bustle may be more than the baby can tolerate. Or it may be that after a busy day of taking in and processing all the sights, sounds, smells and other stimuli in her environment, a baby just needs to unwind with a good cry.

Some perfectly happy babies seem to need to cry themselves to sleep, possibly because of fatigue. If your baby cries for a few minutes before nodding off, don't be concerned. She will eventually outgrow this. What may help is a regular pre-bedtime ritual and enough rest during the day so she isn't overtired at night.

Meanwhile, hang in there. Though you'll be drying some tears for the next eighteen years or so, these probably tearless newborn crying spells are likely to be a thing of the past by the time your baby is three months old. As she becomes a more effective communicator and a more self-reliant individual, and as you become more proficient at understanding her, she will cry less often, for shorter periods, and will be more easily comforted when she does cry.

A sudden bout of crying, however, in a baby who hasn't cried a lot before could signal illness or early teething. Check for fever and other signs that baby isn't well or might be teething, and call the doctor if you note anything out of the ordinary.

COLIC

'My spouse and I haven't had dinner together since our baby was three weeks old. We have to take turns gulping our food and carrying him around while he cries for hours every evening.'

For the parents of a colicky baby, even a steak dinner becomes fast food, choked down to the accompaniment of indigestion-provoking screams. That the doctor promises baby will outgrow colic offers little consolation for their misery.

And if misery likes company, parents of colicky babies have plenty of it. It's estimated that one in five babies have crying spells, usually beginning in late afternoon and sometimes lasting until bedtime, that are severe enough to be labelled colic. Colic differs from ordinary crying (see previous question) in that the baby seems inconsolable, crying turns to screaming, and the ordeal lasts for three hours, sometimes much longer, occasionally nearly round-the-clock. Most often colicky periods recur daily, though some babies take an occasional night off. Doctors usually diagnose colic based on the 'rules of three': at least three hours of crying, at least three days a week, starting at about three weeks of age.

The baby with a textbook case of colic pulls his knees up, clenches his fists and generally increases his activity. He closes his eyes tightly or opens them wide, furrows his brow, even holds his breath briefly. Bowel activity increases and he passes gas. Eating and sleeping patterns are upset by the crying – the baby frantically seeks a nipple only to reject it once sucking is begun or dozes for a few moments only to awaken screaming. But few infants follow the textbook description exactly. No two babies experience exactly the same pattern and intensity of crying and associated behaviour, and no two parents respond in exactly the same way.

Colic generally begins during the second or third week of life (later in preterm infants), and usually gets as bad as it's going to get by six weeks. For a while, colic seems as though it will stretch on interminably, but by twelve weeks, it usually begins to diminish, and at three months (again, later in preterm babies) most colicky infants appear miraculously cured – with just a few continuing their problem crying through the fourth or fifth month. The colic may abate suddenly or gradually, with some good and some bad days, until they are all good.

Though these daily screaming periods, whether marathon or of more manageable duration, are usually dubbed 'colic', there is not a clear definition of exactly what colic is or how it differs, if it does, from other types of problem crying. Definitions and differences, however, matter very little to parents who are desperately trying to calm their infant during these prolonged crying spells.

What causes colic remains a mystery. Theories, however, abound. Many of the following now have been totally or partially rejected: colicky babies cry to exercise their lungs (there is no medical evidence of this); they cry because of gastric discomfort triggered by allergy or sensitivity to something in their mothers'diets if they are breastfeeding or in their formula if they are bottle-fed (this is only occasionally a cause of colic); they cry because of parental inexperience (colic is no less common in second or subsequent babies, though parents may handle the crying with more aplomb); colic is hereditary (it does not appear to run in families); colic is more common in babies whose mothers had complications in pregnancy or childbirth (statistics don't bear this out);

exposure to fresh air stirs up colic (in practice, many parents find that fresh air is the only way they can quiet their crying babies).

The latest research seems to point to a number of potential reasons why colic may occur in some babies:

◆ Overload. For the first few weeks of life, babies are able to block out the extraneous stimuli in their environment, probably so they can focus on sleeping and eating. Once they become more aware of the world around them, they sometimes take in more stimuli than they can handle. Bombarded all day long with sensations (new sounds, sights and smells), they can reach the early evening hours at sensory overload – overstimulated and overwhelmed. The result in babies who are particularly sensitive to stimuli (in some cases because they're extra alert): lots of crying, and sometimes colic. Fortunately, once babies acquire the ability to tune out the environment before overload occurs (usually by three months, occasionally not until five), bouts of colic end. In the meantime, if you think this might be the cause of your baby's colic, the try-everything approach (rocking, bouncing, driving, swinging, singing) may actually make things worse. Instead, watch how your baby responds to certain stimuli and steer clear of the offending ones (if baby cries harder when you rub or massage him, limit that kind of touching during colic; instead, try swinging him in a swing once he's old enough; see page 332).

◆ Immature digestion. Another theory is that a baby's immature digestive tract contracts violently when gas is passed, causing pain and, not surprisingly, lots of crying. When gas seems to be pulling the colic trigger, there are medications that may help (see page 185).

◆ Reflux. Recent research has found that one common cause of colic may be reflux. This form of reflux irritates the oesophagus (much like heartburn in an adult), causing discomfort and crying. If reflux seems to be the cause of the colic in your baby, some of the treatment tips on page 560 may help.

◆ Environment. One factor that does seem to contribute to an increase in colicky behaviour, though the reason for it isn't clear, is tobacco smoke in the home. And the more smokers in a household, the greater the likelihood of colic and the worse the colic will be.

◆ Milk supply problems. Insufficient milk or other breastfeeding problems is another possible cause of colic. Milk supply often diminishes in the early evening, just the time when the baby starts crying. If this is the cause of your baby's colic, improved breastfeeding technique or supplementation with pumped milk usually corrects the problem.

◆ Parental tension. The theory that babies are colicky because their parents are tense is a more controversial one. Though many experts believe it's more likely that it's the baby's crying that makes a parent tense, some insist that a parent who is very anxious may unconsciously communicate this to the baby, making him cry. It may be that although parental anxiety doesn't cause colic, it can make it worse.

What's reassuring about colic is that babies who have these crying spells do not seem to be any the worse for the wear (though the same can't always be said for their parents), either emotionally or physically – they thrive, usually gaining as well as or better than babies who cry very little, and display no more behavioural problems than other children later on. Children who cry vigorously as infants appear, in fact, more likely to be vigorous and active problem solvers as toddlers than those with limp cries. And most reassuring of all is the certainty that the condition won't last for ever. In the meantime, the tips on the following pages should help you deal with the problem. (See page 745 if you have an older child who's having trouble coping with baby's colic.)

SURVIVING COLIC

'This is our first baby and she cries all the time. What are we doing wrong?'

Relax. You're not guilty. The theory that a baby's colic is somehow the fault of the parents just hasn't held up. And, in fact, your baby would probably be doing just as much crying if you were doing everything right (which, of course, no human parent does, even with the benefit of experience). Colic, the latest research indicates, has to do with baby's development and not yours.

The 'rightest' thing you can do is to try to cope with your baby's crying as calmly and rationally as possible, since your tenseness will only compound your baby's. Keeping your cool in the face of colicky fire isn't easy, but knowing that you're not at fault can help. So can the tips you'll find in the next answer.

'Sometimes when I'm rocking the baby through his third hour of colic, and he won't stop screaming, I have this terrible urge to throw him out the window. Of course I don't – but what kind of parent am I to even think such a thing?'

The colic carry. *Some colicky babies are soothed by the pressure applied to their abdomen when they are carried in this position.*

You're a perfectly normal one. Even those otherwise qualified for sainthood couldn't survive the agony and frustration of living with a baby who won't stop crying without experiencing some feelings of anger – even fleeting animosity – towards him. And though few would admit it freely, many parents of chronic criers regularly have to fight off the same kinds of horrifying impulses you've been feeling. (If you find such feelings are more than momentary, and/or if you're afraid that you might really hurt your baby, get help immediately.)

There's no question that parents get the worst of colic. Though it can safely be said that the crying doesn't seem to hurt baby, it certainly does leave its mark on mum and dad. Listening to a crying baby is irritating and anxiety-provoking. Objective studies show that everyone, even a child, responds to the constant crying of a young infant with a rise in blood pressure, a speeding up of the heartbeat, and changes in blood flow to the skin. If the baby was born

PRESCRIPTION FOR COLIC

The desperate parent of a colicky baby often turns to the doctor for a magic potion (or, failing that, a prescription) to stop the crying. Unfortunately, there is no medicine that is known to completely cure colic in all infants, and because all prescription medications have side effects, most doctors prefer not to pick up their prescription pad routinely when treating these chronic criers. There is, however, one medicine for infants, widely used to treat colic in Europe, that may reduce or alleviate symptoms in some colicky babies. Its active ingredient is simethicone, the same antigas ingredient found in many adult preparations.

Though there is no clear scientific consensus that gas is the cause of infant colic, it is recognized that many colicky infants do seem gassy (whether this is a cause of the crying or an effect isn't clear), and studies show that reducing the gas may reduce the discomfort (and the crying). Because the body doesn't absorb the product, it is completely safe and has no side effects. If your colicky baby seems gassy, ask the doctor about simethicone drops. They are available under such brand names as Infacol and Dentinox Colic Drops.

Also promising, according to research, are probiotic drops. They appear to reduce – sometimes dramatically – crying in colicky babies, probably because they soothe gassy tummies. Ask your baby's doctor about the latest information on probiotic drugs. There are also herbal remedies that have been touted as cures for colic by both parents and doctors. However, many paediatricians caution that their safety is questionable. Don't give your baby medication, herbal or otherwise, without talking to your baby's doctor.

---

prematurely, was poorly nourished in the uterus or if the mother had toxaemia (preeclampsia/eclampsia), the pitch of his cry may be unusually high and particularly hard to tolerate.[5]

In order to survive the two or three months of colicky behaviour with some semblance of sanity, try the following:

Take a break. If you're the one who's been left holding the crying baby seven nights a week at colic time, the strain is going to take its toll not only on your parenting but on your health and your relationship with your spouse as well. So if there are two parents at home, make sure colic duty is divided up equally between the two of you (an hour on, an hour off, a night on, a night off; or whatever arrangement you find works best). A fresh set of arms (and a different rocking rhythm) sometimes even induces calm in a crying baby, which may make switching off frequently your best bet.

Then, make sure that you both take a break together occasionally – preferably at least once a week. Rely on paid help (but make sure you hire someone who is endlessly patient and experienced with crying babies) or impose on relatives or friends (but not relatives or friends who drop direct or indirect hints that the crying is your fault – it isn't). Go out to dinner (even if you're breastfeeding, you should be able to squeeze in a restful meal at a local restaurant), visit with friends, go to the gym, get a couple's massage or just take a long, quiet walk.

If you're the only parent in the house

---

5. If a baby's cry is inexplicably high-pitched, check with the doctor; such a cry could indicate illness.

(either all or some of the time), you'll need to call on help even more often; coping with a crying infant for hours a day every day is more than anyone can handle alone. Again, look to a baby-sitter, if you can afford one, a willing relative or friend (grandparents sometimes have a magical touch with fussy babies; friends who've been there and done that with their own children can offer perspective and experience). Even a young teenager whom you wouldn't consider leaving alone with your colicky infant can hold him or push him in the pushchair while you take a break nearby.

Give baby a break. Sure, it's important to respond to baby's crying, which is an infant's sole form of communication. But once you've met all his needs (feeding, burping, changing, comforting, and so on) without perceptibly altering his level of screaming, you can give him a break from you – by putting him down in his cot or cradle (on his back) for a little while. It won't hurt him to cry in his bed instead of your arms for ten or fifteen minutes while you do something relatively relaxing, such as lying down; checking e-mail; doing some yoga, visualization or meditation; watching television; or reading a few pages of a book (see Tune Out, below). In fact, it will do him good if you're a little less ragged and a little more refreshed when you pick him up again where you left off.

Tune out. To lessen the impact of your baby's wails, use earplugs – they won't block out the sound entirely, just dull it so it will be more tolerable. Tucked in your ears, they can help you relax during a break from baby or even while you're walking the floor with him. Or drown out the racket by listening to music on a portable CD player.

Get physical. Exercise is a great way to work off tension, something you've got plenty of. Work out at home with baby early in the day (see page 687), swim or exercise at a health club (wallop a punching bag if they have one) that has child-care services or take the baby for a brisk walk outdoors in his pram when he's fussy (which may help calm him while it calms you).

Talk about it. Do a little crying yourself – on any willing shoulder: your spouse's, your doctor's, a family member's, a friend's, even a stranger in a parenting chat room. Talking about it may not cure the colic, but you may feel a little better after sharing your saga. Most beneficial may be discussing your situation with other parents of colicky babies, particularly those who have weathered the storm successfully and are now sailing on clear waters; you may find some who are – or have been – in the same boat as you in parenting chat rooms. Just knowing you're not alone in the world of inconsolable babies can make a world of difference.

If you really feel violent, get help. Almost everyone is irritated by a constantly crying baby. But for some people, such crying finally becomes more than they can bear. The result is sometimes child abuse. You may be even more likely to cross that line if you're suffering from untreated (and possibly undiagnosed) postnatal depression (see page 676). If your thoughts of hurting your baby are more than fleeting, if you feel about to give in to the urge to strike or shake your baby or harm him in any way, get help *immediately*. Go to a neighbour's, if you can, and hand the baby over until you can collect yourself. Then call someone who can help you – your spouse, a relative, a close friend, the baby's doctor or your own or a helpline such as that run by

Serene (formerly known as Cry-sis), which provides emotional support and practical advice to parents dealing with excessive crying (020 7404 5011). Even if your powerful feelings don't lead to child abuse, they can start eroding your relationship with your baby and your confidence in yourself as a parent unless you get counselling (and if you're suffering from postnatal depression or psychosis, appropriate treatment) quickly.

SPOILING BABY

'We always pick our baby up when she cries. Are we spoiling her?'

Not sparing the comfort won't spoil the baby. In fact, studies show pouring on the comfort now – by picking her up within a couple of minutes whenever she cries and catering to all her needs – not only won't turn out a spoiled brat, it will turn out a happy, more self-reliant child who in the long run will cry less and demand less attention. She will also have a closer attachment to you (or to whoever it is who responds to her) and be more trusting. An additional plus: since she'll come calmly to breast or bottle, without a bellyful of air swallowed while screaming, she will have better feeding sessions.

Realistically, you won't always be able to pick up your baby the moment she starts crying (there will be times when you're in the bathroom, on the phone or taking dinner out of the oven). And there will be times when you'll need to take a break during colicky crying. Again, no harm done – as long as you're responding promptly most of the time.

DUMMY

'My baby has crying jags in the afternoon. Should I give him a dummy to comfort him?'

It's easy, it's quick, and for many babies it turns on the comfort and turns off the tears more reliably than a dozen hoarse choruses of 'Rockabye Baby'. Yet is the dummy the perfect panacea for crying babies that weary parents like you are searching for?

Probably not. Though it may come in handy in the short term (and may be nothing short of indispensable for babies who have a strong sucking need but haven't yet figured out how to get their fingers in their mouths), and is recommended for reasons of safety when baby is sleeping (keep reading to find out why), the benefits of the dummy don't come without some drawbacks. Consider the following before deciding whether or not to pop in a dummy, and, if you do, when to begin and how long to use it:

♦ Early dummy use can interfere with breastfeeding. Because of the potential for teat confusion, it's not a good idea to introduce a breastfeeding baby to the dummy until breastfeeding is well established. It shouldn't be used at all for a baby who isn't gaining weight at an adequate clip or one who is a poor nurser, because it may give him so much sucking satisfaction that he loses interest in suckling at the breast. Some studies have suggested that dummies may shorten the duration of breastfeeding, though it's hard to determine whether the dummy is actually the cause of early weaning or if dummy use is a marker of breastfeeding difficulties to begin with. Bottom line: if you're going to give a dummy to your breastfed baby, wait until he's nursing and gaining weight well.

♦ The dummy is in the parent's control. That can be a good thing – as when you've fed, rocked, sung, and pushed the pram for hours, yet nothing but

COPING WITH CRYING

No medication, pharmaceutical or herbal remedy, or treatment approach is a sure cure for a baby's crying, and some may actually worsen it. To complicate matters more, what may be soothing to one baby may step up squalling in another. But there are a number of strategies that may work – at least some of the time. When trying out various methods of baby calming, stick to one at a time, being sure to give each a fair trial before switching to another – otherwise, you may find you are trying, trying, trying and baby is crying, crying, crying. Here are a few tricks you can pull out of your parental hat the next time the crying starts:

Respond. Crying is your baby's only way of wielding any control over a vast and bewildering new environment, of communicating, of making things happen: 'When I call, someone answers'. If you regularly fail to respond, the baby may feel not only powerless but also worthless ('I'm so unimportant that no one comes when I call'). Though it may sometimes seem that you're responding in vain because no matter what you do, nothing helps, responding promptly to your baby's calls will eventually reduce crying. And, in fact, studies show that babies whose parents responded to them regularly and promptly in infancy cry less as toddlers. In addition, crying that's been left to intensify for more than a few minutes becomes harder to interpret – the baby becomes so upset, even he or she doesn't remember what started all the fuss in the first place. And the longer baby cries, the longer it takes to stop the crying. Of course, you don't always have to drop everything to answer baby's call if you're in the middle of taking a shower, draining the spaghetti or answering the doorbell. Baby's being left to cry for a couple of extra minutes now and then won't prove harmful – as long as the infant can't get into trouble while waiting for you. A ten- or fifteen-minute break taken from a colicky marathon of crying won't hurt baby, either – again, as long as he or she is in a safe place. (For particularly difficult cases of inconsolable crying, some experts suggest setting up a routine in which you let baby cry for ten or fifteen minutes in a safe place like his cot, pick him up and try to soothe him for another fifteen minutes, then put him down and repeat. If you're comfortable with this, it apparently won't cause any problems.)

Don't worry about spoiling your baby by responding promptly. You can't spoil a young infant. And more attention doesn't lead to increased dependency. In fact, quite the opposite is true: babies whose needs are readily met are likely to grow into more secure and less demanding children.

Assess the situation. Before deciding your baby is crying just for crying's sake, determine if there's a simple and remediable underlying cause. If you think it may be hunger, try breast or bottle, but don't make the mistake of invariably responding to tears with food. Even at this tender age, food should be a response to a need for food, not attention or comfort. If you suspect fatigue, try rocking baby to sleep – in your arms, a pram, a cradle or a baby carrier. If a wet nappy may be triggering the crying, change it. If baby seems too warm (perspiration is a clue), take off a layer or two of clothing, open the window, or turn on a fan or air conditioner. If cold may be the problem (neck or body feels cold to the touch), add a layer or turn up the heat. If baby began to cry when clothes were stripped off for a bath (most newborns dislike being naked), quickly cover him with a towel or blanket. If you think baby's being in the same position for too long may be causing discomfort, try a new position. If he's been staring at the same view for the last half hour, try changing it. If you've been inside all day, venture outside (weather permitting).

Get close. In societies where babies are carried papoose style, long periods of crying or fussiness in healthy children are unknown. This traditional wisdom seems to translate well in our culture, too; research has shown that babies who are carried in the arms or in a baby carrier for at least three hours every day cry less than babies who aren't carried as often. Not only does carrying your baby give him or her the pleasure of physical closeness to you (and after nine months of constant closeness, that may be just what baby's crying for), but it may help you tune in better to baby's needs.

Swaddle. Being tightly wrapped is very comforting to some young infants, at least during times of colicky distress. A few, however, intensely dislike swaddling; the only way you'll know which holds true for your baby is to give swaddling a try the next time colic begins (see page 144).

Give a cuddle. Like swaddling, cuddling gives many babies a sense of security; hold baby pressed close to your chest, encircled snugly by your arms. (And, as with swaddling, some babies prefer more freedom of movement and will balk at being held tightly.)

Try a little comfort. Comfort for a newborn comes in different packages. In addition to holding, wearing and cuddling your baby, try any or all of the following:

- Rhythmic rocking, in your arms, a pram, a cradle, a vibrating infant seat, automatic baby swing (when baby's old enough; see page 332). Some babies respond better to fast rocking than to slow – but don't rock or shake your baby vigorously, since this can cause serious whiplash injury. For some babies, rocking side to side tends to stimulate, rocking back and forth to calm. Test your baby's response to different kinds of rocking.

- Walking the floor with baby in a carrier or swing, or simply in your arms. Tried and true, it's tiring but it often works.

- A warm-water bath. But only if your baby likes the bath; some babies only scream louder when they hit the water.

- Singing. Learn whether your baby is soothed by soft lullabies, sprightly rhymes or pop tunes, and whether a light, high-pitched voice or a deep, strong one is more pleasing. If you hit on a tune your baby likes, don't hesitate to sing it over and over – most babies love repetition.

- Rhythmic sounds. Many babies are calmed, for example, by the hum of a fan, vacuum cleaner or tumble dryer, a tape recording of uterine gurglings, a parent's repeated 'sh' or a record that plays soothing nature sounds, such as waves breaking on the beach or wind blowing through trees.

- Laying on the hands. For babies who like to be stroked, massage can be very calming (though it can cause increased screaming in those who don't). You may find it relaxing to both of you to administer the massage lying on your back, baby face-down on your chest. (See page 301 for tips on baby massage.)

Add a little pressure. On baby's tummy, that is. The 'colic carry' (see illustration, page 184) or any position that applies gentle pressure to baby's abdomen (such as across an adult lap, with belly on one knee and head on the other), can relieve discomfort that might be contributing to the crying. Some babies prefer being upright on the shoulder, but again with pressure on their abdomens while their backs are being patted or rubbed. Or try this gas reliever: gently push baby's knees up to his or her tummy and hold for ten seconds, then release and gently straighten them; repeat several times.

Resort to ritualism. For babies who thrive on routine, having as regular a schedule as possible (feeding, bathing, changing, outing, and so on up to bedtime ritual) may reduce crying. If this seems to be the case with your baby (and you won't know unless you check the theory out), be consistent even to the method you use for soothing baby or reducing crying – don't go for a walk one day, ride around in the car the next, and use a baby swing the third. Once you find what works, stick with it most of the time.

Satisfy with sucking. Babies often need sucking for its own sake, rather than simply for nourishment. Some babies appreciate your help in getting their fingers (particularly their thumbs) to their mouths for their sucking enjoyment. Others prefer grown-up pinkies. Still others find pleasure in a dummy (as long as you give it only to calm baby after you've attended to other needs and once breastfeeding is well established).

Start fresh. A parent who's been struggling for an hour to soothe a sobbing newborn will almost invariably start to show signs of stress and fatigue, which the infant is certain to sense and respond to with more crying. Hand baby over to another pair of arms for a fresh start – the other parent's, a relative's or friend's, a sitter's – and the crying may cease.

Seek fresh air. A change to an outdoor locale will often miraculously change a baby's mood. Try a trip in the car, the baby carrier, or the pushchair. Even if it's dark out, baby's sure to find distraction in the twinkling of street and car lights. The motion will also almost certainly prove soothing. (If crying doesn't stop during a car ride, it can distract the driver – in that case, head home and try another trick.)

Control air. A lot of newborn discomfort is caused by swallowing air. Babies will swallow less of it if you keep them upright as much as possible during feeding and burping. The right-size teat hole on a bottle will also reduce air intake; be sure it isn't too large (which promotes gulping of air with formula) or too small (struggling for formula also promotes air swallowing). Hold the bottle so that no air enters the teat (or use an angled bottle or one with disposable liners), and be sure the formula is neither too hot nor too cold (though most babies do fine with unheated formula, a few seem disturbed by it). Be sure to burp baby frequently during feedings to expel swallowed air. One suggested pattern for burping: every 15 ml (½ fl oz) or every 30 ml (1 fl oz) when bottle feeding, between breasts when breastfeeding (or more often if baby seems to be gulping a lot or seems in discomfort mid-breast), and, in both cases, after feeding.

plunking that dummy in your baby's mouth will generate calm. Or it can become a bad thing – as when plunking that dummy in your baby's mouth becomes just a little too easy, and when what starts out as baby's crutch quickly becomes yours. The well-meaning parent who offers the dummy to make sure his or her baby has adequate opportunity to suck may soon be finding it convenient to pop in the dummy the moment the baby becomes fussy, instead of trying to determine the reason for the fussing or if there might be other ways of placating him. A parent may use it to get the baby off to sleep instead of spending time cuddling, to ensure quiet while on the phone instead of picking him up and consoling him, to buy his silence while grocery shopping instead of involving him in the interaction. The result may be a baby who can be happy only with something in his mouth, and who is unable to comfort himself any other way.

◆ Dummies at night can mean less sleep for everyone. Used at bedtime, a dummy can interfere with a baby's

Be entertaining. In the early months, some infants are content to sit and watch the world go by, while others cry out of frustration and boredom because there is, as yet, so little they are able to do on their own. Toting them around and explaining what you're doing as you go about your business, and making an extra effort to find toys and other objects in the environment for them to look at and later swat at and play with, may help keep them busy. On the other hand, an overstimulated baby may be more prone to crying, so know when to stop sending in the clowns and start bringing on the quiet comfort.

Excise excitement. Having a new baby to show off can be fun – everyone wants to see the baby, and you want to take him or her everywhere to be seen. You also want to expose baby to new experiences, to stimulating environments. That's fine for some babies, too stimulating for others (particularly young ones). If your baby is colicky, limit excitement, visitors and stimulation, especially in the late afternoon and evening.

Do a diet check. Be sure your baby isn't crying because of hunger. Lack of adequate weight gain or signs of failure to thrive (see page 159) can clue you in. Increasing baby's intake may eliminate the crying. If baby is bottle fed, ask the doctor whether the crying might be due to an allergy to the formula (though this isn't a likely scenario unless crying is accompanied by other signs of allergy). If you're breastfeeding, you might consider doing a check of your own diet, since there's the very slight possibility that the crying might be triggered by baby's sensitivity to something *you're* eating. See pages 171 and 172 if you suspect allergy.

Check with the doctor. While the odds are that your baby's daily screaming sessions are due to normal crying or colic, it's a good idea to discuss it with the doctor to make sure there's no underlying medical problem. Describe to the doctor the crying, its duration, intensity, pattern and any variation from the norm – all aspects that may provide clues to an illness.

Look for relief. This is one time it doesn't make sense to say, 'I'd rather do it myself'. Take advantage of any and every possibility for sharing the burden.

Wait it out. Sometimes nothing relieves colic but the passing of time. Living with it will be a struggle, but it may help to remind yourself (over and over and over again): This, too, shall pass – usually by the time baby's three months old.

learning to fall asleep by himself – which ultimately can mean less sleep all around the house. It can also interrupt his sleep when he loses it in the middle of the night and can't get back to dreamland without it – who do you think will have to rise to put it back in his mouth?

♦ Dummies can be a hard habit to break. Used temporarily, to satisfy the need for sucking when it's at its most intense, a dummy's harmless – and can help parents and baby over what would otherwise be a tough time. Used longer, it can become addictive for both – and a habit that can be increasingly tricky to kick as a malleable baby turns into a fiercely inflexible toddler.

In the long run, it's probably better for babies to learn – at least to some extent – to comfort themselves (or to be comforted by their parents) than to rely often on artificial aids such as a dummy. A thumb (or a fist) can do the job of providing extra sucking for comfort as well as a dummy, but it's in the baby's control, not the parents' (which may make it a harder habit to break). It's there whenever he needs it; can be plucked out when he wants to smile, coo, cry or otherwise express himself; and it won't cause nipple confusion.

Still, if you're desperate for some relief from your son's crying, and the dummy seems to do the trick – don't hesitate to use it. Give it a try, too, if your child has such a strong sucking need that you're finding your nipples have become human dummies (or baby is taking too much formula because he won't let go of the bottle teat). But use it wisely. *Never* attach a dummy to the cot, pram, playpen or pushchair or hang it around your baby's neck or wrist with a ribbon, string or cord of any kind – babies can be strangled this way. Use it in moderation and only when your baby really seems to need it (each time you consider plugging it in, you might ask yourself first whether it's you or the dummy baby wants). And to avoid development of a habit that's hard to break, plan to begin pulling the plug by the time he's three to six months old. Another reason to wean from the dummy sooner than later: long-term use of a dummy into the toddler years has been linked to recurrent ear infections.

Using a dummy at night and at nap times, on the other hand, does appear to be a smart move: research has linked dummy use during sleep with a reduced risk of SIDS. So even if you don't use one while baby's awake, consider offering it when he's ready to snooze. A dummy at night isn't a must, so don't worry if your baby doesn't like it (some babies don't), or if it falls out while he sleeps (it will).

HEALING OF THE UMBILICAL CORD

'The cord still hasn't fallen off my baby's belly button, and it looks really awful. Could it be infected?'

Healing belly buttons almost always look and smell worse than they actually are. What constitutes 'perfectly normal' in medical terms can actually send the weak-of-knee to the floor as fast as the climactic scene in a horror film.

Infection of the cord stump is unlikely, especially if you've been taking care to keep it dry. (Some doctors still recommend using alcohol swabs to promote healing and prevent infection, but studies show that the cord heals as well, and, in some cases, even faster, without the alcohol.) If you note redness in the surrounding skin (which could be due to irritation from alcohol applications as well as infection) or a discharge from the navel or from the base of the umbilical cord, particularly a foul-smelling one, check with your doctor. If infection is present, antibiotics will probably be prescribed to clear it up.

The cord, which is shiny and moist at birth, usually dries up and falls off within a week or two, but the big event can occur earlier, or even much later – some babies don't seem to want to give them up. Until it does drop off, keep the site dry (no tub baths), exposed to air (turn nappy down so it doesn't rub), and cleaned with alcohol *if recommended* (but try to protect the surrounding skin, perhaps coating with a baby lotion prior to swabbing or applying alcohol just to the base of the cord – not to the skin – with a cotton swab). When it does fall off, you might notice a small raw spot, or see a small amount of blood-tinged fluid oozing out. This is normal, and unless it doesn't dry up completely in a few days, there is no need for concern. If it is not completely closed and dry two weeks after the stump falls off, call the doctor. Occasionally, an umbilical granuloma (a small piece of scar tissue that looks bright red and moist) can develop after the cord has fallen off. It's usually treated with silver nitrate (to dry it out), tied off with a suture, and allowed to wither and drop off. If it doesn't, it can be removed (a very minor procedure).

UMBILICAL HERNIA

'Every time she cries, my baby's navel seems to stick out. What does that mean?'

It probably means that your baby has an umbilical hernia – which (before you start worrying) is absolutely nothing to worry about.

Prenatally, all babies have an opening in the abdominal wall through which blood vessels extend into the umbilical cord. In some cases (for black babies more often than white), the opening doesn't close completely at birth. When these babies cry, cough or strain, a small coil of intestine bulges through the opening, raising the umbilicus and often the area around it, in a lump that ranges from fingertip to lemon size. While the appearance of such a lump (especially when it's tagged with the term *hernia*) might be alarming, it's rarely cause for concern. The intestine almost never strangulates (resulting in the blood supply to the intestine being cut off) in the opening, and in most cases, the hernia eventually resolves without intervention. Small openings usually close or become inconspicuous within a few months, large ones by age two.

The best treatment for an umbilical hernia is usually no treatment at all. Home remedies that press the lump down (such as bellybands or binders) are ineffective and in some cases potentially harmful. Surgery to correct umbilical hernias is not recommended unless the opening in the abdomen is very large, is growing larger, or bothers baby. Often the paediatrician will suggest waiting until the child is six or seven before considering surgery, because most hernias will have closed by then. If, however, you see signs of strangulation – the lump does not recede after crying, can't be pushed in, suddenly becomes larger, is tender, baby is vomiting – go to A&E. Immediate surgery may be needed.

CIRCUMCISION CARE

'My son was circumcised yesterday and there seems to be oozing around the area today. Is this normal?'

Not only is a little oozing normal, it's a sign that the body's healing fluids are heading to the site to begin their important work. Soreness and, sometimes, a small amount of bleeding are also common after a circumcision and nothing to be concerned about.

Using double nappies for the first day will help to cushion the penis and also to keep the baby's thighs from pressing against it; this isn't usually necessary later. Usually, the penis will be wrapped in gauze by the doctor or *mohel* (a ritual circumciser of the Jewish faith). Some doctors recommend putting a fresh gauze pad, dabbed with petroleum jelly or other ointment, on the penis with each nappy change; others don't think it's necessary as long as you keep the area clean. You'll also need to avoid getting the penis wet in a bath (you probably won't be dunking your baby yet anyway, because the umbilical cord is not likely to have fallen off at this point) until healing is complete.

SWOLLEN SCROTUM

'Our son's scrotum seems huge. Should we be concerned?'

Probably not. A boy's testicles are encased in a protective pouch called the scrotum, which is filled with a bit of fluid to cushion them. Sometimes a child is born with an excessive amount of fluid in the scrotal sac, making it appear swollen. Called hydrocele, this condition is nothing to worry about since it gradually resolves during the first year, almost always without any treatment.

You should, however, point out the swelling to your doctor to be sure what you see isn't an inguinal hernia (more likely if there is also tenderness, redness, and discolouration; see page 231), which can either resemble a hydrocele or occur along with it. By examining your son, the doctor can determine if the scrotal swelling is due to excess fluid or if there is a hernia involved.

HYPOSPADIAS

'We were just told that the outlet in our son's penis is in the middle instead of the end. What will that mean?'

Every so often, something goes slightly awry during prenatal development of the urethra and the penis. In your son's case, the urethra (the tube that carries both urine and semen, but not at the same time) doesn't run all the way to the tip of the penis but opens elsewhere. This condition is called hypospadias and it affects approximately 1 in 200 newborn boys. First-degree hypospadias, in which the urethral opening is at the end of the penis but not in exactly the right place, is considered a minor defect and requires no treatment. Second-degree hypospadias, in which the opening is along the underside of the shaft of the penis, and third-degree hypospadias, in which the opening is near the scrotum, can be corrected with reconstructive surgery.

Because the foreskin may be used for the reconstruction, circumcision, even ritual circumcision, is not performed on a baby with hypospadias.

Occasionally, a girl is born with hypospadias, with the urethra opening into the vagina. This, too, is usually correctable with surgery.

SWADDLING

'I've been trying to keep my baby swaddled, like they showed me in the hospital. But she keeps kicking at the blanket, and it gets undone. Should I stop trying?'

The first few days of life on the outside can be a little disorienting – and even a little unsettling. After spending nine months snugly enveloped in the uterine cocoon, a newborn must adjust to the suddenly wide-open spaces of her new environment. Many child-care experts feel the transition can be made more comfortable if the security and warmth of the newborn's former home is simulated by swaddling, or wrapping, her in a receiving blanket. Swaddling also keeps the infant from being disturbed by her own jerky movements while she sleeps, keeps her more comfortable and content on her back, and keeps her warm in the early days when her thermostat is not at peak efficiency. (Though to avoid overheating, a baby should never be swaddled in a warm room.)

Just because a baby is swaddled in the hospital, however, doesn't mean it needs – or likes – to be swaddled at home. Many babies will continue to derive comfort from swaddling (and hence will sleep better) for a few weeks, some even longer. It may also help calm some colicky infants. On the other hand, some babies seem perfectly content without swaddling or obviously disturbed by it right from the start. A good rule: if swaddling seems to feel good to your newborn, do it; if it doesn't, don't.

All babies eventually outgrow the

need for swaddling once they become a little more active – and make this clear by trying to kick off the wrapping. At this point, swaddling during naps becomes potentially unsafe, since a kicked-off blanket poses a suffocation risk. For that reason, and because swaddling can interfere with a baby's ability to practise motor skills, babies shouldn't be swaddled once they become more active – unless they really seem to need that 'wrapped up' feeling during colic spells, in which case swaddling should be limited to those hours only.

KEEPING BABY THE RIGHT TEMPERATURE

'It seems too hot out for a sweater and hat, but when I bring my baby out in just his T-shirt and nappy, everyone who sees us comments that he's underdressed.'

As far as well-meaning strangers on buses, in stores and on the street are concerned, new parents (even if they're on their second or third child) can do no right. So get used to the criticism. But, for the most part, don't let it affect how you take care of your baby. Grandmothers and grandmotherly types will go to their graves claiming otherwise, but once a baby's natural thermostat is properly set (within the first few days of life), you don't normally need to dress him any more warmly than you dress yourself. (And, in fact, prior to that, too much clothing, especially in mild weather, can be as taxing to the newborn's heat-regulating mechanism as too little.)

So, in general, use your temperature comfort to gauge baby's (unless you're the kind of person who's always warm when everybody else is cold, or always cold when everybody else is warm). If you're unsure, don't check his hands for confirmation (as those 'well-meaners' will, with disapproving clucks of 'See! His hands are cold!'). A baby's hands and feet are usually cooler than the rest of his body, again because of an immature circulatory system. Don't take the fact that your baby sneezes a few times to mean he's cold either; he may sneeze in reaction to sunlight or because he needs to clear his nose.

But while you shouldn't listen to strangers, do listen to your baby. Babies will usually tell you that they are too cold (as they tell you most everything else) by fussing or crying. When you get this message (or if you're just not sure whether you've dressed him appropriately), check the nape of the neck, arms, or trunk (whichever is easiest to reach under baby's clothing) with the back of your hand for a temperature reading. If baby feels comfortably warm, maybe it's a hungry or tired cry you're hearing. (And if he's sweaty, he's probably complaining that he's overdressed; take a layer off.) If he's cool, add clothing or covering, or turn up the thermostat. If a young baby seems extremely cold, get him to a warm place right away, because his body probably can't produce enough heat to rewarm him even if he has a lot of covering. In the meantime, put him close to the warmth of your body, under your shirt if necessary.

The one part of a baby that needs extra protection in all kinds of weather is his head – partly because a lot of heat is lost from an uncovered head (especially a baby's head, which is disproportionately large for his body) and partly because most babies have very little protection in the way of hair. On even marginally cool days, a hat is a good idea for a baby under a year old. In hot, sunny weather, a hat with a brim will protect baby's head, face and eyes – but even with this protection (plus sunscreen), exposure to full sun should be brief.

A young baby also needs extra protection from heat loss when he's sleeping. In deep sleep, his heat-producing mechanism slows down, so in cooler weather, bring along an extra blanket or covering for his daytime nap in the pram. If he sleeps in a cool room at night, a blanket sleeper over his pyjamas will help him stay warm (quilts and duvets are unsafe coverings for a sleeping baby). Don't, however, put a hat on baby when you put him or her to sleep indoors – it could lead to overheating.

When it comes to dressing baby in cold weather, the layered look is not only fashionable, it's sensible. Several light layers of clothing retain body heat more efficiently than one heavy layer and the outer layers can be peeled off as needed when you walk into an overheated store or board a stuffy bus, or if the weather takes a sudden turn for the warmer.

An occasional baby falls outside the norm for body temperature control – just as the occasional adult does. If your baby seems cooler than you do, or warmer, all the time, then accept that fact. You may find in talking to your in-laws that your spouse was the same way as a baby. That means, for the cooler baby, more coverings and warmer clothes than you would usually need. For the warmer baby (you'll probably discover this because of heat rash even in the winter), it means fewer coverings and lighter clothes.

TAKING BABY OUT

'It's been ten days since I brought my baby home from the hospital and I'm starting to go stir-crazy cooped up in the house. When can I take her out?'

Unless your hospital and your home are connected by subterranean tunnel, you've taken your baby outside already. And barring a blizzard, a rainstorm or significantly subfreezing temperatures, you could conceivably have continued to take her outside every day since. The old wives' tales (which continue to be perpetuated by even not-so-old mothers and mothers-in-law) that have kept newborns and new parents captives in their own homes for two weeks postpartum and more aren't valid. A healthy, full-term baby is hardy enough to weather a stroll through the park, a quick trip to the supermarket, even a lengthy excursion to visit grandmother (though in flu season, you might want to limit baby's exposure to indoor crowds and the germs they carry, for the first six to eight weeks). Assuming you're up to the exercise (you're likely to need to spend a lot of time off your feet for at least the first postpartum week), feel free to plan that first escape from the confines of your home.

When you take baby out, dress her appropriately, protect her from weather extremes and always take along an extra covering if there's a possibility of a change for the cooler in the weather. If it's windy or rainy, use a rain cover on the pushchair or pram; if it's very chilly or extremely hot and humid, limit the amount of time your baby spends outdoors – if you're freezing or sweltering, she is, too. Avoid more than brief exposure to direct sunlight, even in mild weather. And, most importantly, if your outing is in a car, be sure your baby is properly harnessed in her rear-facing infant safety seat.

EXPOSURE TO OUTSIDERS

'Everybody wants to touch our son. The postman, the bus conductor, old women in stores, visitors we have in our home. I'm always worried about germs.'

There's nothing that cries out to be squeezed more than a new baby. Baby cheeks, fingers, chins, toes – they're all irresistible. And yet resist is just what most parents would like outsiders to do when it comes to their newborns.

Your fear that baby can pick up germs this way is a legitimate one. A very young infant is more susceptible to infection because his immune system is still relatively immature and he hasn't had a chance to build up immunities. So, for now at least, politely ask strangers to look but not to touch – particularly baby's hands, which usually end up in his mouth. You can always blame it on the doctor: 'The paediatrician said not to let anyone outside the family handle him yet'. As for friends and family, ask them to wash their hands before picking up baby, at least for the first month. And skin-to-skin contact should obviously be avoided with anyone who has a rash or open sores.

No matter what you do or say, expect that every once in a while your baby will have some physical contact with strangers. So if a friendly bank clerk tests your child's grasp on his finger before you can stop the transaction, just pull out a baby wipe and discreetly wash off baby's hands. And be sure to wash your own hands after spending time outdoors and before handling your baby. Germs from outsiders (and from door handles or shopping trolleys) can easily be spread from your hands to your baby.

As your baby gets older, however, he needn't – and shouldn't – be raised in an overly sterile environment. He needs to be exposed to a wide variety of 'bugs' in order to start building up immunities to those common in your community. So loosen up a little and let the germs fall where they may after the first six to eight weeks.

INFANT ACNE

'I thought babies were supposed to have beautiful skin. But my two-week-old seems to be breaking out in a terrible case of acne.'

It's unfair and usually inopportune (arriving just in time for a visit from the grandparents or the first formal portrait), but many babies go through bouts with 'adolescent' skin before they're a month old, let alone on the precipice of puberty. Infant acne, which affects around 40 per cent of all newborns, usually begins at two to three weeks and can often last until baby is four to six months old. No one knows for sure the cause of baby acne, but it is believed that such complexion problems have the same cause as many of the complexion problems of teenagers: hormones.

In the case of newborns, however, it's not their hormones that are causing the problems, but those of their mothers that are still circulating in their systems. These maternal hormones stimulate baby's sluggish sweat glands, causing pimples to crop up. Another reason for infant acne is that the pores of newborns aren't completely developed, making them easy targets for infiltration by dirt and the resultant blossoming of blemishes.

Don't squeeze, scrub with soap, slather with lotions, or otherwise treat your newborn's acne. Just wash it with water two or three times daily, pat it dry and it will clear within a few months, leaving no lasting marks.

SKIN COLOUR CHANGES

'My baby suddenly turned two colours – reddish blue from the waist down and pale from the waist up. What's wrong with her?'

Watching your baby change colour before your eyes can be frightening. And yet there's virtually nothing to fear when a newborn suddenly takes on a split-colour appearance, either side to side or top to bottom. As a result of her immature circulatory system, blood has simply pooled on half of your baby's body. Turn her gently upside down (or, if the colour difference is side by side, over) momentarily and normal colour will be restored.

You may also notice that your baby's hands and feet appear bluish, even though the rest of her body is pink. This, too, is due to immature circulation and usually disappears by the end of the first week.

'Sometimes when I'm changing my new baby I notice his skin seems to be mottled all over. Why?'

Purplish (sometimes more red, sometimes more blue) mottling of a tiny baby's skin when he's chilled or crying isn't unusual. These transient changes are yet another sign of an immature circulatory system, visible through baby's still very thin skin. He should outgrow this colourful phenomenon in a few months. In the meantime, when it occurs, check the nape of his neck or his midsection to see if he is too cool. If so, increase his clothing or covering. If not, just relax and wait for the mottling to disappear, as it probably will in a few minutes.

HEARING

'My baby doesn't seem to react much to noises. In fact, she sleeps right through the dog's barking and my older daughter's tantrums. Could her hearing be impaired?'

It's probably not that your baby doesn't hear the dog barking or her sister screaming, but that she's used to these sounds. Although she saw the world for the first time when she exited your uterus, it wasn't the first time she heard it. Many sounds – from the music you played on the stereo to the honking horns and screeching sirens on the street – penetrated the walls of her peaceful uterine home and she became accustomed to them.

Most babies will react to loud noise – in early infancy by startling, at about three months by blinking, at about four months by turning towards the source of the sound. But those sounds that have already become a part of the background Muzak of a baby's existence may elicit no response – or one so subtle the untrained eye misses it, such as a change in position or activity.

Most newborns are screened for hearing problems (see page 95). So it is likely that yours was screened and found to be fine. You can confirm this by asking your baby's doctor if the test was performed and what the results were.

If you're still concerned about your baby's hearing, try this little test: clap your hands behind her head and see if she startles. If she does, you know she can hear. If she doesn't, try again later; children (even newborns) have a wonderful way of ignoring or blocking out their environment at will and she may have been doing just that. A repeat test may elicit the response you want. If it doesn't, try to observe other ways in which your baby may react to sound: is she calmed or does she otherwise respond to the soothing sounds of your voice, even when she isn't looking directly at you? Does she respond to singing or music in any way? Does she startle when exposed to an *unfamiliar* loud noise? If your baby seems never to respond to sound, discuss this with her doctor as soon as it's practical. The earlier a child's hearing deficit is diagnosed and treated, the better the long-range outcome.

Testing is particularly important for high-risk infants, including those who weighed under 2.5 kg (5½ lb) pounds or had complications during delivery, those exposed in the uterus to drugs or infections (such as rubella) that can cause hearing problems, those with a family history of deafness and those with other serious abnormalities.

LOUD MUSIC

'My spouse likes to play loud rock music on the stereo. I'm afraid that it might damage our daughter's ears.'

All ears, young and old, have a lot to lose when they're exposed for long periods of time to loud music (whether rock, classical or any other type), namely, a certain amount of their hearing capacity. Though some ears are more naturally sensitive and prone to damage than others, in general the hearing of babies and small children is most susceptible to the harmful effects of overly loud sound. Damage to the ears can be either temporary or permanent, depending on the noise level and the duration and frequency of exposure.

How loud is dangerously loud? While a baby's crying might signal that music (or another noise) is too loud for her, don't wait for her protests before turning the volume down; a baby's ears don't have to be 'bothered' to be harmed. According to UK law, where the workplace noise level exceeds 90 decibels – a level that can easily be exceeded by a stereo set – an employer must provide hearing protection. If you don't have the equipment to measure the decibels your stereo is putting out when your spouse plays the stereo, you can set the volume safely by maintaining a level that can easily be talked over – if you have to shout, it's too loud.

VISION

'I put a mobile over my baby's cot, hoping the colours would be stimulating. But he doesn't seem to notice it. Could something be wrong with his vision?'

It's more likely there's something wrong with your mobile – at least with where it's hung. A newborn baby focuses best on objects that are between 20 and 35 cm (8 and 14 in) away from his eyes, a range that seems to have been selected by nature not randomly, but by design – it being the distance at which a nursing infant sees his mother's face. Objects closer to or further away from a baby lying in his cot will be nothing but a blur to him, although he will fixate on something distant that is bright or in motion if there is nothing worth looking at within his range of vision.

In addition, he will spend most of his time looking to his right or to his left, rarely focusing straight ahead in the early months. A mobile directly above his cot is not likely to catch his fancy, whereas one hung to one side or the other may. Few babies, however, show any interest at all in mobiles until they are three to four weeks old and many not until even later. (For safety reasons, remember to remove mobiles and gyms from the cot by the time baby can get up on his hands and knees, usually around four to six months.)

So your newborn can see, but not the way he will in three or four months. If you want to evaluate your baby's

KEEPING BABY SAFE

Babies are, despite their fragile appearance, pretty hardy. They don't 'break' when you pick them up, their heads don't snap off when you forget to support them, and they weather most falls without major injury. But they can be vulnerable. Even very young ones, who seem too tiny to get into trouble, do – sometimes the very first time they turn over or reach for something. To protect your baby from accidents that don't have to happen, be sure to follow *all* of these safety tips *all* of the time:

◆ In the car, always buckle your baby into an infant safety seat – no matter how far you're going or how fast or slow you'll be driving. Wear a seat belt yourself, and make sure whoever's doing the driving does, too; no one's safe unless the driver is. And never drink and drive (or drive when you're very tired or taking medication that makes you sleepy), or let baby ride with anyone who does. (See page 132 for more on safety for baby in the car.)

◆ If you bathe baby in a large tub, put a small towel or cloth at the bottom to prevent slipping. Always keep one hand on baby during the bath.

◆ Never leave your baby unattended on a changing table, bed, chair or sofa – not even for a second. Even a newborn who can't roll over can suddenly extend his or her body and fall off. If you don't have safety straps on your changing table, you should always keep one hand on your baby.

◆ Never put baby in an infant (or car) seat or carrier on a table, counter or any elevated surface; never leave baby unattended in a seat on *any* surface, even the middle of a soft bed (where suffocation is a risk should baby tip over).

◆ Never leave a baby alone with a pet, even a very well behaved one.

◆ Never leave baby alone in a room with a sibling who is under five years old. A game of peekaboo affectionately played by a preschooler could result in tragic suffocation for an infant. A loving but overly enthusiastic bear hug could crack a rib.

◆ Don't leave the baby alone with a sitter who is younger than fourteen, or whom you don't know well, or whose references you haven't checked. All sitters should be trained in infant safety and CPR.

vision, hold a penlight to one side of his line of vision, about 25 to 30 cm (10 to 12 in) from his face. During the first month, a baby will generally focus on the light for a brief period, long enough for you to know he's seeing it. By the end of the first month, some babies will follow as you move the light slowly towards the centre of their field of vision. Generally, not until three months will a baby begin to follow an object in a full 180-degree arc, from one side to the other.

Your baby's eyes will continue maturing during the first year. He probably will be farsighted for several months and not be able to perceive depth well (which may be why he's a perfect candidate for falling off changing tables and beds) until nine months. But though his vision isn't perfect now, he does enjoy looking at things – and this pastime is one of his most important avenues to learning. So provide him with plenty of visual stimuli. But don't overload his circuits – one or two

- Never jiggle or shake your baby vigorously (even in play) or throw him or her up into the air.

- Never leave baby alone at home, even while you move the car, or check the washing in the garden; it takes only seconds for an accident to happen.

- Never leave a baby or child alone in a car. In hot (or mild) weather, even keeping the windows down might not prevent the baby from succumbing to heat stroke. In any weather, a child snatcher on the prowl could quickly make off with the car's precious cargo.

- Never take your eyes off your baby when you're shopping, going for a walk, or sitting at the playground. A pushchair or pram makes an easy target for abduction.

- Avoid using any kind of chain or string on baby or on any of baby's toys or belongings – that means no necklaces, strings for dummies or rattles, no religious medals on chains, no ribbons longer than 15 cm (6 in) on cots or cradles. Make sure the ends of strings in hoods, gowns and trousers are knotted so they can't slip through, and never leave cords, string, ropes or chains of any kind around where baby might get to them. Be sure, too, that baby's cot, playpen and changing table are not within reach of electric cords (which present double danger), telephone cords, or venetian blind or drapery cords. All of these items can cause accidental strangulation.

- Don't place filmy plastics, such as dry cleaner bags or plastic bags, on mattresses or anywhere baby can get at them.

- Never leave an unattended infant within reach of pillows, toys or plush items, or let baby sleep on a sheepskin, plush-top mattress, beanbag, waterbed or a bed wedged against the wall. Always remove bibs and any hair ties or hair clips before putting baby down to sleep. Also consider keeping a fan on in your baby's room while he or she is sleeping; research suggests that the circulating air may reduce the risk of SIDS.

- Remove cot gyms when baby can pull up so they won't be used as a climbing step.

- Do not place a baby on any surface next to an unguarded window, even for a second, and even asleep.

- Use smoke detectors and carbon monoxide detectors in your home, and install them according to fire department recommendations.

eye-catchers at a time are about all he can handle. And because his attention span is short, change the scenery frequently.

Most young babies like to study faces – even crudely drawn ones and even their own in a cot mirror (though, of course, they won't recognize it as their own for many months to come). They prefer to gaze at things that are highly contrasted, such as black and white or red and yellow; complex objects to simple ones. They love looking at light: a chandelier, a lamp, a window (especially one through which light is filtered via the slats of vertical or horizontal blinds), will all attract their rapt scrutiny; and they are usually happier in a well-lighted room than in a dim one.

Vision screening will be part of your baby's regular checkups. But if you feel that your baby doesn't seem to be focusing on objects or faces or doesn't turn towards light, mention this to your doctor or health visitor at the next visit.

PHOTO FLASHES

'I've noticed that our baby blinks when the flash from our camera goes off. Could it be hurting his eyes?'

Only the most sought-after celebrities are as hounded by the popping of a camera's flash as a newborn baby whose paparazzi parents are determined to capture in pictures every detail of his first days of life. But, unlike celebrities, infants can't hide behind dark glasses when the flashing starts. To protect your baby's eyes against the possibility of injury from a flash that's too near him and from too intense and too close exposure to the camera lights, it's a good idea to take a few precautions during photo sessions. Try to keep the camera at least 100 cm (40 in) from baby and if your photographic equipment allows, bounce the light off a wall or ceiling instead of in baby's face. If you failed to take such precautions during previous shoots, don't worry. The risk of harm is exceedingly small.

CROSSED EYES

'The swelling is down around my baby's eyes. Now she seems cross-eyed.'

Babies are very obliging: they always give their parents something new to worry about. And most parents worry plenty when they notice their babies' eyes appear to be crossed. Actually, in most cases, it's simply extra folds of skin at the inner corners of the eyes that make the babies look cross-eyed. When the folds retract as baby grows, the eyes begin to seem more evenly matched. For extra reassurance, mention your concern at baby's next checkup.

During the early months, you may also notice that your baby's eyes may not work in perfect unison all the time. These random eye movements mean she's still learning to use her eyes and strengthening her eye muscles; by three months, coordination should be much improved. If it isn't, or if your baby's eyes always seem to be out of sync, then talk to her doctor about the problem. If there is a possibility of true crossed eyes (strabismus, in which the baby uses just one eye to focus on what she's looking at and the other seems aimed anywhere), consultation with a paediatric ophthalmologist is in order. Early treatment is important, because so much that a child learns she learns through her eyes and because ignoring crossed eyes could lead to 'lazy' eye, amblyopia (in which the eye that isn't being used becomes lazy and consequently weaker, from disuse).

TEARY EYES

'At first, there were no tears when my baby cried. Now her eyes seem filled with tears even when she's not crying. And sometimes they overflow.'

Tiny tears don't start flowing out of the tiny eyes of newborns until close to the end of the first month. That's when the fluid that bathes the eye (called tears) is produced in sufficient quantity by the glands over the eyeballs. The fluid normally drains through the small ducts located at the inner corner of each eye, and into the nose (which is why a lot of crying can make your nose run). The ducts are particularly minute in infants, and in about 1 per cent of babies – yours included – one or both are blocked at birth.

Since a blocked tear duct doesn't drain properly, tears fill the eyes and often spill over, producing the perpetually 'teary-eyed' look even in happy babies. But the clogged ducts are nothing to worry about; most will clear up by themselves by the end of the first year without treatment, though your baby's doctor may show you how to gently massage the ducts to hasten the clearing. (Always wash your hands thoroughly first before using massage; if baby's eyes become puffy or red, stop massaging and inform the doctor.)

Sometimes, there is a small accumulation of yellowish white mucus in the inner corner of the eye with a tear duct blockage, and the lids may be stuck together when baby wakes up in the morning. Mucus and crust can be washed away with water and sterile absorbent cottonwool balls. A heavy, darker yellow discharge and/or reddening of the whites of the eye, however, may indicate infection or another condition that requires medical attention. The doctor may prescribe antibiotic ointments or drops, and if the duct becomes chronically infected, may refer your baby to an ophthalmologist. Call the doctor immediately if a tearing eye seems sensitive to light or if one tearing eye looks different in shape or size from the other.

SNEEZING

'My baby sneezes all the time. He doesn't seem sick, but I'm afraid he's caught a cold.'

Hold off on the chicken soup. What your baby's caught isn't likely to be a cold but some amniotic fluid and excess mucus in his respiratory passages – a very common occurrence in young babies. And to clear it out, nature has provided him with a protective reflex: sneezing. Frequent sneezing (and coughing, another protective reflex) also helps the newborn to get rid of foreign particles from the environment that

make their way to his nose – much as sniffing pepper makes many adults sneeze. Your baby may also sneeze when exposed to light, especially sunlight.

FIRST SMILES

'Everybody says that my baby's smiles are 'just gas', but he looks so happy when he does it. Couldn't they be real?'

They read it in books and magazines. They hear it from mothers-in-law, friends with children, their paediatricians, perfect strangers in the park. And, yet, no new parent wants to believe that baby's first smiles are the work of a passing bubble of gas, rather than of a wave of love meant especially for mummy or daddy.

But, alas, it appears from scientific evidence so far to be true: most babies don't smile in the true social sense before four to six weeks of age. That doesn't mean that a smile is always 'just gas'. It may also be a sign of comfort and contentment – many babies smile as they are falling asleep, as they urinate or as their cheeks are stroked.

When baby does display his first real smile, you'll know it, and you'll melt accordingly. In the meantime, enjoy those glimpses of smiles to come – undeniably adorable no matter what their cause.

HICCUPS

'My baby gets the hiccups all the time – and for no apparent reason. Do they bother him as much as they do me?'

Some babies aren't just born hiccupers, they're hiccupers before they're born. And chances are, if your baby hiccuped a lot inside of you, he'll hiccup plenty in the first few months on the outside, too. But a newborn's hiccups, unlike the adult variety, don't have a known cause, though theories abound. One is that they are another of baby's reflexes, though they're frequently triggered by giggling later on. Another theory is that infants get hiccups when they gulp down formula or breast milk, filling their tummies with air. Unlike adult hiccups, they're not bothersome, at least not to baby. If they are to you, try letting your baby nurse or (if he's bottle fed) suck on a bottle, which may quell the attack.

USING DETERGENT ON BABY'S CLOTHES

'I've been using baby soap flakes to wash my daughter's clothes. But nothing seems to come clean, and I'm also getting tired of doing her loads separately. When can I start using our usual detergent?'

Although manufacturers of special baby laundry soaps wouldn't want it to get around, many babies probably don't need their clothes washed separately from the rest of the family's. Even the high-potency detergents that really get clothes clean, eliminating most stains and odours (the kind babies are very good at generating), aren't irritating to most infants when they're well rinsed. (Rinsing is most thorough, and stain-fighting powers are most effective, with liquid detergents.)

To test your baby's sensitivity to your favourite laundry detergent, add one garment that will be worn close to baby's skin (such as a T-shirt) to your next family load, being careful not to overdo the detergent or underdo the rinse. If baby's skin shows no rash or irritation, go ahead and wash her clothes with yours. If a rash does appear, try another detergent, preferably one without colours and fragrances, before deciding you have to stick with baby soap flakes.

One extra laundry step you may want to consider is pre-spotting to avoid those telltale yellow spit-up stains. Better still, tackle spit-up while it's still fresh.

What it's Important to Know: BABIES DEVELOP DIFFERENTLY

From the day a baby's born, the race is on – and it's a sure bet that most parents, rooting their offspring on from the starting line, will be disappointed if their entry doesn't make a good showing. If the child development chart shows that some babies start turning over at ten weeks, why hasn't their baby accomplished it by twelve weeks? If the baby in the next pushchair at the park grabbed an object at three and a half months, why hasn't their baby done it by then? If grandma insists all of her children sat up by five months, why is theirs still slumping at six?

But in this race, the child who comes in first in mastering early developmental skills doesn't necessarily finish in the money, while the one who moseys along developmentally doesn't necessarily finish out of it. Though the very alert baby may indeed turn out to be a bright child and a successful adult, attempts to measure infant intelligence and correlate it with intelligence in later years have not

TODAY'S SLOWER BABIES

Something you should definitely keep in mind when your compulsion to compare gets the best of you (and it will): babies today are developing later in some major gross motor skill categories than they used to. Not because they're less naturally precocious, but because they're spending less time on their tummies. Putting babies to sleep on their backs dramatically reduces the risk of SIDS, but it also temporarily slows motor development. With little opportunity to practise those skills babies used to practise on their tummies (such as rolling over and crawling), more babies are accomplishing these skills later.

Many are even skipping the crawling stage entirely, which isn't a problem unless a baby is skipping other developmental milestones as well, such as rolling over, sitting up, and so on. Parents can help their babies along by making sure they spend plenty of supervised playtime on their bellies from an early age. In the US the AAP recommends playing tummy time with baby 2 to 3 times each day for about 3 to 5 minutes, increasing the amount of time each time while the baby still enjoys the activity. There are tummy-time play mats available but a blanket and a soft, rolled towel under baby's chest (if you want – it's not necessary) will work just as well. Remember: *Back to sleep, tummy to play.*

been fruitful. The baby who seems to be a little slow, it appears, can also turn out to be bright and successful. Studies have shown, in fact, that one in seven children gains forty IQ points from the middle of the third year to the age of seventeen. That means an 'average' toddler can become a 'gifted' teenager.

Part of the difficulty, of course, is that we don't know how intelligence manifests itself in infancy, or even if it does. And even if we did know, it would be difficult to test for it because infants are nonverbal. We can't ask questions and expect answers, we can't assign a passage for reading and then test for comprehension, we can't present a problem to assess reasoning power. About all we can do is evaluate motor and social skills – and these just aren't equitable with what we later think of as intelligence. Even when we evaluate early developmental skills, our results are often in question; we never know whether a baby is not performing because of inability, lack of opportunity, hunger, fatigue or a momentary lapse in interest.

Anyone who's spent any time at all around more than one baby knows that children develop at different rates. Many of these differences are due more to nature than to nurture. Each individual seems to be born programmed to smile, lift his or her head, sit up and take first steps at a particular age. Studies show that there is little we can do to speed up the developmental timetable, though we can slow it down by not providing an adequate environment for development, by lack of stimulation or opportunity, by poor diet, by poor health care (certain medical or emotional problems can hamper development), and by simply not giving enough love and attention.

Infant development is usually divided into four areas:

Social. How readily your baby learns to smile, coo and respond to the human face and voice tells you something about him or her as a social being. Though some babies are naturally more serious than others, and some more social, a

WHAT MONTH IS IT, ANYWAY?

Trying to figure out what month baby's in – and which one you should be reading right now? Here's how it works: The 'First Month' chapter covers your baby's progress from birth to the first-month birthday; the 'Second Month' chapter gives you the low-down on your one-month-old (until he or she turns two months old), and so on – with the first year's expectations ending as baby blows out those first birthday candles.

major delay in this area could indicate a problem with vision or hearing, or with emotional or intellectual development.

Language. The child who has a large vocabulary at an early age or who speaks in phrases and sentences before the usual time is probably going to have a way with words. But the child who makes requests with grunts and gestures into the second year may catch up and do just as well or even better later on. Since receptive language development (how well baby understands what is said) is a better gauge of progress than expressive language development (how well baby actually speaks), the child who 'understands everything' but says very little is not likely to be experiencing developmental delay. Again, very slow development in this area occasionally indicates a vision or hearing problem and should be evaluated.

Large motor development. Some babies seem physically active from the first kicks in the womb; once born, they hold their heads up early, sit, pull up and walk early, and may turn out to be more athletic than most. But there are slow starters who end up excelling on the football field or tennis court, too. Very slow starters, however, should be evaluated to be certain there are no physical or health impediments to normal development.

Small motor development. Early eye-hand coordination, and reaching for, grasping and manipulating objects before the average age may predict a person will be good with his or her hands. However, the baby who takes longer to become skilled in this area is not necessarily going to be 'all thumbs' later on.

Most indicators of intellectual development – creativity, sense of humour and problem-solving skills, for example – don't usually become apparent until towards the end of the first year at the earliest. But, eventually, given plenty of opportunity, encouragement and reinforcement, a child's various inborn abilities will combine to create the adult who is a talented painter, a resourceful mechanic, an effective fund-raiser, a savvy stockbroker, a sensitive teacher, an all-star footballer.

The rate of development in the various areas is usually uneven. One child may smile at six weeks but not reach for a toy until six months, while another may walk at eight months but not talk until a year and a half. When an occasional child does develop evenly in all areas, this may provide a clearer clue to future potential. A child who does everything early, for instance, is likely to be brighter than average; the child who seems extremely slow in every area may have a serious developmental or health problem, in which case professional assessment and intervention (which can make a tremendous difference) is necessary.

Though children develop at different rates, each child's development –

assuming no environmental or physical barriers exist – follows the same three basic patterns. First, the child develops from the top down, from head to toes. Babies lift their heads up before they can hold their backs up to sit, and hold their backs up to sit before they can stand on their legs. Second, they develop from the trunk outwards to the limbs. Children use their arms before they use their hands, and their hands before they use their fingers. Development progresses not surprisingly, from the simple to the complex.

Another aspect of infant learning is the deep concentration directed towards learning a particular skill. A child may not be interested in beginning to babble while practising to pull up. Once a skill is mastered, another moves to centre stage, and the baby may seem to forget the old, at least for a while, so involved is he or she in the new. Eventually, your baby will be able to integrate all the various skills and use each spontaneously and appropriately.

But, in the meantime, don't worry when he or she seems to forget what was recently learned or looks at you blankly when called on to perform the most recently acquired skill.

No matter what your child's rate of development, what is accomplished in the first year is remarkable – never again will so much be learned so quickly. Enjoy this time, and let your baby know you're enjoying it. By accepting your baby's timetable as okay, you will be letting your child know that he or she is okay, too. Avoid comparing your child with other babies (yours or anyone else's) or with norms on developmental charts. The monthly development charts in this book are not meant to inspire such competition (or worry), in parents of babies who aren't achieving at the highest level. Rather, they're meant to give parents an idea of the wide range of normal, so they can be sure their babies don't have any developmental lags that might need looking into.

◆ ◆ ◆

CHAPTER 6

The Second Month

Chances are there have been plenty of changes around your house in the last month (and we're not just talking nappy changes). Changes in your baby, as he or she progresses from cute-but-unresponsive blob to an increasingly active and alert tiny person (who sleeps a little less and interacts a little more). And changes in you, as you begin feeling less the bungling beginner and more the (semi)-seasoned veteran. After all, you've probably got one-handed nappy changing down pat, you're a pro at burping (baby), and you can latch that little mouth onto your breast in your sleep (and often do). Of course, that still doesn't mean you're home free. While life with baby may be settling into a somewhat more predictable (though exhausting) routine, crying spells, cradle cap and nappy contents may still be keeping you guessing (and making frequent calls to the doctor). But as your baby and your parental poise grow, you'll be better equipped to face those everyday challenges without breaking a sweat. It might also help to keep in mind that you'll be getting a reward this month for all those sleepless nights: your baby's first truly social smile!

What Your Baby May Be Doing

All babies reach milestones on their own developmental time line. If your baby seems not to have reached one or more of these milestones, rest assured, he or she probably will very soon. Your baby's rate of development is normal for your baby. Keep in mind, too, that skills babies perform from the tummy position can be mastered only if there's an opportunity to practise. So make sure your baby spends supervised playtime on his or her belly. If you have concerns about your baby's development, check with the doctor. Premature infants generally reach milestones later than others of the same birth age, often achieving them closer to their adjusted age (the age they would be if they had been born at term), and sometimes later.

By two months, your baby . . . should be able to:

By the end of this month, most babies are able to lift their head to a 45-degree angle.

- smile in response to your smile
- respond to a bell in some way, such as startling, crying, quieting

. . . will probably be able to:

- vocalize in ways other than crying (e.g., cooing)
- on stomach, lift head 45 degrees

. . . may even be able to:

- hold head steady when upright

- on stomach, raise chest, supported by arms
- roll over (one way)
- grasp a rattle held to backs or tips of fingers
- pay attention to an object as small as a raisin (but make sure such objects are kept out of baby's reach)
- reach for an object
- say 'Ah-goo' or similar vowel-consonant combination

. . . may possibly be able to:

- smile spontaneously
- bring both hands together
- on stomach, lift head 90 degrees
- laugh out loud
- squeal in delight
- follow an object held about 15cm (6 in) above the baby's face and moved 180 degrees (from one side to the other), with baby watching all the way

What You Can Expect at This Month's Checkup

Each practitioner will have a personal approach to well-baby checkups. The overall organization of the physical exam, as well as the number and type of assessment techniques used and procedures performed, will also vary with the individual needs of the child. But, in general, you can expect the following at a checkup when your baby is about two months old:

- Questions about how you and baby and the rest of the family are doing at home, and about baby's eating, sleeping, and general progress.
- Measurement of baby's weight, length and head circumference, and plotting of progress since birth.
- Physical exam, including a recheck of any previous problems.

MAKING THE MOST OF THOSE MONTHLY CHECKUPS

Even healthy babies spend a lot of time at the doctor's clinic. Well-baby checkups, which are scheduled every month or two during the first year, allow the doctor to keep track of your baby's growth and development, ensuring that everything's on target. But they're also the perfect time for you to ask the long list of questions you've accumulated since your last visit, and to walk away with a wealth of advice on how to keep your 'well baby' well.

To make sure you make the most of a well-baby visit:

♦ Time it right. When scheduling appointments, try to steer clear of nap time, lunchtime and any time your baby's typically fussy. And go for an empty waiting room, avoiding peak hours at the doctor's surgery, if possible. Mornings are usually quieter because older children are in school – so, in general, a prelunch appointment will beat the four o'clock rush. And if you feel you'll need extra time (you have even more questions and concerns than usual), ask for it so it can be scheduled into the visit. That way, you won't feel quite as hurried.

♦ Fill 'er up. A hungry patient is a cranky and uncooperative patient. So show up for your well-baby visits with a well-fed baby (once finger foods have been started, you can also bring a snack along for the waiting room). Keep in mind, however, that overfilling the tank just before the appointment may mean baby will be ripe for spitting once the exam begins.

♦ Dress for undressing success. When choosing baby's wardrobe for the visit, think easy-on, easy-off. Skip outfits with lots of tiny buttons or poppers that take forever to do and undo, or snug clothes that are difficult to pull on and off. And don't be too quick to undress; if your baby hates being naked, wait until the exam is about to begin before stripping down.

♦ Write it down. Remember those two hundred questions you wanted to ask the doctor? You won't, once you've spent twenty minutes in the waiting room and another twenty in the exam room trying to keep your baby (and yourself) calm. So instead of relying on your memory, bring a list you can read off. Pack a pen, too, so you can write down the answers to those questions, plus any other advice and instructions the doctor dispenses. You can also use it to record baby's height, weight, immunizations received that visit, and so on.

♦ Make baby comfortable. Few babies enjoy the poking and prodding of a doctor's exam – but most enjoy it even less when it takes place on a cold, uncomfortable exam table. Ask the doctor if he or she can perform most of the exam while baby's on your lap.

♦ Trust your instincts. Your doctor sees your baby only once a month – you see your baby every day. Which means that you may notice subtle things the doctor doesn't. If you feel something isn't right with your child – even if you're not sure what it is – make sure the doctor knows. Remember, you don't need a medical degree to be a valuable partner in your baby's health care. Sometimes the keenest diagnostic tool is a parent's intuition.

◆ Developmental assessment. The examiner may actually put baby through a series of 'tests' to evaluate head control, hand use, vision, hearing and social interaction or may simply rely on observation plus your reports on what baby is doing.

◆ Immunizations, if baby is in good health and there are no other contraindications. See recommendations, page 227.

◆ Guidance about what to expect in the next month in relation to such topics as feeding, sleeping and development, and advice about infant safety.

Questions you may want to ask, if the doctor hasn't already answered them:

◆ What reactions, if any, can you expect baby to have to the immunizations? How should you treat them? Which reactions should you call about?

Also raise concerns that have come up over the past month about baby's health, feeding issues or family adjustment. Jot down information and instructions from the doctor. Record all pertinent information (baby's weight, length, head circumference, birthmarks, immunizations, illnesses, medications given, test results, and so on) in a permanent health record.

Feeding Your Baby:
INTRODUCING . . . THE BOTTLE

Sure, breastfeeding's ideal – the very best way to feed a baby. But as easy and practical as it is (now that you've, hopefully, got the hang of it), it does have its limitations, the most significant one being: you can't breastfeed your baby unless you're with your baby.

In some cultures, mothers and babies are never further than a baby sling apart, making round-the-clock breastfeeding not just doable but incredibly efficient, and making introducing the bottle completely unnecessary. But in our culture, even young babies are often apart from their mothers at a long enough distance and for a long enough time to require one or more supplementary feedings (that is,

---

BOTTLE-FREE

Not bringing on the bottle? That's fine too; there's no rule that says a baby must be introduced to the bottle. There are a number of reasons some mothers choose to keep their babies bottle free:

◆ They have a baby who rejects the bottle. Mothers who don't have a compelling reason to supplement may then choose not to push the bottle agenda.

◆ Concern that if baby becomes dependent on a bottle, weaning will have to be accomplished twice: first from the breast, then from the bottle. These mothers usually start their babies on a cup as soon as they can sit supported, and use a cup for supplementary feedings of breast milk, and later for other drinks.

SUPPLEMENTATION MYTHS

MYTH: Supplementing with formula (or adding cereal to a bottle) will help baby sleep through the night.
Reality: Babies sleep through the night when they are developmentally ready to do so. Bringing on bottles of formula or introducing cereal prematurely won't make that bright day (the one when you'll wake up realizing you had a full night's sleep) dawn any faster. Researchers have found no relationship between night-time food and sleep.

MYTH: Breast milk alone isn't enough for my baby.
Reality: Exclusively breastfeeding your baby for six months provides him with all the nutrients he needs. After six months, a combo of breast milk and solids can continue nourishing your growing baby well without adding formula.

MYTH: Giving formula to my baby won't hurt my milk supply.
Reality: Any time you give something other than breast milk to your baby (formula or solid food), your milk supply diminishes. The less breast milk your baby takes, the less milk your breasts make. But waiting until breastfeeding is well established can minimize the effect supplementary bottles of formula have on breastfeeding.

the replacement of breastfeeding sessions with a bottle of either expressed breast milk or formula).

Though plenty of mothers choose not to introduce the bottle at all, and can manage to stick close enough to baby enough of the time that they don't ever have to, most do introduce a bottle at some point (so they can have an occasional afternoon or evening away from baby, because they're going back to work, or because the baby is not gaining sufficient weight on breast milk alone, for instance).

Even if you don't plan on giving bottles regularly, it may be a good idea to express and freeze enough breast milk to fill six bottles – just in case. This will give you a backup supply if you become sick, you're temporarily taking medication that might pass into your milk, or you're called out of town unexpectedly. Even if your baby has never taken a bottle, it may be easier for him or her to accept one if it's filled with familiar breast milk rather than with unfamiliar formula. See page 156 for freezer time limits on breast milk; as batches of the emergency cache expire, you may need to replace them with fresh ones.

What's in the Bottle?

Breast milk. Filling a bottle with expressed breast milk is usually uncomplicated (once you've mastered the art of pumping) and allows a mother to feed her baby a breast milk–only diet – even when she and baby are apart. (To avoid nipple confusion, wait until breastfeeding is well established before bringing on the bottle; see page 86).

Formula. Supplementing with formula, while obviously as easy as opening a can, may have drawbacks if started too early on in the breastfeeding relationship. When breastfeeding is going well, a bottle of formula can interfere with the breast milk supply and actually create

WINNING BABY OVER

Ready to offer that first bottle? If you're lucky, baby will take to it like an old friend – eagerly latching on and lapping up the contents. Or, maybe more realistically, he or she may take a little time to get warmed up to this unfamiliar food source. Keeping these tips in mind will help win baby over:

◆ Time it right. Wait until your baby is both hungry (but not frantically so) and in a good mood before attempting to initiate the bottle.

◆ Hand it over. The first few bottles are more likely to be accepted if they are offered by someone other than you – preferably when you're not in the same room for baby to complain to. The substitute feeder should cuddle and talk to the baby during the feeding, just as you would when nursing.

◆ Keep it covered. If you have to offer that first bottle yourself, it may help to keep your breasts well camouflaged (don't try to bottle feed braless or in a low-cut blouse; think heavy sweaters instead) and to distract the baby with background music, a toy or another form of entertainment. Too much distraction, however, and your baby may want to play, not drink.

◆ Pick the right teat. If your baby tries out the teat, then drops it with seeming disapproval, try a different type of teat the next time. For a baby who uses a dummy, a teat that is similar in shape may work.

◆ Be a sneak. If you're meeting resistance to the bottle, sneak it in during sleep. Have your bottle giver pick up your sleeping baby and try to give the bottle then. In a few weeks baby may accept the bottle when awake.

---

problems where there weren't any. When breastfeeding isn't going well, a bottle of formula can make existing problems even worse. Once breastfeeding is well established (usually around six to eight weeks), however, many women find they can successfully combine breastfeeding and formula feeding (see page 85).

MIX IT UP

Don't have enough expressed milk to make up a complete bottle? No need to throw all that hard work down the drain. Instead, mix formula with the expressed milk to fill the bottle. Less waste – and your baby will be getting enzymes from the breast milk that will help digest the formula better.

Some women choose not to supplement with formula for other reasons, including the desire to breastfeed for the recommended one year or longer (studies show a significant relationship between formula supplementation and early weaning) and to prevent or delay allergy from cow's milk formula when there's a family history of allergies.

MAKING THE INTRODUCTION

When to begin. Some babies have no difficulty switching from breast to bottle and back again right from the start, but most do best with both if the bottle isn't introduced until at least three weeks, preferably five weeks. Earlier than this, bottle feedings may interfere with the

SUPPLEMENTING WHEN BABY ISN'T THRIVING

Occasionally, formula supplementation is recommended because baby isn't doing well on breast milk alone. This often leaves a mother feeling conflicted. On the one hand, she hears that giving a bottle in such a situation may totally wipe out her chances of breastfeeding successfully; on the other, she's told by the doctor that if she doesn't start supplementing her baby's diet with formula, the health consequences could be serious. The best solution in many such cases is the supplemental nutrition system, shown on page 161, which provides a baby with the formula he or she needs to begin thriving, while stimulating mum's breasts to produce more breast milk.

successful establishment of breastfeeding, and babies may experience nipple confusion because dining at breast and bottle call for different sucking techniques. Much later than this, many babies reject rubber 'nipples' in favour of their beloved mama's familiar fleshy ones.

How much breast milk or formula to use. One of the beauties of breastfeeding is that baby eats to appetite, not to a specified amount of formula you're pushing. As soon as you start using a bottle, it's easy to succumb to the numbers game. Resist. Tell your baby's care provider (and yourself) to give your baby only as much as he or she wants, with no prodding to finish any particular amount. The average 4-kg (9-lb) baby may take as much as 170 ml (6 fl oz) at a feeding, or less than 60 ml (2 fl oz).

Getting baby used to the bottle. If your schedule will require your regularly missing two feedings during the day, switch to the bottle one feeding at a time, starting at least two weeks before you plan to go back to work. Give your baby a full week to get used to the single bottle feeding before moving on to two. This will help not only baby but also your body adjust gradually, if you are planning to supplement with formula rather than breast milk. The wonderful supply-and-demand mechanism that controls milk production will cut back as you do, making you more comfortable when you're finally back on the job.

Keeping yourself comfortable. If you plan to give a bottle only occasionally, nursing thoroughly on (or expressing from) both breasts before going out will make fullness and leakage less of a problem. Be sure your baby won't be fed too close to your return (less than two hours is probably too close) so that if you are uncomfortably full, you can nurse as soon as you get home.

Whether you choose to supplement with breast milk or formula, you should keep in mind that it will probably be necessary for you to express milk if you will be away from your baby for more than three or four hours, to help prevent clogging of milk ducts, leaking and a diminishing milk supply. The milk can be either collected and saved for future feedings or disposed of.

What You May Be Concerned About

SMILING

'My son is five weeks old, and I thought he would be smiling real smiles by now, but he doesn't seem to be.'

Cheer up. Even some of the happiest babies don't start true social smiling until six or seven weeks of age. And once they start smiling, some are just naturally more smiley than others. You'll be able to distinguish the first real smile from those tentative practice ones by the way the baby uses his whole face – not just his mouth. Though babies don't smile until they're ready, they're ready faster when they're talked to, played with and cuddled a lot. So smile at your baby and talk to him often, and very soon he'll be matching you grin for grin.

COOING

'My six-week-old baby makes a lot of breathy vowel sounds but no consonants at all. Is she on target speechwise?'

With young babies, the 'ayes' – and the *a*'s, *e*'s, *o*'s and *u*'s – have it. It's the vowel sounds they make first, somewhere between the first few weeks and the end of the second month. At first the breathy, melodic (and adorable) cooing and throaty gurgles seem totally random, and then you'll begin to notice they're directed at you when you talk to your baby, at a stuffed animal who's sharing her playpen, at a mobile beside her that's caught her eye, at her own reflection in the cot mirror, or even at a duck on the bumper. These vocal exercises are often practised as much for her own pleasure as for yours; babies actually seem to love listening to their own voices. In the process, baby is also making verbal experiments and discovering which combinations of throat, tongue and mouth actions make what sounds.

For mummy and daddy, cooing is a welcome step up from crying on the communication ladder. And it's just the beginning. Within a few weeks to a few months, baby will begin adding laughing

---

LOOK WHO'S TALKING

Think those adorable 'ba-ba-ba's are just baby babble? They're actually the beginnings of spoken language – baby's first attempts at figuring out how the other half (the adult half, that is) speaks. But here's an interesting baby factoid that researchers (who have spent a great deal of time studying what comes out of the mouths of babes) have uncovered: these early articulations of language typically come out of the right side of baby's mouth (the side controlled by the left side of the brain, the hemisphere that's in charge of language). When babies babble just for pleasure's sake (not for language

practice), they get the whole mouth moving. When they smile, they apparently use the left side of the mouth (which is mission control for emotions).

But before you try this at home with your baby, here's something else you need to know: the differences in mouth movements are so subtle that you'd have to have a PhD in linguistics to distinguish a left movement from a right. So leave such analyses to the folks in the lab. Instead, sit back and enjoy all those adorable sounds – no matter which side of baby's mouth they come out of.

HOW DO YOU TALK TO A BABY?

The roads to communication with a baby are endless, and each parent travels some more than others. Here are some you may want to take, now or in the months ahead:

Do a running commentary. Don't make a move, at least when you're around your baby, without talking about it. Narrate the dressing process: 'Now I'm putting on your nappy . . . here goes the T-shirt over your head . . . now I'm buttoning your dungarees'. In the kitchen, describe the washing of the dishes, or the process of seasoning the pasta sauce. During the bath, explain about soap and rinsing, and that a shampoo makes the hair shiny and clean. It doesn't matter that your baby hasn't the slightest inkling of what you're talking about. Blow-by-blow descriptions help get you talking and baby listening – thereby starting him or her on the path to understanding.

Ask a lot. Don't wait until your baby starts having answers to start asking questions. Think of yourself as a reporter, your baby as an intriguing interviewee. The questions can be as varied as your day: 'Would you like to wear the red trousers or the green dungarees?' 'Isn't the sky a beautiful blue today?' 'Should I buy green beans or broccoli for dinner?' Pause for an answer (one day your baby will surprise you with one),

and then supply the answer yourself, out loud ('Broccoli? Good choice').

Give baby a chance. Studies show that infants whose parents talk *with* them rather than *at* them learn to talk earlier. Give your baby a chance to get in a coo, a gurgle or a giggle. In your running commentaries, be sure to leave some openings for baby's comments.

Keep it simple – some of the time. Though right now your baby would probably derive listening pleasure from a dramatic recitation of Hamlet's soliloquy or an animated assessment of the economy, as he or she gets a bit older, you'll want to make it easier to pick out individual words. So at least part of the time, make a conscious effort to use simple sentences and phrases: 'See the light', 'Bye-bye', 'Baby's fingers, baby's toes', and 'Nice doggie'.

Put aside pronouns. It's difficult for a baby to grasp that 'I' or 'me' or 'you' can be mummy, or daddy, or grandma, or even baby – depending on who's talking. So most of the time, refer to yourself as 'mummy' or 'daddy' (or 'grandma') and to your baby by name: 'Now Daddy is going to change Amanda's nappy'.

Raise your pitch. Most babies prefer a high-pitched voice, which may be why women's

---

out loud (usually by three and a half months), squealing (by four and a half months), and a few consonants to her repertoire. The range for initiating consonant vocalizations is very broad – some make a few consonant-like sounds in the third month, others not until five or six months, though four months is about average.

When babies begin experimenting with consonants, they usually discover one or two at a time, and repeat the

same single combination (*ba* or *ga* or *da*) over and over and over. The next week, they may move on to a new combination, seeming to have forgotten the first. They haven't, but since their powers of concentration are limited, they usually work on mastering one thing at a time. They also love repetition.

Following the two-syllable, one-consonant sounds (*a-ga, a-ba, a-da*) come singsong strings of consonants (*da-da-da-da-da-da*) called 'babble,' at six months

voices are usually naturally higher-pitched than men's, and why most mothers' (and fathers') voices climb an octave or two when addressing their infants. Try raising your pitch when talking directly to your baby, and watch the reaction. (A few infants prefer a lower pitch; experiment to see which appeals to yours.)

Bring on the baby talk . . . or not. If the silly stuff ('Who's my little bunny-wunny?') comes naturally to you, babble away in baby talk. If it doesn't, feel free to skip it (see next page). If you're big on baby talk, don't forget to throw some correct, more adult English into your conversations with your infant, too, so that he or she won't grow up thinking all words end with a *y* or *ie*.

Stick to the here and now. Though you can muse about almost anything to your baby, there won't be any noticeable comprehension for a while. As comprehension does develop, you will want to stick more to what the baby can see or is experiencing at the moment. A young baby doesn't have a memory for the past or a concept of the future.

Imitate. Babies love the flattery that comes with imitation. When baby coos, coo back; when he or she utters an 'Ahh', utter one, too. Imitation will quickly become a game that you'll both enjoy, and which will set the foundation for baby's imitating your language – it will also help build self-esteem ('What I say matters!').

Set it to music. Don't worry if you can't carry a tune – little babies are notoriously undiscriminating when it comes to music. They'll love what you sing to them whether it's a current hit, an old favourite or just some nonsense you've set to a familiar tune. If your sensibilities (or your neighbours') prohibit a song, then singsong will do. Most nursery rhymes entrance even young infants (invest in an edition of *Mother Goose* if your memory fails you). And accompanying hand gestures, if you know some or can make some up, double the delight. Your baby will quickly let you know which are favourites, and which you'll be expected to sing over and over – and over – again.

Read aloud. Though at first the words will have no meaning to baby, it's never too early to begin reading some simple rhyming stories or board books out loud. When you aren't in the mood for baby talk and crave some adult-level stimulation, share your love of literature (or recipes or gossip or politics) with your little one by reading what you like to read, aloud.

Take your cues from baby. Incessant chatter and song can be tiresome for anyone, even an infant. When your baby becomes inattentive to your wordplay, closes or averts his or her eyes, becomes fussy or cranky, or otherwise indicates the verbal saturation point has been reached, give it a rest.

on the average. By eight months, many babies can produce word-like double consonants (*da-da, ma-ma, ha-ha*), usually without associating any meaning with them until two or three months later. (To fathers' delight and mothers' dismay, *da-da* generally comes before *mama*.) Mastery of *all* the consonants doesn't come until much later, often not until four or five years of age – occasionally even later.

'Our baby doesn't seem to make the same kind of cooing sounds that his older brother made at six weeks. Should we be concerned?'

Some normal babies develop language skills earlier than average, some later. About 10 per cent of babies start cooing before the end of the first month and another 10 per cent don't start until nearly three months, the rest somewhere in between. Some start with strings of consonants before the four and a half month mark; others don't string consonants until past eight months. The early verbalizers may end up very strong in language skills (though the evidence isn't that clear); those who lag far behind, in the lowest 10 per cent, may have a physical or developmental problem, but this isn't clear either. Certainly, it's too early to be concerned that this might be the case with your baby, since he's still well within the norm.

If it seems to you over the next several months that your baby consistently, in spite of your encouragement, falls far below the monthly milestones in each chapter, speak to your doctor about your concerns. A hearing evaluation or other tests may be in order. It may turn out that you are so busy that you aren't really noticing your baby's vocal achievements (this sometimes happens with second children) – or that everyone else in the household (including his older brother) is making so much noise he can't get a coo in edgeways. In the less likely case that there actually is a problem, early intervention is often able to remedy it.

BABY TALK

'Other parents seem to know how to talk to their babies. But I don't know what to say to my six-week-old, and when I try, I feel like an absolute idiot. I'm afraid that my inhibitions will slow down his language development.'

They're tiny. They're passive. They can't talk back. And, yet, for many novice mothers and fathers, newborn babies are the most intimidating audience they'll ever face. The undignified, high-pitched baby talk that seems to come naturally to other parents eludes them, leaving them tongue-tied – and feeling guilty over the awkward silence that envelops the nursery.

Though your baby will learn your language even if you never learn his, his speech will develop faster and better if you make a conscious effort at early communication. Babies who aren't communicated with at all suffer not just in language development but in all areas of growth. But that rarely happens. Even the parent who is bashful about baby talk communicates with his or her baby all day long – while cuddling him, responding to his crying, singing him a lullaby, saying, 'It's time for a walk', or muttering, 'Oh, not the phone again'. Parents teach language when they talk to each other as well as when they talk to their baby; babies pick up almost as much from secondhand dialogue as they do when they're part of a conversation.

So although it's not likely that your baby is going to spend the next year in the company of a silent parent, there are ways to expand your baby-word power, even if you're the kind of adult to whom baby talk doesn't come naturally. The trick is to start practising in private, so the embarrassment of gurgling and babbling to your baby in front of other adults won't cramp your conversation style. If you don't know where to begin, use the tips on the opposite page as a guideline. As you grow more comfortable with baby talk, you'll likely find yourself slipping into it unawares, even in the company of adults ('Doesn't that risotto look yummy-yummy for the tum-tummy?').

A SECOND LANGUAGE

'My wife is French, and she wants to speak French to our baby exclusively; I speak English. I think it would be wonderful for our daughter to speak a second language, but wouldn't it be confusing at this age?'

Because fluency in another language isn't necessary to function and succeed in most parts of our country (as it is elsewhere in Europe), Britons are sadly lagging behind the rest of the world in the ability to converse in anything other than their own native tongue. It's generally agreed that teaching a child a second language gives her an invaluable skill, and may help her to think in different ways, possibly even improving her future academic performance in other areas. If the language is one that her forebears spoke or some of her relatives speak, it also gives her a significant link with her roots.

There is less agreement on just when to introduce the second language, however. Most experts suggest beginning as soon as a baby is born so that the second language is 'acquired' along with the first, not 'learned', as it would be when introduced later. Others believe that this puts the child at a disadvantage in both languages – though probably for only a short time. They generally recommend waiting until a child is two and a half or three before putting on the Berlitz. By this time she usually has a

UNDERSTANDING YOUR BABY

It'll probably be almost a year before your baby speaks that first word – two years or more before words are strung into phrases and then sentences, perhaps a year or longer before most of those sentences are easily comprehensible. But long before your baby is communicating verbally, he or she will be communicating in a variety of other ways. In fact, look and listen closely now and you'll find that your baby's already trying to speak to – not in so many words, but in so many behaviours and gestures.

No dictionary of baby communication can tell you what your baby's saying. Rather, the key to understanding this nonverbal communication is observation – patient, careful observation. Observing your child will speak volumes about his or her personality, preferences and needs, months before your child can speak at all. For example, does your baby wiggle and fuss uncomfortably when she's undressed before her bath? That may mean that she dislikes the cold air on her naked body – or just doesn't like the sensation of being naked at all. Keeping her covered as much as possible before lowering her into the bath will help ease her discomfort.

Or does your baby make coughing sounds around the time he's ready for a nap? Coughing might be your baby's way of telling you that he's getting tired – long before early fatigue melts down into crankiness.

Or does your baby frantically stuff her fist into her mouth when she's due for a feeding, before she starts wailing loudly? That could be her hunger cue – her first message to you that she's ready to eat (the second, crying, will make the feeding much more difficult for both of you to accomplish). By observing your baby's behaviours and gestures, you'll notice patterns that will start to make sense – and will help you make sense of what baby's telling you.

And listening to what baby tells you not only makes your job easier (you can provide what baby wants promptly, rather than figuring it out through trial, error and tears) but also lets your baby know that what he or she has to say matters, an important first step on the road to becoming a confident, secure, successful and emotionally mature person.

MAKING THE MOST OF THE FIRST THREE YEARS

Your baby won't remember much, if anything, about the first three years of life, but according to researchers, those three years will have a huge impact on the quality of your child's life – in some ways more than any of the others that follow.

What makes those first three years – years filled primarily with eating, sleeping, crying and playing, the years before formal learning even begins – so vital to your child's ultimate success in school, in a career, in relationships? How can a period of time when your child is so clearly unformed be so critical to the formation of the human being your child will eventually become? The answer is fascinating, complex and still evolving. Here's what scientists believe so far.

Research shows that a child's brain grows to 90 per cent of its adult capacity during those first three years – granted, a lot of brain power for someone who can't yet tie his or her shoes. During these three phenomenal years, brain 'wiring' occurs. ('Wiring' is when the crucial connections are made linking brain cells.) By the third birthday, somewhere around one thousand trillion connections will have been made.

With all this activity, however, a child's brain is very much a work in progress at age three. More connections are made until age ten or eleven, at which point the brain starts specializing for better efficiency, eliminating connections that are rarely used (this pattern continues throughout life,

which is why adults end up with only about half the brain connections a three-year-old has). Changes continue to take place well past puberty, with important parts of the brain still continuing to change throughout life.

While your child's future – like his or her brain – is far from fully cast at age three, it does appear that those early years do form the mould that will shape the person he or she will become. And the greatest influence during those formative years is you. Research shows that the kind of care a child receives during that time determines to a large extent how well those brain connections will be made, how much that little brain will develop, how successful, how content, how confident, and how competent to handle life's challenges that child will be.

Feeling daunted and overwhelmed by the task that's been handed you? Don't be. Most of what any loving parent does intuitively (with no training, without the addition of flash cards or special mind-expanding programmes) is exactly what your child – and your child's brain – needs to develop to his or her greatest potential. Consider:

◆ Every time you touch, hold, cuddle, hug, or respond to your baby with warm responsive care (all things you do anyway), you're positively affecting the way your child's brain forms

pretty good grasp of English but is still able to pick up a new language easily and naturally.

Whether you start now or in a couple of years, there are several approaches to encouraging a child to pick up a second language. One parent can speak English and the other the foreign tongue (as your spouse suggests), or both parents can speak the foreign

language (with the expectation the child will pick up English in school and elsewhere), or a grandparent, sitter, or au pair can speak the foreign language and the parents English (usually the least successful of the methods). None of the methods of teaching a second language is particularly successful if the 'teacher' isn't fluent in the language.

Experts recommend you forget

connections. By reading, talking, singing, making eye contact or cooing to your baby, you're helping your baby's brain reach its full potential. And through your positive parenting, you'll be teaching your child social and emotional skills that will actually boost your child's intellectual development as he or she gets older; the more socially and emotionally confident a child is, the more likely that child will be motivated to learn and to take on new challenges with enthusiasm and without fear of failure.

- Children whose basic needs are met in infancy and early childhood (she's fed when hungry, changed when wet, held when frightened) develop a sense of trust in others and a high level of self-confidence. Researchers have found that children reared in such nurturing environments have fewer behavioural problems in school later on, and are emotionally more capable of positive social relationships.

- By monitoring and helping to regulate your baby's impulses and behaviours during the early years (explaining she can't bite, telling him not to grab a toy), you will eventually teach your child self-control. Setting limits that are fair and age-appropriate and enforcing them consistently will enable your child to be less likely to be anxious, frightened, impulsive or to rely on violent means to resolve conflicts later on in life, say researchers. He or she will also be more

capable of intellectual learning because of the solid emotional foundation you have provided.

- Likewise, any caregiver who spends a significant amount of time with your child should provide the same kind of stimulation, the same kind of responsiveness, the same kind of positive discipline. High-quality child care will help ensure that your baby's brain gets what it needs: lots of nurturing.

- Routine medical care is important, too, ensuring that your child will be screened regularly for any medical or developmental issues that could slow intellectual, social or emotional growth. It will also allow for early intervention should a problem be uncovered, which could prevent that problem from holding your child back.

And here's probably the most important thing to keep in mind. Helping your child reach his or her potential is different from trying to change the person your child is; encouraging intellectual development is different from pushing it; providing stimulating experiences is different from scheduling in the kind of overload that leads to burnout. It's easy to avoid crossing that line from just enough parental interaction and involvement to too much by taking your cues from your baby – who, when it comes to getting what he or she needs, can be wise even beyond your years. Watch and listen carefully, and you'll almost always know what's best for your child.

---

about 'giving lessons in' a second language and instead immerse your child in it – play games (and, as you child grows, computer games) in it, read books in it (many popular children's books have been translated from English into other languages), sing songs in it, listen to CDs and watch DVDs in it, visit with friends who are fluent in it, and, if possible, visit places where the language is spoken.

Whoever is speaking the second language should speak it exclusively to the child, resisting the temptation to resort to English or to translate if the child seems to be struggling with comprehension. Expect your child to go through some periods of mixing the two languages in the beginning, but, eventually, a separation of the two will occur. During the school years, the child should

be taught to read and write in the second
language in order for it to take on greater
usefulness and significance. If classes
aren't available at school, tutoring or
computer-programmed learning may be
a good idea.

COMPARING BABIES

*'I get together regularly with a parents'
group, and inevitably they all start
comparing what their babies have been
doing. It makes me crazy – and worried
about whether my son is developing
fast enough.'*

If there's anything more anxiety
provoking than a roomful of pregnant
women comparing bellies, it's a roomful
of recently delivered parents comparing
babies. Just as no two pregnant bellies
are exactly alike, neither are any two
babies. Developmental norms (such as
those found in each chapter of this
book) are useful for comparing your
baby to a broad range of normal infants
in order to assess her progress and identify any lags. But comparing your baby
with someone else's child, or with an
older one of your own, can only result in
a lot of unnecessary fears and frustrations. Two perfectly 'normal' babies can
develop in different areas at completely
different clips – one may forge ahead in
vocalizing and socializing, another in
physical feats, such as turning over.
Differences between babies become
even more marked as the first year progresses – one baby may crawl very early
but not walk until fifteen months,
another may never learn to crawl at all
but suddenly start taking steps at ten
months. Then, too, a parent's assessment of her baby's progress is highly
subjective – and not always completely
accurate. One may not even recognize
baby's frequent coos as the beginnings
of language, while another may hear

one coo and swear, 'He said "dada"!'

All of this said, it's easier to intellec-
tualize that comparing babies isn't a
good idea than to actually stop doing it
or avoid those who do. Many compulsive comparers can't sit next to another
parent-with-baby on a bus, in a doctor's
waiting room, or at the park without
launching an assault of outwardly innocent queries that lead to the inevitable
comparisons ('What an adorable baby!
She's sitting already? How old is she?').
The best advice, if you can't completely
manage to 'mind your own baby', is to
remember how meaningless these comparisons really are. Your baby, like your
belly before him, is one of a kind.

IMMUNIZATION

*'My baby's doctor says that
immunization is perfectly safe. But I've
heard a few stories about serious
reactions, and I worry about my
daughter getting the injections.'*

We live in a society that considers
good news to be no news. A story
on the positive effects of immunizations
cannot compete with one on the
extremely rare instances of serious complications associated with them. So it is
likely that today's parents have heard
more about the risks of immunization
than the benefits. And, yet, as your
doctor has doubtless told you, for most
infants those benefits continue to far outweigh the risks.

Not too many years ago in the
United Kingdom, the most common
causes of infant death were infectious
diseases, such as diphtheria, typhoid
and smallpox. Measles and whooping
cough were so common that all children
were expected to get them, and thousands, especially infants, died or were
permanently handicapped by these illnesses. Parents dreaded the coming of

IMMUNIZATION MYTHS

Most worries about immunization – though perfectly understandable – are unfounded. Don't let the following myths keep you from immunizing your baby:

MYTH: Giving so many injections together isn't safe.
Reality: Studies have shown that vaccinations are just as safe and effective when given together. There are many combination vaccines that have been used routinely for years (MMR, DTaP). Recently approved and already in use by many doctors is the Pediarix vaccine that combines DTaP, polio and hep B in a single injection. Researchers are continuing to develop combo vaccines that may become approved for use in the near future. The best part about these combination vaccines: fewer total injections for your baby – something you're both likely to appreciate.

MYTH: Injections are very painful for a baby.
Reality: The pain of a vaccine is only momentary and, compared to the pain of the serious diseases the immunization is protecting against, insignificant. And there are ways of minimizing the pain your baby feels. Studies show that babies who get injections while they are being held and distracted by their parents cry less, and those who are breastfed immediately before or during the immunization experience less pain. You can also ask your baby's doctor about giving a sugar solution just before the injection or using an anaesthetic cream an hour earlier (which the doctor will have to prescribe).

MYTH: If everyone else's children are immunized, mine can't get sick.
Reality: Some parents believe that they don't have to immunize their own children if everyone else's children are immunized – since there won't be any diseases to catch. That theory doesn't hold up.

First of all, there's the risk that other parents are subscribing to the same myth, which means their children won't be immunized, either, creating the potential for an outbreak of a preventable disease. Secondly, unvaccinated children put vaccinated children at risk for the disease as well (vaccines are about 90 per cent effective; the high percentage of immunized individuals limits the spread of disease) – so not only might you be hurting your child, you might also be hurting your child's friends. Thirdly, unvaccinated children can catch whooping cough (pertussis) not only from other unvaccinated children, but also from adults. That's because the vaccine that protects against it isn't given after age seven; immunity has largely worn off by adulthood; and the disease, while still highly contagious, is so mild in adults that it's usually not diagnosed – which means that adults who don't realize they have whooping cough can inadvertently spread it to babies, who are much more vulnerable to its effects.

MYTH: One vaccine in a series gives a child enough protection.
Reality: Researchers have found that skipping vaccines puts your child at increased risk for contracting the diseases, especially measles and pertussis. So if the recommendations are for a series of injections, make sure your child receives *all* the necessary injections so he or she is not left unprotected.

MYTH: Multiple vaccines for such young babies put them at increased risk for other diseases.
Reality: There is no evidence that multiple immunizations increase the risk for diabetes, infectious disease or other illnesses. Neither is there any evidence to date that there is a connection between multiple vaccines and allergic diseases such as asthma.

summer and the infantile paralysis (polio) epidemics that seemed invariably to arrive with it, killing or disabling thousands of infants and children. Today, smallpox has been virtually eliminated, and diphtheria and typhoid are extremely rare. Only a small percentage of children are stricken with measles or whooping cough each year, and infantile paralysis is a disease parents are not only no longer afraid of, but often aren't even familiar with. A British baby is now much more likely to die because of not being strapped into a car seat than from a communicable disease. Without a doubt, immunization has made childhood safer for children.

Immunization is based on the fact that exposure to weakened or dead disease-producing microorganisms (in the form of vaccines) or to the poisons (toxins) they produce, rendered harmless by heat or chemical treatment (then called toxoids), will cause an individual to produce the same antibodies that would develop if the person had actually contracted the disease. Armed with the special memory that is unique to the immune system, these antibodies will 'recognize' the specific microorganisms, should they attack in the future, and destroy them.

Even the ancients recognized that when people survived a particular disease, they weren't likely to contract it again, and those who had recovered from the plague were sometimes called upon to care for new victims. Although some societies attempted crude forms of immunization, it wasn't until Edward Jenner, a Scottish physician, decided to test the old belief that a person who contracted the lesser disease cowpox would never get smallpox, that modern immunization was born. In 1796, Jenner smeared pus from the sores of a milkmaid infected with cowpox on two small cuts in the arm of a healthy eight-year-old boy. The child developed a slight fever a week later, then a couple of small scabs on his arm. When exposed to smallpox later, he remained healthy. He had become immune.

The immunization process has come a long way since that early experiment. The first widely administered type of immunization, the smallpox vaccination, was so successful that it is no longer considered necessary. For now, at least, the disease seems to have been eradicated from the entire globe. Plenty of progress has been made with other serious scourges as well, and it's hoped that immunization will someday wipe out most of them, too.

But while immunization clearly saves thousands of young lives each year, it's not perfect. Though most children have only a mild reaction to certain vaccines, some become ill, a very few seriously so. Some types of vaccine have been suspected of causing, on rare occasions, permanent damage, even death. Still, the tremendous benefits of protection from serious disease far outweigh the very small risks of immunization for all but high-risk children – clearly making vaccination the very best bet for your baby. And as minimal as the risks are, they can be reduced even further by taking precautions to make sure your baby is safely vaccinated. Here's how:

- Be sure the doctor gives your baby a thorough checkup before giving a vaccination to be certain no serious illness is developing that is not yet apparent; injections should be postponed when a baby is significantly ill. (A mild illness, such as a cold, is not reason to postpone an injection.)

- Read the information that should be provided by the doctor each time a routine vaccine is given to your child. And find out more about the evidence on MMR vaccinations from the Department of Health at www.immunisation.nhs.uk and from the UK Vaccinations Group at www.uvig.org.

♦ Observe your baby carefully for 72 hours after the vaccination (especially during the first 48), and report any severe reactions (see page 228) or very unusual behaviour to the doctor *immediately*. Also report any less severe reactions at your next visit.

♦ Ask the doctor to enter the vaccine manufacturer's name and the vaccine lot/batch number in your child's records, along with any reactions you report. Be sure to get a copy of the information for your own records as well.

♦ When the next injection is scheduled, remind your baby's doctor about any previous reactions to the vaccine.

♦ If you have any fears about vaccine safety, discuss them with your baby's doctor.

THE ABCS OF DTaPS ... AND MMRS ... AND IPVS. ...

It helps to know what the needle that's headed your baby's way is loaded with. The following is a guide to immunizations your child will probably receive in the first year and beyond. For the latest information on immunizations visit www.immunisation.nhs.uk.

Diphtheria, tetanus, acellular pertussis vaccine (DTaP). Immunization against diphtheria, tetanus and pertussis (whooping cough) is crucial, since all can cause serious illness and death.

Up to a quarter of children who get DTaP have very mild local reactions where the injection was given, such as tenderness, swelling or redness, usually within two days of having the injection. Some children are fussy or will lose their appetite for a few hours or perhaps a day or two. Fever is also a common reaction. These reactions are more likely to occur after second and third doses than after the first dose. Occasionally, a child will have a more serious side effect, such as a fever of over 40°C (104°F). Rarely, a child will cry continuously (for three or more hours) after receiving the DTaP. Even rarer are convulsions, which can result not from the vaccine itself but rather from a high fever accompanying it in a few children (see page 228). Research has shown that any seizures resulting from such vaccine-induced fever do not lead to lasting problems; a suggested link between these seizures and autism has not been found. Research also shows that there is no correlation between the vaccine and a greater risk of SIDS.

In certain circumstances, a doctor may decide to omit the pertussis vaccine (and just administer the DT) if the baby's previous reactions to DTaP were severe. And a doctor may delay giving the DTaP (or not give it at all) if a child had a severe allergic reaction to the first DTaP dose, a high temperature following the DTaP, or any other severe reaction, including seizures.

Most doctors will postpone the injection for a baby who is significantly sick. Though a few doctors will also delay giving a DTaP (or other) injection because of a mild cold, this isn't considered necessary – and could result in a child ending up incompletely immunized. After all, many babies who attend day care or who have an older sibling have frequent colds – sometimes one after another during the 'cold season'.

Finding symptom-free windows of opportunity to vaccinate these babies according to schedule often proves impossible. Delaying injections because of mild fevers, ear infection, and most cases of gastrointestinal upset is also not usually considered necessary or wise.

Polio vaccine (IPV). Immunization has virtually eliminated polio (aka infantile paralysis), once a dreaded disease, from the United Kingdom. The vaccine is not known to produce any side effects except for a rare allergic reaction. The doctor will likely delay administering the IPV if your child is very ill. A child who had a *severe* allergic reaction to the first dose generally won't be given subsequent doses.

Measles, mumps, rubella (MMR). Children get two doses of the MMR, the first between twelve and fifteen months, and the second at three years and four months or soon after (though it can be administered anytime as long as it is twenty-eight days after the first). Measles, though often joked about, is in reality a serious disease with sometimes severe, potentially fatal, complications. Rubella, also known as German measles, on the other hand, is often so mild that its symptoms are missed. But because it can cause birth defects in the foetus of an infected pregnant woman, immunization in early childhood is recommended – both to protect the future foetuses of girl babies and to reduce the risk of infected children exposing pregnant women, including their own mothers. Mumps rarely presents a serious problem in childhood, but because it can have severe consequences (such as sterility or deafness) in adulthood, early immunization is recommended.

Reactions to the MMR vaccine are generally very mild and don't usually occur until a week or two after the injection. About 1 in 5 children will get a rash or slight fever lasting a few days from the measles component. About 1 in 7 will get a rash or some swelling of the neck glands, and 1 in 100, aching or swelling of the joints from the rubella component, sometimes as long as three weeks after the injection. Occasionally, there may be swelling of the salivary glands from the mumps component. Much less common are tingling, numbness or pain in the hands and feet, all difficult to discern in infants, and allergic reactions. Large studies have not shown a link between the MMR vaccine and autism.

Caution should be taken in administering MMR to a child sick with anything but a mild cold, one with an impaired immune system (from medication, cancer or another condition), one who has recently had a blood transfusion, one who has a severe allergy to gelatin or the antibiotic neomycin, or one who had a severe allergic reaction after the first dose of MMR.

Varicella vaccine (Var). Varicella, or chicken pox, until recently one of the most common childhood diseases, is usually a mild disease without serious side effects. There can be complications, such as Reye's syndrome and bacterial infections (including group A strep); and the disease can be fatal to high-risk children, such as those with leukaemia or immune deficiencies, or those whose mothers were infected with varicella just prior to delivery. For the majority of children in the UK the chicken pox vaccine is not considered necessary, however, so is not routinely given.

It appears that the vaccine prevents chicken pox in 70 to 90 per cent of those who are vaccinated. The small percentage who do get chicken pox after receiving the vaccine usually get a much milder case than if they had not been immunized.

The varicella vaccine is very safe.

RECOMMENDED IMMUNIZATION SCHEDULE

Each vaccination is given as a single injection into the muscle of the thigh or upper arm

When to immunize	Vaccination given	What vaccination protects against
2 months	DTaP/IPV/Hib	Diphtheria Tetanus Pertussis (whooping cough) Polio *Hemophilus influenzae* b (Hib)
	Pneumoccal conjugate vaccine (PCV)	Pneumococcal infection
3 months	DTaP/IPV/Hib	Diphtheria Tetanus Pertussis (whooping cough) Polio *Hemophilus influenzae* b (Hib)
	MenC	Meningitis C
4 months	DTaP/IPV/Hib	Diphtheria Tetanus Pertussis (whooping cough) Polio *Hemophilus influenzae* b (Hib)
	MenC	Meningitis C
	PCV	Pneumococcal infection
Around 12 months	Hib	*Hemophilus influenzae* b (Hib)
	MenC	Meningitis C
Around 13 months	MMR	Measles Mumps Rubella (German measles)
	PCV	Pneumococcal infection
3 years and 4 months or soon after	DTaP/IPV	Diphtheria Tetanus Pertussis (whooping cough) Polio
	MMR	Measles Mumps Rubella (German measles)
Girls aged 12 to 13 years	HPV	Cervical cancer caused by human papillomavirus types 16 and 18
13 to 18 years	Td/IPV	Diphtheria Tetanus Polio

WHEN TO CALL THE DOCTOR AFTER AN IMMUNIZATION

Though severe reactions to immunizations are exceedingly rare, you should call the doctor if your baby experiences any of the following within two days of the injection:

◆ High fever (over 40°C/104°F)

◆ Crying that lasts longer than three hours

◆ Seizures/convulsions (jerking or staring) – usually because of fever and not serious

◆ Seizures or major alterations in consciousness within seven days of injection

◆ An allergic reaction (swelling of mouth, face or throat; breathing difficulties; immediate rash)

◆ Listlessness, unresponsiveness, excessive sleepiness

Should you note any of the above symptoms following an injection, call the doctor. This is not just for your baby's sake, but also so that the doctor can report the adverse response. Collection and evaluation of such information may help reduce future risks.

Rarely, there may be redness or soreness at the site of the injection. Some children also get a mild rash (about five spots) a few weeks after being immunized.

Hemophilus Influenzae b vaccine (Hib). This vaccine is aimed at thwarting the deadly *hemophilus influenzae* b (Hib) bacteria (which has no relation to influenza, or 'flu') that is the cause of a wide range of very serious infections in infants and young children, including meningitis and epiglottis (a potentially fatal infection that obstructs the airways) septicaemia (blood infection), cellulitis (skin and connective tissue infection), osteomyelitis (bone infection), and pericarditis (heart membrane infection).

The Hib vaccine appears to have few, if any, side effects. A very small percentage of children may have fever, redness and/or tenderness on the site of the injection.

As with other vaccines, Hib vaccine should not be given to a child who is very ill (mild illness isn't a problem), or who might be allergic to any of the components (check with the doctor).

Hepatitis vaccines. Hepatitis B (hep B), a chronic liver disease, can cause liver failure and liver cancer in future years. It is recommended that the vaccine is given to all babies whose mothers or close family have been infected with hepatitis B. Four doses are needed: the first at birth (it may be delayed for premature infants), the second at 1 month old, the third at 2 months, and a booster dose and blood test at 1 year. Side effects – slight soreness and fussiness – are not common and are short-lived. The vaccine for hepatitis A (hep A), which also affects the liver, is recommended for at-risk children age 12 to 23 months.

Pneumococcal conjugate vaccine (PCV). The pneumococcus bacterium is a major cause of illness among children, responsible for some ear infections, meningitis, pneumonia, blood infections and other illnesses. Side effects, such as low-grade fever or redness and tenderness at the injection site, are occasionally seen and are not harmful.

Influenza. In the UK, the influenza, or 'flu', vaccine is currently only recommended for children at high risk for flu complications. But studies in the United States indicate that even healthy children under age two are at increased risk for hospitalization from flu-related complications. The vaccine is especially important for those at high risk – those with serious heart or lung disease, those with depressed immune systems, asthma, HIV, diabetes and those with sickle-cell anaemia or similar blood diseases. The flu vaccine should not be given to anyone who has had a severe allergic reaction to eggs. High-risk children may, instead, be given antiviral medications to prevent development of influenza.

If for some reason any of your baby's vaccinations are postponed, immunization can pick up where it left off; starting over isn't necessary. Work with the doctor to get your child caught up as soon as possible.

CRADLE CAP

'I wash my daughter's hair every day, but I still can't seem to get rid of the flakes on her scalp.'

Don't pack away those dark-shouldered outfits yet. Cradle cap, a seborrheic dermatitis of the scalp common in young infants, doesn't doom your daughter to a lifetime of dandruff. Mild cradle cap, in which greasy surface scales appear on the scalp, often responds well to a brisk massage with mineral oil or petroleum jelly to loosen the scales, followed by a thorough shampoo to remove them and the oil. Tough cases, in which flaking is heavy and/or brownish patches and yellow crustiness are present, may benefit from the daily use of an antiseborrheic shampoo that contains sulfur salicylates (make sure you keep it out of baby's eyes) after the oil treatment. (Some cases are aggravated by the use of such preparations. If your baby's is, discontinue use and discuss this with the doctor.) Since cradle cap usually worsens when the scalp sweats, keeping it cool and dry may also help – so don't put a hat on baby unless necessary (such as in the sun or when it's cold outside), and then remove it when you're indoors or in a heated car.

When cradle cap is severe, the seborrheic rash may spread to the face, neck, or buttocks. If this occurs, the doctor will probably prescribe a topical ointment.

Occasionally, cradle cap will persist through the first year – and in a few instances, long after a child has graduated from the cradle. Since the condition causes no discomfort and is therefore considered only a cosmetic problem, aggressive therapy (such as use of topical cortisone, which can contain the flaking for a period of time) isn't usually recommended but is certainly worth discussing with your child's doctor as a last resort.

CROOKED FEET

'Our son's feet seem to fold inwards. Will they straighten out on their own?'

Your son's not alone in his stance; most babies appear bowlegged and pigeon-toed. This happens for two reasons – one, because of the normal rotational curve in the legs of a newborn, and, two, because the cramped quarters in the uterus often force one or both feet into odd positions. When baby emerges at birth, after spending several months in that position, the feet are still bent or seem to turn inwards.

In the months ahead, as your baby's feet enjoy their out-of-utero freedom and as he learns to pull up, crawl and then walk, his feet will begin straightening out. They almost always do so without treatment.

Just to be sure there isn't another cause of your baby's foot position, express your concerns at his next well-baby visit. The doctor probably has already checked your baby's feet for abnormalities, but another check to put your mind at ease won't hurt. It's also routine for the doctor to keep an eye on the progress of a baby's feet to make sure they straighten out as he grows – which they almost certainly will in your son's case.

In the very unlikely event a baby's feet don't appear to be straightening out on their own, casting or special shoes may be recommended at a later date. At just what point treatment is considered will depends on the type of problem and on the doctor's point of view.

UNDESCENDED TESTICLES

'My son was born with undescended testicles. The doctor said that they would probably descend from the abdomen by the time he was a month or two old, but they haven't yet.'

The abdomen may seem a strange location for testicles, but it isn't. The testicles (or testes) in males and the ovaries in females both develop in the foetal abdomen from the same embryonic tissue. The ovaries, of course, stay put. The testes are scheduled to descend down through the inguinal canals in the groin, into the scrotal sac at the base of the penis, somewhere around the eighth month of gestation. But in 3 to 4 per cent of full-term boys and about one third of those that are preterm, they don't make the trip before birth. The result: undescended testicles.

Because of the migratory habits of testicles, it's not always easy to determine that one hasn't descended. Normally, the testicles hang away from the body when they are in danger of overheating (protecting the sperm-producing mechanism from temperatures that are too high). But they slip back up into the body when they are chilled (protecting the sperm-producing mechanism from temperatures that are too low) or when they are handled (again protective, to avoid injury). In some boys the testes are particularly sensitive and spend a lot of time sheltered in the body. In most, the left testicle hangs lower than the right, possibly making the right seem undescended (and making a lot of young boys worry). The diagnosis of undescended testicle or testicles is therefore made only when one or both have never been observed to be in the scrotum, not even when the baby is in a warm bath.

An undescended testicle causes no pain or difficulty with urinating, and as your doctor assured you, usually descends on its own. By age one, only three or four boys in a thousand still have undescended testicles, at which point surgery (a minor procedure) can easily put them in their proper place. Hormone therapy can be tried first, but it isn't usually successful.

PENILE ADHESION

'My son was circumcised as a newborn, and my doctor says he's developed a penile adhesion. What does that mean?'

Whenever tissues of the body are cut, the edges will stick to the surrounding tissue as it heals. After the foreskin of the penis is removed during a circumcision, the circular edge remaining tends to stick to the penis as it heals. If a significant amount of foreskin remains after the circumcision, it, too, can stick to the penis during the healing process, causing the foreskin to reattach. This penile adhesion is not a problem as long as it's gently retracted periodically to prevent it from becoming permanently attached. Ask the doctor how you should do this or if it's really necessary to do at all. When boys, even baby boys, have their normal erections, the sticking skin surfaces are pulled, helping to keep them apart, without any adult intervention. Rarely, if a bridge of skin has permanently attached, a urologist may need to separate the skin and remove the remaining piece of foreskin to prevent the problem from recurring.

INGUINAL HERNIA

'The paediatrician said that my twin boys have inguinal hernias and will have to have surgery. Is this serious?'

A hernia is often thought of as something that develops when a grown man does too much heavy lifting. But even infants too young to lift a finger – never mind a heavy package – aren't too young to experience a hernia. Hernias are not unusual in newborns, particularly boys, and especially those born prematurely (as twins often are).

In an inguinal hernia, a part of the intestines slips through one of the inguinal canals (the same channels through which the testes descend into the scrotum) and bulge into the groin. The defect is often first noted as a lump in one of the creases where the thigh joins the abdomen, particularly when a baby is crying or very active; it often retracts when he is quiet. When the section of the intestines slips all the way down into the scrotum, it can be seen as an enlargement or swelling in the scrotum, and may be referred to as scrotal hernia.

A hernia doesn't usually cause any discomfort, and while it must be treated, it isn't a serious condition and isn't con-

sidered an emergency. Nevertheless, any parent who notices a lump or swelling in their baby's groin or scrotum should report the finding to the doctor as soon as possible. Doctors usually advise repair as soon as the hernia is diagnosed – assuming the baby is fit for surgery. Such surgery is usually simple and successful, with a very short (sometimes one-day) hospitalization. Only very rarely does an inguinal hernia recur following surgery, though in some children another hernia occurs on the opposite side at a later date.

If a diagnosed infant inguinal hernia is not treated, it can lead to the herniated section becoming 'strangulated' – pinched by the muscular lining of the inguinal canal, obstructing blood flow and digestion in the intestines. Vomiting, severe pain, even shock can result. Parents who note a baby suddenly crying in pain, vomiting and not having bowel movements should call the doctor immediately. If the doctor can't be reached, the baby should be taken to the nearest A & E department. Elevating the baby's bottom slightly and applying an ice pack while en route may help the intestine to retract, but don't try to push it back in by hand.

INVERTED NIPPLES

'One of my daughter's nipples sinks in instead of standing out. What's wrong with it?'

It's inverted – not at all uncommon in the nipples of infants. Often, a nipple that is inverted at birth corrects itself spontaneously later. If it doesn't, it won't be an issue until she's ready to nurse her own baby, at which point (if necessary, and it likely won't be) she can take steps to draw the nipple out.

FAVOURING ONE BREAST

'My little girl hardly ever wants to nurse on my left breast, and it's shrunken to be considerably smaller than the right.'

Some babies play favourites. It could be that your baby's more comfortable cradled in your favoured, and probably stronger, arm, so she developed a taste for the breast on that side. Or that you often place her on the left breast, so that your right hand is free for eating, holding a book or the phone, or handling other chores, leaving the right breast to dwindle in size and production (or the reverse, if you're left-handed). Perhaps one breast is the better provider because you favoured it early on in the nursing relationship, for any number of reasons – from the location of the Caesarean incision pain to the location of the TV set in your bedroom.

Whatever the reason, preferring one breast over the other is a fact of nursing for some babies, and lopsidedness a fact of life for their mothers. Though you might try to increase production on the less favoured side by pumping daily and/or starting every feeding with it (if your baby will cooperate), these efforts may not do the trick. In many cases, mothers go through the entire nursing experience with one breast larger than the other (though you'll probably be the only one who notices the difference). The lopsidedness will diminish after weaning, though a slightly greater-than-normal difference may continue.

Very rarely, a baby rejects a breast because it harbours a developing malignancy. So do mention your baby's penchant to your doctor.

USING A BABY CARRIER OR SLING

'We usually carry our son around in a baby carrier. Is this a good idea?'

It's been a good idea for millennia. Baby carriers and slings – cloth sacks that harness infants to their parents or other caregivers – have, in one form or another, been helping transport babies in other cultures since prehistoric times. There are at least three good reasons. Firstly, babies are usually happy riding in a carrier; they enjoy the steady gentle movement and the closeness to a warm body. Secondly, babies tend to cry less if they're carried around a lot – and carrying is made a lot easier with a carrier. And, thirdly, carriers provide parents and other caregivers with the freedom to attend to their daily chores – tote packages, push shopping trolleys or the vacuum cleaner, make phone calls – while carrying baby.

Different kinds of baby carriers come with different benefits; see a discussion of these on pages 56–57. But if baby carriers are a boon to today's parents, they can also be a bane if overused or misused. Keep in mind the following when carrying your baby:

Overheating. On a very warm day, even a scantily clothed baby can simmer in a baby carrier – particularly one that encloses the baby's legs, feet and head or is made from a heavy fabric such as corduroy. Such overheating can lead to prickly heat and even heat stroke. If you use a carrier in warm weather, in overheated rooms, or on a hot bus or tube train (baby carriers should never be used instead of a safety seat in the car), check your baby frequently to be sure he isn't sweating and his body doesn't feel warmer than yours. If he does appear to be overheated, remove some clothing or take him out of the carrier completely.

Understimulation. A baby who's always cooped up in a baby carrier that limits his visual perspective to a chest and, if he looks up, the bottom of a face doesn't have the opportunity he needs to see the world. This is not a major problem in the first few weeks of life, when a baby's interest is usually limited to the most basic creature comforts, but it can be now, when he's ready to expand his horizons. Use a convertible carrier or a sling in which baby can face in for a nap or out for viewing the world, or limit baby's sojourns to times when he will be sleeping or will be pacified only by being carried and you need your arms for other purposes. At other times, use a pushchair or infant seat.

Too much sleeping. Babies who are toted in baby carriers tend to sleep a lot – often a lot more than they need to, with two less-than-desirable results. Firstly, they get used to catnapping on the go (fifteen minutes when you run out to the corner shop, twenty when you walk the dog) rather than taking longer naps in their cots. Secondly, they may become so well rested during the day that they don't rest much at night. If your baby immediately falls asleep when placed in a carrier, limit use to make sure he doesn't nap the day away in it.

Risk of injury. A young infant's neck isn't strong enough yet to support his head when he's jiggled and jostled a lot. Though securing your baby in a baby carrier or sling while you jog may seem like an ideal way of getting your exercise and keeping your baby happy, too, the bouncing could be risky. Instead, strap him in a pushchair when you go for a jog. Also be careful to bend at the knees, *not the waist,* when wearing the carrier – or your baby could slip out.

While judicious use of a baby carrier can make your life easier and your baby's life happier, he won't be ready for a back carrier until he can sit by himself.

THE CHALLENGING BABY

'Our little girl is adorable, but she seems to cry for the least little reason. If it's too noisy, or too bright, or even if she's a little wet. We're going crazy trying to cope with this. Are we doing something wrong?'

No parent expects to have a challenging child. Pregnant daydreams are pink-and-blue collages of a contented infant who coos, smiles, sleeps peacefully, cries only when she's hungry and grows into a sweet-tempered, cooperative child. Bawling, inconsolable babies and kicking, screaming toddlers belong to others – parents who did it all wrong and are paying the price.

And then, for so many parents like you, just weeks after your perfect baby is born, reality does a number on that particular fantasy. Suddenly, it's your baby who's crying all the time, who won't sleep, or who seems perpetually unhappy and dissatisfied no matter what you do. Why shouldn't you wonder, 'What have we done wrong?'

The answer is probably nothing, except perhaps pass on some contributing genes, for a baby's temperament appears to have much more to do with heredity than environment. How the childhood environment is structured, however, can make a difference as to how inborn temperament affects future development. The child who, with help from mummy and daddy, learns to direct and develop 'challenging' inborn personality traits, transforming them from liabilities into assets, can go from impossible problem infant to highly successful adult.

DO YOU HAVE A
CHALLENGING BABY?

The active baby. Babies often send the first clue that they're going to be more active than most right from the uterus; suspicions are confirmed soon after birth when swaddling blankets are kicked off, nappy changing and dressing sessions become wrestling matches, and baby always ends up at the opposite end of the cot after a nap. Active babies are a constant challenge (they sleep less than most, become restless when feeding, can be extremely frustrated until they're able to be independently mobile, and are always at risk of hurting themselves), but they can also be a joy (they're usually very alert, interested and interesting, and quick to accomplish). While you don't want to squelch such a baby's enthusiasm and adventurous nature, you will want to take special protective precautions as well as learn ways to quiet him or her for eating and sleeping. The following tips should help:

◆ Use a blanket sleeper in cold weather and lightweight sleepers in cool weather; limit or avoid swaddling.

◆ Be especially careful never to leave an active baby on a bed, changing table or any other elevated spot even for a second – they often figure out how to turn over very early, and sometimes just when you least expect it. A restraining strap on the changing table is useful but should not be relied upon if you're more than a step away.

◆ Adjust the cot mattress to its lowest level as soon as the active baby starts to sit alone for even a few seconds – the next step may be pulling up and over the sides of the cot. Keep all objects a baby might climb on out of cot and playpen.

◆ Don't leave an active baby in an infant seat except on the floor – they are often

capable of overturning the seat. And of course, baby should always be strapped in.

◆ Learn what slows down your active baby – massage (see page 301), soft music (either your own singing or a CD), a warm bath or looking at a picture book (though active children may not be ready for this as early as quieter children). Build such quietening activities into your baby's schedule before feeding and sleeping times.

The irregular baby. At about six to twelve weeks, just when other babies seem to be settling into a schedule and becoming more predictable, these babies seem to become more erratic. Not only don't they fall into schedules on their own, they aren't interested in any you may have to offer.

Instead of following such a baby's lead and letting chaos take over your home life, or taking the reins yourself and imposing a very rigid schedule that is contrary to the infant's nature, try to find a middle ground. For both your sakes, it's necessary to put at least a modicum of order in your lives, but try as much as possible to build a schedule around any natural tendencies your baby seems to exhibit. You may have to keep a diary to uncover any hints of a recurring time frame in your child's days, such as hunger around 11 AM every morning or fussiness after 7 PM every evening.

Try to counter any unpredictability with predictability. That means trying, as much as possible, to do things at the same times and in the same ways every day. Nurse in the same chair when possible, give baths at the same time each day, always soothe by the same method (rocking or singing or whatever works best). Try scheduling feedings at roughly the same times each day, even if your baby doesn't seem hungry, and try to stick to the schedule even if he or she is hungry between meals, offering a small snack if necessary. Ease rather than force your baby into more of a structured day. And don't expect true regularity, just a little less chaos.

Nights with an irregular baby can be torture, mostly because the baby doesn't usually differentiate them from days. You can try the tips for dealing with night–day differentiation problems (see page 176), but it's very possible they won't work for your baby, who may want to stay up throughout the night, at least initially. To survive, mummy and daddy may have to alternate night duty or share split shifts until things get better, which they eventually will if you are persistent and stay cool.

The poor-adaptability or initial-withdrawal baby. These babies consistently reject the unfamiliar – new objects, people, foods. Some are upset by change of any kind, even familiar change such as going from the house to the car. If this sounds like your baby, try setting up a daily schedule with few surprises. Feedings, baths and naps should take place at the same times and in the same places, with as few departures from routine as possible. Introduce new toys and people (and foods, when baby is ready for them) very gradually. For example, hang a new mobile over the cot for just a minute or two. Remove it and bring it out again in a short while, leaving it up for a few minutes longer. Continue increasing the time of exposure until baby seems ready to accept and enjoy the mobile. Introduce other new toys and objects in the same way. Have new people spend a lot of time just being in the same room with your baby, then talking at a distance, then communicating close up, before they make an attempt at physical contact. Later, when you introduce solids, add new foods very gradually, starting with tiny amounts, and increasing portion size over the span of a week or two. Don't add another food until the last is well accepted. Try to avoid unnecessary changes when making purchases – a new feeding bottle with a different shape or colour, a new gadget on the pushchair, a new dummy. If an item wears out or breaks, try to replace it with an identical or similar model.

The high-intensity baby. You probably noticed it right at the beginning – your baby cried louder than any other child in the hospital nursery. The loud crying and screaming, the kind that can frazzle even the steadiest of nerves, continued when you got home. You can't flip a switch and turn down the volume on your baby, of course – but turning down the volume of noise and activity in the environment may help tone your child down a bit. Also, you will want to take some purely practical measures to keep the noise from bothering family and neighbours. If possible, soundproof your baby's room by insulating the walls with insulating board or padding, adding carpeting, curtains, and anything else that will absorb the sound. You can try earplugs, a white-noise machine, a fan or air conditioner to reduce the wear and tear on your ears and nerves without totally blocking out your baby's cries. As crying lessens in the months ahead, so will this problem, but your child will probably always be louder and more intense than most.

The negative or 'unhappy' baby. Instead of smiling and cooing, some babies just seem grumpy all the time. This is no reflection on the parents (unless, of course, they've been neglectful), but it can have a profound impact on them. They often find it difficult to love their unhappy babies, and sometimes they even reject them. If nothing seems to satisfy your baby (and no medical explanation is uncovered), then do your best to be loving and caring anyway, secure in the knowledge that one of these days, when your baby learns other ways of expression, the crying and general unhappiness will diminish, though he or she may always be the 'serious' type.

The parental role in this metamorphosis – as in most aspects of a child's development – is critical. The first step is to identify which of several different types of personalities that have been linked to difficult behaviour your own baby displays (some display a combination). Your baby seems to be what is known as a low-sensory-threshold baby. A wet nappy, a starched dress, a high neckline, a bright light, a staticky radio, a scratchy blanket, a cold cot – any or all of these may unduly upset a baby who seems to be extra sensitive to sensory stimulation. In some children, all five senses – hearing, vision, taste, touch and smell – are very easily overloaded; in others, just one or two. Dealing with the low-sensory-threshold child means trying to keep the general level of unnecessary sensory stimulation down, as well as avoiding those specific things that you notice bother baby, such as:

◆ Sound sensitivity. As much as is practical (remember, you still have to live in the house, too) lower the sound level in your home. Keep the radio, stereo and TV low, adjust the telephone ring to low, and install carpeting and curtains, where possible, to absorb sound. Speak or sing to your baby softly and have others do the same. Be sure any musical or other sound-producing toys aren't disturbing to baby. If outside noises seem to be a problem, try a white-noise machine or air cleaner in baby's room to block them out.

◆ Light or visual sensitivity. Use room-darkening shades or curtains so baby can sleep later in the morning and nap during the day, and avoid very bright lights in rooms she frequents. Don't expose her to too much visual stimulation at once – hang just one toy in the cot, or put just a couple in the playpen at a time. Select toys that are soft and subtle in colour and design rather than bright and busy.

◆ Taste sensitivity. If your baby is breast-fed and has a bad day after you eat garlic or onions, consider that the unfamiliar taste of your milk may be the cause; if she's bottle fed and seems cranky a lot, try switching to a formula with a different taste (ask your doctor or health visitor for a recommendation). When you introduce solids, recognize the fact that your baby may not relish every taste sensation and may reject strong flavours entirely.

◆ Touch sensitivity. With this princess-and-the pea-like syndrome, some babies lose their composure as soon as they wet their nappies, become frantic when they're too warm or dressed in rough fabrics, scream when they're dunked in the bath or put down on a too-cold mattress or, later, when you tie their shoes over wrinkled socks. So keep clothing comfortable (cotton knits with smooth seams and buttons, poppers, labels and collars that won't irritate because of size, shape or location are ideal), bathwater and room temperatures at levels that keep her happy, and nappies changed frequently.

A small percentage of babies are so oversensitive to touch that they resist being held and cuddled. Don't over-handle such a baby; do a lot of your caressing and interacting with words and eye contact rather than actual physical touching. When you do hold your baby, learn which way seems least annoying (tight or loose, for example). Observe closely to see what feels good and what doesn't.

◆ Smell sensitivity. Unusual odours aren't likely to bother a very young infant, but some children begin to show a negative reaction to certain scents before the end of the first year.

The aroma of frying onions, the smell of a nappy rash ointment, the fragrance of mum's new perfume or dad's new aftershave lotion, can all make such a baby restless and unhappy. If your baby seems sensitive to smells, limit strong odours when you can.

◆ Stimulation sensitivity. Too much stimulation of any kind seems to trigger trouble for some infants. These babies need to be handled gently and slowly. Loud talk, hurried movements, too many playthings, too many people around, too much activity in a day – these can all be upsetting. To help such a baby sleep better, avoid active play just before bedtime, substituting a soothing, warm bath followed by quiet storytelling or lullabies. Soft recorded music can often help such a baby to settle down, too.

Taking the extra steps that keep a very demanding baby happy isn't easy, but it's almost always worth the effort. Keep in mind, however, that there will be times when you won't realistically be able to put baby's special needs first (baby dislikes bright lights and noise, but you have to take him or her to a family Christmas party with you). That's fine, too – though you may have to deal with the crying consequences. Keep in mind, also, that most 'challenging' symptoms tend to lessen considerably as a child gets older.

Before you decide your baby is one of the challenging ones, however, you should be sure that there isn't some underlying physical cause of his or her troubling behaviour. Describe it to the doctor so that any possible medical explanation – illness or allergy, for example – can be ruled out. Sometimes a baby who seems to be especially demanding is simply colicky, teething, ill or allergic to her formula. For descriptions of other types of challenging babies, see the box on page 234.

BABY WON'T SLEEP ON BACK

'I know I should put my baby to sleep on his back to protect against SIDS. But he sleeps terribly in that position. Once, when I put him on his tummy to play, he fell asleep and took his longest nap ever. Is it safe to switch?'

Often babies know what's best for them (as when they stop eating when they're no longer hungry, or they tune out overly enthusiastic parents when they've had too much stimulation). But, unfortunately, not when it comes to sleeping positions. Most babies naturally prefer the tummy position for sleeping; it's more comfortable, it's cozier, and it makes them less likely to startle. And for all those reasons, it also ensures longer sleeps and fewer wakings.

But it's clearly not best for baby. Tummy sleeping is linked to a much higher incidence of SIDS – particularly in babies who are not accustomed to the position (because, like yours, they started out on their backs from birth). Most babies get used to the back position quickly, especially if they've never known another sleeping position; others continue to fuss a bit on their backs; and a few, like yours, don't seem able to settle down for a good night's sleep when they're tummy up. Almost all babies would sleep better on their tummies given the chance, which is one of the reasons why scientists believe SIDS is more likely to strike tummy-sleeping babies. Because infants sleep more deeply on their tummies, their arousal responses are muted, preventing them, scientists theorize, from waking up during episodes of sleep apnea and resuming normal breathing patterns.

The first thing you should do is discuss the problem with your doctor. He or she might want to look into why your baby dislikes the back position so much.

Rarely a baby has a physical or anatomical reason that makes being on his back unusually uncomfortable. Much more likely, your baby just plain doesn't like the way it feels. If that's the case, try some of these tips for keeping your baby happy on his back:

♦ Consider swaddling before bedtime. Research shows that infants who are swaddled before they're put on their backs sleep more contentedly – and cry less. They're also less likely to startle and to be woken up by those normal, jerky movements. But don't swaddle once your baby is active enough to kick off the blanket (loose bedding in the cot poses a safety hazard). Some babies can manage this as early as the second month. Also make sure the room is cool enough when you're swaddling; overheating is another risk factor for SIDS.

♦ Prop up the head of the mattress slightly (with a pillow or rolled blanket *under* the mattress) so baby isn't flat on his back. This may make him more comfortable. But don't prop baby with any pillows or other soft bedding inside the cot.

♦ Slowly train your baby to be more comfortable sleeping on his back. If falling asleep in that position is tough for him, try putting him in his infant seat to sleep or rocking him to sleep before transferring him to the cot once he's asleep (on his back).

♦ Stick with it. Consistency almost always pays off when it comes to babies. Eventually, he'll probably get used to sleeping on his back.

♦ Check again with the doctor if baby's still miserable on his back. If nothing you do seems to make your son a happy back-sleeper, the doctor might suggest letting baby sleep on his side, with a wedge that prevents him from rolling onto his stomach (but not his back). While it's not the recommended sleeping position, it's still safer than tummy down, and may allow you both to get some sleep.

Once your baby can roll over by himself, chances are he'll flip over into his preferred sleeping position even when you've put him down on his back (see page 353).

What it's Important to Know: STIMULATING YOUR BABY IN THE EARLY MONTHS

In our achievement-oriented society, many parents worry about turning out babies who can keep up with the baby down the street – and they begin worrying early. They worry that if he doesn't smile by the time he's four weeks old, he may not get into the right preschool programme. They worry that if she hasn't turned over by two months, she may not make the school tennis team. Somewhat of an exaggeration? Well, somewhat. In fact, there are parents who worry that unless they do everything right, they won't be successful in turning the basically unresponsive lump they just delivered into a candidate for Oxbridge.

Actually, they have little reason to worry. Babies – even those destined to get a first-class degree – develop at different rates, and those who get off to a somewhat slower start often excel later. And parents – even those who are chronically insecure – usually do a thoroughly competent job of stimulating their offspring, often without making a conscious effort.

Yet, as comforting as this knowledge should be, it doesn't always stop the worry. For many parents, there is the nagging fear that doing what comes naturally when it comes to parenting may not be quite enough. So, if you'd like to check what you've already been doing instinctively to see if you're on the right track, the following tips for creating the right atmosphere for learning and for supplying sensory stimulation should be helpful to you. Also see Making the Most of the First Three Years, pages 220–221.

CREATING A GOOD ENVIRONMENT

It's a lot easier than you might think. Here's all there is to it:

Love your baby. Nothing helps a baby grow and thrive as much as being loved. A close relationship with a parent, or parents, and/or a substitute parent is crucial for normal development. Love should be unconditional, too – the no-strings-attached variety. It should be communicated as clearly (though it may not come as easily) during a colic bout or a toddler temper tantrum (and, later, during a teenage tempest) as during a moment of angelic behaviour.

Relate to your baby. Take every opportunity to talk, sing or coo to your baby – while you're changing a nappy, giving a bath, shopping for groceries or driving the car. These casual but stimulating exchanges go further in making a brighter baby than forcing computer learning programmes. And even the most educational toys are useless if baby doesn't have you (the best of all toys) to play with part of the time. Your goal at this point isn't to 'teach' your baby but to be involved with him or her.

Get to know your baby. Learn what makes your baby happy or miserable, excited or bored, soothed or stimulated – paying more attention to that feedback than to the advice of any book or expert. Gear attempts at stimulation to your unique baby. If loud noises and/or roughhousing upset your child, then entertain with soft sounds and gentle play. If too much excitement makes your baby frantic, limit the length of playtimes and the intensity of activity.

Take the pressure off – and have fun. Learning and development aren't hastened by pressure, and they may be hindered. Harmful to baby's self-esteem is the message – no matter how carefully camouflaged – that you're not satisfied with his or her progress up the developmental ladder. Instead of thinking of the times you spend stimulating your baby as educational sessions, relax and enjoy, for both your sakes.

Give your baby space. Adequate attention is vital; too much can be stifling. Though children need to know that help is available when they need it, they need to learn how to seek it out, too. Your constant hovering will also deprive your baby of the chance to look for and find diversion elsewhere – in the friendly-looking teddy bear who's sharing the playpen, in the pattern of light cast by the venetian blinds, in his or her own fingers and toes, in the sound of an aeroplane overhead, a fire engine down the street, the dog barking next door. It may also hamper your baby's ability to play, learn and problem-solve independently later on – all important life skills. (Besides, an overly dependent child will make it difficult for you to turn your attention to anything else.) By all means, spend quality time playing with your child. But sometimes just get baby and toy together, and then move off to watch from the sidelines while they get acquainted.

Follow the leader. And make sure your baby, not you, is in the lead. If he or she is fascinated by the mobile, don't bring out the activity board; instead, focus on the mobile together. Allowing baby to take the wheel once in a while not only enhances learning by taking advantage of the 'teachable moment', but also reinforces baby's budding sense of self-esteem by communicating that his or her interests are worthy of mommy's or daddy's attention.

Let your baby take the lead, too, in deciding when to end a play session – even if it's before the rattle is grasped. Your baby will tell you, 'I've had enough', by turning away, fussing, crying or otherwise showing disinterest or displeasure. Ignoring the message and pressing on deprives a baby of a sense of control, turns off interest in the subject (at least for a while), and ultimately makes playtime a whole lot less fun for both of you.

Time it right. A baby is always in one of six states of consciousness: deep, or quiet, sleep; light, or active, sleep; drowsiness; active wakefulness with interest in physical activity; fussiness and crying; or quiet wakefulness. It's during active wakefulness that you can most effectively encourage physical development and during quiet wakefulness that you can best foster other types of learning (see page 114). Also keep in mind that infants have very short attention spans. A baby who turns you off after two minutes of looking at a book isn't rejecting being read to, but has simply run out of concentration.

Provide positive reinforcement. When your baby starts achieving (when he or she smiles, swats at a rattle, lifts shoulders and arms off the mattress, turns over, or grasps a toy successfully) spur on more efforts with positive reinforcement. Do it with hugs, cheers, applause – whatever is comfortable for you and gets the message across to your baby: 'I think you're terrific'.

PRACTICAL TIPS FOR LEARNING AND PLAYING

Some parents, without ever reading a book about or taking a course in infant stimulation, seem to have an easier time than others initiating learning-playing activities with their babies. And some babies, because they are unusually responsive, are easier to engage in such activities. But any parent-baby team can be successful at learning-playing with a little guidance. The areas to nourish and encourage are:

The sense of taste. Right now you don't have to go out of your way to stimulate this sense. Your baby's taste buds are titillated at every meal on breast or bottle. But as baby gets older, 'tasting' will become a way of exploring, and everything within reach will end up being mouthed. Resist the temptation to discourage this – except, of course, when what goes into the mouth is toxic, sharp or small enough to choke on.

The sense of smell. In most environments, the keen smelling apparatus of infants gets plenty of exercise. There's breast milk, dad's aftershave, Rover scampering nearby, the flowers on your walk together, the chicken roasting in the oven. Unless your baby shows signs of being overly sensitive to odours, think of the various scents as additional opportunities for your baby to learn about the environment.

The sense of sight. Though it was once believed that babies were largely sightless at birth, it's now known that they can not only see but can begin learning from what they see right from the start. Through their sense of sight, they learn very quickly to differentiate between objects and human beings (and between one object or human being and another), to interpret body language and other non-verbal cues, and to understand a little bit more every day about the world around them.

Decorate your baby's room or corner with the goal of supplying stimulating visual surroundings, rather than satisfying your own esthetic. When selecting wallpaper, sheets, wall hangings, toys or books, keep in mind that babies like sharp contrasts, and that designs that are bold and bright rather than soft and delicate are more appealing (black-and-white and other colour-contrasting patterns are favoured for the first six weeks or so, pastels and other colours later).

Many objects, toys among them, can stimulate baby visually (but to avoid confusion and overstimulation, provide only one or two at a time during play sessions):

◆ Mobiles. Figures on a mobile should be fully visible from below (the baby's perspective), rather than from the side (the adult's perspective). A mobile should be no more than 30 to 38 cm (12 to 15 in) over the baby's face, and should be hung to one side or the other of the child's line of vision, rather than straight above (most babies prefer to gaze towards the right, but observe your child to discover a preference).

◆ Other things that move. You can move a rattle or other bright toy across baby's line of vision to encourage tracking of moving objects. Take a field trip to a pet shop and position baby in front of a fish tank or bird cage to view the action. Or blow bubbles for baby.

◆ Stationary objects. Babies spend a lot of time just looking at things. This isn't idle time, but learning time. Geometric patterns or simple faces in black and white, hand drawn or store-bought, are early favourites – but baby will probably also be fascinated by every-day objects you wouldn't glance at twice.

◆ Mirrors. Mirrors give babies an ever-changing view, and most love them. (They especially enjoy looking at and socializing with the 'baby' in the mirror, having no clue yet who that baby is.) Be sure to use safe baby mirrors; hang them on the cot, in the carriage, beside the changing table.

◆ People. Babies delight in looking at faces close up, so you and other family members should spend plenty of time in close proximity to baby. Later, you can also show baby family photos pointing out who's who.

◆ Books. Show baby simple pictures of babies, children, animals or toys and identify them. The drawings should be clear and sharply defined without a lot of extra (for a baby) detail. Boldly illustrated board books are perfect for this.

◆ The world. Very soon your baby is going to take an interest in seeing beyond that little button nose. Provide plenty of opportunity to see the world – from the pushchair, pram or car seat, or by carrying your baby face forward. Add commentary, too, pointing out

LOCATION, LOCATION, LOCATION

Here's something you need to know before offering a rattle or other toy to your baby: Where you offer it from makes all the difference. A baby won't reach for an object proffered from the front, only from the side.

cars, trees, people, and so on. But don't ramble non-stop during every outing; you'll become bored, and baby will start tuning you out.

The sense of hearing. It's through hearing that infants learn about language, about rhythm, about danger, about emotions and feelings – and about so much else that goes on around them. Auditory stimulation can come from almost any source.

♦ The human voice. This, of course, is the most significant type of sound in a new infant's life, so use yours – talk, sing and babble to your baby. Try lullabies, nursery rhymes, nonsense ditties you create yourself. Imitate animal sounds, especially ones your baby regularly hears, such as the barking of a dog or the meowing of a cat. Most importantly, play back for your baby the sounds he or she makes.

♦ Household sounds. Many young babies are captivated by either soft or lively background music, the hum of the vacuum or the blender, the whistle of the kettle or the splash of running water, the crinkling of paper, or the tinkling of a bell or wind chime – though they may become fearful of many such sounds later in the first and second years.

♦ Rattles and other toys that make

gentle sounds. You don't have to wait until your baby is able to shake a rattle independently. In the early months, either do the shaking yourself, put the rattle in baby's hand and help shake it, or attach a wrist rattle. Coordination between vision and hearing will develop as baby learns to turn towards sound.

♦ Music boxes. You'll be surprised at how quickly your baby will learn to recognize a tune; especially nice are music boxes that have visual appeal, but if one is placed within reach, be sure it doesn't have small pieces that can be broken off and mouthed by your baby.

♦ Musical toys. Toys that make music and also provide visual stimulation and practice with small motor skills (such as a bunny that moves and makes music when baby pulls a string) are particularly good. Avoid toys that make loud noises that can damage hearing, and don't place even moderately noisy ones right by baby's ear. Also be sure that the toys are otherwise safe for baby.

♦ Children's tapes and CDs. Try to give them a spin before buying to be sure they're good listening. Infancy is also an ideal time to start exposing your child to classical music (play it softly during playtime in the cot, or during dinner or bath time), although many babies seem to prefer the livelier rhythms of rock, pop or country music. Always watch your baby for reactions to music; if he or she seems disturbed by what you're playing, turn it off. Also, protect your baby's sense of hearing by keeping the volume down.

The sense of touch. Touch, though often underrated, is actually one of a baby's most valuable tools for exploring and learning about the world. It's through touch that a baby learns the softness of mummy and the relative hardness of daddy, that rubbing a teddy bear feels wonderful, that rubbing a stiff brush doesn't feel so good, and most important of all, that those who take care of him are loving – a message you send every time you bathe, change, feed, hold or rock your baby.

You can provide more varied touching experiences for your baby with:

◆ A loving hand. Try to learn how your baby likes to be handled – firmly or lightly, quickly or slowly. Most babies love to be caressed and kissed, to have their tummies tickled or razzed by your lips, to have you blow gently on their fingers or toes. They love the difference between mummy's touch and daddy's, the playful way a sibling hugs them and the expert ease with which grandma rocks them.

◆ Massage. Premature babies who are massaged for at least twenty minutes daily gain weight faster and do better overall than those who aren't (whether it's the massage or the fact that they're handled more is unclear); babies who aren't touched at all don't grow at a normal pace. Discover the kind of strokes your baby enjoys most, and avoid those that seem to annoy (see page 302 for tips).

◆ Textures. Try rubbing a baby's skin with different textures (satin, terry cloth, velvet, wool, fur or absorbent cotton) so he or she can get to know how each feels; later encourage independent exploration. Let baby lie tummy down (while supervised only) on surfaces with different textures: the living room carpet, a terry towel, grandma's faux fur coat, dad's wool sweater, mum's corduroy jacket, the marble-topped coffee table – the possibilities are limitless.

◆ Playthings with texture. Offer toys that have interesting textures to baby. A plush teddy bear and a coarse-haired stuffed doggy; hard wooden blocks and soft stuffed ones; a rough wooden bowl and a smooth metal one; a silky pillow and a nubby one.

Social development. Your baby becomes a social being through watching you, through interacting with you and the rest of the family, and later with others. This isn't the time to begin teaching your baby how to throw a successful dinner party or make interesting small talk over the canapés, but it is time to begin teaching by example how people should behave towards one another. A few years from now, when your growing child talks to friends, teachers, neighbours or begins 'playing house', you'll often hear your example echoed in that tiny voice; hopefully, you'll be pleased (and not shocked or disappointed) by what you hear.

Toys that help babies with social development are stuffed animals, animal mobiles and dolls. Though it will be many months before they'll be able to hug them and play with them, even at this point they can and do begin to socialize with them – just watch an infant converse with animals prancing on the cot bumpers or revolving on a mobile. Later, books and opportunities for make-believe and dress-up play will also help children to develop social skills.

Small motor development. Right now your baby's hand movements are totally random, but in a couple of months, those tiny hands will move with more purpose and control. You can aid in the development of purposeful movement by giving your baby's hands plenty of freedom; don't keep them swaddled or tucked tightly under a blanket (except outdoors in cold weather). Provide a variety of objects that are easy for small hands to pick up and manipulate, that don't require fine dexterity. And since young babies usually won't grasp objects that are directly in front of them, offer these objects from the side.

Give your baby ample opportunity for 'hands-on' experience with the following:

♦ Rattles that fit small hands comfortably. Those with two handles or grasping surfaces will eventually allow a baby to pass the rattle from hand to hand, an important skill; those that baby can mouth will help bring relief when teething begins.

♦ Cradle gyms (they fit across the pram, playpen or cot) that have a variety of parts for baby to grab hold of, spin, pull and poke. Beware of those, however, with strings more than 15 cm (6 in) long, and take down any gym once your baby is able to sit up.

♦ Activity boards that require a wide range of hand movements to operate. Your baby may not be able to intentionally manoeuvre the toy for a while, but even a young infant can sometimes set it in motion accidentally. Besides the spinning, dialing, pushing and pressing skills these toys encourage, they also teach the concept of cause and effect.

Gross motor development. Putting your baby through the paces of an infant exercise video won't increase muscular strength or speed motor development. Good motor skills, well-developed bodies and physical fitness for infants depend instead on the following: good nutrition; good health care (both well baby and sick baby); and plenty of opportunity for self-motivated physical activity. Babies kept cooped up in a swing or baby seat, or harnessed in a pram or pushchair, or swaddled in a blanket or bunting will have little opportunity to learn about how their bodies work. Those who are never put down on their tummy for supervised playtime will be slow to learn to lift their head and shoulders or turn over front to back and may never learn to crawl. Change your baby's position often during the day (propping him up in a sitting position, placing her sometimes on her stomach – supervised – and other times on her back) to maximize the opportunities for physical activity.

Encourage physical development by pulling your baby to a sitting position, letting him or her 'fly' (allowing exercise of arms and legs) or 'ride' (lying face-down lengthways on your shins). Motivate rolling over by putting an interesting object to one side as baby lies on his or her back; if baby turns a bit, then give a little help in going all the way. Encourage creeping by letting baby push off against your hands when lying belly down.

Intellectual development. Encouraging the development of all the senses, as well as small and large motor control, will contribute to your baby's intellectual growth. Talk to your infant a lot, right from the start. Give names to objects, animals and people your baby sees, point out body parts, explain what you're doing. Read nursery rhymes and simple stories, showing your baby the illustrations as you go. Expose your child to a variety of settings (the supermarket, a department store, the museum, the park). Travel on buses, in cars, in taxis. Even at home, vary your baby's point of view: place the baby seat by a window (but *only* if it has a window guard and only when you're supervising closely) or in front of a mirror, lay baby in the middle of the living room carpet to survey the action or in the middle of the bed to watch you fold the laundry, or park the pushchair in the kitchen while you prepare dinner.

Whatever you do, remember the most important rule of stimulating your baby: The play's the thing. And the play should be fun.

♦♦♦

CHAPTER 7

The Third Month

This month, baby's finally starting to discover that there's more to life than eating, sleeping and crying. Not to say that babies this age don't do plenty of all of these (colicky infants generally keep up the late afternoon and early evening crying bouts until the end of the month) – just that they've expanded their horizons to interests beyond. Like their own hands – as far as two- and three-month-olds are concerned, the most fascinating toys ever invented. Like staying awake for longer stretches of play during the day (and hopefully, staying asleep for longer stretches at night). Like keeping mummy and daddy entertained with adorable live shows of smiles, gurgles, squeals and coos that make parenting well worth the price of admission.

What Your Baby May Be Doing

All babies reach milestones on their own developmental time line. If your baby seems not to have reached one or more of these milestones, rest assured, he or she probably will very soon. Your baby's rate of development is normal for your baby. Keep in mind, too, that skills babies perform from the tummy position can be mastered only if there's an opportunity to practise. So make sure your baby spends supervised playtime on his or her belly. If you have concerns about your baby's development, check with the doctor. Premature infants generally reach milestones later than others of the same birth age, often achieving them closer to their adjusted age (the age they would be if they had been born at term), and sometimes later.

By three months, your baby . . . should be able to:

◆ on stomach, lift head up 45 degrees[1]

. . . will probably be able to:

◆ laugh out loud

◆ on stomach, lift head up 90 degrees

---

1. Babies who spend little time on their stomachs during playtime may reach this milestone later, and that's not cause for concern (see page 205).

Many, but not all, three-month-olds can lift their heads to a 90-degree angle.

- squeal in delight

- bring both hands together

- smile spontaneously

- follow an object held about 15 cm (6 in) above baby's face and moved 180 degrees – from one side to the other, with baby watching all the way

... may possibly be able to:

- hold head steady when upright

- on stomach, raise chest, supported by arms

- roll over (one way)

- grasp a rattle held to backs or tips of fingers

- pay attention to an object as small as a raisin (but make sure such objects are kept out of baby's reach)

... may even be able to:

- bear some weight on legs when held upright

- reach for an object

- keep head level with body when pulled to sitting

- turn in the direction of a voice, particularly mummy's

- say 'ah-goo' or similar vowel-consonant combination

- razz (make a wet razzing sound)

What You Can Expect at This Month's Checkup

Just immunizations at this checkup – providing baby is in good health and there are no other contraindications. See the schedule on page 227. Be sure to discuss any reactions to the first round of immunizations beforehand.

Feeding Your Baby:
BREASTFEEDING AND WORKING

It's a responsibility that can't be found in any job description, yet more and more employed mothers are electing to take it on. It cuts into coffee breaks and lunch hours, makes a busy day even busier, and takes plenty of planning and even more dedication. And yet most women who pump on the job so they can keep nursing after they return to work wouldn't have it any other way. For them, the benefits of continued breastfeeding – from the physical (better health for baby) to the emotional (built-in close contact with baby before and after work; a strong link with baby while they're on the job) – are well worth the extra effort. Besides, many find that once they get the hang of it, being a breastfeeding employed mother isn't such hard work after all.

BREASTFEEDING AND WORKING – MAKING THEM WORK FOR YOU

As with everything else that's related to going back to work when you have a young infant, plenty of forethought is necessary. To make nursing and employment work, keep the following in mind:

Wait with the bottle . . . Don't start giving bottles until your milk supply is well established. Starting too soon can lead to nipple confusion (see page 86) and an inadequate milk supply. Wait to introduce the bottle until you've worked out any nursing kinks and feel confident about your milk supply. For most women, that's somewhere around four to six weeks – though some find things going smoothly a bit sooner or later.

. . . but don't wait too long. Though you won't want to bring on the bottle much before four to five weeks, don't wait much longer either – even if you won't be heading back to work for a while. Typically, the older and smarter babies get, the less open they are to trying the bottle. Once you've made the

introduction, get baby used to taking at least one bottle feeding a day – preferably during what will soon be your working hours.

Get an early start. Your first day back on the job will be stressful enough without adding the strain of figuring out how to use a breast pump. So begin pumping a few weeks before you're due back on the job. That way, not only will you be a more confident pumper but also you'll have started collecting a stash of frozen milk by the time you start collecting pay cheques.

Do a couple of trial runs. With child care in place, rehearse your workday game plan, doing everything as you would if you were really going to work (including expressing milk away from home), but leave the house for just a couple of hours the first time, longer the next. Noting what problems arise now gives you time to figure out how they can be handled.

Start off slow. If you're going back to a full-time job, you might try returning on a Thursday or Friday to give yourself a chance to get started, see how things go, and evaluate the situation over the weekend. Beginning with a short week will also be a little less overwhelming than starting out with five days ahead of you.

Work part-time. If you can swing a part-time schedule, at least at first, you'll be able to spend more time strengthening breastfeeding links. Working four or five half-days is more practical than two or three full ones for several reasons. With half-days, you may not have to miss any feedings – and certainly no more than one a day. You'll have little trouble with leakage (your silk blouses will thank you), and probably won't have to do any on-the-job pumping (which means you'll actually get to drink coffee on your coffee break). Best of all, you'll spend most of each day with your baby. Working nights is another option that interferes very little with breastfeeding, especially once baby is sleeping through the night, but it can seriously interfere with two other very important commodities: rest and romance.

Once back on the job, finding the time and the place to pump can be a big challenge for nursing mums. Luckily, pumping is fast becoming a part of business as usual; in some workplaces, it's even encouraged (see box, opposite page). Many women successfully combine nursing, pumping and working. Keeping these tips in mind can help you succeed, too.

◆ Dress for pumping success. Wear clothes that are convenient for pumping. Be sure your top can be lifted or opened easily from the front for pumping at work, and that it won't be stretched out of shape or badly wrinkled by being pulled up. (See page 81). Whatever you wear, line your nursing bra with breast pads to protect your clothing, and carry an extra supply of pads in your bag as replacements for wet ones.

◆ Look for privacy. Pumping at work will be infinitely easier if you have access to a private space, such as your own office with a door you can close, an unused office or conference room, or a discreet (and clean) corner in the ladies' room.

◆ Be consistent. Schedule permitting, try to pump at the same times every day – as close as possible to the times you would be feeding your baby if you were home. That way your breasts will come to anticipate pumping (as they would anticipate nursing) and fill up with milk like clockwork.

◆ Plan for storage. Store freshly pumped milk in the office refrigerator, well marked with your name (so that co-workers won't mistake it for coffee creamer). Or bring a cooler from home with ice packs, or use the attached cooler that comes with many portable pumps. See page 156 for more on storing breast milk.

◆ Use promptly. When you get home, refrigerate the pumped milk, and have the care provider feed it to your baby the next day. This way you should always have a full day's supply available in the fridge.

◆ Schedule in breastfeeding, too. Breastfeeding on schedule will help keep your milk supply up – as well as give you and baby that special time together. Breastfeed before going to work in the morning and as soon as you come home in the afternoon or evening. Ask the care provider not to feed the baby during the last hour of the workday, or to feed baby just enough to take the edge off any hunger.

◆ Take a holiday from bottles on weekends. To keep your milk supply abundant, use weekends and holidays as time for exclusive nursing. Try to go bottle-free as much as possible then, or any other day you're home.

◆ Schedule smart. Arrange your schedule to maximize the number of nursings. Squeeze in two feedings before you go to work, if possible, and two or three (or more) in the evening. If you work near home and can either return during lunchtime for nursing or have the sitter meet you somewhere for a drive-by nursing session with baby (even at your office, if you can arrange it), consider

BREASTFEEDING-FRIENDLY COMPANIES

The days of sneaking breast pumps down the hall to the ladies' room and hiding milk stashes where they won't be poured accidentally into someone else's coffee are gone – at least at some enlightened workplaces. As companies begin to realize that policies which make working parents happier usually make them more productive on the job, more and more are making rooms available for their employees, complete with pumps, refrigerators, and even access to a breastfeeding consultant. These programmes benefit not only the mother (because of decreased stress) and baby (because of the health benefits of breast milk) but also the company; if the baby gets sick less often, the mother is absent from work less often – resulting in a more productive worker.

Even if your company does not have such a programme, there are ways to make your place of work a more nursing-friendly environment. Get together with other breastfeeding mothers in the office (if possible) and lobby for periodic break time, a room for privacy, and other such pumping necessities on the job. Keep track of the amount of time other employees take breaks (for coffee, lunch or smoking) so that if your boss says there's no time in the day to spend on pumping, you're armed with an answer. Alert your employer to the many resources available, from organizations such as the NCT and the La Leche League.

doing this. If your baby is in day care, nurse when you arrive there, or in your car before you go in, if that works better. Also try nursing your baby at pickup time, instead of waiting until you get home.

◆ Stick close to home. If your job entails travel, try to avoid trips that take you away from home for more than a day until your baby is weaned; if you must travel, try to express and freeze in advance enough milk for the duration of your trip, or get your baby accustomed to formula before you plan to go. For your own comfort and to keep up your milk supply, take along a breast pump (or rent one where you'll be) and express milk every three or four hours. When you get home, you may find your milk supply somewhat diminished, but more-frequent-than-usual nursings, along with extra-special attention to diet and rest, should replenish it.

◆ Work from home when you can. Try taking home any work that can be done out of the office (with your employer's blessing). This will give you more flexibility and allow you to be home more of your baby's waking hours. Though you will probably have to relegate most of baby's care to a sitter when you're working in your home, you should be able to nurse as needed.

◆ Keep your priorities straight. You won't be able to do everything and do everything well. Keep your baby and your relationship with your spouse (and any other children you have) at the top of the list. Your job – especially if it means a lot to you, either financially, emotionally or professionally – will probably also have to make the top of the list, but be relentless about cutting corners everywhere else.

• Stay flexible. A (relatively) calm and happy mother is more valuable to your baby's well-being than a diet made up exclusively of breast milk. Though it's entirely possible you'll be able to continue providing all of your baby's milk (as many women do), it's also possible that you won't. Sometimes the physical and emotional stresses of holding a job and nursing curtail a woman's milk supply. If your baby isn't thriving on breast milk alone, try nursing more frequently when you're at home and, if it's feasible, returning home during your lunch break to breastfeed and help rebuild your milk supply. If this doesn't work and you find you can't keep up with working and pumping, it might be best to supplement with formula.

What You May Be Concerned About

ESTABLISHING A REGULAR SCHEDULE

'My mother tells me I have to get my baby on a schedule right away. My sister says to throw away the clock and just meet his needs. What's the right thing to do?'

The right thing to do – as it is when it comes to so many aspects of parenting – is what's right for you and your baby. Though advocates on both sides of this issue would argue otherwise, there are no absolutes that definitively answer the question of whether or not to put babies who are no longer newborns on schedules. That's because every baby, like every parent, is an individual. What works for one parent and baby may not work well for another parent and baby, and may not even work well for two different babies in the same family. There are pros and cons to both philosophies of parenting, and many parents, rather than dogmatically following one method or the other, find a middle ground that's comfortable for them.

By three months, some babies will have established a pretty regular daily rhythm, even without prodding from the parents. Typically, it's something like this: he wakes about the same time each morning, feeds, perhaps stays awake for a short period, takes a nap, wakes again for lunch,. follows with another nap, feeds, then perhaps has a fairly long period of wakefulness late in the afternoon, capped off by a meal and a nap in the early evening. If this nap tends to run past the parents' bedtimes, they may wake him for a feeding before they go to bed, maybe about 11 PM (or as late as they can keep their eyes open). At this point he may go back to sleep again until early morning, since babies this age can often sleep six hours at a stretch, and sometimes more.

Other babies have a more idiosyncratic, yet still somewhat consistent, schedule. One, for example, may wake up at 6 AM, feed, and go back to sleep for an hour or two. Once awake, he may be content to play for a while before nursing, but once he starts nursing, he wants to do so non-stop for the next three hours. After a twenty-minute nap, however, he wakes up ready to play all afternoon with just one nursing period and another five-minute nap. He nurses again at about 6 and by 7 is sound asleep, and he stays that way until mum wakes him for a nightcap before she goes to bed. His isn't the traditional four-hour schedule, but there is still a consistent pattern of sleep-wake-eat to his day.

Parents of such 'regular' babies have an easy time creating a regular routine; even the non-traditional yet consistent routine is still one a parent can plan the day around, if not set his or her watch to. And because the baby's schedule is baby-led, not imposed, parents of these babies needn't feel as if they're being too rigid or not being responsive enough.

But many babies don't fall smoothly into any schedule at all, even past three months. Their wake, eat, and sleep pattern is totally random from day to day. If your baby is one of these, you'll have to decide whether you want to take the initiative by trying to make the parts of his life you do have some control over as organized as possible or whether you want to take a laissez-faire attitude towards scheduling. Here's the rundown on what both approaches might have to offer:

Parenting on schedule. Regular routines give children predictability, stability and security, according to proponents of parenting on schedule. Routines keep the day dependable and calm, providing the order and consistency many babies are naturally comforted by. Establishing a schedule doesn't mean a baby's needs won't be met – they're just met within the framework of a daily routine. And because parents have rights, too, a predictable schedule theoretically allows you and your spouse to make time for each other, away from baby (at home or out), something that relationships thrive on, and that is often unattainable when it's anybody's guess when baby will eat or sleep. Schedules become increasingly important to family stability and to a child's well-being as time goes by. Many

children seem to do perfectly well without a schedule in early infancy, when they're extremely portable and can fall asleep or be fed anywhere. Later, they often begin to respond to irregular mealtimes and sleep times with regular crying and crankiness. And once school starts, children who don't have regular bedtimes often have trouble rising on time or getting enough sleep to get productively through their days.

Scheduling a baby, however, can be taken to the extreme – and shouldn't be. Very young infants (under the age of two to three months) shouldn't be put on a schedule – they should eat and sleep on demand. Even later on, denying your hungry baby the breast or bottle because the clock says he shouldn't be hungry yet is never a good idea (and, if baby's breastfed, can lead to a diminished milk supply and even failure to thrive). Not picking up a crying baby because the schedule says it's 'mummy and daddy time' now can make a child feel helpless, abandoned, insecure and unloved. In other words, a strict schedule can be as stifling as a too lax one can be disorienting.

If you decide on a schedule, how much structure you should build into it should depend on your baby's natural eating and sleeping patterns, his inborn personality (some children naturally seem to need more structure, some less), and the needs of the rest of the family. A schedule shouldn't be thought of as a rigid set of rules to be followed and appointments to be kept, but rather as a flexible timetable around which your and your baby's day revolves.

Parenting on demand. Though much of our society is run on schedules – train timetables, work schedules, class timetables – there are those who function perfectly well without them. If baby thrives without a schedule (seems perfectly contented, active and interested by day, and sleeps well at night) and his parents do, too (they don't mind putting baby's needs first, even when it means that other areas of their lives will take a backseat), then this system can work well. Proponents say that responding to your baby's every need on demand allows you to better understand your baby and foster trust, the foundation of good parent-child communication. That nursing baby whenever he cries for food (even if he just finished eating), letting him sleep whenever he wants to (and letting him stay up when he wants to), and carrying (or wearing) baby as much as possible during the day (or when he demands it) allows him to feel secure and valued as a human being and also reduces fussing and crying. And because it builds in more time together, demand parenting can also help parents get to know their babies better and faster. Families who choose demand parenting feel that scheduling baby for the sake of convenience is a short-term gain far outweighed by the long-term loss.

There can be, however, certain potential pitfalls to raising children in an unstructured environment. Some babies crave schedules right from the start. They become cranky when feedings are late or overtired when naps and bedtimes are delayed. If your baby reacts unhappily to your unscheduled days and nights, it may be that she needs a little more structure, even if you don't. And for some babies, the absence of structure in their lives early on can interfere with their developing, and then exercising, self-discipline later in life. Getting to school on time, completing homework, and getting papers in on schedule can be difficult for children who have never been exposed to any kind of structure previously. Of course, some children continue to thrive in schedule-free homes. And since every child is different, and some can end up being quite different from their parents, there's the distinct possibility that a child raised without a schedule may turn out to be a Type A who creates his own to meet his needs (giving himself the bedtime his parents never did), and the child who's raised by the clock may turn out to be the one for whom schedules never fit.

If you choose to parent on demand, make sure, too, that in keeping up with those of your baby, you don't neglect the demands of your relationship with your spouse. Without a regular bedtime for their babies, parents often find they never spend any time alone. They enjoy their threesome so much in the evening, they sometimes forget the fun two can – and should – have.

Not only isn't there any right or wrong answer when it comes to schedules, what's right or wrong for you and your baby may change as the months pass. You may start out with a schedule, only to find it too confining. Or you may start out with demand parenting, only to find out your baby demands a schedule. Or, like so many other parents, you may ultimately find that middle ground the most comfortable place to be. No matter what your choice, remember that it's no one else's to make. Do what works for you and your baby, and don't worry about what anybody else has to say about it.

PUTTING BABY TO BED

'My baby always falls asleep nursing. Is this a bad habit that needs to be broken?'

DUELLING PARENTING PHILOSOPHIES

Walk into any bookshop, check out any newsstand, or surf any on-line parenting site, and you'll be confronted with a multitude of books, magazines, articles and advice on how to parent your child. You'll be bombarded with dozens of parenting philosophies, each with its own set of doctrines – most of them conflicting – and each claiming to offer the best approach to raising children. Whether the philosophy covers how to feed your baby, how to get your baby to sleep through the night, where your baby should sleep, how your baby should be carried, when your baby should be weaned, or what kind of schedule your baby should be on, they are all based on the same premise: every child has needs, and it's the parents who are there to meet those needs.

The spectrum of advice and philosophies is broad, with many methods pitting their own points of view against others. But most parents follow advice that falls into one of two 'mainstream' philosophies. 'Attachment parenting' promotes nursing on demand, co-sleeping and baby wearing (meeting baby's needs by being in close physical contact with him or her as much as possible). 'Parent-guided parenting' promotes creating a structured environment in which a baby's needs are met in a familiar and routine fashion.

Some parents alternate between philosophies depending on the issue. Some sample a little from each before choosing one they feel they and their babies can live with. Some continue to vacillate between philosophies, never feeling sure enough about any one to settle on it. Many take a little from each or from several to create their own philosophy. Other parents embrace one philosophy with everything they've got, even denigrating those who have chosen to parent in another way.

What many philosophies – and their subscribers – fail to take into account, however, is that there are very few absolutes when it comes to the job of parenting. With the exception of safety and health issues (keeping your child in a car seat, making sure he or she receives regular medical care), there are many good ways to be a good parent. Most doctors will agree that as long as both parents agree on an approach and are consistent in it, any parenting style (or a combination of a few) can work out well for a family. As long as your baby is healthy, safe and content, doing what feels best for your family is always a better idea than dogmatically following a set system – or being made to feel guilty by those who disagree with your style of parenting.

It's an idea that looks good on paper: put a baby to bed when she's awake, not already asleep, so that later, once she's weaned, she'll be able to get to sleep on her own – without the breast or a bottle. In practice, as any mother who's tried to keep her baby from falling asleep while nursing or tried to rouse a baby who's conked out while suckling knows, it's an idea that's not necessarily compatible with reality. There's just very little you can do to keep a nursing baby awake if she wants to sleep. And if you could wake her up, would you really want to?

Teaching your baby to fall asleep without assistance from breast (or bottle) can more practically wait until baby is older – between six and nine months – and nursing less often. And if the habit hangs on, breaking it can certainly be accomplished fairly quickly after your baby has been weaned.

Whenever the opportunity presents itself, however, you might want to consider putting your baby down for a nap or at bedtime while she's still awake – not so awake that sleep will be elusive, but in a state of drowsy readiness. A little rocking, nursing or lullabying can usually bring a baby to this state (but try not to prolong the comforting action to the point of sound sleep).

WAKING UP FOR NIGHT-TIME FEEDINGS

'My friend's baby has been sleeping through the night since he got home from the hospital, but mine is still waking up and eating as often as he did when he was first born.'

In young infants, the habit of feeding frequently at night is often a nutritionally necessary one. Though some babies no longer need night feedings by the third month (and sometimes sooner), most two- or three-month-old babies, particularly breastfed ones, still need to eat once or twice during the night.

But while your baby may still need some middle-of-the-night nourishment, he certainly doesn't need to be chowing down three or four times per evening. Gradually reducing the number of late-show feedings baby's getting won't only help you get more rest now, it's an important first step in preparing him to sleep food free through the night later on. Here's how:

♦ Increase the size of the bedtime feeding. Many sleepy babies nod off before they've totally filled their tanks for the night; restart yours if possible, with a burp or a jiggle or some other ploy, and continue feeding until you feel he's had enough. Don't be tempted to add solids to baby's diet (or put cereal in your baby's bottle) before he or she is developmentally ready in an effort to buy extra hours of sleep. Not only won't it work, giving solids isn't recommended until four to six months.

♦ Wake baby for a feeding before you turn in. A late-evening meal may fill him up enough to last him through your own six or eight hours of shut-eye. Even if he's too sleepy to take a full meal, he may take enough to hold him an hour or two longer than he would have gone without a snack. (Of course, if your baby begins waking more often once you've instituted this procedure, discontinue it. It could be that being awakened by you makes him more prone to waking himself.)

♦ Make sure baby's getting enough to eat all day long. If he isn't, he may be using those night feedings to catch up on calories. If you think this might be the case, consider nursing more frequently during the day to stimulate milk production (also check the tips on page 159). If your baby's on the bottle, increase the amount of formula you give at each feeding. Be aware, however, that for some babies feeding every couple of hours during the day sets up a pattern of eating every two hours, a pattern they continue around the clock. If your baby seems to have fallen into such a schedule, you might want to go for longer, less frequent feedings instead.

♦ Wait a little longer between feedings. If he's waking and demanding food every two hours (necessary for a newborn, but not usually for a thriving three- or four-month-old), try to stretch the time between feedings, adding half an hour each night or every other night. Instead of jumping to get him at the first whimper, give him a chance to try to fall asleep again by himself – he may surprise you. If he doesn't, and fussing turns to crying, try to soothe him without feeding him – pat or rub him, sing a soft, monotonous lullaby, or turn on a musical cot toy. If the crying doesn't stop after a reasonable time (for however long you feel comfortable letting him fuss), pick him up and try soothing him in your arms by rocking, swaying, cuddling or singing. If you're breastfeeding, the soothing tactics have a better chance of success if dad's in charge; a breastfeeding infant who sees, hears or smells his source of food is not easily distracted from eating. Keep the room dark, and avoid a lot of conversation or stimulation.

If baby doesn't fall back to sleep and still demands feeding, feed him – but by now you've probably stretched the interval between feedings by at least half an hour from the previous plateau. The hope is that baby will reach a new plateau within the next few nights and sleep half an hour longer between feedings. Gradually try to extend the time between meals until baby is down to one night-time feeding, which he may continue to need for another one to three months.

◆ Cut down the amounts at the night-time feedings you want to eliminate. Gradually reduce the number of minutes he spends nursing or the millilitres/ounces in his bottle. Continue cutting back a little more each night or every other night.

◆ Increase the amount offered at the night feeding you are most likely to continue (for now). If your baby is getting up at midnight, two and four, for example, you may want to cut out the first and last of these feedings.

This will be easier to do if you increase the amount your baby takes at the middle one, either from breast or bottle. A nip from the breast or 60 ml (2 fl oz) or so from the bottle is not likely to knock him out for long. See the tips for keeping a sleepy baby awake for feeding on page 116.

◆ Don't change your baby during the night unless it's absolutely necessary – a quick sniff can usually tell you when it is. If your baby is between nappy sizes, using the next larger size will provide extra surface area for absorption; or use the special night-time nappies.

◆ Consider some distance. If you're sharing a room or a bed with your baby (and don't want to continue co-sleeping in the long term), now might be a good time to think about splitting up (see page 259). Your nearness may be the reason he's waking so often and why you're picking him up so often. (That said, keep in mind that a parent's proximity may reduce the risk of SIDS during the first six to twelve months.)

By four months, most babies don't really need to be eating at all during the night. (From a strictly metabolic standpoint, babies can usually go through the night without a feeding once they've reached 5 kg (11 lb); whether they will or not is another matter entirely.) If the night-waking habit continues into the fifth or sixth month, you can begin to suspect that your baby is waking not because he *needs* to eat during the night, but because he's become *accustomed* to eating during the night; a stomach that's used to being filled at regular intervals around the clock will cry 'empty' even when it's full enough to last a lot longer. See page 348 for tips on getting an older baby to sleep through the night.

SUDDEN INFANT DEATH SYNDROME (SIDS)

'Since a neighbour's baby died of SIDS, I'm so nervous that I've been waking my baby up several times a night to make sure she's okay. Would it be a good idea to ask the doctor about a monitoring machine?'

The fear that a baby might die suddenly in the middle of the night has plagued parents probably from the beginning of time – long before such deaths were given the medical name sudden infant death syndrome (SIDS). Ancient writings mention such deaths;

the baby described in the Book of Kings as being 'overlaid' by his mother was very likely a victim of cot death.

But unless your baby has experienced an actual life-threatening episode in which she stopped breathing and needed to be revived (in which case, see next page), the chances of her actually succumbing to SIDS are very, very small. And preoccupation with the fear that your child might end up being among those very few is more harmful than helpful – to both of you.

For most parents, no reassurance will totally obviate the need they feel to check their baby's breathing occasionally at night. Many, in fact, don't breathe easily themselves until their babies have

WHAT IS SIDS?

SIDS, or sudden infant death syndrome, also commonly known as cot death, is the sudden and unexpected death of an apparently healthy infant that is unexplained by the baby's medical history, an autopsy or the examination of the scene of death. Though SIDS is the major cause of infant death between the ages of two weeks and twelve months, the risk of the average baby dying of SIDS is very small – the present rate for cot deaths in the UK is 1 per 2,000. And thanks to preventive steps parents can take (see Preventing SIDS, next page), that risk is getting smaller still.

SIDS most often occurs in babies between two and four months, with the majority of deaths occurring before six months. Though it was once believed that victims were 'perfectly healthy' babies stricken without reason, researchers are now convinced that SIDS babies only *appear* healthy and actually have some underlying defect that predisposes them to sudden death. One hypothesis is that the control in the brain that wakes us when breathing conditions are dangerous is

underdeveloped in these babies. Another theory is that SIDS may be caused by an undetected defect in the heart.

There is a higher SIDS risk for babies of women who had poor antenatal care, who smoked during pregnancy (smoking pre- and postnatally increases the risk threefold), or were under age twenty (this may be as much because of the poor ante- or postnatal care or because of smoking as because of age). Premature or low birthweight babies are also at somewhat higher risk.

SIDS is *not* caused by vomiting, choking or minor illnesses. It is also *not* caused by immunizations. Nor is SIDS contagious.

There are many environmental factors that increase the risk of SIDS, including tummy sleeping, sleeping on soft or loose bedding or with pillows or toys, exposure to tobacco smoke, and being overheated. The good news is that all of them can be avoided. In fact, there has been a 65 per cent decrease in the UK in the number of SIDS deaths since 1991.

PREVENTING SIDS

You can reduce the SIDS risk significantly for your baby with these measures:

♦ Put baby to sleep on his or her back. Make sure all of baby's providers, including baby-sitters, day-care workers and grandparents are instructed to do this, too.

♦ Use a firm mattress and tightly fitting sheets for baby's cot. Remove all loose bedding, pillows, fluffy quilts, sheepskins and soft toys from the cot. If you use a blanket, make sure it's a thin one, tuck it in around the mattress, and make sure it reaches only baby's chest level. Or, better yet, skip the blanket and put baby in a one-piece sleeper.

♦ Never allow your baby to get overheated. Don't dress baby too warmly for bed – no hats or extra clothing or blankets – and don't keep his or her room too warm. Your baby should not feel hot to the touch. Overheating increases the risk of apnea, which can lead to SIDS in some babies.

♦ Don't allow anyone to smoke in your home or near your baby.

♦ Consider running a fan in baby's room. Circulating air has been shown to reduce risk.

♦ Offer baby a dummy at sleep times, even if you don't want her using one during the day. (Don't worry if she spits it out during the night or if she refuses to take it.)

Studies report a lowered risk of SIDS among breastfed babies as well as babies that sleep in the same room as their parents (if baby sleeps with you, you'll need to be sure your bed is safe; see page 261) and suggest a lower SIDS incidence among infants who use a dummy. More research needs to be done to confirm these findings.

Devices designed to maintain sleep position (such as wedges) or to reduce the risk of rebreathing air are not recommended, because many have not been sufficiently tested for their safety, and none has been shown to be effective at reducing the risk of SIDS.

passed the one-year mark, the age when infants seem to outgrow the risk of SIDS. And that's okay as long as you don't let worry pervade your life with baby.

Though investing in a monitor – an apparatus that can signal if your baby suddenly stops breathing – may seem like an ideal (if expensive) way of easing your fears, monitoring a normal baby can cause more problems than it solves. The false alarms that are common with monitors result more in worry than relief.

What can make you feel more secure – besides taking all the preventive steps listed above – is learning infant CPR, and being sure that baby-sitters, housekeepers, and anyone else who spends time alone with your baby also knows this lifesaving technique. That way, if your baby

ever does stop breathing, for any reason, resuscitation can be attempted immediately (see page 593). If gnawing fears continue to plague you, look to your baby's doctor for reassurance. If that doesn't calm you down, talk to a therapist who is familiar with SIDS and can help to allay your fears. (Sometimes, postnatal depression can trigger this kind of overwhelming anxiety; see page 676.)

'Yesterday afternoon I went in to check on my baby, who seemed to be taking a very long nap. He was lying in the cot absolutely still and blue. Frantic, I grabbed him and he started breathing again. Now his doctor wants to put him in the hospital for tests and I'm terrified.'

REPORTING BREATHING EMERGENCIES TO YOUR DOCTOR

Though very brief (under twenty seconds) periods of breathing lapse can be normal, longer periods – or short periods in which the baby turns pale or blue or limp and has a very slowed heartbeat – require medical attention. If you have to take steps to revive your baby, call the doctor or emergency services immediately. If you can't revive your baby by gentle shaking, try CPR (see page 593), and call or have someone else call 999. Try to note the following to report to the doctor:

◆ Did the breathing lapse occur when baby was asleep or awake?

◆ Was baby sleeping, feeding, crying, spitting, gagging or coughing when the event occurred?

◆ Did baby experience any colour changes; was he or she pale, blue or red in the face?

◆ Did baby need resuscitation? How did you revive him or her, and how long did it take?

◆ Were there any changes in baby's crying (higher pitch, for example) before the breathing lapse?

◆ Did baby seem limp or stiff, or was he or she moving normally?

◆ Does your baby often have noisy breathing; does he or she snore?

As frightening as the experience may have been for you, you're actually lucky it occurred. Not only did your baby come through it fine, but he gave both you and the doctor warning that it might happen again – and a chance to make sure that it doesn't. And that's exactly why the doctor has suggested hospitalization and tests.

Your son experienced an 'apparent life-threatening event', but that doesn't mean his life is in danger. While an episode of prolonged apnea (when breathing stops for more than twenty seconds) does put an infant at slightly increased risk for SIDS, there's a 99 per cent chance that the risk will never become a reality. As a precaution, and to try to determine what triggered the event, your baby will be evaluated in the hospital through a complete health history and physical exam, diagnostic testing and possibly monitoring for further spells of prolonged apnea. (This kind of evaluation may also be performed on an infant who has no history of apnea but who has had two or more siblings who succumbed to SIDS, or one who died and others who suffered apparent life-threatening events.)

If tests at a local hospital are inconclusive, the doctor may recommend referral to a major SIDS centre. For more information, contact the Foundation for the Study of Infant Deaths at fsid.org.uk.

Sometimes the evaluation uncovers a fairly simple cause for such an event – an infection, a seizure disorder or an airway obstruction – that can be treated, eliminating the risk of future problems. If the cause is undetermined, or if heart or lung problems that put him at high risk for sudden death are discovered, the doctor may recommend putting your baby on a device that monitors breathing and/or heartbeat at home. The monitor is usually attached to the baby with electrodes or is embedded in his cot, playpen or cradle mattress. You, and anyone else who cares for your baby, will be trained in connecting the monitor as well as in responding to an emergency with CPR. The monitor won't give your baby absolute protection against SIDS, but it will help your doctor learn more about his condition and help you feel you are doing something, rather than sitting helplessly. Keep in mind, however, that some research has questioned the effectiveness of monitors; apparently even healthy babies often experience periods of apnea or slowed heart rate that don't increase their risk of SIDS. False alarms are also very common.

Don't let the episode, the hospitalization or any monitoring become the focus of your life. Doing so could turn your probably normal baby into a 'patient', even interfering with his growth and development. Seek help from your doctor or a qualified counsellor if a monitor seems to add to family tension rather than reduce it.

Though criteria may vary from doctor to doctor and community to community, babies who've had no critical episodes since their first usually come off a monitor when they have been free of events requiring prolonged or vigorous stimulation or rescue for two months. More stringent requirements for going off the monitor are usually set for those who have had a second critical episode. Though babies are rarely removed from the monitor until they pass six months, when the peak period for SIDS is over, a total of 90 per cent are off their monitors by the time they reach one year.

'My premature baby had occasional periods of apnea for the first few weeks of her life, but her doctor says that I shouldn't worry, that she doesn't need to be monitored.'

Breathing lapses are very common in premature babies; in fact, about 50 per cent of those born before 32 weeks' gestation experience them. But this 'apnea of prematurity', when it occurs before the baby's original due date is totally unrelated to SIDS; it doesn't increase the risk of SIDS or of apnea, itself, later. So unless your baby has serious apneic episodes after her original due date, there's no cause for concern or follow-up.

Even in full-term babies, brief lapses in breathing without any blueness or limpness or need for resuscitation are not believed by most experts to be a predictor of SIDS risk; few babies with such apnea are lost to SIDS, and most babies who do die of SIDS weren't observed to experience apnea previously.

'I've heard that immunizations can cause SIDS, and I'm really worried about having my baby immunized.'

Research has confirmed that there is no link between the DTaP vaccine and SIDS – and, yet, like many theories that have been disproved, it stubbornly continues to circulate. If you are at all worried, talk to your baby's doctor, who will doubtless make you more comfortable about going ahead with your baby's immunizations.

See page 222 for plenty more reasons why you should have your baby immunized.

SHARING A ROOM WITH BABY

'Our ten-week-old has been sharing our room since birth. We don't really want to continue sharing, so when should we move him to his own room?'

In the first month or two of life, when baby's at the breast or bottle as much as he's in bed, having him within a weary arm's reach makes sense. It may also keep him safer, possibly reducing the risk of SIDS. And some parents find room sharing even beyond then – and well into childhood – convenient, pleasurable or both for all concerned (see next question). But if it's not your plan to continue sharing a room with your baby indefinitely, it's probably a good idea to make the break once he outgrows the physiological need for frequent feedings during the night (anywhere from about two to four months), or when the risk of SIDS decreases (after six months). After that, having your baby for a roommate raises a number of potential problems:

Less sleep for baby. Being in the same room with your baby all night, you're tempted to pick him up every time he whimpers, possibly interrupting his sleep cycles. After all, babies make lots of noises while they sleep, and most of the time, they'll fall right back asleep within minutes, without any prodding. If you pick up baby at the slightest whimper, you may be inadvertently waking him up and interrupting his sleep. In addition, during his lighter phases of sleep, your baby is likely to be wakened by your activity, even if you tiptoe around in soft slippers and climb silently into bed.

Less sleep for parents. The fact that you pick him up more often at night if he's in your room means less sleep not only for him but for you, too. And even if you resist picking him up, you're sure to lie awake waiting for the whimper to turn to a howl. You may also lose a few good nights' sleep over his tossing and turning; babies are notoriously restless sleepers. Some parents, however, aren't bothered by baby's nocturnal movements and find that the benefits of being in a baby-free quiet room are offset by the drawbacks of feeling their way down a dark hallway every time they have to fetch a crying infant from his cot.

Less lovemaking. Sure, you know (or at least you hope) your baby is sleeping when you start to make love. But how uninhibited can you really be when you've got company (breathing loudly, tossing his head back and forth, moaning softly in his sleep) so close by? Of course, this problem can be avoided if you're creative in your choice of lovemaking locales (pull-out sofa, anyone?).

For some kids, more problems adjusting later. Having your baby in your room for an extended period may make it more difficult when you finally do move him to a room of his own. (Not all children have trouble adjusting later on; some just leave their parents' room when they're ready to sleep on their own and never look back.)

Of course, 'a room of his own' isn't possible in every household. If you live in a one-bedroom apartment or a small house with several children, there may be no option but for your baby to share. If that's the case, consider a divider – either a screen, or a heavy curtain hung from a ceiling track (the curtain is also a good sound insulator). Or give your bedroom up to the baby and invest in a sofabed in the living room for you. Or partition off a corner of the living room for the baby and do your late-night TV watching or talking in the bedroom.

If your baby will have to share with another child, how well the sleeping arrangement will work out will depend on how well the two sleep. If either one or both are light sleepers with a tendency to awaken during the night, you may all be in for a difficult period of adjustment until each has learned to sleep through the other's wakings. Again, a partition or curtain may help muffle the sounds, while providing the older child with privacy.

SHARING A BED

'I've heard a lot about the benefits of children sharing a bed with their parents. And with all the night waking our daughter has been doing, it seems like such an arrangement would mean more sleep for everyone.'

For some families, co-sleeping, or sharing a 'family bed', is an unequivocal (and cuddly) joy. For others, it's merely a convenience. For still others, it's a nightmare. Proponents of co-sleeping cite several advantages to the family bed: it cultivates emotional bonds, makes it easy to nurse or comfort a child, and combats loneliness. Supporters also say it reduces the risks of SIDS, though there are no data to show whether SIDS is more likely to occur during co-sleeping or when baby sleeps alone. Those on the other side of the co-sleeping fence believe that having a baby learn to sleep on her own encourages independence; discourages the development of sleep disturbances; averts any danger of suffocation from the pillows and fluffy quilts often found on parental beds; and is more comfortable for the parents (not only because they sleep better, but because there's no risk of rolling over into a pool of spit-up or the contents of a leaky nappy).

While there's no shortage of theories and certainly no shortage of opinions on the issue, the decision of whether to have your baby join you in bed or sleep solo in her cot – like so many decisions you'll make in your tenure as parents – is a very personal

one. And it's a choice best made when you're wide awake (read: not at 2 AM), and with your eyes wide open to the following considerations:

Baby's safety. In the UK, where sleeping accommodations are usually pretty cushy, keeping baby safe in her parents' bed takes extra precautions. A report by the Consumer Product Safety Commission in America linked the family bed (and the hazards that too often lie therein) to numerous infant deaths. Proponents of co-sleeping, however, find the study's data flawed and point out that some babies die while sleeping alone in their cots. And other researchers have found that there is an innate connection between a co-sleeping mother and child, possibly because of the hormone response activated when the mother is in close proximity to, or breastfeeding, her child. These researchers theorize that this response may make a mother who co-sleeps more keenly aware of her child's breathing and temperature throughout the night, allowing her to respond quickly to any significant changes. Not surprisingly, the hormone response is also responsible for the lighter sleep that women who co-sleep experience.

If you choose to co-sleep, make sure your bed and bedding meet the same safety criteria looked for in a cot. A firm mattress (not a pillow top or waterbed) is a must, as are tight-fitting sheets. Avoid plush duvets; keep pillows out of baby's creeping reach; check for entrapment dangers (headboard slats should be no farther apart than 6 cm (2⅜ in); there should be no gaps between the mattress and the frame). Never put baby on a bed that's next to a wall (she could slip between bed and wall and become entrapped) or leave her in a position where she could roll off the bed (this can happen at a very young age) or allow her to sleep with a parent who is intoxicated, is taking medication that induces deep sleep, or is just a very deep sleeper. Never let a toddler or preschooler sleep directly next to your baby. And never smoke, or allow anyone else to smoke, in the family bed, since this can increase the risk of SIDS (as well as fires). A great way to keep your child close and safe is to use a bedside sleeper that attaches to your bed (see page 45).

Family feelings. A baby should come between her parents only if *both* have agreed she belongs there. So make sure you're both onboard with the family bed before you bring baby onboard your bed – and consider both your feelings and your spouse's. Keep in mind, too, that if you co-sleep, you'll need to make other arrangements for intimacy, or three could quickly become a crowd that compromises your 'two's company'.

Sleep – yours and baby's. For some parents, not having to get out of bed for midnight feedings or to calm a crying baby is reason enough to co-sleep. For breastfeeding mums, being able to nurse without having to be fully awake is a real plus. The flip side: though they may never have to leave their beds at night, the sleep co-sleepers do get may be more broken up and, although emotionally satisfying, less physiologically satisfying (parents and children who co-sleep tend to sleep less deeply and sleep less overall). Also, co-sleeping babies wake more often and may have trouble learning how to fall asleep on their own, a skill they'll eventually need. Another possible side effect of frequent awakenings is an increase in night-time breastfeeding – fine when an infant is young, not so fine when she has several teeth. Continuous night feedings – breast or bottle – can lead to dental decay.

The future. In making your decision about the family bed, consider how long (ideally) you'd like the arrangement to continue. Some argue that co-sleeping causes prolonged dependency; others argue the opposite – that co-sleeping promotes independence by giving a child strong feelings of security. Often, the longer it lasts, the tougher the transition to solo sleeping. Switching a six-month-old over to a cot shouldn't take too much effort; moving a baby who's approaching her first birthday may be a little more trying; weaning a toddler or preschooler from your bed may be even more challenging. Some children voluntarily leave around age two or three, many are ready to move on by the time they start school, but a few stay on for the long haul – even through early adolescence.

Whether or not you decide to share your bed with baby at night, you'll still enjoy bringing her in for early morning feedings or cuddling sessions. As your child gets older, you can continue to make family togetherness (if not a family bed) a favourite ritual on weekend mornings – complete with pillow fights.

STILL USING A DUMMY

'I was planning to let my daughter use a dummy only until she was three months old, but she seems so dependent on it, I'm not sure I can take it away now.'

Babies are creatures of comfort. The comfort they crave can come in a number of packages, including a mother's breast, a father with a bottle full of breast milk or formula, a soothing lullaby or a dummy. And the more accustomed they become to a particular source of comfort, the more difficult it becomes for them to do without it. If you don't want to run into the problems that may later be associated with dummy use, now is an ideal time to make a break. For one thing, at this age your baby's memory is short, so she'll easily forget the dummy when it disappears from her life. For another, she is more open to change than an older baby – more likely to accept an alternative route to pacification. A toddler not only won't forget her dummy, but will probably demand its return with a storm of will and temper. And, of course, a habit of three months is easier to break than one that has been building for a year or more.

To comfort your baby without a dummy, try rocking, singing, a clean knuckle for sucking (or help her to find her own fingers) or some of the other techniques listed on page 188. Admittedly, all of these take more time and effort on your part than tucking a dummy in her mouth, but they'll be better for baby in the long run, especially if they are gradually eliminated in favour of letting baby learn to comfort herself (as she could with her own thumb, a 'dummy' that's in her control. (See page 126 for the pros and cons of using a dummy.)

There's no need to give up the dummy at sleep times – in fact, it's still a good idea for baby to put her to bed with her dummy since research has shown that this may reduce the risk of SIDS. So if you can, try limiting dummy usage to nap and bedtime. This way, it won't interfere with socializing and vocalizing during the day.

EARLY WEANING

'I'm going back to work full-time at the end of the month, and I'd like to give up nursing my daughter. Will it be hard on her?'

A three-month-old is, in general, a pretty agreeable and adaptable sort. Even with a budding personality all her own, she's still far from the opinionated (and sometimes tyrannical) toddler she'll eventually turn into. So if you're going to pick a time for weaning from the breast that's going to be easiest for her, this may be it. Though she may thoroughly enjoy nursing, she probably won't cling to it as stubbornly as a six-month-old who's never had a bottle and is suddenly subjected to weaning. All in all, you'll probably find that weaning at three months is less difficult for your baby than it is for you. (Before you make your final decision, though, read over the section on making breastfeeding and working work, page 247; you may find that combining the two occupations for at least another few months – and possibly for the entire first year – may not be as difficult as you think.)

Ideally, mothers who want to wean their babies early should begin giving supplementary bottles, using either expressed milk or formula, by around four to six weeks so the infants become adjusted to suckling on the bottle as well as on the breast. If you haven't, your first step is to get baby acclimatized to an artificial nipple; you may have to try several different styles to find one your baby likes. At this point it would be best to use formula, so that your present breast milk supply will begin to diminish. Be persistent, but don't force the teat. Try giving the bottle before the breast; if your baby rejects the bottle the first time, try again at the next feeding. Bottles may be more acceptable to baby if someone other than mum gives them. (See page 211 for more tips on introducing the bottle.)

Keep trying until she takes at least 30 to 60 ml (1 to 2 fl oz) from the bottle.

THE LONGER
THE BETTER

It's not news that breastfeeding is best for babies – and that even a little breast milk goes a long way when it comes to giving your baby the healthiest start in life. Six weeks of nursing, after all, can offer substantial benefits. But what is news – big news – is the research showing that longer is better, and that those substantial benefits increase substantially when a baby is nursed longer than three months. Which is why breastfeeding should continue, ideally, for at least the first year of life. According to the latest reports from researchers, the many benefits may include:

◆ Fewer battles with the bulge. The longer a baby is breastfed, the less likely he or she is to join the rapidly growing ranks of overweight children and adolescents.

◆ Even fewer tummy troubles. Everyone knows that breast milk is more digestible than formula. But research has shown that infants who are fed only breast milk for the first six months have a lower risk of developing gastrointestinal infections than infants who are supplemented with formula beginning at three or four months. Another digestive plus for older breastfed babies: those who are nursed while solids are introduced (usually at five to six months) are less likely to develop celiac disease, a digestive disorder that interferes with the normal absorption of nutrients from food.

◆ Even fewer ear troubles. Studies have found that babies who are exclusively breastfed for longer than four months suffer from half as many ear infections as their formula-fed peers.

◆ Less to sneeze at. Babies nursed for six months are much less likely to have problems with allergies of all kinds.

◆ Higher IQ for smaller babies. Many studies have pointed to a link between continued breastfeeding and higher IQ. But research has also suggested that breastfeeding exclusively for the first six months boosts the IQs of small full-term babies (those who weighed under 2.7 kg/6 lb at birth).

◆ A lower SIDS risk. The longer babies are breastfed, the lower their risk of succumbing to SIDS.

Of course, though the benefits of continued breastfeeding are compelling, not every mother and baby will be able to keep nursing for as long as is recommended. So it's important to keep in mind that while longer may be better, some breastfeeding is still definitely better than none.

Once she does, substitute a meal of formula for a nursing at a midday feeding. A few days later, replace another daytime breastfeeding with formula. Making the switch gradually, one feeding at a time, will give your breasts a chance to adjust without uncomfortable engorgement. Eliminate the evening breastfeeding last, as this will give you and your baby a quiet and relaxing time together when you get home from work. If you like, you may – assuming your milk supply doesn't dry up entirely, and assuming your baby is still interested – be able to continue this once-a-day feeding for a while (or twice a day, if you'd like to nurse first thing in the morning, too), postponing total weaning until a later date, or until your milk is gone.

SUPPLEMENTING WITH COW'S MILK

'I'm breastfeeding and would like to give my baby a supplement, but formula's so expensive. Can't I give him cow's milk instead?'

Cow's milk is a great drink for little cows and older humans, but it just doesn't have the right mix of nutrients for human babies. It contains more salt (much more) and protein than breast milk or commercial formula, and these excesses put a strain on young kidneys. It is also lacking in iron. The composition of cow's milk varies from that of breast milk (and formula) in a variety of other ways, too. In addition, it causes mild intestinal bleeding in a small percentage of infants. Though the blood lost in the stool is generally not visible to the naked eye, the bleeding is significant because it can lead to anaemia.

So if you're planning to supplement, use either expressed breast milk or a formula recommended by the doctor – until your baby is a year old.

FEWER BOWEL MOVEMENTS

'I'm concerned that my breastfed baby may be constipated. She always had six or eight bowel movements a day, and now she rarely has more than one, and sometimes even misses a day'.

Don't be concerned – be grateful. This slowdown in production is not only normal, but will send you to the changing table less often. Definitely a change for the better.

It's normal for many breastfed babies like yours to start having fewer bowel movements somewhere between one and three months of age. Some will even go several days between movements. That's because as babies get bigger, they need more food, so their bodies digest more of what's going in – resulting in fewer by-products. Others will continue their prodigious production rates as long as they are nursing. That's normal, too.

Constipation is rarely a problem for breastfed babies, and infrequency isn't a sign of it; hard, difficult-to-pass stools are (see page 173).

NAPPY RASH

'I change my baby frequently, but she still gets nappy rash – and I have trouble getting rid of it'.

There's a good reason why your baby (and up to 35 per cent of her comrades-in-nappies) isn't sitting on a pretty bottom. The nappy area is exposed to high moisture, little air, a variety of chemical irritants and infectious organisms in urine and feces, and oftentimes the rubbing of nappies and clothing, it's an easy target for a wide variety of problems. Nappy rash can remain a problem as long as a baby is in nappies, but incidence usually peaks between seven and nine months, when a more varied diet is reflected in the more irritating nature of her stools, and then starts to diminish as baby skin toughens, becoming more resistant to the assaults.

Unfortunately, nappy rash tends to repeat in some babies – perhaps because of an inborn susceptibility, allergic tendencies, an abnormal stool pH (an imbalance between acidity and alkalinity), excessive ammonia in the urine, or simply because once skin becomes irritated, it is more susceptible to further irritation.

The exact mechanism responsible for nappy rash isn't known, but it is believed that it probably begins when a baby's delicate skin becomes irritated by chronic moisture. When the skin is further weakened by friction from a nappy or clothing, or by irritating substances in stool or urine, it is left open to attack by germs on the skin or in the urine or stool. Aggressive and frequent cleansing of the nappy area with detergents or soaps can increase the susceptibility of an infant's skin, as can very tight nappies. The ammonia in urine, once thought to be the major culprit in nappy rash, doesn't appear to be a primary cause, but can irritate already damaged skin. And the rashes do tend to start where urine concentrates in the nappy, towards the bottom with girls and the front with boys.

The term *nappy rash* itself describes a number of different skin conditions in the nappy area. Just what distinguishes one nappy rash from another is not widely agreed on in the medical community (maybe the subject just hasn't aroused enough interest to stimulate serious study and clearer definitions), but they are often described this way:

Chafing dermatitis. This is the most common form of nappy rash and is seen as redness where friction is greatest, but not in a baby's skin folds. It generally comes and goes, causing little discomfort if not complicated by a secondary infection.

Tidemark dermatitis. This is an irritation precipitated by friction from the edge of a nappy rubbing against the skin.

Perianal dermatitis. Redness around the anus usually is caused by the alkaline

stools of a bottle-fed baby and is uncommon among breastfed infants until solids have been introduced.

Candidal dermatitis. Bright red and tender, this uncomfortable rash appears in the inguinal folds (the creases between the abdomen and the thighs), and spreads from that point. Nappy rashes that last more than seventy-two hours often become infected with *Candida albicans,* the same yeast infection responsible for thrush. This type of rash may also develop in a baby on antibiotics.

Atopic dermatitis. This nappy rash is itchy, and may turn up in other parts of the body first. It usually begins to spread to the nappy area between six and twelve months.

Seborrheic dermatitis. This deep red rash, often with yellowish scales, usually starts on the scalp as cradle cap, though it sometimes begins in the nappy region and spreads upward. Like most nappy rashes, it's usually more bothersome to parents than to baby.

Impetigo. Caused by bacteria (streptococci or staphylococci), impetigo in the nappy area occurs in two different forms: bullous, with large, thin-walled blisters that burst and leave a thin yellow-brown crust, or non-bullous, with thick, yellow, crusted scabs and a lot of surrounding redness. It can cover thighs, buttocks and lower abdomen, and spread to other parts of the body as well.

Intertrigo. This type of rash, which manifests itself as a poorly defined reddened area, occurs as a result of the rubbing of skin on skin. In infants it is usually found in the deep inguinal folds between the thighs and the lower abdomen, and often in the armpits.

Intertrigo rash may sometimes ooze white to yellowish matter, and may burn when urine touches it, causing baby to cry.

The best cure for nappy rash is prevention – though it isn't always possible. Keeping the nappy area dry and clean is one of the most important principles of prevention. See page 135 for nappy changing practices that will help you to do this. If preventive measures don't work, the following may help eliminate your baby's simple nappy rash, and will be helpful in warding off recurrences:

Less moisture. To reduce moisture on the skin, change the nappy often, even in the middle of the night if your baby's awake and the nappy very full. Put any plans to try to get her to sleep through the night on hold until the nappy rash has cleared up. For persistent nappy rash, change baby as soon as you're aware that she's wet or had a bowel movement.

Once other fluids besides breast milk or formula are introduced, make sure that less superfluous liquid goes into baby, too (since what goes in must come out). Drinking bottle after bottle of juice leads to excessive urination and more nappy rash. Using a cup for juice can avoid overdosing.

More air. Keep baby's bottom bare part of the time, placing her on a couple of folded cloth nappy or cotton blankets over a plastic or waterproof pad or sheet to protect the surface below. If the nappy rash is really persistent, you might let her sleep the same way, but be sure the room is warm enough so she won't be chilly. If she's in cloth nappies, use breathable nappy wraps, or leave the pants off altogether and put her on a waterproof pad. If she's wearing disposables that have a plastic outer covering, poke a few holes in the outer cover. This will allow some air in, and it will also allow some moisture to seep out – which will encourage more frequent nappy changes.

Fewer irritants. You can't limit the natural irritants such as urine and stool except by changing nappies frequently, but you can limit those that you apply to baby's bottom. Soap can dry and irritate the skin, so use it only once daily. Dove and Johnson's baby soap are among those generally recommended for babies (many so-called 'gentle' soaps aren't), or ask the doctor for a suggestion. For nappy changes when the infant has had a bowel movement, wash skin thoroughly (for about thirty seconds to one minute) with warm water and cottonwool balls instead of nappy wipes. Wipes may contain substances that irritate your baby's skin (different babies are sensitive to different substances); those that contain alcohol are particularly drying. If the ones you're using seem to cause a problem, switch – but don't use wipes at all when your baby has a rash. A really messy movement may be best cleaned by a dip in the bath or sink; a sticky one can be gently removed with baby oil. Be careful to pat baby dry thoroughly after washing.

Different nappies. If your baby has a recurrent nappy rash, consider switching to another type of nappy (from cloth to disposables or vice versa, from one type of disposable to another) to see if the change makes a difference. If you home-launder nappies, rinse them with 120 ml (4 fl oz) of white vinegar or a special nappy rinse and, if necessary, boil them in a large pot for ten minutes.

Blocking tactics. Spreading a thick protective layer of ointment or cream (zinc oxide, Sudacrem or whatever your baby's doctor recommends) on baby's bottom after cleaning it at changing time will prevent urine from reaching it. Make sure, though, before you spread the ointment or cream on baby's bottom, that her skin is completely dry. Otherwise, you'll just be trapping the moisture in, leading to recurrent nappy rashes. If you buy these products in the largest sizes, you'll save money and be more likely to use them liberally – which is best. But don't use the ointment when you're airing baby's bottom.

A little baby cornflour can absorb moisture, keeping baby drier, but don't use a talc-based powder. And don't use medications around the house that have been prescribed for other family members; some combination ointments (those that contain steroids and antibacterial or antifungal agents) are a major cause of allergic skin reactions, and you could sensitize your baby by using them. Besides, they may be too strong for baby's skin.

If your baby's nappy rash doesn't clear up or improve in a day or two, or if blisters or pustules appear, call her doctor, who will try to uncover its cause and then treat it. For seborrheic dermatitis, a steroid cream may be necessary (but it should not be used long-term); for impetigo, antibiotics given by mouth; for intertrigo, careful cleansing plus a hydrocortisone cream and protective ointments; and for candida, the most common nappy infection, a good topical antifungal ointment or cream. Ask how long it should take for the rash to clear, and then report back to the doctor if it isn't better by then or if the treatment seems to make it worse. If the rash persists, the doctor may check for dietary or other factors that may be contributing to it. In rare cases, the expertise of a paediatric dermatologist may be needed to unravel the mystery of a baby's nappy rash.

PENIS SORE

'I'm concerned about a red, raw area at the tip of my son's penis.'

Chances are what you're seeing looks a lot worse than it is, which is probably nothing more than a localized nappy rash. Such a rash is common and can sometimes cause swelling – sometimes enough to prevent a baby from urinating. If it spreads to the urethra it could eventually cause scarring, so you should do everything you can to get rid of the rash as soon as possible. Follow the tips for treating nappy rash given above, adding warm soaks if your baby is having trouble urinating. If you use home-laundered nappies, switch to a nappy service or disposables until the problem has resolved. If the rash persists after two or three days of home treatment, and/or if baby's having problem with urination, call the doctor.

SPASTIC MOVEMENTS

'When my son tries to reach for something, he always misses, and his movements seem so spastic, I'm wondering if there's something wrong with his nervous system.'

Though it has come a long way from the days when you felt little twitches in your uterus, your baby's nervous system is still young and inexperienced, and it hasn't worked out all its kinks. When your baby's arm whips out in the direction of a toy but doesn't land anywhere near its target, the lack of coordination is actually a normal stage in infant motor development. Soon he will gain more control, and the purposeful, clumsy batting will be replaced with skillful reaching movements. And once he gets to the stage when nothing within that cunning reach is safe again, you may look back fondly on a time

NEVER SHAKE A BABY

Some parents assume that shaking a baby is a safer way to discipline – or to let off their steam when they're frustrated or angry – than spanking. That's an extremely dangerous assumption to make. Firstly, babies are too young to be disciplined effectively. Secondly, physical discipline of any kind (including spanking) is never appropriate (see page 452 for appropriate and effective ways of disciplining a toddler). But, most important of all, shaking a baby (whether in anger or fun) can cause serious injury or death. *Never, ever shake a baby.*

when he looked, but wasn't able to touch.

If you'd like some additional reassurance, talk with your baby's doctor at his next checkup.

ROUGHHOUSING

'My spouse loves to roughhouse with our twelve-week-old, and she loves it as well. But I've heard that shaking an infant too much, even in fun, can cause injury.'

Watching the glee in a young baby's face as she's tossed up in the air and caught by her adoring parent, it's hard to imagine that such fun could end in tragedy. And yet it could. Certain types of roughhousing – whether they're done in fun or in anger – can be extremely dangerous for children under two years of age.

There are several types of injuries that can result from throwing a baby in the air or shaking or vigorously bouncing her (as when jogging with her in a front or back baby carrier). One is a type

of whiplash (such as a person can get when rear-ended in an car accident). Because the baby's head is heavy in proportion to the rest of her body and her neck muscles are not fully developed, support for the head is poor. When the baby is shaken roughly, the head whipping back and forth can cause the brain to rebound again and again against the skull. Bruising of the brain can cause swelling, bleeding, pressure and possibly permanent neurological damage with mental or physical disability. Another possible injury is trauma to the delicate infant eye. If detachment or scarring of the retina or damage to the optic nerve occurs, lasting visual problems, even blindness, can result. The risk of damage is compounded if a baby is crying or being held upside down during the shaking, because both increase blood pressure in the head, making fragile blood vessels more likely to rupture. Such injuries are relatively rare, but the damage can be so severe that the risk is certainly not worth taking.

While the vast majority of these injuries occur when a baby is being shaken in anger, they can occasionally happen at play. So avoid roughhousing that vigorously shakes or jostles your baby's unsupported head or neck. Also avoid jogging or other 'bouncing' activities with a young infant in a baby carrier (do your running while pushing baby in a pushchair, instead). That doesn't mean no fun at all – it only dictates more gentle rough stuff. Many babies love 'flying' as they are held securely midtrunk and glided smoothly through the air, participating in cuddlefests, and being chased when they are old enough to crawl. There are some babies, however, both male and female, who dislike any kind of rough handling, and they have the right to even more gentle treatment – even from exuberant family members.

Don't spend time worrying about past roughhousing sessions. If your child hasn't exhibited any symptoms of injury, she clearly hasn't been harmed. If you have any concerns, consult your baby's doctor.

BEING TIED DOWN BREASTFEEDING

'I was happy with my decision not to give our baby supplementary bottles until I realized it's almost impossible to have a long evening out without him.'

Nothing's perfect, not even the decision to breastfeed exclusively. For all its many advantages, it can also be occasionally inconvenient – as when dinner and a movie last longer than the window between two feedings, making dates with your spouse or friends a logistical impossibility. And circumventing those logistics may be especially difficult now, with baby still feeding so often. If you're willing to sacrifice sleep for a few hours out, you may be able to accomplish a late evening on the town by getting your baby down for the night by 8 or 9 PM before heading out (unless it's his habit to awaken again before midnight). Or just stick to dinner *or* a movie for now.

Things will get a little easier once solids are introduced (usually around the sixth month) and when baby starts going for longer stretches at night without nursing. And once you've introduced the cup (around five or six months), your baby will even be able to have a drink if he's thirsty without resorting to a bottle.

In the meantime, if you have a special event you'd like to attend that will keep you from home for more than a few hours in the early evening, try these tips:

♦ Take baby and sitter along, if there's an appropriate place for them to hang out while they're waiting. That way baby can nap in a pram or pushchair while you enjoy the event, slipping out to nurse as needed.

♦ If the event is out of town, take the family along. Either bring your own sitter or hire one where you will be staying. If the place where you're staying is near enough to the event, you can pop in at feeding time.

♦ Adjust baby's bedtime, if possible. If your baby doesn't usually go to bed until after nine, and you need to leave at seven, try to get him to cut down on his afternoon nap and put him to bed a couple of hours early. Be sure to give him a full nursing before you leave, and plan on feeding him again when you return home, if necessary.

♦ Leave a bottle of expressed milk and hope for the best. If your baby wakes up and is really hungry, he may take the bottle. If he doesn't take it, he may scream for a while, but will very likely fall back to sleep eventually – and you can always feed him when you get home. Carry a pager or mobile phone so the sitter can reach you; if the sitter feels baby is so upset that you need to return, you'll need to be ready to do so.

LEAVING BABY WITH A SITTER

'We'd love a night out alone, but we're afraid of leaving our daughter with a sitter when she's so young.'

Go to town – and soon. Assuming you're going to want to spend some time alone together (or just alone) during the next sixteen or so years, getting your baby used to being cared for occasionally by a non-parent will be an important part of her development. And in this case, the earlier she starts making the adjustment, the better. Infants two and three months old may recognize their parents, but out of sight usually means out of mind. And as long as their needs are being met, young babies are generally happy with any attentive person. By the time babies reach nine months (much sooner in some babies), most begin experiencing what is called separation or stranger anxiety – not only are they unhappy being separated from mother or father, they're also very wary of new people. So now's the perfect time to bring a sitter into baby's life – and a little adults-only fun into yours.

At first you'll probably want to take only short outings, especially if you're nursing and have to squeeze your dinner in between baby's meals. What shouldn't be short, however, is the time you spend choosing and preparing the sitter, to ensure your baby will be well cared for. The first night, have the sitter come at least half an hour early so you can fully acclimatize him or her to the eccentricities of your child's needs and habits and so baby and sitter can meet. (See the information on choosing child care, starting on the next page, including the Baby-Sitter Checklist, page 272).

'We almost always take our baby with us when we go out; we leave her with a sitter only when she's asleep, and then only for a couple of hours. Friends say this will make her too dependent.'

Again, you'll need to follow your instincts – not those of your friends. While there are some advantages to getting your baby adjusted to a sitter now (before stranger anxiety rears its unfriendly head), and to having more social outlets (realistically, not every place you'll want to go or every event you'll want to attend will welcome babies), a baby whose mummy or daddy is always around doesn't necessarily become overly dependent. Often, in fact, the child who spends a majority of the time in early infancy with one or both parents turns out to be very secure and trusting. After all, she's likely to have unswerving faith that she is loved, that any sitter her parents leave her with will take good care of her, and that when her parents go out, they will return when they say they will. (Of course, a child who's left with a good sitter can also feel this way.)

So do what makes you most comfortable, not what will satisfy your friends. But as your baby gets older, you might consider at least occasionally leaving her with a sitter when she's awake. If you always leave while she's sleeping, and she ends up waking while you're out, she may panic to find herself in the hands of a stranger.

What it's Important to Know:
THE RIGHT CHILD CARE FOR BABY

Leaving your child with a sitter for the first time can be stressful enough without worrying about whether you're leaving him or her with the right person in the right place. And finding child care that you're confident about is no longer as easy – at least, not for most – as picking up the phone and enlisting grandma or the grandmotherly next-door neighbour. With extended

BABY-SITTER CHECKLIST

Even the best-trained, most experienced baby-sitter needs instructions (after all, every baby and every family has different needs). Before you leave your baby with anyone, make certain that he or she is familiar with the following:

- How your baby is most easily calmed (rocking, a special song, a favourite mobile, a ride in the baby carrier)

- What your baby's favourite toy is

- That your baby should sleep face-up with no pillows or duvets

- How your baby is best burped (over the shoulder, on the lap, after feeding, during feeding)

- How to change and clean baby (do you use wipes or cottonwool balls? an ointment for nappy rash?) and where nappies and supplies are kept

- Where extra clothing is kept in case those baby is wearing get soiled

- How to give the bottle, if your baby is bottle fed or is to get a supplement of formula or expressed milk

- What your baby can and can't eat or drink (making it clear that no food, drink or medicine should be given to your baby without your okay, or the doctor's)

- The set-up of your kitchen, the baby's room, and so on, and any other pertinent facts about your house or apartment (such as a burglar alarm that might go off, and where fire exits are located)

- Any habits or characteristics of your baby that the sitter might not expect (spits up a lot, has a lot of bowel movements, cries when wet, falls asleep only with a light on or when being rocked)

- The habits of any pets you may have that the sitter should be aware of, and rules concerning your baby and pets

- Where the first aid kit (or individual items) is located

- Baby safety rules (see page 200); you might want to photocopy rules and post them in an obvious place for the sitter

- Where a torch is located (or candles)

- Who is cleared by you to visit when you are not at home, and what your policy is on a sitter having visitors

- What to do in case the fire alarm goes off or smoke or fire is observed, or if someone who hasn't been cleared by you rings the doorbell

You should also leave the following for the sitter:

- Important phone numbers (the baby's doctor, your mobile or pager number or place you can be reached, a neighbour who will be home, your parents, the poison control centre, the building superintendent, a plumber or handyman), and a pad and pen for taking messages

- The address of the nearest hospital A&E and the best way to get there

- Cab fare in case of an unexpected emergency (such as the need to take the baby to A&E or the doctor's surgery), and the number to call for a cab

- A signed consent form authorizing medical care within specific limits, if you cannot be reached (this should be worked out in advance with baby's doctor)

It's helpful to combine all the information necessary for caring for your baby – for instance, phone numbers, safety and health tips – in a small loose-leaf binder.

family often living some way away, and many grandmothers (and grandmotherly types) working themselves, the parent who needs a sitter must usually depend on a stranger.

When a grandparent is the sitter, a parent's biggest worry is whether her child will be plied with too many biscuits. Turning your baby over to a stranger (or group of strangers) raises a great many more concerns. Will she be responsible and reliable? Attentive and responsive to your baby's needs? Capable of providing your baby with the kind of play-learning stimulation that will help develop mind and body to their fullest potential? Will her child-care philosophies mesh comfortably with yours, and will she accept your ideas and respect your wishes? Will she be warm and loving enough to act as a parent substitute without presuming to take your place as a parent?

Separating from your baby – whether for a 9-to-5 job or a Saturday-night dinner and a show – will never be easy, especially not the first few times. But for you (and the other nearly 50 per cent, of parents of babies under age one who regularly use child care), separating satisfied that you've left your baby in the best possible hands will help ease both your anxiety and your guilt.

IN-HOME CARE

Most experts agree that if a parent can't be with his or her baby all of the time (because of work, school or other commitments), the next best option is a parent substitute (a nanny, sitter, au pair) who cares for the child at home.

The advantages are many. Baby is in familiar surroundings, with his or her own cot, high chair and toys; is not exposed to a lot of other babies' germs;

and doesn't have to be transported to and fro. He or she also has the complete attention of the care provider, (assuming she hasn't been assigned a multitude of other tasks), and there is a good chance for a strong relationship to develop between baby and sitter.

There are some disadvantages, however. If the care provider is sick, unable to come to work for other reasons, or suddenly quits, there is no automatic backup system. A strong attachment between sitter and an older baby can lead to a crisis if the sitter leaves suddenly, or if the parent develops more than a mild case of envy. For some parents, the loss of privacy if the care provider lives in is an added complication. And home care can be costly, probably more so if you choose a professionally trained nanny, probably less so if you choose a college student, an au pair, or someone with minimal experience.

STARTING THE SEARCH

Finding the ideal care provider can be a time-consuming process, so allow as much as two months for the search. There are several trails you can take to track her down:

The baby's doctor. Probably no one else you know sees as many babies – and their mothers and fathers – as your baby's doctor and health visitor. Ask him or her for nanny recommendations, check the surgery bulletin board for notices put up by care providers seeking employment (some doctors require that references be left at the reception desk when such notices are posted), or put up a notice of your own. Ask around the waiting room, too.

Other parents. Don't pass one by – at the playground, at a baby exercise class, at cocktail parties and business meetings

– without asking if they've heard of, or have employed, a good care provider.

Your local community centre, library, house of worship, preschool. Here, too, the bulletin board can be an invaluable resource. So can your clergyman, who may know of congregants who would be interested in caring for your child.

Teachers of nursery-age children. Preschool teachers often know of, or employ part-time in their programmes, experienced child-care workers. They sometimes are available themselves evenings and weekends.

Nanny agencies and registries. Trained and licensed (and usually expensive) child-care workers and nannies are available through these services; selecting a care provider this way usually eliminates a lot of guesswork and legwork. (But always check references and background yourself, anyway.)

Baby-sitting services. Screened baby-sitters are available through these services, listed in your local classified phone book, for full-time, part-time, or occasional work.

A local hospital. Some hospitals offer baby-sitting referral services. Generally, all sitters referred have taken a baby-sitting course offered by the hospital, which includes baby CPR and other first-aid procedures. At other hospitals and nursing schools, nursing students may be available for baby-sitting jobs.

Local newspapers. Check daily papers and specialized parent papers for ads run by care providers seeking employment, and/or run an ad yourself.

College employment offices. Part-time or full-time, year-round or summer help may be found through local colleges.

Senior citizen organizations. Lively seniors can make terrific sitters – and surrogate grandparents at the same time. (Just make sure they're trained in the 'new' ways of baby care, such as putting baby to sleep on his or her back.)

Au pair or nanny organizations. These services can provide families with a live-in au pair, usually a young person from a foreign country who wants to visit or study in Britain for a year or so, or with a well-trained nanny.

SIFTING THROUGH THE POSSIBILITIES

You won't want to spend endless days interviewing obviously unsatisfactory candidates, so sift them out either through CVs that have come in the post or phone conversations. Before you begin talking to people, develop a detailed job description so you know just what you are looking for. Responsibilities may include such chores as shopping and laundry duties, but be wary of overloading the sitter with activities that will distract her attention from your baby. Also decide how many hours a week you'll need her to work, whether the hours will have to be flexible, and whether and how much you'll pay – both as basic salary and for overtime. In a preliminary phone interview, ask the person's name, address, telephone number, age, education, experience (this may actually be less important than some other qualities, such as enthusiasm and natural ability), salary requirements and benefits (check beforehand to see what the going rate is in your area), and why she wants the job. Explain what the position will entail, and see if she is still interested. Set up a personal interview with those applicants who sound promising.

During interviews, look for clues in a candidate's questions and comments

('Does the baby cry a lot?' might reflect impatience with normal infant behaviour), as well as in her silence (the woman who never says anything about liking kids and never comments on yours may be telling you something) to learn what she's like. To learn more, ask questions such as the following, phrasing them so that they require more than a yes or no answer (it doesn't mean much when you get a 'yes' to 'Do you like babies?'):

◆ Why do you want this job?

◆ What was your last job, and why did you leave it?

◆ What do you think a baby my child's age needs most?

◆ How do you see yourself spending the day with a baby this age?

◆ How do you see your role in my baby's life?

◆ How do you feel about breastfeeding? (This is important, of course, only if you are breastfeeding and intend to continue – which will require her support.)

◆ When my baby starts getting more active and getting into mischief, how will you handle it? How do you discipline young children?

◆ How will you get to work on a daily basis? In bad weather?

◆ Do you have a driver's licence and a good driving record? (If driving will be necessary on the job.) Do you have a car? (If that will be necessary in your case.)

◆ How long do you envision staying with this job? (A long stay can never be guaranteed, but the sitter who leaves as soon as your baby becomes adjusted to her can create a multi-

tude of problems for your entire family.)

◆ Do you have children of your own? Will their needs interfere with your work? Will you be able to come to work, for instance, when they're home sick or off from school? Allowing a caregiver to bring her children along has some benefits and some drawbacks. On the one hand, it gives your child the chance to be exposed to the companionship of other children on a daily basis. On the other hand, it gives your child more of a chance to be exposed to all of these extra germs on a daily basis; and having other children to care for may also affect the quality and quantity of attention the caregiver can give your own baby. It may also result in greater wear and tear on your home.

◆ Will you cook, shop or do housework? (Having some of these chores taken care of by someone else will give you more time to spend with your baby when you're at home. But if the care provider spends a lot of time with these chores, your baby may not get the attention and stimulation he or she needs.)

◆ Are you in good health? Ask for evidence of a complete physical exam and a recent negative TB test, as well as about smoking habits (she should be a non-smoker), alcohol and drug use. This last information will probably not be forthcoming from a drug or alcohol abuser, but be alert for clues, such as restlessness, talkativeness, nervousness, agitation, dilated pupils, poor appetite (stimulants, such as amphetamines or cocaine); slurred speech, staggering, disorientation, poor concentration, and other signs of drunkenness with or without

IS HE MANNY ENOUGH FOR THE JOB?

If it's true what they say (and it is!) that there's nothing that a mother can do that a father can't do equally well if not better (besides breast-feed, that is), then it's also true that there's nothing that a female nanny can do that a male nanny can't do equally well if not better. Which is why more and more men are signing up to provide child care – and why more and more parents are hiring them as nannies. In fact, this newer breed of child-care providers have even had a name coined in their honour: manny. Though still a minority in the child-care business, the ranks of mannies are growing fast. Who says a good manny is hard to find?

the odour of alcohol (alcohol, barbiturates and other 'downers'); pinpoint pupils and craving for sweets (early heroin addiction); euphoria, relaxed inhibitions, increased appetite, loss of memory, possibly dilated pupils and bloodshot eyes (marijuana). A sitter who is trying not to use drugs or alcohol at work may exhibit signs of withdrawal from the abused substance, such as watery, runny eyes, yawning, irritability, anxiety, tremors, chills and sweating.

Of course, many of these symptoms can be signs of illness (mental or physical) rather than drug abuse. In either case, should they show up in a child-care worker, they should concern you. You will also want to avoid someone with a medical condition that could interfere with regular attendance at work.

◆ Have you recently had, or are you willing to take, CPR and baby first-aid training?

Though you'll be asking the questions, the job applicant shouldn't be the only one answering them. Ask these questions of yourself, based on your observations of each candidate, and answer them honestly:

◆ Did the candidate arrive for the interview well groomed and neatly dressed? Though you may not require a freshly starched nanny's uniform on the job, soiled clothes, unwashed hair and dirty fingernails are all bad signs.

◆ Does she seem to have a sense of orderliness that's compatible with your own? If she has to rummage through her handbag for five minutes for her references and you're a stickler for organization, you'll probably clash. On the other hand, if she seems compulsively neat and you're compulsively messy, you probably won't get along either.

◆ Does she seem reliable? If she's late for the interview, watch out. She may be late every time she's due to work. Check this out with previous employers.

◆ Is she physically capable of handling the job? A frail older woman may not be able to carry your baby around all day now, or chase your toddler later.

◆ Does she seem good with children? The interview isn't complete until the applicant spends some time with your baby so that you can observe the interaction, or lack thereof. Does she seem patient, kind, interested, really attentive and sensitive to your baby's needs? Find out more about her aptitude for child care from previous employers.

◆ Does she seem intelligent? You'll want someone who can teach and entertain your child the way you would yourself, and who will show good judgment in difficult situations.

◆ Does she speak English? How well? Obviously, you'll want someone who can communicate with your baby and with you (especially if you speak only English), but there are some benefits to a sitter who has a working understanding of English but isn't a fluent speaker – she might be able to teach your baby a second language at a time when baby is ripe for learning one (see page 218).

◆ Are you comfortable with her? Almost as important as the rapport the candidate has with your baby is the rapport she has with you. For your baby's sake, there needs to be constant, open, comfortable communication between a chosen caregiver and you; be certain this will be not only possible, but easy.

If the first series of interviews doesn't turn up any candidates you feel good about, don't settle – try again. If it does, the next step in narrowing down your selection is to check references. Don't take the word of a candidate's friends or family on her abilities and reliability; insist on the names of previous employers, if any, or if she doesn't have much work experience, those of teachers, clergy or other more objective judges of character. You might also consider hiring an employee-screening firm to do a thorough background check (some, but not all, agencies do thorough prescreens). The prospective employee's permission is needed to do this.

THE BUSINESS OF HIRING A NANNY

Hiring a nanny comes with its share of paperwork. By law, you are required to register with the Inland Revenue as an employer and operate a PAYE (Pay As You Earn) scheme. This involves paying Income Tax and National Insurance Contributions (NIC) deducted from your nanny's gross wage (or added to her net wage) as well as an employer's NIC on top of her wage. To register as a new employer, call the Inland Revenue on 0845 6070143.

GETTING ACQUAINTED

You'd probably be very unhappy if you were left alone to spend the day with a perfect stranger. You can expect your baby, who will experience the added stress of missing mummy and daddy (less so in the early months, more so in the second half of the first year), to be unhappy at first, too. To minimize the misery, introduce baby and sitter in advance. If it's a sitter-for-the-evening, have her come at least half an hour early the first time (an hour if your baby is more than five months old), so that your baby will have some time to adjust. Make the introduction gradually, starting baby off in your arms, moving him or her next to an infant seat or swing so the sitter can approach on neutral territory, then, finally, as baby becomes more comfortable with the newcomer, into the sitter's arms. Then, once the initial adjustment has been made, stay away for just an hour or two. The next time, have the sitter arrive half an hour ahead of your departure once again, and stay out a little longer. By the third time, a fifteen-minute period with you still at home should suffice, and

KEEPING AN EYE ON THE SITTER

Do you ever wonder what really goes on when you're not at home? Does the sitter spend all day providing your baby with loving, nurturing care, or talking on the phone and watching soaps? Does she coo, cuddle and dote on your infant, or leave him or her strapped in an infant seat or crying in the cot? Does she follow your instructions to the letter, or throw them out the window the moment you're out the door? Is she the Mary Poppins you hoped you hired, or the baby-sitter nightmares are made of – or more likely somewhere in between?

To make sure the sitter they've chosen is close to everything they thought she is, or to determine if she's far from it (especially if some red flags have been raised), more and more parents are turning to so-called 'nanny cams' – hidden video surveillance to watch those who are watching their children. If you're considering installing such a system, consider the following first:

♦ The equipment. You can either buy or rent cameras, or hire a service that will set up an elaborate surveillance system throughout your home. The least expensive option – a single camera hidden in a room your baby and the sitter are likely to spend the most time in – can provide you with a glimpse of what goes on while you're away, but not a full picture (abuse or neglect might be occurring in a different room, for instance). A wireless camera hidden inside of a stuffed animal is more expensive but is also more inconspicuous, and since it can be moved from room to room, you'll be able to view different rooms on different days. A system that monitors the entire home will obviously offer the clearest picture of your baby's care but is much more expensive.

Keep in mind, too, that how well the surveillance works will depend on how well you survey it. You'll need to be committed to taping at least several days a week (daily would be best) and watching the tapes regularly, otherwise you might not catch abuse or neglect until days after it occurs.

♦ Your rights – and your nanny's. Your equipment supplier should be able to inform you about the legal considerations of videotaping a sitter at work in your home without her knowledge. The ethical issues are another matter – and very much open for debate. Some parents feel that nanny cams are an invasion of the sitter's privacy; others feel that it's the best investment they can make for the safety of their child.

♦ Your motivation. If you're just eager for some peace of mind, a nanny cam might just buy it. On the other hand, if you're already feeling uncomfortable enough about the child-care provider you've hired that you're compelled to spy on her with a nanny cam, perhaps that person shouldn't be in your home at all. In that case, you might be wiser to trust your instincts, save your money, and find your baby a sitter you have confidence in.

If you do decide to install a nanny cam, don't use it as a way of screening prospective child-care providers. Any baby-sitter should be thoroughly pre-screened *before* she's left home alone with your baby.

after that sitter and charge should be bosom buddies. (If they aren't, consider whether you've chosen the right sitter.)

The daily sitter needs an even greater introduction period. She should spend at least a full paid day with you and the baby, becoming familiar not only with your baby but also with your home, your child-care style, and your household routines. That will give you a chance to make suggestions, and her a chance to ask questions. It will also give you a chance to see the sitter in action – and a chance to change your mind about her if you don't like what you see. (Don't judge the sitter on baby's reaction but rather on how the sitter responds to it. No matter how good a sitter is, children – even very young children – often protest being with one as long as a parent is around.)

Your baby will probably adjust to a new care provider most easily when he or she is under six months old, and will take much longer once stranger anxiety appears on the scene (usually sometime between six and nine months; see page 430).

THE TRIAL PERIOD

Always hire a child-care provider on a trial basis so that you can evaluate her performance before deciding whether you want to keep her on for the long term. It's fairer to her and to you if you make clear in advance that the first two weeks or month on the job (or any specified period) will be a trial period. During this time, observe your baby. Does he or she seem happy, clean, alert when you come home? Or more tired than usual, and more cranky? Does it seem a nappy change has been made fairly recently? Important, too, is the care provider's frame of mind at day's end. Is she relaxed and comfortable? Or tense and irritable, obviously happy to be relieved of her charge? Is she eager to tell

you about her day with the baby, reporting the infant's latest achievements, as well as any problems she's noted, or does she routinely tell you only how long the baby slept and how much of the bottle was emptied – or, worse, how long the baby cried? Does she keep in mind that this is still *your* baby, and accept the idea that you make the major decisions about her care? Or does she seem to feel that she's in charge now?

If you're not happy with the new caregiver (or if she's clearly not happy with the job), start a new search. If your evaluation leaves you uncertain, you might try arriving home early and unannounced to get a look at what's really happening in your absence. Or you could ask friends or neighbours who might see the sitter in the park, at the supermarket or walking down the street how she seems to be doing. If a neighbour reports your usually happy baby is doing a lot of crying while you're away, that should be a red flag. Another option: considering video surveillance with a 'nanny cam' (see box, opposite page).

If everything and everyone seems to be fine except you (you're anxious every time you leave your baby, you're miserable while you're away, you keep looking for fault in a sitter who's doing a good job), it's possible that it's the arrangement, not the sitter, that isn't working out. Rather than subjecting your baby to a series of sitters (if, from your point of view, the right full-time sitter seems not to have been born yet), perhaps you should reconsider your decision to go back to work.

GROUP DAY CARE

A good day-care programme can offer some significant advantages. In the best of them, trained personnel provide a well-organized programme specifically geared to a baby's development and growth, as well as opportunities for play and learning with other babies and children. Because such facilities are not dependent on one person, as in-home care is, there is generally no crisis if a teacher is sick or leaves, though the baby may have to adjust to a new one. It is also usually more affordable than in-home care, making it not only the best option but also the only option for many parents.

The disadvantages for babies, however, can also be significant. Firstly, not all programmes are equally good. Even in a good one, care is less individualized than it is in a baby's own home, there are more children per caregiver, and teacher turnover may be high. There is less flexibility in scheduling than in a more informal setting, and if the centre follows the school calendar, it may be closed on holidays when you're working. The cost, though typically less expensive than good in-home care, is still usually fairly high, unless subsidized by government or private sources (as in corporate day care). Possibly the greatest disadvantage is the increased rate of infection among children in day-care situations. Since many employed parents don't have another option when their children have colds and other minor ills, they often send them to the centre anyway – which is why babies who attend them end up with more than their share of ear infections and other bugs.

Certainly, there are some excellent day-care facilities; the trick may be to find such a facility in your area that you can afford and that has space for your baby.

WHERE TO LOOK

You can get the names of local day-care facilities (which may be non-profit, cooperative or for profit) through recommendations from friends whose parenting style is similar to yours by speaking to your health visitor, calling your local council education department or by asking at your local community centre or house of worship. You can also ask your baby's doctor for a suggestion or check the phone book or a local parenting newspaper for child-care referral services or day-care centres themselves. Once you have a few possibilities, you'll need to start evaluating them.

WHAT TO LOOK FOR

Day-care centres have to be registered with, and inspected by, the local authority, but do range in quality from top-of-the-line to bottom-of-the-barrel, with most falling in the mediocre middle. If you'll accept only the best for your baby, you'll have to examine every aspect of each possibility. Look for:

A trained and experienced staff. The 'head' teachers, at least, should have degrees in early childhood education; the entire staff should be experienced in caring for infants. Too often, because of the low pay, day-care workers are people who are in the job because they are qualified for nothing else; in that case, it's likely they aren't qualified for child care, either. The staff turnover should be low; if there are several new teachers each year, beware.

A healthy and safe staff. Ask if all childcare workers have had complete medical checkups, including a TB test, and thorough background checks.

A good teacher-to-baby ratio. There should be at least one staff person for every three infants. If there are fewer, a crying baby may have to wait until someone is free to meet his or her needs.

Moderate size. A huge day-care facility might be less well supervised and operated than a smaller one – though there are exceptions to this rule. Also, the more children, the more chance for the spread of illnesses. Whatever the size of the facility, there should be adequate space for each child. Crowded rooms are a sign of an inadequate programme.

Separation of age groups. Infants under one year should not be mixed with toddlers and older children, for safety, health, attention and development issues.

A loving atmosphere. The staff should seem to genuinely like children and caring for them. Children should look happy, alert and clean. Be sure to visit the facility unannounced in the middle or towards the end of the day, when you will get a more accurate picture of what the centre is like than you would first thing in the morning. (Be wary of any programme that does not allow unannounced parent visits.)

A stimulating atmosphere. Even a two-month-old can benefit from a stimulating atmosphere, one where there is plenty of interaction – both verbal and physical – with caregivers, and where age-appropriate toys are available. As children become older and developmentally advanced, there should be plenty of appropriate toys to play with, as well as exposure to books, music and the out-of-doors. The best programmes include occasional 'field trips': three to six children along with one or two teachers go to the supermarket, the park or other places a baby might go with a stay-at-home parent.

Parent involvement. Are parents invited to participate in the programme in some way; is there a parent board that makes policy?

YOUR CHILD AS A BAROMETER OF CHILD CARE

No matter which child-care alternative you choose for your baby, be alert to signs of discontent: sudden changes in personality or mood, clinginess, fretfulness that doesn't seem attributable to teething, illness or any other obvious cause. If your baby seems unhappy, check into your child-care situation; it may need a change.

A compatible philosophy. Are you comfortable with the day-care centre's philosophy – educationally, religiously, ideologically?

Adequate opportunities for rest. Most infants, in day care or at home, still take a lot of naps. There should be a quiet area for such napping in individual cots, and children should be able to nap according to their own schedules – not the school's.

Security. The doors to the facility should be kept locked during operating hours, and there should be other security measures in place (a parent or visitor sign-in sheet, someone monitoring the door, requesting ID when necessary). The centre should also have a system in place for pickups that protects children (only those on a list pre-approved by you should be able to pick up your child).

Strict health and sanitation rules. In your own home, you needn't be concerned about your baby putting everything in his or her mouth; in a day-care centre, with a convergence of children, each with his or her own set of germs, you should be. Day-care centres can become a focus for the spread of many intestinal and upper respiratory illnesses. To minimize germ spreading and safeguard the health of the children, a well-run day-care centre will have a medical consultant and a written policy that includes:

♦ Caregivers must wash hands (with liquid soap) thoroughly after changing nappies or don a fresh pair of disposable gloves for each change. Hands should also be washed after helping children use the toilet, wiping runny noses or handling children with colds, and before feedings.

♦ Nappy changing and food preparation areas must be entirely separate, and each should be cleaned after every use.

♦ Nappies should be disposed of in a covered container, out of the reach of children.

♦ Toys must be rinsed with a sanitizing solution between handling by different children, or a separate box of toys must be kept for each child.

♦ Stuffed animals should not be shared and should be machine-washed frequently.

♦ Teething rings, dummies, flannels, towels, brushes and combs should not be shared.

♦ Feeding utensils must be washed in a dishwasher or, better still, must be disposable (infant bottles should be labelled with their owners' names so they aren't mixed up).

♦ Food preparation for infants on solids must be carried out under sanitary conditions.

♦ Immunizations must be up-to-date for all babies.

♦ Children who are moderately to severely ill, particularly with diarrhoea, vomiting, high fever and certain types of rashes, must be kept at home (this isn't always necessary with colds, since the cold is contagious before it is evident) or in a special infirmary section of the facility.

♦ There should be a policy about dosing children who attend with medication.

♦ When a baby has a contagious illness, all the parents of children in the centre must be notified by the centre; in cases of *Hemophilus influenzae,* immunization or medication may be given to prevent spread of the disease.[2]

Also check with your local council to be sure there are no outstanding complaints or violations against the centre.

Strict safety rules. Injuries, mostly minor, are not uncommon in day-care facilities. But the safer the facility, the safer your baby will be. The top hazards are climbers, slides, hand toys and blocks, other playground equipment, doors and indoor floor surfaces. Even a crawling baby can get into trouble with these; all babies can get into trouble with small objects (that can be choked

2. Cytomegalovirus (CMV) is easily transmitted among babies in child care because of the frequent contact of caregivers with virus-laden urine and saliva. Since there is a very remote risk of infecting an unborn baby if the mother is infected, take precautions. If you know you are not immune to CMV (most women are), and you are pregnant again or planning to become pregnant again soon, be particularly careful to wash your hands after nappy changes; don't kiss your child on the lips or eat his or her leftovers. (If you are immune, you can't 'catch' CMV and don't have to take special precautions. There is also no risk to the foetus – and no need for precautions – after the 24th week of pregnancy.)

on or swallowed), sharp objects, poisonous materials, and so on. A child-care centre should meet the safety requirements you maintain in your own home:

◆ Infants should be put to sleep on their backs.

◆ Cots, changing tables, high chairs, playpens and other furnishings should meet safety criteria.

◆ Mattresses should be firm; no pillows, fluffy bedding or toys should be used in cots.

◆ Open stairways should have safety gates on them; watch, too, for doors that can slam on little fingers or can open on little faces.

◆ Windows above ground level shouldn't be able to be opened more than 15 cm (6 in) and/or should have window guards.

◆ Special precautions should be taken to protect children from radiators and other heating devices, electrical outlets, cleaning materials and medications (often teachers have to dispense these to children recovering from illnesses or those with chronic problems).

◆ Floors should not be littered with toys that can trip a newly toddling twelve-month-old or caregiver carrying an infant.

◆ Materials used by older children (paints, clay, toys with small or sharp parts) should be kept out of reach of babies.

◆ Smoke detectors, clearly marked fire escape routes, fire extinguishers and other fire safety precautions should be in evidence.

◆ Staff should be trained in CPR and first aid, and a fully equipped first-aid kit should be readily available.

SAFE SLEEPING

If you're leaving a young infant in the care of someone else – whether a sitter, grandparent, friend or day-care provider – be sure he or she is aware of the 'back-to-sleep, tummy-to-play' policy. All babies should nap on their backs (unless a medical condition dictates otherwise) on a safe surface and should spend some wakeful time on their tummies (but only under constant supervision).

Careful attention to nutrition. All meals and snacks should be healthy, safe and appropriate for the ages of the children being served. Parental instructions regarding formula (or breast milk), foods, and feeding schedules should be followed. Bottles should never be propped.

CHLDMINDERS

Many parents feel more comfortable leaving a baby in a family situation in a private home with just a few other children than in a more impersonal day-care centre; and for those who can't arrange for a sitter in their own homes, childminder is often the best choice.

Childminders should be registered with their local authority and, as part of the registrations process, are subjected to a police check. Their homes are also inspected annually to ensure they are safe and secure and there are regulations, too, about the number of children they can have in their care.

There are many advantages to such care. Childminders can often provide a warm, home-like environment at a lower cost than other forms of care. Because there are fewer children than in a day-care centre, there is less exposure to infection and more potential for stimulation and individualized care (though this potential is not always realized). Flexible scheduling – early drop-off or late pickup when that's necessary – is often possible.

The disadvantages vary from situation to situation. The care provider may be untrained, lacking in professional child-care experience, and may have a child-rearing philosophy that differs from the parents'. If she or one of her children is ill, there may be no backup. And though the risk may be lower than in a larger day-care facility, there is always the possibility of germs spreading from child to child, especially if sanitation is lax. See the section on group day care, starting on page 279, for tips on what to look for and look out for when checking out home day care.

CORPORATE DAY CARE

A common option in European countries for many years, day-care facilities in or adjacent to a parent's place of work are much less common in the United Kingdom, though more and more companies have started to offer such services. It's an option many parents would choose if they had it.

The advantages are extremely attractive. Your child is near you in case of emergency; you can visit or even breastfeed during your lunch hour or coffee break; and since you commute with your child, you spend more time together. Such facilities are usually staffed by professionals and are very well equipped. Knowing your child is nearby and well cared for may allow you to give fuller attention to your work. The cost for such care, if any, is usually low.

There are some possible disadvantages. If your commute is a difficult one,

It may be hard on your child to weather on a daily basis – and hard on you if there's a lot of struggling on and off of buses or tubes with changing bags and pushchairs. Sometimes seeing you during the day, if that's part of the programme, makes each parting more difficult for your baby, especially during times of stress (and, later, separation anxiety). And visiting, in some cases, may take your mind from your work.

Corporate day care, of course, should meet all the educational, health and safety standards of any child-care facility. If the one set up by your employer doesn't, then speak to those responsible for the facility about what can be done to make the programme better and safer. Rallying other parents around the cause may help, too.

BABIES ON THE JOB

Very occasionally, a parent is able to take her or his baby to work, even when no day care is provided. And, occasionally, the situation works. It works best before a baby is mobile and if colic is not a problem – and, of course, when the parent has the space for a portable cot and other baby paraphernalia near her or his work area and the support of both employer and co-workers. Ideally, you should also have a sitter on the spot, at least part of the time, or a lot of flexible time; otherwise, baby may actually end up getting less attention and stimulation than he or she might in another child-care situation. Keeping baby on the job usually works best, too, if the atmosphere in the workplace is relaxed; a high stress level can have a negative impact on baby. When it does work, this kind of situation can be perfect for the nursing mum, or for any parent who wants to stay on the job and keep baby close, too.

WHEN YOUR CHILD IS SICK

No parent likes to see his or her baby sick, but the working parent particularly dreads that first sign of fever or upset stomach. He or she knows that caring for a sick baby may present a great many problems, the central ones being who will take care of the baby, and where?

Ideally, either you or your spouse should be able to take time off from work when your child is ill, so that you can administer care yourself at home. After all, as anyone who's ever been a sick child knows, there's nothing quite the same as having your mummy or daddy around to hold your hot little hand, wipe your feverish brow and administer specially prescribed doses of love and attention. Next best is having a trusted and familiar sitter or another family member you can call upon to stay with your baby at home. Some day-care centres have a sick-child infirmary, where a child is in familiar surroundings with familiar faces. There are also special sick-child day-care facilities, both in homes and in larger freestanding centres sprouting up to meet this need; but in these, of course, the child has to adjust to being cared for by strangers in a strange environment when he's or she's least able to handle change. Some corporations, in order to keep parents on the job, actually pay for sick-child care, such as space in a sick child day-care centre or for a sick-baby nurse to stay with the child at home (which will also require adjustment to an unfamiliar caregiver).

◆ ◆ ◆

CHAPTER 8

The Fourth Month

Someone's all smiles this month – and as a result, chances are you'll be, too. Your infant is just entering what might be considered the golden age of babyhood – a period of several enchanted months when good humour reigns during the day, more sleep is happening at night, and independent mobility has yet to be achieved (which means your baby will continue to stay pretty much where you put him or her, limiting mischief and mayhem; enjoy this while it lasts). Sociable and interested, eager to strike up a cooing conversation, to watch the world go by, and to charm anyone within radius, babies this age are an undeniable delight to be around.

What Your Baby May Be Doing

All babies reach milestones on their own developmental time line. If your baby seems not to have reached one or more of these milestones, rest assured, he or she probably will very soon. Your baby's rate of development is normal for your baby. Keep in mind, too, that skills babies perform from the tummy position can be mastered only if there's an opportunity to practise. So make sure your baby spends supervised playtime on his or her belly. If you have concerns about your baby's development (because you've noticed a missed milestone or what you think might be a developmental delay), don't hesitate to check it out with the doctor at the next well-baby visit – even if he or she doesn't bring it up. Parents often notice nuances in a baby's development that doctors don't. Premature infants generally reach milestones later than others of the same birth age, often achieving them closer to their adjusted age (the age they would be if they had been born at term), and sometimes later.

By four months, your baby . . . should be able to:

◆ on stomach, lift head up 90 degrees[1]

◆ laugh out loud

---

1. Babies who spend little time on their stomachs during playtime may reach this milestone later, and that's not cause for concern (see page 205).

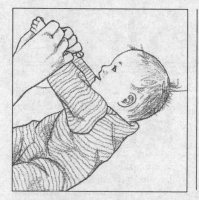
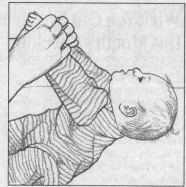

At the beginning of the fourth month, most babies still cannot keep their head level with their body when they are pulled to a sitting position (left). Their heads usually fall backwards (right).

♦ follow an object in an arc about 15 cm (6 in) above the face for 180 degrees (from one side to the other)

. . . will probably be able to:

♦ hold head steady when upright

♦ on stomach, raise chest, supported by arms

♦ grasp a rattle held to backs or tips of fingers

♦ pay attention to an object as small as a raisin (but keep such objects out of baby's reach)

♦ reach for an object

♦ squeal in delight

. . . may possibly be able to:

♦ keep head level with body when pulled to sitting

♦ roll over (one way)

♦ turn in the direction of a voice, particularly mummy's

♦ say 'ah-goo' or similar vowel-consonant combinations

♦ razz (make a wet razzing sound)

. . . may even be able to:

♦ bear some weight on legs when held upright

♦ sit without support

♦ object if you try to take a toy away

♦ turn in the direction of a voice

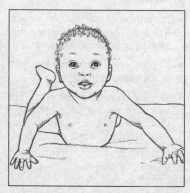

Many, but not all, four-month-olds can raise up on their arms.

What You Can Expect at This Month's Checkup

You've probably thought of a few questions since last month's checkup. Here's your opportunity to ask them. Since immunizations are on the agenda at this visit, try (if possible) to get your questions answered before the injections are administered, so that baby will still be calm, and preferably dressed.

Each practitioner will have a personal approach to well-baby checkups. The overall organization of the physical exam, as well as the number and type of assessment techniques used and procedures performed, will also vary with the individual needs of the child. But, in general, you can expect the following at a checkup when your baby is about four months old:

◆ Questions about how you and baby and the rest of the family are doing at home, and about baby's eating, sleeping and general progress, as well as child care if you are working out of the house.

◆ Measurement of baby's weight, length and head circumference, and plotting of progress since birth.

◆ Physical exam, including a recheck of any previous problems.

◆ Developmental assessment. The examiner may actually put baby through a series of tests to evaluate head control, hand use, vision, hearing and social interaction, or may simply rely on observation plus your reports on what baby is doing.

◆ Third round of immunizations, if baby is in good health and there are no other contraindications. See the recommended schedule on page 227. Be sure to discuss any reactions to the previous rounds of immunizations beforehand.

◆ Guidance about what to expect in the next month in relation to such topics as feeding, sleeping, development and infant safety.

Questions you may want to ask, if the doctor hasn't already answered them:

◆ What reactions can you expect baby to have to the third round of immunizations? How should you treat them? Which reactions should you call about?

◆ When is a good time to start solids?

Also raise concerns that have arisen over the past month. Mention any developmental delays or missed milestones you may have noticed. Jot down information and instructions from the doctor. Record all pertinent information (baby's weight, length, head circumference, birthmarks, immunizations, illnesses, medications given, test results, and so on) in a permanent health record.

Feeding Your Baby:
THINKING ABOUT SOLIDS

The messages that a new parent receives about when to start feeding solids are many, and often confusing. Baby's grandmother: 'I started you before you were four months. What are you waiting for?' To back up her argument, she points to the obvious: 'You're healthy, aren't you?' A well-meaning friend insists that starting solids earlier will help any baby sleep through the night. Her proof positive: a baby who's slept through since his first spoonful of cereal. The health visitor issues instructions to wait until baby is six months, citing the most recent recommendations and research.

Whom do you listen to? Does mother know best? Or friends? Or the health visitor? Actually, your baby does – nobody can tell you when to start giving solids better than he or she can. Though the guidelines offered up by the medical community are certainly valid (probably more so than those offered up by grandma and friends), and should be used to set parameters – an infant's individual development should be at least one of the deciding factors in promoting a baby to a more varied diet.

Very early introduction to solids isn't believed to be physically harmful in most cases, though it can occasionally trigger allergies. But it isn't wise, for a number of reasons. Firstly, a young baby's digestive system – from a tongue that pushes out any foreign substance placed on it, to intestines lacking many digestive enzymes – is developmentally unready for solids. Secondly, solids aren't necessary early on – babies can fill all their nutritional needs for the first six months of life from breast milk or formula alone.

Bringing on the solids too soon can also undermine future eating habits (baby may reject the cereal initially simply because he or she isn't ready, then may reject it later because of prior parental pushing).

On the other hand, waiting too long – until late into the second half of the first year – can also lead to potential pitfalls. An older baby may resist being taught the new (and challenging) tricks of chewing and swallowing solids, preferring to cling to the tried-and-true (and easy) methods of tummy satisfaction: nursing or bottle feeding. And, like habits, tastes may be tougher to change at this point; unlike the more malleable six-month-old, the ten- or eleven-month-old may not be as open to opening wide for solids when he or she is so used to liquids.

To decide if your baby is ready for the big step into the world of solid foods (most will be between four and six months), look for the following clues, then consult the doctor:

◆ Your baby can hold his or her head up well. Even strained baby foods should not be offered until a baby holds his head up well when propped to sit; chunkier foods should wait until a baby can sit well alone, usually not until seven months.

◆ The tongue thrust reflex has disappeared. This is a reflex that causes young infants to push foreign matter out of their mouths (an inborn mechanism that protects them from choking on foreign bodies). Try this test: place a tiny bit of infant rice cereal thinned with breast milk or formula in your baby's mouth from the tip of a baby spoon or your finger. If the food comes right back out again with the tongue, and continues to after several tries, the thrust is still present and baby isn't ready for spoon feeding.

♦ Baby reaches for and otherwise shows an interest in table foods. The baby who grabs the fork out of your hand or snares the bread from your plate, who watches intently and exhibits excitement with every bite you take, is telling you he or she's eager to sample more grown-up fare.

♦ The ability to execute back-and-forth movements with the tongue, as

well as up-and-down ones, is present. You can discover this by observation.

♦ Baby is able to open his or her mouth so that food can be taken from a spoon.

There are instances, however, when even a baby who seems developmentally ready for solids may have to wait – most often because there is a strong history of allergy in the family. Until more is known about the development of allergies, it is generally recommended that children in such families be breastfed for most of the first year, with solids added very cautiously, starting at six months. For more on starting solids, see page 309.

What You May Be Concerned About

REJECTION OF THE BREAST

'My baby was doing very well at the breast – now, suddenly, he's refused to nurse for the past eight hours. Could something be wrong with my milk?'

*S*omething is probably wrong – though not necessarily with your milk. Temporary rejection of the breast, also called a nursing strike (even in non-union babies), is not unusual and almost always has a specific cause, the most common of which are:

Mother's diet. Have you been indulging in pasta al pesto or another dish redolent with garlic? Feasting your chops and chopsticks on stir-fried chicken? Honouring Saint Patrick with corned beef and cabbage? If so, your baby may simply be protesting the spicy and/or strong flavours your diet is imparting to

his milk. If you figure out what turns your baby off, avoid eating it until after you've weaned him. Many babies, on the other hand, don't mind the strong spices in their mother's milk, especially if they became accustomed to those flavours in utero through highly seasoned amniotic fluid; some especially relish the taste of spicy breast milk.

A cold. Babies who can't breathe through stuffy noses can't nurse and breathe through their mouths at the same time; understandably, they opt for breathing. Gently suction baby's nostrils with an infant nasal aspirator, or ask your baby's doctor about nose drops.

Teething. Though most babies don't begin the struggle with teeth until at least five or six months, a few begin teething much earlier, and a very occasional baby actually sprouts a tooth or two in the first four months. Nursing often puts pressure on swollen gums, making suckling painful. When budding teeth are the cause of breast rejection, a baby usually starts nursing eagerly, only to pull away in pain.

An earache. Because ear pain can radiate to the jaw, the sucking motions of nursing can make discomfort worse. See page 555 for other clues to ear infection.

Thrush. If your baby has this fungal infection in his mouth, nursing may be painful. Be sure the condition is treated so that the infection isn't passed on to you through cracked nipples, or spread elsewhere on the baby (see page 122).

Slow let-down. A very hungry baby may grow impatient when milk doesn't flow immediately (in some women let-down may take as long as five minutes to occur), and may push away the nipple in a fury before let-down begins. To avoid this problem, express a little milk before you pick him up, so that he'll get something for his efforts the moment he starts to suck.

A hormonal change in you. A new pregnancy (unlikely now if you're nursing exclusively, more possible if you've started your baby on supplemental formula feedings) can produce hormones that change the taste of the breast milk, causing baby to reject the breast. So can the return of menstruation, which again isn't usually an issue until partial weaning begins.

Tension in you. Maybe you're stressed because you've recently returned to work. Maybe it's because it's bill-paying time, or because the dishwasher just broke – again. Maybe it's just because you've had a really bad day. Whatever the reason, if you're worried or upset you may be communicating your tension to your baby, making him too

agitated to nurse. Try to relax yourself before offering the breast.

Readiness for weaning. This couldn't be the case yet – though in a baby approaching his first birthday, breast rejection might be his way of saying, 'Mummy, I've had it with nursing. I'm ready to move on.' Ironically, babies seem to do this when their mothers are not the least bit interested in weaning, rather than when mum's ready to quit nursing.

Once in a while, there appears to be no obvious explanation for a baby's turning down the breast. Like an adult, a baby can be 'off his feed' for a meal or two. Fortunately, this kind of hiatus is usually temporary. In the meantime, these suggestions may help you ride out the nursing strike:

♦ Don't try substitutes. Offering a bottle of formula when your baby balks at the breast could exacerbate the problem by decreasing your milk supply. Most nursing strikes, even 'long-term' ones, last only a day or two.

♦ Try some breast in a bottle. Express some milk and give it to your baby in a bottle if he continuously rejects the breast (though this won't work if it's something in the milk that's bothering him). Again, the strike's likely to last only a day or two, after which your baby will be ready to take milk from the source again.

♦ Try, try again. Even if he rejects it for a few feedings, chances are he'll surprise you and start right back where he left off.

♦ Slow down on solids. If you've started your baby on solid food, he may be eating too much, curbing his appetite for breast milk. At this age, breast milk is still more important than any solids, so cut down on the amount of solids you're feeding and always offer the breast first.

If rejection of nursing continues, or if it occurs in connection with other signs of illness, speak to his doctor.

WRIGGLING AT CHANGING TIME

'My daughter won't lie still when I'm changing her – she's always trying to turn over. How can I get her to cooperate?'

As far as cooperation during nappy changes is concerned, you can expect to receive less and less as the months go by. The indignity of nappy changing, teamed with the turtle-on-its-back frustration of being temporarily immobilized, may set off a battle with each change. The trick: be quick (have all the changing paraphernalia ready and waiting before you lay baby on the table), and provide distractions (a mobile above the changing table, a music box, preferably one that's also visually tempting, a rattle or other toy to occupy her hands and, hopefully, her interest). Engaging your baby in a song or a cooing conversation may also divert her long enough to get the job done.

PROPPING BABY

'I had my baby propped up in his pushchair, and I was scolded by two older women who insisted he was too young to sit up.'

If your baby wasn't old enough to sit up, he'd tell you so. Not in so many words, of course, but by slumping down or sliding off to one side when you tried to prop him. Though you shouldn't attempt to prop a younger infant whose

Propping baby up to a sitting position will offer him or her a welcome change of perspective, and it will also help build the muscles and experience needed for unassisted sitting.

neck and back need more support than he would get with propping, a three- or four-month-old who holds his head up well and doesn't crumble when propped up is ready (and often very eager) for such a position. (Specially designed head supports are available to keep babies' heads upright when propped.) Babies will usually signal when they've had enough of sitting by complaining or beginning to slump.

Besides providing a welcome change of position, sitting allows a baby an expanded view of the world. Instead of just the sky or the inside of the pushchair, an upright baby can see passersby (including those who are sure to chew you out), shops and homes, trees, dogs, other babies in pushchairs, children walking home from school, buses, cars – and all the other amazing things that inhabit his growing universe. He's also likely to stay happy longer than he would lying down, which will make outings more pleasant for both of you.

BABY'S STANDING

'My baby likes to "stand" on my lap. She cries if I make her sit down. But I've heard that standing so early can make her bowlegged.'

Babies usually know what they're ready for better than anyone else. And many babies of your daughter's age are ready, and eager, for supported lap 'standing'. It's fun, it's good muscle-building exercise, it's an exciting change from lying on her back or slumping in an infant seat – and it certainly does not cause bowleggedness.

On the other hand, any baby who doesn't seem to want to stand shouldn't be pushed into doing so until she's ready. A baby who's allowed to set her own developmental pace will be happier and healthier than one whose parents try to set it for her.

BABY FUSSING IN INFANT SEAT

'I really need to keep my baby in the infant seat once in a while so I can get things done. But she fusses as soon as I put her in.'

Some babies are perfectly content to sit in an infant seat and watch the world (and their parents) go by; others – usually those born with more get up and go than they are able to get up and go with yet are bored and frustrated by stints in the seat. Your baby may be among those who resent and resist such confinement – in which case, keeping her content in infant seats (and car seats, and other places of enforced confinement) may be ever-challenging. To give yourself a fighting chance:

◆ Limit the captivity. Reserve the infant seat for times when you absolutely need your baby safely confined and near your side (as when you're cooking).

◆ Try a change of scenery. An infant seat with a view is less likely to provoke instant rejection. Place the seat on the floor in front of a mirror (baby may enjoy interacting with her reflection), or in a safe spot next to you (there's nothing more fascinating than a parent in action).

◆ Add some entertainment. A toy bar can turn an ordinary infant seat into a personal entertainment centre, particularly if toys are rotated to keep interest up and boredom from setting in. If toys seem to make baby fussier, it may be because she's over-tired or overstimulated, in which case removing the entertainment may calm her.

◆ Make a motion. Turning on the rocking motion may soothe your baby while she's in the seat (though some babies are actually upset by the movement; as always, take your cues from her reaction).

◆ Let her loose. While younger infants are often satisfied to sit, older ones begin craving some freedom of movement. So instead of plunking her in the infant seat, try placing her on a blanket – tummy down – on the middle of the floor. This may not only placate her, but give her a chance to practise such skills as rolling over and creeping. The downside to this option while you're trying to get things done: for safety's sake, you'll have to stay close by to supervise her efforts – which will limit the chores you can tackle.

◆ Consider a different approach to confinement. It's possible your baby has outgrown the infant seat, both physically and developmentally. If you need to keep her in one place sometimes, try a well-stocked playpen or an ExerSaucer instead (but limit use of both; see pages 397 and 329).

BABY UNHAPPY IN CAR SEAT

'My son cries every time I strap him into the car seat, making driving miserable for both of us.'

Though the purr of the car's engine and the motion of driving are both soothing and sleep-inducing to many infants (some of whom will drop off to dreamland the moment the key's in the ignition), not all babies (or their parents) agree that getting there is half the fun – especially when getting there means being strapped into a car seat. Rest assured that your son's not the only confinement-phobic baby on the block staging his own version of *Mutiny on the Motorway*. Fussing in the car seat is common behaiour, particularly once children start becoming older and more active, and especially while they're still forced to face the rear of the car. Of course, since riding unconfined is not only unsafe but illegal, letting him loose on the open road isn't an option. Instead, try these suggestions for subduing the car seat rebellion:

◆ Create a diversion. If your baby tends to wail the moment he spies the car seat, keep him busy while you're buckling him up. Start singing a favourite song or holding up a favourite toy for him to look at as you attempt the dreaded procedure. With any luck, he won't notice what you're doing until the dirty work's done.

● Make him comfortable. Harness straps should be tight enough to ensure safety (you shouldn't be able to fit more than two fingers between baby and harness), but not so tight that they pinch or dig into baby's skin. Straps that are too loose, in addition to being unsafe, may also allow your son to slide around, which may add to his discomfort. And if he still doesn't fill up the whole car seat, use inserts specially designed for smaller babies to make him more comfortable and less apt to flop from side to side. Also check the temperature in the back to make sure it's not too hot or too cold (a blast of air-conditioning blowing on his face may upset him, for instance; if so, repositioning the vent may do the trick).

◆ Block the sun. Many babies are unsettled by having the sun in their eyes; you may have it made if baby's in the shade. So pull up the canopy on the seat, or invest in a window shade, available at baby stores.

◆ Drive him with distraction. Put on some soothing music or a CD of lively children's songs for you to sing along with. Equip the seat with car-safe toys that can't be dropped (and rotate these often so baby won't get bored). Place a specially designed mirror on the seat back in front of him (the view from a rear-facing car seat would bore anyone to tears); not only will the reflection entertain him, but if you position the mirror in the right way, you'll be able to see his face in your rearview mirror.

◆ Let him know you're there. It's lonely sitting in the backseat, especially while baby's still in a rear-facing position. So do a lot of talking and singing (yes, even over the crying); the sound of your voice may eventually calm him down.

◆ Try a little companionship. When two adults are in the car, one can buckle in next to baby and offer some live entertainment and reassurance. Older siblings can do the same (all children under the age of thirteen should ride in the backseat, anyway).

◆ Bring the car seat home. You may be able to desensitize your son to the car seat by strapping him in at home for short periods of time, while lavishing him with toys and attention (to ensure a positive experience).

◆ Give it time, but don't ever give in. Eventually, your baby will come to accept the car seat (though he may never actually enjoy the ride in it). But giving in to his protests – even once, even just for a short ride – is not only incredibly dangerous (it takes only a moment for a crash to occur and for an unrestrained child to be injured or killed) but a strategic error, since it opens the door to future concessions.

THUMB SUCKING

'My son has taken to sucking his thumb. At first I was happy because it was helping him sleep better, but now I'm afraid it's going to become a habit I won't be able to break him of later on.'

It isn't easy being a baby. Every time you latch on to something that gives you the comfort and satisfaction you're searching for, somebody wants to take it away from you – sometimes without good reason.

Virtually all babies suck on their fingers at some time during the first year of life; many even begin the habit in the uterus. That's not surprising. An infant's mouth is an important organ, not just for eating but for exploration and pleasure, too (as you will soon discover, to your dismay, when everything baby picks up goes into his mouth, whether it's a rattle or a long-deceased insect he's unearthed at the bottom of a cupboard). But even before a baby can reach for objects, he discovers his hands – and how natural to put the newly discovered hands into that wonderful sensory cavity, the mouth. The first time, the hands may make it to the mouth by random chance, but the baby quickly learns that a mouthful of fingers provides a pleasurable sensation. Soon he's mouthing his fingers regularly. Eventually, many babies decide that the thumb is the most efficient and satisfying finger to suck on (maybe it's the most succulent) and switch from finger mouthing to thumb sucking. Some stick with one or two fingers, or even a whole fist.

At first you may think the habit is cute, or even be grateful that your baby has found a way to pacify himself without your help. Then, as the weeks pass and the habit intensifies, you begin to worry, envisioning your little boy trooping off to school with his thumb firmly implanted in his mouth, ridiculed by his classmates, reprimanded by his teachers. Will you have to make monthly trips to the orthodontist for the work necessary to straighten the bite deformed by thumb sucking, or, worse, weekly trips to the therapist to try to uncover the underlying emotional problems that made him suck on his thumb in the first place?

Well, stop worrying and start letting your baby indulge himself. There is no evidence that thumb sucking is in itself a sign of emotional neediness. Nor – if it ceases by age five – does it appear to do damage to the alignment of permanent teeth; any distortion of the mouth that does occur before that time returns to normal when the habit is ended. Since most children generally put the habit aside by age four to six, many experts say attempts to wean a child from the thumb don't need to begin before then.

Some studies show that nearly half of all children do some thumb or finger sucking past infancy. The behaviour peaks on average between eighteen and twenty-one months, though some have already abandoned the habit by then. Nearly 80 per cent give it up by age five, and 95 per cent by age six, usually on their own. Those who use it to help themselves get off to sleep or to comfort themselves in times of stress hang on to the habit longer than those to whom it is simply a form of oral gratification.

In the meantime, let your baby suck away. Be sure, however, that if he is breastfed, he isn't sucking his thumb to compensate for suckling he isn't getting at the breast; if he seems to want to nurse a little longer at each feeding, let him. And if thumb sucking seems to become the focus of his daily activities, preventing him from using his hands for other explorations, occasionally remove his finger from its station long enough to distract him with toys, with finger or hand games ('this little piggy', 'patty-cake', or 'so big', for instance), or by holding his hands and letting him stand, if he likes that.

CHUBBY BABY

'Everybody admires my chubby little daughter. But I am secretly afraid she's getting too fat. She's so round, she can hardly move.'

With dimples on her knees and her elbows, a belly to rival any Buddha's, an extra chin to chuck and an endearing amount of pinchable flesh on her cheeks, she's the picture of baby cuteness from head to chubby toes. Yet is the plump baby also the picture of health? Or is she on her way to becoming a fat child and an obese adult? With childhood obesity in the UK reaching epidemic proportions, that question has generated a great deal of interest among parents, doctors and researchers.

One study has already found that babies who put on weight speedily in their first six months may be at an increased risk of obesity as early as age three. But even without the benefit of research, there are clearly disadvantages to extreme chubbiness early on. The baby who is too plump to budge may become a victim to a vicious cycle of inactivity and overweight. The less she moves, the fatter she gets; the fatter she gets, the less she can move. Her inability to move makes her frustrated and fussy, which may lead her parent to overfeed her to keep her happy. If she stays overweight through age four, a problem that is becoming more and more common among British children, the odds that she will be an overweight adult grow greatly.

Before you make a reservation at the fat farm for your baby, however, be certain she is indeed overweight and not just nicely rounded (remember, since babies haven't yet developed much in the way of muscle, even a slim one will sport soft padding; all babies need a certain amount of 'baby fat'). Some parents, fearful that obesity will creep up on their offspring, misguidedly attempt to keep their perfectly normal babies thin by underfeeding them – which can be even more dangerous than overfeeding, leading to a failure to thrive and, possibly, to future eating disorders. Before you jump to any conclusions or take any action, compare her growth with the curve on the height-weight chart on page 788. If her weight seems consistently to be

HOLD THE JUICE

There's nothing more wholesome for a baby than a bottle of juice, right? Actually, that's wrong. Studies show that infants who drink too much juice – particularly apple juice – may become malnourished. That's because juice (which isn't very nutritious to begin with) can drown tender appetites for the breast milk or formula that should be the mainstay of a baby's diet in the first year of life. Excessive juice consumption can also lead to diarrhoea and other chronic tummy troubles, as well as tooth decay (a problem that's especially common among babies who take bottles or sippy cups of juice to bed or suck on them all day long).

Many doctors recommend that fruit juice not be given at all to infants under six months. After six months, parents should avoid giving any juice at bedtime, and only small amounts during the day (no more than 120 to 180 ml/4 to 6 fl oz total daily for children up to the age of six). Mixing the juice at least half-and-half with water will help ensure that your child won't take in too much of the stuff, while minimizing the effects on tummy and teeth. (Get your baby used to such a mixture from the start, and the watered-down taste won't be an issue later on.)

Your choice of juice matters, too. White grape, studies show, is less likely to cause stomach upset than that baby-standard apple, especially for babies who suffered from colic. Later on, look for juices that have something to offer besides calories – added calcium and vitamin C, for instance.

---

moving upwards faster than her height (if they're both moving up quickly, you probably just have a bigger-than-average baby on your hands), discuss this with her doctor.

Unlike the prescription for a chubby adult, the prescription for a chubby baby is not usually a diet. Instead of trying to get an overweight baby to lose weight, the goal is to slow down the rate of gain. Then as she grows taller, she will slim down – something many babies do without intervention as they become more active. Some of the following tips may help not only if your baby is already overweight, but also if you have good reason to believe she's on her way:

♦ Use feeding only to assuage hunger, not to meet other needs. A baby who's fed for all the wrong reasons (when she's hurt or unhappy, when her parent is too busy to play with her, when she's bored in the pushchair) will continue to demand food for the wrong reasons, and as an adult may eat for the same wrong reasons. Instead of feeding her every time she cries, comfort her with a hug or a soothing song. Instead of propping her up with a bottle, prop her in front of a mobile or a music box when you're too busy to play with her; wear her in a baby carrier while you go about your routine; or let her watch what you're doing from her infant seat. Instead of always plying her with teething biscuits to quiet her in the supermarket, attach a toy to her pushchair to keep her occupied while you shop. In spite of what your mother may have believed, constantly pushing food on your baby is not a positive way to express love.

♦ Make dietary adjustments, if necessary. One reason that breastfed babies are less likely to become overweight is that breast milk automatically adjusts to a baby's needs. The lower-fat, lower-calorie foremilk, which comes at the beginning of a feeding, encourages the hungry baby to suckle. The higher-fat, higher-calorie hindmilk, which comes at the end of a feeding, tends to dampen the appetite, sending the message, 'You're feeling full.' If that isn't discouragement enough, and baby continues to nurse away, the breast slows down the amount of milk produced towards the end of the feeding. Suckling for suckling's sake can go on without an excess of calories being consumed. Though baby formulas aren't customized in the same way, if your baby is gaining weight too quickly and is extremely overweight, her doctor may recommend switching to a lower-calorie formula. Before you make such a switch, however, be certain you are not underdiluting the ready-to-mix formula you are presently using – which could increase its calorie count considerably. Don't decide to overdilute it, either, without the doctor's okay. Or to switch to skimmed milk. Babies, even overweight ones, need the cholesterol and fat in breast milk and formula until they're a year old, and the same from whole cow's milk between their first and second birthdays.

♦ Try water, the ultimate calorie-free beverage. Most of us tend to drink too little water. Infant diets (because they are entirely, or almost entirely, liquid) don't require supplementation with water. But water can be very useful for the overweight older baby who wants to keep sucking after her hunger is satisfied, or who is thirsty rather than hungry in hot weather. Instead of breast or formula, offer a bottle or cup of plain water (with no sugar or other sweetening added) when your baby seems to be looking for a nibble between meals – that is, within an hour or two of a previous feeding. (Getting your baby used to the taste, or rather the non-taste, of water early on will make it more likely that she'll have the healthy habit of drinking water later.)

♦ Don't give solids prematurely as a way to encourage sleeping through the night – it doesn't work and may lead to overweight. (Instead, try the tips for helping baby to sleep through the night on page 254.)

♦ Evaluate your baby's diet. If you've already started your baby on solids (on your own, or as recommended by her doctor) and she's taking more than just a few spoonfuls of cereal, check to see if she seems to be drinking as much breast milk or formula as before. If she is, this is probably the reason for excessive weight gain. Cut back on solids if you've started them prematurely, or cut them out entirely for a month or two (most experts recommend not beginning solids until closer to six months anyway). Later, as more solids are added, the amount of breast milk or formula should usually be reduced gradually and the emphasis placed on solids such as vegetables, yoghurt, fruits, cereals and breads. If baby is taking juices (which she shouldn't be before the age of six months, and which can lead to weighty problems at any age; see box, opposite page), dilute them, half-and-half with water. And don't put thin cereal or other solids in a bottle for feeding – babies take too much that way.

♦ Get your baby moving. If your baby can 'hardly move', encourage activity. When you change her nappy, touch

HOW DOES YOUR BABY GROW?

How does a baby grow? Quite contrary to the fears of nervous parents who scan weight and height charts for signs that all is well, usually in a pattern that's normal for him or her.

A baby's future height and weight are to a great extent preprogrammed at conception. And assuming antenatal conditions are adequate, and neither love nor nutrition is lacking after birth, most babies will eventually realize that genetic potential.

The programming for height is based primarily on the midpoint between the father's height and the mother's. Studies show that, in general, boys seem to grow up to be somewhat taller than this midpoint, girls somewhat shorter.

Weight also seems to be preprogrammed, to a certain extent. A baby is usually born with the genes to be slim, stocky or a happy medium. But the eating habits learned in infancy and fostered throughout childhood can help to fulfil this destiny or defeat it.

Growth charts, like the one in the Ready Reference section in the back of this book, shouldn't become a source of anxiety for parents – it's too easy to misread or misinterpret them. But they are useful in telling parents and doctors when a baby's growth is departing from the norm, and when an evaluation, taking into account parental size, nutritional status and general health, is necessary. Since growth often comes in spurts during the first year, one measurement that seems to show too little growth or too much may not be significant. It should, however, be viewed as a red flag. A two-month halt to weight gain may indicate only that baby is slowing down because he or she is genetically destined to be small (particularly if growth in the height department is also easing off), but it can also indicate that baby is being underfed or is ill. A weight gain that is double what is normal during the same two months (if it is not accompanied by a similar jump in height) may just be baby's way of catching up if birth-weight was low or weight gain has been slow so far, but it can also be a sign that baby is just plain eating too much.

her right knee to her left elbow several times, then the reverse. With her grasping your thumbs and your other fingers holding her forearms, let her 'pull up' to a sitting position. Let her 'stand' on your lap – and bounce, if she likes. (See page 302 for other tips on getting your baby moving.)

THIN BABY

'All the other babies I see are all roly-poly; mine is long and thin – the 75th percentile in height and the 25th in weight. The doctor says he's doing just fine and I shouldn't worry, but I do.'

Thin continues to be in – everywhere but in the nursery. While the lean look is favoured on adults, plumpness is what many look for and love in babies. And, yet, though they might not win as many nappy commercial roles as their roly-poly peers, slender babies are usually as healthy, sometimes more.

In general, if your baby is alert, active, and basically content, is gaining weight steadily, and if his weight, though on the low side of average, continues to keep pace with his height, there is, as the doctor has pointed out, no cause for concern. There are often factors that affect a baby's size about which you can do very little. Genetic factors, for example – if you and/or your spouse are thin and small-boned, your baby is likely to be, too. And activity factors – the baby-on-the-go is usually leaner than the inactive one.

There are, however, a few reasons for thinness that do need remedying. A major one is underfeeding. If a baby's weight curve keeps dropping off for a couple of months, and if the loss isn't compensated for by a jump the following month, the doctor often will consider the possibility that the child is not getting enough to eat. If you're breastfeeding and this is the case, the tips on page 158 should help get baby gaining again. If you're bottle feeding, you can try, with the doctor's approval, diluting the formula a little less. Either way, supplementing with solids once the doctor green-lights them can help fill baby out.

Don't underfeed intentionally. Some parents, eager to get their babies started on the path towards a future of slimness and good health, limit calories and fat in infancy. This is a very *dangerous* practise, since infants need both for normal growth and development. You can start them on the road to good eating habits without depriving them of the nourishment they need now.

Be sure, too, that your baby isn't one who is either so sleepy or so busy that he forgets to demand his meals regularly. Between three and four months old, an infant should be eating at least every four hours during the day (usually at least five feedings), though he may sleep through the night without waking to eat. Some breastfed babies may still be taking more feedings, but fewer feedings could mean your baby isn't eating enough. If your baby's the kind who doesn't make a fuss when he's not fed, take the initiative yourself and offer meals to him more often – even if it means cutting short a daytime nap or interrupting a fascinating encounter with his cot gym.

Rarely, a baby's poor weight gain is related to the inability to absorb certain nutrients, a metabolic rate that is out of kilter, or an infectious or chronic disease (in which case you would probably notice other symptoms). Such illness, of course, requires prompt medical attention.

HEART MURMUR

'The doctor says my baby has a heart murmur but that it doesn't mean anything. Still, it's scary.'

Any time the word *heart* is part of a diagnosis, it's scary. After all, the heart is the organ that sustains life; any possibility of a defect is frightening, particularly to the parents of an infant whose life is just beginning. But in the case of a heart murmur, there is, in the vast majority of cases, really nothing to worry about.

When the doctor tells you your baby has a heart murmur, it means that on examination, abnormal heart sounds, caused by the turbulence of the flow of blood through the heart, are heard. The doctor can often tell just what kind of abnormality is responsible for the murmur by the loudness of the sounds (from barely audible to almost loud enough to drown out normal heart sounds), by their location, and by the type of sound – blowing or rumble, musical or vibratory – for example.

Most of the time, as is likely in your baby's case, the murmur is the result of irregularities in the shape of the heart as it grows. This kind of murmur is called 'innocent' or 'functional', and can usually be diagnosed by the baby's doctor by simple surgery examination with a stethoscope. No further tests or treatments or limitations of activities are necessary. More than half of all children have an innocent murmur sometime during their lives, and it is likely to come and go throughout childhood. But the existence of the murmur will be noted on your baby's record so other doctors who examine him at a later date will know it has always existed. Very often, when the heart is fully grown (or sometimes earlier), the murmur will disappear.

If you're worried no matter what anyone says, you can ask your baby's doctor to tell you exactly what type of murmur your baby has and whether or not it can be expected to cause any problems, now or in the future, and to explain just why you have nothing to worry about. If the answers aren't reassuring enough, ask for a referral to a paediatric cardiologist for consultation.

BLACK STOOL

'My daughter's last nappy was filled with a black stool. Could she be having a digestive problem?'

More likely she's been having an iron supplement. In some children, the reaction between the normal bacteria of the gastrointestinal tract and the iron sulfate in a supplement causes the stool to turn dark brown, greenish or black. There's no medical significance in this change, and no need to be concerned by it since studies show that small amounts of iron don't increase digestive discomfort or fussiness. On the other hand, for most babies an iron supplement isn't recommended (breastfed infants get enough iron from breast milk; bottle-fed babies get enough from iron-fortified formula; fortified cereal provides iron later). So unless your baby's doctor has prescoted one, you should discontinue dosing baby. If your baby has black stools and isn't taking a supplement, check with her doctor.

BABY MASSAGE

'I've heard that massage is good for babies. Should I massage my son?'

Massage is no longer for adults only. For some years it's been known that premature newborns do better with therapeutic massage – they grow faster, sleep and breathe better, and are more alert. Now it appears that massage also benefits healthy infants – and healthy children, as well.

There are a number of reasons why you should consider laying the hands on your baby. We know that being held, hugged and kissed by a parent helps a baby thrive and enhances parent-child bonding. But the therapeutic touch of massage may do that and even more, possibly strengthening the immune system; improving muscle development; stimulating growth; easing colic, teething pain and tummy troubles; promoting better sleep patterns; stimulating the circulatory and respiratory systems; and decreasing stress hormones (yes, babies have those too). And a loving touch (whether in the form of massage or just a lot of hugging and holding) has also been shown to decrease aggressive tendencies in children. What's more, baby's not the only one who stands to benefit; massaging an infant is actually relaxing for parents, too – and has been found to relieve symptoms of postnatal depression.

If you'd like to learn how to rub your baby, get a book or video, or take a class with a massage therapist familiar with baby massage. Or try these tips:

Pick a time that's relaxing for you. The massage won't have the desired effect if the phone's ringing, dinner's burning on the stove, and you have two loads of laundry going. Choose a time when you're unhurried and unlikely to be interrupted, and take the phone off the hook or turn off the ringer and let voice mail or the answer phone take a message (a ringing phone – even one answered by machine – is distracting).

Pick a time that's relaxing for baby. Don't massage baby when he's hungry or full. Right after a bath is a perfect time, when baby has already started to relax (unless he hates the bath and it leaves him riled). Before playtime is another possibility, since babies have been shown to be more focused and attentive after a massage.

Set a relaxing scene. The room you select for the massage should be quiet and warm, at least 24°C (75°F) (since baby will be undressed except for a nappy). Dim the lights to reduce stimulation and enhance relaxation, and add soft music if you like. You can sit on the floor or bed, and lay baby on your lap or between your open legs; use a towel, blanket or a pillow covered by a towel or blanket under baby.

Lubricate, if you like. You can give your baby a dry rub, or use a little baby oil, vegetable oil or baby lotion (but not on baby's head). Warm the oil or lotion a little between your hands before you start rubbing.

Experiment with techniques. In general, babies prefer a gentle touch – but not so light that it's ticklish. Here are a few ideas to get you started:

◆ Gently place both of your hands on either side of your baby's head and hold for a few seconds. Then stroke the sides of his face, continuing down the sides of his body to his toes.

◆ Make tiny circles on baby's head with your fingers. Smooth baby's forehead by gently pressing both hands from centre outwards.

◆ Stroke baby's chest from the centre outwards.

◆ Stroke baby's tummy from top to bottom using the outer edge of one hand, then the other, in a circular motion. Then, let your fingers do the walking across your baby's tummy.

◆ Gently roll baby's arms and legs between your hands or use firmer, deep strokes to 'milk' baby's arms and legs. Open those curled-up hands and massage those little fingers.

◆ Rub baby's legs up and down, alternating hands. When you get down to the feet, massage them, uncurling and stroking baby's toes.

◆ Turn baby on his tummy, and stroke his back from side to side, then up and down.

While you work, talk or sing softly. Always keep one hand on baby.

Take your cues from baby. He will tell you whether you're rubbing him the right way or not. He'll also tell you when to keep rubbing, and when it's time to end the massage session.

EXERCISE

'I've heard a lot about the importance of exercising your baby. Is it really necessary for me to take my little girl to an exercise class?'

Britons are increasingly becoming extremists. Either they're totally sedentary, getting all their exercise by turning on the TV and reaching for a beer, or they embark on an overly rigorous jogging programme that lands them injured in the sports specialist's surgery within a week. And either they confine their babies to a stationary life in high chairs, pushchairs and playpens, or they rush out and enroll them in exercise classes the moment they can lift their heads, in hopes of creating a fit-for-life infant athlete.

But extremism in the pursuit of good health tends to be ineffective, and is usually doomed to failure. Moderation is a much better goal to aim for, in your lifestyle and your baby's. So instead of ignoring your baby's physical development or pushing her beyond her abilities, take the following steps to start her on the road to fitness:

Stimulate body as well as mind. Many parents make an effort to teach their children intellectual matter from the cradle but figure the physical will take care of itself. And, for the most part, it will – but paying a little extra attention to it will remind both you and your baby of its importance. Try to spend some part of your playtime with your baby in physical activity. At this stage, it may be nothing more than pulling her to a sitting position (or a standing one, when she's ready), gently raising her hands over her head, 'bicycling' her legs by bending her knees up to meet her elbows in a rhythmic way, or holding her up in the air with your hands around her middle, making her flex her arms and legs.

Make the physical fun. You want her to feel good about her body and about physical activity, so be sure she enjoys these little sessions – and certainly don't be serious about them yourself. Talk or sing to her and tell her what you're doing. She'll come to identify little rhythmic ditties (such as 'Exercise, exercise, how I love my exercise') with the fun of physical activity.

Don't fence her in. A baby who's always strapped safely into a pushchair or an infant seat or snuggled into a baby carrier, without opportunity for physical explorations, is well on her way to becoming a sedentary – and a physically unfit – child.

Even an infant who's too little to crawl can benefit from the freedom to move that a blanket on the floor or the centre of a large bed (with constant supervision, of course) can offer. On their backs in such a position, many three- and four-month-olds will spend great stretches of time attempting to turn over (help them practise by slowly turning them over and back again). On their bellies, many will inch around, exploring with their hands and mouths, pushing their bottoms up in the air, raising their heads and shoulders. All of this activity naturally exercises tiny arms and legs – and is impossible to duplicate in a confined space.

Keep it informal. Exercise classes or taped programmes for infants are not necessary for good physical development, and if they're the wrong kind or are used in the wrong way, they can be detrimental. Babies, given the opportunity, naturally get all the exercise they need. That said, such activities can be fun for both of you – an opportunity to play and interact with other parents and other babies, and to try things you might not be able to try at home. If you do choose to take your baby to an exercise programme, check the programme first for the following:

◆ Do teachers have good credentials? Is it safe? Ask your baby's doctor for an evaluation before you sign up. Also observe. Any programme that encourages exercises that jostle or shake babies is a dangerous one (see page 269). Beware, too, of classes that are high-pressure, rather than fun, encouraging competition instead of individual growth.

◆ Do babies seem to be having fun? If an infant isn't smiling or laughing while exercising, she isn't enjoying it. Beware especially if the babies seem confused or frightened, or pressured to do things that make them uncomfortable.

- Is there plenty of age-appropriate equipment for your baby to play with – for instance, at this age, brightly coloured mats, inclines to creep up, balls to roll, toys to shake?

- Are babies given plenty of opportunity for free play – explorations made on their own and with you? Most of the class should be devoted to this, rather than structured group activities.

- Is music an integral part of the programme? Babies like music and rhythmic activities, such as rocking and singing, and the two go together well in an exercise programme.

Let baby set her pace. Pushing a baby to exercise, or to do anything else she isn't ready for or in the mood for, can set up very negative attitudes. Begin exercise with your baby only when she seems receptive, and stop when she tells you, by her indifference or fussiness, that she's had enough.

Keep her energized. Good nutrition is as important to your baby's good physical development as exercise. Once solids are introduced (with the doctor's permission, of course), start her on the First-Year Diet (see page 312) so that she has the energy needed for fun and games and the nutrients for optimal development.

Don't be an unfit parent. Teach by example; the family that exercises together stays fit together. If your child grows up watching you walking half a mile to the shops instead of driving, doing daily aerobics in front of the TV instead of munching crisps, swimming laps in the pool instead of sunbathing alongside it, she's more likely to enter adulthood with good feelings about fitness that she can pass on to her own offspring.

What it's Important to Know:
PLAYTHINGS FOR BABY

Walking into a toy store is like walking into a carnival in full swing. With every aisle vying for attention with its selection of eye-catching wares, bombarding the senses and sensibilities with an endless array of colourful boxes and displays, it's hard to know where to start. And though such trips can bring out the child in any adult, for parents several responsibilities come along with the joys of choosing toys.

To make sure you don't succumb to the prettiest packages and the most alluring gimmicks the toy industry has to offer, and end up with a vast collection of the wrong toys for your baby, consider these questions when contemplating a purchase – or when deciding whether to keep out, shelve or return to the store playthings that have come as gifts:

Is it age-appropriate? The most obvious reason for making sure a toy you purchase is age-appropriate is so that your baby will appreciate it and enjoy it fully now. A less apparent reason, though, is just as important. Even an advanced baby who might be interested in a toy that's classified as appropriate for older children, and who might even

For a baby, playtime is learning time. A game of peekaboo will elicit delighted giggles from a three- or four-month-old, and it will help teach the important lesson of object permanence: when mummy hides her face behind her hands, she's still there.

manage to play with it on a primitive level, could be harmed by it, since age-appropriateness also takes safety into consideration. Giving your baby toys before he or she is ready for them has another disadvantage, as well; it's possible that by the time baby is ready for them, he or she will also be bored by them.

How can you tell if a toy is appropriate for your baby? One way is the age range listed on the packaging, though your baby may be able to appreciate a particular toy a little earlier or a little later than average. Another is to observe your child with the toy – if you have the toy already or can try it out at a friend's house or the store. Is he or she interested in it? Does he or she play with it the way it's meant to be played with? The right toy will help your baby to perfect skills already learned or promote the development of new ones just about to be tackled. It will be neither too easy (which encourages boredom) nor too difficult (which promotes frustration).

Is it stimulating? Every toy doesn't have to bring your baby one step closer to that college acceptance letter; babyhood (and childhood) are times for just plain fun, too. But your baby will have more fun with a toy if it's stimulating to the sense of sight (a mirror or a mobile), hearing (a music box or a clown with a bell in his belly), touch (a cradle gym or activity board) or taste (a teething ring, or anything else that's mouthable) than if it's merely cute. As your baby grows, you will want toys that help a child learn hand-eye coordination, large and small motor control, the concept of cause and effect, colour and shape identification and matching, auditory discrimination, spatial relationships and those that stimulate social and language development, imagination and creativity.

Is it safe? This is perhaps the most significant question of all, since toys (not including bikes, sleds, Rollerblades, scooters and skateboards, which cause hundreds of injuries of their own) are responsible for over 100,000 injuries a year. In selecting playthings for your baby, look for the following:

♦ Sturdiness. Toys that will break or fall apart easily can often cause injury to a young child.

♦ Safe finish. Be sure that the paint or other finish isn't toxic.

♦ Safe construction. Toys with sharp edges or breakable parts are unsafe.

♦ Washability. Toys that can't be washed can become breeding places for bacteria – a problem for infants, who put everything in their mouths.

♦ Safe size. Toys that are small enough to pass through a small-parts tester or a toilet paper tube or have small removable parts or parts that can be broken off, present a serious choking

SUITABLE FOR CUDDLING

Nearly every stuffed animal your baby will encounter will be lovable and huggable. Here's how to make sure those teddies, giraffes, bunnies and doggies are as safe as they are cute:

◆ Eyes and noses on animals should not be made of buttons or other small objects that could fall off (or be pried or chewed off) and pose a choking hazard. Screen for buttons elsewhere, too (such as on a teddy bear's braces).

◆ No wire should be used to attach parts (such as ears). Even if the wire is covered by fabric, it could be chewed off or worn off and pose a puncture hazard.

◆ No strings should be attached – that goes for bows around the bunny's neck, a leash on the dog, and so on – longer than 15 cm (6 in).

◆ Look for sturdy construction; seams and connections that are tightly sewn. Check periodically for wear that could allow stuffing to come out (which would pose a choking hazard).

◆ All stuffed animals should be washable, and should be washed periodically so germs don't collect on them.

◆ Never place stuffed animals in baby's cot; they can pose a suffocation hazard.

hazard. Ditto toys that pieces can be chewed off of once teeth have emerged.

◆ Safe weight. Toys that can harm your baby if they fall on him or her are unsafe.

◆ No strings attached. Toys (or anything else) with strings, cords, or ribbons longer than 15 cm (6 in) should never be left anywhere near a baby because of the strangulation risk. Toys can be attached to cots, playpens and elsewhere with plastic links that are not only safe, but bright and attractive playthings in themselves.

◆ Safe sound. Loud sounds – for example, from toy guns, model planes or motorized vehicles – can damage baby's hearing, so look for toys that have musical or gentle sounds rather than sharp, loud or squeaky ones.

Do you approve of it philosophically? This is less of a problem in infant toys than it will be later, but it's not too early to think about the subliminal message a toy is sending, and to consider whether that message agrees with your values. Don't let society – at least the part of society that creates some of the TV-generated toy mayhem for children – decide what you want your baby to play with.

◆ ◆ ◆

The Fifth Month

J ust when you thought things couldn't get any better (and baby couldn't get any cuter and more endearing), they do. During the fifth month, your baby continues being endlessly entertaining company – picking up new tricks almost daily, never seeming to tire of social interaction with his or her most favourite companions (you!). And with a (relatively) longer attention span, the interaction's a lot more dynamic than it was even a couple of weeks ago. Watching that little personality unfold is fascinating, as is baby's growing captivation with the world around him or her. Baby's doing more than looking at that world now – he or she is touching it, too, exploring everything that's within reach with those hands, and everything that can fit (and many things that can't), with that mouth.

What Your Baby May Be Doing

A ll babies reach milestones on their own developmental time line. If your baby seems not to have reached one or more of these milestones, rest assured, he or she probably will very soon. Your baby's rate of development is normal for your baby. Keep in mind, too, that skills babies perform from the tummy position can be mastered only if there's an opportunity to practise. So make sure your baby spends supervised playtime on his or her belly. If you have concerns about your baby's development (because you've noticed a missed milestone or what you think might be a developmental delay), don't hesitate to check it out with the doctor at the next well-baby visit – even if he or she doesn't bring it up. Parents often notice nuances in a baby's development that doctors don't. Premature infants generally reach milestones later than others of the same birth age, often achieving them closer to their adjusted age (the age they would be if they had been born at term), and sometimes later.

By five months, your baby . . . should be able to:

◆ hold head steady when upright

◆ on stomach, raise chest, supported by arms

By the month's end, a few babies will be able to manage unassisted sitting when propped up by their hands, but most will still tumble forward from this position.

- pay attention to an object as small as a raisin (but keep such objects out of baby's reach)
- squeal in delight
- reach for an object
- smile spontaneously
- smile back when you smile
- grasp a rattle held to backs or tips of fingers
- keep head level with body when pulled to sitting

... will probably be able to:

- roll over (one way)[1]
- bear some weight on legs
- say 'ah-goo' or similar vowel-consonant combinations
- razz (make a wet razzing sound)
- turn in the direction of a voice

... may possibly be able to:

- sit without support

... may even be able to:

- pull up to standing position from sitting
- stand holding on to someone or something
- object if you try to take a toy away
- work to get to a toy out of reach
- pass a cube or other object from one hand to the other
- look for dropped object
- rake with fingers a tiny object and pick it up in fist (keep all dangerous objects out of baby's reach)
- babble, combining vowels and consonants such as ga-ga-ga, ba-ba-ba, ma-ma-ma, da-da-da

What You Can Expect at This Month's Checkup

Most doctors do not schedule regular well-baby checkups this month. On the bright side, that means no injections for another month; on the downside, you won't be able to see how far baby's growth shot up on the charts. Keep your list of questions for next month, but don't hesitate to call the doctor in between visits if there are any concerns that can't wait until then.

---

1. Babies who spend little time on their stomachs during playtime may reach this milestone later, and that's not cause for concern (see page 205).

Feeding Your Baby: STARTING SOLIDS

It's the moment you've been waiting for. As daddy stands by with the video camera, ready to capture the momentous event, baby is decked out in a freshly laundered bib, propped up and secured in that spanking new high chair. As the camera rolls, baby's first bite of solid food – heaped on the engraved sterling silver spoon from Great-Aunt Alice – is lifted from the bowl to baby's mouth. Baby's mouth opens, then, as the food makes its bizarre first impression on inexperienced tastebuds, screws itself into a knot of displeasure, and spews the alien offering onto chin, bib and high chair tray. Cut!

The challenge to get your child to eat (or at least eat what you'd like him or her to eat), a challenge that's likely to continue as long as you share the same dining table, has begun. But it's more

GOOD EARLY FOODS TO OFFER BABY

Before the gastronomic world can be a baby's oyster (or fillet or lasagne), the land of bland must be conquered. Which means baby must take baby steps at the table – steps that are listed below in the order they're generally suggested (though the times for introduction might be later in a baby with a history or a family history of allergy). The foods, which can be prepared at home or purchased ready to use, should at first be very smooth in texture – strained, puréed or finely mashed, and thinned with liquid if necessary to the consistency of thick cream. The texture should continue to be smooth until the sixth or seventh month, becoming progressively thicker as baby becomes a more experienced eater. Babies usually take less than half a teaspoon at first, but many work up to two to three tablespoons, sometimes more, in a surprisingly short time. Food can be served cold or at room temperature (which most babies prefer) or slightly warmed, though heating is usually done more for the adult's taste than the baby's – and is largely an unnecessary hassle.

4 to 6 months	6 months	7 to 8 months	9 months
Rice cereal	Barley cereal	Chicken	Yoghurt (whole milk)
	Oat cereal	Turkey	Cheese (such as
	Apples purée	Lamb	Gruyère,
	Bananas	Beef	Emmenthal,
	Pears	Avocado	Cheddar)
	Peaches	Egg yolk	Pasta
	Peas		Beans
	Carrots		Tofu
	Green beans		
	Sweet potato		
	Squash		

than a matter of promoting good nutrition; it's one of instilling healthy attitudes towards mealtimes and snack times. As important as ensuring that the food that goes into your baby's mouth is wholesome is ensuring that the atmosphere in which the food is eaten is pleasant and non-combative.

In the first few months of solid feedings (which should begin when baby's ready, somewhere between the ages of four and six months), the actual quantity of food consumed is not of great significance as long as breast or bottle feeding is continued. Eating at first is less a matter of gaining sustenance than of gaining experience – with eating techniques, with different flavours and varying textures, with the social aspects of dining.

OPENING NIGHT – AND BEYOND

Bringing out the video equipment isn't the only preparatory step you'll have to take to ensure a memorable first eating experience. You'll also want to pay attention to the timing, setting and props to make the most of this feeding – and future ones.

Time it right. If you're breastfeeding, the show should go on when your milk supply is at its lowest (in most women this is late in the afternoon or early in the evening). If, on the other hand, your baby seems hungriest in the morning, you might offer solids then. Don't worry if the menu is cereal and the serving time is 6 PM; baby will hardly be expecting steak.

Humour your headliner. You've slotted a 5 PM performance only to find that the star is cranky and overtired. Postpone the show. You can't introduce your baby to anything new, food included, when he or she is out of sorts. Schedule meals for times when your baby is usually alert and happy.

Don't open to a full tummy. Whet baby's appetite before offering the solids, but don't drown it. Start off with an appetizer of a small amount of formula or breast milk. That way, your baby won't be too ravenous to put up with the new experience, and won't be so satiated that the next course will have no appeal. Of course, babies with small appetites may do better starting solids hungry; you'll have to see which works best for yours.

Be ready for a long production. Don't try to schedule baby's meals in five-minute segments between other chores. Baby feeding is a time-consuming process, so be sure to leave plenty of time for it.

Set the stage. Holding a squirming baby on your lap while trying to deposit an unfamiliar substance into an unreceptive mouth is a perfect script for disaster. Set up a sturdy high chair or feeding seat (see page 329) several days before the first feeding experience and allow your baby to become comfortable in it. If your baby slides around or slumps, pad it with a small blanket, quilt or some towels, or if the seat allows, put it in a semi-reclining position. Fasten the restraining straps for baby's safety and your peace of mind. If your baby can't sit up at all in such a chair or seat, it's probably a good idea to postpone solids for a bit longer.

Also be sure you have the right kind of spoon. It doesn't have to be a family heirloom, but it should have a small bowl (perhaps a demitasse spoon) and, possibly, a plastic coating, which is easier on baby's gums. Giving baby a spoon of his or her own to hold and attempt to manoeuvre discourages a tug-of-war over each spoonful, and also gives your budding individualist a sense of independence. A long handle is good for your feeding baby, but choose a short one with a curved handle for baby's use to avoid unintended pokes in the eye. If your young gourmand insists on 'helping' you with your feeding spoon, let a little hand hold on to the spoon as you firmly guide it to the target – most of the time you'll get there.

Finally, use a big, easy-to-clean, easy-to-remove, comfortable bib. Depending on your preference, it can be made from firm or soft plastic that can be wiped or rinsed off, cloth or plastic that can be tossed into the wash, or be a paper disposable. You may not be concerned about your baby getting cereal stains on almost-outgrown sleepers now, but if the bib habit isn't instilled early, it is often difficult (if not impossible) to instill later. And don't forget to roll up long sleeves. An at-home alternative to the bib (room temperature permitting) is to let baby eat topless, in a nappy only. You'll still have to do some wiping off (of baby's face, neck, tummy, arms, legs), but stains won't be a problem.

Play a supporting role. If you give your baby a chance to run the show, your chances of succeeding at feeding are much improved. Before even attempting to bring spoon to mouth, put a dab of the food on the table or high chair tray and give baby a chance to examine it, squish it, mash it, rub it, maybe even taste it. That way, when you do approach with the spoon, what you're offering won't be totally foreign. Though offering new food in a bottle (with a large-holed teat) might seem like a good way to give baby a chance to self-feed, it's not recommended. Firstly, it reinforces the bottle habit and doesn't teach a baby

how to eat grownup-style, which after all is what early feedings are all about. And, secondly, because babies tend to eat too much this way, it can lead to excessive weight gain.

Start with coming attractions. The first several meals won't be real meals at all, but simply the prelude for those to come. Start with a quarter to a full teaspoon of the selected food. Slip just the tiniest bit of it between baby's lips and allow some time for baby to react. If the flavour finds favour, the mouth will probably open wider for the next bite, which you can place farther back (but not so far back that baby gags) for easier swallowing. Even if baby seems receptive, the first few tries may come sliding right back out of his or her mouth; in fact, the first few meals may seem like total flops. But a baby who is ready for solids will quickly start taking in more than he or she is spitting out. If the food continues to slide out, baby is probably not developmentally prepared for the big time yet. You can continue wasting time, effort, food and laundry at this fruitless pursuit – or wait a week or two, then try again.

Know when to end the show. Never continue a meal when your baby has lost interest. The signals will be clear, though they may vary from baby to baby and meal to meal: fussiness, a head turned away, a mouth clamped shut, food spit out or food thrown around.

If your baby rejects a previously enjoyed food, taste it to be sure it hasn't gone bad. Of course, there may be another reason for the rejection. Maybe your baby's tastes have changed (babies and young children are very fickle about food); maybe he or she is out of sorts or just not hungry. Whatever the reason, don't force the issue or the food. Try another selection, and if that doesn't go over, bring down the curtain.

NOT THIS YEAR, BABY

These foods will have to stay off baby's menu for at least the first year:

Nuts and peanuts (see box, page 494)
Chocolate
Egg whites
Honey (see box, page 315)
Cow's milk

Some doctors okay these foods during the last few months of the first year; others recommend holding off on them until baby's birthday, especially if there's a family history of allergy:

Wheat
Citrus fruits and citrus juice
Tomatoes
Strawberries

FOODS TO PREMIERE WITH

Everyone agrees that the perfect first liquid for baby is mother's milk. But is there a perfect first solid? Though there's little substantial scientific evidence that points to any single, best first solid food, and many babies seem to do as well on one as on another (assuming it's appropriate fare for an infant), there is one clear first-food front-runner, and a couple of runners-up, listed below. Ask your health visitor for a recommendation. Keep in mind that you won't be able to accurately assess baby's reaction to first-time foods by his or her expression – most babies will initially screw up their mouths with shock no matter how pleased they are with the offering, particularly if the taste is tart. Instead go by whether baby opens up for an encore.

Rice cereal. Because it is easily thinned to a texture not much thicker than milk, is very easily digested by most infants, is not likely to trigger an allergic reaction, and provides needed iron, iron-enriched baby rice cereal is probably the most commonly recommended first food. Mix it with formula, breast milk or water. Resist the temptation to stir in mashed bananas, apple purée or fruit juices, or to buy prepared cereal with fruit (even down the road, after you've introduced these fruits), or your baby will quickly come to accept only sweet foods, rejecting all else.

Fruit. Many babies are started off on finely mashed or strained banana (thinned with a bit of formula or breast milk if necessary) or apple purée. True, most take to these foods eagerly, but they also then tend to refuse less sweet foods, such as vegetables and unsweetened cereals, when they are offered later. Therefore, while some fruits make good early foods, they aren't necessarily the best first foods.

Vegetables. Vegetables are, in theory, a good first food – nutritious and not sweet. But their strong, distinctive flavours make them less appealing to many babies than cereal or fruit, so they may not create a positive attitude towards the gastronomic experience. It's smart, however, to introduce them before fruit, while baby's palate is more receptive to less-sweet tastes. The 'yellows', such as sweet potatoes and carrots, are usually more palatable (as well as more nutritious) than such 'greens' as peas or green beans. Again, good to introduce early, but probably not first.

EXPANDING BABY'S REPERTOIRE

Even if your baby devours her very first serving of breakfast cereal, don't plan on presenting her with a lunch of yoghurt and runner beans and a dinner of strained meats and sweet potatoes. Each new food you introduce to your baby, from the first one on, should be offered alone (or with foods that have already passed muster) so that if there's a sensitivity or allergy to it, you will recognize it. If you're starting with cereal, for example, give it exclusively, at least for the next three or four days (some doctors recommend five days). If your baby has no adverse reactions to it (excessive bloating or gassiness; diarrhoea or mucus in the stool; vomiting; a rough rash on the face, particularly around the mouth or around the anus; a runny nose and/or watery eyes or wheezing that doesn't seem to be associated with a cold; unusual night wakefulness or daytime crankiness), you can assume he or she tolerates the food well.

If you spot what you think is a reaction, wait a week or so and try the food again. The same reaction two or three times is a good indication that your baby has a sensitivity to the food. Wait several months before introducing it again, and in the meantime try the same procedure with a different new food. If your baby seems to have a reaction to several foods or if there is a history of allergy in your family, wait a full week between new foods. If every food you try appears to cause a problem, talk to the baby's doctor about waiting a few months before reintroducing solids.

Introduce each new food in the same cautious manner, keeping a record of the food, the approximate amounts taken, and any reactions (memory can fail). Be sure to begin with single foods – just strained carrots or strained peas, for example. Baby food companies make special single-food beginner lines for this purpose (which also come in small jars to avoid waste). Once a baby has taken both peas and carrots without a hitch, it's fine to serve them up as a combo. Later, as baby's repertoire expands, a new food that isn't packaged solo can be introduced in a medley along with already accepted vegetables.

Some foods, because they are more allergenic than others, are best introduced later. Wheat, for example, is usually added to the infant diet after rice, oats, and barley have been well accepted. Occasionally, this happens as late as the eighth month, although the okay is usually given earlier for babies with no signs and no family history of food allergy. Citrus juices and fruits are introduced after other fruits and juices, seafood after meat and poultry. Egg yolks (scrambled, or hard-boiled and mashed) aren't usually given until at least the eighth month; the whites, which are much more likely to provoke an allergic reaction, are often not given until near the end of the year. Chocolate, nuts and peanuts have a high allergenic potential and usually aren't given in the first year (and in some cases much later; see page 494 for the complete low-down on nuts and peanuts).

FIRST-YEAR DIET FOR BEGINNERS

Right now your baby is only dabbling in solids; most nutritional requirements are still being filled with breast milk or formula. But from the sixth month on, breast milk or formula alone won't be enough to meet all your baby's needs, and by the end of the

WHO'S COUNTING?

You may have noticed that when it comes to the Baby Daily Dozen, there aren't any suggested serving sizes – or any recommended number of daily servings. That's because the Baby Daily Dozen is offered only as a general guide to the type of foods your brand-new eater should be sampling, not as a dietary bible for parents to stick to strictly. In fact, trying to keep a running tab – or to cram a certain number of servings of each food group into your baby every day – is a sure way to drive yourself crazy (not to mention to set the stage for food squabbles in the high chair and, later, at the table). Babies are all over the appetite map at this stage of the game, when eating is still more for practise and pleasure than for filling nutritional requirements. Some babies eat a lot all the time, some eat very little most of the time, others eat like a mouse one day and a horse the next. Some are varied and adventurous eaters, others are particularly picky. But presented with wholesome foods and allowed to follow their appetite, almost all healthy babies eat as much as they need to grow and thrive. No pushing, no measuring, no counting necessary.

So your baby ate his or her way through a bread box of Whole Grains today, but completely snubbed the Protein? Had a bellyful of Calcium, but balked at the Green and Yellow Fruits and Vegetables? No problem. Just keep offering baby a wide variety of foods each day (as they're introduced), and let his or her appetite determine how much or how little of each is actually eaten.

---

year, most of baby's nutrition will come from other sources. So it's not too early to start thinking in terms of good nutrition when planning your baby's meals now, using a simplified Baby Daily Dozen (see opposite page) once your baby begins taking a variety of foods – usually at about eight or nine months. Don't bother worrying about serving sizes or number of servings yet (see box, above). Instead, focus on making meals fun and nutritious – the best way to help ensure a healthy diet now and healthy eating habits later. (You'll find recipes for the beginning eater starting on page 754.)

THE BABY DAILY DOZEN

Calories. You don't need to count your baby's calories to tell if he or she is getting enough – or too many. Is he or she unpleasingly plump? Too many calories are the likely reason. Very thin or growing too slowly? Then caloric intake is probably insufficient. Right now most of the calories that keep baby thriving come from breast milk or formula; gradually more and more of them will come from solid foods.

Protein. Baby's still getting most of the protein he or she needs from breastmilk or formula. But since that picture will change once those first birthday candles are blown out, now's a good time for baby to start sampling other protein foods. As they're introduced, these can include egg yolk, meat, chicken and tofu. Calcium foods (see below) can double as excellent protein sources.

Calcium foods. Again, baby's getting the lion cub's share of calcium from breast or bottle (about 450 ml/16 fl oz) fills those needs until the first birthday, but

NO HONEY FOR YOUR LITTLE HONEY

Honey not only offers little more than empty calories, it also poses a health risk in the first year. It may contain the spores of *Clostridium botulinum,* which in this form is harmless to adults but can cause botulism (with constipation, weakened sucking, poor appetite and lethargy) in babies. This serious though rarely fatal illness can lead to pneumonia and dehydration. Some doctors okay honey at eight months; most recommend waiting till year's end.

many babies drink far more than that – and that's fine). But baby-friendly calcium foods, such as hard cheese (Gruyère, Emmenthal, Cheddar, Edam are good choices) and plain whole milk yoghurt, are yummy, nutritious additions once they're introduced.

Whole grains and other concentrated complex carbohydrates. These high-chair favourites will add essential vitamins and minerals, as well as some protein, to baby's daily intake. Good options, as they're introduced, include baby cereal, whole-grain bread, whole-grain cereals (particularly those baby can self-feed, such as Cheerios), cooked whole-grain cereal, pasta (bite-sized are always a big hit), puréed cooked lentils, beans, peas or soya beans.

Green leafy and yellow vegetables and yellow fruit. There are dozens of delicious vitamin A–rich fruits and vegetables under the green and yellow rainbow – experiment (as the doctor okays them) to see which ones your baby likes. Choose from winter squash, sweet potatoes, carrots, yellow peaches, apricots, cantaloupe, mango, broccoli and kale (all puréed at first, chunky later). As baby moves on to finger foods, ripe fruits can be served in cubes.

Vitamin C foods. Most doctors don't okay citrus, that vitamin C standard, until the eighth month at least; in some cases, the OJ may have to wait until after the first birthday. In the meantime, baby can take his or her C in mango or cantaloupe, broccoli, cauliflower and sweet potato. Keep in mind, too, that many baby foods and juices are enriched with vitamin C.

Other fruits and vegetables. Still room in that cute little tummy? Fill 'er up with any of the following: unsweetened apple purée, mashed banana, puréed peas or green beans, mashed potatoes.

High-fat foods. Babies who take most of their calories in the form of breast milk or formula get all the fat and cholesterol they need. But as the switch to a more varied diet takes place and a baby spends less time at bottle or breast, it's important to make sure that fat and cholesterol intake doesn't dip too low. That's why most dairy products (cottage cheese, yoghurt, hard cheese) you serve baby should be full-fat or made from whole milk. Unhealthy fats (those found in fried and many processed foods) are another story, however. Loading baby up with too many of those fats can lead to an unbalanced diet, unneeded weight and tummy troubles (since they're hard to digest). It can also set up unhealthy eating habits that'll be hard to break later on.

Iron foods. Bottle-fed babies get their full share of iron from fortified formula; after six months, breastfed babies need another source. Fortified baby cereal can fill the bill easily; additional iron can come from such iron-rich foods as meat, egg yolks, wheat germ, whole-grain breads and cereals, and cooked dried peas and other legumes, as they are introduced into the diet. Serving up iron-rich foods with a vitamin C food (a little cantaloupe alongside the rice cereal, for instance) increases absorption of this important mineral.

Salty foods. Pass on the salt shaker when you're preparing baby's food. Since their kidneys can't handle large amounts of sodium (and because acquiring a taste for salty foods in the high chair can lead to unhealthy eating habits later on), babies shouldn't have added salt in their diet. Most foods contain some sodium naturally (particularly dairy foods and many vegetables), so baby can't possibly come up short.

Fluids. During the first five to six months of life, virtually all of a baby's fluids come from bottle or breast. Now small amounts will start to come from other sources, such as juices and fruits and vegetables. As the quantity of formula or breast milk taken begins to decrease, it's important to be sure that the total fluid intake doesn't. In hot weather it should increase, so offer water and fruit juices diluted with water when temperatures soar.

DOUBLE-DUTY JARS

Use empty baby food jars, thoroughly washed in a dishwasher or by hand with washing-up liquid in very hot water, for heating and/or serving small portions of baby foods. Heat by placing the open jar in a small amount of hot water rather than in the microwave oven (it may heat foods unevenly). Even if you're in a hurry (when won't you be?), always test heated food to make sure it isn't too hot for baby's tender mouth.

Vitamin supplement. Vitamin/mineral supplements are generally not needed for healthy infants (though there are exceptions; breastfed babies, for instance, need a vitamin D supplement). But if your doctor recommends it, or if you'll feel better giving it (as a little extra vitamin/mineral insurance), give only vitamin/mineral drops especially formulated for infants. These drops should contain no more than the recommended daily allowance of vitamins and minerals for babies. Don't give any other supplements without the doctor's approval. See page 168 for more.

What You May Be Concerned About

TEETHING

'How can I tell if my baby's teething? She's biting on her hands a lot, but I don't see anything on her gums.'

When the teething fairy visits, there's no telling how extended or how unpleasant her stay will be. For one child it may be a long, drawn-out, painful affair. For another it may seem to pass with a single wave of the wand in the middle of a restful night. Sometimes a lump or a ridge seems visible in the gum for weeks or months; sometimes there seems to be no visible clue at all until the tooth itself appears.

On average the first tooth arrives sometime during the seventh month, although it can rear its pearly white head as early as three months, as late as twelve or, in rare instances, even earlier or later. Tooth eruption often follows hereditary patterns, so if either parent teethed early or late, their baby may do likewise. Symptoms of teething, however, often precede the tooth itself by as much as two or three months. These symptoms vary from child to child, and opinions as to exactly what these symptoms are and how painful teething actually is vary from doctor to doctor. A teething baby may experience any or all of the following:

Drooling. For a lot of babies, starting at anywhere from about ten weeks to three or four months of age, the tap's on. Teething stimulates drooling, more in some babies than in others.

Chin or face rash. In a prolific drooler, it's not unusual for a dry skin rash or chapping to develop on the chin and around the mouth because of irritation from constant contact with saliva. To help prevent this, gently pat away the drool periodically during the daytime. Should a patch of dry skin appear, keep it well lubricated with a mild skin cream (ask the doctor for a recommendation).

A little cough. The excess saliva can cause baby to gag or cough occasionally. This is nothing to worry about, as long as your baby seems otherwise free of cold, flu or allergy symptoms. Often babies will continue the cough as an attention getter or because they find it an interesting addition to their vocalization repertoires.

Biting. In this case, taking a nip is not a sign of hostility. A teething baby will gum down on anything she can get her mouth on – from her own tiny hand, to the breast that feeds her, to a perfect stranger's unsuspecting thumb. The counterpressure will help relieve the pressure from under the gums.

Pain. Inflammation is the protective response of the tender gum tissue to the impending tooth, which it considers an intruder to fend off. It causes seemingly unbearable pain in some babies, but almost none in others. Discomfort is often worst with the first teeth (apparently most babies become accustomed to the sensations of teething and learn to live with them) and with the molars (which, because of their greater size, seem to be more painful, but which, fortunately, you won't have to think about until sometime before or after baby's first birthday).

Irritability. As inflammation increases and a sharp little tooth rises closer to the surface, threatening to erupt, the ache in baby's gum may become more constant. Like anyone with chronic pain, she may be cranky, out of sorts, not 'herself.' Again, some babies (and their parents) will suffer more than others, with irritability lasting weeks instead of days or hours.

Refusal to feed. A teething baby may appear fickle when it comes to nursing. While she craves the comfort of something in her mouth – and may seem to want to nurse all the time – once she begins to suck, and the suction created increases her discomfort, she may reject the breast or bottle she so passionately desired only moments before. With each repetition of this scenario (and some babies repeat it all day long when they're teething), she (and mother) become more frustrated and more miserable. A baby who's started solids may lose interest in them for the time being; this needn't be a source of concern, since your baby is still getting almost all of her necessary nutrition and needed fluids from nursing or formula, and her

TEETHING CHART

This illustrates the most common pattern of tooth eruption. While most babies do sprout their pearly whites by the book, a few seem to teethe to a different drummer - beginning with their top teeth instead of their bottom ones, for instance. Very rarely a tooth (or pair of teeth) never comes in - in which case the doctor will probably refer your baby to a paediatric dentist or to a general dentist who treats a lot of children. If your baby is an early or late teether now, the same is likely to be true with the second set of teeth.

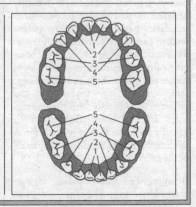

appetite will pick up where it left off once the tooth comes through. Of course, if your baby refuses more than a couple of feedings or seems to be taking very little for several days, a call to the doctor is in order.

Diarrhoea. Whether this symptom actually has a relationship to teething or not depends on whom you ask. Some parents insist that every time their babies teethe, they have loose bowel movements. Some doctors believe that there appears to be a connection – perhaps because the excess saliva swallowed loosens the stool. Other doctors refuse to acknowledge a link, at least for the record – probably not because they are entirely sure it doesn't exist, but because they fear that legitimizing the theory could cause parents to overlook possibly significant gastrointestinal symptoms, attributing them to teething. So though it may be that your baby will have looser movements with teething, you should report actual diarrhoea that lasts more than two bowel movements

to her doctor whenever it occurs.

Low-grade fever. Fever, like diarrhoea, is a symptom that doctors are hesitant to link to teething. Experts say that it's a coincidence that fever sometimes accompanies teething. After all, the first teeth usually come in around six months, the same time that babies lose their immunities from their mothers, making them more susceptible to fevers and infections. Still, some acknowledge that a low-grade fever (under 38.3°C/101°F, rectally) can occasionally accompany teething as a result of inflammation of the gums. To play it safe, treat fever with teething as you would low-grade fever at any other time, calling the doctor if it persists for three days (see page 565 for more about fevers).

Wakefulness. Babies don't teethe only during the daylight hours. The discomfort that has her fussing during the day can keep her awake at night. Even the baby who has been sleeping through the night may suddenly begin night waking again. To avoid her lapsing back into old habits (which will continue long after the teething pain is gone), don't rush in at the first peep. Instead, see if she can settle herself back down quickly. If she can't, try some comfort that doesn't involve feeding (some gentle lullabies and patting may do the trick). Night waking, like many other teething problems, is more common with first teeth and with molars.

Gum haematoma. Occasionally, teething initiates some bleeding under the gums, which may appear as a bluish lump. Such haematomas are nothing to worry about, and most doctors recommend allowing them to resolve on their own without medical intervention. Cold compresses may lessen discomfort and speed the resolution of gum haematomas.

Ear pulling; cheek rubbing. Pain in the gums may travel to the ears and cheeks along nerve pathways they share, particularly when the molars begin pushing their way in. That's why some babies, when they are teething, pull at an ear or rub a cheek or the chin. But keep in mind that babies also tug at their ears when they have ear infections. If you suspect an ear infection (see page 555), teething or no, check with the doctor.

There are probably as many home-tested treatments for teething discomfort as there are grandmothers. Some work, some don't. Among the best that old wives and new medicine have to offer are:

Something to chew on. This is not for nutritive benefits but for the relief that comes from counterpressure against the gums – which is enhanced when the object being chewed is icy cold and numbing. A frozen bagel (once wheat has been introduced), a frozen banana (admittedly messy in the hands of a baby), a clean flannel with an ice cube tightly wrapped and secured inside (but watch to make sure the ice cube doesn't come loose), a chilled carrot with the thin end sliced off (but don't use carrots once teeth are actually in and can chip off chokable bits), a bumpy rubber teething ring or other teething toy, even the plastic railing of a cot or playpen, will all provide a wholesome chew. If you use any food to soothe a teething baby, be sure your baby has it only in a sitting position and while under adult supervision.

Something to rub against. Many babies appreciate a grown-up finger rubbed firmly on the gum. Some will protest the intrusion at first, since the rubbing seems to hurt at the start, and then calm down as the counterpressure begins to bring relief.

Something cold to drink. Offer your baby a bottle of icy cold water. If she doesn't take a bottle or is bothered by the sucking, offer the soothing liquid in a cup – but remove any ice cubes first. This will also augment the teething baby's fluid intake, important if she is losing fluids through drooling and/or loose movements.

Something cold to eat. Once they've been introduced, apple purée, puréed peaches or yoghurt, chilled in the freezer, may be more appealing to a teething baby than warm or room-temperature foods.

Something to relieve the pain. When nothing else spells relief, baby paracetamol should do the trick. Check with your doctor for the right dose, or see page 764 if he or she is not available. Or you can try a topical numbing agent or pain reliever as recommended by your doctor. Avoid giving any other medication by mouth or rubbing anything on baby's gums unless recommended by the doctor. This caveat includes brandy or any other alcoholic beverage. Alcohol, even in drops, can be extremely harmful to an infant.

CHRONIC COUGH

'For the last three weeks my baby has had a little cough. He doesn't seem sick, and he doesn't cough in his sleep – he almost seems to be coughing on purpose. Is this possible?'

Even as early as the fifth month, many babies have begun to realize that all the world's a stage, and that nothing beats an admiring audience. So when a baby discovers that a little cough – either triggered by excess saliva or stumbled upon in the ordinary course of vocal experimentation – gets a lot of attention, he often continues this affectation purely for its effect. As long as he's otherwise healthy, and seems in control of the cough rather than vice versa, ignore it. And though your little thespian may never lose his flair for the dramatic, he will probably give up this attention-getter as he (or his audience) becomes bored with it.

EAR PULLING

'My daughter has been pulling at her ear a lot. She doesn't seem to be in any pain, but I'm worried that she might have an ear infection.'

Babies have a lot of territory to conquer – some of it on their own bodies. The fingers and hands, the toes and feet, the penis or vagina, and another curious appendage, the ear, will all be subjects of exploration at one time or another. Unless your baby's pulling and tugging at her ear is also accompanied by crying or obvious discomfort, fever, and/or other signs of illness (see page 555 if it is), it's very likely that it's only a manifestation of her curiosity, not a symptom of an ear infection. Some babies may also fuss with their ears when teething or when they're tired.

Redness on the outside of the ear isn't a sign of infection, just a result of constant manipulation. If you suspect a problem, do check with the doctor.

Peculiar mannerisms such as ear pulling are common and fairly short-lived; each is replaced by a newer and more exciting one once baby outgrows or grows tired of it.

NAPS

'My baby is awake more during the day now and I'm not sure – and I don't think he is either – how many naps he needs.'

It's inevitable. The first couple of weeks home from the hospital the proud mum and dad, eager to begin active parenting, stand expectantly over their new baby's cot, waiting for him to wake from what seems like endless slumber. Then, as he spends more time awake, they begin to wonder, 'Why doesn't he ever sleep?'

Though the typical baby in the fifth month takes three or four pretty regular naps of an hour or so each during the day, some babies thrive on five or six naps of about twenty minutes each, and others on two longer ones of an hour and a half or two. The number and length of naps your baby takes, however, are less important than the total amount of shut-eye he gets (about fourteen and a half hours a day on average during the fifth month, with wide variations). Longer naps are more practical for you – and nobody needs to tell you this – because they allow you longer stretches in which to get things done. In addition, the baby who gets into catnapping during the day may follow the same pattern during the night, waking up frequently.

You can try to encourage longer naps by:

◆ Offering a comfortable place to nap. Letting baby sleep on your shoulder will result not only in a stiff shoulder for you, but in a shorter nap for him. A cot, pram or pushchair will keep baby down longer.

◆ Keeping the room temperature comfortable, neither too hot nor too cold, and the clothing appropriate.

◆ Timing it right. Don't let baby fall asleep just before mealtime (when his empty stomach is likely to rouse him prematurely), when his nappy needs changing (he won't sleep long if his bottom is drenched), when company (and noise) is expected, or any other time when you know the nap is destined not to last.

◆ Avoiding predictable disturbances. You will quickly learn what disturbs your baby's sleep. Maybe it's wheeling his pushchair into the supermarket. Or moving him from car seat to cot. Or the dog's shrill yap. Or the telephone in the hallway near his room. By trying to control the circumstances under which your baby sleeps, you may be able to minimize these disturbances – though, of course, you can't (and shouldn't try to) eliminate all noise.

◆ Keeping baby awake for longer periods between naps. Your baby should now be able to stay awake for about two and a half to three hours at a stretch. If he does, he's more likely to take a longer nap. Try any of the infant-stimulating ideas on pages 238 and 364 to increase stay-awake time.

Though many babies regulate themselves pretty well when it comes to getting their quota of sleep, not every baby gets as much as he needs. It may

be that yours isn't napping enough or getting enough total sleep if he frequently seems cranky. If you believe your baby needs more sleep, you will have to intervene to increase sleeping time. But if your baby sleeps very little and seems perfectly happy, you will have to accept the fact that he's one of those babies who just don't need a lot of shut-eye.

ECZEMA

'My daughter has begun to break out in a red rash on her cheeks. It must be itchy, because she keeps trying to scratch it.'

This sounds like a classic case of infantile eczema, also known as atopic dermatitis. Eczema is a skin condition that is believed to be a type of allergic reaction. Though it is present at birth in some babies, it typically shows up between two and six months of age. Its onset is often triggered when a baby is put on solids or switched from breast milk to formula or from formula to cow's milk (at a year). It's less likely in babies who are breastfed exclusively, and more common in those with family histories of eczema, asthma or hay fever. In formula-fed babies, the rash usually first appears around three months of age.

A bright red, scaly rash commonly starts on the cheeks and often spreads elsewhere, most frequently to the area behind the ears and to the neck, arms and legs. (It doesn't usually spread to the nappy area until between six and eight months.) Small papules, or pimples, develop and fill with fluid, then ooze and crust over. The severe itching causes children to scratch, which can lead to infection. Except for the very mildest, self-limiting cases, eczema requires medical treatment to prevent complications. It clears by eighteen months in about half the cases, and usually becomes less severe by age three in the others. Approximately one in three children with eczema, however, will develop asthma or other allergies later or continue to combat eczema into adulthood.

The following are all-important in the handling of eczema:

Clip nails. Keep your baby's fingernails as short as possible to minimize the damage caused by scratching her rash. You may be able to prevent her from scratching while she's sleeping by covering her hands with a pair of socks or mittens.

Curtail bathing. Since prolonged contact with soap and water increases skin dryness, limit baths to no more than ten or fifteen minutes, using an extra-mild soap (Dove or Johnson's, for example). Don't allow baby to soak in soapy water, and as soon as baby is out of the water, use a moisturizer. Chlorinated and salt water can make eczema worse; if that's the case with your baby, you may need to limit dips in pools or at the beach.

Lubricate lavishly. Spread plenty of rich hypoallergenic skin cream (one that her doctor recommends) after baths while the skin is still damp. Don't, however, use oils or petroleum jelly (such as Vaseline).

Control the environment. Because excessive heat, cold or dry air can worsen eczema, try to avoid taking your baby outdoors in extremes of weather; keep your home neither too warm nor too cold, and use a humidifier to keep the air moist.

Keep it cotton. Perspiration can make eczema worse, so avoid synthetics, wool and overdressing in general. Also avoid itchy fabrics and clothing with rough seams or trims, all of which can exacerbate the condition. Soft cotton clothing, loosely layered, will be most comfortable and least irritating. When your baby plays on carpeting, which can irritate the skin, too, place a cotton sheet under her.

Control diet. Under the doctor's supervision, eliminate any food that seems to trigger a flare-up or a worsening of the rash.

Get medical treatment. Eczema that comes and goes in infancy usually leaves no lasting effects. But if the condition continues into childhood, affected skin can become thickened, depigmented and cracked. Therefore treatment is essential – and will usually include a steroid cream (or the newer non-steroidal tacrolimus ointment or pimecrolimus cream for children over age two) to spread on the affected areas, antihistamines to reduce the itching, and antibiotics if a secondary infection develops.

USING A BACK CARRIER

'Our baby is getting too big to lug around in a front baby carrier. Is it safe to use a back carrier?'

Once your baby can sit independently, even briefly, he's ready to graduate to a back carrier – assuming it suits you both. Some parents find the conveyance a comfortable and convenient way to carry their babies; others find it awkward and a strain on the muscles. Some babies are thrilled by the height and the bird's eye view a back carrier affords, others are frightened by the precarious perch. To find out whether a back carrier is right for you and your baby, take him for a test ride in a friend's or in a store floor sample before buying.

If you do use a back carrier, always be certain baby is fastened in securely. Also be aware that the position allows a baby to do a lot more behind your back than sightseeing – including pulling cans off the shelves in the supermarket, knocking over a vase in the gift shop, plucking (and then munching) leaves off shrubs and trees in the park. Keep in mind, too, that acquiring this backpack will require you to judge distances differently – when you back into a crowded lift or go through a low doorway, for example.

GRATUITOUS ADVICE

'Every time I go out with my son, I have to listen to at least a dozen strangers tell me that he's not dressed warmly enough, what I should do for his teething, or how I could make him stop crying. How am I supposed to handle all this unwanted advice?'

When it comes to the raising of a baby, everybody thinks they know best – or, at least, better than baby's mum or dad. And that includes the chiding voices of experience that chorus around the pushchair every time you leave your home.

While you may, if you're really discriminating, be able to glean an occasional bit of genuine know-how from those well-meaning know-it-alls, most of what you'll hear is best dismissed. Of course, dismissing it graciously is the tricky part. You could come back with a snide retort ('Don't you think he'd tell me if he weren't warm enough?') or spend ten minutes trying to back up your parenting position with facts ('Actually, research shows that babies don't need to be dressed any more warmly than adults'). But smarter in most situations is to plaster on a

smile, nod appreciatively, issue a perfunctory thank you, and move on as speedily as you can. That way, the advice givers will be able to go about their business thinking they've helped you ('Another baby saved from cold fingers!'); you'll have the satisfaction of knowing otherwise. By letting those strangers speak their piece without letting what they have to say get under your skin, you'll both have a better day.

If the advice that's been offered seems as if it may actually have some validity, but you're not sure, check it out with your baby's doctor or with another reliable source.

STARTING THE CUP

'I don't give my baby a bottle, but the doctor said I can give her juice now. Is it too early to start her on the cup?'

Whether baby is started on the cup in the fifth month, the tenth month or the eighteenth month it's a sure thing she'll eventually get all of her fluids from one. But teaching her to drink from a cup early offers certain important advantages. For one, she learns that there's a route to liquid refreshment other than the breast or bottle, an alternative that will make it easier to wean her from either or both. For another, it provides an additional way to give fluids (water, juice and, after a year, milk) when a mum isn't available to nurse, or when a bottle isn't handy.

Another advantage of early cup training: a five-month-old infant is markedly malleable, open to new experiences. But wait until your baby's first birthday to introduce a cup, and you'll likely encounter considerable resistance. Not only will she be stubbornly set in her ways, but she's apt to sense that giving in to a cup will lead to her having to give up

SIPPY SAFETY

To hear parents who've become dependent on them (or have kids who've become dependent on them), they're the greatest invention since Velcro. They look harmless enough – cups with spouts. And their list of benefits is compelling: Since they're practically spillproof and unbreakable, there's no more crying over spilt milk or juice, fewer cleanups, and less laundry; unlike other cups and glasses, they can be used in the car, at play, in the pushchair, and – here's the biggie for busy parents – without supervision.

But research has pointed to some potential pitfalls in sippy cup use, too. Because they're more like a bottle than a cup in the way liquid is extracted from them (it's a slower process, allowing the liquid to spend more time pooling in the mouth and on teeth), extended, frequent use can lead to tooth decay. This is especially true if the sippy cup is used (as it so often is) between meals and between brushings, and even more likely a risk if it's carried around all day for round-the-clock nipping (the way a bottle might be). Another problem when they're carried around all day is that they become a breeding ground for bacteria (particularly if a child has a 'favourite' that doesn't often get washed thoroughly because it's always being used, or if the cup gets left in a toy pile one day and retrieved and drunk from again the next day). Still another issue: like a child nipping all day from a bottle full of juice, a child drinking all day from a sippy cup full of juice may drown his or her appetite for food and/or take in too many superfluous calories, and/or suffer from chronic diarrhoea. A fourth problem that has been suggested is that kids who use sippy cups exclusively are slower in speech development, or are more likely to have temporary speech impediments. The theory goes that the sippy method of drinking – unlike drinking from a regular cup or with a straw – doesn't give the mouth muscles the workout they need. More research needs to be done before that theory is given universal credence; in the meantime, it's food (or drink) for thought.

Still, sippy cups offer a terrific transition from breast or bottle to traditional cups, minimize mess, and are an undeniable convenience on the road. To eliminate the potential risks that go along with those benefits:

◆ Don't start with a sippy. Make sure your baby has at least begun to learn the fine art of sipping from a spoutless cup – an important skill to master – before you bring on the sippy. Then use both, rather than switching over to the sippy full-time.

◆ Limit sippy sipping to meal and snack times. Don't let your child drag the sippy cup around the house and the playground; don't always use a sippy to placate your baby in the car or pushchair. Limits help protect teeth and speech, prevent overdosing on juice, and keep sippy use from slipping into sippy abuse.

◆ Buy multiples. Many children play favourites – and will demand the same sippy cup at every sitting. To make sure you have one to use while others are in the dishwasher, buy several of the style your child favours.

◆ Fill it with water. If the sippy becomes a comfort object (much as a bottle can), don't deny the comfort, but fill it with water instead of juice. That will avert many of the problems associated with sippy cup use.

◆ Know when to stop. Once your child can easily and proficiently sip from a glass or cup, ditch the sippy.

her bottle or breast. And even if she accepts the cup, it may be a while before she becomes skilled at using it, which means that it could be weeks or months before she will be able to drink significant amounts from it – and consequently weeks or months before you can wean her.

To ease your baby into using the cup early and successfully:

Wait until she can sit supported. Babies as young as two months can be started on the cup, but gagging will be less of a problem once a baby can sit up with support.

Choose a safe cup. Even if you're holding the cup, baby may knock it down or swat at it impatiently when she doesn't want any more, so be sure the cups you use are unbreakable. A cup that is weighted at the bottom will not tip over easily, a definite plus. A paper or plastic cup, though unbreakable, won't work for training because – much to baby's delight – it's crushable or crackable.

Choose a compatible cup. The type of cup preferred differs from child to child, so you may have to experiment with several to find one yours really likes. Some children favour a cup with one or two handles they can grip; others prefer a cup without handles. (If such a cup tends to slip from baby's wet little hands, wrap a couple of strips of adhesive tape around it, changing the tape when it becomes ratty.) A cup with a spouted lid (known in baby and toddler circles as a 'sippy cup') theoretically offers a nice transition from sucking to sipping (probably more so for babies who've taken a bottle than for those who are used to a human nipple), but some children just don't like it – perhaps because they find the liquid more difficult to get at, perhaps because they want to drink from a cup that's just like mummy's or daddy's. And though there will be fewer major spills at the start with a sippy cup (and probably none with the many spillproof varieties), baby will eventually have to face the hurdle of learning to do without its protection – which may result in more spills later on. (Plus, there are other sippy cup issues to consider; see box, previous page.)

Protect all concerned. Teaching your baby to drink from a cup won't be a neat affair; for quite some time you can expect more to drip down her chin than into her tummy. So until she becomes proficient, keep her covered with a large absorbent or waterproof bib during drinking lessons. If you are feeding her on your lap, protect it with a waterproof square or apron.

Get baby comfortable. Seat her so she feels secure – on your lap, in an infant seat or propped up in a high chair.

Fill it up with the right stuff. It's easiest and least messy to start with water. Once that's mastered (sort of), you can move on to expressed breast milk or formula (but not regular cow's milk until age one), or (once it's introduced) diluted juice. Play it by baby's tastes; some children will initially accept only juice in a cup and not milk, others take only milk.

Use the sip-at-a-time technique: Put just a small amount of fluid in the cup. Hold the cup to baby's lips and slowly pour a few drops into her mouth. Then take the cup away, giving her a chance to swallow without gagging. Stop each session when your baby signals she's had enough by turning her head, pushing the cup away, or starting to fuss.

Even with this technique, you can still expect that almost as much liquid will exit your baby's mouth as enters it. Eventually, with plenty of practise, patience and perseverance, more will hit its mark than not.

FEEDING BABY SAFELY

Food poisoning is one of the most common illnesses in the United Kingdom. And it's also one of the most easily prevented. Other hazards that originate at the feeding table (glass splinters, passing of cold germs) can also be avoided. To make sure you do everything you can to make eating safe for your baby, take the following precautions every time you prepare food:

◆ Always wash your hands with soap and water before feeding baby; if you touch raw meat, poultry, fish or eggs (all of which harbour bacteria) during the feeding, wash them again. Wash your hands, too, if you blow your nose or touch your mouth. If you have an open cut on your hand, cover it with a plaster before feeding your baby.

◆ Store dry baby cereals and unopened baby food jars in a cool, dry place away from extremes of heat (over the stove, for example) or cold (as in an unheated cellar).

◆ Wipe the tops of baby food jars with a clean cloth or run them under the tap to remove dust before opening.

◆ Make sure the button is down on safety lids before opening a jar for the first time; when opening listen for the 'pop' to make sure the seal was intact. Discard or return to the store any jar that has a raised button or that doesn't pop. If you use ordinary canned foods for an older baby (or anyone else), discard cans that are swollen or leaky. Don't use foods in which a liquid that should be clear has turned cloudy or milky.

◆ If a jar is hard to open, run warm tap water over the neck or pry the side of the lid open with a bottle opener until you hear a pop; don't tap the top, as this may splinter glass into the contents.

◆ Whenever you use a can opener, make sure it's clean (wash it in the dishwasher), and discard it when it begins to look rusty or you can't get it clean.

◆ Don't feed baby directly out of a baby food jar unless it's the last meal from that jar, and don't save a bowl of food baby's eaten from for the next meal, since enzymes and bacteria from baby's saliva will begin 'digesting' the food, turning it watery and causing it to spoil more quickly.

◆ Remove one serving at a time from a jar of baby food with a clean spoon. If baby wants a refill, use a fresh spoon to scoop it out.

Encourage participation. Your baby may try to grab the cup from you, with an 'I'd rather do it myself' attitude. Let her try. A very few babies can manage a cup even at this early age. Don't get upset if she spills it all – that's part of the learning process. She can also learn by sharing the job, holding the cup along with you.

Take no for an answer. If your baby resists the cup, even after a few tries, and even after you've tried several different liquids and several different types of cups, don't pressure her to accept it. Instead, shelve the project for a couple of weeks. When you try again, use a new cup and a little fanfare ('Look what Mummy has for you!') to try to generate excitement. Or you might try letting your conscientious objector handle an empty cup as a toy for a while.

◆ After you've taken a serving out of a jar, recap the remainder and refrigerate until it's needed again; if it hasn't been used within three days for juices and fruits, and two days for everything else, discard it.

◆ It's not necessary to heat baby food (adults may have a preference for warm meats and vegetables, but babies have developed no such taste bias), but if you do, heat only enough for one meal and discard any unused heated portion. Do not heat baby's food in a microwave oven; though the container may stay cool, the inside continues cooking for a few minutes after you take it out, and may get hot enough to burn baby's mouth. Heat instead in an electric feeding dish or in a heat-resistant glass bowl over simmering water (hot water feeding dishes won't heat foods but will keep them warm). When testing the temperature, stir up the food, then splash a drop on the inside of your wrist rather than taking a taste from baby's spoon; if you taste, use a fresh spoon for baby.

◆ When preparing fresh baby foods, be certain utensils and work surfaces are clean. Keep cold foods cold and warm foods warm; foods spoil fastest between 15.5° and 49°C (60° and 120°F), so don't keep baby's food at those temperatures for more than an hour. (For adults, the safe period is closer to two or three hours.)

◆ When the doctor okays eggs for your baby, cook them well before serving. Raw or uncooked eggs can harbour salmonella. (To be extra safe, you can use pasteurized eggs.)

◆ Do not give baby unpasteurized juice, milk, cheese or other 'raw' dairy products.

◆ Peel vegetables and fruit, when possible, unless they are certified organically grown, and wash all fruits and vegetables well. Melons should be scrubbed before slicing into them.

◆ When tasting during food preparation, use a fresh spoon each time you taste, or wash the spoon between tastings.

◆ *When in doubt* about the freshness of a food, *throw it out.*

◆ On an outing, take unopened jars or dehydrated baby food (to which you can add fresh water). Carry any open jars or containers of anything that needs refrigeration in an insulated bag packed with ice or an ice pack, if it will be more than an hour before you serve it. Once the food no longer feels cool, don't feed it to the baby.

FOOD ALLERGIES

'Both my spouse and I have a lot of allergies. I'm worried that our son may have them, too.'

Unfortunately, it isn't just the better traits – lustrous locks, long legs, musical ability, mechanical aptitude – that are inheritable. The less desirable ones are, too, and having two parents with allergies does make a baby much more likely to develop them than if he has two allergy-free parents. But that doesn't mean your baby is destined for a lifetime of hives and sneezing. It does mean you should discuss your concerns with your baby's doctor, and if necessary with a specialist in paediatric allergies.

A baby becomes allergic to a substance when his immune system becomes sensitized to it by producing antibodies. Sensitization can take place the first time his body encounters a substance or the hundredth time. But once

It does, antibodies rev into action whenever the substance is encountered, causing any one of a wide range of physical reactions, including runny nose and eyes, headache, wheezing, eczema, hives, diarrhoea, abdominal pain or discomfort, violent vomiting and, in severe cases, anaphylactic shock. There is even some evidence that allergy may also manifest itself through behavioural symptoms, such as crankiness.

The most common food offenders include milk, eggs, peanuts, nuts, wheat, corn, fish, shellfish, berries, peas and beans, chocolate and some spices. In some cases even a tiny amount of a food causes a severe reaction; in others, small amounts don't seem to cause a problem at all. Children often outgrow some food allergies but later develop hypersensitivities to other substances in the environment, such as household dusts, pollens and animal dander.

Not every adverse reaction to a food or other substance, however, is an allergy. In fact, in some studies of children, specialists were able to confirm allergy in fewer than half the subjects – all of whom had been previously diagnosed as 'allergic'. What appears to be an allergy may sometimes be an enzyme deficiency. Children with insufficient levels of the enzyme lactase, for example, are unable to digest the milk sugar lactose, and thus react badly to milk and milk products. And those with celiac disease are unable to digest gluten, a substance found in many grains, and thus appear to be allergic to those grains. The workings of an immature digestive system or such common infant problems as colic may also be misdiagnosed as allergy.

For infants in families with a history of allergy, doctors generally recommend the following precautions:

Continued breastfeeding. Bottle-fed babies are more likely to develop allergies than breastfed infants – probably because cow's milk is a relatively common cause of allergic reaction.[2] If you are nursing your baby, continue, if possible, for the entire first year. The later cow's milk becomes a mainstay of his diet, the better. Using a soya-based formula when a supplement is needed is often suggested in allergic families, but some babies turn out to be allergic to soya, too. For those babies, a protein hydrolysate formula will be needed.

Delaying solids. It's now believed that the later a baby is exposed to a potential allergen, the less likely it is that sensitization will take place. So most doctors recommend postponing the introduction of solids in babies of allergic families – usually until at least six months, and occasionally later.

More gradual introduction of new foods. It's always wise to introduce new foods to a baby one at a time, but this is especially important in allergic families. It may be recommended that you give each new food every day for an entire week before starting another. If there is any kind of adverse reaction – looser movements, gassiness, rash (including nappy rash), excessive spitting up, wheezing or runny nose – it's generally advised that the food be discontinued immediately and not be resumed for several weeks at least, at which time it may be accepted without distress.

Introduction of less allergenic foods first. Baby rice cereal, the least likely cereal to cause allergy, is usually recommended as a starter food. Barley and oats are less allergenic than, and are generally given before, wheat and corn. Most fruits

---

2. Occasionally, breastfed babies can have an allergic reaction to nuts, egg or cow's milk protein from their mothers' diet that has been passed through the breast milk (see pages 91 and 171).

and vegetables cause no problems, but parents are often advised to hold off on introducing berries and tomatoes. Shellfish, peas and beans can also wait. Most of the other highly allergenic foods (nuts, peanuts, some spices and chocolate) can usually be introduced after three years of age.

Elimination diets and special liquid diets can be used to diagnose allergies, but they are complicated and time-consuming. Skin tests for food allergies are not highly accurate; a person can have a positive skin test to a particular food, yet have no reaction at all when he eats it. 'Food sensitivity' screening tests that claim to diagnose allergies from blood samples are even less accurate and extremely expensive.

Happily, many childhood allergies are outgrown (though certain food allergies, such as those to peanuts, nuts, shellfish and fish tend not to be). So even if your baby turns out to be hypersensitive to milk, wheat or other foods, he may no longer be in a few years – or even less.

FEEDING CHAIRS

'So far I've been feeding my baby on my lap, but it's very messy. When can I put her in a high chair?'

There's no perfectly neat way to feed a baby (you'll be a two-ply, jumbo-roll paper-towel family for many months to come). But the messiest, and most logistically challenging, is the baby-on-the-lap manoeuvre; a feeding chair of some kind will make the job much more efficient. While a baby still needs some support to sit, an infant seat (with baby strapped in and under your *constant* supervision) can double as a feeding seat. Once she can sit up fairly well by herself, it's time to switch to a high chair. See page 310 for more on keeping a baby from slipping, sliding and slumping in her new seat, and page 330 for Feeding Chair Safety Tips.

WALKERS

'My daughter seems very frustrated that she can't get around yet. She's not content to lie in her cot or sit in her infant seat, but I can't carry her all day. Can I put her in a walker?'

Life can be frustrating when you're all revved up with no place to go (or, at least, no way to get there without a grown-up's help). Such frustrations are often at a peak from the time a baby begins to sit fairly well until she can get around on her own (by crawling, creeping, cruising or whatever method she's first able to come up with). The obvious solution used to be a walker – a seat set inside a table framework on four wheeled legs that allowed babies to zoom around the house long before they achieved independent mobility. But because walkers are the cause annually of thousands of head injuries that require medical treatment, and thousands more that are kissed-and-made-better at home, they are no longer recommended and, in fact, the AAP has called for a ban on the manufacture and sale of all mobile walkers. (If you still decide to use a walker, see the box on page 332.)

A somewhat safer choice is a stationary walker (like the ExerSaucer), which allows baby some movement with less potential risk than the mobile walker. But there's plenty of downside to these, too. First, babies whose frustrations lie in not being able to get from A to B without hitching a ride from mum or dad won't be any less frustrated in a walker that doesn't move. They might even be more frustrated; since the ExerSaucer moves only in circles, it may fuel their fury ('I'm moving but I'm not getting

FEEDING CHAIR SAFETY TIPS

Feeding baby safely doesn't just mean introducing new foods gradually. In fact, feeding baby safely begins even before the first spoon is filled – when baby's placed in a feeding chair. To help make sure every mealtime passes safely, follow these rules:

ALL FEEDING CHAIRS

♦ Never leave a young baby unattended in a feeding chair; have the food, bib, paper towels, utensils and anything else necessary for the meal ready so that you don't have to leave your child alone while you fetch them.

♦ Always secure the safety or restraining straps, even if your baby seems too young to climb out. Be sure to fasten the strap at the groin to prevent him or her from slipping out the bottom. (Many newer seats have crotch guards to prevent slipping – but do be sure to use the strap as well to prevent baby from climbing out.)

♦ Keep all chair and eating surfaces clean (wash with detergent or soapy water and rinse thoroughly); babies have no compunctions about picking up a decaying morsel from a previous meal and munching on it.

HIGH CHAIRS, BOOSTER SEATS AND LOW FEEDING TABLES

♦ Always be certain slide-off trays are safely snapped into place; an unsecured one could allow a lunging and unbelted baby to go flying out headfirst.

♦ Check to be sure that a folding-type chair is safely locked into the open position and won't suddenly fold up with baby in it.

♦ Place the chair away from any tables, counters, walls or other surfaces that baby could possibly kick off from – causing the chair to tumble.

♦ To protect baby's fingers, check their whereabouts before attaching or detaching the tray.

HOOK-ON SEATS

♦ Use the seat only on a stable wooden or metal table; do not use on glass-topped or loose-topped tables, tables with the support in the centre (baby's weight could topple it), card tables or aluminum folding tables, or on a table leaf.

♦ If a baby in a hook-on seat can rock the table, the table isn't stable enough; don't attach the seat to it.

♦ Avoid using place mats or tablecloths on the table; they can interfere with the gripping power of the seat.

♦ Be certain any locks, clamps or snap-together parts are securely fastened before putting your baby in the seat; always take your baby out of the seat before releasing or unfastening it. Always be sure the clamps are clean and functioning properly.

♦ Don't put a chair or other object under the seat as a safeguard should baby fall, or position the seat opposite a table brace or leg; a baby can push off against such surfaces, dislodging the seat. And don't allow a large dog or older child under the seat while baby is in it, because they might also dislodge it from below.

anywhere!'). In addition, some studies have shown that both walkers and ExerSaucers can cause temporary delays in development if they're overused; babies who spend a lot of time in them, according to the research, sit, crawl and walk later than babies who don't. That's not surprising if you consider that a baby trapped in a walker (or in an infant seat or swing) doesn't have the opportunity to flex those muscles necessary to practise and master those skills. In fact, babies use a different set of muscles to stay upright in a walker than they do to stay upright for walking. Research also shows that because babies can't see their feet in a walker or ExerSaucer, they're deprived of the visual clues that would help them figure out how their bodies walk through space (a key part of learning how to walk). What's more, they don't learn how to balance themselves and how, when balance fails them, to fall and pick themselves back up – also vital steps in becoming a solo walker.

If you do choose to use a stationary walker, follow these tips for keeping baby both happy and safe while she's in it:

Take your baby for a test drive. The best way to assess your baby's readiness for a stationary walker is to let her try one out. If you don't have a friend whose baby has one, go to a store and let your baby try out a floor model. As long as she seems happy and doesn't slump pitifully in it, she's ready for a stationary walker.

Don't walk out while she's 'walking'. A stationary walker isn't a substitute for supervision. Leave your baby in her ExerSaucer only when she can be watched.

Don't let her walk around the clock. Limit baby's time in the ExerSaucer to no more than thirty minutes per session.

Every baby needs to spend some time on the floor, practising skills that will eventually help her to crawl, such as lifting her belly off the ground while on all fours. She needs the opportunity to pull up on coffee tables and kitchen chairs in preparation for standing and, later, walking. She needs more chances to explore and handle safe objects in her environment than a walker of any kind allows. And, she needs the interaction with you and others that free play requires and allows; stationary walkers (like infant seats and playpens) should not become baby-sitters.

Don't wait until she can walk before you take away the walker. As soon as your baby can get around some other way – crawling or cruising, for instance – put away the stationary walker. Its purpose, remember, was to ease your baby's frustration at being immobile. Keeping her in the walker not only won't help her to walk sooner, but its constant use may cause 'walking confusion' (much as giving a baby a bottle before she's learned to suck at the breast can cause nipple confusion), because standing and moving in a walker (even a stationary one) and walking solo require different body movements.

JUMPERS

'We received a jumping device, which hangs in the doorway, as a gift for our baby. He seems to enjoy it, but we're not sure if it's safe.'

Most babies are ready and eager for a workout long before they're independently mobile – which is why many enjoy the acrobatics they can perform in a baby jumper. But the joy of jumping doesn't come without potential problems. For one, some paediatric orthopaedic specialists warn that too much jumper use

REDUCING WALKER RISKS

Mobile walkers pose many safety risks (as well as developmental ones; see previous page). If you do choose to use a walker that moves, keep in mind that it doesn't grant *you* freedom of movement – you must stay nearby and supervise closely *every moment your baby is in it.* To further ensure safety, you should:

Only use one that meets safety standards. Walkers must be wider than a 91.5-cm (36-in) doorway or have a braking device that stops the walker if any of the wheels drop lower than the riding surface (for example, at the beginning of a staircase). Don't borrow one that doesn't include these features.

Do your childproofing early. Most any trouble a crawling or walking baby can get into, a baby in a walker can get into, too. A push off the wall and a couple of quick strides, and baby could end up at the other end of the room – and out the door or down a flight of stairs. So even if your baby can't get around without the help of a walker, he or she should be considered as hazardous to his or her own health as a mobile baby. Read Making Home Safe for Baby (page 402), and make all necessary adjustments before you let baby loose in the walker.

Keep dangers out of walker's way. The most potentially dangerous place for a baby in a walker is at the top of a flight of stairs; don't let your baby roam freely near a stairway in the walker, even if it is protected with a closed safety gate. Although most walker/stairway injuries occur on staircases where there is no safety gate or where a gate is left open, some do take place when a gate is not fastened to the wall securely. It's best, therefore, when your baby is in the walker, to block off entirely – with a closed door or heavy obstacles – areas leading to staircases. Other hazards to the walker-walking baby, which should be removed or blocked off before letting him or her loose, include room thresholds, changes in grade (as from carpet to linoleum or patio to grass), toys left on the floor, loose area rugs and other low obstructions that can topple the walker.

Other risks that can be encountered by a child in a walker: dangling cords that can topple appliances over, tablecloths that can be tugged off (bringing everything on a table, including hot dishes, down on baby).

---

can cause certain kinds of injuries to bones and joints. For another, baby's exhilaration with the freedom of movement a jumper affords can quickly turn to frustration as he discovers that no matter how or how much he moves his arms and legs, he's destined to stay put in the doorway.

If you do opt to use the jumper, make sure your doorways are wide enough. As with any baby-busying device (a walker, a swing, a dummy, for example), be sure that you use it to meet your baby's needs, not yours; if he's unhappy in it, take him out immediately. And never leave your baby unattended in the jumper – even for a moment.

BABY SWING

'My baby loves being in her infant swing – she can spend hours in it. How much time can I allow her to spend in the swing?'

You probably love having your baby in the swing nearly as much as she loves being in it. After all, it keeps her busy when you're busy, holds her when your arms are otherwise occupied – and calms her down when nothing else will.

But while being in the swing of things is entertaining and soothing for baby – and convenient for you – it comes with a downside. Too much swinging can prevent your baby from practising important motor skills, such as creeping, crawling, pulling up and cruising. It can also cut down on the amount of contact your baby has with you – both physical (the kind she gets from being held by you) and emotional (the kind she gets from playing with you).

So keep on swinging, but with restrictions. Firstly, limit swinging sessions to no longer than thirty minutes at a time, twice a day. Secondly, place the swing in the room you'll be in and keep interacting with your baby even as she swings – play peekaboo behind the tea towel while you're making dinner, sing songs while you're going through the post, swoop down for an occasional cuddle while you're talking on the phone. If she tends to fall asleep in the swing (who can blame her?), be sure to complete the transfer to the cot before she nods off – not only so that her head doesn't droop, but so that she'll learn to fall asleep without motion. And, thirdly, keep these safety tips in mind whenever she swings:

◆ Always strap baby in to prevent falls.

◆ Never leave your baby unattended while she's in the swing.

◆ Keep the swing at least arm's length away from objects that your baby can grab on to – such as curtains, floor lamps, soft furnishings cords – and away from dangerous items a baby can reach for – such as sockets, the oven or stove, or sharp kitchen utensils. Also keep the swing away from walls, cabinets or any surface your baby might be able to use to push off from with her feet.

◆ Once your baby reaches the manufacturer's weight limit recommendation, usually 6.8 to 9 kg (15 to 20 lb), pack up the swing.

What it's Important to Know:
ENVIRONMENTAL HAZARDS AND YOUR BABY

It's a natural impulse – one that you share with most members of the animal kingdom: to keep your offspring safe and sound. Birds do it by feathering their nests atop trees, far from predatory beasts that might feast on their unborn flock. Alligator and crocodile mothers cover their buried clutches of eggs with vegetation that radiates heat as it rots, keeping nest temperatures within tolerable limits. Penguin mothers and fathers cuddle their eggs on their feet to keep them above the frozen land. Mother bears, wolves and foxes build dens to shelter their vulnerable young from the elements. As a human, you do it by babyproofing the house, using car seats when you drive, choosing safe baby furnishings – and protecting your child from environmental hazards.

So you read the paper, you turn up the volume when a report about these hazards comes on the TV, you skim through child-care books and, if you're like most parents, you do a fair amount of worrying. (And if you're like some parents, a whole lot of worrying.) But is the world around your baby really as dangerous as you've heard? On the other hand, can it be as safe as you'd like? Though you certainly have it easier in your quest to shelter your brood than your furry and feathered friends do, you still have your work cut out for you. It may not be a jungle outside where you live, but protecting your baby from the potential hazards in his or her environment isn't a walk in the park, either.

Fortunately, there are many more factors influencing a child's long-term well-being that are within your control than factors that aren't. Ensuring adequate well-baby and sick-baby care from birth, for instance. Getting baby off to the best nutritional start possible. Not letting anyone smoke around your baby. Encouraging healthy lifestyle habits, such as exercise and good diet, and discouraging unhealthy ones, such as smoking and alcohol abuse, through example. Take care of these, and you're already doing an excellent job of protecting your young.

But there are some hazards in our environment that aren't completely within our control and that, despite best efforts, can be controlled only partially or indirectly. And though most of these pale in significance when compared to the factors that are within your control, they do pose some risk. In general, the risks are greater for babies and young children, for a few reasons. One reason is their smaller body size – the same dose of a hazardous substance in a child is more powerful than it would be in an adult. And since, kilogram for kilogram of body weight, they drink more water, eat more food and breathe more air, they actually take in more toxins. Another is the fact that their organs are still growing and

maturing and thus are more vulnerable to environmental assaults. Their propensity for putting their hands in their mouths also increases the risk for them (since they touch almost everything, and since more things that they touch will ultimately end up in their mouths and thus their systems), as does the fact that they're built close to the ground and often play there, too (they're nearer to the toxins in dust, soil, carpets and grass). Yet another reason is that today's child is looking forward to a longer life span than earlier generations did, and since the damage often takes many years to develop, there are more years available in which it can develop.

Even so, the relative risks are small and in most cases – particularly when viewed with some perspective – not worth losing sleep over. It's important to keep in mind, too, that no matter how hard parents try, it's just not possible to create a completely risk-free environment for their offspring. But following that natural instinct to protect, by taking all the steps you can to minimize the hazards in your child's life, makes sense. It'll also help you sleep better at night. Here's how.

HOUSEHOLD PEST CONTROL

Household pests are aesthetically unappealing and annoying, and in some cases can even transmit disease or inflict painful and dangerous bites. But most of the pesticides used in the home to eliminate pests are dangerous poisons, particularly in the hands (or mouths) of infants and toddlers. You can minimize the risk while achieving the benefits of keeping home and hearth free of infestation with the following:

Blocking tactics. Use window screens, and screen or otherwise close off entry points for insects and vermin.

Sticky insect or rodent traps. Not dependent on killer chemicals, these trap crawling insects in enclosed boxes (roach traps) or containers (ant traps), flies on old-fashioned fly paper, mice on sticky rectangles. Because human skin can stick to these surfaces (the separation can often be painful), these traps, when open, must still be kept out of the reach of children or put out after they are in bed at night and taken up before they are up and around in the morning. Those used for rodents have the disadvantage of prolonging the death.

Box traps. The tenderhearted can catch rodents in box traps and then let the victims loose in fields or woods far from residential areas, though this isn't always easy. Because these rodents can bite, the traps should be kept out of the reach of children or put out when children are not around.

Safe use of chemical pesticides. Virtually all, including the much-touted boric acid, are highly toxic not just to pests but to humans as well. If you opt to use them, *do not* spread them (or store them) where babies or children can get to them or on surfaces where food is prepared. Always use the least toxic substance (check with your local council or health department). If you use a spray, keep the children out of the house while spraying and for the rest of the day, at least. Better still, have the spraying done while you're on holiday, visiting grandma or otherwise away from home. When you return, open all the windows to air out the house or apartment, and scrub all surfaces that baby might touch or that come into contact with food.

LEAD

For years it has been known that large doses of lead could cause severe brain damage in children. Now it is also recognized that even in relatively small doses, lead can reduce IQ, alter enzyme function, retard growth, damage the kidneys, and also cause learning and behaviour problems, hearing and attention deficiencies. It may even have negative effects on the immune system.

It makes sense, then, for parents to know what sources of lead are in their baby's environment and what can be done to minimize exposure.

Lead paint. In spite of legislation prohibiting its use, lead paint continues to be the major source of a child's exposure to lead. Many older homes still harbour lead paint, often containing very high concentrations of lead beneath layers of newer applications. As paint cracks or flakes, microscopic lead-containing particles are shed. These end up on baby's hands, toys, clothing – and eventually in his or her mouth. If there is the possibility of lead in your house paint, check with your local council to get advice on whether and how to remove it. And be certain that any painted object – toy, cot, or anything else your baby comes in contact with – is lead free. Be particularly wary of antique items, as well as those that are imported or were purchased outside the United Kingdom.

Drinking water. It is estimated that the water in thousands of British homes is probably contaminated with lead. The lead usually leaches into the water in buildings where there are lead pipes or where pipes are soldered with lead, especially where the water is particularly corrosive. Since most of the contamination occurs once the water has entered

UNSUITABLE FOR DIGGING?

Most sand sold for sandpits is perfectly safe and ready for your child's digging pleasure. But an occasional batch of sand may be contaminated with a type of asbestos called tremolite. The tremolite fibres float in the air and can cause serious illness if inhaled. The problem is more severe indoors, where sand tends to be dry and dusty, than outdoors, where it is often damp. Though it's virtually impossible for you to learn if the sand your baby digs in (at home or at a day-care centre or in the playground) is contaminated, you can determine if it is dusty and possibly risky to breathe. Return or get rid of the sand (or if it's from a playground, frequent a safer sandpit) if it makes a cloud of dust when you dump a bucketful or if, when you mix a spoonful in a glass of water, the water remains cloudy once the sand settles. Find another source, preferably ordinary beach sand (a lot of play sand is ground-up stone or marble).

---

individual buildings rather than in the public water supply, most communities haven't made major efforts to correct the problem. If you're concerned that your drinking water may be contaminated by lead (or other hazardous substance), have it tested by the local water authority or department of health if they do such testing, or by a registered private testing agency. If lead is found, you can install a reverse osmosis filter (which removes the lead) on your kitchen sink, or use bottled water for drinking and formula preparation. Letting the tap water run for at least three minutes also makes it safe for drinking or cooking, though it's admittedly wasteful. Avoid using water from the hot tap for cooking, since it leaches more lead; don't boil water longer than five minutes, which concentrates the lead.

Soil. Lead house paint that flakes off, industrial residue, dust from the demolition of houses that have been painted with lead can all end up contaminating the soil. Though you needn't be fanatic, do try to keep your baby from ingesting fistfuls of the stuff.

In addition to keeping your child away from known sources of lead, you should also try to increase his or her resistance to lead poisoning with good nutrition, particularly adequate levels of iron and calcium. And ask the doctor about screening tests for lead.

OTHERWISE CONTAMINATED WATER

Most tap water in Britain is fit to drink, but a small percentage contains substances that pose significant health risks. Water systems purified with activated charcoal rather than chlorine are believed to provide safer water, but only a few water districts presently use this type of purification. Well water, too, is often contaminated. If you suspect your water is not safe, check with your local council about how to have it tested. Should it turn out to be contaminated, a water purifier can often make it safe to drink. Which type of purifier will be best for your home will depend on the contaminants in your water and how much you can spend.

POLLUTED INDOOR AIR

Most babies spend a great deal of time indoors, so the quality of the air they breathe there is extremely significant. To keep baby's air clean and safe, watch out for the following indoor air risks:

Carbon monoxide. This colourless, odourless, tasteless but treacherous gas (it can cause lung ailments, impair vision and brain functioning, and is fatal in high doses) that results from the burning of fuel can seep into your home from many sources: improperly vented woodstoves or kerosene heaters (have your local fire station check venting); slow-burning woodstoves (speed up burning by keeping the damper open); poorly adjusted or unvented gas stoves or other appliances (have adjustment checked periodically – the flame should be blue – and install an exhaust fan to the outside to remove fumes); gas ranges each time they are turned on (an electric ignition reduces the amount of combustion gases released); fireplaces with residue-blocked chimneys (fires should never be left to smolder and chimneys should be cleaned regularly); an attached garage (never leave a car idling, even briefly, in a garage that shares a wall or ceiling with your home, since the fumes can seep through). For safety, install a carbon monoxide detector on each floor of your home, not too close to major appliances (as you would with smoke detectors).

Benzopyrenes. A long list of respiratory illnesses (from eye, nose and throat irritation to asthma and bronchitits to emphysema and cancer) can be linked to tar-like organic particles that result from the incomplete combustion of tobacco or wood. To prevent your baby's exposure, allow no tobacco smoking in your home, be sure the flue that vents smoke from a wood fire does not leak, vent combustion appliances (such as tumble dryers) to the outdoors, change air filters on various appliances regularly, and increase ventilation in your home.

Particulate matter. A wide variety of particles, invisible to the naked eye, can fill the air in our homes. They come from such sources as household dust (which can trigger allergies in susceptible children), tobacco smoke, wood smoke, unvented gas appliances, kerosene heaters and asbestos construction materials. The same precautions (no smoking, proper venting, filter changing) discussed above can minimize this threat. Air-filtering units can often remove many of these particles and are particularly useful if someone in the family has allergies. If you find asbestos in your home that may need removal, get professional assistance in dealing with it before particles begin to fly.

Miscellaneous fumes. Fumes from cleaning fluids, from some aerosol sprays (if they contain fluorocarbons, they can also be hazardous to the environment), and from turpentine and other painting-related materials can be highly toxic. If you use these substances at all, always use the least toxic product (water-based paints, beeswax floor waxes, paint thinners made from plant oils), use it in a well-ventilated area (even better, outdoors), and never use it when infants or children are nearby. Store these, like all other household products, safely out of reach of curious little hands. They are best stored in outdoor storage areas where, if they begin to evaporate, fumes won't seep into living areas.

A SAFER WALK ON THE WILD SIDE

Be extra careful if your baby wants to get up close and personal with the goats and sheep at the petting zoo or farm. Though they're cute and cuddly, these animals can also carry the dangerous *E. coli* bacteria, which they can pass on to little petters. *E. coli* infection causes severe diarrhoea and abdominal cramps, and in some cases it can be fatal. So be sure you wash your baby's hands with soap and water (most petting zoos have a sink handy right outside for this purpose), or with an antibacterial wipe or gel after any petting session. If you didn't take these precautions in previous visits but your baby didn't have any subsequent symptoms, there's no need to worry. Just take the precautions next time.

Formaldehyde. With so many products in our modern world containing formaldehyde (from the resins in particle-board furniture to the sizing in decorator fabrics and the adhesives in carpeting), it isn't surprising that the gas, which causes nasal cancer in animals and respiratory problems, rashes, nausea and other symptoms, is everywhere. To minimize the potential risk, look for products that are formaldehyde free when building or furnishing your home. To reduce the effects of formaldehyde already in your home, seal such materials as particle-board with an epoxy sealer – or, even simpler and nicer, invest in a small indoor garden. Fifteen or twenty house-plants can apparently absorb the formaldehyde gas in an average-size house. But make sure they're not plants that are poisonous if ingested, just in case baby ends up doing some munching.

Mould. Fungi, which thrive in damp locations such as cellars, are known to cause breathing problems, croup, bronchitis and other illness in infants. Look out for wet spots and mould in your home and take steps to eliminate them. Also consider measuring household fungi levels if your baby has been experiencing breathing problems.

Radon. A colourless, odourless, radioactive gas that is a naturally occurring product of the decay of uranium in rocks and soil. Of the 34,000 deaths from lung cancer each year in the UK, around 5 per cent are attributable to radon. Breathed in by unsuspecting residents of homes in which it has accumulated, it exposes the lungs to radiation, which over many years can lead to cancer.

Accumulation of radon occurs when the gas seeps into a home from decaying rocks and soil beneath it and is retained because of poor ventilation in the structure.

Taking the following precautions can help prevent the serious consequences of radon exposure:

♦ Before you buy a home, especially in a high-radon area, have it tested for radon contamination. Your local council can give you information on the radon levels in your area and where to turn for testing.

♦ If you live in a high-radon area, or suspect your home may be contaminated, have it tested. Ideally, testing should take place over a several-month period to obtain an average. Levels are usually higher in seasons when windows are closed.

♦ If your home turns out to have high levels of radon, consult your local council for help in locating a radon-abatement company in your community, and ask them for any written material they have on radon reduction. The first step will probably be to seal cracks and other openings in the foundation walls and floors. More important will be increasing ventilation by opening windows; installing vents in crawl spaces, attics and other closed spaces; and eliminating airtight weather stripping and air-to-air heat exchangers. In some cases, a housewide ventilation system may be needed.

CONTAMINANTS IN FOOD

In this world of mass production, manufacturers have learned to use chemicals of various sorts to make the foods they produce look better, smell better, taste better (or, in the case of processed foods, at least more like the real thing), and last longer. But even foods that haven't passed through a manufacturing plant are often contaminated – by pesticides or other chemicals used in growing or storing, or picked up incidentally from water or soil. In many cases, the risks from such chemicals to humans are either unknown or believed to be small. Nevertheless, it's prudent to protect your child (who is, again, more vulnerable to these chemicals than adults are) by following these basic rules when selecting and preparing foods:

◆ Stay away from processed foods with a lot of chemical additives, at least when shopping for baby. Not only are such foods usually less nutritious than fresh, but the chemicals they contain may be of questionable safety. Though many common food additives are believed to be safe, others may not be. Be particularly wary of foods containing any of the following: brominated vegetable oils

(BVO), butylated hydroxyanisole (BHA), butylated hydroxytoluene (BHT), caffeine, monosodium glutamate (MSG), propyl gallate, quinine, saccharin, sodium nitrate and sodium nitrite, sulfites, and artificial colours and flavours. Considered questionable are carrageenan, heptyl paraben, phosphoric acid and other phosphorus compounds.

◆ Don't serve up artificial sweeteners to your baby. Plenty of questions about the safety of some sweeteners still need to be answered. Though some appear to be safe (especially sucralose, or Splenda, a low-calorie sweetener made from sugar), since they're designed for calorie restriction (and babies should never be on a calorie-restricted diet), they don't have a place in a baby's diet.

FOOD HAZARDS IN PERSPECTIVE

Though it makes sense to limit chemicals in your family's diet when you can, fear of additives and chemicals can so limit the variety of foods your family eats that it can interfere with good nutrition. It's important to remember that a well-balanced, nutritious diet, high in whole grains and fruits and vegetables (especially cruciferous ones like broccoli, cauliflower and Brussels sprouts, and those high in vitamin A, such as green leafies and deep yellows), will not only provide the nutrients needed for growth and good health, but will also help to counteract the effects of possible carcinogens in the environment. So limit chemical intake when practical, but don't drive yourself and your family crazy in the process.

OUT OF THE MOUTHS OF BABES

It's not just those handfuls of dirt from the park, or the dried flowers on display at the department store, that you need to keep out of baby's mouth. There are plenty of foods (besides those listed on page 312), as well as drinks and other ingestibles that don't belong in a baby's diet, including:

◆ Unpasteurized (raw) dairy products, juice or cider. These can contain dangerous bacteria that can cause life-threatening illness in babies and young children.

◆ Smoked or cured meats, such as hot dogs and bacon. Usually high in fat and cholesterol as well as in nitrates and other chemicals, these should be served to babies rarely, if at all. (Cold cuts must always be heated until steaming to protect against the bacterial infection listeria.)

◆ Smoked fish, such as smoked salmon or trout. There are two reasons why these

shouldn't find their way onto the high chair tray: one, they're usually cured with nitrites to protect freshness. Two, they may be contaminated with listeria.

◆ Any fish that might be contaminated with high levels of mercury, including shark, swordfish, king mackerel and tilefish, as well as any fish from contaminated waters. Because tuna can also contain a fair amount of mercury (canned contains somewhat less than fresh), the amount of this fish a baby or young child eats should also probably be limited. It's also recommended that a child's intake of freshwater fish caught recreationally (as opposed to commercially) be limited to 55 g (2 oz) (cooked weight) a week. Your local council health department should be able to give you more information on which fish are safe and which aren't at any particular time in your community, which should never be served to a child and which

◆ Buy organic, when possible. (But don't worry when it's not possible, since risks from chemical residues are generally believed to be small.) Locally grown produce in season tends to be safest, since large quantities of chemicals aren't needed to preserve it during shipping or storage. Also safer are foods with heavy protective husks, leaves or skin (such as avocado, melon and bananas) that keep out pesticides. Produce that doesn't look perfect (has blemishes) may also be safer, since it's usually chemical protection that keeps foods looking beautiful.

◆ Peel fruits and vegetables that aren't certified organic before using (par-

ticularly those with a waxy finish), or thoroughly wash with water and, possibly, an all-natural produce wash (but rinse very thoroughly), scrubbing with a stiff brush when feasible. Don't try the brush on lettuce or strawberries; do use it on apples and courgettes.

◆ Keep your child's diet as varied as possible once a wide range of foods has been introduced. Variety adds more than spice to life – it adds a measure of safety (not to mention better nutrition by providing a wide range of vitamins and minerals from different sources). Instead of always offering apple juice, vary the juices from day to day (apple one

should be served only occasionally. For the latest on fish safety, contact the Food Standards Agency on 0207 276 8829 or at www.food.gov.uk.

◆ Raw fish, such as in sushi. Young children don't chew well enough to destroy the parasites that might dwell therein and that could cause serious illness; they're also at greater risk from the illnesses themselves.

◆ Foods or beverages, such as coffee, tea, cocoa and chocolate that contain caffeine or related compounds. Caffeine can make a baby jittery; worse, it can interfere with absorption of calcium and can replace worthwhile dietary items.

◆ Imitation foods, such as non-dairy creamers (full of fat, sugar and chemicals) and fruit 'drinks' (which contain little actual juice, unneeded sugar and, often, plenty of chemicals).

◆ Herbal teas. These often contain questionable substances (comfrey tea, for example, contains a carcinogen) and frequently have unwanted, even dangerous, effects on the body. Use only those recommended by your doctor.

◆ Alcoholic beverages. No one would put this in a baby's regular diet, but some do think it's fun to give a baby a sip – a dangerous game, because alcohol can be poisonous for a baby. Same goes for putting a drop on baby's gums during teething.

◆ Tap water that is contaminated with lead, PCBs or any other hazardous material. Check with your local water authority, or have your water tested privately if you suspect contamination

◆ Vitamin supplements, other than those designed for infants (and given as directed by your baby's doctor). Excessive vitamins can be particularly harmful to babies, whose bodies don't process them as quickly as do adult bodies.

---

day, grape the next, apricot the third and pear the fourth). Vary the protein foods, cereals and breads, and fruits and vegetables you serve, too. Though this won't always be easy – many young children fall into, and won't be coaxed from, food ruts – it's important to make the effort.

◆ Limit your baby's intake of animal fat (other than that in dairy products or formula), because the fat is where chemicals (antibiotics, pesticides and so on) are stored. Trim fats from meat; trim fat and skin from poultry. And keep portions of beef, pork and chicken small. When possible, choose dairy products that are labelled 'organic'; choose meat and poultry raised without chemicals or antibiotics.

◆ Follow the guidelines in the box above for fish safety.

◆ Once they have been introduced into baby's diet, feed foods that are believed to have protective effects against environmental toxins. These include cruciferous vegetables (broccoli, Brussels sprouts, cauliflower, cabbage), cooked dried peas and beans, foods rich in beta carotene (carrots, pumpkin, sweet potatoes, broccoli, cantaloupe), and those high in fibre (whole grains, fresh fruits and vegetables).

ORGANIC FOODS – GROWING AVAILABILITY

Organically grown foods have become increasingly widely available over the last decade, and are now sold in most supermarkets. But for many shoppers, it still isn't possible to fill their shopping trolleys with only the purest organic foods. Not enough of them are being produced, and what is available is often expensive.

As demand grows, so will supply. And as supply grows, the prices will continue to drop. Fortunately for young children and their parents, more and more jarred organic baby foods are already available. Everything a fledgling eater can desire can be found in an organic line, from beginner cereals and strained fruits, vegetables and meats, to combination main courses. Even organic formula is now available.

Buying organic, when you can find what you need and can afford the often higher prices, serves a couple of purposes. One, of course, is protecting your family from unwanted chemicals. The second purpose is to encourage supermarkets to stock organic products – from dairy products to meat to baked goods to produce. If organic foods are not available in your neighbourhood, ask your supermarket or produce store to carry them; consumer interest will help bring the supply up and the prices down. And, again, don't worry if you can't find or can't afford organic produce – just wash thoroughly and peel when possible.

In taking your precautions, don't forget to keep your perspective. Even by the gloomiest estimates, only a small percentage of cancers are caused by chemical contamination of foods. The risks to your child's health from tobacco, alcohol, poor diet, lack of immunization, or ignoring safety precautions in the car are considerably greater.

See, keeping your baby safe isn't so tough after all.

ARE YOUR BABY BOTTLES SAFE?

Bisphenol A (BPA), a chemical that may be toxic in humans, is found in many polycarbonate plastic products, including some baby bottles. While many experts believe that the levels of exposure through food packaging do not pose immediate health risks, some research suggests that BPA may linger in the body longer than previously thought. Consequently, many baby bottle companies are voluntarily avoiding the use of the chemical in their products. Research continues to examine the matter, and until it is conclusive, as a precaution use glass bottles or plastic bottles made without polycarbonate materials. Also avoid heating formula in polycarbonate plastic containers.

◆ ◆ ◆

The Sixth Month

Baby is personality plus these days – and it's a personality all his or her own. Socializing with mum, dad, and just about anyone who passes by the pushchair or sling is still high on baby's list of favourite activities, and you'll find the long sentences of babble, punctuated by giggles and coos, more and more scintillating. Games of peekaboo delight, as does shaking a rattle (or anything else that makes noise). The passion for exploration continues, and extends to your face, which baby will pull at as if it were a favourite toy (your glasses, earrings and hair aren't safe for now). At some point this month it'll be time to break out the bib and high chair (if you haven't already) for a first encounter with solids. *Bon appétit!*

What Your Baby May Be Doing

All babies reach milestones on their own developmental time line. If your baby seems not to have reached one or more of these milestones, rest assured, he or she probably will very soon. Your baby's rate of development is normal for your baby. Keep in mind, too, that skills babies perform from the tummy position can be mastered only if there's an opportunity to practise. So make sure your baby spends supervised playtime on his or her belly. If you have concerns about your baby's development (because you've noticed a missed milestone or what you think might be a developmental delay), don't hesitate to check it out with the doctor at the next well-baby visit – even if he or she doesn't bring it up. Parents often notice nuances in a baby's development that doctors don't. Premature infants generally reach milestones later than others of the same birth age, often achieving them closer to their adjusted age (the age they would be if they had been born at term), and sometimes later.

By six months, your baby . . . should be able to:

◆ keep head level with body when pulled to sitting

Some babies can pick up small and possibly dangerous objects with their fists – so be careful not to leave such things within reach.

- say 'ah-goo' or similar vowel-consonant combinations

. . . will probably be able to:

- bear some weight on legs when held upright
- sit without support
- turn in the direction of a voice
- razz (make a wet razzing sound)

. . . may possibly be able to:

- stand holding on to someone or something

- object if you try to take a toy away
- work to get a toy that's out of reach
- pass a cube or other object from one hand to the other
- look for dropped object
- rake with fingers a tiny object and pick it up in fist (keep all dangerous objects out of baby's reach)
- babble, combining vowels and consonants such as ga-ga-ga, ba-ba-ba, ma-ma-ma, da-da-da
- feed self cracker or other finger food

. . . may even be able to:

- creep or crawl[1]
- pull up to standing position from sitting
- get into a sitting position from stomach
- pick up tiny object with any part of thumb and finger (keep all dangerous objects out of baby's reach)
- say 'mama' or 'dada', indiscriminately

What You Can Expect at This Month's Checkup

Each practitioner will have a personal approach to well-baby checkups. The overall organization of the physical exam, as well as the number and type of assessment techniques used and procedures performed, will also vary with the individual needs of the child. But, in general, you can expect the following at a checkup when your baby is about six months old:

- Questions about how you and baby and the rest of the family are doing at

---

1. Babies who spend little time on their stomachs during playtime may reach this milestone later, and that's not cause for concern (see page 205).

home, and about baby's eating, sleeping and general progress, and about child care, if you are working.

♦ Measurement of baby's weight, length and head circumference, and plotting of progress since birth.

♦ Physical exam, including a recheck of any previous problems. Mouth will probably be checked now and at future visits for the arrival, or imminent arrival, of teeth.

♦ Developmental assessment. The examiner may rely on observation plus your reports on what baby is doing, or may actually put baby through a series of evaluation 'tests', such as head control when pulled to sitting; vision; hearing; ability to reach for and grasp objects, to rake at tiny objects, to roll over and bear some weight on legs; and social interaction and vocalization.

♦ Immunizations, if not given before and if baby is in good health and there are no other contraindications. The recommended schedule is given on page 227, but this can vary depending on the situation. Be sure to discuss any

reactions to previous immunizations beforehand.

♦ Possibly, a haemoglobin or haematocrit test to check for anaemia (usually by means of a pinprick on the finger), particularly for low-birthweight babies.

♦ Guidance about what to expect in the next month in relation to such topics as feeding, sleeping, development and safety.

Questions you may want to ask, if the doctor hasn't already answered them:

♦ How can you help baby to sleep through the night?

♦ What foods can be introduced to baby now?

Also raise concerns that have come up over the past month. Jot down information and instructions from the doctor. Record all pertinent information (baby's weight, length, head circumference, immunizations, illnesses, medications given, foods that can now be introduced, and so on) in a permanent health record.

Feeding Your Baby:
COMMERCIAL OR HOME-PREPARED BABY FOODS

Before commercial baby food found its way onto supermarket shelves, there was no other choice: feeding your baby meant making your own baby food. Today, parents can still opt to do it themselves (something that food processors and blenders have

made about as easy as pushing a pulse button), or select from the now vast variety of ready-to-feed foods.

Will the spoon you'll be piloting into baby's mouth be filled with jarred or heaped with homemade? The choice is yours.

FOOD FOR THOUGHT

Could the food that fills your baby's tummy also build his or her brain? That's the idea behind commercial baby foods that are enriched with DHA and ARA, brain-boosting fatty acids that are in breast milk and are added to some formulas. The source of the DHA depends on the manufacturer, so check the labels before you buy. All-vegetable is probably best for a young baby – fish oils cannot only contain ocean contaminants, but they can taste a little, well, fishy, and products made from enriched egg yolks aren't appropriate until eggs are introduced into baby's diet. How effective these foods are in increasing a child's brainpower is still being researched, but since such fatty acids are also heart-healthy, there's certainly no harm – and potentially plenty of benefits – in choosing them for your baby. The only downside: these foods, like the specially-fortified formulas, can be pricey.

Once baby's menu has expanded beyond baby food, you'll find many foods are enriched with DHA. Nature provides many sources, too (besides breastmilk), including salmon and other oily fish. DHA can also be made in the body from other fats, such as canola oil and the fats found in soybeans and linseed.

COMMERCIAL BABY FOOD

Convenience may come with a nutritional compromise in other parts of the supermarket (where ready-to-serve items are often overprocessed, oversugared and oversalted), but not in the baby food aisle. The convenience that was always a plus still is; foods come in ready-to-feed baby-portion jars, reclosable for refrigerated storage of leftovers. But today's baby foods come with other pluses as well. Most varieties contain no added salt; sugar and fillers are rarely added to single-ingredient foods. Since the fruits and vegetables are cooked and packed soon after picking, they retain a reliably high proportion of their nutrients. The foods are consistent in texture and taste, and because they're prepared under strictly sanitary conditions (conditions that would be difficult to duplicate in your home), you can trust their safety. They're also relatively economical, particularly if the time you save by using them is valuable to you, and when you consider that less food is likely to be wasted than when you prepare large batches of food for baby.

The advantages of using commercial baby foods are greatest in the early months of feeding solids. The strained varieties are the perfect consistency for beginners, and single-ingredient starter foods make it easy to screen for allergies. Although major manufacturers do offer graduated textures for use as babies are ready for them, many families dispense with commercially prepared foods as soon as their offspring are able to handle softly cooked, mashed, coarsely chopped or flaked foods from the family menu. That's because offering table foods earlier on – rather than sticking with baby foods – is more likely to produce a more amenable eater (in other words, one who eats what the rest of the family is eating). Even so, ready-to-eat foods for older babies and toddlers may continue to provide convenience when the family's on the road, visiting friends or eating out, or when the family menu's not appropriate or baby-friendly.

While most baby foods geared to beginning eaters are completely wholesome, it's always smart to check the label just to be sure (especially when baby graduates to 'toddler' foods, which may not be as reliably wholesome). Look out for ingredients your baby doesn't need, such as sugar or corn syrup, salt and modified food starch or other thickeners. Screen, too, for ingredients that your baby hasn't been introduced to yet, such as eggs (which can turn up in unlikely places). Keep in mind, also, that infants – whose taste buds are still unspoiled – are completely content with unsweetened cereals, fruits and other desserts; the sugar that's often added to such products is not only unnecessary, but can undermine a baby's taste for the more delicate flavour of natural sweetness. The same is true of foods that have salt added. Adults who are accustomed to foods that are heavily seasoned with these may find unsweetened, unsalted baby foods bland; babies, on the other hand, will find them just right.

Organic baby foods, once very expensive and not widely available, are now multiplying in the marketplace. Choose these when you can, but be reassured that commercial products – even those that aren't certified organic – are usually free of additives and pesticide residues.

HOME-PREPARED BABY FOODS

Not pressed for time? Feeling motivated? Like the idea of doing it yourself? While commercial baby foods are better than ever, preparing your baby's meals from scratch – some or all of the time – is a wonderful option. Just be sure to follow these guidelines:

◆ When introducing a new food, prepare and serve it without any added ingredients, including sugar, salt or other seasonings. If you're cooking for the whole family, remove baby's portion before adding these.

◆ Cook and serve baby's food without added fat.

◆ Steam, pressure-cook or waterless-cook vegetables, exposing them to a minimum of light, air, heat and water.

◆ To preserve vitamins, boil, microwave or bake potatoes in their skins, then peel after cooking.

◆ Don't cook in copper pots, as this may destroy vitamin C.

◆ Don't cook acidic foods (such as tomatoes, once they're introduced) in aluminium, since they can cause small quantities of aluminium to dissolve and be absorbed into the food.

◆ Don't add bicarbonate of soda; it may preserve colour, but it depletes vitamins and minerals.

◆ Soak dried legumes (peas or beans) overnight; or for a quicker method, boil them for two minutes, then let them stand for an hour, and cook in the soaking water.

◆ Follow the principles of safe food preparation in Feeding Baby Safely on page 326.

For the first several weeks of feeding solids, or at least until baby is seven months old, the food you serve should be finely puréed, and strained or sieved (though you can mash bananas and thin

ATTENTION DO-IT-YOURSELFERS

Feel like giving your food processor a workout? Preparing homemade baby foods is easier than ever. Turn to page 754 for recipe ideas.

with liquid). For convenience, you can prepare a batch of carrots, peas or other vegetables, then freeze in ice cube trays. Once they're frozen, keep individual cubes stored in airtight freezer bags.

Before using, thaw in the refrigerator, in a double boiler, in a microwave (at 'defrost', not 'cook', setting), or under cold water (still in the plastic bag) – not at room temperature.

What You May Be Concerned About

STILL NOT SLEEPING THROUGH THE NIGHT

'My baby's still getting up twice a night, and she won't go back to sleep without nursing. Will we ever get any sleep?'

Your baby will continue to awaken several times a night for the rest of her life, as we all do. But until she learns how to fall back to sleep on her own, neither you nor she will be able to get a good night's sleep.

Helping her to fall back to sleep – with a breast, a bottle, a dummy, rocking, patting, rubbing, singing, sleep tapes – will only postpone her learning how to do it herself. The moment will eventually come when it will no longer be practical or possible for you to be her sandman. If you make that moment now, not only will you get more sleep, so will she.

Before you begin, you'll need to take a close look at baby's sleep habits, including whether she's napping too much during the day. Another important first step will be weaning baby off all middle-of-the-night feedings (see page 254). If baby's been falling asleep at the breast or bottle, try to establish a bed-time routine that puts the bedtime feeding before the bath and other rituals. That way, you'll be able to put her in the cot awake, which will help her begin the process of learning how to fall asleep on her own.

Then you'll need to decide which approach you'll want to take to get your baby on the road to sleeping independence. Keep in mind that, as always, the same route won't work for every parent and every baby. Read about them all before you decide which is more likely to lead to a better night's sleep for your family. Then stay flexible; if the method you opt for doesn't end up working for you and your baby (once you've given it a fair shot), you'll need to move on to Plan B.

Cold turkey. For those parents desperate and determined to get that good night's sleep sooner rather than later, letting a baby cry it out almost always works. Though some recommend utilizing this method as early as three months, it's best to wait until baby's closer to six months. By that point, most babies no longer require night-time nutrition breaks – unless they were born prematurely and are still catching up. And while a younger infant cries to communicate basic needs, older babies are becoming more sophisticated in their motivations. As long as crying results in being picked up, rocked, fed, they'll keep it up. When they find it no longer works, most will give up on night-time crying, usually within three or four nights. (See below for ways of making the crying easier to cope with for you.)

If you're philosophically opposed to this approach, don't try it. Parenting that goes against parental instincts is rarely successful. Instead, provide your baby with a back-to-sleep crutch, such as sleep-inducing music, a dummy, a nursing – or anything else you choose – for as long as necessary, or move on to the plan below.

Gradual withdrawal. If you're uncomfortable with cold-turkey tactics, there are other 'conditioning' methods that work in much the same way but allow you and your baby to move more slowly. Here's a sampling of different approaches:

♦ 'Ferberizing', named for Dr Richard Ferber, the author of *Solving Your Child's Sleep Problems*, works like this: the first night, put your baby down awake, provide a gentle pat and a whispered 'Good night. I love you', and then leave the room. Don't stay with her long enough for her to fall asleep, and don't pick her up. If she begins to cry, as she almost certainly will, let her cry for five minutes, then go back in and pat and reassure her again. (If mum is associated with feedings, it may be better for dad to provide this soothing.) Repeat this as long as she cries, stretching the periods you leave her alone by five minutes or so each time, until she falls asleep. Extend the periods she spends by herself by a few more minutes each night.

The crying will be somewhat easier to tolerate if you block some of it out. Try earplugs, the white-noise whir of a fan, background Muzak, low-volume TV or radio, or anything else that can take the edge off the crying without blocking it out entirely. If you have an intercom to baby's room, lower the volume so the crying won't be such an earful. If at any time your baby's crying changes, however, do check to be sure she hasn't pulled herself up and become stranded, unable to get down or has got into some other kind of trouble. If she does have a problem, make her comfortable again, give her a loving pat and a few gentle words, and leave.

Generally, the period of crying diminishes nightly over three nights. And somewhere between the fourth and seventh night – if you're lucky, and most parents will be – you may hear just a little fussing or a few minutes of crying (don't go in) and then blessed silence.

Another variation on the same concept, which works better for some older babies and is more comfortable

IT'S ALL IN THE TIMING

One major change or stress in your baby's life at a time is plenty. If your baby's already dealing with one such disruption – whether it's teething, mum going back to work, a new baby-sitter, or a bout with an ear infection – wait until he or she is feeling settled again before launching any sleep-through-the-night campaigns. It makes sense to wait, also, if you're planning a family trip in the near future (travel is almost certain to derail your efforts). Keep in mind that even babies who have mastered sleeping through the night may begin waking anew during times of change or stress (it would be smart to offer comfort again only for as long as the issue continues, otherwise baby will continue waking long after it has ended). Night waking may also start up again when a baby has just passed a major developmental milestone – such as learning to crawl or walk – since baby's compulsion to practise the new skill may interfere temporarily with sleep.

WHAT WILL THE NEIGHBOURS THINK?

It's hard enough for you to listen to your baby crying in the middle of the night – but what about the neighbours? If you live in an apartment or otherwise in earshot of the folks next door, letting your baby cry for any amount of time during the night may seem decidedly unneighbourly. Here's how to make a sleeper out of your baby without making enemies out of your neighbours:

◆ Give fair warning. Let your neighbours know what's in store ahead of time (rather than at 3 AM, when they call to complain). Tell them your plan (to teach baby how to sleep through the night by letting her cry for short periods each night) and how long you think it will take (hopefully, not more than a week).

◆ Apologize in advance (and if that doesn't work, buy their forgiveness). Chances are, they won't be thrilled at the prospect of broken sleep (after all, broken sleep comes with your territory as new parents – not theirs). Neighbours who have children of their own (and have done their own share of walking the floor with sobbing infants) may be empathetic – and may even offer some coping suggestions. Childless neighbours may be less

understanding. Apologies may be accepted more graciously if accompanied by a small disturbing-the-peace offering (a bottle of wine, a basket of fruit and cheese, a box of imported truffles – or, in tough cases, all three). If your neighbours have a sense of humour (which they hopefully do), you might offer up a set of earplugs or a pair of earmuffs.

◆ Close the windows. Make sure baby's cries can't travel out an open window and down the street.

◆ Take some muffling measures. Hang blankets on the wall in baby's room, or over any windows that are adjacent to the neighbour's. If possible, put baby's cot in a carpeted room (which will offer better sound insulation than a room with bare floors).

◆ Don't feel too bad. Some amount of noise comes with apartment living – chances are you've put up with your share of yapping dogs, slamming doors, midnight footsteps, blaring music, and crack-of-dawn vacuum cleaners. A good neighbour (hopefully the kind you have) will be just as tolerant of your crying baby.

for some parents, is to reassure your baby from a chair near her cot until she falls asleep each evening (again, without picking her up). Move the chair a little farther away each night, until you're at the doorway. Finally, move out the door – at which point, baby should be able to fall asleep without you present. Keep in mind, however, that for some babies, parents won't be out of mind unless they're out of sight; in that case, this approach will definitely not work.

◆ A programme called 'systematic awakening' may work as well as 'Ferberizing', though perhaps a bit more slowly, and allows you to skip the potentially long bouts of crying. Keep a diary of your baby's night-time awakenings for a week so you will have an idea of the usual times. Then, set your alarm clock for about half an hour before you expect the first howl. At the alarm, get up, wake the baby and proceed with what you usually do when the waking is spontaneous

SLEEP SHARING

Don't feel the need to push the independent sleep agenda at this early age? Dislike the idea of letting your baby cry or of trying to manipulate her natural sleep patterns? Prefer to be there for your baby whenever he or she wakes, rather than having to drag yourself out of bed to dispense comfort? Believe that happiness (in the middle of the night) is a warm baby? Then co-sleeping may be for you.

Sharing a bed with your baby doesn't mean that you're giving up on the idea of independent sleeping entirely (all kids eventually learn to sleep on their own, and some do so voluntarily by the time they're three, just that you're shelving it until you and baby feel ready to tackle it. Fans of bed sharing say that babies who sleep with their parents have positive feelings about sleep (though those who don't bed-share can also have these feelings). The presence of parents – their touch, smell and sound –

gives babies a reassuring message that falling asleep or resettling back into deep sleep after awaking from a light sleep is safe. When the time comes for them to move into their own beds, they're not fearful of sleep or of the dark (though some may ultimately have difficulty weaning themselves off the company).

Co-sleeping, part of the attachment parenting philosophy, also encourages night-time nursing for as long as baby requests it, which can be well into toddlerhood or even the preschool years. (Do keep in mind, though, that frequent night feedings, once teeth appear, can contribute to tooth decay.) It's also important – for the sake of family harmony – that both parents are onboard with co-sleeping; otherwise a baby can literally come between you. Be sure that any co-sleeping you do is done with safety in mind; see page 261.

(change, feed, rock, or whatever). Anticipate each usual waking in the same way. Gradually expand the time between these systematic wakings and then begin to eliminate them. Within a few weeks, according to proponents of this programme, you should be able to begin phasing them out entirely.

◆ The method of reinforcing sleep rhythms involves never letting your baby become overtired. Being exhausted is the root of all sleep problems, according to this view. If you anticipate your infant's natural sleepiness (both at naptime and bedtime) and put her down accordingly (in the cot – not in the pushchair on the run), your baby will fall asleep easily (because she'll be tired, but not overtired) and will sleep well.

Sleep begets sleep, and as long as you never wake your sleepy baby (over four months), even during naptime, your baby will sleep well through the night. If there are night wakings, briefly respond to your baby to provide reassurance, but let her fall asleep on her own.

◆ Wean baby off bedtime sleep aids, so middle-of-the-night wake-ups won't be so challenging to her. This approach (which has been referred to as 'kinder, gentler Ferberizing') calls for helping baby kick those parent-assisted habits (that bottle, that breast, that twenty-minute rocking) that have helped her to fall asleep up until now. While some babies can drift off at the bottle or breast or in mum's or dad's arms at naptime and bedtime and still manage to go back to sleep without these aids in the middle of the night, others can't. If your child is one of these, you will have to change her going-to-bed patterns. Give feedings well before an intended nap or bedtime and then, later, when she seems sleepy, put her into her cot drowsy but awake – after a relaxing bedtime routine. Most babies will have trouble getting to sleep this way at first, but almost all will succeed after a few chances to learn self-soothing techniques. As long as your child is falling asleep on her own, it's okay to respond to her during night wakings, but not by picking her up or feeding her. Your voice and presence, plus perhaps a rub, should reassure your child to the point of calm, but not sleep. Leave your baby so that she can actually fall asleep on her own, a skill that will come in handy in the wee hours.

Whichever getting-baby-to-sleep-through-the-night method you choose, remember that they all share two very important rules: be consistent with the method, and give it a chance to work. If you don't stick with it long enough to see a difference, you'll never know whether the failure lies with the method or your follow-through. Use each technique faithfully for a solid two weeks before you give up on it. Skip from method to method, or enforce the method of choice only sporadically, and your baby's confusion will only compound her sleep issues.

Another point to keep in mind as nightfall approaches: even if you're opposed to letting your baby cry herself to sleep, you shouldn't make a habit of leaping to her side at her first whimper. Doing so may actually wake her up. Babies often cry out during light sleep, and sometimes fall back into a deep sleep without any help. Or they wake momentarily before settling themselves

back down on their own. Some babies always cry for a few minutes before falling asleep (as a means of self-comfort) and also when waking at night. Unless your baby's launched into full-fledged screaming, wait a few minutes to see if the whimpers subside before going in to offer comfort.

EARLY RISING

'At first we were grateful that our son was sleeping through the night. But with him waking up like clockwork at five every morning, we almost wish he'd wake up in the middle of the night instead.'

With a night waker, at least there's the promise of another few hours of sleep once baby beds down again. But with a baby who greets his parents alert and energetic, ready and eager to start every day when even the cockerels are still snoozing, there's no hope of further rest until night falls once more. And yet this rude awakening is faced daily by countless parents.

It probably isn't realistic to expect your early riser to sleep in past six or seven (at least not until he's a teenager, at which point you'll probably have to drag him out of bed each morning just to get him to school on time). But it may be possible to reset your little alarm clock at least a bit later:

Keep out the dawn's early light. Some babies (like some adults) are particularly sensitive to light when they're sleeping. Especially when the days are longer, keeping baby's room dark can buy a little extra sleep for everyone. Invest in room-darkening shades or lined curtains, to prevent the dawn's early light from waking baby.

Keep the traffic out. If your baby's window faces a street that carries a lot of traffic in the early morning hours, the noise could be waking him prematurely. Try keeping his window closed, hanging a heavy blanket or curtains at the window to help muffle sound, or moving him, if possible, to an off-street room. Or use a fan or a white-noise machine to drown out street noises.

Keep baby up later at night. Early to bed often means early to rise. So try putting your baby to bed ten minutes later each night, until you've gradually postponed his bedtime an hour or more. To make this work, it will probably help to move his naps and meals forward simultaneously and at the same pace.

Keep baby up later during the day. Some early risers are ready to go back to sleep in an hour or two. Early naps lead to early bedtime, which inevitably continues the cycle of early waking. To break the cycle, postpone baby's return to the cot by ten minutes more each morning until he's napping an hour or so later, which may eventually help him to extend his night's sleep.

Keep daytime sleeping down. A baby needs only so much total sleep – an average of fourteen and a half hours at this age, with wide variations in individual babies. Maybe yours is getting too much sleep during the day and thus needs less at night. Limit daytime naps, cutting one out or shortening all of them. But don't cut out so much daytime sleep that your baby's actually overtired (and less likely to sleep well) by bedtime.

Keep him waiting. Don't rush to greet him at the first call from the cot. Wait five minutes first. If you're lucky, he may cuddle up and go back to sleep, or at least amuse himself while you catch a few more moments of rest.

Have entertainment standing by. If keeping the room dark doesn't help, try letting a little light seep through so that he can play while he waits for you. An activity centre and/or a cot mirror can keep him busy for a few minutes. If you leave any toys in his cot, make sure they're safe for him to be left alone with (no plushes, no sharp edges, no small pieces).

Keep him waiting for breakfast. If he's used to eating at five-thirty, hunger will regularly come to call at that time. Even if you're getting up with him then, don't feed him right away. Gradually postpone breakfast, so that he's less likely to wake up early for it.

All these efforts may, unfortunately, be fairly futile. Some babies just need less total sleep; some are early-morning people from early on. If yours turns out to be one of these, you may have no choice but to rise and shine early until he's old enough to get up and make his own breakfast. Until then, turning in earlier yourselves, and sharing the predawn burden by taking turns getting up with your baby (this will work only if mummy's presence isn't required for nursing), may be your best survival technique.

TURNING OVER DURING THE NIGHT

'I always put my baby on her back to sleep. But now that she knows how to roll over, she flips over and sleeps on her stomach. I'm worried about the risk of SIDS.'

Once babies learn to flip, there's just no keeping them on their backs if they prefer their bellies. And not only is there no point in trying to keep your baby on her belly, there's no point in worrying if you can't. Experts agree that a baby who is able to change positions easily is at a significantly decreased risk for SIDS. That's for two reasons: one, because the high-risk period for SIDS is generally passed by the time a baby can turn over; two, because a baby who can flip is better equipped to protect herself from whatever it is about tummy sleeping that increases SIDS risk.

You can – and according to experts, you should – keep putting your baby to bed on her back until her first birthday. But don't lose any sleep over her position if it changes during the night. Be sure, however, that her cot is safe; continue to follow the tips for preventing SIDS on page 257, such as using only a firm mattress and avoiding pillows, blankets, duvets, and plush toys.

BATHING IN THE BIG TUB

'Our baby is far too big now for his baby bath. But I'm terrified of washing him in our bath – and he seems to be, too. The one time I tried it, he screamed so much, I had to take him out. How am I supposed to bathe him?'

Taking the plunge into the family bath may seem a frightening prospect for both baby and you; he is, after all, still such a little – and slippery – fish for such a big pond. But if care is taken both to prevent accidents (see box, next page) and to alleviate baby's fears, the big bath can turn into a veritable water wonderland for the five- or six-month-old, and bathtime into a favourite (if wet) family ritual. To ensure a happy water baby, see the basic tips on bath bathing in the Baby Care Primer, page 127, and try the following:

Let your baby test the waters in a familiar boat. For a few nights before he graduates from it, bathe him in his baby bath placed in the empty grownup bath. This way the new bath won't seem quite so formidable when it's filled with water – and him.

Take a dry run. If he's willing, put him in the bath (on a large bath towel or a bath seat to minimize slipping) without water and with a pile of toys. That way he can become accustomed to the scenery while it's dry – and hopefully discover how much fun the bath can be. If the room is nice and warm and he's a baby who's comfortable being naked, let him play in there undressed. Otherwise, keep his clothes on. As in any bath situation, don't leave his side for a moment.

Use a stand-in. While someone else holds baby, give a demonstration bath to a washable doll or stuffed animal in the bath, with a comforting running commentary each step of the way. Make it look as if everybody involved is having a good time.

Avoid the big chill. Babies dislike being cold, and if they associate being chilled with being bathed, they may rebel against bathing. So be sure that the bathroom is comfortably warm. If your bathroom isn't adequately heated, you might want to warm the room by running a hot shower first. Don't remove baby's clothes until the bath is filled and you are ready to slip him into it. Have a large, soft towel, preferably with a hood, ready to wrap him in as soon as you lift him from the water. Dry baby thoroughly, being sure to get into the creases, before unwrapping and dressing him.

Keep entertainment on hand. Make the bath a floating playground for your baby so that he'll be diverted while you take care of bathing business. Specially designed bath toys (particularly those that bob atop the water) and plastic books are great, but so are plastic

SAFE BIG-BATH BATHING

To make sure bath by time is not only fun but safe, follow these important tips.

Wait until baby's a sitting duck. You'll both be more comfortable with big-bath bathing if your baby's capable of sitting alone, or with only minimal support.

Take a safe seat. A wet baby is a slippery baby, and even a solid sitter can take a slide in the bath. And though a momentary slip under the water wouldn't be physically harmful, it could generate a long term fear of baths. (Of course, if he slips and you're not there, the consequences could be much more serious.)

A bath seat can provide an alternative to the old one-hand-on-baby-at-all-times manoeuvre, but many experts feel they don't keep baby safe enough. If you do choose to use a bath seat, be sure the one you use comes with rubber suction cups that attach it securely to the bottom of the bath (but do not use it if your bath has a textured or non-skid bottom). Never use the seat as a substitute for your complete and constant supervision. Some seats have foam pads to place under baby so he or she won't slide around during bath time. If yours doesn't, put a clean flannel or small towel under baby's bottom to achieve the same effect. Rinse, squeeze and hang the cloth to dry, or use a fresh one each bath time to prevent germs. If the seat has a foam pad, dry it in the dryer between uses for the same reason. If you're not using a bath seat, be sure the bath bottom is lined with a rubber bath mat or skidproof stick-ons to prevent slipping.

Be prepared. Towel, flannel, soap, shampoo, bath toys, and anything else you'll need for baby's bath should be on hand *before* you put baby in the bath. If you do forget something and you have to get it yourself, *bundle baby in a towel and take him or her with you.* Also prepare by removing everything from tubside that's potentially dangerous in baby's curious hands, such as soap, razors and shampoo.

Be there. Your baby needs adult supervision every moment of every bath – and will continue to for the first five years of bathing. *Never leave him in the bath unattended,* even in a baby seat (he or she could slip out or climb out), even for a second. Keep this startling statistic in mind when the phone or doorbell rings, a pot boils over on the stove, or anything else threatens to take your attention away from your baby: half of all accidental infant drownings take place in the bath.

Do the elbow test. Your hands are much more tolerant of heat than a baby's sensitive skin. Test the water with your elbow or wrist or a bath thermometer before dunking baby. While it should be comfortably warm, it should not be hot. Turn the hot water tap off first, so that any drips from the tap will be cold and baby won't be scalded. Setting the hot water tank at 49°C (120°F) or below will also prevent scalds. A safety cover on the bath spout will protect baby from burns and bumps.

containers of all shapes and sizes. To avoid mildew buildup on bath toys, towel off after use and store in a dry container or a mesh bag. Clean water-retaining bath toys at least once a week with a mixture of one part chlorine bleach to fifteen parts water (be sure to rinse well) to reduce any buildup of bacteria that can cause infections.

Let baby make a splash. But don't make one yourself. For most babies, splashing is a large part of bathtime fun, and the wetter a baby can make you, the happier he'll be. But while he almost certainly will like to make a splash, he may not like to be the target of one. Many a baby has been turned off to the bath with a single playful splash.

Use the buddy system. Some babies are more amenable to a bath if they've got company. Try bathing with your baby, but at bath temperatures geared to his comfort. Once he becomes adjusted to these duet baths, you can try him solo.

No swimming after eating. Whether your mother's ubiquitous summer chant was medically sound is debatable. But it may make sense not to bathe your baby directly after meals, because the increase in handling and activity could cause spitting up.

Don't pull the plug until baby is out of the bath. Not only can it be a physically chilling experience to be in an emptying bath, it can be a psychologically chilling one, too. The gurgling sound can frighten even a young infant, and an older baby or toddler who sees the water rushing down the drain may fear that he's going down next.

Be patient. Eventually, your baby will take to the bath. But he'll do it faster if he's allowed to do it at his own pace, and without parental pressure.

BOTTLE REJECTION IN A BREASTFED BABY

'I'd like to give my baby an occasional bottle of expressed milk to free me up a little, but she refuses to drink it. What can I do?'

Your baby wasn't born yesterday. And unlike a relative newcomer, she's developed a strong sense of what she wants, what she doesn't want, and how she can best go about getting things her way. What she wants: your nice, soft, warm breasts. What she doesn't want: a fabricated rubber or plastic teat. How she can best go about getting things her way: crying for the former, and rejecting the latter.

Waiting this long to introduce a bottle into your baby's life has turned the odds against you; the introduction is better made no later than six weeks (see page 213). But it's still possible that you'll be able to win her over by following these tips:

Feed her on an empty stomach. Many babies will be more receptive to the bottle as a source of nourishment when they're in the market for something nourishing. So try offering the bottle when your baby is really hungry.

Or feed her on a full stomach. With some babies, offering a bottle when they are looking for a breast makes them feel hostile towards the impostor and perhaps a little betrayed by the bottle giver. If this is the case with your baby (and you'll find out only through trial and rejection), don't offer the bottle when she's at her hungriest; instead, offer it casually between nursings. She may be more in the mood to experiment and be ready for a snack.

Feign indifference. Instead of acting as though there's a lot at stake (even if there is), act as if the bottle issue is no biggie, no matter what her response.

Let her play before she eats. Before attempting to get down to business with the bottle, get her hands on it. If she's had a chance to explore it on her own, she may be more likely to let it into her life and, hopefully, into her mouth. She may even put it there herself – as she does everything else.

Banish your breast. And the rest of you, when the bottle is launched. A breastfed baby is more likely to accept a bottle given by father, grandma or another care provider when mother is well out of smelling distance. At least until bottle feeding is well established, even the sound of your voice may spoil baby's appetite for a bottle.

Try a favourite fluid. It's possible that baby's objecting not to the bottle, but the fluid inside it. Some infants will take to a bottle better if it's filled with familiar breast milk, but others, reminded of breast milk's original source, are more comfortable with another drink. Try formula or diluted apple or white grape juice instead.

Sneak it in during sleep. Have your bottle giver pick up your sleeping baby and try to offer the bottle then. In a few weeks the bottle may be accepted awake.

Know when to surrender – temporarily. Don't let the bottle become the object of a battle, or your side doesn't stand a chance of winning. As soon as your baby raises objections to the bottle, take it away and try again another day. Perseverance – while retaining your nonchalant attitude – may be all that's necessary. Try the bottle once every few days for at least a couple of weeks before you consider admitting defeat.

Should defeat become a reality, however, don't give up hope. There's another alternative to your breasts: the cup. Most babies can master a cup, even at five or six months, and happily take supplementary feedings from it (see page 324); many become proficient enough cup drinkers by the end of the first year (sometimes as early as eight or nine months) to be weaned directly from the breast to the cup – which saves their parents the extra step of weaning from the bottle.

CHANGES IN BOWEL MOVEMENTS

'Since I started my breastfed baby on solids last week, his bowel movements have been more solid – which I would expect – but they are also darker and smellier. Is this normal?'

Alas, the time when everything that passed through your baby came out sweet and innocent is past. For the parent of a breastfeeding baby, the change from soft, mustardy, non-offensive stools to thick, dark, smelly ones can be something of a shock. But, though the change may not be aesthetically pleasing, it is normal. Expect your baby's stools to become increasingly adult-like as his diet does – though a breastfed baby's may remain somewhat softer than a bottle-fed's up until weaning.

'I just gave my baby carrots for the first time, and his next bowel movement was bright orange.'

What goes in must come out. And in babies, with their immature digestive systems, it sometimes doesn't change very much in the process. Once they start solids, stools seem to vary movement to movement, often reflecting the most recent meal in colour or texture. Later, foods not chewed thoroughly – especially those that are harder to digest – may come out whole or nearly so. As long as bowel movements don't also contain mucus and aren't unusually loose, which might signal gastrointestinal irritation (and the need to

BABY'S FIRST TOOTHBRUSH

When it comes to choosing a toothbrush for your baby, looks aren't everything – though favourite characters and bright colours are always a plus. Quality counts, too. Bristles should be soft so they don't injure tender gums; once they become rough around the edges (which will happen pretty quickly if baby likes to chomp down on them), it's time for a change. Even a toothbrush that still looks new should be changed after two to four months; that's because, over time, bacteria from the mouth accumulate on the brush.

withhold the offending food for a few weeks), you can continue his newly varied diet without concern.

BRUSHING BABY'S TEETH

'My daughter just got her first tooth. The doctor said I should start brushing it now, but that seems silly.'

Those tiny pearls that bring so much pain before they arrive and so much excitement when they first break through the gums are destined for extinction. They can all be expected to fall out during the early and mid school years, to be replaced by permanent teeth. So why take good care of them now?

There are several reasons: first of all, since they hold a place for the permanent teeth, decay and loss of these first teeth can deform the mouth permanently. Then, too, your baby will need these primary teeth for biting and chewing for many years; bad teeth could

interfere with good nutrition. And healthy teeth are also important for the development of normal speech and appearance – both important to a child's self-confidence. The child who can't speak clearly because of faulty teeth, or who keeps her mouth shut to hide decayed or missing teeth, doesn't feel good about herself. Finally, if you start your child brushing early, good dental habits are likely to be second nature by the time that second set of teeth comes in.

The first teeth can be wiped with a clean damp gauze pad, flannel or disposable finger brush designed for the purpose, or brushed with a very soft, tiny infant toothbrush (with no more than three rows of bristles) moistened with water. A dentist (you'll need to secure one for your baby soon anyway) or a pharmacist can recommend a brush and help you locate the finger brushes. Wiping will probably do a more thorough job until the molars come in, but brushing will get baby into an important habit she'll need for a lifetime of good dental hygiene, so a combination of the two is probably best. Wipe or brush after meals and at bedtime. But be gentle – baby teeth are soft. Lightly brush or wipe the tongue, too, since it harbours germs (but brush only the front of the tongue; going too far back can trigger gagging).

No toothpaste is necessary for baby's teeth, though you can flavour the brush with a tiny bit of toothpaste (use one that's formulated for infants and toddlers and that doesn't contain fluoride) if it makes her more interested in brushing. If you're using fluoridated toothpaste, add only a pea-size dab to the brush. Many babies love the taste of toothpaste, and since they swallow instead of spitting it out once the brushing's done, they could end up taking in too much fluoride.

Most older babies and toddlers are eager to 'do it themselves'. Once she has the dexterity, which won't be for many months yet, you can let your baby brush on her own after meals, adding a more thorough cleaning with a gauze pad or finger brush yourself as part of the bedtime ritual. Also let her watch you care for your own teeth. If mummy and daddy set a good dental-care example, she's more likely to be a more conscientious brusher and, later, flosser.

Though brushing and flossing will continue to be important throughout your baby's life, proper nutrition will have equal impact on her dental health, starting now (actually, it started before she was born). Ensuring the adequate intake of calcium, phosphorus, fluoride and other minerals and vitamins (particularly vitamin C, which helps to maintain the health of gums) and limiting foods high in refined sugars (including commercial teething biscuits) or sticky natural sugar (such as dried fruit, even raisins) can help prevent the miseries that accompany a mouthful of cavities and bleeding gums. Ideally, limit sweets (even healthy ones) to once or twice a day, since the more sugar intake is spread out over the day, the greater the risk to the teeth. Serve them with meals, when they do less damage to the teeth, rather than between meals. Or brush baby's teeth right after the sweets are eaten.

When your baby does have sweets or snacks high in carbohydrates between meals and a brush isn't available, follow them with a piece of cheese (such as Gruyère or Cheddar, once introduced), which seems to be able to block the action of tooth-decaying acids produced by the bacteria in plaque. For further tooth insurance, get your baby used to drinking juice only from a cup now (serve it watered down and only with meals and snacks, not in between),

and never let her go to sleep with a bottle. Limit sippy cup use, too (see page 324).

In addition to good home care and good nutrition, your baby will need good professional dental care to ensure healthy teeth in healthy gums. Now, before an emergency arises, ask your baby's doctor to recommend a reliable paediatric dentist or a general dentist who treats a lot of children and is good with them. If you have a question about your baby's teeth, call or make an appointment as soon as it comes up.

The first routine checkup should take place between the first and second birthday (between age six months and one year for infants at high risk for tooth decay – such as those babies who habitually fall asleep with a bottle of juice or formula, who do a lot of nighttime or naptime nipping, or who spend much of the day with a bottle in their mouths). The earlier the dental visit, the better the chance of preventing dental problems (and dentist-office phobias common in older toddlers visiting a dentist for the first time). Widely spaced teeth, which usually move closer later, are rarely a cause for early intervention.

BABY-BOTTLE MOUTH

'I have a friend whose baby's front teeth had to be pulled because of baby-bottle mouth. How can I prevent this from happening to my little boy?'

There's nothing cuter than a six-year-old whose grin reveals a charming space where his two front teeth used to be. But losing teeth to baby-bottle mouth – long before they're scheduled to fall out – isn't as cute.

Fortunately, baby-bottle mouth is completely preventable. It occurs most often in the first two years of life, when teeth are most vulnerable, and most frequently as a result of a baby's falling asleep regularly with a bottle (or breast) in his mouth. The sugars in whatever beverage he's imbibing (breast milk, formula, fruit juice, cow's milk or sugar drinks) combine with bacteria in his mouth to decay the teeth. The dirty work is abetted during sleep when the production of saliva, which ordinarily dilutes food and drink and promotes the swallowing reflex, slows dramatically. With little swallowing occurring, the last sips baby takes before falling asleep pool in his mouth and remain in contact with his teeth for hours.

To avoid baby-bottle mouth:

♦ Never give glucose (sugar) water, even before baby's teeth come in, so that he won't become accustomed to the sweet taste. The same applies to such sugary drinks as cranberry juice cocktail, fruit punches, fruit drinks, or fruit-juice drinks. Dilute even 100 per cent fruit juices with water. If possible, serve juice only in a cup; that way, baby won't get into the juice bottle habit at all.

♦ Once your baby's teeth come in, don't put him to bed for the night or down for a nap with a bottle of formula, breast milk or juice. An occasional lapse won't cause a problem, but repeated lapses will. If you must give him a bottle to take to bed, make it a bottle of plain water, which will not harm the teeth (and if it's fluoridated, will help strengthen them).

♦ Don't let your baby use a bottle of milk or juice as a dummy, to crawl or lie around with and suck on at will. All-day nipping can be as harmful to the teeth as night-time sucking. Bottles should be considered part of a meal or snack and like these should

routinely be given in the appropriate setting (your arms, a baby seat, a high chair or other feeding chair) and at appropriate times. The same rules should apply to sippy cups (see page 324).

♦ Don't allow a baby who sleeps in your bed to remain at your breast all night, nursing on and off throughout the evening. Breast milk can cause decay as well if the milk is allowed to pool in baby's mouth, as it could during constant night nursing.

♦ Eliminate the bottle at twelve months.

WEANING TO COW'S MILK

'I'm breastfeeding, and want to wean my baby. I don't want to start with formula – can I give him cow's milk?'

Cow's milk shouldn't be served up until the first birthday. Experts recommend that when possible, breastfeeding should continue for at least the first year (and then as long as mutually desirable). When that isn't possible, an iron-fortified infant formula should be the beverage of choice for a baby. (See page 99 for the many reasons why.) Though there are formulas on the market specifically designed for older babies, many doctors don't feel they're necessary. Check with your baby's doctor before deciding which formula to wean to.

When you switch to cow's milk at a year, be sure you use whole milk, rather than skimmed or semi-skimmed. Whole milk is usually recommended until age two, though some doctors okay using semi-skimmed milk after eighteen months.

SALT INTAKE

'I'm pretty careful about how much salt my husband and I get. But how careful do I have to be about the salt in my daughter's diet?'

Infants, like all of us, do need some salt. But also like the rest of us, they don't need a lot of it. In fact, their kidneys can't handle large amounts of sodium, which is probably why Mother Nature made breast milk a very low-sodium drink (with only 5 milligrams of sodium per 250 ml (8 fl oz), as compared to 120 milligrams per 250 ml (8 fl oz), of cow's milk). And there is some evidence that too much salt too soon, especially when there is a family history of hypertension, can set the stage for high blood pressure in adulthood. A high-sodium diet early in life can also nurture a lifelong taste for the salty stuff.

Because too much sodium isn't good for babies, major manufacturers have eliminated salt from their baby food recipes. Parents who prepare their own baby foods should do likewise. Don't assume that runner beans or mashed potatoes won't appeal to your child unless they've been sprinkled with salt just because you like them that way. Give her taste buds a chance to learn what foods taste like unsalted, and she'll develop a healthy preference that'll last a lifetime.

To be sure that your baby doesn't pick up the high-salt habit and to help the rest of the family reduce salt intake, read labels routinely. You'll find large amounts of sodium in the most unlikely products, including breads and breakfast cereals, cakes and biscuits. Since a baby between the ages of six months and one year requires no more than 250 to 750 milligrams of sodium a day, foods that contain 300 or more milligrams per serving will quickly push the intake over this level. When buying for baby, opt for foods with under 50 milligrams per serving most of the time.

CEREAL SNUBBING

'We started our baby on rice cereal, the way you're supposed to, but he didn't seem to like it. So we moved on to vegetables and fruits – which he laps up. Does he need to eat cereal?'

It's not the cereal that babies need, it's the iron it's fortified with. For the formula-fed set, cereal snubbing isn't an issue, since these babies fill their requirement for this vital mineral every time they drink a bottle. Nursing babies, however, need another source of iron once they've reached the six-month mark. Fortunately, while fortified baby cereals are a very popular alternative source of iron (at least, among the majority of beginning eaters and their parents), they're not the only one. Breastfed cereal spurners can easily fill their requirement with an iron supplement. Ask the doctor for a recommendation.

NO MEAT? NO PROBLEM

Got milk, other dairy products and eggs in your vegetarian diet? Then ensuring good nutrition for your baby should be a piece of (cheese) cake. Calcium's certainly not an issue; dairy products have that covered (while also providing plenty of vitamins A, B_{12} and D). Protein's not a problem; dairy products do the trick there, too. (Pesco-vegetarians, those who eat fish but not meat, will have an even easier time on the protein front.) Egg yolks, once they're allowed, offer additional protein, as well as iron; using DHA-rich eggs will serve up essential omega-3 fatty acids, along with their many benefits.

And before you close the pantry door on all cereal, you might want to try offering baby another variety – barley, perhaps, or oat. It's possible that his more adventurous taste buds naturally prefer a slightly stronger taste (rice is definitely the blandest of the bunch). Or consider mixing a small amount of cereal with one of the fruits he enjoys (while that's not recommended for babies who already like their cereal 'straight up', there's no harm in trying such a combo on a baby who has embraced fruit but rejected cereal.)

VEGAN DIET

'We're strict vegans and plan to raise our daughter the same way. Can our diet provide enough nutrition for her?'

What's good for the vegan goose and gander can be good for their gosling, too. Millions of parents who shun animal products raise perfectly healthy offspring without putting milk, meat or fish on the family table. And in the long run, a vegan lifestyle can have positive health benefits – reducing the risk of heart disease, cancer, and other illnesses linked to a high-fat, low-fibre, meat-heavy diet. Still, there are potential pitfalls to feeding a vegan diet to a child; to avoid these, take these precautions:

♦ Breastfeed your baby. Continuing to breastfeed for at least a year, if possible, will ensure that your infant will get all the nutrients she needs for the first six months and most of what she needs for the first year – assuming you're getting all the nutrients you need (including folic acid and vitamin B_{12} in a supplement) to produce high-quality breast milk.

If you can't breastfeed, be certain that the soya formula you choose is one recommended by your baby's doctor.

♦ Supplement, if needed. Discuss with your baby's doctor whether your breastfed baby should be receiving an infant vitamin-mineral supplement that contains iron, vitamin D, folic acid and vitamin B_{12} (found only in animal products). (See page 168 for more on vitamin supplements.) A supplement will definitely be necessary when your baby is weaned from formula or breast milk.

♦ Be selective. Serve only whole-grain cereals and breads once your baby has graduated from beginner baby cereals. These will provide more of the vitamins, minerals and protein ordinarily obtained from animal products than would their refined-white-flour counterparts.

♦ Turn to tofu. Use tofu and other soya-based products to provide added protein when your baby moves on to solids. Near the end of the first year, brown rice cooked fairly soft, mashed chickpeas or other legumes (beans and peas), and high-protein or whole-grain pastas can also be added to the diet as sources of protein. And don't forget to bring on the edamame (soya beans), mummy (and daddy). Cooked until very soft and shelled, served puréed at first, mashed later, these soya beans are tasty and full of protein.

♦ Concentrate on calories. Growing babies need plenty of calories to grow on, and getting enough fuel is more difficult on a diet that's limited to plant food. Keep an eye on baby's weight gain to make sure enough calories are being taken; if it seems to be slacking, boost her breast milk intake and focus on higher-calorie plant foods, such as avocados.

♦ Keep the calcium coming. Once you

wean your baby, making sure she gets the calcium she needs for strong and healthy bones and teeth will be a little trickier for you than it is for parents who dish out dairy to their children. Good vegetarian sources of this vital mineral include juice that's fortified with calcium, tofu prepared with calcium (but watch out for the many soybean beverages and frozen desserts that contain little or no calcium), as well as broccoli and other green leafies. Since those and many other non-dairy calcium foods are not standard favourites with the high chair set, you may also have to add a calcium supplement to your daughter's diet if you prefer not to feed her milk. Check with her doctor.

♦ Don't forget the fat – the good fat, that is. Foods like salmon and other fish, as well as DHA-rich eggs, will provide essential omega-3 fatty acids. Vegans who never eat animal products at all have to look elsewhere for these good fats. Because vegetables provide no preformed DHA, talk to the doctor about DHA supplements (such as those added to infant formulas).

ANAEMIA SCREENINGS

'I don't understand why the doctor wants to test my son for anaemia at the next visit. He was premature, but is very healthy and active now.'

Thanks to iron-fortified formula and baby cereals, anaemia is rare in well-fed babies these days (only 2 or 3 in 100 middle-class infants become anaemic). Consequently, routine screening for anaemia (a low supply of protein in the red blood cells) is no longer considered absolutely necessary. But because babies with mild anaemia typically don't display the trademark symptoms of the

condition (paleness, weakness and/or irritability) – and, in fact, most are apparently healthy and active – the only way to diagnose it is with a blood test. Which is why some doctors may continue to perform the test (between six and nine months for premature infants and between nine and twelve months for others), just to be on the safe side.

The most common cause of anaemia in babies is iron deficiency – usually occurring in babies born with poor iron stores, such as premature infants who didn't have time before birth to lay down sufficient reserves and those whose mothers didn't get enough iron during pregnancy. Full-term babies are generally born with stores of iron built up during the last few months of pregnancy that carry them for the first few months of life. After that, as babies continue to require the mineral in large quantities to help expand their blood volume to meet the demands of rapid growth, they need a source of iron in the diet, such as iron-fortified formula (for bottle-fed babies) or iron-fortified baby cereal. And though breastfeeding exclusively for the first four to six months is considered the best way to nourish your baby, and the iron in breast milk is very well absorbed, breastfeeding alone does not ensure adequate iron intake after six months.

Typically, the full-term baby who develops iron-deficiency anaemia is one who depends mainly on breast milk (after six months), cow's milk or a low-iron formula for nourishment, and takes very few solids. Because the anaemia tends to slacken his appetite for solids, his sole source of iron, a cycle of less iron/less food/less iron/less food is set up, making the situation worse. Prescribed iron drops usually quickly correct the condition.

To help prevent iron-deficiency anaemia in your baby, try the following:

- Be sure that if your baby is bottle-fed, he's getting a formula fortified with iron.

♦ Be sure that if your baby is breastfed, he is getting iron in some supplementary form (such as an iron-fortified cereal or vitamin drops containing iron, if recommended by your doctor) after six months. And feed a vitamin C food at the same time, when possible, to improve iron absorption.

♦ As your baby increases his intake of solids, be sure to include foods rich in iron (see page 315).

♦ Avoid feeding too much bran to your baby (in bran muffins or bran cereal, for instance), since it can interfere with iron absorption.

SHOES FOR BABY

'My baby's not walking yet, of course, but I don't feel she's completely dressed without shoes.'

Although socks or booties or, weather permitting, bare feet are best for your baby at this stage of development, there's nothing wrong with outfitting her little tootsies in snappy footwear on special occasions – as long as it's the right kind. Since your baby's feet aren't made for walking (at least not yet), the shoes you buy shouldn't be, either. Shoes for infants should be lightweight, made of a breathable material (leather or cloth, but not plastic), with soles so flexible that you can feel baby's toes through them (hard soles are absolutely out). Shoes with stiff ankle support (high-tops) are not only unnecessary and unhealthy for feet now, but will be when baby starts walking, too. And considering how quickly first shoes will be outgrown, it makes sense that they also be inexpensive.

For tips on choosing shoes once baby is walking, see page 448.

If stimulating a baby in the first few months of life takes ingenuity, stimulating a baby who's approaching the half-year mark takes sophistication. No longer is baby physical, emotional and intellectual putty in your hands.

What it's Important to Know:
STIMULATING YOUR OLDER BABY

Now he or she is ready and able to take an active role in the learning process and to coordinate the senses – seeing what's being touched, looking for what's being heard, touching what's being tasted.

The same basic guidelines discussed in Stimulating Your Baby in the Early Months (see page 238) will continue to apply as you approach the second half of baby's first year, but the kinds of activities you can provide are greatly expanded. Basically, they will be directed at these areas of development:

Large motor skills. The best way to help baby develop the large motor strength and coordination necessary for sitting, crawling, walking, throwing a ball and riding a tricycle is to provide plenty of opportunity. Frequently change your baby's position – from back to tummy, from propped-up to prone, from the cot to the floor – to provide the chance to practise feats of physical prowess. As your baby seems ready (which you may not know until you try), provide the opportunity to do the following:

Babies love a lap to stand on. Pulling baby up to this position not only entertains but also helps develop the leg muscles baby will need to pull up, and later stand, unassisted.

♦ Stand on your lap and bounce

♦ Pull to sitting

♦ Sit in a 'frog' position (like a tripod)

♦ Sit upright, propped with pillows if necessary

♦ Pull to standing, holding on to your fingers

♦ Pull to standing in a cot or playpen, or on other furniture

♦ Lift up on all fours

Small motor skills. Developing the dexterity of baby's little fingers and hands will eventually lead to the mastering of many essential skills, such as self-feeding, drawing, writing, brushing teeth, tying shoelaces, buttoning a shirt, turning a key in a lock, and so much more. Proficiency develops more quickly if babies are given ample chance to use their hands, to manipulate objects of all kinds, to touch, explore and experiment. The following will help hone small motor skills:

♦ Activity boards – a variety of activities give baby plenty of practise with small motor skills, though it will be months before most babies can conquer them all.

♦ Blocks – simple cubes of wood, plastic or cloth, large or small, are appropriate at this age.

♦ Soft dolls and stuffed animals – handling them builds dexterity.

♦ Real or toy household objects – babies usually love real or toy telephones (with cords removed), mixing spoons, measuring cups, strainers, pots and pans, paper cups, empty boxes.

♦ Balls – of varying sizes and textures, to hold, to squeeze; they are especially fun once baby is able to sit up and roll them or crawl after them.

♦ Finger games – at first you'll be the one to play clap hands, patty-cake, the itsy-bitsy spider, and similar games, but before you know it, baby will be playing along. After you do a demonstration or two, assist baby with the finger game while you sing along.

Social skills. The middle of the first year is a very sociable time for most babies. They smile, laugh, squeal and communicate in a variety of other ways and are willing to share their friendliness with all comers – most haven't yet developed 'stranger anxiety.' So this is a perfect time to encourage socialization, to expose your child to a variety of people of different ages – from other babies to the elderly. You can do this while shopping, when having friends over or while visiting them, by joining a baby group, even by having baby fraternize with his or her image in the mirror. Teach through example a simple greeting like 'hi' and some of the other basic

HOW DO YOU SPEAK TO YOUR BABY NOW?

Now that your baby hovers on the brink of learning your language, what you say to him or her takes on new meaning. You can help your baby's language skills along in the following ways:

Slow down. When baby is starting to try to decode your jargon, fast talk will slow those efforts. To give your baby the chance to begin picking out words, you must speak more slowly, more clearly and more simply.

Focus on single words. Continue your running commentaries, but begin emphasizing individual words and simple phrases commonly used in baby's everyday life. At feeding time, when you say, 'I'm putting juice in the cup', hold up the juice and add, 'Juice, here is the juice', and the cup, and say, 'Cup'. Always pause to give baby plenty of time to decipher your words before going on to say more.

Continue to downplay pronouns. Pronouns are still confusing for your baby, so stick to 'This is Mummy's book', and 'That is Jordan's doll.'

Emphasize imitation. Now that the number of sounds your baby makes is growing, so is the fun you can have imitating each other. Whole conversations can be built around a few consonants and vowels. Baby says, 'Ba-ba-ba-ba', and you come back with an animated 'Ba-ba-ba-ba.' Baby replies, 'Da-da-da-da', and you respond, 'Da-da-da-da.' If baby seems receptive, you can try offering some new syllables ('Ga-ga-ga-ga', for example), encouraging imitation. But if the role reversal seems to turn baby off, switch back again. In not too many months, you'll find your baby will begin trying to imitate your words – without prompting.

Talk it up. Talk to your baby about everything – and anything – as you go about your day together. Be natural in your conversation, but with a baby-friendly inflection (not to be confused with 'baby talk').

See box on pages 216–217 for more on talking to your baby.

Build a repertoire of songs and rhymes. You may find it tedious having to repeat the same nursery rhyme or little ditty a dozen times a day every day. Your baby, however, will not only love the repetition, but learn from it. Whether you lean on Mother Goose, Dr Seuss, or your own creativity matters not; what counts is consistency.

Use books. Baby's not ready for listening to stories yet, but simple rhymes in books with vivid pictures often catch even a young infant's attention. Do plenty of pointing out of single objects, animals or people. Start asking, 'Where is the dog?' and eventually baby will surprise you by placing a pudgy finger right on Spot.

Wait for a response. Though baby may not be talking yet, he or she is starting to process information, and often will have a response to what you say – even if it's just an excited squeal (when you've proposed a walk in the pushchair) or a pouty whimper (when you've announced it's time to come off the swing).

Be commanding. In time, your baby will learn to follow simple commands such as 'Kiss Grandma', or 'Wave bye-bye', or 'Give Mummy the dolly' (add 'please' if you want the word to eventually come naturally to baby). But keep in mind that baby won't follow through on your requests for months to come, and even when he or she begins to, the response won't be consistent or immediate (baby may wave bye-bye, but not until five minutes after your friend has left the building). Don't show disappointment when baby doesn't perform. Instead, help your child to act out your request (waving bye-bye yourself), and eventually he or she will catch on. Once that happens, try not to treat your baby like a trained seal, asking for performances of the latest 'trick' whenever there's an audience (as tempting as it will be to show baby off).

social graces, such as waving bye-bye, blowing a kiss, and saying thank you.

Intellectual and language skills. Comprehension is beginning to dawn. Names (mummy's, daddy's, sibling's) are recognized first, followed by basic words ('no', 'bottle', 'bye-bye', for example), and soon thereafter, simple, often heard sentences ('Do you want to nurse?' or 'Make nice to the doggy'). This receptive language (understanding what they hear) will come before spoken language. Other types of intellectual development are also on the horizon. Though it won't seem so at first, your baby is taking the first steps towards acquiring the skills of rudimentary problem solving, observation, and memorization. You can help by doing the following:

◆ Play games that stimulate the intellect (see page 433), that help baby observe cause and effect (fill a cup with water in the bath and let baby turn it over – 'See, the water falls out'), that explain object permanence (cover a favourite toy with a cloth and then have baby look for it – 'Where did the choo-choo go?' – or play peekaboo behind your hands, a book, a menu).

◆ Continue sharpening baby's auditory perception. When a plane goes by overhead or a fire engine speeds down the street, sirens screaming, point them out to baby: 'Is that an aeroplane?' or 'Do you hear the fire engine?' will help tune your child in to the world of sounds. Emphasizing and repeating the key words ('aeroplane', 'fire engine') will also help with word recognition. Do the same when you turn on the vacuum cleaner or the water in the bath, when the kettle whistles or the doorbell or phone rings. And don't overlook those favourite funny noises – razzes on baby's belly or arm, clicks with your tongue and whistles are all educational, too, encouraging imitation, which in turn encourages language development.

◆ Introduce concepts. Point out: this teddy is soft, that coffee is hot, the car goes fast, you got up early, the ball is under the table. While using objects, describe what they're for: this broom is for sweeping, this water is for washing and drinking, this towel is for drying, this soap is for washing. At first your words will be meaningless to baby, but eventually, with lots of repetition, the concepts will start to crystallize.

◆ Encourage curiosity and creativity. If your child wants to use a toy in an unusual way, don't be discouraging or try to redirect him or her. Give your child a chance to experiment and explore – whether that means pulling up tufts of grass in the garden or squeezing out a wet sponge in the bath. A baby will learn volumes more through experience than through instruction, and this kind of play and exploration is absolutely free.

◆ Encourage a love of learning. Though teaching specific facts and concepts to your child is important, equally important is teaching how to learn and imparting a love of learning. Remember that learning is always more effective when it's interactive and when it's fun.

◆ ◆ ◆

The Seventh Month

Baby's still a social animal, but those one-on-one interactions now sometimes take a backseat to exploration – a passion fuelled not only by a growing curiosity but by a budding sense of independence (something you're going to be seeing a lot more of in the months to come). With this desire to be his or her own person will come a desire to get around independently. The days of being able to plop your baby down in the middle of the floor and know she'll still be in the same spot five minutes later are coming to a close – if they're not over already. Before you know it, baby will be twisting, rolling, creeping and probably crawling from one end of the room to the other – and beyond (though some babies skip the creeping/crawling stage, particularly if they haven't spent much time on their bellies). With independent mobility imminent, it's time to do a thorough childproofing of your home, if you haven't done it yet.

What Your Baby May Be Doing

All babies reach milestones on their own developmental time line. If your baby seems not to have reached one or more of these milestones, rest assured, he or she probably will very soon. Your baby's rate of development is normal for your baby. Keep in mind, too, that skills babies perform from the tummy position can be mastered only if there's an opportunity to practise. So make sure your baby spends supervised playtime on his or her belly. If you have concerns about your baby's development (because you've noticed a missed milestone or what you think might be a developmental delay), don't hesitate to check it out with the doctor at the next well-baby visit – even if he or she doesn't bring it up. Parents often notice nuances in a baby's development that doctors don't. Premature infants generally reach milestones later than others of the same birth age, often achieving them closer to their adjusted age (the age they would be if they had been born at term), and sometimes later.

By seven months, your baby . . . should be able to:

◆ feed self a cracker

◆ razz (make a wet razzing sound)

◆ coo or babble when happy

◆ smile often when interacting with you

. . . will probably be able to:

◆ sit without support

◆ bear some weight on legs when held upright

◆ object if you try to take a toy away

◆ work to get a toy that's out of reach

◆ look for dropped object

◆ rake with fingers an object and pick it up in fist (keep all dangerous objects out of baby's reach)

◆ turn in the direction of a voice

◆ babble, combining vowels and consonants such as ga-ga-ga, ba-ba-ba, ma-ma-ma, da-da-da

◆ play peekaboo

. . . may possibly be able to:

◆ creep or crawl[1]

◆ pass a cube or other object from one hand to the other

◆ stand holding on to someone or something

. . . may even be able to:

◆ pull up to standing position from sitting

◆ get into a sitting position from stomach

◆ play patty-cake (clap hands) or wave bye-bye

◆ pick up tiny object with any part of thumb and finger (keep all dangerous objects out of baby's reach)

◆ walk holding on to furniture (cruise)

◆ say 'mama' or 'dada' indiscriminately

What You Can Expect at This Month's Checkup

Most doctors do not schedule regular well-baby checkups this month. Do call the doctor if there are any concerns that can't wait until next month's visit.

Feeding Your Baby: MOVING UP FROM STRAINED FOODS

Whether baby's passage to solids has been smooth or bumpy sailing so far, another channel awaits crossing: the one between strained foods and foods with coarser textures. And whether baby has proven to be an eager and adventurous gourmand or a hard-to-please, fussy eater, whether he or

---

1. Babies who spend little time on their stomachs during playtime may reach this milestone later, and that's not cause for concern (see page 205).

she eats solids like a veteran or is a newcomer to the high chair, it's best to make that crossing sooner rather than later. As noted before, once your baby gets on in months, new experiences are more likely to be rebuffed than embraced.

Which is not to say the time has arrived for a family junket to your favourite steakhouse. Even when the first couple of teeth are in place, babies continue to chew with their gums – which are no match for a hunk of meat. For now, coarsely puréed or mashed foods, which have just a touch more texture than strained, will fill the bill of baby's fare.

You can use the commercial 'seventh-month' foods, or mash baby's meals from what you serve the family, as long as they have been prepared without added salt or sugar. You can try regular homemade porridge thinned with formula or breast milk (but, remember, unlike baby porridge, it usually has no added iron); mashed small-curd cottage cheese (preferably unsalted); scraped apple or pear (scrape tiny bits of fruit into a dish with a knife); mashed or coarsely puréed cooked fruit (such as apples, apricots, peaches, plums); and vegetables (such as carrots, sweet and white potatoes, cauliflower, squash). By seven months, you can usually add meat and skinless poultry (puréed, ground or minced very fine) and small flakes of soft fish. When the doctor okays starting egg yolk (it will probably be suggested you wait on the white, which is very allergenic), serve it hard-cooked and mashed, scrambled, or in French toast or pancakes. Watch out for strings from fruits (such as bananas and mangoes), vegetables (such as broccoli, runner beans and kale), and meats. And be sure to check fish very carefully for bones that might be left after mashing. (See page 309 for more on when specific foods are typically introduced.)

Some babies can also handle bread and crackers by seven months (assuming there is no issue with allergies, wheat can be added to their diets by then), but make your selections carefully. They should be whole grain, prepared without much added sugar or salt, and easy to gum. Ideal starters are whole-wheat bagels that have been frozen (they're hard, but whatever baby manages to scrape off will be mushy) and unsalted rice cakes (they crumble easily but dissolve on the tongue, and are loved by most babies). Once these are handled well, baby is ready for whole-grain breads. To decrease the risk of choking, remove crusts, and serve sliced bread in cubes, rolls or loaves in hunks; avoid commercial white breads, which tend to turn pasty when wet and can cause gagging or choking. Give bread and crackers – and all finger foods – only when your baby is seated upright and only under your supervision. And be sure you know how to deal with a choking incident (see page 593).

What You May Be Concerned About

PICKING UP BABY

'I pick my baby up the minute he cries, and end up carrying him around with me much of the day. Am I spoiling him?'

Even though it's hard to spoil a baby this age, there are a lot of good reasons why you might want to slow down on your pickups. Playing 'baby taxi' – picking up your little one the moment you're hailed by a wave of that little arm or a whimper of boredom – can be time-consuming (sounds as if you're already 'on duty' throughout your baby's waking hours). But carrying baby around the clock not only prevents you from getting things done, it can prevent him from getting things done. In your arms your baby doesn't have the opportunity to practise skills, such as creeping and crawling, that will eventually allow him to get around without a free ride. It also doesn't give him a chance to learn how to flex his muscles of independence in other important ways, such as learning how to keep himself entertained for short periods of time and how to enjoy his own good company (skills essential to his budding self-esteem). Finally, it keeps him from learning another lesson that will be invaluable in his development as a caring human being: that other people, even parents, have rights that matter. Because babies and small children are normally and necessarily egocentric, this concept will be hard to grasp at first. Introducing it now, however, will help ensure that you'll raise a child who won't always put his needs before those of others – in other words, a child who's not spoiled.

Sometimes babies cry to be picked up not just because they're looking for a ride, but because they crave comfort and attention – both of which they still need in generous doses. So the first thing you should do is determine whether your baby's getting enough of those precious commodities. Consider: have you actually sat down to play with your son several times during the day, or has most of your interaction consisted of dropping him into the playpen with a toy, leaving him in the ExerSaucer while you start dinner, or strapping him in the car seat for a drive to the supermarket? If so, he may have come to the conclusion that being carted around in your arms, while not all that stimulating, is preferable to no attention at all.

Next, see if your baby has physical needs. Is his nappy soiled? Is it time for lunch? Is he thirsty? Tired? If so, satisfy his needs, then go on to the next step.

Move him to a new location: the playpen, if he was in the cot; the stationary walker, if he was in the playpen; the floor, if he was in the stationary walker. This may satisfy his wanderlust.

Then, be sure he has toys or objects to entertain him – pots and pans, a cuddly stuffed animal, or an activity board – you know what he likes. Since his attention span is short, have two or three playthings within reach; too many toys at his disposal, however, will overwhelm and frustrate him. Provide a fresh selection when he seems to be getting restless.

If he continues to cry for a taxi, try distracting him. Get down on his level for a few minutes, and engage him in an activity without picking him up. Show him how to stack some blocks, point out 'eyes-nose-mouth' on the stuffed animal, spin the cylinder and turn the dial on the busy box to get him started, and challenge him to do the same.

If he's momentarily diverted, and even if he's still voicing halfhearted objections, tell him you have work to do and move off to do it casually and without hesitation. Stay within view, chatting or singing to him if it seems to help; but move out of eyeshot (but not earshot and only if he's in a safe playpen, cot or baby-proofed room) if your presence increases his dissatisfaction. Before you do, poke your head around a corner, playing peekaboo, to show him that when you disappear, you return.

Leave him to his own devices a little longer each time, letting him object a little longer if necessary. But always return to his side when he becomes mildly fussy – to reassure him, play with him for a few minutes, and start the process over. Gradually lengthen the time between pickups, but don't wait until he's screaming to pick him up – the idea is to encourage him to play on his own, not to give him the feeling that he's being ignored or that crying is the only way to get your attention.

Keep your expectations realistic; most babies won't play for more than a few minutes on their own, and even very independent ones need frequent changes of scenery and toys. Remember, too, that many babies who can't yet crawl may be frustrated by the fact that they can't yet get from here to there on their own; until they can, hitching a ride on mum or dad is their only ticket to mobility.

Don't feel guilty about trying to get your son to spend a little time on his own; if you do, you'll be transmitting the message that playing alone is a punishment (it isn't), rather than something that's fun to do once in a while (it should be). But also don't forget that your baby is still a baby – who needs plenty of hugging, holding and being carried around.

GRANDPARENTS SPOILING BABY

'My parents live nearby and see my daughter several times a week. When they do, they stuff her with sweets and give in to her every whim. I love them, but I don't love the way they spoil her.'

Grandparents have the best of all worlds: they can have the joy of indulging a baby without the misery of living with the consequences. They can watch with pleasure as their grandchild relishes the sugary cookies they've plied her with, but don't have to struggle with a fussy – and unhungry – baby come mealtime. They can keep her up through her nap time, so they'll have more time to play, but don't have to deal with her crankiness afterwards.

Is it an inalienable right of grandparents to spoil their grandchildren? To some extent, yes. They've paid their dues as the heavies during your childhood, weaning you from your beloved bottle, cajoling you to eat the spinach you despised, battling with you over curfews. Now that it's your turn to play the heavy, they've earned the cushy job of spoilers. While there's less concern about spoiling in the first year than there will be later, it's a good idea to set up some sensible guidelines (to be agreed upon by all, hopefully) now:

◆ Wider latitude can be given to grandparents whose longitude is distant from yours. Grandparents who get to indulge in person only rarely – seeing your baby only two or three times a year, on holidays or special occasions – can't possibly spoil her but should be given almost every opportunity to try. If baby misses a nap or stays up past her bedtime when your folks are on a two-day, half-birthday visit, or if she is toted around royally much more than you'd prefer while visiting them for the holidays, don't worry. Let her (and them) enjoy the special treatment, and rest assured that your daughter will quickly return to her normal routine when the visit's over.

◆ Grandparents who live near Rome should do as the Romans do – most of the time. It is possible for grandparents who live in the same town, and especially for those who live in the same house, to overdo the overindulgence, making life miserable not only for the baby's parents but for baby as well. Mixed signals – mother and father won't pick her up at every whimper, grandmother and grandfather will – make for a confused and unhappy baby. On the other hand, a child will readily learn that the ground rules can vary with the territory: she can mush the food all over the table at grandma's, but not at home. So even close-by grandparents need to be allowed some leeway – in areas of lesser consequence.

◆ Certain parental rules must be inviolate. Since it's the parents who live with their child on a twenty-four-hour-a-day basis, it's the parents who must lay down the law on more significant issues. It's the grandparents, near or far, who must abide by those rules, even if they don't necessarily agree with them. In one family, a bone of contention may be the bedtime hour; in another, sugar and junk foods in the diet; in yet another, how much TV the children are permitted to watch (not an issue yet with a six- or seven-month-old, but one that will enter the picture soon enough). Of course, if the parents wish to stand firm on every issue, then the grandparents should be allowed to negotiate on occasion.

◆ Certain grandparental rights must be inviolate. The right to give gifts, for example, that the parents might not have chosen – either because they're very expensive, or frivolous, or, in the parents' opinion, tasteless. And to give them more often than mummy and daddy might. (Though gifts that are unsafe should be taboo, and those that violate parental values should be negotiated prior to purchase.) In general, to indulge (yes, spoil) their grandchildren with a little extra of everything – love, time, material things. But not to the point where this spoiling regularly violates parental rules.

If grandparents overstep the boundaries of fair grandparenting; if they ignore or openly flout all the rules you have so thoughtfully set up and try consistently to follow, it's time to open an honest dialogue. Keep the exchange on a loving and light level. Explain (even if you have before) how much you want them to spend time with the baby, but how their breaking the rules you've established is confusing her and upsetting her schedule and the family equilibrium. Tell them you are willing to be flexible on certain issues, but that on others they will have to do the bending. Remind them that when they were parents, they made their own rules; it's your turn to do likewise. If that doesn't work, leave this book, open to Grandparents Spoiling Baby, in a place where they can't miss it.

If any of your differences centre on life-and-death issues (your father refuses to recognize the importance of using the car seat to go around the corner, your mother-in-law smokes while holding the baby in her arms), emphasize the seriousness of the problem, explaining the potential risks and health consequences of their actions, using this book and other resources to make your case more convincing and objective. If they still won't see things your way, lay down the law (no trips in the car with them unless they use a car seat, no smoking around the baby, period).

BABY'S ACTING UP WITH YOU

'The baby-sitter tells me that my baby is just wonderful with her, but he always starts to act up the minute I walk in the door after work. I feel I must be a terrible parent.'

Don't be disheartened – be flattered. The fact that most babies and toddlers, and even older children, are more likely to act up with their parents than with other care providers is a sign that they are more comfortable and secure with their parents. Think of it this way: You're doing such a good job as a parent that your baby is confident that your love is unconditional. He can let his true-blue colours show without risking loss of that love.

Timing may also have something to do with the nightly meltdown. Your homecoming probably coincides with what's typically a baby's crankiest time of the day – early evening – when fatigue, overstimulation and hunger can get the best of even the most cheerful cherub. After a hard day on the job and possibly a difficult commute, you may be frazzled on your return, too – something baby's keen mood radar is sure to pick up on. Your high stress level intensifies his, his reinforces yours – and pretty soon you're both in a lousy frame of mind. If you're generally pretty distracted when you walk in the door (you have to change your clothes, the post has to be sorted, dinner has to be started), your baby's 'acting up' may also be a call for the attention he's craving, attention that's often in short supply at this time of day. For babies who have trouble with change (and more do as they approach their first birthdays), this changing of the guardians can itself be unsettling, provoking a temper tempest.

To ease the transition when you return home each night, try the following tips:

◆ Don't come home to a starving, exhausted baby. Have the sitter feed your baby a meal of solids within an hour of your return. (If you'll want to breastfeed soon after you arrive, however, make sure baby hasn't just had a bottle.) A nap later in the afternoon may also help keep the crankies at bay; but make sure baby's not napping so late that he won't be able to bed down at a reasonable hour. Suggest that the sitter reserve the time before your return for quiet activities so that he won't be overstimulated when you walk in the door.

◆ Relax before you return. If you've been stuck in traffic for an hour, sit in your car and do a few relaxation exercises before you walk in the door. Instead of spending your commute on the bus or tube thinking about the work you left undone on your desk, use it to empty your mind of worries and fill it with thoughts that soothe you.

◆ Relax when you return. Don't rush to start dinner or check e-mail or fold laundry the moment you put down your bag or briefcase. Instead, take fifteen minutes to unwind with your baby, giving him your completely undivided attention, if possible. If your baby seems to be the kind who hates transitions, don't rush the baby-sitter out the door. Reinsert yourself into your baby's day gradually, so that he can get used to the idea that a change is about to take place; when he feels more comfortable, then the baby-sitter can exit.

◆ Include baby in your chores. Once you're both feeling more relaxed, go about your homecoming chores, but include baby in the proceedings. Plunk him in the middle of your bed (supervised) or on the floor while you change your clothes. Hold him on your lap while you check e-mail. Sit him in his high chair with a few toys while you start dinner; chat with him as you chop vegetables.

♦ Don't take it personally. Almost all parents who work experience the homecoming meltdown. Those who have children in day care may experience it at pickup time, on the way home, or when they arrive home.

Is My Baby Gifted?

'I don't want to be a pushy parent. But I don't want to neglect my daughter's talents if she's gifted. How can you tell an ordinary bright baby from a gifted one?'

First of all, it's important to keep in mind that every child is gifted in some way. Maybe it's an ear for music. An artistic flair. Social prowess. Athletic ability. Mechanical genius. Maybe it's a combination of several gifts. Even among children whose gift is exceptional intellectual ability, there are differences. Some are good with numbers, others with spatial relations, still others have a way with words. Some are creative; others excel at organization.

Whatever talents emerge in your child, they'll develop more fully if you nurture and encourage them from early on – which it sounds like you're eager to do. But nurturing and encouraging, as you've wisely noted, are very different from pushing and demanding. Appreciating your child for the special person she is, rather than trying to mould her into the person you'd like her to be, is the very best way to help her use the gifts she's been blessed with.

Though IQ testing can measure intellectual ability later in childhood, determining whether a baby is intellectually gifted is difficult and, on the whole, unnecessary. After all, all babies – no matter what their futures hold academically – should receive the stimulation they need to grow and develop to their potential. And that stimulation doesn't need to come (and really shouldn't come) in the form of special classes and educational computer programmes (see pages 447 and 502). Talking to your baby (and listening when she tries to 'talk' back), reading to her, playing with her, listening to music together, providing her with a variety of interesting experiences, and letting her know that she's loved (no matter how she performs) will give her the foundation she'll need to thrive now and succeed later on.

Still, there are clues to intelligence in the first year that you can look for in your baby:

Uniformly advanced development. A baby who does everything 'early' – smiles, sits, walks, talks, picks up objects with a pincer grasp, and so on – is probably going to continue to develop at an advanced clip, and may turn out to be exceptionally gifted. Though early language ability, particularly the use of unusual words before the end of the first year, is the trait noted most frequently by parents in their gifted children, and is probably indicative of high intelligence, some gifted children are not verbal until fairly late.

Good memory and powers of observation. Gifted children often amaze their parents with the things they remember, often long before most babies have exhibited much memory at all. And when things differ from what they recollect (mummy's got her hair cut, daddy's wearing a new coat, grandpa's wearing a patch on his eye after surgery), they notice immediately.

Creativity and originality. Though most babies under a year are not competent problem solvers, the gifted child may surprise parents by being able to figure out a way to get to a toy that's stuck behind a chair, reach a high shelf in the bookcase (pile up books from lower shelves to climb on, perhaps), or use sign language for a word that's beyond their linguistic abilities (such as pointing to her own nose to indicate that the animal in the book is an elephant, or to her ears if it's a rabbit). The baby on the way to being a gifted child may also be creative in play, using toys in unusual ways, using non-toys creatively as playthings, enjoying playing 'pretend'.

Sense of humour. Even in the first year, a bright child will notice and laugh at the incongruities in life: grandma wearing her glasses on top of her head or daddy tripping over the dog and spilling his glass of juice, for example.

Curiosity and concentration. While all babies are intensely curious, the very gifted are not only curious but have the persistence and concentration to explore what it is they are curious about.

Ability to make connections. The gifted child, more so and earlier than other children, will see relationships between things and will be able to apply old knowledge to new situations. A baby nine or ten months old may see in the store a book that daddy's been reading at home and say, 'Da-da'. Or, accustomed to pushing the button for the lift in her apartment house, she sees an lift in a store and looks for the button.

Rich imagination. Before a year, the gifted child may be able to pretend (to drink a cup of coffee or to rock a baby) and soon after that may become heavily involved in making up stories, games, pretend friends, and so on.

Difficulty sleeping. Gifted children may be so involved in observing and learning that they have trouble tuning out the world, so they don't sleep as much – a trait that can exasperate parents.

Perceptiveness and sensitivity. Very early the gifted child may notice when mummy is sad or angry, may note that daddy has a boo-boo (because he's wearing a plaster on his finger), may try to cheer up a crying sibling.

Even if your baby displays many or all of these traits, it's much too early to tag her with a 'gifted' label. It's also much too early to decide a child isn't traditionally 'gifted' (again, all children are 'gifted' in some way). Some very smart children get to a slower start than their peers when it comes to one or more areas of development, yet manage to zoom ahead later on.

To bring out the best in your baby, love her, don't label her. Provide her with an environment that allows her gifts to grow, but don't forget to cherish her (and let her know that you cherish her) unconditionally for who she is – not just what she's capable of.

NOT SITTING YET
'My baby hasn't started sitting up yet, and I'm worried that she's slow for her age.'

Because normal babies accomplish different developmental feats at different ages, there's a wide range of 'normal' for every milestone. Though the 'average' baby sits unsupported somewhere around six and a half months, some normal babies sit as early as four months, others not until nine. And since your child has a long way to go before she reaches the outer limits of that range, you certainly don't have to worry about her lagging behind.

A child is programmed by genetic factors to sit, and to accomplish other major developmental skills, at a certain age. Though there may not be much a parent can do (or should do) to speed up the timetable, there are ways to avoid slowing it down. A baby who is propped up often at an early age, in an infant seat, a pushchair, or a high chair, gets a lot of practise in a sitting position before she's able to support herself, and may sit sooner. On the other hand, a baby who spends a majority of her time lying on her back or in a baby carrier, and is rarely propped to sit, may sit very late. In fact, babies in other cultures who are constantly worn in baby carriers often stand before they sit, so accustomed are they to the upright position. Another factor that might slow sitting (and other large motor skills) is being overweight. A roly-poly baby is more likely than a leaner child to roll over when attempting a sitting position.

As long as you're giving your baby plenty of opportunities to practise, chances are she'll be sitting pretty sometime during the next two months. If she doesn't, and/or if you feel she's developing slowly in several other ways, consult her doctor.

BITING NIPPLES

'My daughter now has two teeth and seems to think it's fun to use them for biting my nipples during nursing. How can I break her of this painful habit?'

There's no need to let your baby have her fun at your expense. Since a baby can't bite while actively nursing (her tongue comes between teeth and breast), biting usually signals that she's had enough milk and is now just toying with you. It's possible the fun began when she accidentally bit down on your nipple, you let out a yelp, she giggled, you couldn't help laughing, and she continued the game – biting you,

watching for a reaction, smirking at your mock 'No', and seeing through your feeble attempts to keep a straight face.

So instead of encouraging her hijinks with laughter (or with overreaction, which may also invite a repeat performance), let her know that biting isn't acceptable with a firm, matter-of-fact 'No!' Remove her promptly from the breast, explaining that 'Biting hurts mummy – ouch!' If she tries to hang on to your nipple, use your finger to break her grip. After a few such episodes, she'll catch on and give up.

It is important to nip the nibbling habit now, to avoid more serious biting problems later. It's not too soon for her to learn that while teeth are made for biting, there are things that are appropriate to clamp down on (a teething ring, a piece of bread or a banana) and things that are not (mother's breast, brother's finger, daddy's shoulder).

SNACKING

'My baby seems to want to eat all the time. How much snacking is good for him?'

With their own mothers' pronouncements about snacking ('Not before dinner, dear, it'll spoil your appetite!') still ringing in their ears, parents are sometimes reluctant to dole out between-meal goodies to their children on demand, even as they themselves choose to snack the day away. Yet snacks, in moderation, actually play an important supporting role to those three daily squares, especially when it comes to babies.

Snacks are a learning experience. At mealtimes, baby usually is spoon-fed from a bowl; at snack time he has the opportunity to pick up a piece of bread or cracker with his fingers and get it to and into his mouth himself – no small

DINNER AND A BABY

Have reservations about eating out with your baby? Actually, the restaurant may, too – that is, if you don't come prepared. Before you secure a table for two 'and a high chair', check out these restaurant survival tips:

◆ Call ahead. Not just for those reservations (or to find out if the coast is clear; you won't want to choose a restaurant with a wait), but to find out what baby supplies and accommodations are on hand. For instance, are there high chairs? Clip-on feeding chairs? Booster seats probably won't work until baby's closer to a year. Is the kitchen flexible when it comes to ordering; for instance, will they serve up tiny portions of unadulterated meat and vegetables for baby (mashed potatoes without salt and pepper, chicken breast without the sauce) – without charging full price? Children's menus are a plus if they offer more than hot dogs, fries and chicken fingers. Listen carefully when you call. Not just to the answers to your questions, but to the attitude they're tendered with – which can speak volumes about how welcome you and your baby will really be.

◆ Get an early start. Plan to dine on baby's schedule, not yours, even if that means being the earliest birds to catch the early bird special. (Another plus to early eating: the waiting staff isn't frazzled yet, the kitchen isn't fried, there are fewer diners to annoy with baby's cup banging.)

◆ Ask for a 'quiet table in the corner'. Not for the romance, obviously (which definitely won't be on the menu), but so that your group won't offend fellow diners or get in the way of harried waiting staff. You'll also appreciate the privacy if you'll be spending much of the meal nursing.

◆ Make it snappy. Let's face it, even four-star dining can fizzle into fast food when baby's at the table. So it makes sense to prefer quick-paced restaurants, where more time can be spent eating than waiting. Order the entire meal promptly (hopefully you've scanned the menu before sitting down), and ask that baby's food be brought out as soon as possible.

◆ Come prepared. Gone are the days when you could leave for a restaurant with just your credit card. You'll also need to pack:

❖ A bib to keep baby clean, as well as some wipes. If the restaurant is carpeted, a square of clear plastic to spread under baby's chair will be appreciated by those who will have to pick up the mess after you're done.

❖ Toys, books and other diversions to keep baby busy between courses (and when the flaked fish has lost its

accomplishment considering how tiny his mouth is and how primitive his coordination.

Snacks fill a void. Babies have small stomachs that fill quickly and empty quickly, and can rarely last from meal to meal, as adults can, without a snack in between. And as solids become the most significant part of your baby's diet, snacks will be needed to round out nutritional requirements. You'll find it almost impossible to give baby his Daily Dozen in just three meals a day.

Snacks give baby a break. Like most of us, babies need a break from the tedium of work or play (their play *is* their work), and a snack provides this breather.

appeal). Don't take them out, however, until they're needed (baby will probably be content to play with a spoon, flirt with the waiting staff, and point at the light fixtures for the first few minutes), and then bring them on one at a time. No more tricks in your bag? Try a game of peekaboo with the menu or with a napkin.

❖ Jarred food, if junior's not on the table variety yet, or if you fear there won't be any baby-friendly offerings on the menu, or just to supplement what's offered.

❖ Snacks, especially finger foods that will keep those fingers (and that attention) occupied. Nibbles can also be a lifesaver when the meal takes longer than expected to arrive, or when baby bores of table food. But keep these in reserve, too, until they're needed.

◆ If you don't see it, ask for it. Just because it's not on the menu doesn't mean it's not in the kitchen. Good choices, depending on what's been introduced so far, include: cottage cheese, wholemeal bread or rolls, cheese, hamburger (cooked through and crumbled), diced chicken (roasted, grilled or poached), soft fish (cooked through, flaked and carefully screened for bones), mashed or boiled potato or sweet potato, peas (mash them), well-cooked carrots and runner beans, pasta, melon.

◆ Keep baby seated. Never let a child crawl or walk around a restaurant, even one that's relatively empty. Such exploration could result in injury, damages, or both should a waiter bearing a heavy tray of food or drink be tripped up by having baby underfoot. If baby's restless while waiting for food, it's time for one adult to step outside with baby. If baby's finished and you're not, parents may have to take turns (assuming two are on the scene) eating while the other does the 'baby walk'.

◆ Be sensitive to those around you. Maybe the table next to you can't get enough of your baby's adorable smile. Or maybe it's occupied by a couple who's spending good money on a sitter to get away from babies for the night. Either way, be quick to exit for a stroll if baby is crying loudly, practising those ear-piercing shrieks, or otherwise disturbing the peace of the restaurant.

◆ Know when to call it a meal (i.e: when baby's had his or her fill of sweet potatoes and has begun flinging what's left at the next booth); lingering over dessert and coffee is a pleasure of the past for most parents of young children.

◆ Tip, please. The most important tip of all will be the one you leave the waiter (who will be left to scrape mashed peas off the table and carrots off the floor). Especially if you hope to be welcomed back to the same restaurant again (but, in fairness to waiters everywhere, even if you won't be returning), tip generously.

Snacks provide oral gratification. Babies are very orally oriented – everything they pick up goes right to the mouth. Snacking gives them a welcome chance to put things in their mouths without being chastised.

Snacks smooth the way for weaning. If you didn't offer your baby a snack in the form of solids, the odds are good he would insist on one in the form of a breast or a bottle. Snacks will lessen the need to nurse frequently, and eventually – when the time comes – help to make weaning a reality.

For all its virtues, however, snacking can have some drawbacks. To reap the benefits of snacking without stumbling into the pitfalls, remember these pointers:

Snack by the clock. Mum was right. Snacks that come too close to mealtime can interfere with a baby's appetite for meals. Make an attempt to schedule snacks about midway between meals to avoid this problem. Non-stop snacking gets baby accustomed to having something in his mouth all the time, a habit that could be hazardous to the waistline should it be perpetuated into childhood and adulthood. And having the mouth continuously full of food can also lead to tooth decay – even a healthy starch like wholemeal bread turns to sugar when exposed to saliva in the mouth. One snack in the morning, one in the afternoon, and if there's a long span between dinner and bedtime, one in the evening should suffice. Make an exception, of course, if a meal is going to be delayed longer than usual and baby's clearly hungry.

Snack for the right reasons. There are good reasons to snack (as discussed above) and not-so-good reasons. Avoid offering snacks if baby's bored (distract her with a toy), hurt (soothe him with a hug and a song), or has accomplished something that should be rewarded (try verbal praise and an enthusiastic round of applause).

Snack in place. Snacking should be treated pretty much as seriously as mealtime eating. For reasons of safety (a baby eating lying on his back, crawling around, or walking can choke too easily), etiquette (good table manners are best learned at the table), and consideration for the housekeeper (you, or whoever does the cleaning will appreciate not finding crumbs on the sofa and spills on the carpet), snacks should be given while baby is sitting, preferably in his feeding chair. Of course, if you're out and baby is in his pushchair or car seat at snack time, you can serve it up there. But don't give him the idea that a snack is his compensation for serving time in these confining quarters; being strapped into a pushchair or car seat should not be a signal to bring on the crackers and the sippy cup.

GRAZING

'I've heard that grazing is the healthiest way for anyone to eat, particularly a young child. Should I feed my son this way?'

Left to their own devices, most young children would choose the cow's preferred feeding style – grazing – over the modern human's habit of eating meals. They'd be happiest snacking the day away, nibbling crackers and sipping juice as they play, without ever actually sitting down to square one. But though some suggest that light all-day munching is a healthier way to fill nutritional requirements than the old three-meals-a-day-plus-snacks standard, others disagree. Consider the following:

Grazing interferes with proper nutrition. A heifer who grazes in fields of clover gets most of the nourishment she needs that way. But while it's possible that a baby who does nothing but graze all day on favourite finger foods will get his Daily Dozen, it's not likely. Nutritional requirements are filled much more efficiently when meals are taken, along with two or three nutritious snacks.

Grazing interferes with play. Always having a cracker or breadstick in hand (like always having a bottle) limits the amount and kind of playing and exploring a baby can do. And as he becomes mobile, crawling or toddling around with food becomes dangerous because of the risk of choking.

Grazing interferes with sociability. A baby whose mouth is always full of food can't practise his language skills. If he never sits down for meals, he misses out on the social side of dining.

Grazing interferes with the development of good table manners. Children won't learn table manners munching a biscuit on the sofa, sipping formula on the bed or chomping cheese on the carpet.

Grazing contributes to tooth decay. Even wholesome snacks can become a veritable feast for cavity-causing bacteria when left in the mouth all day. Sucking all day from a bottle or sippy cup – a favourite with young snackers – filled with juice can also lead to decay (see page 324).

TEETH COMING IN CROOKED

'My baby's teeth are coming in crooked. Does this mean that he'll eventually need braces?'

Don't make an appointment for the orthodontist yet. The way those first baby teeth come in is no indication of smiles to come. In fact, baby teeth often appear crooked, particularly the front bottom ones, which frequently form a V when they poke through. The top front teeth may also seem huge in comparison to those below. And in some babies, the top teeth come in before the bottom teeth, but that's also nothing to worry about.

By the time your baby reaches two and a half, he'll likely be the proud owner of a full set of baby teeth – twenty in all. And though they'll probably have evened out by then in proportion and formation, don't worry if they haven't. Crooked baby teeth don't predict crooked adult teeth.

TOOTH STAINS

'My daughter's two teeth seem to be stained a greyish colour. Could they be decaying already?'

Chances are, what's keeping your baby's pearly whites a dismal grey isn't decay, but iron. Some children who take a liquid vitamin and mineral supplement that contains iron develop staining on their teeth. This doesn't harm the teeth in any way and will disappear when your child stops taking liquid and begins taking chewable vitamins. In the meantime, brushing your baby's teeth or cleaning them with gauze (see page 358) right after giving her supplement will help minimize staining.

If your baby hasn't been taking a liquid supplement, and especially if she's been doing a lot of sucking on a bottle of formula or juice at bedtime, the discolouration might suggest decay. It could also be the result of trauma, or a congenital defect in the tooth enamel. Discuss this with her doctor or a dentist.

What it's Important to Know:
PUTTING THE SUPER IN BABY

So you've heard about the flashy new educational toy lines sure to boost your baby's mental development and send those fine motor skills soaring off the charts? The CDs and DVDs that'll have your six-month-old channelling Einstein and Mozart (not to mention achieving a reading age of ten by his or her second birthday)? The classes (in art, music, language – you name it) practically guaranteed to turn out a pint-sized prodigy? Maybe you're wondering how parents could buy into these baby-whiz products and programmes – how they could push their little ones so intensely. And at the same time, maybe you're also wondering whether you should be doing the same with yours.

Before you rush out to sign up for the local baby genius class, read on. Though it might be possible – and let's face it, even a little satisfying – to teach an infant a wide variety of skills long before they are ordinarily learned (including how to recognize words), the majority of experts agree that there is no evidence that intense early learning actually provides a long-term advantage over more traditional learning patterns.

In other words, your baby should be spending his or her first year being a baby. And babyhood comes with quite a course load of its own – not just intellectual but emotional, physical and social, as well. During those twelve months, babies have to learn to build attachments to others (mummy, daddy, siblings, sitters, and so on), to trust ('When I'm in trouble, I can depend on mummy or daddy to help me'), to grasp the concept of object permanence ('When daddy hides behind the chair, he's still there, even though I don't see him'). They need to learn to use their bodies (to sit, stand, walk), their hands (to pick up and drop, as well as to manipulate), and their minds (solving problems such as how-to-get-that-truck-from-the-shelf-I-can't-reach). They'll need to learn the meanings of hundreds of words and, eventually, how to reproduce them using a complicated combination of voice box, lips and tongue. And they'll need to learn something about who they are ('What kind of person am I? What do I like, what don't I like, what makes me happy or sad?'). With so many lessons lined up already, it's likely that academic add-ons might overload baby's circuits, maybe even forcing some of these important areas of learning (including those critical emotional and social ones) to be neglected.

Your best bet is to try to produce not a superbaby, but a pretty terrific child – one who reaches his or her maximum potential at a rate that's personally appropriate. Not necessarily by signing him or her up for classes or bringing home armloads of educational toys, but by standing by to offer plenty of encouragement as baby tackles the ordinary (but extraordinary!) tasks of infancy; by nurturing baby's natural curiosity about the world around him or her (whether it's a dust ball on the floor or a cloud in the sky); by exposing him or her to a stimulating variety of settings (stores, zoos, museums, petrol stations, parks and so on); by talking about people you see ('That lady is very old', 'That man has to ride around in a chair because he has a boo-boo on his leg', 'Those children are going to school'); and by descoting how things work ('See, I turn on the tap and water comes out'), what they are used for ('This is a chair. You sit in a chair'), and how they differ ('The horse has a long flowing tail and the pig has a little curly one'). Providing your baby with an environment that's language rich (by spending plenty of time talking, singing songs, and reading books) will boost language skills immeasurably – but keep in mind that it's more important for your baby to know that a dog barks, eats, can bite, has four legs and has fur all over than to be able to recognize that the letters *d-o-g* spell dog.

If your baby does show an interest in words, letters or numbers, by all means nurture that interest. But don't suddenly forsake trips to the playground so you and baby can spend all your time with a pile of flash cards. Learning – whether it's how to recognize a letter or how to throw a ball – should be fun. But there is little fun for either of you in a pressured environment in which you're faced with a never-ending list of goals that must be met (there'll be plenty of time for that later, when homework overtakes your home). Take your cues from your baby; let him or her set the pace. When it seems as though your little scholar has had it up to his or her nappy with your educational agenda, it's time to switch gears.

◆ ◆ ◆

CHAPTER 12

The Eighth Month

Seven- and eight-month-old babies are busy babies. Busy practising skills they've already mastered (such as crawling, perhaps) and skills they're eager to master (such as pulling up). Busy playing (which, with vastly improved dexterity in those chubby little fingers and hands, is at least twice as much fun, and, with greater ability to focus, is at least twice as absorbing). Busy exploring, discovering, learning and, as a budding sense of humour emerges, laughing, a lot. This month, baby contin-ues to experiment with vowels and con-sonants and may even string together those combos you've been waiting for ('ma-ma' or 'da-da') by month's end. Comprehension is still very limited, but baby's starting to pick up the meaning of a few words – fortunately 'no', a word that will come in handy in the months to come, will be one of the first understood (if not complied with). Socializing with a mirror is a favourite activity, though baby doesn't yet recognize who that 'friend' in the reflection actually is.

What Your Baby May Be Doing

All babies reach milestones on their own developmental time line. If your baby seems not to have reached one or more of these mile-stones, rest assured, he or she probably will very soon. Your baby's rate of devel-opment is normal for your baby. Keep in mind, too, that it may have been slowed down in certain departments (such as crawling) if baby didn't spend much time playing on his or her belly. (Some babies skip crawling altogether, and that's fine, too.) If you have concerns about your baby's development (because you've noticed a missed mile-stone or what you think might be a developmental delay), don't hesitate to check it out with the doctor at the next well-baby visit – even if he or she doesn't bring it up. Parents often notice nuances in a baby's development that doctors don't. Premature infants gener-ally reach milestones later than others of the same birth age, often achieving them closer to their adjusted age (the age they would be if they had been born at term), and sometimes later.

By eight months, your baby . . . should be able to:

◆ bear some weight on legs when held upright

◆ feed self a cracker

◆ rake with fingers an object and pick it up in fist (keep all dangerous objects out of baby's reach)

◆ turn in the direction of a voice

◆ look for a dropped object

. . . will probably be able to:

◆ pass a cube or other object from one hand to the other

◆ stand holding on to someone or something

◆ object if you try to take a toy away

◆ work to get a toy that's out of reach

◆ play peekaboo

◆ get into a sitting position from stomach

. . . may possibly be able to:

◆ creep or crawl[1]

◆ pull up to standing position from sitting

By the eighth month, a few babies can pick up small objects using the thumb and forefinger.

◆ pick up tiny object with any part of thumb and finger (keep all dangerous objects out of baby's reach)

◆ say 'mama' or 'dada' indiscriminately

. . . may even be able to:

◆ play patty-cake (clap hands) or wave bye-bye

◆ walk holding on to furniture (cruise)

◆ stand alone momentarily

◆ understand 'no' (but not always obey it)

What You Can Expect at This Month's Checkup

Most doctors do not schedule regular well-baby checkups this month. That's probably just as well, since most babies this age don't enjoy holding still for them – or for anything. Do call the doctor if there are any concerns that can't wait until next month's visit.

---

1. Babies who spend little time on their stomachs during playtime may reach this milestone later, and that's not cause for concern (see page 205).

Feeding Your Baby:
FINALLY – FINGER FOODS

For most parents, the novelty of feeding their babies soon wears as thin as the rice cereal they've been struggling to direct into those little mouths. The lips willfully clenched, the head turned away just at the critical moment (splat!), the pudgy hand intercepting and overturning the spoon just before it reaches its destination (more splat!), and the sheer tedium of repeating this messy ritual three times a day (splat! splat! splat!), makes these parents ready to relinquish the role they couldn't wait to take on a few months earlier. Fortunately, the opportunity to throw in the spoon presents itself fairly quickly. Most babies are not only eager but able to begin finger foods by the time they are seven to eight months old.

The transition is more sudden than gradual. Once babies discover they can get food into their mouths independently, the number of foods that they can expertly express to the mouth increases rapidly. At first, most babies hold the rice cake or piece of bread in the fist and munch on it that way, not having learned yet to coordinate individual fingers for pickup and transport. When the problem of how to get that last piece of food wrapped tightly in the palm into the mouth arises, they may demonstrate their frustration with a tearful outburst. The solution for some is to open the hand flat against the mouth, for others to put the food down and pick it up again with more of it exposed.

The ability to position an object between thumb and forefinger in the pincer grip doesn't develop in most babies until between nine and twelve months of age – though some perfect their pincers earlier and others later. Once this skill is mastered, it allows a baby to pick up very small objects, such as peas and pennies, and bring them to the mouth, considerably expanding the dining repertoire – and the risk of choking.

Learning to handle finger foods is usually the first step on the road to dinner table independence. At first, finger foods merely supplement a young child's diet; as facility with self-feeding grows, a large proportion of the daily intake will be delivered by baby's own hand. Some will learn to wield a spoon respectably well by the middle of the second year or even sooner, and will switch to this more civilized style of eating; others will continue to get most of their meals to their mouths (even such dubious finger fare as porridge and cottage cheese) via the fingers for a long time to come. A few, usually those who were never allowed to do it themselves because of the time or mess involved, will insist on being fed long after they are capable of feeding themselves.

The foods that qualify for first finger-food honours are those that baby can gum to swallowable consistency or that will dissolve in the mouth without chewing, and that have been well received in puréed form on earlier tries. Most of these foods should be cut into manageable cubes or chunks – pea size for firmer items, marble size for softer foods. Good choices include a wholemeal bagel, wholemeal bread or toast, rice cakes or other crackers that become mushy in the mouth; oat cakes, wheat or rice puffs; tiny cubes of natural (but pasteurized) cheese, such as Gruyère, Cheddar, Edam, Havarti; chunks of ripe banana, very ripe pear, peach, apricot, cantaloupe or honeydew melon, or mango; small chunks of cooked-to-very-tender carrot, white or sweet potato, yam, broccoli or cauliflower (flowerets only), peas (cut in half or crushed); flakes of grilled, baked or poached fish (but screen *carefully* for bones); soft meatballs (cook in sauce or soup so they don't get crusty); well-cooked pasta of various sizes and shapes (break up before or cut after cooking, as necessary) if they contain no ingredients that baby isn't allowed yet; scrambled or hard-boiled egg yolk (and once baby can have the whites, whole eggs); cubes of soft-cooked French toast or wholemeal pancakes (again, made at first with yolk only, then, as whites are introduced, with whole eggs). About the same time you add finger foods, you can add more texture to the other foods baby is eating by using commercial toddler foods, or table foods that are chopped or mashed but that contain small, soft chunks baby can gum.

To serve finger foods, scatter four or five pieces onto an unbreakable plate or directly onto baby's feeding tray, and replace as baby eats them. Beginning eaters, confronted by too much food, especially all in one spot, may respond either by trying to stuff all of it in their mouth at once or by sending it all to the floor with one deft swipe. As with other foods, finger foods should be fed only to a baby who is seated, and not to one who is crawling, cruising or toddling around.

Because of the danger of choking, don't give your baby foods that won't dissolve in the mouth, can't be mashed with the gums, or can be easily sucked into the windpipe. Avoid uncooked raisins, popcorn, nuts, whole peas, raw firm-fleshed vegetables (carrots, peppers) or fruits (apples, unripe pears, grapes), chunks of meat or poultry, or hot dogs (most varieties are too high in sodium and additives, anyway).

Once the molars come in (the first teeth are for biting, and don't improve your child's ability to chew), somewhere around the end of the year for early teethers, foods that require real chewing can be added, such as raw apples (cut into very small pieces) and other firm-fleshed raw fruits and vegetables, small slices of meat and poultry (cut across the grain), and seedless grapes (skinned and halved). But hold off until age three on such common choking hazards as raw carrots, popcorn, nuts and hot dogs. Introduce them only when your baby is chewing well.

No matter what the texture, there are some types of food that you shouldn't be in a hurry to introduce your baby to: junk foods that offer little nutrition, foods prepared with lots of added sugar or salt, and refined breads or cereals. Your child will certainly meet up with them soon enough, but hopefully by then the wholesome early eating experiences you've been providing will have laid a solid foundation for future dietary habits. That doesn't mean that your child won't ever have a taste for chips, white bread and doughnuts – just that he or she will also have a taste for the good stuff.

What You May Be Concerned About

BABY'S FIRST WORDS

'My baby has started saying "ma-ma" a lot. We were all excited until we read that she's probably just making sounds without understanding their meaning. Is that true?'

Only your baby knows for sure, and she isn't telling, at least not yet. Just when a baby makes the transition from sounds that mimic real words but have no meaning to meaningful speech is difficult to pinpoint exactly. Your baby may just be practising her 'm' sounds now, or she may be calling for mummy, but it really doesn't matter which. The important thing is that she's vocalizing and attempting to imitate sounds she hears. Many babies, of course, say 'da-da' first – not a sign of favouritism, just a reflection of the consonant a baby has found easiest to pronounce initially.

In many languages the words for male and female parents sound very similar. Daddy, pappa, papa, pita, vater, abba. Mummy, mama, mommy, maataa, mutter, imma. It's a good bet that they all developed from babies' earliest mouthing of syllables, picked up on by eager parents trying to recognize their baby's first word. When, long ago, a young Spanish baby uttered her first 'ma-ma', complaining in the fashion typical of babies, her proud mother probably was certain she was calling *'madre'*. And when an early French infant first vocalized 'pa-pa', his father probably puffed up his chest and said, 'He's trying to say *père*'.

When the first real word is spoken varies a great deal, and is, of course, subject to less-than-objective parental interpretation. According to the experts, the average baby can be expected to say what she means and mean what she says for the first time anywhere between ten and fourteen months. A small percentage of children start a couple of months earlier and some perfectly normal babies don't utter a single recognizable word until midway through their second year, at least as far as anyone can tell. Often, however, a baby may already be using syllables, alone and in combination, to represent objects ('ba' for bottle, 'ba-ba' for bye-bye, or 'daw' for dog), but her parents may not be tuned in enough to notice until the enunciation becomes clearer. A child who is very busy developing motor skills – one who, perhaps, crawls and walks early, is involved in learning to climb stairs and ride a play fire engine – may be slower than less active babies in starting to vocalize. This is nothing to worry about as long as it's clear from behaviour that a lot of the familiar words he or she hears are being understood.

Long before your baby utters her first word, she will be developing her linguistic skills. First, by learning to understand what is said. This receptive language starts developing at birth, with the first words your baby hears. Gradually, she begins to sort out individual words from the jumble of language around her, and then one day, about the middle of the first year, you say her name and she turns around. She's recognized a word. Pretty soon thereafter she should begin to understand the names of other people and objects she sees daily, such as mummy, daddy, bottle, cup, bread. In a few months, or even earlier, she may begin to follow simple commands, such as 'Give me a bite', or 'Wave bye-bye' or 'Kiss Mummy'. This comprehension moves ahead at a much faster pace than speech itself and is an important forerunner to it. You can encourage both receptive and spoken language development every day in many ways (see page 366).

SIGNING WITH BABY

'Some of my friends are using baby signs to communicate with their baby – and it seems to work. But I've also heard that using sign language with my son can slow down the process of learning to speak. I'm confused'.

You can see it in sandpits and pushchairs across the country: babies are talking. Not in so many words, but in so many signs. Sign language, once used only among the deaf, is becoming a popular form of communication between children who can hear but can't yet speak and their parents, who are anxious to understand them.

Though baby signing as a movement is relatively new, preverbal babies have always used hand gestures and motions in an effort to express what they weren't able to through speech. A baby who points to the refrigerator when he's hungry or thirsty or to his coat when he wants to go outside is communicating through signs. So is a baby who pulls his ear when he sees a bunny in a book, or waves to let his parents know that he wants to go bye-bye. Hand games, like 'patty-cake', and finger songs, like 'itsy-bitsy spider', have been favourites for generations because they allow babies to play along even though they're not able to sing along.

But the signs babies use instinctually aren't always readily comprehended by their parents. This communication gap results in frustration on both sides as babies struggle to be understood and parents struggle to understand. That's why some linguistic experts have proposed a system of parent-baby communication that bridges that gap: baby signing.

Baby signing offers many advantages. The most notable, of course, is that as it increases comprehension – allowing a nine- or ten-month-old baby to let his parents know exactly what he needs and wants long before he's able to express it in words – it decreases frustration. Better communication leads to smoother interaction (read: fewer temper tantrums), putting more quality into their quality time together. Knowing that he's understood also bolsters a child's self-esteem ('What I have to say matters'), making him not only a more confident person but a more confident communicator. This confidence translates, eventually, in an increased motivation to speak. (Think about it this way: if you were struggling to speak the language in a foreign country, and the natives took pains to understand you, you'd be more motivated to continue your efforts.) Research disputes the idea that babies who use signs will be slower in their development of spoken language skills; in fact, two-year-olds who signed as babies have, on average, a bigger vocabulary than those who did not use baby signs.

The advantages of baby signing, however, seem mostly to be short-term. Though the child who has signed certainly has an easier time communicating early on, that edge, most research shows, doesn't seem to last into the school years. Once a child can speak and be understood, the benefits of having used signs diminish and eventually disappear. So don't use baby signs because you think it will make your son smarter or more developmentally advanced; use it, if you choose to, because it will help you communicate better with him now.

If you'd like to use baby signs, here's how:

◆ Get an early start on signing. Begin as soon as your baby shows an active interest in communicating with you – at least by eight or nine months, though there's no harm in getting into the signing habit earlier. Most babies will start signing back somewhere between ten and fourteen months.

◆ Sign what comes naturally. Develop a natural sign language that works for you and your baby. Any simple gesture that fits a word or phrase well can work (flapping arms for 'bird', for instance, or scratching under the arms for 'monkey'; hands together and supporting a tilted head for 'sleep', a rubbed belly for 'hungry', a cupped hand placed up to the mouth for 'drink', a finger touched to the nose for 'smell'). Although you can use deaf signing, some experts believe it is not as easy for babies to learn as a natural sign language.

◆ Give your baby the signs he needs. The most important signs to develop and learn will be the ones your baby requires to express his everyday needs, such as hunger, thirst and fatigue.

◆ Sign consistently. By seeing the same signs over and over, your baby will come to understand them and imitate them quickly.

◆ Speak and sign at the same time. To make sure your baby learns both the sign and the spoken word, use both together.

◆ Sign up the whole family. The more people in your baby's life who can speak his language, the happier he'll

be. Siblings, grandparents, care providers and anyone else who spends a lot of time with your baby should be familiar with at least the most important signs.

◆ Follow your baby's signs. Many babies invent their own signs. If yours does, always use the signs of his design, which are more meaningful to him.

◆ Don't push the signs. Signing, like all forms of communication, should develop naturally and at a child's own pace. Babies learn best through experience, not through formal instruction. If your baby seems frustrated by the signs, resists using them, or just shows signs of sign overload, don't force the agenda.

While signing can make life a little easier during the preverbal stage, it's certainly not necessary for good parent-child communication, vital for a good parent-child relationship, or critical for language development. So if an official signing system doesn't feel comfortable for you or seem to work for your baby, don't feel compelled to create or use it. Parents have been figuring out what their children have to say for millennia without the benefit of formal baby signs (usually because they become adept at reading a variety of non-verbal signals, from gestures to grunting) – and you can, too.

BABY'S NOT CRAWLING YET

'My sister's baby started crawling at six months. My son's almost eight months, and he hasn't shown any interest in crawling. Is he delayed developmentally?'

Some babies start off dragging themselves around on their belly. While many graduate to hands-and-knees crawling, a few will cling to creeping until they're up on their feet.

Hands-and-knees locomotion is the classic crawling technique. Some babies are so content zipping around this way that they don't bother with walking for months to come.

A cross between crawling and walking, the hands-and-feet posture may be one that baby settles on at first and sticks with, or one that evolves into a precursor of walking.

It's never fair to compare, but especially when it comes to crawling, which is considered only an optional skill and not one by which overall development can be gauged. Some babies crawl as early as six months (especially if they've spent plenty of supervised playtime on their bellies), but closer to nine months is typical. More babies are crawling later these days (because of less time spent on their bellies), and a significant minority never crawl at all. Neither is cause for concern as long as other important developmental milestones are being reached (such as sitting – a skill babies must master before they can even tackle crawling). Those who opt not to crawl are limited in mobility only briefly – until they figure out how to pull up, to cruise (from chair to coffee table to sofa), and finally to walk. In fact, many babies who never take to crawling end up walking earlier than proficient crawlers, who may be content for months on all fours. Because crawling, unlike sitting or pulling up, is not a predictable part of the developmental pattern, it isn't included on most assessment scales.

Even among babies who do crawl, styles vary. Moving about on the belly, or creeping, is usually a precursor to moving about on the hands or knees, or crawling, though some babies stick to creeping. Many begin crawling backwards or sideways, and don't get the hang of going forwards for weeks. Some scoot on one knee or on their bottom, and others travel on hands and feet, a stage that many babies reach just before walking. The method a baby chooses to get from one point to another is much less important than the fact that he's making an effort to achieve independent locomotion. (If, however, he does not seem to be using both sides of his body – arms and legs – equally, check with his doctor.)

Some babies don't crawl because they haven't been given the chance. A baby who passes most of his day confined in a cot, pushchair, sling and/or playpen or lying on his back won't learn how to raise himself on all fours or put his hands and knees in motion. Be sure your baby spends plenty of supervised time on his tummy (don't worry about dirt as long as the floor has been swept or vacuumed free of small particles and cleared of dangerous objects). To encourage him to move forward, try putting a favourite toy or interesting object a short distance ahead of him. Do cover his knees, however, since bare knees on a cold, hard floor or a scratchy carpet can be uncomfortable and might even discourage your baby from attempting to crawl. Wean him from the stationary walker if he's using one, and limit playpen exile to times when you can't supervise him.

One way or another, in the next few months, your baby will be taking off – and off into trouble – and you'll be left wondering, 'Why was I in such a hurry?'

SCOOTING

'Our little girl scoots around on her bottom instead of crawling. She gets around, but it looks strange.'

For a baby eager and determined to get from one place to another, form and grace are of little consequence. And they should be to you, too. As long as your baby is attempting to get around on her own, it doesn't matter how. You need be concerned only if your baby seems unable to coordinate both sides of her body, in other words, can't move her arms and legs in sync. This could be a sign of a motor disability, for which early treatment can be very helpful.

MESSY HOUSE

'Now that my son is crawling around and pulling up on everything, I can't keep up with the mess he makes. Should I try to control him – and the mess – better, or give up?'

Clutter may be your worst enemy, but it's an adventurous baby's best friend. A home that is kept compulsively tidy provides about as much interest and challenge to a baby who's newly mobile as a pond would to Christopher Columbus or a suburban car park to Michael Schumacher. Within the parameters of reason (you needn't let baby dismantle your cheque book or reprogramme your Palm Pilot) and safety, your child needs to flex and extend his curiosity as he exercises his muscles. Letting him roam – and mess – freely is as important to his intellectual growth as it is to his physical development. Accepting this reality is important to your mental health; parents of young children who fight it, struggling to keep the house as neat as it was prebaby, are in for a disappointment – as well as overwhelming frustration and anxiety.

You can, however, take some steps to make coping with the reality easier:

Start with a safe house. While it may be okay for him to scatter underwear on the bedroom floor or build a house of napkins on the kitchen linoleum, it isn't okay for him to clang liquor bottles together to see what happens or to empty the chlorine cleanser on the rug. So before you let your baby loose, be sure to make the house safe for him and from him (see page 402).

Contain the chaos. The compulsive side of you will be a lot happier if you try to confine the mess to one or two rooms or areas in the home. That means letting your baby have free run only in his own room and perhaps the kitchen, family room or living room – wherever you and he spend the most time together. Use closed doors or baby-safe gates to define the areas. If you have a small flat, of course, you may not be able to place such restrictions on your baby; instead, you may have to resign yourself to daily messes and nightly cleanups.

Also reduce the potential for mess by wedging books in tightly on shelves accessible to your baby, leaving a few of his indestructible books where he can reach them and take them out easily; sealing some of the more vulnerable cabinets and drawers (especially those that contain breakables, valuables or hazards) with childproof safety locks; keeping most knickknacks off low tables, leaving only a few you don't mind him playing with. Set aside a special drawer or cabinet for him to call his own, and fill it with such fun items as paper cups and plates, wooden spoons, a metal cup or pot, plastic measuring cups and empty boxes.

Don't feel guilty about not letting your baby adorn the bathroom with lipstick or shaving cream, tear the pages out of your favourite books, empty boxes of cereal all over the kitchen floor, and generally redecorate your home as he pleases. Setting limits will not only help save your sanity but also help your

baby's development – children really do thrive when limits are set for them – and teach him the important lesson that other people, even parents, have possessions and rights, too.

Restrain yourself. Don't follow your baby around as he wreaks havoc, putting away everything he takes out. This will frustrate him, giving him the sense that everything he does is not only unacceptable but essentially in vain. And it will frustrate you if he immediately redoes the damage you've just undone. Instead, do the serious cleaning up twice a day, once at the end of his morning play period while he's napping or in his playpen or high chair, and once at the end of the afternoon or after he's in bed.

Teach him a lesson in neatness – over and over again. Don't do your intensive cleanups with him around. But do pick up a couple of things with him at the end of each play session, making a point (even if he's not old enough to get the point) of saying, 'Now, can you help Daddy pick this toy up and put it away?' Hand him one of the blocks to put back into the toy chest, give him a pot to return to the cupboard or some crumpled paper to throw into the wastebasket, and applaud each effort. Though he will be messing up a lot more often than he'll be cleaning up for years to come, these early lessons will help him to understand – eventually – that what comes out must go back in.

Let him make a mess in peace. Don't complain constantly about the mess baby is making or make him feel that expressing his natural and healthy curiosity ('If I turn this cup of milk over, what will happen?' 'If I take all these clothes out of the drawer, what will I find underneath?') is bad or means that he is bad. If it was something you would rather not see happen again, let him know – but as a teacher, not a judge.

You can't beat him, but don't join him. Don't decide that since you're fighting a losing battle anyway, you might as well let the mess mount and learn to ignore it. Living that way won't help your morale and will be of no benefit to your baby. Though it's healthy for a baby to be allowed to make a mess, it isn't healthy for him to always be surrounded by disorder. It will give him a sense of security to know that even though he leaves an untidy world at bedtime, it will be returned to order come morning. And it will also make making a mess more fun and more fulfilling – what challenge is there, after all, in messing up a room that's already a mess?

Set aside a sanctuary. You won't always be able to keep up with damage left behind by your junior hurricane, but do try to preserve a place of calm in the midst of the storm – your bedroom or living room, for instance – either by not permitting baby to play there or by making sure that it invariably gets picked up in the afternoon or evening. Then, at the end of every day, you will have a haven to escape to.

Play it safe. An exception to a let-the-mess-fall-where-it-may attitude should be made when it presents a threat to safety. If baby spills his juice or empties the dog's water bowl, wipe it up immediately. Fresh spills turn an uncarpeted floor into a skating rink where falls are inevitable. Also pick up sheets of paper and magazines as soon as baby is through with them, and keep traffic lanes (stairways, especially) clear of toys, particularly those with wheels, at all times.

EATING OFF THE FLOOR

'My baby is always dropping her cracker on the floor and then picking it up and eating it. It seems so unsanitary – is it safe?'

Even if you don't keep your floors 'clean enough to eat off', it's safe for your baby to picnic on them. There are germs on the floor, but not in significant numbers. And for the most part, they're germs your baby has been exposed to before, particularly if she frequently plays on the floor. The same is generally true of floors in other people's homes, supermarkets and department stores, although if your child's recycling a cracker off a foreign floor offends your aesthetic sense, there's nothing wrong with throwing it in the bin and replacing it with a fresh one. But keep in mind that every encounter with a virus or bacterium builds immunity and makes your baby stronger, so don't worry the next time your baby gums the shopping trolley handle.

There are exceptions, however. Although bacteria don't have a chance to multiply much on dry surfaces, they can multiply very rapidly on those that are damp or wet. If you have the choice (in other words, if you can intercept an item before it lands in her mouth), don't let her eat food that's been dropped in the bathroom, in puddles or on other damp or wet surfaces. Moisture on food itself can also be a problem. A cracker or any food that's been mouthed for a time, then left (even in a clean place) for a few hours while bacteria multiply, isn't fit for consumption. So don't leave wet discards lying around where your baby can pick them up again. You won't always have the choice, of course; babies often reclaim long-lost foodstuffs (or sippy cups filled with three-day-old juice) and thrust them in their mouths before you can stop them. Fortunately, they rarely become ill as a result. Another exception: if your home has old lead paint that is in poor repair on the walls, floor picnics won't be safe for your baby (see page 335).

Outdoors, too, you need to be vigilant. Though many a baby has dropped a bottle in the street and then returned it to her mouth without ill effect, there is certainly more risk of picking up nasty germs where dogs defecate and urinate and people expectorate. Replace or rinse any food, bottle, dummy, or toy that has fallen into the street, especially if the ground is damp. Use wipes to clean a teat or toy when running water is not available. In playgrounds, where dogs aren't allowed and where adults usually have more sense than to spit, there's probably less to worry about as long as the ground isn't wet – a quick brush-off of surface dirt should suffice. But even there, puddles can harbour dangerous disease-causing germs, and babies as well as their toys and snacks should be kept away from them. To avoid having to choose between appeasing a screaming baby and playing it safe by discarding a snack that you aren't sure is sanitary, always carry extras.

Do try to wash baby's hands often (a good habit for her to get into early on anyway) or use wipes or antibacterial gels if there's no soap and water nearby.

EATING DIRT – AND WORSE

'My son puts everything in his mouth. Now that he plays on the floor so much, I have less control over what goes in. What's safe and what isn't?'

Into the mouths of babes goes anything and everything that fits: dirt, sand, dog food, insects, dustballs, rotten food, even the contents of a soiled nappy. Though it's obviously best to avoid his sampling from such an unsavoury smorgasbord, it's not always possible. Few babies get through the creepy-crawly stage without at least one oral encounter with something his parents consider revolting; some can't even get through a single morning.

But you've got a lot less to fear from what's unsanitary than from what's used to sanitize. A mouthful of dirt rarely hurts anyone, but even a lick of some cleansers can cause serious damage. You can't keep everything out of baby's inquisitive grasp, so concentrate on substances with the most harmful potential (see page 405 for a list), and concern yourself less with the occasional bug or clump of dog hair that finds its way into his mouth. If you do catch him with the cat-that-is-about-to-swallow-a canary look, squeeze his cheeks with the thumb and forefinger of one hand to open his mouth, and sweep the object out with a hooked finger.

Of most concern – in addition to obviously toxic substances – are foods that are in the process of spoiling. Illness-causing bacteria or other microorganisms can multiply rapidly at room temperature, so be sure to keep food that's gone bad or is about to – most often found in pet feeding bowls, in the kitchen garbage and on an unswept kitchen or dining room floor – out of baby's reach.

You should also be very careful not to let your baby mouth items small enough to swallow or choke on – buttons, bottle caps, paper clips, safety pins, pet kibble, coins, and so on. Before you put your baby down to play, survey the floor for anything that's less than 3.5 cm (1⅜ in) in diameter (about the diameter of a toilet paper tube) and remove it. Also put out of reach items that are potentially toxic, such as cleaning supplies. See Making Home Safe for Baby (page 402) for additional tips on what should be kept away from baby.

GETTING DIRTY

'My daughter would love to crawl around at the playground if I let her. But the ground is so dirty . . .'

Break out the stain remover, and break down your resistance to letting your daughter get down and dirty. Babies who are forced to watch from the sidelines when they'd really like to be in the scrimmage are likely to stay spotless but unsatisfied. Children are eminently washable. The most obvious soil can be removed with baby wipes or premoistened towelettes while you're still at the playground or in the garden, and ground-in dirt will come off later in the bath. So ignore the slight to your sensibilities and, checking first to be sure there's no broken glass or dog droppings in her path, allow your little sport a carefully supervised crawl around. If she gets into something really dirty, give her hands a once-over with a baby wipe and send her on her way again.

Not all babies enjoy getting dirty; some would rather be spectators than players. If yours is one of these, be sure she isn't hesitating because she thinks you don't want her to get dirty. Encourage her to gradually become more active, but don't force her.

Soft shoes will protect her feet when she's crawling on concrete; on grass in warm weather, bare feet are fine. It will be easier on her knees (though a challenge to your laundering skills) if she wears trousers or dungarees during these excursions. If you take pride in her looking fresh and clean in public, keep a set of play clothes in your changing bag and change her into them before handing over her travelling papers; then wash her up and put her back into clean clothes before you set off again.

ERECTIONS

'When I'm changing my baby, he sometimes gets an erection. Am I handling his penis too much?'

As long as you're handling his penis only as much as it needs to be handled to be cleansed at nappy changes and bath times, you're not handling it too much. Your son's erections are the normal reaction to touch of a sensitive sexual organ – as are a little girl's clitoral erections, which are less noticeable but probably as common. A baby may also have an erection when his nappy rubs against his penis, when he's nursing or when you're washing him in the bathtub. All baby boys have erections sometimes (though their parents may not be aware of them), but some have them more often than others. Such erections require no particular notice on your part.

DISCOVERING GENITALS

'My daughter has recently started playing with her genitals whenever her nappy is off. Is this normal at such an early age?'

If it feels good, humans do it. Which is what Mother Nature banked on when she created genitals; if she made them pleasurable to touch, they would be touched, at first by their owner and eventually, when the time was ripe, by a member of the opposite sex – thereby ensuring the perpetuation of the species.

Babies are sexual beings from birth or, more accurately, from before birth – male foetuses have been observed having erections in the uterus. Some, like your baby, begin fledgling explorations into their sexuality in the middle of the first year, others not until year's end. This interest is as inevitable and healthy a part of a baby's development as fascination with fingers and toes was earlier. Trying to stifle such curiosity (as generations past have felt obliged to do) is as misguided as stifling her interest in fingers and toes.

No matter what anyone may tell you, there is no harm – either physical or psychological – in babies or children touching their own genitals. Making a baby or child feel that she's 'dirty' or 'bad' for engaging in such play, however, can be harmful and have a negative effect on future sexuality and self-esteem. Making self-stimulation taboo can also make it more inviting.

The fear that fingers that touch their genitals aren't clean enough to go into their mouths is also unfounded; all the germs that are in a baby's genital area are her own and pose no threat. If, however, you see your little girl probing with very dirty hands, it would be a good idea to wash them, to avoid the possibility of a vaginal infection. A boy's genitals are not susceptible in the same way, but both boys and girls should have their hands washed after they've touched a soiled nappy area.

When your baby gets old enough to understand, you will want to explain that this part of her body is private, and that though it's okay for her to touch it, it isn't okay for her to touch it in public or to let anyone else touch it.

PLAYPEN USE

'When we bought our playpen a couple of months ago, our baby just couldn't seem to get enough time in it. Now he screams to get out after only five minutes.'

A couple of months ago, the playpen didn't seem confining to your baby; on the contrary, it seemed his own personal amusement park. Now he's beginning to realize that there's a whole world – or at least a family room – out there, and he's game to take it on. The four walls that once enclosed his paradise now represent frustrating barriers to him, keeping him on the inside looking out.

Take your baby's hint and start using the playpen for emergency duty only, for those times when he needs to be penned in for his own safety or, briefly and not too often, for your convenience – while you mop the kitchen floor, put something in the oven, answer the phone, go to the bathroom or straighten up for last-minute company. Limit the time he's sentenced to it to no more than five to fifteen minutes at a stretch, which is about as long as an active eight-month-old will tolerate it. Vary the company he has to keep, rotating his stock of toys frequently so he won't become bored prematurely. If he prefers to be able to see and hear you as he plays, keep the pen near you; if he seems contented longer when you're out of sight, keep it in the next room (but make sure he's within earshot and check on him frequently). If he protests before he's done his time, try giving him some novel playthings – a few pots and pans, perhaps, or an empty plastic bottle or two (without the cap) – anything he doesn't usually play with in this setting. If that doesn't work, parole him as soon as you reasonably can.

Be alert to the possibility of a jail-break. The extremely agile and resourceful baby may be able to escape by climbing on large toys – so keep them out of the playpen. Also avoid hanging toys across the top.

'My daughter could stay in the playpen all day if I let her, but I'm not sure I should.'

Some placid babies seem perfectly happy to stay in the playpen for hours on end, even late into the first year. Maybe they just don't know what they're missing, or perhaps they're not assertive enough to demand their freedom. But though such a situation lets a parent accomplish plenty, it prevents a baby from accomplishing enough, intellectually or physically. So encourage your baby to see the world from a new perspective. She may be hesitant at first to leave the playpen, a little uneasy about losing the security of its four walls. Sitting with her on the wide-open floor, playing with her, giving her a favourite toy or a favourite blanket, or cheering on her attempts at crawling will make the transition easier.

READING TO BABY

'I'd like my daughter to develop an interest in reading. Is it too early to start reading to her?'

In an age when television seduces children away from books easily and early, it's probably never too soon to start reading to a child. Some even believe there's value in reading to a baby still in the uterus, and many begin their babies on books shortly after birth. But it isn't until some time in the second half of the first year that a baby becomes an active participant in the reading process, if only by chewing on the corners of the book to start with. Soon she begins to pay attention to the words as you read them (at this point, to the rhythm and sounds of the words rather than their meanings) and to the illustrations (enjoying the colour and patterns, but not necessarily relating the pictures to known objects).

To make sure your baby catches the bookworm early, use the following strategies:

Read to yourself. Reading to your baby will have less impact if you yourself spend more time in front of the TV than behind a book (or newspaper, or magazine). Though it's hard for parents of young children to find a spare moment for a quiet read, it's worth the effort; as with any behaviour, desirable or undesirable, children are much more likely to do as you do than to do as you say. Read a few pages out loud from a propped-up book while you nurse or give your baby a bottle, read a book in her room while she plays, keep a book on your bedside table for reading before you fall asleep and for showing your baby ('This is Daddy's book').

Start a juvenile collection. There are thousands of children's books on the shelves of bookshops, but only a limited number are appropriate for a beginner. Look for the following:

♦ Sturdy construction that defies destruction. Sturdiest are books with laminated cardboard pages with rounded edges, which can be mouthed without disintegrating and turned without tearing. Laminated or soft cloth books are good, as long as they can lie flat. A plastic spiral binding on a board book is a plus, since not only does it allow a book to lie flat when open, but also baby can play with the fascinating spiral design (make sure it's flexible, not rigid, so little fingers can't be pinched). Vinyl books are good for bath time, one of the few times some very young children sit still long enough for a reading session. To keep these free of mildew, dry thoroughly after each bath, and store in a dry place.

♦ Illustrations that include bold, bright, realistic pictures of familiar subjects, particularly animals, vehicles, toys and children. The pictures should be simple, not cluttered, so that baby won't be overwhelmed.

♦ Text that is not too complicated. Rhymes have the best chance of holding a baby's attention when you're reading to her since she's listening largely for ear appeal, not comprehension, and it'll be many months before she'll be able to follow a story line. One-word-on-a-page books are good, too, since they help her to increase her comprehension vocabulary and eventually her spoken vocabulary.

♦ Activity tie-ins. Books that stimulate games like peekaboo, touch-and-feel books that encourage learning about textures, and books that have surprises hidden under little flaps encourage audience participation.

♦ Discardable reading matter. Babies also like to handle and look at magazines with a lot of full-colour illustrations, so instead of recycling old ones, keep a rainy-day collection for your baby. Of course, when she's through with them, you'll probably have to recycle them anyway.

Learn to read parent-style. Yes, you know how to read aloud, but when you read to a baby, you need to read with style. Tempo, tone and inflection are important; read slowly, with a lilting singsong voice and exaggerated emphasis in the right places. Stop at each page

to stress salient points ('Look at the little boy rolling down the hill', or 'See the baby doggie laughing?') or to show her animals or people ('That's a cow – a cow says 'moo',' or 'There's a baby in a cradle – the baby's going 'sleepytime').

Make reading a habit. Build reading into baby's agenda, doing a few minutes at least twice a day, when she's quiet but alert, and when she's already been fed. Before nap time, after lunch, after bath and before bed are all good reading times. But keep to the schedule only if baby's receptive; don't push a book on her when she's in the mood to practise crawling or to make music with two pot covers. Reading should never be a chore.

Keep the library open. Store precious, destructible books on a high shelf for parent-supervised reading sessions, but keep a small (to prevent baby from being overwhelmed) rotating (to prevent baby from becoming bored) library of babyproof books where she can reach and enjoy them. Sometimes a baby who resists being sat down for a reading session with mummy or daddy will be happy to 'read' to herself, turning pages and looking at pictures at her own pace.

LEFT- OR RIGHT-HANDEDNESS

'I've noticed that my baby picks up and reaches for toys with either hand. Should I try to encourage him to use his right?'

We live in a world that's not equal-handed when it comes to handedness – catering to the right-handed among us, leaving lefties to fend for themselves. Most doors, irons, potato peelers, scissors and table settings are designed for righties. And lefties are destined to bump elbows at the dinner table, to shake with what to them is the 'wrong' hand, and wear their watch on what is considered the 'wrong' wrist. In the past, some parents, reluctant to relegate their children to this minority status, routinely tried to force right-handedness onto lefty-prone offspring.

Experts once believed that such parental pressure to change what is most probably a genetically determined trait led to stuttering and a variety of learning disabilities. Now, though they still don't recommend trying to change a child's natural handedness, they suspect that several traits are genetically intertwined with left-handedness. Many of these appear to be related to differences between lefties and righties with respect to development in the right and left hemispheres of the brain. In lefties, the right side of the brain is dominant, making them excel in such areas as spatial relations, which may be why they are overrepresented in such fields as sports, architecture and art. Since more boys than girls are left-handed, it is also theorized that levels of testosterone, a male hormone, somehow affect brain development and handedness. Much more study is needed before we fully understand what makes a person left- or right-handed and just how handedness affects various areas of one's life.

Most babies use both hands equally at first; a small minority show a preference for one hand or the other before 18 months, and a few seem to favour one hand at first, and then switch, but the majority of children will not show a preference until 18 to 24 months. What's important is letting baby use the hand he's most comfortable with, not the one you would like him to use. Since about 70 per cent of the population is strongly right-handed (10 per cent are

left-handed, and the other 20 per cent is ambidextrous), you can assume, until he demonstrates otherwise, that your baby will be, too. Offer things to his right hand. If he reaches over and grabs them with his left, or takes them with his right and then passes them to his left, so be it. If you're concerned that he's showing a preference this early on, bring it up with the paediatrician at the next visit.

CHILDPROOFING YOUR HOME

'I always said that a baby wasn't going to change the way we live. But with our daughter's crawling around, many of the valuable things we've collected over the years are at risk. Should I pack them away, or try to teach her to stay away from them?'

Many china shops would be as happy to host a bull as a seven- or eight-month-old baby. And, indeed, your breakable valuables might stand as much of a chance of surviving in a living room with your baby as they would in a ring with El Toro.

So if you don't want to see the Baccarat bowl you picked up in Paris or the Wedgwood vase your best friend gave you for a wedding gift shattered at your baby's feet, put them well out of reach until she's old enough and responsible enough to treat them with respect – which may not be for a couple of years. Do likewise with objects (of art or otherwise) that are heavy enough to hurt her should she pull them down.

Still, your family shouldn't spend the next years in a house stripped bare of objects – for your child's sake as much as for yours. If you want her to learn to live with the finer and more fragile things in life, she should be

COT SAFETY NOW

As baby becomes more active and adventurous, a whole world opens up, and along with it, a whole lot of potential for getting into trouble. And though the cot may seem like the very safest haven for your little explorer, it won't be long before he or she will be capable of scaling its four rails. While some babies never attempt an escape from their cots, many do, so it's wise to begin taking measures to prevent one now:

◆ If you haven't done so already, lower the mattress as far as it can go. Also check the mattress supports periodically to be sure they're not loose; if they are, an active baby can push the mattress down and get hurt.

◆ Consider removing the bumpers, which some babies figure out how to climb on to facilitate their escape. (Some parents of restless sleepers prefer to keep the bumpers in place to protect their babies' heads from bumps.)

◆ Don't leave big toys in the cot that baby can pile up and use as a stepping stool to freedom – and trouble. Take down any mobiles that baby could pull up on.

◆ Continue to avoid using pillows and fluffy duvets in the cot; not just because of the SIDS danger (which is still present but much smaller), but because a clever baby (aren't they all?) can pile them up to use as a ladder.

◆ Pull the cot at least 30 cm (12 in) away from all furniture and walls to avoid giving your baby a leg up on climbing. As always, make sure the cot isn't within reach of a curtain or window blind cord (all cords should be tied up anyway).

◆ Once baby's pulling up, he or she will probably use the cot railing as a teething biscuit. If the railing is wood and you'd like to protect it from your baby and your baby from it, install a teething rail.

◆ If, no matter what, your baby does try to escape the cot, consider putting some pillows or fluffy blankets on the floor next to the cot to cushion his or her landing.

◆ When baby reaches 89 cm (35 in), it's time to graduate to a bed.

exposed to some even at this age. Leave a few of the sturdier and less pricey pieces in your collection within your baby's reach. When she reaches, firmly tell her, 'No, don't touch that. That's Mummy and Daddy's.' Hand her a toy and explain that it is *hers.* If she persists in reaching for the forbidden object, take it away (too many nos begin to lose their effect) and put it out another day. Though you can't count on compliance

now (young babies have short memories), eventually your child will understand. As she gets older, you can host practise sessions – when she can hold and appropriately fondle breakable objects while you supervise closely, giving her valuable experience in the handling of valuables. Once she can be trusted to steer clear or handle with care, you can bring on the Baccarat and Wedgwood.

What it's Important to Know:
MAKING HOME SAFE FOR BABY

Put a fragile day-old baby next to a sturdy seven-month-old and the newborn will seem, in comparison, so helpless, so much more vulnerable to harm. But, in reality, it's the older baby who's more vulnerable. Newly acquired skills unmatched by good judgment, in fact, make babies in the second half of their first year extremely hazardous to their own health. And once babies are able to get around alone, the average home becomes as dangerous for them to explore as it is exciting.

An independently mobile baby in a home that hasn't been babyproofed is an accident waiting to happen – and happen again. It usually takes a combination of factors to trigger an accident or injury, including a dangerous object or substance (in the case of a baby, perhaps a staircase or drug), a susceptible victim (your baby's a prime one) and possibly environmental conditions (ungated steps, an unlocked medicine chest) that allow victim and danger to come together. In the case of baby injuries, it may also hinge on the faltering vigilance – sometimes only for a moment – of a parent or other care provider.

To minimize the possibility of an injury, all of these factors must be modified in some way. Dangerous objects and substances must be removed from reach, the susceptible baby has to be made less susceptible by gradual safety training, the hazardous environment must be modified (with gates on stairs, locks on cabinets) and, possibly most important of all, care providers must be ever on the alert, especially at times of stress, when most accidents occur.

Because a great many injuries occur at the homes of others – particularly the homes of grandmas and grandpas – you should extend many of these safety measures to homes baby visits often and offer this chapter as reading material to those who frequently care for your child. Here's how to modify the factors that contribute to accidents.

CHANGE YOUR WAYS

Since modifying baby's behaviour will be a long, slow educational process, which can begin now but won't be complete for many years, it's your behaviour that will have the most impact on the safety of your child at this stage.

◆ Be eternally vigilant. No matter how carefully you attempt to childproof your house, remember that you can't make it completely accident-proof. Your attention, or that of another care provider, must be continuous, especially if yours is a particularly resourceful child.

◆ Don't let your attention be diverted in midactivity when using household cleaning products, medicines, electrical appliances or any other potentially hazardous object or substance when your baby is on the loose. It takes no more than a second for baby to get into serious trouble. Very dangerous items – such as power tools – should not be used while baby's on the loose unless a second adult is on baby watch.

◆ Be particularly alert during times of stress and stressful times of day. It's when you're distracted (the phone's ringing, the television's blaring, dinner's boiling over on the stove) that you're likely to forget to take the knife off the table, strap baby into the high chair or close the stair gate.

♦ *Never* leave baby alone in a car or in your home, not even for a moment. Don't even leave him or her alone in a room of your home (except in a playpen or cot, or in a *thoroughly* babyproofed room and then only for a few minutes while you're in earshot, unless he or she is sleeping). Do not leave a baby alone, even 'safely' enclosed in a cot or playpen, awake or asleep, with a preschooler (they often don't know their own strength or realize the possible consequences of their actions) or with a pet (even a docile one).

♦ Choose appropriate clothing. Use only flame-retardant sleepwear; be sure that pyjama feet aren't too floppy, trouser cuffs too long, or socks or slippers too slippery for a baby who is pulling up or starting to walk. Avoid long scarves or sashes that can trip baby up, entrap him or her, or pose a strangling risk; likewise shun strings over 15 cm (6 in) long (remove them from sweats, hoods of jackets and other clothes).

♦ Become familiar, if you aren't already, with emergency and first-aid procedures (see pages 575–602). You can't always prevent injuries, but knowing what to do if a serious one occurs can save lives and limbs.

♦ Give your baby plenty of supervised freedom. Once you've made your baby's environment as safe as possible, avoid hovering (though not watching). Though you want your child to be safety-conscious, you don't want to discourage the normal experimentation of childhood. Children, like adults, learn from their mistakes; never allowing them to make a mistake can prevent growth. And a child who is afraid to run, climb or try new things misses out not only on the education that comes through free play, but on a lot of the fun of childhood as well.

CHANGE YOUR BABY'S SURROUNDINGS

Until now, your baby has seen your home mostly from your arms, at your eye level. Now that he or she is beginning to get a look at it from down on all fours, you will have to begin looking at it from that perspective, too. One way to do this is to actually get down on the floor yourself; from there, you will see a multitude of dangers you may not even have realized existed. Another way is to examine everything that is within 90 cm (3 ft) above the floor – the usual range of a baby's reach.

Changes throughout the home. As you tour your home, look at and alter as necessary the following:

♦ Windows. If they are above ground level, install window guards according to manufacturer's directions; or adjust them so they can't open more than 15 cm (6 in). Keep climbable furniture away from windows.

♦ Cords to blinds or curtains. Tie them up so baby can't become entangled, and avoid loops; do not place a cot or playpen, or a chair or bed baby can climb on, within reach of any cords.

♦ Electrical cords. Move them out of reach, behind furniture so that baby won't mouth them, risking electric

POISON CONTROL

Children, particularly very young ones, do a lot of their discovery of the world orally. Virtually anything they pick up will go right to the mouth. They haven't yet learned to categorize substances or objects as 'safe' or 'unsafe' – everything is merely 'interesting'. Nor are their tastebuds sophisticated enough to warn them, as ours do, that a substance is dangerous because it tastes terrible.

To protect your innocents from perils, follow these rules without fail:

◆ Lock all potentially poisonous substances out of reach and out of sight of your baby – even crawlers can climb up on low chairs and stools or cushions.

◆ Follow all safety rules for administering or taking medicines (see page 538).

◆ Avoid buying brightly coloured or attractively packaged household cleansers, laundry detergents and other substances. They will attract your baby. If necessary, cover illustrations with black tape (but don't cover instructions or warnings). Also avoid toxic substances with attractive food fragrances (such as mint, lemon or apricot).

◆ Purchase products with child-resistant packaging, when possible.

◆ Make it a habit to return hazardous items to safe storage immediately after each use; don't put a spray can of furniture polish or a box of mothballs down 'just for a minute' while you answer the phone.

◆ Store food and non-food items separately, and never put non-edibles in empty food containers (bleach in an apple juice bottle, for example, or lubricating oil in a jam jar). Babies learn very early to identify where their food comes from, and won't understand why they can't drink what's in the juice bottle or lick what's in the jam jar.

◆ Avoid buying and displaying non-foods that look like foods (such as wax or glass fruit).

◆ Discard potentially poisonous substances. Empty them as instructed on the label,

shock, or tug at them, pulling lamps or other heavy items down; don't put them under carpets, where they could overheat and cause a fire.

◆ Electrical sockets. Cover with socket covers or place heavy furniture in front of them to prevent baby from inserting something (such as a hairpin) or probing with a drooly finger and getting a shock.

◆ Unstable furnishings. Put rickety or unstable chairs, tables or other furniture that might topple if baby pulls on it out of the way for the time being; securely fasten to the wall bookcases or other structures that baby could pull down.

◆ Dresser drawers. Keep them closed (and, if possible, safety-latched) so baby won't climb in them and pull the dresser down or the drawers out and on top of himself or herself; if the dresser isn't stable, consider fastening it to the wall.

◆ Painted surfaces within baby's reach. Be sure they are lead free; if they aren't or if you aren't sure, repaint or wallpaper. If testing shows lead in the paint, get expert advice on the best way to proceed.

rinsing the containers before discarding unless the label instructs otherwise, and putting them out in a tightly closed dustbin immediately. *Never* dump them in a wastebasket or kitchen bin.

♦ Choose the *relatively* less hazardous product over the one with a long list of warnings when possible. Among those household products generally considered less hazardous: non-chlorine bleaches, vinegar, soda crystals, lemon oil, beeswax, olive oil (for furniture), non-chemical flypaper, mineral oil (for lubrication, not internal use), compressed air drain openers (rather than corrosive liquids or granules).

♦ Put POISON labels on all poisonous products. If you can't locate such labels, simply put an X of black tape on each product (but don't cover instructions or warnings). Eventually, your child will also come to recognize that these products are unsafe.

♦ Think of all of the following as potentially poisonous if swallowed by your baby (those that are asterisked probably shouldn't be in your home at all):

Alcoholic beverages
Ammoniated mercury (not useful medicinally)*
Antifreeze
Aspirin or paracetamol
Boric acid
Camphorated oil
Chlorine bleach
Cosmetics
Dishwasher detergents
Drain cleaners
Furniture polish
Insect or rodent poisons
Iron pills or drops (even baby's own)
Kerosene
Lye*
Medicines of all kinds (children's varieties that smell and taste good can be especially tempting)
Mothballs
Mouthwash
Nail-care products
Perfume
Petroleum*
Turpentine (not useful)
Oil of wintergreen (not useful medicinally)
Sleeping pills
Tranquillizers
Weed killers

♦ Ashtrays. Put them out of reach so baby won't touch a hot butt or sample a handful of ashes and butts; better still, for your baby's health as well as safety, banish tobacco from your home entirely.

♦ Houseplants. Keep them out of baby's reach, where baby can't pull them down on himself or herself or nibble on them; be especially wary of poisonous plants (see page 415).

♦ Loose knobs on furniture or cabinets. Remove or secure any that are small enough to be swallowed (smaller than baby's fist) or cause choking.

♦ Radiators. Put barriers around them or radiator covers over them during the heating season.

♦ Stairs. Put a gate at the top and another three steps up from the bottom.

♦ Banisters and railings. Be sure the gap between upright posts on stair or balcony railings is less than 10 cm (4 in), and that none is loose. If the gap is too large, install a Plexiglas, clear plastic or mesh barrier across the railing.

♦ Fireplaces, heaters, stoves, floor furnaces. Put up protective grilles or other barriers to keep small fingers from hot surfaces (even the grille on a floor furnace can get hot enough to cause second-degree burns) as well as fire. Unplug heaters when not in use, and whenever possible store them where children can't get at them.

♦ Tablecloths. If they hang over the side of the table and are not well anchored, remove them until your baby knows not to pull up on them or, alternatively, keep baby off the floor when you have a cloth on the table.

♦ Glass-topped tables. Either cover with a heavy table pad or put them out of reach temporarily.

♦ Sharp edges or corners on tables, chests, and so on. If baby can bump into them, cover them with home-made or purchased cushioned strips and corner guards.

♦ Scatter rugs. Be sure they have non-skid backings; don't place them at the top of stairs or allow them to remain rumpled.

♦ Floor tiles and carpets. Repair all loose areas to prevent tripping.

♦ Rubber ends from door stoppers. Remove because they pose a chok-ing risk. Or, remove the entire stopper completely and install a v-shaped hinge pin at the top of the door.

♦ Heavy knickknacks and bookends. Place them where baby can't reach out and pull them over; babies have more strength than you may think.

♦ Toy chests. These should have light-weight lids with safety closing mechanisms (or no lids at all), as well as ventilation holes (in case baby should become locked in). Better still, don't use toy chests at all. In general, open shelves are safer for toy storage.

♦ Cot. Once your baby starts showing interest in pulling up (don't wait until the feat has been achieved), it's time to make some adjustments; see page 401.

♦ Floor clutter. Try to keep it out of traf-fic lanes to prevent tripping. Wipe up spills and pick up papers immediately.

♦ Garage, cellar and hobby areas. Lock securely and keep children out, since these areas usually contain a variety of hazardous implements and/or poisonous substances.

♦ Other areas with hazardous or breakable objects, such as a living room housing a collection of fine teacups. Put up a gate or other bar-rier to keep baby out, or lock objects up.

Also be alert to the host of haz-ardous items found in the typical home and see that they are safely stored, gen-erally in childproof drawers, cabinets or chests or on absolutely out-of-reach shelves (you'd be surprised at how high some babies can manage to climb). When you're using such items, be sure baby can't get at them when you turn your back, and always be sure to put them away as soon as you've finished with them or as soon as you spot one that has been left out. Be particularly careful with:

♦ Sharp implements such as scissors, knives, letter openers, razors (don't leave these on the side of the basin or in the wastebasket), and blades.

♦ Swallowable notions such as mar-bles, coins, safety pins, and anything else smaller than 3.5 cm (1⅜ in) in diameter (about the diameter of a toilet paper tube).

- Pens, pencils and other writing implements (substitute chunky non-toxic crayons).[2]

- Sewing and knitting supplies, particularly pins and needles, thimbles, scissors, yarn and buttons.

- Lightweight plastic bags such as produce bags, dry-cleaning bags and packaging on new clothing (babies can suffocate if such a bag is placed over the face).

- Incendiary articles such as matches and matchbooks, lighters and hot cigarette butts. (For that matter, any cigarette is hazardous – both as a poison and as a chokable.)

- Tools of your trade or hobbies: paints and thinners, if there's an artist in the house; pins and needles if someone sews; woodworking equipment if there's a carpenter; and so on.

- Toys meant for older children. Toys that belong to older siblings generally should not be played with by babies or toddlers under three; this includes building sets with small pieces, dolls with small accessories, bikes and scooters, miniature cars and trucks, and anything with sharp corners, small pieces, removable or breakable small parts, or electrical connections.

- Button batteries: the disc-shaped type used in watches, calculators, hearing aids, cameras, and so on (they are easy to swallow, and can release hazardous contents into baby's oesophagus or stomach).

- Food fakes of wax, papier-mâché, rubber or any other substance that isn't safe for a baby or child to mouth (a wax apple, a candle that smells and looks like an ice-cream sundae, a child's eraser that smells and looks like a ripe strawberry).

- Cleaning materials.

- Glass, china or other breakables.

- Lightbulbs, especially small ones, such as those in night-lights, that a baby can mouth and break.

- Jewellery, particularly beads, which can be pulled apart; and small items such as rings (all are attractive to baby and easily swallowed). Babies shouldn't wear jewellery, for the same reason.

- Mothballs (they're poisonous).

- Shoe polish (besides making a mess, it can make baby sick).

- Perfumes and all cosmetics (they are potentially toxic); vitamins and medicines.

- Toy whistles (baby can choke on them, and on the small ball inside should it come loose).

- Keep the purses or bags of guests out of your child's reach. They may contain toiletries, medications or other items that aren't safe for baby.

- Balloons (uninflated or burst, they can be inhaled and cause choking).

- Small, hard finger foods, such as nuts or raisins, popcorn or hard sweets that may be left around in sweet dishes (baby can choke on them). Ditto pet kibble.

---

2. Some children enjoy using pencils or pens just like mummy and daddy; if your baby does, allow such use only when he or she is safely seated and you can supervise closely.

◆ Guns and ammunition, real or toy (if you must have them in the home).

◆ Lye and acid; for example, some drain-cleaning products (better not to have these in your home at all).

◆ Alcoholic beverages (an amount that merely relaxes you could make your baby deathly ill).

◆ Strings, cords, cot gyms, tape cassettes, or anything else that could get tangled around a baby's neck and cause strangulation.

◆ Anything else in your home that would be dangerous if mouthed or swallowed by a baby. See list of poisons, page 405.

Fire-safety changes. Hearing that a child or children perished in a fire is upsetting enough. To know that the fire could have been prevented, or could have been discovered before it spread to fatal proportions, is even more disturbing. Check every corner of your home for possible fire hazards to be sure 'it can't happen here':

◆ Be sure your baby's and children's sleepwear meets safety standards for flame resistance.

◆ If smoking is permitted in your home, dispose of all cigar or cigarette butts, ashes, pipe ashes and used matches carefully and never leave them where a baby can get at them. Any smokers in your home should make a habit of disposing of butts immediately, and you should empty ashtrays promptly when you have smoking guests.

◆ Do not permit anyone (visitors included) to smoke in bed or while falling asleep on the sofa.

◆ Keep matches and lighters out of the reach of children and babies.

◆ Do not allow rubbish to accumulate (especially combustibles such as paint or paint rags).

◆ Avoid using flammable liquids, kerosene as well as commercial products, for spot removal on clothing. Another reason to avoid these: they are poisonous if ingested.

◆ Don't let anyone (adult or child) near a fireplace, wood-burning stove, candle or space heater while wearing trailing sleeves, dragging scarves or hanging shirttails, any of which could unintentionally catch fire.

◆ Keep candles out of reach of curious hands in places where they won't be knocked over, and be sure to blow them out before leaving the room. Keep Christmas tree lights high enough so a child can't reach one and pull the whole tree down.

◆ Cover halogen bulbs with a safety shield.

◆ Have your heating system checked annually, be careful not to overload electrical circuits, always remove plugs from sockets properly (don't jerk the cord), and check electric appliances and cords regularly for wear and/or loose connections. If you have fuses rather than circuit breakers, use only 15-amp fuses for lighting; never substitute anything else for a fuse.

◆ Avoid using space heaters when there are children in the house. If you must use them, be sure they turn off automatically if toppled or if something is placed against them. And don't leave baby unsupervised around one.

◆ Place extinguishers in areas where fire risk is greatest, such as in the kitchen, near the fireplace or wood-

SAFETY EQUIPMENT

There's more to buying for baby than cute clothes, plush pushchairs, and the latest car seat. You'll also need to fill your shopping trolley with the following childproofing essentials, to make your home safe for baby:

- Cupboard and drawer locks (to keep kitchen cabinets and drawers safe from prying fingers)
- Cupboard latches (to do likewise)
- Oven guards
- Doorknob guards (to make it difficult for little ones to open doors)
- Clear plastic corner cushioning (to soften corners of tables)
- Edge cushions (to do same for sharp edges)
- Socket plugs or covers
- Bath spout safety cover
- Non-skid decorations for bath bottoms
- Skid-resistant step stool
- Kidproof patio door locks
- Potty proofer (suction cups or latch to keep lid down when not in use)

---

burning stove and in the garage. Check the pressure gauge at least yearly or, preferably, two times a year (you can do it when you change the batteries on your smoke detectors). Buy only those that have been tested by an independent laboratory and label for the type (ordinary combustible, flammable liquids or electrical) and size of the fire they can extinguish. (In an emergency, bicarbonate of soda can be used for putting out kitchen fires.) Try to put out a fire only if it is small and contained (such as one in your oven, a frying pan or a wastebasket) and if you are between the fire and an exit. If it is not contained, get out of the house instead.

- Install fire and smoke detectors as recommended by your local fire station, if you haven't already. Check monthly to see that they are in good working order and that batteries haven't run down.

- Install rope ladders at selected upper-floor windows to facilitate escape; teach older children and adults how to use them. Practise getting down holding a doll.

- Devise an escape plan and practise it so that everyone who lives or works in your household will know how to get out safely and quickly in an emergency and know where to meet other family members. Assign parents and other adults to evacuate specific children. Be sure everyone (including baby-sitters) knows that the priority in case of fire is to evacuate the premises immediately – without worrying about dressing, saving valuables or putting out the fire. (The only exception is a well-contained fire that can be put out with a fire extinguisher.) Most deaths occur from suffocation or burns due to hot fumes and smoke, not from direct flame. The fire department should be called as soon as possible from a mobile phone street phone or a neighbour's house.

Changes in the kitchen. Make a special tour of the kitchen, one of the most intriguing places in the house to your newly mobile baby – and also one of the most dangerous. You can make it safer by taking the following steps:

♦ Attach child-guard latches to drawers or cabinets that contain anything off-limits to little ones, such as breakable glass items, sharp implements, hazardous cleaning compounds, medicines or dangerous foodstuffs (such as nuts or popcorn – on which a baby could choke – and hot peppers). If your baby figures out how to unlatch the safety latches (some very wily ones do), you will have to relegate all dangerous items to out-of-reach storage areas or just keep your baby out of the kitchen entirely with a gate or other barrier. What is truly out of reach will change as your baby gets older, so your storage arrangement may have to as well.

♦ Set aside at least one cupboard (baby is less likely to catch his or her fingers in a cupboard than in a drawer) for your little explorer to enjoy freely. Some sturdy pots and pans, wooden spoons, strainers, tea towels, plastic bowls, and so on can provide minutes-at-a-time of entertainment and may satisfy your baby's curiosity enough to keep him or her out of forbidden places.

♦ Keep the handles of pots and pans that are on the stove turned towards the rear and out of baby's reach, and use back burners whenever possible. If controls are on the front of the oven, erect some sort of barrier to keep them untouchable, or snap on oven knob covers. An appliance latch will keep conventional and microwave ovens inaccessible.

♦ Keep the dishwasher door tightly closed at all times. A baby who uses an open door to pull up on can

encounter numerous dangers, including knives.

♦ Don't sit baby on a countertop near electrical appliances, the stove or anything else that might be hazardous – or you may find him or her with fingers in the toaster, hands on a hot pot, or a knife heading for an open mouth the moment you turn your back.

♦ Be sure not to leave a hot beverage or a bowl of soup at the edge of a table where your baby can reach it.

♦ Keep boxes of cling film, foil, greaseproof paper, baking parchment or any other box with a serrated edge (that could easily cut little fingers) in a locked drawer or in a high cupboard.

♦ Keep plastic bags out of reach.

♦ Place refrigerator magnets high enough so your child can't reach them – or don't use them at all. They pose a choking risk.

♦ Keep rubbish in a tightly covered container that baby can't open or under the sink behind a securely latched door. Children love to rummage through rubbish, and the dangers – from spoiled foods to broken glass – are many.

♦ Clean up all spills promptly – they make for slippery floors.

♦ Empty buckets of water immediately after you're finished with them; a baby or toddler can tumble in and drown.

♦ Follow the safety rules for selecting, using and storing kitchen detergents, scouring powders, silver polishes and all other cleaning supplies (see page 404).

Changes in the bath. Nearly as alluring to a baby as the kitchen, and equally dangerous, is the bathroom. One way to keep it off-limits is to put a hook and eye or other latch high up on the door, and to keep it latched when not in use. Baby-safe the bathroom by taking the following precautions:

◆ Keep all medications (including over-the-counter ones such as antacids), mouthwashes, toothpaste, vitamin pills, hair preparations and sprays, skin lotions and cosmetics safely stored out of baby's reach.

◆ Keep the lower shelves of the bathroom closets and cabinets free of cottonwool balls, swabs or anything else that may pose a choking hazard to young children.

◆ Don't use, or let anyone else use, a hair dryer near your baby when he or she is in the bath or playing with water. Don't blow-dry baby's hair.

◆ Never leave small electrical appliances plugged in when you aren't using them. A baby could dunk a hair dryer in the toilet and get a fatal electric shock, switch on a razor and get cut, or get burned on a curling iron. Unplugging appliances won't be enough if your child has good manual dexterity (those little whizzes often figure out how to plug in an appliance, with possibly disastrous results). Better not to leave these appliances out at all.

◆ Keep the water temperature in your home set at or below 49°C (120°F) to avoid accidental scalding, and always turn off the hot water tap before the cold. Routinely test bathwater temperature with your elbow before putting baby in the bath. If your bath doesn't have a non-skid finish, add some skidproof stick-ons.

◆ If you live in a multifamily dwelling – such as a block of flats – you may not have access to the water heater or ability to set it to a safe temperature. Check with the landlord. If the temperature is not set safely, look into installing an antiscald plumbing device on the bathtub, where tap water scalds are most common. (Some housing codes may require it.)

◆ When not in use, keep the toilet lid closed with suction cups, latches or another device made expressly for this purpose. Most babies see the toilet as a private little swimming pool, and love to play in it any chance they get. Not only is this unsanitary, but an energetic toddler could topple in headfirst, with catastrophic results.

◆ Invest in a protective cover for the bath spout to prevent bumps or burns should baby fall against it.

◆ Do not leave your baby in the bath unattended, even once he's sitting well, and even in a special bath seat. This rule should be in force until your child is five years old.

◆ Never leave water in the bath when it's not in use; a small child may topple into the bath at play, and a drowning can occur in as little as a couple of *centimetres/inches* of water.

Changes for a safer outdoors. Though most injuries to infants occur in the home, serious ones can also occur in your own garden or someone else's – as well as on local streets and playgrounds. Many of these accidents are relatively easy to prevent:

◆ Never let an infant or toddler play outdoors alone. Even a baby in a safety harness, napping in a pram or pushchair, needs to be watched almost constantly – he or she could suddenly wake and become tangled in the harness while struggling to be free. A sleeping baby who is not strapped needs to be under someone's watchful eye full-time. Any child left alone for any amount of time can be harmed by an unleashed pet, or become a victim of abduction.

♦ Keep swimming or wading pools and any other water catchments (even if filled with only a couple of centimetres/inches of water) inaccessible to babies and toddlers – whether they are crawling, walking independently or navigating a walker. Fence a swimming pool on all sides with a self-closing, self-latching gate and consider installing a pool alarm. Keep gates or doors to the pool locked at all times; empty and turn wading pools upside down, and drain any other areas where water can accumulate before allowing baby to play nearby.

♦ Check public play areas before letting your baby loose. Though it's fairly easy to keep your garden free of dog droppings (they can harbour worms), broken glass and other dangerous debris, park attendants may find it more difficult to do so.

♦ It's not enough to plead, 'Please don't eat the daisies!' Avoid planting, or at least fence in where baby definitely can't reach them, poisonous plants (see box, page 415). Also begin teaching your baby that eating plants, indoors or out, is a no-no; even if a plant isn't poisonous, stop any leaf or flower nibbling immediately.

♦ Be sure that outdoor play equipment is safe. It should be sturdily constructed, correctly assembled, firmly anchored, and installed at least 1.8 m (6 ft) from fences or walls. Cap all screws and bolts to prevent injuries from rough or sharp edges, and

check for loose ones periodically. Avoid S-type hooks for swings (the chains can swing out of them and they can catch clothing), and rings anywhere on the equipment that are between 12.5 and 25 cm (5 and 10 in) in diameter, since a child's head might become entrapped. Swings should be of soft materials (such as leather or canvas rather than wood or metal) to prevent serious head injuries. The best surfaces for outdoor play areas are 30 cm (12 in) of sand, mulch, wood chips, pea gravel or a shock-absorbent material, such as rubber paving blocks. Openings in guardrails and spaces between platforms and between ladder rungs should measure less than 9 cm (3½ in) or more than 23 cm (9 in) so that children do not get trapped in those openings.

CHANGE YOUR BABY

Injuries are much more likely to happen to those who are susceptible to them and, of course, babies easily fall into that category. But it isn't too early to begin safety-proofing your baby even as you safety-proof your home. Teach your baby about dangers whenever you encounter them. Pretend to touch the point of a needle, for example, saying 'Ouch', and pulling your finger away quickly in mock pain. Build and use a vocabulary of warning words ('Ouch', 'Boo-boo', 'Hot', 'Sharp') and phrases ('Don't touch', 'That's dangerous', 'Be careful', 'That's an ouch', 'That will give you a boo-boo'), so that your baby will automatically come to associate them with dangerous objects, substances and situations. At first your little dramatizations will seem to be going right over your little one's head – and they will be. But gradually the brain will begin storing the information, and one day it will be apparent that your lessons have taken hold. Begin teaching your baby now about the following:

Sharp or pointy implements. Whenever you use a knife, scissors, razor or letter opener in front of your baby, be sure to mention that it is sharp, that it's not a toy, that only mummy and daddy or other grown-ups can touch it. As your child becomes older and gains better small motor control, teach cutting with a child's safety scissors and a butter knife. Finally, advance to supervised use of the 'adult' versions of these implements.

Hot stuff. Even a seven- or eight-month-old will begin to catch on when you consistently warn that your coffee (or the stove, a lit match or candle, a radiator or heater, a fireplace) is hot and shouldn't be touched. Very soon the word 'hot' will automatically signal 'Don't touch' to your baby. Illustrate your point by letting him or her touch something hot, but not hot enough to burn – the very warm outside of your coffee cup, for example. When a child is old enough to strike a match or carry a cup of coffee, he or she should be taught the safe way to do so.

Steps. Parents are often advised to put up safety gates at stairways in homes where there are babies who are beginning to be mobile – either independently or in walkers (see page 329 for why mobile walkers are not advisable). On the one hand, this is an important safety precaution and one that too few families take. On the other hand, the baby who knows nothing about steps besides that they are off-limits is the one who is at greatest risk of falling the first time an open stairway is discovered. So put a gate at the top of every stairway of more than three steps in your home – getting down is much trickier, and thus much more hazardous, for a baby than getting up. But also put a gate three steps up from the bottom so that baby can practise going up and down under safe conditions. When he or she becomes proficient, open the gate occasionally to let baby tackle the full flight as you stand or crouch a step or two below, ready to lend support if a little foot or hand slips. Once going up is mastered, teach baby how to come down safely – a much more challenging task and one that may take several months to achieve. Children who know how to climb up and down steps are much safer should they happen upon an unprotected stairway, which every child does now and then, than those with no climbing experience. But continue to keep the gates in place, fastening them when you're not around to supervise, until your child is a very reliable step climber (somewhere around two years of age).

Electrical hazards. Electrical outlets, electric cords and electrically operated appliances all have great appeal for curious little minds and hands. It's not enough to distract a baby on the way to probing an unprotected socket or to hide all the visible cords in your home; it's also necessary to repeatedly remind the baby of their dangerous potential ('Ouch!'), and to teach older children respectful use of electricity and the risks of mixing it with water.

Baths, pools and other watery attractions. Water play is fun and educational; encourage it. But also teach a baby not to get into the bath, a pool, a pond or any other body of water without mummy or daddy or another grown-up – and that includes babies and children who have gone through swimming classes. You can't sufficiently 'waterproof' a young child, so you can never leave one alone near water, but you can begin to teach some water safety rules.

Poisonous substances. You're always careful about locking away household cleansers, medicines, and so on. But your parents are visiting and your dad leaves his heart medicine on a living room table. Or you're at your sister's house, and she has chlorine bleach and dishwasher detergent in an unlatched cabinet under the kitchen sink. You're asking for trouble if you haven't begun to teach your baby the rules of substance safety. Repeat these messages over and over again:

♦ Don't eat or drink anything unless mummy or daddy or another grown-up you know gives it to you (this is a difficult concept for a baby, but an important one for all children to learn eventually). Don't eat or drink anything that isn't 'food' or 'drink'.

♦ Medicine and vitamin pills are *not* sweets, though they are sometimes flavoured to taste that way. (Never refer to baby's medicine or vitamin drops as 'yummy'.) Don't eat or drink them unless mummy or daddy or another grown-up you know gives them to you.

♦ Don't put anything in your mouth if you don't know what it is.

♦ Only mummy or daddy or another grown-up can use medicine, scouring powder, spray wax or any other potentially poisonous substance. Repeat this every time you take or give a medication, scrub the bath, polish the furniture, and so on.

There are dangers outside your home, too, that your baby needs to be prepared for:

Street hazards. Begin teaching street smarts now. Every time you cross a street with your baby, explain about listening and watching for cars, about crossing at the green and not in between, and waiting for the 'green man'. If there are driveways in your neighbourhood, then you should explain that it's necessary to 'stop, look, and listen' at them, too. Once your child is walking, teach him never to cross without holding on to an adult's hand – even if there's no traffic. It's a good idea to hold hands on the pavement, too, but many toddlers love the freedom of walking on their own. If you permit this (and you probably will have to at least some of the time), you will have to keep an eye on your child literally every second – that's all it takes for a child to dart into the path of an oncoming car. Infractions of the don't-go-in-the-street-alone rule deserve a sharp reprimand.

Be sure, too, that your baby knows not to leave the house or apartment without you or another adult. Every once in a while a toddler toddles alone out the front door and into trouble. An out-of-reach lock will help prevent this potential tragedy.

Car safety. Be certain that your baby not only becomes accustomed to sitting in a car seat in the rear, but as he or she gets older, understands the reason why it's essential. Allow an exception even once and your child will find it very difficult to accept that using a car seat is non-negotiable. Also explain other car safety rules, such as no throwing toys around and no playing with door locks or window buttons.

Playground safety. Even a baby can begin learning playground safety rules. Teach yours not to twist a swing (when they or someone else is on it, or even if it's empty), push an empty swing or walk in front of a moving one. Observe these rules yourself, and regularly mention them to your baby. Also explain

RED LIGHT ON GREENERY

Many common house and garden plants are poisonous when eaten. Since plant leaves and flowers are no exception to a baby's everything-in-the-mouth-that-fits rule, poisonous varieties must be off-limits for babies. Place houseplants high up, where leaves or flowers can't fall on the floor below, and where baby can't get to them by pulling up, crawling or climbing. Better still, give poisonous houseplants to childless friends. Label with the accurate botanical name any houseplant you do keep, so that if your baby accidentally ingests some leaves or flowers or berries, you will be able to supply the accurate information to your doctor. Place all plants, even non-poisonous ones, where they can't be toppled with a tug.

The following houseplants are poisonous, some in very small doses:

Dumb-cane, English ivy, foxglove, hyacinth bulbs (and leaves and flowers in quantity), hydrangea, iris rootstalk and rhizome, lily of the valley, philodendron, Jerusalem cherry.

Outdoor plants that are poisonous include:

Azalea, rhododendron, caladium, daffodil and narcissus bulbs, daphne, poison ivy, foxglove, hyacinth bulbs (and leaves and flowers in quantity), hydrangea, iris rootstalk and rhizome, Japanese yew seeds and leaves, larkspur, laurel, lily of the valley, morning glory seeds, oleander, privet, rhubarb leaves, sweet peas (especially the 'peas', which are the seeds), tomato plant leaves, wisteria pods and seeds, yews.

Christmas favourites holly and mistletoe, and to a lesser extent, poinsettia (which is irritating but not poisonous), are also on the danger list.

---

that it's necessary to wait until the child ahead of you is off the slide before going down, and that it is unsafe to climb up from the bottom.

Kids learn volumes through their parents' example. So the best way to teach your baby about safe living is to practise it yourself. Make a habit of buckling your seat belt and obeying traffic signals, and your child will be likely to grow up with the same good safety habits.

◆ ◆ ◆

CHAPTER 13

The Ninth Month

There just aren't enough waking hours in the day for a busy eight-month old who's on the go – or attempting to be on the go – every chance he or she gets. Baby's also a budding comedian (who'll do anything for a laugh), an avid mimic (who delights in copying sounds you make), and a born performer ('And for an encore, I think I'll do that fake cough – again'). He or she is capable of understanding more complex concepts, such as object permanence – that when something is covered up, such as a daddy behind a menu, it's still there – and is becoming much more sophisticated in his or her play. But this new maturity comes with a price: stranger anxiety. Once happy in just about any pair of cozy arms, baby has all of a sudden become pretty picky about the company he or she keeps. Mummy, daddy and favourite baby-sitter only need apply.

What Your Baby May Be Doing

All babies reach milestones on their own developmental time line. If your baby seems not to have reached one or more of these milestones, rest assured, he or she probably will very soon. Your baby's rate of development is normal for your baby. Keep in mind, too, that it may have been slowed down in certain departments (such as crawling) if baby didn't spend much time playing on his or her belly. (Some babies skip crawling altogether, and that's fine, too.) If you have concerns about your baby's development (because you've noticed a missed milestone or what you think might be a developmental delay), don't hesitate to check it out with the doctor at the next well-baby visit – even if he or she doesn't bring it up. Parents often notice nuances in a baby's development that doctors don't. Premature infants generally reach milestones later than others of the same birth age, often achieving them closer to their adjusted age (the age they would be if they had been born at term), and sometimes later.

By nine months, your baby . . . should be able to:

◆ work to get a toy that's out of reach

◆ look for dropped object

. . . will probably be able to:

◆ pull up to standing position from sitting

◆ creep or crawl[1]

◆ get into a sitting position from stomach

◆ object if you try to take a toy away

◆ stand holding on to someone or something

◆ pick up tiny object with any part of thumb and finger (keep all dangerous objects out of baby's reach)

◆ say 'mama' or 'dada' indiscriminately

◆ play peekaboo

. . . may possibly be able to:

◆ play patty-cake (clap hands) or wave bye-bye

◆ walk holding on to furniture (cruise)

◆ understand 'no' (but not always obey it)

. . . may even be able to:

◆ 'play ball' (roll ball back to you)

◆ drink from a cup independently

◆ pick up a tiny object neatly with tips of thumb and forefinger (keep all dangerous objects out of baby's reach)

◆ stand alone momentarily

◆ stand alone well

◆ say 'dada' or 'mama' discriminately

◆ say one word other than 'mama' or 'dada'

◆ respond to a one-step command with gestures ('Give that to me', said with hand out)

What You Can Expect at This Month's Checkup

Each practitioner will have a personal approach to well-baby checkups. The overall organization of the physical exam, as well as the number and type of assessment techniques used and procedures performed, will also vary with the individual needs of the child. But, in general, you can expect the following at a checkup when your baby is about nine months old:

◆ Questions about how you and baby and the rest of the family are doing at home, and about baby's eating, sleeping and general progress. Questions about child care, if you are working.

◆ Measurement of baby's weight, length and head circumference, and plotting of progress since birth.

◆ Physical exam, including a recheck of any previous problems.

◆ Developmental assessment. The examiner may actually put baby

---

1. Babies who spend little time on their stomachs during playtime may reach this milestone later, and that's not cause for concern (see page 205).

through a series of 'tests' to evaluate baby's ability to sit independently, to pull up with or without help, to reach for and grasp objects, to rake at and pick up tiny objects, to look for a dropped or hidden object, to respond to his or her name, to recognize such words as 'mummy', 'daddy', 'bye-bye', and 'no', and to enjoy social games such as patty-cake and peekaboo, or may simply rely on observation plus your reports on what baby is doing.

◆ Immunizations, if not given before and if baby is in good health and there are no other contraindications. Be sure to discuss previous reactions, if any, beforehand.

◆ Possibly, haemoglobin or haematocrit test to check for anaemia (usually by means of a pinprick on the finger).

◆ Guidance about what to expect in the next month in relation to such topics as feeding, sleeping, development and child safety.

Questions you may want to ask, if the doctor hasn't already answered them:

◆ What new foods can be introduced to baby now? When can citrus, fish, meats, egg whites be introduced, if they haven't been already?

◆ When should you consider weaning from the bottle, if your baby is bottle-fed, or from the breast?

Also raise any concerns that have come up over the past month. Jot down information and instructions from the doctor. Record all pertinent information (baby's weight, length, head circumference, immunizations, foods introduced, test results, illnesses, medications given, and so on) in a permanent health record.

Feeding Your Baby:
ESTABLISHING GOOD HABITS NOW

We've all met them. The beleaguered parents who moan when their preschoolers clamour for the sugar-coated cereal in the supermarket, groan when they howl for chips instead of a sensible lunch at a restaurant, roll their eyes when they reject the sandwich on wholemeal offered at a friend's house or insist on a fizzy drink instead of juice at dinner. Like all parents, they'd like their children to eat more nutritiously, but deep down inside they're convinced they'd be fighting a losing battle. Aren't kids, after all, born with a preference for junk foods?

Surprisingly, no. A child's palate is actually born a clean slate; the tastes that develop depend on the foods introduced, even in those first months of eating. How your child will ultimately eat – whether he or she will choose sandwiches on white bread or wholemeal, find snack satisfaction in an apple or a bag of crisps, breakfast happily on the kind of cereal that comes with raisins or hold out for the kind that comes with chocolate will be influenced primarily by the foods you set on his or her high chair tray now.

So that you don't end up bemoaning your child's eating habits later, start feeding your baby right, right from the start.

Keep white out of sight, most of the time. A preference for wholemeal over white is a form of discrimination that's actually good to teach young children. Though a child who's weaned on whole grains won't necessarily grow up without a taste for white, he or she is more likely to opt for the good stuff when given the choice – or, at least, be less likely to reject it when it's served. Select whole-grain products at the supermarket, bake with whole-grain flours at home, and order whole-grain breads, when possible, in restaurants.

Don't cut that sweet tooth yet. The longer you hold off introducing really sweet foods, the more opportunity your baby will have to establish tastes for foods that are savoury or tart. Don't assume that baby won't eat cottage cheese or natural yoghurt unless it's been mixed with mashed ripe banana, or cereal unless it's been sweetened with apple purée or strained peaches; babies whose taste buds haven't been sweet-talked will not only accept such foods 'straight', they'll learn to love them. Serve fruits, but as a dessert – after you've offered something that isn't sweet, like vegetables (which you should serve early and often). Gradually introduce sweeter treats (preferably ones sweetened with fruit juice instead of sugar), but don't get into the habit of doling out the biscuits instead of fresh fruit in the afternoon, topping off every meal with a sweet, or spreading jam on every cracker you hand your baby. Realistically, your baby's more likely to experience the sweeter side of life sooner if there are older siblings in the house (little sibs always want some of what the big kids are getting); otherwise, you may be able to hold off on the sweets until the first birthday or even later.

Serve the milk straight. When the doctor okays cow's milk – usually at one year – give it to your baby straight. Chocolate milk is loaded with calcium, but also with sugar. Consider, too, that any time you disguise the flavour of milk (even if it's in a wholesome smoothie), you'll be sabotaging your baby's taste for the pure thing. Save such strategies for the 'No milk!' rebellions of the toddler and preschool years.

Save the salt. Babies don't need salt in their foods beyond what is found there naturally. Don't salt food you prepare for baby, and be particularly careful not to serve up salty snacks, which can give your child an unhealthy taste for foods high in sodium.

Spice baby's diet with variety. It's not surprising that so many young children spurn unfamiliar foods. In most cases, their parents have served up the same old, same old from early on (the same cereal every morning for breakfast, the same varieties of baby food for lunch and dinner day in and day out), never offering a change of pace or a chance to sample anything different. Be adventurous in feeding your baby (within the parameters set by the doctor or mandated by your baby's age). Try different types of whole-grain cereals, served hot and cold; varieties of whole-grain breads (oat and rye, as well as wheat) in different forms (rolls, bagels, sliced loaves, crackers and later pittas); different shapes of pastas; dairy products in different forms (yoghurt, cottage cheese, Gruyère and Cheddar); vegetables and fruits beyond carrots, peas and bananas (sweet potato cubes, ripe cantaloupe melon and mango slivers, split fresh blueberries, and so on).

Variety now is no guarantee that your child won't go through a macaroni-and-cheese-only phase – most children do at one time or another. But a familiarity with a wider range of foods will breed a broader diet base and, in the long run, better nutrition.

Make exceptions. We all crave what's forbidden; it's a fact of human nature. Ban junk food entirely, and it will only become more appealing to your child. So once he or she is old enough to understand the concept of 'once in a while', allow occasional treats. As long as they're not a part of your child's daily diet – and are not served up instead of good foods – they won't compromise nutrition.

Do it yourself. Children are much more likely to practise what their parents practise than practise what their parents preach. Stock the house with healthy foods and take obvious pleasure in eating them yourself, and you can expect your child to follow in your wholesome footsteps.

Of course, while you're practising, it doesn't hurt to do a little casual preaching, too. Start teaching your child from an early age that sugar isn't good for you, but fruit is, and that wholemeal bread is better for your body than white.

What You May Be Concerned About

FEEDING BABY AT THE TABLE

'We've been feeding our son separately, and putting him in the play yard while we eat. When should he start eating with us?'

Feeding themselves and their babies at the same time is a juggling feat most parents can't master – at least not gracefully, or without having to pop a couple of antacid tablets after every meal. So until your baby is a competent self-feeder, you might want to continue giving him his meals separately. But that doesn't mean he shouldn't begin to sit in on some adult meals (as long as your schedules permit) for practise in table manners and sociability. Whenever it's practical and desirable, draw his high chair up to the table at your mealtime, or set him up safely in a hook-on dining seat, give him his own place setting (non-breakable dishes and a spoon only) and some finger foods, and include him

in the table conversation. But don't forget to reserve some late dinners for adults only in order to keep (or put back) the romance in your lives.

LOSS OF INTEREST IN NURSING

'Whenever I sit down to breastfeed my son, he seems to want to do something else – play with my buttons, pull up on my hair, look at the television screen, anything but nurse.'

In the early months, when a breastfeeding baby's whole world seems to revolve around his mother's nipples, it seems implausible that a time will ever come when he will be uninterested in nursing. And, yet, though many babies remain passionate about breastfeeding until weaning, a few display waning interest and concentration somewhere around the ninth month. Some simply begin to refuse the breast entirely; others nurse seriously for a minute or two and then pull away; still others are easily distracted during nursing, either by what's going on around them or by their desire to practise their newfound physical prowess. Sometimes the boycott is just transient. Maybe baby is going through a readjustment in his nutritional needs, or perhaps he's put off by the altered taste of your breast milk brought on by hormonal changes during your menstrual period or from the garlicky pasta al pesto you dined on the previous night. Or maybe his lost appetite is temporarily due to a virus or a bout of teething.

Or it could be that he's slowly losing interest in breastfeeding. Though baby often knows what's best for him, unfortunately, this is another case in which he doesn't. It's best – when possible – for baby to continue nursing at least until his first birthday. So don't give up on breastfeeding without a civilized fight. If he continues the nursing strike, strike back with these tips:

◆ Try some peace and quiet. An increasingly curious eight- or nine-month-old baby is easily distracted by just about anything – from the television, to the siren of a fire engine outdoors, to the dog passing by. To maximize baby's concentration on the task at hand, nurse in a dimly lit, quiet room. Stroke him and cuddle him gently as he nurses, to relax him.

◆ Nurse when he's sleepy. Breastfeed first thing in the morning, before all his busy-baby cylinders kick in. Breastfeed after a warm bath at night. Or after a relaxing massage (see page 301). Or right before nap time. If he's tired enough, he might not know what hit him – or he might not care.

◆ Or nurse on the run. Some babies prefer to know that they're part of

GOT MILK? NOT YET

Thinking of switching your baby from breast milk or formula to cow's milk? Think again. Cow's milk isn't appropriate for nine-month-old humans (see page 265 for the reasons why). Whole milk yoghurt and hard cheese are fine additions to your baby's diet (unless a family history of allergy has prompted your baby's doctor to hold off on these, too), and some doctors will allow *small* amounts of whole milk mixed in cereal or even a little in a cup for practise. But wait until the doctor gives the green light before substituting the white stuff for breast milk or formula. When you do make the switch, make sure your baby gets only whole milk until the second birthday (unless the doctor recommends otherwise).

the action – that way they can be sure they're not missing something. If that's the case with your little bundle of energy, nurse while you're walking around the house; securing baby in a sling will be easier on your arms.

If your baby still seems lackadaisical about nursing, he may truly be on the verge of giving up the breast. Though *you* may not be ready for this milestone to take place, there may be absolutely nothing you can do about it. As many mothers before you have learned, you can lead a baby to the breast, but you can't make him drink.

Ideally, you should continue to pump milk to feed your baby until at least the end of the first year. If you don't feel up to pumping your baby's entire intake, you'll need to switch to formula. You can serve up the breast milk or formula in a bottle, if he's already taking one, though a few babies this age who balk at breastfeeding will also balk at sucking from a rubber teat. If that's the case with your baby, or if he's never taken a bottle (there's not much point in starting one now, since experts recommend that weaning from the bottle begin at a year anyway), try serving the breast milk or formula in a cup, at least some of the time. This often satisfies babies who just won't take their feedings lying down. Babies who were started on the cup earlier are often very proficient by this age; those who weren't often catch on quickly.

If you do end up weaning entirely, try to keep the process gradual – for your baby's health as well as your own comfort. Gradual weaning will allow baby time to increase his intake of formula before he gives up breast milk entirely. And it will give your breasts the chance to reduce production slowly to avoid painful engorgement. (See page 476 for tips on weaning; if your baby absolutely refuses to take any breast-feedings, see page 477 for making abrupt weaning easier.)

FUSSY EATING HABITS

'When I first introduced solids, my daughter seemed to love everything I gave her. But lately, she won't eat anything but bread.'

To hear their parents tell it, some children (up until adolescence, when a week's worth of groceries lasts three days) live on nothing but air, love and the occasional crust of bread. But in spite of parental concerns, even picky eaters manage to drink and nibble enough during the day to thrive. Children are programmed to eat what they need to live and grow – unless something happens to alter that programming early in their eating history.

At this stage of development, most babies are still getting a major portion of their needed nutrition from breast milk or formula, and this is usually rounded out by whatever bits of solid foods they get during the day. But at nine months, nutritional requirements are beginning to increase and the need for milk begins to decrease. To be sure that your baby's intake continues to meet her requirements, incorporate the following into your feeding strategy:

Let them eat bread. Or cereal, or bananas, or whatever food they favour. Many babies and toddlers seem to be on a food-of-the-week (or month) plan, refusing to eat anything but a single selection during that time. And it's best to respect their dietary preferences and aversions, even when taken to extremes: cereal for breakfast, lunch and dinner, for example. Eventually, if given a chance to do so on her own – and if offered a wide variety of foods to choose from – a child will expand her repertoire of tastes.

Add on when you can. While you shouldn't push food on your baby, there's nothing wrong with trying to sneak it by her. Spread the bread with mashed banana or cottage cheese, or melt a thin slice of Gruyère on it. Or turn it into French toast, or 'eggy bread' (using only the yolks), served whole or cut into small pieces. Or try baking and buying breads that incorporate other nutritious ingredients, such as pumpkin, carrot, cheese or fruit. If it's cereal your baby craves, slip in a serving of fruit in the form of a diced banana, apple purée or cooked diced peaches, or diced cooked dried fruit (which will also add iron). If bananas are her passion, try serving them conspicuously with a small amount of cereal or cottage cheese, or mashing them on bread.

Omit the mush. Your baby's recent rebellion may simply be her way of telling you that she's had it with the mushed and the mashed and is ready for more grown-up fare. Changing to chunky foods and finger foods that are soft enough for her to manage but intriguing enough in taste and texture to satisfy her maturing palate may turn her into the epicure you seek.

Vary the menu. Maybe your baby's just tired of the same old meals; a change may be just what she needs to spark her appetite; see page 419.

Turn the tables. Perhaps it's just a newly emerging streak of stubborn independence that's keeping her mouth clenched at mealtime. Hand her the responsibility of feeding, and she may open her mouth eagerly to a wide range of food experiences she would never take from the spoon you offer. (For appropriate choices for the self-feeding baby, see page 386.)

Don't drown her appetite. Many babies (and toddlers) eat very little because they're drinking too much juice, formula or breast milk. Your baby should have no more than 120 to 170 ml (4 to 6 fl oz) of fruit juice and no more than 480 to 680 ml (16 to 24 fl oz) of formula (or, after the first birthday, milk) a day. If she wants to drink more than that, give her water or watered-down juice, spreading the servings out over the day. If you're breastfeeding, you don't know exactly how much milk she's taking, but you can be pretty sure that nursing her more than three or four times a day will interfere with her appetite; cut back.

Attack snacks. What do parents do when baby refuses breakfast? Ply her

> ## SOME CEREAL WITH THAT BUTTERNUT SQUASH?
>
> Has your baby moved on from the strained and the bland to new and interesting tastes and textures? Good for your little gourmand! But in your excitement to encourage variety and adventure in the high chair, don't forget to include some iron-enriched cereal in your baby's daily diet. As ho-hum as it may be, it's the easiest way (unless your baby is formula-fed) of ensuring adequate iron intake.

with snacks all morning, of course, which means she isn't likely to have any appetite for lunch. And what happens after lunch is turned down? Baby's hungry again in the afternoon, snacking continues, and there's no room for dinner. Avoid this appetite-sabotaging cycle by limiting snacks to one midmorning and one midafternoon, no matter how little your child eats at mealtimes. You can, however, increase the amount fed at snack time by a bit in order to tide baby over from a light or skipped meal to the next feeding time.

Keep smiling. The easiest way for you to lay the foundation for a permanent feeding problem is to frown with displeasure when your baby turns her head away from the oncoming spoon, to comment unhappily when she comes out of the high chair with her tummy as empty as when she went in, or to spend half an hour trying to guide a couple of spoonfuls into her closed mouth with cajoling, pleading or 'choo-choo train' tricks. She needs to feel she's eating because she's hungry, not because you want her to. So at all costs – even at the cost of some missed meals – don't make eating (or not eating) an issue. If she clearly doesn't want any more, or doesn't want to eat at all, remove the dish and end the meal without further ado.

Of course, short-term appetite loss can accompany colds and other acute illnesses, particularly when fever is present. Rarely, a baby will show a chronic lack of appetite due to anaemia (see page 363) or malnutrition (both uncommon among middle-class British babies) or other illness. If your baby's loss of appetite is accompanied by lack of energy, lack of interest in her environment, a slowdown in development, insufficient weight gain or a marked change in personality (sudden irritability or nervousness, for instance), check with her doctor.

SELF-FEEDING

'Every time the spoon comes near my baby, she grabs for it. If her bowl is near enough, she dips her fingers in and makes a mess trying to feed herself. She's getting nothing to eat and I'm getting frustrated.'

It's clearly time to pass the spoon to a new generation. Your baby is expressing her desire to be independent, at least at the table. Encourage rather than discourage her. But to minimize the mess and keep her from going hungry until she can pass muster with Miss Manners, pass the responsibility on gradually, if possible.

Begin by giving her a spoon of her own while you continue feeding her. She may not be able to do much more than wave it around at first, and when she does fill it and get it to her mouth, it will usually be upside down. Still, wielding a spoon may keep her content enough to let you take care of most of the meal, at

least for a while. The next step is to provide finger foods that she can feed herself while you spoon-feed her. The combination of finger foods and a personal spoon (and/or a cup to take swigs from) usually keeps a baby occupied and happy enough for mum or dad to get the rest of the meal into her, but not always.

Some babies insist on doing it all themselves; if this is the only way your baby will eat, let her. Mealtimes will take longer and be messier at first, but the experience will make your child a more proficient self-feeder sooner. (Spreading newspaper or a plastic mat on the floor beneath baby's chair will at least make cleanup easier.)

Whatever you do, don't let mealtime become battle time, or you'll risk setting her up for permanent eating problems. When self-feeding degenerates into all play and no eating (some play is normal), pick up the spoon and take over the feeding. If your baby balks, it's time to wipe the carrots off the chin and the yoghurt from between the fingers and call it a meal.

STRANGE STOOLS

'When I changed my baby's nappy today, I was really puzzled. Her stool seemed to be filled with grains of sand. But she never plays in a sandpit.'

Just when you're getting bored with changing nappies, another surprise turns up in one. Sometimes it's easy to figure out what went into baby to produce the change in her stools. Halloween orange colour? Probably the carrots. Frightening red? Maybe beetroot or beetroot juice. Black specks or strands? Bananas. Small dark foreign objects? Usually blueberries or raisins. Light green pellets? Perhaps peas. Yellow ones? Sweetcorn. Seeds? Very likely tomatoes, cucumbers or melon from which the seeds were not completely removed. Because babies don't chew thoroughly and their digestive tracts are not fully mature, what goes in often comes out largely unchanged in colour and texture.[2] Sandy stools, such as those in your baby's nappy, are fairly common, not because babies snack from the sandpit (though they do, given a chance) but because certain foods – particularly Cheerios and similar oat cereals, and pears – often appear sandy once they've passed through the digestive tract.

Odd changes in the stool come not just from natural items in your baby's diet but also from those synthesized in the food lab (most of which aren't appropriate for babies but nevertheless sometimes find their way into small tummies). Such products have been known to colour stools such dramatic hues as fluorescent green (from a grape-flavoured beverage) and shocking pinkish red (from berry-flavoured cereal).

So before you panic at the sight of what's filling your baby's nappy, think about what's been filling her tummy. If you're still puzzled, show a sample to the doctor.

CHANGES IN SLEEP PATTERNS

'Suddenly my daughter doesn't want to nap in the morning. Is one nap a day enough for her?'

Though one nap a day may not be enough for the exhausted parents, it is all many babies need as they approach their first birthday. A few babies even try to give up both naps at this time. Most often it is the morning nap that goes first, but occasionally it's the after-lunch siesta. The babies of some lucky parents continue to nap twice a day well into the second year, and this is perfectly normal, too, as long as it doesn't seem to be interfering with a good night's sleep. If it does seem to be, baby should be weaned down to one nap.

How much a baby sleeps is of less consequence than how well she functions on the sleep she's getting. If your baby refuses to go down for a nap or naps but seems cranky and overtired by dinnertime, it may be that she needs the extra sleep but is protesting because she doesn't want to waste precious time – that she could use for activity and exploration – on sleep. Not getting needed naps makes for a less happy, less cooperative baby during the day, and often one who goes to bed less easily and sleeps less well at night; being overtired and overcharged, she has a difficult time settling down and staying down.

If your baby doesn't seem to be getting the naps she needs, make a special effort to encourage her. Try putting her down – fed, changed and relaxed by a little quiet play and quiet music, and perhaps a massage (see page 301) – in a dark room with no distractions. Don't give up immediately if she doesn't fall asleep; some babies need more time to settle down during the day. If that doesn't work, you may need to resort to walking her in the pushchair or driving around with her in the car. (Many city babies do all their napping in the pushchair, suburban babies in the car.) If necessary, and if you've chosen this method for night-time sleep also, try sleep training your baby (see page 348) before giving up on getting her to nap, but not for as long as you would at night. More than twenty minutes of crying, and there goes her nap time.

---

2. Squashing or splitting raisins, berries, peas and sweetcorn kernels will make them not only easier to digest but safer to eat.

'We thought we'd done everything right. Our baby always went to sleep without a fuss. Now he seems to want to stay up and play all night.'

It's something like making a sudden move from a small town to the big city. A couple of months ago, there wasn't much to keep your baby up at night. Now, with so many discoveries to make, toys to play with people to interact with and physical accomplishments to fine-tune (who wants to lie down when you're just learning to stand up?), your baby doesn't want to take time out to sleep.

Unfortunately, this is yet another case in which baby doesn't know what's good for him. As with not sleeping enough during the day, going to sleep too late at night can make him overtired, which, in turn, can keep him from settling down well at all. Children who aren't getting adequate sleep are more likely to have trouble falling asleep and to wake up during the night. They may also be cranky during the day and more prone to accidents.

If your baby isn't going to sleep readily at night, be sure he's napping sufficiently during the day (see pages 320 and 425). Next, establish a bedtime routine; if you've already established one but have been adhering to it half-heartedly, enforce it. If a baby-sitter or grandparents will be putting baby to bed occasionally, make sure they are familiar with the rituals.

If you aren't certain what to include in a bedtime routine, you can try some or all of the following:

A bath. After a day of cleaning the floor with his knees, massaging his scalp with mashed banana and rolling in the sand-pit, a baby needs a bath. But the evening bath does more than get a baby clean – it relaxes him. Warm, soothing waters wield magical, sleep-inducing powers; don't waste them by giving baby his bath earlier in the day. You might also want to try baby bedtime lotions or bath soaps enriched with lavender and camomile, known for their soothing and relaxing properties.

A sleep-inducing atmosphere. Dim the lights, turn the TV off, send older children from the room, and keep other distractions to a minimum.

A story, a song, a cuddle. After your baby's been changed and pyjamaed, settle down together into a comfortable chair or sofa, or on baby's bed once he's graduated to one. Read him a simple story, if he will sit still for one, in a soft monotone rather than a lively, animated voice. Or, if he prefers, let him look at some picture books himself. Sing quiet songs and lullabies, cuddle, but save rougher fun (such as wrestling matches and tickling sessions) for other times. Once baby's motor is turned on, it's hard to turn off. If your baby enjoys massage, now would be a great time to relax him with one. Research suggests that babies who are massaged before bed produce more of the sleep-inducing hormone melatonin.

A light for the wary. Some babies are afraid of the dark. If yours is one of them, give him a night-light to keep him company.

Good-byes. Put a favourite toy or animal to bed. Encourage your baby to wave bye-bye to it, as well as to stuffed animals, siblings, mummy and daddy. Share good-night kisses all around, tuck baby into his cot, and make your departure.

If he cries when you leave the room, return for a moment to be sure he's okay, kiss him again, then leave. If he continues crying, and if you've chosen this route, you will probably need to try one of the getting-baby-to-sleep-through-the-night methods beginning on page 348. They are likely to work but may be harder on you now that he's not only older but wiser. At this age, he will probably know how to get you back into the room, or at least how to make you feel guilty if you don't return. He may repeatedly pull up and scream until you help him to get down again. Or he may start calling 'ma-ma' or 'da-da', making it difficult for you not to respond. And rather than being calmed by a visit, as a younger baby might, he will probably be all the angrier when you leave him again. Your best bet with such a little wiseguy might be to try to stay away entirely while he gets himself back into the habit of going to sleep on his own.

'We haven't been able to set up a bedtime routine for our baby because he always falls asleep nursing before we start.'

If your baby routinely falls asleep with the last nursing of the evening, go through the entire go-to-bed routine – including the good-nights – before settling down to nurse. Or if you'd like to try to break him of the nursing-to-sleep habit, try nursing him before his bath under conditions not conducive to sleep – with plenty of noise, light and activity, and the promise of a bath and story ahead. If he falls asleep in spite of all your efforts, try waking him for the bath. If that doesn't work, go back to nursing after the bedtime rituals, and try again in a couple of weeks.

'We really want our baby to learn how to fall asleep on her own when she wakes during the night. But now that she's teething, I feel guilty letting her cry.'

There are plenty of ways to comfort a teething baby – but, unfortunately, they all involve rushing to her side. Easy enough if you've made the decision to co-sleep, not so easy if you're committed to getting her to sleep on her own. Here's the problem: while the worst of teething pain usually lasts just a few nights (and wakes baby only briefly and sporadically), having you around at night can quickly become a habit that's hard for baby to break. In other words, teething pain will keep your baby up for a short time; knowing that you'll appear when she cries may keep her up indefinitely.

It's a good idea to peek in on your baby when she cries during the night to make sure she hasn't pulled up and stranded herself in a standing position, unable to get back down – as often happens at this age. It's also fine to offer her some quiet comfort (as much as you like, for as long as you like): a little patting, a soft lullaby, a teething ring. But if your goal is to get her to fall back asleep on her own, try not to pick her up. See if she can settle back down by herself (if your presence invariably prevents that, consider staying out of her room).

If she seems inconsolable nightly, ask her doctor about the possibility of giving her a dose of baby paracetamol before she goes to bed. Do be sure, however, that your baby's night waking isn't prompted by illness – an ear infection, for example, the pain of which often worsens at night – which such pain medication could mask.

PULLING UP

'Our baby just learned to pull up. He seems to love it for a few minutes but then starts screaming. Could standing be hurting his legs?'

If your child's legs weren't ready to hold him, he wouldn't be pulling up. He's screaming out of frustration, not pain. Like most babies who've just learned to stand, he's stranded in this unfamiliar position until he falls, collapses or is helped down. And that's where you come in. As soon as you notice frustration setting in, gently help him down to a sitting position. Slowly does it – so that he can get the idea of how to do it himself, which should take a few days, or at most, a few weeks. In the meantime, expect to spend a lot of time coming to the rescue of your baby-in-distress – perhaps even in the middle of the night, if he decides to practise pulling up then.

'My baby is trying to pull up on everything in the house. Should I be concerned for her safety?'

As babies learn to pull up, then cruise, and finally walk, they enter a stage when they have more brawn than their brains can be responsible for – putting them at high risk of injury. Nerve-racking as it may be for you, your almost-toddler needs plenty of opportunity to explore the world around her. Your job is to make that world as safe as possible.

Be especially certain now that anything she might attempt to pull up on (get down on her level if necessary to determine what that might be) is secure. Unstable tables, bookcases, dressers, chairs and floor lamps should be anchored to the wall (and dresser drawers safety-latched), put away or kept out of baby's reach for the time being; cords for appliances should be hidden or secured to the wall so that baby can't pull up on them, bringing heavy equipment down on herself. Corners and sharp edges on remaining coffee or end tables should be cushioned in case baby falls against them (she probably will, and often). Breakable or dangerous knickknacks she couldn't reach before should be stowed now. If you have a dishwasher, keep it closed when you're not using it (it's easy to pull up on an open one, and the contents – such as knives, glasses and remnants of detergent – can pose a threat). To prevent slips and trips, be sure that electrical cords are out of the way, that papers are not left lying around on the floor, and that spills on smooth-surfaced floors are wiped up quickly. And to be sure her feet won't sabotage her, keep her barefoot or in skidproof socks or slippers, rather than in smooth-soled shoes or slippery socks.

When a child begins pulling up, cruising around the room – from chair to table to wall to sofa to daddy's legs, for example – can't be far behind. As always, increased mobility means the potential for increased danger. To protect your cruising baby, make sure that every corner of every room in your home (except those behind always-closed and latched doors) is thoroughly babyproofed. If you didn't attend to this when your baby began crawling, or if she never crawled, see page 402 for tips on making home safe for baby.

FLAT FEET

'My baby's arches look totally flat when he stands up. Could he have flat feet?'

In babies, flatness is the rule, not the exception. And it's a rule that you're not likely to find an exception to. There are several reasons: first of all, since young babies don't do much walking, the muscles in their feet haven't been exercised enough to fully develop the arches. Secondly, a pad of fat fills the arch, making it difficult to discern, particularly in chubby babies. And when babies begin to walk, they stand with feet apart to achieve balance, putting more weight on the arch and giving the foot a flatter appearance.

In most children, the flat-footed look will slowly diminish over the years, and by the time full growth is attained, the arch will be well formed. In only a small percentage will the feet remain flat (not a serious problem, anyway), but that's something that can't be predicted now.

WALKING TOO EARLY?

'Our baby wants to walk all the time, holding on to the hands of any willing adult. Will walking before she's ready hurt her legs?'

It's more likely to hurt your backs than her legs. If your baby's legs weren't ready for this kind of prewalking activity, she wouldn't be clamouring for it. Like early standing, early walking (assisted or unassisted) can't cause bowleggedness (actually a normal characteristic of babies under two) or any other physical problem. In fact, both these activities are beneficial, since they exercise and strengthen some of the muscles used in walking solo. And if she's barefoot, they will help strengthen her feet as well. So as long as your backs hold out, let her walk to her legs' content.

A baby who doesn't want to 'walk' at this stage, of course, shouldn't be pushed into it. As with other aspects of development, just follow your half-pint-size leader.

SLOW DEVELOPMENT

'Our baby has begun only recently to sit well by himself – much later than our friends' babies. Should we be worried?'

Each baby's rate of development is predetermined primarily by his genes, which determine how quickly his nervous system develops. He is programmed to sit, pull up, stand, walk, smile his first smile and say his first word at a certain age. Few develop at a uniform rate in all areas; most are faster in some and slower in others. One baby might, for example, be quick to smile and talk (social and language skills) but not pull up until nearly a year (a gross motor skill). Another might walk (a gross motor skill) at eight months, yet not exhibit a pincer grasp (a fine motor skill) until after his first birthday. The rate at which motor skills develop is in no way related to intelligence. Keep in mind, too, that development of certain skills can be slowed down because a baby hasn't had enough opportunity to practise them. This is certainly true of sitting; if your baby spent a great deal of time on his back, strapped into an infant seat, or secured in a baby carrier or sling, he may not have had much chance to figure out how to get himself into a sitting position.

Doing even most things later than other children, as long as development falls within the wide range considered normal (as is definitely the case with sitting) and progresses from one step to the next, is not usually a matter for concern. When a child routinely reaches developmental milestones long after other children, however, a consultation with his doctor is in order. In most cases, such a consultation will put a parent's fears to rest. Some children mature slowly yet are perfectly normal. Occasionally, further workups will be necessary to determine whether or not a problem really exists, which it sometimes does.

Once in a great while, the baby's doctor is not concerned but the parents have some lingering doubts in spite of every reassurance. Their best route to peace of mind: a referral to a developmental specialist. Sometimes the baby's doctor, who sees him only for brief evaluations, misses signs of poor development that a parent sees or senses and that an expert doing a lengthier workup can pick up. The consultation serves a dual purpose. Firstly, if parental concern turns out to be truly unnecessary, worry, at least about development, can be cast aside. Secondly, if there does turn out to be a problem, early intervention can make a tremendous difference.

FEAR OF STRANGERS

'Our little girl has always been friendly and outgoing. But when my in-laws – whom she always loved to play with – came in from out of town yesterday, she broke into tears every time they came near her. What's come over her?'

Maturity – of a very immature sort. Though she'll show a definite preference for her mother and father after the first couple of months, a baby under six months or so will generally respond positively to almost any grown-up. Whether they are familiar adults or strangers, she lumps them pretty much into the category of people who are capable of taking care of her needs. Often, as a baby approaches eight or nine months, she begins to realize which side her teething biscuit is really buttered on; that mother and father, and possibly another familiar person or two, are her primary caretakers; and that she ought to stick close to them and steer clear of anyone who might try to separate her from them. ('Stranger anxiety', the official term for this phenomenon, can begin at six months or even earlier.) During this time, even once-beloved grandparents (and occasionally even

beloved baby-sitters) may suddenly be rejected, as baby clings desperately to her parents (particularly the parent who provides the most care).

Wariness of strangers may disappear quickly or not peak until somewhat past a year; in about two in ten babies it never develops at all (possibly because these babies adjust easily to new situations of all kinds) or passes so quickly it isn't noticed. If your baby does exhibit stranger anxiety, don't pressure her to be sociable. She'll come around eventually, and it's best that she does on her own terms. In the meantime, warn friends and family that she's going through an apprehensive stage (which they shouldn't take personally) and that quick advances will frighten her. Suggest that instead of trying to hug her or pick her up immediately, they try to break down her resistance slowly – by smiling at her, talking to her, offering her a plaything – while she sits securely on your lap. Eventually, she may warm up, and even if she doesn't, at least there won't have been any tears and bad feelings along the way.

If it's a longtime baby-sitter your child suddenly doesn't want to go to, the odds are that once you leave the house – no matter how hysterical baby may be in your presence – she will quiet down. If it's a new sitter, you may have to spend some additional orientation time before your baby will be willing to stay with the newcomer. If your baby is truly inconsolable when left with a sitter, new or old, then it's time to reevaluate your child-care situation. Maybe the sitter is not giving your baby the kind of attention and love she needs, even if she seems caring when you're around. Or it may simply be a case of extreme stranger anxiety. Some infants, particularly those who are breastfed, can cry for hours when mummy is gone, even when daddy or grandma is the baby-sitter. In such a case, you may have to limit time away from your child, if possible, until this 'missing mummy' phase has passed. If it isn't possible (you work outside the home and must leave her with a sitter or in day care), make yourself as available to her as you can when you are around.

SECURITY OBJECTS

'For the last couple of months, our baby has become more and more attached to his blanket. He even drags it around when he's crawling. Does this mean he's insecure?'

He is a little insecure, and with good reason. In the last couple of months he's discovered he's a separate person, not an extension of his parents' arms. The discovery is undeniably exciting (so many challenges!), yet more than a little frightening (so many risks!). Many babies, when they realize that mummy and daddy may not always be available to lean on from now on, become attached to a transitional comfort object (a soft blanket, a cuddly stuffed animal, a bottle, a dummy) as a sort of stand-in. Like parents, the object offers comfort – particularly appealing when a baby is frustrated, sick, tired, exploring new horizons or making transitions of any kind – but, unlike parents, it's under the infant's control. For the baby who has trouble separating from his parents, taking the security object to bed makes going to sleep alone easier.

Sometimes a baby who hasn't become attached to a security object earlier will do so suddenly when confronted with a new and unsettling situation (a new sitter or day-care centre, moving to a new home, and so on). The transitional comfort object is usually given up sometime between the ages of two and five (about the same time that thumb sucking, another comfort habit, is abandoned), but often not until it is lost, disintegrates or in some other way becomes unavailable. Some children mourn for a day or two but then get on with their lives; others hardly note the passing of their old friend.

Though parents (or other care providers) should never tease or scold a baby or child about a security object or pressure him to give it up, it is often possible to set some limits early on that will make the habit less objectionable and help to prepare a baby for the inevitable separation:

◆ If the habit is in its early stages and is not yet deeply entrenched, you can try to head off future hassles by limiting its use to home or to bedtime. (But don't forget to take it along on overnights and holidays.) If it's already a habit baby can't seem to live without, don't worry about setting any limits; let him take his comfort to go (in the pushchair, in the car, to day care, wherever).

◆ Before the object begins to take on a grubbiness that your baby can smell, wash it. Otherwise, he may become attached as much to the odour as to the object itself, and complain strenuously if it returns from the wash smelling like springtime. If you can't get it away from him during waking hours, wash it while he's asleep.

◆ If the object is a toy, you might want to invest in a duplicate. This will give you a ready replacement in case of loss, let you wash them alternately, and allow you to rotate the items so that neither becomes too grimy. If it's a blanket, you could also consider purchasing a duplicate, or you might try cutting it into several sections so that lost or threadbare pieces can be replaced as needed.

- Though the less said about the object, the better, as your child gets bigger you can remind him now and then that when he's 'big' he won't need his blanket (or other object) any more.

- Although an empty bottle or a bottle of water is acceptable, don't let your baby use a bottle (or sippy cup) of juice or milk as a comfort object. Sucking on such liquids for long periods at a time – particularly at night – can cause dental decay and interfere with a baby's getting adequate solids.

- Make sure your baby is getting the comfort (and love and undivided attention) he needs from you, too, not only in the form of plenty of hugs and kisses, but with frequent talking and playing sessions.

Though attachment to a comfort object is a normal developmental step for many (though far from all) babies, a child who becomes so obsessed with the object that he doesn't spend enough time interacting with people, playing with toys, or practising physical feats may have some emotional needs that aren't being met. If this seems to be the case with your baby, check with his doctor.

No Teeth

'Our baby is almost nine months old and still doesn't have a single tooth. What could be holding her teething up?'

Enjoy those toothless grins while you can, and be reassured that there are many nine-month-olds who are all gums – even a few who finish their first year without a single tooth with which to bite into their birthday cake – but that the tooth fairy comes to visit every baby eventually. Though the average baby cuts a first tooth at seven months, the range is from two months (occasionally earlier) to twelve (sometimes later). Late teething is usually hereditary, and is no reflection on your baby's development. (Second teeth will probably come in later, too.) Toothlessness needn't interfere, incidentally, with a baby's moving on to chunkier foods; the gums are used for chewing in toothed and toothless babies alike until molars arrive in the middle of the second year.

Still Hairless

'Our daughter was born bald and still has little more than peach fuzz. When will she get some hair?'

To parents tired of hearing 'What a cute little boy' whenever they're out with their cute little girl, and eager to make a definitive gender statement with long hair and bows, that continued cue-ball look can be frustrating. But, like toothlessness, hairlessness at this age is not unusual – and not permanent. Hairlessness is most common among fair babies with light hair and is not a forecast of scanty hair later in life. In time your daughter's hair will come in (though perhaps not in quantity until sometime late in the second year). For now, be thankful that you don't have to wrestle with a tangled headful of hair during shampoos and comb-outs.

What it's Important to Know: GAMES BABIES PLAY

When it comes to baby care, a lot has changed since our great-grandmother's mothering days. Yet with all that's new, there are some things that never get old – especially the games that babies love.

Time-honoured as any heirloom, the peekaboos and this-little-piggies that brought squeals of delight to your great-grandmother's baby are guaranteed to do the same for yours. But such games do more than entertain; they improve socialization skills, teach such concepts as object permanence (peekaboo), coordination of words and actions (the itsy-bitsy spider), counting skills (one, two, buckle my shoe), and language skills (eyes, nose, mouth).

Chances are that even if you haven't heard a nursery game in decades, many your mother played with you will come back to you now that you're in her shoes. If they don't, ask for a replay of her favourites (a mother never forgets). Tap, too, the resources of older relatives for venerable folk songs, nursery rhymes, and games that might otherwise be lost.

Refresh your memory, or learn a few new games from the list below.

Peekaboo. Cover your face (with your hands, the corner of a blanket, a piece of clothing, a menu in a restaurant, or by hiding behind a curtain or the foot of the cot) and say, 'Where's Mummy?' (or 'Daddy'). Then uncover your face and say, 'Peekaboo, I see you!' Or say 'Peekaboo' when you cover your face, 'I see you' when you uncover it. Either way, be ready to repeat and repeat until you collapse; most babies have a voracious appetite for this game.

Clap hands. While you sing – 'Clap, clap, clap your hands, clap your hands together' (or any other ditty) – take your baby's hands and show him or her how to clap. At first, your baby's hands will probably not open wide, but the ability to hold the hands flat will finally come, though maybe not until the end of the year; don't push it. It may also be a while before your baby can clap independently, but that, too, will come. During the interim, he or she may enjoy holding your hands and patting them together.

You can add a hiding game to the clapping by singing, 'Clap your hands, one-two-three, play a clapping game with me. Now your hands have gone away, find your hands so we can play'. Or you can try clapping feet, for a change of pace. Or you can use this rhyme: 'Pat-a-cake, pat-a-cake, baker's man, Bake me a cake as fast as you can. Pat it and prick it, and mark it with a 'B', and put it in the oven for baby and me!' (Or substitute baby's name, as in: 'and mark it with a 'C' and put it in the oven for Caitlin and me!'.)

The itsy-bitsy spider. Use your fingers – the thumb of one hand to the pointer finger of the other – to simulate a spider climbing up an invisible web, and sing: 'The itsy-bitsy spider went up the water spout'. Then, use your fingers to imitate rain falling, and continue: 'Down came the rain and washed the spider out'. Throw your arms up and out for 'Out came the sun and dried up all the rain'. And then back to square one, the spider goes back up the web and you end with, 'And the itsy-bitsy spider went up the spout again'.

This little piggy went to market. Take baby's thumb or big toe and start with, 'This little piggy went to market'. Move on to the next finger or toe, 'This little piggy stayed home'. And the next, 'This little piggy had roast beef' (or if you're a vegetarian, 'pizza'); fourth finger, 'This little piggy had none'. As you sing the final line, 'This little piggy cried wee, wee, wee, all the way home', run your fingers up baby's arm or leg to under the arms or neck, gently tickling all the way. (If your baby doesn't like tickling, just use a stroking motion instead.)

So big. Ask, 'How big is baby?' (or use child's name, the dog's name, or a sibling's name), help your child to spread his or her arms as wide as possible, and exclaim, 'So big!'

Eyes, nose, mouth. Take both baby's hands in yours, touch one to each of your eyes, then both to your nose, then to your mouth (where you end with a kiss), naming each feature as you move along: 'Eyes, nose, mouth, kiss'. Nothing teaches these body parts faster.

Ring-a-round o' rosies. Try this one once your baby is walking. Hold hands with him or her (invite a sibling, playmate or other adult to join the circle, when possible) and walk around in a circle, singing, 'Ring-a-ring o' roses, A pocket full of posies, A-tishoo! A-tishoo! We all fall down!' – at which point you all collapse down on the floor.

One, two, buckle my shoe. When climbing stairs or counting fingers, sing: 'One, two, Buckle my shoe. Three, four, Knock at the door. Five, six, Pick up sticks. Seven, eight, Lay them straight. Nine, ten, A big fat hen.'

Pop goes the weasel. You can turn slowly in a circle with baby if you're standing, or rock him or her back and forth if you're seated, as you sing, 'Half a pound of tuppenny rice, Half a pound of treacle, That's the way the money goes . . .' Then, 'Pop goes the weasel!' as you gently bounce baby with the pop. Once baby is familiar with the song, wait a moment or two before the bounce and the 'punchline' to give him or her a chance to do the popping (remember, a baby's reaction time is likely to be delayed a few beats to allow for processing).

◆ ◆ ◆

CHAPTER 14

The Tenth Month

The only thing about baby that's slowing down this month is his or her rate of growth, and along with it, the appetite that fuels it. Which is just as well, since babies-on-the-go would much rather explore the living room than sit still for stints in the high chair. Like any good explorer, baby's determined to reach previously uncharted territory – which often means doing some climbing. Unfortunately, the ability to climb comes long before the ability to climb back down – often leaving baby stranded. (Such advanced explorations also put baby at increased peril, so don't let your vigilance falter.) Baby understands 'no' but may just be starting to test your limits by defying it – or may already be quite adroit at tuning the word out. Memory improves, and fears (which go hand in hand with increased cognitive skills) begin to multiply – of the vacuum cleaner, for instance, which may have to be used only when baby's sleeping.

What Your Baby May Be Doing

All babies reach milestones on their own developmental time line. If your baby seems not to have reached one or more of these milestones, rest assured, he or she probably will very soon. Your baby's rate of development is normal for your baby. Keep in mind, too, that it may have been slowed down in certain departments (such as crawling) if baby didn't spend much time playing on his or her belly. (Some babies skip crawling altogether, and that's fine, too.) If you have concerns about your baby's development (because you've noticed a missed milestone or what you think might be a developmental delay), don't hesitate to check it out with the doctor at the next well-baby visit – even if he or she doesn't bring it up. Parents often notice nuances in a baby's development that doctors don't. Premature infants generally reach milestones later than others of the same birth age, often achieving them closer to their adjusted age (the age they would be if they had been born at term), and sometimes later.

Many ten-month-olds have gained 'cruise control', the last step before unassisted walking. With one hand holding cautiously on to home base, they reach first with their other hand, then with a foot, towards another piece of furniture. Ensure sure footing by letting baby cruise only around steady chairs and tables.

By ten months, your baby . . . should be able to:

◆ stand holding on to someone or something

◆ pull up to standing position from sitting

◆ object if you try to take a toy away

◆ say 'mama' or 'dada' indiscriminately

◆ play peekaboo

◆ exchange back-and-forth gestures with you

. . . will probably be able to:

◆ get into a sitting position from stomach

◆ play patty-cake (clap hands) or wave bye-bye

◆ pick up tiny object with any part of thumb and finger (keep all dangerous objects out of baby's reach)

◆ walk holding on to furniture (cruise)

◆ understand 'no' (but not always obey it)

. . . may possibly be able to:

◆ stand alone momentarily

◆ say 'dada' or 'mama' discriminately

◆ point to something to get needs met

. . . may even be able to:

◆ indicate wants in ways other than crying

◆ 'play ball' (roll ball back to you)

◆ drink from a cup independently

◆ pick up a tiny object neatly with tips of thumb and forefinger (keep all dangerous objects out of baby's reach)

◆ stand alone well

◆ use immature jargoning (gibberish that sounds as if baby is talking in a made-up foreign language)

◆ say one word other than 'mama' or 'dada'

◆ respond to a one-step command with gestures ('Give that to me' – with hand out)

◆ walk well

What You Can Expect at This Month's Checkup

Most doctors do not schedule regular well-baby checkups this month. Do call the doctor if there are any concerns that can't wait until the next visit.

Feeding Your Baby:
WHEN TO WEAN

Those early days of breastfeeding – when you fumbled through every feeding session, when you spent as much time nursing sore nipples as you did nursing your baby, when let-down often let you down – are now just a blur. These days, breastfeeding is second nature for both you and baby – something you can both do in your sleep (and probably often do). You feel as if you've been breastfeeding forever – and, in a way, you wish that you could breastfeed forever. And at the same time, maybe you're wondering whether it's almost time to think about calling it quits.

When to wean? That's a question with no definitive answers, not even from 'the experts'. Ultimately, Mum, it's up to you, though you'll probably want to consider many factors in making your decision:

The facts. You've heard this one before (over and over again): though any amount of breastfeeding is better than none, it is recommended that breast-feeding continue – ideally – for at least a full year, and then for as long as baby and mother both want to keep it up. Waiting until the first birthday to wean means that the baby who has never taken a bottle (at least of formula) can move directly from breast milk to cups of whole milk, without an interim switch to formula.

Many women choose to continue nursing into the second year and beyond, and that's fine. But since their busy toddlers need more protein, vitamins and other nutrients than breast milk alone can provide, they need to do their share of eating (and milk drinking) too.

Though some have speculated that continuing to breastfeed into the toddler and even the preschool years may limit a child's social and emotional development, there's been absolutely no evidence to back such theories up. Older children who breastfeed are just as likely to be secure, happy and independent as those who wean earlier.

If you decide to continue breast-feeding past the first birthday, there are a couple more facts to consider. Firstly, all-night nipping (something co-sleeping toddlers may indulge in) may, like prolonged bottle feeding at night, lead to dental decay – though breastfed children develop, as a group, fewer cavities than those who bottle feed. Secondly, doing a lot of sucking lying down (also more common at night) may lead to an increased risk of ear infection – though, again, as a group, breastfed children have fewer such infections. Avoiding these pitfalls is simple: nurse at bedtime but not during the night.

Your feelings. Are you still enjoying breastfeeding as much as ever? Are you in absolutely no hurry to give up this special part of your relationship with baby? Then continue as long as you and baby like.

Or are you starting to grow weary of hauling your breasts in and out of your shirt all day (and perhaps all night) long? Are you beginning to yearn for some of the freedom and flexibility that seem unattainable while you're still nursing (though nursing an older child generally ties you down less)? Are you uncomfortable about the prospect of nursing an older child? If you're starting to have mixed feelings about breastfeeding, your baby's radar will certainly pick them up. He or she may even take it as a personal rejection, rather than a rejection of the nursing experience. So weaning – again, preferably after the first birthday – may be the way to go.

Your baby's feelings. Some babies are self-weaners. Through their actions and reactions (restlessness and indifference at the breast, nursing that is erratic and brief) they show that they're ready to move on to other ways of obtaining liquid nourishment. Keep in mind, however, that it's possible to misinterpret a baby's signals. At five months, lack of interest in nursing may be only a sign of your baby's growing interest in the environment; at seven months, it may suggest a craving for physical activity that outweighs any craving for food; at nine months or later, it often signifies growing independence and maturity. At any age, it could be a response to illness or teething. At no age should it be construed as a rejection of you, only of the milk you provide. (Babies who seem to be losing interest in nursing can often be convinced to continue; those who are easily distracted can often be redirected back on task; see page 421 for tips.) A baby is most likely to self-wean somewhere between nine and twelve months. If your baby's attachment to the breast doesn't show any signs of letting up by the age of eighteen months (and this is not uncommon), it's possible that he or she will never be the one to take the initiative in weaning.

Your situation. Although it is recommended that babies continue breastfeeding at least for a full year, sometimes that's not practical or desirable. Sometimes work gets in the way and the logistics of expressing milk to fill daytime bottles begin to take their toll. Sometimes, it's other activities (from school to sports to lovemaking) that a woman finds conflicting with a nursing schedule. If breastfeeding just isn't fitting in with your life or your lifestyle any more, consider weaning – either fully or partially. When possible, however, don't try to wean during another major change in your life or baby's (see below). Illness or the need for travel may also call for weaning; in that case, there may be no choice but to wean suddenly.

Your baby's situation. The best time to wean a baby is when all's quiet on the home front. Sickness, teething, moving, holidays, your return to work, a change of sitters, or any other kind of change or stress in a baby's life suggests putting weaning on hold, so he or she won't be saddled with an additional strain.

Your health. If you're perpetually exhausted and there seems to be no explanation other than the physical and emotional demands of nursing, you may want to discuss with your doctor the advisability of weaning so that you can recoup your strength. Before you do, however, be sure that it isn't some easily remedied problem, such as inadequate nourishment and/or insufficient rest, that's kayoing you.

Your baby's health. Sometimes the supply of breast milk seems to diminish excessively as a baby gets older. If your baby is gaining weight poorly, is lethargic, irritable or shows other signs of failure to thrive (your doctor will be able to determine if this is the case), your breast milk may not be meeting its quota of nutritional needs. Consider adding more solids, supplementing with formula, or weaning completely. Often a weaned baby takes a sudden interest in other forms of nourishment that didn't appeal when the breast was available, and begins to thrive anew.

Your baby's other sources of nourishment. If your baby has been accepting bottles all along, weaning to a bottle at any point will be relatively easy. Likewise, if your baby has learned to take fluids from a cup with fair skill, weaning directly to a cup (bypassing the bottle) will be possible at year's end. If, on the other hand, your baby resists taking milk from any source but your breast, weaning will have to wait until either the bottle or cup is mastered.

Your baby's age. If neither of you wants to put a time limit on nursing, your baby's age isn't an issue – just keep it up as long as you like. If, on the other hand, you're feeling ready, here's something to contemplate. Even if they don't take the initiative, most babies are more readily weanable around the first birthday, when a switch to whole cow's milk in a cup can take place (no formula

necessary). Most have less need for sucking, resist being held or sitting still for feedings (some even prefer to nurse standing up), and are generally more independent. They may also be less set in their ways at this age than they will be as toddlers, making them (relatively) easier to wean.

Making the decision to wean is only one step in the long process of switching a baby from the breast to other sources of nourishment – a process that already began with the first sip from the bottle or the first spoonful of solids. Whenever and however it comes for you, weaning is bound to be a time of mixed emotions. On the one hand, you'll likely be somewhat relieved to be relieved of your nursing duties – excited by the prospect of more freedom (a late night out on the town, a weekend away). You'll no doubt be proud of your offspring's new step on the road to growing up. But, at the same time, you'll probably be more than a little misty at the end of this chapter in your child's life, at the loosening ties, at the knowledge that your baby will never depend on you as much again.

Whether early or late, weaning is an inevitable milestone in a child's development – as they say, nobody goes off to college still breastfeeding. Your child (even if he or she is a really ardent nurser) probably won't end up missing breastfeeding for more than a brief time, and will likely move on more quickly than you'd really like. And you, too, will survive this monumental moment in mothering – though you'll probably continue to experience pangs when you watch other mothers nurse, even years later.

What You May Be Concerned About

MESSY EATING HABITS

'My son doesn't eat anything until he's smushed it, smashed it and rubbed it into his hair. Shouldn't we try to teach him some table manners?'

Eating with the average nine- or ten-month-old is enough to make anyone lose his appetite. There's as much playing with the food as eating it, and it's not unusual for more of it to end up *on* baby (and his clothes, his high chair and the family dog who's waiting eagerly below) than *in* him.

That's because mealtimes are no longer just for nourishment but for exploring and discovering as well. As in the sandpit and the bath, baby's finding out about cause and effect, about textures, about temperature differences. When he squeezes yoghurt in his fist, mashes sweet potatoes into the table, slings a glob of porridge from his high chair tray, rubs banana into his T-shirt, blows bubbles in his cup of juice, crumbles crackers with his fingers – a mess for you but a learning experience for him.

Expect the mealtime mayhem, and your need for paper towels by the case-ful, to continue for months to come until your child has learned everything he can about the fascinating physical properties of food and is ready to start consistently eating it instead. That doesn't mean you have to grin (if you can) and bear it without taking some steps in defense of your sensibilities and your home and preparing your baby for a future of respectable (well, at least somewhat respectable) table manners:

Use cover-ups. An ounce of protection is worth a pound of paper towels. Use all the protective measures available to you: spread newspaper all around the base of the high chair or table, to be dumped after the meal. Outfit baby in a wipe-clean bib that covers his front and shoulders (a spill-catching pocket, which keeps the cereal and sweet potatoes from landing on his legs and the floor, is a plus), or use disposable bibs (which can also come in extra handy for meals on the go). Roll baby's sleeves up past the elbow to keep them dry and relatively clean. (Room temperature permitting, it may be more sensible to feed baby seriously messy foods in a nappy only.)

Thwart unwanted advances. You don't want to inhibit your baby's experimentation, but you also don't want to make it too easy for him to play demolition dining room. So give him his food in a bowl, rather than a flat plate from which food can be pushed off easily. Or put it directly on his high chair tray (making sure that it's completely clean). Using a bowl that attaches to table or tray with suction cups gives additional protection, but it will work only on a non-porous surface such as plastic, and only if the surface and the suction cups are clean. To minimize spills, consider offering mealtime beverages in a sippy cup until baby becomes more proficient with a regular cup. If he prefers to drink without a spout, put just 30 ml (1 fl oz) or so of liquid in a regular cup, and hand it to him whenever he's ready for a drink, but keep it out of reach between sips. Don't offer more than one bowl of food at a time, and don't serve more than two or three items in the bowl – babies tend to be overwhelmed by too many choices and react by playing and tossing instead of eating. All utensils and dishes should be non-breakable, for both safety and economy.

Remain neutral. As you have probably already learned, babies are natural-born performers. If you respond by laughing at their high chair antics, you'll only encourage more of the same. Criticism often has the same effect. So scoldings and warnings to 'stop that now!' not only won't curb the behaviour, they'll probably step it up. The best policy: don't comment on manners. If, however, your baby does take a few neat bites, with either the spoon or his fingers, praise him generously. Let him know whenever possible that neatness counts.

Retaliate with silverware. Even though he may do nothing with it but bang it on the tray (while he continues to use his other hand for the transport of food), put a spoon in your baby's hand at the beginning of the meal, and also periodically during the proceedings. Eventually (though not for some months to come), he'll get the idea of actually using it to eat with.

Don't resort to a hostile takeover. Desperate parents tend to take desperate actions – in this case, taking the feeding, and thus the ability to mess, completely out of their baby's control. But while such a takeover will result in neater mealtimes, it will also result in a baby who's delayed in learning how to feed himself and who, as a result, is also slow to develop polite table manners and good eating habits.

Be a model leader. It's not lectures that will teach your baby good table manners in the long run, but what he observes at family meals. If other family members eat with their fingers, shovel food in without a breath, chew loudly, reach for food instead of asking for it to be passed; if everyone talks with their mouths full or, worse, no one talks at all during the meal, your baby will cultivate these habits instead of the ones you hope to instill.

Know when to call a cease-fire. When the amount of time spent playing with the food begins to significantly outweigh the time spent eating it, it's time to call it quits. Clear the table and remove your baby from his high chair as soon as this moment arrives. It's unlikely that baby will protest (boredom with mealtime has prompted this behaviour in the first place), but if he does, distract him with a toy or activity.

HEAD BANGING, ROCKING AND ROLLING

'My son has taken to banging his head on the wall or the side of his cot. Though it's painful for me to watch him, he doesn't seem to be in pain at all – in fact, he seems quite happy'.

It sounds as though your son has discovered that he's got rhythm, and this is his way of expressing it – at least until he takes to dancing or playing his toy drum set. Head banging (like head rolling, rocking and bouncing, all of which are also common at this age) is a rhythmic movement, and rhythmic movements, especially of their own making, are fascinating to babies. Though most infant rock 'n' rollers rock when they hear music during waking hours, there seems to be more to such pursuits than simple fun. It's suspected that some of these children may be trying to reproduce the feeling of being rocked by mummy or daddy. Or that teething infants may be trying to cope with the pain – in which case rocking continues only as long as the teething, unless by that time it has become a habit. For those who bang, rock or roll at nap time, bedtime and when they awaken in the middle of the night, these activities appear to be a sleep aid and perhaps a way of releasing tensions built up during the day. The behaviour is sometimes triggered, or increased, by stress (weaning, learning to walk, getting a new sitter, and so on) in a child's life. Though boys and girls are equally likely to rock or roll, head banging is much more common in boys.

Rocking usually begins somewhere around six months, banging usually not until about nine months. These habits can last a few weeks or months, or a year or more. But most children abandon them by the time they are three years old without parental intervention. Scolding, teasing or otherwise drawing attention to the behaviour not only does no good, it may make the problem worse.

Though it may be hard to believe, rocking, rolling and even head banging are not ordinarily hazardous to your baby's health. Neither are they, in a normally developing child, associated with neurological or psychological disorders. If your baby seems otherwise happy, isn't banging his head in anger, and isn't constantly bruising himself (an occasional black-and-blue mark isn't a cause for concern), there is nothing to worry about. But if these activities are taking up a good deal of your baby's time, if he seems to display other unusual behaviour, is developing slowly, or seems unhappy most of the time, do talk to his doctor about the problem.

You can't force a baby to give up one of these habits before he's ready, but the following tips may make it easier for both you and your baby to live with the habit and to eventually ease him out of it:

♦ Give your baby extra love, attention, cuddling and rocking during the day and at bedtime.

♦ Supply other – and to you, more acceptable – rhythmic activities for your baby during the day. Possibilities include: rocking in a rocking chair with him or showing him how to rock in a child-size one of his own; giving him one or more toy instruments, or just a spoon and pot, with which he can make sounds; pushing him on a swing; dancing to lively music and playing patty-cake or other finger or hand games, especially to music.

♦ Allow your baby plenty of time for active play during the day and ample opportunity to wind down before bedtime.

♦ Establish a regular, soothing presleep routine that includes quiet games, hugging, a little massage (see page 301), and perhaps some rocking (though not to the point of sleep).

♦ If your baby does most of his head banging in the cot, don't put him down until he's sleepy.

♦ If your baby rocks or bangs in his cot, minimize the danger to furniture and walls (which is usually much more serious than any damage to baby) by setting the cot on a thick rug and removing the casters so the cot won't bounce across the floor. Place the cot as far from the wall or other furniture as possible, and if necessary, pad the outsides of the cot to soften the impact. Remember to check the cot periodically for loose bolts, too, if your baby is a banger.

♦ You can try to protect your baby's head by placing bumpers in the cot (or putting them back in if you've removed them) and a mat on the floor where he likes to bang if it isn't already carpeted – but the odds are good he won't be satisfied with the cushioned blows and will make his way to a harder surface.

HAIR ROLLING AND PULLING

'When my daughter is sleepy or cranky, she pulls at a lock of her hair.'

Hair stroking or pulling is another way that a baby or a young child releases tension or tries to re-create the soothing comfort she received as an infant during nursing or bottle feeding, when she would stroke her mother's breast or cheek or pull at her hair. Since she's more likely to crave this comfort during times of stress, especially when she's overtired or cranky, she's more likely to indulge during those times.

Occasional hair twirling, stroking, or pulling, which is often accompanied by thumb sucking, is common, and can linger into childhood without ill effect. Continuous or vigorous tugging at the hair, or hair pulling that results in lost patches of hair, should, obviously, be stopped. These tips may help:

- Provide your child with more comfort and attention, especially at times of increased stress.

- Get her hair cut in a short style, so she won't be able to get a good grip on it.

- Give her something else to pull on – a long-haired stuffed animal, for instance.

- Engage her in other activities that keep her hands occupied, particularly when she starts pulling.

If all else fails, seek advice from her doctor.

TEETH GRINDING

'I often hear my son grinding his teeth when he's down for a nap. Is this harmful in any way?'

Like head banging or rolling, hair pulling or thumb sucking, teeth grinding is often a way some babies discharge tension. To minimize grinding, reduce the tension in your baby's life when possible, and be sure that he has plenty of other outlets for releasing it – such as physical activity and toys that encourage banging. Lots of love and attention before nap or bedtime can also decrease the need for teeth grinding by helping a baby unwind. In most cases, the habit is relinquished as a baby's coping skills improve, and before any damage is done to the teeth.

Tension isn't always the cause of teeth grinding. Sometimes a baby accidentally discovers the mannerism when experimenting with his new teeth, enjoys the sensation and sound of it, and adds it to his growing repertoire of skills. But, before long, the thrill is gone and he loses interest in his dental orchestra.

If you find that your baby's teeth grinding is becoming more frequent, rather than diminishing, and you're concerned that he might begin to do damage to his teeth, consult his doctor or a dentist.

BITING

'My baby has started biting us playfully – on the shoulder, the cheek, any soft, vulnerable area. At first we thought it was cute. Now we're beginning to worry that he's developing a bad habit – and, besides, it hurts!'

THE BABY SOCIAL SCENE

Now that your baby is ready for more entertainment than you alone can provide, joining a play group will offer the added stimulation he or she craves. But the benefits of a play group aren't just for baby. In fact, you probably have more to gain from joining up than baby does. Advantages of a play group include:

Adult conversation. Your child's babbles may be the sweetest sounds to your ears, but if you're like most parents, especially stay-at-home ones, chances are you also long for a little adult dialogue. Meeting regularly with other parents will provide you with the opportunity to speak and be spoken to in full sentences.

Entertainment for baby. While it's still too early in your child's social career to expect him or her to play in a group situation, by the end of the first year, most babies become more capable of some type of meaningful interaction with their peers – usually in the form of parallel play (playing side by side). There's also plenty of entertainment value for baby in just watching other babies at play – and if the group is at someone else's house, trying out new and exciting toys.

Establish friendships. And that goes for both of you. If the group is a success, your baby may have a chance to pal around with the same children on a regular basis for years. The friendships forged at a play group may continue in the form of play dates long after school and other commitments start interfering with regular meetings of the original group. And if the play group is a neighbourhood one, many of the same children may end up in your baby's future classes – a familiarity that can breed comfort on that first day of school. As for you, the opportunity to create a whole new network of like-minded friends may be especially welcome, particularly if your old network hasn't entered the baby phase of life yet.

Resources and referrals. Whether you're in the market for a new doctor or are wondering when and how to wean, chances are someone in the group will have advice or a recommendation.

Support from those who know. Meeting regularly with other parents can remind you that you're not the only one who has a) a baby who won't sleep b) no time for romance with your spouse c) career frustrations d) a breeding farm for dust bunnies in your living room or e) all the above.

There are many ways to find a play group to join. Ask around; or look for flyers promoting them in neighbourhood stores, your local library, community centre, house of worship, hospital or doctor's surgery, or check out the local parents' paper.

If you (and a group of friends) would rather start fresh with a group of your own, you'll have a number of things to consider first, including:

◆ What will the age range of children be? They don't all have to be exactly the same age, but at this point a spread of a few months is better than a spread of a year or more. This will ensure that they'll be able to play with the same toys and relate on somewhat the same level.

◆ How often will the group meet – weekly, twice a week, every other week?

◆ What time and day are most convenient for you and the other parents? Once you pick a schedule, try to hold to it as much as possible. Consistency is an important ingredient-in a successful play group. Avoiding nap time and typically cranky times (such as late afternoon) is also wise.

◆ Where will the group meet? In one person's home or rotating from home to home? At a local park or community centre? Rotating the location keeps things exciting for the baby group members while sharing the responsibilities that come with hosting the group equally among all the grown-up group members. It also means that the children will have a chance to play with plenty of different toys. Shifting the location to a playground or park when the weather is favourable (or to a community centre or museum when it isn't) will provide a nice change of pace for everyone involved.

◆ How many participants will there be? Will there be a limit on the number of parents and babies who can attend? Too many parents and babies (say fifteen babies) can make a group extremely tumultuous; too few (just two or three babies) may provide too little stimulation. (Keep in mind that not every member will show up at every group meeting, thanks to colds, doctor's appointments and other scheduling conflicts.)

◆ Will there be refreshments? Will the host parent be solely responsible for providing a snack? If there are children with food allergies in the group, will those be respected? Will there be rules restricting sugary foods and drinks, or will the snack choice be up to the discretion of the host?

◆ Will the group offer structured parent-child activities, or will it be a playtime for children and social time for adults? Keep in mind that parents may have to spend a great deal of time serving as referees and peacekeepers until the children are old enough (think at least three or four) to play nicely on a consistent basis.

◆ Will there be guidelines about discipline and behaviour expectations? You'll probably want to specify that parents are responsible for monitoring the behaviour of their own offspring only.

Once you've defined the parameters of the group, promoting it is the next step. Pass the word around to friends and neighbours, post flyers, advertise in your community newspaper or parents' paper, approach other parents in your local playground. Once you have a few interested parents, you're ready to play (you can always add more members later).

Along with all the fun, there are some potential risks to joining or starting a play group. For one, seeing other babies your child's age every week could lead you to worry unnecessarily about how he or she is developing relative to other children. (The solution: remember – and repeat this often to yourself – that the range of what's normal is very wide when it comes to a baby's physical, verbal and social development.) Another is the likelihood that your child will share at least as many germs as toys with other group members. (This is just an inevitable result of group activities in early childhood, nothing to be concerned about, and is actually likely to result in fewer colds later on in life. But it will help somewhat to put a 'sick babies stay at home' statute in the group bylaws.) Another potential risk is that you might unwittingly put social pressure on your child. Play groups should be fun, not stressful. If your child wants to participate, that's great. If not, that's fine, too.

Keep in mind, also, that while joining or starting a group can offer many benefits, it's by no means a requirement of the early years. Your baby may enjoy playing with other babies but certainly doesn't need to. If both of you get plenty of stimulation without a play group, or if you work and can't find time in your schedule for one, or you dislike structured group experiences and would prefer impromptu get-togethers with other parents and children, don't feel obliged to play along with the group concept.

It's only natural for your baby to test his new set of chompers on every possible surface, you included. But it's also only natural for you not to want to be bitten – and to want to put a stop to it. Biting can become a bad habit and, as more teeth come in, increasingly painful for its victims.

The biting at first is playful and experimental; baby has absolutely no idea he's hurting anyone with it. After all, he's bitten down on many a teething ring, sucked on many a stuffed toy and chewed on many a cot rail without a single complaint. But a human reaction makes for interesting cause and effect, and often encourages more cause (biting) in the pursuit of more effect (reaction). He finds the expression on mummy's face when he bites down on her shoulder funny, the startled look and mock 'Ouch!' from daddy hilarious, and the 'Isn't that cute, he's biting me', from grandma a definite sign of approval. Oddly enough, even an angry 'Ouch!' or stern reprimand can reinforce the biting habit, because the baby either finds it amusing or sees it as a challenge to his emerging sense of independence, or both. And biting him back can make matters worse; not only is it cruel, but there's the not-so-subtle implication that what's good for you is fair play for him. For the same reason, love bites from parents or grandparents can also trigger biting.

The most effective way to respond is to remove the little biter calmly and matter-of-factly from the part he's biting, with a firm 'No biting'. Then quickly divert his attention with a song, a toy, or other distraction. Do this each time he bites and he will eventually get the message.

BLINKING

'For the last couple of weeks, my daughter has been blinking a lot. She doesn't seem to be in any discomfort, and she doesn't seem to have trouble seeing, but I can't help worrying that there's something wrong with her eyes.'

It's probably more likely that there's something right with her curiosity. She knows what the world looks like through open eyes, but what if she closes her eyes partially, or if she opens and shuts them quickly? The results of her experimentation may be so intriguing that she may keep the 'blinking' up until the novelty wears off. (When she gets older, somewhere around age two, she will probably try similar experiments with her ears, putting her fingers in them or covering them with her hands to see what happens to sound.)

Of course, if your baby seems to have difficulty recognizing people and objects, or if blinking or squinting seem to be triggered by a sensitivity to normal (not uncomfortably bright) daylight, check with the doctor right away. Otherwise, if the blinking habit hasn't run its course by the time your baby goes for her next checkup, mention it to the practitioner.

Squinting is another temporary habit that some babies cultivate, also for the change of scenery. Again, it shouldn't concern you unless it's accompanied by other symptoms or is persistent – in which case, check with her doctor.

BREATH HOLDING

'Recently my baby has started holding his breath during crying spells. Today he held it so long he actually passed out. Could this be dangerous?'

Invariably, it's the parents who suffer most when a child holds his breath.

While the adult witnessing the ordeal is likely to remain shaky for hours, even a baby who turns blue and passes out during a breath-holding session recovers quickly and completely, as automatic respiratory mechanisms click into place and breathing resumes.

Breath-holding spells are usually precipitated by anger, frustration or pain. The crying, instead of letting up, becomes more and more hysterical; baby begins to hyperventilate, then finally stops breathing. In mild events, the lips turn blue. In more severe instances, baby turns blue all over and then loses consciousness. While he's unconscious, his body may stiffen or even twitch. The episode is usually over in less than a minute – long before any brain damage can occur.

About one in five infants holds his breath at one time or another. Some have only occasional episodes, others may have one or two a day. Breath holding tends to run in families and is most common between six months and four years, though it can occasionally begin earlier or continue later.

Breath holding can usually be distinguished from epilepsy (they are in no way related) by the fact that it is preceded by crying and the fact that baby turns blue and loses consciousness before stiffening or twitching. In epilepsy, there is usually no precipitating factor, and the child doesn't ordinarily turn blue before a seizure.

No treatment is necessary for a child who has passed out from breath holding. And though there's no sure cure for the condition – other than the passing of years – it is possible to head off some of the temper tantrums that can result in a breath-holding episode:

◆ Be sure your baby gets enough rest. A baby who is overtired or overstimulated is more susceptible than a well-rested one.

◆ Choose your battles. Too many nos can lead to too much frustration for baby.

◆ Try to calm baby before hysteria sets in, using music, toys or other distractions (but not food, which will create another bad habit).

◆ Try to reduce the tension around baby – yours and everyone else's – if this is at all possible.

◆ Respond calmly to breath-holding spells; your anxiety can make them worse.

◆ Don't cave in after a spell. If your baby knows he can get what he wants by holding his breath, he will repeat the behaviour frequently, especially as he becomes a more manipulative toddler.

◆ Some research has shown that breath-holding spells sometimes stop when a child begins receiving an iron supplement; check with the doctor to see if this might be a good treatment option for your baby.

If your baby's breath-holding spells are severe, last more than a minute, are unrelated to crying, are not related to pain or frustration, or have you worried for any other reason, discuss them with his doctor as soon as possible.

STARTING CLASSES

'I see so many advertisements for classes for babies that I feel as if I'm depriving my baby if I don't enroll her in at least one.'

With thirteen years of school ahead of your child (as many as seventeen if you count those nursery years, much more than that if you're talking university), there's really no need to rush into enrollment. Especially when you consider that babies learn best not through instruction (especially formal instruction) but through experience: the kind of experience they get when they have plenty of time and opportunity to explore the world their way, with just a little help from their adult friends. In fact, being expected to learn a certain way, at a certain time, at a certain place or at a certain pace can dampen a child's natural enthusiasm for learning – and for the new experiences that ultimately will help her learn the most. Too many structured activities and classes too early can also lead to burnout by the time a child actually begins formal schooling.

Certainly, your baby doesn't need to be taking art or music or swimming classes at her age – and won't be left 'behind' if she's the only baby on the street who doesn't. (In fact, she may actually be the baby on the street who ends up enjoying these activities most, simply because she wasn't pushed into participating in them so early on in life.) But while classes aren't necessary for babies, there can be benefits – for both of you – to joining some baby group activities. After all, it's nice for your child to play near other children – she probably isn't yet ready to play *with* them – and to spend time with and get to know other adults. It's even nicer for you to have a chance to talk to other parents, sharing common concerns and experiences and picking up some new ideas for playing with your child.

There are some ways for you to reap group benefits for your baby without the potential pitfalls of premature matriculation:

♦ Take her to a local playground. Even if she isn't walking, she will enjoy the baby swings, small slides and the sandpit and she will especially enjoy watching other children.

♦ Start or join a mother and baby group. If you don't know other parents with babies your daughter's age, post recruitment notices in the doctor's surgery, in a local parents' paper, at your house of worship, even in the supermarket. Such groups, which usually meet weekly in homes or at playgrounds, are often very informal and provide an ideal introduction to group activities (see box, page 444).

♦ Enroll her in an informal baby exercise, music, art or movement class, observing the guidelines on page 302. Just remember, in any class your baby or toddler is involved in, fun – not learning – should be the operative word.

SHOES FOR WALKING

'Our baby has just taken her first steps. What kind of shoes does she need now?'

The best shoes for a new walker are no shoes. Experts agree that the feet, like hands, develop best when they are bare, not covered and confined; walking barefoot helps build arches and strengthen ankles. And just as your baby's hands don't need gloves in warm weather, her feet don't need shoes indoors and on safe surfaces outdoors, except when it's cold. Even walking on uneven surfaces, such as sand, is good for her feet since it makes the muscles work harder.

But for safety and sanitation (you wouldn't want her to step on broken glass or in dog droppings), as well as appearance, your baby will need shoes for most excursions, as well as for special occasions (what's a party dress without Mary Janes?). Choose shoes that are closest to no shoes at all by looking for the following:

Flexible soles. Shoes that bend fairly easily when the toe is bent up will interfere least with the foot's natural motion. Your best bet is to look for leather or rubber soles that bend easily. Many doctors recommend canvas shoes for their flexibility, but some maintain that traditional first-walker shoes are even more flexible and babies are therefore less likely to fall in them. Ask your baby's doctor for a recommendation, and test those available at your local store before making your selection.

Low cut. Though high-top shoes may stay put better than low ones, most experts believe they are too confining and interfere with ankle movement. They certainly shouldn't be used to prop up a baby who is not yet ready to walk.

Porous and flexible uppers. To stay healthy, feet need to breathe and to get plenty of exercise. They breathe best, and have the most freedom of movement, in shoes of leather, cloth or canvas. Plastic or imitation leather is usually stifling and sometimes stiff, and tends to cause the feet to sweat excessively. Avoid 'running' shoes with wide bands of rubber around them, since they can also increase sweating. If you purchase rain shoes or boots that are made of plastic or rubber for your baby, use them only when needed, and take them off as soon as she is indoors.

Flat, non-skid bottoms with no heels. A beginning walker has enough difficulty maintaining her balance without having to contend with slippery soles. Rubber or composition soles, particularly when they are grooved, usually provide a less slippery surface than leather, unless it is scored or grooved. If an otherwise appropriate pair of shoes is too slippery, rough up the soles a bit with sandpaper or a few strips of adhesive tape.

Firm counters. The back of the shoe (above the heel) should be firm, not flimsy. It's best if the top edge is padded or bound and the back seam smooth, with no irregularities that could cause irritation to the back of your baby's heel.

Roomy fit. Shoes are better too large than too small, but of course 'just right' is the best fit of all. Though shoes can't provide as much foot freedom as going bare, too-tight shoes provide no freedom at all. If the shoes are to be worn with thick socks, be sure to bring a pair along when trying them on. Have feet measured, and test new shoes (both of them) for size when the baby is standing with her full weight on her feet. The top of the shoe shouldn't gape open while she's standing (though it's okay if it does when she walks), nor should her heels slip up and down with each step. To check the width, try to pinch the shoe at its widest point. If you can grasp a tiny bit of it between your fingers, the width is fine; if you can pinch a good piece of shoe, it's too wide; and if you can pinch none at all, it's too narrow. To check the length, press your thumb down between your baby's toes and the end of the shoe. If there's a thumb's width (or about 1.3 cm/½ in), the length is right. The back of the shoe should be snug but not tight. If baby's heel slips out easily, the shoe is too big; if the shoe pinches the heel, the shoe is too small. Once you've purchased a pair of shoes for your baby, check the fit every few weeks, since babies outgrow shoes quickly, sometimes within six weeks, often within three months. When that distance at the toe shrinks to less than half a thumb's width, start to think about new shoes. Reddened areas on baby's toes or feet when shoes are removed are also a sign of poor fit.

Standard shapes. Unusual styles – such as cowboy boots or pointy-toed party shoes – may make a fashion statement, but they can also distort the foot as it grows. Look instead for a shoe with a broad instep and toe and a flat-as-a-pancake heel.

Durability is not a requirement in children's shoes because they are (all too rapidly) outgrown. Because of the high price of children's shoes and their brief life span with each child, the temptation is great to pass shoes on to younger siblings – but resist. Shoes mould to the shape of the wearer's foot, and wearing shoes moulded by someone else is not good for little feet. Make an exception only for those shoes (such as dress-up shoes) that have no more than light wear, have held their shape, and aren't run down at the heel area.

A good shoe is only as good as the sock in it. Socks, like shoes, should fit well and be of a material (such as cotton) that allows feet to breathe. Socks that are too tight can cramp foot growth; those that are too long can wrinkle and cause irritations or blisters, though neatly folding up the tip of a too long sock before putting on the shoe can often solve the problem of wrinkling. Stretch-to-fit socks usually do fit well, but be alert for the point at which they become too small and begin squeezing, usually indicated by marks left on baby's feet. Touch-sensitive babies will appreciate a seam that's at the base of the toes rather than at the tip, where it can rub.

HAIR CARE

'Our daughter was born with a headful of hair and it's got quite straggly and hard to manage.'

To the parents of countless hairless nine-month-olds, yours would be a problem they'd love to have. But handling an unruly head of superfine hair, particularly when it belongs to a squirming, uncooperative baby, could make any stylist want to throw in the comb. Things will probably get worse before they get much better; for some toddlers and preschoolers, every shampoo and comb-out is reason for a tantrum. But short of resorting to a short haircut (which, if you're brave enough, may be the best way to go), you can get the best grooming results with the least struggle by using the following tips:

◆ Untangle hair before beginning to shampoo, to prevent even worse tangles afterwards.

◆ Try using a shampoo-conditioner combination, or a spray-on detangler that doesn't need to be rinsed out. Comb-outs will be much easier.

◆ Use a wide-tooth comb or a brush that has bristles with plastic-coated tips for comb-outs on wet hair. A fine-tooth comb tends to tear the ends and also pulls more.

◆ Untangle from the ends up, keeping one hand firmly on the roots as you work, to minimize the pulling on baby's scalp and the pain that comes with it.

◆ Don't use a hair dryer on baby's hair.

◆ Don't braid baby's hair or pull it tightly into a ponytail or pigtails, since these styles can lead to patches of baldness or thinning of hair. If you do make ponytails or pigtails, make them loose, and tie them with special protective clips or coated bands rather than with regular rubber bands or clips, both of which can pull out and damage hair. Don't use clips small enough (or with parts small enough) to pose a choking hazard (see page 406). Take bands and clips out before you put baby to bed.

- ◆ Trim hair (or have it trimmed at a salon that specializes in children's cuts and patience) at least every two months, for healthier growth. Trim fringes when they reach the brows.

- ◆ Plan hair grooming for a time when your baby isn't tired, hungry or cranky. Make it more pleasant by getting her occupied with a toy before beginning, possibly a long-haired doll and a comb. Or set her up in front of a mirror so she can watch you work on her hair; eventually, she may learn to appreciate the end result, making the sessions more tolerable.

FEARS

'My baby used to love to watch me turn on the vacuum cleaner; now he's suddenly terrified of it – and anything else that makes a loud noise.'

That's because he's wising up. When your baby was younger, loud noises didn't frighten him – though they may have momentarily startled him – because he didn't perceive the possibility they might be attached to something dangerous. Now, as his understanding of the world grows, so do his fears.

There are any number of things in a baby's everyday life that, though innocuous to you, can trigger terror in him: sounds, such as the roar of a vacuum cleaner, the whir of a blender, the barking of a dog, the whine of a siren, the flushing of a toilet, the gurgle of water draining from the bath; having a shirt pulled over his head; being lifted high in the air (especially if he's begun to

climb, pull up or otherwise develop depth perception); being plunked down in a bath; the motion of a wind-up or mechanical toy.

Probably all babies experience fears at some point, though some overcome them so quickly their parents are never aware of them. Children who live in a lively, active environment, particularly one with older siblings, tend to experience these fears earlier, as well as get rid of them earlier.

Sooner or later, most children leave the fears of late babyhood and toddlerhood behind. Till then, you can help your baby deal with his fears (which will likely multiply in the next year) in these ways:

Don't force. Making your baby come nose to nozzle with the vacuum cleaner not only won't help, it may intensify his fear. Though his phobia may seem irrational to you, it's very legitimate to him. He needs to wait and confront the noisy beast on his own terms and in his own time, when he feels it's safe.

Don't resort to ridicule. Making fun of your child's fears, calling them silly or laughing at them, will only serve to undermine his self-confidence and his ability to deal with them. Take his fears seriously – he does.

Do accept and sympathize. By accepting your baby's fears as real, and offering comfort for them as needed, you'll help him overcome them faster. If he wails when you switch on the vacuum cleaner (or flush the toilet, or turn on the blender) be quick to pick him up and give him a great big reassuring hug. But don't overdo the sympathy or you may reinforce the idea that there is something to be afraid of.

Do reassure and support, then build confidence and skills. Though you should sympathize with his fears, your ultimate goal is to help him conquer them. He can do this only by becoming familiar with the things he fears, learning what they do and how they work, and gaining some sense of control over them. Let him touch or even play with the vacuum when it's turned off and unplugged – he is probably as fascinated with the machine as he is afraid of it.

Once he becomes comfortable playing with the vacuum when it's off, try holding him securely in one arm while you vacuum with the other – if this doesn't upset him. Then show him how to turn the machine on himself, with a little help from you if the switch is tricky. If it's the toilet's flush he fears, have him throw some paper in and encourage him to flush it down himself when he feels ready. If it's the draining bath, let him watch the water drain when he is safely out of it, fully dressed and, if need be, in your arms. If dogs are his nemesis, try playing with one while your baby watches from a distance and from a safe spot – perhaps from your spouse's lap. When he's finally willing to approach a dog, encourage your baby (while you hold him) to make 'nice doggy' to a dog you know is gentle and won't suddenly snap.

What it's Important to Know:
THE BEGINNING OF DISCIPLINE

You applauded wildly your baby's first successful attempt at pulling up, and cheered proudly from the sidelines as creeping finally became crawling. Now you're wondering what all the celebration was about. Along with the new mobility has come a talent for getting into trouble to rival that of Dennis the Menace. If your baby's not adroitly turning off the TV, he or she is triumphantly sliding the tablecloth (along with the fruit bowl atop it) from the dining room table, gleefully unravelling whole rolls of toilet paper, or industriously emptying the contents of drawers, cupboards and bookshelves onto the floor. Before, all you had to do to keep both baby and home from harm was to deposit your child in a safe spot; now, no such haven exists.

For the first time, you're likely to be upset by, rather than proud of, your offspring's exploits. And for the first time the question of discipline has probably come up in your home. The timing is right. Waiting to introduce discipline into a child's life much later than ten months could make the task much more difficult; trying to have done so much earlier, before memory was developed, would have been futile.

Why discipline a baby? First of all, to instil a concept of right and wrong. Though it'll be a long time before your child will fully grasp it, it's now that you should begin to teach right from wrong by both example and guidance. Secondly, to plant the seeds of self-control. They won't take root for a while, but unless they do eventually, your child won't be able to function effectively. Thirdly, to teach respect for the rights and feelings of others, so that a child will grow from a normally self-centred baby and toddler into a sensitive and caring child and adult. And, finally, to protect your baby, your home and your sanity – now and in the months of mischief ahead.

As you embark on a programme of child discipline, keep the following in mind:

- Though the word *discipline* is associated with punishment in many minds, it actually comes from the Latin word for 'teach'.

- Every child is different, every family is different, each situation is different. But there are universal rules of behaviour that apply to everyone, at all times.

- Until infants understand what is safe and what is not, or at least which actions are permissible and which are not, their parents have total responsibility for keeping the environment safe, as well as for safeguarding their own belongings and those of others.

- Withdrawal of parental love threatens a child's self-esteem. It's important to let children know that they are still loved unconditionally, even when their behaviour is disapproved of.

- The most effective discipline is neither uncompromisingly rigid nor overly permissive. Strict discipline that relies entirely on parental policing rather than encouraging the development of self-control usually turns out children who are totally submissive to their parents but totally uncontrollable once out of reach of parental or other adult authority. On the other hand, overly permissive parents aren't likely to turn out well-behaved children, capable of coping in the real world, either. Their over-indulged children are often selfish, rude and unpleasant, quick to argue, slow to comply. Both extremes of discipline can

leave a child feeling unloved. Strict parents may seem cruel, and thus unloving; permissive parents may seem not to care. A more nurturing brand of discipline falls somewhere in between – it sets limits that are fair, and enforces them firmly but lovingly.

That's not to say that there aren't normal variations in discipline styles. Some parents are simply more relaxed and some more rigid. That's okay as long as neither goes to the extreme.

- Effective discipline is individualized. If you have more than one child, you almost certainly noticed differences in personality from birth. Such differences will affect how each child is best disciplined. One, for instance, will refrain from playing with an electric socket after a gentle remonstrance. Another won't take your warning seriously unless there is a toughness – or perhaps fear – in your voice. A third may need to be physically removed from the source of danger. Tailor your style to your child.

- Circumstances can alter a child's response to discipline. A child who ordinarily requires strong admonitions may be crushed if scolded when tired or teething. Switch gears, if need be, to meet your child's immediate needs.

- Children need limits. They often can't control themselves or their impulses and become frightened at the loss of control. Fair, age-appropriate limits, set by parents and lovingly and consistently enforced, provide a comforting tether to keep children secure and steady while they explore and grow. Stretching those limits because he or she's 'just a baby' isn't fair to your child or to those whose rights are being violated. Tender age – at least after ten months – shouldn't guarantee carte blanche to pull a sibling's hair or tear up mummy's magazine before she's read it. Planning ahead and teaching baby to live with limits from an early age can help calm some of the turmoil of the terrible twos. It will also be necessary for success in a society that is full of limits – at school, work and play.

Just which limits you set depends partly on your priorities. In some homes, keeping shoes off the sofa and not eating in the living room are paramount issues. In others, staying out of mummy's or daddy's desk is high on the list. In most families, common courtesy and simple etiquette – using 'please' and 'thank you', sharing, respecting other people's feelings – are key expectations. Set rules you will enforce carefully, and limit their numbers. Too many rules means too little opportunity for a baby to learn from his or her own explorations and mistakes.

Keep your baby's age in mind as you set – and eventually enforce – the rules that apply to him or her. While it may be reasonable to expect a three-year-old to say 'please' and 'thank you' or to put away toys, it obviously isn't reasonable to expect a one-year-old to. Expecting more than your child can deliver will invariably result in failure.

It's easier, of course, to talk about setting and enforcing limits for babies than to actually follow through. It's tempting to give in to an adorable tot who gives you an impish smile when you say 'No!' or to a sweet, sensitive one who breaks into tears at the very sound of the word. But steel yourself and remember it's for your child's own good. It may not seem vital now to stop your baby from taking the crackers into the living room, but if he or she doesn't learn to follow at least a few rules now, it will be harder to handle the many that will be faced later. You can continue to expect protestations, but gradually you will find that more and more, your child will accept limits matter-of-factly.

◆ A baby who gets into trouble isn't 'bad'. Babies and young toddlers don't know right from wrong, so their actions can't be considered naughty. They learn about their world by experimenting, observing cause and effect, and testing the adults in it. What happens when I turn over a glass of juice? Will it happen again? And again? Or what's inside the kitchen drawers, and what will happen if I take it all out? What will mummy's reaction be?

Repeatedly telling your child that he or she is bad can damage the ego and interfere with self-confidence and achievement down the road. And the child who hears 'You're a bad boy [or girl]!' over and over may fulfill the prophecy in later years ('If they say I'm bad, I must be bad'). Criticize your baby's actions but not your baby ('Biting is bad', not 'You're bad').

◆ Consistency is important. Once you've made a fair number of age-appropriate rules, enforce them consistently. There's nothing more unsettling to a young child than rules that apply only sometimes, or that vary depending on whether mummy or daddy or the baby-sitter's on duty. If shoes on the sofa are forbidden today but permitted tomorrow, or if hand washing before dinner was compulsory yesterday but overlooked today, the only lesson learned is that the world is confusing and rules are meaningless.

♦ Follow-through is crucial. Looking up from your book long enough to mutter 'No' to a baby who's tugging at the television wires but not long enough to make sure that he or she stops is not effective discipline (plus, it isn't safe). If your actions don't speak at least as loud as your words, your admonitions will lose their impact. When the first no is ineffective, take immediate action, especially in such a dangerous situation. Put down your book, pick up your baby and move him or her away from the tempting TV wires – preferably far away, into another room. Then take your baby's mind off the television with a favourite plaything. For most babies, what's been taken out of sight is quickly out of mind – though a few may try to return to the scene of the crime, in which case you may have to block it off. Distraction, when it works, also allows a baby who feels that 'No' is a challenge to his or her ego to save face.

♦ Babies and young toddlers have limited memories. You can't expect them to learn a lesson the first time it's taught, and you can expect them to repeat an undesirable action over and over again. Be patient, and be prepared to repeat the same message – 'Don't touch the TV' or 'Don't eat the dog food' – every day for weeks before it finally sinks in or the fascination is lost.

♦ Babies enjoy the 'no game'. Most babies love the challenge of a parent's 'No!' as much as the challenge of climbing a flight of stairs or fitting a circle into a shape sorter. So no matter how your baby goads you,

don't let your 'No!' deteriorate into a game or a fit of laughter. Your baby won't take you seriously.

♦ Too many nos lose their effectiveness and are demoralizing. You wouldn't want to live in a world ruled by an unforgiving dictator whose three favourite words were 'No! No! No!' And you shouldn't want your baby to live in one either. Limit the nos to those situations in which baby's wellbeing or that of another person or of your home is threatened. Remember that not every issue is worth a fight. Fewer nos will be needed if you create a childproof environment (see page 402) in your home, with plenty of opportunities for exploration under safe conditions.

Along with each no, try to offer a yes in the form of an alternative: 'No, you can't play with Daddy's book, but you can look at this one', or 'You can't empty the cereal shelf, but you can empty the pots and pans shelves'. Instead of 'No, don't touch those papers in Mummy's desk' to the baby who already has emptied several items on the floor, try 'Those papers belong in Mummy's drawer. Let's see if we can put the papers back and close the drawer'. This face-saving approach gets the message across without making your baby feel 'bad'.

Once in a while, when the stakes aren't high or when you realize you've made a mistake, let baby win. An occasional victory will help make up for the many losses he or she must take each day.

♦ Children need to be allowed to make some mistakes, and to learn from them. If you make it impossible for your child to slip up (stashing away all knickknacks, for instance), you won't have to say no very often, but you will also miss important chances to teach. Allow room for errors (though you'll want to avoid those that are dangerous and/or expensive through prudent childproofing), so that your baby can learn from them.

◆ **Correction and reward work better than punishment.** Punishment, always of questionable value, is particularly useless for young children, since they don't understand why they're being punished. A baby is too young to associate a time-out in the playpen with having just dumped the salt out of the salt shaker, or to understand that a bottle is being withheld because he or she bit a sibling. Instead of punishing misbehaviour, catch your baby being good. Positive reinforcement, rewarding and praising good behaviour, works much better. It builds, rather than smashes, self-confidence and encourages more good behaviour. Another productive approach, one that teaches that actions have consequences, is to have the perpetrator help remedy the results of the offence – wipe up the spilt milk, pick up the scattered tea towels, hand you the books to put back on the shelf.

◆ **Anger triggers anger.** Indulge in an angry outburst when your baby breaks a favourite sweet dish by tossing it like a ball across the room, and he or she is likely to follow in fury, rather than respond with remorse. If necessary, take a few moments to temper your temper before addressing the guilty party. Once your cool is collected, explain to your baby that what he or she did was wrong, and why. ('That wasn't a toy, it was Mummy's dish. You broke it and now Mummy's sad'.) This is important to do even if the explanation seems to be sailing clear over your baby's head, or if distraction has already set in.

Try to remember at moments of high anxiety (it won't always be easy) that your long-term goal is to teach right behaviour, and that screaming or swatting will teach wrong behaviour, setting poor examples of what's appropriate when you're angry.

Don't worry if you occasionally find it impossible to put the brakes on your anger. As a human parent, you're allowed your share of mistakes and weak moments, and your baby needs to know that. As long as your tirades are relatively few, far between and short-lived, they won't interfere with effective parenting. When they occur, be sure to apologize: 'I'm sorry I yelled at you, but I was very angry'. Adding 'I love you' and a hug will not only be reassuring but will let your baby know that sometimes we get angry at people we love and that such feelings are okay.

◆ **Discipline can be a laughing matter.** Nothing lightens life like humour – and it's also a surprisingly effective disciplinary tool. Use it liberally in situations that would otherwise lead you to exasperation, for instance, when baby refuses to allow you to put a snowsuit on him. Instead of doing fruitless combat over shrill screams of protest, head off the tantrum and the struggle with some unexpected silliness. Suggest, perhaps, that you put the snowsuit on the dog (or the cat, or the dolly or on yourself), and then pretend to do so. The incongruity of what you are proposing will probably take your baby's mind off objections long enough for you to accomplish your goal.

Humour can be brought into a variety of disciplinary situations.

TO SMACK OR NOT TO SMACK

Though smacking has been passed on from generation to generation in many families, many experts agree that it is not, and never has been, an effective way to discipline a child. Children who are smacked may refrain from repeating a misdemeanour rather than risk another smacking, but they obey only as long as the risk is present. Smacking may stop a child's undesirable action in its tracks, but it won't change behaviour. It doesn't teach children how to differentiate right from wrong (only what they get smacked for and what they don't get smacked for) – which is, after all, the most important goal of discipline.

Research shows that the short-term benefit of smacking – instant obedience (for the moment) – is definitely outweighed by the potential long-term risks. Smacking has been shown to promote violence, aggression and other antisocial behaviour. For another, smacking teaches children that the best way to settle disputes is with force, and denies them the chance to learn (through a parent's example) alternative, less hurtful routes to dealing with anger and frustration. It also represents an abuse of power by a very large, strong party against a very small, weak one (a model you don't want your child to follow later on in the playground). And it can lead to serious injury of a child, often unintentionally, particularly when it is done in anger. Smacking after the anger is cooled, though it may do less physical damage, seems even more questionable than lashing out in the heat of the moment. It is certainly more cruelly calculated, and it is even less effective in correcting behaviour. In fact,

experts say there's often a grey area between when smacking ends and child abuse begins.

Advocates for a ban on smacking argue that it has negative consequences and is no more effective than other forms of discipline. They recommend that parents use methods other than smacking to discipline their children, such as consequences: time-outs (when the child is old enough to understand the meaning of time-outs) or positive reinforcement. If smacking is done spontaneously out of anger, parents should later explain calmly why they did it, the specific behaviour that provoked it, and how angry they felt, as well as issue an apology (again, this is for children who are old enough to understand).

If it's inadvisable for a parent to smack a child, it is even more inadvisable for another person to do so. Though with a parent a child is usually secure in the knowledge that the smacking has been given by someone who cares, with someone outside the family there's generally no such security. Sitters, teachers and others who tend to your child should be instructed *never* to strike him or her or administer any form of physical punishment.

Some experts (and parents) would agree that a sound smack on the hand or the bottom may be warranted in a dangerous situation to get a serious message across to a child too young to understand words – for example, when a toddler wanders out into the street or approaches a hot stove and a stern reprimand doesn't do the trick. Once comprehension is established, however, physical force is no longer justifiable.

Issue requests while pretending you're a dog or a lion, Pooh, or another of your child's favourites; perform unpopular chores with silly-song accompaniments ('This is the

way we wash the face, wash the face'); carry baby to the dreaded changing table (carefully supported) upside down; make silly faces in the mirror with baby instead of chiding,

'Don't cry, don't cry'. Taking each other less seriously more often will add sunshine to your days, particularly as the sometimes stormy second year approaches. Stay serious, however, when a dangerous situation is involved, since then even a smile can be fatal to the effectiveness of the lesson you are trying to teach.

◆ Accidents require different treatment from intentional wrongdoings. Remember, everyone's entitled to mistakes, but babies, because of their emotional, physical and intellectual immaturity, are entitled to a great many more of them. When yours knocks over a cup of milk while reaching for a slice of bread, 'Oops, the milk spilled. Try to be more careful, honey' is an appropriate response. But when the cup is upended intentionally, 'Milk is to drink, not to spill. Spilling makes a mess and wastes the milk. See, now there's no more' is more fitting. In either case, it also helps to hand baby a paper towel to help in the cleanup, to fill cups with only small amounts of liquids in the future, and to be sure that your baby has plenty of opportunity to pursue his or her experiments with pouring fluids in the bath or other acceptable surroundings.

◆ Parents have to be the adults in the family. That means staying calm when your almost-toddler throws a tantrum, apologizing when you've made a mistake, not always demanding things your way when they could just as easily be done your baby's way – in general, acting your age while baby acts his or her age.

◆ Children are worthy of respect. Instead of treating your baby as an object, a possession or even 'just a baby', treat him or her with the respect you would accord any other person. Be polite (say please, thank you and excuse me), offer simple explanations (even if you don't think they'll be understood) when you forbid something, be understanding of and sympathetic to your baby's wants and feelings (even if you can't permit acting them out), avoid embarrassing your baby (by scolding in front of strangers), and listen to what he or she is trying to say. In this pre-verbal stage, when grunts and pointing are the main modes of communication, listening is a challenge, and it continues to be so until speech becomes clear and language is well developed (somewhere between three and five) – but making that effort is important. Remember, it's frustrating for baby, too. (See Signing with Baby, page 389, for ways to bridge this communication gap.)

◆ There should be a fair distribution of rights between parents and child (or children). It's easy, when a baby is young, for parents to err in this area, going to one extreme or the other. Some abrogate all their rights in favour of their child – they base their lives on baby's schedule, drop everything at baby's first whimper, always put baby's needs before their own – and end up teaching their child that his or her rights are the only ones that matter. Others live their lives as though they were still childless. Without much thought to their infant's needs, they drag an overtired baby to parties, skip story time in favour of a football game and opt for hanging around the house on a Sunday afternoon over a trip to the playground. These parents teach their child that his or her rights don't matter at all. To be fair, family life should be neither completely baby-focused or completely parent-centric. A balance is what's needed.

◆ Nobody's perfect – and nobody should be expected to be. Avoid setting standards that your baby can't possibly live up to. Children need all the years that childhood provides to develop to the point at which they can behave as adults. And as they grow and mature, they also need to know that you don't expect perfection at any age. Praise particular achievements rather than make sweeping pronouncements about your child's nature: 'You were very good in the store' rather than 'You're the best baby in the world'. Since no one can be 'good' all the time, such overlavish praise on a regular basis can make a child fear that your expectations can't possibly be lived up to. It can also help create a praise junkie, always dependent on that cheer, that pat on the back, to feel good about him or herself.

Neither should you expect perfection from yourself. Parents who never lose their temper, never yell and never even have the remotest desire to slug a difficult toddler don't exist. And verbally venting your feelings of anger and frustration occasionally (without acting on that slugging impulse; see box, previous page) may be better than keeping them bottled up inside. Bottled-up anger has a way of bursting out inappropriately, often far out of proportion to the crime of the moment.

If, however, you find yourself losing your temper at your baby too often, try to determine the underlying cause. Are you angry about being responsible for all the child-care chores? Are you really angry at yourself or someone else, and taking it out on baby? Have you set too many limits or provided too many opportunities for baby to get into trouble? If so, try to remedy the situation.

◆ Children need to know they have some control over their lives. For good mental health, everyone – even a baby – needs to feel as though he or she calls at least some of the shots. It won't always be possible for baby to have his or her way, but when it is appropriate, allow it. Give your baby a chance to make some choices – the cracker or the piece of bread, the swing or the baby slide, the bib with the elephant or the one with the clown. Just don't offer too many choices (which will only overwhelm baby), and know when a choice isn't baby's to make (when it comes to sitting in the car seat, for instance).

◆ ◆ ◆

The Eleventh Month

You may have a Baby Houdini on your hands this month, whose major preoccupations are getting into things he or she shouldn't be getting into and getting out of things he or she shouldn't be getting out of. There's no shelf too high, no cabinet handle too unwieldy to deter a ten-month-old baby on a mission of seek and (what seems like) destroy. Accomplished as an escape artist, baby will now try to wriggle his or her way out of nappy changes, pushchairs, high chairs – in other words,

any confining situation. Along with great physical advances (including, for a few, those momentous first steps) come remarkable verbal strides – not so much in the number of words spoken but in the number of words understood. Looking at books becomes a much more interesting and enriching experience as baby begins to recognize and even point to familiar pictures. In fact, pointing becomes a favourite activity no matter what baby's doing – just one way he or she is able to communicate without words.

What Your Baby May Be Doing

All babies reach milestones on their own developmental time line. If your baby seems not to have reached one or more of these milestones, rest assured, he or she probably will very soon. Remember that some babies zoom ahead in certain areas (large motor skills, for example) while they lag a bit in others (verbal skills, perhaps). Your baby's rate of development is normal for your baby. If you have concerns about your baby's development (because you've noticed a missed milestone or what you think might be a developmental delay), don't hesitate to check it out with the doctor at

the next well-baby visit – even if he or she doesn't bring it up. Parents often notice nuances in a baby's development that doctors don't. Premature infants generally reach milestones later than others of the same birth age, often achieving them closer to their adjusted age (the age they would be if they had been born at term), and sometimes later.

By eleven months, your baby . . . should be able to:

- get into a sitting position from stomach

- pick up tiny object with any part of thumb and finger (as always, make sure dangerous objects stay out of baby's reach)

- understand 'no' (but not always obey it)

...will probably be able to:

- play patty-cake (clap hands) or wave bye-bye

- walk holding on to furniture (cruise)

- point or gesture to something to get needs met

...may possibly be able to:

- pick up a tiny object neatly with tips of thumb and forefinger (again, keep all dangerous objects out of baby's reach)

- stand alone momentarily

- say 'dada' or 'mama' discriminately

- say one word other than 'mama' or 'dada'

. . . may even be able to:

- stand alone well

- indicate wants in ways other than crying

- 'play ball' (roll ball back to you)

- drink from a cup independently

- use immature jargoning (gibberish that sounds as if baby is talking a made-up foreign language)

- say three or more words other than 'mama' or 'dada'

- respond to a one-step command without gestures ('Give that to me' – without hand out)

- walk well

What You Can Expect at This Month's Checkup

Most doctors do not schedule regular well-baby checkups this month – again, just as well, since babies this age do not appreciate the holding still required during a doctor's visit. Those with stranger anxiety may also not appreciate the doctor, no matter how warm and friendly. Do call the doctor if there are any concerns that can't wait until next month's visit.

Feeding Your Baby:
WEANING FROM THE BOTTLE

Ask most paediatricians when a baby should be weaned from the bottle and the majority will say by age one – and definitely no later than eighteen months. Ask most parents when they actually weaned their baby off a bottle, and the majority will say . . . much later than that. There are a host of reasons why parents (and babies) hang on to the bottle for longer than doctors recommend, reasons ranging from convenience for the parents, to comfort for the baby, to less mess for everyone involved. Throw in a dose of parental weariness and infant attachment, and it's no wonder millions of two- and three-year-olds still haven't kicked the bottle habit.

But here's the message about bottles most experts would like parents to pay attention to: weaning by age one – or as soon as possible after the first birthday – is best for your baby. And there are many good reasons why. First of all, as with many other attachment objects of baby-hood (such as a dummy, being rocked to sleep, and so on), old habits die hard. And the older the habits (and the baby) are, the harder it is to break them. Weaning a fairly flexible one-year-old is like taking candy from a baby compared to tussling with a strong-willed two-year-old over the bottle.

Secondly, when an older baby uses a bottle, he or she runs the risk of developing tooth decay from bottle feeding, and not only because there are now teeth to decay. While an infant is usually fed in his or her parents' arms – and the bottle removed when the feeding ends – a mobile toddler often totes the bottle wherever he or she goes. This drinking-on-the-go and nipping-all-day-long allows the milk or juice to bathe teeth in sugar, with cavities the potential result.

Thirdly, toddlers who are bottle drinkers end up drinking more juice or milk than they should, filling up on too many liquids and taking in too few solids. Not only do these toddlers become fussy eaters (not surprising, since their tummies are always full of juice and milk), but they can end up missing out on important nutrients. If their bottles are filled with juice – particularly apple juice – they can also end up with chronic diarrhoea.

And if you're still not convinced to switch to a cup in the next month or two, consider these developmental drawbacks: a toddler who's constantly toting and nipping from a bottle has only one hand free for playing and exploring – and a mouth too full to speak out of.

If your baby hasn't been introduced to a cup yet, see page 323 for tips on how to begin. While introducing the cup is relatively easy – albeit messy – getting your baby to give up the bottle entirely and take all his or her liquid from a cup is a little more challenging. Following these suggestions can make the switch from all bottle to all cup a little smoother:

Time it right. Don't wean your baby from the bottle if he or she is sick, very tired or even hungry. A cranky baby won't take kindly to your weaning attempts. And wait until baby has settled down again after a big move, new baby-sitter arrangements, or any other stressful time.

Go slow. Unless you're planning on making your baby kick the bottle habit cold turkey – a technique better suited for an older toddler or preschooler whose help can actually be enlisted in the plan – the best way to transition from a bottle to a cup is by slowly phasing out the bottles while phasing in the cup. There are a number of ways to do this:

◆ Drop one bottle-feeding session at a time and replace it with a cup. Allow a few days or a week before replacing the next one with a cup. The middle-of-the-day bottle will be easier to cut out first. The morning and bedtime ones are usually harder to give up.

◆ Put less formula or milk (formula for babies under a year, whole milk for those over a year) in each bottle than your baby normally takes and top off each bottle feeding with a cup.

Slowly decrease the amount of formula or milk in the bottle while you increase the amount of formula or milk in the cup.

◆ Serve only water in the bottle, starting with one feeding at a time. Save milk, formula or juice for the cup. Your baby might find that the bottles aren't worth it any more. But do make sure your baby's getting enough total formula or milk, or enough in the way of other calcium foods.

Keep it out of sight. Out of sight, out of mind – hopefully. Keeping the bottle away from your baby (during the feeding you're replacing with a cup) will make craving it less likely. Hide it in the cupboard, put it on a high shelf, and when you're down to the last feeding and ready to call it quits entirely, throw it away. At the same time, make sure your baby sees his or her cup around the house often – in the refrigerator, on the kitchen counter, on the dining room table.

Make it exciting. Give your baby cups with bright colours, adorned with his or her favourite characters, or see-through so he can watch the liquid swish around – whichever type makes it more thrilling to use.

Expect a mess. Unless you're using a nonspill sippy cup (which you shouldn't use all the time; see box, page 324), you should expect lots of wet accidents until your baby has mastered drinking from the cup well. Allow your baby to experiment (and to do it himself or herself) – and protect your floors, walls and yourself with newspapers, aprons and towels. Don't be tempted to take the cup away and manoeuvre it yourself into baby's mouth in order to cut down on mess. The

bottle was in baby's control; the cup needs to be, too.

Expect less. Less milk, that is. Expect your baby to take less formula or milk during the weaning process. Once he or she gets used to taking in all his or her daily liquid from a cup, the amount he or she consumes will increase.

Teach by example. Babies at this age love imitating adults (particularly adults they love). Take advantage of this urge to mimic and drink from a cup along with your baby (or have older siblings pitch in with drinking duty).

Be positive. Every time your baby uses a cup, apply positive reinforcement. Clap when your baby holds the cup (even if he or she doesn't drink from it). Cheer when baby takes a sip.

Be patient. Like Rome, weaning from a bottle won't be conquered in a day. Allow several weeks, even a month or two, for the entire process to be completed. The first few days will be rough, but, like most things in parenting, being consistent (by not caving in and giving your baby his bottle back) and giving it time will allow for a much smoother transition. And if it takes a long time because your child is really attached to the bottle, don't stop trying. It's okay if it takes longer – as long as the eventual goal is met.

Give extra love. For many babies, the bottle provides not only nourishment but also comfort. As you limit the amount of time your baby has the bottle, be prepared to shower him or her with extra hugs, extra play sessions, an extra bedtime story on your lap, another stuffed animal to help your baby feel secure and comforted.

What You May Be Concerned About

BOWED LEGS

*'My baby just started taking
steps and she seems to be
bowlegged.'*

Bowed until two, knock-kneed at four, a small child's legs certainly won't give a supermodel a run for her money. But even the legs that grace fashion's top catwalks were probably bowed when they took their first steps. Almost all children are bowlegged (their knees don't touch when they stand with feet together) during the first two years of life. Then, as they spend more time walking, they become knock-kneed (their knees meet, but their ankles don't). Not until the teen years do the knees and ankles align and the legs appear to be shaped normally. Special shoes or orthotics (bars, braces or other orthopaedic appliances) aren't needed and won't make a difference in this normal progression.

Occasionally, a doctor will note a true abnormality in a child's legs. Perhaps just one leg is bowed, or one knee turns in, or perhaps the baby is knock-kneed (though sometimes a baby only looks that way because of very chubby thighs), or normal bowing becomes progressively more pronounced once walking begins. In such cases, or if there is a history of bowlegs or knock-knees in adults in the family, the baby may need further evaluation, either by the baby's doctor or by a paediatric orthopaedist. Depending upon the particular case, treatment may or may not be recommended. Fortunately, rickets, once the most common cause of permanently bowed legs, is fairly rare in the United Kingdom today, thanks to the fortification of formula, milk, and other dairy products with vitamin D.

PARENTAL NUDITY

*'I sometimes dress in front of my
baby, but I'm starting to wonder how
long I should let him see me naked.'*

You've got some time before you'll have to start retreating behind closed doors to do your dressing and undressing. Experts agree that up until the preschool years, parental nudity won't affect a child in any way. (Beyond the age of three or four, however, the consensus changes. At that point, some believe, it may be less healthy for children to see parents of the opposite sex fully undressed.) Certainly, an infant under a year is too young to be stimulated by seeing his mother undressed (though a breastfeeder may smack his lips at the sight of his favourite milk machine). He's also too young to remember, years later, what he's seen. In fact, he's as unlikely to notice anything special about mum's birthday suit as he is about her best dress, and will probably largely ignore it.

If your baby is curious about what he views, however, and wants to touch your pubic hair or pull at your nipples, feel free to end any explorations that bother you. Be matter-of-fact, and don't overreact. His interest in the private parts of your body is, after all, no less wholesome than his interest in the public parts, such as your nose or ears (though he may be even more fascinated by the private parts since they're usually kept under wraps). 'That's Mummy's' is a response that will help a baby begin to understand the concept of body privacy and help him keep his private parts private later on – but one that won't instil guilt.

The same, of course, applies to a baby girl and her father – nudity now is not an issue (though covering up is fine, too).

FALLS

'I feel as though I'm living on the brink of disaster ever since my little boy started to walk. He trips over his own feet, bangs his head on table corners, topples off chairs . . . .'

This is an age that many parents fear neither they nor their babies will survive. Split lips, black eyes, bumps, bangs, bruises and countless close calls for baby. Frazzled nerves and skipped heartbeats for mummy and daddy.

Yet babies keep going back for more. And a good thing, too, or they'd never learn to get around on their own – or, in fact, learn much of anything at all. Though horse riding can be mastered, according to the old adage, with just seven falls, mastery of walking and climbing takes a good deal more – with seven or more falls not being uncommon in the space of a single morning. Some children learn caution fairly quickly. After the first topple off the coffee table, they retreat for a few days and then proceed more carefully. Others (those who will probably always enjoy living life on the edge, much to their parents' chagrin) seem as though they will never learn caution, never know fear, never feel pain; five minutes after the tenth topple, they're back for number eleven.

Learning to walk is a matter of trial and error or, more accurately, step and fall. You can't, and shouldn't try to, interfere with the learning process. Your role, other than that of proud but nervous spectator, is to do everything possible to ensure that when your baby falls, he falls safely. While taking a tumble on the living room rug can bruise his ego, tumbling down the stairs can bruise a lot more. Bumping into the rounded edge of the sofa may draw some tears, but colliding with the sharp corner of a glass table may draw blood. To decrease the chance of serious injuries, be sure that your house is safe for your baby (see page 402). And even if you have removed the most obvious hazards from your toddler's path, remember that the most important safety feature in your home is you (or whoever else is minding your child). While your child needs plenty of freedom for exploration of the world around him, it should be permitted only under very close and *constant* adult supervision.

Even in the most conscientious of homes, however, serious injuries can happen. Be prepared for this possibility by knowing just what to do if one should occur; take a baby-resuscitation course and learn the first-aid procedures beginning on page 575 (they're dark at the top for quick flipping).

Parental reaction often colours a baby's response to mishap. If each fall brings one or more panicked adults rushing to his rescue, chorusing, 'Are you okay? Are you okay?' between gasps and shudders, your fallen soldier is likely to overreact as much as those around him – shedding as many tears when he's not really hurt as when he really is – and may soon become overcautious or lose his sense of adventure, perhaps even to the point of hesitating to attempt normal physical developmental hurdles. If, on the other hand, the adult's reaction is a calm 'Oops, you fell down! You're all right. Up you go', then the child is likely to turn out to be a real trouper, taking minor tumbles in stride and getting right back on his feet without missing a beat.

NOT PULLING UP YET

'Although she's been trying for some time, my baby hasn't yet pulled up to stand. I'm worried that she's not developing normally.'

For babies, life's a never-ending series of physical (and emotional and intellectual) challenges. The skills that adults take for granted – rolling over, sitting up, standing – are for them major hurdles to be confronted and scaled with no small effort. And no sooner is one challenge met than another looms ahead.

As for pulling up, there will be babies who will master this skill as early as five months and those who will wait until well after the first birthday, though most will fall (or rather, stand) somewhere between the two developmental extremes. A baby's weight may have an impact on when she first pulls up; a heavier baby has more baggage to take with her than does a lighter one, and so the effort needed may be greater. On the other hand, a strong and well-coordinated baby may be able to pull up early no matter how much she weighs. The baby who's cooped up in a pushchair, baby carrier or mesh-sided playpen much of the day won't be able to practise her pull-ups. Nor will a baby want to practise if she is surrounded by fragile furniture that buckles under her every attempt to steady herself. Slippery shoes or socks can also hamper efforts to pull up, and can cause falls that dampen enthusiasm for the activity – bare feet or slipper-socks with non-skid soles give baby a better foot to stand on. You can encourage your baby to try to pull up by putting a favourite toy in a place where

she has to stand to get to it. Also, help her to pull up in your lap frequently, which will build her leg muscles as well as her confidence.

The average age for passing the pulling-up milestone is nine months – and most, but certainly not all, children have accomplished the skill by twelve months. Of course, it's a good idea to check with the doctor if your child hasn't successfully pulled up by her first birthday, just to rule out the possibility of a problem. Right now, all you need to do is sit back and wait for her to stand – in her own good time. Children gain confidence from being allowed to progress at their own pace, from discovering 'I can do it myself'. Trying to force a child to stand or walk before she's ready could set her back rather than move her forward.

BABY TOOTH INJURIES

'My son fell and chipped one of his baby teeth. Should I take him to the dentist?'

Since those cute little pearly whites will fall out someday anyway to make room for permanent teeth, a small chip in a baby tooth is usually nothing to worry about – and pretty common, considering the number of tumbles the typical fledgling toddler takes in the course of a day. Still, it's a good idea to make sure you're not dealing with anything that's more than cosmetic. First, do a quick check of the tooth. If there seem to be any sharp edges, give the dentist a call when you have a chance. He or she may want to smooth out the edge or fix it with a plastic filling or crown. Call the dentist right away, however, if baby seems to be in any pain (even days later), if the tooth appears to have shifted position or become infected (swollen gums can tip you off to this), or if you see a pink spot in the centre of the chipped tooth. Any of these symptoms might indicate that the fracture has gone into the nerve. In such a case, the dentist will need to determine – by taking an X-ray – if the tooth should be extracted or if nerve treatment (a baby root canal) is needed. An injury to the nerve, if left untreated, can damage the permanent tooth that is already forming in your baby's mouth. Either way, try to smile – chances are there will be plenty more bumps for your baby on the road to walking!

CHOLESTEROL IN BABY'S DIET

'My wife and I are very careful about cholesterol in our diets, but when we asked our doctor whether we should start our son on skimmed milk at a year, he said no, only whole milk. Does this mean we don't have to worry about his cholesterol at all?'

A child in the first and second years of life is in an enviable position – at least from the point of view of parents who miss their daily bacon and eggs. Not only are fat and cholesterol not hazardous to a baby's health, they're believed to be essential for proper growth and for development of the brain and the rest of the nervous system.

Still, though you should plan to include whole milk and whole milk dairy products (including whole milk yoghurt and cheeses) in your baby's diet until his second birthday, it also makes sense to take steps to help ensure a healthier cardiovascular future by instilling heart-smart eating habits now:

Don't butter baby up. If your baby becomes accustomed to bread, pancakes, vegetables, fish and other foods cooked and served without added butter or margarine now, he won't crave that buttery taste later on. And if, when he's older, he wants to spread his bread, less will likely be more. (To keep the family's cholesterol down, when shopping for margarine, choose those that are low in trans fatty acids; generally, softer margarines are heart-healthier than block varieties.)

Forgo the frying. Fried foods shouldn't be a regular part of anyone's diet. Serve or order baked potato (or oven chips) instead of chips for your baby, grill the chicken breast or bake the nuggets instead of frying, pan-fry the fish in a non-stick frying pan or bake it in the oven. When you cook with fats, opt for those high in polyunsaturates, such as olive, rapeseed, safflower, sunflower, corn or soya oil, over saturated fats, such as palm or coconut oil, hydrogenated vegetable shortening or fat, coconut butter or animal fats.

Be picky with your protein. Red meat's fine for baby (and, in fact, is a good source of iron). But it's also important for your child to get a taste for protein sources that are low in cholesterol and fat (such as fish, skinless poultry, dried beans and peas, and tofu) – if only so your child won't grow up spurning anything but hamburger. It's okay to avoid red meat entirely, but then be certain your baby has other sources of iron in his diet. Eggs are a great source of protein for baby; choosing omega-3-rich eggs will offer brain-boosting and heart-healthy fatty acids, too.

Favour fish. There's no heart-healthier food than fish, particularly those varieties that are high in omega-3 oils (such as salmon and sardines) – which makes the fish habit a good one to catch early on. Introduce your baby to a variety of fresh fish, particularly those that have a pleasingly mild taste and an easily chewable texture. (Some fish are better for baby than others, and some should be avoided altogether because of mercury contamination; see page 340). Always screen carefully for bones when serving your baby the catch of the day.

Look at the label. Most of the fat and cholesterol in the diets of both adults and children is hidden in prepared foods. Crisps and other snack foods are, not surprisingly, a major source of dietary fat, but so are cakes and pastries. To avoid hidden unhealthy fats, read labels carefully. Look for products made either without fat or without saturated fats or oils.

Take it slow on fast foods. They may be finger-licking good, but most fast foods are high in fat, cholesterol and sodium, and low in important nutrients and fibre. They can also be pretty addictive. Holding off on serving your baby fast foods will keep him from getting hooked on them at an early age. Another reason not to rush into fast food: most fast foods are nutritionally inappropriate for babies. Though burgers prepared at home are fine, fast-food varieties generally contain too much sodium. Ditto fast-food chicken nuggets, that perennial preschool favourite; baby will be better off nibbling on homemade ones (baked in the oven) or on wholesome brands bought at the health food market. Same with chips; there's no need to give baby a taste for them this early in life, especially since they're loaded with salt and unhealthy fats. If you do visit fast-food restaurants as a family, do so infrequently, and choose from the menu carefully. Good options for babies include grilled chicken and plain baked potatoes.

GROWTH SWINGS

'The health visitor just told me that my son has dropped from the 90th to the 50th percentile in height. She said not to worry, but it seems like such a big drop.'

Healthy babies and children come in all sizes. When a doctor or health visitor assesses a child's progress, she looks at more than the curve of his growth chart. Are both height and weight keeping pace fairly closely? Is baby passing developmental mileposts (sitting, pulling up, for example) at about the right time? Is he active and alert? Does he appear happy? Does he seem to relate well to his parents? Are hair and skin healthy-looking? Apparently, the health visitor is satisfied with the way your baby is growing and developing, and unless you have some reason (other than this drop in height) to believe something's amiss, you should take your cues from that assessment.

The most common reason for such a growth shift at this time is that a baby who was born on the large side is just moving closer to his genetically predestined size. If both parents are not very tall, you shouldn't expect your son to stay in the 90th percentile – chances are he won't. Height, however, isn't inherited through a single gene. So a child with a 1.8-m (6-ft) father and a 1.5-m (5-ft) mother isn't likely to reach adulthood exactly the same height as one or the other. More likely, he will end up somewhere in between. (Each generation is, however, on the average, a little taller than the previous one.)

Occasionally, what appears to be a sudden growth shift is just the result of a measuring error – one made at this last visit or at a previous one. Babies are usually measured while they're lying down, and a baby's wriggling can easily yield inaccurate results. When a child graduates to upright measurement, he may actually appear to lose a few centimetres/an inch or so in height because his bones settle a little when he stands.

Because keeping thorough health records is important, jot down your baby's statistics at each checkup. Then do your very best to forget about them. As you will soon realize, kids grow up too fast anyway.

What it's Important to Know: HELPING BABY TO TALK

You've come a long way, baby. From a newborn whose only way of communicating was crying, and who understood nothing but his or her own primal needs; to a six-month-old who was beginning to articulate sounds, comprehend words, and express anger, frustration and happiness; to an eight-month-old who was able to convey messages through primitive sounds and gestures; and now, to a ten-month-old who has uttered (or will soon utter) his or her first real words. And yet with all the accomplishments already behind your baby, still more astounding growth is around the bend. In the months to come, your baby's comprehension will increase at a remarkable rate; by around a year and a half, there will be a dramatic expansion also in the number of words spoken.

Here's how you can help your baby's language development:

Label, label, label. Everything in your baby's world has a name – use it. Verbally label objects in baby's home environment (bath, toilet, kitchen sink, oven, cot, lamps, chair, sofa and so on); play 'eyes-nose-mouth' (take baby's hand and touch your eyes, your nose and your mouth, kissing the hand at the last stop), and point out other body parts; point to birds, dogs, trees, leaves, flowers, cars, trucks and fire engines while you're out walking. Don't leave out people – point out mummies, daddies, babies, women, men, girls, boys. Or baby – use his or her name often to help develop a sense of identity.

Listen, listen, listen. As important as what you say to your baby is how much you let your baby say to you. Even if you haven't identified any real words yet, listen to the babble and respond: 'Oh, that's very interesting', or 'Is that so?' When you ask a question, wait for an answer, even if it's just a smile, excited body language, or undecipherable babble. Make a concerted effort to pick out words from your baby's verbal ramblings; many 'first words' are so garbled that parents don't notice them. Try to match baby's unrecognizable words with the objects they may represent; they may not even sound remotely correct, yet if the child uses the same 'word' for the same object consistently, it counts. When you have trouble translating what your baby's asking for, point to possible candidates ('Do you want the ball? the bottle? the puzzle?'), giving him or her a chance to tell you whether you've guessed right. There will be frustration on both sides until baby's requests become more intelligible, but your continuing to attempt to act as interpreter will help speed language development as well as provide baby with the satisfaction of being at least somewhat understood.

Concentrate on concepts. So much of what you take for granted, baby has yet to learn. Here are just a few concepts you can help your baby develop; you can probably think of many more. Be sure to say the word for the concept as you and baby act it out.

- *Hot and cold:* Let baby touch the outside of your warm coffee cup, then an ice cube; cold water, then warm water; warm porridge, then cold milk.

- *Up and down:* Gently lift baby up in the air, then lower to the ground; place a brick up on the dresser, then put it down on the floor; take your baby up on the slide, then down.

- *In and out:* Put bricks in a box or bucket, dump them out; do the same with other objects.

- *Empty and full:* Show baby a container filled with bathwater, then one that's empty. A bucket filled with sand, then an empty one.

- *Stand and sit:* Hold baby's hand, stand together, then sit down together (use ring-a-ring o' roses to help with this concept).

- *Wet and dry:* Compare a wet flannel and a dry towel; baby's just-shampooed hair with your dry hair.

- *Big and little:* Set a large ball beside a small one; show baby that 'daddy (or mummy) is big and baby is little' in the mirror.

Explain the environment and cause and effect. 'The sun is bright so we have light'. 'The refrigerator keeps food cold so it will taste good and stay fresh'. 'Mummy uses a little brush to brush your teeth, a medium brush to brush your hair, and a big brush to scrub the floor'. 'Flip the wall switch up and the room becomes light, down and it's dark'. And so on. An expanded awareness and understanding of his or her surroundings, as well as sensitivity to other people and their needs and feelings, is a far more important step towards your baby's eventual mastery of language and reading than learning to parrot a lot of meaningless words.

Become colour conscious. Start identifying colours whenever it's appropriate. 'See, that balloon is red, just like your shirt', or 'That truck is green; your pushchair is green, too', or 'Look at those pretty yellow flowers'. Keep in mind, however, that most children don't 'learn' their colours until sometime around age three.

Use double-speak. Use adult phrases, then translate them into baby shorthand: 'Now you and I are going for a walk. Daddy, Connor, go bye-bye'. 'Oh, you've finished your snack. Brandon made all gone'. Talking twice as much will help baby understand twice as much.

Don't talk like a baby. Using simplified grown-up talk, rather than baby talk, will help your baby learn to speak correctly faster: 'Abby wants a bottle?' is better than 'Baby wanna baba?' Forms like 'doggie' or 'dolly', however, are fine to use with young children – they're naturally more appealing.

Introduce pronouns. Though your baby probably won't be using pronouns correctly for a year or more, the end of the first year is a good time to start developing familiarity with them by using them along with names. '*Daddy* is going to get *Josh* some breakfast – *I'm* going to get *you* something to eat'. 'This book is *Mummy's* – it's *mine* – and that book is *Olivia's* – it's *yours*'. This last also teaches the concept of ownership.

Urge baby to talk back. Use any ploy you can think of to try to get your baby to respond, in either words or gestures. Present choices: 'Do you want bread or crackers?' or 'Do you want to wear your Mickey Mouse pyjamas or the ones with aeroplanes?' and then give baby a chance to point to or vocally indicate the favoured selection, which you should then name. Ask questions: 'Are you tired?' 'Would you like a snack?' 'Do you want to go on the swing?' A shake of the head will probably precede a verbal yes or no, but it still represents a response. Get baby to help you locate things (even if they aren't really lost): 'Can you find the ball?' Give baby plenty of time to turn up the item, and reward with cheers. Even looking in the right direction should count – 'That's right, there's the ball!'

Never force the issue. Encourage your baby to talk by saying, 'Tell Mummy what you want' when he or she uses non-verbal communication (pointing or other signs, grunting) to indicate a need. If baby grunts or points again, offer a choice; for instance, 'Do you want the bear or the dog?' If you still get a non-verbal response, name the item yourself, 'Oh, it's the dog you want', and then hand it over. *Never* withhold something because your child can't ask for it by name or because he or she pronounces the name incorrectly. Eventually, the verbal responses will outnumber the non-verbal.

Keep directions simple. Sometime around the first birthday (often before), most toddlers can begin following simple commands, but only if they're issued one step at a time. Instead of 'Please pick up the spoon and give it to me', try 'Please pick up the spoon', and when that's been done, add 'Now, please give the spoon to Daddy'. You can also help your baby enjoy early success in following commands by giving commands that he or she is about to carry out anyway. If, for example, your baby is reaching for a cracker, say 'Pick up the cracker'. These techniques will help develop comprehension, which must precede speech.

Correct carefully. Very rarely will a young child say even a single word perfectly, and none say everything with adult precision. Many consonants may be beyond your baby's capability for the next several years or more, and the ends of words may be omitted for at least many more months ('mo mi' may mean 'more milk' and 'go dow' 'go down'). When your baby mispronounces a word, don't correct as if you're a demanding schoolteacher – too much criticism could prompt a baby to give up trying. Instead, use a more subtle approach, teaching without preaching to protect your baby's tender ego. When baby looks up at the sky and says, 'Moom, tar', respond with, 'That's right. There's the moon and the stars'. Though baby mispronunciations are adorable, resist the temptation to repeat them, which will be confusing (baby's supposed to be learning how they should sound).

Expand your reading repertoire. Rhymes are still favourites with babies entering their toddler years, as are books with pictures of animals, vehicles, toys and children. A few children are ready for very simple stories, though most won't be willing to sit still for them for several months yet. Even those who are ready usually can't handle more than three or four minutes with a book at this age – their attention span is still short. You'll hold it longer if you make reading interactive, a process baby can participate in fully. Stop to discuss the pictures ('Look, that cat is wearing a hat!'), ask your child to point to familiar objects (naming them will come later), and name those he or she hasn't seen before or doesn't remember. Eventually (fairly soon for some children), your child will be able to fill in last words of rhymes or sentences in favourite books.

Think numerically. Counting may be a long way off for baby, but the concept of one or many isn't. Comments like 'Here, you can have one biscuit', or 'Look, see how many birds are in that tree', or 'You have two kitty cats' will start to inculcate some basic mathematical concepts. Count, or recite, 'One, two, buckle my shoe', as you climb the stairs with your baby, particularly once he or she can walk up while you hold both hands. Sing number rhymes, such as 'Baa, baa, black sheep' (when you get to the 'three bags full' hold up three fingers, then bend down one finger at a time as you 'distribute' the bags), or 'This old man, he played one, he played knickknack on my thumb'. Integrate counting into your baby's life: when you do your sit-ups, count them out in one through tens; when you're adding flour to the biscuit dough, count out the spoonfuls one by one as you add them; when you're adding banana to your baby's cereal, count out the slices.

Use signs. Many parents enjoy using signs and hand motions for words with their baby to encourage communication, enhance understanding, and even, as some studies show, promote language development. For more on using baby signs, see page 389.

◆ ◆ ◆

CHAPTER 16

The Twelfth Month

L ife's a game to baby these days, or actually, due to a still relatively short attention span, many different games played in rapid succession. One game that will soon become particularly engaging: dropping things (baby's finally figured out how to let go of objects), seeing them fall, watching mummy or daddy pick them up, and then repeating the sequence over and over – preferably until parental backs are aching and parental patience worn thin. Push toys may become great favourites; as baby struggles to master the most challenging large motor skill of all – walking – these toys can offer the security he or she needs to stand and, eventually, put one foot in front of the other. This month you may also notice signs that your baby – small and cute though he or she still is – won't be a baby much longer. Slowly but surely you'll begin to glimpse behaviours (a growing independence, the dawn of negativity, primitive temper tantrums, a my-way-or-the-highway mind-set) that foreshadow the theme of the year that lies ahead: I Am Toddler, Hear Me Roar.

What Your Baby May Be Doing

A ll babies reach milestones on their own developmental time line. If your baby seems not to have reached one or more of these milestones, rest assured, he or she probably will very soon. Your baby's rate of development is normal for *your* baby. If you have concerns about your baby's development (because you've noticed a missed milestone or what you think might be a developmental delay), don't hesitate to check it out with the doctor at the next well-baby visit – even if he or she doesn't bring it up. Parents often notice nuances in a baby's development that doctors do not. Premature infants generally reach milestones later than others of the same birth age, often achieving them closer to their adjusted age (the age they would be if they had been born at term), and sometimes later.

By twelve months, your baby . . . should be able to:

♦ walk holding on to furniture (cruise)

YOU KNOW YOUR BABY BEST

Maybe you don't have a degree in child development, but when it comes to your child's development, even the experts agree that you're something of an expert. Unlike a doctor or health visitor, who usually sees your baby only once a month or less – and who sees hundreds of other babies in between – you see your baby every single day. You spend more time interacting with your baby than anyone else. You probably notice nuances in your baby's development that others might miss.

Whenever you have a concern about your child's development – whether it's because some areas are lagging, or because a skill that was mastered seems to have been forgotten, or just because you've got a nagging feeling that something's not quite right – don't keep it to yourself. Child development experts believe that parents are not only their children's best advocates but can be key in the early diagnosis of developmental disorders, such as autism. Early diagnosis can lead to the kind of early intervention that can make an enormous difference in the long-term developmental future of a child with autism or another developmental disorder.

To help parents help their children better, doctors have pinpointed a number of developmental red flags to look out for as early as twelve months. Hopefully your baby's doctor will screen for these red flags as well during well-baby checkups. But if you notice your one-year-old doesn't exchange back-and-forth sounds with you, doesn't smile or gesture with you, fails to establish and maintain eye contact with you, doesn't point or use other gestures to get needs met, doesn't enjoy playing social games such as peekaboo or patty-cake, fails to respond when you call his or her name, or doesn't look when you point at something, let the doctor know. It could be that nothing at all is wrong. But further assessment, and perhaps referral to a specialist, can help determine whether there is reason for concern.

- use a few gestures to get needs met

. . . will probably be able to:

- play patty-cake (clap hands) or wave bye-bye (most children accomplish these feats by thirteen months)
- drink from a cup independently
- pick up a tiny object neatly with tips of thumb and forefinger (many babies do not accomplish this until nearly fifteen months; continue to keep all dangerous objects out of baby's reach)
- stand alone momentarily (many don't accomplish this until thirteen months)
- say 'dada' or 'mama' discriminately (most will say at least one of these by fourteen months)
- say one word other than 'mama' or 'dada' (many won't say their first word until fourteen months or later)

. . . may possibly be able to:

- 'play ball' (roll a ball back to you; many don't accomplish this feat until sixteen months)
- stand alone well (many don't reach this point until fourteen months)
- use immature jargoning (gibberish that sounds like a foreign language; half of all babies don't start

jargoning until after their first birthday, and many not until they are fifteen months old)

◆ walk well (three out of four babies don't walk well until thirteen and a half months, and many not until considerably later. Good crawlers may be slower to walk; when other development is normal, late walking is rarely a cause for concern)

. . . may even be able to:

◆ say three words or more other than 'mama' or 'dada' (a good half of all babies won't reach this stage until thirteen months, and many not until sixteen months)

◆ respond to a one-step command without gestures ('Give that to me' – without hand out; most children won't reach this stage until after their first birthday, many not until after sixteen months)

What You Can Expect at This Month's Checkup

Each practitioner will have a personal approach to well-baby checkups. The overall organization of the physical exam, as well as the number and type of assessment techniques used and procedures performed, will also vary with the individual needs of the child. But in general, you can expect the following at a checkup when your baby is about twelve months old:

◆ Questions about how you and baby and the rest of the family are doing at home, and about baby's eating, sleeping and general progress.

◆ Measurement of baby's weight, length and head circumference, and plotting of progress since birth.

◆ Physical exam, including a recheck of any previous problems. Now that baby can pull up, feet and legs will be checked when standing supported or unsupported, and walking if baby walks.

◆ A test to check for anaemia, if not performed earlier.

◆ Developmental assessment. The examiner may actually put baby through a series of 'tests' to evaluate baby's ability to: sit independently, pull up and cruise (or even walk), reach for and grasp objects, pick up tiny objects with a neat pincer grasp, look for dropped or hidden objects, respond to his or her name, cooperate in dressing, recognize and possibly say such words as *Mama, Dada, bye-bye* and *no*, and enjoy social games such as patty-cake and peekaboo; or he or she may simply rely on observation plus your reports on what baby is doing.

◆ Immunizations, if not given before and if baby is in good health and there are no contraindications. Be sure to discuss previous reactions, if any, beforehand. (A test for tuberculosis will be performed only if your child is at high risk of having come into contact with an infected person. It may be given before, or at the same time as, the MMR vaccine.)

- Guidance about what to expect in the next months in relation to such topics as feeding, sleeping, development and child safety.

- Recommendations about supplemental fluoride, if needed.

You may want to ask these questions if the doctor hasn't already answered them:

- What new foods can be introduced to baby now? When can wheat, citrus fruits, fish, meats, tomatoes, strawberries and egg whites be introduced, if they haven't been already?

- When should you consider weaning from the bottle, if your baby is bottle-fed, or from the breast, if you haven't weaned yet? When can whole milk be introduced?

- Should you take your baby to the dentist? Most experts recommend that children have their first dental visit sometime between their first and second birthdays (sooner if they're at high risk for tooth decay).

- Also raise concerns that have arisen over the past month. Jot down information and instructions from the doctor. Record all pertinent information (baby's weight, length, head circumference, immunizations, test results, illnesses, medications given, and so on) in a permanent health record.

Feeding Your Baby:
WEANING FROM THE BREAST

Weaning may be just around the corner, or months (or even years) down the line. Either way, it's a big step on that long road to independence – a step that means your child will never again be quite so dependent on you for a meal (though you can almost certainly look forward to many years of 'Mum, I'm hungry! What's for dinner?'). It's also a step that's almost as big for you as it is for your child, and one you'll want to be prepared for physically and emotionally. For support and strategy dealing with this major milestone, whenever it comes, read on.

WEANING FROM THE BREAST

As the task of weaning your baby looms as large as any child-care challenge you've faced so far, it may be comforting to know that you've probably already begun the process. The first time that you offered your baby a sip from a cup, a nip from a bottle or a nibble from a spoon, you took a step towards weaning. You've been taking baby steps ever since.

Weaning is basically a two-phase process:

Phase One: Getting baby accustomed to taking nourishment from a source other than your breasts. Since it can take a breastfeeding baby a month or

KEEPING YOURSELF COMFORTABLE

Often mums have a harder time with weaning than their babies do – both physically and emotionally. Gradual weaning late in the first year or after the first birthday is likely to prevent any major physical discomfort. You probably won't experience much, if any, engorgement (if you do, see tips below). Taking weaning slowly will also lessen the emotional impact on you – though, realistically, it won't eliminate it entirely. Weaning, like menstruation, pregnancy, childbirth and the postpartum period, is a time of hormonal upheaval, and the result is often mild depression, irritability and mood swings. The feelings are often exaggerated by a sense of loss and sadness over giving up this most special relationship with your baby, especially if you don't plan on having any more children. (In a few women, post-weaning depression, similar to postnatal depression, can be severe and requires immediate professional help; see page 676 for the warning signs.)

If weaning must be accomplished suddenly, especially in the early months when the milk supply is at its most copious, discomfort for the mother can be considerable. Extreme engorgement accompanied by fever and flu-like symptoms may result, and the chance of breast infection and other complications is much greater than with gradual weaning. Hot compresses and/or hot showers plus paracetamol may relieve some of the pain. Expressing just enough milk to relieve engorgement, but not enough to stimulate renewed production, may also help. Check with your doctor if symptoms don't diminish after twenty-four hours.

Sudden weaning can also be stressful to a baby. If you must wean without any prior preparation, be sure to give your child plenty of extra attention, love and cuddling, and try to minimize other stresses in his or her life. If you have to be away from home, see that daddy, grandma, another relative or a doting baby-sitter remembers to do the same.

Several weeks after weaning, your breasts may seem totally empty of milk. But don't be surprised if you're still able to express small amounts of milk months, even a year or more, later. This is perfectly normal. It's also normal for breasts to take time to return to close to their former size, often ending up somewhat larger or smaller. Frequently, they are less firm, as much because of hereditary factors and pregnancy as nursing.

---

more to catch on to drinking from a cup (and some a considerable time before they're even willing to give such alternative methods of feeding a try), it's best to introduce them well before you hope to complete weaning.[1] That's why it's a good idea to begin Phase One of weaning now, even if you're not planning to wean until age one or later.

The longer you wait to introduce a breast substitute (the cup being the ideal one at this age), the slower and more difficult weaning may prove to be. That's because the older a baby gets, the more stubbornly opposed to change he or she becomes. If your baby proves particularly inflexible on the cup issue, you may need to break down resistance by:

---

1. If you do decide to wean *to* a bottle, remember that it's a good idea to wean *from* the bottle by the first birthday or shortly after, in order to avoid the problems of tooth decay from baby-bottle mouth (see page 461).

MILK SENSE

Thinking about weaning from breast or formula at baby's first birthday? Not sure what kind of milk should be filling those cups and bottles once you do? Experts recommend whole milk – which provides the extra fat and cholesterol very young children need for optimal brain and nervous system development until they're twenty-four months old. And not just any whole milk will do. For safety's sake, choose only pasteurized (not raw) milk for your child.

Once you've replaced breastfeeding on demand or calibrated baby bottles with cup feeding, you may also be wondering how you'll be able to tell whether your baby's getting enough milk. The fact is, most young children who are offered a well-balanced choice of healthy foods and are allowed to eat to appetite will end up, on average, getting everything they need nutrientwise, including calcium. They'll drink enough milk (and/or eat enough calcium-providing foods) each day (or most days) without their parents keeping track of the exact amount

If you'd like to be sure that's the case with your baby, you can try this experiment: Measure out 680 ml (24 fl oz) of milk each morning for a week (baby's daily requirement plus a little extra to allow for spillage). Pour it into a clean jar and refrigerate. Serve all your baby's milk (for cereal, drinking, mashing with potatoes or other vegetables) from this supply. If it's gone at the end of most days, baby's meeting his or her requirement. Don't worry if it isn't completely drained every day, or if, once or twice during the week, plenty of milk is left over, especially if baby's also getting calcium (and protein) in other forms (such as cheese and yoghurt). If, however, baby seems to be regularly rejecting calcium- and protein-providing foods, talk to the doctor to see if you need to push the agenda a little more.

Be aware, too, that milk-loving toddlers can actually guzzle too much of that good thing, leaving little room for other foods in the diet. If your child regularly drinks much more than 680 ml (24 fl oz) of milk a day, particularly if he or she seems to be seriously slacking off in the solids department, you may need to cut down on the white stuff.

◆ Letting baby go hungry. The idea isn't to starve baby, just to get to the point where hunger wears him or her down some. Try skipping (or postponing) one breastfeeding session a day and offering the cup. Given no other alternative, baby may decide to take a sip.

◆ Staying out of the picture. As when you were introducing the bottle (if you did), baby's more likely to be amenable to the cup when mum's not the one offering it.

◆ Varying the contents of the cup. Some babies are more likely to consider the cup if it's filled with familiar breast milk. Others are more open to the experience if it doesn't remind them of breastfeeding. In that case, substitute formula (before age one) or a juice-water mixture. After a year (and the doctor's go-ahead), you can switch directly to whole cow's milk.

◆ Varying the cups. If you've been trying a regular cup, try a sippy cup. If you've been trying a sippy cup, try switching to a regular cup. Cups decorated with characters are almost certain to be more appealing.

◆ Persevering. Be patient and nonchalant (as if you couldn't care less whether baby took the cup or not), and give it time. Eventually, all children learn to drink from a cup.

Phase Two: Cutting back on breastfeedings. Unlike a smoker giving up cigarettes or a chocoholic giving up chocolate, cold turkey isn't the best route for a baby giving up the breast. Nor is it best for the mother whose breasts are being retired. For the baby, it's too unsettling. For the mother, there are not only the emotional issues (compounded by the sudden hormonal havoc that will result) but the physical ones. Leaking, engorgement, clogged ducts and infection are all more likely if nursing stops suddenly. So unless illness, a sudden need for travel without baby, or some other event in your lives makes hurried weaning necessary, take it slowly. Wean gradually, beginning at least several weeks – and up to many months – before your targeted weaning completion date. Postpone the process entirely at a time of change (major or minor) in your baby's life – such as when a new baby-sitter is taking over, mummy is returning to work, or the family is moving to a new house.

The most common approach to weaning is to begin dropping feedings one at a time, waiting at least a few days, but preferably a week, until your breasts and your baby have adjusted to that loss before imposing another. Most mothers find it's easiest to omit first the feeding baby seems least interested in and takes the least amount at, or the one that most interferes with her own day. In the case of a mother who works outside the home, that's often the midday feeding. With babies under six months, who are mostly dependent on milk for their nourishment, each dropped breastfeeding should be replaced by formula. With older babies and toddlers, a snack or meal (with a drink in a cup) can replace the nursings, as appropriate.

If you've been breastfeeding on demand, and demand has been quite erratic around the clock (in other words, baby's been taking the snack bar approach), you may have to become a little more regimented – getting down to a fairly regular schedule and a somewhat reduced number of feedings before you can get serious about weaning.

No matter what a mother's schedule, the early morning and late evening feedings – which provide the most comfort and pleasure for both mother and baby – are usually the last to go. Some women, in fact, continue to give one or both of these feedings to their otherwise weaned babies for weeks or even months, just for the joy of it. (This option isn't available for everyone; some women find that their milk supply diminishes rapidly once they cut nursing back that far.)

For some women, particularly those who are at home full-time, cutting down on all feedings, rather than cutting out individual feedings, is a method that works well. Here's how it works: to start, the baby is given 30 ml (1 fl oz) of formula (or whole cow's milk if baby's already passed his or her first birthday) from cup or bottle prior to each breastfeeding, and then allotted less time at the breast. Gradually, over the course of several weeks, the amount in the cup or bottle is increased and time at the breast for each feeding is decreased. Eventually the baby is taking adequate quantities of formula or milk, and weaning is accomplished.

Occasionally illness, a bout of painful teething or a disorienting change of locale or routine (such as might occur on holiday) can lead to backsliding, with baby demanding the breast more often.

Be understanding and don't worry – such a setback will be only temporary. Once baby's life is back to normal, you can begin your mission anew.

Keep in mind that nursing is only one part of your relationship with your baby. Giving it up won't weaken the bond or lessen the love between you. In fact, some women find that the relationship is enhanced as they spend less time nursing and more time actively interacting.

During weaning or once weaned, your baby may turn to other sources of comfort, such as the thumb or a blanket. This is normal and healthy. He or she may also hunger for extra attention from you, so give it freely. Most babies don't, however, seem to miss breastfeeding for very long. Some, in fact, move on so quickly that it takes their mothers – often still misty-eyed themselves as they think back on the good old days of nursing – aback.

What You May Be Concerned About

THE FIRST BIRTHDAY PARTY

'Everyone in the family is gearing up for my daughter's first birthday. I want the party to be special, but I don't want it to be too much for her.'

Many parents, caught up in the excitement of planning a party for baby's first birthday, seem to lose track of the fact that baby is still – in many ways – a baby. The gala they so painstakingly stage is rarely suitable for the guest of honour, who is likely to end up cracking under the pressure (of too many guests, too much excitement, the wrong kind of entertainment) and spending much of her celebration in tears.

To plan a first birthday party to remember, instead of one you'd rather forget, follow this strategy:

Keep the invites light. A room too crowded even with familiar faces will probably overwhelm your birthday pixie, with clinging and weeping the likely results. Save the long guest list for her wedding, and keep this crowd intimate, limiting it to a few family members and close friends. If she spends time with other babies her age, you may want to invite two or three; if she doesn't, the occasion of her first party probably isn't a good time to launch her social career.

Ditto the decor. A room decorated with all that your local party store has to offer, and then some, may be your dream but your baby's nightmare. Too many balloons, streamers, banners, masks and hats, like too many people, may prove too much for a one-year-old to handle. So decorate with a light hand, perhaps in a theme you know she'll appreciate (a favourite character, for example, or colourful teddy bears). If balloons will round out your party picture, remember to dispose of them postparty – tiny tots can choke on the rubber scraps left after balloons go pop.

Time it right. Scheduling is everything when it comes to a baby's party. Try to orchestrate the big day's activities so that baby is well rested, recently fed (don't hold off her lunch figuring she'll eat at the party), and on her usual schedule. Don't plan a morning party if she usually naps in the morning, or an early afternoon party if she usually conks out after lunch. Inviting a tired baby to participate in the festivities is inviting disaster. Keep the party brief – an hour and a half at the most – so she won't be a wreck when the party's over or, worse, in the middle of it all.

Let her eat cake. But make sure it's not the kind of cake she shouldn't eat (one with chocolate, nuts or honey). Instead serve up a carrot or banana cake topped with unsweetened fresh whipped cream or cream cheese frosting – shaped like, or decorated with, a favourite character if you're doing the baking and you're feeling artistic. Serve your confection à la mode if you like, with ice cream. Cut the cake at your baby's usual snack time, if possible, keeping toddler portions small to avoid waste. Finally, if you choose to put out party nibbles, choose them with safety as well as nutrition in mind. A birthday party's no time to risk a baby's choking on popcorn, peanuts, cocktail sausages, grapes, raw vegetables or small chunky pretzels. Also for safety's sake, insist that all young guests do their eating sitting down.

Don't send in the clowns. Or magicians, or any other paid or volunteer entertainment that might frighten your baby or a playmate. One-year-olds are notoriously sensitive and unpredictable. What delights them one minute may terrify them the next. Also don't try to organize the toddler set into formal party games – they're not ready for that yet. If there are several young guests, however, do have a selection of toys out for non-structured play, with enough of the same items to avoid competition. Simple, safe favours such as brightly coloured large rubber balls, board books or bath toys are a fun extra and

can be handed to young guests just before the gifts are opened.

Don't command a performance. It would be nice, of course, if baby would smile for the camera, take a few steps for the company, open each present with interest and coo appreciatively over it – but don't count on it. She might learn to blow out the candles if you give her enough practice during the month before the party, but don't expect complete cooperation, and don't put the pressure on. Instead, let her be herself, whether that means squirming out of your arms during that party pose, refusing even to stand on her own two feet during the step-taking exhibition, or opting to play with an empty box over the expensive gift that came in it.

Record it for posterity. The party will be over much too quickly, and so will your baby's childhood. Recording the occasion in pictures or on video will be well worth the effort.

NOT YET WALKING

'Today is my son's first birthday, and he hasn't even attempted to take his first step. Shouldn't he be walking by now?'

It may seem appropriate for a baby to take his first steps at his first birthday party (and great adult entertainment, to boot), but few babies are willing or able to oblige. Though some start walking weeks, or even months, earlier, others won't totter towards the momentous milestone until much later (sometimes when mum and dad aren't around). While passing the first birthday without a step may be a disappointment to the relatives, and especially those who've dragged out the video equipment to capture history in the making, it in no way signals a developmental problem.

The majority of children, in fact,

HANDLE WITH CARE

Now that your toddler is on two feet, or almost so, you may be tempted to try out that favourite childhood activity: holding hands (one parent on each side) and being swung through the air. Resist. Because of a young child's still rather loose joints, swinging him by the hands or suddenly twisting or tugging an arm (to get him or her moving faster) can result in a very painful (if easy-to-repair) dislocated elbow or shoulder.

don't start walking until after their first birthday. And the age at which a child first steps out, whether nine months, fifteen months, or even later, is no reflection on his intelligence or his future success in any area (even athletics).

When a baby walks is often related to his genetic makeup – early (or late) walking runs in families. Or to his weight and build – a wiry, muscular baby is more likely to walk earlier than a placid, plump one, and a child with short, sturdy legs before one with long, slender ones that are difficult to balance on. Or to personality – a child who's a risk-taker is more likely to rise to the challenge of walking sooner than a child who's naturally cautious. It may also be related to when and how well he learns to crawl. A child who is an ineffective crawler or who doesn't crawl at all sometimes walks before the baby who is perfectly content racing about on all fours.

A negative experience – perhaps a bad fall the first time a tentative one-year-old let go of a parent's hand – can also delay those first steps. In such a case, the child may not take a chance again until he's very steady, at which point he may take off like a pro, rather than with the stiff awkwardness of an amateur. The child who's been pressured by overeager parents to endure walking practice sessions several times daily may rebel (particularly if he has a stubborn streak) and walk independently later than he would have if he had been allowed to do it on his own terms and at his own pace. The first steps of a baby who's had his energy zapped by an ear infection, the flu or other illness may be put on hold until he's feeling better. A child who's been virtually waltzing from room to room may suddenly regress to the two-step-and-tumble when under the weather, only to rebound just as quickly once he's feeling himself again.

A baby who's always corralled in a mesh playpen (in which he may not be able to pull up to a standing position), strapped in a pushchair or otherwise given little chance to develop his leg muscles and his confidence through standing and cruising may walk late. In fact, he may develop slowly on other fronts as well. Give your baby plenty of time and space for practising pulling up, cruising, standing and stepping in a room that doesn't have scatter rugs or a slippery floor to slip him up, and which has plenty of safe-for-pulling-up-on furniture arranged close enough together for confident transfers or very short toddles. He'll do best if he's barefoot, since babies use their toes for gripping when they take their first steps; socks are slippery, shoes too stiff and heavy.

Though many perfectly normal, even exceptionally bright, babies don't walk until the second half of their second year, particularly if one or both parents didn't, a baby who isn't walking by eighteen months should be examined by his doctor to rule out the possibility that physical or emotional factors are interfering with walking. But even at that age – and certainly at twelve months – a child's not walking yet isn't cause for alarm.

INCREASED SEPARATION ANXIETY

'We've left our baby with a sitter before. But now he makes a terrible fuss every time we start walking out the door.'

When it comes to a one-year-old separated from his parents for the evening, absence doesn't just make the heart grow fonder, it makes the wails grow louder. And your baby is by no means alone in this sentiment. Separation anxiety affects most babies and toddlers to some degree, and some to a very pronounced degree.

Though it may seem like your child's regressing – after all, a baby-sitter's never bothered him before – separation anxiety actually is a sign that your child's maturing. Firstly, he's becoming more independent, but with strings attached (to you). As he ventures off to explore the world on two feet (or on his hands and knees), he takes comfort in knowing that you're just a toddle away should he need you. When he separates from you (as when he leaves your side to explore the playground), it's on his own terms. When you separate from him (as when you leave him with a baby-sitter for a movie and dinner), it's not. Enter anxiety. Secondly, he's now able to comprehend the complex (for a baby) concept of object permanence – that when someone or something isn't visible, it still exists. When he was younger and you left, he didn't miss you; if you were out of sight, you were out of mind. Now when you're out of sight, you're still very much on his mind – which means he *can* miss you. And because he hasn't yet grasped the even more complicated concept of time, he has no idea when, or even if, you're coming back. Enter more anxiety. Improved memory – another sign of maturation – also plays a role. Your baby recalls what it means when you put on your coat and say 'bye-bye' to him. He's now able to anticipate that you will be gone for some indefinite length of time when you walk out the door. A child who hasn't been left often with a baby-sitter (and seen his parents return often) may also wonder whether you'll ever return. Enter still more anxiety.

While some babies can show signs of separation anxiety as early as seven months, it usually peaks between twelve and eighteen months for most. But, as with everything in child development, the timing of separation anxiety varies from child to child. Some babies and toddlers never experience it at all, while some suffer the anxiety much later, around three or four years of age. For some it lasts just a few months; for others it continues for years, sometimes continuously, sometimes on and off. Certain life stresses, such as moving, a new sibling, a new baby-sitter, even tension at home can trigger a first episode of separation anxiety or a brand-new bout of it.

Separation anxiety most commonly strikes when you leave your child in another care provider's hands – when you're heading off to work, going out for the evening, or dropping your baby off at day care. But it can also happen at night when you put your baby to bed (see page 486). No matter what the trigger, the symptoms are the same: he'll cling to you for dear life (with superhuman baby strength that makes those arms and sticky fingers particularly difficult to pry off of you), cry uncontrollably, resist all attempts by the baby-sitter to calm him down, and make it perfectly clear to you that he doesn't want you to leave. All of which will leave you feeling guilty and upset, wondering whether the separation is worth the anxiety it's causing for both of you.

But as unsettling as it is for you, separation anxiety is a normal part of your baby's development as normal as learning to walk and talk. Helping him learn how to handle separations well now will help him handle them better as he turns into a toddler.

To minimize baby's anxiety and your guilt, and to maximize his adjustment to being left with a sitter and separated from you, follow these steps before stepping out:

◆ Make sure you're leaving your baby with a sitter who not only is reliable but also will be understanding, patient, responsive and loving, no matter how difficult he becomes during the separation.

◆ Have the sitter arrive at least fifteen minutes before you're planning to leave (earlier if it's her first time sitting for your baby), so that the two of them can get involved in an activity (playing with the shape sorter or a puzzle, building with bricks, putting teddy to bed) while you're still bustling around. Keep in mind, however, that your baby may refuse to have anything to do with the sitter (even if she's a familiar one) while you're still home. After all, consenting to playing with her might mean he's consenting to being left with her. Don't worry; once you've left, he'll almost certainly agree to join in the fun.

◆ If possible, try to schedule departures after naps and mealtimes. Babies are more susceptible to any kind of anxiety when they're tired or hungry. (They're always much more susceptible, too, when they're sick – though if you simply can't cancel your plans, there may not be much you can do about this.)

◆ Give your baby advance notice of your departure. If you try to avoid a scene this time by sneaking out of the house while he's not looking (or when he's sleeping), he'll panic when he notices you're gone (or when he wakes up and you're not there). He may also begin to fear that you'll leave without warning at any time, and he may respond with excessive clinginess. Instead, tell him ten to fifteen minutes before you leave that you'll be going out. Give him more time than that and he might forget, less and he won't have a chance to adjust.

◆ Take your baby's anxiety seriously. Calmly and lovingly (but without a hint of distress) tell your baby you know he's upset and that he doesn't want you to leave, but that you'll be back soon.

◆ Make a happy ritual out of leaving, with a hug and kiss from both of you. But don't prolong the good-byes or make them overly sentimental. Keep a smile on your face, even if he's tearful, and try to look as if you're taking it all in stride. (If you seem upset, he'll figure there's actually something to fear in this situation.) If there's a window, he and the sitter can wave to you as you leave.

◆ Reassure him you'll be back. 'See you later, alligator' is a good light phrase to use that he can begin to associate with your leaving and coming back. One day he'll be able to respond happily with 'After a while, crocodile'.

◆ Once you leave, leave. Repeated appearances at the door after you've already 'left' will make it harder on you, your baby, and the sitter.

◆ If possible, start with short separations. Limit the first one to an hour or two. Once he's confident that you will return, he may be comfortable enough with these short outings to be ready for longer ones. Increase the time you spend away by fifteen-minute increments, until you can stay away several hours at a time. As your baby gets used to being separated, you can extend your outings.

◆ Let baby know when you'll be back. Though your baby won't yet understand, it's a good idea to start plugging in concepts of time he will eventually be able to relate to: 'I'll be back after your nap' or 'I'll be back when you're eating supper' or 'I'll see you when you wake up'.

Remember that separation anxiety doesn't last forever. All too quickly, your child will learn to separate easily and painlessly from you. Possibly, for you, a little too easily and painlessly. One day, when your teenager heads off to school with a perfunctory 'bye' and (if you ask really nicely) an even more perfunctory kiss, you'll look back fondly on the days when you couldn't pry those little fingers and arms off your leg.

ATTACHMENT TO THE BOTTLE

'I was hoping to wean my son from the bottle at a year, but he's so attached to it I can't even get it away from him for a minute, much less permanently.'

Like a favourite teddy bear or blanket, a bottle is a source of emotional comfort and gratification for a small child. But unlike cuddly security objects, a bottle can be harmful if used improperly or used much past a baby's first birthday.

Which means you're right, there's no time like the present for weaning. For the complete low-down on why it's wise to wean now, see page 461. For tips on how to wean gently, see page 462.

DON'T HAVE A COW

Your one-year-old is ready to graduate from formula to milk. Only problem is, he's allergic to cow's milk, and your doctor has suggested that you substitute soya milk. But you worry that your toddler won't get enough fat in his diet, since soya milks only have about half the fat of whole milk. Stop the worrying. While it's true that soya milk alone wouldn't provide all the fat a child under the age of two needs for optimum brain development, milk won't be the only source of fat in your toddler's diet. He'll be getting plenty of fat from a balanced diet that includes meat, fish, poultry and oils used in cooking. (Do ask your doctor about how your toddler can best meet all his fat requirements with other foods). After his second birthday, his fat requirements will be trimmed, anyway, to about the same as an adult's.

PUTTING THE WEANED BABY TO BED

'I've never put my daughter to bed awake – she's always been nursed to sleep. How am I going to get her to sleep at night once she's weaned to a cup?'

How easy it's always been for your baby to suckle her way blissfully into dreamland. And how easy for you to nurse your way hassle-free to a peaceful evening. From now on, however, if you're serious about weaning your baby from her nightcap, bedding her down is going to take a little more effort on both sides of the cot rail.

Like a habit for any sleep aid – from

pills to late-night talk shows – a bedtime nursing habit can be broken. Once it is, your child will have mastered one of life's most valuable skills, the ability to fall asleep on her own. To make this goal a reality, follow this plan, starting well before you plan to wean:

Keep the old rituals. A bedtime routine, with each item on the agenda carried out in the same order each evening, can work its soporific magic on anyone, adult or child. If you haven't instituted a ritual yet for your baby, do so at least two weeks before you plan to wean her off the night-time feeding. Also make sure environmental conditions are conducive to sleep: the bedroom dark unless baby prefers a night-light, neither too warm nor too cold, and quiet; the rest of the house maintaining a business-as-usual hum that lets her know you're there if she needs you. (See page 426 for more tips on making a baby sleepy; also see the next question.)

Add a new twist. A few days to a week before W day, add a bedtime snack to your baby's ritual (if it's not already on the schedule). She can eat the snack after she's in pyjamas and while you're reading to her. Keep it light but satisfying (a whole-grain mini-muffin and a half cup of milk (once she's reached her first birthday), perhaps, or a piece of cheese and a rice cake), and let her enjoy it on your lap if she likes. Not only will the mini-meal eventually come to take the place of the nursing she'll be giving up, but the milk will have a sleep-inducing effect. Of course, if you've been brushing baby's teeth earlier in the evening, you will now have to move this part of the routine to after her snack. If she's thirsty once her teeth have been cleaned, offer her water.

Break the old habit, but try not to replace it with a new one. Your baby may find an easy route to slumber in rocking, singing or other sleep aids. But if you'd like her to develop sleeptime self-sufficiency, you'll need to let her figure out how to fall asleep on her own. Do plenty of cuddling during the bedtime routine, then put her down dry, happy (hopefully), snug and drowsy – but awake.

If you'd like to stay a while, patting and reassuring her, that's fine. See page 348 for more tips on helping a baby fall asleep on her own.

Expect some crying. Possibly, lots of it at first. Chances are your baby will resist this bold new approach to bedtime – loudly. Few babies will accept the switch without a fight, though some may accept it much more readily if mum (and her breasts, constant reminders of what was) isn't the one doing the bedding down. But expect, too, that baby will adjust fairly quickly to a bedtime without nursing, as she will to all aspects of weaning.

BEDTIME SEPARATION ANXIETY

'Our baby used to fall asleep easily and sleep through the night. But suddenly he clings to us and cries when we put him down – and also wakes up crying during the night.'

Separation anxiety, the familiar gremlin of the daylight hours that usually peaks between twelve and fourteen months, can also come out at night. In fact, since separating at night leaves a baby completely alone, it can become even more anxiety-provoking than daytime separation. The result: another saga in the continuing story of the young and the restless.

Fortunately, it's a story that doesn't have to continue. For parents who co-sleep, there's no issue, since there's no separation. For parents who wish to keep (or make) their bed their own, there are solutions for night-time separation anxiety. To help your baby conquer his fears of being alone:

♦ Know that it's normal. Most babies who experience separation anxiety by day will also experience it by night. It doesn't mean that your baby's feeling unloved or uncared for, or that you're doing something wrong. It means that he's growing up, but still has a ways to grow. (See page 483 for more on separation anxiety.)

♦ Have a peaceful prelude to bedtime. Keep the hour or two leading up to bedtime as calm, reassuring, and nurturing as possible, especially if you've been at work all day, but even if you've just been busy around the house. Try to give your baby as much attention as you can, putting other matters (such as making and eating your dinner or catching up on paperwork) on hold until he's asleep. This will help keep his stress level low before bedtime, while storing up some reserves of mummy and daddy attention.

♦ Rely on routines. A bedtime ritual isn't just sleep-inducing – it's comforting at a time in your baby's life when comfort is derived from consistency. Each night it reassures your child that the same events will take place in the same sequence (no surprises means fewer anxieties). A bedtime routine can also become the start of a night-time cycle that your child will come to anticipate (instead of fear), predictably beginning with a bath leading to sleep, and ending with waking up in the morning.

Be sure not to stray from the routine in even the smallest way – switching the bath with the snack, or skipping the lullaby. A baby's comfort comes from knowing *exactly* what he can expect. (See page 426 for more on bedtime rituals.)

♦ Bridge the gap with a transitional object. Sometime around the first birthday, when transitions become so difficult for toddlers to make, a transitional (or comfort) object often helps bridge the gap. It could be a favourite small stuffed animal, a small blanket (for clutching; big blankets for covering are still not recommended at this age; see page 500), or even a cot-safe memento of you (such as a T-shirt you've worn). Not all young children derive comfort from such an object – but many do. Armed with the object, leaving you (and making that tricky transition from being awake to being asleep) can be less stressful.

♦ Be reassuring but not sentimental. Give your baby a hug and kiss before you put him down in his cot, then say your good night. Consistency is important here, too; it's best if you keep the parting words as routine as the rest of the bedtime ritual (something like 'Nighty-night, sleep tight, see you in the morning light'). A loving but light tone in your voice will help; if your baby senses that you're anxious about leaving, he will be, too.

If your baby cries, continue calmly and quietly reassuring him – gently putting him back down if he's pulled up. But don't pick him up, don't turn on the light, and don't stay until he's asleep. Use this strategy, too, if your baby wakes up again during the night. Be consistent in your approach to comfort – using the same techniques, the same words – but also try to do progressively less each night (offering the comfort first from cotside, then from a few feet away, then from the doorway). A phrase like 'Mummy (or Daddy) is right here. Go back to sleep. I'll see you in the morning' will reinforce the message that night will end predictably with day.

◆ Be consistent. This deserves repeating. And repeating. Without consistency, life is confusing for young children. And without consistency, parenting techniques are doomed to failure. With resolve on your part, your baby will learn to handle night-time separation anxiety – and stop fighting bedtime and sleep.

◆ Try not to feel guilty. Staying with your child all night won't help him overcome night-time separation anxiety (any more than avoiding leaving him with a baby-sitter would help him overcome separation anxiety during waking hours) – a consistent routine, lovingly enforced, will.

Some babies also begin to wake up at night when they're cutting their molars. If that seems to be the case, see page 427.

SHYNESS

'My husband and I are very outgoing; we're sort of surprised to see how shy our daughter is.'

A baby's tentative nature around new situations and new people at this age is usually a result not of true shyness but of normal, developmentally appropriate behaviour. Several factors contribute to this behaviour, which is common in almost-toddlers and young toddlers:

◆ Stranger anxiety. Some babies start exhibiting this reticence around anyone but mummy and daddy as early as seven months, but many don't start shying away from strangers until closer to the first year (see page 430).

◆ Separation anxiety. Situations that require socializing often require separating from mummy and daddy. Clinging at a play group or when a family friend tries to pick your daughter up isn't necessarily a sign that she's shy – just that she's anxious about venturing off without you at this point in her development (see page 483).

◆ 'Unfamiliar' anxiety. For a newly mobile baby, the world is an exciting place to explore, but it can also be a scary one. The independence that comes with standing on your own two feet is exhilarating, but at the same time can be unnerving. In the face of so much change, older babies and young toddlers often shrink away from the unfamiliar, deriving comfort from continuity and consistency. This hesitant behaviour can easily be interpreted as shyness.

◆ Social anxiety. What may appear to be shyness may actually just be a lack of social experience. This is especially likely if your daughter has done most of her socializing with you or with a single care provider, and hasn't been exposed from an early age to group situations (such as day care). It's too soon to assume that your seedling won't – with plenty of practice and a minimum of pushing – eventually blossom socially. By the third birthday, many toddlers who started out 'shy' make rapid progress in the art of socializing.

Of course, some children are more shy by nature, others more outgoing. In fact, research shows that many personality traits are at least partially predestined by genetics. Some researchers have found shyness to be 10 per cent the result of nature (with the remaining 90 per cent determined by nurture); others feel that genetics plays an even greater role. Even if it's a trait parents don't display themselves, it's one that they carry to their child's conception. Though it's possible for parents to help modify shyness in their child – and to help her become a part of the party, if not the life of it – it's not possible for them to wipe it out entirely. Nor should that be the goal. Shyness should be respected as part of a child's personality.

Though many 'shy' children retain an inner core of reserve all their lives, most turn out to be fairly extroverted adults. It's not parental prodding and pressure to perform socially that brings a timid child out of her shell, but a generous supply of loving nurturing and support. Drawing attention to a child's shyness ('Oh, she's so shy!') will only reinforce it; presenting it as a shortcoming will only undermine her self-confidence, which in turn will make her more unsure of herself in social situations. On the other hand, boosting her self-esteem will help her feel more at ease with herself. In turn she will feel more at ease with others, which will eventually help diminish her shyness.

For now, encourage your daughter in social situations. (Sit down with her on the floor so she'll feel more comfortable playing at a peer's birthday party; hold her securely when friends approach to say hello to her.) But don't push. Allow your daughter to respond to people on her own terms and at her own pace – while letting her know that you're always there for her if she needs a leg to cling to or a shoulder to hide her head in.

SOCIAL SKILLS

'We've been involved in a play group for the last few weeks, and I've noticed that my child doesn't play with the other children. How can I get her to be more sociable?'

You can't, and you shouldn't try. Though a child is a social being from birth, she isn't capable of being truly sociable until at least the age of eighteen months – as you'll see if you peek in at any group of babies and young toddlers 'at play'. Though tots at a play group may interact (often just long enough to grab another child's shovel or shove a peer away from a push toy that's caught their eye), most of their play is done in the parallel mode – they'll play side by side but not together. They may enjoy watching other children at play, but not necessarily join in with them. Naturally and normally egocentric, they're not yet able to recognize that other children might make worthy playmates. In fact, they still see them largely as objects – moving, interesting objects, but objects nonetheless.

All of which is completely age appropriate. While one-year-olds who have had plenty of group play practice may progress faster in the sociability department, every child will eventually progress. Pushing your daughter to play with other children in her group will only cause her to withdraw from such situations altogether. For best results, provide your daughter with the opportunities to socialize, and then let her socialize at her own pace.

SHARING

'My little boy belongs to a play group. He and the other children seem to spend most of their time fighting for the same toys. When will things get better?'

You and the other parents can look forward to playing play group referee for at least two more years. It's not until the second half of the second year that a child even begins to understand the idea that an item he covets can belong to someone other than himself – a necessary concept to grasp before sharing can make sense, which it begins to sometime around age three. Until that bright day of social enlightenment dawns, 'mine' will be the sole article of possession in his vocabulary. For now, your son's own needs and desires will be the only ones that matter to him, and he will continue to treat his peers as objects without needs and desires of their own. Not surprisingly, he won't be the only one. Because this self-absorbed behaviour is completely age appropriate (babies and toddlers need to learn about and care about themselves before they can learn about and care about others), each child in his play group will continue to believe that his or her right to play with any or all toys is absolute.

Later on in the second and third years tactics of compromise – such as setting a timer so that three children can take turns playing with the same fire engine – will help encourage sharing and help keep the peace, but they are far too sophisticated for a young toddler to comprehend or comply with. A better approach would be to have multiples of the same toys or same types of toys available at play group sessions (which will cut down on the tugs-of-war). Failing that, distraction by an adult – diverting attention away from the disputed toy to another toy or activity – usually does the trick.

Teaching sharing by example every chance you get (when you offer your son a chance at your magazine, let him know that you're 'sharing my magazine'; when you give him a bite of your sandwich, tell him you're 'sharing my sandwich') won't turn your child into a model of generosity overnight, but it will slowly reinforce the values you hope to pass on. Pushing your child to share, on the other hand, will only injure his fledgling sense of self by implying that his needs are less significant than those of others. It may also turn him into a hoarder. A child who feels his possessions are always up for grabs will be less likely to share them freely, more likely to guard them jealously.

It's also important to keep your perspective when your child refuses to let a guest so much as touch his trucks or teddy bears, won't share a single one of his cookies with a child in the park, and howls when his younger cousin is given a ride in his pushchair. How often do you, after all, let a friend – much less a stranger – drive your car, borrow a treasured necklace or take your place in a favourite armchair?

HITTING

'My son is in a play group with a few children who are slightly older than he is. Some of them hit when they don't get their way, and my son has started doing it, too. How should I handle this?'

First, it would help to understand why your son hits. Hitting, like other forms of aggressive behaviour, is common among one-year-olds for many reasons. For one, it's a form of communication. Still lacking the vocabulary that will one day allow your child to say, 'You make me so mad!' or 'Give me back my truck!' hitting can express what words can't yet. For another, it's a way of releasing frustration. Frustration at being such a small fish in an increasingly bigger pond; frustration at being largely unable to control and manipulate his environment (and those in it); frustration in his still limited skills (that can't seem to keep pace with what he'd like to accomplish). Add to these factors a toddler's natural egocentricity (which causes a young child to treat his peers as objects, and which goes hand in hand, or fist in fist, with a lack of empathy), a fundamental lack of impulse control (he doesn't think before he strikes), a shortage of social skills (these don't come as standard equipment in a human; they must be learned and practised over time), and a knack for imitation (it's likely he picked up his slugging habit from fellow sluggers), and it's not surprising your son's play group has turned into a boxing match. The interesting reaction that hitting elicits (usually crying) encourages frequent rematches.

But just because the hitting is understandable doesn't mean it's acceptable. Long before a child is capable of understanding that he's actually hurting someone when he hits, he's capable of understanding that hitting is not allowed. When your child hits (or bites, or displays another form of undesirably aggressive behaviour), respond immediately, firmly and calmly. Anger is likely only to reinforce your son's ire. Slapping or spanking will teach him only that violence is a good way to resolve a dispute (or to express anger). Overreacting to the incident will probably only encourage a repeat performance in a quest for more attention. Instead, say simply, 'No hitting. Hitting hurts' and remove your child promptly from the scene of the scuffle. Without any further remonstrations, distract him with a toy or activity. Then, prepare to repeat the entire sequence many dozens of times before

the message starts to seep in. (Keep in mind that even once your son does begin to understand that hitting is not acceptable, a lack of impulse control will occasionally compel him to throw a punch anyway.)

In the meantime, always make sure that play sessions with other children are carefully supervised. Even though a toddler's right hook rarely packs enough power to do harm to a playmate, there's always the chance that a child might use more than a fist to strike with. There's much more risk of injury from a foot, a toy, a rock or a stick.

Also, since normal toddler aggression can be aggravated by a lack of sleep and by hunger, make sure your son shows up for his play group rested and fed.

'FORGETTING' A SKILL

'Last month my daughter was waving bye-bye all the time, but now she seems to have forgotten how. I thought she was supposed to move forwards developmentally, not backward'.

She *is* moving forwards developmentally, on to other skills. It's very common for a baby to practise perfecting a skill almost continuously for a while – to her delight and everyone else's – and then, once she's mastered it, to put it aside while she takes on a new challenge. Though your baby has tired of her old trick of waving bye-bye, she's more than likely excited by those she's rehearsing now, perhaps barking every time she sees a four-legged animal and playing peekaboo and patty-cake. All of which she will eventually temporarily retire once they, too, lose their allure. Instead of worrying about what your baby seems to have forgotten, tune in to and encourage her in whatever new skills she's busy developing.

You need to be concerned only if your baby suddenly seems unable to do many things she did formerly, and if she isn't learning anything new. If that's the case, check with the doctor.

A DROP IN APPETITE

'All of a sudden, my son seems to have no interest in his meals – he only picks at his food and can't wait to get out of the high chair. Could he be sick?'

More likely Mother Nature has placed him on a maintenance diet. Because if he continued eating the way he did early on in life, and continued gaining at the same rate, he would soon resemble a small blimp instead of a small toddler. Most babies triple their birthweight in the first year; in the second year they add only about a third of their weight. So a decline in appetite now is your baby's body's way of ensuring this normal decline in the weight gain rate.

There are also other factors that may affect your baby's eating habits now. One is increased interest in the world around him. During most of his first year of life, mealtimes – whether spent in your arms or in a high chair – were highlights of his existence. Now they represent an unwelcome interruption in 'a day in the life of a fledging toddler', who'd rather be on the go than sitting still for a bowl of cereal (so many things to do, so many places to see, so much mischief to make – so little time in a day!).

Growing independence can also influence a child's reaction to the food placed in front of him. The baby in the throes of becoming a toddler may decide that he, not you, should be the arbiter of the dinner table. In the next months, wide taste swings may rule – cheese on everything one week, rejection of anything vaguely cheesy the next. And it's better to accept baby's dictatorial menu planning (as long as he has only nutritious choices to point to) than to fight it. Eventually, eating eccentricities will diminish (though they will almost certainly get worse before they get better). Control of the spoon may also be an issue for your increasingly independent descendent; if you haven't yet handed over the job of feeding to your son, now would be a good time. Let him self-feed (as well as he can) with a spoon of his own and a variety of finger foods.

Maybe your baby's on a feeding strike because he dislikes being exiled to the high chair. If so, try seating him at the family table in a safely secured clip-on dining chair. Or maybe he can't sit still as long as the rest of the family. In that case, don't put him in the seat until his food is served, and release him as soon as he starts to get restless (but keep an eye on him while you finish your meal); or serve him before you eat.

Some babies lose their appetites temporarily during teething bouts, particularly when they're cutting their first molars – and that's nothing to worry about. If your baby's loss of appetite is accompanied by irritability, finger chewing and other symptoms of teething, you can be pretty sure that it will pass once the discomfort eases. Don't worry, either, if baby's loss of appetite is accompanied by signs of mild illness, such as a cold or fever. That's typical and, once the illness has passed, it's likely his appetite will return to normal. But do check with the doctor if baby's weight gain stops altogether, if he looks very thin, if he seems weak, apathetic and irritable, or if he has particularly dry, brittle hair and dry skin with little tone.

Though there's nothing you can do (or should do) about an appetite that's slacking off as a result of your baby's normal growth slowdown, there are ways to make sure he eats what he needs in order to grow (see the next question).

PICKY EATING

'I'm afraid my baby's not getting enough protein or vitamins because she won't eat meat or vegetables.'

Parents of picky eaters (in other words, most parents of older babies and toddlers), relax. Firstly, the nutritional requirements for a one-year-old are surprisingly small, meaning they're easily filled. Secondly, those requirements don't just come in the most obvious packages (protein in meat and fish, vitamin A in broccoli). They also come in some unexpected and unexpectedly toddler-friendly ones:

◆ Protein. Your baby can get adequate protein while still turning up her nose at meat and poultry – and even at fish. Cottage cheese, hard cheeses, milk, yoghurt, eggs, whole-grain cereals and breads, wheat germ, beans and peas, and pastas (especially high-protein brands) all provide protein. In fact, a full day's protein requirement for a one-year-old can be met with 600 ml (21 fl oz) of milk and 2 slices of wholemeal bread; *or* 480 ml (16 fl oz) of milk and 25 g (1 oz) of Gruyère; *or* 240 ml (8 fl oz) of milk, 240 ml (8 fl oz) of yoghurt, 1 small bowl of porridge and 1 slice of wholemeal bread; *or* 240 ml (8 fl oz) milk, 45 g (1½ oz) cottage cheese, 1 bowl of Cheerios and 2 slices of wholemeal bread.

If your baby doesn't like protein foods straight, try a little sleight of hand. Make fruit smoothies with yoghurt or milk; pancakes with milk,

eggs and wheat germ; French toast with wholemeal bread, eggs and milk (the longer the bread soaks in the egg/milk mixture, the more it will absorb); add cheese to scrambled eggs; top high-protein pasta with meat sauce and grated cheese. Also see recipes beginning on page 754.

◆ Vegetable vitamins. You can serve up all of the vitamins in vegetables in a variety of tempting disguises: courgette muffins, carrot cake, tomato or cheese-and-finely-minced-broccoli or cauliflower sauce on pasta, veggie pancakes, vegetables tossed with cheese sauce or in a noodle casserole. Sometimes cooked vegetables served with a dip (a cold yoghurt one, or a warm cheese one, for example) – because they're fun to eat – are more acceptable to a fussy one-year-old. (This is especially true when a child's hungry, so consider serving cooked veggies and dip as an appetizer.) Or skip the vegetables entirely for now (though you should continue to offer them when you're eating them). Many fruity favourites, including cantaloupe melon, mangoes, peaches and apricots, provide the vitamins found in less-loved green-leaf and yellow vegetables. Sweet potato, though technically a vegetable, tastes like a fruit when it's baked until soft and cubed.

Also keep the following points in mind when feeding the picky eater:

Let baby's appetite be your guide. Let him eat heartily when he's hungry, and let him pick when he's not. Never force. But do sharpen his appetite for meals by limiting snacking just before them.

Don't dampen tiny appetites. Large amounts of juice (more than 120 to 170 ml/4 to 6 fl oz a day) can fill a baby up, leaving no room for nutritious solids.

GOING NUTS?

When it comes to peanut butter, most children – and their parents – are big fans. Kids love it for its taste. Parents love it because it's an inexpensive and versatile source of protein, fibre, vitamin E and minerals that even the finickiest child will eat without a fight.

But food allergies in general and peanut allergy in particular are on the rise among children, forcing this lunch-box favourite to take some heat. While when to introduce nuts to your baby's diet is up for debate, if there's no history of food allergy in your family, your doctor will probably give you the go-ahead on smooth peanut butter once baby has reached the first birthday (to minimize the choking risk, spread very thinly, never allow eating by the finger or the spoonful,

and wait until age four before bringing on the chunky variety). If there is a family history of allergies (peanut or other foods), peanut products should be withheld until you get the green light from the doctor – probably not until age two, possibly not until age three, four or even later.

These guidelines apply to ground or finely chopped nuts. Whole nuts pose a choking risk and should not be given until a child is four or five.

Researchers are developing treatments for peanut allergies that involve giving increasing doses of peanuts, building the child's tolerance. These studies are preliminary and researchers caution that parents should NOT try to treat their child's allergy on their own.

Ditto for too much formula or milk, which can easily spoil a tender appetite. So be strict about juice limits, and don't offer more formula or milk than a baby this age needs (see box on page 478). Switching from bottle to cup will make enforcing such limits a lot easier.

Have baby make dinner. Or at least let him help. The more involved a child is in the process that brings a meal to his high chair, the more likely he is to actually consume it. So if he's interested, have him help pick out the green beans in the supermarket and plunk them into the plastic bag. Scrub a carrot with a soft brush. Or tear the lettuce into the bowl. A sense of ownership in the meal ('I made it!') may induce him to sample foods he might otherwise have rejected. Later on, try planting a small vegetable garden together (if you have the room and the motivation) and bringing the harvest to the dinner table. Cultivating a green thumb may just break down his resistance to all things green.

Don't give up. Just because your baby won't eat his meat (or chicken or fish) and spinach (or broccoli or carrots) today doesn't mean he won't eat them tomorrow. Make them available to him at the family table – but don't ever force him to eat them – in various forms regularly. One day he may surprise you by helping himself.

Don't be concerned with whether he's getting a balanced meal – or even a balanced day every day. Look instead to his food intake over the week to gauge whether he's getting as much of the Daily Dozen as possible (see page 314).

INCREASE IN APPETITE

'I thought a one-year-old's supposed to experience a drop in appetite. My daughter's has seemed to increase substantially. She's not fat, but I can't help worrying that she will be if she keeps eating at this rate.'

Chances are she's eating more because she's drinking less. Babies who are either just, or just about, weaned from the breast or bottle to the cup are likely to be getting less of their total caloric intake from milk and other liquids, and they may compensate by stepping up their intake of solids. Though it may seem that your daughter is taking in more calories, she probably is taking in the same number or less, only in a different form. Alternatively, it could be that she's eating more because she's going through a growth spurt or because she's become more active – possibly because she's walking a lot – and her body needs the extra calories.

Healthy babies, when allowed to eat as dictated by their appetites – hearty or not – without parental interference, continue to grow at a normal rate. If your daughter's weight and height curves aren't suddenly parting company, there's no need to worry that she's overeating. Pay more attention to the quality, rather than the quantity, of her intake; make sure that her robust appetite isn't squandered on nutritionally frivolous foods and that her diet isn't overloaded with high-fat fare (which *could* lead to obesity). Take note, too, of her motivation for eating. If she seems to be eating out of boredom, for instance, instead of hunger, you can help by making sure she has plenty to keep her busy outside the kitchen between meals. You can also avoid setting up bad eating habits – don't always give her a snack for the pushchair or car seat, for instance, or when she's crying in the supermarket. Or if you suspect she's eating out of a need for emotional gratification, make sure she gets enough attention and tender loving care. When she falls and hurts herself, give her a hug instead of a biscuit.

REFUSING TO SELF-FEED

'I know my son is perfectly capable of feeding himself – he's done it several times. But now he absolutely refuses to hold his bottle, pick up a cup or try a spoon.'

The inner struggle between wanting to remain a baby and wanting to grow up has only just begun for your child. Finally capable of taking care of one of his needs, he's not sure he wants to if it means giving up the secure and cushy role of baby. As with all aspects of separation, it's one clouded with ambivalence.

Don't force your baby to grow up too soon. When he wants to feed himself, let him. But when he wants to be fed, feed him. Eventually the big boy will triumph over the baby, if you let the two of them battle it out in the natural course of things – although the inner conflict (and that ambivalence) will likely recur in every stage of his development into adulthood and at every separation. In the meantime, present him with every opportunity to be self-sufficient. Make the bottle, the cup and the spoon available to him without insisting he use them. Offer him finger foods often, at meals as well as snack times. Few children at this age are really competent with a spoon, and most will make their first ventures into self-feeding with the five-pronged utensils that are conveniently attached to their wrists. Also make sure that you don't unconsciously discourage these efforts by insisting on some semblance of neatness (that won't be on the table for many months to come).

When he does feed himself, reinforce his decision by sticking around to give him plenty of encouragement, praise and, especially, reassuring attention. He needs to know that giving up being fed by mummy or daddy doesn't have to mean giving up mummy or daddy.

GROWING INDEPENDENCE

'My little girl can't seem to make up her mind what she wants. One minute she's chasing me around the house, hanging on my legs while I'm trying to get work done. The next, she's trying to get away from me when I sit down to hug her.'

Feeling conflicted is part of being a normal one-year-old. Like the baby who refuses to self-feed, your daughter is split between a craving for independence and a fear of paying too high a price for that independence. When you're busy with something other than her, especially when you're moving about faster than she can follow, she worries that she's losing her hold on you and the love, sustenance, comfort and safety that you represent, and she responds by clinging. On the other hand, when you make yourself more available, she's able to play hard to get and to test out her independence in the security of your presence.

As she becomes more comfortable with her independence and more secure in the fact that you'll be her mummy and daddy no matter how grown-up she becomes, she'll be less clingy. But this inner battle will manifest itself repeatedly for years to come, probably even when she's a mum herself.

In the meantime, you can help her to strike out on her own by making her feel more secure. If you are in the kitchen peeling carrots and she's across the divider in the family room, chat with her, stop periodically and visit with her, or invite her to help you, stationing her high chair next to you at the sink, for example, and giving her some cour-

gettes and a soft vegetable scrub brush. Support and applaud your baby's steps towards independence, but be patient, understanding and welcoming when she stumbles and rushes back to the solace of your arms.

Also be realistic in terms of the amount of time you can humanly supply in response to her demand. There will be moments when you'll have to let her hang on your legs crying while you get dinner on the table and moments when you will be able to provide only intermittent bursts of attention while you take care of the bills. As much as it's important for her to know that you'll always love her and will meet her needs, it's important for her to know that other people – you included – have needs, too.

NON-VERBAL LANGUAGE

'Our little girl says very few words, but she seems to have developed a system of sign language. Could her hearing be bad?'

It probably isn't that your child's hearing is bad, but that her resourcefulness is good. As long as your child seems to understand what you say and tries to imitate sounds, even unsuccessfully, her hearing is almost certainly normal. Her use of signs or other, more primitive, ways of expressing needs and thoughts (such as grunting) is merely an inventive way of coping with a temporary handicap: a limited comprehensible vocabulary. Some children simply have more difficulty forming words at this age than others; for many the difficulty continues, usually well into their preschool years and sometimes into nursery and infant school. They may be saying 'wove' for 'love' or 'toof' for 'tooth' when most of their agemates are speaking very clearly.

To compensate for the inability to communicate verbally, many of these children develop their own forms of language. Some, like your child, are good at talking with their hands. They point to what they want and push away what they don't. A wave is bye-bye, a finger pointed up is up, a finger pointed down is down. They may bark to indicate a dog, point to their nose to 'say' elephant or to their ears for rabbit. Some hum songs to communicate: 'Rock-a-bye Baby' when they are sleepy, 'Rain Rain Go Away' when it's pouring out, the theme to their favourite show when they want to watch TV. (See page 389 for more on signing with your baby.)

Since this takes a lot of creativity and a strong desire to communicate – both good qualities to cultivate – you should do your best to decipher your child's special language and to show her you do understand. But don't forget that the ultimate goal is real speech. When she hums a lullaby, say, 'Do you want to go to sleep?' When she points to the milk, respond, 'You'd like a glass of milk? Okay'. If she points to her ears when she sees a rabbit in her storybook, reply, 'You're right! That's a rabbit. A rabbit has long ears.'

If, however, she doesn't seem to hear you calling from behind her or from another room, or to understand simple commands, then you should ask the doctor about testing her hearing.

GENDER DIFFERENCES

'We're trying very hard not to raise our children in a sexist way. But we find that no matter how we try, we can't induce our son to be nurturing with dolls – he prefers to throw them against a wall.'

You're making the same discovery that many well-meaning parents, determined to avoid moulding their offspring into homemade sexual stereotypes, make. Sexual equality is an ideal whose time has come, but sexual sameness is an idea whose time can never come – at least as long as Mother Nature continues to have some say in the matter. Boys and girls, it appears, are as much moulded in the womb as in the playroom and garden.

The differences between the sexes, scientists believe, begin in the uterus when sex hormones such as testosterone and oestradiol begin to be produced. Male foetuses receive more of the former and females more of the latter. This apparently makes for somewhat different brain development and different strengths and approaches to life.

Though much more work needs to be done before scientists can spell out all the differences precisely, it's clear some differences exist from birth on. Even before they've come home from the hospital, girls may focus longer on faces, particularly talking faces. Girls react more to touch, pain and noise; boys react more to visual stimuli. Girls are more sensitive but are more easily soothed and comforted; boys tend to cry more and be more irritable. These and all differences, of course, apply for boys and girls as groups and not necessarily as individuals. Some girls may have more 'masculine' traits than some boys, and some boys more 'feminine' traits than some girls.

It's also apparent early on that boys have more muscle mass, larger lungs and hearts, and a lower sensitivity to pain, while girls have more body fat, a different shape to their pelvises and a different way of processing oxygen in their muscles, giving them less stamina than boys later in life. Girl babies, however, are definitely not the weaker sex — they tend from the start to be healthier and hardier than boys.

From early on, it seems, girls generally show more interest in people, boys in things, which may be why more girls like dolls and dress-up play, while more boys prefer trucks and fire engines. But does the fact that a girl dotes on dolls while a boy plays with trucks mean that their destinies are preordained? Partly, yes – girls will grow up to be women and boys will grow up to be men. But much in their attitudes will depend on their parents' attitudes; much in their behaviour will depend on the example their parents set. It is possible to raise children who are not 'sexist' in their points of view, who have respect for both males and females, who will choose their future life roles not on the basis of stereotypes (of any kind) but on the basis of their own personal strengths and desires – and who, no matter what their gender, will be nurturing in their relationships. Following these tips will help you meet those goals:

♦ Remember that the fact that there are innate differences between males and females in no way means that one sex is in any way better or worse, stronger or weaker. Differences are enriching, sameness is limiting. Pass this attitude on to your children.

♦ Treat your children as individuals. While as a group men have more muscles and are more aggressive than women, there are some women who have more muscle and are more aggressive than some men. If you have a daughter who has more 'male' traits or a son with more 'female' ones, don't berate or belittle them – and don't try to force a change, either. Encourage them to use their strengths, not suppress them.

Accept, love, support and encourage your child just as he or she is.

♦ Modify extremes. Accepting your child as he or she is doesn't mean never helping him overcome behaviours that could hold him back in life. If a child is overly aggressive, you should teach him to tone the aggression down. If, on the other hand, he is overly passive, you can encourage assertiveness.

♦ Select toys not because you're trying to either make or break a stereotype, but because you truly believe your child will enjoy them and benefit from them. If a child uses a toy differently from the way you expect (boys and girls will use the same toys in different ways, and even within each sex the use will vary), accept that. Remember, a boy never has to rock a doll to sleep to become a nurturing father; the example of a nurturing father (or another nurturing man in his life) will have far more impact.

♦ Don't fall unconsciously into sexist traps. Don't tell your sobbing toddler not to cry because he's a big boy and then cuddle his sister when she's tearful. Don't limit your compliments to a daughter to 'How pretty you look', and to a son to 'You climb so well', or 'What a big boy you are'. Say these things, by all means, when appropriate. But also compliment a boy on his being sweet to his sister and a girl for throwing a ball well. Do this because a child's personality is made up of many facets, all of which need nurturing.

♦ Try to avoid making value judgments about different types of skills or roles in life. If, for example, you give your children the impression that child care is a job that commands low respect, neither boys nor girls will come to value it as adults. If you give them the idea that going to an office to work is somehow more worthwhile than working as a full-time parent or working in a non-office environment, they won't value the latter choices, either.

♦ Divide family chores according to abilities, interests and time, rather than according to a preconceived stereotype or in order to break such a stereotype. That means the best cook should do most of the cooking (the other partner can do the dishes and clean up), and the best bookkeeper should take care of the finances. Jobs no one wants to do can be rotated, apportioned by agreement, or relegated on the spur of the moment ('Honey, can you take out the rubbish, please?'), but this latter system can fail miserably unless it's carefully monitored (as when nobody takes out the rubbish).

♦ Set an example. Decide which qualities in both males and females you and your spouse value most, and try to cultivate them in yourselves as well as in your children. Young children develop their gender identity partly through play with those of their own sex and partly through identification with the parent of the same sex. Again, dolls won't teach a little boy as much about nurturing as a nurturing daddy (or other important man in his life) will. A bat and ball are less likely to encourage a little girl to develop her physical aptitude than a mother who jogs every day.

SWITCHING TO A BED

'We're expecting a second baby in six months. When and how should we switch our son from his cot to a bed?'

THE TODDLER YEARS ... CONTINUED

Think you've seen negativity? Believe you've glimpsed willfulness? That's just a preview of the toddler years – when these toddler-centric behaviours and more will enchant and exasperate, delight and dumbfound, fascinate and frustrate, test both your resourcefulness and your patience as a parent. From food fetishes to ritualism, toddlers have a unique way of approaching life that keeps their parents guessing – and looking for advice on the best way to handle their quirky and fiercely independent offspring. Since so many toddler behaviours begin appearing late in the first year, you'll be able to glean some tips for tackling toddlerhood in this chapter. But for much more help on many more topics, read *What to Expect the Toddler Years*.

Whether or not your child is ready for a bed depends more on his age, size, development and spirit of adventure than on whether or not there's a new sibling on the way. The generally accepted rule: if a child is 89 cm (35 in) tall or can climb out of a cot on his own (or has tried and almost succeeded), he's ready for a bed. Some particularly agile children can climb out of a cot before they reach the 89-cm (35-in) cutoff; others, less daring, may never even try. (Even a child who's taller than 89 cm (35 in) but is perfectly content in his cot – and isn't trying to escape it – doesn't have to move out until he's ready.)

Since your older child will still be very young when your new baby is born, it's unlikely that he will be ready for the big move into a 'big boy' bed. Even if he is, he may feel displaced if you switch him out just as the new baby arrives. A better idea might be to move him now to a cot that can convert to a junior bed when he's ready.

USING A PILLOW

'I haven't given my baby a pillow or a blanket in her cot because of the risk of SIDS. But now that she's eleven months old, I'm wondering if it's safe to let her sleep with them.'

For you, a bed might not be a bed without a pillow (or two or three) to rest your head on, and a fluffy duvet to cuddle beneath. But for a baby who has slept flat and uncovered on the mattress since birth, pillows and blankets aren't an issue – what she doesn't know can't bother her or keep her up at night. And that's just as well. While the time of greatest risk for suffocation and SIDS has passed, most experts advise not handing out a pillow until your baby moves to a bed, or somewhere between eighteen and twenty-four months. By then, even the slight remaining risk is gone. Another piece of advice you might consider sleeping on: some experts say sleeping flat is better for everyone – baby and adult.

As for the blanket, the same advice holds true – later is better than sooner. Though some parents start tucking in their babies with a blanket closer to twelve months, most experts advise holding off until at least midway through the second year. The risk of using a blanket, especially with an active baby, is less of suffocation and more that she might get tangled up in the blanket when she stands up in the cot, leading to falls, bruises and frustration. Many parents opt instead for the one-piece footed pajamas on top of lightweight cotton

ones to keep their babies warm on cold nights.

When you do decide to throw in the pillow and blanket, don't let your preference for fluffy bed accessories guide your selection. Choose a 'toddler' pillow that's smaller and very flat and a blanket that is lightweight.

WATCHING TV

'I feel very guilty because I have begun turning on a cartoon for my child when I start to prepare dinner. She seems to love it, but I'm concerned she'll become addicted to TV.'

You're not the only one who's concerned – most experts are, too. Excessive TV viewing by children is linked to obesity and poor school performance. Because it can reduce interaction among family members (particularly if it's turned on during mealtimes or if children have TVs in their rooms), it can also promote a communication gap. Perhaps worst of all, it can create a picture of the world that is distorted and inaccurate and confuse a child's developing value system by establishing norms of behaviour and belief that are not accepted in the real world.

Programming designed for children is, of course, much better for kids than programming designed for older viewers. Though there's still plenty that's unworthy of the young viewers it is meant to attract, programming for children is a lot better than it used to be, thanks to the efforts of watchdog agencies. Most programming geared to the youngest audiences is high quality, offering a good dose of education along with its entertainment value. Many shows strive to teach not just numbers and letters but such positive values as sharing, cooperation, self-control, racial tolerance, environmental awareness and kindness towards others. Some also have an inter-active component, making television viewing somewhat less of a passive activity.

There has been very little research done on the effect of television on babies and toddlers, but one study does suggest that while television is not harmful to young children, it also doesn't do much by way of helping them boost language and visual motor skills either. Based on this and other evidence, many experts concur that even the best that television has to offer isn't very good for one-year-olds. Most experts recommend that parents hold off on television viewing for children under two. Before then, babies and toddlers need and appear to benefit most from person-to-person interaction with a parent or other care provider – the kind of interaction that helps make those critical brain connections, the kind of interaction that nurtures a child's social, emotional and intellectual devel-opment. Though television may promote learning, it doesn't allow young children to learn from experience and hands-on explorations, which is how they learn best.

Probably the greatest potential prob-lem with plunking your baby down in front of the television is how easily it can become a habit. Not so much for your baby (who at this age can still be swiftly distracted by any number of other activi-ties), but for you. Many harried parents use the TV as a baby-sitter, and though it's completely understandable (TV can keep a young child engaged – and in one spot – while mum or dad fixes dinner, catches up on e-mail or talks on the phone), and perhaps sometimes unavoid-able, it's not wise to do it on a regular basis. It's just too easy for those 'five min-utes while I empty the dishwasher' to lapse into twenty, then a half hour, then an hour, and then . . . you get the picture.

Besides, experts strongly advise that if a young child does watch television, she's much better off watching it side by side with a parent – who can make the experi-ence more educational and interactive by asking questions, pointing out images, discussing themes – something that's not possible when the parent's using TV to baby-sit.

Some families will decide that wait-ing until a child is two to introduce the television just isn't realistic (especially when there are older siblings in the home). Whenever television does become a part of your child's life, try to set strict limits from the start. A single non-commercial show of redeeming value is plenty to begin with. Avoid keeping the television on for your own entertainment during your child's waking hours, especially during meal-times, when family interaction can be lost to its mesmerizing effect. Though it won't always be practical, watch along-side her whenever you can, reinforcing what she sees on the screen – much as you would reinforce what she sees on a page during story time.

Rather than relying on TV as your toddler's only audiovisual entertainment, turn also to audiotapes and CDs; they require visual imagination (something television doesn't), stimulating creativity and, when they're musical, providing opportunities for self-expression through song and dance.

And if you need another reason to avoid or limit television watching now, here's one: it will never again be easier to do. The first two years are about the only time you'll be able to avoid strug-gles over television with your child. Once your toddler reaches preschool – and the influences of peers in more television-lenient households – the age of media innocence will be over for good.

MULTIMEDIA FOR BABIES

'I've seen computer programmes and websites geared specifically for babies. Should I give my son some screen-time already?'

In a culture where preschoolers who can't yet read are likely to be at least as computer literate as their parents, it was only a matter of time before software use trickled down to the nappy set. Yet 'lapware', so called because it's designed for children so young that they still need to sit on an adult's lap to see the screen and reach the keyboard, is quickly gaining popularity among parents eager to provide their progeny with the techno head start they never had.

Lapware programmes and websites, geared mostly to the nine- to twenty-four month age group, include such baby-and-toddler-friendly and educational activities as sorting objects, listening to animal sounds, dressing characters, putting together simple puzzles, playing hide-and-seek and listening to stories. Some software and sites actually allow parents to integrate family photographs and voices into the programme, much to the delight of the young participants. Baby keyboards, with large, brightly coloured buttons, invite banging away; a ball-and-spinner, easier to manipulate than a mouse, takes into account the limited fine-motor skills of users.

It's educational, it's fun, and many young children love it, clamouring for a turn at the computer every chance they get. But lapware – along with educational television shows and DVDs – has been a subject of debate among childhood development experts. Many experts agree that for children under the age of two, there's no such thing as 'educational' media (even if it's marketed as such), and that the best bet for helping develop your child's brain is plenty of parental interaction. In fact, a recent study has found no evidence that exposing infants and toddlers to television improves their language and visual motor skills at age three.

Which is not to say that lapware is harmful, either. But before you turn on the computer consider the potential benefits and downsides to lapware. On the plus side, he'll become familiar with computers at an early age, which could give him valuable skills to build on, and possibly a technological edge later on (though learning these skills a little later on, in the preschool and kindergarten years, will probably give him just as much of an edge). Lapware can provide him with a fine-motor workout and, through graphics and games, plenty of the stimulation he craves. It may also promote learning (though less than reading to him, playing non-computer games with him or sharing a variety of experiences outside of the home with him might). Computer play for babies also taps into their natural desire to mimic others in the household, just as serving dinner from a play kitchen or jabbering into a play telephone would. Finally, because it requires the participation of an adult – or at least, his or her lap – lapware, unlike television (which parents can simply park babies and toddlers in front of) encourages parents and young children to spend 'quality time' together, learning and having fun (though, again, such 'quality time' can be afforded through numerous technology-free activities).

The downside to feeding your child a diet of computer chips this early in life? For one thing, unlike other kinds of play, computer play doesn't challenge baby's brainpower all that much. When he's putting together a puzzle on the living room floor, he has to visualize how the piece will fit, then turn the piece in his hand to reflect that image, and then manipulate it into the board. When he's putting together a puzzle on the computer, he can do it by randomly hitting keys on the keyboard, which cause the on-screen action to occur. Creativity isn't nurtured, either, through lapware. While the scope of your child's vision on a computer screen is limited to what the software or website provides, his imagination is limitless when he role-plays with a family of teddy bears or a kid-sized garage full of cars. What's more, too much time at the computer can limit the opportunity children have to learn critical real-life skills that can't come from cyber experiences, such as self-control and getting along with others. Occasional interface with a machine is fine, but what young children really need is interface with people. Though more interactive than television typically is, computer play is still much more passive than other types of play. This makes it particularly inappropriate for an active one-year-old who wants to be (and should be) on the go most of his waking hours, exploring the world up close and personally. Though lapware does guarantee time spent together, some experts suggest that a computer can actually come between a parent and child. According to these experts, one-on-one activities that are free of technological interference – such as reading to your child, dancing or rolling a ball with your child, playing dolly tea party with your child – put a lot more quality in 'quality time' than computer use does. Besides, they wonder – what's the rush?

While there's not yet enough evidence to prove that computer programmes and websites hinder or harm brain development in toddlers and babies, you may want to proceed with caution, keeping these guidelines in mind:

◆ Remember the 'lap' in lapware. Never strap your baby into a chair and plop him in front of a computer.

◆ Don't 'byte' off more than baby can chew. Limit usage to ten to fifteen minutes at a time. Too much time spent on the computer can result in too little time spent working on social, emotional, physical and intellectual development. It prevents baby from learning the old-fashioned way – by doing. Also beware of forcing a child who has tired of banging on the keyboard – and would prefer to be banging on a junior workbench – to sit still for more computer time than he has the patience or attention span for.

◆ Use it for the right reasons. It's entertaining, somewhat stimulating, borderline educational. But it won't raise your baby's IQ, give him a lasting edge in school, or turn him into a techno-whiz kid.

And, certainly, if you opt out of the baby-technology craze and reserve your lap time for sessions with *Each Peach, Pear, Plum* and rounds of 'Itsy-Bitsy Spider' (not to mention good, old-fashioned cuddling), don't worry that you're depriving your child of the preparation he'll need to succeed in a wired world. There's plenty of time to hook him up.

HYPERACTIVITY

'My daughter is on the go all day long – crawling, walking, climbing, always moving. I'm afraid she may turn out to be hyperactive.'

Observing the frenetic pace that the average toddler sets, it's easy to see why so many parents of one-year-olds wonder the same thing you're wondering. But not to worry. What seems an abnormally high activity level to someone who has never tried to keep up with a toddler before is much more likely to be a normal one. After many months of frustration, the mobility your child struggled so hard to attain is finally hers. It's no wonder that she's a perpetual motion machine – off and running (or toddling or crawling or climbing) every chance she gets. As far as she's concerned, the day's too short for all the expeditions she wants to take.

This is way too early to worry about true hyperactivity (officially labelled ADHD, or Attention Deficit Hyperactivity Disorder). Such a diagnosis is contemplated only in the early school years when it's clear that a child's attention span has not grown appropriately with her. For now, your daughter's fleeting attention span and propensity for perpetual motion are as appropriate for her age as are messy eating habits. When winding down your perpetual-motion machine becomes necessary at bedtime, a soothing, warm bath and some quiet activities, such as a massage (if she likes it) and a little quiet reading or singing, can do the trick.

NEGATIVISM

'Ever since my son learned to shake his head and say no, he's been responding negatively to everything – even to things I'm sure he wants.'

Congratulations – your baby is becoming a toddler. And with this transition comes the beginning of a behaviour pattern you're going to see a lot more of, with increasing intensity, in the next year or so: negativism.

As hard as it is to be on the receiving end of it, negativism is a normal and healthy part of a young child's development. For the first time, he's able to be his own person rather than your malleable baby, to exert some power, test his limits and challenge parental authority. Most importantly, he's able to express opinions of his very own clearly and distinctly. And the opinion, he's discovered, that has the most impact is 'No!'

Fortunately, at this stage of negativism, your child isn't likely to mean 'no' as fiercely as he expresses it. In fact, he's often likely not to mean it at all – as when he says no to the banana he was just clamouring for, or shakes his head when you offer the ride on the swing that you know he really wants. Like pulling up or taking steps, learning how to say no and how to shake his head are skills – and he needs to practise them, even when they're not appropriate. That babies invariably shake their heads no long before they nod their heads yes has less to do with negativism than with the fact that it's a less complex, more easily executed movement that requires less coordination.

True negativism can sometimes be avoided with a little clever verbal manipulation on your part. If you don't want to hear a no, don't ask a question that can be answered with one. Instead of 'Do you want an apple?' try 'Would you like an apple or a banana?' offering one in each hand for your baby to point to it. Instead of 'Do you want to go on the slide?' ask 'Would you like to go on the slide or the swing?' Be aware, however, that some young children will answer even multiple-choice questions with a no.

Occasionally, an eleven- or twelve-month-old will even act out a primitive version of the 'terrible twos' tantrum. These are usually laughable, though laughing at them (or at the vigorous use of no and of head shaking) will only prolong the behaviour and encourage repetition. Though it won't always work later on (an older toddler can keep a tantrum going full steam until he or his parent drop), ignoring a year-old baby's tirade will usually result in his giving up the struggle and sheepishly picking himself up to go play with a toy. Distraction, a big hug or a little humour can work well, too.

The nos will probably have it in your household for at least another year, and they'll probably intensify before they taper off. The best way to weather this stormy period is to pay little mind to negative behaviour; the more you fuss over baby's nos, the more nos you'll hear. Keeping negativism in perspective while keeping your sense of humour may not help check the nos, but it may aid your ability to cope with them.

What it's Important to Know: STIMULATING YOUR ONE-YEAR-OLD

First words. First steps. With these two feathers in the toddler's cap, or nearly so, the learning game becomes more exciting than ever before. The world is growing by leaps and bounds; give your one-year-old a chance to explore and learn about it, while promoting his or her continued physical, social, intellectual and emotional development, by offering the following:

Safe space to walk in – both indoors and out. The rookie walker usually objects to being strapped in a pushchair or backpack, so use these only when necessary. Encourage baby to walk as often as possible, but keep an eagle eye out for dangers, especially near streets, roads and driveways. For the baby who isn't quite walking yet, put some enticing objects up out of reach, to provide incentive for pulling up and/or cruising. Push toys can also help steady a baby who's uncertain about standing or walking.

Safe space for supervised climbing. Babies love to climb steps (when you're not supervising, a gate is a must), clamber up a slide (stay right behind, just in case), manoeuvre onto a low chair or off the bed. Let them – but stand by and be ready to come to the rescue if need be.

Encouragement to be physically active. The inactive baby may need a little coaxing to become more active. You may need to get down and crawl yourself, playfully challenging your child to come crawling or walking after you ('Try and catch me!') or move away from you ('I'm gonna get you!'). Put toys or other favourite objects out of reach and encourage some sort of locomotion to retrieve them. The fearful baby may need some moral – and physical – support. Encourage, but don't push. Climb up and slide down the slide with a timid child until he or she is comfortable enough to go it alone. Stroll with the tentative walker, lending a hand (or two) for support. Go on a 'big kid' swing together until your little kid is willing to risk the baby swing solo.

A varied environment. The baby who sees nothing but the inside of his or her own home, the family car and the supermarket is going to be a very bored baby (not to mention how bored the care provider will be). There's an exciting world outside the door, and your baby should see it daily. Even going out

THE EYES HAVE IT . . . ALREADY

All parents hope that their children will look to them for direction. Well, according to some interesting research, children do look to their parents (and other adults) for direction – and a lot earlier than previously believed. Scientists found that twelve-month-old babies were more likely to look in the direction of an object if an adult looked at it first. According to the researchers, this shows that babies this young understand the significance of eyes – and begin to look to them for social cues. (The question is, does the experiment work with sixteen-year-olds?)

in the rain or snow (barring flooding or blizzard conditions) can be a learning experience. Give your baby a tour of area playgrounds, parks, art museums (toddlers are usually fascinated by paintings and statues), a children's museum (if you're lucky enough to have one nearby), toy stores, restaurants (pick those that welcome children), pet shops and shopping centres or other busy business areas with lots of store windows to peer into and lots of people to see.

Pull-and-push toys. Toys that need to be pushed or pulled provide practice for those who've just begun to walk, and confidence (and physical support) for those just tottering on the brink. Riding toys babies can sit astride and propel with their feet may help some children walk, though others find walking independently easier.

Creative materials. Scribbling with crayons provides tremendous satisfaction for many year-old babies. Taping the paper to a table, the floor or an easel will keep it from sliding all over, and confiscating the crayons as soon as they are used where they shouldn't be or if baby decides to chew on one will help teach their proper use. Don't allow pens and pencils, except under close supervision, since the sharp points can spell disaster if baby waves it near his or her eyes. Finger painting can be fun for some, while others are uncomfortable with the messy fingers that are an occupational hazard of the art. (Though hand washing demonstrates that the condition is only temporary, some children continue resisting the medium.) Musical toys can be fun, too, but look for those with fairly good quality sound. Baby can also learn to improvise musically, with a spoon on a pot bottom, for instance, if you demonstrate first.

Putting-and-taking toys. Babies love to put things in and take them out, although the latter skill develops before the former. You can buy putting-and-taking toys, or just use objects around the house such as empty boxes, wooden spoons, measuring cups, paper cups and plates and napkins. Fill a basket with a variety of small items (but not small enough for baby to put in her mouth and choke on) for starters. Be ready to do most of the putting in until baby becomes much more proficient. Sand or, if you're in the house, raw rice or water (you can limit its indoor use to the bath and baby's high chair) allow for putting in and taking out in the form of pouring – and most toddlers love both materials, but they require constant supervision.

Shape-sorters. Usually long before babies can say circle, square or triangle, they have learned to recognize these shapes and can put them in the proper openings in a shape-sorter toy. These

SAFETY REMINDER

Your baby is getting smarter and more coordinated all the time – but it will be a long while before judgment catches up with intelligence and motor skills. Since baby is now capable of thinking up and acting on new ways of getting into trouble, it's those smarts and skills that put him or her at even more risk than before.

So as baby enters the second year of life, be sure to continue your constant vigilance as well as all the safety precautions you have already put into effect. But also do a second safety inventory, taking into account the fact that your toddler is now, or will soon be, a proficient climber. This means that virtually nothing in your home that is not behind lock and key or safety latch is safe from tiny hands. In your survey, look not only to things that your one-year-old can reach from the floor, but also anything he or she could conceivably get to by climbing. Removing or safeguarding all items that might be hazardous to baby (or vice versa) would be wise. Consider, too, that toddlers can be quite resourceful in obtaining what they want – piling up books to reach a shelf, pulling over a chair to reach a window, standing on a toy to reach the kitchen counter. Also be sure that anything baby might climb on – chairs, tables, shelves – is sturdy enough to hold his or her weight. Continue setting limits ('No, you can't climb on that!'), but don't, just yet, depend on your still-very-young child to remember today's prohibition tomorrow.

toys also teach manual dexterity and, in some cases, colours. Be aware, however, that baby may need many demonstrations and much assistance before mastery of shape-sorters is achieved.

Dexterity toys. Toys that require turning, twisting, pushing, pressing and pulling encourage children to use their hands in a variety of ways. Many parental demonstrations may be needed before babies are able to handle some of the more complicated manoeuvres, but once mastered, these toys provide hours of concentrated play.

Bath toys for water play. These teach many concepts, and allow the joy of water play without a mess all over the floor or furniture. The bath is also a good place for blowing bubbles, but you'll probably have to do the blowing yourself for a while yet.

Follow-the-leader play. Daddy starts clapping, then mummy. Baby is encouraged to follow suit. Then daddy flaps his arms, and mummy does, too. After a while, baby will follow the leader without prodding, and eventually will be able to take the lead.

Books, magazines, anything with pictures. You can't have a live horse, elephant and lion in your living room – but you can have all of them, and more, visit your home in a book or magazine. Look at and read books with your baby several times during the day. Each session will probably be short, maybe no more than a few minutes, because of your child's limited attention span, but together they will build a firm foundation for later enjoyment of reading.

Materials for pretend play. Toy dishes, kitchen equipment, pretend food, play houses, trucks and cars, hats, grown-ups' shoes, sofa cushions – almost anything can be magically transformed in an imaginative toddler's world of make-believe. This kind of play develops social skills as well as small-motor coordination (putting on and taking off clothing, 'scrambling' eggs or 'cooking' soup), creativity and imagination.

Patience. Though the skills babies on the brink of toddlerhood display have advanced by leaps and bounds over what they were at six months, their attention spans haven't kept pace. Some toys may hold their attention for an extended period, but they'll have only fleeting interest in most activities. The attention span may be shorter still when the activity requires sitting still, as for a story. Be understanding of these limitations, don't push your one-year-old beyond them, and definitely don't worry – as babies grow, so do their attention spans.

Applause (but not standing ovations). Cheer your baby on as new skills are mastered. Achievement, while satisfying, often means more when accompanied by recognition. But be wary of cheering too much or too often, otherwise baby may become an applause junkie – dependent on the cheers and unable to challenge him- or herself unless they're forthcoming. Self-satisfaction (being proud of his or her own accomplishment) is also important, and sometimes it should be all baby needs.

◆ ◆ ◆

Part 2

OF SPECIAL
CONCERN

CHAPTER 17

A Baby for All Seasons

No matter what time of year your baby was born in, there will be four seasons in his or her first twelve months. And as those seasons change – with sun, wind, heat, cold, rain and, in some climates, snow coming and going with them – a wide range of new questions may come to mind. Questions that don't necessarily apply to a particular month of a baby's life but to a particular season of the year – questions about feeding, dressing, and playing in weather extremes, about sunburn and frostbite, about window screens and fireplace screens, about Christmas decorations and maybe even about swimming lessons. Read on to make sure you and your baby are prepared for all seasons.

What You May Be Concerned About in Summer Weather

KEEPING BABY COOL

It's summertime and the dressing is easy. Or is it? Here's a common summer sighting: a parent in shorts, a tank top and sandals pushing a pram holding an infant dressed for an arctic winter. The fact is that babies – even very new babies – don't need to be dressed any more warmly in warm weather than adults do. Not only is adding extra clothing unnecessary, it can be risky and can lead to such undesirable consequences as prickly heat and, in extreme cases, heatstroke.

Unless you've got an unreliable personal thermostat (you're always warm when everyone else is cool, or you're always cool when everyone else is warm), feel free to dress your baby as you would yourself. If you're comfortable in shorts and a tank top, your baby will be fine in the junior equivalent. If you're sweltering in a sweater, your baby will be, too. Lightweight, loose-fitting, light-coloured clothing will be most comfortable when temperatures soar; a lightweight porous cap, hat or bonnet will protect baby's head without overheating it. Materials should be absorbent to soak up perspiration, but when clothing becomes damp, it should be changed – so routinely carry along an extra set of clothes for baby.

A SUMMER RASH

It's what many babies are wearing every summer season: heat rash. Also known as prickly heat, its telltale tiny red spots on the face, neck, armpits and upper torso are caused when perspiration builds up because of clogged sweat-gland ducts. Though the rash usually fades on its own within a week, you can treat baby with a cool bath (as always, use a very mild soap), but avoid powders or lotions that can further block the sweat from flowing. Call the doctor if pustules, increased swelling or redness develop – these symptoms may indicate a yeast or bacterial infection.

While a baby carrier or sling constructed of heavyweight fabric can keep baby warm in the winter, it can keep him or her sweltering in the summer, especially if it covers baby head to toe. Lack of ventilation in combination with your body warmth and a high outdoor temperature could add up to excessive heat within the confines of the carrier.

Indoors in hot weather, your baby will enjoy the cooling effects of an air conditioner or fan as much as you do. Just be sure neither blows directly on the baby, that the room temperature doesn't drop much below 22°C (72°F), and that cooling equipment and its electrical cords are out of baby's reach. A nappy alone will do for sleeping on hot nights, but a lightweight sleeper may be needed if the air conditioner is running.

Cool hands or feet are not a sign that your baby is chilly, but perspiration (check the neck, head, underarms) is a sign of being too warm.

HEATSTROKE

Though parents commonly worry about their babies being too cold, they often don't realize that being too hot can be just as dangerous. In the first year of life babies are particularly susceptible to heat because their temperature-regulation systems aren't yet matured

and it's difficult for them to cool themselves effectively. As a result, overheating can lead to serious, even fatal, heatstroke. Heatstroke typically comes on suddenly. Signs to watch for include hot and dry (or, occasionally, moist) skin, very high fever, diarrhoea, agitation or lethargy, confusion, convulsions and loss of consciousness. Should your baby exhibit such symptoms, summon emergency medical help immediately and follow the first-aid procedures on page 586.

As with most other medical emergencies, the best treatment is prevention. You can prevent heatstroke in these ways:

♦ *Never* leave an infant or child in a parked vehicle in warm or hot weather, even for a moment. (Keep in mind that infants and children should never be left alone in parked cars no matter what the weather.) Even with the windows open, the interior temperature can rise rapidly and dangerously. When the outdoor temperature is 35.5°C (96°F), for example, temperatures in the car can shoot up to more than 40.5°C (105°F) within fifteen minutes *when the windows are rolled halfway down,* and to nearly 65.5°C (150°F) if the windows are closed. Babies can die quickly under these conditions.

- Don't bundle up a baby who has a fever with blankets or heating pads. A child with a fever needs cooling down, not heating up. 'Sweating it out' is not a recommended treatment in any type of weather.

- Dress baby lightly in hot weather, and avoid direct sunlight. Beware of overheating in a baby carrier.

- Always be sure that your child gets extra fluids in hot weather.

TOO MUCH SUN

There was a time when children who were tanned from hours of frolicking in the hot sun of a summer afternoon were considered healthy; children who were pale from too much time spent indoors were considered 'sickly'. The sun's rays, it was believed, were as wholesome as apple pie and as restorative as a week in the country.

Today, it's known that sunshine isn't quite what the doctor ordered. In fact, it's what doctors now routinely order their patients to stay away from. Too much unprotected time in the sun can lead to skin cancer (including the potentially fatal melanoma), brown spots and premature wrinkling and aging of the skin. Though a tan looks 'healthy', it's actually a sign of injury to the skin and is that sensitive organ's way of trying to protect itself against further damage.

Excessive exposure to the sun's rays has also been strongly linked to the development of cataracts (they are much more common in sunny climes), and has been found to reduce body levels of beta-carotene (a substance in the body believed to be protective against cancer). If that's not enough to make you take a dim view of bright sunshine, consider this: it can also precipitate certain other diseases, or make them worse, among

them herpes simplex and some other viral skin diseases; vitiligo (white, or depigmented, spots on the skin); PKU; and photosensitive eczema. For those taking certain antibiotics (such as tetracycline) or other medications, it can cause serious side effects. A pretty long rap sheet for what was once considered an all-purpose panacea.

Daily sessions of direct sunshine were once crucial to healthy growth and development in childhood, for it was the only available source of vitamin D, which is needed for building strong bones. Today, infant formulas and some dairy products are fortified with the vitamin, and it is also found in the supplements that exclusively breastfed babies are given. So parents needn't sacrifice the future of their children's skin to ensure them the required dose of vitamin D.

To be certain your baby doesn't suffer the consequences of too much sun, keep in mind the following sun-safety facts and sun-safety tips.

SUN-SAFETY FACTS:

- Infants are particularly susceptible to sunburn because of their thin skin. A single episode of severe sunburn during infancy or childhood doubles the risk of the most deadly of skin cancers, malignant melanoma. Even seemingly innocent tanning without burning in the early years has been linked to basal cell and squamous cell carcinomas, the most common types of skin cancer, as well as to premature aging of the skin. The sun is believed responsible for at least 90 per cent of all skin cancers, most of which could have been prevented.

- There is no such thing as a safe tan, no matter how gradually acquired. Nor does a base tan protect the skin from further damage.

WHAT TO LOOK FOR IN SELECTING A SUNSCREEN

High SPF. Sunscreens are labelled with a sun protection factor, or SPF, from 2 to as high as 50. The higher the number, the greater the protection. An SPF of at least 15 is recommended for babies and children, though a 30 to 45 is best for those with very fair or sensitive skin. Do not use tanning products on babies or children; they don't protect at all.

Effectiveness. Look for a product that contains ingredients that screen out both the short ultraviolet (UVB) rays of the sun that burn and can cause cancer, as well as the longer ultraviolet (UVA) rays that tan, can cause long-term skin damage and enhance the cancer-causing effects of the UVB rays.

Safety. Some sunscreen ingredients are irritating to or cause allergic reactions in some people, particularly infants with tender skins. Most common offenders are PABA (para-aminobenzoic acid) and forms of PABA (padimate O or octyl dimethyl PABA, for example), fragrances, and colourings. To be extra safe, do a 'patch test' with a new sunscreen on your baby's forearm forty-eight hours before using it all over his body. Once you've begun using a product, if your baby develops an itchy red rash or any other kind of skin reaction, or if his or her eyes seem irritated, try another product, preferably one that is designed for use by infants or is hypoallergenic. If your child has sensitive skin, look for a product with the active ingredient titanium dioxide, a chemical-free block.

Protection in the water. When your baby is going to be in the water, select a product that is waterproof (which means it will retain its effectiveness after four twenty-minute dunkings) or water resistant (it will retain effectiveness after two such dunkings).

♦ Fair-skinned individuals with light eyes and hair are most susceptible, but no one is immune from the hazardous effects of the sun's rays.

♦ The nose, lips and ears are the parts of the body most susceptible to sun damage.

♦ The sun's intensity is greatest, thus its rays most dangerous, between 10 AM and 3 PM (or 11 AM and 4 PM daylight savings time).

♦ Fully 80 per cent of the sun's radiation penetrates cloud cover, so protection is needed on cloudy days as well as on clear ones.

♦ Water and sand reflect the sun's rays, increasing the risk of skin damage and the need for protection at the beach, swimming pool or lake.

♦ Wet skin allows more ultraviolet rays to penetrate than dry skin – so extra protection is needed in the water.

♦ Extreme heat, wind, high altitude and closeness to the equator also accentuate dangers of the sun's rays, so take extra precautions under such conditions.

♦ Snow on the ground can reflect enough of the sun's rays on a bright day to cause a sunburn.

SUN-SAFETY TIPS:

♦ Avoid exposing babies under six months to strong sunlight, particularly at the height of the sun's intensity in summer or in climates that are warm year-round. Protect these young infants with a sunshade or parasol on pushchairs or prams.

◆ If adequate shade is not available, apply sunscreen on baby's face, hands and body at least fifteen (but preferably thirty) minutes before sun exposure. Slather on generously for older babies; use in smaller amounts on infants under the age of six months (but continue to limit exposure to direct sunlight). Avoid getting sunscreen into baby's mouth or eyes, or on the eyelids. For extra protection on very sensitive areas, such as lips, nose and ears, ask the doctor about using a sun-blocking lip balm or stick, or zinc oxide. Use waterproof sunscreen if baby will be going in the water.

◆ Reapply sunscreen every two to three hours, more often during water play or if baby is sweating a lot. Carry sunscreen in your changing bag in case you need it unexpectedly.

◆ Initial protected exposures to the sun should be for no more than a few minutes and can gradually be increased, by a couple of minutes a day, up to twenty minutes.

◆ In the sun, all babies and children should wear light hats with brims to protect eyes and face, and shirts to protect the upper body, even when they're in the water. Clothing should be of lightweight, tightly woven fabrics. Two thin layers may protect better than one, since the sun's rays can pass through some fabrics – but be wary of overdressing.

◆ Sun exposure damages the eyes as well as the skin. Children who spend a lot of time in the sun should wear protective sunglasses that filter harmful rays. So once baby's eight or nine months old (especially if he or she is a regular at the playground), it's time to bring out the shades. Look for those that are labelled '100% UV protection' and meet European safety standards. Getting baby in the sunglasses habit early on will help with compliance later.

◆ During hot weather, try to schedule most outdoor activity for early morning or late afternoon. Keep children out of the midday sun whenever possible.

◆ If your child is taking any medication, be sure that it doesn't cause increased sensitivity to sunlight before allowing sun exposure.

◆ Set a good example by protecting your own skin from the ravages of the sun's rays, with a hat, sunscreen and shades.

SIGNS OF SUNBURN

Many parents assume their babies are fine in the sun as long as there is no reddening of the skin. Unfortunately, they're mistaken. You can't see sunburn when it's occurring, and when you do see it, it's too late. It's not until two to four hours following exposure that the skin becomes red, hot and inflamed, and the colour doesn't peak at lobster red until ten to fourteen hours after exposure. A bad sunburn will also blister and will be accompanied by localized pain and, in the most severe cases, headache, nausea and chills. Redness usually starts to fade and symptoms diminish after forty-eight to seventy-two hours – at which point the skin, even in fairly mild cases, may start to peel. Occasionally, however, discomfort may continue for a week to ten days. See page 580 for tips on treating sunburn.

INSECT BITES

Though most insects are harmless, their bites and stings almost always cause pain or uncomfortable itching, and can occasionally transmit serious disease or cause a severe allergic reaction. So it makes sense to protect your baby from bugs and their bites whenever you can. (For treating insect bites, see page 576.)

STING OR BITE PROTECTION

Bees and other stinging insects. Keep baby out of areas where bees congregate, such as clover or wildflower fields, fruit orchards or near birdbaths. Protect baby even in your own garden, especially on bright, warm days or after a heavy rain. If you discover a beehive or a wasp nest in or near your home, have it removed by an expert. To avoid attracting bees, dress your family for outdoor play in white or pastels rather than dark or bright colours or flowered prints. Don't use fragrant powders or lotions, cologne or scented hair spray.

Mosquitoes. They breed in water, so, if you live somewhere where they are prevalent, drain puddles, birdbaths, gutters and other areas and things that collect water near your home, such as toys left outdoors, swing sets and pool covers. Keep baby indoors at dusk when mosquitoes swarm, and be sure windows are screened and screens kept in good repair. A mosquito net over baby's pushchair can help protect infants. For babies over six months, use an insect repellent formulated for children, or those made with citronella or soybean oil (though these products are less effective than ones containing DEET; see below). Follow manufacturer's directions when applying repellent, use sparingly, avoid getting it on baby's hands or face, and wash it off with soap and water when you get inside. Lotion formulas are easier to control; a spray's fumes can be inhaled and get into the eyes.

Deer ticks. Before outings in high tick areas, apply an insect repellent containing low concentrations (30 per cent or less) of DEET (if baby is over two months old) to clothing and sparingly to uncovered skin. To prevent ingestion, don't put it on baby's hands. Check family, pets and gear frequently for the pinhead-size ticks. (They are easier to spot on light-coloured clothing and cling less to tight weaves.)

All biting or stinging insects. Keep arms, legs, feet and head covered in areas where such insects might be lurking. Where ticks are prevalent, tuck trouser cuffs into socks.

SUMMER SAFETY

The arrival of summer signals a whole new set of injury possibilities. The following precautions will help minimize the chance that the possibilities will become realities:

♦ Because warm weather often means open windows, be sure to install window guards that meet safety standards for emergency exiting on all windows in your home. Don't depend on screens, since they can be easily pushed out by a baby. If window guards aren't in place in your home, or where you're visiting, open windows no more than 15 cm (6 in) (and be sure they can't be pushed open further), or open them only from the top. You can also buy window stops that can be added to the frame to prevent the window from opening more than 10 cm (4 in). Some new windows come with the window stops already

WATER, BABY?

During the dog days of summer (which can start in spring and last through the autumn in some areas), or in a climate that's warm year-round, your little puppy needs more fluids to replace those lost through perspiration. Babies under the age of six months who are exclusively breastfed can almost always get all the additional fluids they need by nursing more often, but ask the doctor whether you should offer a little water on very hot days. For the very young formula-fed baby, the doctor might suggest giving water between bottles of formula – but again, do so only if recommended. For older babies, offer small amounts of water or diluted fruit juice in cups or bottles. (Giving too much water isn't good for babies; see page 167.)

Once they've been introduced, juicy fruits such as melons, peaches and tomatoes can provide additional fluids. Do not serve drinks that are sweetened with sugar, such as fizzy drinks, juice drinks or punches, since they increase thirst (and aren't appropriate for babies, anyway), or drinks that contain added salt (such as special athletic drinks).

---

installed. Don't put furniture, or anything else a baby can climb, under windows.

- Doors, too, are often left open in warm weather, inviting crawlers to crawl and toddlers to toddle out and into trouble. Be sure to keep all doors, including sliding doors and screens, locked.

- Outdoors, never take your eyes off the baby who can crawl or toddle, and be especially watchful around swings and other playground equipment. Be sure any equipment in your own garden is at least 1.8 m (6 ft) from fences or walls, and that there is protective surfacing (rubber, sand, pea gravel, wood chips or bark) under it. Babies under a year should be placed only in seat swings that have seat belts and crotch straps or in specially designed infant bucket-type swings. Don't use metal slides in warm weather without feeling them first – in the sun they can get hot enough to cause burns.

- Don't put baby down in deep grasses or underbrush or anywhere there could possibly be poison ivy or where he or she might get a hand on or nibble at other poisonous flowers, shrubs or trees. When in wooded areas, be sure your baby is protected with cover-up clothing. If your baby accidentally has contact with poison ivy, or some other poisonous plant, remove all clothing while protecting your own hands with gloves or paper towels. Wash baby's skin thoroughly with soap and water as soon as possible – preferably within five minutes. Anything else that might have touched the plants (clothing, buggy, even the dog) should be washed, too. Shoes should be washed, if they're washable, or at least wiped down thoroughly. Should a reaction occur, apply calamine or another soothing lotion to relieve itching (see page 588).

- Since warm weather also brings out the barbecues, take steps to protect babies from accidental burns. Keep grills out of reach of small hands. Be sure there are no chairs or anything else on which a baby can climb to reach these hot attractions. Tabletop grills should be placed only on stable surfaces. Remember that coals can stay hot for a long time. To reduce the risk of burns, drench the coals with water when the cooking is complete, then dispose of them where your child can't get to them. Never use grills in an enclosed space, both because of the risk of carbon monoxide poisoning and the potential fire hazard.

WATER BABIES

Parents, eager to 'waterproof' their babies as well as to give them a competitive edge over their pint-size peers, are often enticed to enroll their babies in swimming classes. But according to safety experts, swimming classes are not a good idea for babies. Though it is easy to teach crawlers to float – young children float naturally because they have a higher proportion of body fat than adults – it's unlikely they could use this skill in a life-threatening situation. Nor do infant swimming lessons make children better swimmers in the long run than do lessons taken later on in childhood. There is, in fact, some question as to whether children under three can benefit at all from swimming classes. In addition, there are potential health risks. For one, if babies are allowed to put their heads under water, 'water intoxication' is a possibility (see page 518). For another, early exposure to public pools could increase the risk of such infections as diarrhoea (because of germs swallowed along with pool water), swimmer's ear (because of water entering the ear) and swimmer's itch and other skin rashes.

That doesn't mean you shouldn't try to help your baby to feel comfortable in water – an important first step in water safety training. Before you take the plunge with your baby, however, do acquaint yourself thoroughly with the following points. Keep them in mind, too, if you plan on enrolling your baby in a swimming class:

♦ A baby should not be taken into a pool or other large body of water until good head control is achieved – that is, when the head can be lifted to a 90-degree angle routinely. Before this skill is mastered, usually by four or five months of age, the head might accidentally bob under the water.

♦ A baby with any kind of chronic medical problem, including frequent ear infections, should have the doctor's okay before you allow water play. A baby with a cold or other illness (especially diarrhoea) should be temporarily barred from water activities, other than in the bath, until recovery is complete.

♦ The baby who likes and is used to water is probably less safe near it than one who is afraid of it. So don't leave a child, even one who has had 'swimming' lessons, or is wearing water wings or another flotation device, unattended near water (a pool, hot tub, bath, lake, ocean, puddle) for *any* period of time. Drowning can occur in less time than it takes to answer the phone and in only a couple of centimetres/inches of water. If you must leave the waterside, even for a second, take baby with you.

♦ All infant water activity should be on a one-to-one basis with a responsible adult. The adult should not be fearful of the water, because such fear could be passed on to the infant.

♦ Swimming instructors of infants should be qualified to teach swimming to babies and should be certified in infant CPR. Any class

AS THE FOOD TURNS

For adults, spoiled food can spoil a summer day. For babies and small children, the food poisoning it causes can be much more dangerous. So take special precautions with baby's food in warm weather, when soaring temperatures can cause bacteria to multiply much more quickly. Follow the tips on pages 326 and 327 to reduce the risk of food poisoning. Keep several small ice packs in the freezer, ready to go. On outings, use one to keep formula, breast milk, opened jars of juice or baby food, or perishable table foods chilled, or tote beverages in a thermos or in a jar with added ice cubes (for juice only, since formula or breast milk shouldn't be diluted by melted ice). A soft-sided six-pack cooler gives extra protection on longer outings and is easy to carry. Don't use any food or drink (except for unopened juice boxes and baby food jars) once it's no longer cool to the touch.

should be age and developmentally appropriate. Be wary of any instructor or programme that claims that they will 'drown-proof' your baby or toddler.

◆ A baby who is fearful of the water or resistant to being dunked should not be forced to participate in water play.

◆ Water in which an infant plays should be comfortably warm. In general, babies like water between 29° and 30°C (84° and 87°F). Infants under six months should never be dunked in water cooler than this. Air temperature should be at least 1.7°C (3°F) warmer than water temperature, and water play

should be limited to thirty-minute sessions to avoid chilling. Also, to reduce the risk of infection, pool water should be properly chlorinated, and natural bodies of water should be unpolluted and certified by local authorities as safe for family swimming.

◆ Infants in nappies should wear either waterproof pants that have snug elastic around the leg or disposable nappies specially designed for use in the water. You don't have to worry too much about urine leakage, but it makes sense to exit even a chlorinated pool when baby has had a bowel movement.

◆ An infant's head or face should not be submerged. Though babies instinctively hold their breath under water, they continue to swallow. Swallowing large quantities of water, which many babies do during water play, can dilute the blood, leading to 'water intoxication'. This watering down of the blood can dangerously reduce the levels of sodium. The resultant swelling of the brain can cause restlessness, weakness, nausea, muscle twitching, stupor, convulsions and even coma. Babies are much more susceptible than adults to water intoxication because of a smaller blood volume (it doesn't take a huge quantity of water to dilute it) and because they tend to swallow anything in their mouths. Water intoxication is a deceptive condition. Since a baby doesn't show any signs of trouble while in the water, and symptoms may not appear until three to eight hours after its ingestion, the illness is often not associated with swimming. Submersion also increases the risk of infection, particularly of the ears and sinuses, as well as of hypothermia (dangerously low body temperatures).

◆ Tubes, water wings, Lilos or other flotation devices lend a false sense of security to a baby and parent. It takes but a moment for a little one to slip from a tube or tumble off a float. Safety-approved vests should be worn around the water by babies and young children, but even these should never replace constant adult supervision.

◆ A toy bobbing in a pool can become a fatal attraction to a curious child. Keep all objects out of the pool when not in use.

◆ A pool, wading pool or fountain with a missing drain cover should not be used until the drain is repaired. A baby or young child could be seriously injured by the force of the suction.

◆ Adults supervising babies or children near water should be familiar with resuscitation techniques (see page 593), preferably through a hands-on course. Rescue equipment, such as life preservers, and a CPR-technique poster should be displayed near any swimming area. A phone should be readily available for emergency calls.

What You May Be Concerned About in Winter Weather

KEEPING BABY WARM

Baby, it's cold outside. Just as when it's warm outside, your own comfort can be your guide to dressing older babies and children. But infants under six months – because they have a greater ratio of body surface to body weight and because they can't yet shiver to generate heat – need a little more protection in cold weather than you do.

Even when the weather is only slightly cool, a young baby should wear a hat to help retain heat (much of the body's heat is lost via the head). When the temperature is near freezing, a hat, mittens, warm socks and booties, and a scarf or neck warmer should be standard issue. When the wind is biting or temperatures are very low, a scarf can be wrapped around the face or a knitted mask hat slipped over it, but be careful not to block the nose (and be sure any scarves are tied up well so they can't

get caught in pushchair wheels or playground equipment). A raincover will keep wind and snow out of a pushchair or pram and warmth in. But even a well-bundled baby shouldn't be out in very cold weather for long periods.

In cold weather, a lot of lightweight layers (polyester fleece is a great choice) are more effective and less restrictive than a couple of heavy garments. If at least one layer is wool, baby will be warmer. Down or imitation down makes for a warm snowsuit or bunting.

The following cold weather tips will also help to keep your baby cozy and comfortable:

◆ Be sure your baby has recently had a meal or snack before going out – it takes a lot of calories to maintain body heat in cold weather.

◆ If any of your baby's clothes should

CHANGEABLE WEATHER

If there's any kind of weather that puzzles even those who top best-dressed lists, it's that neither-here-nor-there weather so common in the spring and autumn. For the inexperienced parent of a young baby, the puzzle is even more complex. How do you piece together an outfit from baby's cupboard when the day dawns like a lamb but is expected to roar like a lion by sundown (or vice versa)?

In general, the layered look is the key to dressing for success in changeable weather. Most practical are lightweight layers, which can be easily added or subtracted as the weather unpredictably zigzags from warm to cool and back again. An extra sweater or blanket is always a sensible take-along in case the mercury takes a sudden sharp dip. A hat is a good idea for a young baby in almost any weather – a very light one with a sunshade when it's balmy, a warmer one on blustery days. An older baby can go hatless when temperatures are 15° to 24°C (60° to 75°F) or so and sun or wind isn't excessively strong. And remember, once your baby's thermostat becomes well regulated (at about six months), let your own comfort be your baby-dressing guide. A quick check of baby's arms, thighs or nape of the neck (but not the hands or feet, which are almost always cool in young babies) will tell you if baby's comfortable. If you find these body parts are cool and/or if baby is fretful, he or she may be chilly.

become wet, get indoors and change them immediately.

◆ A baby who's on two feet should wear waterproof, lined boots when walking in wintry weather. The boots should be roomy enough to allow air, which will offer some extra insulation, to circulate around stockinged feet.

◆ In a car, remove your baby's hat and one or more layers of clothing, if possible, to prevent overheating; if not, take care to keep the car cool. Also remove some clothing on a warm bus or train.

◆ In windy weather, use a mild moisturizing lotion or cream on baby's exposed skin to keep it from chapping.

◆ Don't worry if your baby's nose runs when outdoors in cold weather (you can't catch a cold from being cold). The cilia, or little hairs, which ordinarily move nasal secretions to the back of the nose instead of letting them drip out are temporarily paralyzed by the cold. Once indoors, the running should stop. A little cream or Vaseline under the nose (not in it) will help prevent chapping.

FROSTBITE

While you needn't worry about your baby's nose running, you'd better be concerned if the nose (or ears, cheeks, fingers or toes) becomes very cold and turns white or yellowish grey. This indicates frostbite, which can cause very serious injury. Frostbitten body parts must be rewarmed immediately. See page 584 for how to do this.

After prolonged exposure to cold weather, a baby's body temperature may drop below normal levels. This is a medical emergency – no time should be wasted in getting a baby who seems unusually cold to the touch all over, even under clothing, to the nearest A&E department. In the meantime, remove wet clothes, wrap baby in warm blankets or any available cloth, give a warming drink, if possible (breast milk, warm formula, warm soup), and keep baby close to your body (for warmth).

Prevent such cold weather emergencies by dressing your baby adequately, protecting exposed areas of skin, and limiting the time your baby spends outdoors in extreme weather.

SNOW BURN

It isn't just the baby tagging along to tropical beaches for the winter holidays who is in danger of suffering a sunburn in winter – a baby enjoying a white Christmas is, too. Since snow reflects up to 85 per cent of the sun's ultraviolet rays, even a weak winter's sun can burn a baby's sensitive skin if it bounces off a snowy landscape first. So be sure to protect your baby's skin with clothing, a brimmed hat and sunscreen whenever you'll be spending a lot of time in sun and snow.

KEEPING BABY WARM INDOORS

In cold weather, baby's room should be kept at between 20° and 22°C (68° and 72°F) by day, and about 20°C (68°F) by night. If indoor temperatures are higher than this, the arid heated air can dry the mucous membranes of the nose, making them more vulnerable to cold germs, and also dry the skin, making it itchy. At night, keep baby toasty with flannel cot sheets, which tend to stay comfortable to the touch even on cold nights. Keep in mind that extra covering (for safety's sake this

should come in the form of fleecy-footed sleeper pyjamas) is needed during sleep when metabolism slows. But try not to make the common mistake of overdressing your baby for bed (and if he or she awakens in the night damp with perspiration, that's what you're doing).

DRY SKIN

Few people of any age are exempt from the dry, itchy skin of winter. Though most people assume that merely protecting babies from the cruel assaults of wind and cold outdoors will keep their skin soft and supple, this isn't so. The major cause of winter dry skin is found indoors, not out. In most homes, once the heating season begins, the indoor air becomes hot and dry. It's this hot, dry air that is a major contributor to skin dryness in winter. You can help counteract this effect in these ways:

Up the moisture in your home. Get a humidifier for your heating system, or at least one for your baby's room. See page 42 for which type to buy.

Up the moisture inside your baby. Babies (and all of us) get moisture for the skin from inside as well as out. Be sure your baby is getting enough fluids.

Up the moisture on baby's skin. Smoothing a good-quality baby lotion on baby's damp skin right after the bath will help retain the moisture. Ask the doctor to recommend a particular product, or select one that is labelled hypoallergenic.

Reduce the soap. Soap is drying. It rarely needs to be used on tiny infants – except once a day in the nappy area. Crawlers may need a sudsing on knees, feet and hands. But in general, use very little soap; particularly avoid using bubble bath or liquid soap to make bubbles in baby's bath, since soapy water is more drying than clear water. Use a gentle soap or moisturizing skin cleanser; ask the doctor for a recommendation.

Turn down the heat. The hotter the house, the drier the air (assuming no humidity is being returned to the air as the house is heated). For babies more than a few weeks old, the home need not be warmer than 20°C (68°F). If baby seems chilled at this temperature, it's better to add layers of clothing rather than degrees of heat.

FIREPLACE FIRES

Before there were televisions, there were fireplaces to draw families together on a cold winter's evening. Even today, a roaring fire can rival whatever prime time has to offer, bringing warmth to both body and spirit. The trick, however, when babies and young children are part of the family circle, is to keep them safe when near the fire. Keep the fireplace covered, even once the fire's out (embers can stay hot for hours), with a screen that's too heavy for even strong and persistent little hands to move. If you can't protect a baby or toddler from hot surfaces with appropriate barriers, then you shouldn't use the fireplace. For added protection, teach your baby early on that fire is 'hot!' and that touching it can cause pain. Be sure, too, that the flue is clear so fumes don't fill the room and you don't start a chimney fire. If baby or other family members have a chronic respiratory condition – such as asthma – consult with the doctor about whether fireplace use may worsen the problem.

CHRISTMAS HAZARDS

Nothing is more wondrous to a young child than a home that's been decked out for Christmas. But if proper precautions aren't taken, nothing can turn out to be more dangerous. Concealed in many idyllic living-room scenes are a host of hazards. All of the following are potential threats to your baby. Some should be used with care, others shouldn't be used at all – at least until your child is older, wiser and less vulnerable.

Mistletoe and Jerusalem cherry. Both of these can be deadly if eaten. Do not bring them into your home or let your baby play near them when visiting.

Holly. This plant is only slightly poisonous (large quantities must be consumed for a baby to suffer serious consequences), but it's wise to keep it out of baby's reach. Christmas cactus is safe, however.

Poinsettia. This holiday beauty can cause local irritation to the mouth, and perhaps serious stomach upset if large quantities are ingested. Keep it out of reach.

Evergreens. A cut tree should be fresh and kept well watered; any dry greens should be discarded to avoid a fire hazard. Artificial trees don't let you off the safety hook entirely: choose one that's labelled 'fire-resistant', and never use electric lights on a metallic tree. Don't allow unsupervised play around a tree; pulling up on a branch could lead to baby pulling down the tree.

Pine needles. Sweep these up regularly, and if possible, keep pine trees, wreaths and branches out of reach of babies and toddlers. Pine needles can cause a persistent croupy cough if they lodge in the trachea; seek medical help if you suspect this.

Snow-scene paperweights. Although the liquid inside these is not poisonous, once broken, it can become contaminated with germs; discard if the paperweight becomes cracked.

Angel hair. This is spun glass, which can irritate skin and eyes and cause internal bleeding if swallowed; use high up and out of baby's reach, if at all.

Artificial snow spray or flocking. These can aggravate a respiratory problem; don't use if anyone in your family has one.

Tree lights. Because young children may bite these enticing ornaments and suffer internal cuts, hang them high out of reach. Keep cords out of reach, too. Be particularly careful with small blinking lights, which contain a chemical that is hazardous if ingested.

Candles. Light them and keep them completely out of baby's reach – and, of course, away from curtains or other flammable materials. Never leave them lit and unsupervised; make sure they're thoroughly extinguished before leaving the house or retiring at night. If you display them in a window, be sure curtains are securely tied back.

Mini-decorations. Very small tree ornaments, tree lights or any items smaller than the diameter of a toilet paper tube (or with parts that small that can be broken or pulled off) can cause choking. Don't use these, or use them only where you're sure baby can't get to them.

Tinsel, glass or plastic ornaments and Styrofoam. All of these decorative items are alluring choking hazards. If a piece is bitten off, it can become stuck in the throat or, depending on what the ornament is made of, cause internal bleeding.

Tree preservatives. If you use these, make sure a curious baby can't dip into the tree container for an unusual – and unhealthy – snack.

Gifts. Sure, the presents you've stacked up for baby are perfectly safe and appropriate for his or her play, but there's a good chance that the gifts you're giving to other family members aren't. So after the unwrapping, be sure all gifts that aren't baby-friendly are stashed out of reach.

Food and drink. It isn't just what sets the scene that can be dangerous; what sets the table can be, too. Every year, hundreds of young children are rushed to A&E after downing a martini, beer or cupful of eggnog or spiked punch left carelessly within their reach. Others choke on olives, nuts, cocktail sausages, hard sweets and other favorite adult nibbles. So play it safe when you're hosting a Christmas party. Be sure that alcoholic drinks or inappropriate edibles aren't left around, even briefly, on coffee or end tables where even moderately active crawlers can get to them. Keep in mind that no matter what the season, certain foods – such as fruitcake that's been soaking in liquor, popcorn, chocolate, nuts and anything containing honey – are off-limits to babies.

UNDER WRAPS

When it comes to holiday gift wrapping, all that glitters isn't necessarily safe. They're festive, but those ribbons, bows, and figurines – and even the wrapping paper – can pose a choking and/or suffocation danger to a curious baby who's exploring under the tree. So keep wrapped gifts – and ripped off wrapping – under wraps, out of baby's reach.

So deck the halls, feast and celebrate with care. But don't stop there. Just in case a mishap should occur in spite of all your precautions, prepare for the holidays by becoming familiar with first-aid and CPR techniques, if you aren't already.

SAFE GIFT GIVING

First on any parent's list when doing Christmas toy shopping should be safety. As tempting as toy stores are at this time of year, resist them until you've completely familiarized yourself with the tips for buying safe and worthwhile playthings for your baby, starting on page 304. Remember, manufacturers can't always be counted on to produce what's best for your baby – particularly during the holiday season you, the buyer, must beware.

What it's Important to Know: THE SEASON FOR TRAVEL

In the days before parenthood, any season was the season for a trip. Summer excursions to a friend's beach house, winter holidays with parents in the Caribbean, whirlwind ski weekends squeezed in between busy work weeks, leisurely tours of Paris in the spring, escape weekends to the Canary Islands when the streets back home were covered with ice, or to the mountains when they were steaming with heat and humidity.

But now what? Considering the effort involved in taking your baby across town on a simple shopping expedition – the hours of planning, the exacting execution, and the 9 kg (20 lb) of baby, equipment, and supplies lugged on your aching shoulders – the logistics of a two-week holiday, or even a two-day trip to grandma's, might seem too overwhelming to consider attempting.

Yet you needn't wait until your children are old enough to carry their own luggage to satisfy your wanderlust or grandma's pleas for a visit. Though holidays with baby will rarely be restful and will always be a challenge, they can be both feasible and enjoyable.

PLANNING AHEAD

The days of spur-of-the-moment weekend getaways, when a restless spirit and a few garments and toiletries flung into an overnight bag took you where you wanted to go, ended abruptly with your baby's arrival. Now you can expect to spend more time planning a trip than taking one. Sensible preparatory steps for any trip with baby include:

Underschedule yourself. Forget itineraries that will take you through six scintillating cities in five whirlwind days. Instead, set a modest pace with plenty of unscheduled time – for an extra day on the road should you end up needing it, an extra afternoon at the beach or morning by the pool should you end up wanting it.

Update passports. You won't be able to take your baby abroad on your passport. These days every traveller, no matter what age, needs his or her own. For information on obtaining a passport for your baby, ask at your local Post Office.

JUST THE TWO OF YOU?

These days, security's tighter than ever, even when it comes to travelling with a baby. If you're taking your child overseas alone, you may need permission in writing from his or her other parent to do so – or proof that you are the sole guardian. Policies vary from country to country (and may even vary from day to day, depending who's on duty at an entry point), so do your homework well before departure day. You should check with the airline you're flying and your travel agent, as well as with the foreign consulate or embassy of the country you'll be travelling to. Bring more than you think you'll need (for instance, have the letter of permission notarized), just in case you're asked for it.

Take medical precautions. If you're going abroad, check with the doctor to be sure baby's immunizations are up-to-date. If you're heading for exotic destinations, ask the doctor if you and your baby may need specific immunizations (against yellow fever, for example) or prophylactic treatments (to prevent hepatitis A and/or malaria). For the latest information on these and other precautions you may need to take before a trip, visit the Department of Health's website at www.doh.gov.uk. Or ask the doctor for a referral to a travel clinic for specific advice about and protection from disease at exotic destinations.

Before taking an extended trip, schedule a well-child checkup if it's been a while since the last one. In addition to providing assurance that your baby's in good health, the visit will give you an opportunity to discuss your proposed trip with the doctor and ask any questions that might otherwise keep you up while you're away – when it may be impossible, or at least impractical, to pick up the phone and call the surgery. If your baby has had a checkup within the previous month, a telephone consultation may be all that's needed.

If your baby takes medication, be sure you have enough for the trip, plus a prescription in case the supply is lost, spilled or otherwise meets with calamity. If a medication needs to be refrigerated, keeping it on ice continuously may be difficult, so ask the doctor if it's possible to substitute another medication that needn't be kept cold. Since a stuffy nose can make a baby miserable, interfere with sleep and cause ear pain when flying, also ask the doctor to recommend a decongestant in case your older baby should come down with a cold. If you are going to a place where 'traveller's stomach' might be a problem, stock up on paediatric rehydration fluids. For any medication you are taking along, be sure you know the safe dosage for a child your baby's age, as well as the conditions under which it should be administered and the possible side effects. Also useful, especially for extended trips: the name of a doctor at your destination or destinations. Of course, you can also call your baby's doctor for medical advice no matter where in the world you are.

Time your trip. What hour of the day or night you begin your journey will depend on, among other things, baby's schedule and how he or she reacts to changes in it, your mode of travel, your destination and how long it will take to get there. If you're travelling west by plane, for example, it might make sense to plan to arrive around baby's bedtime. Assuming a nap has been taken en route, the excitement and chaos of arrival will probably make it possible to keep baby awake a couple of hours past the usual bedtime. This may enable baby to sleep until a relatively respectable 5 or 6 AM rather than rising raring to go at an indecent 3 or 4 AM. (Of course, you will also have to pray trains and planes will be on schedule.)

Consider the advantages of travelling at off-peak times, when there are more likely to be empty seats for your baby to crawl over and fewer fellow passengers who might be disturbed.

If your baby habitually falls asleep in the car and you're planning a long-distance car trip, plan, if possible, to do most of your driving when he or she would ordinarily be asleep – during nap times or at night. Otherwise, you may arrive at your destination with a baby who's slept all day and is ready to play all night. If your baby sleeps well on trains or planes, but is fussy when awake in such confined quarters, coordinate nap time with travel time. But if your baby is always too excited to sleep in such environments, plan to travel after nap time to avoid crankiness during the trip.

It may seem that getting to your destination as quickly as possible makes the most sense. But it doesn't always. For an active baby, for example, a connecting flight with some time to let off steam between legs of the trip may be better than a long non-stop.

Order ahead. When flying, don't plan on feeding even an older baby from a standard airline selection, since the food offered is usually not appropriate for babies. These days, many airlines are cutting costs by cutting back on extras, but you may still be able to place a special order, such as a cottage cheese and fruit platter and wholemeal bread, with your older baby. Even once you've put in your order, however, plan to take along a substantial stash of snacks. When flights are delayed or special

orders go astray (not unheard of these days), long waits between meals can make baby, and everyone else in the vicinity, miserable. For flights on which no meals are served – just those little bags of almonds baby can't dip into – make sure you take along enough food to keep the peace until landing.

Some airlines, particularly on overseas flights, offer baby foods, bottles, nappies and carrycots. Ask about these when you make your reservations.

Arrange for suitable seating. If you're travelling by air, either fly off-peak and have the airline save an empty seat for you, or take advantage of the 50 per cent discount offered for children under two. Bring along baby's rear-facing car seat (make sure it meets approved safety standards), and use it – laps aren't safe during takeoff, landing or turbulence.

An aisle seat for you (so you can pace up and down, when necessary) and a window for the baby (interesting if there are clouds or sunsets to watch) are ideal, but not always possible. Whatever you do, don't accept seats in the middle of a wide-centre section, not just for your sake, but for the sake of those seated around you.

Though you can, and should, reserve space on many trains in this country, you can't reserve specific seats. But you can reserve sleeper compartments on some long-distance runs. Such compartments give you a measure of privacy, something you may really appreciate when spending long hours on a train with a baby.

Book in advance. You may assume that when travelling by road in off-peak seasons, hotel reservations won't be necessary, but this can't always be guaranteed. So plan ahead where you will be stopping overnight, allowing more time to get there than you could ever possibly imagine needing, and reserve a hotel room with a cot (make sure it meets the standards on page 44, or if you can, bring a safe carry cot).

Choose a helpful hostelry. Whenever possible, look for a hotel that caters to the needs of families; many do not. One clue to what you can expect is whether or not cots and baby-sitters are available. You will probably have an uncomfortable stay at a hotel without such amenities. You will probably feel unwelcome, as well.

Equip yourself. Getting around, especially if you're travelling without another adult or with more than one child, will be easier if you have the right equipment:

◆ A baby carrier, if baby is small. It will free your hands to juggle luggage – important when boarding and disembarking. But don't forget to bend at the knees when picking up that collection of bags, so baby doesn't fall out.

◆ A lightweight and very compact buggy, for an older baby. You can hang totes from the handles, but be careful not to let the buggy tip backwards. Most airlines will let you drop off your buggy at the gate right before you step on the plane and will return it at your destination, as soon as you step off the plane.

◆ A portable baby seat – a cloth one adds almost no weight to your luggage.

◆ An safety-approved car seat. You can carry it on and use it in flight when travelling by plane. If you're travelling by train and plan on renting a car at your destination, you can rent a car seat, too – but be sure to reserve the age-appropriate seat at the time you reserve the car.

You can also rent or borrow other equipment, such as cots, playpens, high chairs and feeding seats, at the other end. Try to make these arrangements in advance.

Don't rock the boat before you set sail. To avoid unnecessary problems on your trip, avoid unnecessary changes just before it. Don't try weaning your baby, for instance, just prior to departure – the unfamiliar surroundings and changes in routine will be hard enough to deal with without adding other stresses. Besides, no other way of feeding baby on the road is as easy for you or as comforting for baby as breastfeeding. Don't introduce solids close to departure, either. Beginning to spoonfeed is enough of a challenge (for both of you) at home. If your baby is ready for finger foods, however, consider introducing them pretrip. Portable nibbles are great for keeping babies occupied and happy en route.

If your baby isn't sleeping through the night, now is not the time to try to remedy the situation. There's likely to be some regression into night waking during a trip (and for a while, upon return), and letting baby cry it out in a hotel room or at grandma's will enhance neither your holiday nor your welcome.

Confirm. The day before your departure, confirm all your reservations if they haven't already been confirmed, and call to check departure times before leaving home. You don't want to arrive at the airport to find your flight's been cancelled or delayed four hours, or at the train station to find the train is going to be late.

PACKING WISELY

While virtually everything, including the kitchen sink (for rinsing off dropped bottles and dousing stains), might come in handy on your trip, packing it all would obviously not be advisable. Neither, however, would be starting out perilously underpacked. Instead, strive for a happy (albeit heavy) medium, taking only what you absolutely need, being as efficient as possible in your selection: travel sizes of liquid baby soap, paracetamol or ibuprofen, toothpaste, and the like; the extra-trim and extra-absorbent variety of disposable nappies; mix-and-match clothes in bright patterns that conceal stains well and thus hold out longer between launderings, in lightweight fabrics that will dry fast if you need to rinse them out.

You can pack less if you'll be somewhere where you can fill in the blanks (like a T-shirt from a souvenir shop), but if you'll be hiking in the Dales or camping in Snowdonia, everything that you could conceivably end up needing should end up in your backpack. Keep in mind that airline regulations currently limit the amount of liquids you can carry on the plane. Check out the government's public services website Directgov for up-to-date regulations (www.direct.gov.uk). For the typical trip, you will probably want to pack the following:

A changing bag. It should be lightweight, plastic-lined, have outside compartments for storing tissues, wipes, bottles and other needed-in-a-hurry items, and have a shoulder strap so you won't need to tie up a free hand carrying it. The items you may want to keep handy in the bag include:

◆ A light jacket for baby (waterproof nylon with a hood is best, since it doubles as a raincoat) or sweater in case the car, train, plane or bus is chilly.

◆ Enough disposable, extra-trim, extra-absorbent nappies for the first leg of your journey, and then some more, in case of a delay or a bout of traveller's tummy. Plan on buying nappies as you go rather than carrying cases with you from home, unless you're travelling by car and have the room, or unless you won't be able to purchase them at your destination.

◆ Baby wipes for your hands (and baby's) as well as the obvious. They can also serve to sanitize the arm of the plane seat that baby seems intent on chewing or the train window that he or she is set on licking clean and to outsmart spills on clothing or upholstery before they set into stains.

◆ Nappy rash ointment or cream, since unfamiliar foods, fewer nappy changes and warm weather can all prompt an outbreak of nappy rash.

◆ A large waterproof bib, or a pack of disposable ones, to protect clothing. Just in case you accidentally leave the plastic bib in a restaurant or run out of throwaways, bring along a safety pin with which to fasten a restaurant napkin over baby's clothes.

◆ Some reclosable plastic bags to hold leaky bottles, dirty bibs or clothing, and soiled nappies when a dustbin isn't immediately available.

◆ Sunscreen, if your destination will be sunny or snowy.

◆ A light blanket or quilt for baby to nap on or play on en route and in homes that you visit. Or take along a shawl you can wear on your shoulders and use for baby when necessary.

◆ A small waterproof lap pad or changing pad to protect hotel beds and other surfaces when baby needs a change.

◆ A comfort object, if your baby has one (and maybe an extra, in case you lose it).

◆ A pair of socks or booties for a barefoot baby, in case you run into some heavy air-conditioning.

◆ Plastic socket covers if your baby is a crawler or walker, to babyproof hotel rooms or homes you're visiting. You may also want to take a toilet lock if your baby is into water play. (Some hotel chains offer babyproofing kits.)

◆ A generous supply of snacks and beverages. Don't rely on being able to find appropriate food for your baby on the road, in the air or on the rails. Bring along enough food and drink for one or two more meals than you anticipate feeding, just in case. Depending on baby's culinary repertoire, take along baby food (dehydrated, if you must travel light); whole-grain crackers; small containers of bite-size dry cereal for nibbling; ready-to-use formula for the bottle baby in disposable bottles; watered-down juice in a small bottle or thermos with a cup (if there's a favourite sippy cup in your baby's life, bring that, too). Carry the 85-g (3-oz) baby food jars to provide variety and avoid waste.

◆ Plastic spoons stashed in a plastic bag, for feeding baby en route.

◆ Paper towels, unrolled, which are more practical, stronger and usually more absorbent than napkins.

◆ Something old and something new to entertain your baby – the old for comfort and reliability; the new for excitement and challenge. A small activity board and a brightly illustrated board book are good choices for an older baby; a mirror, rattle and a musical stuffed animal for a younger one. Leave at home toys with a lot of pieces that can get lost or which are too bulky for easy packing and use in tight spaces – as well as toys that make noise (and headaches). For a teether, be sure to take a couple of items to gnaw on.

◆ A small purse. Since you have a limited number of hands, carrying a separate handbag will be virtually impossible as well as a little risky (you'll most likely look distracted and disorganized enough to qualify as easy prey for a pickpocket). Instead, keep personal items, plane, train or bus tickets, and your wallet, with ID, money, credit cards, medical insurance information and copies of medication prescriptions, as well as baby's doctor's phone number and the names of recommended doctors at your destination, in a small, easy-to-identify-by-feel purse in the changing bag. Or, as an alternative, keep your wallet handy in your pocket (if all of your travel outfits have safe, deep pockets, you'll find life much easier).

◆ A mobile phone, to use in case of emergencies, medical or otherwise.

◆ If you still have room (and motivation), a square metre of clear heavy-duty plastic to protect hotel furniture and rugs during feedings, and to serve as unobtrusive protection under baby's high chair in restaurants.

A bag for baby's clothing. Ideal for baby's travel wardrobe is a small, lightweight, soft-sided carry-on with a shoulder or backpack strap. Since it can be kept handy in car, plane or train, you'll be able to get at a fresh outfit without any fuss and without rummaging through your own suitcase in public. If you choose to pack baby's clothes in your suitcase, however, and that bag won't be available while you're travelling (because it's going to be either checked through on the plane, train or bus, or buried in the car trunk), make sure you keep an extra outfit or two for baby in the changing bag.

A medical and toiletry bag. This bag should be inaccessible to a curious baby at all times (in overhead compartments on trains and planes, for example), and should preferably be difficult for a child to open. Ideally, it should have a waterproof and washable interior as well as a shoulder strap. Keep this bag with you as you go so that medications will be available, if needed, and to protect liquids from damage by freezing in the cargo compartment of planes. It can contain:

♦ Any prescription medicines and vitamins to last your trip; baby paracetamol or ibuprofen; any other medication recommended by the doctor.

♦ For outdoor trips, insect repellent, calamine lotion, bug-bite medicine and a bee-sting kit if baby is allergic.

♦ A first-aid kit containing plasters and self-adhesive gauze pads; antiseptic cream; elastic bandages for sprains; thermometer; tweezers; baby nail clipper.

♦ Liquid baby soap, which serves as a cleanser for both hair and skin. The soaps found in hotel rooms aren't usually gentle enough for babies.

♦ Baby's toothbrush, finger brush or gauze pads for tooth wiping, if teeth are in.

♦ Multipurpose pocketknife, with can opener and scissors (but don't try to carry this on an aeroplane; it will be confiscated).

♦ A night-light, if your baby likes to sleep with one.

GETTING THERE IS HALF THE FUN?

Not likely. But you can at least try to ensure that it will be half the hassle. Whether you will be going by land, air or rail, there are several ways of making your trip easier.

If you're flying. Planes have the advantage for family travel of usually being the fastest commercial way of getting from one point to another. You can make a flying trip pleasant (at least relatively so) as well as comfortable, if you:

♦ Consider requesting bulkhead seats. They offer more leg and manoeuvring room and privacy, though less storage space for changing bags etc. Another plus is: no seat in front of yours for baby to bang on; no passengers in front of you for baby to annoy.

♦ Arrive early enough to take care of preboarding details like luggage and seats, and to get through security screenings, but not so early that you have an uncomfortably long wait in the air terminal.

♦ Preboarding is an advantage offered on some airlines to those travelling with children, allowing them to settle in and stow luggage in overhead compartments before the rush. However, if you have a baby who you expect will be fidgety in close quarters (remember, you won't be able to walk the aisles while they're being used for boarding), you may want to wait and board last. If you're travelling with another adult, ask if one of you can board with the luggage while the other spends some extra time with baby in the open spaces of the waiting area.

- Coordinate feedings with takeoff and landing. Children are more prone than adults to the ear pressure, and sometimes pain, caused by cabin-air-pressure changes during ascent and descent. Bottle feeding (with expressed breast milk or formula) or offering finger foods or a dummy encourages frequent swallowing, which helps prevent the painful pressure buildup and the crying that usually accompanies it. Nursing isn't practical during these times, since baby should be buckled up for safety's sake.

- If your baby does do a lot of loud complaining, accept a kind hand from friendly fellow passengers if offered, and disregard those who give you dirty looks.

- Give your baby a lot to drink during the flight; air travel is dehydrating. If you're nursing, be sure you, too, take extra fluids – but remember, beverages with caffeine or alcohol don't count.

- If your baby prefers warmed feedings, you can ask flight attendants if it's possible for them to warm bottles and baby food for you (without their tops). But remember to shake or stir thoroughly and to carefully double-check the temperature before serving to prevent scalding accidents, since microwaves can heat unevenly. Keep in mind, too, that on busy flights, attendants may not be able to help you out with these services.

- If you're travelling alone, feel free to ask an attendant to hold baby while you use the lavatory – but try to wait until service has been completed.

- Deplane last, to avoid the squeeze and to be sure you have time to gather up all your belongings. (Let anyone who is meeting you know that you will be last off the plane.)

If you're going by train. Travelling by train, though slower than by plane, allows children a little more mobility. Your family train trip will be easier if you remember to:

- Board as early as possible to find a plum seat. A good choice is the four-seater unit at either end of most cars, which allows families to spread out comfortably. If the train is crowded because you'll be travelling at peak time and your trip is long, it may make sense to buy a seat for your baby. If you have only one seat, it's a toss-up whether to favour the window seat (so baby can watch the scenery go by) or the aisle (so you can get up frequently for walks if baby is fidgety).

- Be sure to have a baby carrier if you're travelling alone and baby can still ride in one; without it you may find it impossible to go to the bathroom. (Don't park your baby even briefly with any stranger, no matter how friendly.)

- If your train ride will be a long one, have a varied collection of toys so you can pull out a new one when your baby tires of the old. Or do some sightseeing. Looking out of the window, pointing out cars, horses, cows, dogs, people, houses, sky and clouds, is an onboard activity that has saved many a parent at the bottom of his or her bag of tricks.

- Be sure to have plenty of snacks on hand for you and baby. Queues for food on trains are often long, and it would not be unusual to finally reach the buffet counter only to find that the chicken sandwich you were counting on was sold out.

AT HIGH ALTITUDES

If you're heading to an area high above sea level, there are certain precautions that need to be taken. Because the sun's rays are more intense at higher altitudes, you need to be particularly conscientious about using sunscreens and limiting sun exposure. Because fluid requirements are increased, your older baby will need additional fruit juice or water daily while you remain at the higher altitude.

In a baby who is anaemic, the reduced level of oxygen in the air may increase heart and respiratory rates and cause fatigue. This is nothing to be concerned about unless your baby has an infection or other medical condition, such as a heart ailment – in which case you should consult the doctor before making the trip. But do schedule frequent rest stops.

If you're driving. Driving is slower than other forms of transport, more taxing on you if you're the driver, and most confining to baby. But it does give you the luxury of going at your own pace, stopping when and where you'd like, and having ready transport at your destination. Make family car travel safer, more pleasant and more comfortable in these ways:

◆ Be sure that there are seat belts for all adults and older children, car seats for younger ones, and that the car never moves until all are safely secured and all doors locked (see pages 132–133 for more on car seat safety).

◆ Take frequent breaks (every two hours or so is ideal), since babies become restless sitting in car seats for very long stretches. When you do stop, take baby out for some fresh air, and if he or she's mobile, a crawl or walk. Use rest stops for nursing, too.

◆ Alternate roles. For a change of pace and companionship for everyone, alternate driving with sitting in the back entertaining baby.

◆ Attach playthings to baby's car seat with plastic links (or strings no longer than 15 cm/6 in so that you won't have to unbelt repeatedly to retrieve tossed toys.

◆ If you're driving in cold weather, especially if a storm is predicted, bring along extra clothing and blankets in case you get stranded. A car can quickly turn into a deadly icebox in subfreezing temperatures.

◆ Never leave a baby in a parked car in hot or even warm weather. Even with the windows open, the car can rapidly become a deadly oven. For that matter, never leave a baby or child in a car alone – no matter what the weather.

AT HOTELS OR OTHER HOMES AWAY FROM HOME

The first overnighter away from home with your baby can be a little unnerving. But you'll all sleep better if you take the following precautions:

◆ Upon arrival at your destination, do a safety check of the room you'll be staying in – especially if your baby is mobile. Some family-friendly hotel chains offer childproofing kits; otherwise you may have to bring your own equipment. Be sure open windows, electrical cords, glasses and so on (see pages 403–408) aren't accessible. Cap exposed sockets and keep the bathroom door closed. Check the cot for safety (see page 401). If there's a minibar in the room, either ask that it be emptied or make sure it's securely locked.

◆ If you put baby on the bed for a nappy change or play, use a waterproof pad – to protect the bed from baby and baby from a probably unsanitary bedspread.

◆ When you're feeding baby in the room, spread newspaper or a plastic square on the floor to protect carpeting – for courtesy's sake, and so you won't be stuck for damages.

◆ Don't confine an active baby. Crawling under your supervision is okay unless the carpet is visibly dirty; exploratory toddling is fine, too, but again under a watchful adult eye. Be sure to do a thorough check under the bed to make sure there are no hazardous (or unsanitary) objects lurking beneath.

◆ Arrange for baby-sitters through the hotel. Most hotels and resorts offer some type of baby-sitting. But what they offer can vary wildly. It might be a hotel chambermaid looking to make some extra cash; it might be a list of phone numbers of baby-sitting agencies in the area (you're on your own to call and hire); or it might be an onsite child-care programme (most common with big resorts that cater to families). Treat any baby-sitter on the road as you would on your home turf: interview the person (or at least the service), if possible, and make sure any baby-sitter you hire has been vetted. Meet them at the concierge's desk, so you'll be sure you've got the right person.

HAVING FUN

You've planned, you've packed, you've lugged and you've travelled. Now it's time to have fun. Here are some general guidelines for ensuring a bon voyage with baby:

◆ Be realistic about the itinerary. You just won't be able to keep up the same pace with a baby in tow as you would on a trip for adults only. Overschedule, and you'll end up underenjoying.

◆ Be flexible about the itinerary. If you'd planned to drive straight through from London to Edinburgh, but baby's had it with the car seat by York, consider adding an overnight stop. If you've scheduled two days of sightseeing in Athens, but baby's crankiness is ruining the ruins for all of you by the first morning, postpone the Parthenon until another day.

◆ Stick to sites where baby won't be confined or required to be silent for long periods of time. Outdoor monuments, parks, zoos and even some museums can be interesting to babies and young children – even if they spend most of their time just looking at other people. Hire a baby-sitter, if possible, when you want to go to the opera, a concert or the theatre.

◆ Remember whose needs must come first – if anyone's going to have a good time. If baby doesn't nap or eat on time, or is repeatedly subjected to uncustomarily late bedtimes, everyone will suffer the consequences. In fact, the only schedule you shouldn't be flexible about is baby's. Do what the Romans do, by all means, but only if your baby can adjust easily.

◆◆◆

CHAPTER 18

When Baby is Sick

There's nothing quite as pathetic, vulnerable and helpless-looking as a sick baby. With the exception of a sick baby's parents.

An infant's illness, even a mild one, usually hits mummy and daddy harder than it does baby, especially when it's a first illness in a first child. There's the anxiety when the initial symptoms appear, the alarm when they seem to worsen or others develop, the indecision over whether or not to call the doctor and when (children almost invariably get sick in the middle of the night or on weekends, outside of usual surgery hours), the pacing while waiting for the doctor's callback (interminable, even if it's only fifteen minutes), the ordeal of administering medicine, and the worry, worry, worry.

Believe it or not, things do get better. With experience, parents learn to handle a feverish infant or a vomiting baby with less panic and more self-assurance. To reach that point more quickly, it will help to learn how to evaluate symptoms, how to take and interpret a baby's temperature, what to feed a sick child, what the most common childhood illnesses are, and how to recognize and handle a real emergency.

Before Calling the Doctor

Most doctors want to hear from you if you think your baby is really sick – no matter what the time of day or night. But before you dial that probably already familiar number, be sure you're armed with a written list of all the information your baby's doctor might need to know in order to accurately assess the situation.

Start with symptoms. In most simple illnesses, only two or three symptoms will be present – in some cases, maybe just one – but running down the list that follows will ensure you haven't missed anything. Be prepared to tell the doctor when symptoms first appeared; what, if anything, triggered them; what exacerbates or alleviates them (keeping baby upright reduces the coughing, for example, or eating increases vomiting); and which home remedies or over-the-counter medications you've tried treating them with. It will also be helpful to let the doctor know if your baby

PARENT'S INTUITION

Sometimes you can't put your finger on any specific symptom, but your baby just doesn't seem 'right' to you. Put a call in to the doctor. Most likely you'll be reassured, but it's also possible that your parent's intuition will have picked up something subtle that needs attention.

has been exposed to a cousin with chicken pox, a sibling with diarrhoea, or anyone else with a communicable illness, if he or she has recently been injured, as in a fall, or has been recently sick. And don't assume baby's notes are in the doctor's hand. Mention baby's age, any chronic medical problems and any medications he or she is taking.

Have handy the name and phone number of an open pharmacy in case the doctor needs to phone in a prescription, and a pad and pen for jotting down any instructions you receive.

Temperature. The old lips-on-the-forehead technique for checking for fever is notoriously unreliable (though more reliable than a hand), especially if you've had a cold or hot drink recently or if you've just come in from the heat or the cold. While you might consider screening for fever this way (particularly if you're not near a thermometer; keeping in mind the method is more likely to be accurate in the absence of fever than in its presence), don't rely on it for accurate readings. Instead, turn to a thermometer if you suspect a fever in your baby (see page 567). Remember that in addition to illness, readings can be affected by such factors as room or air temperature (a baby's temperature is likely to be higher after spending the morning in an overheated apartment than after coming in from the snow);

level of activity (exercise, energetic play and vigorous crying can all raise temperature); and time of day (temperatures tend to be higher later in the day). If baby's forehead is cool, assume there's no significant fever.

Heart rate. In some cases, knowing what your baby's heart rate is may be useful to the doctor. If your baby seems very lethargic or has a fever, take the upper arm (or brachial) pulse (see illustration, page 536). The normal range in infants is much higher than it is for older children and adults, between 120 and 140 beats per minute when baby is awake (though the rate can go as low as 70 beats per minute when baby is asleep, and higher than 170 when he or she is crying).

Respiration. If your baby has difficulty breathing, is coughing, or seems to be breathing rapidly or irregularly, check respirations by counting how many times in a minute his or her chest rises and falls. Breathing is more rapid during activity (including crying) than during sleep, and may be speeded up or slowed down by illness. Newborns normally take about 40 to 60 breaths per minute; one-year-olds only 25 to 35. If your baby's chest doesn't seem to rise and fall with each breath, or if breathing appears laboured or raspy (unrelated to a stuffy nose), report that information to the doctor, too.

Respiratory symptoms. Is your baby's nose runny? Stuffy? Is the discharge watery or thick? Clear, white, yellow or green? Is there a cough? Does it seem dry, hacking, heavy, crowing? Does the cough bring up any mucus? (Sometimes mucus will be brought up with a forceful cough.) Is baby wheezing (a whistling sound, mostly on breathing out)? Does he or she have stridor (a grunting sound from below the voice box)?

Practise taking the brachial pulse when your baby is healthy and calm.

Behaviour. Is there any change from the norm in your baby's behaviour? Would you describe your child as tired and lethargic, cranky and irritable, inconsolable or unresponsive? Or is baby his or her usual jolly self? Can you elicit a smile (if baby has started smiling already)?

Sleeping. Is baby unusually drowsy or sleeping much more than usual? Or is he or she having trouble sleeping?

Crying. Is baby crying more than usual? Does the cry have a different sound or intensity – is it high-pitched, for instance?

Appetite. Is baby eating as usual? Refusing the breast or bottle and/or turning down solids? Or eating normally?

Skin. Does baby's skin appear different in any way? Is it red and flushed? White and pale? Bluish or grey? Is it moist and warm (sweaty) or moist and cool (clammy)? Or unusually dry? Are lips, nostrils or cheeks excessively dry or cracking? Are there spots or lesions anywhere on baby's skin – under the arms, behind the ears, on limbs or trunk, or elsewhere? How would you

describe their colour, shape, size, texture? Does baby seem to be trying to scratch them?

Mouth. Is there swelling on the gums where teeth might be trying to break through? Any red or white spots or patches visible on the gums, inside the cheeks, or on the palate or tongue?

Throat. Is the arch framing the throat reddened? Are there white or red spots or patches?

Fontanel. Is the soft spot on top of your baby's head sunken or bulging?

Eyes. Do baby's eyes look different than usual? Are they glassy, vacant, sunken, dull, watery or reddened? Do they have dark circles under them, or seem partially closed? If there is a discharge, how would you describe the colour, consistency and quantity?

Ears. Is baby pulling or poking at one or both ears? Is there a discharge from either ear?

Digestive system. Has baby been vomiting? How often? Is there a lot of material being vomited, or are baby's heaves mostly dry? How would you describe the vomitus (like curdled milk, mucus-streaked, pinkish, bloody?) Is the vomiting forcible? Does it seem to project a long distance? Does anything seem to trigger the vomiting – eating, for example? Has there been any change in baby's bowel movements? Is there diarrhoea, with loose, watery mucus or bloody stools? Are movements more frequent, sudden and forceful? Or does baby seem constipated? Is there an increase or decrease in saliva? Or any apparent difficulty swallowing?

Urinary system. Are baby's nappies less wet than usual? Or do they seem wetter? Is there any noticeable change in odour or colour (dark yellow, for example, or pink)?

Abdomen. Does your baby's tummy seem different in any way – flatter, rounder, more bulging? When you press it gently, or when you bend either knee to the abdomen, does baby seem to be in pain? Where does the pain seem to be – right side or left, upper or lower abdomen?

Motor symptoms. Has your baby had, or is he or she having, chills, trembling, stiffness or convulsions? Does the neck seem to be stiff or difficult to move; can the chin be bent to the chest? Does there seem to be any difficulty in moving any other part of the body?

How Much Rest for a Sick Baby?

Babies have a lot to learn, but when it comes to their own bodies, they can often teach their parents a thing or two. You can trust your baby to tell you how much rest he or she needs during an illness, not in words, naturally, but in actions. A very sick infant will give up the usual daily pursuits in favour of needed rest, whereas one who is just mildly ill or on the way to recovery will be active and playful. In either case, there's no need to impose restrictions of your own. Just follow baby's lead. (If anyone needs a rest when a baby's sick, it's the parent.)

Feeding a Sick Baby

Loss of appetite often accompanies illness. Sometimes, as in the case of digestive upsets, that's good, since an eating slowdown gives the stomach and intestines a break while they recover. Sometimes, as when there's a fever, it's not so good, since decreased appetite means baby's not getting the additional calories needed to fuel the fever that fights the infection.

For most minor illnesses that don't affect the digestive system, no special diet is necessary (except as noted under specific illnesses). But several general rules apply when feeding any sick baby:

Stress fluids. If your baby has a fever, a respiratory infection (such as a cold,

influenza or bronchitis), or a gastrointestinal illness with diarrhoea, fluids – which help prevent dehydration – should take precedence over solids. Babies on breast milk or formula alone should suckle as often as they like, unless the doctor recommends otherwise. Older babies can also be given clear fluids and foods with high water content (juices, juicy fruits, soups, gels and frozen-juice desserts, if they've been introduced). Offer fluids frequently throughout the day, even if baby takes no more than a sip at a time. Rehydration fluids may be recommended by the doctor if there has been a lot of diarrhoea or vomiting and/or if baby seems to be dehydrated.

Play favourites. When you're sick, certain foods appeal, others don't. Be especially respectful of your baby's tastes when his or her appetite has been rendered tender by illness. If that means nothing but breast milk or formula and bananas for four days, that's okay.

Don't force. Even if your baby hasn't taken a bite in twenty-four hours, don't force. Babies tend to take what they need when they need it. Once your baby recovers from the illness, his or her appetite is sure to recover, too. In fact, babies usually make up for missed meals big-time after they've been sick, eating ravenously and quickly regaining lost weight. Do let the doctor know about this loss of appetite, however.

When Medication is Needed

Few babies manage to get through their first year without coming down with an illness or condition that requires medication. Whether that medication is prescribed or recommended by your baby's doctor, you'll need to know a lot more than which chemist to pick it up at. To make sure your baby gets the right treatment, you'll have to ask the right questions.

WHAT YOU SHOULD KNOW ABOUT THE MEDICATION

Either the doctor or the pharmacist (or the drug insert that the pharmacy supplies with the medication) will be able to answer the following questions. Since you'll be likely taking the information in while holding a crying baby (and/or at 3 AM, in a sleep-deprived haze), don't rely on your memory. Jot the responses down so you'll be able to refer to them later.

♦ What is the generic name of the drug? The brand name, if any?

♦ What is it supposed to do?

♦ What is the appropriate dose for your baby? (Be ready with your baby's approximate weight so that, if necessary, the doctor can calculate the dose accordingly.)

♦ How often should the medication be given; should baby be awakened in the middle of the night for it?

♦ Should it be taken before, with or after meals?

♦ Should it be washed down only with certain liquids and not with others?

♦ What common side effects may be expected?

♦ What possible adverse reactions could occur? Which should be reported to the doctor? (Remind the doctor of any previous reactions.)

♦ If your child has a chronic medical condition, might the drug have an undesirable effect on it? (Be sure to remind the prescribing doctor of the condition, since he or she may not have your baby's notes to hand.)

♦ If your child is taking any other medication, could there be any adverse interaction?

- How soon can you expect to see an improvement?

- When should you contact the doctor if there is no improvement?

- When can the medication be discontinued?

GIVING MEDICATION CORRECTLY

Medicines are meant to cure or relieve symptoms, but when used improperly, they can do more harm than good. Always observe these rules when giving medication:

- Don't give a baby under three months of age any medication (not even an over-the-counter one) not prescribed for him or her by a doctor.

- Don't use a drug if its expiration date has passed, or if it has changed in texture, colour or odour. Wrap expired medicines securely and place them in the dustbin.

- Measure medications meticulously according to the directions the baby's doctor has given you, or according to label directions on over-the-counter products. Use a calibrated spoon, dropper, plastic oral syringe or special cup (all are usually available from your pharmacy) to get precise measurements; kitchen spoons are variable, so you're better off not using them.

- Keep a record of the time each dose is given so you will always know when you gave the last dose. This will minimize the risk of missing a dose or doubling up accidentally. (Since infants tend to keep drugs in their systems longer than older children or adults, the medication in their systems can quickly build up to an overdose level.) But don't worry about being a little late with a dose; get back on schedule with the next dose.

- Check the bottle label for care and storage directions, and follow them. Some medicines need to be stored in the refrigerator or at cool temperatures, and some must be shaken before use.

- If directions on the label conflict with the doctor's instructions and/or those received from the pharmacist, call the pharmacist or doctor to resolve the conflict *before* giving the medication.

- Always read the label before giving a medication, even when you're sure you have the right bottle. If it's dark in the room, check the label in the light first.

- Don't give medicines prescribed for someone else (even a sibling) to your baby without the doctor's approval. Don't use even a medicine previously prescribed for your baby without the doctor's okay.

- Don't administer medication to a baby who is lying down; this could cause choking. Instead, elevate your infant's head slightly, or sit your older baby up.

- Don't put medicine in a bottle of juice or formula unless your doctor recommends it. Your child may not consume the whole bottle and won't get the entire medication dose. Also, some medications become less effective when mixed with the acid in juices.

- Always give antibiotics for the prescribed length of time, unless the doctor advises otherwise, even if your baby seems completely recovered.

♦ If your baby is having an adverse reaction to a medication, stop it temporarily and check with the doctor right away.

♦ Don't continue giving a medicine beyond the time specified by the doctor; don't start giving one again after discontinuing it without checking with the doctor first.

♦ Record any medication you give your baby, the illness it was given for, the length of time it was taken, and any side or adverse effects in your baby's health history for future reference (see page 558).

HELPING THE MEDICINE GO DOWN

Learning how to give medication correctly is only the first step for parents, and usually the easiest. Actually giving it is another story. As far as many children are concerned, the cure is almost always worse than the illness, and without their cooperation, getting the medicine down can be a dreaded ordeal. And even when medicine does go down, it often comes right back up – all over baby, parent, furniture and floor.

If you're lucky, your baby will be one of those few who delight in the medicine-giving ritual and even in the strange, syrupy taste of vitamins, antibiotics or pain relievers – and who opens up like a little sparrow at the first sight of a medicine dropper. If you're not so lucky (and, unfortunately, the odds are against you here), you'll have an infant who clamps down tight when presented with a dose of anything. There is probably nothing that will make administering

medicine to such a baby a pleasure, but these tips will help get more medicine down with less trouble:

♦ Unless you're instructed to give the medication with or after meals, plan on serving it up just before feeding. Firstly, because baby is more likely to accept it when hungry, and, secondly, because if baby does vomit it right back up, less food will be lost.

♦ Chill the medication if this won't affect its potency (ask your pharmacist); the taste may be less pronounced when it's cold.

♦ Ask the pharmacy if they can mask the bad taste of a medication with a flavouring. (Keep in mind that any medication should be kept safely out of baby's reach, but especially one that baby loves the taste of.)

♦ Ask the pharmacist for a medicine spoon or plastic syringe, which will allow you to squirt the medicine deep into baby's mouth; but don't squirt more than a baby can swallow at one time. If your baby rejects medication from a dropper, spoon or syringe and likes a teat instead, try putting the dose in a bottle teat or medicine dummy so baby can suck it out. Follow this with water from the same teat so any medication remaining in the teat can be rinsed out in the baby's mouth.

♦ Aim a spoon towards the back of the mouth, a dropper or syringe between molars or rear gum and cheek, since the taste buds are concentrated at the front and centre on the tongue (and the trick here is to avoid them as much as possible). But avoid letting the dropper or spoon touch the back of the tongue, where it could set off a gagging reflex.

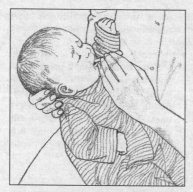

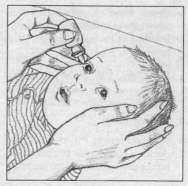

Use a medicine spoon or dropper to ease medications into baby's mouth.

Keeping baby's head steady when using eye drops will help ensure that at least some of the medicine will hit its mark.

♦ As a last resort, mix the medication with a small amount (1 or 2 teaspoons) of strained fruit or fruit juice, but only if the doctor or pharmacist hasn't ruled out such a mix. Don't dilute the medicine in too large a quantity of food or juice because then your baby may not finish it all. Unless your baby is generally tentative about new foods, use an unfamiliar fruit or juice for mixing, since the medicine may impart an unpleasant taste to a familiar one, causing baby to reject it in the future.

♦ Paracetamol that comes in 'sprinkle caps', is tasteless, and can be emptied into a spoonful of juice or fruit can make giving this medicine much easier.

♦ Enlist help when you can. Holding a wriggly, uncooperative baby while trying to bring a spoon filled to the brim with medicine to an unwilling mouth would be a challenge even for an octopus parent, and can sometimes be next to impossible for the two-armed variety. If your spouse (or another assistant) isn't around to hold baby, try using an infant seat or a high chair as your extra pair of hands; but be sure to strap your baby in before you begin.

If you have to go it alone with no seat to hold baby, try this procedure with a young medicine resister: first, premeasure the medicine and have it ready to use on a table within reach in a dropper, syringe, medicine cup or medicine spoon (which shouldn't be filled to the brim). Sit in a straight chair and position baby on your lap, facing forward. Put your left arm across baby's body, holding his or her arms securely. Take hold of his or her jaw with your left hand, your thumb on one cheek, your index finger on the other. Tilt baby's head backwards slightly and depress cheeks gently to open the mouth. With your right hand (reverse hands if you're left-handed), administer the medicine. Keep baby's cheeks slightly depressed until the medicine is swallowed. Speed is essential to the success of this manoeuvre; should it take longer than a few seconds, your baby will begin to fight being held down.

- Gently blow on your baby's face when giving the medicine. It will trigger the swallowing reflex in young babies.

- If any liquid leaks out of your baby's mouth, use your finger to push it back in. Your baby will likely suck the rest off your finger.

- If every dose is a battle, ask the doctor if it's possible to prescribe a higher concentration of the medicine or a different medication that requires fewer doses per day.

- Approach your baby confidently with medicine – even if past experience has taught you to expect the worst. If baby knows you're anticipating a battle, you're sure to get one. You may get one anyway, of course, but a confident approach could swing the odds in your favour.

The Most Common Infant Health Problems

Infants in their first year of life are generally healthy, and most of the illnesses to which they are susceptible are one-time affairs (see the chart starting on page 766 for details on these). But there are some illnesses that are so common, or that tend to recur so frequently in some babies, that parents need to know as much as possible about them. They include allergies, the common cold, constipation, ear infections, and gastro-intestinal illnesses with diarrhoea and vomiting.

ALLERGIES

Symptoms: Depend on the organ or system inflamed by the hypersensitivity. The following are common body systems affected, and the related symptoms and conditions:

- The upper respiratory tract: runny nose (allergic rhinitis), sinusitis (though not in infants), earache (otitis media), sore throat (as much the result of mouth breathing of dry air as from allergy), postnasal discharge (a dripping of mucus at the back of the nose into the throat that can trigger a chronic cough), spasmodic croup. When swelling occurs in the throat, breathing can be hampered.

- The lower respiratory tract: allergic bronchitis, asthma.

- The digestive tract: watery, sometimes bloody diarrhoea; vomiting; gassiness.

- The skin: atopic dermatitis, including such itchy rashes as eczema (see page 321), hives (blotchy, itchy, raised red rash) and facial oedema (swelling of the face, particularly around eyes and mouth, which is not as itchy as hives).

- The eyes: itching, redness, watering and other signs of allergic conjunctivitis.

Season: Any time of year for most allergies; spring, summer or autumn for those related to pollens.

HAVING A PET IS NOTHING TO SNEEZE AT

To minimize the risk of developing an allergy to pets, parents and doctors have long believed that babies born to a family with a history of allergies should keep their distance from pets – which meant that these children grew up with Spot in their books, but not in their homes. However, a growing body of evidence now suggests that having pets in the home may actually protect children from pet allergies. Researchers have found that babies who live with cats or dogs from the first year of their life are less likely to show a pet allergy by the age of seven. And two or more pets in the home appear to protect even better than one.

Since researchers don't yet know why having a pet seems to protect children from developing allergies, it's not likely that doctors are going to issue a general 'buy a pet' recommendation to families with allergy histories any time soon. And keep in mind, too, that although having a pet or two might prevent young children from developing allergies, flying fur can definitely bring on sneezes and wheezes in any family member who already has an allergy – in which case you *will* need to keep Fido in the doghouse.

Cause: The release of histamine and other substances by the immune system in response to exposure to an allergen in babies who are hypersensitive to the allergen or a similar one (the sensitization occurs at an earlier exposure). The tendency towards allergy runs in families. The way allergy is manifested is often different in different members of the family – one has hay fever, another asthma and a third breaks out in hives upon eating strawberries.

Method of transmission: Inhalation (of pollen or animal dander, for example), ingestion (of milk or egg whites), injection (penicillin shot or insect sting) or contact (laundry soaps, paint) with the allergen.

Duration: Variable. The duration of a single allergic episode may vary from a few minutes to several hours or several days. Some allergies, such as an allergy to cow's milk, are outgrown; others change, as children get older, from one kind of allergy to another. Many allergic people have allergies of one kind or another all their lives.

Treatment: The most successful treatment for allergy, though also often the most difficult, is to remove the offending allergen from the sufferer's life. Here are some ways in which you can remove allergens from your child's environment, whether your child is definitely allergic (difficult to determine since skin tests are not very accurate in children under eighteen months) or only possibly so:

♦ Food allergens (see *Dietary changes,* page 545).

♦ Pollens. Pollen allergy is rare in infants, but if you and the doctor suspect pollen allergy (the clue is the persistence of symptoms as long as pollen is in the air, and their disappearance when it is gone), keep your child indoors most of the time when the pollen count is high or when it is particularly windy during pollen season (spring, late summer or autumn, depending on the type of pollen), give daily baths and shampoos (to remove pollen), and use an air-conditioner in warm weather rather than opening the windows and admitting the pollen. If you have a pet, the animal can also pick up pollen when outdoors, so you should bathe him or her frequently, too.

- Pet dander. Sometimes pets themselves cause an allergy. If this is the case, or might be, try to keep your animal and your baby in different rooms, or keep the animal outside. (In severe cases, the only solution may be to find the pet another home.) Since horsehair can also trigger allergy, don't buy a horsehair mattress for your baby's cot.

- Dust mites. These microscopic critters are no problem for most people, but for someone with a hypersensitivity to mites, it can mean misery. Limit your baby's exposure, even if you just suspect this allergy, by keeping the rooms he or she lives in as dust-free as possible.

Dust often with a damp cloth or furniture spray when baby is not in the room, vacuum rugs and upholstered furniture and damp-mop floors often; avoid chenille bedspreads, carpeting, curtains, and other dust catchers where baby sleeps and plays; wash stuffed toys frequently; keep clothing in plastic garment bags; put filters over hot-air vents; install an air filter. You can also buy a vacuum or air cleaner with a high-efficiency particulate arresting (HEPA) filter to trap dust mites and other allergens. Any curtains, throw rugs or other such items you do have should be washed at least twice a month, or packed away. Since dust mites survive on moisture from the air, keep humidity low.

- Moulds. Control moisture in your home by using a well-maintained dehumidifier, providing adequate ventilation, and by venting steam from your kitchen, laundry, and baths. Areas where moulds are likely to grow (dustbins, refrigerators, shower curtains, bathroom tiles, damp corners)

IS IT AN ALLERGY – OR JUST INTOLERANCE?

Sit down at a dinner party these days, and you might get the impression that the rate of food allergies has reached epidemic proportions. Between those who decline the soup ('dairy') to those who beg off on the bread ('wheat'), more and more diners are passing on foods they believe they're 'allergic' to. But the fact is that true food allergies involving the immune system are relatively uncommon. Most food 'allergies' are really sensitivities or intolerances to a food. Here's the difference: someone with an allergy to a food must avoid it completely (especially when the allergy causes severe reaction), even in minuscule amounts. Someone with an intolerance doesn't have to be as vigilant about avoiding the offending food (since the reactions generally aren't more than uncomfortable), and can sometimes eat small (or even moderate) quantities of it without feeling the effect. While a baby who is merely lactose intolerant (lacks the enzyme needed to digest milk sugar) may suffer from abdominal pain, gassiness and possibly diarrhoea when fed milk, a baby with a true milk allergy will also have blood and/or mucus in the stool. So if your baby experiences what seems to be 'allergic' symptoms after eating certain foods, check with the doctor, who may be able to determine whether your baby is actually allergic or simply sensitive.

should be cleaned meticulously with an anti-mould agent. Outdoors, be sure drainage around your home is good, that leaves and other plant debris are not allowed to pile up, and that, if possible, plenty of sun hits the garden and house to prevent damp areas from spawning mould. Keep baby's sandpit covered in the rain.

♦ Bee venom. Anyone allergic to bee venom should avoid outdoor areas known to have bee or wasp populations. If your baby has an allergy to bee venom, any caregiver should be equipped with and know how to use a bee-sting kit.

♦ Miscellaneous allergens. Many other potential allergens and irritants can also be removed from your child's world: wool blankets (cover them or use cotton or synthetic blankets); down or feather pillows (use foam or hypoallergenic polyester-filled ones when baby's old enough to use one); tobacco smoke (allow no smoking in the house at all, or near baby in other locations); perfumes (use unscented wipes, sprays, and so on); soaps (use only hypoallergenic types); detergents (you may have to switch to an unscented detergent or use baby soap flakes for the laundry).

Since an allergy is a hypersensitive (or oversensitive) reaction of the immune system to a foreign substance, desensitizing (usually via gradually increased injected doses of the offending allergen) is sometimes successful in eliminating allergies – particularly to pollen, dust and animal dander. Except in severe cases, however, desensitization is not usually started until a child is four years old. Antihistamines and steroids may be used to counteract the allergic response and bring down the swelling

of mucous membranes in both infants and children.

Dietary changes:

♦ Elimination of possible dietary allergens, always using nutritionally equivalent substitutes (see The Daily Dozen on page 314). Remove a suspected food allergen (cow's milk, wheat, egg whites and citrus are among the possibilities) from your baby's diet under medical supervision; if symptoms disappear within a few weeks, you probably have discovered the culprit. You get further confirmation if the symptoms recur when the food is returned to the diet (but try this only at the doctor's suggestion). Substitute (as needed) oat, rice and barley flours for wheat; soya or hydrolysate formula[1] for cow's milk formula; egg yolks for whole eggs; and mangoes, cantaloupe melon, broccoli, cauliflower and red peppers for citrus.

Prevention:

♦ Breastfeeding for at least six months – preferably for a year – may help. This is especially important if there is a family history of allergy.

♦ Later introduction of solids, not until at least six months, and then with caution (see page 313). Even later introduction of the most common offenders (cow's milk, egg whites, wheat, chocolate, citrus, peanuts, nuts, shellfish). Careful observation for reactions when food is introduced.

♦ Scientists are making progress towards finding a cure for food allergies. Preliminary studies show that slowly introducing allergens like

---

1. About 40 per cent of babies allergic to cow's milk are also allergic to soya, so hydrolysate formula is usually a safer bet. *Do not* use so-called soya milks, since they do not provide adequate nutrition for infants.

COLD OR ALLERGY?

Symptoms of colds and allergies are so similar, it's hard to tell them apart. But with a little medical detective work, you'll be able to uncover the cause of your baby's congestion. If you answer yes to one or more of these questions, chances are, you're dealing with an allergy:

♦ Are the symptoms lasting more than ten to fourteen days? (Though this can also indicate that a cold has turned into a secondary infection; check with the doctor.)

♦ Is your baby's nose always stuffy or running?

♦ Is the mucus that drains from your baby's nose clear and thin (instead of yellow or green and thick)?

♦ Does your baby seem to be constantly rubbing, pulling or pushing his or her nose?

♦ Does your baby sneeze a lot?

♦ Are your baby's eyes watery and red? Does your baby rub them often (when he or she's not tired)?

♦ Does your baby have a rash?

---

peanuts and eggs may help children build a tolerance. More study is needed (see page 494).

Complications:
♦ Asthma

♦ Anaphylactic shock, which can be fatal without treatment (but is extremely rare)

When to call the doctor: Soon after you suspect an allergy. Call again whenever your child has new symptoms. Call immediately if there are any signs of asthma (wheezing), difficulty breathing, or signs of shock (disorientation, panting, rapid pulse rate, pale, cold, moist skin, drowsiness or loss of consciousness).

Chance of recurrence: Some allergies disappear in adulthood never to return; others return under different guises.

Conditions with similar symptoms:
♦ The common cold (like allergic rhinitis); see box, above

♦ Bronchitis (but a child who seems to have repeated bouts of this disease probably has asthma)

♦ Gastrointestinal illnesses (similar to digestive tract symptoms)

♦ Food sensitivities (similar to digestive tract symptoms); see box, page 544

THE COMMON COLD OR UPPER RESPIRATORY INFECTION (URI)

The common cold is even more common among the very young. That's because babies and small children haven't yet had the chance to build up immunities against the many different cold viruses. So be prepared to have at least a few run-ins with a runny nose during the first couple of years, probably more if your child attends day care or has older siblings.

Symptoms:
♦ Runny nose (discharge is watery at first, then thicker and yellowish)

♦ Sneezing

♦ Nasal congestion

TAKING THE BITE
OUT OF THE FLU BUG

Most people consider flu just one step up from a cold, at least for the young and healthy. A few feverish, bedridden days off from work or school, some chills, a lingering cough. Miserable and annoying, yes, but dangerous, no – unless you're elderly or sick.

These days, the medical community is trying to change that perception, urging parents to line young children up for flu injections right alongside their grandparents and great-grandparents. While it's true that serious illness and complications from the flu are highest in folks over the age of 65, rates of flu infection are actually highest among children. And for babies and toddlers, the flu bug can bite harder than parents might expect. In fact, children between six and twenty-three months who come down with the flu often need to be hospitalized.

Luckily, there is a vaccine available for babies over six months old that pro-tects against the flu (see page 228). The vaccine is usually offered beginning in October (the flu season in the United Kingdom generally runs from November through April). Protection develops within two weeks and lasts up to a year. Babies need two flu injections – given at least one month apart – the first time they get vaccinated.

As yet, there is no vaccine for babies under six months old. Until scientists develop one, parents can protect their babies from exposure to the virus by get-ting flu injections themselves and by immunizing older siblings and other household members. Remember, too, that even if your family has been vaccinated, it's important to wash hands thoroughly and often to prevent the spread of the many other common viruses that cause colds and flulike illnesses.

For more on the symptoms of the flu, see page 774.

Sometimes:

♦ Dry cough, which may be worse when baby is lying down

♦ Fever

♦ Itchy throat

♦ Mild fatigue

♦ Loss of appetite

Season: All year round, but more common when older children are in school.

Cause: More than 100 different viruses are known to cause colds.

Method of transmission: Usually spread from hand to hand.

Incubation period: One to four days.

Duration: Usually three to ten days, but in small children colds can linger longer.

Treatment: No known cure, but symptoms can be treated, as necessary:

♦ Suctioning of mucus with a nasal aspirator (see illustration, page 550). If mucus is hardened, before suctioning soften with over-the-counter saline nose drops. This may be necessary to help baby to feed as well as to sleep. (If baby resists being suctioned, you can use the saline drops alone to loosen the mucus so that it can drip out or be swallowed.)

♦ Humidification (see page 763) to help moisten the air, reduce congestion and make breathing easier for baby.

TREATING BABY'S SYMPTOMS

SYMPTOM	APPROPRIATE TREATMENT
Cough	Humidified air*
	Increased fluids*
	Reduction of dairy products, for older babies in whom milk products seem to increase mucus production
	Cough medication (but only if prescribed, since such treatment is usually inappropriate for babies)
Croupy cough	Abundant steam*
	A trip outdoors
Diarrhoea	Possible dietary changes (see page 554)
	Antidiarrhoeal medicine (but only if prescribed, since such treatment is usually inappropriate for babies)
Ear pain	Pain reliever, such as paracetamol or ibuprofen
	Local dry heat to ear (warm water in a hot water bottle)
	Decongestant (but only if prescribed, since such treatment is usually inappropriate for babies)
	Antibiotics, only if prescribed for infection
	Ear drops, only if prescribed
Fever	Increased fluids (see page 572)
	Adequate calorie intake, if possible
	Antifever medication, such as paracetamol or ibuprofen, as recommended by doctor
	Tepid bath or sponging (best if used in conjuction with fever-reducing medication; see page 572)
	Light clothing and cool room temperature (see page 572)
Itching	Calamine lotion or lotion containing pamoxine (but avoid topical antihistamines)
	Comfortably warm bath (test with your elbow or wrist)
	Soothing tepid bath*
	Colloidal oatmeal bath

*See Ready Reference (page 763) for tips on carrying out this treatment.

SYMPTOM	APPROPRIATE TREATMENT
Itching (cont.)	Prevention of scratching and infection (keep fingernails short and clean; cover hands with socks or mittens during sleep)
	Pain reliever, such as paracetamol (but *not* aspirin; see page 573)
	Oral antihistamine (but only if prescribed, since such treatment is usually inappropriate for babies)
Nasal congestion	Humidified air*
	Saltwater irrigation*
	Nasal aspiration*
	Head elevation
	Increased fluids*
	Saline (saltwater) nose drops
	Decongestant (but only if prescribed, since such treatment is usually inappropriate for babies)
	Medicated nose drops, only if prescribed
Pain or discomfort from minor injury	Comfort (cuddling)
	Distraction
	Pain reliever, such as paracetamol or ibuprofen
	Local heat or cold, as appropriate
Sore throat	Soothing, non-acid foods and beverages
	Pain reliever, such as paracetamol or ibuprofen
	Fever treatment, if needed
Teething pain	Comfort (cuddling)
	Something cold (and safe) to gum, such as a frozen teething ring
	Pressure on gums (see page 319)
	Pain reliever, such as paracetamol or ibuprofen, or topical pain reliever only if recommended by the doctor
Vomiting	Increased fluids, in small sips (see page 554)
	Restricted diet (see page 554)

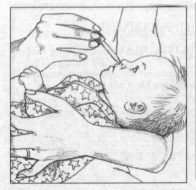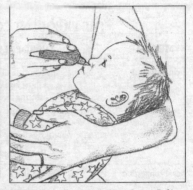

For a baby who's having trouble breathing through a stuffy nose, saline drops (left) to soften the mucus and aspiration (right) to suction it out will bring welcome relief.

♦ Letting baby sleep with head elevated (by raising the head of the cot mattress with a couple of pillows or other supports *under* the mattress; never put any pillows in the cot with baby) to ease breathing.

♦ Decongestants, only if recommended by the doctor (they rarely are for infants), to try to make eating and sleeping easier; they are usually ineffective and can make some babies irritable.

♦ Nose drops that do not contain medication, if recommended by the doctor, to ease congestion. But follow directions carefully because these drops can have side effects and an overdose can be harmful. Use for more than a few days can cause a rebound reaction and make baby feel worse.

♦ Petroleum jelly (Vaseline) or similar ointment applied *lightly* to outside of, and under, nose to help prevent chapping and reddening of skin. But be careful to not let it get into the nostrils, where it could be inhaled or block breathing.

♦ Cough medicine, but only to ease a dry cough that interferes with sleep, and only if it is prescribed by the doctor (many doctors question both the effectiveness and safety of giving cough suppressants to young children). *Antibiotics will not help* and should not be used unless there is secondary bacterial infection.

Dietary changes: Baby can continue a normal diet (though many have a loss of appetite), with the following exceptions:

♦ Increased intake of fluids to help replace those lost through fever, mouth breathing or runny nose. If baby is old enough, drinking from a cup may be more comfortable than

THE HAND-WASHING SOLUTION

The best way to prevent the spread of any kind of infection is frequent hand washing, after nappy changing, after toilet use or nose blowing, before food handling, and so on. Wash with soap and hot water for at least ten seconds.

THE FREQUENT COLD PROGRAMME

Does it seem as if your baby has enrolled in the frequent cold programme – catching every cold the older siblings come down with, or bringing one home from day care every other week? Don't worry. Though they'll try your patience and are rough on your baby's nose, such frequent mild illnesses won't do any harm – and can actually do some good.

The perks? Frequent colds (and ear infections and bouts with other bugs) boost your child's immune system, making your child less susceptible to infection later in life. In fact, babies in day care (who catch illness more often than those at home) are much less susceptible to colds and other infections as they get older and enter school.

Frequent colds also appear to have absolutely no effect on your baby's future development. Researchers have found that children who come down with multiple colds, ear infections and diarrhoea are no less prepared for preschool and have just as many social skills as their peers who were sick less often. (Plus, these children are already good at sharing – their germs, at least.)

trying to nurse or bottle feed with a stuffy nose.

◆ If recommended by baby's doctor, reduce intake of dairy products (but not of breast milk or formula), since it is possible they may thicken secretions.

Prevention: Careful hand washing for all the family, especially when someone has a cold, and particularly before handling baby or baby's things. Coughs and sneezes should be covered.

Complications: Colds sometimes progress to ear infections or bronchitis. (In infants and young children, viral bronchitis is the natural extension of a cold into the larger breathing tubes of the lungs. It usually does not require separate treatment, and gets better by itself. If, however, a cough far outlasts a cold's other symptoms, let the doctor know.) Less often, a cold can lead to pneumonia or sinusitis.

When to call the doctor:

◆ If this is a first cold; if your baby is under three months old and has a fever over 38°C (100.4°F)

◆ If the temperature goes up suddenly or a fever continues for more than two days

◆ If a dry cough lasts more than two weeks, is interfering with baby's sleep, causes choking or vomiting, becomes thick and productive (mucus is coughed up) or wheezy, or if breathing difficulties develop. A cough that lasts more than three weeks in an infant or six in an older baby may require consultation with a specialist

◆ If a thick, greenish yellow nasal discharge develops and lasts more than a day, or if the discharge is streaked with blood

THE SUDDEN COUGH

If your baby or young child suddenly begins coughing uncontrollably and does not seem to have a cold or other illness, consider the possibility that an inhaled object could be the cause. See page 593 for emergency treatment.

COMPLEMENTARY AND ALTERNATIVE MEDICINE

Most parents wouldn't consider treating a baby's symptoms with anything stronger than paracetamol without first placing a phone call to the doctor. Some won't even reach for the Infant Calpol without the doctor's okay. Yet many of the same parents wouldn't hesitate to visit the local health food store to look for a holistic remedy for their baby's cold, flu or constipation – or think twice about dosing baby with an herbal remedy without checking in with the doctor first.

They have plenty of company. According to some estimates, up to 40 per cent of parents have joined the ranks of those choosing alternative therapies for their children. Whether it's a dose of echinacea to nip a cold in the bud, a sniff of lavender to relieve stress, a bottle of camomile to soothe a colicky baby, or a visit to the chiropractor to prevent recurrent ear infections, complementary and alternative medicine (CAM) has clearly found its way into the nursery.

But the question is – is the nursery any place for CAM? For years, alternative medicine – and those who practised it – was considered the province of fringe practitioners. Today, it's being integrated in one form or another into almost every area of traditional medicine, from cardiology to oncology. Unfortunately, however, the study of CAM in paediatric practice has lagged seriously behind.

Virtually no CAM therapies have been tested on children, making determining which treatments are safe for the littlest patients and which aren't an imprecise science – even for scientists. For parents, who have only anecdotal information to go on, the answers are even more elusive.

Some study is under way; much more needs to be done. In the meantime, here's what you need to consider before taking a CAM approach to your child's health. Firstly, unlike over-the-counter and prescription medicines, herbal remedies are not rigorously regulated by government. They haven't been tested for effectiveness, safety, or proper dosing, even in adults. Secondly, 'natural' doesn't necessarily mean safe. Herbal remedies are not necessarily any safer than pharmaceutical preparations, and in some cases may be a lot less safe. In fact, some herbal remedies can actually cause serious side effects in children; others may interfere with traditional care a child is receiving – interacting badly with a prescribed medication, for instance. Thirdly, while there are almost certainly CAM therapies that are beneficial, proceeding with any treatment – traditional or alternative – without consulting a knowledgeable doctor is unwise and potentially unsafe. If you're considering using a CAM therapy on your baby, always check with his or her doctor first.

◆ If there is an unusual amount of crying (with or without tugging at the ears)

◆ If there is a complete loss of appetite

◆ If baby seems really out of sorts

Chance of recurrence: Since having a cold caused by one virus doesn't make baby immune to a cold caused by another, babies, who haven't had the chance to build up immunities to the more than 100 viruses that exist, can have one cold right after another.

Conditions with similar symptoms:
◆ Rubella and chicken pox begin with cold-like symptoms; check those diseases (see table starting on page 766) for additional symptoms

- ◆ Respiratory allergies
- ◆ Influenza

CONSTIPATION

This problem is rare in breastfed babies (even if they move their bowels infrequently and their movements seem difficult to expel), because their movements are never hard. (In a breastfed newborn, infrequent movements – no matter how soft – can be a sign that baby isn't getting enough to eat; see page 158.) Constipation can, however, plague formula-fed infants.

Symptoms: Infrequent bowel movements with stools that are hard (often small pellets) and hard to pass; infrequency alone, however, is not a sign of constipation and may be your baby's normal pattern.

- ◆ Stool streaked with blood, if there are anal fissures (cracks in the anus caused by the passage of hard stool)

- ◆ Gastric distress and abdominal pain

- ◆ Irritability

Season: Any time

Cause: A sluggish digestive tract, illness, insufficient fibre in diet, not enough to drink, insufficient activity or an anal fissure that makes defecation painful; rarely, a more serious medical condition.

Duration: May be chronic or occur just occasionally.

Treatment: Though constipation is not unusual in bottle-fed infants, symptoms should always be reported to the doctor, who can, when necessary, check for any abnormalities that might be causing it. Occasional constipation or mild chronic constipation is usually treated with dietary changes (see below); an increase in

exercise may help (in infants, try moving the legs in a bicycle fashion when you see your baby having difficulty with a movement). Do not give laxatives, enemas, or any medication without the doctor's instructions.

Dietary changes: Make these only after consultation with baby's doctor:

- ◆ If they've been introduced, give 30 to 60 ml (1 to 2 fl oz) of prune or apple juice by bottle, cup or spoon.

- ◆ For a baby on solids, increase intake of fruits (other than banana) and vegetables.

- ◆ In older babies, cut back on dairy products (but not breast milk or formula).

Prevention: When solids are added to baby's diet, be sure to include mostly whole grains, plus plenty of fruits and vegetables. Also be sure fluid intake is adequate and that baby has plenty of opportunity for physical activity.

Complications:
- ◆ Fissures

- ◆ Impacted stool (stool that is not passed naturally and may be painful to remove manually)

- ◆ If it continues chronically through the toddler and preschool years, difficulty with toilet training can result.

When to call the doctor: If your baby seems to be constipated often or regularly; if the problem suddenly arises when it has not been noted before; or if there is blood in the stool.

Chance of recurrence: The problem can become a 'habit' if it isn't dealt with when it first occurs.

Conditions with similar symptoms:
♦ Intestinal obstructions or abnormalities

DIARRHOEA

This problem, too, is unusual in breastfed babies because there appear to be certain substances in breast milk that destroy many of the microorganisms that cause diarrhoea.

Symptoms:
♦ Liquidy, runny stools (not seedy like a breastfed baby's stools)

Sometimes:
♦ Increased frequency

♦ Increased volume

♦ Mucus in stool

♦ Blood in stool

♦ Vomiting

Cause: Very varied:
♦ Gastrointestinal infection (viruses, most often rotavirus; also bacteria, parasites)

♦ Sometimes, another infection

♦ Teething (possibly)

♦ Sensitivity to a food in the diet

♦ Too much fruit or juice (particularly apple or pear)

♦ Antibiotic medication (feeding yoghurt with live cultures to a baby on antibiotics may prevent this type of diarrhoea)

Method of transmission: Infectious cases can be transmitted via the faeces-to-hand-to-mouth route. Also transmitted by contaminated foods.

Incubation period: Depends on the causative organism.

Duration: Usually anywhere from a few hours to several days, but some cases can become chronic if the cause is not discovered and corrected.

Treatment: Depends on the cause, but most common approaches are dietary (see below). Sometimes medication may be prescribed. Do not give antidiarrhoeal medication to an infant without the doctor's approval – some can be harmful to young children. Protect baby's bottom from irritation by changing nappies as soon as possible after they're soiled and by spreading on a thick ointment after each change. If nappy rash develops, see page 265.

A very sick baby may need hospitalization to stabilize body fluids.

Dietary changes:
♦ Continuing breast or formula feedings in most cases is best. Since a baby with diarrhoea may develop a temporary lactose intolerance, a switch to a soya-based, lactose-free formula may be recommended if the diarrhoea doesn't improve on baby's regular formula.

♦ High fluid intake (at least 60 ml/2 fl oz an hour) to replace fluids lost through diarrhoea. To augment breast milk or formula, a rehydration fluid (such as Dioralyte), available over the counter at any pharmacy, is sometimes recommended. Offer a few sips by spoon, cup or bottle every two or three minutes, working up to 225 ml (8 fl oz) between loose bowel movements. Do not give sweetened drinks (such as colas), undiluted fruit juices, athletic drinks, glucose water or homemade salt-and-sugar mixtures.

♦ Continuation of solids, if baby takes them regularly. The sooner a baby is fed, the less severe the diarrhoea will be. Starchy foods such as mashed banana, white rice or rice cereal, potatoes, pasta or dry white toast, depending on baby's usual diet, are all good choices. Small amounts of protein foods (such as chicken) are also appropriate. Steer clear of other fruits (besides bananas) and vegetables in the short term.

♦ If there is vomiting, solid feeding is usually not resumed until vomiting has stopped. But do offer sips of clear fluids (diluted juices or oral rehydration fluid, if prescribed). Offering small amounts (no more than a tablespoon or two at a time, less for a very young infant) will greatly increase the chance that it will be held down. Once vomiting has stopped, foods can be added as above.

♦ When stool begins to return to normal, usually after two or three days, the doctor will recommend that you begin to return your baby to a regular diet but continue limiting dairy products (other than breast milk and formula) for another day or two.

♦ In diarrhoea that lasts for two weeks or more in a bottle-fed infant, the doctor may recommend a change in formula.

Prevention: Diarrhoea can't always be prevented, but risks can be reduced:

♦ Attention to sanitary preparation of foods (see page 326).

♦ Careful hand washing by baby's care providers after handling nappies and going to the bathroom.

♦ The dilution of fruit juices taken by babies; limiting total intake to no more than 120 to 170 ml (4 to 6 fl oz) a day; switching to white grape juice (see box, page 556).

Complications:
♦ Nappy rash

♦ Dehydration, if diarrhoea is severe and left untreated

When to call the doctor: One or two loose stools is not a cause for concern. But the following indicate diarrhoea that may need medical attention:

♦ You suspect baby may have consumed spoiled food or formula.

♦ Baby has had loose, watery stools for 24 hours.

♦ Baby is vomiting (more than the usual spit-up) repeatedly, or has been vomiting for 24 hours.

♦ There is blood in baby's stools.

♦ Baby is running a fever or seems ill.

♦ Call *immediately* if baby shows signs of dehydration: significantly decreased urine output (nappies aren't as wet as usual and/or urine is yellow); tearless and sunken eyes; a sunken fontanel ('soft spot'); dry skin; scanty saliva.

Chance of recurrence: Likely, if cause has not been eliminated, some babies are more prone to diarrhoea.

Conditions with similar symptoms:
♦ Food allergies

♦ Food poisoning

♦ Enzyme deficiencies

MIDDLE EAR INFLAMMATION (OTITIS MEDIA)

Babies and young children are more susceptible to earaches of all kinds, for a variety of reasons. Most outgrow the susceptibility.

A BETTER JUICE FOR YOUR SICK BABY?

A sick tummy got your baby down? It may be time for a change of juice. Researchers have found that children recover more quickly from diarrhoea when they drink white grape juice than when they stick to those high chair standards, apple and pear. They're also less likely to experience a recurrence on the white grape. Apparently, the sugar and carbohydrate composition of white grape juice is better for the digestive system (and a lot less challenging in the laundry department than its purple cousin).

Apple and pear juices naturally contain sorbitol (an indigestible carbohydrate that can cause gas, bloating and discomfort) and a higher amount of fructose than glucose, while white grape juice is sorbitol free, and has an even balance of fructose to glucose.

Before switching to white grape juice, though, discuss it with the doctor, who might recommend water or rehydration liquids instead. In some cases, too much of any type of juice can cause tummy troubles.

Symptoms: In acute otitis media (AOM), infection of the middle ear, symptoms include:

Usually:

◆ Ear pain, often worse at night (babies sometimes pull or rub or hold their ears but often give no indication of pain except for crying, and sometimes not even that; crying when sucking on breast or bottle may indicate ear pain that has radiated to the jaw)

◆ Fever, which may be slight or very high

◆ Fatigue and irritability

◆ Runny nose and congestion (often, but not always)

Sometimes:
◆ Nausea and/or vomiting

◆ Loss of appetite

Occasionally:
◆ No obvious symptoms at all

On examination, the eardrum appears pink (during the early stages of infection), and then red and bulging (later on). In many cases, AOM will get better without treatment (though the decision of whether to treat or to 'wait and see' should be left to the doctor; see page 557 for more on treatment). Sometimes, however, if the infection is left untreated, pressure can burst the drum, releasing pus into the ear canal and relieving pressure. The eardrum heals eventually, but treatment helps to prevent further damage.

In serous otitis media (SOM), also known as otitis media with effusion, or fluid in the middle ear, symptoms include:

Usually:
◆ Hearing loss (temporary but can become permanent if condition persists for many months untreated)

Sometimes:
◆ Clicking or popping sounds on swallowing or sucking (as reported by older children)

♦ No symptoms at all, other than the fluid in the ear

Season: All year round, but much more common in winter.

Cause: Usually bacteria or viruses, but allergy can also cause middle ear inflammation. Babies and young children may be most susceptible because of the shape and size of their eustachian tubes; because they are more likely to get respiratory infections, which usually precede ear infections; because they have immature immune response; or because they are often fed while lying on their backs. The eustachian tubes, which drain fluids from the ears down the back of the nose and the throat and keep the middle ear ventilated with air, are shorter in a baby than in an adult, so germs can easily travel through them into the middle ear. And because the tubes are horizontal rather than vertical (as in adults), drainage is poor, especially in infants who spend a lot of time on their backs. The small diameter also makes the tubes more subject to blockage (by swelling from allergy or from an infection, such as a cold, by a malformation, or by enlarged adenoids). This blockage causes fluid buildup, which makes an excellent breeding place for infection-causing bacteria, causing serous otitis media.

Method of transmission: Not direct (you can't 'catch' an ear infection), but children in day care may be more vulnerable simply because they get more colds, which can lead to ear infections. There may be a family disposition to ear infections.

Incubation period: Often follows a cold or the flu.

Duration: Can be as short as a few days; can become chronic.

Treatment: Ear infections require consultation with a doctor; do not try to treat on your own. Treatment may include:

♦ Antibiotics, when deemed necessary (sometimes they absolutely are necessary, sometimes they aren't; see below). When antibiotics are prescribed, always give for the full time prescribed – usually five or ten days – to avoid reinfection chronic infection or antibiotic resistance. Decongestants are not usually helpful.

♦ Watchful waiting in situations that do not require immediate antibiotic treatment. Research has shown that most uncomplicated cases of acute otitis media clear up within four to seven days without treatment. Ask your doctor whether antibiotics are absolutely necessary for your baby's particular infection.

♦ Ear drops, if doctor recommended.

♦ Baby paracetamol or ibuprofen for pain and/or fever.

♦ Heat applied to the ear in the form of a heating pad set on low, a hot-water bottle filled with warm water, or warm compresses (see page 764) – any of which can be used while you are trying to reach the doctor.

♦ Periodic ear exams until the ear (or ears) is back to normal, to be sure the condition has not become chronic.

♦ Elimination or treatment of allergies related to repeated ear infections.

Dietary changes: Extra fluids for fever. If antibiotics are prescribed, whole milk yoghurt with active cultures (if dairy products have been introduced) can help prevent stomach distress often caused by such medications.

YOUR BABY'S HEALTH HISTORY

If there isn't adequate space in your new arrival's baby book, buy a notebook to use as a permanent health history. Record all your baby's birth statistics, as well as information about each illness, medications given, immunizations, doctors, and so on. What follows is a sample of the kinds of things to include.

AT BIRTH

Weight: Length: Head circumference:

Condition at birth:

Apgar score at one and five minutes:

Results of other tests:

Any problems or abnormalities:

INFANT ILLNESSES
(for each illness record the following information)

Date began: Date recovered:

Symptoms:

Doctor called:

Diagnosis:

Instructions:

Medications given: How long:

Side effects:

IMMUNIZATIONS

Type: Received: Reactions:

Prevention: A sure way to prevent otitis media is not yet known. Recent research, however, suggests that the following may reduce the risk of ear infections in babies:

◆ Overall good health through adequate nutrition and rest, and regular medical care

◆ Breastfeeding for at least six months, preferably the entire first year

◆ Flu injection, pneumococcal vaccine (see page 228)

◆ A more upright feeding position, especially when a baby has a respiratory infection

◆ Using angled bottles, instead of the traditional straight ones

◆ A slightly elevated sleeping position when a baby has a cold (put a couple of pillows *under* the head of the mattress, not under baby's head)

◆ Having baby suck on a bottle or dummy during plane takeoffs and especially landings, when most ear problems occur because of air pressure changes

◆ Limiting the use of a dummy during the day, and taking a dummy out of your baby's mouth once he or she is asleep

◆ Low-dose prophylactic (given to prevent infection) antibiotics for children with frequent ear infections during the height of the otitis media season, or just when the child comes down with a cold, to prevent a secondary ear infection

◆ Smoke-free living space (second-hand smoke can lead to more congestion, which can lead to SOM)

◆ Home child care rather than group day-care situations, where children are more likely to come down with otitis media

Complications:
Among others:
◆ Chronic otitis media with hearing loss

◆ Mastoid infection (a rare condition in which the mastoid bone of the skull becomes infected)

◆ Meningitis, pneumonia

When to call the doctor: Initially, as soon as you suspect your baby may have an earache. Again if symptoms do not seem to begin clearing within two days, or if baby seems worse. Even if no ear infection is suspected, call if baby suddenly doesn't seem to be hearing as well as usual.

Chance of recurrence: Some babies never have an ear infection, others have one or two in infancy and then no repeats, and still others have them repeatedly on into toddlerhood and the preschool years.

Conditions with similar symptoms: A foreign object in the ear, swimmer's ear and referred pain from respiratory infection can mimic an earache. Teething sometimes causes referred pain to the ear.

GASTROESOPHAGEAL REFLUX (GER)

There has been an apparent dramatic increase in the number of babies with GER recently – not because more babies are developing the condition but because more are being correctly diagnosed. Doctors believe that many babies who were labelled colicky in the past were actually suffering from GER. It's a common condition in babies under a year of age, and even more common in premature babies.

Symptoms: GER is similar to heartburn (acid reflux) in adults. The acid in the stomach backs up into the oesophagus or even up to the back of the throat, causing frequent spitting up or vomiting and irritation of the oesophagus, indicated by unrelenting crying and discomfort. Symptoms include:

◆ Sudden or inconsolable crying, severe pain and arching during feeding

◆ Excessive spitting up or vomiting

◆ Extremely forceful vomiting

◆ Vomiting hours after eating

◆ Erratic feeding patterns such as refusing food or constant eating or drinking

◆ Slow weight gain

◆ Poor sleep habits

◆ Gagging or choking

◆ Frequent burping or hiccupping

◆ Difficult or noisy swallowing

◆ Excessive drooling

Sometimes:

◆ Chronic coughing, recurrent croup

◆ Frequent red or sore throat

◆ Frequent ear infections

◆ Respiratory problems including wheezing, laboured breathing, asthma, bronchitis, pneumonia and apnea

Season: Any time.

Cause: GER is the return of stomach contents into the oesophagus. Normally during swallowing, the oesophagus propels food or liquid down to the stomach by a series of squeezes. Once food has entered the stomach, it is mixed with acid to start digestion. When this mixing occurs, the circular band of muscles at the lower end of the oesophagus becomes tight, keeping the food from backing up. In premature and some term infants, the junction between the stomach and oesophagus is underdeveloped and it sometimes relaxes when it should be tightening. This relaxation of the muscles allows the liquid and food to come back up. Reflux of the acidic stomach content irritates the lining of the oesophagus and causes a form of heartburn.

Duration: GER usually begins between two and four weeks of age and can last until the child is one or two years old. Symptoms peak around four months and begin to subside around seven months when the baby begins to sit upright and take more solid foods.

Treatment: Mild forms of GER are common, usually require no treatment and subside on their own over a period of months. For more serious GER, treatment is aimed not at curing the illness but at making baby feel better until he or she outgrows it. Use the strategies for prevention (below) to help ease your baby's discomfort. Medications that reduce stomach acid, that neutralize stomach acids or that increase stomach motility are sometimes helpful but should be given only if the doctor prescribes or recommends one for your baby. If the condition is serious and other forms of treatment have failed, surgery may be performed to tighten the lower oesophageal sphincter.

Dietary changes:

♦ Avoid overfeeding. Offer smaller amounts of breast milk, formula or solid food more frequently.

♦ When the infant is old enough to eat solids, serve thicker, rather than thin, watered-down foods. Gravity holds down heavier foods more easily. Also, avoid acidic (once introduced) or fatty foods in large quantities.

Prevention: GER can't always be prevented, but there are things you can do to reduce its severity:

♦ Breastfeed for as long as possible. GER is usually much less severe in breastfed babies because breast milk is more easily and more quickly digested than formula and acts as a natural antacid. If you are breastfeeding, eliminate caffeine (a known contributor to reflux) from your diet.

♦ Make feedings as calm and quiet as possible, avoiding interruptions.

♦ Burp your baby frequently.

♦ Prop your baby upright during feeding and for one to two hours after feedings. If possible, do this in a quiet place. If your baby falls asleep after a feeding, put him or her to bed flat, but at an incline. You can do this by placing a couple of pillows under the head of the mattress or using a slanted wedge pillow specially designed for babies with GER (Velcro straps keep baby from sliding down).[2]

----

2. Though changing an infant's position during and after a feeding may work for some babies, there is some evidence suggesting that placing an infant upright may actually worsen reflux. Talk to your doctor to determine what is best for your baby.

♦ Try offering a dummy after feedings; sucking on a dummy often eases reflux.

♦ Avoid playing or jostling the baby immediately after feedings. Don't give baths after feeding.

♦ Don't smoke around baby. Nicotine stimulates gastric acid production.

Complications:

♦ Failure to thrive

♦ Severe choking spells

♦ Wheezing, aspiration pneumonia and other lung problems

♦ Apnea

When to call the doctor:

♦ If GER is severe enough to interfere with weight gain or sleep.

♦ If your baby seems to be in a lot of pain.

Chances of recurrence: The good news is that almost all babies with GER will outgrow it. And once they do, it usually doesn't recur. Occasionally, reflux can continue into adulthood.

Conditions with similar symptoms:

♦ Viral or bacterial infections

♦ Asthma

♦ Pyloric stenosis

♦ Metabolic diseases

♦ Hirshsprung's disease

URINARY TRACT INFECTION (UTI)

Urinary tract infections (UTIs) are bacterial infections of the urinary tract (kidneys, ureters, bladder and urethra).

Symptoms: Symptoms of a UTI can be hard to recognize in a baby or young child, but they're important to look for when a child is sick with a fever and urination appears painful. Symptoms include:

- Unexplained fever in a baby

- Crying, irritability, holding the genitals or showing other signs of pain when urinating

- Stomach or back pain (hard to detect in infants)

- Foul-smelling urine

- Cloudy urine

- Bloody (brown, red or pink) urine

- More frequent than usual urination

- Nausea, vomiting or diarrhoea with other urinary symptoms

- Decreased appetite or lack of interest in eating

- Irritability

- Poor growth in an infant

Season: All year round.

Cause: The urinary tract includes the kidneys, the bladder, the tubes that carry urine from the kidneys to the bladder (ureters) and the tube that carries urine from the bladder to outside of the body (urethra). Urinary tract infections occur when bacteria (or, more rarely, a virus or fungus) begin to grow in the urinary tract. UTIs are common in young children because the urethra is very short, providing bacteria with easy access to the bladder.

Method of diagnosis: The doctor will need to perform a urine culture on sterile urine to determine if the child does indeed have a UTI. To do this on a young baby, the doctor may place a plastic bag over the genitals to collect the urine. This method of collection isn't very accurate because bacteria (from the rectum, from the environment) can contaminate the sample. A better way of collecting a urine sample for culture is by inserting a catheter up the urethra and retrieving urine directly from the bladder.

Method of transmission: The bacteria can come from the skin around the rectum and genitals and then travel up the urethra to the bladder. Some UTIs are caused by bacteria in the blood moving through the kidneys.

Duration: Depends on the type of infection and how severe it is.

Treatment: Most UTIs are effectively treated with antibiotics.

Dietary changes:

- Increase fluid intake

Prevention: Some children are prone to UTIs because of their anatomy. Preventive measures include:

- When changing a nappy, always wipe from front to back, even for boys.

- Make sure your baby gets a lot of fluids to help flush unwanted bacteria out of the body.

- Avoid bubble baths and perfumed soaps, which can irritate the genitals, especially in girls.

- Some studies suggest that cranberry juice is effective against UTIs, but the studies have all been done on adults, not children; consult with your baby's doctor.

- Possibly, circumcision for boys. Some research shows that uncircumcised boys are slightly more prone to UTIs.

Complications: Untreated urinary infections can lead to kidney infections, which, if left untreated, can cause serious damage.

When to call the doctor: If your baby has a fever for a few days without any signs of a cold (such as runny nose), if urination seems to be painful, or if your baby is experiencing any of the symptoms listed above.

Chances of recurrence: Can recur at any time.

RESPIRATORY SYNCYTIAL VIRUS (RSV)

RSV is the leading cause of lower respiratory tract infections in infants and young children. Approximately two-thirds of infants are infected with RSV during their first year. For most babies, RSV infection causes no more than a minor illness. In certain high-risk babies, however, RSV may lead to something much more serious.

Symptoms: In most infants, the virus causes symptoms resembling those of the common cold, including:

- Nasal congestion
- Runny nose
- Low-grade fever
- Decreased appetite
- Irritability

In some infants, it can sometimes cause lower respiratory (lung) symptoms (bronchiolitis):

- Rapid breathing
- Flaring of the nostrils
- Rapid heart rate
- Hacking cough
- Grunting
- Noticeable bluish colour in the skin around the mouth (cyanosis)
- Wheezing sound when breathing
- Skin between the ribs is sucked in with each breath
- Lethargy, sleepiness, dehydration

Season: Peaks between October and April.

Cause: RSV is such a common virus that nearly all adults and children are affected by it sooner or later. A normal cold virus or mild RSV infection affects just the nose and upper part of the lungs. But these symptoms can worsen rapidly in some babies, as the virus infects the lungs, inflaming the lower part of the lungs and the smallest inner branches of the airways, making it difficult to breathe (such an infection is called bronchiolitis). For most babies, the illness is mild. But babies at risk (such as premature babies whose lungs are underdeveloped and who have not yet received enough antibodies from their mothers to help them fight off RSV disease once they've been exposed to it) are more likely to get severe bronchiolitis and end up in the hospital. Those considered at higher risk include babies who:

- Were born prematurely
- Have pre-existing lung disease
- Are not breastfed
- Are exposed to tobacco smoke
- Were one in a multiple birth (such as twins), since they're more likely to be premature
- Were born within six months of the RSV season (birthday in April or later)

- Attend day care (because these babies are more likely to be exposed to RSV infection in the first place)

- Have school-age siblings; again, because exposure is more likely

Method of transmission: RSV is highly contagious and is transmitted by direct hand contact from infected individuals. The infection can also be spread through the air, by coughing and sneezing. RSV can survive for four to seven hours on surfaces such as cots and countertops.

Method of diagnosis: Diagnosis is generally made by nasal swab, with a chest X-ray to confirm the diagnosis.

Incubation period: Four to six days from exposure.

Duration: Children with mild RSV bronchiolitis are treated at home and improve within three to five days, though they may remain contagious for up to a week.

Treatment: For those whose RSV has caused more severe bronchiolitis:

- Oxygen administration if there is respiratory distress or blood oxygen levels are low. Rarely, infants may need to be briefly placed on a ventilator.

- Salbutamol, a medication that opens up the airways and is given through a nebulizer, may help. The nebulizer machine turns liquid medicine into a mist that is then inhaled.

- Steroids have been found to decrease inflammation in the lungs and are sometimes used to treat severe RSV bronchiolitis.

- Antibiotics are not effective because RSV is a virus, not a bacteria.

Dietary changes: As with the common cold, be sure your baby gets plenty of fluids.

Prevention:
- Breastfeed, if possible.

- Make hand washing a priority around the house.

- Keep older siblings away from the baby as much as possible if they have a runny nose, cold or fever.

- Do not take a high-risk baby out to crowded areas such as shopping centres during RSV season.

- Do not smoke around your baby.

- A medication is available to prevent RSV (but not treat it). The shot, called Synagis, does not give long-term protection and must be administered monthly during RSV season to high-risk infants in the hospital. It is also extremely expensive.

Complications:
- High-risk children who are infected with RSV disease often need to be hospitalized

- Dehydration

- Respiratory failure

When to call the doctor:
- If your infant has any symptoms of bronchiolitis (see page 766).

- If a fever persists for more than four to five days and/or remains elevated despite giving paracetamol.

- If your infant has changes in breathing pattern (rapid breathing, wheezing or if the skin between the ribs is sucked in with each breath) or is difficult to console.

Chances of recurrence: Almost all children recover fully with no lasting effects. Reinfection throughout life is common, though lower respiratory tract symptoms are most common in infants and toddlers and most marked in the first infection. In older children, RSV is indistinguishable from the common cold.

Conditions with similar symptoms:
◆ Common cold

◆ Asthma (though less often in younger infants)

◆ Pneumonia

◆ Gastric reflux with aspiration of the stomach contents may also produce the symptoms of bronchiolitis, but cold-like symptoms do not precede respiratory distress in these cases.

What it's Important to Know: ALL ABOUT FEVER

Though you may remember your mother standing over you, thermometer in hand, concern in her voice, announcing, 'You've got a fever, I'd better call the doctor', fever hasn't always been considered cause for alarm. The ancients welcomed an elevated temperature because they were convinced that it burned out bad 'humours'. Hippocrates, too, speculated that fevers did more good than harm. In the Middle Ages, fever was actually induced on occasion to fight syphilis and certain other infections. And in fact, fever was believed so beneficial historically that it wasn't even treated until about 100 years ago, when aspirin, with its fever-reducing capabilities, came on the scene. With the advent of aspirin, however, came a reformulating of medical opinion about fever. Throughout much of the twentieth century, even the slightest rise in temperature became a cause for worry, and a high fever for all-out panic.

Oddly enough, as it turns out, Hippocrates and the other ancients had a better notion of what fever is all about than did the modern medical community of a few generations ago. Research has confirmed that most fevers serve to heal, rather than harm – that they exist in a sense to burn out, if not the bad humours, at least the bad germs that invade and threaten the body. Instead of being a condition to be feared and fought, fever is now recognized to be an important part of the body's immune response to infection. Fever is not a disease; rather, it is a sign of illness – and a sign of the body's effort to overcome the illness.

Here's how scientists now believe fever plays its role. In response to invaders such as viruses, bacteria and fungi, white blood cells in the body produce a hormone called interleukin, which travels to the brain to instruct the hypothalamus to turn up the body thermostat. At higher body temperatures, the rest of the immune system is better able to fight infection. Viruses and bacteria grow best in cooler temperatures, so a fever actually makes the body

CONVULSIONS IN A FEVERISH BABY

A fever occasionally causes convulsions in infants and young children, usually at the very onset of the fever. Though febrile convulsions are frightening for parents, doctors now believe they are not dangerous. (See page 571 for safe handling of convulsions.) Studies have shown that children who have simple, brief febrile convulsions show no neurological or mental impairment later on. Babies who have once had convulsions with a fever have a 30 to 40 per cent greater chance of a repeat episode, and medical treatment doesn't affect that risk. Nor does treatment of a fever during the illness seem to reduce the incidence of seizures in these predisposed children, probably because the convulsions almost always occur just as the fever rises at the onset of an illness, before treatment can be given.

less hospitable to infection. Fever may also lower iron levels while increasing the invaders' need for that mineral – in effect starving them. And when it's a virus that has launched the attack, fever helps enhance the production of interferon and other antiviral substances in the body.

When a person's body temperature suddenly rises a couple of degrees above normal (37°C (98.6°F) taken orally), he or she often feels, paradoxically, chilled. The chilling serves to encourage a further rise in temperature in several ways. The involuntary shivering that usually occurs signals the body to turn its thermostat up still another notch and prompts the fever sufferer to take other measures that raise the body temperature: drink hot drinks, throw on another blanket, put on a sweater. At the same time, outlying blood vessels constrict to reduce heat loss, and body tissues – such as stored fat – are broken down to produce heat (which is why it is important to take in extra calories during a fever).

An estimated 80 to 90 per cent of all fevers in babies are related to self-limiting viral infections (they get better without treatment). Most doctors today don't recommend trying to reduce such fever in babies over six months unless it is 38.9°C (102°F) (rectally) or more, and some wait for significantly higher temperatures before they advise parents to break out the medicine dropper as long as baby doesn't seem to be in discomfort. (For guidelines on when to call the doctor with fever, see page 570.) They may, however, suggest the use of baby paracetamol or ibuprofen even with lower temperatures to relieve aches and pains, make a baby more comfortable, improve sleep and, sometimes, to make a nervous parent feel better. But while the fever may not need treatment, the illness that's triggering the fever may. For instance, illness caused by bacteria usually needs to be treated with antibiotics, which will wipe out the infection (thereby indirectly lowering temperature). Depending on the illness, the antibiotic selected, the child's level of comfort and the height of the fever, antibiotics and fever reducers may or may not be prescribed simultaneously.

Unlike most other infection-related fever, fever related to shock from a generalized bacterial invasion of the body, as in septicemia (blood poisoning), requires immediate medical treatment to lower the body temperature. So does fever related to heatstroke.

Normally, body temperature is at its lowest (as low as 35.5°C/96.5°F taken orally) in the middle of the night (between 2 AM and 4 AM), is still relatively low (as low as 36.1°C/97°F) on getting up in the morning, then slowly rises over the day until it peaks (at about 37.2°C/99°F) between 6 and 10 in the evening. It tends to be slightly higher in hot weather, lower in cold, and higher during exercise than at rest. It's more volatile and subject to greater variation in babies and young children than in adults.

Fevers behave differently in different illnesses. In some, a fever may remain persistently elevated until a baby is well; in others it will be consistently lower in the morning and higher in the evening, spike (shoot up) periodically, or come and go with no obvious pattern. The pattern sometimes helps the doctor to make a diagnosis.

When fever is part of the body's response to infection, temperatures above 40.5°C (105°F) are rare and those beyond 41.1°C (106°F) unheard of. But when fever is the result of the failure of the body's heat-regulation mechanism, as in heatstroke, temperatures can soar as high as 45.5°C (114°F). Such temperatures can occur when the environment is very hot and the body can't cool itself effectively. This can occur either through an internal abnormality or, more commonly, through overheating caused by an external heat source, such as a sauna or a hot tub, for example, or the inside of a parked car in warm weather (air temperatures inside the car can quickly shoot up to 45°C (113°F) even with the windows open 5 cm/2 in and the temperature outside a moderate 29.4°C/85°F). Overheating can also result from strenuous physical activity in hot or humid weather, or from being overdressed in warm weather. Infants and the elderly are most susceptible to heat illnesses because their temperature-regulation mechanisms are less dependable. Fever due to the failure of heat regulation is an illness in itself, and not only is it apparently not beneficial, it is dangerous and requires immediate treatment. Extremely high temperatures (over 41.1°C/106°F), whatever their cause, require immediate treatment to prevent damage to the brain and other organs. It's believed that when a fever is that high it ceases to be beneficial, and its positive effects on the immune response may be reversed.

TAKING BABY'S TEMPERATURE

Most doctors prefer a more accurate indicator of a baby's condition than a parent's kiss (though the kiss will still be welcomed by a baby who's not feeling well). Enter the thermometer.

Taking the temperature during the course of an illness can help answer such questions as 'Has the treatment effectively lowered the temperature?' or 'Has the fever risen, meaning a turn for the worse?' But keep in mind that while temperature readings can be useful, they needn't be taken every hour on the hour. In most cases, once in the morning and once in the evening is adequate. Take it in between only if baby suddenly seems sicker. If baby seems better, and your lips testify that the fever has broken, you don't really need a second opinion from the thermometer.

Temperatures are most often taken through the mouth, the rectum, the armpit (axilla) or the ear. Since putting a thermometer in a baby's mouth is dangerous (most doctors do not recommend taking oral temperatures until a child is four or five), you'll go one of the other routes for now.

FEVER DOESN'T TELL THE WHOLE STORY

Fever isn't the only indication of illness – and on its own can be an unreliable measure of how sick a baby really is. A baby who's running a moderately high fever but is cheerful and active is likely to be less sick than a baby who's running a low-grade fever (or no fever at all) but is clearly out of sorts and lethargic. After taking a baby's temperature, also take a look at other measures of well-being, including how a baby looks, is behaving and is eating.

Before you start. Try to keep your baby calm for half an hour before temperature taking, since crying or screaming could turn a slightly elevated temperature into a high one. (Though it's necessary to withhold hot or cold drinks or foods before taking an oral temperature, as they too could affect temperature readings, this precaution isn't necessary when taking rectal, axillary or tympanic temperatures.)

Choosing a thermometer. The use of glass mercury thermometers is no longer recommended because of the dangers of mercury exposure. Instead, choose from the following:

◆ *Digital thermometers.* These are safe, easy to use, readily available and relatively inexpensive. They can be used to take a rectal, oral or axillary (armpit) reading (but don't use the same thermometer for oral and rectal). With a digital thermometer, you'll have your reading in about 20 to 60 seconds – a real advantage when you're dealing with a squirming infant. Look for a thermometer that has a flexible tip for extra comfort. If

you want, you can use disposable covers available in chemists, but they are not necessary.

◆ *Dummy thermometers.* Shaped like a dummy, and designed to give an oral reading in a baby too young to use an oral thermometer, these usually read between 0.1° and 0.25°C (0.2° and 0.5°F) lower than rectal thermometers. And since they require an average of three minutes to get a reading, they are difficult to use with an uncooperative baby and therefore are not very reliable.

◆ *Tympanic thermometers.* These thermometers, which measure the temperature in the ear, are fairly expensive. And even though they provide a reading in just seconds, they're difficult to position and use correctly – especially in a young baby. In general, a reading from the ear is less reliable than an axillary (armpit) one, and neither is as accurate as a rectal reading – still considered the gold standard. Ear readings may be even less accurate in young infants, who have very narrow ear canals; most experts agree that you should hold off using an ear thermometer until your baby is at least three months old, preferably over a year. Wax in the ear can also interfere with the temperature reading, no matter what a child's age. If you do have a tympanic thermometer, ask the doctor for a demonstration on proper use.

◆ *Temporal artery thermometers.* These measure temperature with a transducer that rolls across the forehead, and have been shown in studies to be very accurate (though still not as accurate as a rectal). They're easier to use than in the past and more widely available but can be more expensive than other types.

The rectal method.

Taking the temperature.

♦ *Rectal:* Prepare the thermometer by lubricating the sensor tip with Vaseline and bare baby's bottom, speaking reassuringly as you do. Then turn baby onto his or her tummy on your lap (which allows the legs to hang down, making insertion easier) or on a bed or changing table (where a small pillow or folded towel under the hips will raise the baby's bottom slightly for easier insertion). To distract baby, try singing a couple of favourite songs, or putting a favourite book or toy in baby's line of vision. Spread the buttocks with one hand, exposing the anus (the rectal opening). With the other, slip about 2.5 cm (1 in) of the tip of the thermometer into the rectum, being careful not to force it. Hold the thermometer in place until it beeps, using your other fingers to press the buttocks together to keep the thermometer from sliding out and to keep baby from wriggling. Remove the thermometer immediately, however, if baby begins to show very active resistance.

♦ *Axillary or underarm:* An axillary reading is useful when a baby has diarrhoea or won't lie still for a rectal or if only an oral thermometer (which should *never* be used rectally) is available. You can use a digital rectal or oral thermometer for an underarm reading. Remove baby's shirt so it won't come between the thermometer and baby's skin, and be sure the armpit is dry. Place the tip of the thermometer well up into the armpit and hold the arm snugly over it, gently pressing the elbow against baby's side. Distract baby as needed.

♦ *Tympanic:* This thermometer takes a great deal of skill to use correctly. Ask the doctor for a demonstration.

Reading the thermometer. A rectal temperature is the most accurate since it picks up temperatures from the body's core. Temperatures obtained rectally, as they are most frequently in infants, are usually one-half to a full degree higher than those determined orally; axillary readings are about one degree lower than an oral temperature. The norm for an oral reading is 37°C (98.6°F); the norm rectally is 37.5°C (99.6°F); and 36.3°C (97.6°F) is normal for an axillary reading. A fever of 39°C (102.2°F) taken rectally is roughly

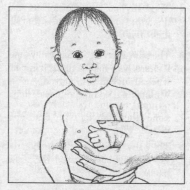

The underarm method.

equivalent to 38.4°C (101.2°F) taken orally and 37.9°C (100.2°F) by an armpit reading.

Storing the thermometer. After use, wash the thermometer with cold soapy water, rinse and swab the sensor tip with alcohol. Be careful not to wet the digital display, on/off button or battery cover.

EVALUATING A FEVER

Behaviour is a better gauge of how sick an infant is than body temperature. A baby can be seriously ill, with pneumonia or meningitis for example, and have no fever at all, or have a high fever with a mild cold.

Under the following circumstances a baby with a fever requires immediate medical attention (call the doctor even in the middle of the night, or go to an A&E department if the doctor can't be reached):

♦ The baby is under two months old with a fever of over 37.9°C (100.2°F) rectally.

♦ A baby over two months has a fever over 40.5°C (105°F) rectally.

♦ The baby has a convulsion for the first time (the body stiffens, eyes roll, limbs flail).

♦ The baby is crying inconsolably (and it clearly isn't colic), cries as if in pain when touched or moved, or is whimpering, non-responsive or limp.

♦ The baby has purple spots anywhere on the skin.

♦ The baby is having difficulty breathing once you've cleared the nasal passages.

♦ The baby's neck seems stiff; baby resists having the head pulled forward towards the chest.

♦ The onset of fever follows a period of exposure to an external heat source, such as the sun on a hot day or the closed interior of a car in hot weather. Heatstroke is a possibility (see page 586), and immediate emergency medical attention is indicated.

♦ A sudden increase in temperature occurs in a baby with a moderate fever who has been overdressed or bundled in blankets. This should be treated as heat illness.

♦ The doctor has instructed you to call immediately should your baby run a fever.

♦ You feel something's very wrong, but you just don't know what.

Under the following conditions a baby with fever needs medical attention as soon as practical:

♦ The fever is over 38°C (100.4°F) rectally for babies two to six months or

---

BEFORE THAT FIRST FEVER

The best time to ask the doctor what to do when your baby has a fever is *before* that first fever strikes – especially because it's most likely to strike (call it another Murphy's Law of Parenting) in the middle of the night. The two-month well-baby visit is a good time to set up or review that protocol. Find out, for instance, when to call the doctor, when to give medication, and what other methods of reducing a fever you should try.

HANDLING FEBRILE CONVULSIONS

Convulsions due to fever usually last only a minute or two. Should your baby have one, keep calm (remember, such convulsions are not dangerous) and take the following steps. Keep baby unrestrained in your arms or on a bed or another soft surface, lying on one side, with head lower than body if possible. Don't try to feed or put anything into baby's mouth, and remove anything (like a dummy) that might be in it. Babies often lose consciousness during a seizure, but they usually revive quickly without help. When a seizure has ended, the baby often wants to sleep.

Once the seizure has stopped you should call the doctor. (Any seizure that lasts five minutes or more requires immediate emergency help – dial 999.) If you don't reach help immediately and he or she is more than six months old (as most babies who have convulsions are), you can dose with paracetamol or ibuprofen to try to lower the temperature while you're waiting (but not while baby is convulsing). You can also give a sponge bath. But don't put baby in the bath to try to reduce the fever, since another seizure could occur and water could be inhaled.

over 39.2°C (102.6°F) for babies older than six months (or whatever temperature your baby's doctor recommends you call at). Though such a temperature is not in itself an indicator of a baby's being very sick (babies can run fevers of 40°C (104°F) with minor illness), check with the doctor, just in case. *Remember, younger babies need medical attention for any fever over 39°C (102.2°F).*

◆ The baby has a chronic illness, such as heart, kidney or neurological disease, or sickle-cell or other chronic anaemia.

◆ The baby is having febrile convulsions and has had convulsions with a fever in the past.

◆ The baby exhibits signs of dehydration: infrequent urination, dark yellow urine, scant saliva and tears, dry lips and skin, sunken eyes and fontanel.

◆ The baby's behaviour seems uncharacteristic: he or she is excessively cranky; lethargic or excessively sleepy; unable to sleep; sensitive to light; crying more than usual; refusing to eat; pulling at ears.

◆ A fever that has been low grade for a couple of days spikes suddenly; or a baby who has been sick with a cold for several days suddenly begins to run a fever (this may indicate a secondary infection, such as otitis media or pneumonia).

◆ A fever isn't brought down by fever-reducing medication.

◆ A low-grade fever (under 38.9°C (102°F) rectally) with mild cold or flu symptoms lasts for more than three days.

◆ A fever lasts more than twenty-four hours when there are no other detectable signs of illness.

TREATING A FEVER

If your baby has a fever, take these measures as needed, unless the doctor has recommended a different course of action.

Keep baby cool. Contrary to popular belief, keeping a feverish baby warm with blankets, heavy clothing or an overheated room is not a safe practice. These measures can actually lead to heatstroke by raising body temperature to dangerous levels. Dress your baby lightly to allow body heat to escape (no more than a nappy is needed in hot weather) and maintain room temperature at 20° to 21.1°C (68° to 70°F) (when necessary to keep the air cool, use an air conditioner or fan if you have one, but keep baby out of the path of the air flow).

Increase fluid intake. Because fever increases the loss of water through the skin, it's important to be sure a feverish baby gets an adequate intake of fluids. Give young infants frequent feedings of breast milk or formula. For older babies, offer good sources of fluids often. These include (if they're been introduced) diluted juices and juicy fruits (such as citrus and melons), water, clear soups and gelatin desserts (see pages 758–759). Encourage frequent sipping but don't force. If baby refuses to take any fluids for several hours during the day, inform the doctor.

Give fever-reducing medication, if necessary. The decision of whether (and when) to give a fever-reducing medication to your baby should be based on the doctor's recommendations (which you've hopefully secured in advance). In general, most doctors are comfortable having parents give paracetamol to infants over two months old when they have a high fever (over 38°C/100.4°F rectally for babies two to six months; over 39.2°C/102.6°F for babies older than six months) before they contact the doctor. If the fever goes down after

giving the medicine and there are no other indications that baby needs immediate medical attention (see Evaluating a Fever, page 570), contact the doctor as soon as practical (in the morning if the fever began in the middle of the night, for instance). If the temperature does not go down, or if it goes up, or if baby seems very uncomfortable, call the doctor right away – even if it's the middle of the night.

Sponging. Once a routine treatment for fever, sponging is now recommended only under certain circumstances, such as when fever-reducing medication isn't working (the temperature isn't down an hour after it is given); when trying to lower the body temperature of a baby under six months old without medication; or when trying to make a very feverish baby more comfortable.

Only tepid or lukewarm water (body temperature, neither warm nor cool to the touch) should be used for sponging. Using cool or cold water, or alcohol (once a popular fever-reducing rub), can raise rather than lower temperatures by inducing shivering, which prompts the confused body to turn up its thermostat. In addition, the alcohol fumes can be harmful if inhaled. Using hot water will also raise body temperatures and could, like overdressing, lead to heatstroke. You can sponge a feverish baby in the bath or out, but in either case the room should be comfortably warm and draught free. (If sponging seems to upset your baby, discontinue it.)

♦ Sponging out of the bath. Have three flannels in a basin of tepid water ready before you begin. Spread a waterproof sheet or pad, or a plastic tablecloth, on the bed or on your lap; place a thick towel over it and place baby, face-up, on top of the towel. Undress baby and cover with a light

PARACETAMOL
OR IBUPROFEN?

There are many kinds of pain relievers and fever reducers on the market, but only two should be considered for young children: paracetamol (Calpol and generic store brands) and ibuprofen (Nurofen and generic store brands). Giving aspirin to children became taboo after children who took aspirin to treat the symptoms of viral infections such as the flu were found to have a greater risk of contracting Reye's syndrome, a rare and potentially fatal disorder affecting the brain and liver. Because of this increased risk, the BMA advises against giving aspirin to children unless a doctor specifically prescribes its use.

Both paracetamol and ibuprofen work as well as aspirin to relieve pain or fever (and also taste good to many children), though they work differently in the body and have different side effects. For many years, paracetamol was the first choice for non-aspirin pain relief. Then over-the-counter ibuprofen liquids became available, and many paediatricians started to recommend them because they're slightly more powerful and longer lasting (with dosing every 6 to 8 hours compared to every 4 to 6 hours with paracetamol).

Paracetamol for infants is most widely available as a liquid syrup, but can also be obtained in drops, sprinkle or suppository form (which can come in handy when a child with a stomach flu needs to take fever medication but is vomiting, or when a baby refuses medication by mouth). Ibuprofen is also available in liquid or drop form. *Ibuprofen should be given only to children older than six months, and it should never be given to children who are dehydrated or vomiting continuously or who have abdominal pain.*

There are few side effects to these medications when used properly – and that's the critical part. Although paracetamol is considered safe when used as recommended, taking it regularly for longer than a week at a time can be dangerous. A large overdose of paracetamol (about 15 times the recommended dose) can cause fatal liver damage, which is probably why infant liquid paracetamol comes in such tiny bottles (and why all medicines should be stored out of baby's reach). The biggest drawback to ibuprofen is the potential for stomach irritation. To avoid this side effect, give your baby the medicine with a meal or drink.

The practice of alternating doses of paracetamol and ibuprofen to treat fever in children had been recommended by some paediatricians, but most doctors now agree that doing so long-term isn't beneficial and could be harmful. There have been some cases of kidney problems caused by long-term combination therapy with these two drugs.

If your child is over six months and has pain or fever, start with whichever of the two medications is in your medicine cabinet (if your baby is younger than six months, stick to paracetamol). If that doesn't do the job, try the other one, as long as you make sure to give correct doses, wait until it's safe to give another dose of medication (at least 4 hours with paracetamol, at least 6 hours with ibuprofen), and follow the recommended schedule according to the instructions on the label and advice from the doctor. And when you're not using them, keep them (like all medications) safely locked away, out of the reach of babies and children.

swaddling blanket or towel. Wring out one flannel so it won't drip, fold it, and place it on baby's forehead (remoisten if it begins to dry at any point during the sponging). Take another flannel and begin lightly rubbing baby's skin, exposing one area of the body at a time and keeping the rest lightly covered. Concentrate on the neck, face, stomach, inside of the elbows and knees, but also include the area under the arms and around the groin. The blood brought to the surface by rubbing will be cooled as the tepid water evaporates on the skin. When the rubbing flannel begins to dry out, switch it with the third flannel. Continue rubbing and sponging your baby, alternating flannels as needed, for at least twenty minutes to half an hour (it takes this long to lower body temperature). If at any time the water in the basin cools to below body temperature, add enough warm water to raise it again.

♦ Sponging in the bath. For many babies, baths are soothing and comforting, especially when they are sick. If yours is one of these, do the sponging in the bath. Again, the water should be body temperature, and you should sponge and rub for at least twenty minutes to half an hour

to bring the temperature down. Do not put a baby who has had a febrile convulsion in a bath for sponging.

What not to do. As important as knowing what to do when your baby has a fever is knowing what not to do:

♦ Do not force rest. A really sick baby will want to rest, in or out of the cot. If yours wants out, moderate activity is okay, but discourage strenuous activity as this could raise body temperature further, especially in a warm room.

♦ Do not overdress or bundle a baby warmly.

♦ Do not cover baby with a wet towel or wet sheet, since this could prevent heat from escaping through the skin.

♦ Do not 'starve a fever'. Fever raises the caloric requirement, and sick babies in fact need more calories, not fewer.

♦ Do not give aspirin or paracetamol when heatstroke is suspected. Instead, see page 586.

♦ ♦ ♦

CHAPTER 19

First Aid Do's and Don'ts

oo-boos happen. Even when you're conscientious, even when you're painstakingly careful and ever vigilant, even when you've taken all the precautions and then some. Hopefully, most of the boo-boos that happen in your baby's life will be small (the kiss-and-make-better variety). Still, you'll need to know how to respond in the event of a bigger mishap, and how to care for injuries (such as cuts, bruises, burns and breaks) that need more treatment than a cuddle – and that's what this chapter is for. It will be even more helpful if reinforced with a live first-aid course. But don't wait until baby tumbles down the stairs or chews on a rhododendron leaf to look up what to do in an emergency. Now – before those incidents happen – become as familiar with the procedures for treating common injuries as you are with those for bathing baby or changing a nappy, and review less common ones when appropriate (snakebite, for example, if you visit a desert area or before you go on a camping trip). See that anyone else who cares for your baby does the same.

Below are the most common injuries, what you should know about them, how to treat (and not treat) them, and when to seek medical care for them. Types of injuries are listed alphabetically (abdominal injuries, bites and broken bones, for example), with individual injuries numbered for easy cross-reference.

A grey bar has been added to the top of these pages, making them easy to flip to in an emergency.

ABDOMINAL INJURIES

1. Internal bleeding. A severe blow to your baby's abdomen could result in internal injury. The signs of such injury would include: bruising or other discoloration of the abdomen; vomited or coughed-up blood that is dark or bright red and has the consistency of coffee grounds (this could also be a sign of baby's having swallowed a caustic substance); blood (it may be dark or bright red) in the stool or urine; shock (cold, clammy, pale skin; weak, rapid pulse; chills; confusion; and possibly nausea, vomiting and/or shallow breathing). Seek emergency medical assistance by calling 999. If baby appears to be in shock (No. 46), treat immediately. Do not give food or drink.

2. Cuts or lacerations of the abdomen. Treat as for other cuts (Nos 49, 50). With a major laceration, intestines may protrude. Do not try to

put them back into the abdomen
Instead, cover them with a clean, moistened flannel or nappy and get
emergency medical assistance immediately.

BITES

3. Animal bites. Try to avoid
moving the affected part. Call the
doctor immediately. Wash wound gently
and thoroughly with soap and water. Do
not apply antiseptic or anything else.
Control bleeding with pressure (Nos 49,
50, 51), and apply a sterile bandage. Try
to restrain animal for testing, but avoid
getting bitten. Dogs, cats and bats may
be rabid, particularly in other countries,
especially if they attacked unprovoked.
Infection (redness, tenderness, swelling)
is common with cat bites and may
require antibiotics.

Low-risk dog bites (bites from a dog
that is known not to have rabies) do not
usually require antibiotics, but it's important to consult your baby's doctor for any
animal bite, to decide on the need for
antibiotics. *Call the doctor immediately* if
redness, swelling and tenderness develop
at the site of the bite.

4. Human bites. If your baby is
bitten by a sibling or another child,
don't worry unless the skin is broken. If
it is, wash the bite area thoroughly with
mild soap and cool water by running tap
water over it, if you can, or by pouring
water from a jug or a cup. Don't rub the
wound or apply any spray or ointment
(antibiotic or otherwise). Simply cover
the bite with a sterile dressing and call
the doctor. Use pressure to stem the
bleeding (No. 50), if necessary.
Antibiotics may be prescribed to prevent infection.

5. Insect stings or bites. Treat
insect stings or bites as follows:

- Scrape off the honeybee's stinger
  immediately, by scraping it horizon-
  tally with the edge of a blunt butter
  knife, a credit card or your fingernail, or gently remove it with
  tweezers or your fingers. (Try not to
  pinch the stinger, because doing so
  could inject more venom.) Then
  treat as below.

- Remove ticks *promptly,* using blunt
  tweezers or your fingertips protected
  by a tissue, paper towel or rubber
  glove. Grasp the bug near the head
  as close to baby's skin as possible and
  pull upwards, steadily and evenly.
  Don't twist, jerk, squeeze, crush or
  puncture the tick. *Don't* use such
  folk remedies as Vaseline, petrol or a
  hot match – they can make matters
  worse.

- Wash the site of a minor bee or
  wasp sting, or an ant, spider or tick
  bite with soap and water. Then
  apply ice or cold compresses (see
  page 762) if there appears to be
  swelling or pain.

- Apply calamine lotion to itchy bites,
  such as those caused by mosquitoes.

- If there seems to be extreme pain
  after a spider bite, apply ice or cold
  compresses and *call 999 for emergency help.* Try to find the spider and
  take it to the hospital with you (avoid
  being bitten yourself), or at least be
  able to describe it; it might be poisonous. If you know the spider was
  poisonous – a black widow, brown
  recluse spider, tarantula or scorpion,
  for example – *get emergency treatment immediately,* even before
  symptoms appear.

- Watch for signs of hypersensitivity,
  such as swelling of the face, lips or
  tongue, hoarse voice or any shortness
  of breath, following a bee, wasp or

hornet sting. If baby exhibits such symptoms after a first sting he may develop allergies to the venom, in which case a subsequent sting could be fatal if immediate emergency treatment is not administered. Should your baby's reaction to a sting be anything more than pain or swelling at the immediate site of the sting, report this to the doctor, who is likely to recommend allergy testing. If allergy is diagnosed, it will probably be necessary for you to carry a bee-sting emergency kit with you on outings during bee season.

♦ It's possible, of course, for sensitization to bee venom to occur without a previously noticed reaction, especially in a baby. So if after a sting your baby should break out in hives all over the body, experience difficulty breathing, hoarseness, coughing, wheezing, severe headache, nausea, vomiting, thickened tongue, facial swelling, weakness, dizziness or fainting, *get immediate emergency medical attention.*

6. Snakebite. It's rare for a baby in the UK to be bitten by a poisonous snake, but such a bite is very dangerous. If you suspect your baby has been bitten by a snake, seek medical treatment immediately and call NHS direct (0845 4647) for treatment recommendations. Because of an infant's small size, even a tiny amount of venom can be fatal. Following such a bite, it is important to keep the baby and the affected part as still as possible. If the bite is on a limb, immobilize it, with a splint if necessary, and keep it below the level of the heart. Use a cool compress, if available, to relieve pain, but *do not* apply ice or give any medication without medical advice. *Get prompt medical help;* and be ready to identify the variety of snake if possible. If you will not be able to get medical help within an hour, apply a loose constricting band (a belt, tie or hair ribbon loose enough for you to slip a finger under) 5 cm (2 in) above the bite to slow circulation. (Do not tie such a band around a finger or toe, or around the neck, head or trunk.) Check pulse (see page 599) beneath the band frequently to be sure circulation is not cut off, and loosen it if the limb begins to swell. Make a note of the time it was tied. *Do not* suck out the venom by mouth and *do not* make an incision of any kind, as these are not medically approved treatments. If baby is not breathing, give CPR (see page 596). Treat for shock (No. 46), if necessary.

Even if you suspect the snake was not poisonous, call NHS Direct and your doctor to be certain.

7. Marine animal stings. Such stings are not usually serious, but an occasional baby or child will have a severe reaction. Medical treatment should be sought immediately as a precaution. First-aid treatment varies with the type of marine animal involved, but, in general, any clinging fragments of the stinger should be gingerly brushed away with a clean nappy or piece of clothing (to protect your own fingers). Treatment for heavy bleeding (No. 51), shock (No. 46) or stopped breathing (see page 600), if needed, should be begun immediately. (Don't worry about light bleeding; it may help purge toxins.) The sting of a stingray, lionfish, catfish, stonefish or sea urchin should be soaked in very warm water, if available, for 30 minutes, or until medical help arrives. The toxins from the sting of a jellyfish or Portuguese man-of-war can be counteracted by applying alcohol, diluted ammonia or meat tenderizer. (Pack a couple of alcohol pads in your beach bag, just in case.)

BLEEDING
See Nos 49, 50, 51

BLEEDING, INTERNAL
See No. 1

BROKEN BONES OR FRACTURES

8. Possible broken arms, legs, collarbones or fingers. It's hard to tell when a bone is broken in a baby. Signs of a break include: a snapping sound at the time of the injury; deformity (although this could also indicate a dislocation, No. 17); inability to move or bear weight on the part; severe pain (persistent crying could be a clue); numbness and/or tingling (neither of which a baby would be able to tell you about); swelling and discoloration. If a fractured limb is suspected, don't move the child (if possible) without checking with the doctor first – unless necessary for safety. If you must move baby immediately, first carefully try to immobilize the injured limb by splinting it in the position it's in with a ruler, a magazine, a book or other firm object, padded with a soft cloth to protect the skin. Or use a small, firm pillow as a splint. Fasten the splint securely at the break and above and below it with bandages, strips of cloth, scarves or neckties, but not so tightly that circulation is hampered. Check regularly to be sure the splint doesn't cut off circulation. If no potential splint is handy, try to splint the injured limb with your arm. Though fractures in small children usually mend quickly, medical treatment is necessary to ensure proper healing. Take your child to an A&E department.

9. Compound fractures. If bone protrudes through the skin, don't touch it. Cover the injury with sterile gauze or with a clean cloth nappy; control bleeding with pressure (Nos 50, 51) and get emergency medical assistance. Do not give baby food or drink.

10. Possible neck or back injury. If neck or back injury is suspected, don't move baby *at all*. Call for emergency medical assistance. Cover and keep child comfortable while waiting for help and, if possible, put some heavy objects (such as books) around the child's head to help immobilize it. Don't give food or drink. If there is severe bleeding (No. 50), shock (No. 46) or absence of breathing (see page 600), treat these immediately.

BRUISES, SKIN
See No. 47

BURNS AND SCALDS

Important: If a child's clothing is on fire, use a coat, blanket, rug, bedspread or your own body to smother the flames.

11. Limited burns from heat. If it's an extremity (arm, leg, foot, hand, finger) that has been burned, immerse the part in cool water (if possible, and if baby is cooperative, hold it under running cool water). If baby's face or trunk is burned, apply cool compresses (10° to 15.5°C/50° to 60°F). Continue until baby doesn't seem to be in pain any more, usually about half an hour. Don't apply ice, butter or ointments to the burn, all of which could compound the skin damage, and don't break any blisters that form. After soaking, gently pat burned area dry and cover with nonadhesive material (such as a non-stick bandage, or in an emergency, aluminum foil). Burns on the face, hands, feet or

BE PREPARED

- Discuss with your baby's doctor what the best plan of action would be in case of injury – calling the surgery, going to an A&E department or following some other protocol. Recommendations may vary, depending upon the seriousness of the injury, the day of the week and the time of day.

- Keep your first-aid supplies (see page 41) in a childproof, easily manageable kit or box so they can be moved as a whole to an accident site. Make sure you have a charged cordless or mobile phone handy, so that it can be taken to the site of injury in or around your home.

- Near each telephone in your home, post the numbers of the doctors your family uses, the nearest hospital A&E department (or the one you plan on using) and your pharmacy, as well as the number of a close friend or neighbour you can call on in an emergency. Keep a card with the same listings in your changing bag.

- Know the quickest route to the A&E department or other emergency medical facility.

- Take a course in baby CPR, and keep your skills current and ready to use with periodic refresher courses and regular home practice on a doll. Also become familiar with first-aid procedures for common injuries.

- Keep some cash reserved in a safe place in case you need cab fare to get to A&E or a doctor's surgery in an emergency.

- Learn to handle minor accidents calmly, which will help you keep your cool should a serious one ever occur. Your manner and tone of voice (or those of another caregiver) will affect how your baby responds to an injury. Panic or worry on your part could upset your baby. A baby who is upset is less likely to cooperate in an emergency and will be harder to treat.

- Remember that TLC (tender loving care) is often the best treatment for minor injuries. But tailor your comfort to the hurt's degree of seriousness. A smile, a kiss and a little reassurance ('You're all right') are all a little bump on the knee may need. But a painful pinched finger will probably warrant a heavy dose of kisses and some distraction. In most cases, you will need to calm a baby before giving first aid. Only in life-threatening situations (which are fortunately rare, and in which babies are not usually up to being uncooperative) will taking some time to quiet baby interfere with the outcome of treatment.

---

genitals should be seen by a doctor immediately. Any burn, even a minor one, on a child under a year old warrants a call to the doctor.

12. Extensive burns from heat. Keep baby lying flat. Remove any clothing from the burn area that does not adhere to the wound. Apply cool wet compresses (you can use a flannel) to the injured area (but not to more than 25 per cent of the body at one time). Keep the baby comfortably warm, with extremities higher than heart if they are burned. Do not apply pressure, ointments, butter or other fats, powder or boric acid soaks to the burn. If baby is conscious and doesn't have severe mouth burns, nurse or give water or another fluid. Transport the child to the A&E department at once or call for emergency medical assistance.

13. Chemical burns. Caustic substances (such as lye and acids) can cause serious burns. Using a clean cloth, gently brush off dry chemical matter from the skin and remove any contaminated clothing. Immediately wash the skin with large amounts of water. Call a doctor or an A&E department for further advice. Get immediate medical assistance if there is difficult or painful breathing, which could indicate lung injury from inhalation of caustic fumes. (If a chemical has been swallowed, see No. 42.)

14. Electrical burns. Immediately disconnect the power source, if possible. Or separate the victim from the source using a dry non-metallic object such as a wooden broom, wooden ladder, rope, cushion, chair or even a large book – but not your bare hands. Initiate CPR (see page 596) if baby is not breathing. All electrical burns should be evaluated by a doctor, so call your baby's doctor or go to A&E at once.

15. Sunburn. If your baby (or anyone else in the family) gets a sunburn, treat it by applying cool tap-water compresses (see page 764) for 10 to 15 minutes, three or four times a day, until the redness subsides; the evaporating water helps to cool the skin. In between these treatments, apply pure aloe vera gel (available in pharmacies or directly from the leaves of an aloe plant if you have one), or a mild moisturizing cream. Don't use petroleum jelly (Vaseline) on a burn, because it seals out air, which is needed for healing. Don't give antihistamines unless they are prescribed by the doctor. For severe burns, steroid ointments or creams may be prescribed, and large blisters may be drained and dressed. A baby pain reliever, such as paracetamol, may reduce the discomfort. If there is swelling, ibuprofen would be a better choice. As with any other burn in a baby, sunburns merit at least a call to the doctor. Extensive sunburn can cause more serious symptoms, such as headache and vomiting, and needs urgent medical evaluation.

CHEMICAL BURNS
See No. 13

CHOKING
See page 593

CONVULSIONS

16. Symptoms of a seizure or convulsion include: collapse, eyes rolling upwards, stiffening of the body followed by uncontrolled jerking movements, and in the most serious cases, breathing difficulty. Brief convulsions are not uncommon with fevers (see page 571). Deal with a seizure this way: clear the area around baby, but don't restrain except if necessary to prevent injury. Loosen clothing around the neck and middle, and lay baby on one side with head lower than hips. Don't put anything in the mouth, including food or drink, breast or bottle. Call the doctor. When the convulsion has passed, sponge with cool water if fever is present, but don't put baby into a bath or throw water in his or her face. If baby isn't breathing, begin CPR (see page 596) immediately.

CUTS
See Nos 49, 50

DISLOCATIONS

17. Shoulder and elbow dislocations are not as common among babies as they are among toddlers, who get them mostly because they are often tugged along by the arm by adults in a hurry (or 'flown' through the air by their arms). A deformity of the arm or the inability to move it, usually combined with persistent crying because of pain, are typical indications. A trip to the doctor's surgery or A&E, where an experienced professional will reposition the dislocated part, will provide virtually instant relief. If pain seems severe, apply a cool compress and a splint before leaving (see pages 762 and 578) but do not give food or drink.

DOG BITES

See No. 3

DROWNING (SUBMERSION INJURY)

18. Even a child who quickly revives after being taken from the water unconscious should get medical evaluation. For the child who remains unconscious, have someone else call for emergency medical assistance, if possible, while you begin CPR (see page 596). Even if no one is available to phone for help, begin CPR immediately and call later. Don't stop CPR until the child revives or help arrives, no matter how long that takes. If there is vomiting, turn baby to one side to avoid choking. If you suspect a blow to the head or a neck injury, immobilize these parts (No. 10).

EAR INJURIES

19. Foreign object in the ear. Try to dislodge the object with these techniques:

♦ For an insect, use a torch to try to lure it out.

♦ For a metal object, try a magnet to draw it out (but don't insert the magnet in the ear).

♦ For a plastic or wooden object that can be seen and is not deeply lodged in the ear, dab a drop of quick-drying glue (don't use one that might bond to the skin) on a straightened paper clip and touch it to the object. Do not probe into the inner ear. Wait for the glue to dry, then pull the clip out, hopefully with the object attached. Don't attempt this if there's no one around to help hold the baby still.

If the above techniques fail, don't try to dig the object out with your fingers or an instrument. Instead, take baby to the doctor's surgery or A&E.

20. Damage to the ear. If a pointed object has been pushed into the ear or if your baby shows signs of ear injury (bleeding from the ear canal, sudden difficulty hearing, swollen earlobe), call the doctor.

ELECTRIC SHOCK

21. Break contact with the electrical source by turning off the power, if possible, or separate the child from the current by using a dry, non-metallic object such as a wooden broom, wooden ladder, robe, cushion, chair, or even a large book. Call for emergency medical assistance, and if baby isn't breathing, begin CPR (see page 596).

EYE INJURY

Important: Don't apply pressure to an injured eye, touch the eye with your fingers, or instill medications without a doctor's advice. Keep baby from rubbing the eye by holding a small cup or glass over it or by

Baby won't enjoy an eye bath, but it's crucial for washing away a corrosive substance.

restraining baby's hands, if necessary.

22. Foreign object in the eye. If you can see the object (lash or grain of sand, for example), wash your hands and use a moist cottonwool ball to gently attempt to remove it from baby's eye, while someone else holds the baby still (attempt this only in the corner of the eye, beneath the lower lid, or on the white of the eye; stay away from the pupil to avoid scratching the cornea). Or try pulling the upper lid down over the lower for a few seconds. If those techniques don't work, and if baby is very uncomfortable, you can also try flushing the object out by pouring a little tepid (body temperature) water from a jug, cup or bottle into the eye while someone holds baby still (but be careful not to get water into baby's nose).

If after these attempts you can still see the object in the eye or if baby still seems uncomfortable, proceed to the doctor's surgery or A&E, since the object may have become embedded or scratched the eye. Don't try to remove an embedded object yourself. Cover the eye with a sterile gauze pad taped loosely in place, or with a few clean tissues or a clean handkerchief, to alleviate some of the discomfort en route. Do not apply pressure.

23. Corrosive substance in the eye. Flush the eye immediately and thoroughly with plain lukewarm water (poured from a jug, cup or bottle) for 15 minutes, holding the eye open with your fingers. If just one eye is involved, keep baby's head turned so that the unaffected eye is higher than the affected one and the chemical runoff doesn't drip into it. Don't use drops or ointments, and don't allow baby to rub the eye or eyes. Call the doctor or A&E for further instructions.

24. Injury to the eye with a pointed or sharp object. Keep baby in a semi-reclining position while you seek help. If the object is still in the eye, do not try to remove it. If it isn't, cover the eye lightly with a gauze pad, clean flannel, or facial tissue; do not apply pressure. In either case, get emergency medical assistance immediately. Though such injuries often look worse than they are, it's wise to consult an ophthalmologist any time the eye is scratched or punctured, even slightly.

25. Injury to the eye with a blunt object. Keep baby lying face-up. Cover the injured eye with an ice pack or cold compress (see page 762). If the eye blackens, if baby seems to be having difficulty seeing or keeps rubbing the eye a lot, or if an object hit the eye at high speed, consult the doctor.

FAINTING/LOSS OF CONSCIOUSNESS

26. Check for breathing, and if it is absent begin CPR *immediately* (see page 596). If you detect breathing, keep baby lying flat, lightly covered for

TREATING A YOUNG PATIENT

Babies are rarely cooperative patients. No matter how uncomfortable the symptoms of their illness or how painful their injuries, they're likely to consider the treatment worse. Because of their limited comprehension, it won't help to tell them that applying pressure to a bleeding cut will make it heal faster or that the ice pack will keep a bruised finger from swelling. Your best approach when trying to treat a baby is to use distraction.

Entertainment (begun before the treatment and, hopefully, before the tears have started) in the form of a favourite music box or audiotape; a toy dog that yaps and wags its tail; a choo-choo train that can travel across the coffee table; or a parent or sibling who can dance, jump up and down, or sing silly songs can help make the difference between a successful treatment session and a disastrous one. You can also try sailing some boats in the soaking water; taking a teddy bear's temperature; giving a doll a dose of medicine; putting an ice pack on a stuffed doggie's boo-boo.

How forceful you will have to be about treatment will depend on the severity of the injury. A slight bruise may not warrant upsetting yourself and a baby who's rejecting the ice pack. A severe burn, however, will certainly merit the cold soaks, even if baby screams and thrashes during the entire treatment. In most cases, try to treat at least briefly: even a few minutes of soaking will reduce inflammation of a burn; even a few minutes of ice on a bruise will reduce swelling. Know when to call it quits. When baby's upset outweighs the benefits of the treatment, abandon it.

warmth if necessary. Loosen clothing around the neck. Turn baby's head to one side and clear the mouth of any food or objects. Check briefly to see if baby could have got into a medicine or household cleanser (if so, call for emergency medical assistance. Don't give anything to eat or drink. Call the doctor immediately.

FINGER AND TOE INJURIES

27. Bruises. Babies, ever curious, are particularly prone to painful bruises from catching fingers in drawers and doors. For such a bruise, soak the finger in iced-water. As much as an hour of soaking is recommended, with a break every 15 minutes (long enough for the finger to rewarm) to avoid frostbite.

Unfortunately, few babies will sit still for this long, though you may be able to treat for a few minutes by using distraction or force. A stubbed toe will also benefit from soaking, but again it often isn't practical with a baby who won't cooperate. The bruised fingers and toes will swell less if kept elevated – again, not likely to happen when the victim is a baby.

If the injured finger or toe becomes very swollen very quickly, is misshapen or can't be straightened, suspect a break (No. 8). Call the doctor immediately if the bruise is from a wringer-type injury or from catching a hand or foot in the spokes of a moving wheel.

28. Bleeding under the nail. When a finger or toe is badly bruised, a blood clot may form under the nail, causing painful pressure. If blood oozes out from under the nail, press on it to encourage the flow, which will help to relieve the pressure. Soak the injury in iced water if baby will tolerate it. If the pain continues, a hole may have to be made in the nail to relieve the pressure. Your doctor can do the job or may tell you how to do it yourself.

29. Torn nail. For a small tear, secure with a piece of adhesive tape or a plaster until the torn nail grows to a point where it can be trimmed. For a tear that is almost complete, trim away along the tear line and cover with a plaster until the nail is long enough to protect the fingertip once again.

30. Detached nail. The nail will fall off by itself; it's not necessary to pull it off. Soaking the finger or toe is not recommended because constant moisture of a nail bed without the protection of a nail increases the risk of fungal infections. Do make sure, however, to keep the area clean. Antibiotic ointments can be applied but are not always necessary (ask your baby's doctor). Cover the nail bed with a fresh plaster often, but once the nail starts growing back in, plasters are not necessary. It usually takes four to six months for a nail to grow all the way back. If the redness, heat and swelling of infection occur at any point, call the doctor.

FROSTBITE AND HYPOTHERMIA

31. Babies are extremely susceptible to frostbite, particularly on fingers and toes, ears, nose and cheeks. In frostbite, the affected part becomes very cold and turns white or yellowish grey. Should you note such signs in your baby, immediately try to warm the frosty parts against your body – open your coat and shirt and tuck baby inside next to your skin. As soon as possible, get to a doctor or an emergency room. If that isn't feasible immediately, get baby indoors and begin a gradual rewarming process. Don't put a baby with frostbite right next to a radiator, stove, open fire or heat lamp, because the damaged skin may burn; don't try to quick-thaw in hot water, which can also add to the damage. Do not rub. Instead, soak affected fingers and toes directly in water that is about 38.9°C (102°F) – just a little warmer than normal body temperature and just slightly warm to the touch. For unsoakable parts, such as nose, ears and cheeks, use compresses (wet flannels or towels) of the same temperature, but don't apply pressure. Continue the soaks until colour returns to the skin, usually in 30 to 60 minutes (add warm water as needed), nursing baby or giving warm (not hot) fluids by bottle or cup as you do. As frostbitten skin rewarms it becomes red and slightly swollen, and it may blister. If baby's injury hasn't been seen by a doctor up to this point, it is important to get medical attention now.

If, once the injured parts have been warmed, you have to go out again to take baby to the doctor (or anywhere else), be especially careful to keep the affected areas warm en route, as refreezing of thawed tissues can cause additional damage.

Much more common than frostbite (and much less serious) is frostnip. In frostnip, the affected body part is cold and pale, but rewarming (as for frostbite) takes less time and causes less pain and swelling. As with frostbite, avoid dry heat and avoid refreezing with frostnip. Though a surgery or A&E visit isn't necessary, a call to the doctor makes sense.

After prolonged exposure to cold, a baby's body temperature may drop below normal levels. This is a medical emergency known as hypothermia. No time should be wasted in getting a baby who seems unusually cold to the touch to the nearest A&E department. Keep baby warm next to your body en route.

HEAD INJURIES

Important: Head injuries are usually more serious if a child falls onto a hard surface from a height equal to or greater than his or her own height, or is hit with a heavy object. Blows to the side of the head may do more damage than those to the front or back of the head.

32. Cuts and bruises to the scalp. Because of the profusion of blood vessels in the scalp, heavy bleeding is common with cuts to the head, even tiny ones, and bruises there tend to swell to egg size very quickly. Treat as you would any cut (Nos 49, 50) or bruise (No. 47). Check with the doctor for all but very minor scalp wounds.

33. Possibly serious head trauma. Most babies experience several minor bumps on the head during the first year. Usually these require no more than a few make-it-better kisses from mummy or daddy, but it's wise to observe a baby carefully for 6 hours following a severe blow to the head. Call the doctor or summon emergency medical assistance immediately if your baby shows any of these signs after a head injury:

- Loss of consciousness. If your baby has lost consciousness, call 999 immediately. (A brief period of drowsiness may be common and may be nothing to worry about, but call the doctor to be sure.)

- Convulsions

- Difficulty being roused. Check every hour or two during daytime naps, two or three times during the

Pupils (the dark circle in the centre of the eyeball) should become smaller in response to light (above) and larger once the light is removed (below).

night for the first 6 hours following the injury to be sure baby is responsive; if you can't rouse a sleeping baby, check for breathing: see page 598.

- More than one or two episodes of vomiting

- A depression or indentation in the skull, or so much swelling over the wound that you can't tell whether the skull might be depressed

- Inability to move an arm or leg

- Oozing of blood or watery fluid from the ears or nose

- Black-and-blue areas appearing around the eyes or behind the ears

- Apparent pain for more than an hour that interferes with normal activity and/or sleep

- Dizziness that persists beyond one hour after the injury (baby's balance seems off)

♦ If baby's pupil size is uneven, or pupils don't respond to the light of a penlight by shrinking (constricting; see illustration, page 585) or to the removal of the light by growing larger (dilating). Call 999 immediately

♦ Unusual paleness that persists for more than a short time

♦ Your baby just isn't acting right – seems dazed, confused, doesn't recognize you, is unusually clumsy, and so on

While waiting for help, keep your baby lying quietly, and if vomiting, with head turned to one side. Treat for shock (No. 46), if necessary. Begin CPR (see page 596) if baby stops breathing.

Don't offer any food or drink until you talk to the doctor.

HEAT INJURIES

34. Heatstroke typically comes on suddenly. Signs to watch for include hot and dry (or occasionally, moist) skin, very high fever, diarrhoea, agitation or lethargy, confusion, convulsions and loss of consciousness. If you suspect heatstroke, wrap your baby in a large towel that has been soaked in iced water (dump ice cubes in the sink while it's filling with cold tap water, then add the towel) and summon immediate emergency medical help, or rush baby to the nearest A&E department. If the towel becomes warm, repeat with a freshly chilled one.

HYPOTHERMIA
See No. 31

INSECT STINGS OR BITES
See No. 5

LIP, SPLIT OR CUT
See Nos 35, 36

MOUTH INJURIES

35. Split lip. Few babies escape the first year without at least one cut on the lip. Fortunately, these cuts usually look a lot worse than they are and heal a lot more quickly than you'd think. To ease pain and control bleeding, apply an ice pack. Or let an older baby suck on an ice pop. If the cut gapes open, or if bleeding doesn't stop in 10 or 15 minutes, call the doctor. Occasionally a lip injury is caused by baby chewing on an electrical cord. If this is suspected, call the doctor.

36. Cuts inside the lip or mouth (including tongue). Such injuries, too, are common in young children. An ice pack for young infants, or an ice pop to suck on will relieve pain and control bleeding inside the lip or cheek. To stop bleeding of the tongue, if it doesn't stop spontaneously, apply pressure to cut with a piece of gauze or clean cloth. If the injury is in the back of the throat or on the soft palate (the rear of the upper mouth), if there is a puncture wound from a sharp object (such as a pencil or a stick), or if bleeding doesn't stop within 10 to 15 minutes, call the doctor.

37. Knocked-out tooth. There is little chance that the dentist will try to reimplant a dislodged baby tooth (such implantations often abscess and rarely hold), so precautions to preserve the tooth aren't necessary. But the dentist will want to see the tooth to be sure it's whole. Fragments left in the gum could be expelled and then inhaled or choked on by the baby. So take the tooth along to the dentist or to A&E if you are unable to reach a dentist.

Applying pressure to a cut lip with a piece of gauze held between thumb and forefinger will stop the bleeding.

Pinching the nostrils stems the flow of a bloody nose.

38. Broken tooth. Clean dirt or debris carefully from the mouth with warm water and gauze or a clean cloth. Be sure the broken parts of the tooth are not still in baby's mouth – they could cause choking. Place cold compresses (see page 762) on the face in the area of the injured tooth to minimize swelling. Call the dentist as soon as you can for further instructions.

Nose Injuries

39. Nosebleeds. Keeping baby in an upright position or leaning slightly forward, pinch both nostrils gently between your thumb and index finger for 10 minutes. (Baby will automatically switch to mouth breathing.) Try to calm baby, because crying will increase the blood flow. If bleeding persists, pinch for 10 minutes more. If this doesn't work and bleeding continues, call the doctor – keeping baby upright while you do. Frequent nosebleeds, even if easily stopped, should be reported to baby's doctor.

40. Foreign object in the nose. Difficulty breathing through the nose and/or a foul-smelling, sometimes bloody, nasal discharge may be a sign that something has been pushed up the nose. Keep baby calm and encourage mouth breathing. Remove the object with your fingers if you can reach it easily, but don't probe or use tweezers or anything else that could injure the nose if baby moves unexpectedly or that could push the object farther into the nasal canal. If you can't remove the object, blow through your nose and try to get baby to imitate your action. If this fails, take baby to the doctor or to A&E.

41. Blows to the nose. If there is bleeding, keep baby upright and leaning forward to reduce the swallowing of blood and the risk of choking on it (No. 39). Use an ice pack or cold compresses (see page 762) to reduce swelling. Check with the doctor to be sure there is no break.

POISONING

42. Swallowed poisons. Any non-food substance is a potential poison. If your baby becomes unconscious, and you know of or suspect the ingestion of a dangerous substance, begin emergency treatment immediately. Place baby face-up on a table and check for respiration (see page 598). If there is no sign of breathing, begin CPR promptly. Call for emergency medical assistance after one minute, then continue CPR until baby revives or until help arrives.

Symptoms vary according to the baby's size and the product ingested. (In some cases there may be none at all.) Some common symptoms are: lethargy, agitation, or other behaviour that deviates from the norm; racing, irregular pulse and/or rapid breathing; diarrhoea or vomiting; excessive watering of the eyes, sweating, drooling; hot, dry skin and mouth; dilated or constricted pupils; flickering, sideways eye movements; tremors or convulsions.

If your baby has several of these symptoms (and they cannot be explained in any other way), or if you have evidence that your baby has definitely or possibly ingested a questionable substance, do not try to treat it on your own. Instead, call your doctor or the emergency services *immediately* for instructions. Call even if there are no symptoms – they may not appear for hours. Take with you to the phone the container the suspected substance came in, label intact, as well as any of the remaining contents. Report the name of the substance (or of the plant if your baby ingested greenery) and how much of it you know or believe baby took, if it's possible to determine that. Also be prepared to supply your baby's age, size, weight and symptoms.

Never give activated charcoal (used to absorb the poison) or anything to induce vomiting (including syrup of ipecac) without medical advice. The wrong treatment can do much more harm than good.

43. Noxious fumes or gases. Fumes from petrol, car exhaust and some poisonous chemicals and dense smoke from fires can be toxic. (Every year in the UK more than 50 people die from accidental carbon monoxide poisoning, and symptoms often mimic the flu.) Promptly get a baby who has been exposed to any such hazards into fresh air (open windows or take the child outside). If baby is not breathing, begin CPR (see page 596) *immediately* and continue until breathing is well established or help arrives. If possible, have someone else call the emergency services while you continue CPR. If no one else is around, take a moment to call for help yourself after one minute of resuscitation efforts – and then return immediately to CPR. Unless an emergency vehicle is on its way, transport baby to a medical facility promptly, but not if doing so means discontinuing CPR – or if you were also exposed and your judgment is impaired. Have someone else drive. Even if you should succeed in establishing breathing, immediate medical attention will be necessary.

POISON IVY

44. Most children who come in contact with poison ivy will have an allergic reaction (usually a red, itchy rash, with possible swelling, blistering, and oozing) that develops within 12 to 48 hours and can last from 10 days to 4 weeks. If you know your baby has had such contact, remove his or her clothing, protecting your hands from the sap (which contains the resin that triggers the reaction) with gloves, paper towels or a clean nappy. The rash itself is not contagious and won't spread from person to person or from one part of the body to another once the sap has been washed away (do this as quickly as possible, preferably within 10 minutes).

To prevent resin from 'fixing', wash the skin thoroughly with soap and flush with cool water for at least 10 minutes; rinse thoroughly. In a pinch, use a wipe. Also wash anything else that may have come in contact with the plants (including clothes, pets, pushchair, and so on); the rash-causing resin can remain active for up to a year on such objects. Shoes can be thoroughly wiped down if they aren't washable.

Should a reaction occur, calamine or an anti-itch lotion that contains pramoxine will help relieve the itching, but avoid lotions that contain antihistamines (though the doctor may recommend an oral antihistamine to reduce itching and scratching, or in the case of severe poison ivy or swelling in sensitive areas, a few days of an oral steroid). Paracetamol, ibuprofen, cool compresses and/or an oatmeal bath may also offer relief. Cut your baby's nails to minimize scratching. Contact the doctor if the rash is severe or involves the eyes, face or genitalia.

PUNCTURE WOUNDS
See No. 52

SCRAPES
See No. 48

SEVERED LIMB OR DIGIT

45. Such serious injuries are rare, but knowing what to do when one occurs can mean the difference between saving and losing an arm, leg, finger or toe. Take these steps as needed immediately:

◆ Try to control bleeding. With sterile gauze pads, nappy, sanitary pad or a clean flannel apply heavy pressure to the wound. If bleeding continues, increase pressure. Don't worry about pressing too hard. Do not apply a tourniquet. Keep limb elevated above the heart if possible.

◆ Treat shock if present. If baby's skin seems pale, cold and clammy, pulse is weak and rapid, and respiration is shallow, treat for shock by loosening clothing, covering baby lightly to prevent loss of body heat, and elevating legs on a pillow (or folded garment) to force blood to the brain. If breathing seems laboured, raise baby's head and shoulders slightly.

◆ Reestablish breathing, if necessary. Begin CPR immediately if baby isn't breathing (see page 596).

◆ Preserve the severed limb or digit. As soon as possible, wrap it in a wet clean cloth or sponge, and place in a plastic bag. Pack the bag with ice and tie it shut. Do not place part directly on ice, don't use dry ice and don't immerse it in water or antiseptics.

◆ Get help. Call or have someone else call for immediate emergency medical assistance, or rush to A&E, calling ahead so they can prepare for your arrival. Be sure to take along the ice-packed limb; surgeons may be able to reattach it. During transport, keep pressure on the wound and continue other lifesaving procedures, if necessary.

SHOCK

46. Shock can develop in severe injuries or illnesses. Signs include cold, clammy, pale skin; rapid, weak pulse;

chills; convulsions; and frequently, nausea or vomiting, excessive thirst and/or shallow breathing. Call 999 immediately. Until help arrives, position baby on back. Loosen restrictive clothing, elevate legs on a pillow or folded garment to force blood to the brain, and cover baby lightly to prevent chilling or loss of body heat. If breathing seems laboured, raise baby's head and shoulders very slightly. Do not give food or water or use a hot water bottle to warm a baby in shock.

Skin Wounds

Important: Exposure to tetanus is a possibility whenever the skin is broken. Should your child incur an open skin wound, check to be sure tetanus immunization is up-to-date. Also be alert for signs of possible infection (swelling, warmth, tenderness, reddening of surrounding area, oozing of pus from the wound), and call the doctor if they develop.

47. Bruises or black-and-blue marks. Encourage quiet play to rest the injured part, if possible. Apply cold compresses, an ice pack or cloth-wrapped ice for 30 minutes. (Do not apply ice directly to the skin.) If the skin is broken, treat the bruise as you would a cut (Nos 49, 50). Call the doctor immediately if the bruise is from a wringer-type injury or if it resulted from catching a hand or foot in the spokes of a moving wheel. Bruises that seem to appear out of nowhere or that coincide with a fever should also be seen by a doctor.

48. Scrapes or abrasions. In such injuries (most common on knees and elbows) the top layer (or layers) of skin is scraped off, leaving the area raw and tender. There is usually slight bleeding from the more deeply abraded areas.

Using sterile gauze or cotton or a clean flannel, gently sponge off the wound with soap and water to remove dirt and other foreign matter. If baby strenuously objects to this, try soaking the scrape in the bath, or hold it under running water. Apply pressure if the bleeding doesn't stop. Cover with a sterile non-stick bandage.

49. Small cuts. Wash the area with clean water and soap, then hold the cut under running water to flush out dirt and foreign matter. Apply a sterile non-stick plaster. A butterfly bandage (see illustration opposite) will keep a small cut closed while it heals. To prevent infection, apply an antiseptic solution or ointment; ask the doctor for a recommendation) before putting on the bandage. Check with the doctor about any cuts on a baby's face.

50. Large cuts. With a sterile gauze pad, a fresh nappy, a sanitary pad, a clean flannel or, if necessary, your bare finger, apply pressure to try to stop the bleeding, elevating the injured part above the level of the heart, if possible, at the same time. If bleeding persists after 15 minutes of pressure, add more gauze pads or cloth and increase the pressure. (Don't worry about doing damage with too much pressure.) If necessary, keep the pressure on until help arrives or you get baby to the doctor or A&E. If there are other injuries, try to tie or bandage the pressure pack in place so that your hands can be free to attend to them. Apply a sterile non-stick bandage to the wound when the bleeding stops, loose enough so that it doesn't interfere with circulation. Do not use iodine or other antiseptic without medical advice. Take baby to the doctor's surgery (call first) or A&E for wounds that gape, appear deep, or don't stop bleeding within 30 minutes. Lacerations that involve the face, are

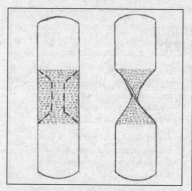

A butterfly bandage keeps a gaping cut closed so it can heal. If you don't have one on hand, trim down a regular plaster and make one complete twist to form a strong butterfly.

longer than 1.3 cm (½ in), are deep, or are bleeding heavily, may require stitches or surgical adhesive.

51. Massive bleeding. Get emergency medical attention by calling 999 or rush to the nearest A&E if a limb is severed (No. 45) and/or blood is gushing or pumping out. In the meantime, elevate limb above the heart if possible, and apply pressure with gauze pads, a nappy, sanitary pad, flannel or towel. Increase the packing and pressure if bleeding doesn't stop. Do not resort to a tourniquet without medical advice, as it can sometimes do more harm than good. Maintain pressure until help arrives.

52. Puncture wounds. Soak the injury in comfortably warm, soapy water for 15 minutes, if possible. Consult the baby's doctor or go to A&E. Do not remove any object (such as a knife or stick) that protrudes from the wound, as this could lead to increased bleeding. Pad it, if necessary, to keep it from moving around. Keep baby as calm and still as possible to avoid thrashing and making the injury worse.

53. Splinters or slivers. Wash the area with clean water and soap, then numb it with an ice pack (see page 763). If the sliver is completely embedded, try to work it loose with a sewing needle that has been sterilized with alcohol or the flame of a match. If one end of the sliver is clearly visible, try to remove it with tweezers (also sterilized by flame or alcohol). Don't try to remove it with your fingernails, which might be dirty. Wash the site again after you have removed the splinter. If the splinter is not easily removed, try soaking in warm, soapy water for 15 minutes, three times a day for a couple of days, which may help it work its way out. If it doesn't, or if the area becomes infected (indicated by redness, heat, swelling), consult the doctor. Also call the doctor if the splinter was deep and your baby's tetanus shots are not up-to-date.

SPLINTERS OR SLIVERS
See No. 53

SUNBURN
See No. 15

SWALLOWED FOREIGN OBJECTS

54. Coins, marbles and similar small round objects. When a baby has swallowed such an object and doesn't seem to be in any distress, it's best to wait for the object to travel through the digestive tract. Most children will pass a small object within two or three days. Check the stool for the object until it's passed. The exception: if baby has swallowed a button battery or magnet consult the doctor right away.

BANDAGING A BOO-BOO

As a parent, you can expect to apply dozens, possibly hundreds, of adhesive plastic strips and bandages over the years, on cuts and scrapes sometimes large, mostly small. These tips make bandaging easier while helping boo-boos get better faster:

◆ Treat the injury appropriately (see individual injuries).

◆ To improve stickability, always apply plasters to clean, dry skin.

◆ If your baby resists bandages or tends to pick them off, or for places where it's hard to get a plaster to stay put, consider applying a liquid, gel or spray bandage. They're expensive, but in some cases, well worth the premium price.

◆ On open wounds, use only sterile bandages or gauze pads that have not been opened prior to use. Don't touch the face of the pad with your fingers; handle only the tape.

◆ Use non-stick pads and/or an antibiotic ointment to prevent the bandage from sticking to the wound. If the bandage does stick, soak it in warm water rather than trying to yank it off.

◆ Except for cuts that need to be held closed, bandage loosely to allow air to enter.

◆ Don't wrap a bandage around a toe or finger so tightly that it cuts off circulation.

◆ Remove the bandage daily to check how the wound is healing (the best time is during or just after a bath, when the bandage is wet and loosened and will slip off without tugging). Rebandage the wound if it still looks raw or open. If a scab has formed on a scrape or if a cut has closed up, continued covering isn't necessary.

◆ Change bandages more often if they become wet or dirty.

If, however, after ingesting such an object, your baby has difficulty swallowing, or if wheezing, drooling, gagging, vomiting or difficulty swallowing develop later, the object may have lodged in the oesophagus. Call the doctor and take your child to A&E immediately.

If there is coughing or there seems to be difficulty breathing, the object may have been inhaled rather than swallowed; in this case, treat it as a choking incident (see below).

55. Sharp objects. Get prompt medical attention if a swallowed object is sharp (a pin, a fish bone, a toy with sharp edges). It may have to be removed in an A&E department using a special instrument.

TEETH, INJURY TO
See Nos 37, 38

TOE INJURIES
See Nos 27, 28, 29, 30

TONGUE, INJURY TO
See No. 36

Resuscitation Techniques for Babies and Children

The instructions that follow should be used only as reinforcement. You must, for your child's safety's sake, take a course in baby CPR (check with your doctor, a local hospital or the Red Cross or St John's Ambulance for the location of a class in your community) in order to be sure you can carry out these life support procedures correctly. Periodically, reread these guidelines or those you receive at the course and run through them step by step on a doll (never on your baby or any other person, or even on a pet) so you will be able to perform them automatically should an emergency occur. Take a refresher course now and then – both to brush up on your skills and to learn the latest techniques.

WHEN BABY IS CHOKING

Coughing is nature's way of trying to dislodge an obstruction in the airway. A baby (or anyone else) who is choking on food or some foreign object and who can breathe, cry and cough forcefully should not be interfered with. When the choking victim is struggling for breath, can't cough effectively, is making high-pitched crowing sounds and/or is turning blue (usually starting around the lips), begin the following rescue procedures. Begin *immediately* if the baby is unconscious and not breathing, *and* if attempts to open the airway and breathe air into the lungs (see pages 597–599, Steps A and B) are unsuccessful.

Important. An airway obstruction may also occur because of such infections as croup or epiglottitis. A choking baby who seems ill needs immediate attention at A&E. *Do not* waste time in a dangerous and futile attempt to try to relieve the problem.

FOR BABIES UNDER ONE YEAR (CONSCIOUS OR UNCONSCIOUS)

1. Get help. If someone else is present, ask them to call 999 or the local emergency number. If you're alone and unfamiliar with rescue procedures, or if you panic and forget them, take the baby to a phone, or take a cordless or mobile phone to where the child is and call for emergency medical assistance *immediately*. It's also recommended that even if you're familiar with rescue procedures, you take the time to call for emergency assistance before the situation worsens (if alone, it's best to attempt rescue procedures for two minutes and then call 999).

2. Position baby. Position the baby face-up on your forearm, place your other hand on top of the baby, using your thumb and fingers to hold the baby's jaw while sandwiching the baby between your arms. Turn the infant over so that he or she is face-down on your forearm. Lower your arm onto your thigh so that the baby's head is lower than his or her chest (see illustration, page 594). If baby is too big for you to comfortably support on your forearm, sit in a chair or on your knees on the floor and place baby face-down across your lap in the same head-lower-than-body

Back blows can often expel an inhaled object.

position. You can give back blows effectively whether you stand or sit, as long as the baby is supported on your thigh.

3. Administer back blows. Give five consecutive forceful blows between baby's shoulder blades with the heel of your free hand while supporting the arm that is holding the baby on your right thigh.

4. Administer chest thrusts. If there is no indication that the obstruction has been dislodged or loosened (forceful coughing, normal breathing, the object shoots out), place the baby in a face-up position. Put your free hand and forearm along the baby's head and back so that the baby is sandwiched between your two hands and forearms. Continue to support the baby's head between your thumb and finger from the front while you cradle the back of the head with your other hand. Turn the baby onto his or her back. Lower your arm that is supporting the baby's back onto your opposite thigh. The baby's head should be lower than his or her chest, which will assist in dislodging the object.

Locate the correct place to give chest thrusts by imagining a line running across the baby's chest between the nipples. Place the pads of two or three fingers in the centre of the baby's chest. Use the pads of these fingers to compress to the breastbone 1.3 to 2.5 cm (½ to 1 in) and then let the breastbone return to its normal position. Keep your fingers in contact with the baby's breastbone. Using this method give a total of five chest thrusts.

If baby is conscious, keep repeating the back blows and chest thrusts until the airway is cleared or the baby becomes unconscious. If baby is unconscious, continue below.

5. Do an airway check. If an unconscious baby is not breathing, tilt his or her head back and give two rescue breaths. If the breaths do not go in, reposition the baby's airway by re-tilting the head and try to breathe again. If the breaths still do not make the baby's chest rise, locate the correct hand position for chest compressions. Give 30 chest compressions in about 18 seconds. Each compression should be about 1.3 to 2.5 cm (½ to 1 in) deep.

6. Do a foreign body check. Look in the mouth for a foreign object. If the object is seen, remove it with a sweep of your little finger. Give two rescue breaths.

7. Repeat sequence. If the breaths do not go in, repeat cycles of chest compressions, foreign object check and rescue breaths until the object is removed and the chest clearly rises with rescue breaths, or the baby starts to breathe on his or her own, EMS personnel or another trained responder arrive and take over, or you are too exhausted to continue. If the breaths go in (the chest clearly rises), check for signs of life for no more than 10 seconds.

FOR CHILDREN OVER ONE YEAR (UNCONSCIOUS)

1. Position baby. Place child face-up on a firm, flat surface (the floor is best). Stand or kneel at the child's feet (don't sit astride a small child) and place the heel of one hand on the abdomen in the midline between the navel and the rib cage, fingers facing towards the child's face. Place the second hand on top of the first.

2. Perform chest compressions. With the upper hand pressing against the lower, compress the child's chest, to a depth of about 4 cm (1½ in), 30 times in about 18 seconds to dislodge the foreign object. These thrusts should be gentler than they would be for an adult or older child. Be careful not to apply pressure to the tip of the sternum or to the ribs.

3. Do a foreign body check. If there is no indication that the obstruction has been dislodged or loosened (forceful coughing, normal breathing, the object shoots out), check for a visible obstruction. Open the mouth by placing your thumb in baby's mouth, and grasp the tongue and lower jaw between your thumb and forefinger. As you lift the jaw up, depress the tongue with your thumb and move it away from the back of the throat. If you see a foreign object, attempt to remove it with a sweep of a finger. Do not sweep the mouth if you do not see an obstruction, and do not try to remove a visible obstruction with a pincer grasp, as you might force the object farther into the airway.

4. Give two breaths. If the child is still not breathing spontaneously, tilt the head back slightly and administer two slow mouth-to-mouth breaths, while pinching the nostrils closed. If the chest rises and falls with each breath, the airway is clear. Check for spontaneous breathing, Step B (see page 598) and continue the procedure as necessary.

5. Repeat sequence. If the airway remains blocked, continue repeating the sequence above until the airway is cleared and the child is conscious and breathing normally, or until emergency help has arrived. Don't give up.

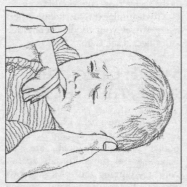

Clearing the baby's mouth of foreign matter.

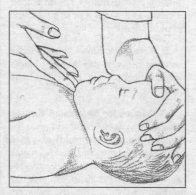

Head tilt/chin lift.

FOR CHILDREN OVER ONE YEAR (CONSCIOUS)

1. Position yourself. To give back blows, stand slightly behind the child and provide support by placing one arm diagonally across the chest and lean the child forward. To administer abdominal thrusts, stand or kneel behind the child (to reach a young child, you'll need either to bend yourself or to elevate the child by placing him or her on a chair or table) and wrap your arms around his or her waist.

2. Give back blows. Firmly strike the child between the shoulder blades with the heel of your other hand five times.

3. Administer abdominal thrusts. Make a fist with one hand and place the thumb side against the child's abdomen just above the navel and well below the lower tip of the breastbone. Grab your fist with your other hand and give five quick, upward thrusts into the abdomen.

4. Repeat if needed. Each back blow and abdominal thrust should be a separate and distinct attempt to dislodge the obstruction. Continue back blows and abdominal thrusts until the object is dislodged and the child can breathe or cough forcefully, or becomes unconscious.

> **Important:** Even if your child recovers quickly from a choking episode, medical attention will be required. Call the doctor or the A&E.

CARDIOPULMONARY RESUSCITATION (CPR): RESCUE BREATHING AND CHEST COMPRESSION

Begin the protocol below only on a baby who has stopped breathing, or on one who is struggling to breathe and turning blue (check around the lips and fingertips).

If a baby is struggling to breathe but hasn't turned blue, call for emergency medical assistance immediately. Meanwhile, keep baby warm and as quiet as possible, and in the position he or she seems most comfortable.

To determine if resuscitation is necessary, survey your toddler's condition with Check, Call, Care.

STEP 1: CHECK THE SCENE, THEN THE BABY

Try to rouse a baby who appears to be unconscious by calling by name loudly, 'Hannah, Hannah, are you okay?' several times. If that doesn't work, try tapping the soles of baby's feet. As a last resort, try gently tapping baby's shoulder – do not shake.

Step 2: Call

If you get no response, have anyone else present call for emergency assistance while you continue to Step 3 without delay. If you are alone – give about 2 minutes of care, then call 999. If you can, periodically call out to try to attract help from neighbours or passersby. If, however, you are unfamiliar with CPR or feel overwhelmed by panic, go to the nearest phone immediately – with your baby, if there are no signs of head, neck, or back injury. Better still, bring a cordless or mobile phone to baby's side, and call 999. The dispatcher will guide you as to the best course of action.

Important: The person calling for emergency medical assistance should be certain to stay on the phone as long as necessary to give complete information to the dispatcher. This should include: name, age, and approximate weight of the baby; any allergies, chronic illnesses, or medications taken; present location (address, cross streets, flat number, best route if there is more than one). Also tell them the condition (is baby conscious? breathing? bleeding? in shock? is there a pulse?); cause of condition (fall, poison, drowning, etc.), if known; phone number if there is a phone at the site. Tell the person calling for help not to hang up until the dispatcher has concluded questioning and to report back to you after completing the call.

Step 3: Care

Move baby, if necessary, to a firm, flat surface. Quickly position the child face-up, head level with heart, and proceed with the A-B-C survey below.

If there is a possibility of a head, neck or back injury – as there may be following a fall or auto accident – go to Step B to look, listen and feel for breathing before moving the child. If breathing is present, leave the baby where he or she is unless there is immediate danger (from traffic, fire, an imminent explosion) at the present site. If breathing is absent and rescue breathing cannot be accomplished in the baby's present position, roll the baby as a unit to a face-up position, so that head, neck and body are moved as one, without twisting, rolling or tilting the head.

A. Clear the Airway

Use the head-tilt/chin-lift technique described below to try to open the airway, unless there is a possibility of a head, neck or back injury – in which case, try to minimize movement of the head and neck when opening the airway. Tilt the head and lift the chin to open the airway.

Important: The airway of an unconscious baby may be blocked by a relaxed tongue or by a foreign object. It must be cleared before baby can resume breathing.

Head tilt/chin lift. Place the hand nearest baby's head on the baby's forehead and one or two fingers (not the thumb) of the other hand under the bony part of the lower jaw at the chin. Gently tilt baby's head back slightly by applying pressure on the forehead and lifting the chin. Do not press on the soft tissues of the underchin or let the mouth close completely (keep your thumb in it if necessary to keep the lips apart). Baby's head should be facing the ceiling in what is called the neutral position, with the chin neither down on the chest nor pointing up in the air.

Important: Even if the baby resumes breathing immediately, get medical help. Any baby who has been unconscious, has stopped breathing (even briefly) or has nearly drowned requires prompt medical evaluation.

B. CHECK FOR BREATHING

1. After performing the head-tilt/chin-lift technique, look, listen and feel for no more than 10 seconds to see if the baby is breathing. Can you see the chest rising and falling? Can you hear or feel the passage of air when you place your ear near the child's nose and mouth?

If normal breathing has resumed, maintain an open airway with the head-tilt/chin-lift technique as you continue to look for other life-threatening conditions. You can now activate the emergency medical system: if breathing has resumed, and no one has yet called for help, call 999 now.

If the baby regains consciousness as well (and has no injuries that make moving inadvisable), turn him or her on one side. A spate of coughing when the baby starts to breathe independently may be an attempt to expel an obstruction. Do not attempt to interfere with the coughing. If breathing hasn't resumed or if the baby is struggling to

breathe and has bluish lips and/or a weak, muffled cry, you must try to get the air into the lungs immediately. Continue with Step 2 below.

Important: If emergency medical assistance has not yet been summoned and you are alone, continue trying to attract neighbours or passersby as you work.

2. Maintain an open airway with the head tilt/chin lift with your hand on the forehead.

Important: If vomiting should occur at any point, turn the child on one side and clear the mouth of vomit with a finger sweep. Reposition child and resume rescue procedure. If there is a possibility of neck or back injury, be very careful to turn the child as a unit, carefully supporting head, neck and back, as you do; do not allow the head to roll, twist or tilt.

3. Take a breath through your mouth and place your mouth over baby's mouth and nose, forming a tight

In rescue breathing for infants, both mouth and nose must be covered.

seal (see illustration, page 598). If the baby is over a year old, pinch the nose shut with the thumb and forefinger of the hand that is maintaining the head tilt and, after taking a breath, make a complete seal around the baby's mouth with your mouth.

4. Blow two slow breaths (lasting 1 second each) into the baby's mouth. Pause between rescue breaths to let the air flow out. Observe with each breath whether the baby's chest rose. If it did, allow it to fall again before beginning another breath. After two successfully delivered breaths, move on to Step C.

> ***Important:*** Remember, a small baby needs only a small amount of air to fill the lungs. Though blowing too lightly may not expand the lungs fully, blowing too hard or too fast can force air into the stomach, causing distension.

5. If the chest doesn't rise and fall with each breath, your breaths may have been too weak or the baby's airway may be blocked. Readjust the baby's head to try to open the airway by tilting the chin upward a bit more (Step B-1) and give two more breaths. If the chest still does not rise with each breath, it is possible the airway is obstructed by food or by a foreign object – in which case, move quickly to dislodge it, using the procedure described in When Baby is Choking on page 593. If the chest does rise, indicating the airway is open, move on to Step C.

C. CHECK CIRCULATION

1. As soon as you've determined that the airway is clear, as evidenced by the successful delivery of two breaths,

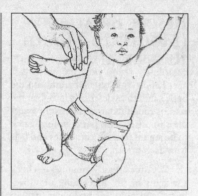

Checking brachial pulse in infants.

check for a pulse at the carotid artery using your index and middle fingers for no more than 10 seconds. (The carotid pulse is located on the side of the neck between the trachea and the neck muscles). With an infant under a year, try to find the brachial pulse in the arm closest to you: keeping one hand on the baby's head to maintain an open airway, use the other to pull baby's arm away from the body and turn it palm up. Use your index and middle fingers to try to locate the pulse between the two muscles on the inside of the middle arm, between the shoulder and the elbow; see illustration.

2. If you can't locate a pulse, proceed with CPR (see page 600) immediately. If you find a pulse, the child's heart is beating and CPR is not necessary. Perform rescue breathing if breathing has not resumed.

RESCUE BREATHING (MOUTH-TO-MOUTH RESUSCITATION)

1. Give one rescue breath into the baby's mouth as described in B-4, at the rate of roughly one breath every 3 seconds (or 20 breaths per minute). Watch to be sure the child's chest rises and falls with each breath.

2. After about 2 minutes, recheck for signs of life (breathing or movement) and pulse for no longer than 10 seconds to make sure the heart is still beating. If there is no pulse, go to CPR. If the baby had begun to breathe independently, continue to maintain an open airway and check breathing and pulse frequently while waiting for help to arrive; keep the baby warm and as quiet as possible. If there are signs of life but no breathing, continue rescue breathing.

3. If you're alone, give care for about 2 minutes before calling 999. If one is available, bring a cordless or mobile phone to the baby's side. If one isn't available and there is no evidence of head or neck injury, carry the baby to the phone, supporting the head, neck and torso. Continue rescue breathing as you go. Quickly and clearly report to the dispatcher, 'My baby isn't breathing,' and give all pertinent information the dispatcher requests. Don't hang up until the dispatcher does. Continue rescue breathing immediately on hanging up. If you can't move the baby, dash to the phone alone and explain the situation, then hurry back to resume rescue breathing.

Important: Continue rescue breathing until the scene becomes unsafe, the child begins to breathe on his own, you are too exhausted to continue, or another trained responder takes over for you.

CHEST COMPRESSIONS (CPR): BABIES UNDER ONE YEAR[1]

If, after following Steps 1-2-3 (A-B-C) on page 596, baby is not breathing and has no pulse, begin the following CPR protocol:

Important: In CPR, rescue breaths, which force oxygen into the lungs where it is picked up by the bloodstream, must be alternated with chest compressions, which artificially pump the blood containing oxygen to the vital organs and the rest of the body.

1. With baby still lying on a firm, flat surface, face-up, head level with the heart, continue to maintain baby's head in a neutral position with one hand on forehead (see illustration, page 601). Stand or kneel facing the baby from the side. Bare the baby's chest.

2. Position the three middle fingers of your free hand on baby's chest. Imagine a horizontal line from nipple to nipple. Place the pad of the index finger just under the intersection of this line with the breastbone, or sternum (the flat bone running midline down baby's chest between the ribs). The area to compress is one finger's width below this point of intersection (see illustration, page 601).

---

1. One year is the cutoff chosen for switching from infant to child resuscitation procedures. The child's size may be a factor in some cases, but experts say that a slight error either way is not critical.

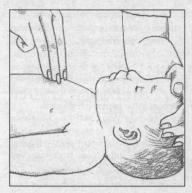

Compressions on infants can be done with two or three fingers.

3. Using two or three fingers, compress the sternum straight down to a depth of 1.3 to 2.5 cm (½ to 1 in) (your elbow should be bent). At the end of each compression, release the pressure without removing your fingers from the sternum and allow it to return to its normal position. Develop a smooth compression-relaxation rhythm that allots equal time to each phase and avoids jerky movements. Compress at a rate of 100 compressions per minute.

4. After 30 compressions, pause with your fingers still in position on the sternum and deliver two slow rescue breaths. Watch for the chest to rise. (If it doesn't, remove your fingers from the breastbone and lift the chin and blow again.) Aim for a rate of 100 compressions per minute, with a rescue breath after every five compressions. Count at a more rapid rate than you would if counting seconds: one, two, three, four, five – breathe.

5. Keep repeating cycles of 30 compressions and two breaths. Continue CPR until emergency personnel arrive and take over.

6. After about a minute of CPR, if you are alone and have not been able to attract anyone who could call for emergency medical assistance up until now, go quickly to a phone (carrying baby with you, if possible, or bringing the phone to where baby is) and summon help; then immediately return to rescue procedures as needed.

> *Important:* Do not discontinue CPR until breathing and heartbeat are reestablished or until medical relief arrives.

CHEST COMPRESSIONS (CPR): CHILDREN OVER ONE YEAR

If, after following Steps 1-2-3 (A-B-C) on page 596, your child over a year is not breathing and has no pulse, begin the following CPR protocol:

1. Position the child. Continue with the child face-up on a firm, flat surface.

2. Position your hands. Locate the correct hand position by placing the heel of one hand on the child's sternum (breast bone) at the centre of his chest. Place your other hand directly on top of the first hand and try to keep your fingers off the chest by interlacing them or holding them upward. Alternatively, you can use a one-handed technique by placing one hand on the child's chest and the other hand on the forehead to maintain an open airway. Position your body correctly by kneeling beside the child, placing your hands in the correct position, straightening your arms and locking your elbows so that your shoulders are directly over your hands.

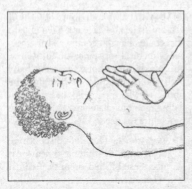

Hand position for CPR compression for children over a year old.

Important: Do not apply pressure to the tip of the sternum. To do so could cause severe internal damage.

3. Begin compressions. Compress the chest smoothly to a depth of about 4 cm (1½ inch) using the heel of the dominant hand. Lift up, allowing the chest to fully return to its normal position, but keep contact with the chest. Repeat compressions, performing 30 compressions in about 18 seconds.

4. After giving 30 compressions, remove your compression hand(s) from the chest, open the airway and give two rescue breaths. After giving the breaths, place your hand(s) in the same position as before and continue compressions. Keep repeating cycles of 30 compressions and two rescue breaths.

If you are alone, give care for about 2 minutes before calling 999. If one is available, bring a cordless or mobile phone to the child's side. If not, and the child is small enough and there is no evidence of head or neck injury, carry him or her to the phone supporting head, neck and torso. Continue rescue breathing as you go. Quickly and clearly report to the dispatcher, 'My child isn't breathing and has no pulse,' and give all pertinent information the dispatcher requests. Don't hang up until the dispatcher does. If you can't move the child, dash to the phone alone and explain the situation, then hurry back to resume basic life support procedures as needed.

Important: Continue CPR until an Automated External Defibrillator becomes available or the emergency services arrive and take over.

◆ ◆ ◆

The Low-Birthweight Baby

Most parents-to-be expect their babies to arrive right around their due date, give or take a couple of days or weeks. And the majority of babies do arrive on schedule, allowing them plenty of time to prepare for life outside the uterus and their parents plenty of time to prepare for life with a baby.

But about 130 times a day in the UK, that vital preparatory time is cut unexpectedly – and sometimes perilously – short when baby is born prematurely and/or too small. Some of these babies weigh in at just a few grammes/ounces under the low-birthweight (2.5 kg/5 lb 8oz) cutoff, and are able to quickly and easily catch up with their full-term peers. But others, robbed of many weeks of uterine development, arrive so small that they can fit in the palm of a hand; and it can take months of intensive medical care to help them do the growing they were supposed to have done in the womb.

Many parents, too, are far from ready when birth comes too early. For them, the first postpartum days, sometimes weeks or months, are filled not with learning to change nappies, getting adjusted to having a baby in the house and writing thank you notes, but with reading hospital charts, learning to feed baby through a tube, and getting adjusted to *not* having a baby in the house.

Though the low-birthweight baby (whether born early or not) is still at higher risk than larger babies, rapid advances in medical care for tiny infants have made it possible for the great majority of them to grow into normal, healthy children. But before they are carried proudly home from the hospital, a long road often lies ahead for these babies and their parents.

If your baby has arrived too soon and too small, you'll find the information and support you'll need to navigate that road in the pages that follow.

Feeding Your Baby:
NUTRITION FOR THE PRETERM OR
LOW-BIRTHWEIGHT INFANT

Learning to eat outside the womb isn't easy at first, even for a full-term baby – who must master the fine points of nursing from a breast or a bottle. For preterm babies, the challenges increase exponentially – and the younger and smaller the baby, the greater the challenges. Those who are born just three or four weeks early are usually able to breastfeed or take the bottle right after birth – again, after mastering those fine points. But babies born before 36 weeks have special nutritional needs that traditional feeding can't satisfy – not only because they're born smaller, but because they grow at a faster rate than full-term babies do, may not be able to suck effectively and/or may have immature digestive systems.

For one thing, these littlest babies need a diet that mirrors the nutrition they would be receiving if they were still in utero, and that helps them gain weight quickly. For another, these nutrients need to be served up in the most concentrated form possible, because premature and low-birthweight babies can take only tiny amounts of food at a time – partly because their stomachs are so small, and partly because their immature digestive systems are sluggish, making the passage of food a very slow process. And since they can't always suck well or even suck at all, they can't take their meals from a bottle or a breast – at least not right away. Luckily, breast milk, fortified breast milk, or specially designed formulas can usually provide all the nutrients premature babies need to grow and thrive.

As a parent of a premature infant, you will find that feeding and monitoring weight gain will become some of the most consuming aspects of caring for your baby in the hospital – both in terms of time and emotion. The neonatologists and nurses will do everything they can to ensure that your premature baby receives the proper nutrition needed to gain weight. Just how your baby receives that nutrition depends on how early he or she was born:

IV feeding. When a very small newborn is rushed to the intensive care nursery, an intravenous solution of water, sugar and certain electrolytes is often given to prevent dehydration and electrolyte depletion. Very sick or small babies (usually those who arrive before 28 weeks' gestation) continue to receive nutrition through their IV. Called total parenteral nutrition (TPN) or parenteral hyperalimentation, this balanced blend of protein, fat, sugar, vitamins, minerals and IV fluids is given until the baby can tolerate milk feedings. Once your baby is able to begin milk feedings by gavage (see below), TPN will decrease.

Gavage feeding. Babies who arrive between 28 and 34 weeks' gestation and who don't need IV nutrition are fed by gavage – a method not dependent on sucking, since babies this young usually have not yet developed this reflex. (This method is also used to feed babies who started out on TPN but have progressed to the point where they can tolerate milk feedings.) A small flexible tube (gavage

Baby receives feedings through a gavage tube.

tube) is placed into the baby's mouth or nose and passed down to the stomach. Prescribed amounts of pumped breast milk, fortified breast milk or formula are fed through the tube every few hours (see facing page for the advantages of using breast milk). Gavage tubes are either left in place between feedings or removed and reinserted for each feeding. (The tube won't bother your premature baby because the gag reflex doesn't develop until about 35 weeks.)

It may be a relatively long time before you'll be able to feed your baby as you'd always imagined you would, through breast or bottle. Until then, you can still take part in feedings by holding the tube and measuring how much your baby takes; cuddling during tube feedings (if baby can be held); or giving your baby your finger to practise sucking on while he or she's being fed (this helps strengthen the sucking reflex and may also help your baby associate sucking with getting a full tummy).

Nipple feeding. One of the most momentous milestones of your premature baby's stay in the hospital will be

EARLY WEIGHT LOSS

As parents of a premature or low-birthweight baby, you'll be particularly anxious to start seeing the numbers on the scale creeping up. But don't be discouraged if instead your baby seems to be losing weight at first. It's normal for a premature infant (as it is for a full-term baby) to drop quite a few grammes/ounces – typically losing between 5 to 15 per cent of his or her birthweight – before beginning a gain. As with a full-term baby, much of that weight loss will be water. Premature babies don't usually regain their birthweight before they are two or more weeks old, at which point they can begin surpassing it.

the switch from gavage feeding to nipple feeding. When it comes to readiness for this milestone, there can be some big differences among little babies. Some are ready to tackle the breast or bottle as early as 30 to 32 weeks' gestational age. Others won't be ready to take on the nipple until 34 weeks, still others, not until 36 weeks' gestational age.

The neonatologist will consider several factors before giving you the green light to begin breast or bottle feeding: is your baby's condition stable? Can he or she handle being fed in your arms? Have all the other physical requirements been met? (Baby has shown readiness by rhythmically sucking on a dummy or feeding tube, can coordinate breathing and sucking, is awake for longer periods, has active bowel sounds, has passed meconium stools and shows no sign of abdominal distension or infection).

Since nipple feedings are tiring for a small baby, they'll be started slowly – one or two a day, alternated with tube

EXPRESSING MILK
FOR A PREMATURE BABY

The decision to breastfeed a preterm baby is not always an easy one, even for women who planned on nursing at term. A major attraction of breastfeeding, close mother–child contact, is usually absent, at least at first. Instead, a cold impersonal pump stands in the way of an intimate experience, making nursing a mother–machine–child affair. But though almost all women find pumping their breasts exhausting and time-consuming, most persevere, knowing that this is the one way in which they can contribute to the well-being of the baby from whose care they otherwise feel excluded.

The following tips can make the effort to feed a preterm baby in the best possible way more efficient and less tedious:

◆ See page 149 for tips on expressing breast milk. Ask about in-hospital facilities for expressing milk. Most hospitals have a special room (with comfortable chairs and an electric breast pump) set aside for mothers to use.

◆ Begin expressing milk as soon after delivery as possible, even if your baby isn't ready to take it. Express every two to three hours (about as often as a newborn nurses) if your baby is going to use the milk immediately; every four hours or so if the milk is going to be frozen for later use. You may find getting up to pump once in the middle of the night helps build up your milk supply; or you may value a full night's sleep more.

◆ It's likely you will eventually be able to express more milk than your tiny baby can use. Don't cut back, however, figuring you're wasting too much. Regular pumping now will help to establish a plentiful milk supply for the time when your baby takes over where the machine leaves off. In the meantime, the excess milk can be dated and frozen for later use.

◆ Don't be discouraged by day-to-day or hour-to-hour variations in supply. Such variations are normal, although you wouldn't be aware of them if you were nursing directly. Also normal when milk is expressed mechanically are an apparently inadequate milk supply and/or a drop in production after several weeks. Your baby will be a much more efficient stimulator of your milk supply than even the most efficient pump. When actual suckling begins, your supply is almost certain to increase quickly.

◆ When baby is ready for feeding by mouth, try to nurse first, before the baby is given a bottle. Studies show that low-birthweight babies take to the breast more easily than to the bottle. But don't worry if yours does better on the bottle – use it while your baby gets the hang of breastfeeding (begin feeding sessions with nursing, then move to bottle), or use a supplemental nutrition system (see page 161).

feedings. Infants with respiratory problems may have an even harder time, requiring extra oxygen while feeding or experiencing short episodes of apnea (breathing cessation) while sucking (they might concentrate too hard on sucking and forget to breathe). For babies who have trouble mastering the suck, a specially designed dummy may be used to help them practise and perfect their technique before graduating to breast or bottle.

Premature babies who are ready to move on to nipple feedings can be nourished either with breast milk, fortified breast milk or formula:

◆ Breast milk. Breast is best not only when it comes to full-term infants. Most experts favour breast milk over formula for the premature baby, too, and for a number of reasons: First of all, it's custom designed for a premature baby's special nutritional needs. Milk from mothers who deliver early is different than milk from mothers who deliver at term. It contains more protein, sodium, calcium and other nutrients than full-term breast milk does, but less than is found in formula. This premature-baby-perfect balance prevents tiny babies from losing too much fluid, which helps them maintain a stable body temperature. It's also easier to digest and helps babies grow faster. Secondly, breast milk has important substances not found in formula. Colostrum (early breast milk) is extremely rich in antibodies and cells that help fight infection. This is especially important when babies are sick or premature and may have a higher chance of developing an infection. Thirdly, research has shown that breastfed premature babies have a lower risk of developing necrotizing enterocolitis, an intestinal infection unique to premature babies (see page 627); have a better tolerance of feedings, less risk of allergies and enhanced development; and receive all the benefits that a full-term baby gets from breast milk (see page 3). Even if you don't plan to breastfeed long term, providing breast milk for your baby while he or she is in the hospital gives your baby the best possible start at a time when that start has begun too soon.

To ensure your baby is still getting enough nutrition in the early stages of breastfeeding (when baby's suck may still be weak or your breasts not producing sufficient amounts of milk), talk to the doctor about the following supplemental feeding methods that don't interfere with nursing:

◆ nursing with the gavage still in place

◆ using a supplemental nutrition system (see page 161)

◆ using a feeding system taped to your finger (finger feeding)

◆ cup feeding with specially designed cups

◆ syringe feeding

◆ bottle feeding with slower-flow bottle teats

For more on breastfeeding your premature baby, see page 617.

◆ Fortified breast milk. Sometimes, even the milk of a premature baby's mother isn't adequate. Since some babies, particularly very tiny ones, need even more concentrated nutrition – including more fat, proteins, sugars, calcium and phosphorus and, possibly, more of other nutrients such as zinc, magnesium, copper and vitamin B_6 – the breast milk being fed through a tube or a bottle may be fortified with human milk fortifier (HMF) as needed. HMF comes in a powered form that can be blended with breast milk, or in a liquid form for use when adequate amounts of breast milk are not available.

◆ Formula. Babies can do well, too, when they're fed formula specially designed for premature babies. Even if you are breastfeeding, your baby may get additional feedings with a bottle or supplemental nutrition system. Premature babies are fed using small plastic bottles marked in cubic centimetres (cc) or millilitres (ml). The teats are specially designed and require less sucking strength from your baby. Ask a nurse to show you the correct position for bottle feeding a premature baby – it may differ slightly from that for a full-term infant.

FEEDING AT HOME

Once you've arrived home with your premature baby, feedings will be as challenging and time-consuming as they were in the hospital. You'll need to experiment with different teats, bottles, nursing positions, and so on. As a general rule, premature babies need to be fed smaller amounts and more often than full-termers. They feed slowly and tire easily. Depending on your baby's progress, you may or may not need to continue using formula specifically designed for premature babies. Often parents continue to use the same small bottles that were used in the hospital. But keep in mind that what worked in the hospital might not work as well once you're home and your baby continues to grow in both size and maturity.

You can expect to encounter one or all of the following feeding concerns at home (though some lucky parents experience none at all):

♦ Sleepy baby. Many premature babies tire easily and the desire to sleep sometimes overrides the desire to eat. But since all babies, especially those born small, need regular feedings, it is all the more important that

you make sure your baby doesn't sleep through feedings. For tips on how to rouse a sleepy baby, see page 116.

♦ Breath holders. Some premature babies, especially those who were born without good suck-breath coordination, will forget to breathe when feeding. This is tiring for your baby and anxiety-producing for you. If you notice your baby hasn't taken a breath after a number of sucks or looks pale while feeding, remove the nipple from baby's mouth and let him or her take a breath. If your baby seems to be holding his or her breath all the time during feedings, regularly remove the nipple after every three to four sucks.

♦ Oral aversion. Babies who have spent a lot of time in the NICU may have come to associate the mouth with unpleasant experiences (feeding tubes, ventilator tubes, suctioning, and so on) and often develop a strong aversion to having anything in or around their mouths once they are home. To combat this, try to replace the unpleasant oral associations with more pleasant ones. Touch your baby around the mouth in a soothing manner, give your baby a dummy or your finger to suck, or encourage your baby to touch his or her own mouth or suck on his or her thumb or fist.

♦ Reflux. Many premature babies are prone to excessive spitting up or GER because of their immature digestive systems. For tips on coping with spitting up and GER, see pages 170 and 559.

♦ Starting solids. Like full-term babies, premature babies should start receiving solids somewhere between four and six months. But for premature babies, that date is based on their corrected age rather than chronological age (which means a premature baby wouldn't be ready for solids until six to eight chronological months). Because some premature babies experience delays in development, solid feedings should not be started until the baby shows signs of readiness (see page 289), even if the corrected age says 'it's time' for solids. Some have a more difficult time with solids – especially once they graduate to chunkier foods.

What You May Be Concerned About

NEONATAL INTENSIVE CARE UNIT (NICU)

'My baby was rushed to the NICU immediately after birth. What can I expect when I visit him there for the first time?'

A first look at a neonatal intensive care unit can be frightening, especially if your baby is one of the tiny, helpless patients in it. Knowing what you're looking at can keep your fears from overwhelming you. Here's what you can expect in most NICUs:

◆ A main nursery area comprising a large room or a series of rooms, with designated bed areas along the walls. There may also be a couple of isolation rooms in an area separate from the main nursery. Adjoining may be several small family rooms where mothers can express milk (breast pumps are usually provided), and where families can spend cuddling time with their babies as they get stronger.

◆ A bustling atmosphere. There will be many nurses and doctors busily moving about, treating and monitoring babies. Parents may also be caring for or feeding their own infants.

◆ Relative quiet. Though it's one of the busiest places in the hospital, it's typically also one of the quietest. That's because loud noises can be stressful for tiny babies or even harmful to their ears. To help keep the sound level down, you should talk quietly, close doors and isolette portholes gently, and take care not to drop things or place items loudly on the tops of incubators. (One sound that is important for your baby, however, is the sound of your voice; see page 614.) Since still-sensitive eyes need protection, too, NICU staff usually tries to control the brightness in the nursery. Occasionally, however, the lights in certain areas can become intense to allow doctors and nurses to perform procedures.

◆ Strict hygiene standards. Keeping germs that can spread infection (and make sick babies sicker) out of the nursery is a major priority in the NICU. Each time you visit, you'll need to wash your hands with antibacterial soap or sanitizer (there's usually a sink for this purpose right outside the nursery doors). You may be asked to put on a hospital gown, too. If your baby is in isolation, you may also need to wear gloves and a mask.

◆ Tiny babies everywhere. You'll see them in clear incubators or isolettes (cots that are totally closed except for four porthole-like doors that allow you and the staff to reach in and care for your baby) or in open cots. You'll also see some on warming tables under overhead heat lamps. Some babies may be wrapped in cellophane to minimize the loss of fluids and body heat through the skin. This helps premature babies keep warm (particularly those under 1.8 kg/4 lb, who lack the fat necessary to regulate body temperature, even when they're swaddled in blankets).

◆ An endless array of apparatus. You'll notice an abundance of technology near each bed. Monitors that record vital signs (and will warn, by setting off an alarm, any changes that need prompt attention) are hooked up to babies via leads that are either stuck on the skin with gel or inserted by needle just under the skin. In addition to a monitor, your baby may also be linked to a feeding tube, an IV (via the arm, leg, hand, foot or head), a catheter in his umbilical stump, temperature probes (attached to his skin with a patch) and a pulse oximeter that measures the oxygen level in his blood with a small light attached to his hand or foot. A mechanical ventilator (breathing machine) may be used to help your baby breathe normally if he's under 30 to 33 weeks' gestation. Otherwise, he may receive oxygen through a mask or delivered into the nose through soft plastic prongs attached to tubing. There will also be suction set-ups that are used periodically for removing excess respiratory secretions, as well as lights for phototherapy (bililights), used to treat babies with jaundice. (Babies undergoing this treatment will be naked except for eye patches, which protect their eyes from the bililights.)

◆ A place for parents to sit and cuddle their babies. In the midst of all this high-tech equipment, there will likely be rocking chairs where you can feed or hold your baby.

◆ A large team of highly trained medical specialists. The staff caring for your baby in the NICU might include a neonatologist (a paediatrician who has had special training in newborn intensive care); paediatric residents and neonatal fellows (doctors undergoing training); a clinical nurse specialist; a primary nurse (who will most frequently take care of your baby and teach you how to care for him); a nutritionist; a respiratory therapist; other specialists depending on your baby's particular needs; social workers, physical and occupational therapists; X-ray and lab technicians; and lactation specialists.

◆ Being part of the team yourself. Remember that you are one of the most important partners in your baby's care. Educate yourself as much as possible about the NICU's equipment and procedures, and familiarize yourself with your baby's conditions and progress. Ask for explanations of how ventilators, machines and monitors are helping your baby. Request written information that explains the medical jargon you'll be hearing. Learn as much as you can about the routine: visiting hours and visitor restrictions, when nurses change shifts, when doctors make rounds. Find out who will give you updates on your baby's progress and when you'll get them. Give the

PORTRAIT OF A PREMATURE BABY

The parents of full-term newborns may be surprised when they first see their babies. The parents of preterm infants are often shocked. The typical premature baby weighs between 1.6 kg (about 3½ lb) and 1.9 kg (about 4 lb 3 oz) at birth, and some weigh considerably less. The smallest can fit in the palm of an adult hand and have wrists and hands so tiny that a wedding band could be slipped over them. The premature baby's skin is translucent, leaving veins and arteries visible. It seems to fit loosely because it lacks a fat layer beneath it (making it impossible for baby's temperature to self-regulate), and often it is covered with a fine layer of prenatal body hair, or lanugo, that has usually been shed by full-term infants. Because of an immature circulatory system, skin colouring changes when the infant is handled or fed. The baby's ears may be flat, folded, or floppy because the cartilage that will give them shape has yet to develop. The premature baby often lies with arms and legs straight rather than curled or tucked in because of the lack of muscle strength.

Sexual characteristics are usually not fully developed – testicles may be undescended, the foreskin in boys and the inner folds of the labia in girls may be immature, and there may be no areola around the nipples. Because neither muscular nor nerve development is complete, many reflexes (such as grasping, sucking, startle, rooting) may be absent. Unlike term babies, a premature baby may cry little or not at all. He or she may also be subject to periods of breathing cessation, known as apnea of prematurity.

But the physical characteristics of premature babies that make up this portrait are only temporary. Once preterm newborns reach forty weeks of gestation, the time when, according to the calendar, they should have been born, they very much resemble the typical newborn in size and development.

staff your mobile phone and pager numbers, so they can always reach you if necessary.

'The nurses warned me that having my daughter in the NICU would be like being on a roller coaster with all its ups and downs. But I'm surprised at the incredible range of emotions I'm feeling.'

You're not alone. Most parents whose babies are in the NICU experience a wide spectrum of ever-changing emotions, including shock, anger, stress, panic, fear, numbness, frustration, disappointment, confusion, sadness, intense grief and equally intense hope. All for good reason. You may feel overwhelmed by all the medical equipment attached to your baby and the constant activity of nurses and doctors. You may be frightened of the procedures your baby is undergoing or frustrated by feelings of helplessness. You may feel disappointed that your daughter isn't the dimpled, adorable full-term baby you'd been expecting (and envisioning) throughout your pregnancy, frustrated that you can't take her home to begin your life together, and guilty about both emotions. You may also feel guilty for not feeling happy about your baby's birth or guilty about not being able to keep the pregnancy going longer (even if there was absolutely nothing you could have done to prevent your daughter's prematurity). You may feel distraught at the uncertainty of your baby's future, particularly if she's very small or sick. You may even unconsciously distance yourself from her for fear of becoming too attached or because you find bonding difficult to accomplish through the portholes of an isolette. Or, you may feel unexpectedly strong feelings of affection, deepened, instead of compromised, by the challenges you and your baby are facing. You may be angry at yourself for your reactions, at your spouse for not reacting the same way you are, at your family and friends for not understanding what you're going through or for acting as if nothing has happened, at your doctor for not preventing this. Confusing these emotions may be the fact that they may often conflict or fluctuate wildly – for instance, leaving you feeling hopeful one minute, hopeless the next, deeply in love with your baby one day, afraid to love her the next. Compounding them may be the physical exhaustion that comes from keeping a round-the-clock vigil at your baby's bedside, which may be more debilitating still if you haven't yourself recovered from childbirth.

Coping with these emotions may be extremely difficult, but keeping the following in mind may help:

◆ What you're feeling, saying and doing are perfectly normal. Such extreme and sometimes contradictory emotions are experienced by nearly every parent of a premature baby at some time or another (though you may often believe that no one else has ever felt the way you do).

◆ There is no one right way to feel. Your emotions may differ from those of your spouse, the parents of the baby in the next isolette or your friends who've also had premature babies. Everyone will react to it a little differently – and that's normal too.

◆ It's important to express your emotions. Keeping them inside will only make you feel more isolated and helpless. Let the NICU staff know what your feelings and fears are. Not only will they understand what you're going through (since helping parents is almost as important a part of their job as helping babies), they may offer insights that can help you cope.

◆ Don't shut out your spouse. You can both gain strength by leaning on each other. Open communication can also help keep the stress inherent in parenting a premature baby from hurting your relationship.

◆ Support best comes from those who know. Try talking with other parents in the NICU. You'll find that they also feel alone, unsure and scared. Friendships are easily formed in the NICU because other parents need you as much as you need them. Many hospitals make support available through groups run by the NICU social worker, or can hook you up with support families whose babies have left the NICU. No one can relate better to what you're experiencing – and share more wisdom and empathy – than parents who've experienced it themselves. You can find additional empathetic support by joining one of the many parents-of-premature-babies discussion groups on the Internet.

◆ It will take time. You probably won't be on an even emotional keel at least until your baby's on an even physical one. Until then, you'll have good days and bad days (usually corresponding to your baby's ups and downs). Reminding yourself that your feelings are normal – that all parents of premature babies ride an emotional roller coaster until their babies are safely home and completely well – won't make the feelings go away, but it will help give you the perspective you need to cope with them.

If you have another child at home, helping him or her cope with anxiety will be a priority; see page 617.

GETTING OPTIMUM CARE

'How do I know that our premature baby – she's only a little more than 1.14 kg (2½ lb) – is getting the best possible care?'

Though healthy babies, including premature babies who weigh in at close to 2.25 kg (5 lb) or more do well at general hospitals, very small babies (those who are at the highest risk, weighing less than 1.5 kg (3 lb 5 oz) at birth do best at major medical centres. Having your baby at such a facility is the best guarantee you can get of good care. If your baby is not at such a hospital, discuss the possibility of having her transferred to one with her paediatrician and the staff at your current hospital.

Wherever your baby is, however, your input will be important in ensuring optimum care. Become knowledgeable about low-birthweight babies in general, and about any special problems your baby has, by reading books and by asking questions. Whenever you're uncomfortable or unhappy about the course your baby's treatment is taking, raise your concerns with her paediatrician and/or the hospital nurses or neonatologists. You may be satisfied with their explanation, or perhaps things can be done differently. If you aren't satisfied, ask for a consultation with another neonatologist. If you feel uncomfortable challenging doctors, find a friend or relative to act as advocate.

LACK OF BONDING

'We'd expected to bond with our baby right after birth. But since she arrived six weeks early and weighed only 1.6 kg (3½ lb), she was whisked away before we had a chance to even touch her. We're worried about the effect this will have on her – and on our relationship with her.'

During this stressful time, the last thing you need is another worry. And the last thing you need to worry about is bonding at birth. Love and attachment between parent and child develops over many months, even years, blossoming over a lifetime rather than bursting into full bloom during the first few moments of life. So instead of regretting the first few moments (or even days) you've lost, start making the most of the months of parenthood that lie ahead. Though it isn't necessary to begin bonding at birth, you may be able to initiate the process while your baby is still in the hospital. Here's how:

Ask for a picture, along with a thousand words. If your baby has been moved from the hospital you delivered in to another hospital for upgraded intensive care (possibly essential to her survival), and you are not yet able to be discharged, ask that pictures of her be brought to you. Your spouse or the hospital staff can take them, and you can enjoy looking at them until you're able to look at the real thing. Even if more tubing and gadgetry is visible than baby, what you see will likely be less frightening and more reassuring than what you might have imagined. As helpful as a picture may be, you'll still want those thousand words – from your spouse, and later the medical staff – describing every detail of what your baby is like and how she's getting along.

LIGHTS OUT?

For a tiny baby who should still be in the peaceful and relatively dark uterine environment, too much light can be stressful – causing irregular heart rates and decreased sleep – and even harmful to sensitive eyes. It may also keep your baby from opening his or her eyes to look around and interact with you. On the other hand, there's also some evidence that constant dim light poses some problems, too, disturbing body rhythms and slowing development of normal sleep-wake cycles. Research suggests that premature babies who are exposed to natural cycles of light and dark that mimic day-night rhythms gain weight faster than those kept around-the-clock in either bright light or low light. (Ask the neonatologist if this can be done for your baby, if appropriate.)

Most NICUs do their best to keep the lights down to simulate life in the womb, though bright lights may be necessary at least occasionally so that medical personnel can perform procedures. Though there's probably not much you can do about the light level in the NICU, putting a blanket over your baby's isolette when the lights are bright may help somewhat.

Feast with your eyes. Just watching her in her isolette or warming mattress may help bring you closer.

Lay on the hands. Though it may seem that such a tiny and vulnerable infant is better off not being touched, studies have shown that premature infants who are stroked and lightly massaged while they are in intensive care grow better and are more alert, active and behaviourally mature than babies who are handled very little. Start with her arms and legs, since they are less sensitive at first than the trunk. Try to work up to at least 20 minutes of gentle stroking a day. (For some very premature babies, touching is extremely stressful. If the neonatologist suggests that you minimize physical contact, spend as much time as you can with your baby – just without physical contact.)

Kangaroo care. Marsupials have the right idea. Skin-to-skin contact can not only help you get close to your baby, it can help her grow and get better faster. In fact, studies have shown that babies who receive so-called kangaroo care are likely to leave the NICU sooner. To cuddle your baby marsupial-style, place her on your chest under your shirt so that she's resting directly on your skin (she'll probably be wearing only a nappy and hat; the hat prevents heat loss via the head). Loosely place your shirt over her to keep her warm or cover her with a blanket.

Carry on a conversation. To be sure, it will be a one-way conversation at first – your baby won't be doing much talking, or even crying, while she's in the NICU. She may not even appear to be listening. But she will recognize your voices, which she heard in utero, and will be comforted by the familiar sound. If you can't be with your baby as often as you'd like, ask the nurses if you can leave a recording of you talking, singing or reading quietly, which can be played for your baby. (Be sure to speak softly, however, whenever you're around your baby, since her ears are still very sound-sensitive. In fact, for some very small babies, any extra sounds can be extremely disturbing, so check with your baby's doctor about what's good for her and what isn't.)

See eye-to-eye. If your baby's eyes are shielded because she's getting phototherapy for the treatment of jaundice, ask to have the bililights turned off and her eyes uncovered for at least a few minutes during your visit so that you can make eye-to-eye contact, an important part of parent-child bonding.

Take over for the nurses. As soon as your baby's out of immediate danger, the NICU nurse will probably be happy to show you how to change, feed and bathe her. You may even do some simple medical procedures for her. One of the first tasks parents feel comfortable doing is taking the baby's temperature. Caring for her during your visits will help make you more comfortable with the role of parent, while giving you some valuable experience for the months ahead.

Don't hold back. Many parents remain detached from their premature babies for fear of loving and losing. But that's a mistake. Firstly, because the odds are very much with your preterm baby; the great majority survive to be healthy and normal. And secondly, because if you do hold back and the unthinkable happens, you'll always regret the moments you lost. The loss would be harder, not easier, to take.

LONG HOSPITALIZATION

'The first time I saw our baby in the intensive care nursery I was devastated. It's horrible to think that our baby will spend the first weeks – maybe months – of his life in a sterile hospital room.'

Parents of premature babies usually have to wait until their babies reach a gestational age of 37 to 40 weeks before taking them home – about as long as they would have had to wait if the babies had been carried to term. When a premature baby faces other medical challenges besides being small, the wait can be longer still. But no matter how long your baby's hospitalization ends up being, it will likely feel even longer. In order to make the most of that time and to even help it pass somewhat faster, try:

Striking up a partnership. Parents of a premature baby often begin to feel that their baby belongs less to them and more to the doctors and nurses, who seem so competent and do so much for him. But instead of trying to compete with the staff, try working together with them. Get to know the nurses (which will be easier if your baby has a 'primary' nurse in charge of his care at each shift), the neonatologist and the other staff. Let them know you'll be happy to do little chores or errands for your baby, which can save them time, help you pass yours and help you feel less like a bystander and more like an involved participant in his care.

Getting a medical education. Learn the jargon and terminology used in the NICU. Ask a staff member (when he or she has a free moment) to show you how to read your baby's chart; ask the neonatologist for details about your baby's condition and for clarification when you don't understand. Parents of premature babies often become experts in neonatal medicine very quickly, throwing around terms like 'RDS' and 'intubation' with the aplomb of a neonatologist.

Being a fixture at your baby's side. Some hospitals may let you move in, but even if you can't, you should spend as much time as possible with your baby, alternating shifts with your spouse. This way you will get to know not only your baby's condition but your baby as well.

(If you have other children at home, however, they'll also need you now. Be certain that they get a substantial piece of mum and dad's time, too.)

Making your baby feel at home. Even though the isolette's only a temporary stop for your baby, try to make it as much like home as possible. Ask permission to put friendly-looking stuffed animals around your baby and tape pictures (perhaps including stimulating black-and-white enlargements of snapshots of mummy and daddy) to the sides of the isolette for his viewing pleasure. Tuck in a baby music box for a little night and day music or a recording of your voice (if the doctors say it's okay). Remember, however, that anything you put in the baby's isolette will have to be sterilized and should not interfere with life-sustaining equipment. Also be sure to keep noise levels low.

Readying your milk supply. Your milk is the perfect food for your premature baby (see page 607). Until he's able to nurse, pump your breasts for indirect feedings and in order to keep up your milk supply. Pumping will also give you a welcome feeling of usefulness.

Hitting the shops. Since your baby arrived ahead of time, you may not have had time to order baby furniture, layette items and other necessities. If so, now's the time to get that shopping done. If you feel superstitious about filling your home with baby things before baby is discharged from the hospital, put in your orders pending his homecoming. You'll not only have taken care of some necessary chores, you'll also have filled some of the interminable hours of baby's hospitalization and made a statement (at least to yourself) that you are confident of bringing him home.

INTRAUTERINE GROWTH RESTRICTION

'*My baby wasn't premature, but she was just under 2.25 kg (5 lb). The doctor said it was because of intrauterine growth restriction. What does this mean?*'

Intrauterine growth restriction, often shortened to IUGR, appears to be nature's way of ensuring a foetus's survival in a uterus where, for some reason, she is not getting an adequate supply of nutrients through the placenta. The reduction in size allows a baby to get along well on the reduced intake of nutrients. Doctors surmise that this protective mechanism is called into action when the placenta isn't functioning at optimal efficiency, limiting the passage of nutrients to the foetus, or when the mother's nutrition is inadequate, because of illness, poor diet, smoking or other, sometimes unknown, factors.

The baby's brain also appears to be protected by this survival mechanism, usually continuing to grow normally by taking more than its share of nourishment from what is available. That's why most babies with IUGR have heads that are even larger in relation to their bodies than are those of full-size newborns.

Though a low-birthweight baby is at high risk for complications during the early days of life, most will do well with proper care. With good nutrition, preferably beginning with breast milk, you can expect your baby to start thriving. By the end of her first year she'll likely have caught up on many, or even on all, fronts with her peers. But should you decide to become pregnant again, try to determine first, with the aid of your doctor, what might have been responsible for the poor growing environment in your uterus so that your next baby won't have to struggle with the same prenatal problems.

SIBLINGS

'We have a three-year-old daughter, and we don't know what to tell her about her new premature sister.'

Children, even a child as young as yours, are able to understand and handle a lot more than we adults usually give them credit for. Trying to protect your daughter by keeping her in the dark about her new sibling's condition will only make her anxious and insecure – particularly when you and your spouse suddenly, and to her, inexplicably, start spending so much of your time away from home. Instead, enlighten her fully, but on her level. Explain that the baby came out of mummy too soon, before she had grown enough, and has to stay in a special cot in the hospital until she's big enough to come home. With the hospital's okay, take your older daughter for an initial visit, and if it goes well and she seems eager, take her regularly. Children are just as likely to be fascinated by the wires and tubes as they are to be scared, particularly if their parents set the right tone – confident and cheerful rather than nervous and sombre. Have her bring a present for the baby, to be placed in the isolette, which will help her feel that she's a part of the team caring for her new sibling. If she would like to, and if you have the staff's permission, let her scrub up and then touch the baby through the portholes. Like you, she will feel closer to the baby when that homecoming finally takes place if she has some contact now. (Read about sibling relationships in chapter 25.)

BREASTFEEDING

'I've always been determined to breastfeed my baby, and since she was born prematurely, I've been pumping milk to be fed to her through a tube. Will she have trouble switching to nursing later?'

So far, so good. From birth your baby has been provided with the best possible food for a premature newborn – her mummy's milk – in the only way such a tiny baby is able to take nourishment, through a tube. Naturally, you're concerned that she be able to continue to get this perfect food once she graduates to suckling.

Research indicates that you have little to worry about. One study found that premature infants weighing as little as 1.3 kg (nearly 3 lb), were not only able to suckle at the breast but were more successful at it than they were with the bottle. It took these infants between one and four weeks longer to become proficient at sucking from the bottle than at suckling from the breast. In addition, their bodies responded better to breastfeeding. When they nursed, their oxygen levels fluctuated little, whereas during bottle-feeding they showed significant drops in oxygen levels, with these levels staying down for varying periods after feeding. They were also comfortably warmer when being breastfed than when getting the bottle, which is important because premature babies, whose thermostats aren't operative, have trouble keeping themselves warm. This study and others like it show that some preterm infants begin to show the sucking reflex at 30 gestational weeks (though for other babies, the sucking reflex may not be strong enough till later).

Once you do put your baby to the breast, you'll want to make conditions as conducive to success as possible:

◆ Read all about breastfeeding, beginning on page 60, before getting started.

◆ Be patient if the neonatologist or nurse wants your baby monitored for temperature and/or oxygen changes during breastfeeding. This won't interfere with the breastfeeding itself, and it will protect your baby by sounding an alarm in case she is not responding well to the feeding.

◆ Be sure you're relaxed and that your baby is awake and alert. A nurse will probably see to it that she is dressed warmly for this momentous event.

◆ Ask the staff if there is a special nursing area for premature baby mums, a private corner with an armchair for you and your baby, or a privacy screen that can be put up to shield you.

◆ Get comfortable, propping your baby on pillows, supporting her head. Many women find a clutch hold comfortable (see page 66) as well as easy on the nipples.

◆ If your baby doesn't yet have a rooting reflex (she probably doesn't), help her get started by placing your nipple, with the areola, into her mouth. Compress your breast lightly with your fingers to make it easier for her to latch on to (see page 67), and keep trying until she succeeds.

◆ Watch to be sure your baby is getting milk. The first few minutes at the breast, baby's suckling may be very rapid, a non-nutritive motion aimed at stimulating let-down. Your breasts are used to mechanical pumping and will take a while to adjust to the different motions generated by your baby's mouth, but soon you will notice that the movement has slowed and that your baby is swallowing. This lets you know that let-down has occurred, and your baby is getting milk.

◆ If your baby doesn't seem interested in your breast, try expressing a few drops of milk into her mouth to give her a taste of what's in store.

◆ Nurse your baby for as long a period as she's willing to stay at the breast. Experts who've studied breastfeeding of premature babies recommend letting them remain at the breast until they've stopped active suckling for at least two minutes. Small premature babies have been known to nurse for close to an hour before being satisfied.

◆ Don't be discouraged if the first session or first several sessions seem unproductive. Many full-term babies take a while to catch on, and premature babies deserve at least the same chance.

◆ Ask that any feedings at which you cannot nurse be given by gavage (through the nose) rather than by bottle. If your baby is given bottle feedings while you're trying to establish breastfeeding, nipple confusion could interfere with your efforts. If human milk fortifier or other fortification is given to your baby to supplement the breast milk, ask that it, too, be given by gavage or by the supplemental nutrition system (see page 161).

You'll be able to tell how well your baby is doing on the breast by following her daily weigh-in. If she continues gaining about 1 to 2 per cent of her body weight daily, or about 100 to 210 g (3½

TAKING BABY HOME

When will that moment come? Chances are, the momentous homecoming will take place approximately at the same time it would have if your baby had been born full-term, at 40 weeks – though occasionally a baby may be discharged as early as two to four weeks before his or her due date. Most hospitals don't have a specific weight requirement. Instead, babies are usually sent home once they meet the following criteria:

♦ are able to maintain normal body temperature in an open cot

♦ have graduated to breast or bottle feedings only

♦ are gaining weight on breast or bottle feedings

♦ are breathing on their own

♦ show no sign of apnea (pauses while breathing)

---

to 7½ oz) a week, she'll be doing fine. By the time she reaches her original due date, she should be approaching the weight of a full-termer – somewhere around 2.7 to 3.6 kg (6 to 8 lb).

HANDLING BABY

'So far I've handled our baby only through the portholes of her isolette. But I'm worried about how well I'll be able to handle her when she finally comes home. She's so tiny and fragile.'

When your baby finally makes that long-anticipated trip home, she may actually seem pudgy and sturdy to you, rather than tiny and fragile. Like many premature babies, she'll probably be double her birthweight by the time she hits the requisite 1.8 or 2.25 kg (4 or 5 lb) necessary for discharge. And chances are you won't have any more trouble caring for her than most new parents have caring for their full-term babies. In fact, if you have a chance to do some baby care at the hospital (something you should insist on) in the weeks before your baby's homecoming, you'll actually be ahead of the game. Which is not to say it will

be easy – rare is the new parent (of premature baby or full-termer) who finds it so.

If you're wondering how well you and your baby will do without a nurse or neonatologist looking over your shoulder and ready to step in if anything goes wrong, be assured that hospitals don't send home babies who are still in need of full-time professional care. Most NICUs offer parents the opportunity to spend the night with their baby in a family room close to the nursery but without any nursery staff supervision. Still, some parents, particularly those who come home with such extra paraphernalia as breathing monitors or oxygen hoods, find it comforting to hire a maternity nurse who has had experience with premature babies and their medical care to help them through the first week or two. Consider this option if you're anxious about going at it alone.

PERMANENT PROBLEMS

'Though the doctor says our baby is doing well, I'm still afraid that he'll come through this with some kind of permanent damage.'

One of the greatest miracles of modern medicine is the rapidly increasing survival rate for premature infants. At one time, a baby weighing in at 1 kg (about 2 lb 3 oz) had no chance of making it. Now, thanks to the advances in neonatology, many babies who are born even smaller than that can be expected to survive.

Of course, along with this increased survival rate has come an increase in the number of babies with moderate to severe handicaps. Still, the odds of your baby's coming home from his hospital stay both alive *and* well are very much in his favour. Only an estimated 10 per cent of all premature babies and 20 per cent of those between 680 g and 1.6 kg (1½ and 3½ lb) end up with major handicaps. The risks of permanent disability are much greater for those who are born at 23 to 25 weeks and/or weigh less than 710 g (25 oz); still, of the 40 per cent of these infants who survive, more than half do well.

Overall, better than 2 out of 3 babies born prematurely will turn out to be perfectly normal, and most of the others will have only mild to moderate handicaps. Most often the baby's IQ will be normal, though preterm infants do have an increased risk of learning problems.

As your baby grows, it will be important to keep in mind that he will have some catching up to do before his development reaches the normal range for his birth age. His progress is likely to follow more closely that of children of his corrected age; see next question. If he was very small, or had serious complications during the neonatal period, he is very likely to lag behind his corrected agemates too, particularly in motor development.

It may be slower going in the neuromuscular department, too. Some premature babies may not lose such newborn reflexes as the Moro, tonic neck or grasp reflexes as early as term infants, even taking corrected age into account. Or their muscle tone may be abnormal, in some cases causing the head to droop excessively, in other cases causing the legs to be stiff and the toes to point. Though such signs may be a sign that something's wrong in full-term babies, they're usually nothing to worry about in pretermers. (Still, they should be evaluated by the doctor, and physical therapy should be begun if necessary.)

Slow developmental progress in a premature baby is *not* cause for alarm, it is to be expected. If, however, your baby seems not to be making *any* progress week to week, month to month, or if he seems unresponsive (when he's not ill), speak to his doctor. If the doctor doesn't share your concerns but doesn't allay them either, ask for a second opinion. Not infrequently, a parent, who sees her baby day in and day out, catches something the doctor misses. If there turns out to be no problem, which will most often be the case, the second opinion will help to ease your fears. If a problem is discovered, the early diagnosis could lead to treatment as well as ongoing training and care, which may make a tremendous difference in the ultimate quality of your baby's life.

CATCHING UP

'Our son, who was born nearly two months early, seems very far behind compared with other three-month-olds. Will he ever catch up?'

He's probably not 'behind' at all. In fact, he's probably just where a baby conceived when he was should be. Traditionally, in our culture, a baby's age is calculated from the day he was born. But this system is misleading when assessing the growth and development of premature infants, since it fails to take into account that at birth they have not yet reached term. Your baby, for example, was just a little more than *minus* two months old at birth. At two months of age he was, in terms of gestational age (calculated according to his *original* due date), equivalent to a newborn. At three months, he's more like a one-month-old. Keep this in mind when you compare him to other children his age or to averages on development charts. For example, though the average baby may sit well at seven months, your child may not do so until he's nine months old, when he reaches his seventh-month corrected age. If he was very small or very ill in the neonatal period, he's likely to sit even later. In general, you can expect motor development to lag more than the development of the senses (vision and hearing, for example).

Experts use the gestational age, usually called 'corrected age', in evaluating a premature child's developmental progress until he's 2 or 2½ years old. After that point, the two months or so differential tends to lose its significance – there isn't, after all, much developmental difference between a child who is four years old and one who is two months shy of four. As your baby gets older, the behaviour gap between his corrected age and his birth age will diminish and finally disappear, as will any developmental differences between him and his peers (though occasionally, extra nurturing may be needed to bring a premature baby to that point). In the meantime, if you feel more comfortable using his corrected age with strangers, do so. Certainly do so when assessing your baby's developmental progress.

Instead of looking for specific behaviours from your baby at specific times, relax and enjoy his progress as it comes, providing support as needed. If he's smiling and cooing, smile and coo back at him. If he's starting to reach for things, give him the opportunity to practise that skill, too. When he can sit propped up, prop him in different surroundings for a while each day. But always keep his corrected age in mind, and don't rush him or push him.

Use the infant stimulation tips in this book (pages 238, 364, 505), gearing them to your baby's behaviour rather than his age, and be careful to stop when he signals that he's had enough. You can, additionally, encourage motor development by placing your baby on his tummy, facing outwards towards the room rather than towards the wall, as often and for as long as he'll tolerate it (but only when he is carefully supervised). Since premature and low-birthweight babies spend most of their early weeks, sometimes months, on their backs in isolettes, they often resist this 'tummy to play' position, but it's a necessary one for building arm and neck strength.

If, of course, your baby is far behind developmentally even after making allowances for his prematurity, and if he seems to stay that way, read page 474 and check with his doctor.

CAR SEATS

'My baby seems way too small for the infant car seat. Wouldn't she be safer in my arms?'

Every baby, no matter how tiny, must be buckled up safely, securely and snugly each and every time he or she's in a moving vehicle. But parents of low-birthweight babies often find that their especially little babies seem lost in a standard rear-facing infant car seat. When choosing and using a car seat for your premature baby, follow this advice:

PREMATURE BABY VACCINES

For most of your premature baby's first two years, his or her corrected age will be the one that counts most, except in one area: immunizations. Most of a baby's vaccine schedule isn't delayed because of prematurity, so instead of receiving vaccines according to gestational age, he or she will receive them according to birth age. In other words, if your baby was born two months early, he or she will still get those first shots at age two months – not age four months. There are, however, two exceptions. Firstly, doctors will usually wait until a baby weighs 1.5 kg (3 lb 5 oz) before vaccinating (most infants will weigh at least 1.8 kg/4 lb by age two months). Secondly, the hepatitis B vaccine is not given to a premature infant at birth (as it sometimes is for full-termers). Instead, doctors will wait until the baby weighs in at a minimum of 1.95 kg/4 lb 6 oz.

Don't worry about your tiny baby's not being able to produce antibodies to the vaccines. Researchers have found that at seven years, even children who were born extremely small have antibody levels similar to other children the same age.

♦ Select a car seat that will fit your baby. Look for ones that have less than 14 cm (5½ in) from the crotch strap to the seat back. This will help keep your baby from slouching. Also, look for one that measures less than 25.5 cm (10 in) from the lowest harness strap position to the seat bottom so that the harness won't cross over your baby's ears.

♦ Make it fit even better. Roll a towel or small blanket and arrange it so that it pads the seat at the sides of her head, or buy a ready-to-use head roll designed for infant car seats. If there's a big gap between your baby's body and the harness, use a folded towel or blanket to fill it in. But don't place one *under* baby.

Some premature babies have trouble breathing in the semi-propped position the seat requires. One study has shown that these infants may show a decreased oxygen supply while riding in a car seat, and that this deficit may last for as long as thirty minutes or more afterwards. Some may also experience short periods of apnea (breathing cessation) in car seats. Make sure your baby is observed and monitored in the car seat by the hospital staff before going home. In the past, babies who experienced problems in a car seat were encouraged to use a crash-tested infant car bed. These days, however, doctors no longer recommend infant car beds because there doesn't seem to be much benefit to the baby in terms of breathing. Instead, if your baby does experience breathing problems in a car seat, it's best to limit the amount of car travel you do with your baby for the first month or two at home, especially if she has had spells of apnea previously. Or ask her doctor about monitoring her breathing when she's in an ordinary car seat, at least for a while, to see if she is experiencing any problems.

The same breathing problems may occur in young premature babies in infant seats and baby swings, so don't use either without the doctor's approval.

HOME-CARE TIPS FOR PRETERM BABIES

Even once they've reached the age of full-term babies, premature babies continue to need some special care. As you prepare to take your baby home, keep these tips in mind:

◆ Read the month-by-month chapters in this book. They apply to your preterm baby as well as to full-termers. But remember to adjust for your baby's corrected age.

◆ Keep your home warmer than usual, about 22.2°C (72°F) or so, for the first few weeks that your baby is at home. The temperature regulating mechanism is usually functioning in premature infants by the time they go home, but because of their small size and greater skin surface in relation to fat, they may have difficulty keeping comfortable without a little help. In addition, having to expend a great many calories to keep warm could interfere with weight gain. If your baby seems unusually fussy, check the room temperature to see if it's warm enough. Feel baby's arms, legs or the nape of the neck to be sure it isn't too cool in the room. (However, don't overheat the room.)

◆ Buy nappies made for premature babies, if necessary. You can also buy baby clothes in premature sizes, but don't buy too many – before you know it, your baby will have out-grown them.

◆ Sterilize bottles, if you're giving them, by boiling them before the first use and running them through a hot dish-washer after each feeding. Though it may be an unnecessary precaution for a term baby, it's a good one to take for premature ones, who are more susceptible to infection. Continue for a few months, or until baby's doctor gives you the okay to pack away the sterilizer.

◆ Feed your baby frequently, even though this may mean spending most of your time nursing or bottle feeding. Premature babies have very small stomachs, and they may need to fill them up as often as every two hours. They also may not be able to suckle as efficiently or effectively as full termers, and so they may take longer – as long as an hour – to drink their fill. Don't rush feedings.

◆ Ask the doctor if your baby should be receiving a baby multivitamin supplement. Preterm babies can be at greater risk of becoming vitamin deficient than full-termers and may need this extra insurance.

◆ Don't start solids until your doctor gives the go-ahead. Generally, solids are introduced to a preterm infant when weight reaches 5.9 to 6.8 kg (13 to 15 lb), when more than 950 ml (32 fl oz) of formula is consumed daily for at least a week, and/or when the corrected age is six months. Occasionally, when a baby is not satisfied with just formula or breast milk, solids may be started as early as four months, corrected age.

◆ Relax. Without a doubt, your baby has been through a lot – and so have you. But once he or she is home, and once you've taken the above precautions, try to put the experience behind both of you. As great as the impulse may be to hover or overprotect, aim instead to treat your baby like the normal, healthy child he or she is now.

GUILT

'I know that I wasn't as careful during my pregnancy as I should have been. And even though the doctor said it probably wasn't my fault, I can't help blaming myself for my son being born so early.'

There's probably not one mother of a premature baby who doesn't look back and regret something she did during pregnancy that she might have done better – something she fears might have contributed to her baby's early arrival.

Such feelings of remorse are normal but not productive. Besides, it's almost impossible to be sure just what factor or factors are responsible for your baby's early arrival. In many cases, what a mother did or didn't do during pregnancy had no impact (and no expectant woman does *everything* right). Even if you are sure that your behaviour or lifestyle played a part, assigning blame is not going to help your baby. What your baby needs now is a mother who is strong, loving and supportive, not one who is paralyzed by feelings of guilt.

Read chapter 21, which concerns newborns with special needs for some suggestions on how to deal with your feelings of guilt, anger and frustration. It may also help to talk to other parents of premature babies. You will find they share many of your feelings. Some hospitals have parent support groups; others feel parents do better consulting with the staff than with other parents. Do what seems to help you most.

What it's Important to Know: HEALTH PROBLEMS COMMON IN LOW-BIRTHWEIGHT BABIES

Prematurity is risky business. Tiny bodies are not fully mature, many systems (heat regulatory, respiratory and digestive, for example) aren't yet fully operative and, not surprisingly, the risk of neonatal illness is increased. As the technology for keeping such babies alive improves, more attention is being given to these common premature conditions, and completely successful treatment is becoming more and more the norm for many of them. (New treatments are being developed almost daily and so may not be detailed here, so be sure to ask your neonatologist or paediatrician about recent advances.) The medical problems that most frequently complicate the lives of preterm infants include:

Respiratory distress syndrome (RDS). Because of immaturity, the premature lung often lacks pulmonary surfactant, a detergent-like substance that helps keep the air sacs (alveoli) in the lungs from collapsing. Without surfactant the tiny air sacs collapse like deflating balloons with each expiration, forcing the tiny baby to work harder and harder to breathe. Babies who have undergone severe stress in the uterus, usually during labour and delivery, are less likely to lack surfactant, as the stress appears to speed lung maturation.

RDS, the most common lung disease of premature infants, was once frequently fatal, but more than 80 per cent of babies who develop RDS today survive, thanks to an increased understanding of the syndrome and new ways of treatment. Extra oxygen is given via a plastic oxygen hood, or via continuous positive airway pressure (CPAP), which is administered through tubes that fit into the nostrils of the nose or mouth. The continuous pressure keeps the lungs from collapsing until the body begins producing sufficient surfactant, usually in three to five days. For babies with severe RDS, a breathing tube is placed and the baby put on a respirator. Surfactant is then administered directly to the baby's lungs via the breathing tube. Sometimes, when lung immaturity is detected in utero, RDS can be prevented entirely by the prenatal administration of a hormone to the mother, to speed lung maturation and production of surfactant.

A mild case of RDS usually lasts for the first week of life, though if the baby is placed on a respirator, the recovery may be much slower. Babies with severe cases of RDS may be at an increased risk of colds or respiratory illnesses during their first two years of life, a greater likelihood of childhood wheezing or asthma-like illnesses, and a greater likelihood of being hospitalized in their first two years.

Bronchopulmonary dysplasia (BPD). In some babies, particularly those born very small, long-term oxygen administration and mechanical ventilation appear to combine with lung immaturity to cause BPD, or chronic lung disease. The condition, which results from lung injury, is usually diagnosed when a newborn still requires increased oxygen after reaching 36 weeks' gestation. Specific lung changes are generally seen on X-rays, and these babies frequently gain weight slowly and are subject to apnea. Treatment of BPD includes extra oxygen; continued mechanical ventilation; medications such as bronchodilators (to help open the airways) or steroids (to reduce inflammation); limiting fluids or giving diuretics (to reduce fluid); RSV and influenza vaccinations. Recent research suggests nitric oxide may help as well. Some babies will require oxygen at home, and all require a high caloric intake to improve growth. Often the condition is outgrown as the lungs mature, though babies with BPD may be at increased risk for respiratory infections and diseases.

Apnea of prematurity. Though apnea, periods of breathing cessation, can occur in any newborn, this problem is much more common among premature infants. Apnea of prematurity occurs when a preterm baby's immature respiratory and nervous systems cause them to stop breathing for short periods. It is diagnosed when a baby has such periods that last more than 20 seconds or that are shorter but are associated with bradycardia, a slowing of the heart rate. It is also considered apnea if the cessation of breathing is associated with the baby's colour changing to pale, purplish or blue. Almost all babies born at 30 weeks or less will experience apnea.

Apnea is treated by stimulating the infant to start rebreathing by rubbing or patting the baby's skin, administering medication (such as caffeine or theophylline), or by using continuous positive airway pressure (CPAP), in which oxygen is delivered under pressure through little tubes into the baby's nose. Many babies will outgrow apnea by the time they reach 36 weeks' gestation. Occasionally, monitoring at home may be required, though most babies no longer show signs of apnea by the time they are ten weeks past their due date. Apnea of prematurity is not associated with SIDS. If a baby has breathing pauses after apnea goes away, it is not considered apnea of prematurity and is more likely due to some other problem.

Patent ductus arteriosus. While baby is still in the uterus, there is a duct connecting the aorta (the artery through which blood from the heart is sent to the rest of the body) and the left pulmonary artery (the one leading to the lungs) called the ductus arteriosus. This duct shunts blood away from the non-functioning lungs and is kept open during gestation by high levels of prostaglandin E (one of a group of fatty acids produced by the body) in the blood. Normally, levels of prostaglandin E fall at delivery, and the duct begins to close within a few hours. But in about half of very small premature babies (those weighing 1.5 kg/3lb 5 oz), and in some larger babies, levels of prostaglandin E don't drop and the duct remains open or 'patent'. In many cases there are no symptoms, except a heart murmur and a little shortness of breath on exertion and/or blueness of the lips, and the duct closes by itself sooner after birth. Occasionally, however, severe complications occur. Treatment with an antiprostaglandin drug (indomethacin) is often successful in closing the duct; when it isn't, surgery generally does the job.

Retinopathy of prematurity (ROP). This condition, caused by abnormal growth of the blood vessels in an infant's eye, affects 85 per cent of babies born earlier than 28 weeks. Though babies born between 28 and 34 weeks are also at risk (though not at such a high percentage), typically only the smallest preterm babies, no matter what their gestational age, have the highest risk. It was once thought to be caused by excessive oxygen administration, but it is now known that a high level of oxygen is only one of the factors involved, and doctors are still trying to determine what other factors might contribute to ROP. Close monitoring of blood gases in the infant when oxygen therapy is given is now routine and does seem to help minimize the risk of ROP.

Since ROP can lead to scarring and distortion of the retina, increased risk of nearsightedness (myopia), wandering eye (amblyopia), involuntary rhythmic movements of the eye (nystagmus) and even blindness, a newborn with ROP will need to be seen by a paediatric ophthalmologist. Infants with severe ROP may require treatment to stop the progression of the abnormal vessels. With treatment, the inner lining of the eye at the ends of these vessels is killed to prevent further abnormal growth of the blood vessels.

Intraventricular haemorrhage (IVH). IVH, or bleeding in the brain, is extremely common among premature infants because the vessels in their developing brains are very fragile and can bleed easily. Intraventricular haemorrhage strikes 15 to 20 per cent of premature babies weighing less than 1.5 kg (3 lb 5 oz), most often within the first 72 hours of life. The most severe haemorrhages (which strike only 5 to 10 per cent of extremely premature babies) require close observation to correct any further problems that develop – for example, hydrocephalus (blockage of spinal fluid). Regular follow-up ultrasounds are usually ordered for such haemorrhages until they are resolved. Babies with the more severe-grade haemorrhages are also at greater risk for seizures immediately, and handicaps later on. There is no specific treatment for IVH. Surgery will not prevent or

REHOSPITALIZATION

Happily, most premature babies who go home from the hospital stay home. But sometimes, a baby ends up back in the hospital during the first year, usually for the treatment of a respiratory illness or dehydration. When this happens, it's particularly tough on the parents, who have been struggling to put the time spent in the NICU behind them and begin a normal life with their babies. Memories and all-too-familiar emotions may come flooding back if your baby is rehospitalized, from feelings of guilt ('What did I do wrong?') to feelings of fear and panic ('What happens if my baby gets sicker?'). After finally having your baby home and under your care, you may also feel as though you've lost control again.

Try to keep in mind that rehospitalization usually doesn't last long, and that, like your child's stay in the NICU as a newborn, the stay in the hospital (more likely to be in the PICU or paediatric intensive care unit) will also come to an end – at which point you'll be able to bring your baby home once again, this time, hopefully, for good.

cure the bleeding. In mild cases (and most cases are), the blood is absorbed by the body. Usually the follow-up head ultrasound is normal and the baby's development is normal for a preterm baby.

Necrotizing enterocolitis (NEC). NEC is an inflammation of the intestines that doesn't occur until feedings have begun. The cause is unknown, but because the more premature a baby is, the greater the risk of NEC, doctors speculate that the intestines of very premature babies are not developed enough to completely handle digestion. Babies fed breast milk get NEC less often than babies fed formula. The symptoms of this serious bowel disease include abdominal distension, bilious vomiting, apnea and blood in the stool. A baby with necrotizing enterocolitis is usually put on intravenous feedings and antibiotics. If there is serious deterioration of the intestine, surgery is usually performed to remove the damaged portion.

Anaemia. Many premature infants develop anaemia (too few red blood cells) because their red blood cells (like all babies') have a shorter life than red blood cells of adults (this may be exaggerated if the baby's blood type is different from the mother's), they make few new red blood cells in the first few weeks of life (like all infants), and the frequent blood samples that must be taken from the baby to do necessary laboratory tests make it difficult for red blood cells to replenish. Mild anaemia may not need treatment if the number of red blood cells is enough to carry oxygen to meet the baby's needs. Severe anaemia is usually treated by giving the baby a blood transfusion. Since premature babies, whether they're anaemic or not, are born with low levels of iron, they are usually given iron supplements to help them build up the reserves necessary to produce red blood cells.

Infection. Premature infants are most vulnerable to a variety of infections because they are born before the transfer of disease-fighting antibodies from the mother that normally occurs towards the end of pregnancy. Premature babies also have an immature immune system, making it more difficult to fight germs, including those that are introduced via feeding tubes, IV lines and blood tests. Among the infections premature babies are more likely to come down with are pneumonia, urinary tract infections, sepsis (infection of the body or bloodstream) and meningitis. Babies whose blood, urine or spinal fluid cultures come back positive for signs of infection are treated with a full course of IV antibiotics.

Jaundice. Premature babies are much more likely to develop jaundice than are full-term infants. Also, their bilirubin levels (the measure of jaundice) are likely to be higher and the jaundice longer lasting. Read about the condition on page 123.

Hypoglycaemia. Low blood sugar in an infant is often unrecognized and untreated because symptoms may be absent or not apparent. Consequently, it can lead to such serious complications as brain damage. It's most commonly a problem among multiples, when the smaller or smallest baby weighs less than 2 kg (4½ lb), and in babies of diabetic mums (who usually have high, rather than low, birthweights). Hypoglycaemia is routinely screened for during the first 24 to 48 hours, and if it's found, treatment to normalize sugar levels is begun immediately.

Low blood pressure. This condition is common in premature babies after birth because of blood loss before or during delivery, fluid loss after delivery, infection, or medications given to the mother before delivery. Low blood pressure also often accompanies RDS. It is treated by increasing fluids, by giving the baby medications to increase blood pressure, or by giving a blood transfusion, if necessary.

◆ ◆ ◆

CHAPTER 21

The Special Needs Baby

After nine months of hoping for a perfectly healthy baby, it can be devastating to give birth to a child who has special needs. If the condition affecting the baby wasn't detected antenatally, shock can compound feelings of pain and disappointment. But as hopeless – and helpless – as you might feel when you first discover that your baby has been born with a birth defect or a chronic medical problem, it may help to know that with time, such feelings eventually fade. As you learn to cope with the complexities of having a baby with special needs, you'll come to see past the problems to the child underneath – a child who needs, above all, what every child needs: your love and attention.

Keep in mind, too, that medical technology has made tremendous strides in helping improve the prognosis for these babies. In many cases, a birth disorder – even one that seems so frightening at first – is relatively easily corrected with surgery, medication, physical therapy or other treatment. In other cases, the condition – and the outlook for the baby – can be greatly improved. In still other cases, learning to live with a baby's disability – rather than overcome it – becomes the major objective. Even then, parents often find that raising a special needs baby adds another dimension to their lives – initially challenging, ultimately enriching. Though caring for such babies can easily be double the effort, it can also bring double the rewards. As time passes they often discover that their child, in addition to teaching them something about pain, has taught them a lot about love.

While much of the general information in this book is useful to parents of a child born with birth defects, this chapter deals with some of the adjustments and decisions that are unique to their situation. If your baby was also premature, it will be helpful to read chapter 20.

Feeding Your Baby:
CAN DIET MAKE A DIFFERENCE?

All parents want their children, disabled or not, to be the best they can be. Ensuring optimum nutrition – from birth on – is one way to help children develop to their greatest potential, whatever that potential might be. While a good diet can't change the fact that a child has a birth disorder, or may not even improve his or her condition, it can have an impact on general health and can affect behaviour, learning ability and development. There's no evidence, however, that dietary manipulation (feeding a special diet, for example, or giving vitamin megadoses) can significantly improve the medical condition of a child born with a birth disorder, except in cases where the defect is diet related.

For the child with no such unusual dietary needs, the best in nutrition begins with breast milk, when possible, or commercial infant formula, and then the First-Year Diet for Beginners; see page 313.

What You May Be Concerned About

FEELING RESPONSIBLE

'*Our doctor just told us that our baby has a birth defect. I can't help feeling that I'm somehow responsible – that I could have done something to prevent his problem.*'

Parents often feel responsible for the bad things that happen to their children; even a tumble precipitated by a toddler's own normal clumsiness can prompt his parents to beat themselves up ('Why didn't we watch him more carefully?'). When a child is born with a birth disorder, the guilt can be overwhelming and debilitating. But birth disorders are rarely caused by anything a mother or father has done – and unrelieved guilt can prevent you from bonding with and caring for your baby. Accepting that the cause was out of your control can help you begin the process of coming to terms with your baby's disability – a process that must begin before you can start learning to live with and love your newborn.

Speak to your child's doctors for more reassurance. If that's not enough to help you put the guilt behind you, try speaking to other parents who've weathered the same storm. Enquire at the hospital about support groups in your area, or chat on-line with other parents whose babies have the same disability. You'll soon find that the feelings you're experiencing are virtually universal among parents of special needs children. Knowing that you're not alone can help immeasurably.

FEELING ANGRY

'*Ever since I gave birth to my daughter, who has Down's syndrome, I've been angry at everyone – the doctors, my spouse, my parents, other parents with normal babies, even the baby.*'

Why wouldn't you be angry? Your dreams of nine months, or maybe

WHEN THE GUILT IS REAL

Occasionally, as in the case of foetal alcohol syndrome, the development of a birth defect can be traced to a mother's actions, making the guilt that burdens nearly all parents of babies born with birth defects all the more difficult to handle. It's important to remember, however, that alcoholism is as much a disease as diabetes is, that alcoholic mothers drank not because they wanted to hurt their babies but because the disease was controlling them. If your baby's defect can be pinpointed to this type of problem, seek professional help now to deal with it and to prevent any further negative impact on this baby and babies you may have in the future.

It's also important to keep in mind that even when guilt does have a basis, it does no one any good – least of all your baby. Instead of wasting emotional energy berating yourself, concentrate on the positive steps that can be taken to make your baby's future, and your family's, the best it can be.

---

longer, have been shattered. You look around at friends, neighbours, relatives, strangers at the supermarket with their normal babies, and you think bitterly, 'Why not me?' The fact that asking this question yields no satisfying answers further fuels your frustration. You may be angry at the doctor who delivered your baby (even though he or she wasn't at fault), at your spouse (even without logical reason), even at your normal children.

Accept your anger as normal, but also recognize that, like guilt, it isn't a particularly productive emotion. Being angry takes a lot of energy – energy that really should be focused on your baby and her needs. You can't change the past, but you can make a huge difference in your child's future.

NOT LOVING THE BABY

'It's been almost a month since our daughter was born with a birth defect, and I still don't feel close to her. I wonder if I ever will.'

Because bonding is a gradual process, even parents with normal babies often take months to feel really close to their newborns. For parents with dis-

abled infants, who must let go of the idealized baby they were expecting before they can open their hearts to the baby they've actually given birth to, the process is, understandably, even more gradual. And, as is true with parents of normal infants, getting to know your baby is the first step in learning to love your baby. To do this, interact as you would with any newborn – singing lullabies, cuddling, stroking and kissing. Not only will this help you feel closer to your baby, but it will help you look past her birth defect so that you can discover and focus on her endearing qualities (every child has them).

Talking to other parents of babies with similar disabilities will help you realize that your feelings are completely normal and undoubtedly fleeting. If you don't feel closer to your baby as time passes, then seek counselling from someone experienced in working with parents of children with birth defects or join a regular support group. Your doctor or hospital should be able to direct you.

'Doctors tell us our little boy may not make it, so we're afraid to get too attached to him.'

WORKING OUT YOUR FEELINGS

Maybe it's guilt you're feeling, or anger, or frustration. Maybe you're having trouble bonding with your baby or connecting with your spouse. No matter what's getting you down, joining a support group with other new parents who are in the same boat as you (check on-line, at the hospital or with your baby's doctors) can help you work out your feelings with others who know how you're feeling. So can open communication with your spouse, who is faced with the same experience but may be confronting it differently. If these steps don't work, seek professional help as soon as possible to prevent your feelings from interfering with your relationships with your baby, your spouse, and with your other children.

Parents of babies whose lives are in jeopardy – either because they're very small or very sick – often share this fear of loving and losing, and consciously or subconsciously avoid bonding with their newborns. In general, though, parents who allow themselves to get to know their critically ill babies (even if only through the portholes of an incubator) end up having an easier time coping if the child doesn't survive than do those who keep their emotional and physical distance – perhaps because they're better able to grieve. But by far the best reason for showering love on your critically ill infant is that you'll be providing him, in a sense, with a reason for living. The love of his parents can have a significant impact on your baby's will to survive and might actually help to pull him through.

WHAT TO TELL OTHERS

'Our son's birth defect is very obvious. People don't know what to say to me when they see him, and I don't know what to say to them.'

Even people who never seem to be at a loss for words often are when confronted with a child who has a birth defect. They want to say the right thing, but they don't know what the right thing is. They want to be kind and supportive, but they don't know how to be either. They want to congratulate you on the birth of your baby but feel almost as though condolences would be more appropriate. You can help them, and yourself, by acknowledging their discomfort, opening the way for them to express their feelings. If you're feeling able to, let them know you understand if they're uneasy, that most people are at first, and that it's perfectly natural. Beyond this, all that a casual friend needs to be told is that though your newborn has a birth defect, he's yours, you love him and you intend to treat him as normally as possible – and hope that they will do the same.

Of course, this is a rational approach to the situation, and you may not feel rational at first. You may want to ignore the staring strangers, and sometimes even well-intentioned friends and family – or to lash out at thoughtless or tactless remarks. Don't be hard on yourself if you're initially too upset to put others at ease. With time and, if necessary, sensitive individual counselling or group therapy or support, you'll become better able to cope.

Friends and relatives who will be in closer, more frequent contact with your baby will, of course, need to know more. In addition to being encouraged to be open about their feelings, they will have to be educated about your child's problems and special needs. Provide them with reading material or websites about your child's medical problems, ask the baby's doctor to speak with them, encourage them to talk informally to other family members of children with birth defects, or refer them to a support group. Include them in your baby's care – give them the opportunity to hold, change, bathe and play with him. In time they, too, will come to see him as the lovable baby he is.

Sometimes close relatives, particularly grandparents, feel guilty ('Did I contribute a faulty gene?'), or angry ('Why couldn't you give us a healthy grandchild?'), or think they have all the answers ('Feed him this food', 'Go to that doctor'). If your efforts to involve them in your baby's life and educate them about his problems don't help to overcome such attitudes, and if their negative input continues to threaten the delicate equilibrium of your nuclear family, keep lines of communication open, but don't let their problem become yours.

In spite of your best efforts, there will always be people who – because they just don't know any better – will make cruel and insensitive comments, undervalue your child because he is different, and feel uncomfortable around him. There will be times when both you and he will be hurt by their intolerance. As much as you might like to educate the entire world, it isn't possible. You'll just have to learn to hold your head high and ignore the narrow-minded people you can't reach.

Handling It All

'We love our new baby, even with all her problems and the special care she requires, but with another small child to care for and care about at home, I feel totally overwhelmed and unable to cope.'

Raising a child with a birth defect can be both physically and emotionally draining, even for the parent with no other children at home. The pointers in chapters 23 and 24, which can help any new parent, can help you, too. But you'll also need more:

More breaks. If you are a full-time parent (and many parents of disabled children are, choosing to postpone returning to their jobs), then you've got to find ways of getting out of the house, away from the stress of caring for your child day in and day out. Take off at least a few hours a week (an hour or two every day would be even better), leaving the baby with a relative, friend, trusted sitter or maternity nurse. Or take your breaks when your spouse gets home from work each day, and on the weekends when he's not at work. (But also make sure you take some breaks together; a weekly 'date night' is important for all new parents but essential for parents of a special needs baby.) Have lunch with a friend, work out at the gym, see a movie, get a facial or a haircut or just go window shopping – whatever will relax you most and give you the greatest psychic boost. If you have another child, try to take some of your breaks with him or her; both of you will benefit from the one-on-one time that's become so scarce.

More release. Don't bottle up your worries, fears, complaints – air them with your spouse, your own parents or siblings, your best friend, your doctor, other

BE A FRIEND IN DEED

Few people know what to do or say when they hear that a friend, relative, neighbour or casual acquaintance has given birth to a child with a birth defect, a child who is seriously ill, or one who dies at or shortly after delivery. There are no pat answers; every individual and every situation is unique. But in general, these approaches are the ones likely to help the most:

Lend an ear. Don't say, 'I know how you feel', unless you've been there yourself. Don't say, 'You've got to be brave', or offer any other platitudes, as well intentioned as they may be. The new parents in crisis will get plenty of advice from the professionals. What they need from you is unconditional love, unswerving support and a willing ear. Listen to what's on their minds and in their hearts without being judgmental or offering your viewpoints. Let them vent their feelings, whatever those feelings may be (you can expect them to be angry at times, despondent at others) and sympathize with them – this will be the best therapy.

Become informed. If the parents seem to want to talk about their baby's problems, listen. But if they've told the terrible tale too many times already, get your information second- or third-hand from a relative or friend so they needn't relive it again. To be better able to understand what they are going through, read this chapter (and if relevant, the previous one) and get further information, if you feel you need it, from an organization that deals with the baby's specific condition.

Use body language. Often when words fail, the squeeze of a hand, a loving hug, a sympathetic look will get the message that you care across.

Keep in touch. Because you're not sure what to do or say, it's often easier to do or say nothing, avoiding the friend who is going through a crisis. Those who have been on the receiving end of such behaviour almost always say, 'I'd rather hear the wrong words than none at all'. So keep those phone calls, visits and invitations coming. And though you shouldn't force your company on someone who would rather suffer their pain alone, don't give up after one 'We're not up to it yet'. Try again soon.

Help out. There are innumerable chores friends and family can take over when new parents are mourning the loss of an infant or are faced with one who is hospitalized or needs a great deal of attention. Cook a meal, baby-sit for older children, do the laundry, offer to vacuum, wield the dust cloth, or even take over with the baby for an hour or two if possible. Any way in which you can lighten the burden will doubtless be appreciated.

parents in your situation or a professional counsellor if necessary. You may not feel ready to face a support group for parents of children with similar problems at first, but you may find this extremely helpful (not just in terms of emotional support, but for practical and logistical tips) later on. On-line chat rooms, which allow you to get that support any time of the day or night, may be even more convenient.

Keeping a journal is another way to express your feelings and work out your anxieties. Record problems and progress, what you've done and what needs to be done. Seeing your life on paper may help make it seem more manageable.

More help. You can't do it alone. If you can't pay for help with household and child-care chores, you will need to rely

JUST THE FACTS

The Internet has become a valuable source of information and support for parents, particularly for parents of special needs children. Without having to leave their homes, or even their babies' sides, parents who want to learn everything they can about a birth defect or another health problem can access hundreds of resources. Parents who crave the companionship of others who can understand and empathize can join chat rooms, where experiences and insights are shared freely. So, by all means, tap into the Internet for help in coping with your child's disability. But keep in mind that there's plenty of misinformation on the information highway. To make sure you're getting your facts straight, always run what you've learned by a medical professional before accepting it or considering using it in your child's care.

on friends and family more than most. You needn't feel guilty about it, as long as you don't take the time and energy given by others for granted. Though you may feel like the sole beneficiary of their kindness, they also benefit – perhaps even more – by helping.

GETTING THE RIGHT DIAGNOSIS

'According to our family doctor, our son has a very serious congenital disorder. I just can't believe it – everyone in our family is so healthy.'

Serious illness, especially in our children, is difficult to accept. The first reaction is almost always denial: you cling to the hope that someone's made a mistake. The best way to resolve your nagging doubts is to double-check the diagnosis – no one, after all, is infallible. So if you haven't already, do have your child thoroughly examined by an experienced neonatologist (or other appropriate paediatric subspecialist: geneticist, neurologist, cardiologist, for example), one familiar with the condition that's been diagnosed, and be sure that all appropriate tests are carried out, both to verify the diagnosis and to uncover any other problems that may exist. You can help ensure an accurate diagnosis by giving examining doctors as much information as possible about your family's medical history (including any familial genetic disorders) and your pregnancy history and behaviour (including tobacco use, alcohol or drug consumption, medications taken, illnesses, especially with accompanying fevers, and so on). Your candid answers may, in fact, help a doctor to pinpoint an elusive diagnosis.

If the consulting doctor concurs with the first, you can be pretty sure their diagnosis is correct – and taking your child from doctor to doctor won't change the facts. Though there's always that one-in-a-million chance that even several doctors are wrong, the odds are much better that a problem does exist.

But be certain that you're completely clear about what the diagnosis is. The first time parents are told their newborn child has a birth defect, it's not unusual for most of the details to be washed away in a tide of overwhelming shock. What they hear is 'Your child isn't normal'. Beyond that, everything's a blur. So request a second meeting with the doctor when your head is a little clearer (don't expect your thinking to

WHERE TO GO FOR HELP

How can you find the resources that can best help you help your baby? The following organizations are good places to start:

- Association for Spina Bifida and Hydrocephalus
  42 Park Road
  Peterborough PE1 2UQ
  0845 450 7755
  www.asbah.org

- Newlife Foundation for Disabled Children
  Newlife Centre
  Hemlock Way
  Cannock
  Staffordshire
  WS11 7GF
  01543 462777
  www.newlifecharity.co.uk

- Cleft Lip and Palate Assocation (CLAPA)
  First Floor
  Green Man Tower
  332B Goswell Road
  London
  EC1V 7LQ
  0207 833 4883
  www.clapa.com
  Information and counselling for parents, and contacts for local groups

- Down's Syndrome Association
  Langdon Down Centre
  2a Langdon Park
  Teddington
  TW11 9PS
  0845 230 0372
  www.downs-syndrome.org.uk
  Advice on the care of children with Down's syndrome

be very focused for a while). In addition to the information you get from the doctors and/or nurses caring for your baby, seek out information in books, from parents in similar situations, and from organizations concerned with disabled children and/or your baby's particular problem (call for information or visit their websites), or from other resources listed in the box above. Don't rely, however, on advice from well-meaning but uninformed family or friends – it's likely to be based more on mythology than on medicine.

Before you take your baby home, ask his doctor exactly what you can expect (in terms of behaviour, development, medical problems) and what warning signs you need to be on the lookout for, as well as what you and the rest of your family can do to help your baby reach his potential. Take notes so that you'll have them to refer to when you go home.

WHETHER OR NOT TO ACCEPT TREATMENT

'Our baby boy was born without part of his brain. The doctors say he has no chance of living, but they want to operate on him to keep him alive a little longer. We don't know what to do.'

While the issue of whether or not babies who have no hope of long-term survival should be treated and kept on life-support systems has become a major ethical one for society, it is now a painfully personal one for you. Your decision is one that, if at all possible, probably shouldn't be made without first talking it over with your family, a religious counsellor, the baby's doctors and the hospital ethicist, if there is one. In many cases there will be time for such reasoned decision making. Even when there isn't, and time is of the essence, there is usually a chance to talk with your baby's doctors and, possibly, a hospital chaplain. The doctors can usually tell you the quality of life you can expect your child to have if kept alive, and whether treatment will improve the quality of his life or only prolong his dying. The chaplain can explain the religious issues involved, and the ethicist, your legal rights and responsibilities as well as the ethical issues. When you make your decision, consider all the information and counsel you've received, but do what you believe in your heart to be right – because no matter what it is, that's the decision you will be able to live with best.

In some cases, parents of children for whom there is no hope have found some solace in being able to donate some of their baby's organs to save the life of another sick infant. This isn't always feasible – sometimes for medical reasons, sometimes for legal ones – but do ask your doctor and hospital authorities about the possibility of organ donation if it interests you.

GETTING THE BEST CARE AND TREATMENT

'We're determined to give our baby, in spite of his disabilities, the best possible chance in life. But we're not sure how to do it.'

Your determination to help your child greatly increases his chances of enjoying a productive and satisfying life. But there's much more you can do, and the earlier you begin the better. Most babies with serious birth defects get the best start in a major medical centre, but occasionally a community hospital is equipped with an excellent neonatal intensive care unit (NICU). A hospital near your home has the benefit of allowing you to visit regularly, which sometimes will compensate for a lack of scientific sophistication.

Wherever your child is treated, you'll want to have him cared for by a doctor who specializes in dealing with his particular birth defect – though often day-to-day care can be provided by a local paediatrician or family doctor under the supervision of the specialist. For multiple birth defects, a team approach to treatment is best. The team may include doctors from various specialties, psychologists, physiotherapists, nutritionists, social workers, as well as a neonatologist and, usually, the baby's own doctor.

Though excellent medical care and, often, early educational intervention will be crucial to your child's development, in most cases the home environment you create will be even more significant in determining how well he is prepared for life and whether or not he reaches his maximum potential. The primary need of most children born with birth defects is to be treated like other children – to be loved and nurtured, but also to be disciplined and expected to meet standards (which should, of course, take into account their individual limitations). Like other children, they need to feel good about themselves – to know that each step forward, no matter how small, is appreciated and applauded, and that they won't be expected to keep up with the baby next door, only to live up to their own possibilities.

A wide range of therapies, as well as high-tech aids – everything from adapted playground equipment and toys to special education software, cochlear implants (to aid hearing) and robotic devices – are now available to help you help your disabled child grow, develop and enjoy life. Ask a member of your child's care team about them, or check with the appropriate organization for information.

EFFECT OF BABY ON SIBLINGS

'We're worried about how well our normal three-year-old daughter will handle the changes that having a brother with a birth defect will bring to her life.'

Sharing her home with a disabled sibling will undoubtedly bring changes to your daughter's life. And since the sibling relationship is usually the longest-lasting one in the family, those changes will continue to affect her not only as long as she lives in your home, but as long as she and her new brother live. The good news is that the changes can turn out to be largely positive – ultimately, even profoundly positive – if you take steps now and throughout your daughter's childhood not only to help her cope with the challenges of being a sister to a special needs sibling, but to let her know that she's special, too. In fact, having a disabled sibling makes children, on average, more patient and understanding, as well as more adept at getting along with different kinds of people. But being without that much-needed support can force a child to seek parental attention any way she can, putting her at risk for a variety of emotional and behavioural problems, from feeling displaced and devalued, to becoming withdrawn or aggressive, to developing psychosomatic symptoms, to acting up or doing poorly at school.

To make sure the changes in your daughter's life turn out to be largely positive, she will need:

♦ Lots and lots of support. Most children with special needs siblings don't need counselling, just some extra understanding. Much of the support your daughter will need can – and should – come from you,

in the form of unconditional love, generously dispensed. But it can also come from other children who understand how she feels. Many hospitals and organizations sponsor programmes for siblings; check into this possibility in your area. Such a programme gives children a chance to talk about their worries – and swap stories and strategies – in a safe and supportive environment, and to learn that they're not alone.

♦ The facts, on her level. Sometimes, parents try to protect an older sibling by keeping details about the new baby's medical condition away from her, or even avoiding the subject entirely. Since the imagined is always worse than the reality, at least in the minds of small children, this inevitably does more emotional harm than good. Sit your daughter down and share, on a very fundamental level, the facts about your new baby's condition. Invite her questions, and answer them honestly – giving as much information as she asks for, but not more than she can handle. Look for books geared for young children with special needs siblings to help reinforce the facts, as well as to let her know that she's not alone. But while you're letting your daughter know what's different about her new brother, don't forget to point out what's the same: that he has the same blue eyes as she does, that he likes being cuddled and cooed to just like all babies do. Also point out differences that have nothing to do with his birth defect (he has dark hair and she has blonde) so that she learns that there's nothing wrong with being different.

♦ To know it's not her fault. Young children – because they're naturally egocentric – tend to blame themselves for anything that goes wrong in a family. It's important to let your daughter know through reassuring words and actions (for instance, lots of hugs and kisses) that her brother's birth defect is no one's fault, least of all hers.

◆ To know that she doesn't have to be perfect. Some older siblings, when confronted with so much stress at home, feel as though they have to be on their best behaviour – to be the 'perfect child' – in order to compensate for the baby who isn't. Letting your daughter know that she's loved unconditionally, just the way she is, will help her feel secure enough to be herself.

◆ A chance to vent. Every older sibling has her share of ambivalent feelings, even antagonistic feelings, about the new arrival. Your daughter may have more than her share of such feelings – simply because that new arrival has disrupted family-life-as-usual to an even greater extent than most babies do. Encourage her to talk her feelings through without censoring her, letting her know that you have some mixed feelings of your own. Some children will prefer to work out their mixed emotions through dramatic play, others through artwork.

As your daughter reaches school age, her feelings may become complicated by social pressures. She may feel embarrassed by having a disabled sibling or may be teased about it by friends or classmates. Again, letting her talk her feelings through freely (not only with you but, if possible, with other children who face the same challenges) and arming her with coping strategies will help her overcome these hurdles.

◆ As normal a life as possible. In the face of all the upheaval a special needs baby has inevitably brought into your home, it's essential that your daughter's life remain as normal as it possibly can, given the circumstances. Rather than trying to make up for lost attention through expensive presents or elaborate excursions (which may only make her feel less settled), attempt to keep the normal routines that small children find so comforting. If bedtime has always come with a bath and three stories, now would not be the time to cut out the bath or cut down to one story. If she ordinarily has play dates a few times a week or dance class on Mondays, make an effort to keep her accustomed schedule. And, as it becomes feasible, plan family outings that include her new sibling.

◆ Her own life. Many new siblings of normal babies begin to feel that their lives – like their parents' – have taken a backseat once a new baby comes on the scene. When the new baby has special needs, this is even more likely. To protect your child's fledgling sense of self, make sure she has her own space, her own friends, her own identity, her own life. When you start feeling up to it, holding play dates at your home will allow her to feel as though having a disabled sibling is nothing to be ashamed of. But as the baby grows older, don't expect your daughter to always include her special needs sibling in her play or activities.

◆ Time with you alone. Don't forget that your older child's needs – and her need for your attention – are at least as great as those of your special needs baby. Even if your little wheel doesn't squeak (some older siblings bravely try to put their needs on hold when they see how much stress their parents are under), make sure she gets oiling. As impossible as it may sometimes seem, try to devote some uninterrupted time each day to just her: have tea with her teddy bears, read stories or put together a puzzle, push her on the swings at the playground. Taking turns with your spouse on the baby care – and spending one-on-one time with your older child – will help ensure that she'll get what she needs from both of you. When you can't spend time alone with her, try to include her while you're caring for the baby (buying her a doll of her own to care for may help her feel more in control of a situation that's largely out of her control, while giving her the opportunity to work out her feelings through dramatic play).

For a newsletter and more information, ideas and the latest research on the challenges facing siblings of disabled and specialist needs children, contact: Contact a Family, 209–211 City Road, London EC1V 1JN, 0207 608 8700, www.cafamily.org.uk.

EFFECTS ON YOUR RELATIONSHIP

'My spouse and I have cried a lot together since our son was born with a birth defect, but that's been the extent of our relationship. I'm afraid we'll never have emotional energy to spend on each other again.'

All new parents discover that having a baby in the house makes finding time as a twosome challenging. For new parents of babies born with a disability, the challenges are even greater. After all, caring for your baby zaps not just physical strength but emotional reserves as well. You are learning not only to be a parent (a tough enough task for those who come to the job without experience), but a parent of a special needs child. Your days and nights are consumed not only with the normal logistics of life with a newborn, such as feedings and nappy changes, but with endless medical logistics – not to mention endless questions, concerns and worries.

But just because your relationship has been taking a distant backseat to your son's birth doesn't mean it always will. Most couples find that having a special needs child doesn't undermine their relationship; many, in fact, discover that the experience actually strengthens their twosome. To help nurture your relationship as you nurture your newborn, make sure that:

The work is shared. No one can single-handedly care for a disabled child and still have the energy left to be a loving partner to a spouse. If your spouse works all day while you stay at home, let him take over at least some of the baby-care responsibilities in the evening so you can have a break. If he's considering taking on a second job to ease the financial strain of your not working, it might be better for you to take a part-time job and to transfer more of the child-care load to him. Hired or volunteer relief child care, for at least a few hours a week, and/or household help can also ease the burden and free up some time and energy for each other.

Each partner gets enough support from the other. Both of you have hurts that need healing; both of you need to make adjustments in your lives. (Many people fail to realize that the father of a disabled child may be as much in need of emotional support as the mother.) Facing the future as a team will be infinitely more productive and satisfying than facing it as individuals. Share your problems and concerns, and protect each other from outside assault (from overly critical grandparents, for example).

You make time for each other. All new parents need to make a concerted effort to make time alone for each other – or the time just doesn't happen. And as particularly difficult as it may be for you and your spouse, you need to do the same. See page 693–695 for tips.

You give yourselves time. Romance may be the furthest thing from your minds right now, and it may take a few months before any desire returns. This is the rule among most newly delivered couples, and it is even more likely in your situation. So instead of pressuring yourselves to perform sexually when you're not emotionally ready, wait until you are. Remember, you don't have to make love to show love. Hugging and hand-holding – sometimes even a good cry together – may be, more than anything, what both of you need right now.

A REPEAT WITH THE NEXT BABY

'We would like to have another baby within a year or so, but we're afraid that our daughter's birth defect might repeat in our next child.'

As common as this fear is among parents of children born with birth defects, in most cases it is unfounded. Their chances of having a normal baby are often as good as those of other parents. But in order to predict the risk in your particular case, the cause of your baby's problem needs to be determined. There is a wide range of possibilities:

Genetic. If your baby's defect is determined to be genetic (passed on by genetic material from you and/or your spouse), a genetic counsellor or, often, the baby's doctor will probably be able to give you precise odds on the likelihood of a repeat. In some instances, you will also be able to test future foetuses for the defect early in pregnancy, giving you a chance to prepare emotionally and physically – or the option to terminate – should it turn up again.

Environmental. If the birth defect was the result of a one-time event, such as an exposure during pregnancy to infection, chemicals, X-rays, medications or other factors that interfered with normal foetal development, it is not likely to repeat unless the exact set of circumstances recur at the same critical point in pregnancy.

Lifestyle. If the defect can be traced to your smoking, alcohol consumption, drug abuse or poor nutrition, for example, it is not likely to repeat in subsequent pregnancies unless the lifestyle mistakes are repeated.

Maternal factors. If a baby's problems seem related to the mother's age, the shape or size of her uterus or other unchangeable factors, they might repeat, though the risk can sometimes be reduced. For example, if you are past thirty-five and have a Down's syndrome baby, antenatal testing can diagnose the disorder in future pregnancies. Or if your uterus is misshapen, surgery may be able to reshape it. If a medication – either one prescribed for a chronic health problem or taken for an acute illness – might have triggered the defect, avoiding medication or switching to a safer one can prevent a future problem.

A combination of factors. When more than one factor is involved, predicting future outcomes may be more complicated, but the doctor or a genetic counsellor can still be helpful in such cases.

Unknown. Sometimes there is no apparent reason for a baby's birth defect. Usually such cases do not repeat. But if no one can say why your baby was not born completely normal, it would be a good idea to discuss the situation with a doctor familiar with genetic counselling before becoming pregnant again.

If you do decide to become pregnant again, your obstetrician should be completely familiar with your previous history so that you can be monitored throughout pregnancy for any possible problems. But with good medical care and good self-care, your chances of delivering a normal and healthy baby will likely be excellent.

A Different Birth Defect Next Time

'I'm not so worried about having another child with the same birth defect – I can be tested for that. What I'm worried about is having one with a different defect.'

Even if the chances of a repeat of your first child's defect in your next baby may be somewhat higher than average (and this isn't always the case), the same would not be true of other unrelated defects. In fact, you and your spouse have just as good a chance of producing a child free of other birth defects as any other set of parents.

As reassuring as these odds should be, it's normal to still harbour some nagging fears after what you've already gone through. To help ease them, talk to your doctor, consult a genetic counsellor, and follow the precautions listed in the previous question.

What it's Important to Know: THE MOST COMMON BIRTH DISORDERS

If your child hasn't been diagnosed as having a birth disorder but you've noticed symptoms that lead you to look through the information in this chapter, remember: what you notice may indicate something far less serious than you're imagining. But do check with your baby's doctor. It may take more than a phone call to allay your fears; an examination or special testing may be necessary. If a problem does turn up, early recognition and prompt medical attention and therapy can often be beneficial or even correct the problem completely.

AIDS/HIV- Perinatal

What is it? HIV infection usually has no symptoms, but it often eventually causes AIDS, a serious immune disorder.

How common is it? Becoming less common in newborns, since treatment of infected women during pregnancy and of their infants after birth has markedly decreased the rate of transmission from mothers to babies.

What causes it? The human immunod-eficiency virus (HIV), most often passed on from mother to child during pregnancy, childbirth or breastfeeding.

Treatment. Antiviral drugs for HIV positive mother during pregnancy, for child after birth.

Prognosis. Many children survive for several years. Both survival and quality of life are improved with antiviral drug treatment.

ANENCEPHALY

What is it? A neural tube defect in which the failure of the neural groove to close normally early in pregnancy leads to lack of brain development. All or a major part of the brain is absent.

How common is it? Very rare in full-term babies, since 99 per cent of foetuses with the defect are miscarried.

Who is susceptible? Not known.

What causes it? Heredity is probably involved in some way, along with an adverse antenatal environment. Folic acid deficiency in the mother can also cause anencephaly (and other neural tube defects). Incidence has been reduced by use of vitamin supplements containing folic acid before conception and through the first two months of pregnancy, as well as the fortification of cereals and breads with folic acid.

Related problems. All body systems are affected negatively.

Treatment. None, and most doctors agree that no medical intervention is best, though the baby should be kept as comfortable as possible.

Prognosis. The condition is incompatible with life.

AUTISM

What is it? An inability, which dates from birth or develops within the first two and a half years of life, to develop normal human relationships, even with parents. There are great differences among children with autism. Some who are mildly affected may exhibit only slight delays in language and greater challenges with social interactions than is typical. Others who have a more severe form of autism don't smile or respond to parents or anyone else in any way and dislike being picked up or touched. There are often extreme problems in speaking (including strange speech patterns, such as one in which the child echoes the words just heard rather than replying), strange positions and mannerisms, erratic and inappropriate behaviour (compulsiveness and ritualism, screaming fits and arm flapping) and, sometimes, self-destructiveness. The child may have normal intelligence but appear to be retarded or deaf because of a lack of responsiveness. Autism may sometimes be confused with childhood schizophrenia, and occasionally may precede it.

How common is it? Nearly 1 in 100 babies are born with autism.

Who is susceptible? Male children are four times more likely to be autistic than females.

What causes it? Autism has no single cause. Researchers have identified a number of genes that play a role in the disorder. In some children, environmental factors (including maternal smoking while pregnant) also may play a role in development of the disorder. Several studies suggest that autism may be caused by a combination of biological factors, including exposure to a virus before birth, a problem with the immune system or genetics. It is not related to parenting or currently used vaccines.

Related problems. Behaviour and developmental problems.

Treatment. At present there is no cure, but some children can be helped with behaviour modification therapy, stimulation, special training and, sometimes, drugs. Early intervention results in dramatically positive outcomes for young children with autism. With appropriate services, training and information, most families are able to support their child at home. Counselling is often helpful for the rest of the family. Some parents have had success with dietary changes (such as removing sources of gluten and casein from the diet of autistic children), but talk to your doctor before starting any new diet regimen.

Prognosis. Symptoms in many children improve with intervention or as the children age. Some people with autism eventually lead normal or near-normal lives. Outlook is best with early intervention and therapy.

CELIAC DISEASE

What is it? Celiac disease is a digestive disease that damages the small intestine and interferes with absorption of nutrients from food. Children who have celiac disease can't tolerate a protein called gluten, which is found in wheat, rye, barley and possibly oats. When children with celiac disease eat foods containing gluten, their immune systems respond by damaging their small intestines. Symptoms may include chronic diarrhoea, weight loss, pale, foul-smelling stool, unexplained anaemia (low count of red blood cells), gas, fatigue, delayed growth, failure to thrive in infants.

How common is it? As high as 1 in 250 in Europe. Females are affected twice as often as males and whites from northwestern Europe most often. It is rare in blacks, Asians, Jews and others of Mediterranean descent.

Who is susceptible? Children of parents who both carry the gene for the condition.

What causes it? Unclear, but most likely some combination of environmental factors and genetic disposition.

Related problems. Symptoms of malnutrition such as developmental delay, fluid retention, late teething and rickets.

Treatment. Gluten-free diet, which usually begins to work in three to six weeks and which must be followed for life. Nutritional supplementation and, sometimes, steroids may also be prescribed.

Prognosis. Usually, a normal life on a gluten-free diet.

CEREBRAL PALSY

What is it? A neuromuscular disorder caused by damage to the brain. Motor impairment may be mild to disabling. The infant may have difficulty sucking or retaining the nipple; drool constantly; seldom move voluntarily; have arm or leg tremors with voluntary movements; have legs that are hard to separate; have delayed motor development; use only one hand or, later, use hands but not feet, crawl in a strange fashion; and walk on tiptoes. Muscle tone may be excessively stiff or floppy, but this may not be apparent until three months of age or so. Exact symptoms differ in each of the three different types of CP: spastic, athetoid and ataxic.

How common is it? Decreasing in

frequency (except in the tiniest newborns) because of safer childbirth. About 1 in 5000.

Who is susceptible? Premature and low-birthweight babies, boys slightly more often than girls, white infants more often than blacks.

What causes it? In most cases, the cause of cerebral palsy is unknown, though it is sometimes related to insufficient oxygen reaching the foetal or newborn brain. Premature birth, low birthweight, RH or A-B-O blood type incompatibility between mother and foetus, or rubella in early pregnancy are other risk factors. Cerebral palsy may also result from brain or spinal fluid infection.

Related problems. Sometimes, seizures; speech, vision and hearing disorders; dental defects; mental retardation.

Treatment. No cure, but early treatment can help a child live up to potential. May include: physical therapy, braces, splints or other orthopaedic appliances; special furniture and utensils; exercise; surgery, when needed; medication for seizures or to relax muscles if needed.

Prognosis. Varies with case. Child with a mild form, given proper treatment, may live a nearly normal life. Child with a severe form may be completely disabled. Condition does not get progressively worse.

CLEFT LIP AND/OR PALATE

What is it? A split (sometimes extensive, sometimes slight) occurs where parts of upper lip or palate (the roof of the mouth) fail to grow together. Some babies have only cleft lip, more have only cleft palate. About 40 per cent of affected babies have both.

How common is it? About 1,000 children a year, or approximately 1 in 700 births.

Who is susceptible? More common among Asians than those of African descent. Also more common among premature babies and those with other defects.

What causes it? Heredity plays a role in about 1 in 4 cases; after having a baby with a cleft, the odds of having another one increase slightly. But illness, certain medications, lack of essential nutrients (particularly folic acid), and other factors that adversely affect the antenatal environment may also interfere with normal development of lip and palate, possibly in combination with each other and/or heredity.

Related problems. Because sucking is usually difficult, feeding may be a problem, so special procedures are necessary (usually an upright position, small amounts, a teat with large holes or a special syringe). It is possible to breastfeed in some cases, especially when only cleft lip is present. The use of an oral appliance can allow a baby with a cleft palate to breastfeed. Ear infections are also common and need to be controlled.

Treatment. Usually a combination of surgery (sometimes in the first few months of life), speech therapy and dental adjustments (often including braces later in life).

Prognosis. Usually excellent with treatment.

CLUBFOOT AND OTHER FOOT AND ANKLE DEFORMITIES

What is it? An ankle or foot deformity that occurs in three forms. In the mildest form of deformity, metatarsus varus, the front part of the foot is turned inwards. This type may not be diagnosed until the baby is a few months old, though it is present at birth. In the most common type of foot deformity, calcaneal valgus, the foot is sharply angled at the heel and points upwards and outwards. In the most severe and least common, equino-varus, the 'clubbed' foot twists inwards and downwards. If both feet are 'clubbed' the toes point towards each other. Clubfoot and other foot deformities are not painful and do not bother the baby until it's time to stand or walk.

How common is it? Affects 1 to 2 in 1,000 babies.

Who is susceptible? Boys are twice as likely to have a foot or ankle deformity as girls.

What causes it? Not the position in the uterus, as was once believed (cases of this sort correct themselves after birth). Probably a combination of heredity and environmental factors, leading to abnormalities in the muscles or nerves that supply the ankle and foot, in most cases; but some cases are related to spina bifida, nerve diseases or muscle diseases.

Related problems. With clubfoot (the equinovarus deformity), the foot can't move up and down as it normally would in walking; the child walks as though on a peg leg. When both feet are affected, the child may walk on the sides or even tops of feet, leading to damage to this tissue and to abnormal leg development.

Occasionally, there may be other defects as well.

Treatment. Mild cases of foot and ankle deformity may be treated by exercise alone. Plaster casts or surgery are used in more severe cases to force the twisted foot gradually and gently into place so that it can move up and down normally. For clubfoot, early evaluation and treatment by a paediatric orthopaedist is essential for best outcome.

Prognosis. With expert early treatment, most grow up to wear regular shoes, take part in sports and lead active lives.

CONGENITAL HEART DEFECT

What is it? Any heart defect, minor or major, that is present at birth. Though the defects can usually be diagnosed with a stethoscope, further tests such as X-rays, ultrasound and ECGs will be needed to verify abnormalities. Depending on the type of defect, one or more functions of the heart may be adversely affected. Symptoms may show up at birth, or not become apparent until adulthood. Cyanosis, or bluing of the skin, particularly around fingers, toes and lips, is the most common symptom.

How common is it? About 1 out of 145 babies in the UK is born with a heart defect.

Who is susceptible? There's a greater risk among children of mothers who had rubella during pregnancy, Down's syndrome children, and those with affected siblings (though their increased risk is slight).

What causes it? In most cases, scientists just don't know, though genetics appear to play an important role. Certain infections (such as rubella) and some chemicals (thalidomide, amphetamines or alcohol, for example) are capable of causing heart abnormalities antenatally, but such abnormalities may sometimes be the result of a random genetic error.

Related problems. Sometimes poor weight gain and growth, fatigue, weakness, difficulty breathing or sucking (because of weakness from heart failure).

Treatment. The most common heart defect (VSC, or ventricular septal defect) often needs no treatment – if it is small, it often closes by itself. Surgery (either immediately or later in childhood), which varies according to the defect present, and sometimes drugs or a heart transplant can remedy other heart defects. (In some cases, a defect that causes no symptoms may require treatment to prevent problems later in life.) Sometimes a heart defect can be diagnosed before birth and medication given to correct it.

Prognosis. Most congenital heart defects are treatable; only some very serious ones (and these are rare) may be disabling or even fatal. Most children with murmurs can lead normal lives with no restrictions on activities.

CYSTIC FIBROSIS (CF)

What is it? A condition in which there is a generalized dysfunction of the exocrine glands, the glands that discharge their secretions through an epithelial surface (such as the skin, the mucous membranes, the linings of the hollow organs). When sweat glands are affected, perspiration is salty and profuse, and excessive perspiration can lead to dehydration and shock. When the respiratory system is affected, thick secretions may fill the lungs, causing chronic coughing and increased risk of infection. With digestive system involvement, mucus secretions may make first bowel movements after birth difficult to pass, causing intestinal obstruction. The pancreatic ducts may also be obstructed, resulting in deficiencies of the pancreatic enzymes and inability to digest protein and fat. The stools, containing the undigested materials, are usually frequent, bulky, foul-smelling, pale and greasy. Weight gain is poor, appetite may be ravenous, abdomen can be distended, arms and legs thin, and skin sallow. Sweat-test screening is used to pick out possible cases of CF, and lack of meconium bowel movement after birth, salty skin and poor weight gain along with good appetite can be early indications.

How common is it? Relatively rare; about 1 in 2,500.

Who is susceptible? More common in those with central and northern European ancestry than those of African or Asian ancestry.

What causes it? Autosomal recessive inheritance: both parents must pass on recessive genes for a child to be affected.

Related problems. Pneumonia, because of respiratory secretions, is common. Also pancreatic insufficiency, insufficient insulin production, abnormal glucose tolerance, cirrhosis of the liver and hypertension, among others.

Treatment. The earlier the better, to prevent development of symptoms when possible. No cure exists, but treatment helps a child lead a more normal life. For sweat gland malfunction, generous salting of foods and salt supplements during hot weather. For digestive problems, pancreatic enzymes given by mouth with meals and snacks, limitation of fat, supplementation with fat-soluble vitamins (A, D, E and K). For various types of intestinal blockages (meconium ileus, rectal prolapse, and so on) associated with CF, both surgical and non-surgical treatment is available and usually successful. For respiratory problems, copious fluid intake to thin secretions, usually daily respiratory physical therapy (including postural drainage, to help loosen and remove secretions) and oxygen therapy as needed. Room air is best kept cool and dry. Infections are treated with large doses of antibiotics. Initial studies indicate that treatment with anti-inflammatory agents (such as prednisone) may help reduce bouts of illness. A cure may eventually be possible.

Prognosis. Today with early diagnosis, aggressive treatment and strong family support, the prognosis is very good, especially for those with less severe disease.

DEFORMATION

What is it? An abnormality in one or more organs or parts of the body caused by external forces on the foetus, such as crowding in utero.

How common is it? About 2 in every 100 babies has some deformity of this type.

Who is susceptible? An extra large foetus in a crowded uterus, or any foetus in a malformed or small uterus or a uterus having fibroids, an inadequate supply of amniotic fluid, or an unusual placental site; a foetus who shares the uterus with one or more siblings. Deformations are most common in babies of small and first-time mothers, and when there is an abnormal presentation such as a breech.

What causes it? Conditions in the uterus, such as those just mentioned,

that put undue pressure on one or more developing parts of the foetus. In some cases, a combination of heredity and environmental factors, such as infection, drugs and disease.

Related problems. Depends on the abnormality.

Treatment. In most cases, none is necessary since the deformed part will gradually resume normal shape. Some conditions, however, such as scoliosis (abnormal side-to-side curvature of the spine), clubfoot and hip dislocations do require treatment.

Prognosis. Good, for most conditions.

DOWN'S SYNDROME

What is it? A set of signs and symptoms that usually include mild to severe mental retardation, specific facial features (more obvious in some than in others), an oversized tongue and a short neck. They may also include a flat back of the head, small ears (sometimes folded at the tops) and a flat wide nose. Hearing and vision may be poor, and various internal defects (particularly of heart or GI tract) may also exist. Down's syndrome children are often short and have loose muscle tone (responsible for some of the delayed development). They are also usually very sweet and lovable.

How common is it? Down's syndrome affects about 1,000 babies a year, or approximately 1 in 1,000.

Who is susceptible? Babies of parents who have already had a baby with the birth defect, or of a mother or father with a chromosome rearrangement, or of a mother over thirty-five or a father over forty-five to fifty (the risk increases with age). All ethnic groups and economic levels are affected.

What causes it? In 95 per cent of the cases, an extra chromosome contributed by either the mother or the father, so that baby has 47 instead of 46 chromosomes. This cause of Down's syndrome is called Trisomy 21, because three number-21 chromosomes are present (normally there are two). About 4 per cent of the time, certain other accidents affecting chromosome number 21 are responsible. For example, sometimes a piece of a normal chromosome 21 breaks off and attaches to another chromosome in the parent (called translocation). The parent remains normal, because he or she still has the right amount of genetic material. But if this augmented chromosome is passed on to a child, the child can have an excess of chromosome 21 material, resulting in Down's syndrome. Very rarely, an accident during cell division in the fertilized egg results in an extra chromosome in some but not all cells. This is called mosaicism, and affected children may have only some Down's syndrome characteristics, because only some of their cells are affected.

Related problems. Dental problems, poor eyesight and hearing, heart disease, gastrointestinal defects, thyroid dysfunction, early aging (including Alzheimer's disease), higher risk for respiratory illnesses as well as leukaemia and other cancers.

Treatment. Antenatal tests can diagnose Down's syndrome in the foetus. Surgery, after birth, can correct heart and other serious medical abnormalities. Early specialized education programmes improve the IQs of Down's syndrome children who are mildly or moderately retarded.

Prognosis. Most children with Down's syndrome have greater capabilities than previously believed, and early intervention can bring these abilities out, leaving fewer than 10 per cent severely retarded. Many can be mainstreamed to a certain age in school; some even go to college. Most later find places in sheltered homes and workshops; some live and work independently.

FOETAL ALCOHOL SYNDROME (FAS)

What is it? A group of signs and symptoms that develop during gestation in a child whose mother drinks heavily during pregnancy. The most common are low birthweight, mental deficiency, deformities of the head and face, limbs and central nervous system; the neonatal mortality rate is high. Less obvious effects may occur in children of moderate drinkers.

How common is it? Each week in the UK 14 babies are born with FAS.

Who is susceptible? Babies of women who drink heavily. (It is estimated that 30 to 40 per cent of women who drink heavily during pregnancy have babies with FAS.)

What causes it? Ingestion of alcohol – usually five or six drinks of beer, wine, or distilled spirits a day – *during pregnancy*.

Related problems. Developmental problems.

Treatment. Therapy for individual disabilities.

Prognosis. Depends on extent of the problem.

HEART DEFECT – SEE CONGENITAL HEART DEFECT

HYDROCEPHALUS

What is it? Absorption of the fluid that normally bathes the brain is blocked, and the fluid collects. The pressure spreads apart the loosely connected plates of the skull, causing the head to become enlarged. This enlargement is often the first clue to the problem. Often occurs along with spina bifida, or following surgery to close an open spine. The scalp skin may be shiny and thin, neck muscles may be underdeveloped, eyes may look strange, cry may be high pitched, and baby may suffer from irritability, lack of appetite and vomiting.

How common is it? Relatively rare.

Who is susceptible? Not clear, though infants with spina bifida are at increased risk because of associated malformations of the brain stem.

What causes it? At birth, a defect in the membrane that is supposed to absorb cerebrospinal fluid; later, injury or a tumour.

Related problems. Retardation if fluid is not drained away regularly; complications with shunts, including infection and shunt malfunctions.

Treatment. Under anaesthesia, a special tube is inserted through a hole drilled in the skull into the brain to drain the excess fluid, usually into the abdominal cavity. The head gradually returns to normal size, but frequent checkups are necessary to be sure all is going well and the tube has not become blocked.

Doctors are now trying to develop a treatment that doesn't require surgery.

Prognosis. Good if treatment is begun early enough; this can usually prevent retardation and the child can probably lead a normal life. Poor if the problem is well advanced by the time the baby is born. In that case, it can cause various disabilities affecting, among other things, intelligence, language skills, movement, hand-eye coordination and eyesight. It can also be fatal in untreated cases. Treatment before birth is not widely done, and it remains uncertain whether there is any benefit to treating the condition in utero.

MALFORMATION

What is it? An organ or part of the body appears abnormal. Sometimes several organs or body parts are affected, and grouped together, they form a syndrome that indicates a particular condition (such as Down's syndrome). Sometimes there is just one isolated malformation – such as a stunted limb.

How common is it? Probably fewer than 1 in 100 newborns is born with a noticeable malformation, usually a mild one.

Who is susceptible? Those with similar malformations in other family members; those whose parents, most often mothers, are exposed to certain dangerous environmental hazards before or after conception.

What causes it? Abnormal differentiation or organization during the development of the embryo, because of either a genetic or chromosomal abnormality or an environmental factor (such as high-dose radiation or infection).

Related problems. Depends on the malformation(s).

Treatment. Varies with the defect.

Prognosis. Depends on the malformation. (See individual conditions, such as spina bifida, Down's syndrome and so on.)

OPEN SPINE – SEE SPINA BIFIDA

PYLORIC STENOSIS

What is it? A probably congenital condition in which thickening or overgrowth of the muscle at the exit of the stomach causes a blockage, leading to increasingly more severe and more forceful projectile vomiting (spewing 30 cm/12 in or more) usually starting at two or three weeks of age, and accompanied by constipation. The thickening can usually be felt as a lump by the doctor; spasms of the muscle are often visible.

How common is it? Affects 2 per 1,000 births.

Who is susceptible? Males more often than females; sometimes tends to run in families.

What causes it? It isn't known what triggers development.

Related problems. Dehydration.

Treatment. Surgery, after baby's fluid levels have been normalized, is safe and almost always completely effective.

Prognosis. Excellent.

RH DISEASE

What is it? A condition in which a child inherits a blood type from the father that is incompatible with the mother's. If the mother has antibodies to the baby's blood (from a previous pregnancy, an abortion, miscarriage or blood transfusion), these antibodies can attack the baby's red blood cells.

How common is it? Much less common since the development of preventive techniques.

Who is susceptible? A baby who inherits Rh positive blood from his or her father and has a mother with Rh-negative blood.

What causes it? Antibodies in mother's blood attack baby's blood cells, recognizing them as foreign.

Related problems. Severe anaemia and jaundice, leading to possible brain damage or death before or shortly after birth.

Treatment. Often a complete blood transfusion of the baby's blood (an 'exchange transfusion'). Some babies may not need a transfusion immediately but do require one at four to six weeks because of severe anaemia. Prevention, with the injection of a vaccine called Rh immune globulin for Rh-negative mothers within seventy-two hours of the birth (or miscarriage or abortion) of a baby or foetus that is Rh-positive is the best way to prevent the problem in future pregnancies. A dose of the vaccine may also be given about midway during pregnancy.

Prognosis. Usually good, with treatment.

WHEN DIAGNOSIS MAKES ALL THE DIFFERENCE

The availability of newborn screening tests has made early diagnosis of many metabolic disorders possible. The good news: with early diagnosis can come early treatment and, for many babies who might otherwise have died within a few months of birth, the chance to live a completely normal life. Conditions that can be diagnosed and treated include:

◆ Congenital hypothyroidism, which results from an inadequate supply of thyroid hormone and affects 1 baby in 4,000. Oral doses of thyroid medication prevent the stunted growth and mental retardation associated with hypothyroidism.

◆ Congenital adrenal hyperplasia, a condition in which hormone deficiency compromises genital development and kidney function, affects 1 in 5,000 babies, and can be treated with hormone replacement.

◆ Medium chain acyl-coA dehydrogenase deficiency (MCAD) results when the enzyme needed to convert food fat to energy is missing. It affects 1 in 15,000 babies and can lead to severe metabolic problems with otherwise simple illnesses. Since the condition shows up only during prolonged fasting (as might occur if appetite is lost to a virus or other illness), the treatment involves feeding on a regular schedule.

◆ Galactosaemia, in which 1 in 70,000 affected babies can't convert galactose, a milk sugar, into glucose (eventually causing mental retardation and liver disease), can be treated with the elimination of dairy products.

◆ Biotinidase deficiency, which occurs in less than 1 in 60,000 babies, results from the deficiency of biotinidase, an enzyme that recycles biotin (one of the B vitamins). Without treatment (supplementation with biotin), it can cause frequent infections, poor muscle control, seizures, hearing loss and mental retardation.

◆ Maple syrup urine disease (MSUD), which affects 1 in 300,000 babies, occurs when the body is unable to use some components of food protein, and can result in poor feeding, lethargy and, eventually, coma. Given its name because an affected baby's urine smells like maple syrup, MSUD can be treated with a special diet.

◆ Homocystinuria affects about 1 in 344,000 infants and is due to a lack of enzymes in the liver. Untreated, it can lead to skeletal abnormalities, abnormal blood clotting, mental retardation and eye problems. A special diet, combined with dietary supplements, can prevent these symptoms.

◆ Phenylketonuria (PKU), a condition in which the individual is unable to metabolize an amino acid (or 'protein building block') called phenylalanine, affects 1 in 10,000 infants. If left untreated, the buildup of phenylalanine in the bloodstream can interfere with brain development and cause severe retardation. A diet low in phenylalanine (low in high-protein foods such as breast milk, cow's milk or regular cow's milk formula and meat), begun immediately and continued indefinitely, will allow a child with PKU to live a normal life.

SICKLE-CELL ANAEMIA

What is it? An anaemia in which red blood cells (usually round) are abnormal (sickle shaped) and do a poor job of carrying oxygen to body cells, often getting stuck in and blocking blood vessels. Symptoms (such as fatigue, shortness of breath, joint swelling, especially in fingers and toes, and severe bone pain) don't usually appear until six months of age, but testing should diagnose the condition immediately after birth.

How common is it? Almost entirely confined to the black population in the UK, where about 3,000 babies are affected annually.

Who is susceptible? Primarily blacks of African descent, but also whites of Mediterranean/Middle Eastern heritage. Risk is 1 in 4 if both parents are carriers, 4 in 4 if both have the disease.

What causes it? Autosomal recessive inheritance: both parents must pass on recessive genes for child to be affected. Periodic crises can be triggered by infection, stress, dehydration and inadequate oxygen.

Related problems. Poor growth, delayed puberty, narrow body, curved spine and barrel chest; infection, particularly pneumococcal. It can be fatal if untreated.

Treatment. Penicillin daily beginning at two months, at least through age five. Also symptomatic relief: pain relievers, blood transfusions, oxygen, fluids. Full series of immunizations, including pneumococcal vaccine. Parent education and genetic counselling are also important.

Prognosis. Fair. Still, most live past young adulthood, and some reach middle age and beyond. Treatment greatly improves prognosis. Promising research is being done into new and better treatments.

SPINA BIFIDA (OPEN SPINE)

What is it? The bony spine, or backbone, that helps protect the spinal cord is normally open for the first few days of antenatal development but then closes. In spina bifida, the closing is incomplete. The resultant opening can be so slight that it causes no problems and is not noticed except through an X-ray taken later for other reasons, though a small dimple or tufts of hair may be visible on the covering skin. Or it can be large enough that part of the covering of the spinal cord protrudes through, covered by a purplish red cyst or lump (a meningocele), which can range in size from 2.5 to 5 cm (1 to 2 in) in diameter to the size of a grapefruit. If this meningocele is low on the spinal column, it can cause weakness in the legs. In the most severe form of spina bifida, the spinal cord itself protrudes through the opening. It often has little or no skin protecting it, allowing spinal fluid to leak out. The area is often covered with sores, the legs are paralyzed, and bladder and bowel control become a problem later, though some children do attain this control.

How common is it? Affects 1 in 2,000 babies born in the UK, though it has been estimated that 1 in 10 may have hidden spina bifida. The more severe form of the condition is fortunately the least common. There has been a nearly 20 per cent reduction in the number of babies born with neural tube defects such as spina bifida in recent years. This can be attributed to the use of folic acid supplements by mothers before conception and through the first two months of pregnancy, as well as the fortification of breads and cereals with folic acid.

Who is susceptible? Children of mothers who already have an affected child have a 1 in 40 risk; with two affected children in the family, the risk rises to 1 in 5. Cousins of affected children have a two-fold increase in risk.

What causes it? Not known at present. Heredity is probably involved in some way along with an adverse antenatal environment. Nutrition may be involved – specifically a low intake of folic acid.

Related problems. Infection when spine is visibly open. Also hydrocephalus in about 70 to 90 per cent of cases (see page 650). Lower limb paralysis and numbness, impaired bladder and bowel control.

Treatment. None is needed for a slight defect. Cysts can be removed surgically and hydrocephalus can be shunted. But though surgery can remove the most severe cysts and repair the opening, covering it with muscle and skin, the paralysis in the legs can't be cured. Physical therapy, and later leg braces and crutches or a wheelchair, will probably be needed. Casts may be applied to prevent or minimize deformity. Prior to surgery, it is important not to put pressure (even in the form of clothing) on the cyst. Team approach to treatment, with a range of specialists, is usually best. Spina bifida can often be detected through antenatal testing, such as blood tests, ultrasound and amniocentesis. Antenatal surgery to repair spina bifida birth defects is in the experimental phase.

Prognosis. Depends on the severity of the condition. Most children with less severe conditions can have active and productive lives; most females will be able to bear children, but their pregnancies will be in the high-risk category.

TAY-SACHS DISEASE

What is it? Children with this lipid-storage disease, in which there is a congenital deficiency of an enzyme needed for breaking down fatty deposits in the brain and nerve cells, appear normal at birth. But about six months later, when the fatty deposits begin to clog cells, the nervous system stops working and children begin to regress – they stop smiling, crawling and turning over, lose the ability to grasp, gradually become blind, paralyzed and unaware of their surroundings. Most die by age three or four.

How common is it? Rare.

Who is susceptible? Mostly descendants of Central and Eastern European (Ashkenazi) Jews.

What causes it? Autosomal recessive inheritance – one gene from each parent is necessary for child to be affected.

Related problems. Concern about future children; there is a 1 in 4 chance of an affected child with each pregnancy.

Treatment. None, though researchers are trying to find a way of replacing the missing enzyme. Those with Ashkenazi backgrounds should be tested for the gene before conception or during early pregnancy. If both parents have the gene, then amniocentesis can be performed to see if the foetus has inherited the disease.

Prognosis. Disease is invariably fatal.

HOW DEFECTS ARE INHERITED

All the good and beautiful things a baby is are a result of the genes he or she inherited from both parents, as well as the environment in the uterus during the nine months of gestation. But the not-so-good things a baby is born with – a birth defect, for instance – are also a result of genes and/or environment. Usually the genes a parent passes on to a child are inherited from his or her own parents, but occasionally a gene changes (because of an environmental insult or some unknown factor) and this mutation is passed on.

There are several kinds of inherited disorders:

♦ Polygenic disorders (such as clubfoot and cleft lip) are believed to be inherited through the interaction of a number of different genes in much the same way that eye colour and height are determined.

♦ Multifactorial disorders (such as some forms of diabetes) involve the interaction of different genes and environmental conditions (either prior to birth or after it).

♦ Single-gene disorders can be passed on through either recessive or dominant inheritance. In recessive inheritance, two genes (one from each parent) must be passed on for the offspring to be affected. In dominant inheritance, just one gene is needed, and it is passed on by a parent who also has the disorder (by virtue of having the gene). Single-gene disorders can also be sex linked (haemophilia, for example). These disorders, carried in genes on the sex-determining chromosomes (females have two X chromosomes and males one X and one Y), are most often passed from carrier mother to affected son. The male child, having only one X chromosome, has no opposite gene to counteract the one carrying the defect and is affected with the disorder. A female child receiving the gene on an X chromosome from her mother has also received a normal X chromosome from her father, which makes her a carrier but usually leaves her unaffected by the disorder.

THALASSAEMIA

What is it? An inherited form of anaemia in which there is a defect in the process necessary for the production of haemoglobin (the oxygen-carrying red blood cells). The most common form, thalassaemia B, can range from the very serious form, called Cooley's anaemia, to thalassaemia minima, which has no effect but shows up in blood or genetic testing. Even in serious cases, infants appear normal at birth, but gradually become listless, fussy and pale, lose their appetites, and become very susceptible to infection. Growth and development are slow.

How common is it? About 2,800 babies are born with thalassaemia annually in the UK.

Who is susceptible? Most frequently, those of Greek or Italian descent; also those from Middle Eastern, southern Asian and African backgrounds.

What causes it? Autosomal recessive inheritance: an affected gene must be inherited from each parent for the child to have the most serious form.

Related problems. Without treatment, the heart, spleen and liver all become enlarged, and the risk of death from heart failure or infection multiplies.

Eventually bones become brittle, distorting appearance.

Treatment. Frequent blood transfusions of young blood cells, and sometimes bone marrow transplants for children with the most severe form of the disease. Build-up of iron, which can lead to heart failure, can be treated with medication. Antenatal diagnosis is available to determine if a foetus is affected.

Prognosis. Excellent for those with minor forms of the disease; those with moderate disease also become normal adults, though puberty may be delayed. Of those with severe disease, more children are now living into their teens and twenties, though the threat of heart failure and infection are still great.

TRACHEOESOPHAGEAL FISTULA

What is it? A congenital condition in which the upper part of the oesophagus (the tube through which foods move from throat to stomach) ends in a blind pouch and the lower part, instead of connecting to the upper, runs from the trachea (windpipe) to the stomach. Since this makes taking food by mouth impossible, vomiting, choking and respiratory distress occur on feeding. Excessive drooling occurs since saliva can't be swallowed. Food getting into lungs can cause pneumonia, and even death.[1]

How common is it? Affects about 1 in 4,000 live births.

Who is susceptible? Prematurity has been associated with this condition. Often, the first sign is excessive amniotic fluid during pregnancy (because the fluid can't be swallowed by the baby in utero, as it usually is).

What causes it? A defect in development, possibly due to hereditary or environmental causes.

Related problems. A small percentage of babies also have associated malformations, such as heart, spine, kidney and limb abnormalities.

Treatment. Immediate surgery can usually correct condition.

Prognosis. If no other abnormalities exist and surgery corrects the problem, outlook is very good – though there are often long-term problems with reflux.

---

1. There are several other, much less common, deformities of the trachea and oesophagus.

◆ ◆ ◆

CHAPTER 22

The Adopted Baby

Whether you're bringing home a newborn from the local hospital or a nine-month-old from another continent, becoming an adoptive parent is every bit as joyous, life-changing and nerve-racking as becoming a birth parent. Although chances are you've been waiting for this moment even longer than birth parents usually do, you may feel surprisingly unprepared now that it's finally upon you. Along with the excitement and elation you'll feel when you first hold your baby in your arms, you'll probably feel a fair amount of trepidation and uncertainty. Just like birth parents do.

As adopting parents, this chapter is specifically for you. But so is most of the rest of this book. Your baby is like other babies – and you are like other fathers and other mothers.

What You May Be Concerned About

GETTING READY

'My friends who are pregnant are involved in all kinds of preparations – including antenatal classes and looking over hospitals. But I don't know where to start in preparing for our daughter's arrival.'

Instead of surprising parents (of all species) with their babies without benefit of notice, Mother Nature wisely designed 'gestation'. This waiting period before birth (or hatching) was meant to give parents a chance to prepare for the arrival of their offspring. A chance for the mother bird to feather her nest, the expectant lioness to prepare her lair, and nowadays anyway, for the human mother and father to decorate a nursery, take classes, toss around names, make key decisions about breastfeeding and child care and generally prepare themselves emotionally, intellectually and physically for becoming a family.

For the couple about to adopt a baby, the waiting period is not usually a predictable and manageable nine months, as it is for other expectant parents. For some, usually those who go the agency route, the entire process may take years, but the big day itself may arrive unexpectedly, not leaving enough time for reality to set in, much less for preparations to be made – not unlike being told you're pregnant one day and delivering a baby the next. For others, usually those who adopt privately, definite arrangements may be made to adopt a particular baby far in advance of the infant's due date, giving the adoptive parents-to-be the opportunity to go through pre-baby preparations that are not dissimilar in many ways to those of biological expectant parents. But no matter how much or how little time you have between learning you are going to become a parent and the actual arrival of that bundle of joy, there are some steps you can take to make the transition smoother:

Shop ahead. Read chapter 2 of this book. Most of the preparations for the arrival of a baby are the same whether you're adopting or birthing. If you are uncertain as to the date, scout around for the cot, pram, layette and so on in advance. Have everything picked out (brand names, style numbers, sizes) and listed along with the store names and telephone numbers, so that you can call for delivery the moment you hear from the adoption agency. (Check in advance with the stores to be sure that your choices will be in stock.) If you are going the private adoption route and have an approximate arrival date, many stores will allow you to put your order in and then will hold delivery until you call. Such advance purchasing is a lot better than trying to do the shopping after the baby arrives, when you're busy trying to get acquainted and adjusted.

Find out how adoptive parents feel. Talk to other couples you know who have adopted infants (or find adoptive parents on-line) about their concerns, their problems and their solutions. Find a support group for adoptive parents and attend a few sessions – your clergyman, doctor or adoption agency may be able to direct you in locating individuals or groups. Again, you may be able to find some of this support – as well as plenty of other resources – on the Internet. Or look to books for information and strategies.

Find out how newborns feel. Read up on childbirth so that you have some idea of what your baby has gone through when he or she finally does arrive. You'll learn that after a long, hard struggle to be born, babies may be tired – something that birth parents understand because they are tired, too. Adoptive parents, usually exhilarated and excited rather than exhausted by their baby's arrival, might be tempted to overstimulate the newborn rather than allow her needed rest. If you're adopting an older baby, read up on the months that are already behind her, as well as those that are just ahead, keeping in mind that your baby may have some catching up to do developmentally if she has spent her first months in an orphanage or in an unnurturing home environment.

Learn the tricks of the trade. Take a parenting class that gives instruction in basics such as bathing, changing, feeding and carrying baby. Or plan on hiring a maternity nurse who is as good at teaching baby care as she is at practising it, for a day or two, or longer if you prefer, to help out with the basics (see page 16). But be sure whoever you hire will help rather than intimidate.

Take a good look at babies. Visit friends or acquaintances with young babies, or stop in at a hospital nursery at visiting time, so that a newborn won't seem so unfamiliar to you. Read about newborn characteristics in chapter 4. If you're adopting an older baby, pay visits to those who are about the same age as your baby.

ADOPTION MEDICINE

More and more parents today are choosing to adopt babies born in foreign countries where health care practices are often lacking. Though most of the challenges these parents face are no different from those faced by parents who adopt or give birth in this country (a baby is a baby no matter where he or she is born), there may be some concerns or questions unique to foreign adoption to which a regular doctor may not have the answers. Some parents turn for these answers to a paediatrician who specializes in foreign adoption medicine. These doctors have extensive experience in the medical, emotional, developmental and behavioural issues of children born abroad (especially in underdeveloped countries) and adopted by parents in the United Kingdom, and can offer preadoption counselling (includ-

ing an assessment of potential health risks) based on existing medical records. Since those records are often incomplete or nonexistent, paediatricians who specialize in adoption medicine also offer postadoption care, which routinely screens for problems specific to the child's country of origin.

While most adoptive parents do not need a consultation with an adoption medicine specialist, some – particularly those who have reason to be concerned about their new baby's health – will find the service useful. If you feel you might benefit from such a consultation, but don't have an adoption medicine specialist in your area, your GP may be able to confer with one and get responses to your specific concerns.

Consider breastfeeding. Some adoptive mothers are able to breastfeed their babies, at least partially. If you're interested, check with your gynaecologist to discuss the possibility, and see page 661.

NOT FEELING LIKE A PARENT

'Not having gone through pregnancy, I don't feel much like a parent to our son, even when I hold him.'

You don't have to be an adoptive parent to have trouble feeling like a 'real' parent. Most birth parents experience the very same self-doubts as they hold their newborns, who often seem like strangers at first. After all, though the technical part of becoming a parent takes no more than giving birth or signing the final

adoption papers, the emotional part takes a lot more. Bonding with a baby, whether a birth baby or an adopted one, is a process that occurs not in moments but, rather, gradually over days, weeks, even months. Few parents 'feel' like parents during those challenging early days and nights, yet virtually all eventually do – usually once they've mastered some of the basics of infant care and managed to get into a rhythm (you will!) with their new baby.

Keep in mind that while you may have a hard time accepting yourself as a parent, your baby will have no such difficulty. You – who love, shelter and provide for all of his needs – are the real thing to him. And you'll know that long before you hear his first 'Mama' or 'Dada'.

LOVING THE BABY

'I've heard that birth parents fall in love with their babies right in the delivery room. I'm afraid that because I didn't carry and deliver this baby, I'm never going to be able to love her in the same way.'

That all parent-baby love affairs begin in the birthing room is yet another parenthood myth. In fact, your fears are actually shared by a large proportion of birth parents who are surprised and disappointed to find they are not overcome by a great swell of love when they first hold their babies. And neither you nor they have anything to be concerned about. The mother-baby or father-baby love doesn't miraculously reach full bloom at first meeting (or even first few meetings) – it takes time and nurturing to grow.

This love apparently grows for adopting parents just as it does for birth parents. Studies show that adoptive families form good strong bonds, particularly when the child is adopted before the age of two. Adopted children are often more confident than non-adopted children, tend to view the world more positively, feel more in control of their lives, and see their parents as more nurturing than non-adopted children do – perhaps because being an adopted parent, unlike being a birth parent, always happens by choice.

BABY'S CRYING A LOT

'Our baby girl seems to cry a lot. Are we doing something wrong?'

There aren't any healthy new babies who don't cry, and many of them happen to cry a lot – it is, after all, their only way of communicating. But sometimes, crying is increased by overstimulation, or stimulation of the wrong kind. Many adoptive parents are so excited about the arrival of their new babies and so eager to show them off that they expose them to a steady stream of visitors. Just because you aren't exhausted from delivery doesn't mean your baby's not. Give her a chance to rest. Slow down, handle her gently, speak to her quietly. After a couple of weeks in a calm atmosphere, you may find she's crying less. If not, she may have colic, which is no reflection on you or your care, just a very common pattern of behaviour in the first three months of life (see page 182 for more on colic; page 117 for help cracking the crying code.)

POSTADOPTION BLUES

'If postnatal blues are supposed to be hormonal, how come I've been feeling depressed since we brought our son home?'

If the baby blues were triggered solely by hormones, adoptive parents wouldn't suffer from them – yet many do. That's because a wide range of fac-

---

THE WAITING PERIOD

Don't have enough to worry about now that you're a new mother (or father)? Here's something else many adoptive parents need to keep in mind: as soon as the waiting period is over (the time during which the birth mother can change her mind about the adoption), be sure to finalize the adoption in court. Some parents forget to do this in the excitement (and exhaustion) of the newborn period, and thus end up not having legal custody of their children, something that can lead to serious complications later.

tors play a role in the baby blues, and many of them have absolutely nothing to do with hormones.

For instance, whether you adopt or deliver, life as you knew it (from how you spend your days to how you spend your nights, from how you spend your money to how much money you have to spend) will never be the same, and that takes some getting used to. Until you adjust to life with a baby (that is, life without much sleep or much romance, life without free time, life – if you're taking maternity leave – without a career and possibly without a salary), you're bound to feel a little unsettled, a little overwhelmed and a little depressed. Also contributing to the baby blues for many parents (biological and adoptive, mothers and fathers) is the crumbling of confidence – that 'all thumbs, no instincts' feeling – experienced almost universally by first-timers.

Since it is likely that at least some of the causes of your mood slump are the same as for traditional postnatal blues, many of the cures may help you, too. The tips throughout chapter 23 can help you shake the blues and let you enjoy your new role more.

BREASTFEEDING AN ADOPTED BABY

'After years of trying to conceive, we are making our family by adopting. I'm excited about that, but I'm very disappointed that I won't be able to nurse when our baby arrives.'

Once a baby's born, there's just about nothing that a biological mother can do that an adoptive mother can't. In this age of medical miracles, that even goes, to a certain extent, for breastfeeding. Though most mothers of infants who were adopted will never lactate enough to feed their babies exclusively from the breast, a few mums do manage to breastfeed their babies at least partially. Among those adoptive mothers who attempt to induce lactation, even those who fail to produce milk can reap the benefits of the special intimacy nursing builds in.

Breastfeeding will be possible only if the baby you are adopting is a newborn, not yet used to sucking on an artificial nipple, and if you have no medical condition (such as a history of breast surgery) that might prevent you from producing milk.

Before you decide whether breastfeeding your adopted baby is right for you, ask yourself these questions:

Why are you so eager to breastfeed? If you simply want to give your baby the best nutritional start possible and to share the emotional pleasures of nursing with your new arrival, by all means go ahead and give it all you've got. On the other hand, if you're trying to prove your worth as a mother or deny to yourself or to others (consciously or subconsciously), that your baby was adopted, you should reconsider. It's important for you to come to terms with – and feel blessed about – the fact that your baby was adopted; if you don't, you and baby may run into problems later.

How committed are you? Are you willing to put everything else in your life on hold while you try to get lactation going? You may have to nurse almost constantly and face weeks of intense effort and possible frustration, with no results. Are you ready to accept the idea that you may not succeed, and that if you do, you may be able to supply only part of your baby's nourishment?

Will you have support? Ask your spouse and other family members whether they'll be behind you all the way. Without that support, you're much less likely to succeed.

If you're determined to do whatever it takes to try breastfeeding your baby, following these steps will increase your chances of success:

◆ Visit the doctor. See your gynaecologist to discuss your plan and to be sure that no condition exists that will make breastfeeding impossible or especially difficult in your case. Ask for advice on logistics, too. If he or she is unfamiliar with lactation induction, ask for a referral to a doctor who is familiar with it – possibly a paediatrician.

◆ Read up. Chapter 3 will tell you everything you need to know about breastfeeding.

◆ Get help. Call the NCT or the La Leche League in your community and ask them to recommend a breastfeeding consultant who can join your support team.

◆ Get a head start. If you know in advance approximately when your baby will be arriving, begin priming your breasts for that momentous day. About a month or so in advance, start stimulating breastfeeding with a breast pump, preferably an electric one. If you successfully produce milk before your baby arrives, bag it and freeze it for future use. See page 149 for information about expressing milk.

◆ Stimulate while you nurse. Order a supplemental nutrition system (SNS) to be delivered when your baby arrives. An SNS will allow your baby to stimulate milk by suckling while simultaneously being nourished by supplementary formula. Even if you aren't able to get a head

start on milk production (because baby arrives unexpectedly), an SNS will help you catch up, without compromising baby's nutrition. And if you don't end up making enough milk to completely satisfy baby, you can keep using the SNS as long as you breastfeed. See page 161 for more on SNS.

◆ Relax. Get plenty of rest, relaxation and sleep. Even a woman who has just given birth can't produce adequate milk if she's tense and exhausted. Stress can also interfere with let-down, so try to do some serious relaxing before each nursing or breast stimulation session.

◆ Eat right. Follow the Postpartum Diet (see page 669), being particularly careful to get enough calories and fluids and to take a vitamin-mineral supplement.

◆ Don't give up too soon. A pregnant woman's body usually has nine months to prepare for breastfeeding; give yours at least two or three months to get it going. Be persistent.

You'll know your efforts are paying off if you feel the sensation of let-down in your breasts and your baby shows signs of adequate intake (such as contentment after feeding, wet nappies, frequent bowel movements). If he or she doesn't appear satisfied, continue to use the SNS. (See page 158 for more on determining whether or not a baby is getting enough breast milk and on how to increase your milk supply if he or she isn't).

If in spite of all your hard work you don't succeed at producing milk, or don't produce enough to make you the sole supplier of your baby's nourishment (some biological mothers don't, either), you should feel comfortable abandoning your efforts, knowing you and your baby have already shared some of the important benefits of breastfeeding. Or you can continue nursing largely for the pleasure it provides, supplementing your baby's intake of breast milk, if any, with formula, either through the supplemental nutrition system or with a bottle.

GRANDPARENTS' ATTITUDES

'My parents already have three grandchildren they dote on. I'm very upset that they don't seem to be excited about the baby boy we've just adopted.'

It's easy for your parents to become attached to their biological grandchildren. They've borne their own children and slip easily into loving the children their children have borne. But they may be a little unsure whether they will be able to love an adopted grandchild as easily or as well – even as many adoptive parents are unsure – and may stay aloof for fear they will fail. Perhaps, too, they haven't yet resolved any feelings of disappointment (or guilt) they may have had about your not being able to conceive – they may even believe deep in their hearts that you still can. They may feel some anger if you're adopting by choice.

It's understandable that you feel hurt by your parents' seeming lack of interest in your baby, but don't be tempted to retaliate by excluding them from his life. The more you include them, the sooner they will grow to accept and love him.

Ideally, it's best to involve grandparents in preparing for the arrival of their adopted grandchild just as they would be, or have been, involved in preparing for a biological one. Enlist them in shopping for furniture and a layette, in picking out teddy bears and musical mobiles. Consult with them on possible colours for the baby's room, and on possible names for the baby. Choosing a family name for your child may make him feel more like 'real' family to them.

After you bring the baby home, seek your parents' advice on feeding and burping, bathing and changing, even if you don't really need it. If they live nearby, ask them to baby-sit when it's convenient. If you're planning a christening, ritual circumcision or baby naming, invite them to play a major role in the planning and in the celebration themselves. If you're not having a religious ceremony, consider having a 'welcome baby' party for relatives and friends. Being able to show the baby off will make them feel more like grandparents.

If you feel comfortable doing so, talk to them about your perception of their feelings. Tell them that with this kind of new experience, uncertainties are natural – you've had some yourself. If they get a chance to vent their feelings, they may begin to feel more comfortable with them – and with you and the baby. If you can't raise the subject, perhaps a respected relative, family friend, clergy member or doctor can do it for you.

Most of all, give your parents plenty of time to get to know your baby; to know a baby is usually to love him. Be sure that you're not being oversensitive or defensive, and just imagining that your baby is being treated differently. If in the end they still seem not to accept him fully, try to cover your hurt and keep family ties tied, with the hope that closeness will come gradually over the years.

UNKNOWN HEALTH PROBLEMS

'We've just adopted a beautiful little girl. She seems perfect, but I keep worrying that some unknown hereditary problem will surface.'

The genetic makeup of every child, adopted or not, is uncertain. And every parent worries occasionally about possible unknown defects. Fortunately, really serious genetic defects are rare and most parental worry unnecessary. It would be helpful to you, however, to get as complete a health history on both the baby's biological parents if possible, to provide to the baby's doctor and in case of future illness. Also try to arrange, when drawing up adoption papers, for some way to trace the adoptive mother so that should an unlikely crisis arise and your baby needs help from the birth mother (a bone marrow transplant, for instance), you would be able to find her.

But while an adopted baby is not any more likely to have an inherited disorder than is one who isn't adopted, she is more subject to infection. Because she doesn't come equipped with the same germs as her adoptive mother and father, she is less likely than a biological child to have antibodies to infectious organisms in her new environment. Take some extra precautions for the first few weeks, such as washing your hands before handling your baby, her bottle or anything that may go into her mouth or come in contact with her hands, and by limiting visitors. Though the temptation to show her off is great, wait a few weeks before exposing her to large numbers of people. (She can use the rest, too.)

If your baby has come from abroad, she may also be harbouring an infection or parasites that would be rare here. Her doctor should know her country of origin and should check her for diseases indigenous to that area of the world upon her arrival here. Immediate treatment of any problems uncovered will not only assure your baby of a good start in life, but it will also protect the rest of your family.

DEALING WITH FRIENDS AND FAMILY

'A few close friends knew we were going to adopt a baby. But now that she's here we have to tell everyone we know. I'm not sure how to go about this.'

Whether they've adopted or delivered, the traditional way for new parents to spread their happy word is to send announcements to friends and family, and sometimes, to local papers. Exactly how you tell the world is up to you. Though you can specify in the announcement that your baby was adopted, you certainly don't have to. Instead, you can introduce your baby as any other parent would. If she's a newborn, you can announce her birth: 'We're delighted to announce the birth of . . .' If she's an older baby, you can announce her arrival: 'We're thrilled to announce the arrival of . . .' or 'We're proud to announce that . . . has joined our family'. Either way, a picture will be worth a thousand words.

When talking to anyone about your baby, start right off saying 'our baby' or 'my baby'. In referring to the parents who conceived her, use the words 'birth' or 'biological' parents, rather than 'real' or 'natural'. *You* are baby's real parents, and the more you hear yourself say it, the more you – and everyone else – will come to accept it. If you have other biological children, don't call them 'my own' children or let other people refer to them in that way.

ADOPTION ANTIBODIES

If you've adopted an older baby, you'll need to pay extra attention when it comes to vaccinations. Because some adoption agencies don't have accurate records, it's hard to know which, if any, vaccinations your child has already received. If your child has been adopted from abroad, he or she may not have received vaccinations on the United Kingdom vaccination schedule. Even if there is a vaccination record for your overseas baby, a foreign vaccination schedule is no guarantee that your child is adequately protected. That's because the vaccines may not have been properly stored or administered.

To determine your child's level of immunity, your child's doctor can do a blood test to detect if your child has antibodies against a disease. If the test shows a lack of antibodies, the vaccine should then be given to your baby. Don't worry about the potential of your baby's being vaccinated for the same disease twice. Any adverse reactions (which are usually minor and quite rare) are still safer than contracting a disease.

Internationally adopted older babies will also need to be screened for a variety of infectious diseases such as TB and hepatitis B because they are at higher risk of having been exposed to such diseases.

TELLING BABY

'Even though our son is still an infant, I can't help worrying about how and when we're going to tell him that he was adopted.'

It's no longer a question, as it once was, of whether or not to tell a child that he was adopted. Today, experts agree that children need to know and have the right to know about their adoption, and should find out about it from their parents, not through inadvertent slips by relatives or friends. There's also agreement that the best way to tell is by introducing a child, gradually, from infancy on to the fact that he was adopted – so he grows up completely comfortable with the concept.

You can start right now, while your baby is tiny and still doesn't understand what you are saying. Just as a birth parent talks about the day her baby was born, you can talk about the day you brought your baby home: 'That was the best day of our lives!' When you're gurgling and cooing at him, you can say, 'We made our family when we adopted you!' or 'We're so happy that we were able to adopt you and make our family!' Though your baby won't be able to comprehend, even in the simplest terms, what 'adoption' means until he's three or four years old, early exposure to the concept will make it seem natural, and the eventual explanation of it easier to process.

SUPPORT FOR THE ADOPTING FAMILY

Baby on the way – or already arrived? Every new parent can use a little support (make that a lot), and adopting families can find it through these Internet resources:

- www.adoptionuk.org.uk
- www.postadoptioncentre.org.uk
- www.doh.gov.uk/adoption/postadoptioncentres.htm

ADOPTION BENEFITS

It's a growing trend across the country – and this trend is a good one. Some family-friendly employers are beginning to recognize that parents who have adopted a child are just as entitled to benefits as are parents who have given birth to one. These forward-thinking employers offer adoptive parents maternity and paternity benefits that parallel the ones they voluntarily offer birth parents, including paid leave. If your company doesn't offer such perks for adoptive parents (check with personnel to see if it does), you might consider lobbying for them with other adoptive (or just plain supportive) parents.

The rights to paternity leave introduced by the government in April 2003 apply also to a father adopting a child (see page 721).

Another way to help your baby learn about his adoption is to keep a scrapbook that commemorates it. You can include pictures and mementos of his first day with you and his homecoming – as well as some diary entries detailing the event and the emotions you were feeling when you first held him in your arms or first took him home. If you travelled to a foreign country for the adoption, the scrapbook is the perfect place to document the journey – and to give your son a glimpse of his heritage. If the adoption was open, photos of the birth mother (especially if they were taken with you, while you were both waiting for your baby's arrival) can also help make the concept of your baby's adoption more tangible to him. No matter what you include, looking at the scrapbook together is sure to become a favourite activity as your child grows – a special reminder of the special day that he came into your life and 'made' your family.

◆ ◆ ◆

Part 3

FOR THE FAMILY

CHAPTER 23

For Mum: Enjoying the First Year

After nine months of growing a baby and many long hours of birthing it, your body has just endured one of the greatest challenges known to humankind. It's been drained of nutritional reserves, zapped of strength, deprived of rest, pushed to limits you didn't know existed. And as if that's not enough, now that you're finished with the hard work of expecting, you're expected to begin an even tougher job: motherhood.

Because pregnancy, labour and delivery are so physically gruelling, the first six weeks after the birth of a baby are considered a 'recovery period'. But once the fog of the first six postpartum weeks has lifted and the aches and pains of delivery have (mostly) faded, you'll probably begin to feel vaguely human again. You may even begin to feel as though you're falling into a rhythm with your baby (albeit an exhausting rhythm) and that the routines you struggled with before now come to both of you almost easily. Still, even once you've started getting the hang of this parenting thing, many challenges still await you in the first year of your baby's life: from finding time for your spouse to finding time for yourself, from reentering the workplace to reestablishing friendships, from working on that balancing act they call parenthood to recognizing that even professional jugglers drop a few balls from time to time. And just when you're starting to wonder whether your life will ever be the same as it was pre-baby, you may be surprised to suddenly realize that you're really glad it isn't.

What You Should Be Eating: THE POSTPARTUM DIET

If you worked hard to revamp your eating habits during pregnancy, now isn't the time to abandon your newly improved ones, temporarily or permanently. If you didn't eat as well as you might have liked during pregnancy, you couldn't pick a better time to start good habits than now. Though a post-partum diet plan will include a few more perks and a lot more leeway than did the pregnancy one, careful eating will be essential if you're going to keep up your energy level (so you can keep up with your baby), gradually take off that extra weight put on during the nine months of pregnancy, and, if you're breastfeeding, produce enough quality milk.

NINE BASIC DIET PRINCIPLES FOR NEW MOTHERS

Good nutrition helps fuel a speedy recovery from childbirth, while maintaining the abundant energy and optimum health necessary for top-notch mothering. It is also crucial to successful breastfeeding. While neglecting nutrition essentials when you're breastfeeding won't necessarily reduce your milk supply, at least not for a couple of months (even women who are severely under-nourished can often produce milk for a while), it may affect the nutritive value of your milk and shortchange your own body nutritionally. Whether you decide to nurse or not, these nine basic principles can serve as a general guide to eating well during the postpartum period:

Make most bites count. Though the bites you take aren't shared with your baby as directly in the postpartum period as they were during pregnancy (and aren't really shared at all if you're not nursing), it's still important to make as many of them as possible count towards good nutrition. Careful food selection will help ensure a plentiful supply of quality breast milk, enough energy to survive sleepless nights and endless days, and a speedier return to pre-pregnancy shape. Of course, as long as you're taking in your share of nutrients – and not taking in a surplus of calories that might make weight loss elusive – treat yourself now and then to bites that feed only your cravings. You've earned a little indulgence.

All calories are not created equal. No matter who in the family you're feeding, the 2,000 calories in *one* typical fast-food meal aren't nutritionally equal to the 2,000 calories in *three* well-balanced meals. Consider, too: The 235 calories in a sliver of frosted devil's food cake are undeniably delicious, but so are the 235 calories in half a ripe cantaloupe mounded high with chocolate frozen yoghurt – and one (guess which) offers a bounty of nutrition, while the other offers nothing but calories. The same holds true for the 160 calories in ten French fries – nutritionally light-weight when weighed against the 160 calories in a baked potato topped with grated Cheddar cheese and steamed broccoli.

Starve yourself, cheat your baby. Missing meals isn't potentially harmful (as it was when you were pregnant), but a consistently irregular eating schedule can cut into your own reserves, leaving you lagging. If you're breastfeeding, severely inadequate nutrition – such as might develop on certain fad diets (juice fasts, for instance) – could in time seriously reduce your milk supply.

Stay an efficiency expert. To keep your postpartum weight going down and your nutrition up, it's still important to select foods dense in nutrition in relation to their calorie content – turkey over smoked sausage for lunch, pasta with vegetables over pasta with cream sauce for dinner. If your problem is losing too much weight, look for foods high in both nutrition and calories but low in bulk, such as avocado and nuts, but stay away from foods like air-popped popcorn that fill you up without filling you, or your nutritional requirements, out.

Carbohydrates are a complex issue. And complex carbohydrates, unrefined, are just the kind you want to concentrate on postpartum (and beyond, for a lifetime of good nutrition for yourself and your family). Whole-grain breads, cereals and cakes, brown rice, dried beans, peas and other legumes provide fibre (as important now as during pregnancy to ensure regularity) and plenty of vitamins and minerals. They also give you a longer-lasting energy boost than refined carbs do.

Sweet nothings are exactly that. The average Briton consumes almost their entire weight in sugar each year. Some of this comes right from the sugar bowl, sprinkled on cereals and fruits or stirred into coffee or tea. A fair amount is taken, not unexpectedly, in cakes, biscuits, sweets, pastries and pies. But a surprising proportion comes from such unlikely sources as soups, salad dressings, breakfast cereals, breads, hot dogs, luncheon meats, and processed, canned or frozen main courses and side dishes.

If your sugar intake is just average, you're consuming over 800 nutritionless or empty calories a day. For a new mother who wants to make sure she gets her Daily Dozen without gaining a dozen (or more) pounds in the process, having sugary treats occasionally won't create nutritional havoc, but consuming a great many empty calories a day can.

Eat foods that remember where they came from. Foods that are highly processed lose a lot of their nutrition along the way. These foods also often contain unhealthy excesses of saturated fat, sodium and sugar, as well as artificial colours and other chemical additives, none of which enhance the diet, and the last of which can occasionally contaminate breast milk (see page 92). The closer the food you eat is to its natural state, the better for your baby – and for you.

Make good eating a family affair. Include the whole household in your good eating, and your baby will grow up in a home where good nutrition is natural. This may translate to better long-term health (and longer life) not only for you, but for your spouse and your children as well.

Don't sabotage your diet. Though you may enjoy an occasional alcoholic beverage even if you're breastfeeding, too much alcohol can definitely affect you and your baby adversely, as can any amount of tobacco or illicit drug use (see page 90–91).

THE DAILY DOZEN FOR POSTNATAL AND BREASTFEEDING

If you're familiar with the Pregnancy Diet, you already know that you don't have to sit down with a ledger, a calculator and volumes of nutritive value tables before each meal in order to be sure you're getting the nutrients you need (to produce milk and stay healthy yourself if you're breastfeeding, or just to stay healthy if you're not). All you have to do is get your Daily Dozen.

Calories. You'll need to take in enough calories to fuel the energy you'll require as a new mother, but not so many that you can't begin shedding that pregnancy weight. If you're breastfeeding, that breaks down to about 400 to 500 extra calories a day above what you would need to maintain your pre-pregnancy weight (double that if you're breastfeeding twins, and triple that for triplets). You can reduce that number a little after the first six postpartum weeks if you don't seem to be losing weight, but you shouldn't cut calories drastically, as that could cut down on your milk supply.

Even if you're not breastfeeding, you should put serious dieting on hold until after the first six weeks. During that recovery period, you should be able to begin losing that unwanted pregnancy weight while sustaining your energy levels by eating about as many calories as you would need to maintain your pre-pregnancy weight.[1] When recovery is complete and dieting is safer, you can reduce that number by

---

1. To find out how many calories it takes to sustain your pre-pregnancy weight, calculate your pre-pregnancy weight *in pounds* and multiply by 12 if you're sedentary, 15 if you're moderately active, and up to 22 if you're very active.

THE ONE-TWO PUNCH

Want to pack in the nutrition without packing on the weight? Choose foods that efficiently fill more than one requirement in a serving. Many dairy products provide protein and calcium servings, some overachieving fruits and vegetables offer up both yellow or green leafy and vitamin C. A real nutritional superstar? Broccoli, which packs a one-two-three punch (green leafy, vitamin C and, if eaten in somewhat greater quantity, a calcium serving).

---

200 to 500 calories a day, but don't go on a very stringent diet without medical supervision.

Breastfeeding or not, weighing yourself regularly is the best way of determining whether your calorie intake is high, low or just right. As long as you are losing pregnancy weight gradually and stop losing once your desired weight is reached, you're on target. Adjust your calories up or down if you're not. Keep in mind, too, that it's always wiser to increase exercise than to dramatically decrease calories. If you can't put the brakes on a too rapid weight loss, see your doctor.

Protein – three servings daily if you're breastfeeding, two if you're not. Many of these also serve up a calcium requirement. One serving equals any of the following: 2½ to 3 glasses skimmed or semi-skimmed milk; 420 ml (14 fl oz) low-fat yoghurt; 125 g (4½ oz) low-fat cottage cheese; 2 large eggs plus 2 whites; 5 egg whites; 85 to 100 g (3 to 3½ oz) fish, meat or poultry; 140 to 170 g (5 to 6 oz) tofu. Other soya products (including many vegetarian frozen dinners) may also contain plenty of protein;

check labels. Breastfeeding mothers of twins or triplets need an extra serving for each additional baby. Vegans, those vegetarians who eat no animal protein, should add an extra protein serving daily since the quality of vegetable protein is not as high as that of animal protein.

Vitamin C foods – two servings daily if you're breastfeeding, at least one if you're not. Keep in mind that many vitamin C foods also fill the requirement for green leafy and yellow vegetables and yellow fruits. One serving equals any of the following: 3 tablespoons strawberries; ¼ small cantaloupe; ½ grapefruit; 1 small orange; 90 to 120 ml (3 to 4 fl oz) citrus juice; ½ large mango, papaya or guava; 3 tablespoons cooked broccoli or cauliflower; 3 tablespoons shredded raw cabbage; 3 tablespoons cooked kale or kohlrabi; 1 medium green pepper or ½ medium red pepper; 2 small tomatoes or 240 ml (8 fl oz) tomato juice.

Green leafy and yellow vegetables and yellow fruits – at least three servings daily if you're breastfeeding, two or more if you're not. Keep in mind that many of these also fill the requirement for vitamin C. One serving equals any of the following: 2 fresh or dried apricots; ⅛ cantaloupe; ½ mango; 1 large yellow (not white) peach or nectarine; 3 tablespoons cooked broccoli; ½ medium carrot; 8 to 10 large leaves of romaine lettuce; 2 tablespoons cooked greens; ¼ small sweet potato.

Calcium – five servings daily if you're breastfeeding, three plus if you're not. Many of these also serve up a considerable amount of protein. One serving equals any of the following: 35 g (1¼ oz) Gruyère; 40 g (1½ oz) Cheddar; 240 ml (8 fl oz) skimmed or semi-skimmed milk; 150 ml (5 fl oz) calcium-added milk; 120 ml (4 fl oz) evaporated semi-skimmed milk; 55 g (2 oz) non-fat dry milk; 250 g (9 oz) low fat cottage cheese; 170 to 225 g (6 to 8 oz) yoghurt; frozen yoghurt (calcium content varies, so check label or ask for nutritional information); 170 ml (6 fl oz) calcium-fortified orange juice; 7 tablespoons broccoli; 3 tablespoons kale; 2 tablespoons blackstrap molasses (treacle); 170 ml (6 fl oz) canned salmon or 85 g (3 oz) sardines, with bones; tofu (calcium content varies, so check label; a serving should contain about 30 per cent of the daily value – DV); 2 corn tortillas (again, check label). Mothers breastfeeding twins, triplets or more will need an extra calcium serving for each additional baby, and may want to use calcium-enriched dairy products or calcium supplements to get their quota. Vegetarians who don't use dairy products may find it difficult to meet the requirement from purely vegetable sources unless they are fortified with calcium (orange juice, for example) and may need calcium supplements. Though lack of calcium when breastfeeding isn't likely to affect breast milk composition, the calcium drawn from a mother's bones to produce breast milk may make her more susceptible to osteoporosis later in life.

Other fruits and vegetables – two or more servings daily. One serving equals any of the following: 1 apple, pear, banana or white peach; 3 tablespoons fresh cherries or grapes; 3 tablespoons blueberries; 1 slice pineapple; 2 slices watermelon; 5 dates; 3 figs; 1 tablespoon raisins; 3 tablespoons cooked green beans; 6 or 7 asparagus spears; 3 tablespoons cooked Brussels sprouts; 3 tablespoons cooked parsnips, mange-tout or green peas; 1 medium potato; 3 tablespoons fresh mushrooms.

Whole grains and other concentrated complex carbohydrates – six servings daily whether you're breastfeeding or not. One serving equals any of the following: 40 g (1½ oz) cooked brown rice, wild rice, millet, kasha (buckwheat groats), unpearled barley, bulgar or quinoa; 3 tablespoons cooked beans or peas; 1 serving (25 g/1 oz) cooked or ready-to-eat whole-grain cereal; 2 tablespoons wheat germ; 1 slice whole-grain bread; ½ wholemeal bagel or muffin; 1 small or ½ large wholemeal pitta; 1 corn or wholemeat tortilla; 1 serving whole-grain or soya crackers; 2 rice cakes; 25 g (1 oz) whole-grain, soya, or high-protein-type pasta; 55 g (2 oz) air-popped popcorn.

Iron-rich foods – one or more daily. Iron is found in varying amounts in dried fruit, beef, chickpeas and other dried legumes, potatoes in their skins, pumpkin, cooked greens, Jerusalem artichokes, oysters, sardines, soyabeans and soya products, spinach, blackstrap molasses (treacle), carob and liver.[2] It is also found in wheat germ, whole grains and cereals that are iron fortified.

High-fat foods – small amounts daily. While an adequate fat intake was essential during pregnancy, and your body was able to handle even those foods high in cholesterol with impunity, it is now once again necessary for you to consider limiting fat in your diet and carefully selecting the type of fat you do consume. It is generally agreed that the average adult should get no more than 30 per cent of his or her total calories from fat. Those at high risk for heart disease should limit their intake even more rigidly. This means that if your ideal weight is 57 kg (8 st 13 lb), you need

1,875 calories daily, no more than 30 per cent of those, or 62 g, from fat. That's the equivalent of 4½ fat servings (at 14 g each) a day. If you're lighter, you will need fewer servings; if you're heavier, more. You can expect that you will get roughly one serving from dribs and drabs in low-fat foods; the rest can come from fatty foods. High-fat foods that will provide you with one half a fat serving include: 25 g (1 oz) of hard cheese (Gruyère, Cheddar); 2 tablespoons grated Parmesan; 1½ tablespoons single cream, pecans, peanuts or walnuts; 2 tablespoons whipped cream; 1 tablespoon cream cheese; 2 rounded tablespoons soured cream; 240 ml (8 fl oz) whole milk or whole-milk yoghurt; 120 ml (4 fl oz) regular ice cream; 170 g (6 oz) tofu; ¼ small avocado; 1 tablespoon peanut butter; 100 g (3½ oz) dark meat or 200 g (7 oz) light meat turkey or chicken (no skin); 115 g (4 oz) fatty fish (such as salmon); 2 large eggs or 2 large egg yolks; 2 small biscuits or 1 average muffin; 1 slice of cake or 3 biscuits (sizes vary with recipes). Pure fats which provide one full serving include: 1 tablespoon olive, safflower, corn, rapeseed or other vegetable oils, butter, margarine or regular mayonnaise; 2 tablespoons 'light' margarine; 2 tablespoons regular salad dressing.

Salty foods – limited quantities. While it may not have been necessary to limit your sodium intake during pregnancy, it might be smart to start cutting back on the salty stuff now. Read labels to screen for foods high in sodium, and avoid making them staples in your diet. Unless someone in your family is on a sodium-restricted diet, lightly salting to taste when cooking is fine. But remember that any family food you're planning to also feed to your baby should go unsalted to the table – both because infants can't handle a great deal of

2. Eat liver only rarely in spite of its great nutritive value, because it is a storehouse for the chemicals, including questionable ones, to which an animal is exposed.

sodium and because exposing them to salt early will help give them a taste for it.

Fluid – 1.8 litres (64 fl oz) daily whether you're breastfeeding or not. (You may need to drink more if you're breastfeeding twins.) Water, sparkling water, fruit and vegetable juices, and clear soups are all good fluid choices. You can also count milk (which is about ⅔ water); fruits and vegetables with a high water content will add more. But beware of too much of a good thing: excessive fluids (more than 2.7 litres/96 fl oz a day if you're breastfeeding one child) can inhibit breast milk production.

Vitamin supplements. Take a pregnancy/breastfeeding formula daily if you're breastfeeding, not as a replacement for a good diet but as nutritional insurance. The supplement should contain zinc and vitamin K. If you eat no animal products (not even milk and eggs), you should also be certain your supplement contains at least 4 mcg of vitamin B_{12} (which is found naturally only in animal foods), 0.5 mg of folic acid and, if you don't get at least half an hour's dose of sunshine daily, 400 mg of vitamin D.

Even if you're not breastfeeding, you should continue taking your pregnancy vitamins for at least the first six weeks postpartum. After that, a stan-

dard multiple vitamin/mineral supplement will fill in the nutritional gaps if you find you don't always have the time or opportunity to eat as well as you'd like. A supplement designed for women in the childbearing years will provide the extra iron needed to replace iron that might have been depleted with pregnancy and/or postpartum bleeding and will again be lost when menstruation resumes.

IF YOU'RE NOT BREASTFEEDING

Good nutrition is important for all mothers postpartum. Eating well will not only help ensure a speedy recovery, but it will fuel you with the energy you'll need to keep up with a growing baby (and to keep going in that sleep-deprived state they call new parenthood). It will also help ward off a variety of illnesses (from certain cancers to diabetes to osteoporosis) that are known to be diet-related. So even if you're not breastfeeding, continue to eat to your good health, using the Nine Basic Principles and the Daily Dozen as a general guide to generally good nutrition – for your sake as well as your baby's.

What You May Be Concerned About

EXHAUSTION

'I expected to be tired during the first few weeks after my baby's birth, but it's been a few months now since I had my baby and I'm still exhausted.'

Between recovering from the demanding physical biathlon of labour and childbirth, caring for a newborn who hasn't yet figured out the difference between day and night, and adjusting to the round-the-clock responsibilities of parenthood, virtually all new mothers feel like walking (and nappy-changing and breastfeeding) zombies at first. But while the postpartum recovery period is officially over after six weeks, feelings of exhaustion don't usually end with it. Rare is the woman (or man, especially if he's a stay-at-home parent) who escapes continued parental fatigue syndrome during the first year. And it's not surprising. There's no other job as emotionally and physically taxing as parenting in the first year. The strain and pressure are not limited to eight hours a day or five days a week, and there are no lunch hours or coffee breaks to spell relief. For the first-time parent, there's also the stress inherent in any new job: mistakes to be made, problems to solve, a lot to learn. If all this isn't enough to produce exhaustion, the new mother may also have her strength sapped by breastfeeding, by toting around a rapidly growing infant (and accompanying paraphernalia) and by night after night of broken sleep.

The new mother who goes back to work outside the home may also suffer from the kind of fatigue that comes from trying to do two jobs well. She gets up early to attend to several mummying jobs, often including breastfeeding, before she even leaves for her job away from home. When she returns home, she still has baby care and, often, cooking, cleaning and laundry to contend with. To top it all off, she can be up with the baby half the night and still be expected to be alert, cheerful and efficient in the morning. Exhaustion would be inevitable for Supermum herself.

Of course, it's a good idea to see your doctor to be sure there is no medical cause for your exhaustion (such as postpartum thyroiditis). If you get a clean bill of health, be assured that in time, as you gain experience, as your routine becomes routine, and as your baby begins sleeping through the night,

the unrelenting fatigue will gradually fade (though you may not feel totally caught up on your rest until your children are all in school). And your energy level should pick up a bit, too, once your body adjusts to the new demands. In the meantime, there are ways to minimize that night-of-the-living-dead feeling:

- Get all the help you can, and then some. Sign up help, paid or otherwise, to pick up the slack (and the groceries and the house) so you don't have to.

- Share, share alike. Make a list of all of the baby-care tasks and household chores that need to be done, then split them evenly between you and your spouse. Assign according to schedule (if he works during the day, he'll obviously have to do his share in the early morning and at night), preference and ability (keeping in mind that the only way to get really good at a task – whether it's nappy changing or bathing – is to practise, practise, practise). If you are formula feeding, you can switch off on night feedings (one night on, one night off) so you can switch off on getting some sleep. But even if you're breastfeeding, dad can rise to the occasion to do any necessary nappy changing before handing baby to you for a feeding. Or, keep the baby in a cot beside your bed (or, if you're co-sleeping, next to you in bed) so you can just reach over and latch baby on. Once breastfeeding is established, you can also pump a bottle of milk each day for dad to give in the middle of the night while you catch some zzz's.

- Be an equal-opportunity parent. There is nothing, besides breastfeeding, that a father can't do as well or better than a mother. Yet many a

NEWLY DELIVERED?

Then you're bound to have almost as many questions about how to care for yourself as you do about how to care for your newborn. For answers on everything you might encounter (and worry about) during your six-week recovery period – from lochia to haemorrhoids, hair loss to night sweats, that first bowel movement to that first postnatal checkup – read chapters 15 and 16 in *What to Expect When You're Expecting*. Then, when those six weeks are behind you, come back here for answers to all your other questions about the first year postnatal.

new mum doesn't give dad a chance when it comes to baby care – or she stands over his shoulder criticizing so much that he ends up throwing in the nappy. So if it's an 'I'd rather do it myself because I do it better' mentality that's standing between you and some rest, lose it now.

◆ Turn in earlier. It may be stating the obvious, but earlier to bed will make it easier to rise. Don't stay up late to watch the news or surf the Internet. Go to bed as early as possible to get as much sleep (even if it'll be interrupted) as you can.

◆ Nap when the baby naps. As crazy as that sounds (after all, there's laundry, cooking and a thousand other things to do) and as unrealistic as it seems (especially if there's a toddler at home or if older children need homework help), try to rest when baby does, even if it's just for half of baby's nap time. 'Power naps' of even fifteen minutes can be surprisingly refreshing.

◆ Don't forget to feed yourself. Sure, you're busy feeding your baby (if you're nursing, it may seem like you're always busy feeding your baby). But don't neglect your own nutritional needs (which will be even greater if you're breastfeeding). Grazing is fine (what new parent has time for a full-fledged meal during the day?), as long as the snacks you reach for are healthy ones. Keep a supply of easy-to-grab but nutritious foods in stock: cheese sticks, hard-boiled eggs, individual servings of yoghurt and cottage cheese, small pieces of fruit, ready-cut raw vegetables and dip, cereal mix (combine a few of your favourites with some nuts and raisins in single-serving plastic bags), ready-to-eat edamame (soya beans), whole-grain crackers and pretzels, frozen fruit juice pops, frozen yoghurt bars.

◆ Get moving. Though postnatal fatigue is caused by a lack of rest, it can be heightened by a lack of activity – and a lack of fresh air. So try to take a walk with your baby every day (particularly during those afternoon slumps). If the weather's not baby-friendly, try a shopping centre or museum walk instead. Joining a postnatal exercise class or doing some postnatal exercises at home (see page 687) will also give you the lift you're looking for.

POSTNATAL DEPRESSION

'My baby is over a month old and I can't stop feeling depressed. Shouldn't I be feeling better by now?'

If the baby blues (which strike 60 to 80 per cent of women, most commonly in the first postnatal week) don't fade over

GETTING HELP FOR POSTNATAL DEPRESSION

Until recently, postnatal depression was a condition that was largely swept under the rug of medical practise. It was ignored by the public, minimally discussed by doctors, and suffered with unnecessarily in shame and silence by the women who experienced it. This attitude has prevented women from learning about postnatal depression and its highly effective treatments. Worst of all, it has kept women from getting the help they need.

Fortunately, there's been a shift in the way the medical community views and treats PND. Practitioners are becoming better educated about PND – learning how to look for risk factors during pregnancy, to screen routinely for PND during postnatal visits, and to treat it quickly, safely and successfully. Researchers are also looking into other screening tools (such as a simple test in which women are asked a series of questions at their six-week postnatal checkup) to diagnose and treat postnatal depression more quickly.

Postnatal depression is one of the most treatable forms of depression. So if it strikes you, don't suffer with it any longer than you have to. Speak up and get the help you need now.

For more help contact the Association for Postnatal Illness, 145 Dawes Road, London SW6 7EB, 0207 386 0868, apni.org.

---

time, chances are postnatal depression is to blame. True postnatal depression (PND) is less common (affecting about 10 to 20 per cent of women) than the baby blues, much more enduring (lasting anywhere from a few weeks to a year or more), and much more serious. PND may begin at delivery, but more often not until a month or two later; in some it doesn't begin until the first postnatal menstrual period occurs or until weaning (due in part to fluctuating hormones). Women who have had PND before, have a personal or family history of depression or severe PMS, felt depressed during pregnancy and/or had a complicated pregnancy and delivery, or have a sick or difficult baby are more susceptible. Recent research suggests that diabetes during and after pregnancy may also be a factor.

The symptoms of PND are similar to those of the baby blues, though much more pronounced (for more on baby blues, see *What to Expect When You're Expecting*). They include crying and irritability; sleep problems (not being able to sleep or sleeping the day away); eating problems (having no appetite or eating all day); persistent feelings of sadness; an inability or a lack of desire to take care of yourself or your newborn; exaggerated concerns about your baby; and memory loss. If symptoms persist for more than two or three weeks, chances are you have PND and it won't go away without professional help. Don't wait to see if it does.

First, call your doctor and ask for a thyroid test. Irregularities in thyroid hormone levels (very common in the postnatal period) can lead to emotional instability. If those levels check out normally, ask for a referral to a therapist who has a clinical background in the treatment of postnatal depression and make an appointment *promptly*. Antidepressants such as Zoloft or Prozac (which appear to be safe during breastfeeding), combined with counselling, can help you feel better fast. Bright light therapy may bring relief from PND and can be used instead of or in addition to medication. (Recent studies have shown that high-risk women can take antidepressants such as Zoloft or Prozac right after delivery to prevent postnatal depression. Some doctors will even prescribe low doses of antidepressants during the third trimester of pregnancy to women with a history of postnatal depression.)

Whichever treatment route you and your therapist decide is right for your postnatal depression, keep in mind that swift intervention is critical. Without it, PND can prevent you from bonding with, caring for and enjoying your baby. It can also have a devastating effect on your relationship with your spouse and other children, as well as on your own health and well-being.

Some women, instead of (or in addition to) feeling depressed postnatal feel extremely anxious or fearful, sometimes experiencing panic attacks, including rapid heartbeat and breathing, hot or cold flushes, chest pain, dizziness and shaking. These symptoms also require prompt treatment by a qualified therapist.

Much more rare and more serious than PND is postnatal psychosis. Its symptoms include loss of reality, hallucinations and/or delusions. If you are experiencing suicidal, violent or aggressive feelings, or hearing voices or have other signs of psychosis, don't wait – call your doctor *immediately* and insist on getting help right away. Don't let anyone reassure you that these kinds of feelings are normal during the postnatal period – they're not. To be sure you don't act out any dangerous feelings, try to get a neighbour to stay with you while you contact the doctor.

GETTING EVERYTHING DONE

'Now that I have a baby, I'm falling behind on everything: cleaning, laundry, dishes, literally everything. My once immaculate house is now a mess. I've always considered myself a together person – until now.'

Take the responsibility of caring for a newborn baby for the first time. Days and nights that seem to blur together as one endless feeding. Add a few too many visitors, a generous helping of postnatal hormonal upheaval and, possibly, a fair amount of clutter accumulated during your stay in the hospital, or in the last days of pregnancy – when you could barely move, never mind clean. Throw in the inevitable mountain of gifts, boxes, wrapping paper and cards to keep track of. It's only natural to feel that as your new life with your baby is beginning, your old life – with its order and cleanliness – is crumbling around you.

Don't despair. Your inability to keep up with both baby and house during the first weeks at home in no way predicts your future success at the juggling act they call motherhood. Things are bound to get better as you regain your strength, become familiar with the basic baby-care tasks, and learn to be a little more flexible. It will also help to:

Get hold of yourself. Dwelling anxiously on what you have to do makes facing it twice as difficult. So relax. Take a few deep breaths. Then, instead of trying to do it all at once (which you can't), focus on what's really important: getting to know and enjoy your newborn. Banish thoughts of household chores while you're with her (relaxation techniques learned in childbirth class may help you to do this). When you look around later on, the clutter and chaos will still be there, but you'll be better able to deal with it.

Get rest. Paradoxically, the best way to start getting things done is to start getting more rest. Give yourself a chance to recuperate fully from childbirth and you will be better able to tackle your new responsibilities.

Get help. If you haven't already arranged for household help – paid or unpaid – and taken steps to streamline housekeeping and cooking chores, now's the time to do so. Also be sure that there is a fair division of labour (both baby care and household care) between you and your spouse.

Get your priorities straight. Is it more important to get the vacuuming done while baby's napping or to put your feet up and relax so you can be refreshed when she awakens? Is it really essential to dust the bookshelves, or would taking the baby out for a walk in the pram be a better use of your time? Keep in mind that doing too much too soon can rob you of the energy to accomplish anything well, and that while your house will someday be clean again, your baby will never be two days, or two weeks, or two months old again.

Get organized. Lists are a new mother's best friend. First thing every morning, jot down a list of what needs to be done. Divide your priorities into three categories: chores that must be taken care of as soon as possible, those that can wait until later in the day, and those that can be put off until tomorrow, or next week, or indefinitely. Assign approximate times to each activity, taking into account your personal biological clock (are you useless first thing in the morning, or do you do your best work at the crack of dawn?) as well as your baby's

(as best you can determine it at this point).

Though organizing your day on paper doesn't always mean that everything will get done on schedule (in fact, for new parents it rarely does), it will give you a sense of control over what may now seem like a completely uncontrollable situation. Plans on paper are always more manageable than plans flying frenetically around your head. You may even find, once you've made your list, that you actually have less to do than you thought. Don't forget to cross off completed tasks for a satisfying feeling of accomplishment. And don't worry about what's not crossed off – just move those items to the next day's list.

Another good organizational trick of the new mother trade: keep a running list of baby gifts and their givers as they're received. You think you'll remember that your cousin Jessica sent that darling blue-and-yellow sweater set, but after the seventeenth sweater set has arrived, that memory may be dimmed. And check off each gift on the list as the thank-you note is sent, so you don't end up sending two notes to Aunt Karen and Uncle Bob and none to your boss.

Get simplified. Take every shortcut you can find. Make friends with frozen vegetables, your local salad bar, the pizza delivery guy.

Get a jump on tomorrow tonight. Once you've bedded baby down each night and before you collapse onto the sofa for that well-deserved rest, summon up the strength to take care of a few chores so that you'll have a head start on the next morning. Restock the changing bag. Measure out the coffee for the coffee pot. Sort the laundry. Lay out clothes for yourself and the baby. In ten minutes or so, you'll accomplish what would take you at least three times as long with the baby awake. And you'll be able to sleep better (when she lets you) knowing that you'll have less to do in the morning.

Get good at doubling up. Become a master of multitasking. Learn to do two things or more at once. Wash the dishes or chop vegetables for the salad while you're on the phone. Balance your chequebook or fold the laundry while you catch the news on TV. Check your e-mail or help an older child with homework while breastfeeding. There still won't be enough hours in the day, but this way you may only crave 36 instead of 48.

Get out. Plan an outing every day – even if it's just a walk to the shops. The change of pace and space will allow you to return somewhat refreshed.

Get to expect the unexpected. The best-laid plans of mothers often (actually *very* often) go astray. Baby's all bundled up for an outing, the changing bag is ready, your coat is on, and suddenly the distinct gurglings of a bowel movement can be heard from under all baby's gear. Off comes coat, bunting, nappy – ten minutes lost from an already tight schedule. To allow for the unexpected, build extra time into everything you do.

Get the joke. If you can laugh, you're less likely to cry. So keep your sense of humour, even in the face of total disorder and utter clutter; it'll help you keep your sanity, too.

Get used to it. Living with a baby means living with a certain amount of mayhem most of the time. And as baby grows, so will the challenge of keeping the mayhem in check. No sooner will you scoop the bricks back into their canister than she will dump them back out again. As fast as you can wipe mashed peas off the wall behind her high chair, she can redecorate with strained peaches. You'll put safety latches on the kitchen cabinets, and she'll figure out how to open them, covering the floor with your pots and pans.

And remember, when you finally pack your last child off to college, your house will be immaculate once again – and so empty and quiet that you'll be ready to welcome the pandemonium (and dirty laundry) they bring home in the holidays.

NOT BEING IN CONTROL

'For the last ten years I've run my business, my household and every other aspect of my life quite effectively. But ever since I came home with my little boy, I can't seem to get control of anything.'

There's been a coup in your home – as there is in the homes of all new parents. And the man who would be king in your castle isn't a man at all, he's a newborn baby boy. As powerless as he may seem, he is quite capable of disrupting your life and usurping the control you once had over it. He won't care if you customarily take your shower at 7:15 and your coffee at 8:05, if you favour a leisurely cocktail at 6:30 and dinner promptly at 7:00, if you enjoy dancing into the wee hours on Saturday night and sleeping luxuriously late the morning after. He'll demand feedings and attention when he wants them, without first checking your schedule to see if it's convenient. Which means your routine and many of your old, comfortable ways may have to be abandoned for several months, if not several years. The only schedule that will matter, particularly in these early weeks, is his. And that schedule, at first, may have no discernible pattern you can latch onto. Days, and especially nights, may pass as a blur. You may often feel more like an automaton (and if you're breastfeeding, a milk cow) than a person, more servant than master, wielding not the slightest measure of power over your life.

What to do? Hand the sceptre over graciously – at least for now. With the passage of time, as you grow more competent, confident and comfortable in your new role and, as your baby becomes more capable and less dependent, you will regain some (though not all) of the control you've lost.

In other words, you might as well accept the fact that your life will never be quite the same. But then, would you really want it to be?

NOT FEELING COMPETENT

'I really thought I could handle it. But the moment our little girl was handed to me, all my confidence dissolved. I feel as though I'm a total flop as a parent.'

Though the ultimate rewards of parenthood are greater than those of any other occupation, the stresses and challenges are greater, too – particularly at the beginning. After all, there's no other job in the world that thrusts you, without previous training or experience and without supervisory guidance, into fully responsible eighteen-to-twenty-hour shifts. What's more, there's no other job that offers as little feedback during the first weeks to let you know how you're doing. The only person who could possibly give you a job evaluation is a largely unresponsive, unpredictable and uncooperative newborn who doesn't smile when she's satisfied,

doesn't hug you when she's grateful, sleeps when she should be eating, cries when she should be sleeping, hardly even looks at you for more than a couple of minutes, and doesn't seem to know you from the next-door neighbour. A sense of satisfaction in a job completed may seem totally absent. Virtually everything you do – changing nappies, making formula, washing baby clothes, feeding baby – is quickly undone and/or needs redoing almost immediately. It's not surprising that you feel like a flop at your new profession.

Even for a seasoned pro the postnatal period is no picnic. For a novice, it can seem like a never-ending series of blunders, bumbles, mishaps and misadventures. Yet there are better times in sight (though you may have trouble envisioning them); competence at parenting is closer than you'd now imagine. In the meantime, keep these points in mind:

You're unique. And so is your baby. What works for another parent and baby may not work for you, and vice versa. Avoid making comparisons.

You're not the only one. More first-time parents than ever before have had no previous experience with newborns. Even among those who've had some, very few manage to glide through those first weeks as though they'd been doing it all their lives. Remember, parents are not born, they are made on the job. Hormones do not magically transform newly delivered women into able parents; time, trial and error, and experience do. If you have the opportunity of sharing your worries with other new parents, you will be reminded that though you are unique, your concerns as a new parent are not.

You need to be babied. In order to be an effective parent, you've got to baby

WHEN YOU'RE ON YOUR OWN

Whether you are a single mother (or father) by choice or by circumstance, whether you're on your own for the foreseeable future or just until your spouse returns from a long business trip or ships back from overseas duty, being the sole parent – and possibly the sole provider – for your baby is at least twice the work, twice the responsibility and twice the challenge of shared parenting. It can also be isolating, especially when you see couples caring for their babies together (he's closing up the pushchair while she carries the baby onto the bus), while you care for yours on your own (you're struggling to close up the pushchair while you carry the baby onto the bus). It can be lonely, particularly when it's two in the morning and you've been walking the floor with a crying baby for an hour and a half, with no one to hand him or her off to. And it can be frustrating when you read magazines and books (including this one) that offer tip after tip about lightening a new mother's load by 'depending on dad'.

The fact is that there are no easy tips for how to lighten a new mother's load when she's carrying the load by herself. The tips in this chapter apply doubly to you. Also, check out the numerous online resources available for single parents, including: www.oneparentfamily.org.uk; and www.gingerbread.org.uk.

Remember, too, that though being your child's only parent can be twice as challenging, it can also be twice as rewarding, with a bond between the two of you that is at least twice as strong and twice as special. In other words, more than worth that extra effort.

---

yourself a little. Tell yourself, as your own parent would, that you need to eat right and get enough rest, particularly in the postnatal period, and that moderate exercise to keep your energy level up and a bit of relaxation now and then to elevate your spirits are important, too.

You're both only human. There's no such thing as a perfect parent, or a perfect baby – so try to keep your expectations realistic, taking into account that you're both only human.

Your instincts can be trusted. In many cases, even the greenest parent often knows more about what's right for her baby than friends and relatives or baby books.

You needn't go it alone. Realize that you won't always know what to do – no parent does – and that asking for guid-

ance doesn't mean that you're short on instincts, just that you're short on experience. There's a lot of good advice and comforting support out there you can benefit from. Judiciously sift through information acquired from others, test out what seems right for you and your baby, toss what doesn't.

Your mistakes can help you grow, and they won't count against you. Nobody's going to fire you if you make mistakes (though on a particularly bad day you may wish that you could quit). Mistakes are an important part of learning to be a parent. You can expect to continue making them at least until your children are off to college. And if at first you don't succeed, just try, try something else (the baby only screams louder when you rock her in your arms side to side, so try holding her over your shoulder and swaying back and forth).

Your love won't always come easy. It's sometimes difficult to relate lovingly to a newborn – a basically unresponsive creature who takes but doesn't offer much in return (except an endless supply of spit-up and dirty nappies). It may be some time before you stop feeling like a fool babbling in baby talk and crooning off-key lullabies and before you can hug and kiss this tiny bundle naturally and unself-consciously. But it will happen.

Your baby is forgiving. Forget to change her nappy before a feeding. Let soap drip into her eye during her shampoo. Get a T-shirt stuck halfway over her head. Your baby will forgive and forget these and a multitude of other minor mishaps – as long as she gets the message that you love her loud and clear.

The ultimate rewards are unparalleled. Think of parenthood as a long-term project, with results that will be unfolding in the months and years ahead. When you see your baby's first smile, watch her reach for a toy, laugh out loud, pull herself up, say 'Mummy, I love you', you will know that your efforts have paid off, and that you have indeed accomplished something very special.

DOING THINGS RIGHT

'I'm so worried that I'm going to make a wrong move that I spend hours researching every little decision I make about my baby. I want to make sure I do everything right for her, but I'm driving myself and my spouse crazy.'

No parent can do *everything* right. In fact, all parents make their share of mistakes – mostly little ones, occasionally bigger ones – in raising their children. And it's through making a few mistakes

and learning from them (at least some of the time) that you become a more effective parent. Keep in mind, too, that since all parents and babies are different, what's right on target for one set may in some cases be way off base for another.

Even reading all the literature and consulting all the experts won't always give you all the answers. Getting to know your baby and yourself and learning to trust your instincts and good sense is often a better route to making decisions you both can live with. It's true, for example, that some babies love to be snugly swaddled, but if yours cries whenever she's wrapped up tightly in a swaddling blanket, consider that she would rather be free to kick up her heels. The experts may tell you young babies like to listen to high-pitched coos, but if yours clearly responds more positively to a deep voice, come down an octave. Trust yourself and your baby – you may not always be right, but you won't go too far wrong.

ACHES AND PAINS

'I've been having backaches and a nagging pain in my neck, arm and shoulder ever since our son was born.'

New parents don't have to hang out at the local gym to do their share of weight lifting – all they have to do is carry a growing baby and an overstuffed changing bag around all day. But in addition to building muscles, carting this heavy load can also trigger a variety of aches and pains in the neck, arms, wrists, fingers, shoulders and backs of mums and dads – especially if it's done the wrong way.

As long as you remain your son's major source of transport and comfort, you'll be pumping plenty of baby. To minimize the aches and pains:

◆ Take it off. If you haven't yet taken off all of your pregnancy weight, try, gradually, to do so now. Excess weight puts unnecessary strain on your back.

◆ Work out. Exercise regularly, concentrating on those exercises that strengthen the abdominal muscles (which support the back) and those that strengthen the arms.

◆ Assume a comfortable position for feeding baby. Don't slouch, and be sure your back is supported – if you can't slide all the way to the back of the chair, tuck a pillow behind you. Use pillows or armrests, as needed, to support your arms as you hold baby and direct breast or bottle. And don't cross your legs.

◆ Lift and bend smart. You'll be doing more lifting (of baby and baby paraphernalia) and bending (to pick up all those toys strewn on the floor) than ever before. It pays to do it the right way. When lifting baby, put the weight of the load on your arms and legs rather than on your back. Bend at the knees, with your feet shoulder-width apart, not at the waist.

◆ Sleep smart, too. Sleep on a firm mattress, or put a board under an overly soft one. A mattress that sags in the middle will have you sagging, too. Lie on your back or side with your knees bent.

◆ Get a step up. Don't stretch to reach high places; stand on a ladder or footstool instead.

◆ Listen to your mother. Remember all the times she told you, 'Don't slouch. Stand up straight!' You'd be smart to follow that advice now, being extra conscious of your posture. Walk, sit, and lie with your buttocks tucked under, abdomen tilted inwards (this is called a 'pelvic tilt'), and keep your shoulders back instead of slouched.

◆ Make adjustments. If you push a pram or pushchair, be sure the handles are at a comfortable height for you. If they aren't, see if you can have them adjusted, or if they're too short, buy extenders.

◆ Do a lot of switching. If one shoulder starts to ache from the weight of the changing bag, periodically switch shoulders, carry the bag in the crook of your arm for a while, or opt for a backpack. Switch baby from arm to arm, too, rather than always relying on the same one. Instead of walking the floor all night with your colicky baby, alternate time spent rocking in your arms to time spent rocking in an infant swing.

◆ Use a baby carrier or sling – whichever seems easier on your back – to give your aching arms a break.

◆ Turn on the heat. A heating pad or a warm bath can spell relief from muscle discomfort and spasms.

◆ Take a seat. Try not to stand for long periods of time. If you must stand, keep one foot on a low stool with your knee bent. Use a small rug as a cushion underfoot if you're often standing on a hard-surfaced floor.

RETURN OF MENSTRUATION

'I weaned my daughter two months ago and I still haven't had a period. Shouldn't I have by now?'

There aren't any sure formulas for calculating when a nursing mother will resume her periods – and there's a wide range of normal. Some women produce

TIME TO STOCK UP ON TAMPONS?

While there's no telling for sure when your menstruation holiday will end, there are some averages to consider. The earliest a breastfeeding mum might expect her period is six weeks postnatal, though such an early resumption is rare. Up to 30 per cent will get their first period within three months after delivery, just over 50 per cent by the six-month mark. Still others won't be pulling the tampons out of storage until closer to the end of the first year, and a few who continue breastfeeding will be period free well into the second year. Though some women have a sterile first cycle (without an egg being released), the longer that first period is delayed, the more likely it will be a fertile one.

On average, woman who don't breast-feed will find themselves back on schedule sooner. The first period may occur as early as four weeks after delivery (though, again, this is less common); 40 per cent will resume their cycle by six weeks postnatal, 65 per cent by twelve weeks, and 90 per cent by twenty-four weeks.

enough oestrogen to begin menstruating again even before they've weaned their babies, occasionally as early as six weeks to three months postnatal. But others, particularly those who have breastfed for a long time, nursed exclusively or had irregular menstrual periods before pregnancy, will have a holiday from menstruation until several months after they've weaned. Chances are you're just lucky enough to fall into this group. Be sure, however, that you're eating enough and haven't been losing weight too quickly; strenuous dieting, especially when combined with strenuous exercise, can temporarily stall the return of the menstrual cycle. And mention the situation to your doctor at your next checkup, which will probably be scheduled some time after the sixth month postnatal. (See box, above, for more on postnatal periods.)

Keep in mind that just because you're not getting your period doesn't mean you can't get pregnant (it's possible to ovulate before your first postnatal period). See page 697 for information on more reliable means of contraception.

'My first period after the pregnancy was really heavy and painful. Can something be wrong?'

Your cycle's been on hiatus for probably a year or longer, so it's not surprising it has a few kinks to work out on its return. In fact, most women find that their first postnatal period is different from pre-pregnancy periods. Often it's heavier, crampier and longer, though occasionally it's lighter and shorter. Cycles may be irregular, too, for at least a few months. Once your body gets used to ovulating and menstruating again – and once hormone levels finally get back to pre-pregnancy levels – your periods will almost certainly return to business as usual. One plus you can probably look forward to: many women find their periods eventually become less painful and less heavy after they've delivered a baby.

IT'S KEGEL TIME AGAIN

Sure, doing Kegels during pregnancy was a great way to get your perineum in shape for delivery. But there even more reasons to keep your Kegel routine up now that you've delivered – starting, in fact, as soon as you've delivered. These perineum-tightening exercises firm up muscles left slack by delivery, increase circulation to the area (promoting healing), prevent and/or treat urinary and faecal incontinence, and ease haemorrhoids.

In case you've never done a Kegel before or you need a refresher, it's simple:

Firmly tense the muscles that you use to stop the flow of urine. Hold for as long as you can, up to eight or ten seconds, then slowly release the muscles and relax for several seconds. Repeat. Do at least 25 repetitions at various times during the day, while sitting, standing, lying on your back, making love (a great way to mix business with pleasure), queuing at the checkout, talking on the phone, checking e-mail, changing baby's nappy, taking a bath . . . basically any time is Kegel time!

URINARY INCONTINENCE

'Ever since my second child was born, I find that I leak a bit of urine when I cough or laugh or strain to lift something.'

Sounds like stress incontinence, a common symptom in women after childbirth – particularly those who've had more than one child. Annoying, messy and often embarrassing, postnatal stress incontinence is generally a direct result of labour and delivery, when the connective tissues and muscles that support the bladder and urethra are stretched and weakened, allowing urine to leak out whenever the bladder is stressed (as when you cough or sneeze). Pelvic nerves may also be damaged from labour and delivery, compounding the problem.

The good news is that urinary incontinence is usually temporary (though it may last a few months or even longer) and treatable (so you won't have to buy nappies for both you and your baby). Here are some tips to help you regain bladder control:

♦ Do your Kegels. Spreading out Kegel exercises over the course of a day every day for a couple of months (see box, above) may help to strengthen the muscles in the vaginal wall and eliminate the problem. Start off by doing sets of ten, three to four times a day, and work your way up to more. Biofeedback or electrical stimulation may help make Kegel exercises more effective; ask your doctor.

♦ Eat right. Avoid bladder irritants, such as caffeinated beverages, alcohol, carbonated drinks, citrus drinks and spicy foods.

♦ Don't smoke. Nicotine acts directly on the muscles of the bladder, causing them to contract. Smokers also tend to cough often, leading to more urine leakage.

♦ Take off the weight. Too much weight on the bladder can stress the pelvic floor and cause incontinence. If you're overweight, try to shed it.

♦ Don't hold it in. Urinate frequently so your bladder doesn't get too full.

While you're waiting for some improvement, use maxipads or panty liners to absorb the flow of urine. If incontinence continues, consult your doctor. In severe cases, surgery may be needed to remedy the condition.

REGAINING YOUR FIGURE

'I knew I wouldn't be ready for a bikini right after delivery, but I still look six months pregnant a few weeks later.'

Back when you were pregnant, looking the part was half the fun. Remember the thrill of buying your first pair of maternity jeans? The excitement of watching your belly swell from a scarcely noticeable (if you stuck your stomach out) bulge to a larger-than-life watermelon? And the momentous day when you could finally walk down the street confident that everyone you passed could plainly see that you were pregnant and not just plump?

Once delivery day has come and gone, however, looking pregnant quickly loses its appeal. No woman wants to look as though she's still toting a baby in her belly once she's toting a newborn in her arms.

Though childbirth produces more rapid initial weight loss than any diet you'll find on the bestseller list (an average of 5.5 kg/12 lb at delivery), few women are satisfied with the results. Particularly after they catch a glimpse of their postnatal silhouettes in a mirror and see that they still look distressingly pregnant. The good news is that most are able to pack away their pregnancy jeans within the first month or two. The bad news: the old jeans may not fit the way they used to for a while longer.

How quickly you return to your pre-pregnant shape and weight will depend on how much weight you put on during pregnancy – and where it settled. Women who gained the recommended amount of weight on a good diet and at a gradual and steady pace may be able to shed it all, without dieting, by the end of the second month or so postnatal. On the other hand, those whose gain far exceeded that magic number – particularly if they gained the weight in uneven spurts or on a steady diet of junk food – may find the return to pre-pregnancy shape more challenging.

No matter how much you gained and how you gained it, sticking to the Postnatal Diet now should lead to slow, steady weight loss – with no loss of energy. Mums who do not breastfeed can, once the six-week postnatal recovery period has passed, move on to a sensible, well-balanced reducing diet to drop whatever weight remains. Breastfeeding mothers who aren't losing weight can reduce calorie intake by a couple hundred a day and increase activity to encourage weight loss without cutting into milk production. Though some won't manage to lose all of the weight while they're nursing, most will be able to take off any remaining excess once they wean their babies.

Of course, one of the major reasons why most women continue to look a little pregnant well after delivery – and sometimes even after they've lost all the pregnancy weight – doesn't have anything to do with weight gain. It has to do with stretched-out abdominal muscles and skin (see the next question).

GETTING BACK INTO SHAPE

'I've lost all my pregnancy weight, but I still don't look like I did before I got pregnant. How can I get my body back to the way it was before?'

For many women it's not pregnancy weight that keeps them looking pregnant; most is shed without much effort in the first six weeks postnatal. Rather, it's stretched-out abdominal muscles that stand between those new mothers and their old pre-pregnancy profiles.

Unfortunately, simply waiting it out won't work. Pregnancy-stretched muscles regain some of their tone as time goes by, but won't ever return to their pre-pregnancy condition without exercise. Leave your tummy muscles to their own devices, and you'll find that their sagging increases as the years pass, and with each baby you deliver.

Postnatal exercise will do more than help you pull your tummy in. Abdominal routines will improve general circulation and reduce the risk of back problems (which new mothers are more susceptible to, simply because of all the baby toting they do), varicose veins, leg cramps, swelling of ankles and feet, and the formation of clots in blood vessels. Perineal exercises (Kegels) will help you avoid stress incontinence (leaking of urine), which sometimes occurs after childbirth as well as dropping, or prolapse, of the pelvic organs. Plus, they'll tighten your perineum so that making love eventually will be as good or better than ever. Regular exercise will also promote healing of your uterine, abdominal and pelvic muscles, hastening their return to normal and preventing further weakening from inactivity, as well as help your pregnancy-and-delivery-loosened joints tighten back up (or nearly so). If excess weight is a problem, exercise will help you shed it (you can burn the 100 calories of a baked potato in just 20 minutes of brisk walking, even faster if you're power walking). Finally, exercise can provide psychological benefits, improving your ability to handle stress and to relax, while minimizing the baby blues.

If you have the time, opportunity and inclination, sign up for a postnatal exercise class (you can usually bring baby along), or buy a postnatal exercise book or video and fit an at-home programme into your schedule (baby will probably love watching you jump around). If you're currently too exhausted to contemplate an intense exercise programme, regularly doing just a few simple exercises aimed at your particular problem areas (such as tummy, thighs, buttocks) can also get you back into shape. Add a daily brisk walk or other aerobic activity (or combine both, as with pushchair exercise) to your agenda and you will have put together an adequate exercise programme. Before you begin any exercise programme, of course, be sure you have your doctor's okay.

Keep these tips in mind when exercising postnatal:

◆ Stick to a schedule. Exercise done only sporadically is useless and thus a waste of the time you're so short on to begin with. Muscle-toning exercises (leg lifts, sit-ups and pelvic tilts, for example) are best done daily in short takes; two or three 5-minute sessions a day will tone you up better than one 20-minute workout. Once you begin doing aerobic exercises (brisk walking, jogging, bicycling and swimming, for example), aim for at least three 20-minute sessions of sustained activity a week – though 40 minutes four or five times weekly may be a better goal for strengthening bones and preventing osteoporosis later in life.

◆ Don't rush. Muscle-toning exercises are most effective when done slowly and deliberately, with adequate recovery time between repetitions.

A PUSHCHAIR EXERCISE

You've got trainers? You've got a baby? You've got a pushchair? You've got all it takes to try pushchair exercise – a programme designed for new mums. Pushchair exercising is as easy as taking your baby out for a walk in the pushchair; no other equipment is necessary. Begin by strolling for about five minutes at a slow pace, to warm up your muscles. Then work your way to a brisk pace. Because you're pushing, you'll be working harder (especially as your baby gets heavier) than if you were walking without baby or with baby in a carrier. You can also use the pushchair (and the baby) as a resistance apparatus, allowing for numerous stretching and muscle-building exercises. Another plus: the motion will soothe a colicky baby. For more information, check out the websites www.strollercize.com or www.strollerstrides.com.

It's during the recovery periods that muscle buildup occurs.

◆ Start slowly if you haven't exercised recently or are doing unfamiliar exercises. Do only a few repetitions the first day, and increase the number gradually over the next week or two. Don't do more than the recommended amount, even if you feel great. Stop your workout as soon as you begin to tire.

◆ Avoid competitive sports until you get your doctor's okay to participate.

◆ Because your joints are still unstable and your connective tissue lax, avoid jumping; rapid changes of direction; jerky, bouncy or jarring motions; and deep flexion or extension of joints. Also avoid knee-chest exercises, full sit-ups and double leg lifts during the first six weeks postnatal.

◆ Do muscle-toning exercises on a wood floor or tightly carpeted surface to reduce shock.

◆ Do five minutes of warm-ups (very light stretching exercises, slow walking

EASING BACK INTO SEX

Sure, maybe all you really need is each other – and five uninterrupted minutes – to make love in the postnatal period. But to make love and actually enjoy it, taking the following steps may help:

Lubricate. Altered hormone levels during the postnatal period (which may not normalize in the breastfeeding mother until her baby is partially or totally weaned) can make the vagina uncomfortably dry. Use a lubricating product (like K-Y jelly) or lubricating vaginal suppositories until your own natural secretions return.

Medicate. If necessary, ask your doctor to prescribe a topical ooestrogen cream to lessen pain and tenderness.

Warm up. Assuming you have the time, indulge in plenty of foreplay. Think of it as an appetizer that will whet your appetite for the main course.

Loosen up. Try a massage, a shower for two, or anything else that can help you unwind and relax. Or try a glass of wine to take the edge off (but be aware that too much alcohol can interfere with sexual desire and performance).

Exercise. Kegel exercises (see box, page 686) will help to tone the pelvic muscles, which are associated with vaginal sensation and response during intercourse.

Vary positions. Side-to-side or woman-on-top positions allow more control of depth of penetration and put less pressure on a sore perineum. Experiment to find what works best for you.

---

or stationary biking against low resistance) before you begin exercising. Cool down at the end of each session with some gentle stretching exercises, but to avoid damaging still-loose joints, don't stretch to the maximum for the first six weeks.

◆ Get up slowly to avoid dizziness from a sudden drop in blood pressure and, to equalize circulation, keep your legs moving for a few moments (by walking, for example) when you stand up.

◆ Once you begin doing aerobic exercises, be careful not to exceed your target heart rate. Ask your doctor what that is.

◆ Drink plenty of fluids before and after exercising, and if the weather is very hot or you are perspiring a great deal, have something to drink as you

go, as well. Water's the best sports drink; avoid sugar-sweetened beverages, including those marketed especially for athletes.

◆ Don't use your baby as an excuse for not exercising. Most babies love lying on mummy's chest during a calisthenics session; snuggling in a baby carrier while she pedals a stationary bike, works a rowing machine or skiing machine, or walks on a treadmill; and being pushed in the pram or pushchair while mummy walks or jogs. But don't bounce an infant around in a baby carrier while you jog.

There are, alas, some postnatal body changes that will stay with you no matter how many sit-ups and leg lifts you do – and how carefully you monitor your diet. These changes – which may be imperceptible or significant enough to increase a shoe or dress size – are largely due to the loosening of the joints during pregnancy (to make room for delivery) and their tightening up again (though not necessarily in exactly the same configuration) postnatal. Women who have had Caesareans may also note a slight alteration in the shape of the abdomen that won't yield to exercise.

FITTING SEX IN

'We've got the go-ahead on sex – but sex is the last thing I feel like doing now.'

Is the honeymoon over? Has the romance faded now that there's a little fledgling sharing your love nest? Will you ever feel that heady rush of abandon in bed again? For that matter, will you ever stop feeling tired long enough to feel anything else at all?

For most women, even those who lived highly memorable love lives before delivery, doubts that any kind of sexual relationship with their spouse will ever resume, at least on a regular basis, are nagging and numerous. The fact is, many couples find the postnatal period (and sometimes a several-month stretch following it) a sexual wasteland.

There's no shortage of reasons why you may not feel like making love now, among them:

♦ Readjusting hormones can zap sexual desire and response during the post-natal period, especially if you're breastfeeding.

♦ Your libidos (yours and your spouse's) usually lose when they compete with sleepless nights, exhausting days, dirty nappies, and the endless needs of a demanding baby.

♦ Fear of pain, of your vagina being stretched out, or of becoming preg-

> ## SLIGHT SPOTTING ALERT
>
> Occasionally, a couple of months postnatal, a new mother notes very slight spotting after intercourse. This may be due to the growth of skin flaps at the site of an incision or tear. These skin flaps are easily repaired. Report such spotting to your doctor.

nant again too soon may nip any romantic buds before they blossom.

♦ A painful first intercourse postnatal can make the thought of further attempts unappealing. Pain on subsequent tries can make lovemaking extremely awkward and uncomfortable. Such pain may continue for a while even after the perineum is healed.

♦ Discomfort because of decreased vaginal lubrication, a result of hormonal changes during the postnatal period, can also dull desire. The problem usually lasts longer in breast-feeding mothers, but can continue for as long as six months, even in those who are not breastfeeding.

♦ Uneasiness over the sudden lack of privacy, particularly if baby's in the room with you, can help you lose that loving feeling. Even if your head believes what you've heard – that your baby will be oblivious to and unaffected by your lovemaking – your body may balk at the idea.

♦ Mothering may be taking all the loving and nurturing you have to give right now, and you may sometimes be unable to summon any up for anyone else, even your spouse.

◆ Breastfeeding may be satisfying your needs for intimacy (without your realizing it), making you less interested in encounters of the sexual kind.

◆ Leaking of breast milk, stimulated by sexual foreplay, may make either you or your spouse uncomfortable, physically as well as psychologically. Or, with your breasts suddenly serving such a nurturing purpose, you may have trouble with the idea of using them for pleasure.

◆ There are so many other things that you feel you need or want to do that sex may just seem less important now – if you have a spare half hour, lovemaking may not be at the top of the list (or on the list at all).

Still, there's promise for the future. You will surely live to love again, with as much pleasure and passion as ever – and maybe, because you have been brought closer by sharing parenthood, even more. In the meantime, there are many steps you can take to improve both interest and performance right now:

Don't rush it. It takes at least six weeks for your body to recover completely, and sometimes much longer – especially if you had a difficult vaginal delivery or a Caesarean section. Your hormonal balance may not return to normal until you resume menstruating, which, if you are breastfeeding, may not be for several months or more. Don't feel obligated to jump into bed until you feel up to it – mentally, emotionally and physically.

Express love in other ways. Intercourse isn't the only way for a couple to love. If you're not ready to go all the way, try cuddling and caressing in front of the TV, back rubs in bed and hand holding while strolling in the park

with baby. As for any couple getting acquainted (and you, after all, are becoming reacquainted physically), romance en route to the bed is an important first step. If you're not too pooped to pop, you can even try mutual masturbation. But some evenings, there may be nothing more satisfying than the intimacy that is shared lying in each other's arms.

Expect some discomfort. Many women are surprised and disheartened to find that postnatal intercourse can really hurt. If you've had stitches, you may indeed experience some degree of pain or discomfort (ranging from mild to severe) for weeks, even months, after the tissues have outwardly healed. You may have pain with intercourse, though probably less of it, if you delivered vaginally, perineum intact – and even if you had a Caesarean. To minimize pain, try the tips in the Easing Back into Sex box, page 690.

Don't expect perfection. Don't count on perfectly orchestrated orgasms at your very first return engagement. Many usually orgasmic women don't have orgasms for several weeks or even longer when they start making love again. But with time, caring and patience, the thrill does return and sex becomes as satisfying as ever (maybe more, if you've been faithful with your Kegels!).

If you can't beat baby's schedule, work around it. Falling into each other's arms when and where the spirit moves may no longer be possible. Instead, you may have to set your sexual watches according to that spirited little alarm clock in the cot. Baby is napping at 3 o'clock on Saturday afternoon; drop everything and head for the bedroom. Or if the little angel has been predictably sleeping from 7 to 10 every evening, plan ahead for a romantic interlude. If he or she wakes up crying just as your evening is reaching a climax, try to see the humour in the situation. (If you really, really concentrate, you may be able to finish up while you keep your little coitus interrupter waiting for a couple of minutes.) Should sexual encounters with your spouse continue to be less frequent for a while (perhaps even for a long while), strive for quality rather than quantity.

Keep your priorities straight. If making love is important to you, reserve energy for it by cutting corners elsewhere (in areas that won't affect your family's physical or emotional well-being, like housekeeping). If you spend your entire day at full throttle, you won't have the strength left to do anything in bed but close your eyes.

Talk about it. A good sexual relationship is built on trust, understanding and communication. If, for instance, you're too exhausted one night from your 24-hour baby-care shift to feel sexy, don't beg off with a headache. Instead, tell it like it is. If your spouse has been sharing baby-care responsibilities from the beginning, he's very likely to understand (he may, in fact, be too fathered out some nights himself). If he hasn't, this may be the time to explain the many reasons, including this one, why he should be.

Communicate, too, about problems like a dry vagina or pain during intercourse. Let your spouse know what hurts, what feels good, what you'd rather put off until next time.

Don't worry about it. The more you worry about a lack of libido, the less libido you're likely to have. So face the facts of postnatal life, relax and take your sexual relationship one night at a time, confident that the romance will return to your life.

Stretched Vagina

'It seems like my vagina is roomier than before I delivered, and making love is less satisfying for both of us.'

Most women come out of vaginal deliveries roomier than when they went in. Often, the change isn't significant enough to be noticed by either partner. Sometimes, as when conditions were previously too cramped for comfort, it's welcomed. Occasionally, however, a vaginal delivery can leave a woman who was 'just right' before stretched out enough to markedly decrease the pleasure she and her spouse experience during intercourse.

The passing of time may help tighten things up a bit, and so can keeping up with your Kegels. Repeat these multipurpose muscle toners as many times as you can during the day; get into the habit of doing them while you're cooking, watching TV, breastfeeding or reading – even during intercourse.

Very rarely, the muscles don't tighten up satisfactorily. If six months have passed since delivery and you still feel that you're too slack, discuss with your doctor the possibility of surgical repair to snug things up. The procedure is a minor one, but it can make a major difference in your love life.

The State of Your Romance

'My spouse and I are both so busy – with our jobs, our new son, the house – that we rarely find any time for each other. When we do, we're too tired to make the most of it.'

The three that baby makes isn't necessarily a crowd, but caring for that baby can crowd your days and nights so much that you feel as though you have no time left for the company of two. And though it's true that your relationship with your spouse is the most important in your life (babies grow up into children, who grow up and move away from home, but your mate will hopefully be yours into old age), it's also true that it's the easiest in your life to take for granted. Neglect your baby, neglect your jobs, neglect your home, and the consequences would be clear and swift. But the results of neglecting a marriage are often not apparent at first. Still, they can erode a relationship before the partners even realize it.

So start giving your relationship its due. Make a conscious effort to keep the love lights glowing or, if they seem to have flickered out, to rekindle them. Rethink your priorities and reorganize your time in any way you have to, but free some up to spend alone together. For instance, consider putting your baby on a reasonably early-to-bed schedule so that you can settle back for some quality time with each other. Share a leisurely late dinner (no TV, no phone calls, no reading the paper or checking e-mail and, with any luck, no crying baby allowed). A glass of wine may help you unwind (unless it leads to three or four, which may unravel you completely). Candlelight and soft background music will help set the romantic mood.

Every such evening doesn't need to culminate in sex. Indeed, sex may turn out to be a relatively rare treat in the exhausting early months – it may even be a treat you won't be very interested in for a while. Right now, verbal intercourse can be even more beneficial to your relationship than the sexual variety. But resist the temptation to talk exclusively about the baby; that would defeat the purpose of your interlude.

Schedule a romantic night out on the town once a week (if it's the same night each week, with a standing sitter,

you're both less likely to find a reason why you can't make it). Have dinner, see a movie, visit friends or do whatever it is you enjoy doing together most. Also try to arrange for a baby-free hour or two on weekends to pursue a shared interest. Hire a sitter, swap sitting time with a neighbour or enlist a grandparent.

If you can't seem to squeeze a regular rendezvous into your current schedule, it's time to start making your relationship a top priority.

'Ever since our son was born, I've felt that my husband sees me only as the mother of his child, not as a lover.'

Tiny babies can bring some huge changes when they appear on the family scene. From how much (or how little) you sleep to how you spend your money and your free time, to how much money and free time you have, having a baby impacts nearly every aspect of your life, including your romantic life. Almost every couple finds that the dynamics of their relationship undergo significant shifts as they adjust to being both a twosome and a threesome.

Just as you're adjusting to becoming a mother, your mate is adjusting to becoming a father. With so much energy focused on that challenging transition into parenthood, it's not surprising that the romantic side of your relationship has been put on hold. But while many of the changes you've noticed around the house are permanent – at least until baby grows up and leaves the nest – the change in your relationship is not. Once you're comfortable in your new roles as parents, you'll both be able to focus energy on reestablishing your old ones as lovers. Not only are the roles not mutually exclusive – you can be parents and lovers at the same time – but they're mutually beneficial. There's no better way to ensure that a child will grow up in a happy, intact home than by taking the time to nurture the romance that created that child in the first place.

That said, it's not easy to nurture romance when you're so busy nurturing a newborn – or to see each other as lovers when you're so busy learning how to be mothers and fathers. These tips, as well as those above, can help:

Make yourself feel like a woman. Yes, you're preoccupied with baby care – and that leaves you with very little time to care for yourself. But, let's face it, going three days without a shampoo or two days in the same spit-up-stained sweatshirt isn't going to put either one of you in the mood for romance. Spending a half hour perfecting your blow dry and another on your makeup obviously isn't a realistic goal when you're the mother of a newborn, but finding the time for a shampoo, a little mascara and lipstick (and maybe a lot of concealer), a dab of your favourite scent and some fresh clothes might be. Such efforts won't only make you look more attractive, they'll make you *feel* more attractive.

Make him feel like a man. Most new mothers transfer their focus from their partner to their baby, at least initially. That's good for the perpetuation of the species, but not so good for the perpetuation of the relationship. Make it a point to romance your spouse as you would like to be romanced. Hug him unexpectedly from behind while he's washing the dishes, squeeze his hand when he passes the baby shampoo, notice when he comes home with a new haircut, kiss him anytime (and anywhere) at all.

Make time for romance. Choose to share dinner after baby's down for the night, rather than eating on the run while you take turns walking the floor. Keep a bottle of massage oil and a few candles by the bed, and give each other a romantic rubdown after baby has conked out (and before you do). Establish a 'date night' once a week and use it to catch up on each other. Be impulsive, too, indulging in a bubble bath or grabbing a quickie when baby's napping.

THINKING ABOUT THE NEXT BABY

'My daughter is nearly a year old. We're definitely planning to have another child, but we're not sure how far apart to space them.'

Mother Nature notwithstanding, the decision of how many months or years to wait before getting pregnant again is a couple's alone to make, and different couples feel very differently on the subject. Some feel very strongly that they'd like to cluster their children together, one directly after the other. Others feel just as strongly that they'd like several years – or more – of breathing (and sleeping) room between deliveries. And the way couples feel about child spacing before they actually become parents ('Wouldn't it be great to have them just a year apart?') isn't necessarily the way they feel once the reality of endless nappy changes and sleepless nights sinks in ('Maybe we need a break before we try this again'.).

There aren't very many firm facts to help parents out in making their decision. Most experts agree that postponing conception for at least a year after baby number one allows a woman's body to recover fully from pregnancy and childbirth before beginning the reproductive cycle all over again. But that health issue aside, there's little evidence to show that there is an ideal spacing period between children.

PLANNING AHEAD

Thinking about expanding the family again? There are plenty of preconception steps you and your spouse can take to improve your chances of fertility success, as well as the odds of having a safe pregnancy and a healthy baby. For a complete list of tips, see chapter 21 of *What to Expect When You're Expecting.*

Researchers haven't found that spacing affects a child's intelligence or emotional development, the children's eventual relationship (which has more to do with their personalities than their age difference), or the parents' relationship.

The bottom line: it's up to you. The best time for you to add to your family is when you and your spouse feel your family is ready.

Still don't have a clue? There are many questions to ask yourself when deciding how close or how far apart to space your children:

Will I be able to handle the demands of two babies? Children under age three are high maintenance, requiring constant attention and care. If your second baby arrives before your oldest is two years old, you'll be doing double nappy duty, enduring endless sleepless nights and, if they're really close in age, dealing with the more difficult aspects of toddler behaviour (such as tantrums and negativity) in two toddlers at once. On the flip side, although caring for closely spaced children will probably leave you exhausted at first, once the first few years have passed, you'll have put those challenges behind you (unless you decide to start all over again with number three). Though your children won't necessarily be close just because

they're close in age, they're more likely – because of their developmental similarities – to be natural playmates for each other. Another convenience: they'll likely find the same toys, films, activities and holidays interesting.

Do I want to start all over again? Once you're in 'baby mode', it's sometimes easier to just stay that way, consolidating the years spent on baby care. The cot is set up, the baby wipes are in place, the pushchair isn't yet collecting dust in the attic and the safety gates are still up. Spacing children far apart requires you to reorient yourself to the demands of having a baby again, just when your oldest is independently off at school and you're getting your 'life' back in order. Of course, having a new baby a few years after the first allows you ample time to enjoy and shower attention on one child before the arrival of the next. And since the oldest most likely won't be at home all the time, you'll get that same opportunity to provide individual attention to your younger child.

Am I physically ready to go through a new pregnancy? Some women just don't feel ready to go through pregnancy again so soon, especially if their first pregnancy was difficult. Toting a young toddler while also carting around a watermelon-size belly isn't easy; neither is running after your newly mobile fifteen-month-old while you're doubled over in the bathroom with morning sickness. Also take into consideration your feelings about going from a pregnancy to breast-feeding to another pregnancy and breastfeeding again. You may decide that you'd like to give yourself a physical break – to experience a completely baby-free body again before resuming reproduction. On the other hand, women who thoroughly enjoy both pregnancy and breastfeeding may see no reason to postpone further bundles of joy. And parents who would prefer to have their children by a certain age or women who feel that the ticking of their biological clock doesn't give them time to wait, may opt for close spacing simply because it's their best option.

What is best for my children? There's certainly no consensus on this issue – and results can vary widely, depending on the children's temperament, the way sibling conflicts are resolved, the atmosphere around the home, and many more factors. For instance, if there is a very large gap in ages between siblings, they might grow up not feeling like siblings at all – or they might have a very special affection for each other. Siblings spaced far apart may experience less sibling rivalry than those closer in age, since the oldest sibling already has a life outside the home (school, sports, friends), may actually appreciate the new addition more, and may enjoy helping care for the baby. Or she may resent the responsibilities that often come with being the much older child.

If the gap is very small – less than two years – closeness in age won't necessarily guarantee closeness between your children. Because of their developmental similarities, they may be built-in playmates for each other, although they may also, because of their developmental similarities, be more likely to fight. The fact that they'll probably enjoy the same toys might be both a convenience (fewer toys to buy) and a potential nightmare (more tug-of-war over the toys). Having children close in age may minimize the adjustment of the oldest child to a new sibling; feelings of displacement are less common and less pronounced, since the oldest doesn't remember what it was like to be the 'only'. On the other hand, a very young older sibling may resent the sudden shortage of lap space – lap space she still very much needs.

What is best for my personality? If your temperament is easygoing, it may not matter if you've chosen a large gap or small one between children. Having two closely spaced children may not bother you in the least; neither might having to get back into baby mode again after a long hiatus. On the other hand, if you have a hard time dealing with chaos and clutter, a longer interval between children might be best.

How close in age are my siblings to me? The way you grew up may influence how you'd like your family to be structured. If you had a great experience growing up with a brother eighteen months older than you, you might wish the same for your children. If you hated that you went off to college when your younger sister was still in primary school, you may choose to have children closer in age. If you found yourself always fighting with your close-in-age sister, you may choose to space your own kids further apart.

BIRTH CONTROL

'I'm definitely not ready to have another baby yet. What are my options for birth control?'

Okay, maybe sex isn't the first thing on your minds these days – particularly as you spend yet another evening playing 'pass the crying baby' (rock and sing lullabies until your arms are aching and your voice is hoarse, pass the baby to your spouse, rest and repeat). Maybe it's the last thing on your mind most of the time. Yet there will come a night (or a Sunday afternoon when baby's napping) when you'll get the urge to sweep the dummies and burping cloths off the bed and sweep each other off your feet – when lust will return to your life, and passion will pick up where it left off pre-baby.

So be prepared. To avoid back-to-back pregnancies, you'll need to use some form of birth control as soon as you begin having sex again. And because you never know when the urge might first strike, it's good to have that birth control in hand (or by your bed) well in advance of that first amorous advance.

Unless you're a gambling woman (and one who doesn't mind becoming pregnant again right away), counting on breastfeeding to provide birth control is risky, to say the least. Although some women do not begin menstruating while they're nursing exclusively, many do. And since it's possible to ovulate and conceive before ever having that first postnatal period, some women who go that risky route end up going from pregnancy to pregnancy without menstruating in between. In other words, the fact that your periods have been suppressed by breastfeeding doesn't mean you're not capable of conception, or that you should consider yourself 'safe' without birth control.

So you'll need a more reliable form of contraception. Nearly every method of contraception is available to new mothers, though there are many factors (such as whether you're breastfeeding, how much childbirth has changed the size of your cervix) that must be considered before choosing which method is right for you. Don't automatically assume that the type of birth control you used before getting pregnant is the best one to return to postnatal. Your contraceptive needs and concerns may be different now than before. And with today's rapid advances in contraceptives, there may be new options open to you that weren't even on the market before you became pregnant. Be sure to read up on and discuss with your doctor all the birth-control methods

available before selecting the one that's right for you now.

Each of the following methods of birth control has its benefits and drawbacks. Deciding which will work best for you will depend on your gynecological history, your lifestyle, your doctor's recommendation, whether you want to become pregnant again in the future (and how certain you want to be about preventing pregnancy in the meantime), and your own feelings and circumstances. All are effective when used correctly and consistently, though some offer better results than others.

HORMONAL METHODS

Oral contraception. Available by prescription only, oral contraceptives (or 'the Pill') are among the most effective non-permanent methods of birth control, with a success rate of about 99.5 per cent (most failures are due to a user's missing a day or taking pills in the wrong order). Another plus: they allow for spontaneity in lovemaking.

There are two basic types of oral contraception: combination pills (which contain both oestrogen and progestin) and progestin-only pills (minipills). Both work by preventing ovulation and by thickening cervical mucus to keep sperm from reaching an egg, should one be released. They also prevent a fertilized egg from implanting in the uterus. The combination pills are slightly more effective in preventing pregnancy than the mini ones. For maximum efficacy, the minipills must be taken at the same time every day (the combination pills have a slightly longer window).

Some women experience side effects from oral contraception (which vary, depending on which pill they use), most commonly fluid retention; weight changes; nausea; breast tenderness; an increase or decrease in sex drive; hair loss; and menstrual irregularities

HORMONAL CONTRACEPTIVE WARNING SIGNS

The vast majority of women who use hormonal contraceptives do so with very few side effects, most of them mild. But because an occasional serious side effect occurs, you should be alert to the following warning signs, just in case.

If you are taking an oral contraceptive (or using any other hormonal contraceptive) and experience any of the following symptoms, call your doctor immediately. If your doctor can't be reached, go to the nearest A&E.

- ◆ sharp pains in the chest
- ◆ coughing up of blood
- ◆ sudden shortness of breath
- ◆ pain or tenderness in the calf or thigh
- ◆ severe headache
- ◆ dizziness or faintness
- ◆ muscle weakness or numbness
- ◆ disturbed speech
- ◆ sudden partial or complete loss of vision, blurred vision, flashing lights
- ◆ severe depression
- ◆ yellowing of the skin
- ◆ severe abdominal pain

(spotting, breakthrough bleeding or, rarely, amenorrhoea, or total cessation of menstruation). Less common are reports of depression, listlessness or tenseness. After the first few cycles of pill use, side effects often diminish or disappear completely. In general, today's oral contraceptives trigger fewer side effects than pills did years ago. Newer versions of the Pill deliver constant levels of oestrogen and a new type of progestin or use three different levels of oestrogen and progesto, to reduce bloating and PMS. Another option which might be especially appealing to women who aren't fond of that monthly flow, is Seasonale. It comes in a packet with 84 hormone pills and 7 inactive pills; women take the hormones for 12 weeks straight before taking a break for their period (which then only comes four times a year). Some women, however, experience more break-through bleeding with Seasonale than with monthly pills. (Most doctors agree that it's safe to take any monophasic pill continuously – by skipping the inactive pills – to avoid that monthly period.)

Women who are over age thirty-five and heavy smokers may be at increased risk of adverse side effects (such as blood clots, heart attack or stroke) from the Pill. The Pill may also be unsuitable for women with certain medical conditions, including a history of blood clots (thromboses), fibroids, diabetes, hypertension and certain types of cancers. Check with your doctor.

On the plus side, the Pill appears to protect against a whole host of conditions, including pelvic inflammatory disease, non-malignant breast disease, ectopic pregnancy, ovarian and uterine cancer, ovarian cysts and iron-deficiency anaemia (because menstrual flow is lighter); taking it may also reduce the risk of arthritis, possibly osteoporosis, and the incidence of menstrual cramping. Other benefits experienced by some women who take the Pill are diminished premenstrual tension, very regular periods and (with some) clearer skin. There is some controversy about how the Pill affects your breast cancer risk, so talk to your doctor about any concerns you may have.

If you're planning to have another baby, fertility may take longer to return if you're using the Pill than if you're using a barrier contraceptive. Ideally, you should switch to a barrier method (see page 703) about three months prior to the time you plan to try to conceive. About 80 per cent of women ovulate within the first three months after stopping the Pill, 95 per cent within a year.

If you decide to try the Pill, your doctor will help you determine which type and which dose is best for you, based on whether you're breastfeeding (any oral contraception containing oestrogen is not recommended during breastfeeding, but a progestin-only pill is safe to use), as well as on your menstrual cycle, weight, age and medical history. Making sure the Pill that's prescribed works the way it's supposed to is up to you. Take it regularly; if you miss even one pill, or if you have diarrhoea or vomiting (which can interfere with absorption of the Pill by your body), use back-up protection (such as a condom and spermicide) until your next period. See your doctor every six months to one year for monitoring of your health; report any problems or signs of complications that show up between visits, and be sure to inform anyone prescribing medication of any kind that you are on oral contraceptives (some herbs and medications, such as antibiotics, interact adversely with the Pill, making it less effective).

The Pill does not protect against sexually transmitted diseases, so be sure to supplement with a condom if there is a chance of contracting an STD from your partner. Because oral contraceptives increase the need for certain nutrients (though they decrease the need for others), take a daily vitamin supplement that contains B_6, B_{12}, C, riboflavin, zinc and folic acid while on the Pill.

Injections. Hormonal injection, such as Depo-Provera, is a highly effective method of birth control (with a success rate of 99.7 percent) that stops ovulation and thickens cervical mucus to keep sperm and egg from meeting. The injection, given in the arm or buttock, is effective for three months. Depo-Provera is a progestin-only injection, so it is safe for breastfeeding mothers.

As with oral contraception, side effects of hormonal injections can include irregular periods, weight gain and bloating. For some women, periods become fewer and lighter, and many women will have no periods after five years of using Depo-Provera. Other women might experience longer and heavier periods. And, like the Pill, the injection is not for every woman, depending on her specific health and medical condition.

The greatest advantage to the injection is that it prevents pregnancy for twelve weeks, and this can be compelling for someone who doesn't like to have to think about birth control or who often forgets to take a pill or insert a diaphragm. It also protects against endometrial and ovarian cancers. But there are disadvantages, too: having to return to your health-care provider every twelve weeks for another injection, the fact that the effects of the injection cannot be reversed immediately (if you suddenly want to become pregnant) and that it may take up to a year for fertility to return after discontinuing Depo-Provera.

Patch. The Ortho Evra patch, a matchbox-size adhesive patch, delivers the same hormones as the combination pill but in a patch form. Unlike oral contraceptives, the patch maintains a steady state of hormonal levels because it constantly and continuously delivers hormones through the skin. The patch is worn for one week at a time and is replaced on the same day of the week for three consecutive weeks. The fourth week is 'patch free', during which you'll get your period. The patch can be

IUD WARNING SIGNS

Most women who use an IUD find that it provides long-lasting, hassle-free birth control with few if any side effects. However, because the potential for complications exists, a woman wearing an IUD should call her doctor immediately if she experiences any of the following:

♦ cramping, tenderness, sharp pain in the pelvis or lower abdomen (after the discomfort of the initial insertion has passed)
♦ an urge to have a bowel movement associated with lower pelvis pain or cramping

♦ fainting
♦ painful intercourse
♦ pain that radiates down the legs, or pain in the shoulder
♦ a missed or delayed period, followed by spotty, scanty or irregular bleeding
♦ unusual or abnormal vaginal bleeding, with or without pain (other than the not unusual spotting or staining following the initial insertion)
♦ unexplained chills and fever
♦ genital sores or vaginal discharge

changed any time of the day. If you forget to change the patch and leave it on beyond seven days, there is a two-day-grace period during which the hormones are still effective.

The patch can be worn during all kinds of activities – when showering, while exercising, while in a sauna or whirlpool, and so on. Patch adhesion is not affected by humidity or temperature. Most women choose to wear the patch on the buttock or abdomen. It can also be worn on the upper torso (excluding the breasts) or the upper outer arm.

Like other hormonal contraceptives, the patch is highly effective in preventing pregnancy (about 99.5 per cent effective). However, the patch may be less effective in women weighing over 90 kg (14 st 2 lb). Side effects are similar to the Pill, but there may be a greater risk of blood clots with the patch.

Rings. The NuvaRing is a small transparent, flexible plastic ring that can flatten like a rubber band, be inserted into the vagina, and left in place for twenty-one days. Once inserted, the ring

releases a steady flow of low doses of oestrogen and progestin. The exact positioning of the ring within the vagina is not critical for it to work because it is not a barrier method of birth control. You can easily insert the ring yourself once a month and don't have to remember to take a daily pill or insert a diaphragm before intercourse. Once it's removed, you'll get your period. You'll need to insert a new ring one week after the last one was removed (even if your period has not stopped). Studies show that the level of cycle control with the NuvaRing is better than that with the Pill and there is little breakthrough bleeding. Because the hormones are the same as those used in the combination pills, side effects are generally the same, and those women who are advised not to use oral contraceptives are also advised not to use contraceptive rings. The ring is also not for breastfeeding mothers. It has a success rate of 98 to 99 per cent.

Implants. Under-the-skin progestin implants have been shown to be a safe and effective method of birth control (with a success rate of about 99 per cent), but the manufacturer of Norplant has discontinued making it. The next generation of implants includes a one-rod system such as Implanon that is effective for three years and a two-rod system that is effective for five years. It is unclear whether these implants work effectively in overweight women because, so far, clinical trials have not included overweight or obese women in the study samples.

INTRAUTERINE DEVICES (IUD)

The IUD is the world's most commonly used method of reversible birth control for women, yet only 5 or 6 per cent of women in the UK use one. Today's IUDs are considered to be one of the safest methods of birth control – with a pregnancy rate equivalent to that of sterilization (over 99 per cent effective). They're also the most convenient and, for most women, trouble free – definitely worth considering.

IUDs are small plastic devices that are inserted by a doctor into a woman's uterus and are left there for a number of years, depending on the type of IUD. The Copper T 380 IUD, the most effective IUD, with a failure rate of 0.3 per cent, releases copper in the uterus to immobilize sperm. It also prevents implantation in the uterus. The Copper T 380 can be left in for ten years. Other IUDs last for five years.

The major advantage of an IUD is that it offers the ultimate in convenience. Once it is inserted, it can be forgotten about except to check regularly (monthly is a good idea) for the string attached to it. This allows for a completely spontaneous sex life – with no pausing to find and insert a diaphragm or put on a condom, or remembering to take a daily pill. In addition, the IUD does not interfere with breastfeeding nor does it affect the breastfeeding infant.

You can increase the already excellent protection from pregnancy provided by the IUD if you check regularly for the IUD string and if you use condoms and/or spermicides for the first two or three months following insertion (when most failures occur).

The IUD should not be used by a woman who has gonorrhoea or chlamydia, or who is exposed to multiple partners, or has a partner who is. Nor should it be used by a woman with a history of pelvic inflammatory disease (PID) or ectopic pregnancy; known or suspected uterine or cervical malignancy or premalignancy (or even an unexplained abnormal Pap smear); abnormalities of the uterus or an unusually small uterus; menstrual or other bleeding irregularities (the IUD can increase menstrual flow and cramping, though it doesn't always); postnatal or post-abortion infection within the past three months; or by a woman who delivered a baby, experienced a miscarriage or had an abortion within the past six weeks. Allergy or suspected allergy to copper rules out the use of a copper IUD.

Possible complications include cramping (which can be severe) during insertion and, rarely, for a few hours or even days following; uterine perforation (extremely rare); accidental expulsion (it might go unnoticed and leave you unprotected); and tubal or pelvic infections (also rare). Some women may experience spotting between periods during the first few months after insertion. The first few periods may also last longer and be heavier. It's also not unusual for a woman to continue having heavier and longer periods while using an IUD, though the progestin-releasing IUD may lessen the amount of bleeding.

BARRIER METHOD WARNING SIGNS

Check with your doctor if any of the following symptoms occur when using a diaphragm or cervical cap:

- discomfort when the diaphragm or cap is in place
- burning sensations while urinating
- irritation or itching in the genital area
- unusual discharge from the vagina

- irregular spotting and bleeding
- redness or swelling of the vulva or vagina
- sudden high fever
- diarrhoea and/or vomiting
- dizziness, faintness and weakness
- a sunburn-type rash not related to sun exposure

BARRIER METHODS

Diaphragm. The diaphragm is a dome-shaped rubber cap that is placed over the cervix to block the entry of sperm. It is an effective birth-control method when used properly with a spermicidal gel to inactivate any sperm that might get past the barrier (94 per cent effective). Aside from possible increases in urinary tract infections and an occasional allergic reaction triggered by either the spermicide or the rubber, the diaphragm is safe. In fact, used with a spermicide, it appears to reduce the risk of pelvic infections that can lead to infertility. It in no way interferes with breastfeeding or affects a breastfeeding baby.

The diaphragm must be prescribed and fitted by a medical professional. Refitting is essential after childbirth because the size and shape of the cervix may have changed. The diaphragm has the disadvantage of having to be inserted before each intercourse (unless you'll be having an encore sexual performance within a few hours, in which case you just need to add more spermicide), left in for six to eight hours, and removed within twenty-four hours. (Some experts suggest it's prudent to remove it within twelve to eighteen hours, and some recommend women insert their diaphragms nightly when they brush their teeth so they don't forget to use it in a moment of passion). The fact that the diaphragm must be inserted through the vagina makes this method unappealing to some women. The diaphragm needs to be checked periodically for holes.

Cervical cap. The cervical cap is similar to the diaphragm in many ways. It must be fitted by a doctor, must be used with a spermicide, and does its job by preventing the entry of sperm into the uterus. Its success at preventing pregnancy is lower than the diaphragm (approximately 60 to 75 per cent). However, the cap offers a couple of advantages over the diaphragm. Shaped like a large thimble, the pliable rubber cap has a firm rim that fits snugly around the cervix, making it only about half the size of the diaphragm. A convenience plus: it can be left in place for forty-eight hours rather than the twenty-four-hour outside limit recommended for the diaphragm. Some women find that an unpleasant odour can develop when the cervical cap is left in for a couple of days; for others, the insertion process presents problems.

The FemCap, a newer type of barrier contraceptive (with a success rate of 85 per cent), is a silicone dome shaped like a sailor's hat. It fits over the cervix with a brim that seals against the vaginal walls and has a groove that stores the spermicides and traps the sperm. It also has a removal strap.

Vaginal sponge. The vaginal sponge, which currently has limited availability, blocks the entrance to the uterus; it works by keeping sperm from swimming up to meet an ovum and also by absorbing sperm. The sponge requires neither a visit to the doctor nor a prescription, it is relatively easy to use (you insert it yourself, like a diaphragm), it allows for greater spontaneity than other barrier methods (providing continuous protection for a full twenty-four hours after insertion), and has no effect on the breastfeeding infant. The major contraceptive effect of the sponge is probably through the spermicide it releases. It is somewhat less effective than the diaphragm (about 80 per cent effective), but because it contains nonoxynol-9 (a spermicide that acts as a disinfectant), it appears to reduce the risk of contracting such sexually transmitted diseases as gonorrhoea and chlamydia. It can, however, increase the risk of the yeast infection candida. Some people are allergic to the spermicide used, and some women are uncomfortable inserting the sponge into the vagina. It should not be left in longer than recommended, and great care should be taken to remove the entire sponge (a piece left in could cause odour and infection). The sponge can't be reused.

Condoms. A sheath for the penis made of latex or natural skin (from the intestines of a sheep) and often called a rubber, the condom is a very effective birth-control method if used conscientiously, though it is somewhat less foolproof than others (success rate of 86 per cent). Its effectiveness, as well as its ability to combat pelvic infection, is enhanced if it is used with a spermicidal agent or gel, and if care is taken to see that it is undamaged before use. The condom is totally harmless, though the latex or any spermicide used with it may spark an allergic reaction in some people. It has the advantage of not requiring a doctor's visit or prescription, of being easily available and easy to carry, and of reducing the risk of transmitting infections, such as gonorrhoea, chlamydia and AIDS (the latex variety is better at preventing passage of the AIDS virus). Because it in no way interferes with breastfeeding or affects the breastfeeding infant, and because it doesn't require postnatal refitting (as does the diaphragm), it is an ideal 'transitional' method for many couples. Some find, however, that because it must be put on before intercourse (and not until erection), it interferes with spontaneity. Others find that putting on the condom can become an enjoyable part of the lovemaking.

To increase effectiveness, the penis should be withdrawn before the erection is totally lost and while the condom is held on, to avoid leakage. The use of a lubricating cream (or a lubricated condom) will help make insertion more comfortable when the vagina is dry after pregnancy and during breastfeeding. (But don't use oil-based lubricants, such as baby, massage or bath oils, or Vaseline, because they can damage the condom.)

The female condom is a thin lubricated polyurethane pouch that lines the vagina and is held in place by a closed inner ring near the cervix and an outer open ring at the opening of the vagina. The female condom is inserted into the vagina up to eight hours before intercourse and is removed right after sex. The downsides to the female condom are that it is more expensive than the

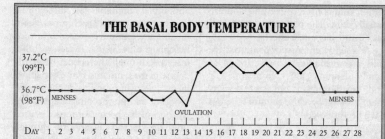

THE BASAL BODY TEMPERATURE

The basal body temperature (BBT): The BBT can help to pinpoint more accurately the period of ovulation during which unprotected intercourse is riskiest. To get the BBT, the woman takes her temperature with a special basal body thermometer every morning immediately on awakening, before speaking or sitting up, etc. (the thermometer should be shaken down and left next to the bed the night before). In most women the temperature will drop and then rise abruptly at the time of ovulation as seen above. Three full days after ovulation, intercourse can be resumed. See next page for more on natural family planning.

male condom, may prevent full sensation, and is clearly noticeable once in place. The good news is that it's more effective than the male condom (success rate of 95 per cent) and, like the male condom, also prevents STDs and HIV.

Spermicide foams, creams, jels, suppositories and contraceptive films. Used alone, these antisperm agents are fairly effective (approximately 72 to 94 per cent) at preventing pregnancies. They are easy to obtain without a prescription and don't interfere appreciably with lovemaking, but they can be messy and inconvenient. They can be inserted up to one hour before intercourse.

EMERGENCY CONTRACEPTION

The emergency contraception pill (ECP) is the only method of birth control that can be used after unprotected intercourse (or as backup when your contraceptive method has failed, as with a broken condom, slipped diaphragm or missed oral contraceptive pills) but before a pregnancy is established.[3] Both the combined oestrogen and progestogen pill and the progestogen-only pill reduce a woman's risk of pregnancy by 75 per cent when taken within seventy-two hours of unprotected sex. The sooner ECPs are taken after unprotected sex, the more effective they are. (Your doctor might also recommend using ordinary birth control pills as emergency contraception, but check with him or her first to confirm the dose you should use.)

ECPs work by temporarily stopping ovulation, or by preventing fertilization. They may also work by preventing a fertilized egg from attaching to the uterus.

Side effects of the combined pill are similar to those associated with combi-

---

3. Emergency contraception pills will not work if you are already pregnant. It is not an abortion pill.

nation oral contraceptive pills and are usually mild. The progestogen-only pill may cause fewer side effects.

Presently, emergency contraceptive pills are available by prescription at family planning clinics, from your GP and, as a last resort, an A&E department, though over-the-counter schemes have been piloted.

STERILIZATION

Sterilization is frequently the choice of couples who feel that their families are complete, don't have a problem with closing (and locking) the door to conception, and are anxious to dispense with contraception altogether. It's increasingly safe (with no known long-term health effects) and virtually foolproof. The occasional failure can be attributed to a slip-up in surgery or, in the case of vasectomy, not using alternative birth control until all viable sperm have been ejaculated. Though sterilization is sometimes reversible, it should be considered permanent.

Tubal ligation is a procedure done under general or epidural anaesthesia in which a small incision is made in the abdomen and the fallopian tubes are either cut, tied or blocked. It does require some down time, usually two days (sometimes more) of only light activity. A vasectomy (the tying or cutting of the vasa deferentia, the tubes that transport sperm from testicles to penis) is a much easier, outpatient procedure done with local anaesthesia, and it carries far fewer risks than tubal ligation. It doesn't (as some men fear) affect the ability to achieve erection or ejaculate. Research has also shown that there is no increased risk of prostate cancer for men with vasectomies.

A newer permanent birth-control option that does not require tubal ligation has also been developed. This type of sterilization requires neither an abdominal incision (as does tubal ligation) nor general anaesthesia. A soft, flexible microinsert is placed into each fallopian tube via a catheter (tube) inserted through the cervix. Over the course of three months, new tissue grows in the fallopian tube (inside the insert), blocking the tubes completely. Another method of birth control must be used until the doctor can confirm through testing that your tubes are effectively blocked (usually after three months).

FERTILITY AWARENESS

Women who prefer not to use hormonal or mechanical contraception can opt for a 'natural' form of birth control (also called 'natural family planning'). This approach relies on the woman becoming aware of a number of body signs or symptoms to determine the time of ovulation. This method works best for those who have regular cycles. But, because of the irregularity of the menstrual cycle in many women, it is the least effective of the various popular birth-control methods.

The more factors a couple takes into consideration, the better the success rate. These factors include keeping track of the calendar rhythm; mucus changes in the vagina (the mucus is clear, has an egg white consistency, and can be pulled into a long string at ovulation); basal body temperature changes (the baseline temperature, measured first thing in the morning, drops slightly just before ovulation, reaches its lowest point at ovulation, and then immediately rises to a high point before returning to the baseline for the rest of the cycle; see diagram, page 705); and cervical changes (the normally firm cervix becomes a little softer). Ovulation predictor kits can also help to pinpoint ovulation (though using them every month to *prevent* pregnancy can get very costly). Saliva tests for ovulation can also help some women predict when ovulation is imminent and are more cost effective. Intercourse is avoided from the first sign that ovulation is about to occur until three days after.

DIAGNOSING A NEW PREGNANCY

'I had a baby about twelve weeks ago, and I started feeling a little queasy yesterday. How soon can you get pregnant again, and if you're breastfeeding, how can you tell?'

A new pregnancy at twelve weeks postnatal is very unusual, particularly in a breastfeeding mother, though it has been known to happen. The fact is that unless you or your partner have been sterilized, you run the risk of conceiving any time you have intercourse, even if you use birth control and especially if you don't. A postnatal pregnancy, however, may be difficult to recognize. This is particularly true if you haven't resumed menstruating, since the first tip-off most women get that they might be pregnant is a missed period. If you're breastfeeding, another pregnancy clue many women rely on – tender and enlarged breasts with more noticeable veins – may be obscured. However, you may begin to notice other clues that you may have conceived once a new pregnancy is established: a diminished milk supply because different sets of hormones operate in pregnancy and breastfeeding (but such a drop in production may also be due to exhaustion, not breastfeeding enough, or other factors); morning sickness or queasiness (which could also result from something you ate or a gastrointestinal virus); or frequent urination (this could instead be due to a urinary tract infection).

If you have any reason to suspect you are pregnant, or even if you're just unreasonably nervous about the possibility, take a home-pregnancy test. In the unlikely event that you turn out to be pregnant, be sure to begin regular antenatal care as soon as possible. A new pregnancy so close to childbirth puts a tremendous strain on the body, and you'll need close medical supervision, extra rest and plenty of good nutrition.

As long as you feel up to it, you can continue breastfeeding your baby while expecting another. If you feel utterly exhausted, you may want to supplement with formula or even wean completely. Discuss the options with your doctor. If you do breastfeed while pregnant, it will be extremely important to consume enough extra calories (about 300 for the foetus and another 200 to 500 for milk production), protein (four servings a day) and calcium (the equivalent of six servings a day), as well as to get plenty of rest.

PASSING GERMS ON TO BABY

'I have a really bad cold. Can my son catch it?'

Germs have a way of making rounds through the family, and later on, when your son is in school, he'll be bringing plenty your way. For now (unless he's already in day care), chances are much better that you or other family members will pass germs on to him.

To minimize the possibility that your baby will catch your cold – or any other infection you or another family member comes down with – wash your hands very thoroughly before handling him or anything that goes into his mouth (including his hands, bottle or dummy, and your nipples), and avoid drinking from the same cup. Keep baby from touching any cold sore or other contagious rash, and steer clear of kissing (as hard as it will be to keep your lips off that yummy face) while you have symptoms of infection. Make sure other family members follow the same rules. By the way, it's fine to continue nursing your baby while you're sick; in fact, breastfeeding strengthens your baby's immune system.

All that said, you'll also have to resign yourself to the fact that few babies escape their first year cold free. Even with all the above precautions, he's likely to succumb to the sniffles at some point – and, because you spend so much close time together and share susceptibility (he receives only immunities from you that you already have), he's actually more liable to catch a cold from you than from a passing sneezer on the street.

FINDING TIME FOR YOURSELF

'I'm so busy taking care of my new daughter's needs that I never have time to take care of my own. Sometimes I don't even have a chance to take a shower.'

Little things can mean a lot to the parent of a young baby. And often these little things that others take for granted – going to the bathroom when you feel the urge, having a cup of coffee while it's still hot, sitting down for lunch – become luxuries you can no longer afford.

Still, it's important to *make* time you can call your own. Not only so that you (and your spouse) will remember that your needs count, but so that your baby, as she grows in awareness, will recognize this, too. 'Mother' needn't be (and really shouldn't be) synonymous with 'martyr'. You don't have to suffer frequent urinary tract infections or constipation from infrequent trips to the bathroom, or

indigestion from eating on the go, or depressingly dirty hair from postponing showers. Though it will, indeed, take a lot of judicious juggling to meet your own needs without neglecting your baby's, it will be well worth it for both of you. After all, a happier parent is a better parent.

How to best make time for yourself will depend on such factors as your schedule, your priorities and just what it is you want to find time for. But the following tips can help put a little more personal time in your life:

Let baby cry. Not for half an hour, but certainly it won't hurt if you put her safely in her cot and let her fuss while you brush your teeth or go to the bathroom.

Include baby. Sit down to lunch with your baby. If she's not yet on solids, put her in a baby seat on the table (only while you're sitting right next to her) and chat with her as you eat. Or take your lunch to the park if she's more content in her pushchair and if weather permits. Place her in her baby seat on the bathroom floor while you attend to personal needs – she'll be getting early potty training while you get relief. Or play peekaboo with her from behind the curtain while you shower.

Depend on daddy. Shower while he breakfasts with her in the morning, or give yourself a facial while he takes her for a walk on Saturday afternoon. Don't feel guilty about turning baby over to him in his spare time; a mother's work (whether full- or part-time) is more consuming and demanding than any paid job. Parenthood is a partnership, and when two parents are on the scene, all the responsibilities of baby care should be shared equally.

Exchange favours. Trade baby-sitting services with other parents who also need to free up some time. Sit for a friend's baby and your own one afternoon or morning a week while she does whatever it is she needs to get done; she reciprocates another day.

Hire help. You may not be able to afford even a part-time baby-sitter, but you probably can afford a responsible teenager to entertain your baby (when you are in the house), while you buy a little time for yourself.

FINDING OUTSIDE INTERESTS

'As much as I'm committed to being a full-time mother, I'm starting to feel suffocated by staying home with my new daughter. There's got to be more to life than changing nappies.'

In the first few months of a baby's life, when the demands of feeding and caring for her are round-the-clock and seemingly endless, about all a new mother has the time or inclination to crave is sleep. But once baby has settled into a routine and mum into a manageable rhythm, the dreary doldrums may settle over the frenetic fog of earlier weeks. Instead of finding yourself with too much to do and not enough time in which to do it, you may find yourself with too much time and not enough to do with it. The challenge gone from getting through a day's baby-care chores, you may well begin to feel like a wind-up mother going mechanically through the motions, and to crave the stimulations and satisfactions of life beyond the four walls of home. Particularly if you were involved in many activities before – a career, hobbies, school, athletics, community work – you may start to feel those four walls closing in, and start doubting your self-worth as well as your decision to stay home with your baby.

Yet a rich, full, satisfying lifestyle and life with baby are not, as they may seem now, mutually exclusive. The important first step towards achieving such a lifestyle is to recognize that woman (or man) cannot live by baby alone. Even if you adore every moment with your baby, you still need intellectual stimulation and the chance to communicate with someone who can say more than *ah-goo, ah-goo* (cute as that may be). There are a variety of ways of achieving these goals, and of reclaiming the sense of self you feel you've lost.

THROUGH YOUR BABY

You can look upon your baby as an obstacle to reentry into the grown-up world – or as a ticket to it. The following will give you a injection at finding adult interaction through your baby:

Play groups. Locate an existing group or seek out mothers interested in joining you to set up a new one up by putting up a notice at your doctor's surgery; at your house of worship; on your building complex, supermarket or community bulletin board. Try for a group with mothers whose interests match yours. See page 444 for more on setting up a play group.

Baby classes. Classes designed for babies are often more valuable for their parents. By signing up for such a class (first making sure it's appropriate and safe for your baby; see page 447), you'll have the weekly opportunity to meet and talk with other women, many of whom have chosen to stay home with their babies.

Parents' discussion groups. Join an established one, or become involved in setting up a new one. Invite guest speakers (a local paediatrician, a nurse, an author, and others who can address your needs as parents and/or as women);

jointly hire a baby-sitter or sitters for the children. Meet in homes, school, a community centre – or wherever there's space available – weekly, every other week or monthly. Joining on-line chats and discussion boards will also help you feel connected, provide you with valuable resources, give you a chance to vent and, most of all, remind you that you're not alone in your situation.

The local playground or play area. Where babies play, parents can't be far behind. The playground is not only a great place for infants (even when too young to be mobile, they find watching the children and the activity fascinating) and older babies (when they can sit well, they usually love the swings, and many can tackle the slide and climbing areas before they are a year old), it is also an ideal place for mothers to meet other mothers and set up 'play dates'. These dates, too, are more for the benefit of the parents at this point than they are for their babies, who aren't yet capable of 'playing together'.

THROUGH PERSONAL ENRICHMENT ACTIVITIES

Being a full-time mother doesn't mean you can't be anything else. Continue to pursue old interests, or find new ones, through any of the following:

A course at a local college. Take it to gain a qualification or just for fun or intellectual enrichment.

An adult education class. These are proliferating all over the country and offer everything from aerobics to Zen.

An exercise class. Challenging the body activates the mind. In addition, an exercise programme, particularly one that offers child care or combines mother exercise with baby exercise, is a good

---

BRING BABY ALONG

More and more colleges, community centres, workplaces and gyms or exercise studios are offering on-site child care, allowing parents to drop baby off while they study, work or work out. Another option if you're taking a class or course: see if there are other parents of infants or young children enrolled, and ask them if they'd like to chip in for a communal sitter.

---

place to meet other women with similar interests.

Active sports. Playing tennis or golf or another favourite sport regularly will help keep both body and mind well toned, as well as provide companionship.

A museum or art gallery. Become a member of a local museum and visit regularly, studying one exhibit each time. (It will be even more fun if you go with another parent.) Added benefits for baby: early exposure to art and artifacts is visually and intellectually stimulating (infants are often fascinated by paintings and sculpture) and will help keep young minds open to them later.

Educational DVDs or CDs. Watch a DVD while doing household chores or breastfeeding; listen to CDs or podcasts while driving; keep up with an old interest or explore a new one (learn a foreign language using computer software, for instance). Educational tapes are often available at no charge at your local library.

Books. They can take you anywhere, anytime. Read while you nurse, on a stationary bike, while baby naps, before bed. You'll not only be entertaining and stimulating yourself by reading but, through your example, you nurture a life-long love of reading in your child. A great way to combine a love of literature and a need for adult companionship is to start or join a book club. If the club is made up of other new mothers and fathers, it can double as a parents' group (where you talk books and babies). Babies can be invited, or the club can hire a sitter or two to care for them while parents chat.

THROUGH GOOD WORKS

If you're not in the paid workforce, then your local charities and community service organizations could use your help. Choose an organization you already belong to or join a new one, and offer your services. If you don't know where to start, you can contact a central clearinghouse for volunteers if there is one in your city, or you can ask at your local school, hospital, house of worship or community centres where volunteers are needed. The possibilities are endless: tutoring a child or adult in English or other subjects; visiting the elderly (they'll doubly appreciate your visit if you bring your baby along); cheering patients at hospitals; acting as a 'big sister' and source of support for a teenage mother or mother-to-be; serving meals at a soup kitchen; and so on.

Or use volunteer work to keep your professional skills from becoming rusty. Teach a course in your area of expertise at your local adult learning centre; write a newsletter; design a website or a direct mail campaign; or provide legal advice pro bono.

THROUGH PAID WORK

Being a full-time mother doesn't mean you can't be a part-time worker. A few hours a week at work related to your present field or a field you'd like to break into can keep you in touch, provide adult contacts and offer escape from your daily routine. See box on pages 718–719 for suggestions on how to find or create such work options, particularly those you can pursue from your home.

FRIENDSHIPS

'I feel uncomfortable with my friends who don't have children, but I don't know any women with young babies, and I feel very lonely.'

Major changes in one's life – a new school, a new job, a new marriage, a move to a new community, a divorce, children leaving the nest, retirement, widowhood – almost always have some effect on relationships. The arrival of a baby is no different. So it's no wonder many women seem uncertain about how to deal with the changing balance of friendships when they become mothers.

Many factors can contribute to changes in your social life post-baby. For one, you undoubtedly have a lot less time and energy for socializing. For another, until you go back to paid employment – whether that's six weeks or six years after your baby is born – you'll feel somewhat removed emotionally as well as physically from the circle of friends that revolved around your job or career. For still another, your interests, if they haven't already, will begin to change. As much as you still might enjoy a conversation centred around foreign policy, films, literature or entertainment gossip, you've probably recently developed an interest in discussing the merits of baby exercise classes or the efficacy of various nappy-rash preparations, sharing thoughts on how to quieten a crying baby or how to get more sleep, bragging about baby's first successful attempt at turning over or cutting a first tooth. Yet another factor upsetting your social life: some single friends seem less comfortable with you. This may be partly because you share less in common and partly because some of them, consciously or unconsciously, are envious of your new family. Finally, friendships that are only job-deep (or partying-deep) often don't have what it takes to survive change.

What most women are searching for is a way to integrate the women they were with the mothers they've become – without diminishing either. That isn't easy. Trying to stay completely within the old circle denies that you're a mother now. Abandoning old friends and spending time only with other new mothers denies the old you. Making new friends while keeping as many of the old as possible will probably be the happiest and most fulfilling of compromises, one which satisfies all the women you are.

See your old friends socially on occasion – for lunch, a drink, a movie. They'll want to hear about your baby and your new lifestyle (but not exclusively), and you'll want to hear what's new and what's the same, at work and with their relationships. Try to stick to subjects you have in common, whatever brought you together in the first place. You may find yourself feeling a little uncomfortable at first, but pretty soon you'll know which friendships are going to continue and which it makes sense to put on hold, except perhaps for birthdays and holidays. You may be surprised to find that one or more old friends become very involved in your new life and offer a great source of support. And those old friends you lose touch with may suddenly seek you out again when they begin to have families of their own.

Making new friends among the new mothers in your community is relatively easy. It only requires your turning up at places where mothers of babies congregate (at playgrounds, exercise classes, mothers' groups, play groups, your house of worship). Seek out those who share not only your interest in babies but also some of your other interests, so that these friendships can be multidimensional and so that you'll have more to talk about than nappies and day care – though you'll find babies will often be the subject of choice.

DIFFERENT MOTHERING STYLES

'My closest friend is relaxed and disorganized, doesn't worry if her seven-month-old doesn't get his lunch until dinnertime, drags him to parties until all hours, and is in no hurry to return to work. I'm compulsive about everything – bedtimes, meals, clean laundry – and I went back to work part-time when my son was three months old. Is either of us doing something wrong?'

Nope – you're each doing what feels right for you, and there's no 'righter' way to to parent than that. Let's face it: you would probably have a nervous breakdown trying your friend's laissez-faire parenting style, and she would do likewise trying yours. The only time you need fear you're doing something wrong is when your baby tells you – by crying a lot, by being unresponsive or by not thriving physically – that he's not satisfied with your approach to mothering. If that happens, you've got to make some adjustments, because babies, like mothers, are individuals, with different styles.

A baby who is happy and healthy is saying to his mother, no matter what her style, 'You're doing a great job!'

JEALOUSY OF DADDY'S PARENTING SKILLS

'I thought that mothers were supposed to be naturally better at parenting than fathers. But my spouse has a way with our son – making him laugh, calming him down, rocking him to sleep – that I don't. And that makes me feel inadequate and insecure.'

Every parent enters parenthood with something to offer his or her baby, with no one contribution more valuable or desirable than another, at least not as far as the little beneficiary is concerned. Some parents are better at the fun-and-games aspects of baby raising (getting a good giggle going, playing peekaboo), some at the nuts-and-bolts tasks (feeding, bathing, getting baby dressed without a struggle). Some, like your spouse, display a knack for building rapport with baby.

It isn't uncommon for one parent to be a little envious of the other's parenting finesse. But it's possible to shake such feelings:

Consider yourself lucky. While many women still complain of spouses who don't do enough, you're fortunate enough to have a partner who's not only happy to do more than his share, but who's gifted at doing it. An involved father can take a lot of the pressure off mum – and can have a dramatically positive effect on his child's development. So let him practise his baby magic whenever possible.

Don't be a female chauvinist. Sexual stereotypes that depict women as naturally better at parenting than men are inaccurate and, ultimately, destructive all around. There is no child-care responsibility – other than breastfeeding – that all mothers are more naturally suited to than all fathers, or vice versa. Some parents (no matter what gender) have a natural knack for parenting skills; some have to work hard at mastering infant care. Given the opportunity and some time, any parent of either sex can overcome a lack of natural aptitude or experience.

Give yourself more credit. You may not realize how much you do for your baby and how well you do it – though your baby almost certainly does, and he couldn't do without you.

Give yourself a chance. Just because certain parenting skills don't come as easily to you as they do to your spouse doesn't mean they'll always be elusive. If you're breastfeeding, you may find that once you've weaned your baby and the distraction of breast milk is past, you'll be able to calm him on your chest as well as daddy does. With practise and a lessening of self-consciousness, you will also learn to sing the lullabies and silly songs your baby loves, to play finger games and make funny faces, and to rock him with a comforting rhythm. But for best results, don't mimic what seems to work for your spouse or compare your technique to his. Instead try doing what comes naturally to you. Your own parenting style will emerge and evolve if you let it.

And remember, no matter how wonderful a relationship dad and baby have developed, there will always be times when no one else will do for your child but you, and you'll hear those soon-to-be familiar words: 'I want my mummy'.

JEALOUSY OF DADDY'S ATTENTION TO BABY

'As terrible as this sounds, I'm finding that I'm jealous of the time my spouse spends with our daughter. I sometimes wish he'd devote half as much attention to me.'

As heartwarming as a budding romance between father and infant may seem to an outsider, it can be genuinely threatening to a woman who's not used to sharing her spouse's affection, particularly if she's enjoyed his especially solicitous attention during nine months of pregnancy.

Although your feelings of jealousy will probably subside on their own once the family dynamics have had some time to work themselves out, there are several steps you can take to deal with them in the meantime:

Be assured. The first thing you need to do to overcome the feelings you're experiencing is to recognize that they're normal and common – not petty, selfish or otherwise shameful. Dump that guilt.

Be grateful. Consider how lucky you are to be with to the kind of man who's eager to spend time with his baby. Take advantage of the time they spend together to catch up on chores or personal needs. Watch with appreciation the love that's blossoming between the two of them, and try to support it. The bonds they're building now will last a lifetime, through the terrible twos and even the turbulent teens, and will make your daughter a better woman (or make your son a better man).

Be a part of it. Father and baby should certainly share some time alone together, but sometimes a third player will be welcome. Join that cuddle fest (he gets the tummy, you get the toes), flop down on the bed beside them as they read a book, sit down and make their two-way game of 'catch' on the rug three-way.

Be honest and open. Don't just sulk from the sidelines when daddy and baby leave you out of the loving action. In the excitement of discovering a new best buddy,

your spouse may not realize that he's been shutting out his (relatively) old one; he may even believe he's helping you out. Tell him, without being offensive or putting him on the defensive, how you feel and exactly what he can do about it (for example, tell *both* of you how pretty you look, give *both* of you a kiss and hug when he comes and goes, snuggle spontaneously with *both* of you). He can't fulfill your needs unless he knows what they are.

Be there for him. Remember, a relationship that works, works two ways. You can't ask your spouse to devote more attention to you without your reciprocating. Make sure you, too, haven't been spending all your time, energy and affection on the baby, unwittingly leaving none for him. Dote on him, and you're bound to find him doting back.

QUALITY TIME

'I hear a lot about the importance of spending quality time with your children. Well, even though I spend virtually all my time with my son, I'm so busy that I'm not sure there's any quality to it.'

Along with the proliferation of the term 'working mother' (a misnomer, since *all* mothers work) came the popularization of the concept of 'quality time': if a mother couldn't spend a lot of time with her child, the least she could do was make the best of the time she did spend with him. The theory seemed to imply that quantity was no longer important. But there's quality in quantity, too. You don't have to drop everything, sit down on the floor, and play with your baby all day long to provide him with quality care. You give quality time every time you change his nappy and smile at him, every time you feed him and talk to him, every time you bathe him and splash around with bath toys. You do it even when you chat with him from the kitchen as he races around on hands and knees, sing to him while you're driving in the car, lean over to tickle him in his playpen as you vacuum by, or sit him down with the shape sorter while you pay some bills.

Quality parenting time is time spent relating to your child in passive as well as active ways, and something that a loving and responsive parent who spends a lot of time with her child can hardly avoid providing. You'll know if you're succeeding just by watching your baby: does he smile, laugh, respond, seem basically content? If the answers are yes, he's getting plenty of quality time.

'As a parent who works outside the house full-time, I worry that I don't spend enough quality time with my daughter.'

When you have limited time to spend with your baby, the impulse is great to make every minute count. Accepting the impossibility of this (there will be moments when you'll need to do things other than child care, moments when she'll want to turn her interests elsewhere; days when you'll be in a lousy mood, days when she'll be) will, ironically, be the first step in ensuring your time with her is well spent. The following are other steps you can take:

Act natural. No need to don your Superparent cape before you walk through the door. All your daughter wants is *you.* There is no need to fill every minute you have with her with stimulating activities. Instead, be spontaneous, and take your cues from your baby (she may be too pooped at day's end for active play). Quality time is time spent together whether it's eating

together, cuddling together or just being together in the same room (even if you're not doing the same thing).

Involve your baby. Take her with you into the bedroom while you change from your work clothes, and otherwise include her in your routine when you get home from work. She can play with the empty envelopes while you open the post, empty the shopping bags while you put away groceries, or bang on pots and pans while you prepare dinner.

Tell her about your day. This will serve two purposes. One, it will ensure that you're communicating with her (she loves to listen to you talk, even if she doesn't understand what you're saying). Two, unloading your day's experiences (in an upbeat voice, even if your day was a downer) will help you unwind and make a faster transition from your job to your home life.

Give your house short shrift. With time at a premium, devote less of it to matters that matter less (cleaning, cooking and clothes care for instance). Take shortcuts in dinner preparation wherever possible (cook double quantities, freeze half to reheat another night; use frozen vegetables; get your green leafies from the ready-to-serve bags). Let the dust accumulate all week, and wait until the weekend to tackle it all at once with your spouse. Or if you can afford it, hire someone to clean once a week. Put the iron in storage and send out your shirts if they have to be perfect.

Keep your dinner on the back burner. Or don't put it on at all until your baby's gone to bed. Late meals may not be best for digestion, but they'll give you more time to spend with your baby while she's awake (give her your undivided attention while she dines) and more time to spend with your spouse when she's asleep.

Though family dinnertimes are important later on, they're not really necessary now. At this age, in fact, meals with baby can be so stressful that instead of enhancing togetherness, they can give it a bad name.

Tune out distractions. You can't give your baby quality time while you're catching the six o'clock news. Save television watching, Net surfing, and phone-call making for after your baby's gone to bed. Let the answerphone pick up the phone to postpone talking to incoming callers until after her bedtime, too.

Don't shut out your spouse. In your quest for quality time with your baby, don't forget time spent as a family. Include your spouse in whatever you're doing with the baby, from bathing to cuddling. Also keep in mind that the time each parent spends with her alone is important, too, giving your baby the benefits of closeness with two unique individuals – and it doubles her quality time.

LEAVING BABY WITH A SITTER

'I don't work outside the home, but I do occasionally leave my nine-month-old son with a sitter, and always feel guilty when I do.'

As every employer knows, no worker can stay on the job round the clock and round the calendar, and still be effective. As a self-employed mother, you'll have to recognize this fact, too. No matter how much you enjoy your child and how much he enjoys you, you'll both benefit from some time apart. Take it – and don't feel guilty.

What it's Important to Know: TO WORK OR NOT TO WORK

For many women, there's no decision to make. Because of a variety of pressures – financial, career, societal – returning to work after their babies are born is the only option. However, for those who have a choice, the process of decision making can be agonizing. Child development experts – because they are in disagreement – offer these mothers little to go on. Some believe there is no harm and possibly some benefit when a mother takes a job and leaves her baby in a child-care situation. Others believe just as strongly that there is the potential for more than a little damage to the infant in a two-paycheque family, and urge that one parent stay at home, at least part-time, until the baby is three years old.

Objective research is no more helpful. Study results are contradictory, primarily because such studies are both difficult to do and difficult to evaluate. (How do you judge the effects on her offspring when a mother holds a paying job? Or doesn't hold one? Which effects are important to evaluate? Which are difficult to quantify? Are there some we can't even predict? Will problems show up early or not until adulthood?) In addition, the research isn't as objective as it should be. It's often coloured by the bias of the researcher. It also rarely shows the whole picture.

With no clear-cut evidence on the long-term risks or benefits of a mother's working outside the home to go on, the full weight of making this decision falls entirely on the parents. If you're pondering the question, asking yourself the following questions may help you sort out the best way to go.

What are your priorities? Consider carefully what is most important in your life. List your priorities in order on paper. They may include your baby, your family, your career, financial security, the luxuries of life, holidays, study – and may be vastly different from those of the woman next door or the woman at the next desk. After charting your priorities, consider whether returning to employment or staying at home will best meet the most important of them.

Which full-time role suits your personality best? Are you at your best at home with the baby? Or does staying home make you impatient and tense? Will you be able to leave worries about your baby at home when you go to your job and worries about your job at the office when you're home with the baby? Or will an inability to compartmentalize your life keep you from doing your best at either job?

Would you feel comfortable having someone else take care of your baby? Do you feel no one else can do the job as well as you can? Or do you feel secure that you can find (or have found) a person (or group situation) that can substitute well for you during your hours away from home?

How do you feel about missing some major milestones? The first time your baby laughs, sits alone, gets up on all fours and crawls, or takes a step – do you think you'll mind hearing about it secondhand, if you happen to be at work when it happens? Will you feel slighted if the baby develops a close bond with the sitter? Do you feel you can learn to tune in to your baby's unspoken needs and feelings by just spending evenings and weekends together? Remember that most mothers who work outside the home manage to build just as strong a relationship with their children as stay-at-home mums. And no matter how close your baby becomes to the sitter, no one can take your place in your child's heart.

How much energy do you have? You'll need plenty of emotional and physical stamina to rise with a baby, get yourself ready for work, put in a full day on the job, then return to the demands of your baby, home and spouse once again (though you'd also need plenty of energy to be a stay-at-home mum). On the other hand, many women – particularly those who really love their work – find their time at the office rejuvenating, a respite from home life that allows them to reenter each night refreshed and ready to tackle the very different challenges of baby care. Keep in mind, however, that what often suffers most when energy is lacking in the two-paycheque family with young children is the relationship between spouses. If you decide to return to work, you'll need to make an effort to nurture that relationship, too.

How stressful are your job and your baby? If your job is low stress and your baby's a piece of cake to care for, the duo may be relatively easy to handle. If your job is high pressure and your baby is, too, will you find yourself unable to cope with both, day in and day out? Of course, how well you handle stress is also an important factor to consider; some women thrive under it.

FAMILY-FRIENDLY WORK

Working doesn't always have to mean 9-to-5 (or 8-to-7). Innovations in the working world can sometimes allow parents more flexibility, making that family-work balancing act somewhat more manageable. Here are some of the many options available:

Part-time. This is an old favourite of working mothers, the twist being that more and more fathers are taking advantage of this kind of work, too. The bottom line: if your skills are valuable to someone full-time, then you hopefully can sell them part-time, either to a current employer, a previous one or someone new. See which option works best for you and your employer – five mornings or afternoons, two full days and one half (they can be consecutive, or spread out during the workweek), some mornings, some afternoons.

Freelance. Freelancing isn't an easy way to earn a living – you'll have to spend time hustling up work before you can get started – but for some mums it's the best way. It allows you to be your own boss and work your own hours.

Telecommuting. So much of today's corporate world runs electronically that many jobs can be done from just about anywhere, including from home. Given the right equipment, you may able to conduct most of your business via e-mail, fax and phone – even videoconference (but remember to change out of your bathrobe and wash the spit-up off your shoulder).

Compressed workweek. For those with stamina, working ten hours a day can give you a full forty-hour week in only four days, leaving you with one day off. You can take the day off in the middle of the week, or opt for a three-day weekend.

Flextime. This is all about flexibility and, if your employer is willing to accommodate, you may be able to devise a schedule that works better for you and your baby than a typical 9 AM to 5 PM. For instance, you can

---

If you do return to employment, will you get adequate support from your spouse or from some other source? No mother can do it all alone – and no mother, whether she works outside the home or not, should be expected to. Will your spouse be doing his share (read: half) of baby care, shopping, cooking, cleaning and laundry? Are you able to afford outside help to take up the slack or to reduce the load for both of you?

What is your financial situation? If you don't work, will it threaten your family's economic survival, or just mean you'll have to cut down on some extras? Are there ways of cutting back so that the loss of your income won't hurt so much? If you go back to work, how much of a dent will job-related costs (clothes, commuting, child care) make in your income? In some cases, once you've added in those costs, working hardly pays.

How flexible is your job? Will you be able to take time off if your baby or your baby-sitter is sick? Or come in late or leave early if there's an emergency at home? Does your job require long hours, weekends and/or travel? Are you willing to spend extended time away from the baby?

How will not returning to your job affect your career? Putting a career on hold can sometimes set you back when you return to the working world. If you suspect this will happen to you (though many women discover when they

work some evening or weekend hours (when your spouse can be on duty at home), so that you can spend some weekdays at home. Or you can work the early shift (6:30 AM to 2:30 PM, perhaps).

Job sharing. Chances are you're not the only working parent at your company who yearns for more time with his or her family. If your employer is amenable (and you can afford to share your salary), consider splitting your job with another employee (you work the mornings while she works the afternoons; you and he alternate Monday-Wednesday-Friday schedules with Tuesday-Thursdays). This way, two part-time employees do the work of one full-timer.

Baby on board. Some parents have managed to mix baby with business – literally – by bringing their offspring to the office. Another option (if you're in the right line of work and you have a baby with the right kind of temperament): take your baby along with you to see clients and on assignments. Business travel is even possible if you bring along or hire baby-sitters wherever you go.

Home-based business. Running a part-time or full-time business out of your home can give you the best of both worlds. If you're an accountant, an advertising copywriter or fund-raiser, find a few clients whose accounts you can handle from your home. If you're a writer, editor or graphic designer, look for freelance assignments. If you have a knack for knitting, design sweaters to sell to baby boutiques. If you make an incomparable carrot cake, package your creations for a local gourmet shop.

Keep in mind that if you do decide to work out of your home – either for yourself or someone else – you may still need a sitter for at least part of your working hours. But you can also plan to work while baby naps and after he or she's bedded down for the night, and (though the logistics won't be easy) to do pickups and deliveries with baby in tow. Getting help with the household chores and shopping will be important, though, so that you won't have to give up too much of your time with baby.

return, that their fears haven't materialized), are you willing to make this sacrifice? Are there ways to keep yourself in touch professionally during your at-home years without making a full-time commitment?

Is there a compromise position? Maybe you can't have it all and remain sane, but you may be able to have the best of both worlds by looking for a creative compromise. The possibilities are endless and depend on your skills and work experience (see box above).

Whatever choice you make, it's likely to require some measure of sacrifice. As committed as you might be to staying home, you may, nevertheless, feel a pang or two (or more) of regret when you talk to friends who are still pursuing

their careers. Or as committed as you might be to returning to your job, you may experience regret when you pass mothers and their babies on their way to the park while you're on your way to the office.

Such misgivings are normal and, since few perfect situations exist in our imperfect world, they're something you'll have to learn to live with. If, however, they begin to multiply and you find dissatisfaction outweighing satisfaction, it's time to reassess the choice you've made. A decision that seemed right in theory when you made it may seem all wrong in practise now – in which case you shouldn't hesitate to reverse or alter it, if at all possible. No decision is final.

And when everything isn't as idyllic as you'd like, remember that children who get plenty of love and attention are very resilient, and likely to grow up happy and secure, whether their mothers work outside the home or not.

WHEN TO RETURN TO YOUR JOB

There's no predictably perfect point at which someone can say, 'Okay, now you can go back to your job. Your baby will be fine and so will you'. If you decide to go back to work during the first year, when you pick up that briefcase or lunchbox will depend in part on your job and the amount of maternity leave you were able to wangle and in part on when you and your baby are ready. All of which is highly personal and highly individual.

If you have the choice, experts suggest that you wait at least until you've 'attached' or 'bonded' with your baby and feel competent as a mother. Bonding can take three months (though if your baby has had colic, you will probably just be starting to become friends at this point), or it can take five or six. Some research suggests that there are benefits to waiting a year, if possible (though, for many parents, this isn't possible), to return full-time.

But, as always, no research – and no expert – can tell you what's right for you and your baby. Ultimately, that's a decision only you can and should make.

◆ ◆ ◆

Becoming a Father

During the nine months of pregnancy, the direct care of your baby was pretty much out of your hands – not by choice, but thanks to the quirks of reproductive biology. You could stand by, offering love and support (and the occasional carton of ice cream) to your pregnant spouse, but you couldn't take over the responsibility of nurturing your baby even for a moment.

Now that the cord's been cut, the rules of the game have changed. No longer do you need special biological equipment in order to care for your baby (though breasts might come in handy). You don't even need experience (like your spouse, you'll learn all you need to know on the job). All you need to be a partner in parenting is enthusiasm, a good sense of humour, a certain amount of stamina (there are a lot of late nights involved) and dogged dedication to the wonderful, unpredictable, exhausting, exhilarating, enlightening, ever-challenging business of raising a child.

What You May Be Concerned About

PATERNITY LEAVE

'I'd like to take some time off when my baby is born, but we're not sure that I should use up all of my holiday entitlement.'

Luckily, most fathers today don't have to choose between enjoying baby's first few weeks of life at home and enjoying a holiday later on. The Employment Act 2002 allows men to take either one or two consecutive weeks' paternity leave without tapping into their holiday entitlement. (To be eligible, you must have worked continuously for your employer for 26 weeks, ending with the fifteenth week before the baby is due.) These days, most employees are entitled to Statutory Paternity Pay (SPP) during their leave: from April 2003, this was £100 a week or 90 per cent of earnings if they are less than £100.

While the laws are slowly changing in response to the needs of new fathers, some men fear that taking this paternity leave will result in hostility from their co-workers and management and don't take advantage of their rights. Some take

DON'T STOP HERE

Sure, this chapter's devoted to the special concerns of new fathers – just as the postnatal chapter (see pages 668 to 720) is devoted to the special concerns of new mums. But that doesn't mean your reading should stop here. Unless you've been around the baby block once or twice before, there's probably lots you (like your spouse) need to learn about the care and feeding of an infant. You'll find what you need to know in the rest of this book (though some things you'll just have to figure out through baby-trial-and-error). So don't stop here – start at the beginning to find out what to expect the first year.

no more than a day or two off, others patch together a few days of holiday and a few sick days to stretch their time at home with baby to a week.

But the trend is definitely moving in the right direction. A growing number of fathers are deciding to take advantage of paternity leave so that they can spend extra time with their new family. And nearly all who do would agree that it is a time not to be missed – no matter what the cost.

To make the most of the rights you do have on the job, and to make the most of the time you have with baby:

◆ Know your rights. Some companies offer more than the law requires. To get the scoop, read the fine print in your company handbook (if there is one) or ask someone in the human resources department of your company.

◆ Sniff around. If you're not sure how family-friendly your company is – and how your employer would react to your taking paternity leave – seek out other men in your company who have successfully (or unsuccessfully) blazed the paternity leave trail. It's possible that you can use their experiences to make your experience a better one.

◆ Stock up on overtime. Some fathers stockpile overtime in the weeks before delivery, and exchange it for time off when baby arrives. Of course, this will work only if your company policy allows it and if you are ordinarily compensated for overtime.

◆ Mix it up. If you can't afford to take all the paternity leave you're entitled to, consider combining it with some accrued holiday time or sick days.

◆ Spread it out. If you'd like to take several weeks off, but your employer isn't happy about your taking them consecutively, try spreading the time out over a longer period. The options are endless: you could take one week off each month, one or two days off each week (choose to take Fridays off, and you have yourself a long weekend), numerous half days. Not only will that kind of schedule interfere less with work, but it'll keep that baby buzz going even longer, and give you an opportunity to spend time with him or her at different stages of development.

◆ Work by phone. Telecommuting is a viable option for many workers, either on a part-time or full-time basis. You could also head to the office for important meetings, as needed.

If it turns out you have to – or choose to – use up your holiday entitlement so that you can be home during those first weeks, keep in mind that the resorts, cruises and tours will still be there next year, but your baby will be a newborn only once. Paternity leave is almost always worth the price of admission.

STAY-AT-HOME FATHER

'My wife and I have decided that I should stay at home with the baby while she works. I'm excited at the prospect of being a stay-at-home father, but also a little nervous.'

Although the Hollywood-generated image of a stay-at-home dad – the bumbling incompetent who turns the white laundry pink, burns dinner, and puts baby's nappy on backwards – is still pretty pervasive, it's just a matter of time before it becomes as outdated as it is unfounded. More and more dads in the UK are bucking the roles traditionally carved out by society to stay at home with their children. Far from bumbling, these full-time dads are proving once and for all that – with the exception of breastfeeding – there's nothing a mother can do that a father can't do at least as well.

For some, it's a choice made out of economic necessity: since their wife earns more money, it makes financial sense for her to become the sole breadwinner while dad becomes the sole bread baker. For others, it's a choice made for career reasons, as when the father's job can be more easily put on hold than the mother's, or when the mother's job means more to her than the father's does to him. Still other fathers choose to stay home because they want to or because their temperaments are better suited to full-time child care than are their spouses'.

While many stay-at-home dads turn in their briefcases when they take on their new responsibilities, some figure

out ways to combine baby with work – by freelancing or telecommuting. Others choose the most challenging scenario of all – dad works the night shift after spending the day with the kids (though this arrangement is physically draining and leaves room for virtually no couple time).

Though there are countless joys and endless satisfaction for the stay-at-home dad to experience (it's often he who gets to see that first real smile or hear that first word), there's also some potential for pitfalls – most shared with stay-at-home mums who temporarily have left their careers behind, some unique to fathers. For one thing, unless they know other stay-at-home fathers, they may feel somewhat isolated. While stay-at-home mums can usually become part of a network of other mums, stay-at-home dads can feel like a fish out of water at play groups, baby classes and other settings where mothers and babies hang out. For another, some men have trouble fielding the insensitive questions and comments they're likely to encounter: 'So when are you going back to work?' or 'Did you get laid off your job?' They may also have self-esteem issues of their own to deal with, if being without a paycheque or a career path leaves them feeling less valued. Suddenly being without the stimulation of a career (and adult conversation) may prove a tough adjustment for any stay-at-home parent – male or female – to make.

Still, most fathers find that the pleasures of stay-at-home parenting make the challenges more than worthwhile. And eventually, many of the challenges become easier to handle. They learn how to proudly confront cocktail party wisecracks. They discover how to blend in with the mums at play groups and playgrounds, or how to seek out the few fathers in their neighbourhood who are also full-time parents. Most importantly of all, they realize that though the job they're doing doesn't come with a paycheque, it comes with more benefits and bonuses than any other.

And as a father opting for full-time parenting today, you're likely to find fewer challenges than those who took on the job even a few years ago. There are support groups for stay-at-home dads to join, as well as chat rooms on-line. There are even conferences and get-togethers where full-time fathers can swap insights and resources.

For more information on being a stay-at-home dad, check out www.home.dad.co.uk.

SPOUSE'S BABY BLUES

'We have a beautiful and healthy baby girl, just what my wife has always wanted. Still, she's been weepy and unhappy ever since she came home from the hospital.'

A number of factors – from a sense of let-down over not being pregnant any more to frustration over still looking as if she is – combine with hormonal upheaval to trigger baby blues in more than half of all newly or recently delivered women. Fortunately, these blues aren't long-lasting. In fact, most 'blue' mums start to feel in the pink within a couple of weeks.

Though hormonal changes may contribute to baby blues, you don't have to be an endocrinologist – only a loving, attentive and supportive partner – to help banish these common mood swings. Try to:

Lighten her load. Fatigue, a major contributor to depression, is an inevitable component of the postpartum period. Be sure that your spouse has all the help she needs (which in the initial few weeks, while she's recovering from labour and delivery, will be a lot) – from you when you're around, and from

others when you're not. Remember that even if you're working full-time (hopefully you've managed to score some paternity leave so you're not working at all right now), being a partner in parenting means sharing equally in all aspects of baby care. And being a partner in life means sharing equally in all aspects of home care – from doing the laundry to vacuuming to shopping to cooking.

Brighten her day – and night. When the new arrival becomes the centre of everyone's attention, the new mother often feels neglected. She may also feel inadequate (having much to learn about the care and feeding of an infant) as well as unattractive (having pregnancy weight still to shed). Here, too, you can make a difference. Compliment her at unexpected moments on how good she is with the baby, how radiant she looks, how slim she looks, how motherhood becomes her. Cheer her up with little gifts – flowers, a pair of earrings, a new CD she can listen to while she's nursing, a pretty nightgown with easy breast-access.

Take her away from it all. Time alone together is critical not only for her sake but also for the sake of your relationship. Make some time daily for the two of you.

Though baby blues will fade on their own (and will fade faster with your help), true postnatal depression, which affects about 10 to 20 per cent of new mothers, won't. PND is a serious condition that needs prompt professional attention. If your wife's depression lasts more than two weeks, is accompanied by sleeplessness (or a desire to sleep around the clock), lack of appetite, expressions of hopelessness and helplessness, anger, extreme anxiety or agitation, or suicidal or violent urges, don't wait any longer for it to pass. Insist that she seek help from her doctor, and that she receive a referral to a therapist who is experienced in the treatment of PND. Don't let anyone reassure you that PND is normal – it isn't. In addition to supportive psychotherapy and medication with antidepressants, the treatment for PND may also include light therapy. (See page 676 for more on PND.)

Once in a while, PND holds off until the new mother weans her breastfed baby. As with any depression, it should be treated promptly.

YOUR DEPRESSION

'How come my wife feels terrific since our son was born, and I'm the one with postnatal depression?'

Short of carrying the foetus and nursing the baby, there's virtually no aspect of parenting fathers can't take part in – including postnatal mood swings. In fact, a full 62 per cent of dads in one study were found to be suffering from the 'baby blues'. And as in women, it's speculated, hormones may be at least partly to blame (research has shown that many men experience a surge in female hormones during their partner's pregnancy and the postnatal period, perhaps as nature's way of bringing out the nurturer in the male of the species). But it's also likely that any number of the following contributing factors (all of which can also affect new mothers) are combining to bring you down at what you may have expected would be one of the highest points of your life:

Financial stress. Rare is the parent who is exempt from financial concerns once there's another mouth to feed, body to clothe, mind to educate and future to plan. The stress can be compounded

when one paycheque in a two-paycheque family suddenly disappears, even temporarily.

Feeling like a third wheel. A father who's become accustomed to being the centre of his spouse's life may be somewhat disheartened to suddenly discover himself on the sidelines, watching her attention being lavished on a noisy newcomer.

A love life lost. With endless nappy changes, feedings and sleepless nights to contend with, sex is probably the last thing on your spouse's mind right now – and possibly yours, too. That can be depressing enough. But so can the fear that romance – and intimacy – may never be completely revived now that the cozy company of your twosome has been invaded by a demanding third party.

Changed relationships. A husband who had been dependent on his wife for the fulfillment of a variety of needs may be upset to find she's suddenly unavailable because she's busy filling someone else's needs. Conversely, a husband used to having his wife depend on him may be unnerved to find that she, having found a dependent of her own, no longer is. Until he adjusts to the changing family dynamics, a new father can feel emotionally out of kilter.

Altered lifestyle. Even if you didn't exactly have a full social calendar before baby's arrival, you can still be depressed about the stay-at-home life now that he's here. At least for a while, even a movie or a dinner with friends may be a seemingly unattainable goal, and staying in night after night can certainly spark a dark mood in anyone but the most confirmed homebody – mother or father.

Sleep deprivation. Though the father who routinely answers his baby's calls is likely to be most worn out by middle-of-the-night wakings, even the father who doesn't is bound to feel the effects of night after night of disturbed sleep. The physical exhaustion soon takes an emotional toll, often in the form of depression.

Being aware of the possible causes of your 'baby blues' may help you to escape, or at least manage, them – particularly if you take steps to modify their effects (see tips throughout this chapter). Adjustment to the demands of parenthood (you'll eventually fall into a rhythm), and to the changes in your lifestyle and in the family dynamics (you'll eventually become accustomed to these, too), will also help you feel better. Then again, it's possible that your depression will linger for a few weeks no matter what you do and then disappear as unexpectedly as it arrived. If it doesn't, and if it starts to interfere with your functioning and/or with your relationship with your wife and/or your child, speak to your family doctor or contact a therapist.

MIXED FEELINGS

'Now that my wife is breastfeeding, touching her breasts during sex makes me uncomfortable.'

Breasts were designed for both fun and function. Although these purposes are not only not mutually exclusive but are actually interdependent in the grand scheme of things (if breast play weren't fun, there wouldn't be as many babies to nurse), they can conflict temporarily during lactation.

Many couples, either for aesthetic reasons (leaking milk, for instance) or because they feel uncomfortable using their baby's source of nourishment for their own sexual pleasure, find breastfeeding a very definite turnoff. Others,

however, find it a sexual turn-on, possibly because of its inherently sensual nature. Either reaction is perfectly normal.

If you feel that your wife's breasts are too functional to be sexy now, if leaking occurs on stimulation and you find that to be unsettling, or if your touching them makes your wife uncomfortable, simply leave them out of sexual foreplay until baby is weaned.

Be sure, however, to be open and honest with your wife now. Taking a sudden, unexplained hands-off approach to her breasts could leave her feeling that becoming a mother has somehow made her unappealing as a lover. Also be sure she gets her full share of foreplay in other ways. Because of vaginal dryness (which is more pronounced in women who breastfeed), fatigue and plenty of other postnatal factors, she may need much more warming up than she did pre-baby.

'The first time we had sex after the baby was born my wife had a lot of pain. Now I'm so afraid of hurting her again that I've been avoiding sex.'

You may hurt her more by avoiding sex than by initiating it. Possibly more than ever before, your wife needs to feel attractive, desirable and wanted – even if she herself is having mixed feelings (either because of fear of pain or lack of desire). Although your intentions are certainly noble, steering away from lovemaking may lead to beneath-the-surface anger and resentment in either or both of you, which could actually put your relationship at risk.

But before you approach her again sexually, approach her verbally. Tell her your concerns, and find out what hers are. Decide together whether you'd like to give lovemaking another shot soon, or whether you'd rather wait a little longer. Whatever you decide, the tips on page 690 will help minimize the pain and

IT TAKES THREE

Thought breastfeeding was just between a mum and her baby? Actually, fathers factor in plenty. Research shows that when fathers are supportive, mums are far more likely to try nursing – and to stick with it. In other words, while it only takes two to breastfeed, it seems to take three to make breastfeeding successful.

maximize the pleasure when lovemaking resumes. (The number one tip being: Bring on the foreplay, and lots of it.) Remember, too, that postponing intercourse does not – and should not – mean postponing intimacy. Right now, as two exhausted parents, you may find just as much fulfillment in a night of cuddling as in a night of lovemaking.

JEALOUSY OF MOTHER'S ATTENTION TO BABY

'I love my new daughter, but I also love my wife, and as much as I hate to admit it, I'm jealous of all the time my wife spends with her. She doesn't seem to have any energy left for me.'

There may be a companionable new twosome in your family, but it doesn't mean that three has to be a crowd. To help you deal with those jealous feelings (which, by the way, are normal and common among new dads, and often among new mums, too), take these steps – they'll also help you preserve and improve your own adult twosome:

Make your feelings known. Perhaps your wife isn't aware that as she's getting to know your baby she's losing touch with you. Let her know you appreciate the terrific job she's doing as a mother,

but remind her that full-grown men, too, need regular doses of tender loving care – though they may not always be as vocal as babies in demonstrating that need.

Make it a love triangle. Join them. As time alone with each other becomes a more and more precious and elusive commodity, concentrate on spending more time together as a family – stretching that mother-baby twosome into a cozy threesome – which you may find will strengthen the bonds between you as a couple. Fully sharing all the responsibilities and joys of baby care will give your wife more time to devote to you, while giving you less inclination (and energy) to feel jealous.

Make yourself useful. Even fathers who believe they're pulling their weight around the home often aren't doing their fair share, which should work out to half of the household responsibilities. The more chores you take over – or do together – the more energy your spouse will have left for you. She'll also be less likely to feel resentment, a sentiment that's bound to have a negative impact on the time you do spend together.

Make a deal. Negotiate for some private time with your wife. Try to arrange to set aside an hour each night (after the baby's asleep and before the television goes on) for the two of you to spend together eating dinner (if it isn't too late), unwinding, chatting (hopefully not just about the baby), getting to know each other again. Bargain to reserve at least one night a month (a weekly date would be better, and a good goal to shoot for as baby gets on a more regular schedule) for a special and romantic evening out.

Make a little love. Romance is a two-way street. It's possible that your wife is feeling as neglected by you, since the baby's been born, as you are by her. So go out of your way to cast that romantic spell: be spontaneous (flowers for no reason), flirtatious (hug her from behind as she bends over to pick up that nappy), lavish her with compliments (especially when she needs them most).

In spite of all your efforts, and even your wife's good intentions, you may find that she still seems distant. That's not unusual in women for anywhere between six weeks to six months after the birth of a baby. This attitude may be part of a built-in protective mechanism that keeps a new mother from cohabiting (and conceiving) too soon after delivery, and ensures that her attention and energies are focused on the newborn. It isn't a reflection on her partner or a barometer of her love for him. Be patient – and be supportive – and it will pass. If, however, you're still having trouble making a love connection well into the second half of the year, and talking about it doesn't help, professional counselling may be needed.

FEELING INADEQUATE AS A FATHER

'I want to be involved with caring for the baby, and I want to help my spouse out. But I've never had any experience with an infant, and I'm feeling completely useless.'

Most new fathers – and most new mothers – feel the same way you do in the first few weeks of parenthood. That's because few parents come on the job with experience and, as a result, few come on with very much in the way of confidence. While most other occupations offer training, support and supervisory guidance, parenting offers none of these – new mums and dads must learn their trade on the job.

And the best way to learn is by doing. The fact is that you don't need

---

A FATHER'S TOUCH

Think only mum has that special touch when it comes to baby? Think again. Research shows that a dad's touch has an equally positive effect on a baby's health, well-being and development (massage has been linked to fewer sleep problems and better digestion in babies, among many other physical and emotional perks). And baby's not the only one who stands to gain when you rub him or her the right way. Fathers who learn to soothe their babies through massage see their own stress levels drop, experience increased self-esteem as parents, and establish warm, positive relationships with their newborns that continue through childhood. For tips on how to give your baby a massage, see page 301.

---

prior experience to succeed at parenting – all you need is the willingness to try and a lot of love to offer. Though those with some baby care under their belts may get off to a faster start, even a novice like you will be running (and rocking and bathing and changing) neck-and-neck with the pros within a couple of months. In the meantime, you needn't worry about your baby's suffering because of your inexperience. First of all, babies are resilient, and a lot tougher than you'd think. Your son won't 'break' if your touch is tentative or awkward. Secondly, he'll be a good sport as you learn. He has no frame of reference, no 'perfect' father to measure you against. As long as his immediate needs are attended to, and he senses your good intentions, he's bound to appreciate you – imperfections and inexperience, crooked nappies and all. (Keep in mind that there's no such thing as a 'perfect' father or mother; even the

---

DADS MATTER

Make room for daddy. It seems that when it comes to a child's development, fathers matter as much as mothers do – and in some respects, even more.

Researchers have found that infants and toddlers whose fathers play with them in a sensitive, supportive and challenging way (talking to a child on his or her own level, encouraging instead of criticizing, and suggesting activities that are truly child-friendly) end up forming closer and more trusting relationships with others when they become teenagers and adults. What's more, the experts concluded that the quality of daddy play is at least as crucial as mother-infant interaction in predicting a child's future emotional and social well being, especially as the teen years roll around.

Kids develop better when their mums don't have a corner on the bonding market, too. According to the experts, children who are well attached to their fathers by age five are more likely to be confident and socially successful at school.

A couple more good reasons to make every day Father's Day.

---

experienced ones make lots of mistakes.)

Don't sell your intuition short, either, because of your gender. Studies show that fathers exhibit the same physiological responses to a baby's crying as mothers, and they can be just as sensitive to a baby's cues (although because they're unfortunately less likely to spend as much time around baby as a mother, they're less likely to sharpen this sensitivity and respond accordingly). Some fathers, in fact, once the initial trepidation has worn off, demonstrate even greater natural ability for parenting than their female partners. Babies aren't blind to this: by their first birthdays, children are as likely to object to being separated from father as from mother, and a full 25 per cent are more likely to go to their dads than their mums when given the choice.

If your spouse has had previous experience caring for babies, or is taking to the job more readily than you, have her show you the ropes. If she's as green as you, learn as you go, together (the tips in the Baby Care Primer, starting on page 127, will help). You'll both be pros the next time around.

UNFAIR BURDEN?

'I work a long day at the office while my wife stays home with our daughter. I don't mind helping out on the weekend, but I resent her pressuring me to give her a hand on weeknights, particularly in the middle of the night.'

Caring for your baby when you come home from work, a time when you used to relax and unwind from the pressures of the day, may seem an unfair burden; it does to many husbands of women who don't work outside the home. But, actually, it's not unfair and it's far from a burden.

Consider these facts. While your job has limited hours – eight, maybe ten a day tops – the job of parenting a new baby is around-the-clock. Which means that your wife works all the same hours you do – and if you don't share in the parenting when you come home, another fourteen or sixteen hours that you don't work. Her daytime workday is at least as physically and emotionally demanding as yours (more so if she's nursing). Though you need to rise in the early light of each morning to start another day of work, so does she, except that unlike you, she won't be able to take lunch hours, coffee breaks and, often, not even bathroom breaks. In other words, she needs relief in the evening more than you need the rest you'll be giving up by sharing the parenting load fully.

Caring for your baby is also an incomparable opportunity. In previous generations, few fathers spent a significant amount of time with their babies. As a member of a more enlightened generation, you're being handed the chance to get to know your daughter as you couldn't otherwise. You may miss the evening news or a before-dinner workout, but you'll find that an even better way to relax and unwind is with your baby. Nothing can make you forget a personnel problem, a botched job or a lost deal faster than conversing in coos with your baby as you change her nappies, watching her splash and giggle in the bath, or rocking her gently to sleep. And while you're forgetting your workaday cares, you'll also be building a collection of moments to remember.

Which is not to say that every moment you spend with your little one, particularly in the middle of the night, will be one you'll want to remember (some will pass in such a thick, sleepy fog that you wouldn't be able to remember them even if you wanted to). Like any job, baby care has its quota of hard work.

Keep in mind, too, next time you walk the floor with your colicky baby, that while baby care now may seem more a chore than a delight, soon the rewards will begin to outweigh the stresses. At first, it will be the smiles and gurgles meant just for you, then a breathless 'da-da' when you come through the door, then a finger raised for your kiss to make a boo-boo better. Later, and for years to come, compensation will come in the form of a closer relationship with your child that will not only bring joy but will also make the more difficult times a little easier.

Of course, sometimes both your spouse *and* you will need a break from child care, so be sure that once in a while there's a night out for just the two of you.

NOT ENOUGH TIME TO SPEND WITH BABY

'I work long hours, often staying late at the office. I want to spend more time with my new son, but I don't seem to have any.'

If there was ever something worth making time for, that little baby of yours is it. As terrific a job of parenting as one parent can do, two can do it twice as well. Baby boys who get lots of attention from their fathers are brighter and happier by the time their half-year birthday rolls around than boys who don't. So it's not just you who stands to lose if you don't spend time with your son. (Little girls, too, grow up more confident when they are close to their dads.)

Research also shows that children who have active and involved fathers learn better, have higher self-esteem, and are less prone to depression than those who don't.

Make more time for your baby, even if it means taking time from other important activities in your life. Organization may help. Try to dovetail your working hours and your baby's waking ones. If you don't have to be in the office until ten, spend the early morning with him. If you don't get home until eight, see if your spouse can arrange his schedule so that he naps early in the evening, then is up for play time with you before bed (of course, this will cut into time alone with her). Or bring some work home so you can leave the office earlier. If a lot of extracurricular activities (whether night-time meetings or weekend sports) keep you from your baby's side, cut back on them.

Especially if you're not able to make a great deal of time for your baby, it's important to make the most of the time you do have. Wield the baby spoon at breakfast, give the bath at night, take the baby to the playground on Saturday morning.

You can also make time for your baby by including him, when feasible, in your other activities. If you've got a few errands to run, strap him in a baby carrier and take him along. If jogging is on your schedule, tuck him in a pushchair and increase your aerobic effort by pushing as you go (but *don't* jog with him in a baby carrier). And if you've got some chores to do or some catch-up work on the computer, prop him securely in a baby seat or tuck him into a baby sling and let him watch as you provide a blow-by-blow description of what you're doing.

◆ ◆ ◆

CHAPTER 25

From Only Child to Older Child

When you brought your first child home from the hospital, you were novices at parenting, with a lot to learn about living with and caring for a new baby. Now, as you're about to bring home your second child, you're seasoned pros who've been there, done that, and lived to tell about it. You know your way around a changing table (in your sleep), don't get flustered when the crying starts, aren't fazed by the sight of an umbilical stump or daunted at the prospect of giving a sponge bath. This time around, it'll be your first born who will have a lot to learn – and a lot of adjustments to make – as he or she makes that difficult shift from only child to older child. Following the suggestions and tips in this chapter won't make that transition effortless for your older child (or for you), but it can help to make it smoother.

The best tip of all? Relax. Children take their cues from the adults around them. If you're anxious about how your child is going to react to a new sibling, your child will be anxious, too.

What You May Be Concerned About

PREPARING AN OLDER CHILD

'We have a two-and-a-half-year-old and we're expecting another baby. How can we best prepare our first child so she won't feel threatened?'

Gone are the days when children sat through mysterious talk about cabbage patches and storks. Today, sibling-to-be preparation is considered nearly as important as childbirth preparation, at least for second-time parents. Instead of being excluded from the excitement that will culminate in the arrival of a new brother or sister, first-borns are often involved in mum's pregnancy from the early months on.

The first step in preparing your child for the fact that she's about to become a big sister is to break the news of the pregnancy. Just when and how to do this depends somewhat on her age. From a young child's perspective, nine months can be nothing short of an eternity, and in the case of your daughter, very close to half of her own life. So that the wait for her sibling won't be interminable, and because most parents-to-be feel more comfortable sharing the news about their pregnancies once the first trimester has been passed, you may want to hold off until the end of the third month or the beginning of the fourth to tell her that a baby's on the way. (If you're anxious about amnio or other test results, you might even want to wait until you've gotten the all-clear.) Just make sure you tell her before she hears it from someone else, or begins to sense that something is wrong or that something's being kept from her (mum's feeling sick, tired and has to go to the doctor; her belly is sud-denly swollen; there are unexplained changes going on around the house). Since young children have little concept of the passing of the time, tying the due date to something concrete ('The baby's coming in the summer, when it's warm out') may make it a little more tangible.

How to break the news? Do it hon-estly, but on her level. Skip over the birds and the bees, the storks and the cabbage patches, and just give her the facts in simple language that she can understand. In figuring out how much information is enough, and how much is too much, let your daughter be your guide. Always start with the most basic facts, something along the lines of: 'We're going to have a baby. The baby is growing inside of mummy, and when it gets big enough to

come out, you'll have a new brother or sister.' Don't volunteer more, but be ready to answer follow-up questions as they come. In your answers, consider using the correct terms for body parts – 'uterus' or 'womb' for baby's location, 'vagina' for baby's exit route. For help finding the right words, and to make this very hard-to-grasp concept a little more real, read your daughter age-appropriate picture books on the subject.

Once the kitten's out of the bag, there are a number of steps you can take to make the expected arrival less threat-ening to the child already in residence – and perhaps even eagerly anticipated:

- Make any planned major changes in your child's life early in the pregnancy if you haven't had a chance to make them before conception. For exam-ple, get her enrolled and settled in a preschool or play group (if this is in your plans, anyway), so that she'll have an out-of-home experience to escape to once the baby's arrived and won't feel she's being displaced because of the baby. Begin toilet train-ing her (if she's ready) or weaning her from the bottle now (if you haven't done this yet), rather than just after your new baby's birth. Any significant changes not made within a month or two of the baby's due date should probably be postponed until a couple of months after the birth, if possible.

- Get your child used to spending a little less time alone with mum. Initiate (or continue) some regular father-firstborn fun activities (Sunday morning breakfast out, Saturday afternoon at the playground, a Tuesday night 'dinner date' at the pizza place). If mum's always in charge of bedtime, now might be a good time to start switching off (you can continue to switch off once baby's born, to make sure you both get plenty of one-on-one with her, and plenty with the new baby). Start leaving her with a baby-sitter for short periods during the day, if you haven't already and will need to after the baby arrives. Be careful, though, not to withdraw too far or too suddenly from your firstborn; she needs to be reassured (through loving actions, not in so many words) that the arrival of a baby won't mean the loss of either of her parents.

◆ Be honest and open about the physical changes mum's undergoing. Explain that you're tired, queasy or grumpy because 'making a baby' is hard work, not because you're sick or sick of her. But don't use the pregnancy as an excuse for not picking her up as much as you used to. Picking up a child is not in any way threatening to your pregnancy unless your doctor has for some reason (such as premature dilatation of your cervix) forbidden it. If you can't pick her up because your back is killing you, blame your back, not the baby (which might set the stage for sibling rivalry), and give her extra hugs from a sitting position. If you need to lie down more often, suggest she lie down with you and nap, read a story or watch TV together.

◆ Introduce your child to the new baby while it's still in the uterus. Show her month-by-month pictures of foetal development that seem appropriate for her age (again, a picture book is ideal). Explain that as the baby grows so will mummy's tummy, and that when the baby is big enough it will be ready to come out. As soon as kicks are easily seen and felt by outsiders, let her experience the baby's movements herself. Encourage her (but don't push her if she resists) to kiss, hug, sing and talk to the baby. When referring to the baby, call it 'our baby' or 'your baby' to give her a sense that it belongs to her as well as to you. If you haven't learned the sex of the baby through ultrasound or amniocentesis, make a game out of guessing whether a brother or sister is on the way.

◆ Take your child to at least one or two antenatal visits (and if she seems interested and isn't disruptive, take her to all of them) so she will feel like more than a player in the unfolding pregnancy drama. Explain that these visits are like checkups for the baby, and that just like at her doctor's checkups, the doctor (or midwife) will be measuring the baby to see how much it's grown and listening to the baby's heartbeat. Hearing the heartbeat for herself will help make the baby more of a reality for her. If an ultrasound photograph has been taken, show her that, too. But be sure to bring a snack and a book or favourite toy to the doctor's surgery in case of a long wait or a waning attention span. And if she decides she doesn't care for a return visit, don't push her to go.

◆ Involve your child in any baby preparations she shows interest in. Let her help you pick out furnishings, a layette and toys. Go through her old toys and baby clothes together (this will also help her understand the concept of growth) to select items which might be recyclable, but don't pressure her to hand down anything until she wants to. Making her the official present opener for the baby (since babies are too little to open their own presents), will help her feel less jealous of the windfall baby is receiving. So will explaining that all babies get lots of presents when they're born, because it's like their 'birth day', and that she did, too.

◆ Familiarize your child with babies in general. Show her photos of herself as a baby, and tell her what she was like (be sure to include some stories that will show her how much she's grown up since then). If possible, take her to a hospital nursery to look at the newborns (so she will know they aren't as cute as older babies). If you have friends with small babies, arrange for the two of you to spend some time with them. Point out babies everywhere – in supermarkets, in the park, in picture books. So that she'll be prepared for reality, explain that babies do very little besides eat, sleep and cry (which they do a lot of), and that they don't make good playmates for quite a while. If you're planning to nurse, explain that baby will drink milk from mummy's breasts (just as she did, if she did), and if you have a friend who is nursing, arrange a casual visit at feeding time. A picture book that gives the lowdown on new babies can also help.

◆ Play up the perks of being a big sister and of being big in general. The more appealing you make the role of big sibling sound, the more she'll look forward to taking it on. Explain all the things that the baby won't know how to do that she'll eventually help teach her. Make a list together of all the things that babies are too young to do that big kids can, like swing on the swings, play with friends and eat ice cream.

◆ In trying to prepare your child, don't raise issues that may never materialize. For instance, don't tell her, 'Don't worry, we'll love you just as much as the new baby', or 'We'll still have

plenty of time for you.' These kinds of comments can bring up concerns that she might not even have thought of yet about how well she'll be able to compete with her new sibling for your love and attention.

◆ If you're planning to have your older child vacate a cot for her expected sibling, do it several months in advance of your due date. If she's not ready for a bed, buy her another cot – preferably one that can convert to a junior bed. (Or let her stay put and buy or borrow a cot for the new arrival.) If you'll be moving her to a different room, do this, too, well in advance, and have her help with the decor and furnishings. Put the emphasis on her graduating to a new bed or new room because she is growing up, rather than on her being displaced from the old by the baby.

◆ If you have a car and your older child has been sitting in the middle backseat, move her car seat to a side backseat now; if she's big enough (see page 54), put her in a belt-positioning booster. Put a doll in a rear-facing infant seat in the middle seat for a few weeks before baby's due to accustom her to a travel companion.

◆ Try out names you're considering on your child, involving her in the selection process. Helping to name the baby will help make her feel closer to him or her. (Of course, it probably wouldn't be smart to give your preschooler complete creative control over the process. You'll have to make the final determination, unless you want your second child named Big Bird or Tinky-Winky.)

◆ If there's a sibling class available in your neighbourhood – some hospitals offer them – enrol your child. It's

READ ALL ABOUT IT

To a young child who's about to become a big brother or sister, a picture book is sometimes worth a thousand parental explanations. Look for books (such as *Why is Mummy's Tummy so Big?*, *What to Expect When Mummy's Having a Baby* and *What to Expect When the New Baby Comes Home*) that are geared to your older child's level, and that will paint a realistic (but age-appropriate) picture of what pregnancy's all about – and what life with a newborn will be like.

important for her to know that there are other children in the same spot that she's in – about to become a big brother or sister to a new sibling.

◆ As your due date draws near, get your child used to the idea that you'll be spending some time at the hospital or birthing centre when the baby arrives. Have her help you pack your suitcase and encourage her to add something of hers that she would like you to take along to keep you company – a teddy bear, a picture of her or a picture she's drawn, for instance. Be sure that whoever is going to be caring for her is fully familiar with her routines, so there won't be any break from them at this sensitive time. Tell her in advance who will be staying with her (daddy, grandma, grandpa, another familiar relative, a regular sitter or a close family friend), and assure her you will come home in a few days. If the hospital permits sibling visits (most do), tell her when she will be able to visit you and the baby. Whether she will be able to visit or

not, a prebirth tour of the hospital, if one can be arranged, will make her feel more comfortable about your being away.

◆ Don't suddenly shower her with gifts or special outings in the weeks before delivery. Instead of making her feel more secure about your love, such unaccustomed overindulgence may well give your child the sense that something terrible is about to happen, and that you're trying to soften the blow. It may also give her the idea that baby's impending arrival is bestowing her with valuable bartering power and lead her to attempt to trade good behaviour for presents and favours in the future. Buy just a couple of small but thoughtful gifts to give her after the baby arrives – perhaps one to give at the hospital and one for when you get home, for her being such a big help while mummy was away. For a fairly young child, a life-like plastic newborn doll is often a good gift. Later on she can bathe, 'nurse', or change her baby doll while you care for the real thing. Shop with her for (and let her wrap) a small gift for the baby 'from her' that she can bring to the hospital on the occasion of their first meeting.

◆ In your efforts to prepare your first child for the birth of your second, don't overdo it. Don't let your pregnancy and the expected family addition become the primary focus of your household or the dominant topic of conversation. Remember that there are, and should be, other concerns and interests in your preschooler's life – and that they deserve your attention, too.

SIBLINGS AT THE BIRTH

'We're delivering our second baby at a birthing centre, and we have the option of having our four-year-old son attend the birth. Should we have him there during delivery?'

Everybody's getting into the act – or, at least, the birthing room – these days. Mothers and fathers are often joined by a host of significant others as they bring a new family member into the world, including their own parents, uncles- and aunts-to-be, close friends and, sometimes, their older children. Always an option at home births and birthing centres, these family-centred deliveries are also being offered in more traditional hospital settings.

But as with most birthing options (at least, those that aren't dictated by medical practice), the decision of whether or not to include your son in the celebration of his sibling's birth is entirely up to you. In making that decision, you'll need to consider your own gut feelings (after all, no one knows your child and what your child can handle as well as you do), as well as the pros and cons presented by experts and parents in both camps. Some experts and parents who've opted to have siblings present at the birth cite numerous benefits, from less rivalry and better attachment between siblings (since the older child is involved from the moment his sister or brother arrives) to less potential for trauma for the firstborn (since he's not deserted while mum and dad go off to pick up his 'replacement'). Other experts and parents believe there are drawbacks, some of them significant, to inviting a sibling to attend the birth – including the fact that the labouring mother may feel uncomfortable, distracted, or inhibited by her older child's presence (she may want to cry out or grunt and may feel hesitant to do so in front of him). If she does end up making noises or faces that aren't familiar to the older child he may be unsettled by them, or he even may be afraid that his mother is in some kind of danger. They also express concern that if an emergency Caesarean becomes necessary or something is significantly wrong with the newborn, the resultant frantic flurry of activity might be truly frightening to the older sibling, particularly if he's very young. Another factor to consider is your child's feelings. If your son has expressed great interest in your pregnancy and has been an eager participant at antenatal visits, he may be a good candidate for the birthing room. If he has seemed blasé or ambivalent (or even antipathetic) about the proceedings so far, he's probably better off sitting it (or sleeping it) out with a favourite grandparent or baby-sitter.

If you're leaning towards having your son attend his sibling's birth (you can change your mind right up to delivery, of course), there are several steps you can take ahead of time to help ensure a positive experience for everyone:

◆ **Prepare.** While the two of you may know what to expect at labour and delivery (having been through it before), your son will have a lot to learn. And what he doesn't know can frighten him unnecessarily. Explain that birthing a baby is hard work, and that mummy may make lots of strange noises, such as grunts, moans, even screams, while she's trying to help the baby come out, and some even stranger faces. Prepare him by demonstrating the noises and faces you may be making (you can even make a game out of the demonstration by having him mimic you). Tell him how the birth will probably take place (in the water, on the bed, while squatting), and explain that there will be some blood (which helps the baby grow, and is normal and nothing to worry about). You might also consider watching DVDs of births together and signing him up for a sibling class that discusses labour and delivery. Both of these will not only prepare him, but give him a chance to find out precisely what he's in for, and allow him to back out if he ultimately feels uncomfortable with the idea of attending the birth.

- Allow for flexibility and choice. While your attendance at the birth is compulsory, keep in mind that your child is a volunteer participant. He should feel free to come and go as he pleases (which is why there should be child care on-site; see below), as well as to change his mind at the last minute if he'd rather look at picture books in the waiting room. Don't pressure him to stay, or make him feel guilty if he opts out of the main event. Remember, too, that even the most enthusiastic older sibling doesn't have the attention span or the physical stamina to endure a marathon labour and delivery. If labour begins in the middle of the night and birth is not imminent, let him get some sleep until you're further along (an overtired sibling will not be a cheerful one).

- Provide diversions and sustenance. The two of you may have nothing on your minds but birthing that baby – but your older child should and will. Bring along a supply of books, toys and other diversions to keep your youngest birth attendant occupied. And because a hungry birth attendant is a cranky one, don't forget to pack a stash of snacks, too.

- Bring along child care. Sign up someone whom your child is comfortable with – a grandparent, aunt or uncle, close family friend, or trusted babysitter – to be in charge of his care while you're in labour. The appointed person should not double as a labour companion (your child's care should be his or her only responsibility) and should be ready to miss the birth if your child backs out at the last minute.

- Build in sibling bonding. Be sure to include your older child in those first few moments of postbirth bonding.

If you decide against having your child present at his sibling's birth – or if he decides to opt out – another possibility is to welcome him into the birthing room to greet his new brother or sister immediately after the actual birth. If that's not possible or practical (or you end up delivering while he's asleep, for instance), remember that bonding with his sibling can begin later on when he visits you at the birthing centre or when you bring the new baby home.

SEPARATION AND HOSPITAL VISITS

'Will visiting me in the hospital make my older child miss me more than if she doesn't see me at all?'

Actually, quite the opposite is true. Being out of your child's sight doesn't mean you'll be out of her mind. Seeing you at the hospital will assure her that you're all right, that you haven't gone off and left her for another child, and that she's still important in your life.

Consider also that it's not just you she'll get to see when she visits the hospital. She'll also be allowed to see, touch and 'hold' her new baby brother or sister, which will give her a sense of reality about this new sibling (who to this point has been a pretty abstract concept). It will also help make her feel included in the new-baby excitement.

Not to say that there won't be some hesitancy when she comes and, possibly, some tears when she leaves. To make the hospital visits – and the separation – go more smoothly:

◆ Be sure your child is prepared in advance for the visit. She should know how long she's going to stay, and that she's going to have to return home without you and the baby. Tell her if regulations will limit her to seeing the baby through the nursery window (such as if the baby's in the Neonatal Intensive Care Unit).

◆ Be sure you're prepared for your child's visit. If you're expecting her to rush headlong into your arms and fall in love at first sight with her new sibling, you may be disappointed. It's very possible that she'll give either you or the baby or both of you the cold shoulder, that she'll seem tentative or out of sorts, and that she'll burst into angry or sorrowful tears upon departure. Such negative or neutral reactions are common, are not a cause for concern, and are – believe it or not – better for her than no visit at all. Keep your expectations realistic, and you'll be pleasantly surprised if all goes smoothly – and won't be unduly upset if it doesn't.

◆ If you leave for the hospital in the middle of the night, or when your older child is in school or otherwise away from home, leave her a note that can be read to her when she wakes up or returns. Tell her that 'our' baby is ready to come out, that you love her, and that you'll see her or speak to her soon. If it's practical (a relative or baby-sitter can come along to stay with her) and possible (the hospital allows it), take her along to the hospi-

tal to await baby's arrival. Have a bag for her, as you do for yourself. It should include a change of clothing, nappies (if she wears them), playthings and snacks you know she will enjoy. If labour is lengthy (it is less likely to be the second time around) and you are confined to the birthing room, have daddy come out and deliver regular bulletins, possibly even have lunch with her in the cafeteria (if there's enough time). Of course, if her bedtime comes up before the baby comes out, you will probably want to have her taken home so she can sleep in her own bed. If she is still around when the baby arrives, try to arrange for her to visit – at least with you, and possibly with her new sibling.

◆ Take a picture of your older child along to the hospital and place it on your bedstand, so she'll know that you've been thinking of her when she comes to visit.

◆ If it's possible, have whoever is bringing your child to visit you stop at a store on the way so that she can buy you and her new sibling small presents. Exchanging gifts (this is the time to give her that little something you picked up for her before delivery) will help break the ice and make her feel important. The practice of giving a gift 'from the baby' is common, but most kids see right through the ploy, and it's not a good idea to start this relationship with a deception, however innocent.

◆ Hold a little 'birth day' party for the new enlarged family in your hospital room. Have a cake (the big sister will probably be pleased that she can have a piece and her new sibling can't), candles (she can blow them out), and a few decorations (let her choose them).

- Have the same person who brings your child to visit take her home. If daddy takes her and then stays on for an extended visit while she's sent home with a grandparent or friend, she may feel doubly deserted.

- Between visits, or if she can't visit, keep in touch by phone (avoiding sensitive times such as right before bed, if you feel that the sound of your voice may upset her) and by writing notes that daddy can read to her. She may feel good, too, about making a drawing or two for you to display in your hospital room. Have daddy or a favourite relative take her out to dinner or on some other special outing so that it will be clear that the new baby isn't the only person everyone is interested in these days – and make sure that conversation during the outing doesn't centre around the baby unless she wants it to.

- Arrange to go home early, if you want to and can, so that your older child can begin sharing in the new-baby experience sooner, and so that the separation time is reduced.

EASING THE HOMECOMING

'How can I make coming home with the baby less traumatic for my older son?'

An older sibling usually has mixed feelings when it comes to the homecoming. On the one hand, he knows that he wants his mother to come home; on the other hand, he's not quite as sure about the baby she's planning to bring with her. In a way he's pumped about having a new baby in the house – it's exciting and different and, if he's old enough, something to boast to his friends about. But at the same time, he's probably at least a little nervous when

he contemplates that great unknown – just how his life is going to change once that baby's carried through his front door and deposited in what used to be his cot.

How you handle the homecoming will influence, at least initially, whether your child's greatest expectations or worst fears about the new baby are realized. Here's how to accentuate the positive and minimize the negative:

- Consider letting your child come home with you. Being a part of the homecoming team, rather than waiting at home, will help him feel less threatened by baby's arrival. It will also increase his sense of excitement, as well as his sense of 'ownership.' So, if possible (and this will work only if a relative or other familiar adult is along, so daddy can be free to take care of any paperwork and carry the suitcase and bags of gifts), have him come to the hospital with daddy to take you and the new baby home.

- If he can't join you at the hospital, have him help with preparations for the baby's arrival at home. While daddy goes to pick you up, a relative or friend can help him lay out nappies and cottonwool balls, make signs or other decorations, bake cakes or other treats, and otherwise set the scene for a festive homecoming. Try to come into the house first (perhaps daddy can wait in the car with the baby) so that you can greet your older child privately for just a few minutes.

- Start right off using the baby's name, rather than always referring to the new sibling as 'the baby'. This will give your older child a sense that this baby is really a person, not just an object.

- Limit visitors for the first few days at home – for your own health and sanity, and for your older child's sake. Even the most well-meaning of visitors tend to go on endlessly about a new baby, all but ignoring the older child. Those visitors you can't deny immediate access to (such as grandparents, aunts and uncles, and close friends) should be briefed in advance not to be overly and obviously effusive towards the baby, and to give plenty of attention to the older sibling. You can also suggest that visitors come when he's in school or after he's gone to bed. Limiting visitors for the first week or so has other benefits – more time for you to regain your strength and more opportunity for the bonding of your expanding family.

- Focus a lot of your attention on your older child, particularly in the early days, when the baby will probably be sleeping or feeding a good deal of the time. Hang his drawings on the refrigerator, applaud toileting if he's new on the potty, tell him how proud you are about his being such a good big brother, sit down and read stories to him whenever you can (nursing sessions are a perfect time for this), be quick with praise and slow with anger. Be wary of worshiping at the new baby's cot ('Oh, look at those tiny fingers!' or 'Isn't she beautiful!' or 'See, she's smiling!'), which could leave your son feeling very much like yesterday's news. But don't go to the other extreme, either, consciously avoiding showing affection for the new baby in front of your older child. Such tactics can confuse or worry him ('I thought we were supposed to love this baby. Is it possible my parents will soon stop loving me, too?') or lead him to jump to anxiety-provoking

conclusions ('They're pretending not to like the baby so I won't know that they really like her more than me'). Instead, relate baby talk to him: 'Look at those tiny fingers; do you believe yours were once so small?' or 'Isn't she beautiful? I think she looks just like you', or 'See, she's smiling at you; I think she loves you already.'

- Some wise visitors remember to bring a small gift for the older child; but should several days pass and truckloads of baby gifts come in with nothing for the older sibling, have grandma or daddy bring home something special just for him. If the influx of gifts really seems excessive, put away those that don't come to his attention. Eventually, those cards and gifts will stop coming.

- If your older child decides he wants to stay home from nursery school for a few days, let him. This will assure him that you aren't pushing him out of the house so you can enjoy the baby without him, while giving him an opportunity to bond with (and adjust to) the baby. Decide in advance just how long his 'holiday' will be, so that he doesn't get the idea that he can stay home permanently. Don't, however, force your child to stay home if he would rather go to school. He may feel the need to be in a place where there is no new baby and where there are other centres of interest.

  Of course, if your older child is in primary school, missing a few days of school might not be an option (or, at least, not one his teacher would appreciate). In that case, find ways to remind him that he's special, too. Pack an I-love-you note in his lunch box, plan an after-school activity or snack for him that makes him feel especially welcome at home.

RESENTMENT

'My toddler is openly resentful of the new baby. She tells me she wants him to go back to the hospital.'

You obviously can't carry out your child's wishes, but you can – and should – let her express them. Though her feelings may seem very negative, the fact that she is able to vent them is actually very positive. Every older sibling feels a certain measure of resentment towards the new intruder (or to her parents for bringing the intruder in). Some just express it more openly than others. Instead of implying to your older child that she's bad to feel that way ('Oh, that's a terrible thing to say about the baby!'), try a little empathy. Tell her that you understand that it isn't always fun to have a new baby in the house – for her or you. Let her talk out her resentment if she needs to. Share some stories about her when she was a new baby, so that she'll begin to see that there's some hope for the baby, too (once the baby gets bigger, he won't need to be held so much; once he learns to communicate in other ways, he won't cry so much; once he gets more grown up, he'll be able to do some things for himself). Then, instead of dwelling on the subject, move on quickly to an activity that's focused on her ('How about if we bundle the baby up and go to the playground together?').

Some children don't feel free to express negative feelings towards a new baby, and it's a good idea to encourage them to talk about how they feel. One way to do that is to confide your own mixed feelings: 'I love the baby, but sometimes I hate having to get up in the middle of the night to feed him', or 'Boy, with our new baby I hardly ever have a free moment for myself'. Another is to tell and/or read stories about older siblings with mixed feelings about new arrivals. If you are an older sibling yourself, you can talk about how you felt when a new baby came to your house.

'My son shows no hostility towards his new sister. But he's been acting very moody and disagreeable with me.'

Some older siblings don't see any point in turning on a newborn (after all, you can't get a rise out of her no matter what you do). The next best target, one they feel they can torment with less guilt and more satisfying results, is mummy or daddy. It is, after all, mummy who's spending hours feeding and rocking the baby, and daddy who's always busy changing and cuddling her – and both of them who are spending much less time focused on him than they used to. A first-born may vent his feelings towards his parents by throwing tantrums, exhibiting regressive behaviour, refusing to eat or rejecting his parents entirely and turning to someone else (a baby-sitter, for instance) as a 'favourite'. This type of behaviour is a common and normal component of the adjustment period.

Don't take your son's disagreeableness personally – and definitely don't scold or punish him for it. For much better results, try to respond with patience, understanding, reassurance and extra attention. Encourage your son to voice his feelings: ('I understand that you must be pretty angry because of all the time I've been spending with the new baby.') And remember, this too will pass – usually within a few months.

'I was all prepared for sibling rivalry when we decided to have another baby. But throughout the pregnancy and in the four months since her brother's arrival, my daughter hasn't shown any jealousy or resentment. Is that healthy?'

Jealousy and resentment are common reactions when a baby arrives on the scene, but they certainly aren't inevitable – or essential for the development of strong sibling ties. A child who seems delighted with a new sibling isn't necessarily hiding brewing hostility, she may just be genuinely thrilled with the new addition, or honestly excited about her role as big sister. Or she may be so completely secure in your love that she's thoroughly unthreatened by the changing family dynamics.

Which isn't to say that she'll never have anything but warm feelings for her baby brother. She may find some solid ground for resentment down the developmental road – once the helpless little newcomer takes to the floors as a crawler, tearing up her books, scattering her bricks on the floor and chewing the fingers off her favourite doll (see page 751).

In the meantime, you should be sure that your older child gets at least as much time and attention as her new sibling, even if she isn't demanding it. If you unintentionally begin to take her for granted because she's being such a good sport about the new baby, she may start to feel neglected and, eventually, resentful. Even wheels that don't squeak, after all, need to be oiled periodically.

And because almost every child experiences some negative feelings towards a sibling somewhere along the way, make sure she knows it's okay to have such feelings, and give her ample opportunity to express them.

EXPLAINING GENITAL DIFFERENCES

'My three-year-old daughter is obsessed with her new brother's penis. She wants to know what it is and why she doesn't have one. I don't know what to tell her.'

Try the truth. As young as your daughter is, if she's old enough to ask questions about her body and her brother's, she's old enough to get some honest answers. It can be quite a shock for a little girl to see something on her baby brother that she doesn't have (or for a little boy to note the absence of a penis on his baby sister). Realize (and make sure she knows) that her interest is not inappropriate; as little scientists, children are curious about everything in their environment, including everything on their bodies and the bodies of those around them. The simple explanation that boys (and men, like daddy) have penises and girls (and women, like mummy) have vaginas is probably all that is needed and will help your child understand one fundamental difference between males and females. Be sure to use the proper names for these body parts just as you would for the eyes, nose or mouth, and add more information only if it's requested. (If she asks why, for instance, you can volunteer that girls have vaginas so that when they grow up they can have babies and boys have penises so they can be fathers.) Should your child ask more in-depth questions than you feel comfortable fielding, look for a book for parents that can help you with the job, and/or for one written and illustrated at your child's level that you can read to her.

NURSING IN FRONT OF AN OLDER CHILD

'I'm planning to nurse my second baby, but I'm worried about doing it in front of my four-year-old son.'

Not to worry. There's absolutely no reason why you shouldn't nurse in front of your son. Rather than being harmful, it's healthy for him to understand that breastfeeding is a normal, natural process – not something to be hidden or ashamed of. In fact, it's more likely to be harmful if you go out of your way to keep your son away from you while you nurse – considering how much time is spent nursing a newborn, you'd be seeing very little of your older child. Besides baby's naptime, there's no more undivided time you can give your son than when you're nursing. Almost any quiet activity, from reading a story to putting together a puzzle, can be pursued during feeding sessions.

If you're uncomfortable about your older child seeing your breasts, nurse discreetly, covering up as much as you feel you need to. But don't overreact if he does catch a glimpse or even reaches a curious hand over for a squeeze. This is a sign of normal curiosity, not of inappropriate sexual interest. Rather than reacting sharply, which could give him the idea that there's something 'bad' about the human body, react nonchalantly. Explain that your breasts are the baby's source of nourishment now (as they were for him when he was a baby), and then divert his attention quickly to another activity.

THE OLDER CHILD WHO WANTS TO NURSE

'My 2½-year-old son, watching me nurse the baby, has been saying he wants some milk, too. I thought the interest would pass if I ignored it, but it hasn't.'

Actually, one way to cure an older sibling of the desire to nurse is to let him know that he can. (But only if the older sib is still very young; a child of four or more needs to understand that nursing is for babies.) Often, just your

okay will be enough, and he won't feel the need to pursue the issue further. If he does, consider letting him – if you're comfortable doing so. He'll feel that he's being given access to this mysterious and special relationship the baby has with you. Chances are one nip is all he'll need to make him realize that babies don't have it so good after all. The warm, watery, unfamiliar, poor-excuse-for-milk fluid he extracts almost certainly won't be worth the effort involved (and he may well give up before the milk ever makes it to his mouth). His feelings of curiosity satisfied, he'll probably never ask to nurse again, and he'll likely feel more sympathy for the baby (who's stuck drinking that stuff when he's guzzling apple juice and 'real' milk and gobbling macaroni and cheese and peanut-butter sandwiches) than jealousy. (Of course, don't try this approach if you're uncomfortable with it; instead, provide other forms of attention.)

If he continues to show an interest in nursing, or if he objects to baby's indulging, it's probably not a breast to suck on that he's after, but a breast (and a mummy) to snuggle up against and some of the attention he feels the baby's always getting when nursing. Including your older child in the nursing sessions may be all that's necessary to quell his interest in taking to the breast.

There are several simple ways to do this. Before you sit down to nurse, for example, say, 'I'm going to give the baby some milk now. Would you like some juice?' or 'Would you like your lunch now, while baby is eating?' Or take the quiet opportunity offered by nursing to read him a story, help him do a puzzle, or listen to music with him (an activity that's good because you don't have to use your hands). Be sure, too, that your first-born gets plenty of hugging and cuddling when you're not feeding the baby.

HELPING SIBLING LIVE WITH COLIC

'Our new baby's constant crying seems to really upset his three-year-old sister. What can I do?'

If there's an innocent bystander in a household with a colicky newborn, it's an older sibling. After all, she didn't ask for this baby (and if she did, she may be regretting that request). With all the attention that's being paid to him, she is likely feeling somewhat threatened and even replaced. And here he is making a terrible racket during what was once one of her favourite parts of the day – dinner (and probably bath and story time) with mummy and daddy. Not only is the crying unbearable for her, so is the upheaval that comes with it. Instead of being a time for eating, sharing and quiet play, early evening turns into a time of disrupted meals, frantic pacing and rocking, and distracted, irritable parents. Worst of all, perhaps, is the helplessness she probably feels. While the adults in the house are able to at least take some action against the colic (as futile as it might be) and commiserate with each other about it, she can only sit by, powerless and miserable.

You can't make colic easy on your older child any more than you can make it easy on yourself. But you can help her cope better, if you:

Talk it out. Explain, on your older child's level, what colic is. Reassure her that it won't last, that once the baby gets used to being in his new and strange world – and learns other ways of communicating – most of the crying will stop. Point out that when she was a new baby she cried a lot (even if she didn't actually have colic). This should give her hope for her new brother, too.

Let her know it's not her fault. Little children tend to blame themselves for everything that goes wrong in a household, from mummy and daddy's arguing to great-grandfather's dying to a new baby's crying. Your older child needs to be reassured that no one is at fault here, least of all her.

Show and tell her you love her. Dealing with a colicky baby can be so distracting – especially in the context of an already busy day – that you may forget to do those special little things that show a toddler or older child you care. So make a point of doing at least one of those things (play 'swimming' in the bath, bake cakes with her, help her paint a mural on an extra-large piece of paper) every day, before the colic session begins. Even during the worst of the storm, make sure you break from the pacing and rocking occasionally to give your daughter a reassuring hug.

Divide the baby, conquer the sibling rivalry. When both parents are home, try taking turns walking the floor with the baby during colic marathons, so that your older child is usually getting the attention of at least one parent. Once in a while, weather permitting, one parent can take baby out for a ride in the pushchair or the car (the motion often helps subdue the colic) while the other parent spends some quality quiet time at home with your daughter. Or one of you can take your daughter out to dinner (for pizza with a side of peace and quiet) or, if it's still light out, for an early evening excursion to the playground while the other toughs it out at home with The Screamer.

Don't sacrifice the rituals. Routines are comforting to young children, and when they're disrupted, it can be enormously unsettling – especially during times when life is more unsettled than usual (as when there's a new, crying baby in the house). Do your best to make sure your daughter's treasured rituals don't fall victim to your baby's colic; if bedtime has always meant a leisurely bath (complete with bubbles and splashing), a cuddlefest and four stories, strive for a leisurely bath, cuddlefest and four stories every night, even when colic's in full swing. Dividing the colic duty will, hopefully, make those routines possible more often than not.

Save some time for her alone. Even if it's only half an hour, try to find some time every day to spend with your older child without baby sibling tagging along. Snatch the time when the baby is napping (this is more important than catching up on paperwork), when your mother or a friend comes by to visit or, if you're able to afford it, when you have a sitter for the baby.

REGRESSIVE BEHAVIOUR

'Ever since her sister was born, my three-year-old daughter has started acting like a baby herself. She talks in baby jargon, wants to be picked up all the time, and even has toileting accidents.'

Even fully grown adults can't help sometimes envying a newborn her undemanding existence ('Oh, that's the life!' they'll sigh as a sleeping baby is wheeled by them in a padded pram). It's not surprising that a youngster, barely out of the pram herself and just beginning to master some of the many responsibilities that come with growing up, would yearn for a return to babyhood when confronted with an infant sibling. Especially when she sees that acting like a baby works very well for her new sister, who is allowed to lie in the lap of luxurious leisure (not to mention the lap of her parent), who is carried everywhere, catered to endlessly, opens her mouth to whimper and receives precisely what she wants when she wants it (instead of receiving a sharp, 'Stop that whining!').

Rather than pressuring your older daughter to 'be a big girl' at this sensitive time, baby her when she wants to be babied – even if it means caring for two 'babies' at once. Give her the attention she is craving (rock her in your arms when she's tired, carry her up the stairs once in a while, feed her when she demands it), and don't chide her when she regresses to one-word sentences (even if it grates on your nerves), wants to take her milk from a bottle (even if she never has before), or if her toilet habits take a sudden turn for the infantile. At the same time, encourage her to act her age by making a big deal about big girl behaviour, for instance, when she cleans up after herself, helps you out with the baby, or goes on the potty. Offering such praise in front of others will reinforce its benefits. Remind her that she was your first baby, and now she's your first big girl. Take every opportunity to point out the special things that she can do that her sister can't, such as enjoying ice cream at a birthday party, zooming down the slide at the playground, or having pizza out with mummy and daddy. Bake with her while baby is napping, enlist her help when food shopping, take her to see a movie while the baby stays with a sitter. In her own time, she will figure out for herself the perks of being the older child and will decide to leave her baby past behind.

SEEING GREEN?

Has a little green monster invaded the nursery since the arrival of your new baby? Or are you just hoping to head off older sibling envy? All the tips in this chapter for dealing with sibling rivalry should help prevent or ease those very normal jealous feelings. It might also help to refer to the infant either by his or her name, or as 'our baby' or 'your baby brother (or sister)' – never as 'my baby'.

Try, too, to avoid commands that make the older child feel as if his or her life revolves around the younger child: 'Keep quiet – baby's sleeping' or 'You can't sit on my lap – baby's nursing' or 'Stop poking the baby – you'll hurt him!' You'll get a better result by limiting 'don't' directives and rephrasing requests more positively: 'Baby's sleeping. Let's see if we can whisper so he won't wake up'. Or 'How about sitting on this chair right next to me so we can be close together while I'm nursing?' Or 'Your baby brother really loves it when you stroke him gently like this'. But remember, too, that a certain amount of jealousy is inevitable and, when you think about it, completely understandable.

THE OLDER SIBLING HURTING THE NEW BABY

'I left the room for a minute and was horrified when I returned to find my older son jabbing his baby sister with a toy. She wasn't hurt this time, but it seemed as though he was trying to make her cry on purpose.'

Although such an assault would seem, on the surface, nothing more than a sadistic attempt to harm an unwanted newcomer, this isn't usually the case. Though there may be an element of hostility involved (and this is only natural, considering the upheaval a newborn causes in an older sibling's life), these seemingly malicious attacks are often merely innocent investigations. Your son may have been trying to make his sister cry not out of malevolence, but out of curiosity to find out how this strange little creature you've brought home works (just as he is constantly examining and probing everything else in his environment). The trick is to react to such a situation without over-reacting. Impress upon your older child, by example and by involving him in baby care when you're around, the importance of being gentle with the baby. When he gets rough, react calmly and rationally, avoiding angry, guilt-provoking recriminations for him (if he's into tormenting you, he will enjoy having triggered your outburst) and hysterical protectiveness for her (which can reinforce any feelings of jealousy). Avoiding the explosive response is even more vital if the baby has actually been hurt; making an older child feel guilty about what he has done, whether it was intentional or not, can leave emotional scars and serves little positive purpose.

But while overreacting to your older child's aggressive behaviour towards his sibling isn't a good idea, neither is ignoring it. Let your child know calmly, empathetically, but in no uncertain terms that hitting or otherwise hurting anyone (baby or otherwise) is unacceptable. Give him alternative ways of venting his mixed (or hostile) feelings that won't harm baby – like using words ('Baby, you make me so mad!'), punching a pillow, pounding play

WIDELY SPACED SIBS

Not all siblings come two or three years apart. Thanks to second marriages, secondary infertility (difficulty getting pregnant a second time), a renewed need to fill an almost-empty nest, and good old-fashioned 'surprises', many brand-new older brothers and sisters are actually *much* older – six, eight, or even ten or more years older.

Waiting many years for a second round of the baby game offers several advantages. For one, older children usually make excellent baby-tenders. While a three-year-old can't be trusted to hold a newborn unsupervised for even a moment, an eight- or nine-year-old can watch a sibling while mum takes a shower or dad finishes the dishes. A teenage sib can even serve as an occasional baby-sitter (if he or she can be persuaded to give up an evening out with friends). Since older children already have a life of their own beyond their home and their parents, they're less likely to be threatened by the baby invasion than a toddler or preschooler would be (and less likely to miss lap time). And because they're in school or activities much of the day, there's more opportunity for parents to focus –

uninterrupted – on the new arrival, and less of that tugged-in-two-directions feeling.

Of course, sibs of all age differences can and do experience rivalry and their share of transition issues when a new baby arrives. (In fact, for those who have enjoyed only-heir status for a decade or more, the transition may be even tougher, though ultimately, the revelation that family life doesn't revolve around him or her may come as a beneficial, if not initially welcome, wakeup call.) And the challenges faced by these widely spaced sibs – and their parents – are much different from those faced by those who are close in age. For instance, older children may not resent the loss of mum's lap, but they may resent that she can't always show up for after-school games or activities because baby has to nap. A preteen may be proud of the new family addition – or decidedly embarrassed (it's proof that his parents had . . . sex!) Logistics of everything – from where to eat (you may be exiled to 'family' restaurants long after the older offspring have graduated to white-napkin establishments) to what music to listen to in the car (the latest

---

dough, jumping up and down, or drawing a picture.

Still, keep in mind that when it comes to an older (but still very young) sibling hurting younger, prevention is preferable to punishment. No matter how well you believe your older child has got the message, don't leave the two of them unsupervised in the same room together again until your older child is of an age – probably around five years old – to understand what damage he can do. Younger children do not really have a sense of the extent of injury they can inflict with their actions, and they can inflict serious harm unintentionally.

DIVIDING TIME AND ATTENTION

'I'm wondering how I can divide myself fairly, so that both my four-year-old son and his new baby brother get the attention they need and the older child won't be jealous.'

As much as a second you (or at least a second pair of arms) would prove helpful at this time in your life, that's obviously not possible. Which means there will be only one of you to go around – leaving you divided at least two ways for many years to come. The question is how to make the division in a

hip-hop single, or yet another chorus of Barney's 'I Love You') to what movies to go to (action thrillers or mousecapades) to which holiday spots to head for (white water river adventures or Disney cruise) – may be complicated by the age spread. Then, of course, there are the late nights on two very different fronts: how do you stay up waiting for your teen's key to turn in the door when you know you'll have to be up again in an hour for baby's next feeding?

To help your older child or children adjust to life with a new baby:

♦ Don't forget to prepare. Just because your firstborn is older and wiser doesn't mean he or she knows anything about newborns. A little Baby basics – in the form of books geared to your child's reading level, visits with friends' babies, a walk down memory lane through his or her own baby book – will help paint a realistic picture of what infants are really like.

♦ Pay attention. The signs that your older child is craving a little mum or dad time may be less obvious than they would be in a toddler or preschooler. But just because your firstborn doesn't cry for it, doesn't mean he or she doesn't need it. In fact, with the stresses of school, peer pressures and growing up weighing heavy, your older child may need your attention more than ever (even as he or she is least likely to admit it). Make time for just the two or three of you – away from the baby. Hire a sitter and take your first-born out to a grown-up dinner and a movie, an afternoon at an amusement park or shopping centre, a few rounds of miniature golf.

♦ Avoid turning your older child into a miniparent. Occasionally asking your old-enough firstborn to watch the baby while you run to the store or the post office is fair. Asking him or her to spend every Saturday night at home sitting for a baby sibling is not. Baby-sitting shouldn't be an obligation that comes with the territory of being a much older child. If you often want to enlist his or her services for the evening, you should ask (not demand), and pay the going rate.

♦ Let your children act their age. Even a teenager is still a child and has every right to act like one. So keep expectations realistic.

way that will be best for your preschooler as well as for his new brother.

Later on in your child-rearing years, the split will have to be pretty much equal; the amount of time you spend with one child will have to be matched fairly evenly by the amount of time you spend with the other (just as every apple or slab of cake will have to be divided precisely to satisfy both children). Now, however, a little lopsidedness in favour of your older child is not only acceptable, it's best. Consider, first, that your older child is used to being an only child who never had to share your attention before. Your baby, on the other hand, is happily unaware of who's getting more of you and will be basically content as long as his needs are being met. Keep in mind, too, that unlike your firstborn, who came home from the hospital to a relatively quiet home, your new baby has been born into a very active household, with plenty of parent-children interaction to keep his senses occupied and stimulated. If he sits on your lap while you're building a brick city or fitting together puzzle pieces with your older son, or nestles in a baby carrier while you push your older son's swing, he's receiving as much stimulation as if you were playing with him directly. Finally, remember that there's another care provider in your home now – your older son – who will be giving lively attention to your baby.

There are a couple of ways to make double duty doable, while preventing excessive jealousy (you probably won't be able to prevent it all). Firstly, you can share your attention with your older child without cutting into your time with the younger by taking care of the needs of both at once (for instance, reading a book to your son while nursing or bottle-feeding his brother). Secondly, you can appoint your first-born your chief assistant. He can fetch nappies for the baby when he's wet, sing and dance for the baby when he's cranky, and help you fold and put away the baby's laundry – matching those little socks is a chore for you, but a challenge and a learning experience for a child. You can also enlist your older child in such 'big boy' chores as dusting, opening vegetable packets, or setting the table. Even when his help isn't all that helpful, acknowledging his efforts ('What a big helper you are!') will make him feel like a valued member of the family – and, especially, of the mummy and daddy team. Feeling useful – and a part of your team – will help keep him from feeling neglected.

But the older sibling needs more than shared time; he also needs an unbroken span of time alone with you every day – more so than your newborn does. Baby's nap time is ideal. So is any time when both parents are home, and baby care can be shared. (Keep in mind that your older child will appreciate time alone with each of you, so switching off with baby makes sense.)

Of course, it isn't always possible to put your older child's needs first, or to give him more than his fair share of attention. Nor is it a good idea, even while the baby's too young to notice or care. Sharing you with the baby is a part

of life with a sibling that your older child will have to learn to accept – and the sooner he learns to accept it, the less rivalry you'll ultimately have to deal with. There will be times – plenty of times – when he'll have to wait while you finish a feeding or a nappy change. It will be easier for him if you continue to remind him of the benefits of being the older child and if you praise him for his independence (when he does something for himself or plays on his own) and his patience (when he waits for your attention without whining). It'll also help if you sometimes turn the tables. So once in a while, say to the baby (even if your child may have doubts about baby's comprehension), 'You're going to have to wait a minute for your nappy change because I have to give your brother his snack', or 'I can't pick you up now because I have to tuck your big brother in'.

SIBLING ATTACHMENT

'I wonder how I can help my older child to feel more connected to his new baby brother.'

Mothers and fathers, who spend many hours a day caring for their newborns, have built-in opportunities for bonding with them. And there's no good reason why siblings can't do the same. With close adult supervision, even the youngest of older siblings can share in baby's care and begin to feel a sense of attachment to the baby – and an easing of postpartum jealousy. Depending on the age of the older child, he can participate in a variety of ways, including the following:

Changing. A school-age child can actually change a wet nappy with mum or dad standing nearby. A toddler can help by fetching a clean one, handing over a baby wipe, patting down the Velcro or tabs or by entertaining the wriggling baby during the process.

Feeding. If your baby is bottle-fed, or takes a bottle occasionally, even a fairly young child can hold it for him. If your baby is on the breast exclusively, your older child can't actually do the feeding, but he can snuggle next to you with a book while you nurse his sibling. Or he can sing to his baby brother while he feeds.

Burping. Even a toddler can gently pat baby's back to bring on an after-meal burp – and he's likely to delight in the results.

Bathing. Bath time can be a fun time for the whole family. An older sibling can pass the soap, flannel or towel, pour rinse water (temperature-tested by an adult) over baby's body (but not head), and entertain baby with his own bath toys or with singing. But don't let a sibling under twelve be baby's only chaperone at bath time – not even for a moment.

Baby-sitting. While an older sibling can't take total responsibility for a younger one until he's a teen (never allow a preschooler to mind a baby alone for even a minute), he can be dubbed 'baby-sitter' when you're close by. Babies find no one quite as amusing as their older siblings, and finding that they have the ability to entertain baby is ego-boosting to senior sibs.

ESCALATING WARFARE

'My daughter was very loving towards her little brother from the time he was born. But now that he's crawling and able to get into her toys, she's suddenly turned on him.'

For many older siblings, a newborn doesn't pose much of a threat. He's helpless, basically immobile, incapable of grabbing away books or breaking up dolly tea parties. Give him several months to develop reaching, crawling, cruising and other motor skills, and the picture takes a turn from the idyllic. Even older children who have been loving (at least most of the time) to a younger sibling up to this point may suddenly begin to display hostility. And you can hardly blame them – a miniature barbarian has just invaded their turf. Their crayon boxes have been looted, their books violated, their dolls plundered.

To defend her turf, an older sibling (tension is usually greatest if the age difference between the two siblings is three years or less) often begins screaming at, hitting, pushing and knocking down the baby. Sometimes there is a mix of affection and aggression in the actions: what begins as a hug ends up with baby on the floor crying. The action often accurately reflects the child's conflicting inner feelings. As the parent, you have to walk a narrow tightrope in such a situation, protecting the younger sibling without punishing the older. Though you should make it clear to your older child that it's not permissible to hurt her younger brother intentionally, you should also make it clear that you understand and empathize with her plight and her frustrations. Try to give her the chance to play without him around part of the time (while he naps, is in the playpen or is otherwise occupied). Particularly when she has guests over, respect her privacy and property and be sure that her younger sibling does, too (by removing the baby whenever necessary). Spend some extra time with her, and intervene on her behalf whenever the baby takes away or tries to destroy her belongings, instead of always urging her to 'let him, he's only a baby'. But do give her plenty of praise on occasions when she comes to this mature realization on her own.

Fairly soon, the tables will turn. Little brother, tired of being pushed around and strong enough to do some intentional pushing (and hair pulling and biting) of his own, will start fighting back. This usually occurs near the end of the first year, and is followed by a couple of years or more of mixed feelings between siblings – a confusing combination of love and hate. You can expect these years, when you'll often feel more like a referee than a parent, to be a constant challenge to your patience and your ingenuity – as well as a joy.

◆ ◆ ◆

Part 4

READY REFERENCE

Baby's First Recipes

Four to Eight Months

STEAMED ANY-KIND-OF-VEGETABLE

MAKES 1 TO 2 CUPS, DEPENDING ON THE VEGETABLE

*1 white potato, sweet potato or acorn
    squash; 3 to 5 carrots; 150 g (5½ oz)
    green beans or shelled peas, well
    scrubbed or rinsed
Water, breast milk or formula (optional)*

1. Remove the peel from the potato, squash or carrots and cut into chunks or slices. Trim the green beans and cut in half. Pour water to a depth of 2.5 (1 in) into a medium-size saucepan and bring to the boil over a high heat.

QUICK TIP

Once baby has been introduced to each type of vegetable or fruit separately, start combining two or more into a vegetable or fruit medley.

---

2. Place the vegetable of choice in a steamer basket and place the basket in the pan. The water level should be below the level of the basket. Cover the saucepan.

3. Lower the heat to a simmer, and steam the vegetable until tender, 7 to 10 minutes for carrots, green beans and peas; 15 to 20 minutes for potatoes and squash.

4. For younger babies, purée the vegetable in blender or food processor, adding a few teaspoons of water, breast milk or formula to thin, if desired.
    For older babies, mash with a fork, leaving soft, small chunks for baby to chew on.

5. Store leftovers, covered, in the refrigerator, for 2 days or in the freezer for up to 2 months.

STEWED ANY-KIND-OF-FRUIT

MAKES 1 TO 2 CUPS, DEPENDING ON THE FRUIT USED

*2 fresh apples, pears, peaches or plums,
or 3 to 5 apricots, well scrubbed,
peeled, cored or pitted and cut into
medium-size chunks*
*Water, apple or white grape juice, breast
milk or formula (optional)*

1. Pour water to a depth of 2.5 cm (1 in) into a medium-size saucepan and bring to the boil over a high heat.

2. Place the fruit of choice in the pan, cover, lower the heat to a simmer and cook the fruit until tender, 7 to 10 minutes.

QUICK TIP

Most fruits, especially when they're well ripened, are naturally sweet. If a fruit purée you are serving tastes a little too tart, add a dash of apple or grape juice – or even juice concentrate. But remember, babies haven't cut that sweet tooth yet and it's probably best to keep it that way for as long as you can, by keeping fruits not too sweet.

QUICK TIP

No time to whip up a fresh batch of steamed vegetables or stewed fruit each day? No problem. You can freeze puréed vegetables or fruits or even stews in an ice cube tray. After they're solid, transfer the individually frozen portions to freezer bags; store for up to two months. Defrost one cube at a time (overnight in the refrigerator) to minimize waste. Each cube-portion equals approximately 1 tablespoon; depending on the age and appetite of your baby; a serving size can be anywhere from one cube to four or more. There's no need to reheat before serving (after defrosting) unless your baby prefers it warm.

---

3. For younger babies, purée the fruit in blender or food processor, adding a few teaspoons of water, juice, breast milk or formula to thin, if desired.

For older babies, mash with a fork, leaving soft small chunks.

4. Store leftovers, covered, in the refrigerator, for 2 days or freeze for up to 2 months.

Six to Twelve Months

LENTIL STEW

MAKES APPROXIMATELY ¼ CUP

25 g (1 oz) dried lentils
*1 small potato, well scrubbed, peeled
and cubed*
*½ teaspoon tomato juice (if tomatoes
have been introduced) or low-
sodium vegetable or chicken broth*
*1 small carrot, well scrubbed, peeled
and sliced*

1. Place all the ingredients in a saucepan and add enough water just to cover.

2. Bring to the boil over a high heat, then lower the heat and simmer the stew until the water is absorbed and the vegetables are cooked, about 30 minutes.

3. Purée the stew and carrots in a blender or food processor, or mash with a fork.

4. Store leftovers, covered, in the refrigerator, for up to 2 days or freeze for up to 2 months.

BABY'S FIRST CASEROLLE

MAKES 4 TO 6 SERVINGS

    1 teaspoon olive oil
    ½ small onion, peeled and chopped
    1 small potato, well scrubbed, peeled
        and cut into small chunks
    1 carrot, well scrubbed, peeled and sliced
    55 g (2 oz) dried lentils
    55 g (2 oz) dried cannellini, or kidney
        beans, quick-soaked (see Note)
    1½ cups low-sodium vegetable stock

1. Preheat the oven to 180°C (350°F).

2. Heat the olive oil in a small saucepan over a medium-low heat. Add the onions and cook until soft, 3 to 5 minutes.

3. Place the onions in an ovenproof casserole dish. Add the remaining ingredients, cover and bake until the lentils and beans are very tender, 1 hour. For younger babies, mash or purée the beans and vegetables.

4. Store leftovers in the refrigerator, covered, for up to 3 days.

Note: To quick-soak beans, place them in 480 ml (16 fl oz) water in a saucepan and bring to a rapid boil. Remove the pan from the heat, cover, and let sit for 1 hour. Then, drain the beans and proceed with the recipe.

Eight to Twelve Months

TOMATO AND CHEESE PASTA

Make sure baby's doctor has given the green light to tomatoes and to wheat before serving this dish.

MAKES APPROXIMATELY 2 SERVINGS

    55 g (2 oz) alphabet (or other small) pasta
    ½ teaspoon olive oil
    1 large ripe tomato, well scrubbed,
        peeled, seeded and finely chopped
    25 g (1 oz) low-fat Cheddar cheese, grated
    1 tablespoon cottage cheese

1. Bring a pot of water to the boil over a high heat. Add the pasta, lower the heat to medium and cook until very tender (*not* al dente). Drain and set aside.

2. Heat the oil in a saucepan over a low heat. Add the tomato and cook until very soft, 2 minutes. Remove the pan from the heat and add the cheeses, stirring until the Cheddar is melted.

3. Pour the sauce over the pasta and cool slightly before serving.

4. Store leftovers, covered, in the refrigerator, for up to 2 days.

BABY'S FIRST CRISTMAS TURKEY

MAKES 1 TO 2 SERVINGS

    1 medium-size slice of cooked turkey,
        cut up
    1 teaspoon water
    30 ml (1 fl oz) fruit-only cranberry sauce

1. Place the turkey and water in a blender or food processor and process to the desired consistency (purée for younger baby, small chunks for older baby).

2. Mix in the cranberry sauce and serve.

EGGY BREAD

Make sure baby's doctor has given the green light to wheat and to egg yolks before serving this dish.

MAKES 1 TO 2 SERVINGS

> 1 egg, beaten (use 2 yolks if egg white has not yet been introduced)
> 1 slice wholemeal bread
> ½ teaspoon rapeseed oil

1. Beat the egg in a large bowl. Dip the bread in the egg, turning it so that both sides are coated and all the egg is absorbed.

2. Heat the oil in a non-stick frying pan over a medium heat.

3. Place the bread in the pan and fry until golden brown on both sides, about 5 minutes.

4. Cut the bread into small pieces, removing the crusts, if necessary, and serve warm.

CROQUE BÉBÉ

Make sure baby's doctor has given the green light to wheat and to egg yolks before serving this dish.

MAKES 1 TO 2 SERVINGS

> 1 egg (use 2 yolks if egg white has not yet been introduced)
> 60 ml (2 fl oz) formula or breast milk
> 1 slice (about 25 g/1 oz) Gruyère or Cheddar cheese
> 1 slice wholemeal bread, cut in half
> Vegetable oil cooking spray

1. Beat the egg and breast milk or formula together in a large bowl.

2. Layer the cheese between the bread portions. Using tongs to hold the pieces together, soak the sandwich in the egg mixture, turning it until the liquid is absorbed.

3. Spray a non-stick frying pan with vegetable oil cooking spray. Heat over a medium-high heat, then reduce the heat to medium, add the sandwich and cook until golden brown on both sides, about 5 minutes. Cut the sandwich into small pieces, removing the crusts, if necessary, and serve warm.

4. This should be served on the day it is prepared. Store leftovers wrapped in aluminum foil to serve later in the day as a snack or another meal. Reheat, if necessary, in a toaster oven preheated to 160°C (325°F).

BANANA FRENCH TOAST

Make sure baby's doctor has given the green light to wheat, egg yolks and citrus before serving this dish.

MAKES 2 TO 4 SERVINGS

> 1 egg (use 2 yolks if egg white has not yet been introduced)
> 2 tablespoons orange juice concentrate (or use extra apple juice if citrus has not yet been introduced)
> 2 tablespoons apple juice concentrate
> ½ small ripe banana, puréed
> 60 ml (2 fl oz) breast milk or formula
> 2 slices wholemeal bread
> Vegetable oil cooking spray

1. Combine the egg, juice concentrates, banana and breast milk in a large bowl and mix well.

2. Place the bread in the concentrate mixture and soak, turning the slices with a fork or tongs, until the liquid is absorbed.

3. Spray a non-stick frying pan with vegetable oil cooking spray. Heat over a medium-high heat, then reduce the heat

to medium-low. Add the bread and cook until golden brown on both sides, about 5 minutes. Cut the bread into small pieces, removing the crusts, if necessary, and serve warm.

4. Store leftovers wrapped in aluminum foil, for up to 2 days or frozen for up to 1 month. Once thawed, reheat in a toaster oven preheated to 160°C (325°F).

FUNNY FINGERS

Make sure baby's doctor has given the green light to wheat before serving this dish.

MAKES 1 TO 2 SERVINGS

Vegetable oil cooking spray
1 small piece (10 cm/4 in long by 5 cm/2 in wide) fresh fish fillet, such as sole, flounder or haddock; or boneless chicken breast; or tofu
15 g (½ oz) fine wholemeal bread crumbs (see Note)
1 tablespoon Parmesan cheese, grated (optional)
½ teaspoon mayonnaise

1. Preheat the oven to 180°C (350°F). Spray a small baking dish with vegetable oil cooking spray. Set aside.

2. Cut the fish (checking carefully for bones), chicken or tofu into 1.3-cm (½-in) strips.

3. Combine the breadcrumbs and cheese in a small bowl, stirring to blend.

4. Rub the mayonnaise on the fish, chicken or tofu strips, then roll them in the crumb mixture.

5. Arrange the strips in the prepared baking dish and bake for 5 minutes. Turn the strips and continue to bake until golden brown and cooked through, about 5 minutes more. Serve warm.

6. Store leftovers wrapped in aluminum foil in the refrigerator for up to 2 days.

Note: To make your own breadcrumbs, toast a piece of wholemeal bread, tear it into pieces and process into crumbs in a blender or food processor. Store in an airtight container for up to 3 days.

FRUIT SUNDAE

Only prepare fruit that's been okayed by the doctor.

MAKES 1 TO 2 SERVINGS

45 g (1½ oz) fresh fruit, such as ripe bananas, cantaloupe, peaches and/or strawberries
60 ml (2 fl oz) whole-milk yoghurt
1 teaspoon juice-sweetened preserves
Oat circles (such as Cheerios)

1. Depending on the fruit, scrub or rinse it well before peeling or removing the rind. Hull the strawberries.

2. Finely chop the fruit or cut into chunks, depending on the age of your baby. Arrange the pieces on a small plate and top with yoghurt, then preserves and finally oat circles.

3. This is best served on the day it is prepared. Store leftovers, covered, in the refrigerator, to serve later in the day as a snack or meal.

APPLE-CRANBERRY CUBES

MAKES 4 SERVINGS

1 tablespoon unflavoured gelatin
60 ml (2 fl oz) water
350 ml (12 fl oz) unsweetened apple-cranberry or other flavour juice
60 ml (2 fl oz) apple juice concentrate

1. Mix the gelatin and the water together in a medium-size bowl; let stand to soften, 1 minute.

2. Meanwhile, bring the apple-cranberry juice to the boil in a small saucepan over a medium heat. Remove the pan from the heat and add the unsweetened juice to the gelatin mixture. Stir until the gelatin is thoroughly dissolved. Stir in the juice concentrate and pour the mixture into an 20-cm (8-in) square baking tin. Refrigerate until firm, then cut into cubes and mound in a dessert dish.

3. Store leftovers, covered, in the refrigerator, for up to 4 days.

BANANA-ORANGE GEL

Make sure your baby has been introduced to citrus before serving this dish.

MAKES 4 SERVINGS

1 tablespoon unflavoured gelatin
60 ml (2 fl oz) water
240 ml (8 fl oz) fresh orange juice
120 ml (4 fl oz) banana-orange juice
concentrate
1 small ripe banana, sliced

1. Mix the gelatin and the water together in a medium-size bowl; allow to stand to soften, 1 minute.

2. Meanwhile, bring the orange juice and juice concentrate to the boil in a small saucepan over a medium heat. Remove the pan from the heat and add the juice mixture to the gelatin mixture. Stir until the gelatin is thoroughly dissolved.

3. Pour half the mixture into a 20-cm (8-in) square baking tin and place in the freezer until thickened, about 10 minutes. Add a layer of sliced banana and cover with the remaining gelatin mixture. Refrigerate, covered, until firm, then cut into squares and serve.

4. Store leftovers, covered, in the refrigerator, for up to 4 days.

PEACHY FROZEN YOGHURT

MAKES 4 SERVINGS

300 ml (10 fl oz) natural whole-milk
yoghurt
170 g (6 oz) well-scrubbed, peeled,
sliced fresh yellow peaches
60 ml (2 fl oz) apple juice concentrate

FABULOUS FINGER FOODS

Let your self-feeder dig into any of the following:

- Cheerios or other low-sugar whole-grain cereal
- Whole-grain toast strips
- Rice cakes
- Digestive biscuits (look for fruit-sweetened ones)
- Unsalted pretzels
- Bagels (a few days old, preferably whole-grain)

- String cheese
- Grated Cheddar cheese
- Very ripe peeled pear, peach, plum, avocado or mango wedges
- Banana slices
- Fork-mashed peas
- Fork-mashed cooked beans (kidney, flageolet, cannellini)
- Mini meat (or minced chicken) balls (poached in broth or sauce so they don't get crusty)
- Flaked fish sticks

MAKES ONE 23-CM (9-IN) SQUARE LAYER
CAKE

> *Vegetable oil cooking spray*
> *275 g (9¼ oz) thinly sliced, scrubbed,*
> * peeled carrots*
> *About 600 ml (20 fl oz) apple juice*
> * concentrate*
> *225 g (8 oz) raisins*
> *285 g (10 oz) wholemeal flour*
> *75 g (2½ oz) wheat germ*
> *2 tablespoons low-sodium baking*
> * powder*
> *1 tablespoon ground cinnamon*
> *60 ml (2 fl oz) rapeseed oil*
> *2 whole eggs*
> *4 egg whites*
> *1 tablespoon vanilla extract*
> *125 g (4½ oz) unsweetened apple purée*
> *Cream Cheese Frosting (recipe follows)*

1. Preheat the oven to 180°C (350°F).
Line two 23-cm (9-in) square cake tins
with greaseproof paper and spray the paper with vegetable oil cooking spray. Set
aside.

2. Combine the carrots with 270 ml
(9 fl oz) of the juice concentrate in a
medium-size saucepan. Bring to the boil
over a high heat, then lower the heat to
medium and simmer, covered, until the
carrots are tender, 15 to 20 minutes.
Transfer the carrot mixture to a blender
or food processor and purée until
smooth. Add the raisins and process until finely chopped. Set the mixture aside
to cool.

3. Combine the flour, wheat germ, baking powder and cinnamon in a large
mixing bowl. Add 300 ml (10 fl oz) of
the remaining juice concentrate (and
any remaining concentrate from the
Cream Cheese Frosting, see recipe below), oil, whole eggs, egg whites and
vanilla and beat just until well mixed.

QUICK MEALTIME IDEAS

- ◆ Cheese omelette or scramble (use only yolks until whites are introduced)

- ◆ Natural whole-milk yoghurt mixed with fruit purées or finely chopped fresh fruit

- ◆ Melted cheese on wholemeal bread

- ◆ Cottage cheese and melon pieces

- ◆ Veggie burger (screen for ingredients baby hasn't been introduced to)

- ◆ Finely mashed tuna fish stuffed in wholemeal pitta

- ◆ Steamed frozen mixed vegetables topped with melted cheese

---

1. Combine all the ingredients in a
blender or food processor and process
until smooth.

2. Pour into an 20-cm (8-in) square baking tin and freeze until mushy. Scrape
the mixture into a large mixing bowl and
beat until fluffy. Repeat the freezing-
beating process once or twice more.
Then freeze until the desired texture is
reached. If the dessert freezes too hard,
allow it to thaw until spoonable.

FIRST BIRTHDAY CAKE

Usually, by the first birthday, egg whites
and wheat have been introduced. If the
doctor has not given them the green light
for your baby, save this recipe for the second birthday, or another occasion.

Fold in the carrot purée and apple purée. Divide the batter between the prepared cake tins, smoothing out the tops with a rubber spatula.

4. Bake until a knife inserted in the centre of the cake comes out clean, 35 to 40 minutes. Place on wire racks and allow to cool briefly in the tins, then turn out onto the racks to cool completely.

5. When cool, frost with Cream Cheese Frosting (see recipe below). Place a layer, top side up, on a platter. Spread some of the frosting over the top of the layer. Place the second layer on top of the first layer, top side up, and use the rest of the frosting to frost the top and sides of the cake.

6. Store any leftovers, loosely covered, in the refrigerator for up to 2 days.

CREAM CHEESE FROSTING

MAKES ENOUGH TO FROST ONE 23-CM (9-IN) SQUARE LAYER CAKE

> *120 ml (4 fl oz) apple juice concentrate*
> *450 g (1 lb) cream cheese, at room temperature*
> *2 teaspoons vanilla extract*
> *75 g (2½ oz) finely chopped raisins*
> *1½ teaspoons unflavoured gelatin*

1. Set aside 2 tablespoons of the juice concentrate. Process the remaining juice concentrate, cream cheese, vanilla and raisins in a blender or food processor until smooth. Transfer to a mixing bowl. Set aside.

2. Stir the gelatin into the reserved 2 tablespoons juice concentrate in a small saucepan; allow to stand to soften, 1 minute. Then, heat to boiling over a medium heat, stirring to dissolve the gelatin.

3. Beat the gelatin mixture into the cream cheese mixture until well blended. Cover and refrigerate just until the frosting begins to set, 30 to 60 minutes. Then frost the cake.

◆ ◆ ◆

Common Home Remedies

Doctors recommend suctioning baby's nose to ease the congestion of a cold. Cold compresses, you hear, are the best way to treat a burn. And steam is ideal for treating a baby with the croup. But just how do you suction a baby's nose? What is a cold compress? And how do you build up enough steam to ease the croup? This guide to home remedies will give you the answers.

COLD COMPRESSES

Fill a basin (a polystyrene bucket or cooler is best) with cold water and a tray or two of ice cubes. Dip a clean flannel into the water, wring it out, and place it over the affected area. Repeat the process when the flannel is no longer cold.

COLD SOAKS

Fill a basin (a polystyrene bucket or cooler is best) with cold water and a few ice cubes. Immerse the injured part for 15 to 30 minutes, if possible. Repeat 30 minutes after first soak, if necessary. Do not apply ice directly to baby's skin.

COOL COMPRESSES

Fill a basin with cool water. Dip a flannel or towel into the water, wring it out, and place it over the affected area. Repeat the process when the flannel is no longer wet and cool.

EYE SOAKS

For eyes, dip a clean flannel in warm, not hot, water (test it for comfort on your inner wrist or forearm) and apply to baby's eye for 5 to 10 minutes every 3 hours.

HEATING PAD

A hot-water bottle, which has no cords or heating element, is usually safer to use with an infant. If you use a heating pad, reread directions before each use, be sure the pad and cord are in good condition, and cover entirely with a cloth nappy if the pad doesn't have a cloth covering. Keep the temperature low, do not leave baby during treatment, and use for no more than 15 minutes at a time.

Hot Compresses

See 'Warm compresses'. Never use hot compresses on a baby.

Hot Soaks

Fill a basin with water that feels comfortably hot on your inner wrist or arm (not to your fingers). Never use water you haven't tested first. Immerse injured part in basin.

Hot-Water Bottle

Fill a hot-water bottle with water that is just a little warm to the touch. Wrap the bottle in a towel or cloth nappy before applying to baby's skin.

Humidifier

See 'Steam'.

Ice Pack

Use a commercial ice pack you keep in the freezer or a plastic bag filled with ice cubes (and a couple of paper towels to absorb the melting ice) and closed with a twist tie or rubber band. You can also use an unopened can of frozen juice concentrate or an unopened packet of frozen food. Do not apply the ice pack directly to a baby's skin.

Increased Fluids

If you are advised to increase fluids: frequently nurse the solely breastfed baby. Give formula to a bottle-fed baby, unless instructed otherwise by the doctor. Give water between feedings for babies older than six months, if recommended by your doctor. When baby is taking juice, dilute to half juice, half water. For an older baby, ask the doctor about rehydration fluids. *Do not* force fluids unless the doctor tells you to. When baby is vomiting, tiny sips of fluids spaced out stay down better than larger quantities. (See specific illnesses for preferred fluids.)

Nasal Aspiration

With baby held upright, squeeze the bulb of an aspirator (see illustration, page 550) and place the tip carefully in one nostril. Slowly release the bulb to draw mucus into it. Repeat with the second nostril. If mucus is dried and caked, irrigate with salt water (see below) and aspirate again.

Saltwater Irrigation

Though it's possible to use a homemade salt solution (add ⅛ teaspoon salt to 120 ml (4 fl oz) cooled boiled water), commercial saline solutions are safer, and worth keeping around the house. Put two drops in each nostril using a clean small dropper to soften crusts and clear congestion. Wait 3 to 5 minutes and suction with a nasal aspirator.

Steam

Use a warm-mist humidifier or a steam vaporizer placed out of baby's reach to moisten the air; or place a bowl of hot water on a hot radiator (out of baby's reach) or a kettle or pot of hot water on the stove in the same room as baby. For quick and abundant steam for a baby with croup (see page 768), close the bathroom door, turn on the hot water in the shower full blast, and fill the room with steam. Remain with baby in the bathroom until the croupy cough stops. If the cough has not improved in 10 minutes, check with baby's doctor.

WARM COMPRESSES

Fill a basin (a polystyrene bucket or cooler is best) with warm, not hot, water (it should not feel uncomfortable on your upper arm), Dip a clean flannel into the water, wring it out, and place it over the affected area.

DOSAGE CHART FOR COMMON INFANT-FEVER MEDICATION*

CALPOL (PARACETAMOL)**	DROPS	SUSPENSION LIQUID
Under 3 months**** 2.7 to 5 kg (6 to 11 lb)	½ dropper	
4 to 11 months**** 5.5 to 7.7 kg (12 to 17 lb)	1 dropper	½ teaspoon
12 to 23 months 8 to 10.5 kg (18 to 23 lb)	1½ droppers	¾ teaspoon
2 to 3 years 11 to 16 kg (24 to 35 lb)	2 droppers	1 teaspoon
NUROFEN (IBUPROFEN)**	**DROPS**	**SUSPENSION LIQUID**
4 to 11 months**** 5.5 to 7.7 kg (12 to 17 lb)	½ dropper	
12 to 23 months 8 to 10.5 kg (18 to 23 lb)	1 dropper	½ teaspoon
2 to 3 years 11 to 16 kg (24 to 35 lb)	2 droppers	1 teaspoon

*Aspirin should not be given without a doctor's recommendation.
**Give medication every 4 hours as needed, but no more than 5 doses in 24 hours.
***Give medication every 6 to 8 hours as needed, but no more than 4 doses in 24 hours.
****Do not give medication to babies under six months old without a doctor's recommendation. If weight range and age don't correlate, use the dosage appropriate for baby's weight.

Common Childhood Infections

Though the doctor will usually be the one to diagnose your baby's illnesses, you may find the basic information in this chart helpful as you try to sort out the possibilities and prepare to seek that medical advice. Symptoms are numbered in the order they can be expected to appear during the course of each illness, and rashes are listed separately for quick and easy comparison. Keep in mind that not every child has a textbook case of every infection – symptoms can vary, as can duration.

The details of how to treat specific symptoms (such as a cough, diarrhoea or an itch, for example) or of how to handle a fever are omitted from the chart to avoid repetition. For information on treating symptoms, see page 548; for treating a fever, see page 572.

Something else to remember: even if this chart tells you everything you want to know about a particular childhood infection, remember that it's no substitute for medical advice. Consult your baby's doctor as recommended.

DISEASE/SEASON/ SUSCEPTIBILITY	SYMPTOMS	
	NON-RASH	RASH
	(numbers indicate order of appearance)	
BRONCHIOLITIS (inflammation of the smaller branches of the bronchial tree) **Season:** Respiratory syncytial viruses (RSV), winter and spring; parainfluenza viruses (PIV), autumn. **Susceptibility:** Greatest in those under 2 years, especially under 6 months, or with a family history of allergy.	1. Cold symptoms. 2. *A few days later:* Rapid, shallow breathing; more pronounced cough; wheezing on breathing out; low-grade fever for about 3 days. *Sometimes:* Chest does not seem to expand with breathing in; pale or bluish colour.	None.
CHICKEN POX (varicella) **Season:** Most commonly, late winter and spring in temperate zones. **Susceptibility:** Anyone not immune.	Slight fever; malaise; loss of appetite.	Flat red spots turn into pimples, then blister, crust and scab; severe itching; new crops continue to develop for 3 to 4 days, mostly on the body.

CAUSE/ TRANSMISSION/ INCUBATION/ DURATION	CALL THE DOCTOR/ TREATMENT/DIET	PREVENTION/ RECURRENCE/ COMPLICATIONS
Cause: Various viruses, most often RSV. **Transmission:** Usually via respiratory secretions by direct contact or on household objects. **Incubation:** Varies with causative organism; usually 2 to 8 days. **Duration:** Acute phase may last only 3 days; cough from 1 to 3 weeks or more.	**Call the doctor immediately** if the child is having trouble breathing **or go to A&E** if the doctor can't be reached. **Treatment:** Bronchodilating drug (to open up breathing tubes). If not successful, hospitalization. **Diet:** If food can be taken by mouth, frequent small meals.	**Prevention:** Good hand washing, limiting exposure of high-risk infants. Monthly injections for very high-risk infants can reduce severity of infection and cut down on hospitalization rates (see page 563 for more). **Recurrence:** Can recur, but symptoms may be milder. **Complications:** Heart failure; bronchial asthma.
Cause: Varicella-zoster virus **Transmission:** Person-to-person via droplets, and airborne; very contagious from 1 to 2 days before onset until all lesions are scabbed. **Incubation:** Usually 14 to 16 days, but can be as short as 11 or as long as 20. **Duration:** First vesicles crust in 6 to 8 hours, scab in 24 to 48; scabs last 5 to 20 days.	**Call the doctor** to confirm diagnosis; **call** if itching turns to pain; **call** if there is fever for more than 3 days; **call immediately** for high-risk children; **call again** if symptoms of encephalitis appear. **Treatment:** for itching (page 548) and fever (page 572). DO NOT GIVE ASPIRIN because of the risk of Reye's syndrome.	**Prevention:** Avoidance of exposure in infants; varicella immunization in those over 12 months. **Recurrence:** Extremely rare, but dormant virus may flare up as shingles later in life. **Complications:** Rarely, encephalitis; anyone on steroids or those who have compromised immune systems can become seriously ill. **In pregnant women,** possible risk to foetus; contact a doctor if exposure occurs.

| DISEASE/SEASON/ SUSCEPTIBILITY | SYMPTOMS | |
	NON-RASH	RASH
	(numbers indicate order of appearance)	
CONJUNCTIVITIS (pink-eye; inflammation of the conjunctiva or lining of the eye)	*Depending on cause, may include:* Bloodshot eyes; tearing; discharge; burning; itching; light sensitivity. Usually begins in one eye, but may spread to the other.	None.
CROUP (acute laryugotracheitis) **Season:** Varies; usually worse at night. **Susceptibility:** Young children.	Hoarseness; sharp, barking cough; crowing or grunting sound on breathing in (stridor). *Sometimes:* Difficulty breathing.	None.
EAR INFECTION (Otitis media) See page 555.		

CAUSE/ TRANSMISSION/ INCUBATION/ DURATION	CALL THE DOCTOR/ TREATMENT/DIET	PREVENTION/ RECURRENCE/ COMPLICATIONS
Cause: Many, including viruses, bacteria, allergens, environmental irritants, blocked tear duct (see page 202), chlamydia. **Transmission:** For infective organisms, eye-hand-eye. **Incubation:** Usually brief. **Duration:** Varies: virus, 2 days to 3 weeks (can become chronic); bacteria, about 2 weeks; others, until allergen, irritant or duct blockage is removed.	**Call the doctor** to confirm diagnosis; **call again** if condition worsens or does not start to improve. **Treatment:** Eye soaks (see page 762); separate sheets and towels to prevent spread of infection; elimination of irritants, such as tobacco smoke, when possible; drops or ointment prescribed for bacterial and herpes infections, possibly for viral conjunctivitis (to prevent secondary infection), and to relieve discomfort of allergic reaction.	**Prevention:** Good hygiene (separate towels when family member is infected); avoidance of allergens and other irritants. **Recurrence:** Some people are more susceptible and more likely to have recurrences. **Complications:** Chronic eye inflammation; eye damage from repeated attacks.
Cause: Usually, virus; sudden attacks at night called 'spasmodic croup'. **Transmission:** Probably, person-to-person; contaminated objects. **Incubation:** 2 days (usually follows cold or flu). **Duration:** May recur over several days.	**Call the doctor immediately** if steam doesn't bring relief; if baby looks blue, has blue lips, is drooling excessively, has stridor or difficulty breathing; or if you suspect an inhaled object. **Initial treatment:** Steam (see page 763). Spasmodic croup usually responds well to a steamy bathroom or going outside and breathing the cold night air. **Follow-up:** Humidifier. Sleep in same room as baby to reassure and to be handy for treating another attack or use a monitor so that you can hear an attack and respond immediately.	**Prevention:** Supply humidified air to baby with cold or flu. **Recurrence:** Tends to repeat in some children. **Complications:** Breathing problems; pneumonia; ear infection about 5 days after recovery.

DISEASE/SEASON/ SUSCEPTIBILITY	SYMPTOMS	
	NON-RASH	RASH
	(numbers indicate order of appearance)	
ENCEPHALITIS (inflammation of the brain) **Season:** Depends on cause. **Susceptibility:** Varies with cause.	Fever; drowsiness; headache, vomiting. *Sometimes:* Neurological impairment.	None.
EPIGLOTTITIS (inflammation of the epiglottis) **Season:** Winter months in temperate climates. **Susceptibility:** Not common in children under 2.	Muffled voice, difficulty breathing and swallowing; drooling. Sudden onset of high fever is typical. Child seems ill. *Sometimes:* Low-pitched cough; protruding tongue; fever.	None.
FIFTH DISEASE/ SLAPPED CHEEK (erythema infectiosum) Season: Early spring. **Susceptibility:** Greatest in children 2 to 12 years old.	*Sometimes:* sore throat, headache, pink eyes, fatigue, mild fever or itching. *Rarely:* Joint pain	1. Intense flush on face (slapped-cheek look). 2. *Next day:* Lacy rash on arms and legs. 3. *3 days later:* Rash on inner surfaces, fingers, toes, trunk and/or buttocks. 4. Rash may reappear on and off with exposure to heat (bathwater, sun) for 2 or 3 weeks.
GASTROINTESTINAL UPSET See **Diarrhoea,** page 554.		

CAUSE/ TRANSMISSION/ INCUBATION/ DURATION	CALL THE DOCTOR/ TREATMENT/DIET	PREVENTION/ RECURRENCE/ COMPLICATIONS
Cause: Often a complication of another viral disease. **Transmission:** Depends on cause; some viruses transmitted via insects. **Incubation:** Depends on cause. **Duration:** Varies.	**Call the doctor immediately or go to A&E** if you suspect encephalitis. **Treatment:** Hospitalization is required.	**Prevention:** Immunization against diseases for which this is a complication (for example, measles). **Recurrence:** Unlikely. **Complications:** Neurological damage; can be fatal.
Cause: Bacteria, most often haemophilus influenzae (Hib). **Transmission:** Probably person-to-person, or inhalation of droplets. **Incubation:** Less than 10 days. **Duration:** 4 to 7 days or longer.	**Call 999 immediately or go to A&E.** While waiting for help, keep baby upright, leaning forward, with mouth open and tongue out. **Treatment:** Hospitalization; establishment of airway; antibiotics.	**Prevention:** Hib immunization. **Recurrence:** Slight possibility. **Complications:** Can be fatal without prompt medical attention.
Cause: Human parvovirus. **Transmission:** Probably person-to-person. **Incubation:** 4 to 14 days; usually 12 to 14. **Duration:** 3 to 10 days, but rash may reappear on and off for up to 3 weeks.	**Call the doctor** only if you need confirmation of diagnosis or if other symptoms occur. **Treatment:** None. **Diet:** No changes.	**Prevention:** None. **Recurrence:** Possible. **Complications:** Only in those who are immune deficient. Pregnant women should let their doctors know if they are exposed because of slight risk to foetus.

DISEASE/SEASON/ SUSCEPTIBILITY	SYMPTOMS	
	NON-RASH	RASH
	(numbers indicate order of appearance)	
GERMAN MEASLES (rubella) **Season:** Late winter and early spring. **Susceptibility:** Anyone not immune.	None in 25 to 50 per cent of cases. 1. *Sometimes:* Slight fever; swollen neck glands.	2. Small (25-mm/1/10-inch), flat, reddish pink spots on face. 3. Rash spreads to body and, sometimes, to roof of mouth.
HAND-FOOT-MOUTH DISEASE **Season:** Summer and autumn in temperate climates. **Susceptibility:** Greatest in babies and young children.	1. Fever; loss of appetite. *Often:* Sore throat and mouth (discomfort nursing); difficulty swallowing.	2. *In 2 or 3 days:* Lesions in mouth; then fingers, maybe feet, buttocks, sometimes arms, legs, and less often face. Mouth lesions usually blister.
HERPANGINA **Season:** Mostly, summer and autumn in temperate climates. **Susceptibility:** Greatest in babies and young children. Occurs alone or with other diseases.	1. Fever (37.8°C to 40°C/100°F to 104°F, even 41.1°C (106°F); sore throat. 1. or 3. Painful swallowing. *Sometimes:* Vomiting; loss of appetite; diarrhoea; abdominal pain; lethargy.	2. Distinct grayish white papules in back of mouth or throat that blister and ulcerate (5 to 20 in number).
HERPES SIMPLEX (cold sores, fever blisters) **Season:** Any, but sunshine can precipitate flare-up of virus. **Susceptibility:** Most primary infections occur in childhood.	*Primary infection:* Fever (can be as high as 41.1°C/106°F); sore throat; swollen glands; drooling; bad breath; loss of appetite. *Often:* No symptoms. *Subsequent flare-ups:* *Possibly:* Headache. Infection can also occur in the eye.	*Primary infection:* Sores in mucous membranes of mouth. *Subsequent flare-ups:* Welt forms on or near lip, tingles and itches, then blisters and oozes (painful stage), finally crusts and scabs (may itch).

CAUSE/ TRANSMISSION/ INCUBATION/ DURATION	CALL THE DOCTOR/ TREATMENT/DIET	PREVENTION/ RECURRENCE/ COMPLICATIONS
Cause: Rubella virus. **Transmission:** 7 to 10 days before rash appears until possibly 7 days after rash appears; via direct or droplet contact. **Incubation:** 14 to 21 days; usually 16 to 18. **Duration:** A few hours to 4 or 5 days.	**Call the doctor** if a non-immune pregnant woman is exposed. **Treatment:** Symptomatic. **Diet:** Extra fluids.	**Prevention:** Immunization (MMR). **Recurrence:** None; one case confers immunity. **Complications:** Very rarely, thrombocytopenia or encephalitis. Risk is primarily to the foetus if a pregnant non-immune woman is exposed.
Cause: Coxsackie virus. **Transmission:** Mouth-to-mouth; faeces-to-hand-to-mouth. **Incubation:** 3 to 6 days. **Duration:** About one week.	**Call the doctor** to confirm diagnosis. **Treatment:** Symptomatic (see page 548). **Diet:** Soft foods will be more comfortable.	**Prevention:** None. **Recurrence:** Possible. **Complications:** None.
Cause: Coxsackie virus. **Transmission:** Mouth-to-mouth; faeces-to-hand-to-mouth. **Incubation:** 3 to 6 days. **Duration:** 4 to 7 but healing can take 2 to 3 weeks.	**Call the doctor** to confirm diagnosis. **Call immediately** if convulsions or other symptoms occur. **Treatment:** Symptomatic (see page 548). **Diet:** Soft foods will be more comfortable.	**Prevention:** None. **Recurrence:** Possible. **Complications:** None.
Cause: Herpes simplex virus (HSV) remains in body and can be reactivated by sun, stress, teething, a cold, fever. **Transmission:** Direct contact with lesion, saliva, stool, urine or eye discharge; or with household articles within hours of contamination. **Incubation:** Possibly, 2 to 12 days. **Duration:** Scab falls off within 3 weeks.	**Call the doctor** only if baby seems ill (unless baby is under 3 months, then call immediately). **Treatment:** Over-the-counter ointment may help (NOT cortisone); antiviral drugs in high-risk children. **Diet:** For primary infection, soft, non-acid foods; during subsequent flare-up, plain yoghurt with live cultures may help.	**Prevention:** Avoid triggering factors when possible. **Recurrence:** Latent infection can flare up anytime. **Complications:** Eye involvement.

DISEASE/SEASON/ SUSCEPTIBILITY	SYMPTOMS	
	NON-RASH	RASH
	(numbers indicate order of appearance)	

DISEASE/SEASON/ SUSCEPTIBILITY	NON-RASH	RASH
HYDROPHOBIA See **Rabies**.		
INFLUENZA (flu) **Season:** More often in cold months; often in epidemics. **Susceptibility:** Anyone, but very old and very young can become sicker.	*Sometimes:* None noted. 1. *Usually, abrupt onset of:* Fever (38°C to 40°C/100.4°F to 104°F); shivering; malaise; dry, unproductive cough; diarrhoea/vomiting. 2. *Often, 3 or 4 days after onset:* Cold symptoms. *Can include:* Intermittent or variable, fever, malaise, headache, mild neck stiffness; and achiness. 3. *Sometimes, for next 1 or 2 weeks:* Productive cough; fatigue. *In some cases:* As disease spreads: headache, fatigue, aches and pains, nervous system involvement. 4. *Late disease, if un-treated:* Chronic arthritis, especially in knees; further central nervous system involvement; *rarely,* heart damage.	None.

CAUSE/ TRANSMISSION/ INCUBATION/ DURATION	CALL THE DOCTOR/ TREATMENT/DIET	PREVENTION/ RECURRENCE/ COMPLICATIONS
Cause: Influenza A, Influenza B. **Transmission:** Inhalation of respiratory droplets; use of contaminated articles. Communicable from 5 days before symptoms appear. **Incubation:** 1 to 2 days. **Duration:** Acute phase, a few days; convalescent phase, 1 to 2 weeks.	**Call the doctor** if baby is under 6 months, if symptoms are severe or continue 3 days, or if fever is over 38.9°C (102°F). **Treatment:** Symptomatic; in severe cases antiviral drugs may be prescribed. DO NOT GIVE ASPIRIN because of the risk of Reye's syndrome. **Diet:** Extra fluids.	**Prevention:** Annual immunization for all infants over 6 months old; avoiding crowds in flu season; hand washing. **Recurrence:** Common. **Complications:** Secondary bacterial infections: otitis media, croup, pneumonia.

DISEASE/SEASON/ SUSCEPTIBILITY	SYMPTOMS	
	NON-RASH	RASH
	(numbers indicate order of appearance)	
MEASLES (Rubeola) **Season:** Winter and spring. **Susceptibility:** Anyone not immune.	1. *For 1 or 2 days:* Fever; runny nose; red, watery eyes; dry cough. *Sometimes:* Diarrhoea; swollen glands.	2. Tiny white spots like grains of sand appear inside of cheeks; may bleed. 3. Dull, red, slightly raised rash begins on forehead, behind ears, then spreads downwards giving a red-allover look.
MENINGITIS (inflammation of the membranes around the brain and/or the spinal cord) **Season:** Varies with causative organism; for Hib, winter. **Susceptibility:** Depends on causative organism; for Hib, greatest for infants and young children.	Fever; high-pitched cry; drowsiness; irritability; loss of appetite; vomiting; bulging fontanel. *In older children, also:* Stiff neck; sensitivity to light; blurred vision and other signs of neurological ills.	None.
MENINGOENCEPHALITIS (a combination of meningitis and encephalitis) See **Meningitis** and **Encephalitis.**		

CAUSE/ TRANSMISSION/ INCUBATION/ DURATION	CALL THE DOCTOR/ TREATMENT/DIET	PREVENTION/ RECURRENCE/ COMPLICATIONS
Cause: Measles virus. **Transmission:** Direct contact with droplets from 2 days before to 4 days after rash appears. **Incubation:** 8 to 12 days. **Duration:** About a week.	**Call the doctor** for diagnosis; **recall immediately** if cough becomes severe, if convulsions or symptoms of pneumonia, encephalitis or otitis media occur, or if fever goes up after going down. **Treatment:** Symptomatic; warm soaks, dim lights if eyes are sensitive (but bright lights are not harmful). **Diet:** Extra fluids for fever.	**Prevention:** Immunization (MMR); strict isolation of infected persons. **Recurrence:** None. **Complications:** Otitis media, pneumonia, encephalitis; can be fatal.
Cause: Most often, bacteria, such as Hib, pneumococcus, or meningococcus; also viruses, which cause less serious disease. **Transmission:** Depends on organism. **Incubation:** Varies with organism; for Hib, probably less than 10 days. **Duration:** Varies.	**Call the doctor immediately** if you suspect meningitis, **or go to A&E** if doctor can't be reached. **Treatment:** For viral meningitis, symptomatic; for bacterial, hospitalization required; antibiotics. **Diet:** Extra fluids for fever.	**Prevention:** PCV immunization; Hib immunization for Hib infections. **Recurrence:** Possible. **Complications:** Viral forms usually do no long-term damage; Hib and other bacterial forms can do lasting neurological damage.

DISEASE/SEASON/ SUSCEPTIBILITY	SYMPTOMS	
	NON-RASH	**RASH**
	(numbers indicate order of appearance)	
MUMPS **Season:** Late winter and spring. **Susceptibility:** Anyone not immune.	1. *Sometimes:* Vague pain; fever; loss of appetite. 2. *Usually:* Swelling of salivary glands on one or both sides of jaw, below and in front of ear; ear pain, pain on chewing, or on taking acid or sour food or drink; swelling of other salivary glands. No symptoms at all in about 30 per cent of cases.	None.
NON-SPECIFIC VIRAL INFECTIONS **Season:** Mostly summer. **Susceptibility:** Mostly young children.	*Varies, but may include:* Fever; loss of appetite; diarrhoea.	Various types of rashes are seen with NSV.
OTITIS MEDIA See page 555.		

CAUSE/ TRANSMISSION/ INCUBATION/ DURATION	CALL THE DOCTOR/ TREATMENT/DIET	PREVENTION/ RECURRENCE/ COMPLICATIONS
Cause: Mumps virus. **Transmission:** Usually 1 or 2 days (but could be as long as 7 days) prior to onset until 9 days after onset, via direct contact with respiratory secretions. **Incubation:** Usually 16 to 18 days, but can be 12 to 25. **Duration:** 5 to 7 days.	**Call the doctor** for diagnosis; **call back immediately** if there is vomiting, drowsiness; possible headache, back or neck stiffness, or other signs of meningoencephalitis either along with or following the mumps. **Treatment:** Symptomatic for fever and pain; cool compresses applied to cheeks. **Diet:** Non-acid, non-sour, soft diet.	**Prevention:** MMR immunization. **Recurrence:** Rare **Complications:** Meningoencephalitis; other complications rare in infants, but can be serious in males after puberty because of swelling of the testicles.
Cause: Various enteroviruses. **Transmission:** Faeces-to-hand-to-mouth; possibly mouth-to-mouth. **Incubation:** 3 to 6 days. **Duration:** Usually a few days.	**Call the doctor** to confirm diagnosis; **call again** if baby seems worse or if new symptoms appear. **Treatment:** Symptomatic. **Diet:** Extra fluids for diarrhoea, fever (see pages 554, 572).	**Prevention:** None. **Recurrence:** Common. **Complications:** Very rare.

DISEASE/SEASON/ SUSCEPTIBILITY	SYMPTOMS	
	NON-RASH	**RASH**
	(numbers indicate order of appearance)	
PERTUSSIS (whooping cough) **Season:** Late winter/early spring. **Susceptibility:** Half of all cases occur in babies under 1 year.	1. Cold symptoms with dry cough; low-grade fever; irritability. 2. *1 or 2 weeks later:* Coughing in explosive bursts with no breaths between; thick mucus expelled. *Often:* Bulging eyes and protruding tongue; pale or red skin; vomiting; profuse sweating; exhaustion. *Sometimes:* Apnea, in infants; hernia, from cough. 3. Cessation of whooping and vomiting; reduced coughing; improved appetite and mood. Mild in immunized children.	None.
PHARYNGITIS See **Sore Throat**		
PNEUMONIA (inflammation of the lung) **Season:** Varies with causative factor. **Susceptibility:** Anyone, but especially the very young, very old and those with chronic illnesses.	*Commonly, after cold or other illness, baby seems suddenly worse, with:* Increased fever; productive cough; rapid breathing; blueness; wheezy, raspy and/or difficult breathing; abdominal bloating and pain.	None.

CAUSE/ TRANSMISSION/ INCUBATION/ DURATION	CALL THE DOCTOR/ TREATMENT/DIET	PREVENTION/ RECURRENCE/ COMPLICATIONS
Cause: Pertussis bacteria. **Transmission:** Direct contact via droplets; most communicable during early stage, less so later; antibiotics reduce period of communicability. **Incubation:** 7 to 10 days; rarely more than 2 weeks. **Duration:** Usually 6 weeks, but can last much longer.	**Call the doctor promptly** for persistent coughing. **Treatment:** Hospitalization for infants; antibiotics (may help reduce symptoms in first stage, communicability later); oxygen; mucus suctioning; humidification. **Diet:** Frequent small feedings; fluid replacement; intravenous feeding if necessary.	**Prevention:** Immunization (DTaP) **Recurrence:** None; one attack confers immunity. **Complications:** Many, including: otitis media; pneumonia; convulsions. Can be fatal, especially in infants.
Cause: Various organisms, including bacteria; fungi, viruses and protozoa, as well as irritation from a chemical or other inhaled substance or object. **Transmission:** Varies with cause. **Incubation:** Varies with cause. **Duration:** Varies with cause.	**Call the doctor** for productive or persistent cough, or if a slightly sick baby seems worse or has increased fever or cough; **call immediately or go to A&E** if baby has difficulty breathing, turns a bluish colour or seems very sick. **Treatment:** Symptomatic. Most cases can be treated at home. Antibiotics, if needed. **Diet:** Fluids; adequate nutrition.	**Prevention:** Hib immunization for Hib infections; protection of susceptible infants against illness. **Recurrence:** Many types can recur. **Complications:** Riskiest for those infants weakened by other illnesses, prematurity or low birthweight.

DISEASE/SEASON/ SUSCEPTIBILITY	SYMPTOMS	
	NON-RASH	RASH
	(numbers indicate order of appearance)	
RESPIRATORY SYNCYTIAL VIRUS (RSV) See page 563.		
REYE'S SYNDROME **Season:** Mostly winter and spring. **Susceptibility:** Mostly children who are given aspirin during a viral illness such as chicken pox or influenza. It's a rare disease.	*1 to 7 days following a viral infection:* Persistent vomiting; lethargy; rapidly deteriorating mental state (irritability, confusion, delirium); rapid heartbeat and respiration. *May progress to:* Coma.	None.
ROSEOLA INFANTUM **Season:** Year-round, but more common in spring and autumn. **Susceptibility:** Greatest in babies and young children.	1. Irritability; loss of appetite; fever (38.9° to 40.5°C/102°F to 105°F). *Sometimes:* Runny nose; swollen glands; convulsions. 2. *On 3rd or 4th day:* Fever drops and baby seems better.	3. Faint pink spots that turn white upon pressure on body, neck, upper arms, and sometimes face and legs. The rash appears after the fever subsides. In some cases, there may be no rash.
SCARLET FEVER (scarlatina) **Season:** Year-round, but more common in cold months. **Susceptibility:** Greatest among school-age children; less common in those under 3 and in adults.	Similar to strep throat, but often heralded by vomiting and characterized by rash. Infants don't usually have a sore or red throat; instead, they're likely to be pale (and, in general, to 'look sick').	Bright red rash on face, groin and under arms; spreads to rest of body and limbs; leaves skin rough, peeling.

CAUSE/ TRANSMISSION/ INCUBATION/ DURATION	CALL THE DOCTOR/ TREATMENT/DIET	PREVENTION/ RECURRENCE/ COMPLICATIONS
Cause: Unknown, but appears to be related to the use of aspirin during such viral illnesses as chicken pox and influenza, which is why it's very important never to give a child aspirin. **Transmission:** Unknown. **Incubation:** Unknown, but seems to occur within days of onset of viral infection. **Duration:** Varies.	**Call the doctor** immediately if you suspect Reye's Syndrome; **or go to A&E.** **Treatment:** Hospital treatment is vital.	**Prevention:** Avoid giving aspirin with viral diseases such as chicken pox or influenza. **Recurrence:** None. **Complications:** Can be fatal, but survivors usually have no lasting problems.
Cause: Human herpes virus, types 6 and 7 (HHV-6, HHV-7) **Transmission:** From respiratory secretions of family members and close contacts, who may themselves be healthy. **Incubation:** 9 to 19 days. **Duration:** 3 to 6 days.	**Call the doctor** to confirm diagnosis; call back if fever persists for 4 or 5 days, if baby develops convulsions or seems ill. **Treatment:** Symptomatic. **Diet:** Increased fluids for fever.	**Prevention:** None known. **Recurrence:** Unusual in otherwise healthy persons. **Complications:** Very rare. Brief febrile seizures occur in 10 per cent of cases because of high fever.
Cause: Streptococcus bacteria. **Transmission:** Direct contact with infected person. **Incubation:** 2 to 5 days. **Duration:** About 1 week in infants under 6 months, but runny nose and general crankiness can last 6 weeks; about 1 to 2 weeks in older babies.	See **Strep Throat.**	**Prevention:** Isolation of infected persons at least until they have had a day or two of antibiotics, and good preventive hygiene. **Recurrence:** Can occur. **Complications:** See **Strep Throat.**

DISEASE/SEASON/ SUSCEPTIBILITY	SYMPTOMS	
	NON-RASH	**RASH**
	(numbers indicate order of appearance)	
SORE THROAT, VIRAL (tonsillitis; pharyngitis) **Season:** Autumn, winter and spring. **Susceptibility:** More often, older children.	Moderate fever (38.3°C to 39.4°C/101°F to 103°F); fatigue; throat pain or discomfort; some difficulty swallowing; irritability and fussiness. Throat appears red and tonsils may be swollen. *Sometimes:* Hoarseness, coughing and conjunctivitis (pink eye), particularly if caused by the adenovirus.	None.
STREP THROAT (streptococcal pharyngitis) **Season:** October through April. **Susceptibility:** Most common in school-age children.	*Chronic strep in infants:* Runny nose; fluctuating temperature; crankiness; loss of appetite; pale appearance. *Strep throat in older children:* High fever; red throat with pockets of pus; trouble swallowing; swollen tonsils and glands; abdominal pain.	Usually none. Scarlatina rash is possible in older children. (See **Scarlet Fever.**)

CAUSE/ TRANSMISSION/ INCUBATION/ DURATION	CALL THE DOCTOR/ TREATMENT/DIET	PREVENTION/ RECURRENCE/ COMPLICATIONS
Cause: Various viruses, most often adenovirus; also enterovirus. (Chronic sore throat may be due to allergy; tobacco smoke, hot, dry air or other factors.) **Transmission:** Depends on causative virus; probably respiratory route with adenovirus. **Incubation:** Depends on causative virus; 2 to 14 days with adenovirus. **Duration:** 1 to 10 days.	**Call the doctor** if you suspect baby has a sore throat so the doctor can determine the cause. **Treatment:** Symptomatic. Paracetamol for pain. (Babies are too young to gargle or to suck on lozenges.) DO NOT GIVE ASPIRIN because of risk of Reye's syndrome. **Diet:** Soft cold foods may be easier for a baby on solids to tolerate. Fluids.	**Prevention:** Isolation of infected person, and good hygiene. In chronic sore throat, the removal of the cause (elimination of smoke in the environment, for instance). **Recurrence:** Possible. **Complications:** Unlikely, except in children with suppressed immunity.
Cause: Group A streptococcus bacteria. **Transmission:** By direct contact with infected individual from 1 day before onset to 6 days after, but antibiotics reduce communicability to 24 hours. Highly contagious. **Incubation:** 2 to 5 days, **Duration:** Usually about 1 week, but the chronic form of strep infection in infants with runny nose and general crankiness can last 6 weeks. About 1 to 2 weeks in older babies.	**Call the doctor** initially for diagnosis (culture of nose or throat will confirm); call again if fever doesn't drop in 2 days, or if new symptoms appear. **Treatment:** Symptomatic. Antibiotics to kill bacteria and prevent complications. **Diet:** Soft, cold foods may be easier for a baby on solids to tolerate. Fluids.	**Prevention:** Isolation of infected persons, and good hygiene. **Recurrence:** Possible. **Complications:** Untreated infection can spread to ears, mastoids, sinuses, skin (impetigo), lungs, brain, kidneys. Rheumatic fever less common but does occur in infants; also joint pain and rashes.

DISEASE/SEASON/ SUSCEPTIBILITY	SYMPTOMS	
	NON-RASH	**RASH**
	(numbers indicate order of appearance)	
TETANUS (lockjaw) **Season:** When more time is spent outdoors. **Susceptibility:** Anyone not immunized.	*Localized:* Spasm and increased muscle tone near the wound. *Generalized:* Involuntary muscle contractions that can arch back, lock jaw, twist neck; convulsions; rapid heartbeat; profuse sweating; low-grade fever; difficult sucking, in infants.	None.
TONSILLITIS See **Sore Throat**.		
UPPER RESPIRATORY INFECTION (URI) See **Common Cold** (page 546) and **Influenza**.		
WHOOPING COUGH See **Pertussis**.		

CAUSE/ TRANSMISSION/ INCUBATION/ DURATION	CALL THE DOCTOR/ TREATMENT/DIET	PREVENTION/ RECURRENCE/ COMPLICATIONS
Cause: Toxin produced by bacteria that spread through the body. **Transmission:** Transmitted via contamination by bacteria from a puncture wound, a burn, a deep scrape or an unhealed umbilical cord. **Incubation:** 3 days to 3 weeks, but an average of 8 days. **Duration:** Several weeks.	**Call the doctor immediately or go to A&E** if unvaccinated baby incurs susceptible wound. **Treatment:** Medical treatment essential: tetanus toxoid to prevent development of disease; tetanus antitoxins; muscle relaxants; antibiotics; respirator.	**Prevention:** Immunization (DTaP); sanitary care of umbilical cord; avoidance of outdoor injuries when possible. **Recurrence:** None. **Complications:** Many, including: ulcers; pneumonia; abnormal heart rate; blood clot in lung. Can be fatal.

Height and Weight Charts

Record your baby's weight and length at birth in a permanent health record, and update his or her progress at each visit to the doctor. To chart measurements on these graphs, find baby's age along the bottom of the chart and weight (in kilograms and pounds) or length (in centimetres and inches) along the side. Put a coloured dot at the point where the two come

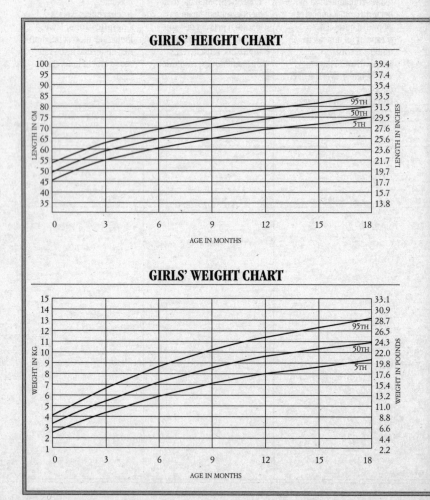

GIRLS' HEIGHT CHART

GIRLS' WEIGHT CHART

together. To see your baby's progress, connect the dots as they are added. Ninety out of every one hundred children fall within the fifth and ninety-fifth percentiles. Though those in the top and bottom five per cent may come by their size genetically and be doing well, some may be growing too slowly or gaining too quickly. If your baby falls into either of

these groups, discuss your concern with baby's doctor. Also, check with the doctor about any sudden variation from the typical pattern (in height or weight or both), though such a variation may be perfectly normal for your baby.

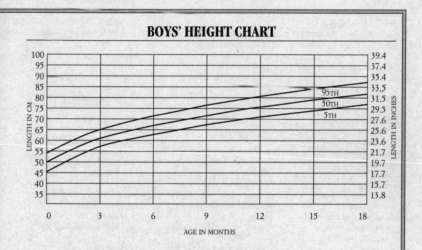

BOYS' HEIGHT CHART

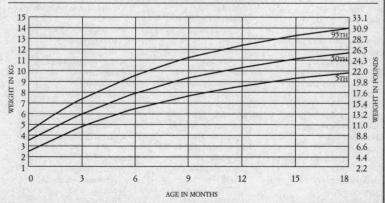

BOYS' WEIGHT CHART

INDEX

A

abdomen, in sick baby 537
abdominal injuries, and first
    aid for 575–6
  pain, and colic 184
  pain, and food allergy 328
  pain, and gastric distress 553
  pain, and lactose intolerance
    544
  pain, and too much formula
    167
  pain, in sick baby 537
  thrusts, for choking child
    595
ABR see auditory brainstem
    response (ABR) hearing
    screening
abrasions, first aid for 590
abscess, breast 83
accidents
  falls 465–6
  parental reaction to 465
  prevention of 400–15
acellular pertussis see DTaP
    (diphtheria, tetanus,
    acellular pertussis)
    vaccine
aches, postpartum 685–6
acne 197
active baby 234
acute otitis media 555–9
  see also ear infection
additives in food 339
  and breastfeeding 92
  see also organic food
ADHD, see Attention Deficit
    Hyperactivity Disorder
    (ADHD)
adoption 657–66
  announcing 664–5
  and baby blues 660–1
  benefits of 666
  and bonding 660
  and breastfeeding 11, 150,
    659, 661–3
  and crying baby 660
  finalizing 660
  foreign, and special medical
    concerns 659

and getting ready 657–9
and grandparents' attitude
    663
and not feeling like a parent
    659
preparing for 657–9
and support for the family
    665
telling baby about 665
and unknown health
    problems 664
and vaccines 665
and waiting period 660
AIDS
  and contraception 704
  maternal, and breastfeeding
    10
  perinatal 642–3
air
  baby swallowing 187; see
    also gas, burping baby
  polluted indoor, minimizing
    risk to baby 337–9
air bags, and car seats 133, 134
air conditioning, and baby 511
airway
  check, when baby is choking
    594, 595
  clearing of, in CPR 594, 596
  suctioning of, at birth 94
alcohol
  abuse 334
  and breastfeeding 91
  dangers of giving, to baby
    341
  and foetal alcohol syndrome
    (FAS) 649
  and teething pain 341
  for umbilical cord care 145,
    192
allergies
  bee venom 545
  and breastfeeding 545
  common 542–6
  or common cold 546
  cow's milk 172, 545
  dust mites 544
  food 327–9
  and HEPA 544
  or intolerance 544
  milk, in breastfed babies 172

miscellaneous 545
mould 544
nut 41, 89, 91
and pets 544
pollen 543–4
prevention from 545
reaction to immunization
    222
and solids, later introduction
    of 545
soya 172
wheat 313
and when to call a doctor
    546
alternative medicine 31, 552
anaemia 627
  screenings 363–4
anencephaly 643
anger, parental, 456, 459
  because of crying baby 184
  because of premature baby
    612–13
animals, see pets
ankle deformities, see clubfoot
antibiotic ointment
  for first aid 592
  and newborn eyes 94, 110,
    111
  and umbilical cord 94
antibiotics
  for baby's ear infection 548
  maternal, and breastfeeding
    10
antibodies
  and breast milk 4
  and colostrum 72
anxiety, and breastfeeding 9
Apgar score 94
Apgar table 97
Apgar test 97
Apgar, Virginia 97
apnea of prematurity 259, 611,
    625–6
apparent life-threatening event
    256
appearance
  of newborn 96
  of premature baby 611
appetite
  drop in 492–3
  erratic 438